THE wallflower
YAMATONADESHIKO SHICHIHENGE

22 - 23 - 24

Tomoko Hayakawa

Translated and adapted by
David Ury

Lettered by
North Market Street Graphics

DEL REY

Ballantine Books · New York

The Wallflower volumes 22, 23, and 24 are works of fiction. Names, characters, places, and incidents are the products of the author's imagination or are used fictitiously. Any resemblance to actual events, locales, or persons, living or dead, is entirely coincidental.

A Del Rey Manga/Kodansha Trade Paperback Original

Published in the United States by Del Rey, an imprint of The Random House Publishing Group, a division of Random House, Inc., New York.

DEL REY is a registered trademark and the Del Rey colophon is a trademark of Random House, Inc.

Publication rights arranged through Kodansha Ltd.

First published in Japan in 2009 by Kodansha Ltd., Tokyo, as *Yamatonadeshiko Shichihenge* volumes 22, 23, and 24.

ISBN 978-0-345-51460-8

Printed in the United States of America

www.delreymanga.com

9 8 7 6 5 4 3 2 1

Translator/Adapter—David Ury
Lettering—North Market Street Graphics

Honorifics Explained

Throughout the Del Rey Manga books, you will find Japanese honorifics left intact in the translations. For those not familiar with how the Japanese use honorifics and, more important, how they differ from American honorifics, we present this brief overview.

Politeness has always been a critical facet of Japanese culture. Ever since the feudal era, when Japan was a highly stratified society, use of honorifics—which can be defined as polite speech that indicates relationship or status—has played an essential role in the Japanese language. When addressing someone in Japanese, an honorific usually takes the form of a suffix attached to one's name (example: "Asuna-san"), is used as a title at the end of one's name, or appears in place of the name itself (example: "Negi-sensei," or simply "Sensei!").

Honorifics can be expressions of respect or endearment. In the context of manga and anime, honorifics give insight into the nature of the relationship between characters. Many English translations leave out these important honorifics and therefore distort the feel of the original Japanese. Because Japanese honorifics contain nuances that English honorifics lack, it is our policy at Del Rey not to translate them. Here, instead, is a guide to some of the honorifics you may encounter in Del Rey Manga.

-san: This is the most common honorific and is equivalent to Mr., Miss, Ms., or Mrs. It is the all-purpose honorific and can be used in any situation where politeness is required.

-sama: This is one level higher than "-san" and is used to confer great respect.

-dono: This comes from the word "tono," which means "lord." It is an even higher level than "-sama" and confers utmost respect.

-kun: This suffix is used at the end of boys' names to express familiarity or endearment. It is also sometimes used by men among friends, or when addressing someone younger or of a lower station.

-chan: This is used to express endearment, mostly toward girls. It is also used for little boys, pets, and even among lovers. It gives a sense of childish cuteness.

Bozu: This is an informal way to refer to a boy, similar to the English terms "kid" and "squirt."

Sempai/
Senpai: This title suggests that the addressee is one's senior in a group or organization. It is most often used in a school setting, where underclassmen refer to their upperclassmen as "sempai." It can also be used in the workplace, such as when a newer employee addresses an employee who has seniority in the company.

Kohai: This is the opposite of "sempai" and is used toward underclassmen in school or newcomers in the workplace. It connotes that the addressee is of a lower station.

Sensei: Literally meaning "one who has come before," this title is used for teachers, doctors, or masters of any profession or art.

-[blank]: This is usually forgotten in these lists, but it is perhaps the most significant difference between Japanese and English. The lack of honorific means that the speaker has permission to address the person in a very intimate way. Usually, only family, spouses, or very close friends have this kind of permission. Known as *yobisute*, it can be gratifying when someone who has earned the intimacy starts to call one by one's name without an honorific. But when that intimacy hasn't been earned, it can be very insulting.

THE wallFLOWER

YAMATONADESHIKO SHICHIHENGE

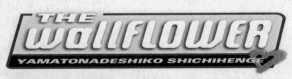

Volume 22

A Note from the Author

♥ VOLUME 21 WAS FULL OF ROMANCE SO I WENT A
LITTLE CRAZY WITH THIS ONE. I PREFER SILLY STORIES TO
ROMANCE ANY DAY, BUT WE CAN'T HAVE THAT NOW, CAN
WE? WE HAVE TO SEE SOME PROGRESSION IN KYOHEI AND
SUNAKO'S RELATIONSHIP. I'M NOT ONE FOR ROMANCE, BUT
I'LL DO MY BEST TO MAKE IT WORK. THANKS FOR ALL YOUR
SUPPORT.

—Tomoko Hayakawa

THE wallflower

YAMATONADESHIKO SHICHIHENGE

ヤマトナデシコ七変化♡

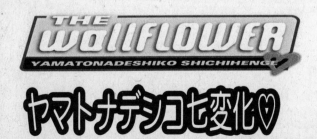

CONTENTS

Chapter 88

THE PRINCESS OF DARKNESS GOES TO THE BEACH

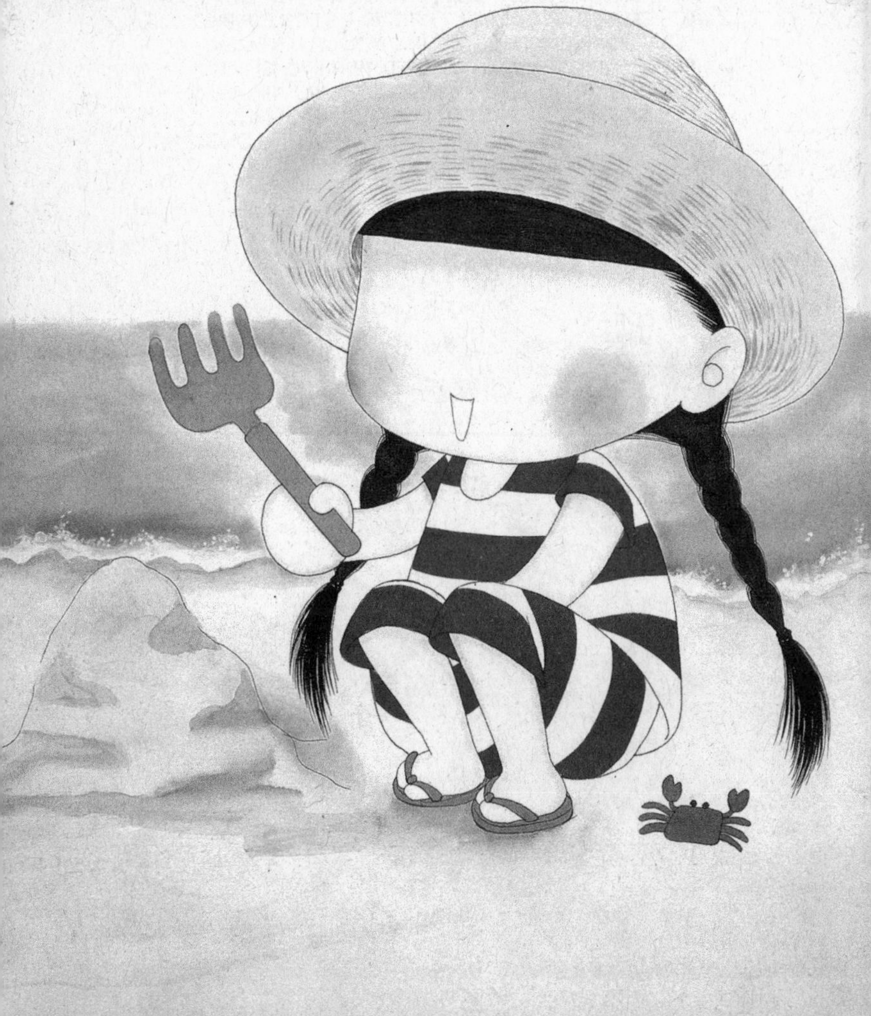

WALLFLOWER'S BEAUTIFUL CAST OF CHARACTERS (?)

SUNAKO IS A DARK LONER WHO LOVES HORROR MOVIES. WHEN HER AUNT, THE LANDLADY, LEAVES TOWN, SUNAKO IS FORCED TO LIVE WITH FOUR HANDSOME GUYS. SUNAKO'S AUNT MAKES A DEAL WITH THE BOYS, WHICH CAUSES NOTHING BUT HEADACHES FOR SUNAKO. "MAKE SUNAKO INTO A LADY, AND YOU CAN LIVE RENT FREE." FOR A MOMENT IT SEEMED THAT KYOHEI HAD FINALLY STARTED TO SEE SUNAKO AS A WOMAN, BUT IT TURNS OUT HE ONLY HAD EYES FOR HER FAMOUS FRIED SHRIMP (TEARS). THE ROAD TO LOVE IS LONG AND PERILOUS....

KYOHEI TAKANO—
A STRONG FIGHTER,
"I'M THE KING"

TAKENAGA ODA—
A CARING FEMINIST

RANMARU MORII—
A TRUE LADY'S MAN

YUKINOJO TOYAMA—
A GENTLE, CHEERFUL, AND
VERY EMOTIONAL GUY

SUNAKO NAKAHARA

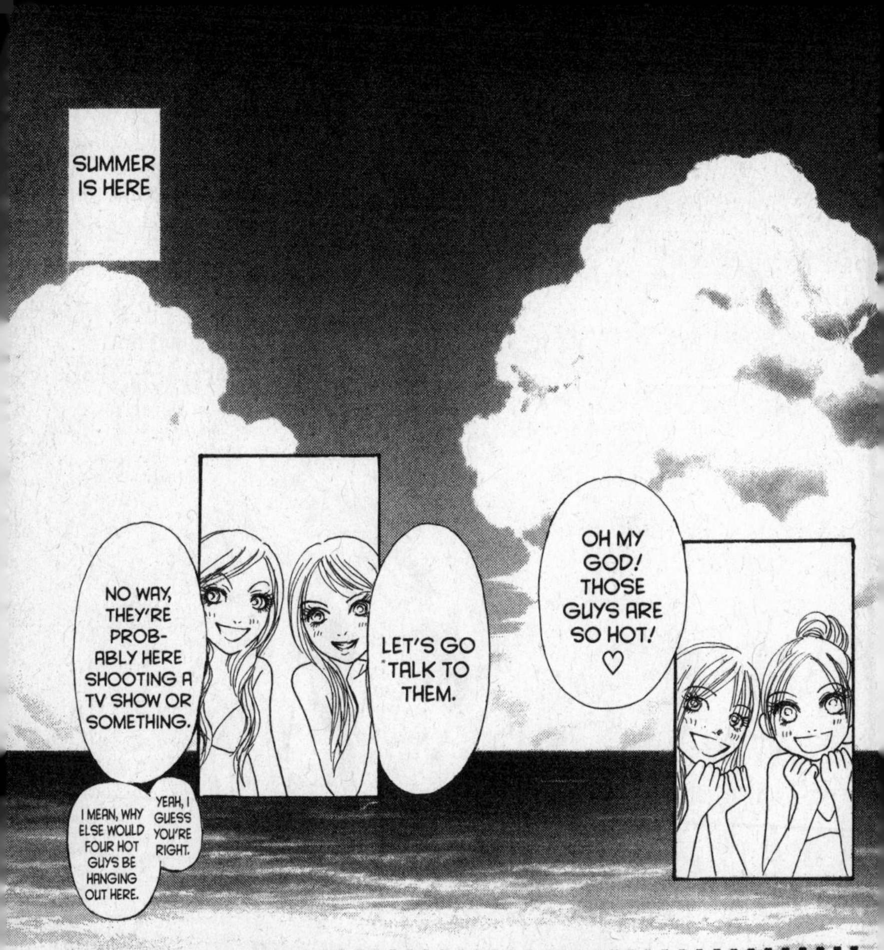
SUMMER IS HERE
OH MY GOD! THOSE GUYS ARE SO HOT! ♡
LET'S GO TALK TO THEM.
NO WAY, THEY'RE PROB-ABLY HERE SHOOTING A TV SHOW OR SOMETHING.
I MEAN, WHY ELSE WOULD FOUR HOT GUYS BE HANGING OUT HERE.
YEAH, I GUESS YOU'RE RIGHT.

BEHIND THE SCENES

I WAS PRETTY DEPRESSED WHEN I WROTE THIS. A LOT OF PEOPLE HELPED CHEER ME UP. (SEE VOLUME 21 ← SHAMELESS PLUG) ONCE I START WORKING ON A STORY, I REALLY HAVE TO MAKE SURE I DON'T GET DEPRESSED, SO I KEEP LOTS OF ITEMS AROUND TO CHEER ME UP. THE SKULLS YOU SEE ON THIS PAGE ARE FROM A ROTEKA CONCERT. THANKS, NEW ROTEKA AND KATARU-KUN. ♥ ♥ ♥ I ALSO HAD A FRIEND, WHO'S A TOTAL STRANGER TO THE MANGA WORLD, HELP ME OUT. (SHE'S SOMEONE I KNOW FROM CONCERTS.) KAI-CHAN LOVES KYO-SAN (THE VOCALIST FROM D'ERLANGER, BUG). IT WAS FUN HAVING YOU AS AN ASSISTANT. ♥ KAI-CHAN'S STARTING TO GET REALLY GOOD AT COLORING.

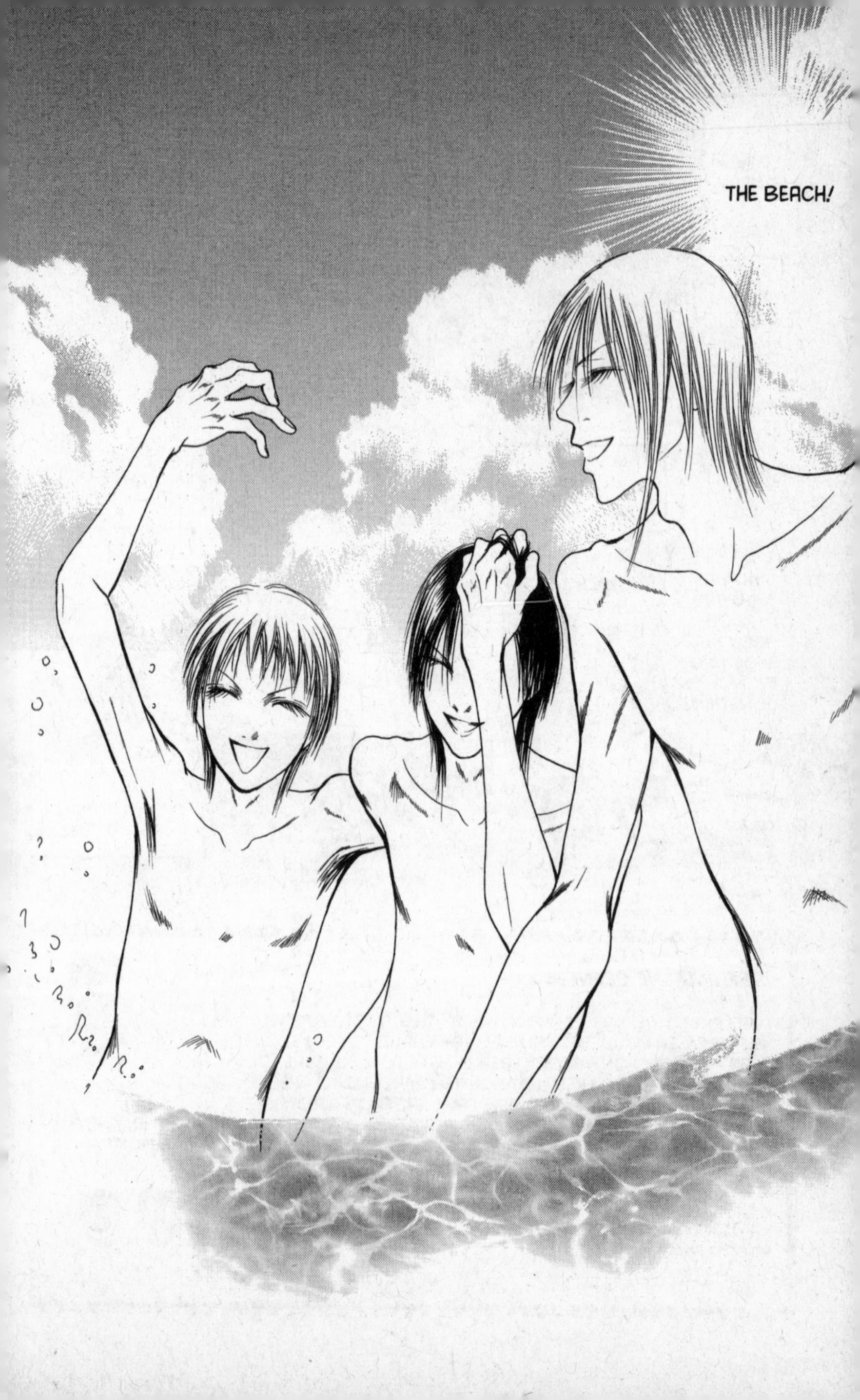
THE BEACH!

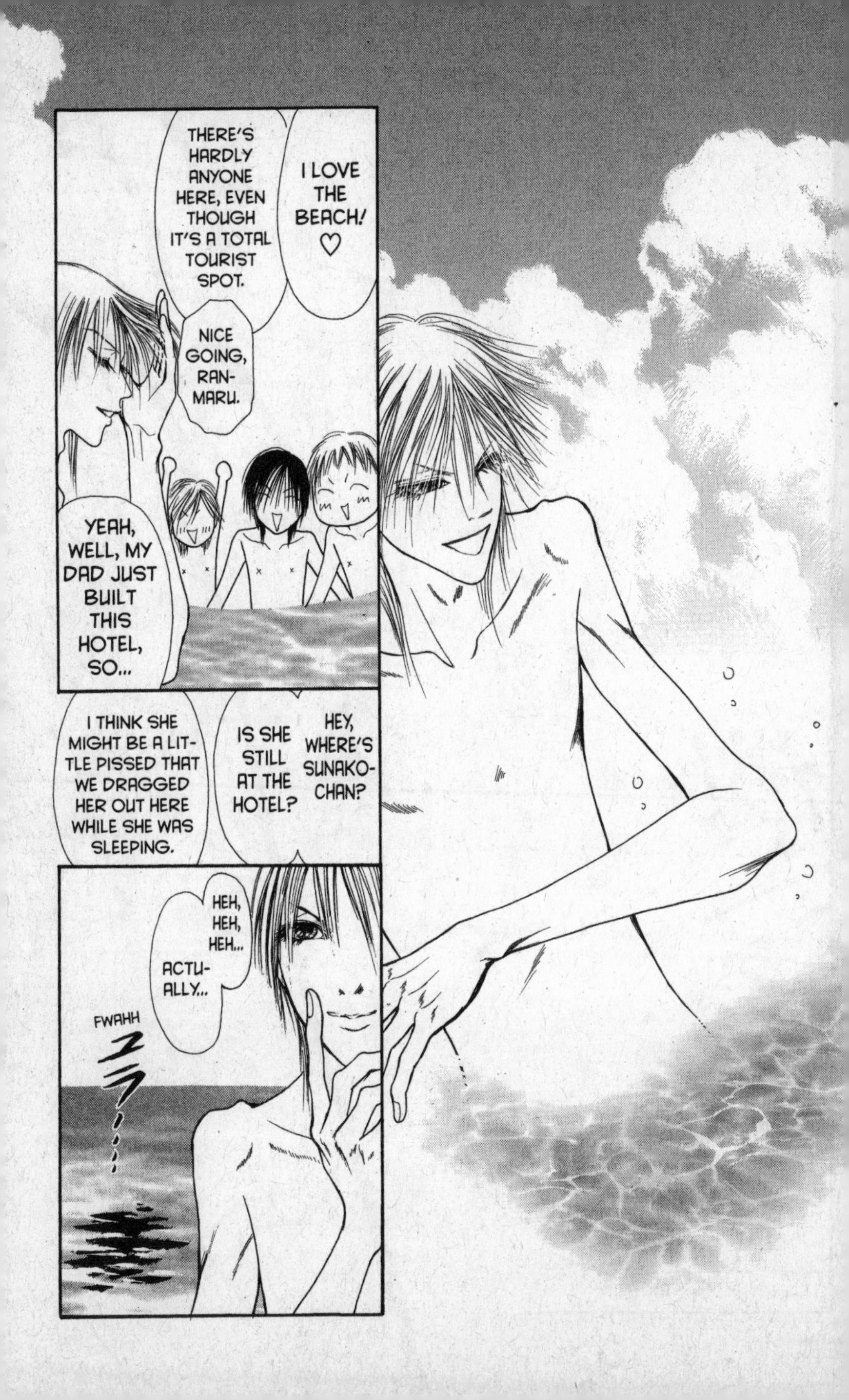
I LOVE THE BEACH! ♡
THERE'S HARDLY ANYONE HERE, EVEN THOUGH IT'S A TOTAL TOURIST SPOT.
NICE GOING, RAN-MARU.
YEAH, WELL, MY DAD JUST BUILT THIS HOTEL, SO...
HEY, WHERE'S SUNAKO-CHAN?
IS SHE STILL AT THE HOTEL?
I THINK SHE MIGHT BE A LIT-TLE PISSED THAT WE DRAGGED HER OUT HERE WHILE SHE WAS SLEEPING.
HEH, HEH, HEH... ACTU-ALLY...
FWAHH

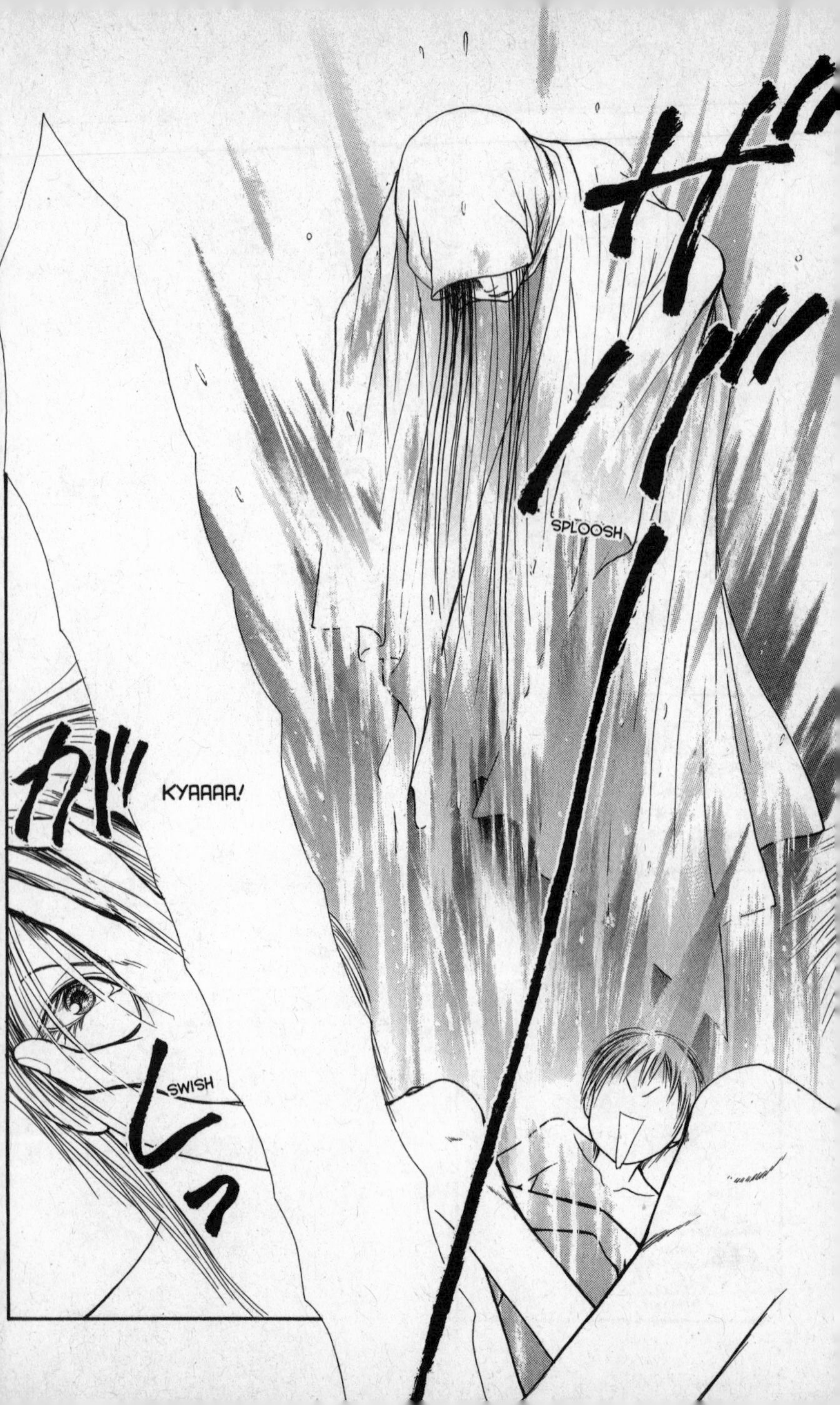
SPLOOSH
KYAAAA!
SWISH

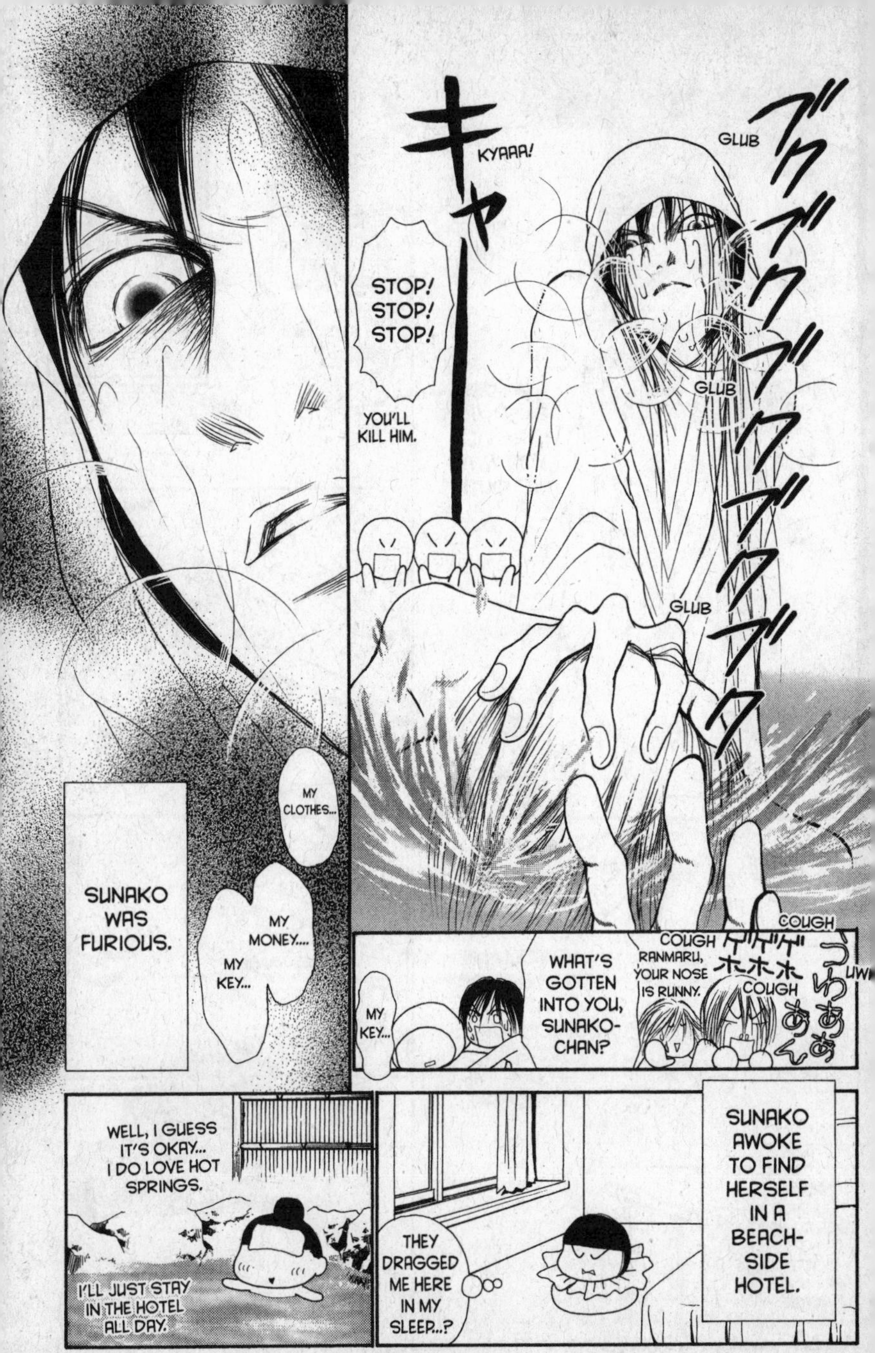

ブクブクブクブクブク
GLUB
キャー
KYAAA!
STOP! STOP! STOP!
YOU'LL KILL HIM.
GLUB
GLUB
うわあああん
UWA
COUGH
ゲホゲホゲホ
COUGH
COUGH
RANMARU, YOUR NOSE IS RUNNY.
WHAT'S GOTTEN INTO YOU, SUNAKO-CHAN?
MY KEY...
MY CLOTHES...
MY MONEY....
MY KEY...
SUNAKO WAS FURIOUS.
SUNAKO AWOKE TO FIND HERSELF IN A BEACH-SIDE HOTEL.
THEY DRAGGED ME HERE IN MY SLEEP...?
WELL, I GUESS IT'S OKAY... I DO LOVE HOT SPRINGS.
I'LL JUST STAY IN THE HOTEL ALL DAY.

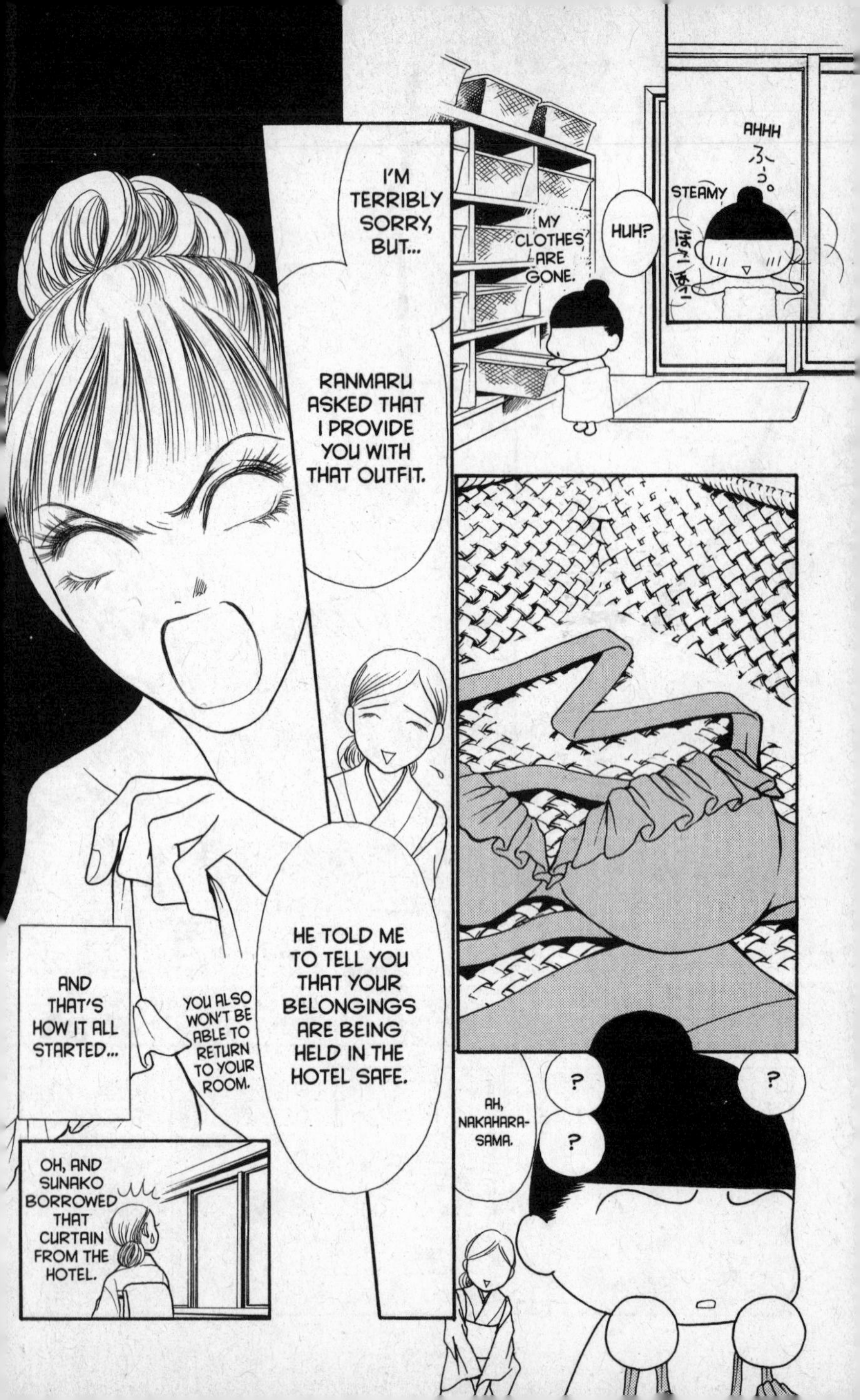
AHHH
ふーっ。
STEAMY
HUH?
MY CLOTHES ARE GONE.
AH, NAKAHARA-SAMA.
?
?
?
I'M TERRIBLY SORRY, BUT...
RANMARU ASKED THAT I PROVIDE YOU WITH THAT OUTFIT.
HE TOLD ME TO TELL YOU THAT YOUR BELONGINGS ARE BEING HELD IN THE HOTEL SAFE.
YOU ALSO WON'T BE ABLE TO RETURN TO YOUR ROOM.
AND THAT'S HOW IT ALL STARTED...
OH, AND SUNAKO BORROWED THAT CURTAIN FROM THE HOTEL.

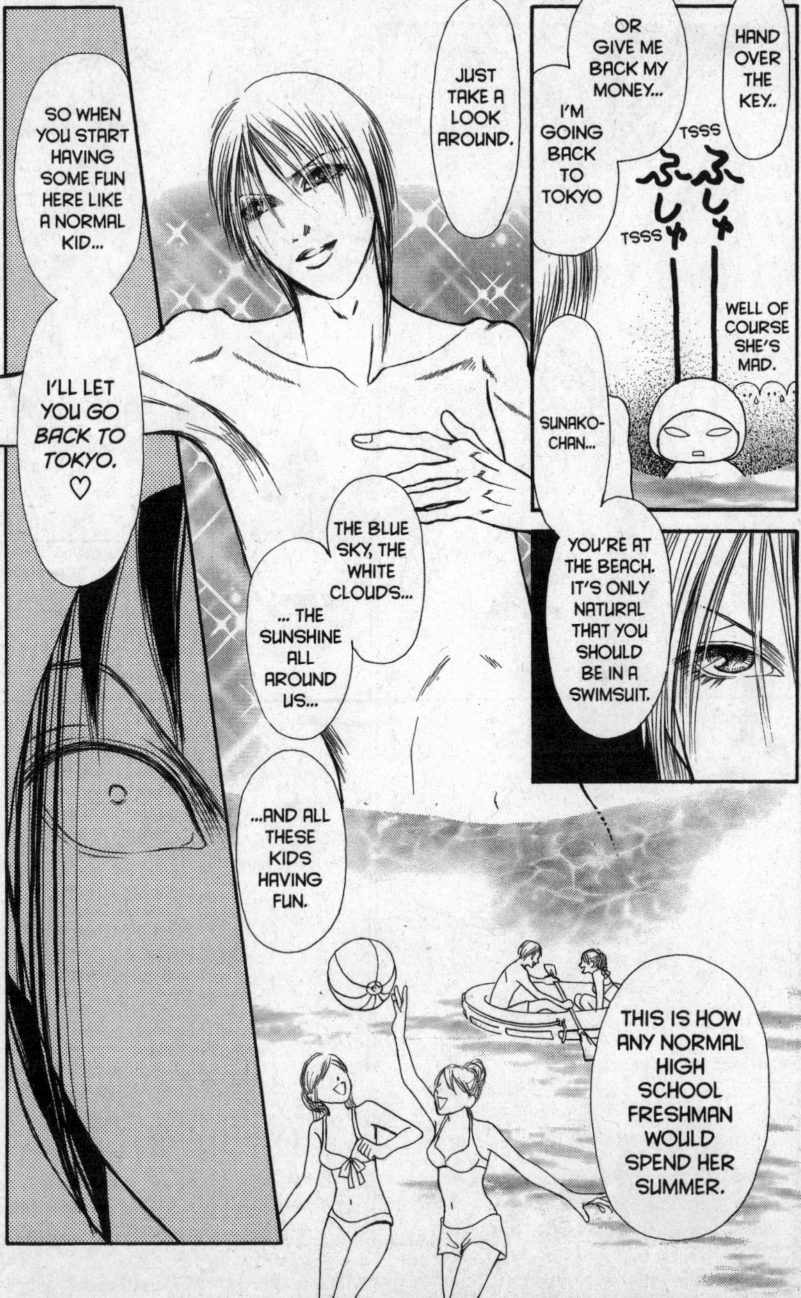
HAND OVER THE KEY..
OR GIVE ME BACK MY MONEY...
I'M GOING BACK TO TOKYO
TSSS
ふしゅ
ふしゅ
TSSS
WELL OF COURSE SHE'S MAD.
SUNAKO-CHAN...
YOU'RE AT THE BEACH. IT'S ONLY NATURAL THAT YOU SHOULD BE IN A SWIMSUIT.
JUST TAKE A LOOK AROUND.
THE BLUE SKY, THE WHITE CLOUDS...
... THE SUNSHINE ALL AROUND US...
...AND ALL THESE KIDS HAVING FUN.
THIS IS HOW ANY NORMAL HIGH SCHOOL FRESHMAN WOULD SPEND HER SUMMER.
SO WHEN YOU START HAVING SOME FUN HERE LIKE A NORMAL KID...
I'LL LET YOU GO BACK TO TOKYO. ♡

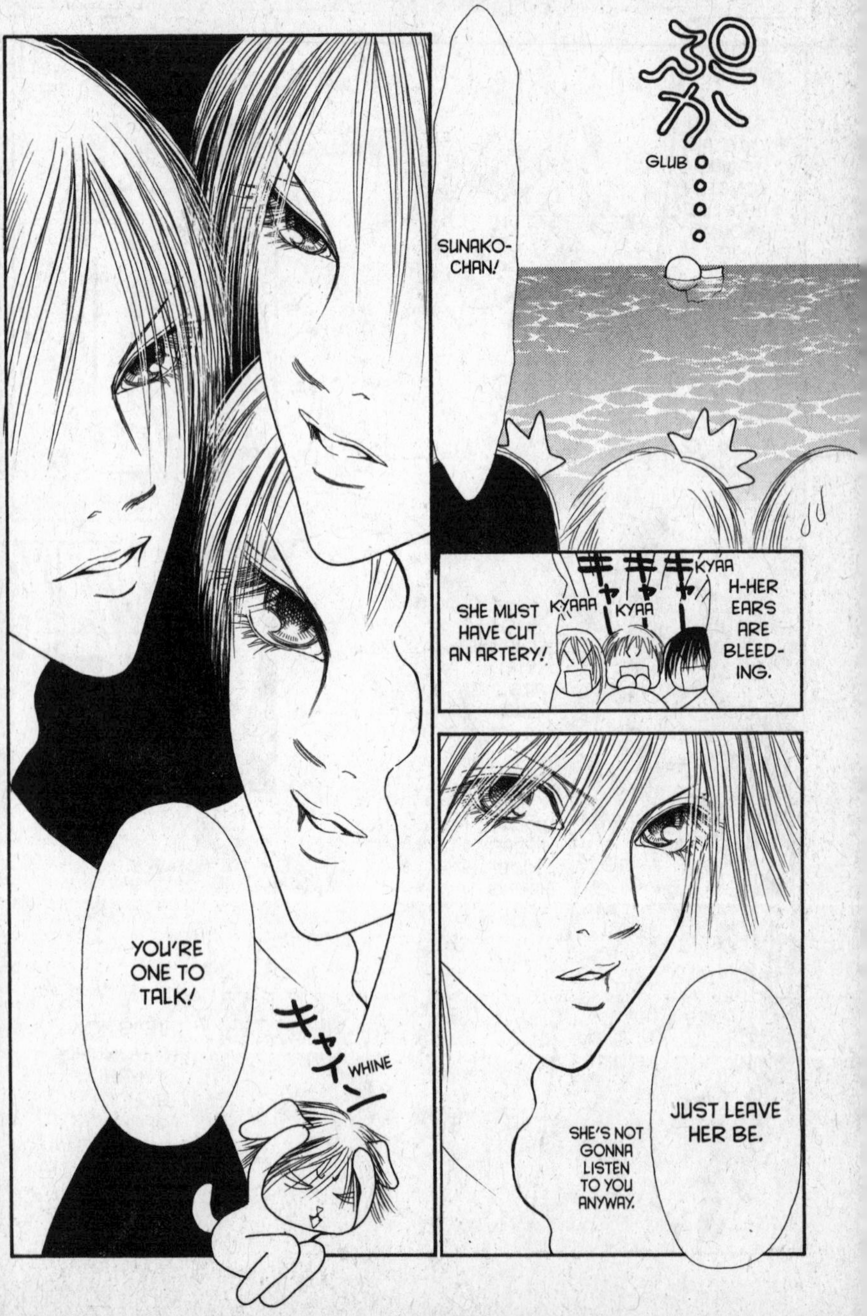
ぷか
GLUB
SUNAKO-CHAN!
H-HER EARS ARE BLEED-ING.
キャ KYAA
キャ KYAA
キャ KYAAA
SHE MUST HAVE CUT AN ARTERY!
JUST LEAVE HER BE.
SHE'S NOT GONNA LISTEN TO YOU ANYWAY.
YOU'RE ONE TO TALK!
キャイン WHINE

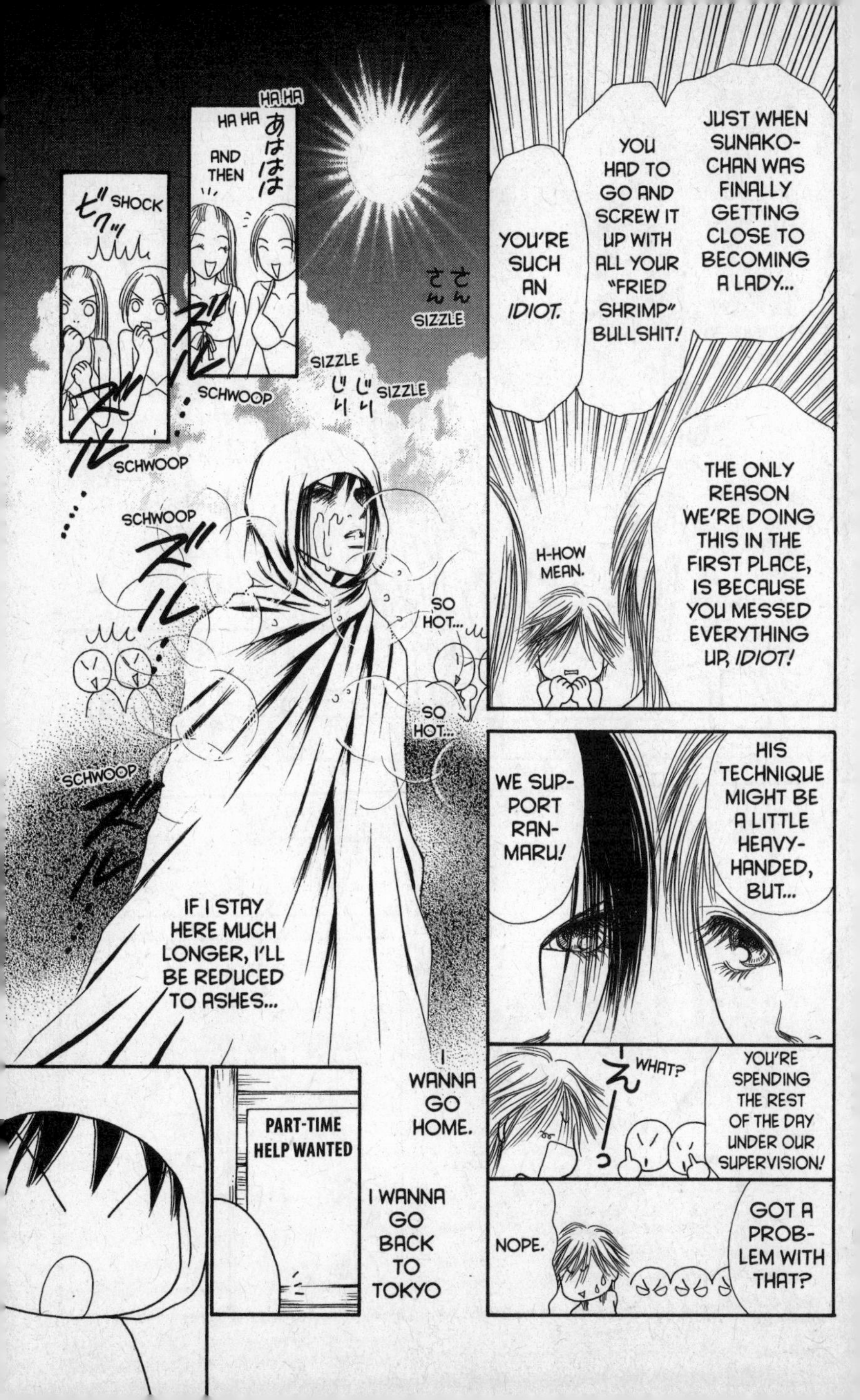
JUST WHEN SUNAKO-CHAN WAS FINALLY GETTING CLOSE TO BECOMING A LADY...
YOU HAD TO GO AND SCREW IT UP WITH ALL YOUR "FRIED SHRIMP" BULLSHIT!
YOU'RE SUCH AN *IDIOT.*
THE ONLY REASON WE'RE DOING THIS IN THE FIRST PLACE, IS BECAUSE YOU MESSED EVERYTHING UP, *IDIOT!*
H-HOW MEAN.
HIS TECHNIQUE MIGHT BE A LITTLE HEAVY-HANDED, BUT...
WE SUPPORT RANMARU!
YOU'RE SPENDING THE REST OF THE DAY UNDER OUR SUPERVISION!
えー!
WHAT?
GOT A PROBLEM WITH THAT?
NOPE.
さんさん
SIZZLE
あははは
HA HA
HA HA
AND THEN
ビクッ
SHOCK
じりじり
SIZZLE
SIZZLE
ズル
SCHWOOP
SCHWOOP
SCHWOOP
SCHWOOP
SO HOT...
SO HOT...
IF I STAY HERE MUCH LONGER, I'LL BE REDUCED TO ASHES...
I WANNA GO HOME.
I WANNA GO BACK TO TOKYO
PART-TIME HELP WANTED

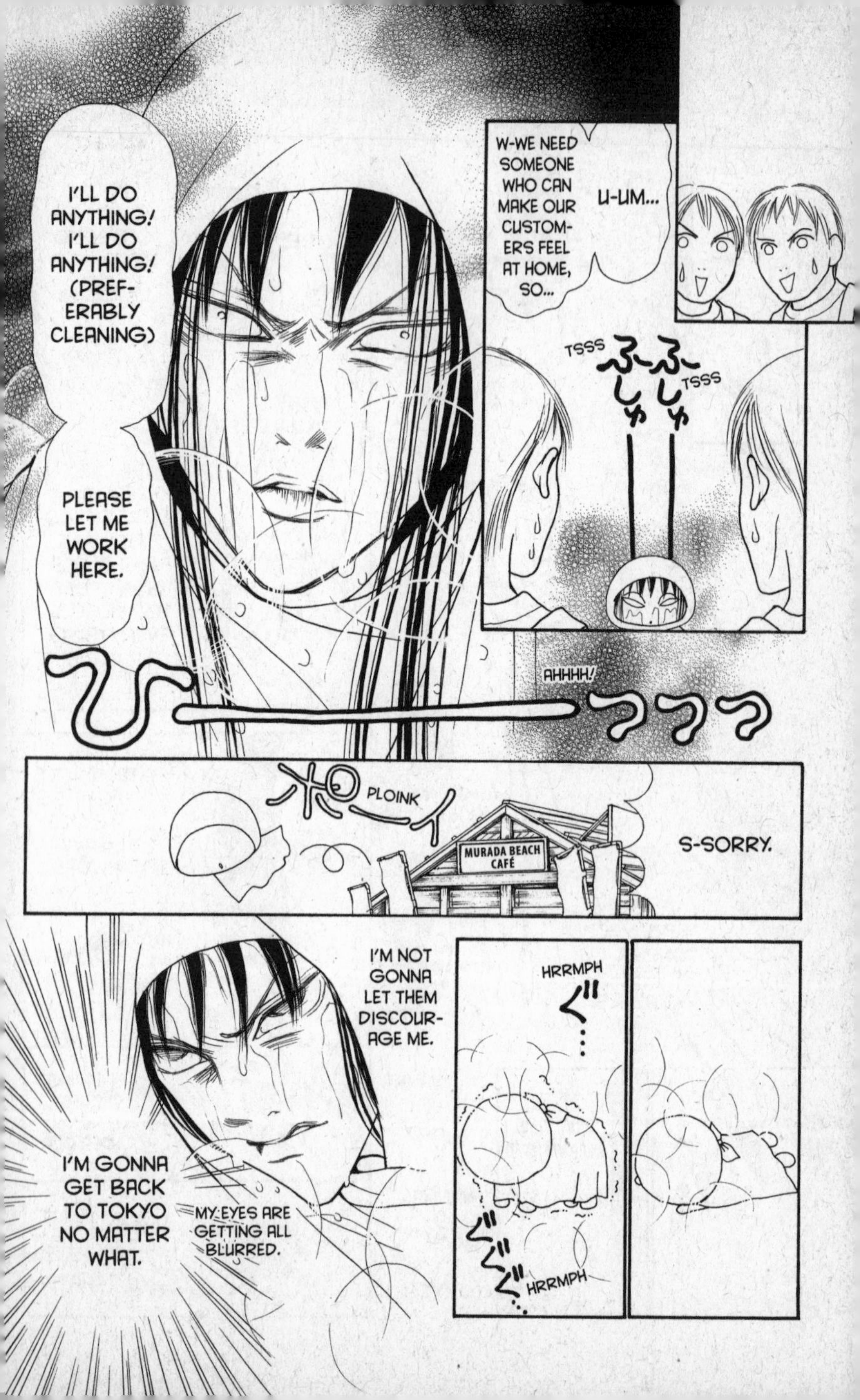
U-UM...
W-WE NEED SOMEONE WHO CAN MAKE OUR CUSTOM-ER'S FEEL AT HOME, SO...
ふーしゅ TSSS
ふーしゅ TSSS
I'LL DO ANYTHING! I'LL DO ANYTHING! (PREF-ERABLY CLEANING)
PLEASE LET ME WORK HERE.
ひーっっっ
AHHHH!
S-SORRY.
ポーイ PLOINK
MURADA BEACH CAFÉ
ぐ… HRRMPH
ぐぐぐ… HRRMPH
I'M NOT GONNA LET THEM DISCOUR-AGE ME.
I'M GONNA GET BACK TO TOKYO NO MATTER WHAT.
MY EYES ARE GETTING ALL BLURRED.

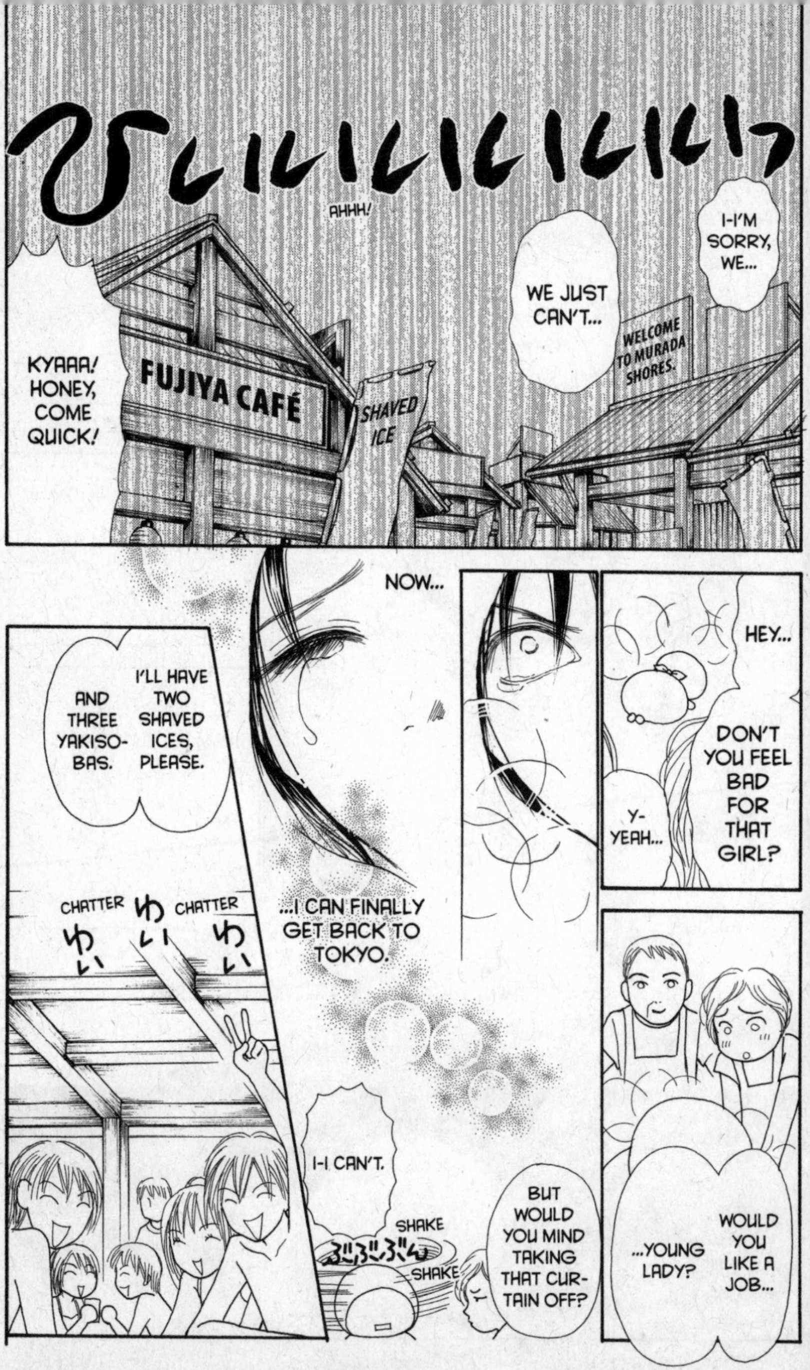
I-I'M SORRY, WE...
WE JUST CAN'T...
WELCOME TO MURADA SHORES.
AHHH!
SHAVED ICE
FUJIYA CAFÉ
KYAAA! HONEY, COME QUICK!
HEY...
DON'T YOU FEEL BAD FOR THAT GIRL?
Y-YEAH...
NOW...
...I CAN FINALLY GET BACK TO TOKYO.
I'LL HAVE TWO SHAVED ICES, PLEASE.
AND THREE YAKISOBAS.
CHATTER
CHATTER
WOULD YOU LIKE A JOB...
...YOUNG LADY?
BUT WOULD YOU MIND TAKING THAT CUR- TAIN OFF?
I-I CAN'T.
SHAKE
SHAKE

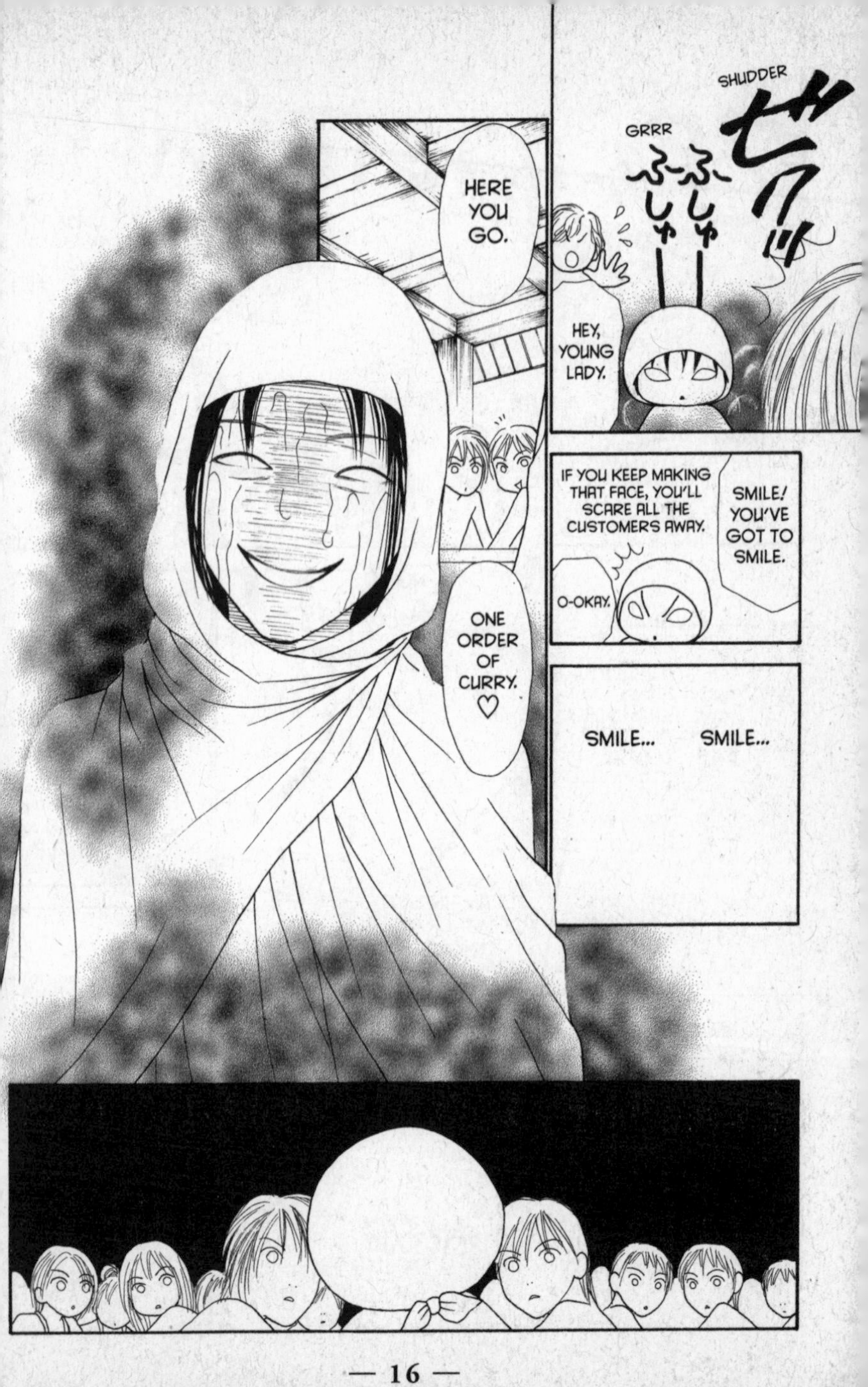
SHUDDER
GRRR
HEY, YOUNG LADY.
SMILE! YOU'VE GOT TO SMILE.
IF YOU KEEP MAKING THAT FACE, YOU'LL SCARE ALL THE CUSTOMERS AWAY.
O-OKAY.
SMILE... SMILE...
HERE YOU GO.
ONE ORDER OF CURRY. ♡

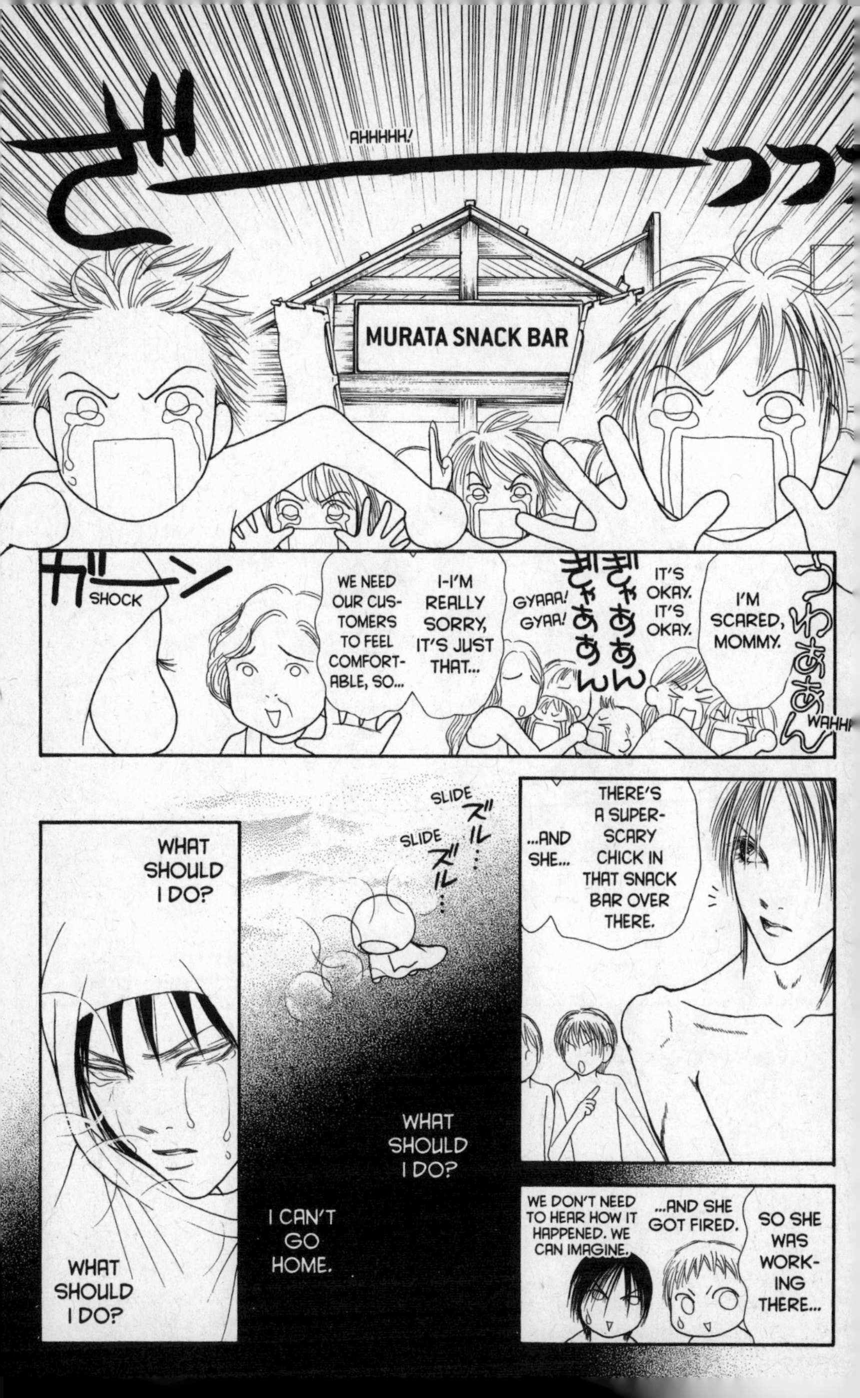
AHHHHH!
MURATA SNACK BAR
WAHHH
I'M SCARED, MOMMY.
IT'S OKAY. IT'S OKAY.
GYAAA! GYAA!
I-I'M REALLY SORRY, IT'S JUST THAT...
WE NEED OUR CUSTOMERS TO FEEL COMFORTABLE, SO...
ガーン
SHOCK
THERE'S A SUPER-SCARY CHICK IN THAT SNACK BAR OVER THERE.
...AND SHE...
SO SHE WAS WORKING THERE...
...AND SHE GOT FIRED.
WE DON'T NEED TO HEAR HOW IT HAPPENED. WE CAN IMAGINE.
ズル...
SLIDE
ズル...
SLIDE
WHAT SHOULD I DO?
I CAN'T GO HOME.
WHAT SHOULD I DO?
WHAT SHOULD I DO?

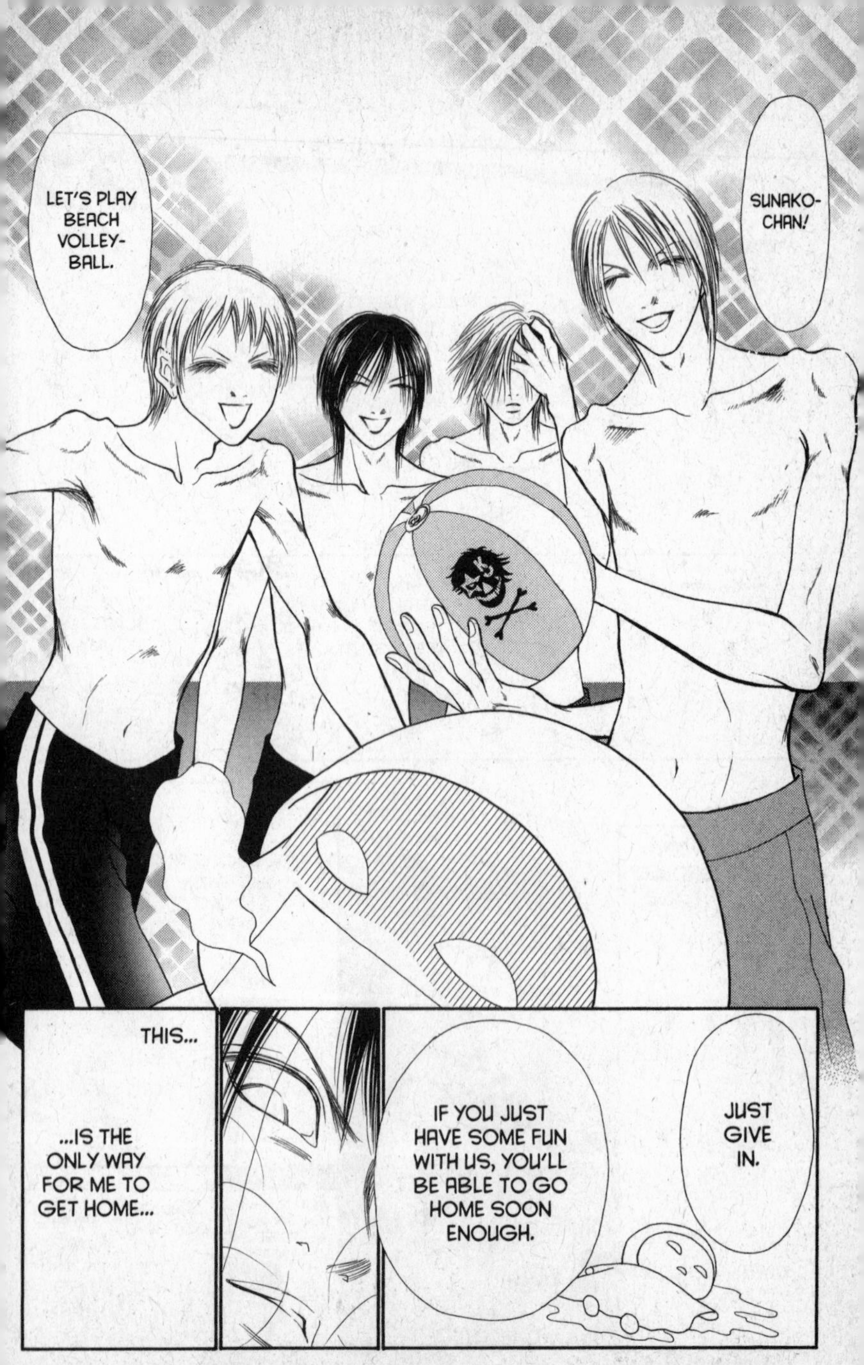
SUNAKO-CHAN!
LET'S PLAY BEACH VOLLEY-BALL.
JUST GIVE IN.
IF YOU JUST HAVE SOME FUN WITH US, YOU'LL BE ABLE TO GO HOME SOON ENOUGH.
THIS...
...IS THE ONLY WAY FOR ME TO GET HOME...

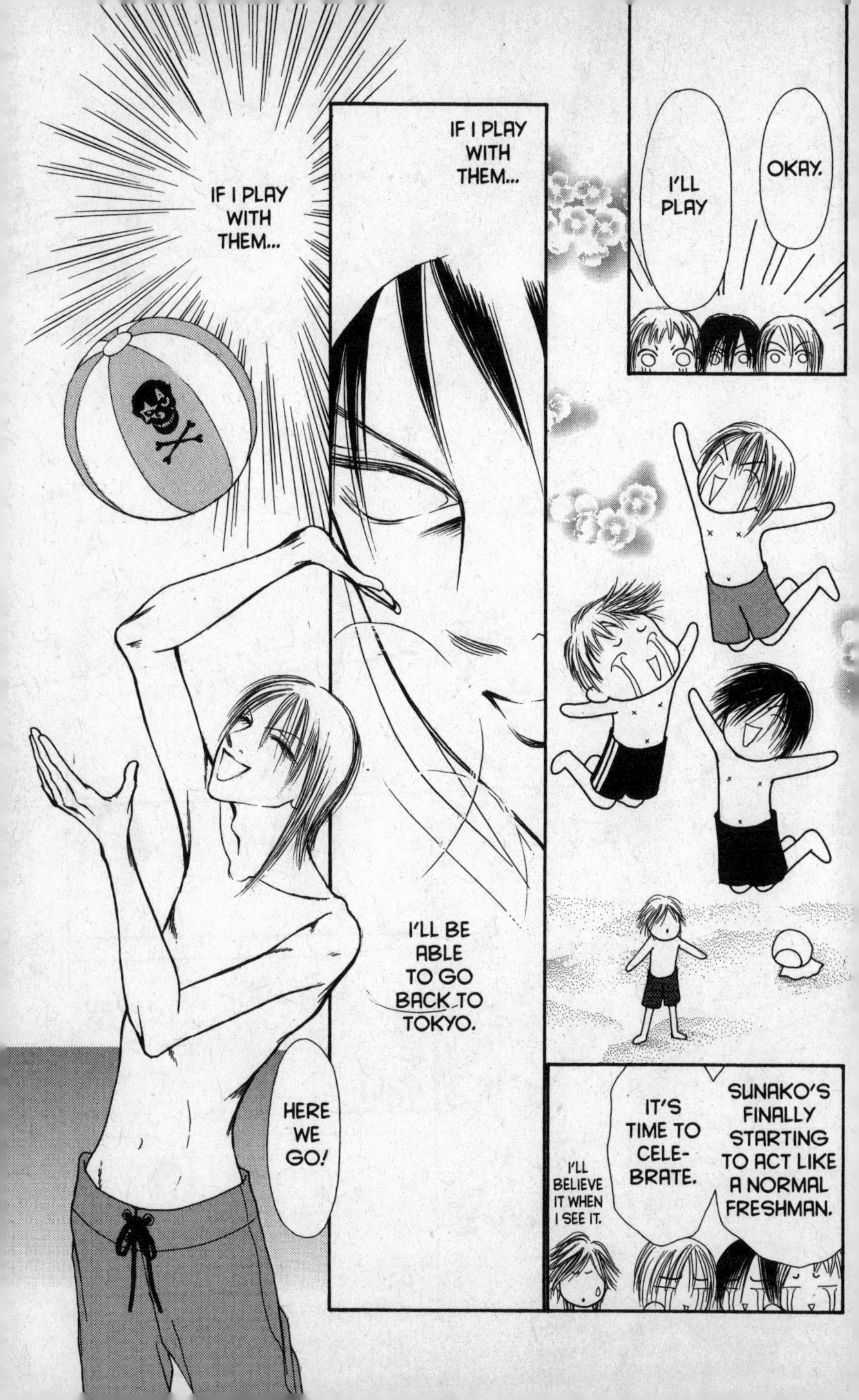
OKAY.
I'LL PLAY
SUNAKO'S FINALLY STARTING TO ACT LIKE A NORMAL FRESHMAN.
IT'S TIME TO CELE-BRATE.
I'LL BELIEVE IT WHEN I SEE IT.
IF I PLAY WITH THEM...
I'LL BE ABLE TO GO BACK TO TOKYO.
IF I PLAY WITH THEM...
HERE WE GO!

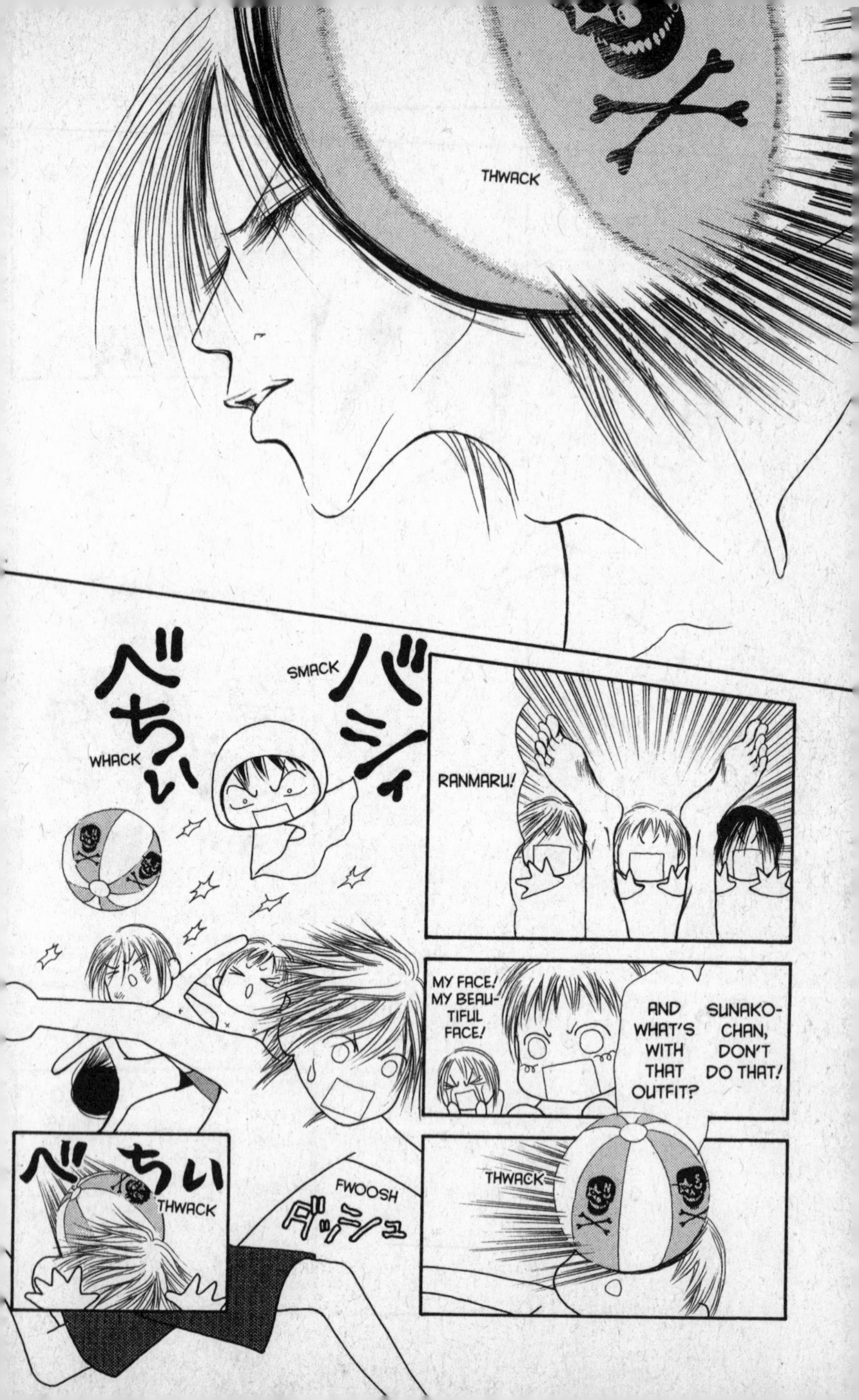
THWACK
RANMARU!
SUNAKO-CHAN, DON'T DO THAT!
AND WHAT'S WITH THAT OUTFIT?
MY FACE! MY BEAU-TIFUL FACE!
THWACK
バシィ
SMACK
べちぃ
WHACK
ダッシュ
FWOOSH
べちぃ
THWACK

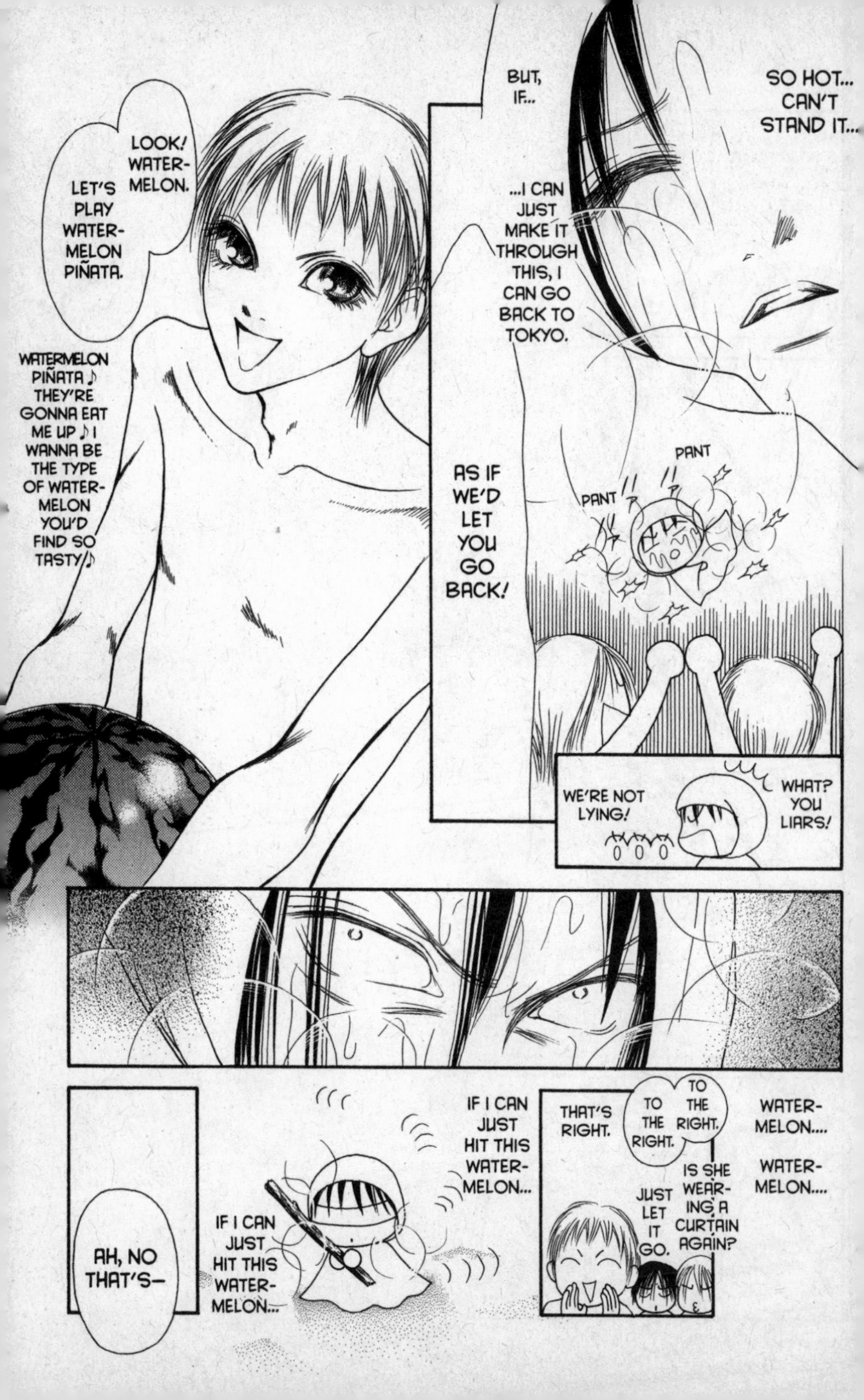
SO HOT... CAN'T STAND IT...
BUT, IF...
...I CAN JUST MAKE IT THROUGH THIS, I CAN GO BACK TO TOKYO.
PANT
PANT
AS IF WE'D LET YOU GO BACK!
WHAT? YOU LIARS!
WE'RE NOT LYING!
LOOK! WATER-MELON.
LET'S PLAY WATER-MELON PIÑATA.
WATERMELON PIÑATA♪ THEY'RE GONNA EAT ME UP♪I WANNA BE THE TYPE OF WATER-MELON YOU'D FIND SO TASTY♪
WATER-MELON....
WATER-MELON....
TO THE RIGHT.
TO THE RIGHT.
THAT'S RIGHT.
IS SHE WEAR-ING A CURTAIN AGAIN?
JUST LET IT GO.
IF I CAN JUST HIT THIS WATER-MELON...
IF I CAN JUST HIT THIS WATER-MELON...
AH, NO THAT'S—

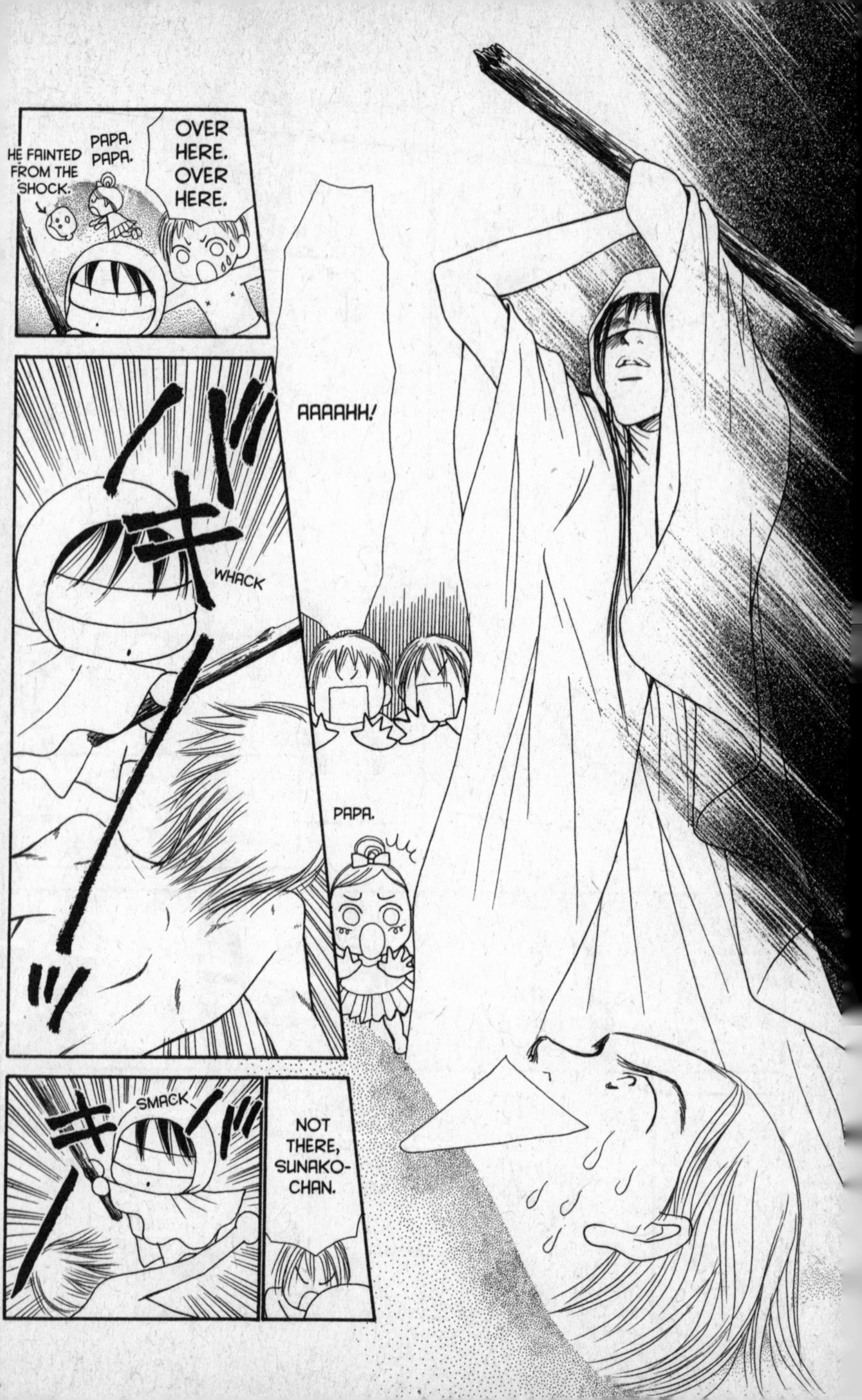
AAAAAH!
PAPA.
OVER HERE. OVER HERE.
PAPA. PAPA.
HE FAINTED FROM THE SHOCK.
WHACK
NOT THERE, SUNAKO-CHAN.
SMACK

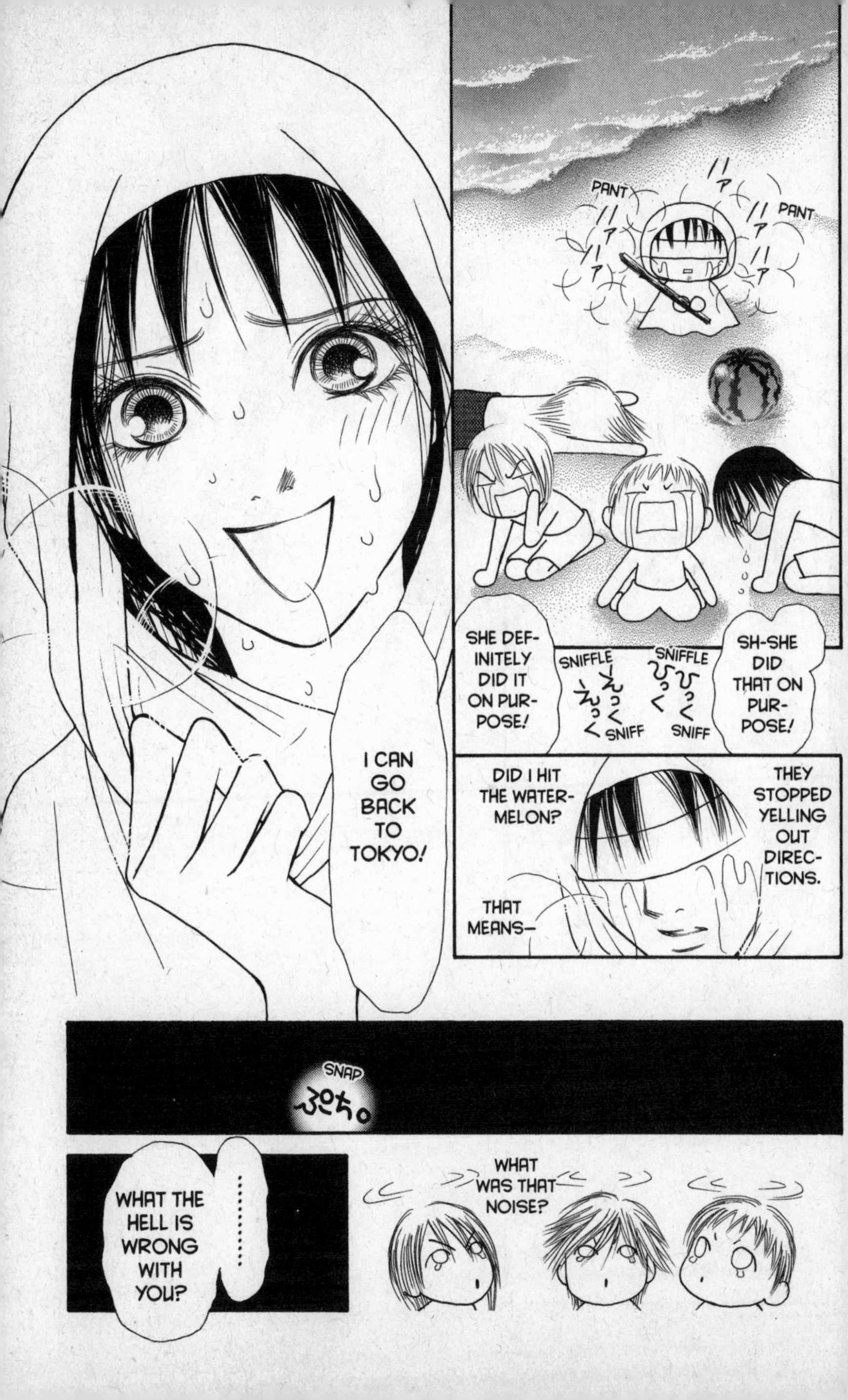
PANT
ハァ ハァ
PANT
ハァ ハァ
SH-SHE DID THAT ON PUR-POSE!
SNIFFLE ひっく ひっく SNIFF
SNIFFLE えっく えっく SNIFF
SHE DEF-INITELY DID IT ON PUR-POSE!
THEY STOPPED YELLING OUT DIREC-TIONS.
DID I HIT THE WATER-MELON?
THAT MEANS—
I CAN GO BACK TO TOKYO!
SNAP
ぷち。
WHAT WAS THAT NOISE?
......
WHAT THE HELL IS WRONG WITH YOU?

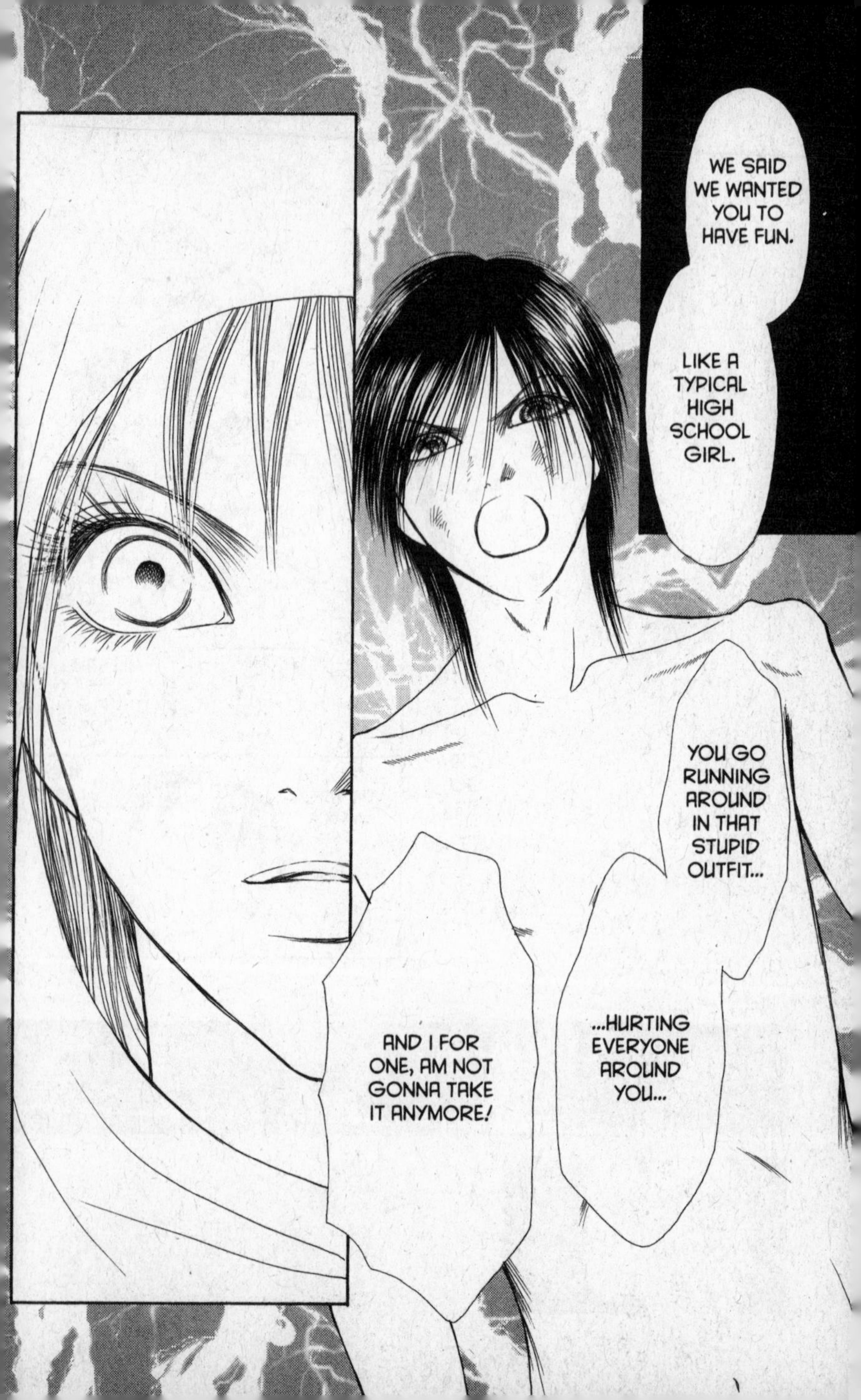
WE SAID WE WANTED YOU TO HAVE FUN.
LIKE A TYPICAL HIGH SCHOOL GIRL.
YOU GO RUNNING AROUND IN THAT STUPID OUTFIT...
...HURTING EVERYONE AROUND YOU...
AND I FOR ONE, AM NOT GONNA TAKE IT ANYMORE!

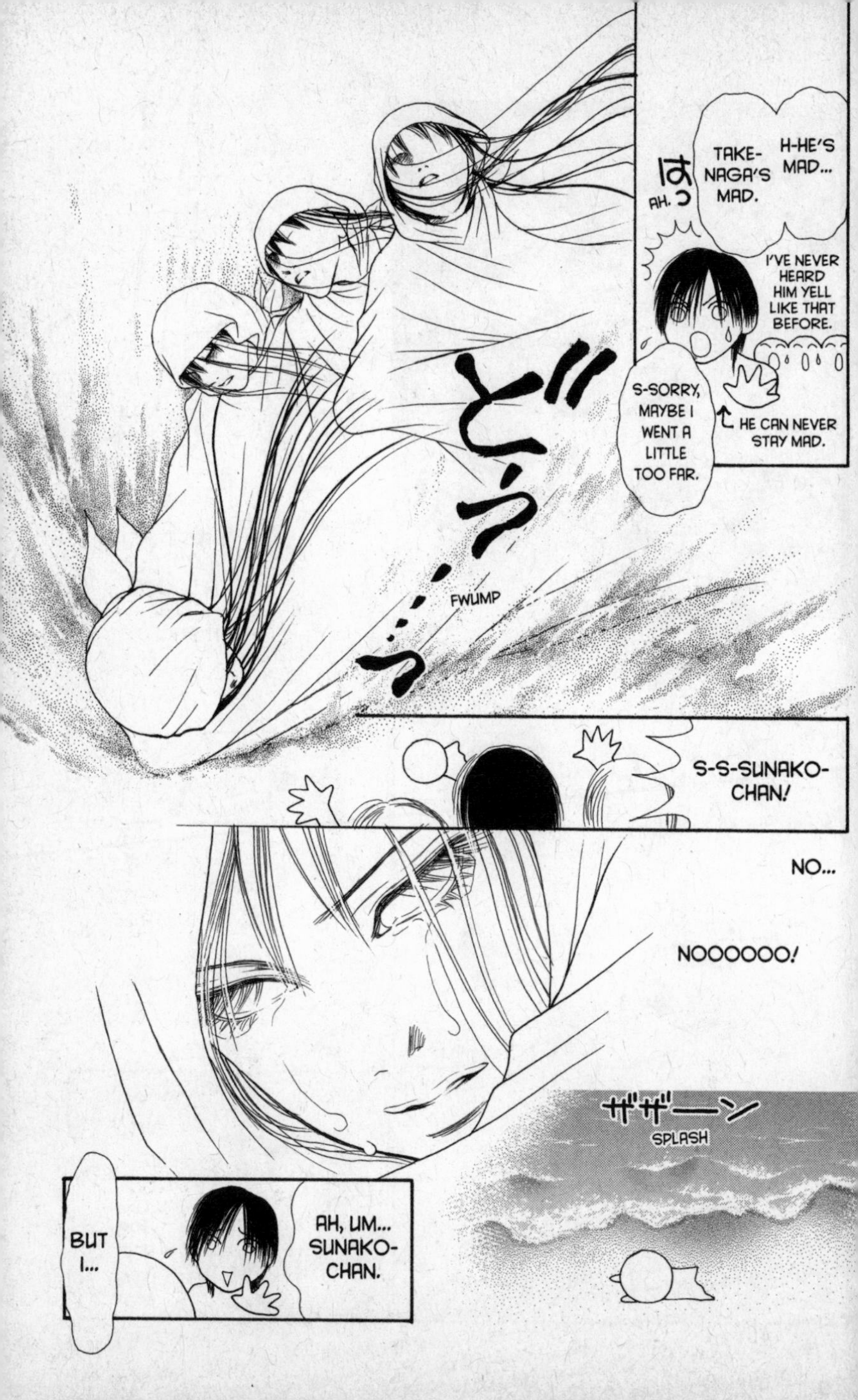

H-HE'S MAD... TAKE-NAGA'S MAD.
はっ
AH.
I'VE NEVER HEARD HIM YELL LIKE THAT BEFORE.
S-SORRY, MAYBE I WENT A LITTLE TOO FAR.
HE CAN NEVER STAY MAD.
どう…っ
FWUMP
S-S-SUNAKO-CHAN!
NO...
NOOOOOO!
ザザーン
SPLASH
AH, UM... SUNAKO-CHAN.
BUT I...

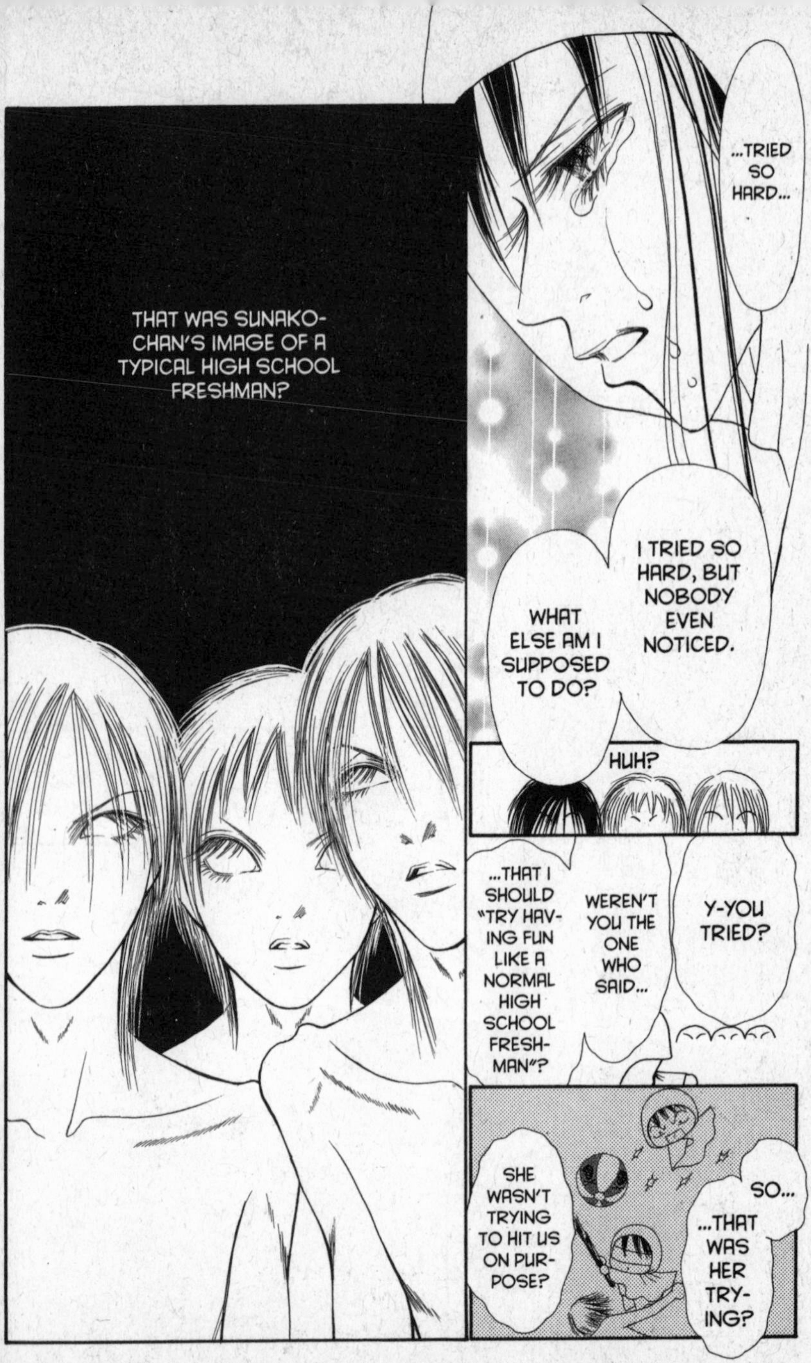
...TRIED SO HARD...
I TRIED SO HARD, BUT NOBODY EVEN NOTICED.
WHAT ELSE AM I SUPPOSED TO DO?
HUH?
Y-YOU TRIED?
WEREN'T YOU THE ONE WHO SAID...
...THAT I SHOULD "TRY HAVING FUN LIKE A NORMAL HIGH SCHOOL FRESHMAN"?
SO...
...THAT WAS HER TRYING?
SHE WASN'T TRYING TO HIT US ON PURPOSE?
THAT WAS SUNAKO-CHAN'S IMAGE OF A TYPICAL HIGH SCHOOL FRESHMAN?

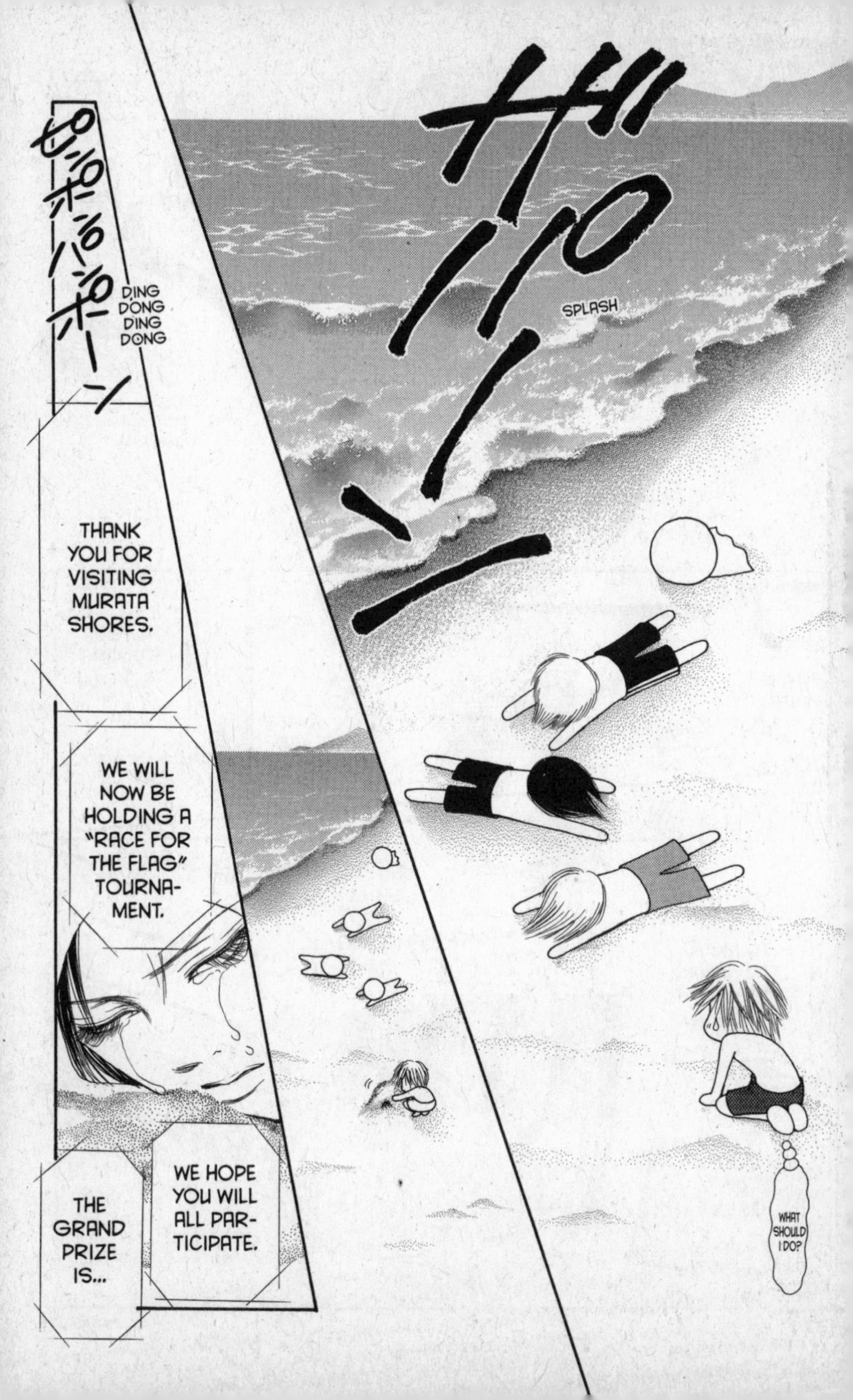
ザパーン
SPLASH
WHAT SHOULD I DO?
ピンポンパンポーン
DING DONG DING DONG
THANK YOU FOR VISITING MURATA SHORES.
WE WILL NOW BE HOLDING A "RACE FOR THE FLAG" TOURNAMENT.
WE HOPE YOU WILL ALL PARTICIPATE.
THE GRAND PRIZE IS...

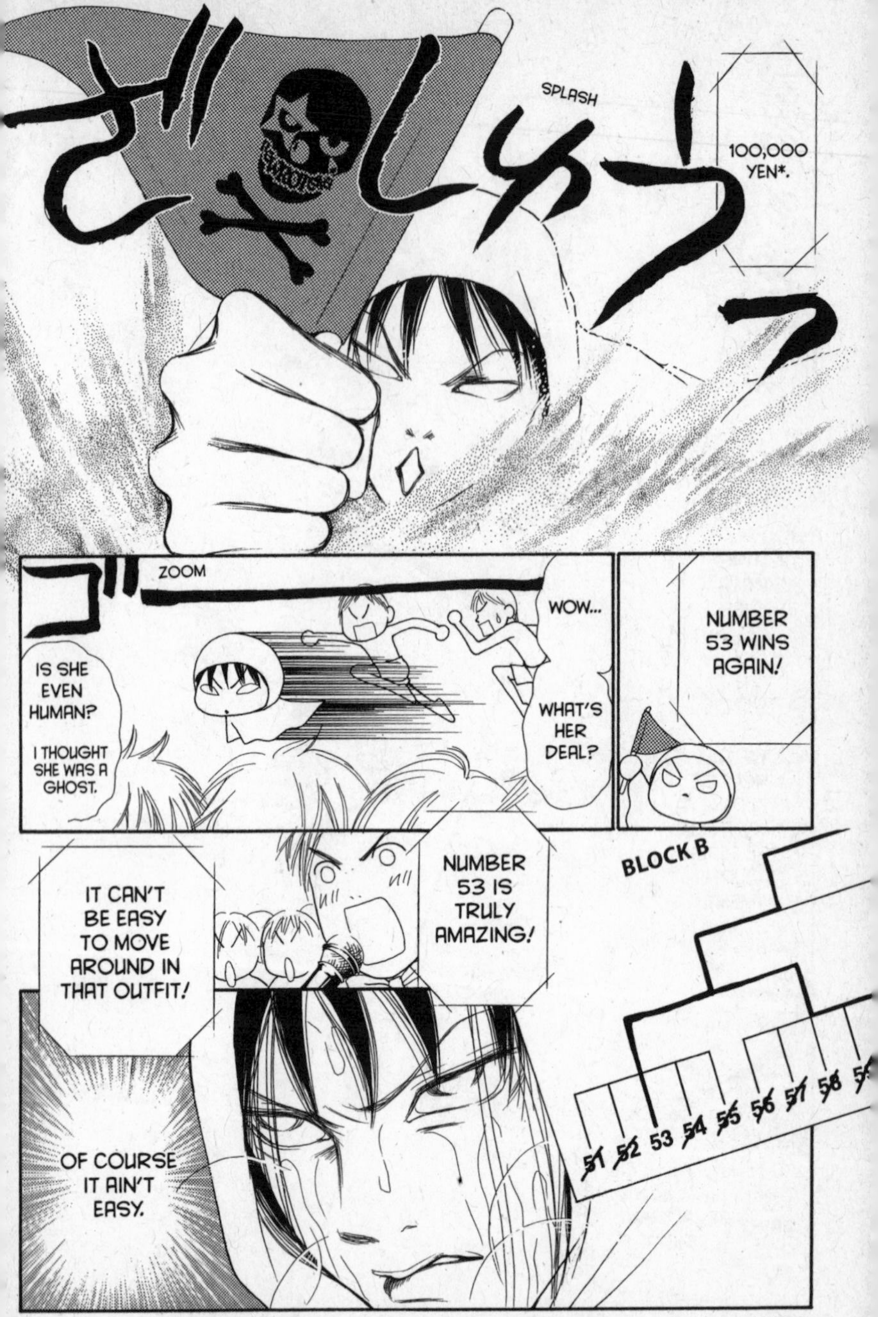
100,000 YEN*.
SPLASH
NUMBER 53 WINS AGAIN!
WOW...
WHAT'S HER DEAL?
ZOOM
IS SHE EVEN HUMAN?
I THOUGHT SHE WAS A GHOST.
BLOCK B
51 52 53 54 55 56 57 58
NUMBER 53 IS TRULY AMAZING!
IT CAN'T BE EASY TO MOVE AROUND IN THAT OUTFIT!
OF COURSE IT AIN'T EASY.

*$1000

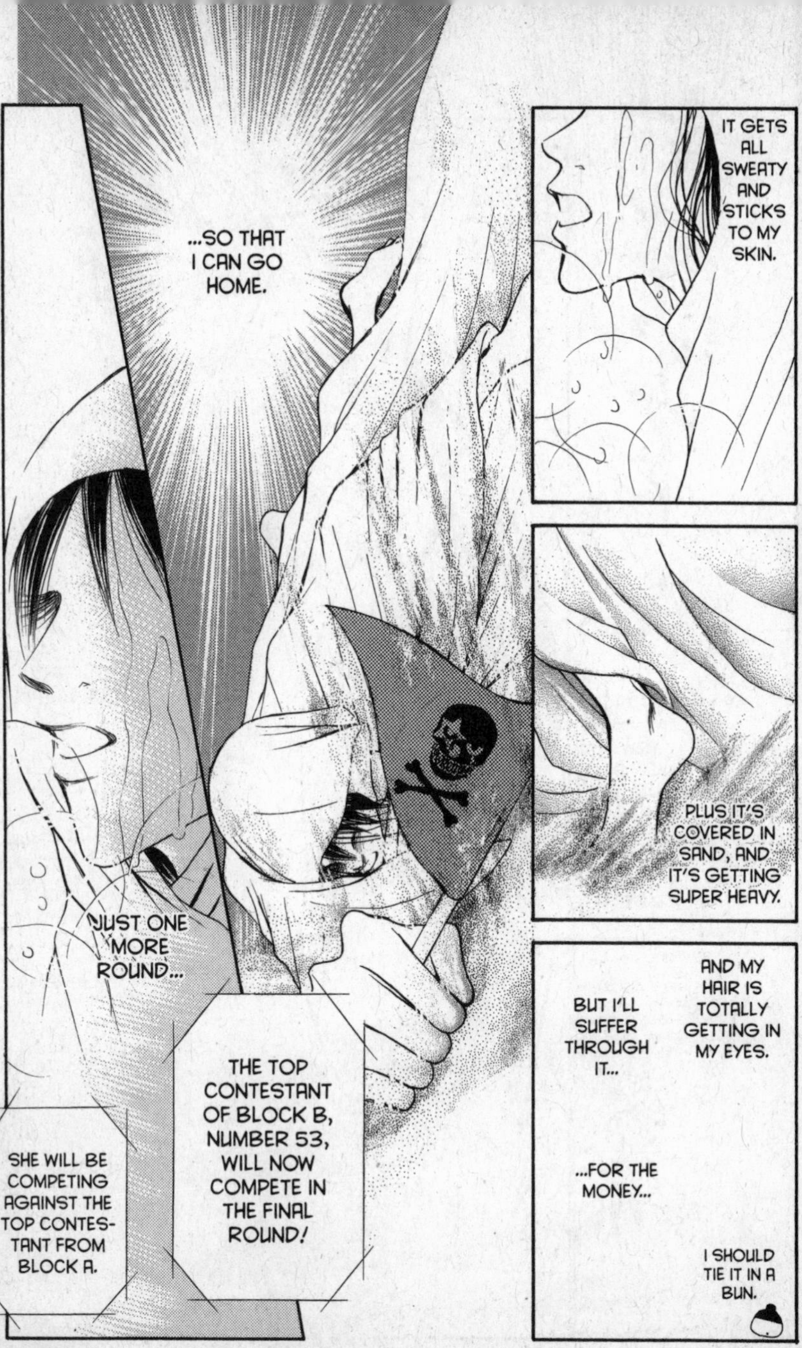
IT GETS ALL SWEATY AND STICKS TO MY SKIN.
PLUS IT'S COVERED IN SAND, AND IT'S GETTING SUPER HEAVY.
AND MY HAIR IS TOTALLY GETTING IN MY EYES.
BUT I'LL SUFFER THROUGH IT...
...FOR THE MONEY...
I SHOULD TIE IT IN A BUN.
...SO THAT I CAN GO HOME.
JUST ONE MORE ROUND...
THE TOP CONTESTANT OF BLOCK B, NUMBER 53, WILL NOW COMPETE IN THE FINAL ROUND!
SHE WILL BE COMPETING AGAINST THE TOP CONTES-TANT FROM BLOCK A.

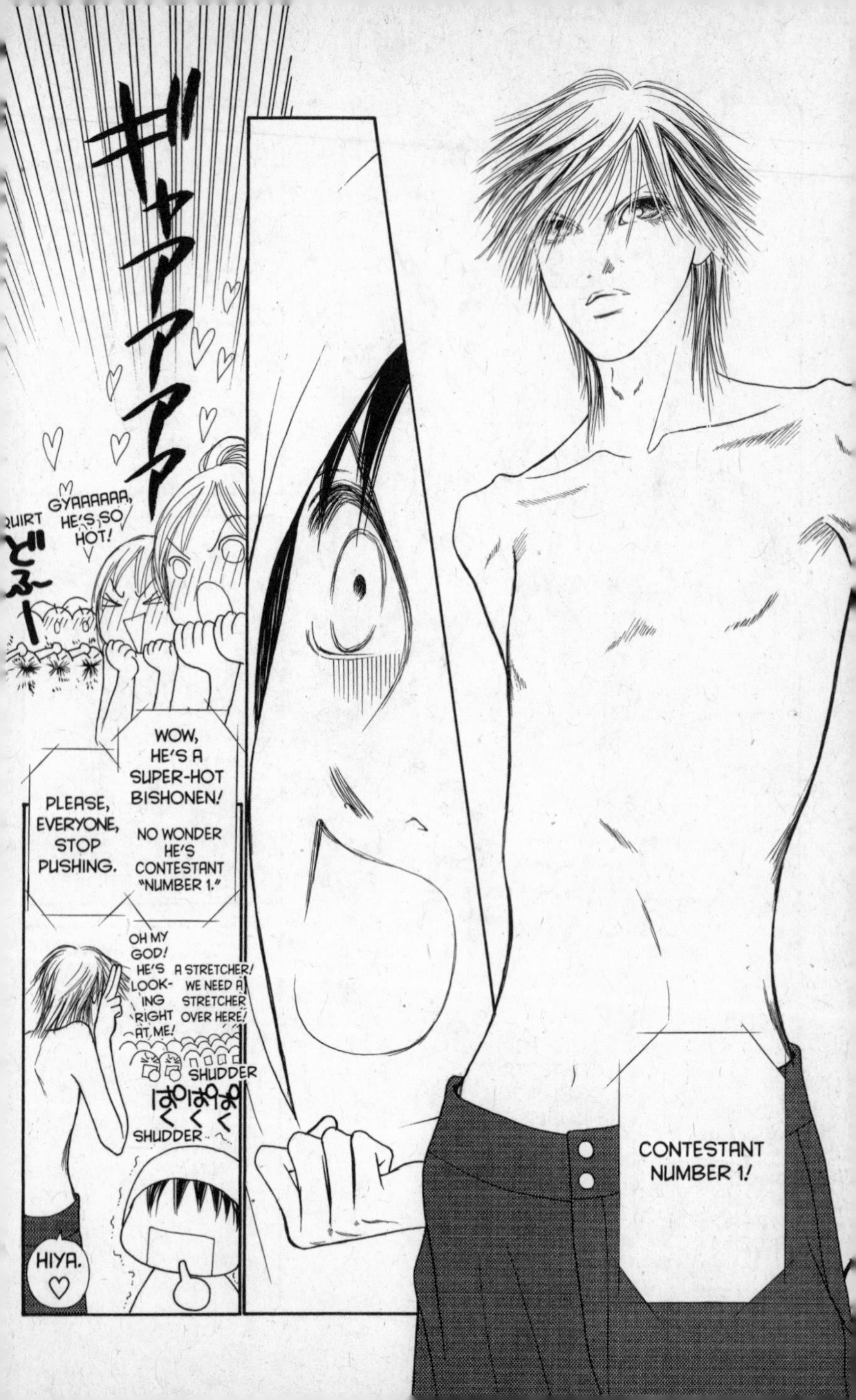
CONTESTANT NUMBER 1!
ギャアアアア
GYAAAAAAA, HE'S SO HOT!
QUIRT
どふー
WOW, HE'S A SUPER-HOT BISHONEN!
NO WONDER HE'S CONTESTANT "NUMBER 1."
PLEASE, EVERYONE, STOP PUSHING.
OH MY GOD! HE'S LOOK-ING RIGHT AT ME!
A STRETCHER! WE NEED A STRETCHER OVER HERE!
SHUDDER
ぱくぱくぱく
SHUDDER
HIYA. ♡

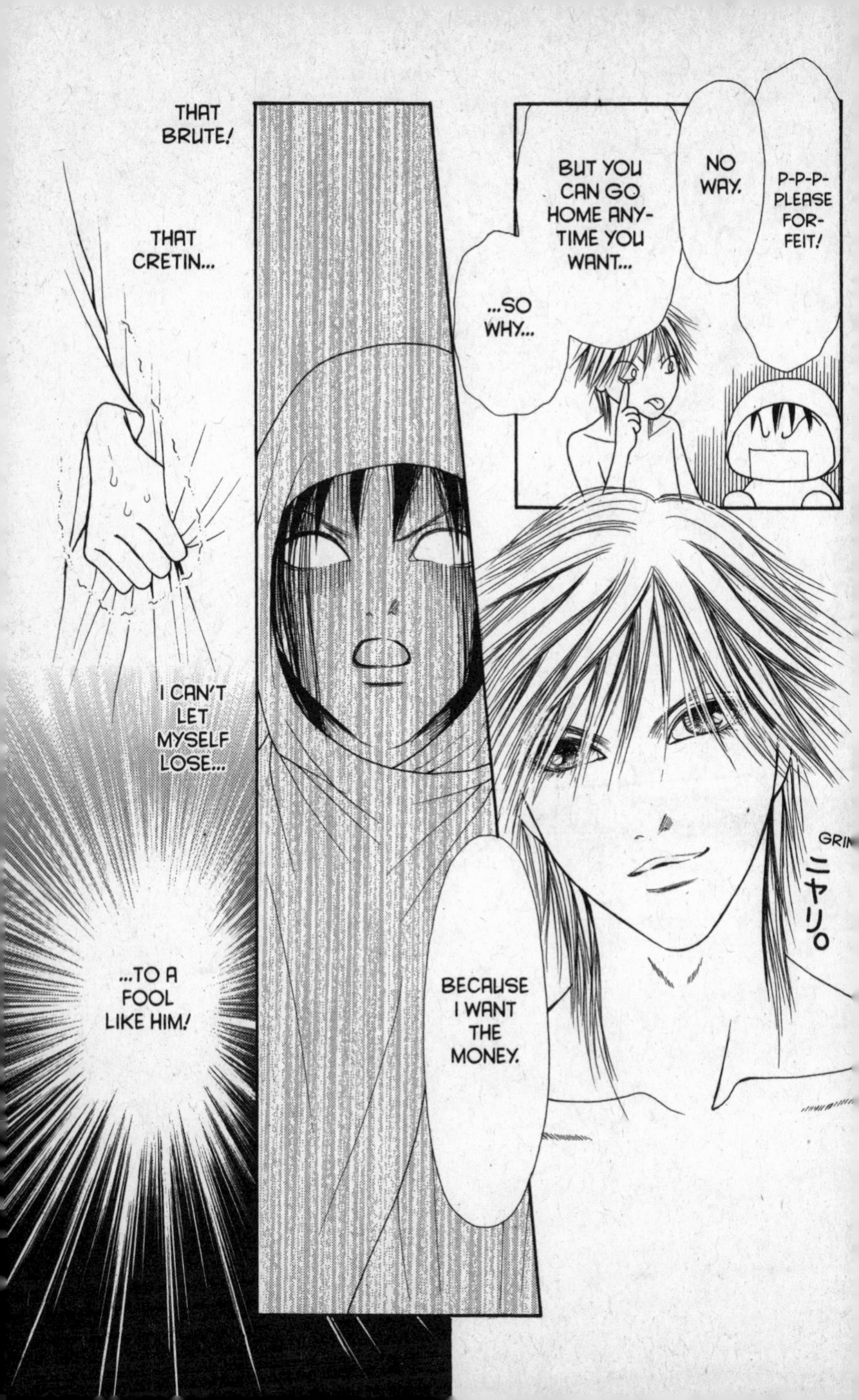
P-P-P-PLEASE FOR-FEIT!
NO WAY.
BUT YOU CAN GO HOME ANY-TIME YOU WANT...
...SO WHY...
GRI
ニヤリ。
BECAUSE I WANT THE MONEY.
THAT BRUTE!
THAT CRETIN...
I CAN'T LET MYSELF LOSE...
...TO A FOOL LIKE HIM!

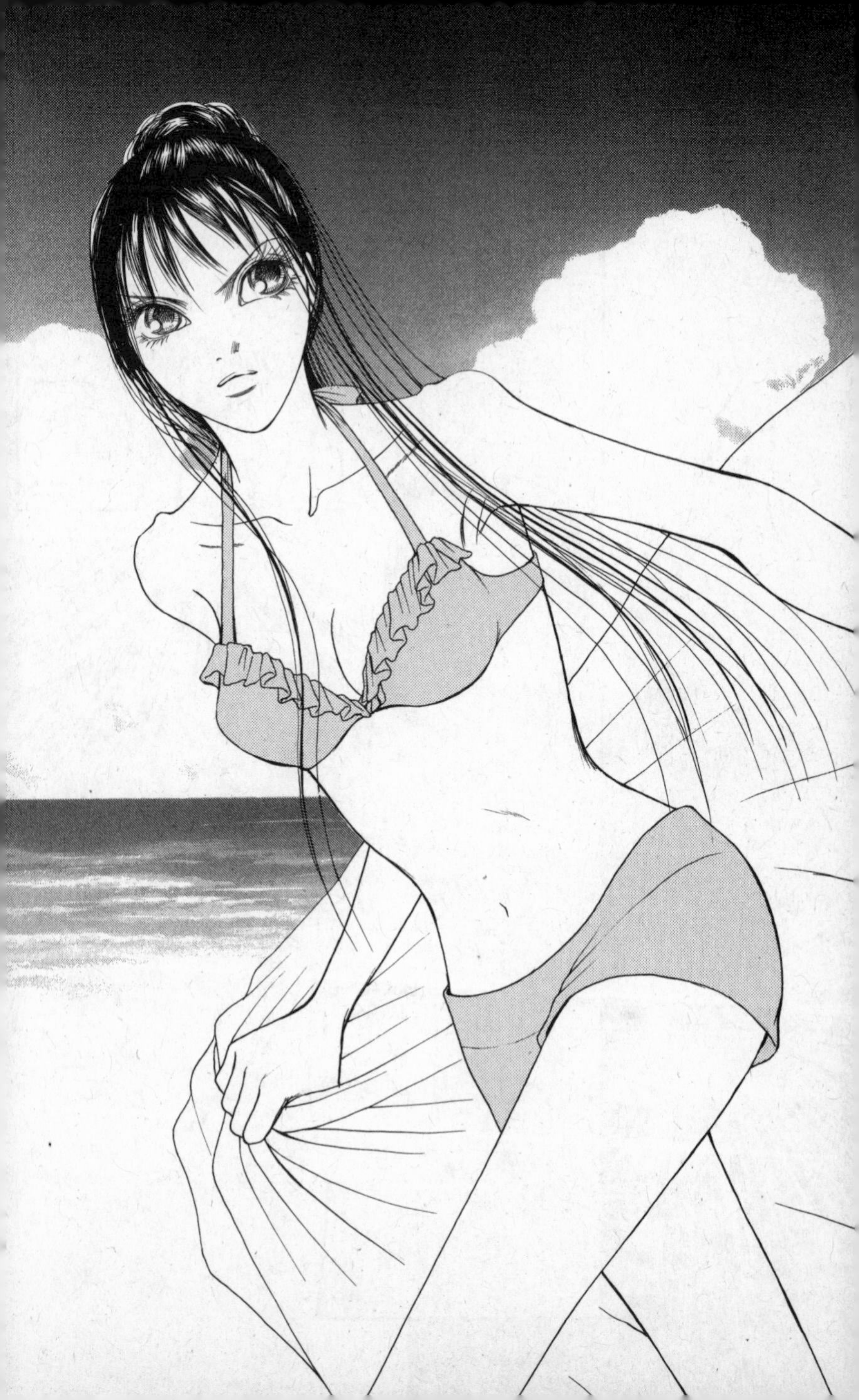

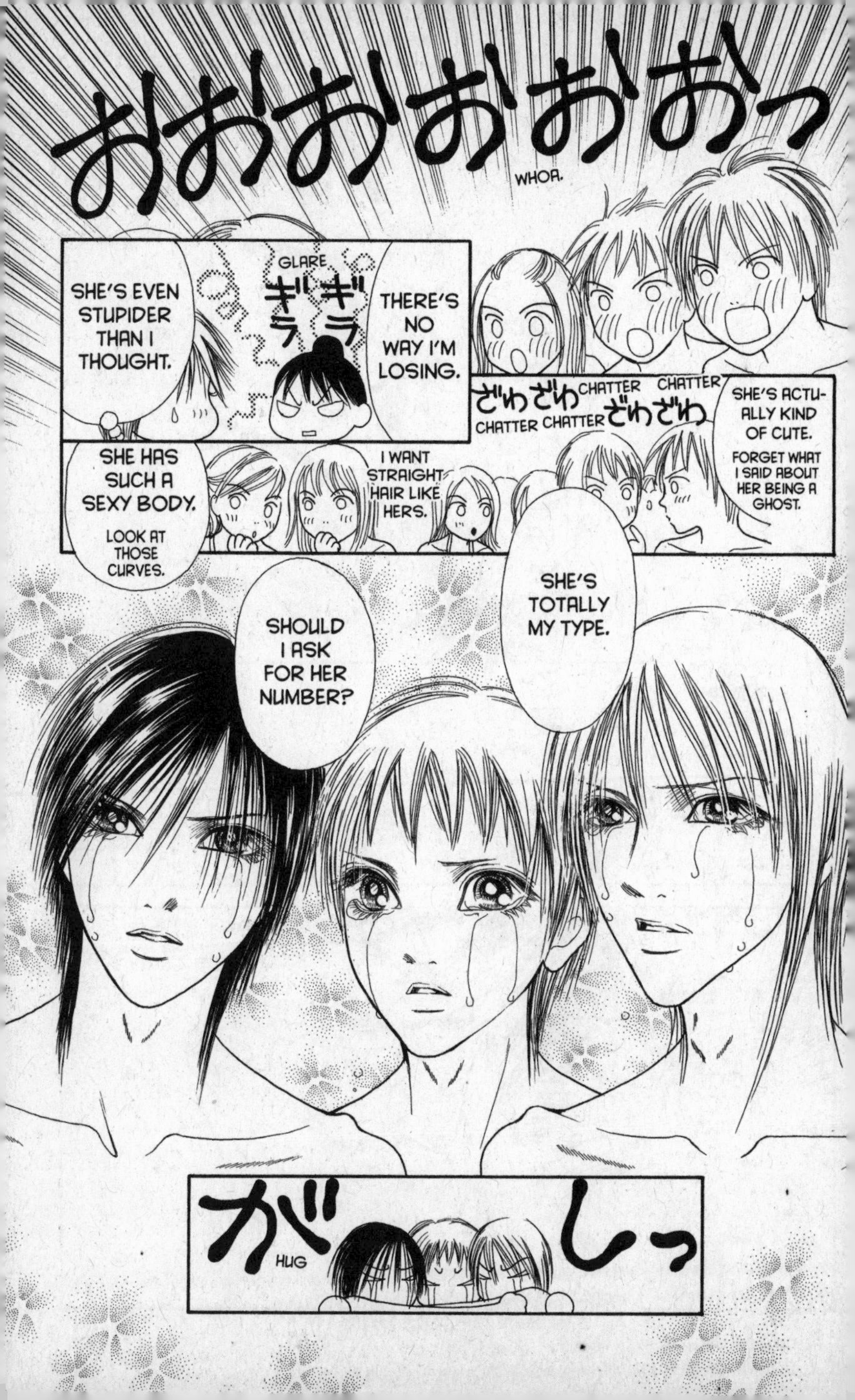
おおおおおっ
WHOA.
ざわざわ CHATTER CHATTER
ざわざわ CHATTER CHATTER
SHE'S ACTUALLY KIND OF CUTE.
FORGET WHAT I SAID ABOUT HER BEING A GHOST.
THERE'S NO WAY I'M LOSING.
ギラギラ GLARE
SHE'S EVEN STUPIDER THAN I THOUGHT.
I WANT STRAIGHT HAIR LIKE HERS.
SHE HAS SUCH A SEXY BODY.
LOOK AT THOSE CURVES.
SHE'S TOTALLY MY TYPE.
SHOULD I ASK FOR HER NUMBER?
がしっ HUG

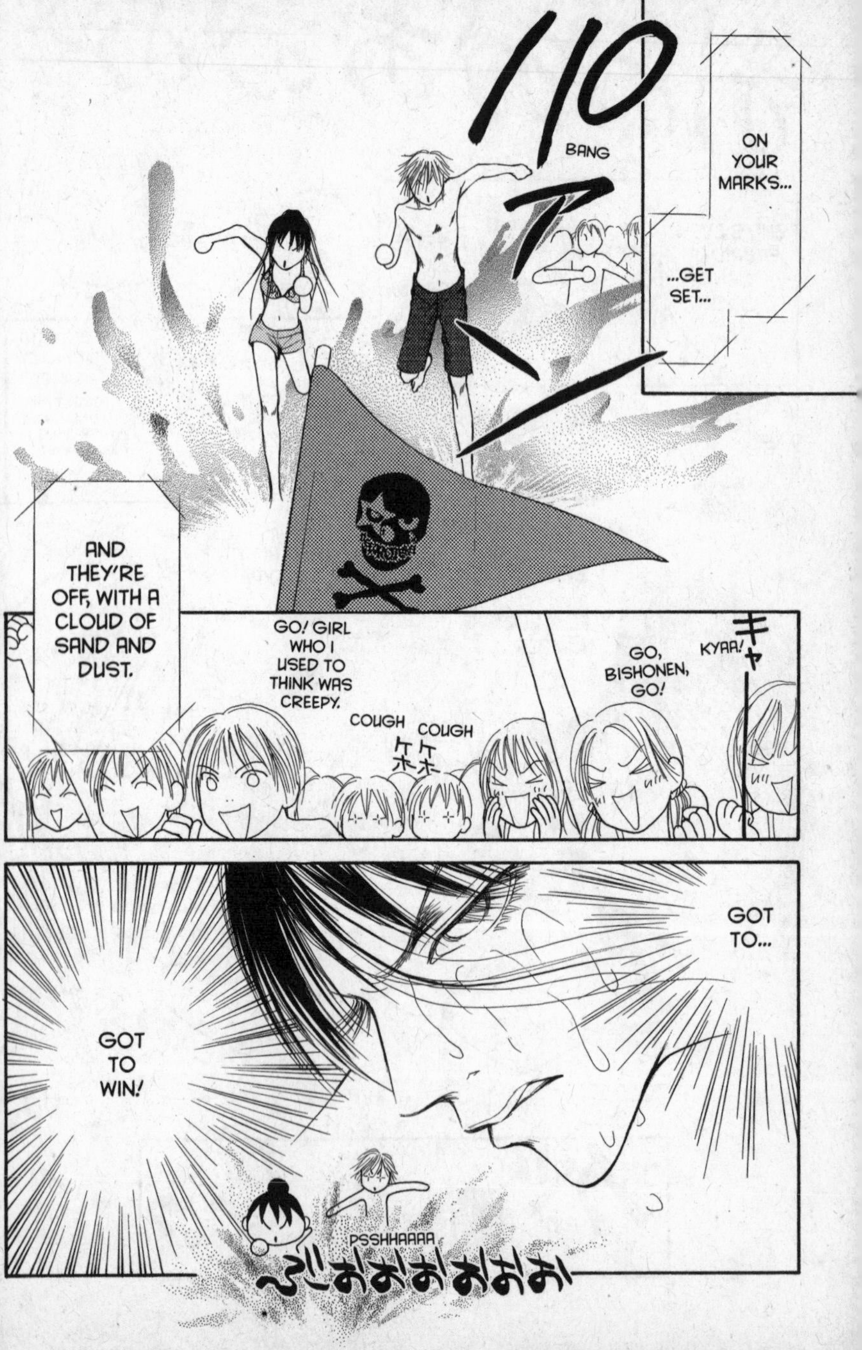
ON YOUR MARKS...
...GET SET...
BANG
AND THEY'RE OFF, WITH A CLOUD OF SAND AND DUST.
KYAA!
GO, BISHONEN, GO!
COUGH COUGH
GO! GIRL WHO I USED TO THINK WAS CREEPY.
GOT TO...
GOT TO WIN!
PSSHHAAAA

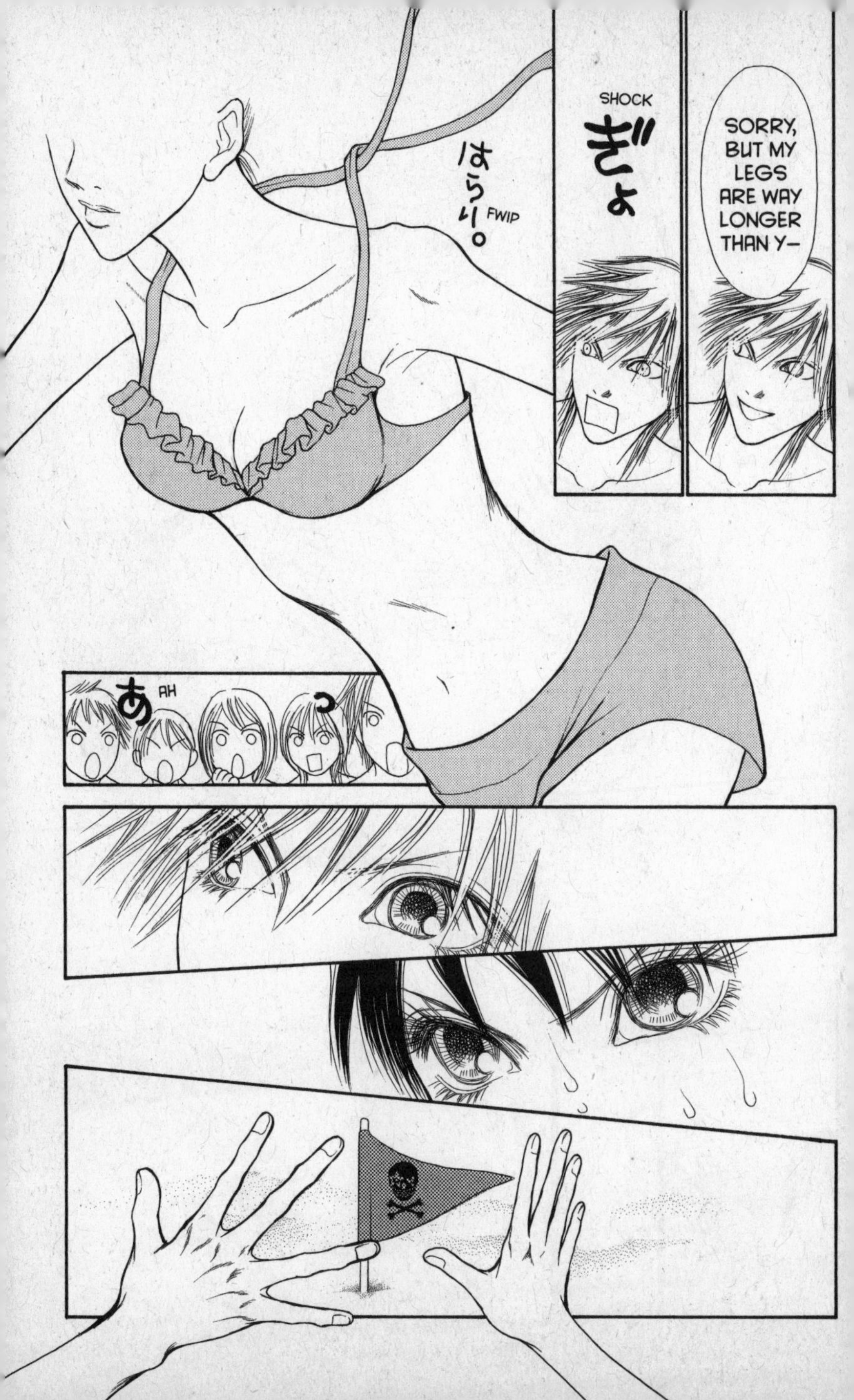
SORRY, BUT MY LEGS ARE WAY LONGER THAN Y—
SHOCK
ぎょ
はらり。
FWIP
あっ
AH

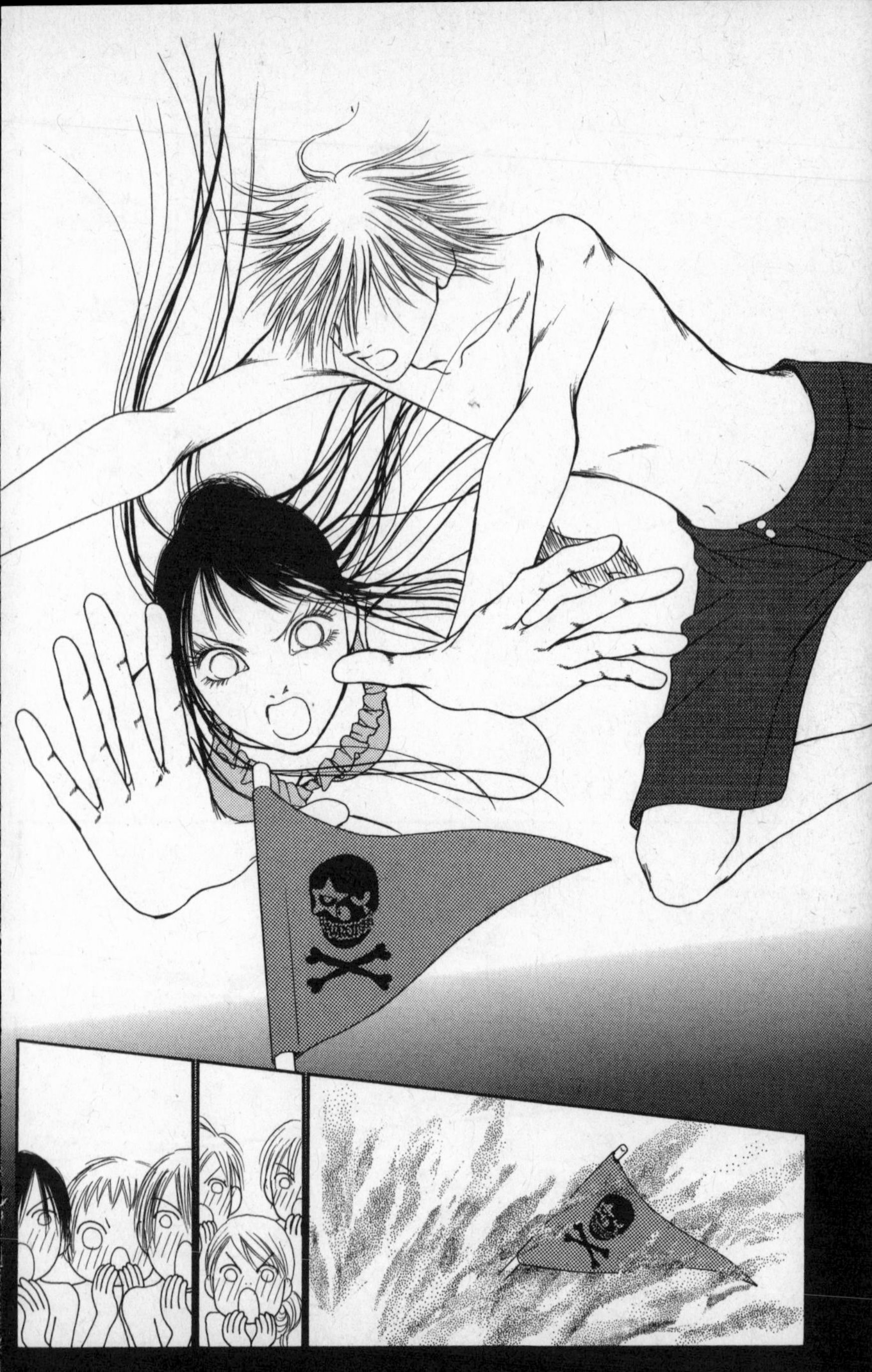

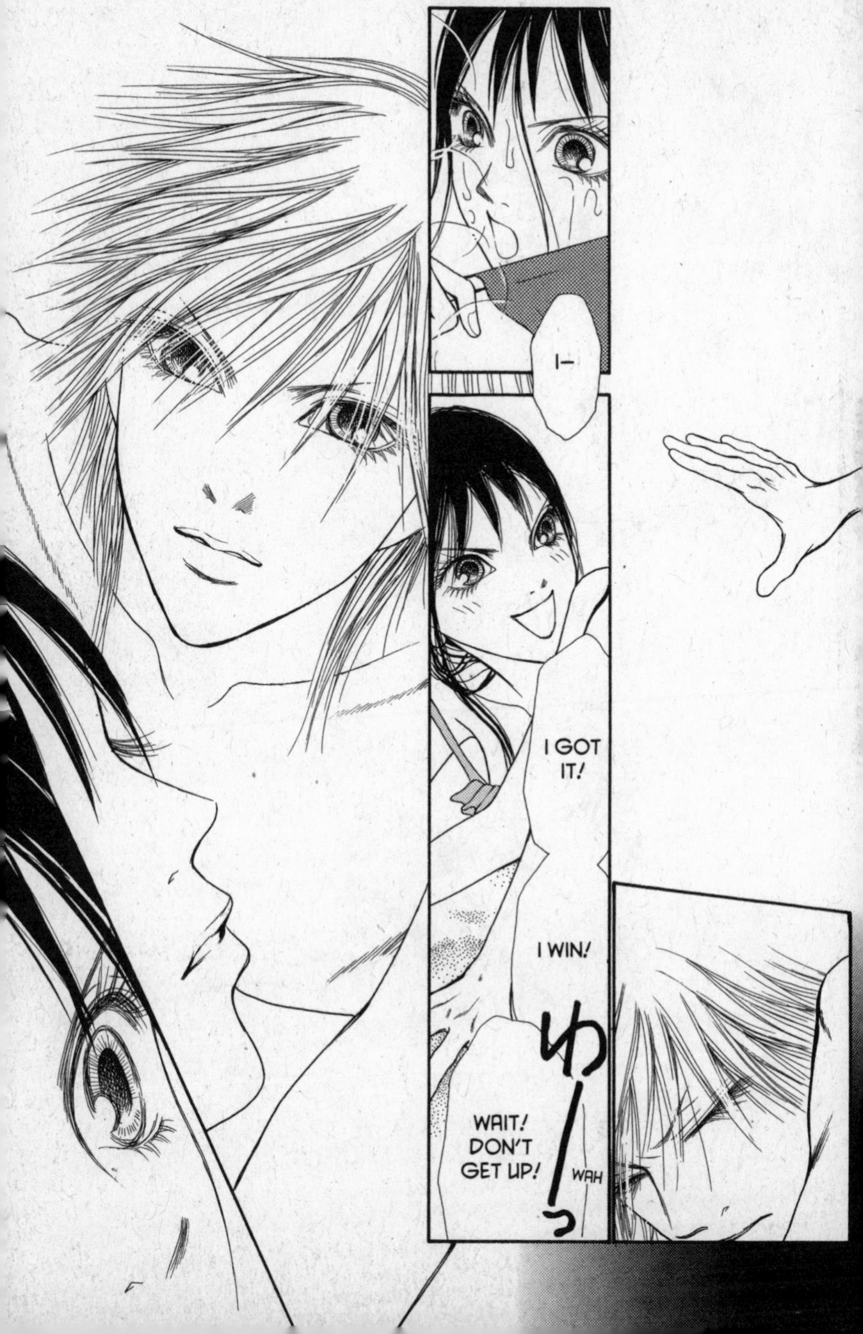

I—
I GOT IT!
I WIN!
ゆーっ
WAH
WAIT! DON'T GET UP!

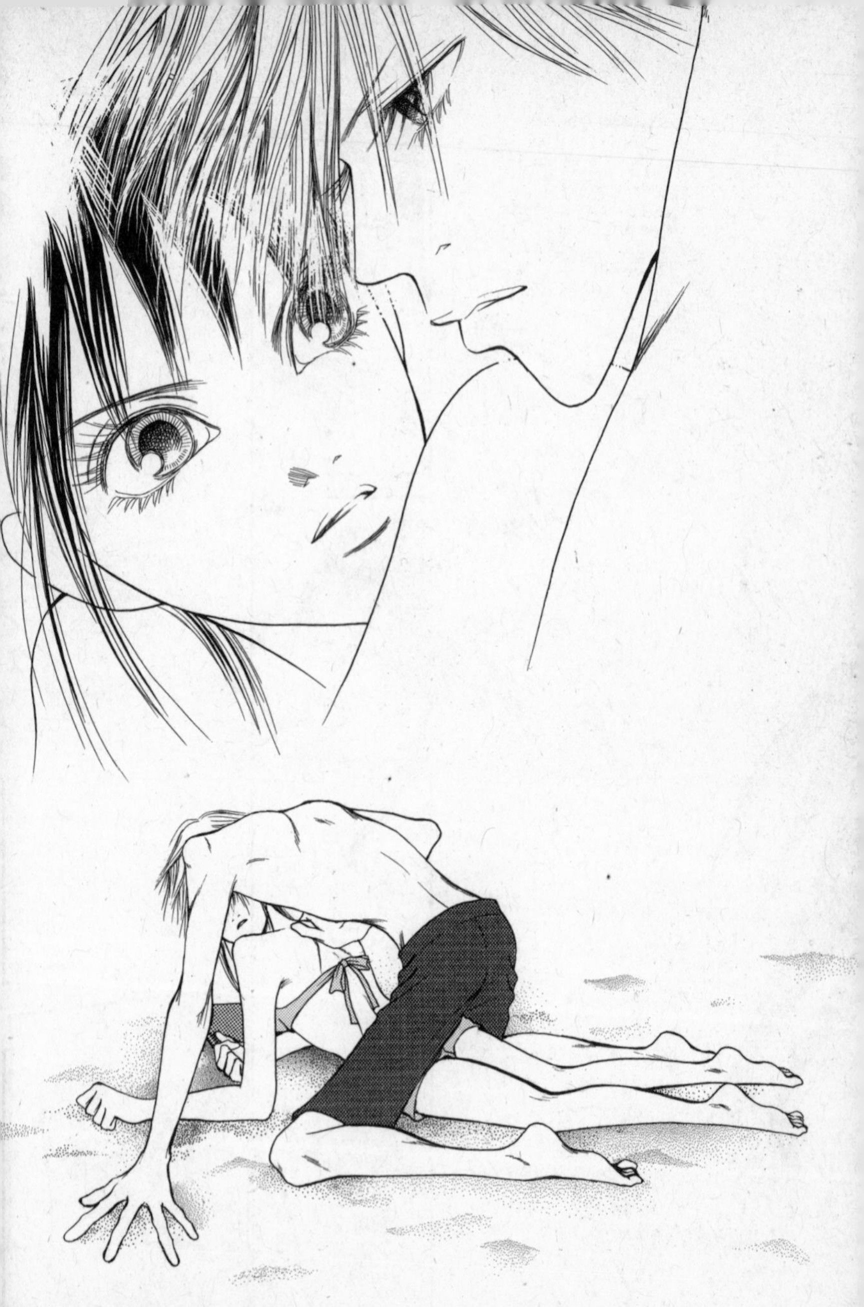

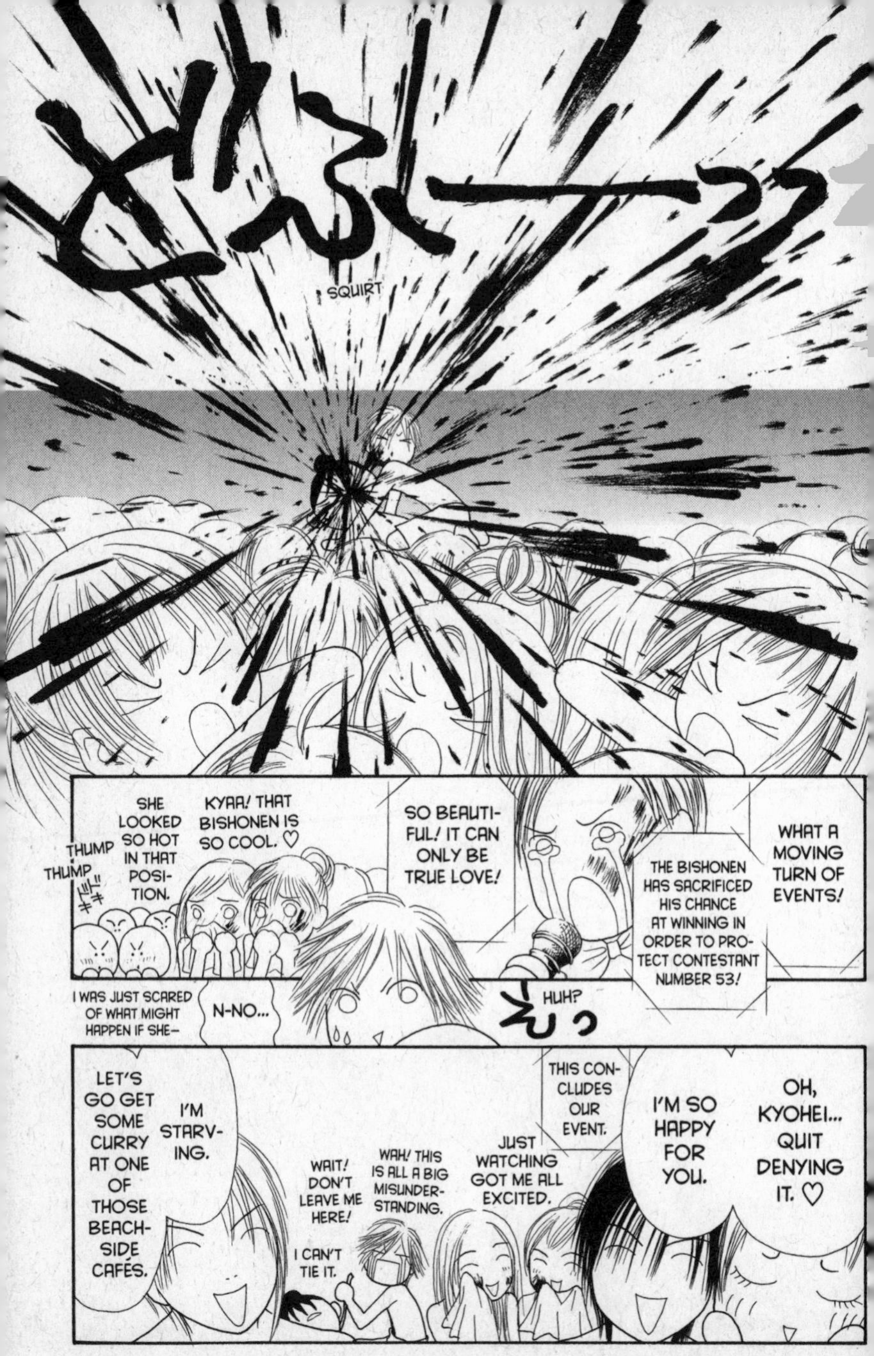
SQUIRT
WHAT A MOVING TURN OF EVENTS!
THE BISHONEN HAS SACRIFICED HIS CHANCE AT WINNING IN ORDER TO PROTECT CONTESTANT NUMBER 53!
SO BEAUTIFUL! IT CAN ONLY BE TRUE LOVE!
KYAA! THAT BISHONEN IS SO COOL. ♡
SHE LOOKED SO HOT IN THAT POSITION.
THUMP THUMP
ドキ
えっ
HUH?
N-NO...
I WAS JUST SCARED OF WHAT MIGHT HAPPEN IF SHE—
OH, KYOHEI... QUIT DENYING IT. ♡
I'M SO HAPPY FOR YOU.
THIS CONCLUDES OUR EVENT.
JUST WATCHING GOT ME ALL EXCITED.
WAH! THIS IS ALL A BIG MISUNDERSTANDING.
WAIT! DON'T LEAVE ME HERE!
I CAN'T TIE IT.
I'M STARVING.
LET'S GO GET SOME CURRY AT ONE OF THOSE BEACHSIDE CAFÉS.

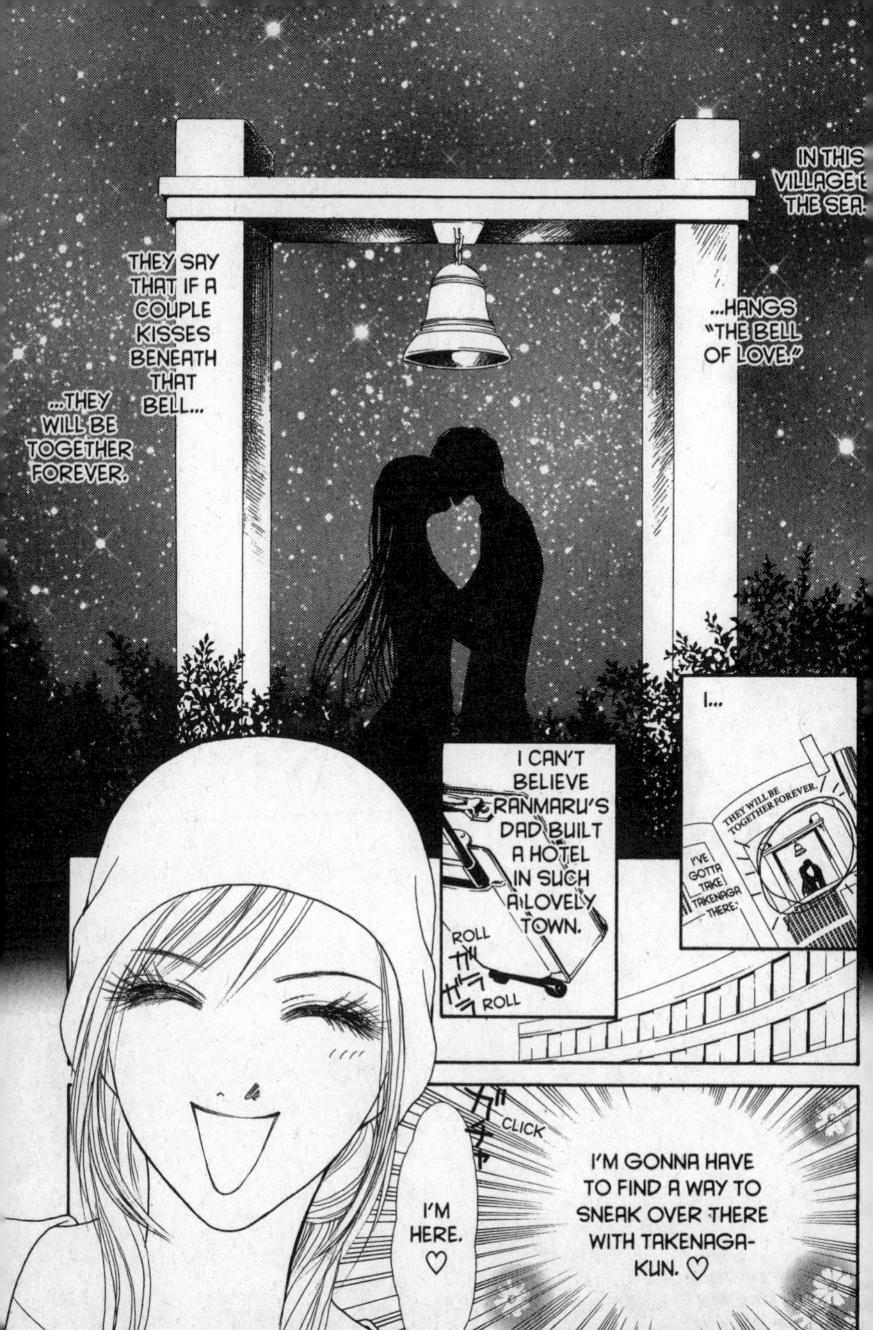
IN THIS VILLAGE B THE SEA.
...HANGS "THE BELL OF LOVE."
THEY SAY THAT IF A COUPLE KISSES BENEATH THAT BELL...
...THEY WILL BE TOGETHER FOREVER.
I...
THEY WILL BE TOGETHER FOREVER.
I'VE GOTTA TAKE TAKENAGA THERE.
I CAN'T BELIEVE RANMARU'S DAD BUILT A HOTEL IN SUCH A LOVELY TOWN.
ROLL
ROLL
CLICK
I'M GONNA HAVE TO FIND A WAY TO SNEAK OVER THERE WITH TAKENAGA-KUN. ♡
I'M HERE. ♡

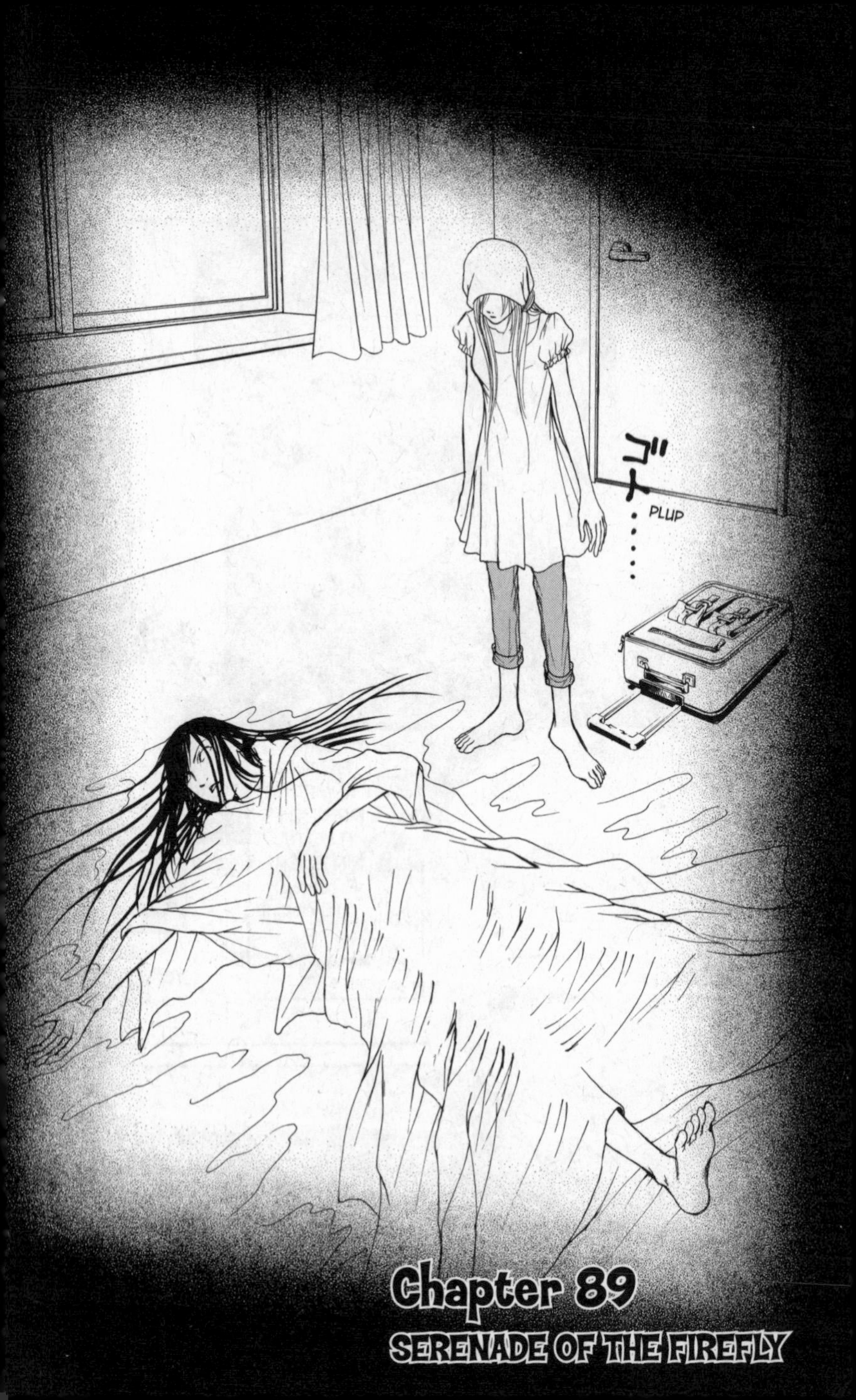
ゴト
PLUP

Chapter 89
SERENADE OF THE FIREFLY

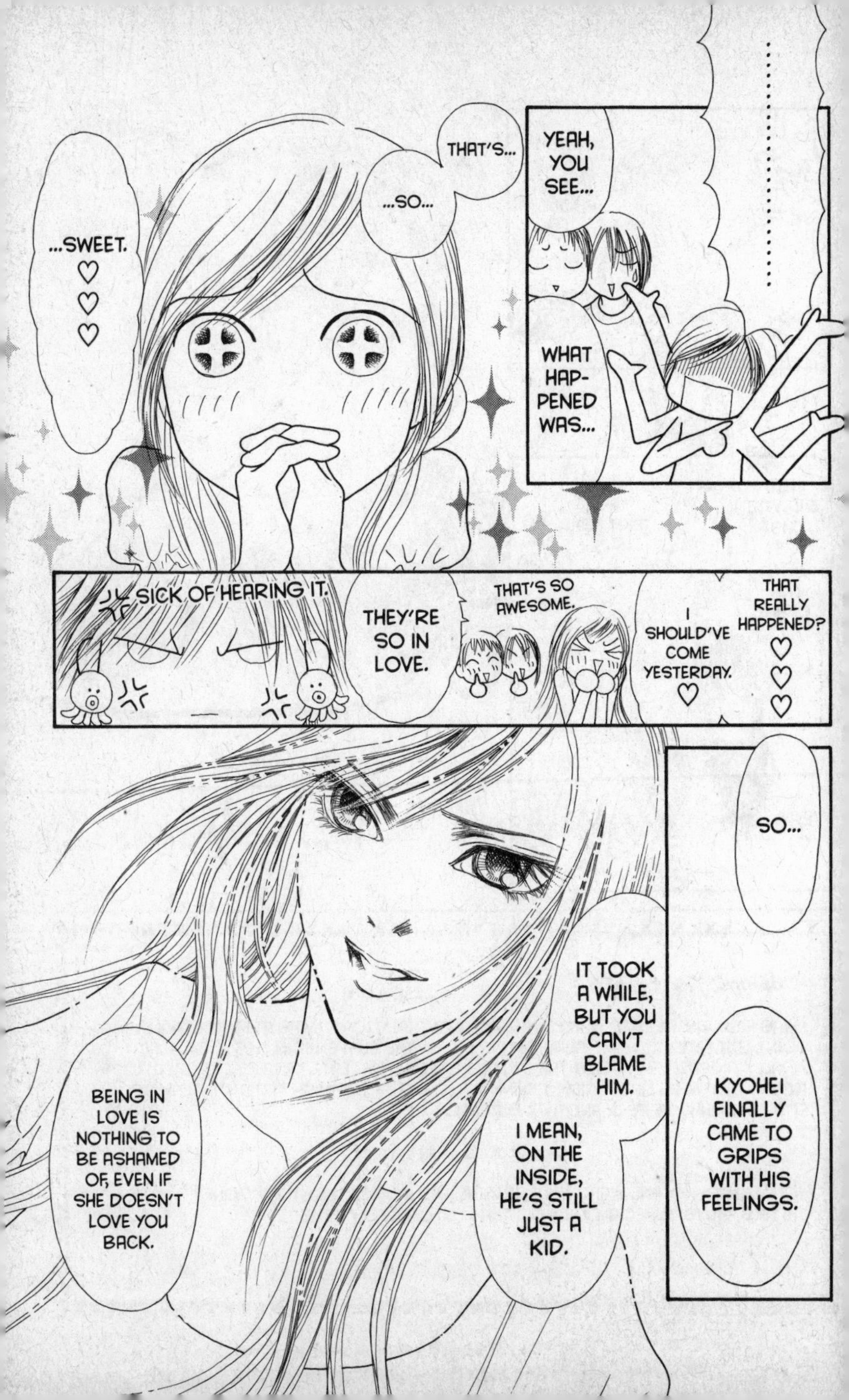

....
YEAH, YOU SEE...
WHAT HAPPENED WAS...
THAT'S...
...SO...
...SWEET. ♡ ♡ ♡
THAT REALLY HAPPENED? ♡ ♡ ♡
I SHOULD'VE COME YESTERDAY. ♡
THAT'S SO AWESOME.
THEY'RE SO IN LOVE.
SICK OF HEARING IT.
SO...
KYOHEI FINALLY CAME TO GRIPS WITH HIS FEELINGS.
IT TOOK A WHILE, BUT YOU CAN'T BLAME HIM.
I MEAN, ON THE INSIDE, HE'S STILL JUST A KID.
BEING IN LOVE IS NOTHING TO BE ASHAMED OF, EVEN IF SHE DOESN'T LOVE YOU BACK.

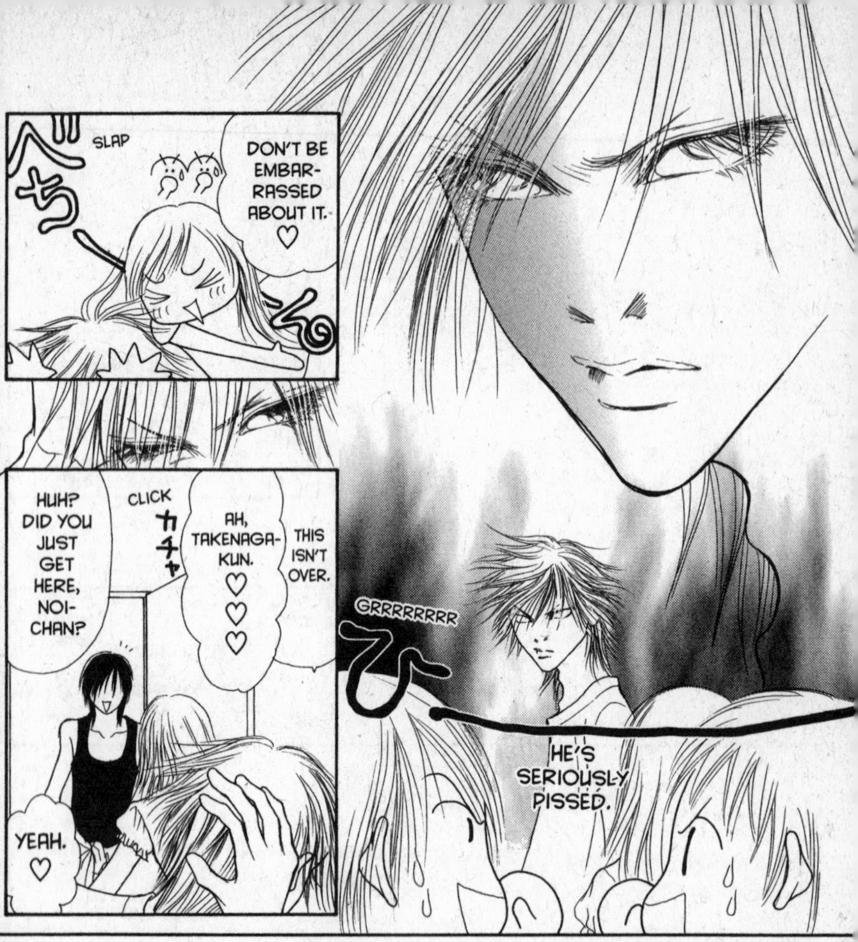
GRRRRRRRR
HE'S SERIOUSLY PISSED.
DON'T BE EMBARRASSED ABOUT IT. ♡
SLAP
THIS ISN'T OVER.
AH, TAKENAGA-KUN. ♡ ♡ ♡
CLICK
HUH? DID YOU JUST GET HERE, NOI-CHAN?
YEAH. ♡

BEHIND THE SCENES

I WAS STILL DEPRESSED WHEN I WAS WRITING THIS STORY. I WAS AT MY BREAKING POINT. BUT I HAD TO MAKE SURE THAT I KEPT UP THE SUSPENSE IN THIS STORYLINE. I FINALLY FINISHED, BUT I GOT THE STORY IN A FEW DAYS LATE. I REALLY LET MY EDITORS DOWN. THEY WERE LIKE "I DIDN'T THINK YOU'D ACTUALLY FINISH." I DIDN'T THINK SO EITHER. IT MUST'VE BEEN ANOTHER MIRACLE.

↑ WHAT DO YOU MEAN "ANOTHER"?

TOMMY, NABEKO, AND KAI-CHAN REALLY HELPED ME GET THE STORY DONE. THANKS, GUYS. ESPECIALLY TOMMY. THANKS FOR EVERYTHING.

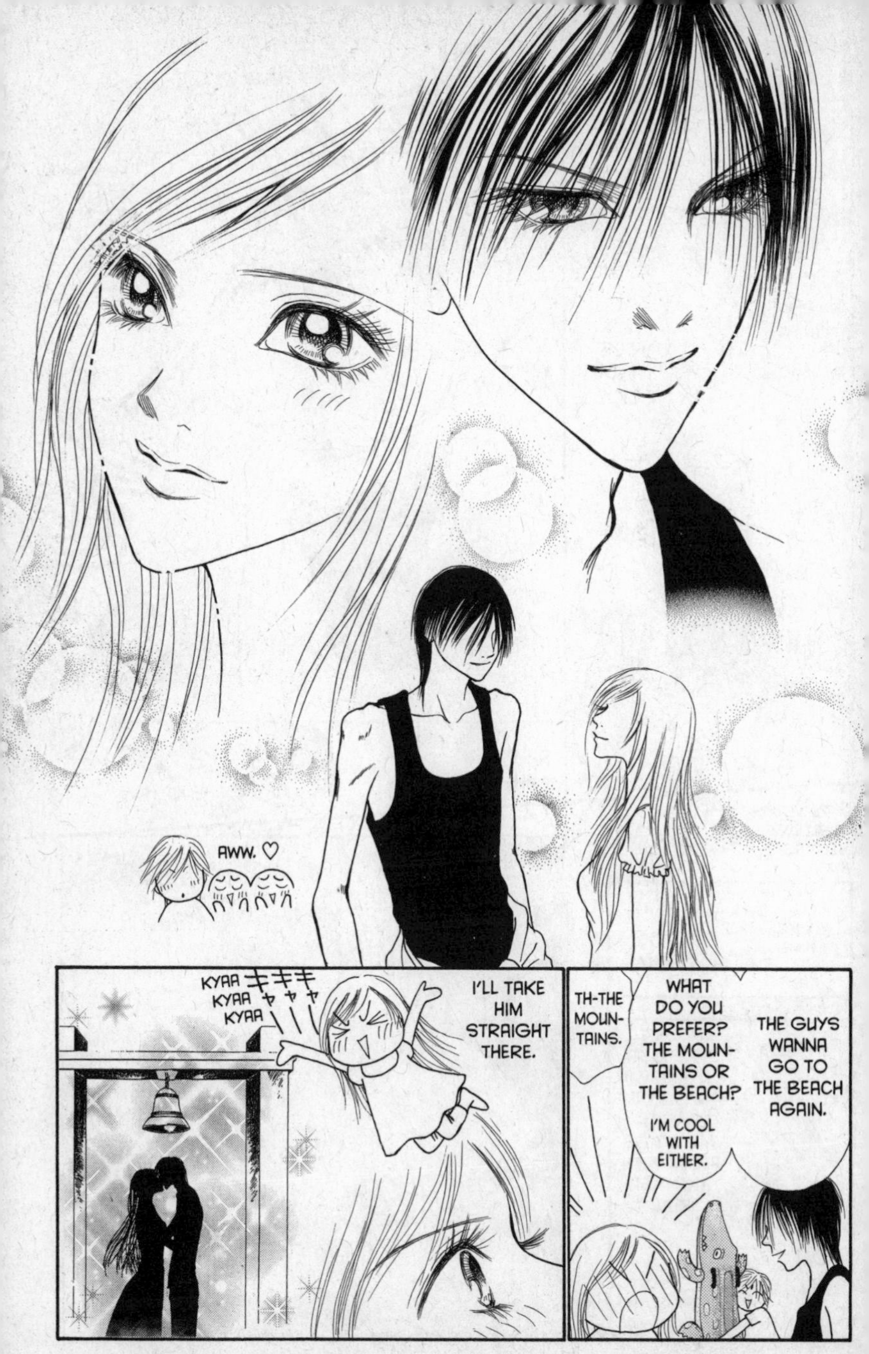
AWW. ♡
THE GUYS WANNA GO TO THE BEACH AGAIN.
WHAT DO YOU PREFER? THE MOUN-TAINS OR THE BEACH?
I'M COOL WITH EITHER.
TH-THE MOUN-TAINS.
I'LL TAKE HIM STRAIGHT THERE.
KYAA KYAA KYAA
キャ キャ キャ

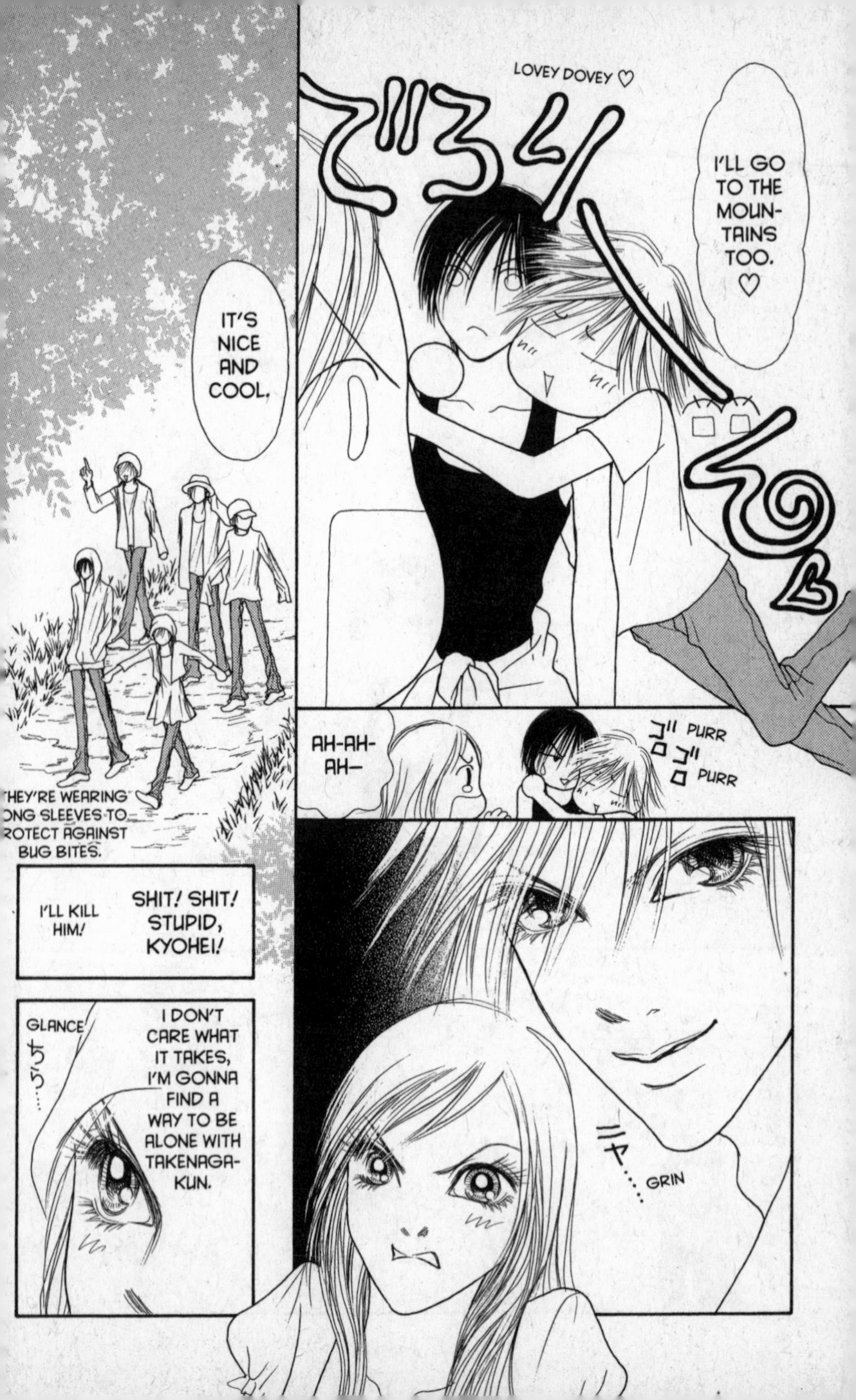
LOVEY DOVEY ♡
I'LL GO TO THE MOUN-TAINS TOO. ♡
PURR
PURR
AH-AH-AH—
GRIN
IT'S NICE AND COOL.
THEY'RE WEARING ONG SLEEVES TO ROTECT AGAINST BUG BITES.
SHIT! SHIT! STUPID, KYOHEI!
I'LL KILL HIM!
I DON'T CARE WHAT IT TAKES, I'M GONNA FIND A WAY TO BE ALONE WITH TAKENAGA-KUN.
GLANCE

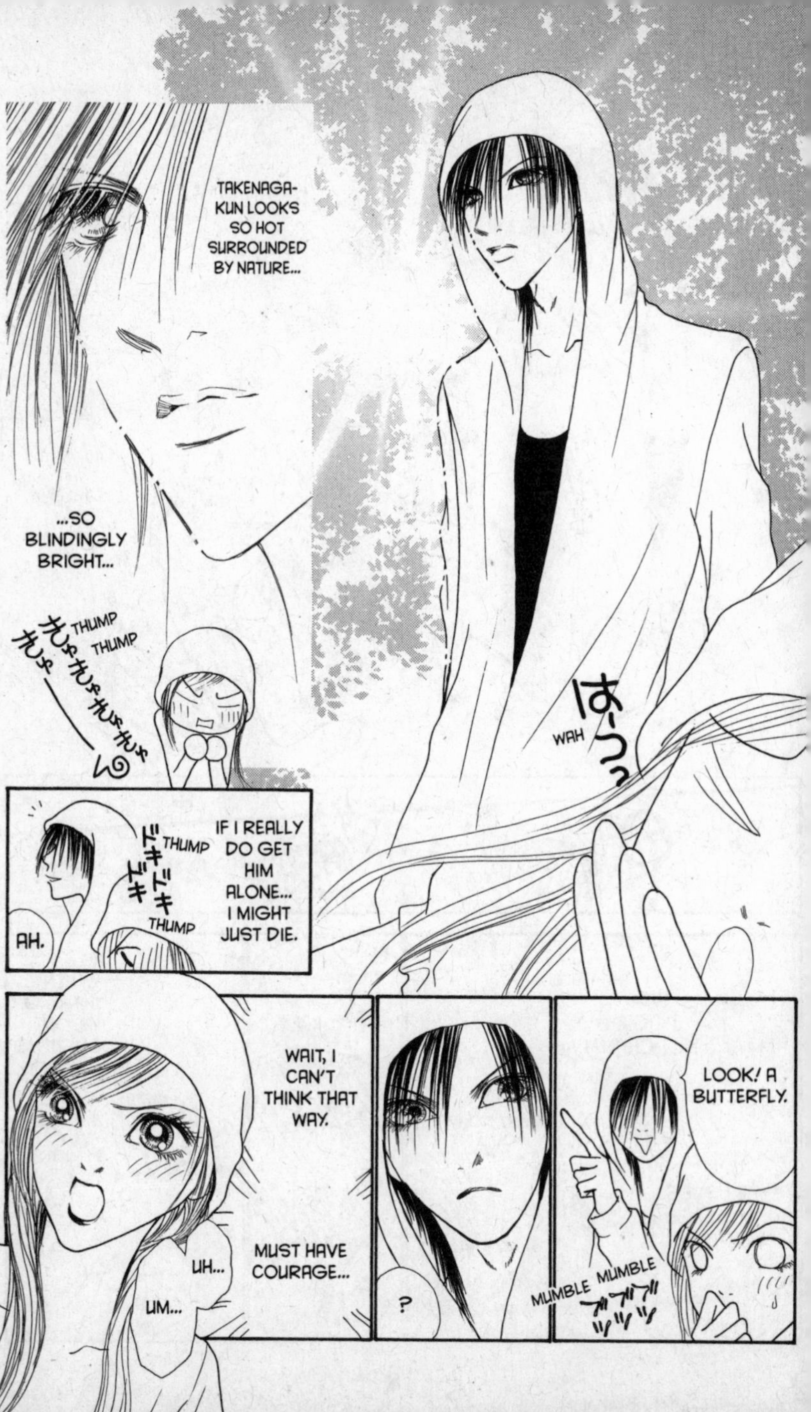
はーっ
WAH
TAKENAGA-KUN LOOKS SO HOT SURROUNDED BY NATURE...
...SO BLINDINGLY BRIGHT...
きゅきゅきゅきゅきゅきゅーん
THUMP THUMP
IF I REALLY DO GET HIM ALONE... I MIGHT JUST DIE.
ドキドキ
THUMP THUMP
AH.
LOOK! A BUTTERFLY.
MUMBLE MUMBLE
ブツブツ
?
WAIT, I CAN'T THINK THAT WAY.
UH...
UM...
MUST HAVE COURAGE...

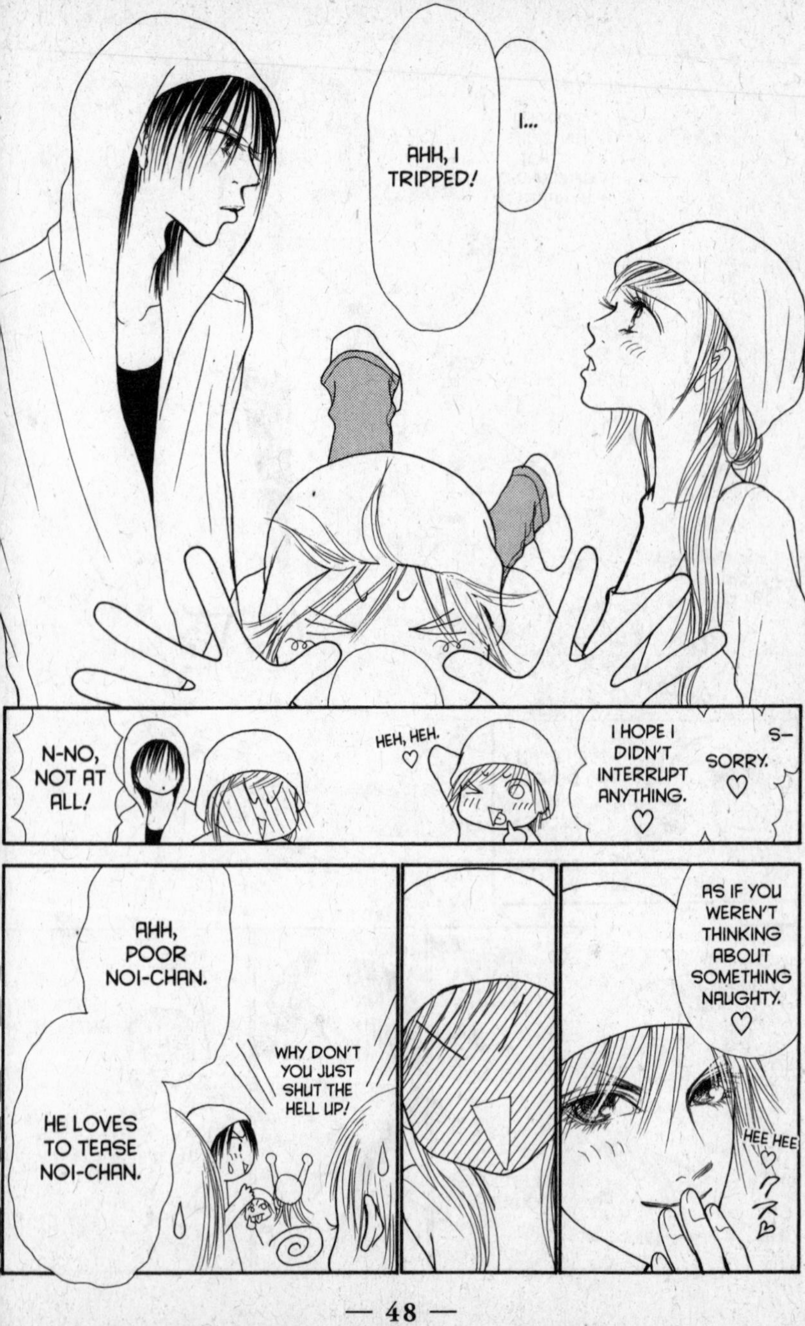
I...
AHH, I TRIPPED!
S— SORRY. ♡
I HOPE I DIDN'T INTERRUPT ANYTHING. ♡
HEH, HEH. ♡
N-NO, NOT AT ALL!
AS IF YOU WEREN'T THINKING ABOUT SOMETHING NAUGHTY. ♡
HEE HEE ♡
クス♡
WHY DON'T YOU JUST SHUT THE HELL UP!
AHH, POOR NOI-CHAN.
HE LOVES TO TEASE NOI-CHAN.

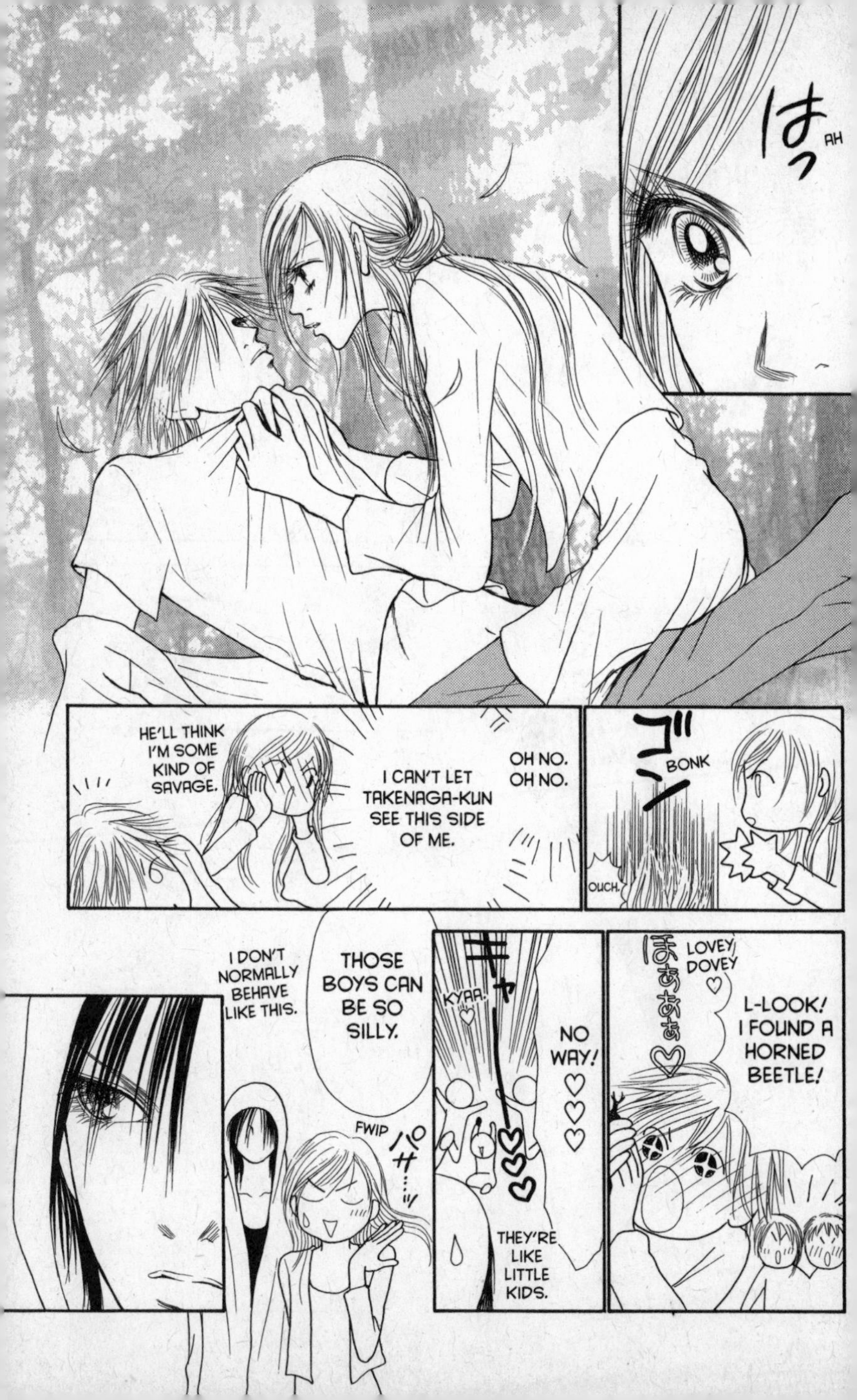
はっ
AH
ゴン
BONK
OUCH.
OH NO. OH NO.
I CAN'T LET TAKENAGA-KUN SEE THIS SIDE OF ME.
HE'LL THINK I'M SOME KIND OF SAVAGE.
ほあああ♡
LOVEY DOVEY ♡
L-LOOK! I FOUND A HORNED BEETLE!
キャー
KYAA! ♡
NO WAY! ♡♡♡
THEY'RE LIKE LITTLE KIDS.
THOSE BOYS CAN BE SO SILLY.
I DON'T NORMALLY BEHAVE LIKE THIS.
パサ…ッ
FWIP

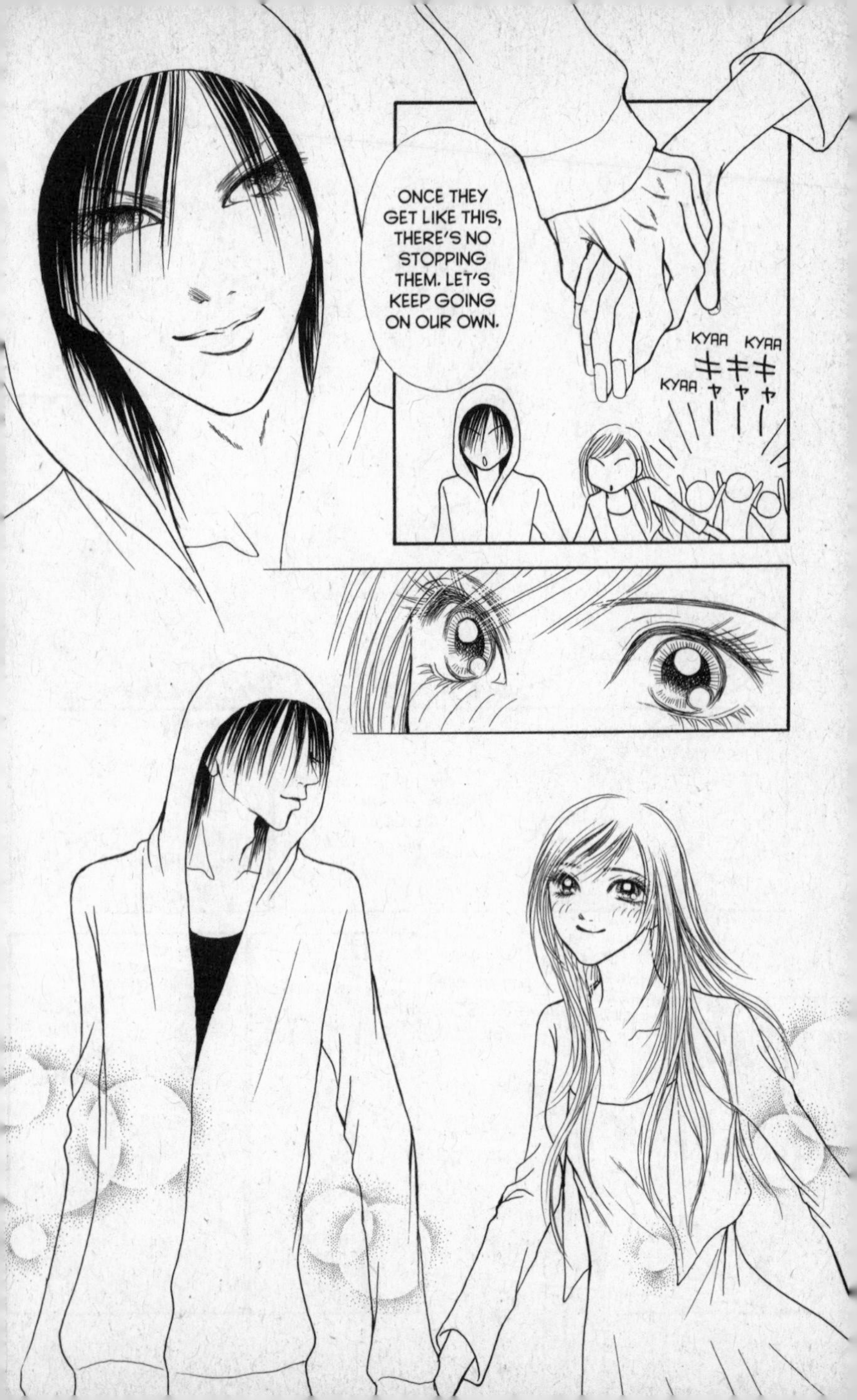
ONCE THEY GET LIKE THIS, THERE'S NO STOPPING THEM. LET'S KEEP GOING ON OUR OWN.
KYAA
KYAA
KYAA
キャー
キャー
キャー

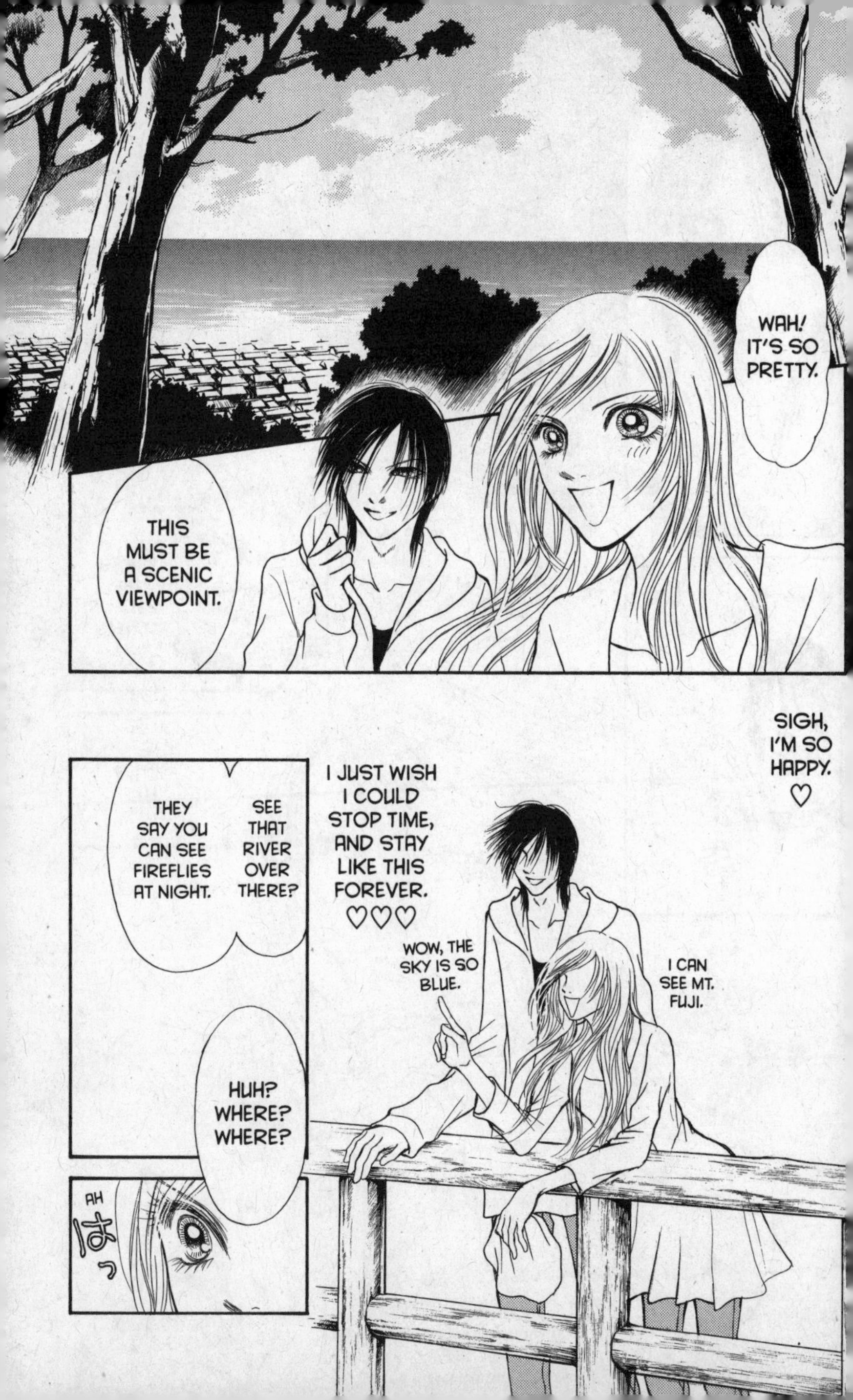
WAH! IT'S SO PRETTY.
THIS MUST BE A SCENIC VIEWPOINT.
SIGH, I'M SO HAPPY. ♡
I JUST WISH I COULD STOP TIME, AND STAY LIKE THIS FOREVER. ♡♡♡
I CAN SEE MT. FUJI.
WOW, THE SKY IS SO BLUE.
SEE THAT RIVER OVER THERE?
THEY SAY YOU CAN SEE FIREFLIES AT NIGHT.
HUH? WHERE? WHERE?
はっ
AH

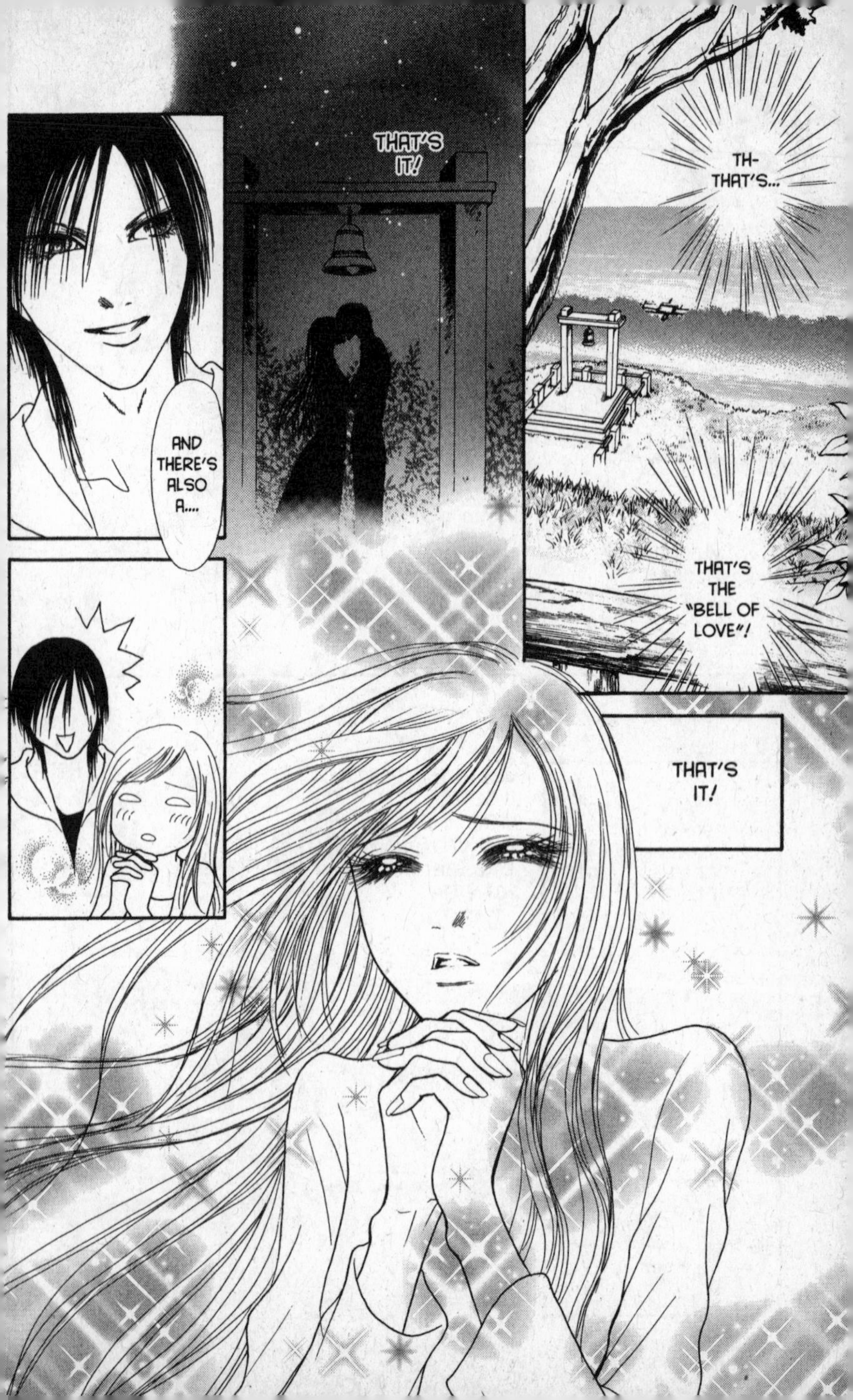
TH-THAT'S...
THAT'S THE "BELL OF LOVE"!
THAT'S IT!
AND THERE'S ALSO A....
THAT'S IT!

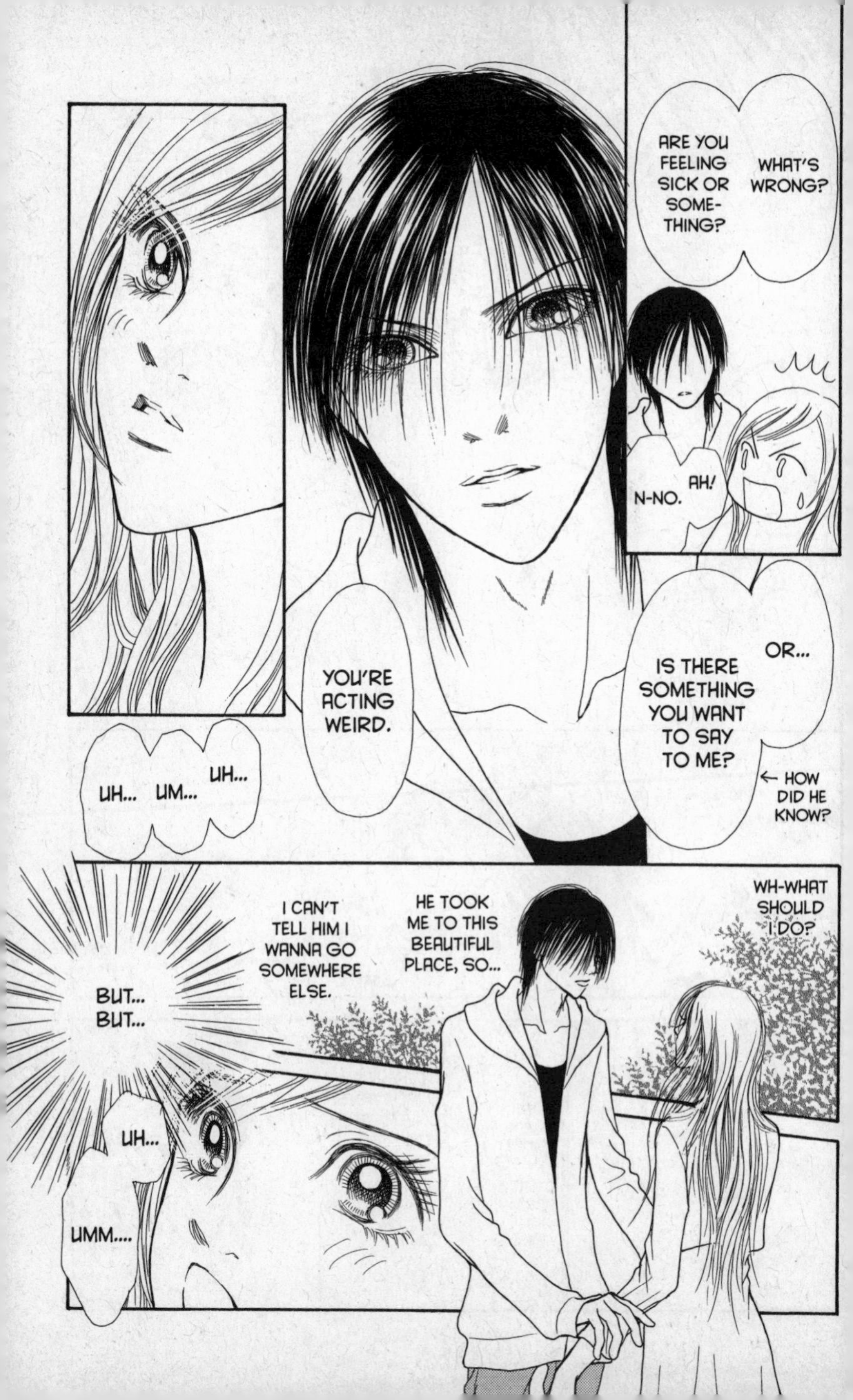
WHAT'S WRONG?
ARE YOU FEELING SICK OR SOME-THING?
AH!
N-NO.
OR...
IS THERE SOMETHING YOU WANT TO SAY TO ME?
← HOW DID HE KNOW?
YOU'RE ACTING WEIRD.
UH... UM... UH...
WH-WHAT SHOULD I DO?
HE TOOK ME TO THIS BEAUTIFUL PLACE, SO...
I CAN'T TELL HIM I WANNA GO SOMEWHERE ELSE.
BUT... BUT...
UH...
UMM....

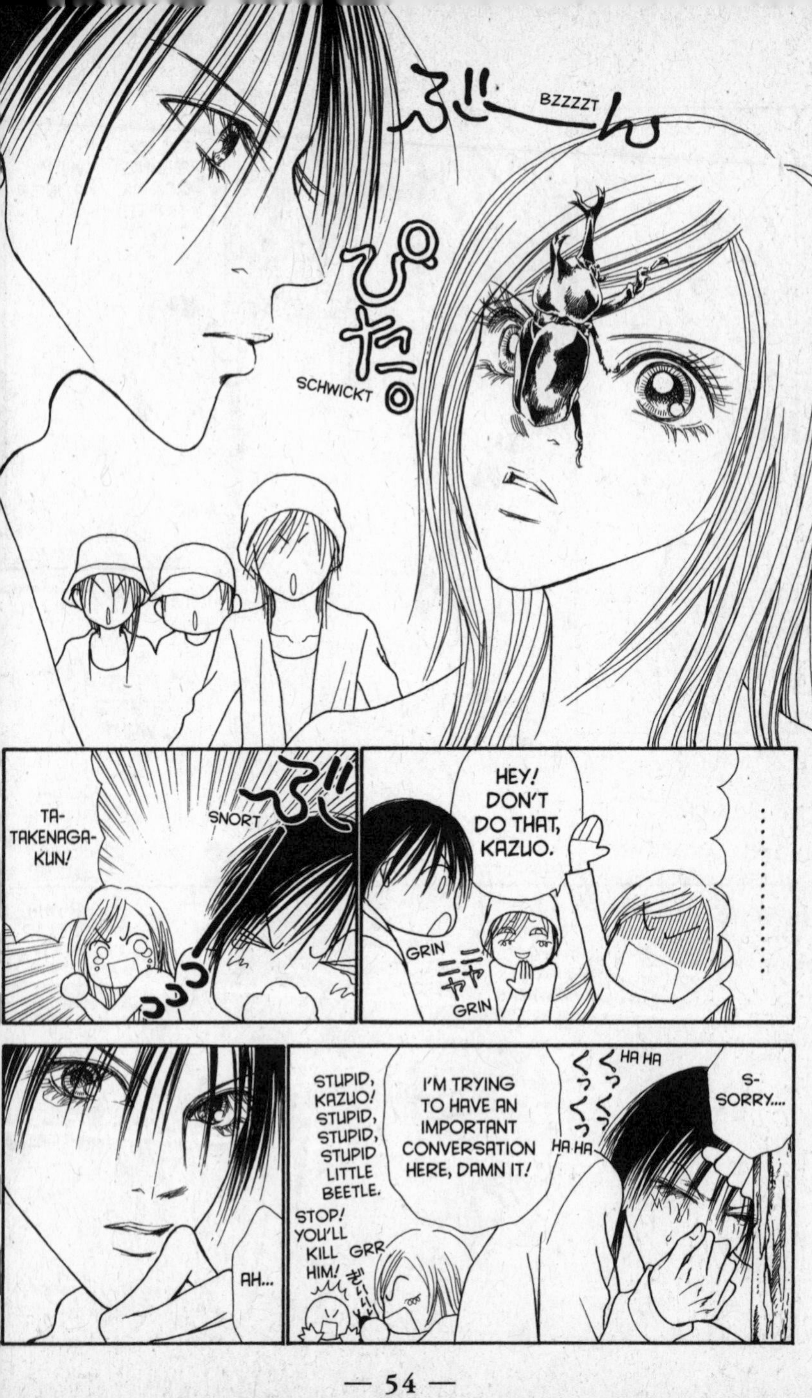
BZZZZT
SCHWICKT
......
HEY! DON'T DO THAT, KAZUO.
GRIN
GRIN
SNORT
TA-TAKENAGA-KUN!
S-SORRY....
HA HA
HA HA
I'M TRYING TO HAVE AN IMPORTANT CONVERSATION HERE, DAMN IT!
STUPID, KAZUO! STUPID, STUPID, STUPID LITTLE BEETLE.
STOP! YOU'LL KILL HIM!
GRR
AH...

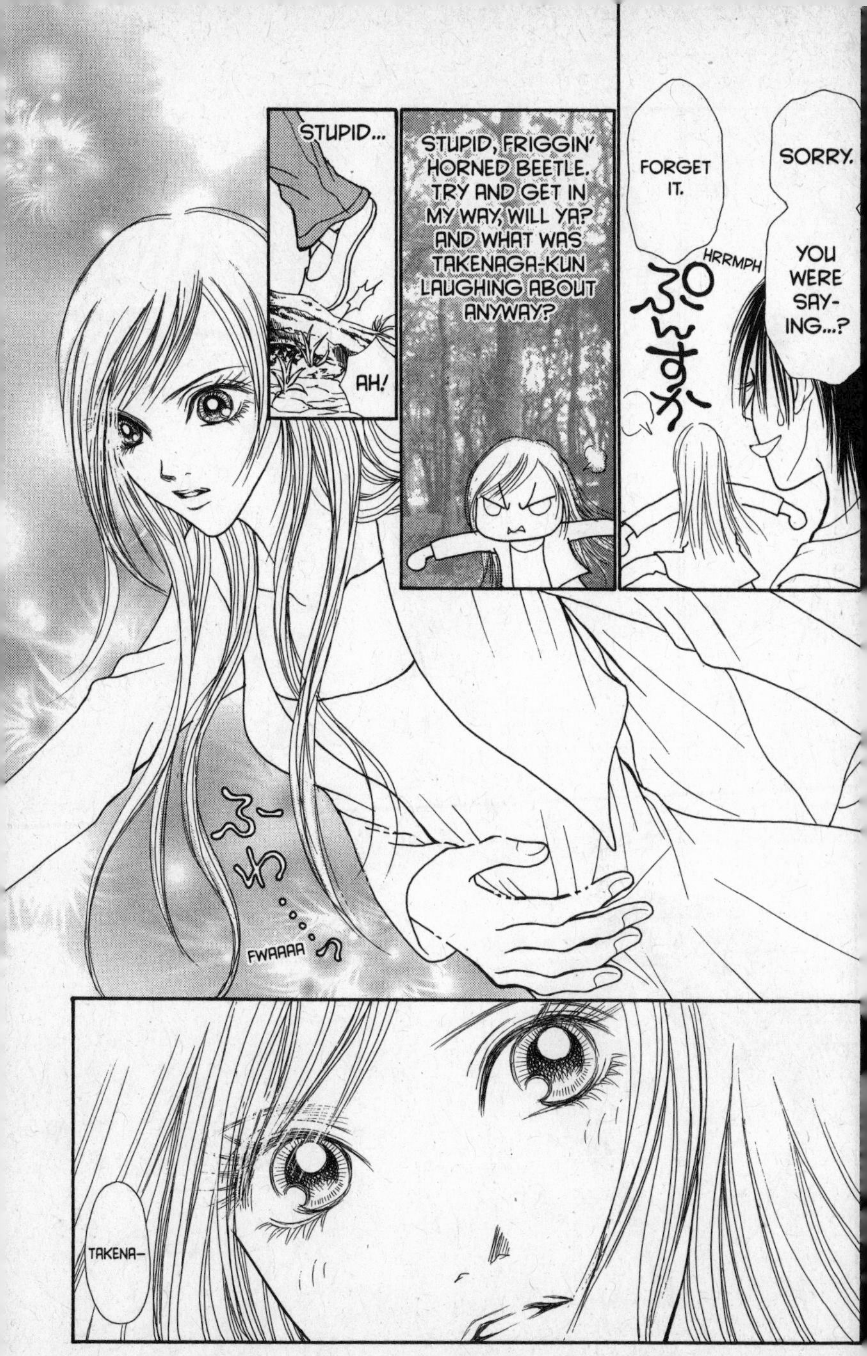
SORRY.
YOU WERE SAYING...?
FORGET IT.
HRRMPH
ふんすか
STUPID, FRIGGIN' HORNED BEETLE. TRY AND GET IN MY WAY, WILL YA? AND WHAT WAS TAKENAGA-KUN LAUGHING ABOUT ANYWAY?
STUPID...
AH!
ふ～わ……ん
FWAAAA
TAKENA-

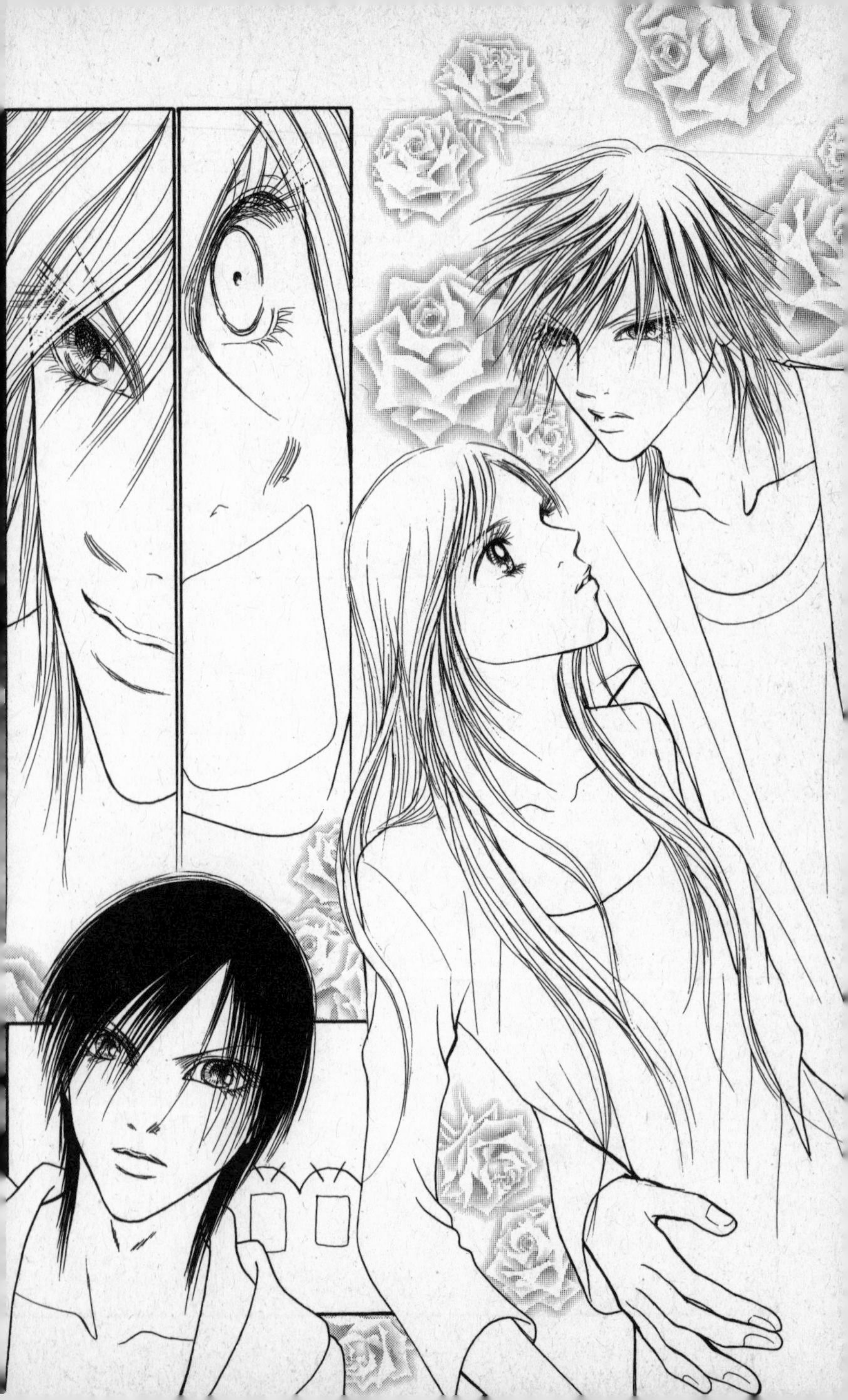

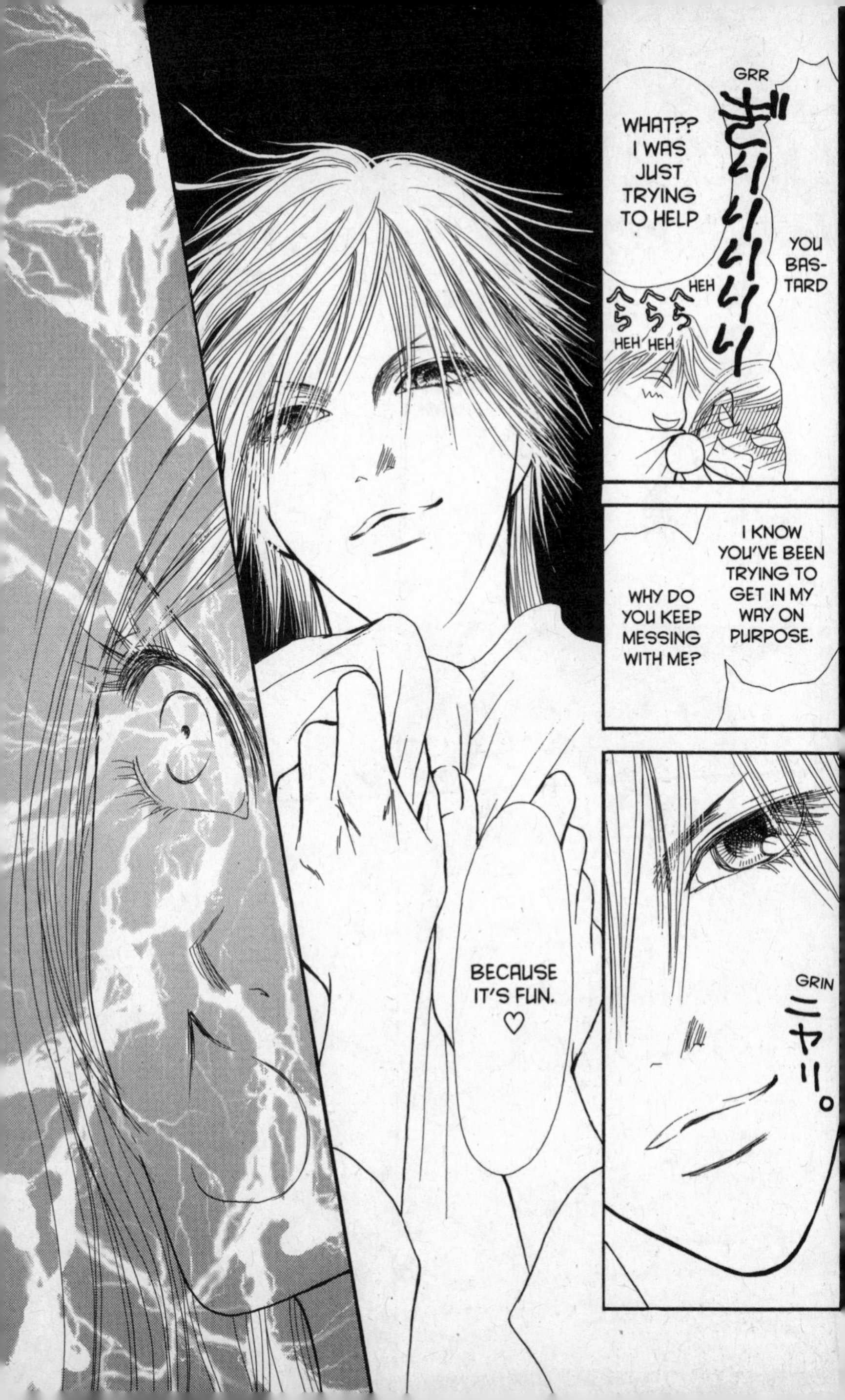
GRR
ぎりりりりりり
YOU BAS-TARD
WHAT?? I WAS JUST TRYING TO HELP
HEH HEH HEH
へらへらへら
I KNOW YOU'VE BEEN TRYING TO GET IN MY WAY ON PURPOSE.
WHY DO YOU KEEP MESSING WITH ME?
GRIN
ニヤリ。
BECAUSE IT'S FUN. ♡

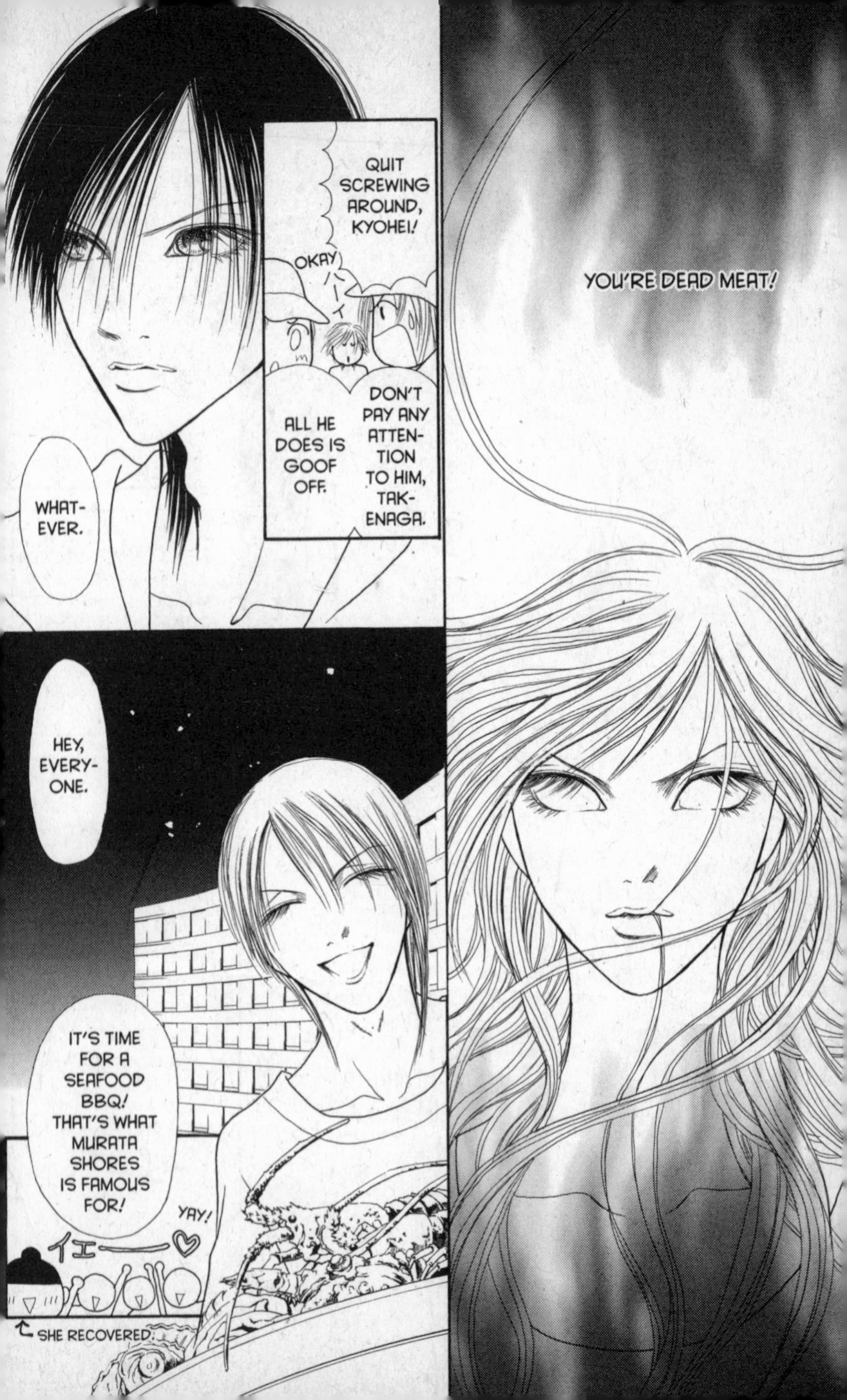
YOU'RE DEAD MEAT!
QUIT SCREWING AROUND, KYOHEI!
OKAY
ハーイ
DON'T PAY ANY ATTENTION TO HIM, TAKENAGA.
ALL HE DOES IS GOOF OFF.
WHATEVER.
HEY, EVERYONE.
IT'S TIME FOR A SEAFOOD BBQ! THAT'S WHAT MURATA SHORES IS FAMOUS FOR!
YAY!
イエー♡
SHE RECOVERED.

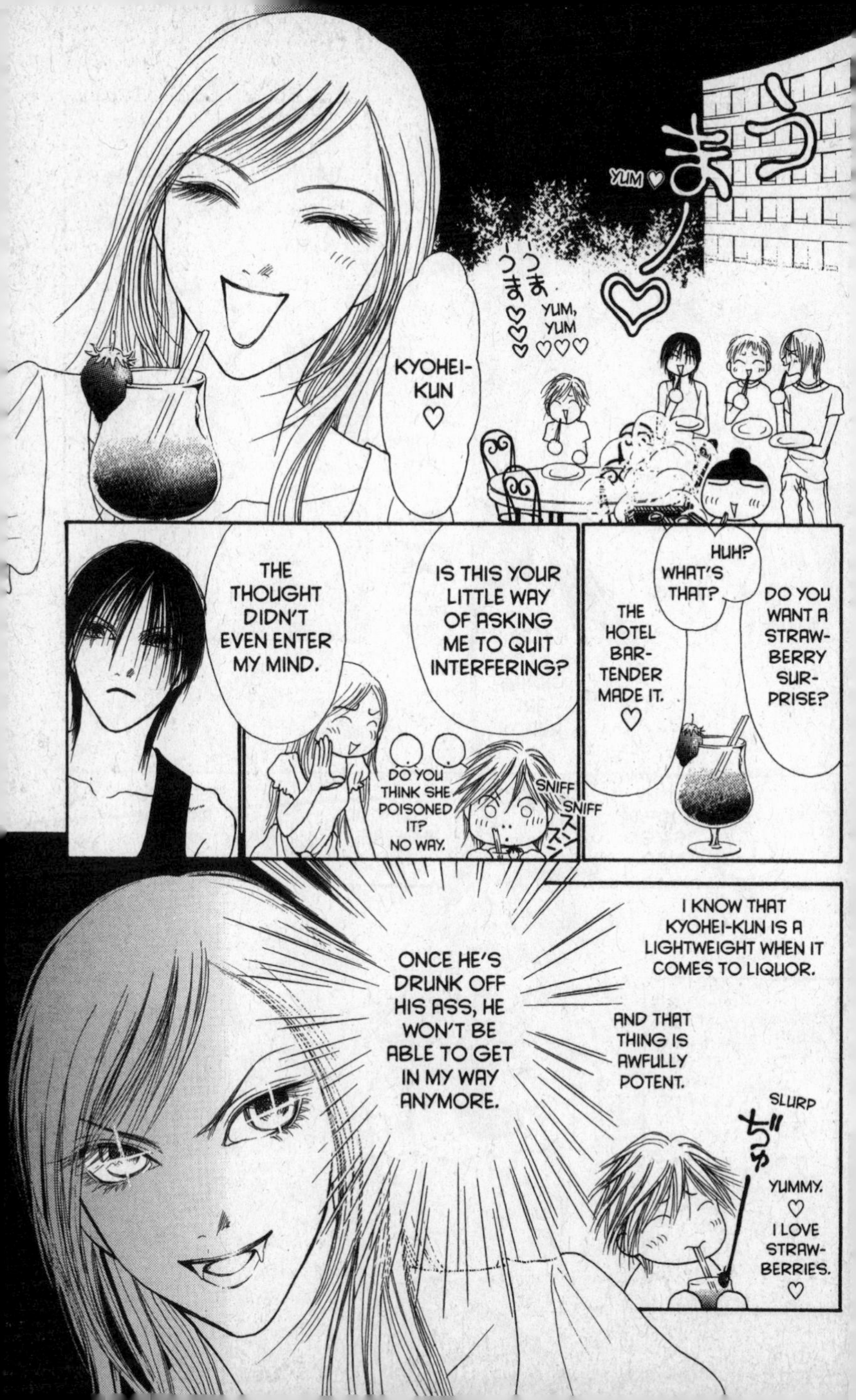
YUM ♡
YUM, YUM ♡♡♡
KYOHEI-KUN ♡
DO YOU WANT A STRAWBERRY SURPRISE?
HUH? WHAT'S THAT?
THE HOTEL BARTENDER MADE IT. ♡
IS THIS YOUR LITTLE WAY OF ASKING ME TO QUIT INTERFERING?
SNIFF SNIFF
DO YOU THINK SHE POISONED IT? NO WAY.
THE THOUGHT DIDN'T EVEN ENTER MY MIND.
I KNOW THAT KYOHEI-KUN IS A LIGHTWEIGHT WHEN IT COMES TO LIQUOR.
AND THAT THING IS AWFULLY POTENT.
ONCE HE'S DRUNK OFF HIS ASS, HE WON'T BE ABLE TO GET IN MY WAY ANYMORE.
SLURP
YUMMY. ♡ I LOVE STRAWBERRIES. ♡

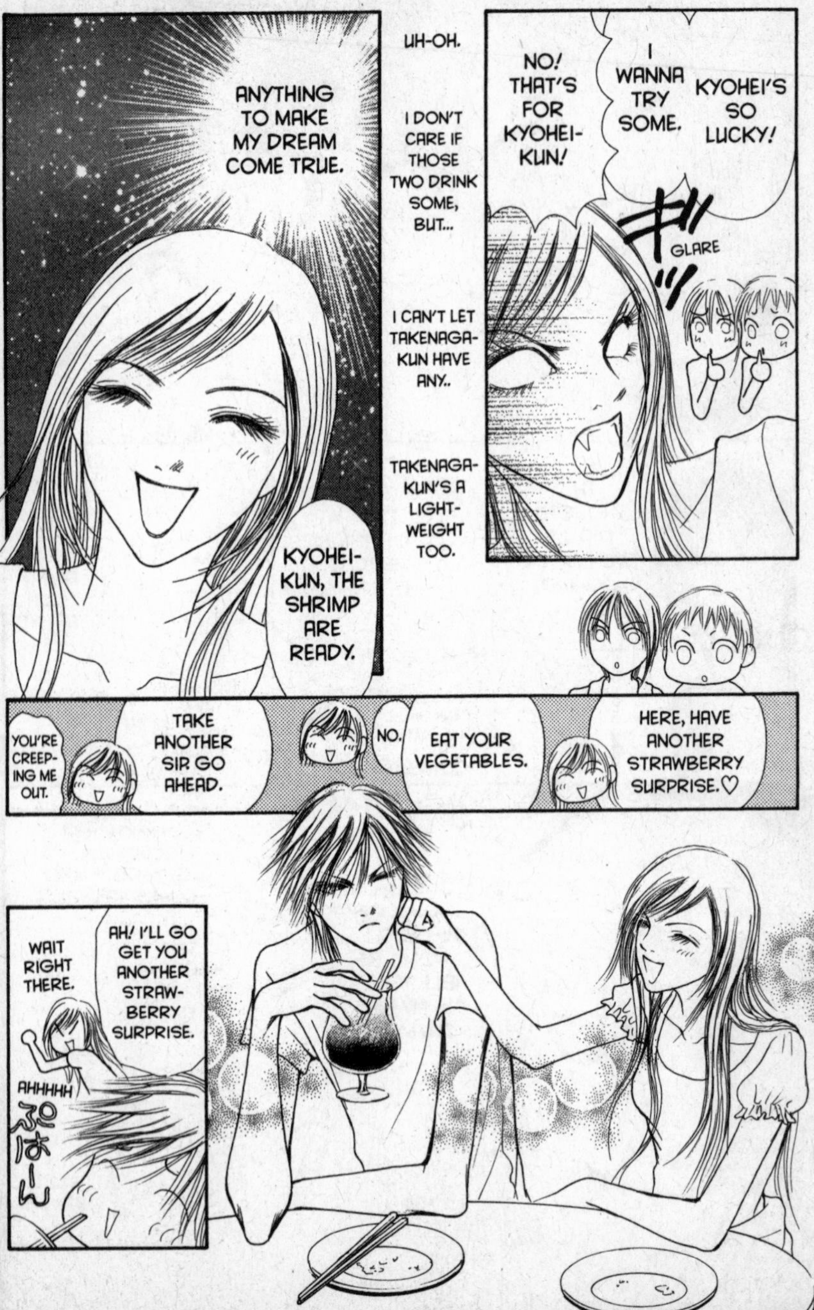
KYOHEI'S SO LUCKY!
I WANNA TRY SOME.
NO! THAT'S FOR KYOHEI-KUN!
GLARE
UH-OH.
I DON'T CARE IF THOSE TWO DRINK SOME, BUT...
I CAN'T LET TAKENAGA-KUN HAVE ANY..
TAKENAGA-KUN'S A LIGHT-WEIGHT TOO.
ANYTHING TO MAKE MY DREAM COME TRUE.
KYOHEI-KUN, THE SHRIMP ARE READY.
HERE, HAVE ANOTHER STRAWBERRY SURPRISE.♡
EAT YOUR VEGETABLES.
NO.
TAKE ANOTHER SIP. GO AHEAD.
YOU'RE CREEPING ME OUT.
AH! I'LL GO GET YOU ANOTHER STRAW-BERRY SURPRISE.
WAIT RIGHT THERE.
AHHHHH
ぷはーん

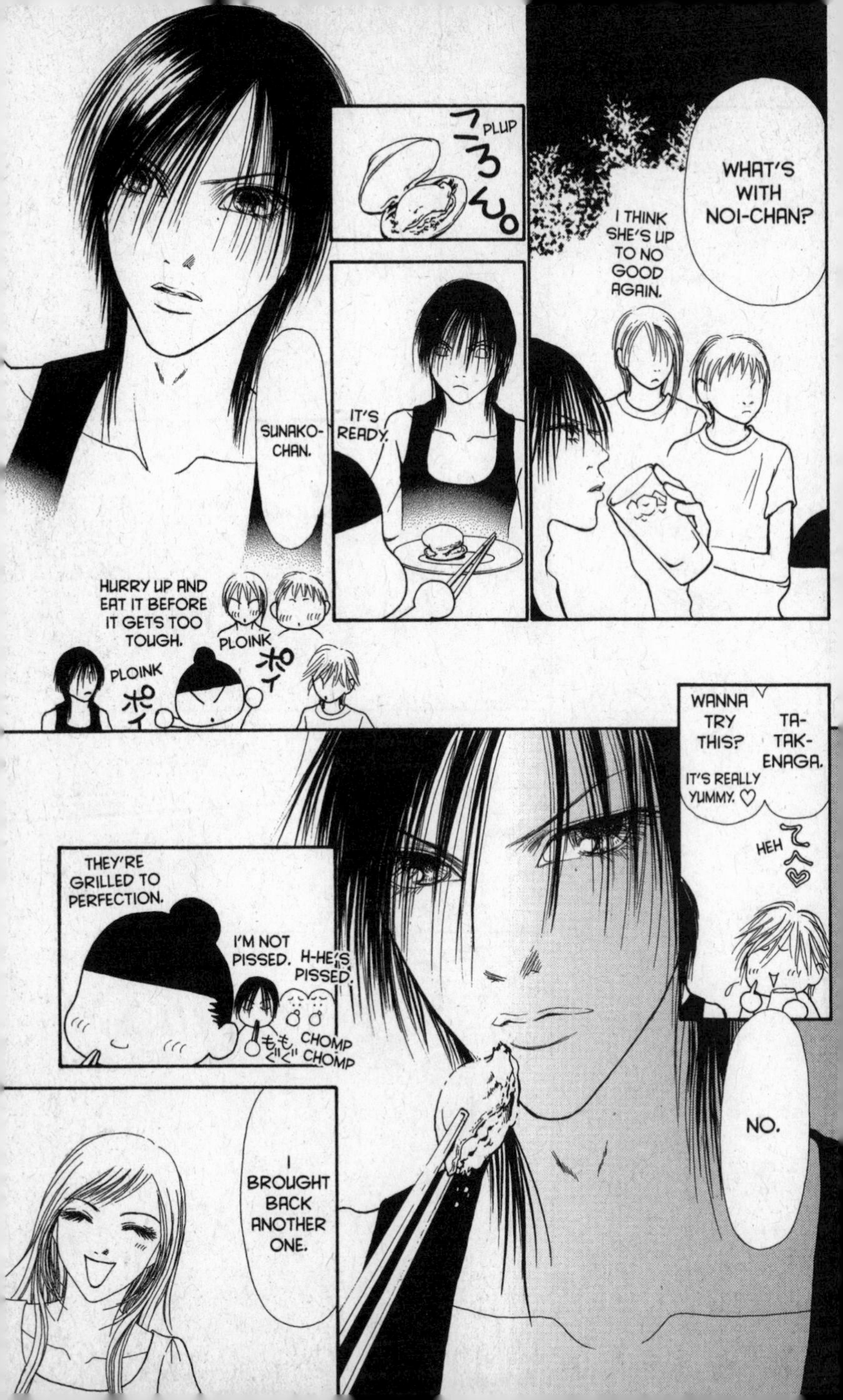

WHAT'S WITH NOI-CHAN?
I THINK SHE'S UP TO NO GOOD AGAIN.
ころんっ
PLUP
IT'S READY.
SUNAKO-CHAN.
HURRY UP AND EAT IT BEFORE IT GETS TOO TOUGH.
ポイ
PLOINK
ポイ
PLOINK
WANNA TRY THIS?
TA-TAK-ENAGA.
IT'S REALLY YUMMY. ♡
てへ
HEH
NO.
THEY'RE GRILLED TO PERFECTION.
H-HE'S PISSED.
I'M NOT PISSED.
もぐもぐ
CHOMP CHOMP
I BROUGHT BACK ANOTHER ONE.

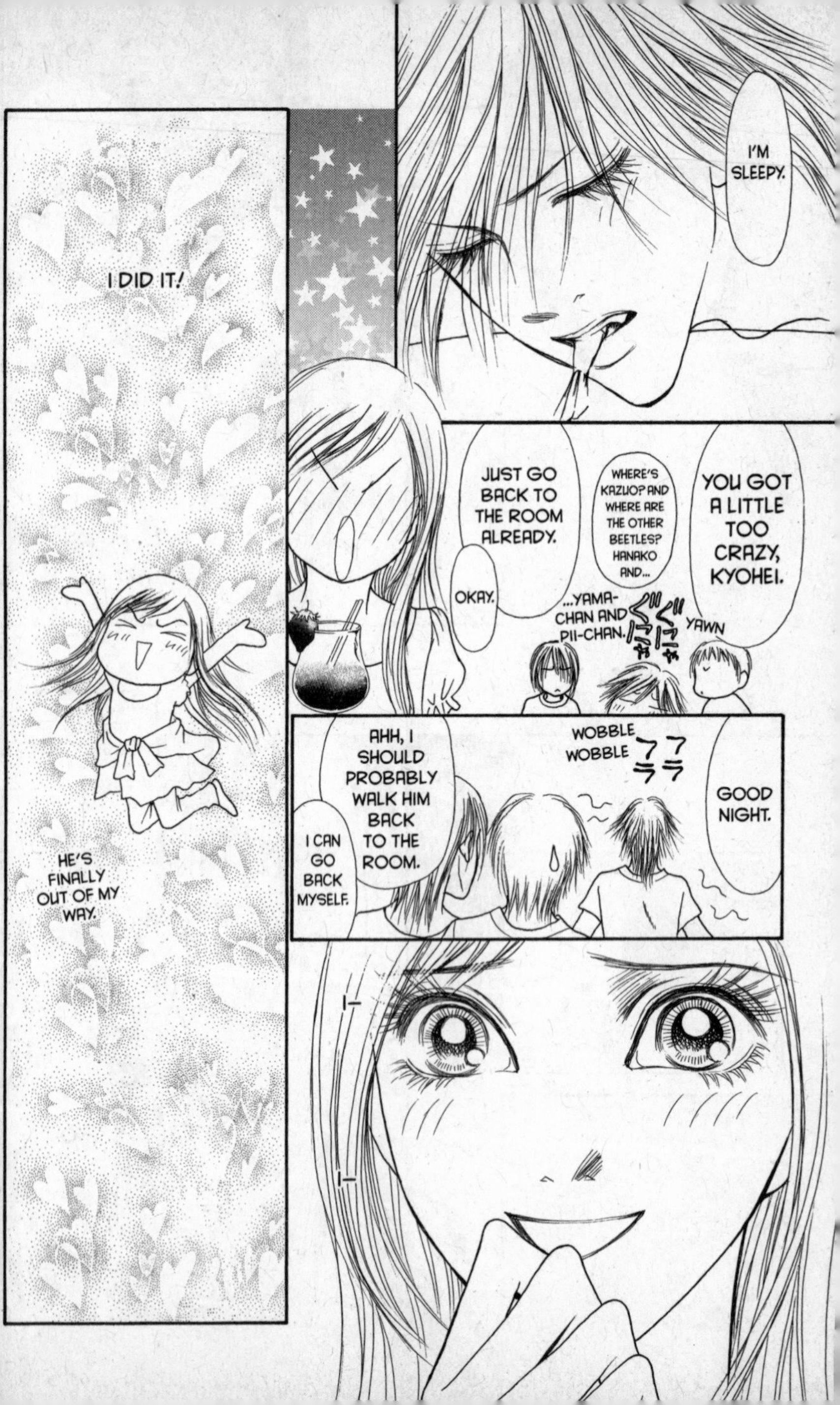
I'M SLEEPY.
YOU GOT A LITTLE TOO CRAZY, KYOHEI.
WHERE'S KAZUO? AND WHERE ARE THE OTHER BEETLES? HANAKO AND...
...YAMA-CHAN AND PII-CHAN.
YAWN
JUST GO BACK TO THE ROOM ALREADY.
OKAY.
GOOD NIGHT.
WOBBLE WOBBLE
AHH, I SHOULD PROBABLY WALK HIM BACK TO THE ROOM.
I CAN GO BACK MYSELF.
I—
I—
I DID IT!
HE'S FINALLY OUT OF MY WAY.

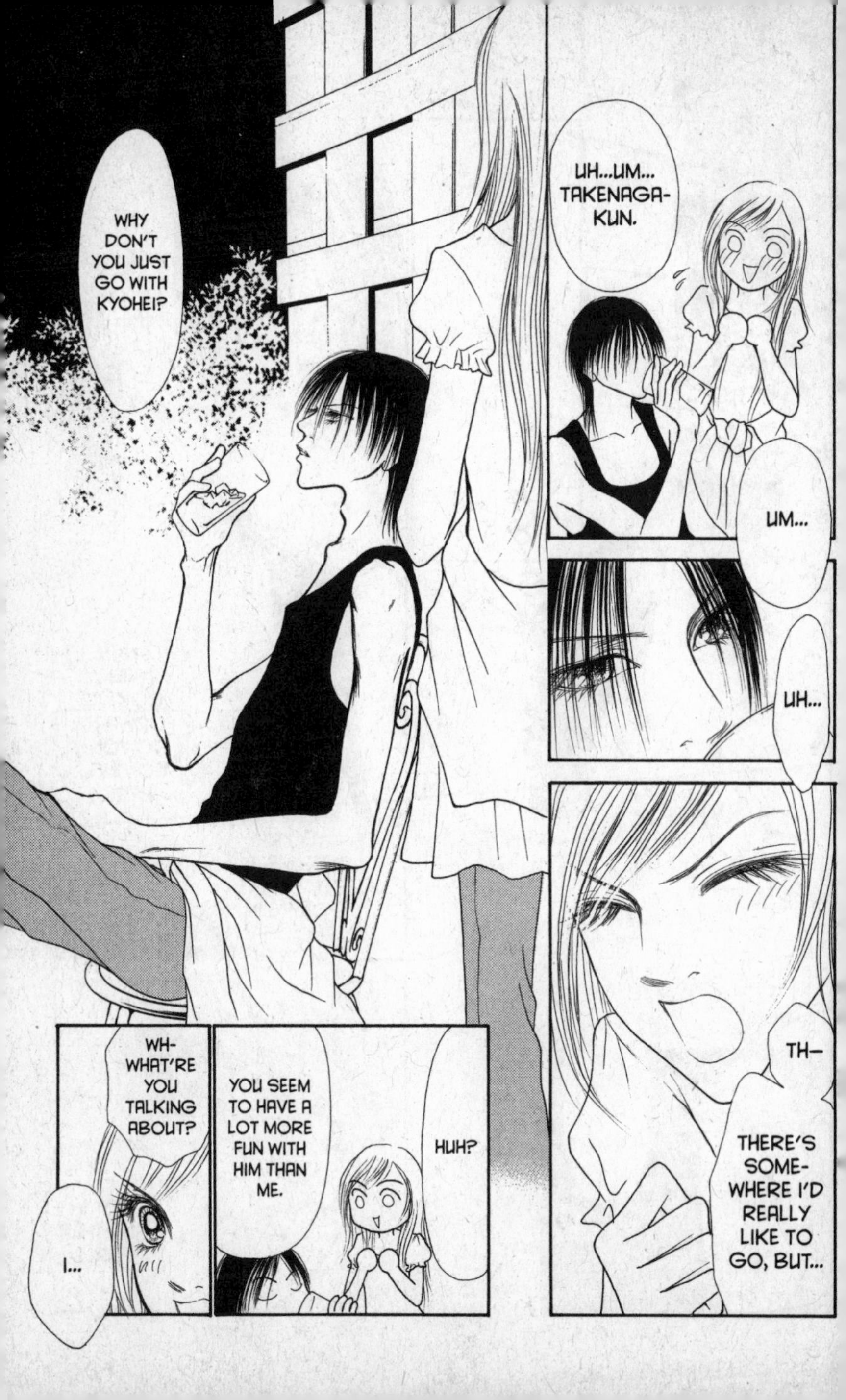
UH...UM... TAKENAGA-KUN.
UM...
UH...
TH—
THERE'S SOMEWHERE I'D REALLY LIKE TO GO, BUT...
WHY DON'T YOU JUST GO WITH KYOHEI?
HUH?
YOU SEEM TO HAVE A LOT MORE FUN WITH HIM THAN ME.
WH-WHAT'RE YOU TALKING ABOUT?
I...

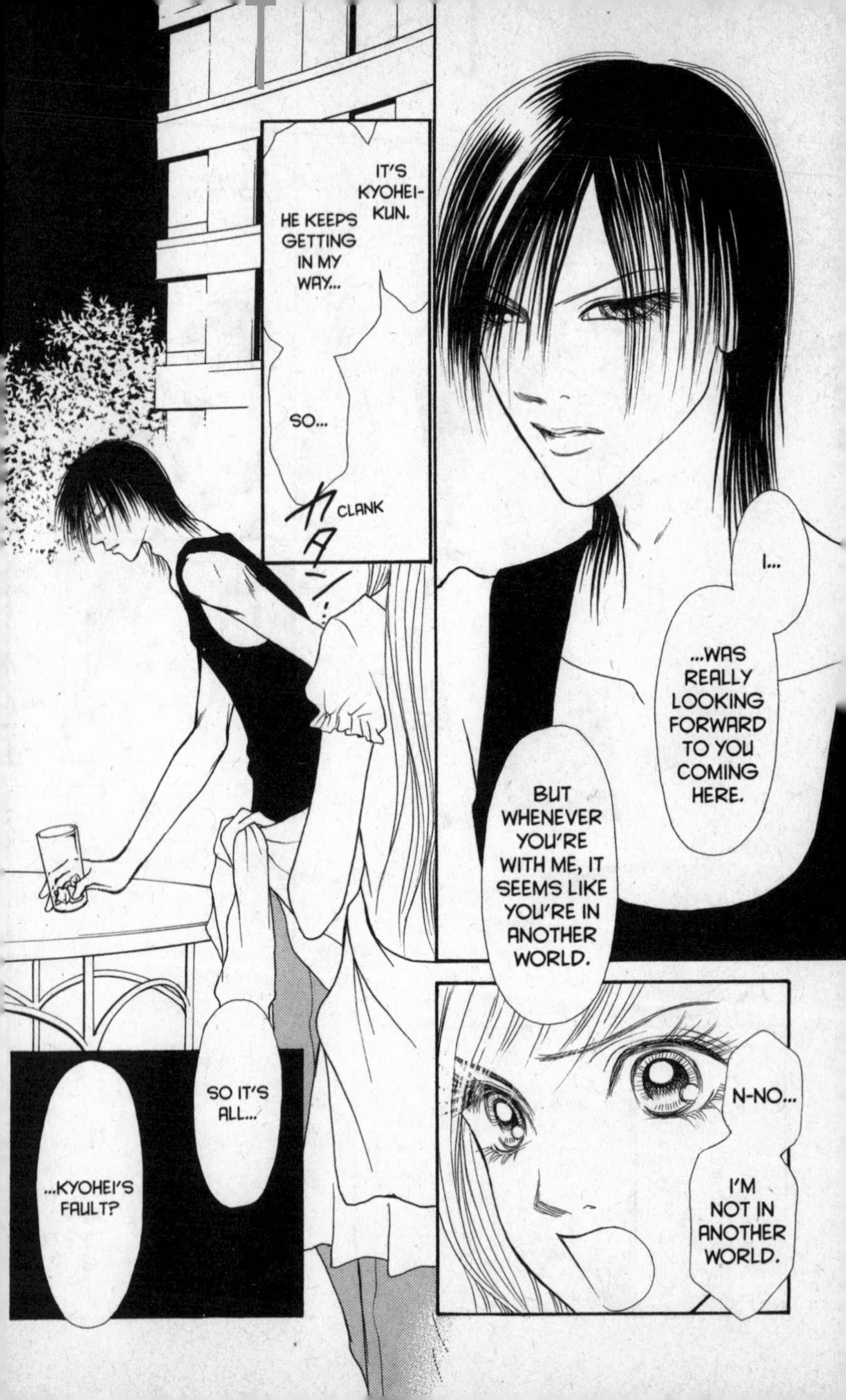

I...
...WAS REALLY LOOKING FORWARD TO YOU COMING HERE.
BUT WHENEVER YOU'RE WITH ME, IT SEEMS LIKE YOU'RE IN ANOTHER WORLD.
N-NO...
I'M NOT IN ANOTHER WORLD.
IT'S KYOHEI-KUN.
HE KEEPS GETTING IN MY WAY...
SO...
CLANK
SO IT'S ALL...
...KYOHEI'S FAULT?

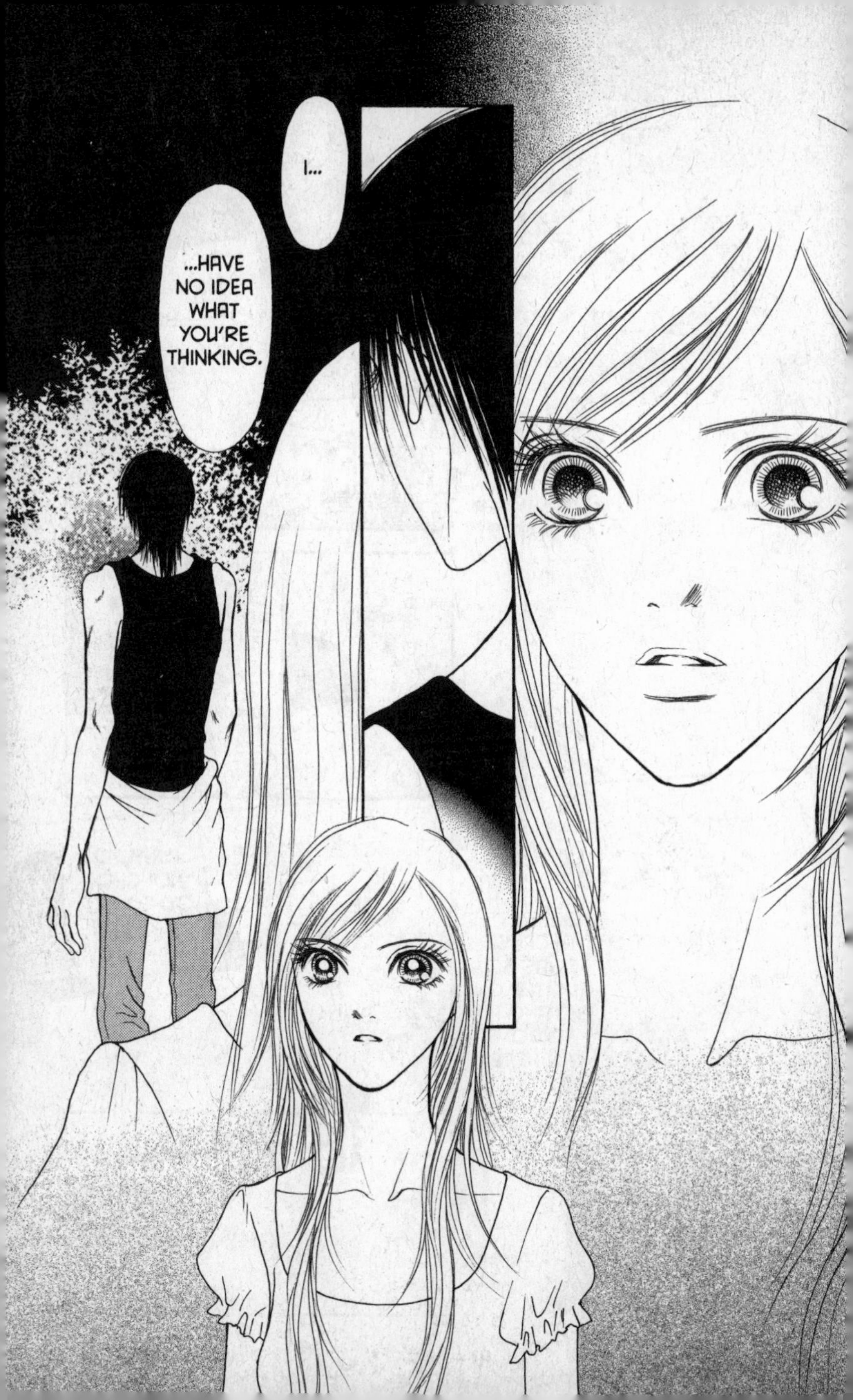
I...
...HAVE NO IDEA WHAT YOU'RE THINKING.

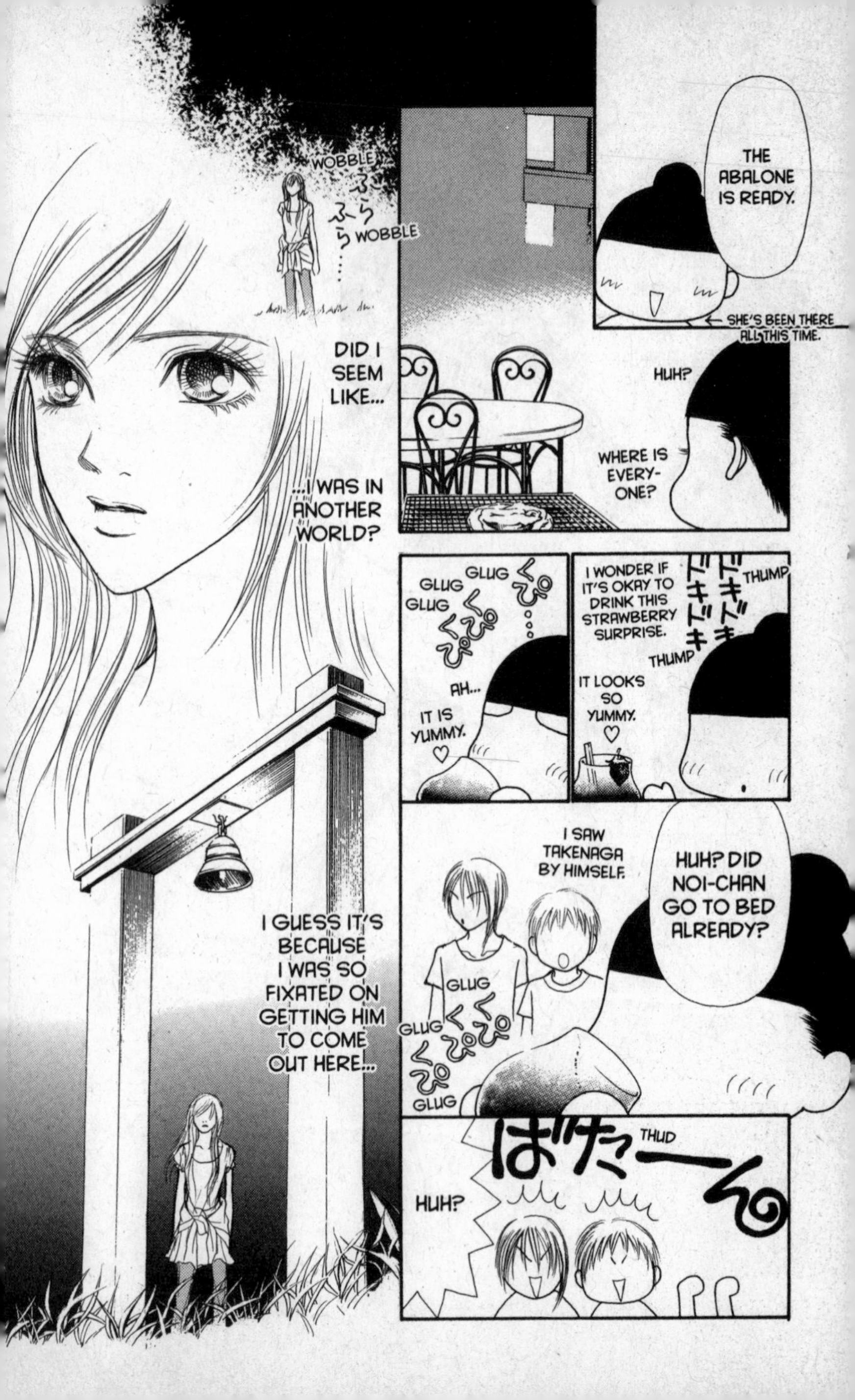
THE ABALONE IS READY.
SHE'S BEEN THERE ALL THIS TIME.
HUH?
WHERE IS EVERY-ONE?
I WONDER IF IT'S OKAY TO DRINK THIS STRAWBERRY SURPRISE.
THUMP
THUMP
IT LOOKS SO YUMMY. ♡
GLUG GLUG GLUG
AH...
IT IS YUMMY. ♡
HUH? DID NOI-CHAN GO TO BED ALREADY?
I SAW TAKENAGA BY HIMSELF.
GLUG GLUG GLUG
THUD
HUH?
WOBBLE
WOBBLE
DID I SEEM LIKE...
...I WAS IN ANOTHER WORLD?
I GUESS IT'S BECAUSE I WAS SO FIXATED ON GETTING HIM TO COME OUT HERE...

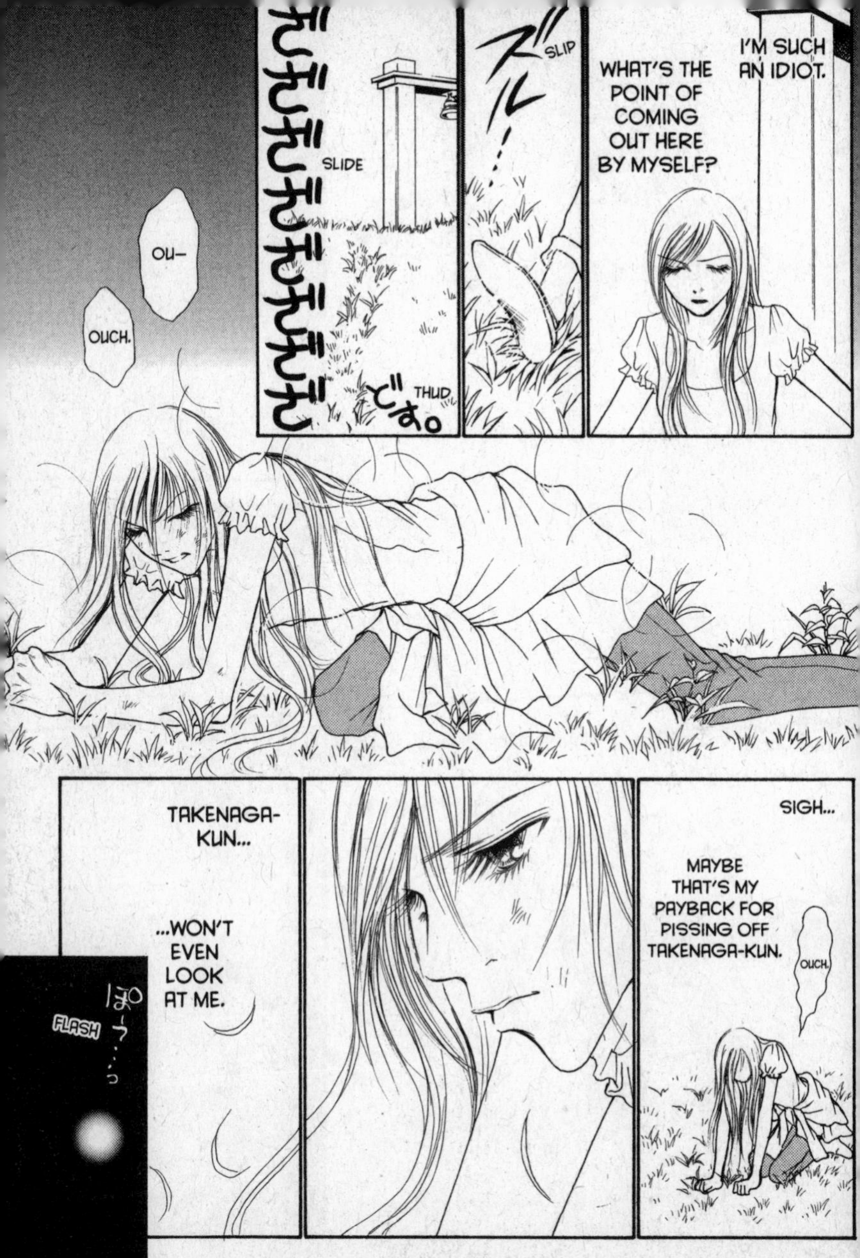

I'M SUCH AN IDIOT.
WHAT'S THE POINT OF COMING OUT HERE BY MYSELF?
ズル…
SLIP
SLIDE
どす。
THUD
OU–
OUCH.
SIGH...
MAYBE THAT'S MY PAYBACK FOR PISSING OFF TAKENAGA-KUN.
OUCH.
TAKENAGA-KUN...
...WON'T EVEN LOOK AT ME.
FLASH

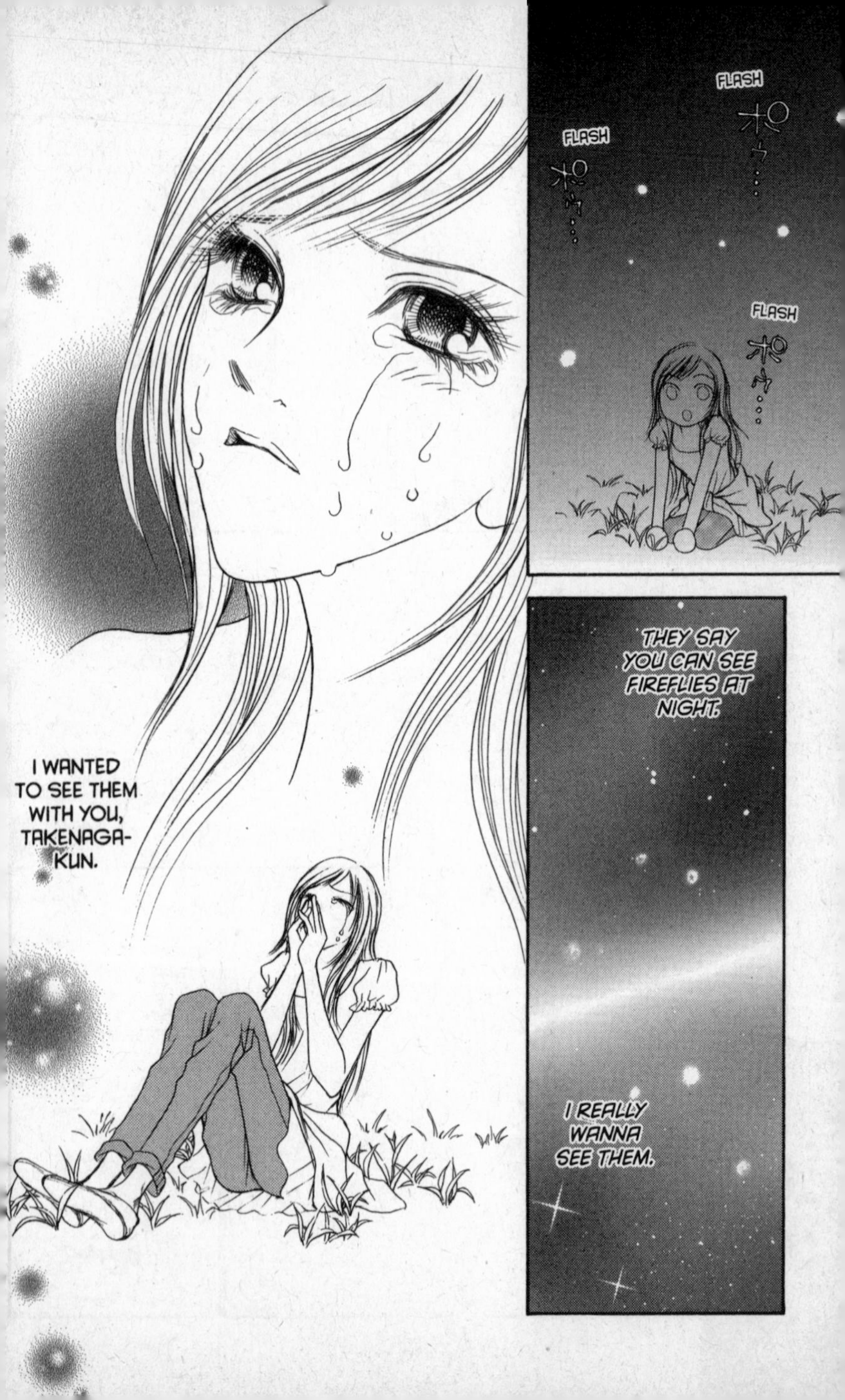
FLASH
FLASH
FLASH
THEY SAY YOU CAN SEE FIREFLIES AT NIGHT.
I REALLY WANNA SEE THEM.
I WANTED TO SEE THEM WITH YOU, TAKENAGA-KUN.

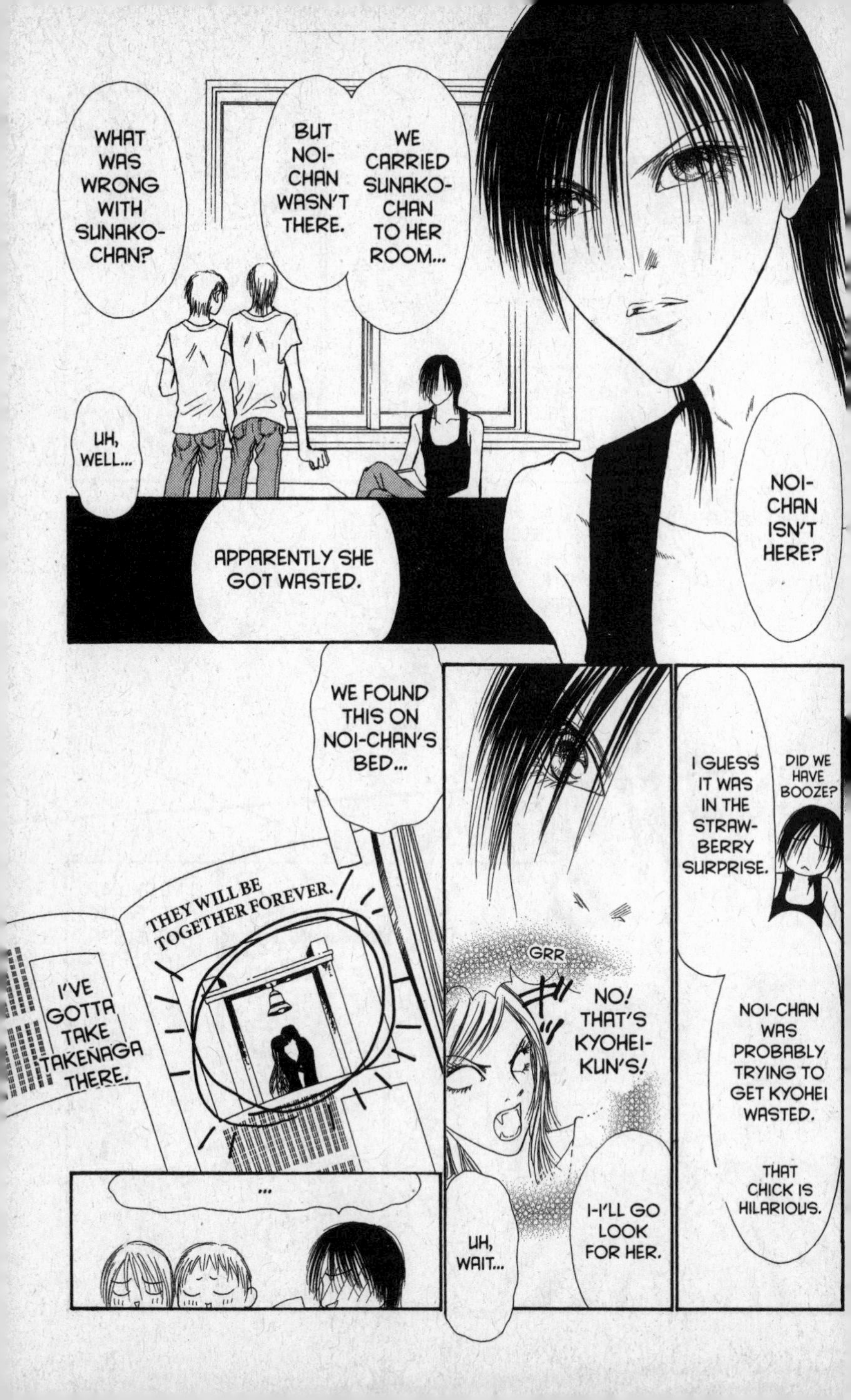
NOI-CHAN ISN'T HERE?
WE CARRIED SUNAKO-CHAN TO HER ROOM...
BUT NOI-CHAN WASN'T THERE.
WHAT WAS WRONG WITH SUNAKO-CHAN?
UH, WELL...
APPARENTLY SHE GOT WASTED.
DID WE HAVE BOOZE?
I GUESS IT WAS IN THE STRAWBERRY SURPRISE.
NOI-CHAN WAS PROBABLY TRYING TO GET KYOHEI WASTED.
THAT CHICK IS HILARIOUS.
GRR
NO! THAT'S KYOHEI-KUN'S!
I-I'LL GO LOOK FOR HER.
UH, WAIT...
WE FOUND THIS ON NOI-CHAN'S BED...
THEY WILL BE TOGETHER FOREVER.
I'VE GOTTA TAKE TAKEÑAGA THERE.
...

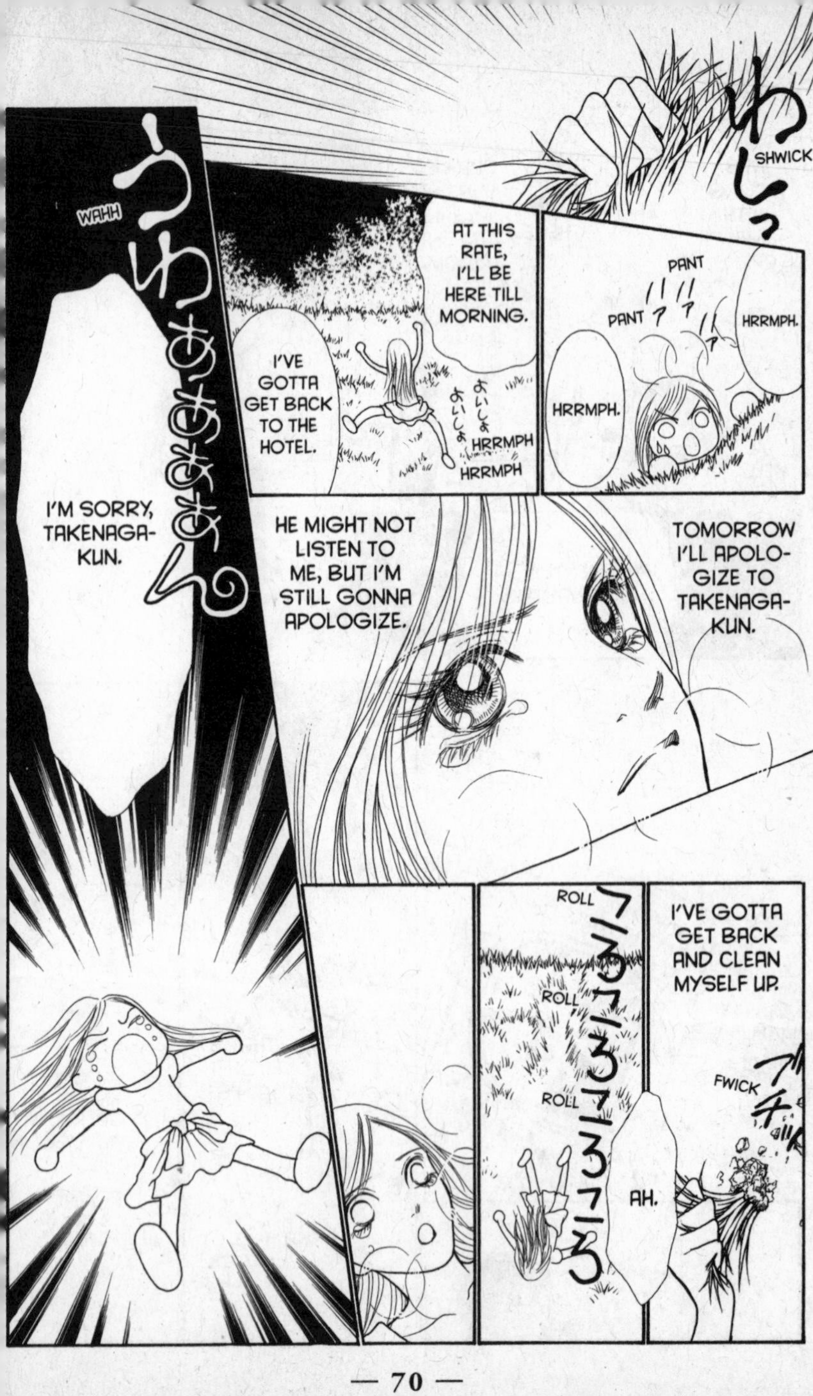
SHWICK
PANT
PANT
HRRMPH.
HRRMPH.
AT THIS RATE, I'LL BE HERE TILL MORNING.
I'VE GOTTA GET BACK TO THE HOTEL.
HRRMPH
HRRMPH
TOMORROW I'LL APOLOGIZE TO TAKENAGA-KUN.
HE MIGHT NOT LISTEN TO ME, BUT I'M STILL GONNA APOLOGIZE.
I'VE GOTTA GET BACK AND CLEAN MYSELF UP.
FWICK
AH.
ROLL
ROLL
ROLL
WAHH
I'M SORRY, TAKENAGA-KUN.

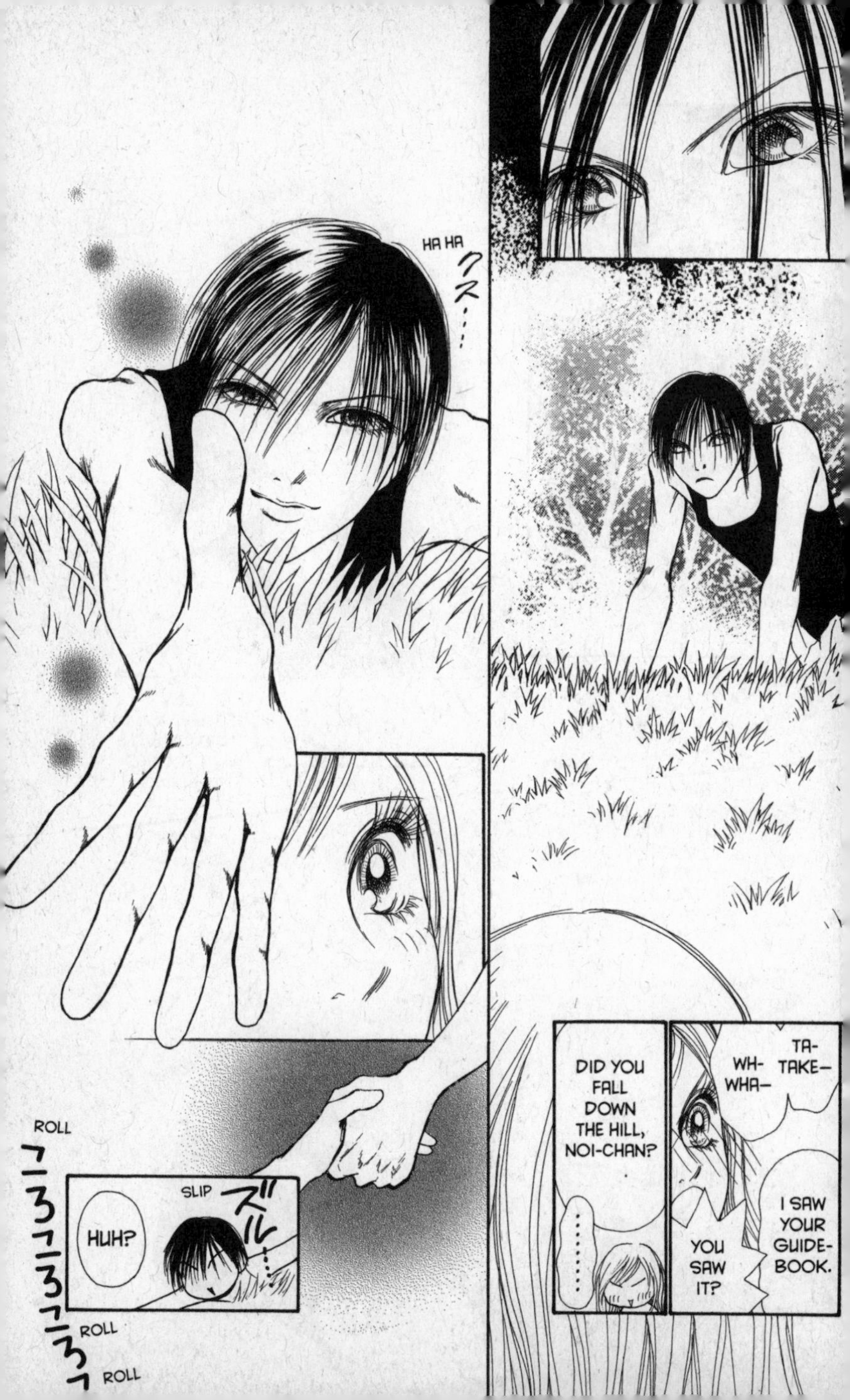
TA-
TAKE—
WH-
WHA—
I SAW YOUR GUIDE-BOOK.
YOU SAW IT?
DID YOU FALL DOWN THE HILL, NOI-CHAN?
......
HA HA
クス…
SLIP
ズル…
HUH?
ROLL
ROLL
ROLL

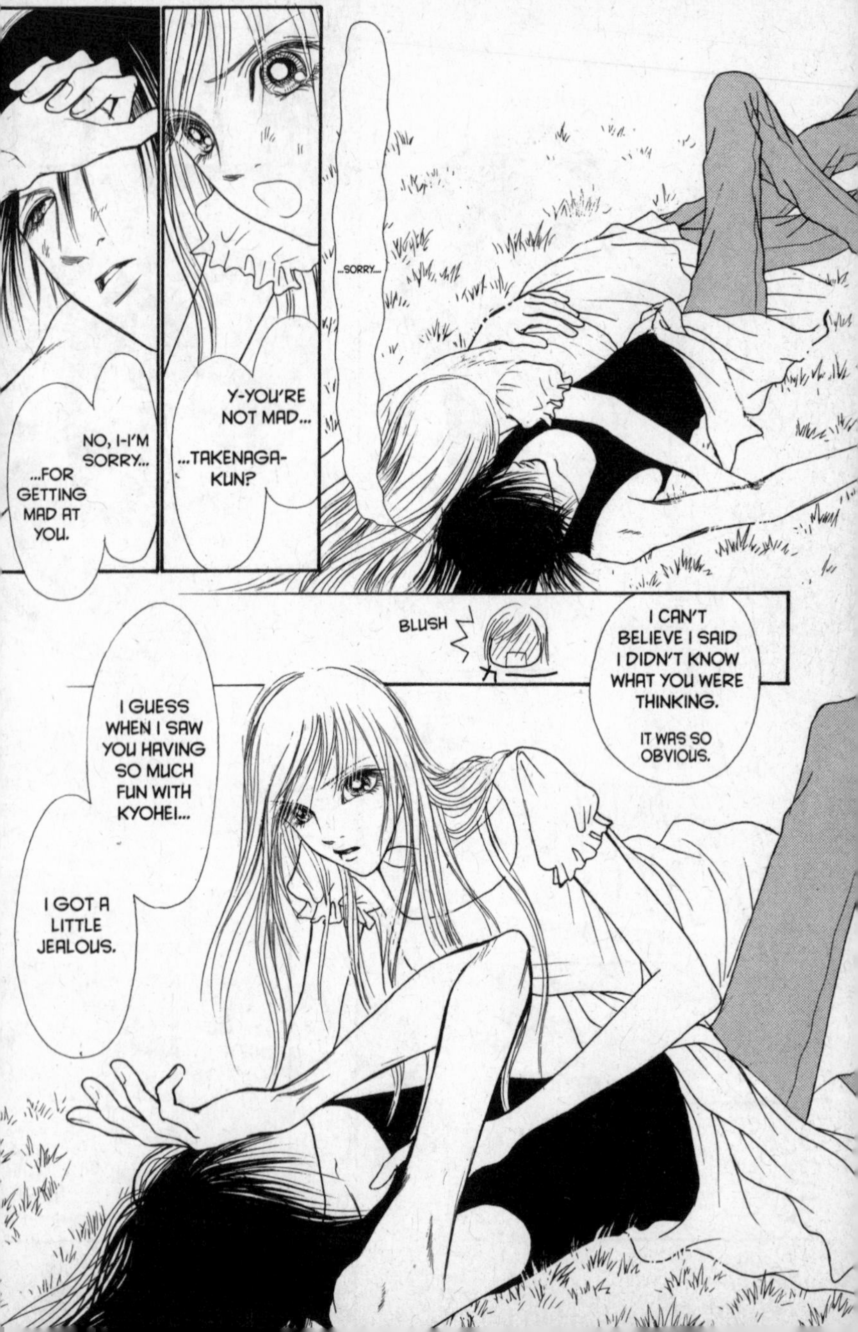
...SORRY...
Y-YOU'RE NOT MAD...
...TAKENAGA-KUN?
NO, I-I'M SORRY...
...FOR GETTING MAD AT YOU.
I CAN'T BELIEVE I SAID I DIDN'T KNOW WHAT YOU WERE THINKING.
IT WAS SO OBVIOUS.
BLUSH
I GUESS WHEN I SAW YOU HAVING SO MUCH FUN WITH KYOHEI...
I GOT A LITTLE JEALOUS.

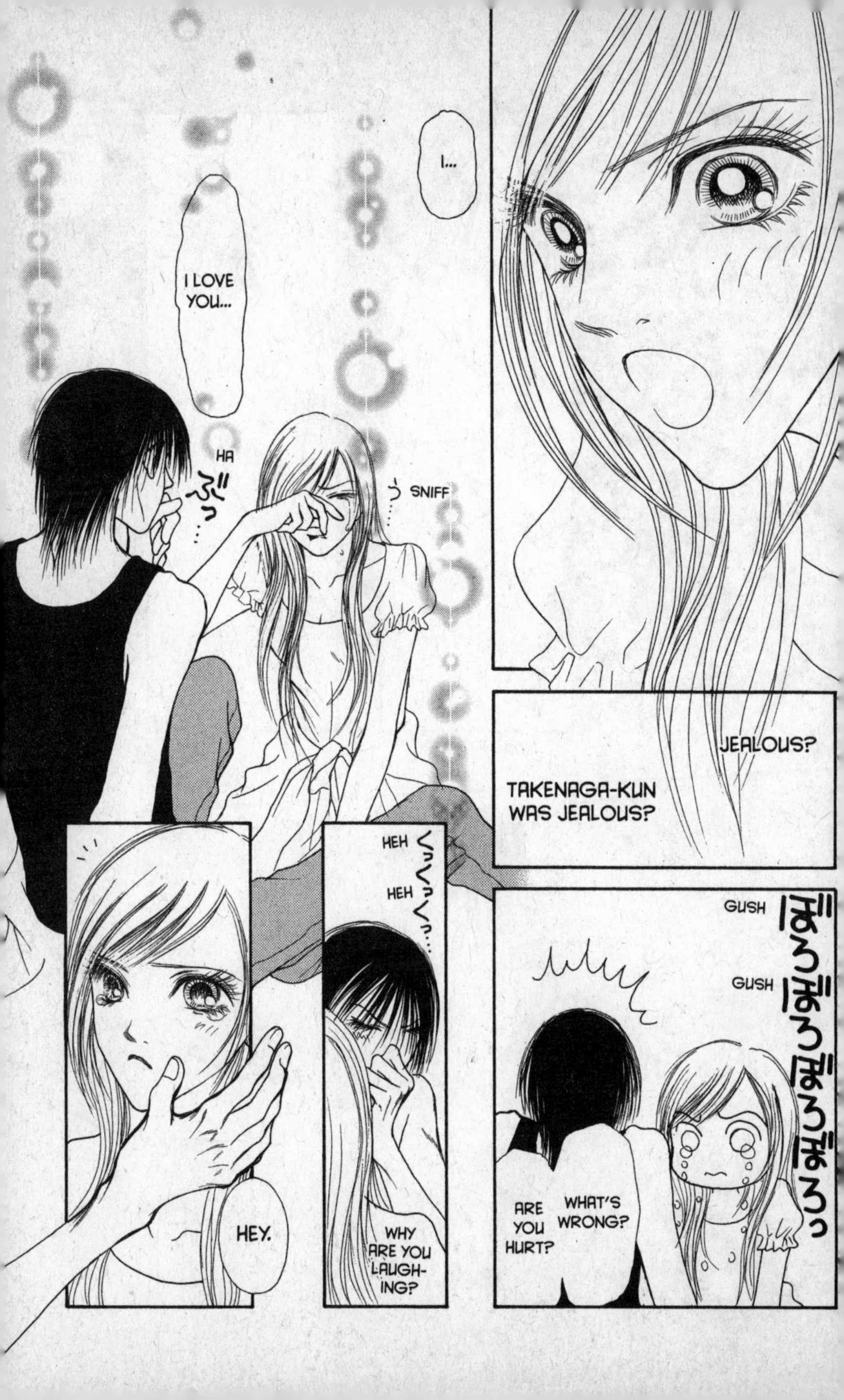
I...
I LOVE YOU...
SNIFF
HA
ぶっ…
JEALOUS?
TAKENAGA-KUN WAS JEALOUS?
GUSH
GUSH
ぼろぼろぼろぼろっ
WHAT'S WRONG?
ARE YOU HURT?
HEH
HEH
WHY ARE YOU LAUGHING?
HEY.

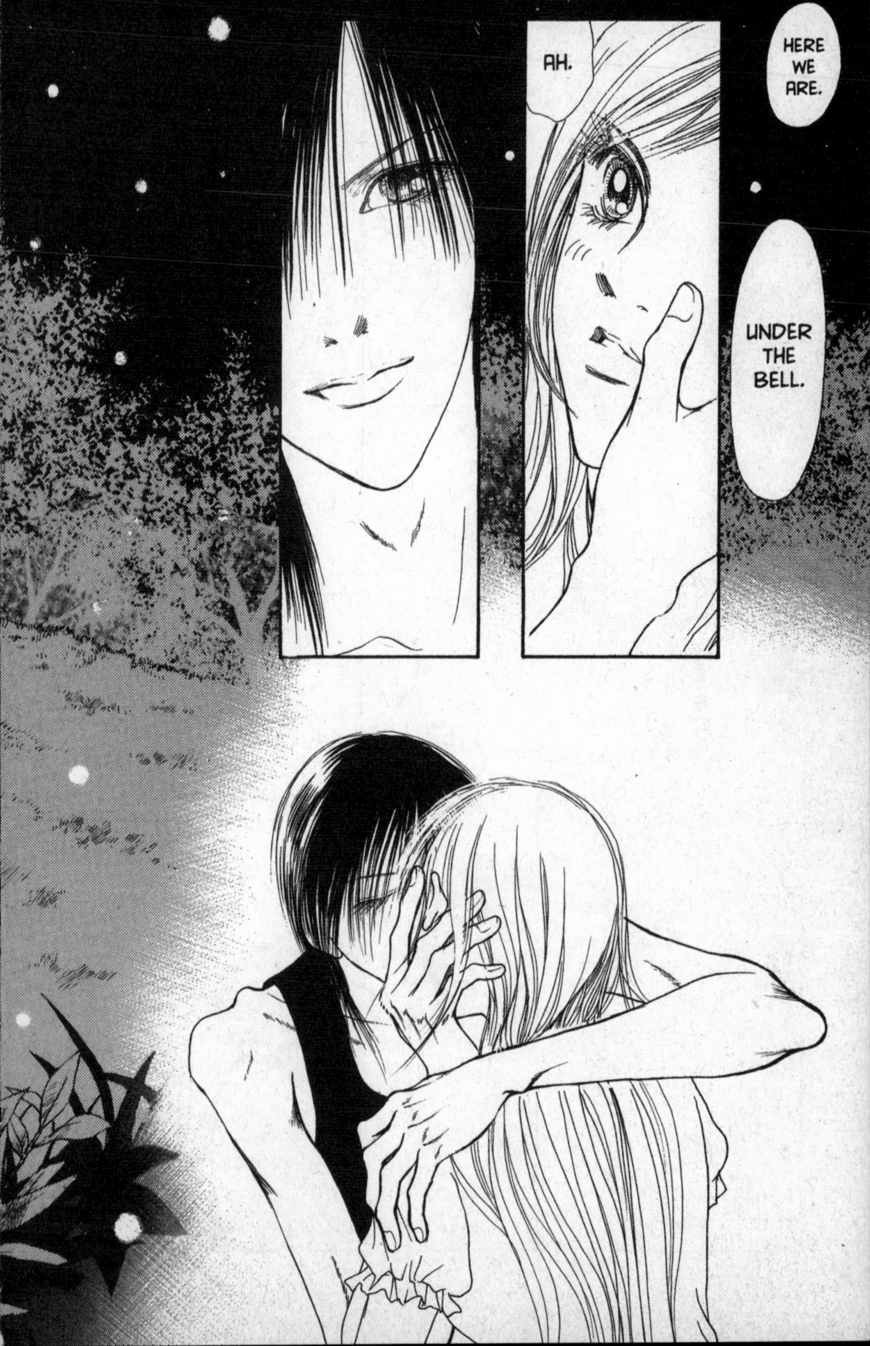
HERE WE ARE.
UNDER THE BELL.
AH.

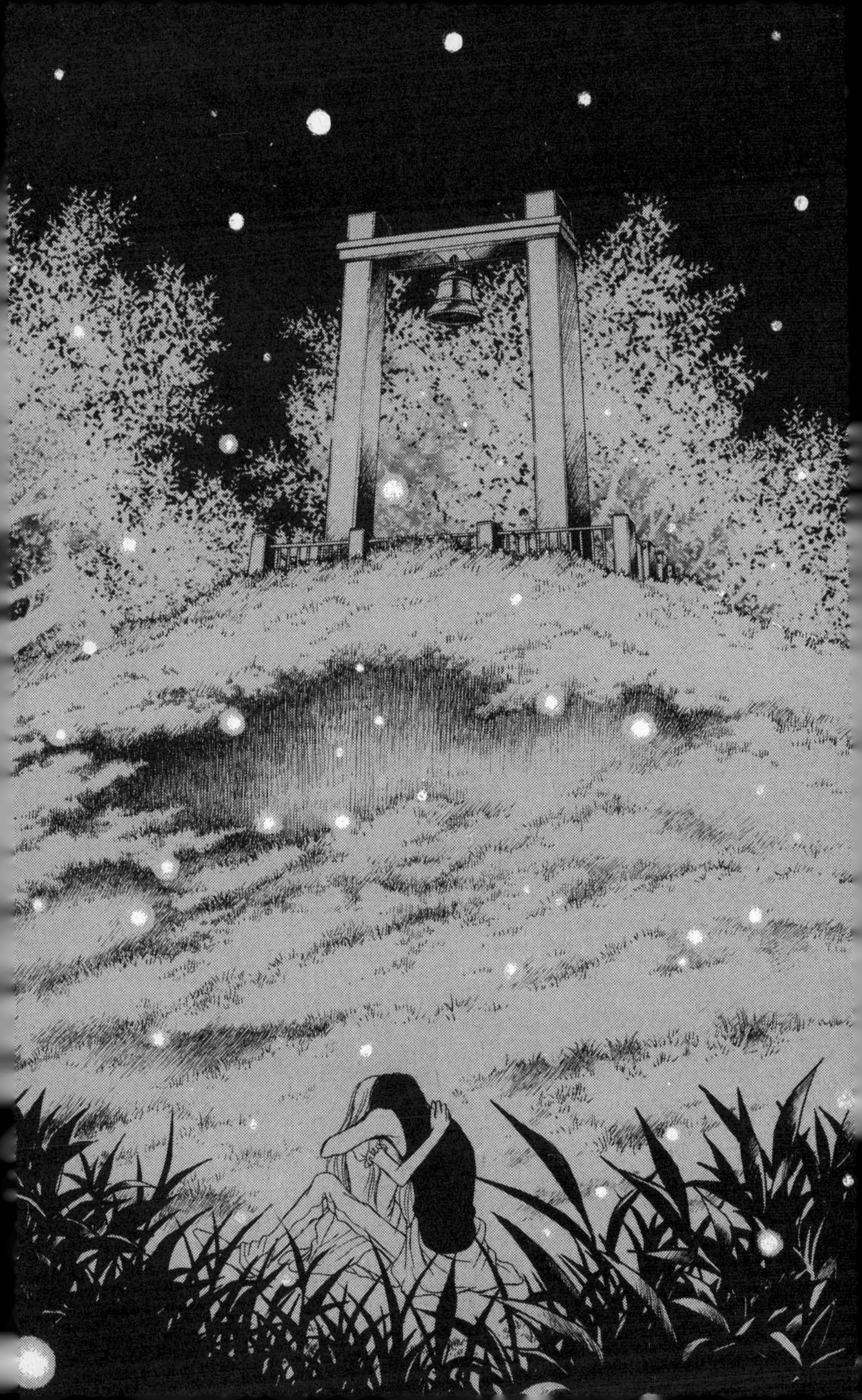

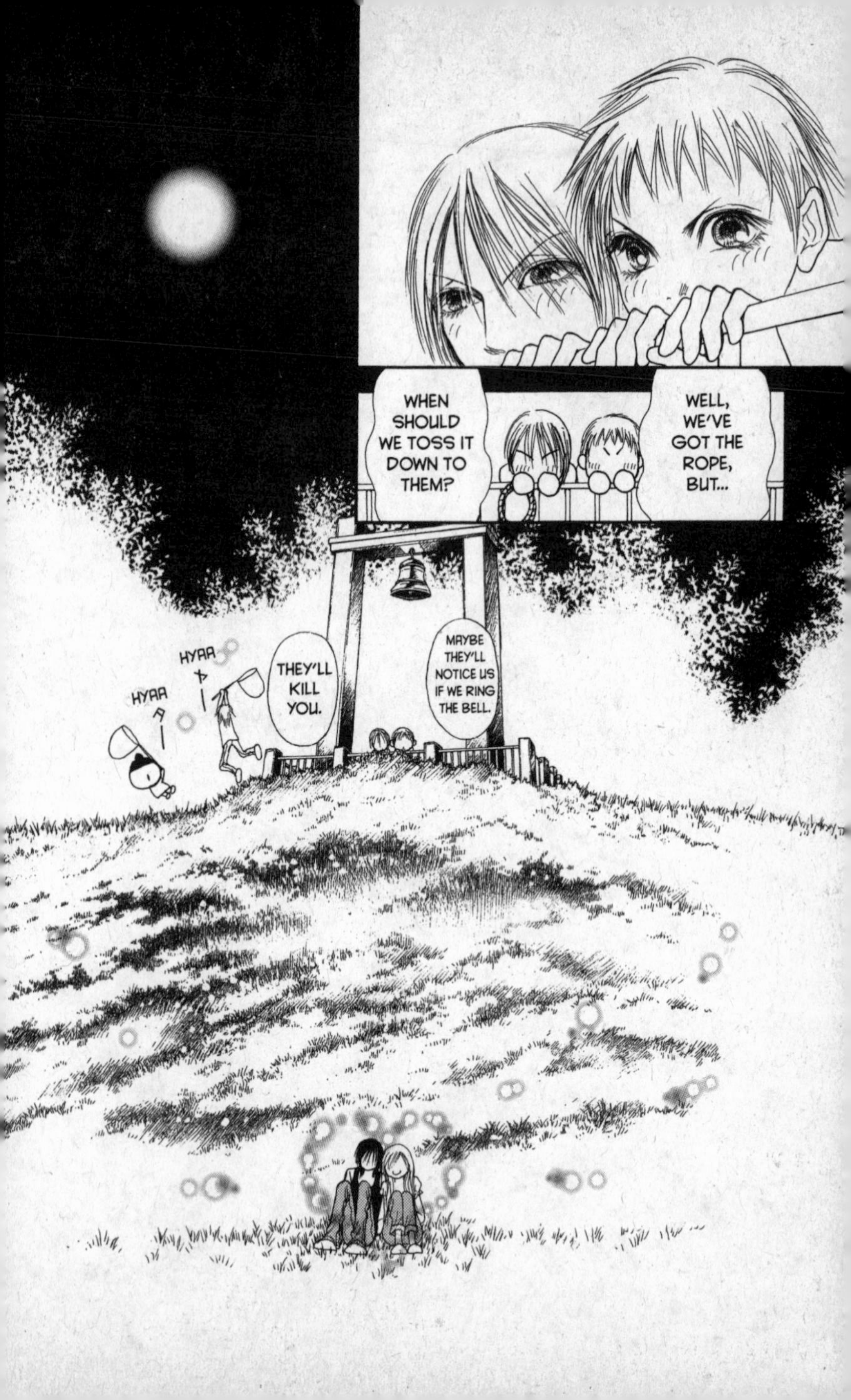
WELL, WE'VE GOT THE ROPE, BUT...
WHEN SHOULD WE TOSS IT DOWN TO THEM?
MAYBE THEY'LL NOTICE US IF WE RING THE BELL.
THEY'LL KILL YOU.
HYAA
HYAA

IS ANY-
BODY
THERE?
HELLO! HELLO!

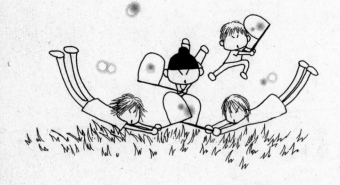

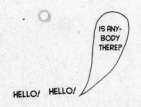

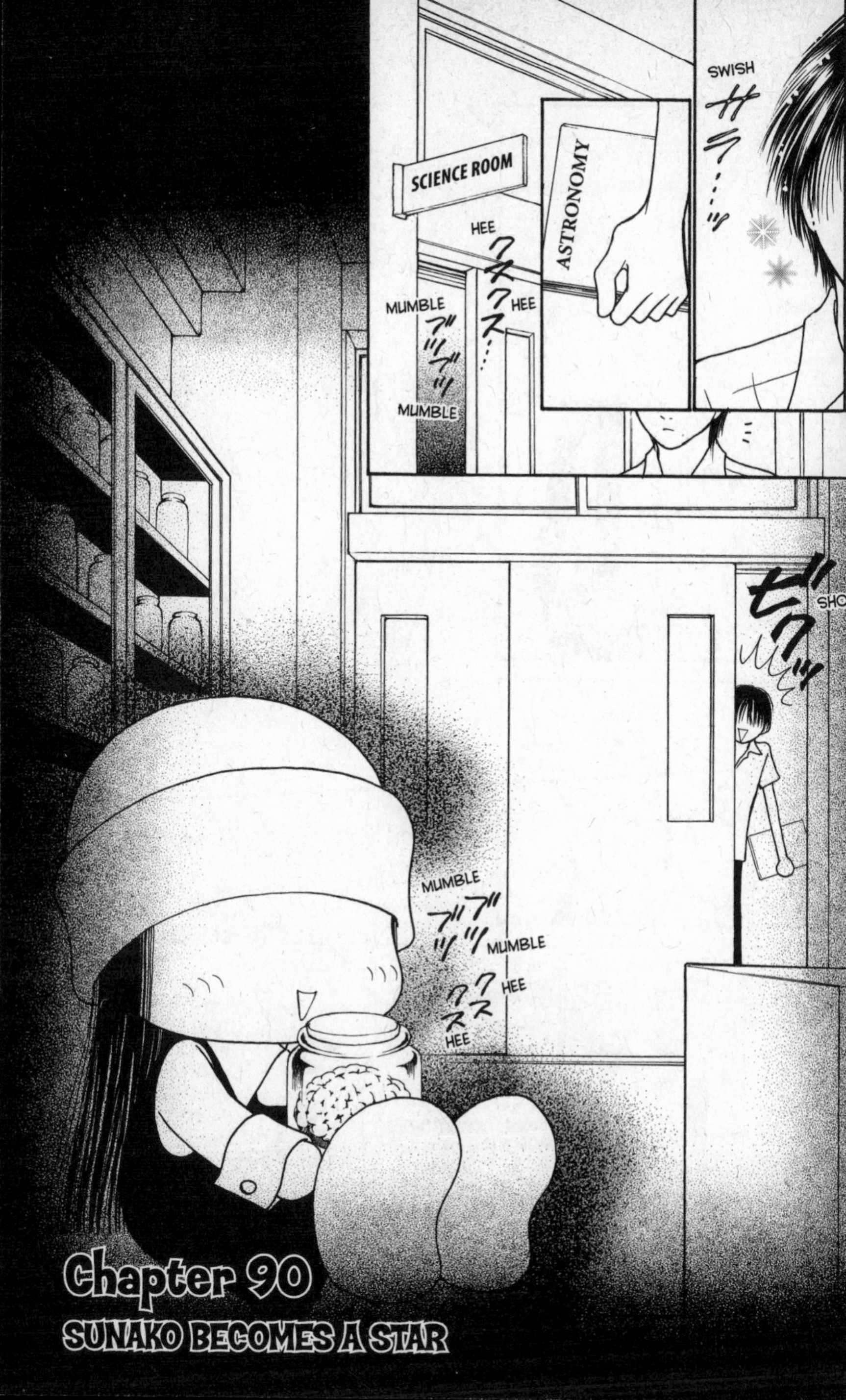
SWISH
サラ…ッ
ASTRONOMY
SCIENCE ROOM
HEE
クスクス…
HEE
MUMBLE
ブツブツ
MUMBLE
ビクッ
SHO
MUMBLE
ブツブツ
MUMBLE
HEE
クスクス
HEE

Chapter 90

SUNAKO BECOMES A STAR

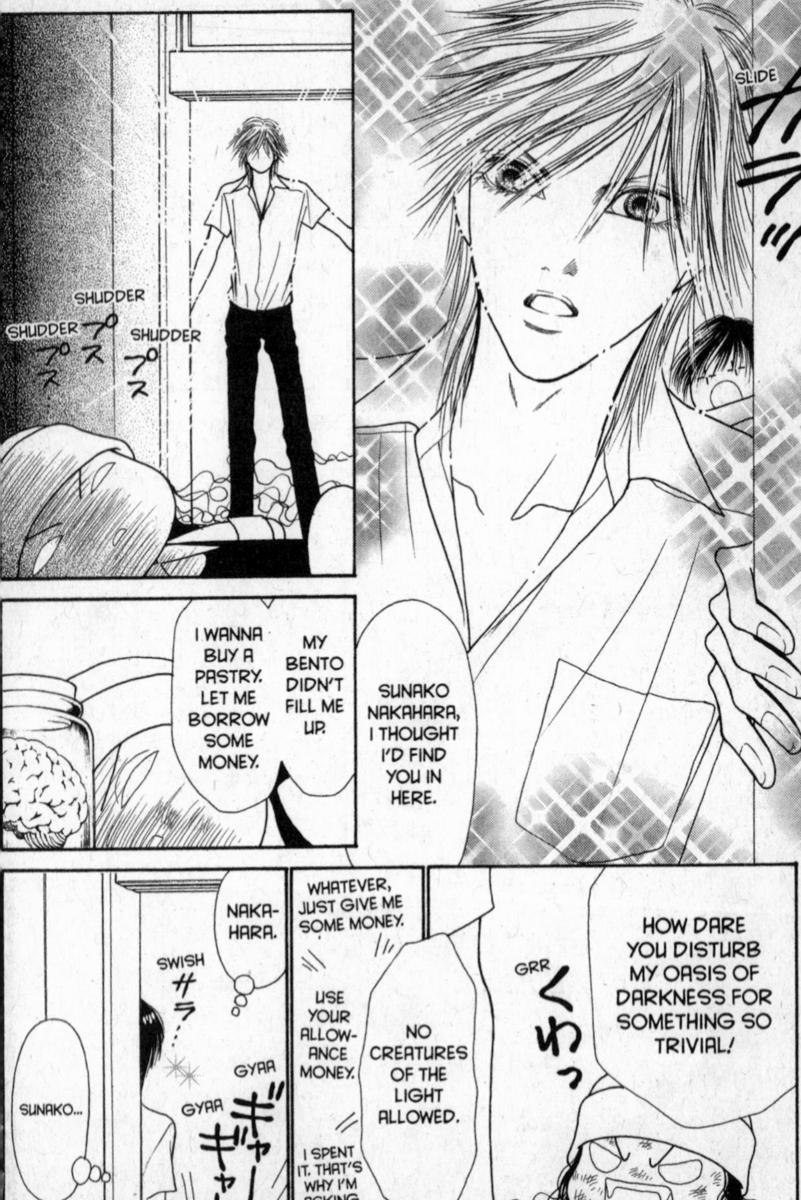
SLIDE
SUNAKO NAKAHARA, I THOUGHT I'D FIND YOU IN HERE.
SHUDDER
SHUDDER
SHUDDER
MY BENTO DIDN'T FILL ME UP.
I WANNA BUY A PASTRY. LET ME BORROW SOME MONEY.
HOW DARE YOU DISTURB MY OASIS OF DARKNESS FOR SOMETHING SO TRIVIAL!
GRR
NO CREATURES OF THE LIGHT ALLOWED.
WHATEVER, JUST GIVE ME SOME MONEY.
USE YOUR ALLOWANCE MONEY.
I SPENT IT. THAT'S WHY I'M ASKING YOU.
NAKAHARA.
SWISH
GYAA
GYAA
SUNAKO...

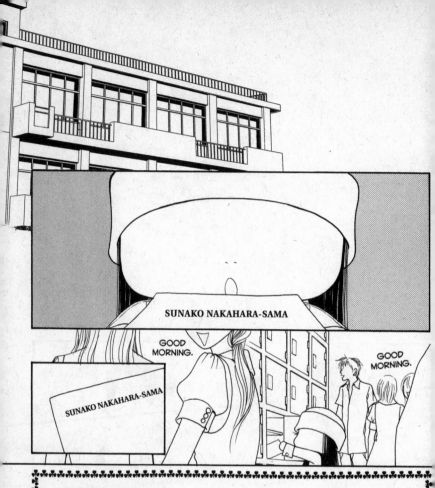

SUNAKO NAKAHARA-SAMA

SUNAKO NAKAHARA-SAMA

GOOD
MORNING.

GOOD
MORNING.

BEHIND THE SCENES

AROUND THE TIME I WAS WRITING THIS STORY, THINGS FINALLY WENT BACK TO NORMAL. I WAS MY USUAL SELF AGAIN. BUT I HAD TO RELY ON OTHER PEOPLE TO CHEER ME UP. I WANT TO THANK EVERYBODY WHO HELPED ME SO, SO MUCH. ♥ ♥ ♥

BEFORE I WENT BACK TO WORK, I SAW A SPECIAL SCREENING OF THE MOVIE *ATTITUDE*. (WITH A Q&A ♥) IT WAS DYNAMITE TOMMY-SAN'S DIRECTORIAL DEBUT. A-CHAN FROM NEW ROTEKA WAS PRETTY MUCH THE MAIN CHARACTER, AND I WAS SUPER EXCITED. ♥ AHH, HE'S SO HOT. ♥ ♥ ♥ A-CHAN. ♥

THE Q&A SESSION WITH A-CHAN, KATARU-KUN, AND TAKEIRI-SAN WAS REALLY FUN. ♥ ♥ ♥ THANKS FOR EVERYTHING, DYNAMITE TOMMY-SAMA.

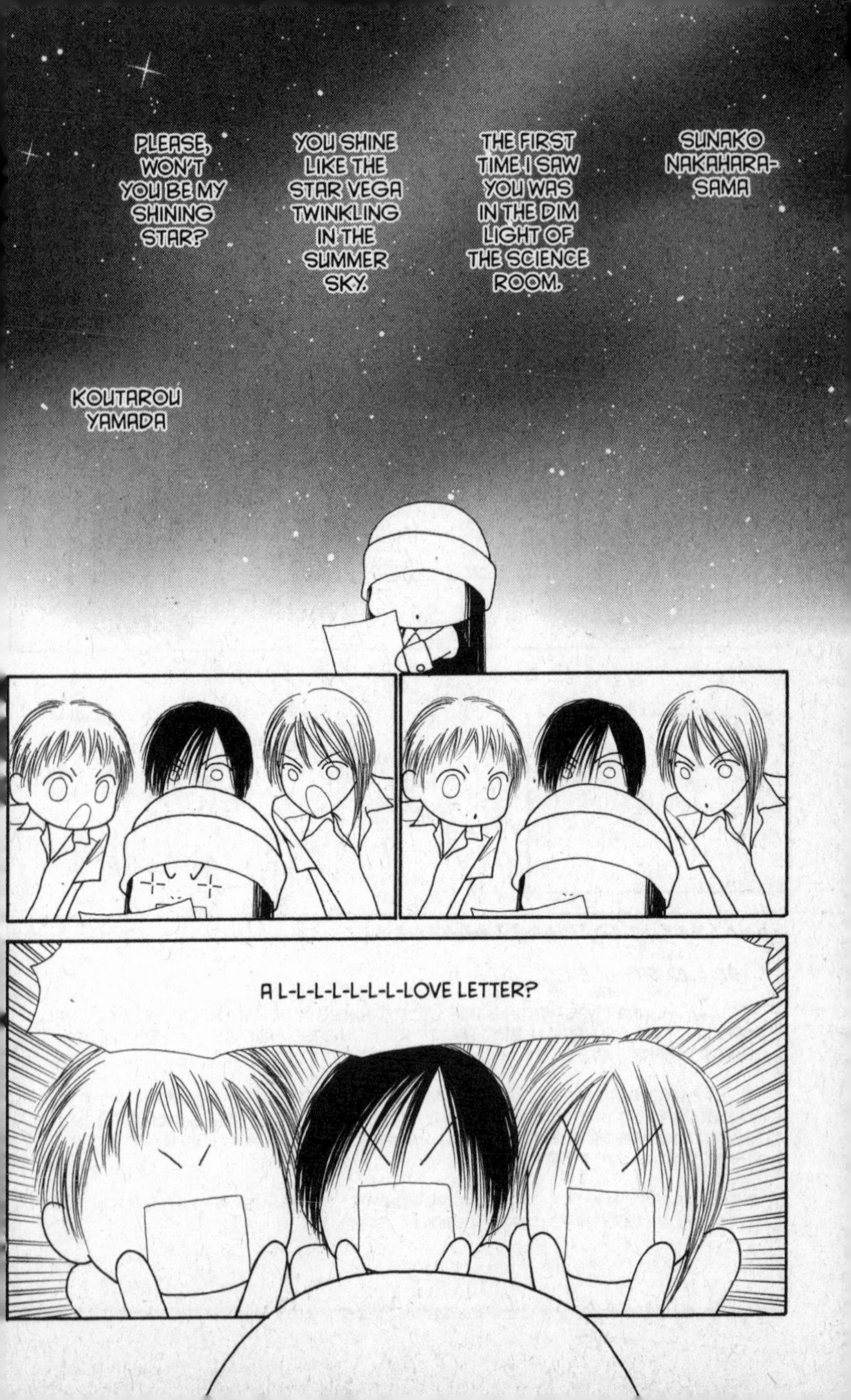
SUNAKO NAKAHARA-SAMA
THE FIRST TIME I SAW YOU WAS IN THE DIM LIGHT OF THE SCIENCE ROOM.
YOU SHINE LIKE THE STAR VEGA TWINKLING IN THE SUMMER SKY.
PLEASE, WON'T YOU BE MY SHINING STAR?
KOUTAROU YAMADA
A L-L-L-L-L-L-L-LOVE LETTER?

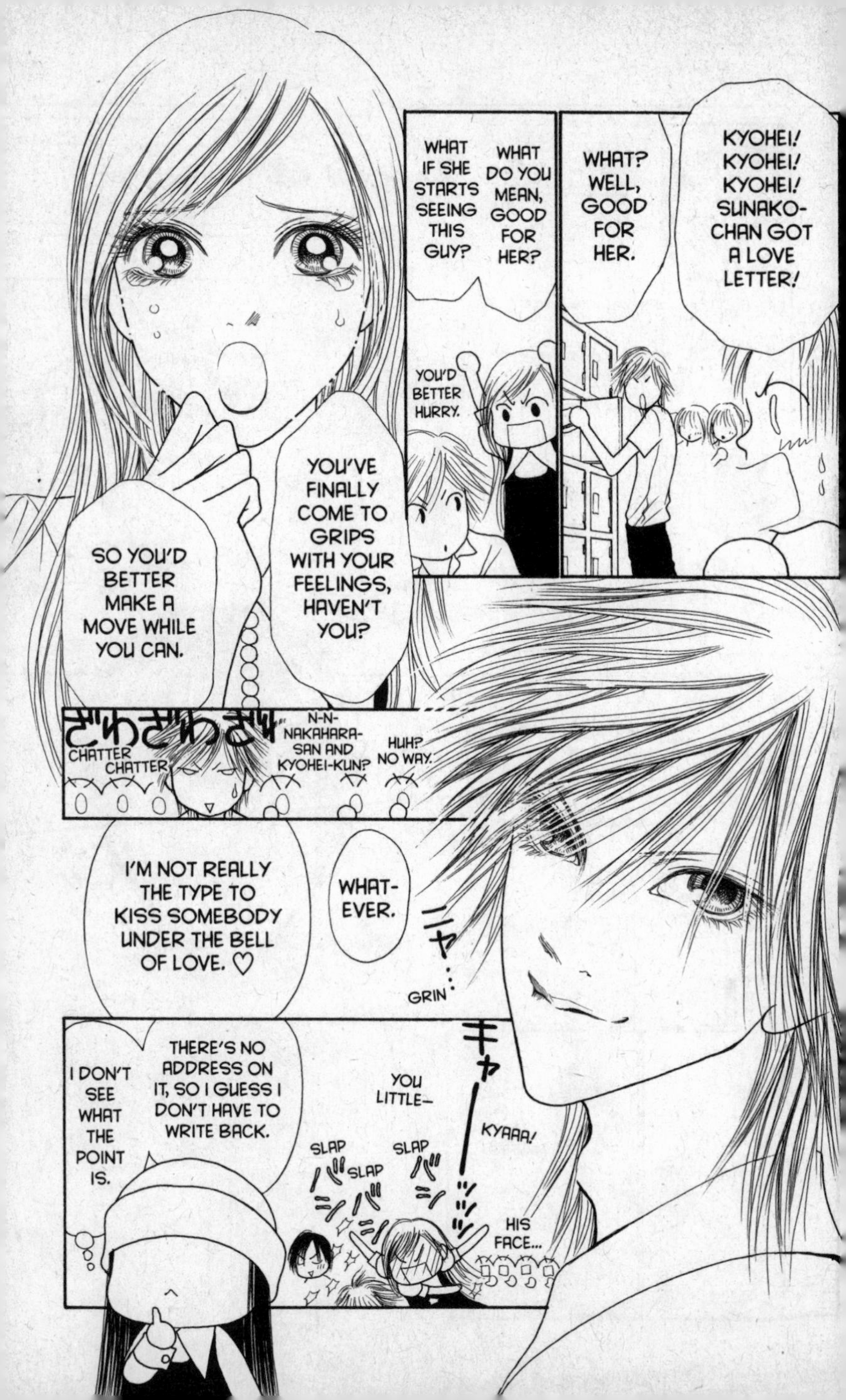
KYOHEI! KYOHEI! KYOHEI! SUNAKO-CHAN GOT A LOVE LETTER!
WHAT? WELL, GOOD FOR HER.
WHAT DO YOU MEAN, GOOD FOR HER?
WHAT IF SHE STARTS SEEING THIS GUY?
YOU'D BETTER HURRY.
YOU'VE FINALLY COME TO GRIPS WITH YOUR FEELINGS, HAVEN'T YOU?
SO YOU'D BETTER MAKE A MOVE WHILE YOU CAN.
HUH? NO WAY.
N-N-NAKAHARA-SAN AND KYOHEI-KUN?
ざわざわざわ
CHATTER CHATTER
WHAT-EVER.
I'M NOT REALLY THE TYPE TO KISS SOMEBODY UNDER THE BELL OF LOVE. ♡
ニヤ…
GRIN
キャー ツツツ
KYAAA!
HIS FACE...
YOU LITTLE—
SLAP
SLAP
SLAP
THERE'S NO ADDRESS ON IT, SO I GUESS I DON'T HAVE TO WRITE BACK.
I DON'T SEE WHAT THE POINT IS.

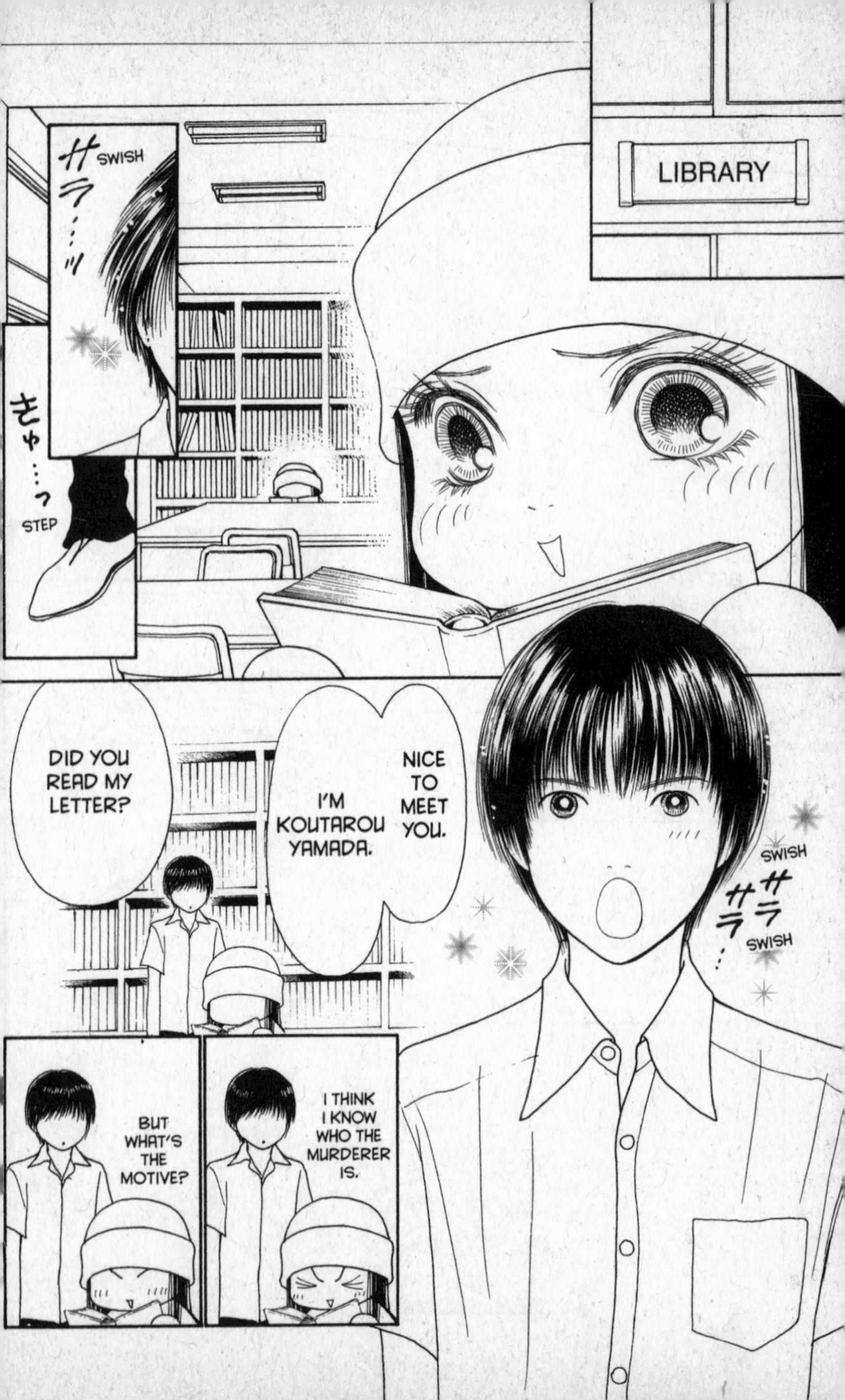
LIBRARY
サラ…ッ SWISH
きゅ…っ STEP
サラ サラ… SWISH SWISH
NICE TO MEET YOU.
I'M KOUTAROU YAMADA.
DID YOU READ MY LETTER?
I THINK I KNOW WHO THE MURDERER IS.
BUT WHAT'S THE MOTIVE?

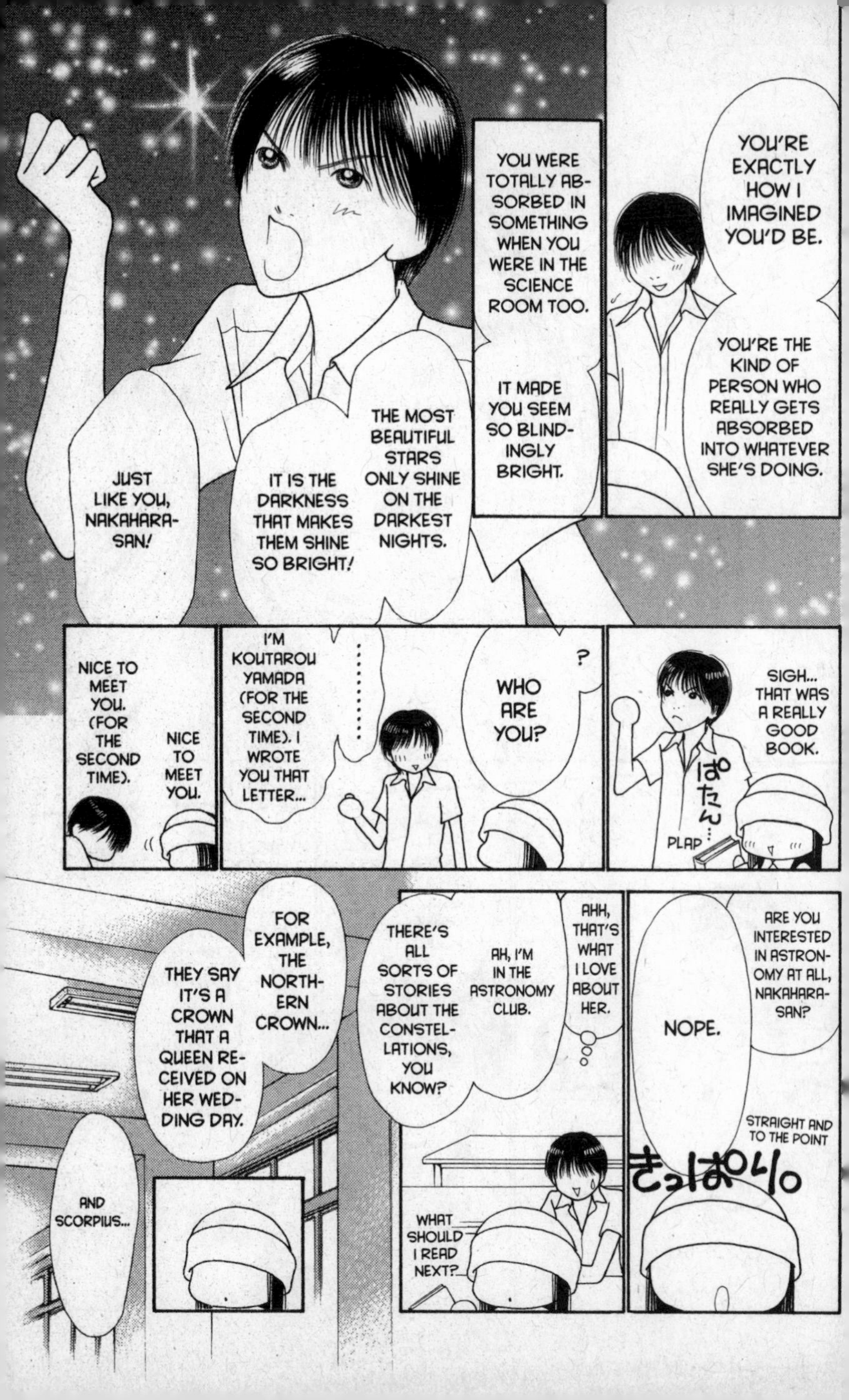
YOU'RE EXACTLY HOW I IMAGINED YOU'D BE.
YOU'RE THE KIND OF PERSON WHO REALLY GETS ABSORBED INTO WHATEVER SHE'S DOING.
YOU WERE TOTALLY ABSORBED IN SOMETHING WHEN YOU WERE IN THE SCIENCE ROOM TOO.
IT MADE YOU SEEM SO BLINDINGLY BRIGHT.
THE MOST BEAUTIFUL STARS ONLY SHINE ON THE DARKEST NIGHTS.
IT IS THE DARKNESS THAT MAKES THEM SHINE SO BRIGHT!
JUST LIKE YOU, NAKAHARA-SAN!
SIGH... THAT WAS A REALLY GOOD BOOK.
ぱたん…
PLAP
?
WHO ARE YOU?
......
I'M KOUTAROU YAMADA (FOR THE SECOND TIME). I WROTE YOU THAT LETTER...
NICE TO MEET YOU.
NICE TO MEET YOU. (FOR THE SECOND TIME).
ARE YOU INTERESTED IN ASTRONOMY AT ALL, NAKAHARA-SAN?
NOPE.
STRAIGHT AND TO THE POINT
きっぱり。
AHH, THAT'S WHAT I LOVE ABOUT HER.
AH, I'M IN THE ASTRONOMY CLUB.
THERE'S ALL SORTS OF STORIES ABOUT THE CONSTELLATIONS, YOU KNOW?
WHAT SHOULD I READ NEXT?
FOR EXAMPLE, THE NORTHERN CROWN...
THEY SAY IT'S A CROWN THAT A QUEEN RECEIVED ON HER WEDDING DAY.
AND SCORPIUS...

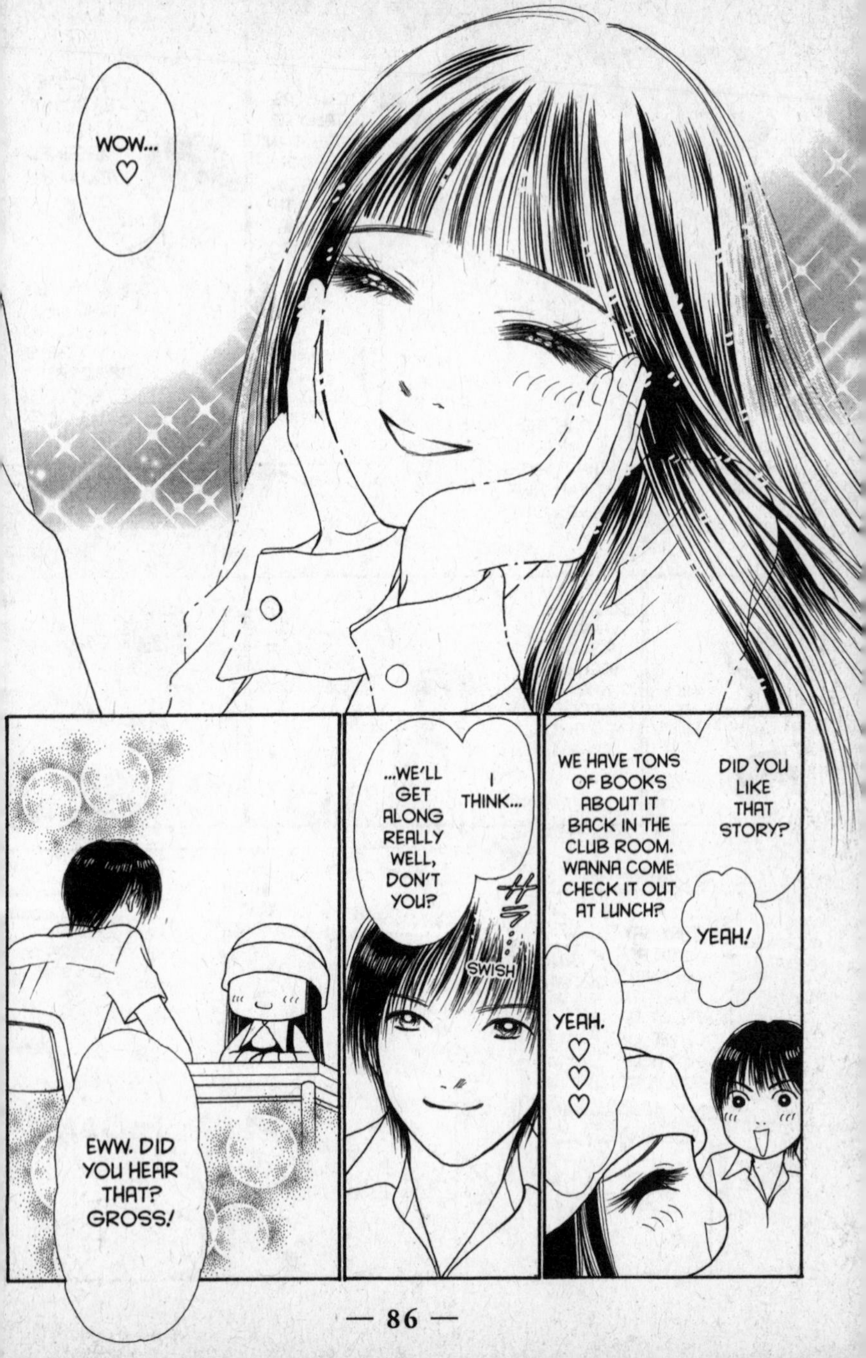
WOW... ♡
DID YOU LIKE THAT STORY?
WE HAVE TONS OF BOOKS ABOUT IT BACK IN THE CLUB ROOM. WANNA COME CHECK IT OUT AT LUNCH?
YEAH!
YEAH. ♡ ♡ ♡
I THINK...
...WE'LL GET ALONG REALLY WELL, DON'T YOU?
SWISH
EWW. DID YOU HEAR THAT? GROSS!

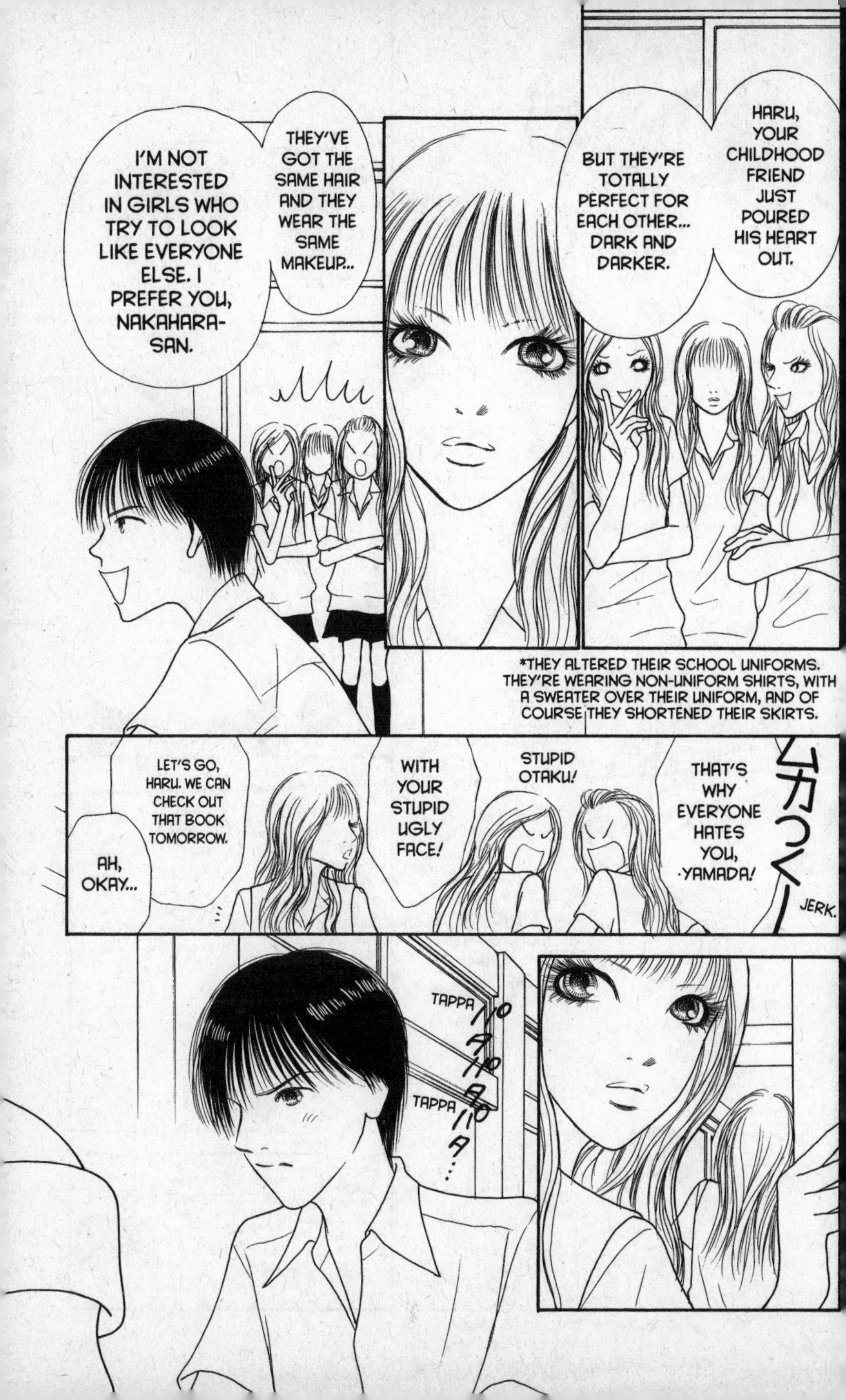
HARU, YOUR CHILDHOOD FRIEND JUST POURED HIS HEART OUT.
BUT THEY'RE TOTALLY PERFECT FOR EACH OTHER... DARK AND DARKER.
THEY'VE GOT THE SAME HAIR AND THEY WEAR THE SAME MAKEUP...
I'M NOT INTERESTED IN GIRLS WHO TRY TO LOOK LIKE EVERYONE ELSE. I PREFER YOU, NAKAHARA-SAN.
*THEY ALTERED THEIR SCHOOL UNIFORMS. THEY'RE WEARING NON-UNIFORM SHIRTS, WITH A SWEATER OVER THEIR UNIFORM, AND OF COURSE THEY SHORTENED THEIR SKIRTS.
ムカつく
JERK.
THAT'S WHY EVERYONE HATES YOU, YAMADA!
STUPID OTAKU!
WITH YOUR STUPID UGLY FACE!
LET'S GO, HARU. WE CAN CHECK OUT THAT BOOK TOMORROW.
AH, OKAY...
パタパタパタ...
TAPPA
TAPPA

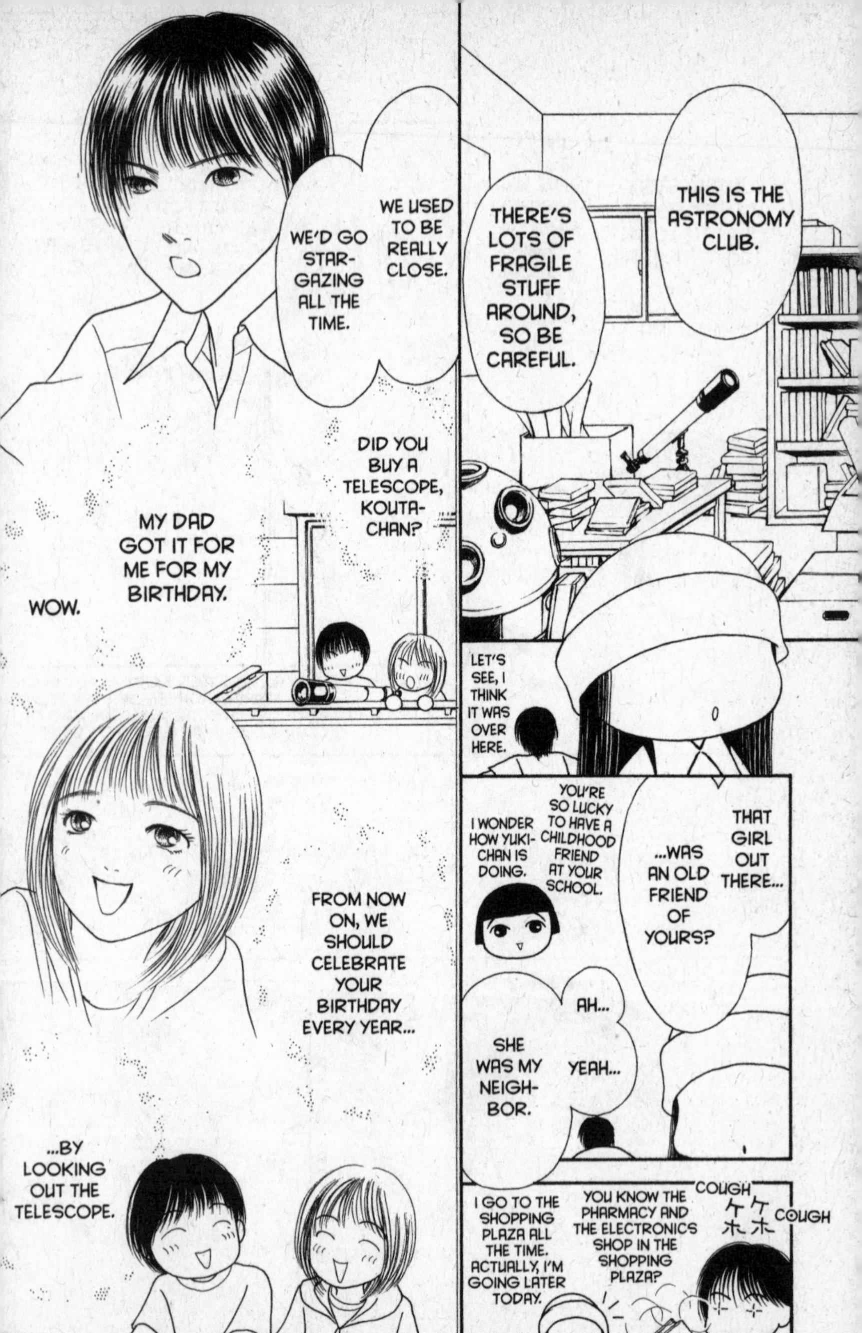
THIS IS THE ASTRONOMY CLUB.
THERE'S LOTS OF FRAGILE STUFF AROUND, SO BE CAREFUL.
LET'S SEE, I THINK IT WAS OVER HERE.
THAT GIRL OUT THERE...
...WAS AN OLD FRIEND OF YOURS?
AH...
YEAH...
SHE WAS MY NEIGHBOR.
YOU'RE SO LUCKY TO HAVE A CHILDHOOD FRIEND AT YOUR SCHOOL.
I WONDER HOW YUKI-CHAN IS DOING.
COUGH ケホ ケホ COUGH
YOU KNOW THE PHARMACY AND THE ELECTRONICS SHOP IN THE SHOPPING PLAZA?
I GO TO THE SHOPPING PLAZA ALL THE TIME. ACTUALLY, I'M GOING LATER TODAY.
WE USED TO BE REALLY CLOSE.
WE'D GO STAR-GAZING ALL THE TIME.
DID YOU BUY A TELESCOPE, KOUTA-CHAN?
MY DAD GOT IT FOR ME FOR MY BIRTHDAY.
WOW.
FROM NOW ON, WE SHOULD CELEBRATE YOUR BIRTHDAY EVERY YEAR...
...BY LOOKING OUT THE TELESCOPE.

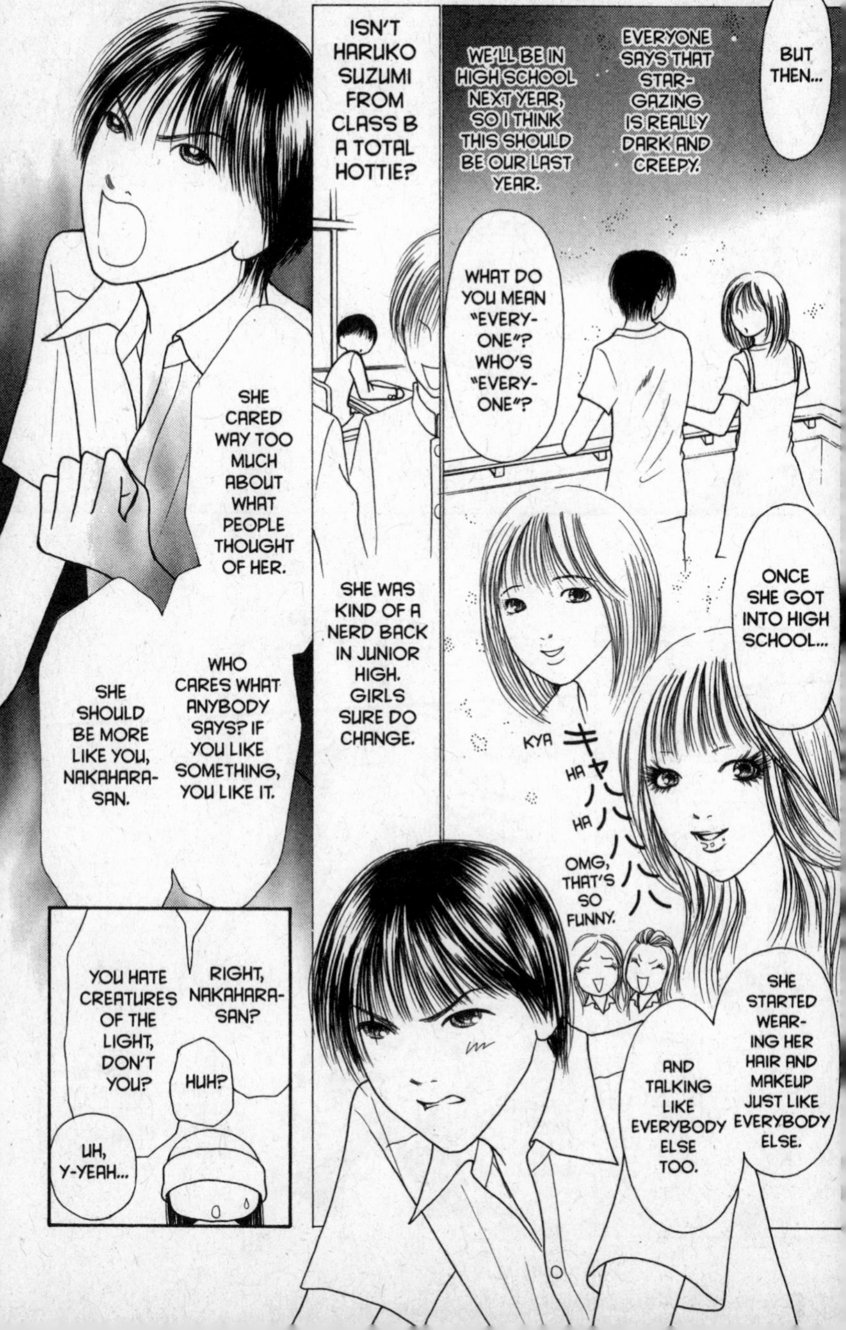
BUT THEN...
EVERYONE SAYS THAT STAR-GAZING IS REALLY DARK AND CREEPY.
WE'LL BE IN HIGH SCHOOL NEXT YEAR, SO I THINK THIS SHOULD BE OUR LAST YEAR.
WHAT DO YOU MEAN "EVERY-ONE"? WHO'S "EVERY-ONE"?
ONCE SHE GOT INTO HIGH SCHOOL...
KYA
キャハハハハ
HA
HA
OMG, THAT'S SO FUNNY.
SHE STARTED WEAR-ING HER HAIR AND MAKEUP JUST LIKE EVERYBODY ELSE.
AND TALKING LIKE EVERYBODY ELSE TOO.
ISN'T HARUKO SUZUMI FROM CLASS B A TOTAL HOTTIE?
SHE WAS KIND OF A NERD BACK IN JUNIOR HIGH. GIRLS SURE DO CHANGE.
SHE CARED WAY TOO MUCH ABOUT WHAT PEOPLE THOUGHT OF HER.
WHO CARES WHAT ANYBODY SAYS? IF YOU LIKE SOMETHING, YOU LIKE IT.
SHE SHOULD BE MORE LIKE YOU, NAKAHARA-SAN.
RIGHT, NAKAHARA-SAN?
YOU HATE CREATURES OF THE LIGHT, DON'T YOU?
HUH?
UH, Y-YEAH...

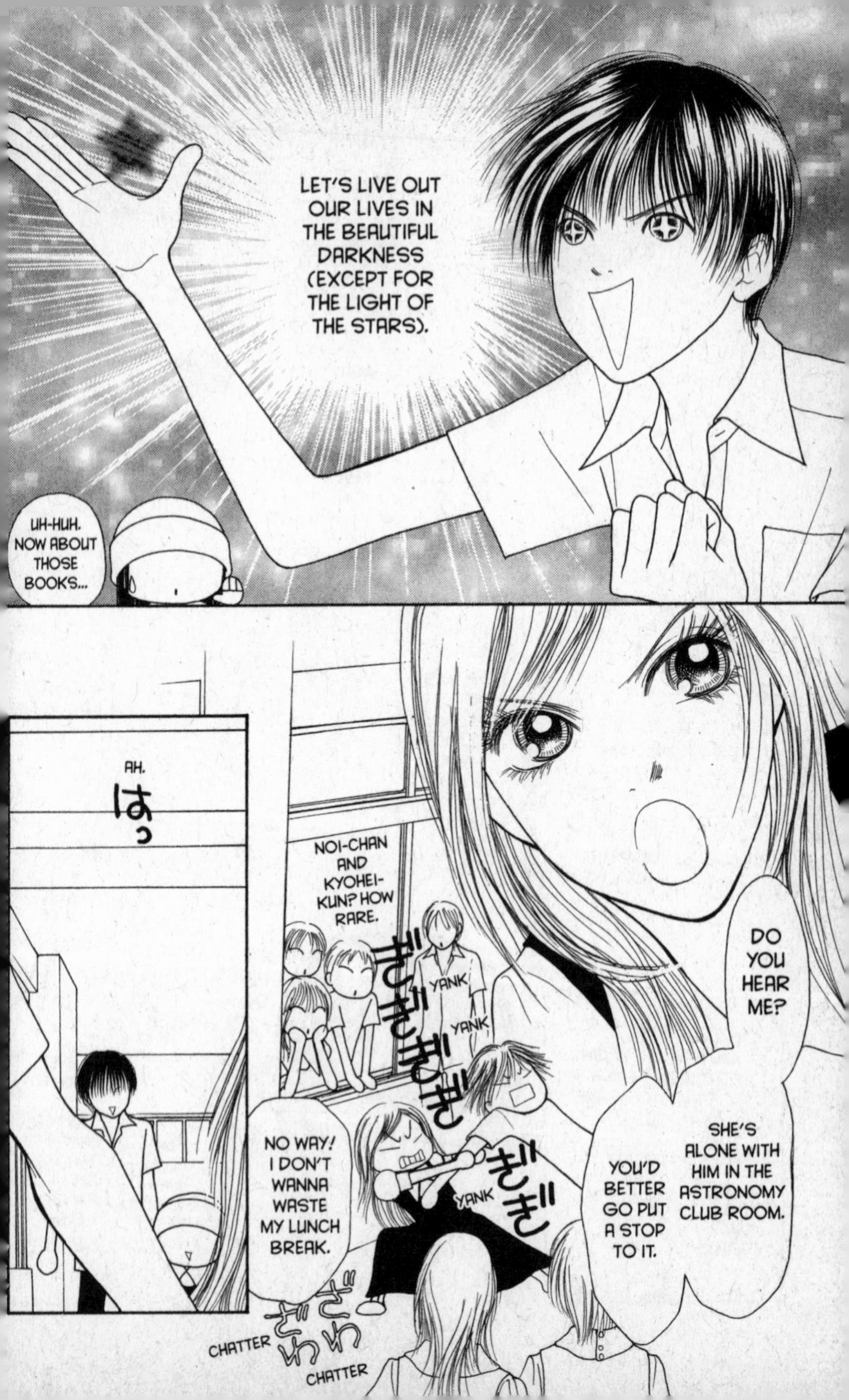
LET'S LIVE OUT OUR LIVES IN THE BEAUTIFUL DARKNESS (EXCEPT FOR THE LIGHT OF THE STARS).
UH-HUH. NOW ABOUT THOSE BOOKS...
DO YOU HEAR ME?
SHE'S ALONE WITH HIM IN THE ASTRONOMY CLUB ROOM.
YOU'D BETTER GO PUT A STOP TO IT.
NOI-CHAN AND KYOHEI-KUN? HOW RARE.
ぎぎぎぎ
YANK
YANK
ぎぎ
YANK
NO WAY! I DON'T WANNA WASTE MY LUNCH BREAK.
ざわざわ
CHATTER
CHATTER
AH.
はっ

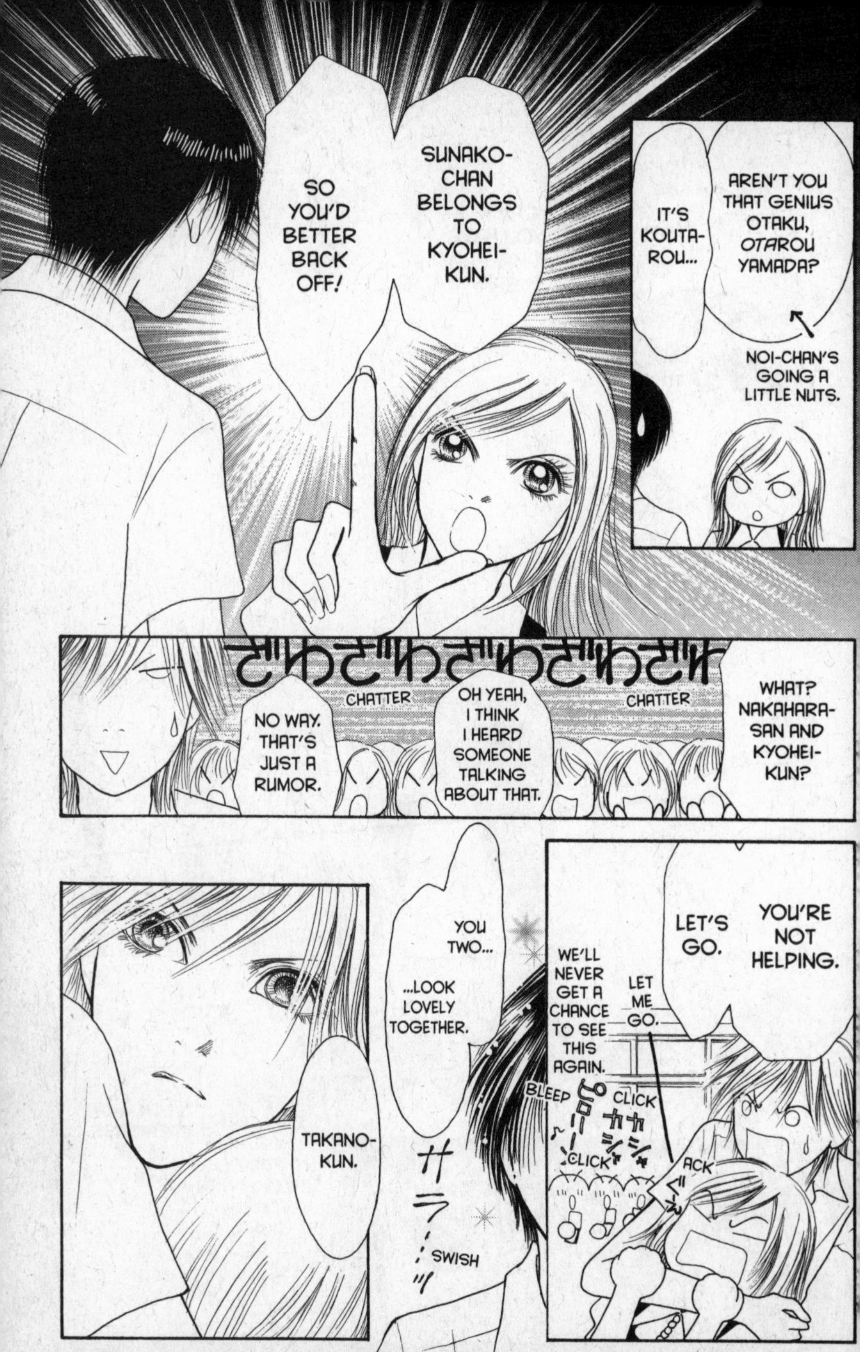
AREN'T YOU THAT GENIUS OTAKU, OTAROU YAMADA?
IT'S KOUTA-ROU...
NOI-CHAN'S GOING A LITTLE NUTS.
SUNAKO-CHAN BELONGS TO KYOHEI-KUN.
SO YOU'D BETTER BACK OFF!
WHAT? NAKAHARA-SAN AND KYOHEI-KUN?
ざわざわざわざわざわ
CHATTER
OH YEAH, I THINK I HEARD SOMEONE TALKING ABOUT THAT.
CHATTER
NO WAY. THAT'S JUST A RUMOR.
YOU'RE NOT HELPING.
LET'S GO.
LET ME GO.
WE'LL NEVER GET A CHANCE TO SEE THIS AGAIN.
CLICK
BLEEP
CLICK
ACK
YOU TWO...
...LOOK LOVELY TOGETHER.
TAKANO-KUN.
SWISH

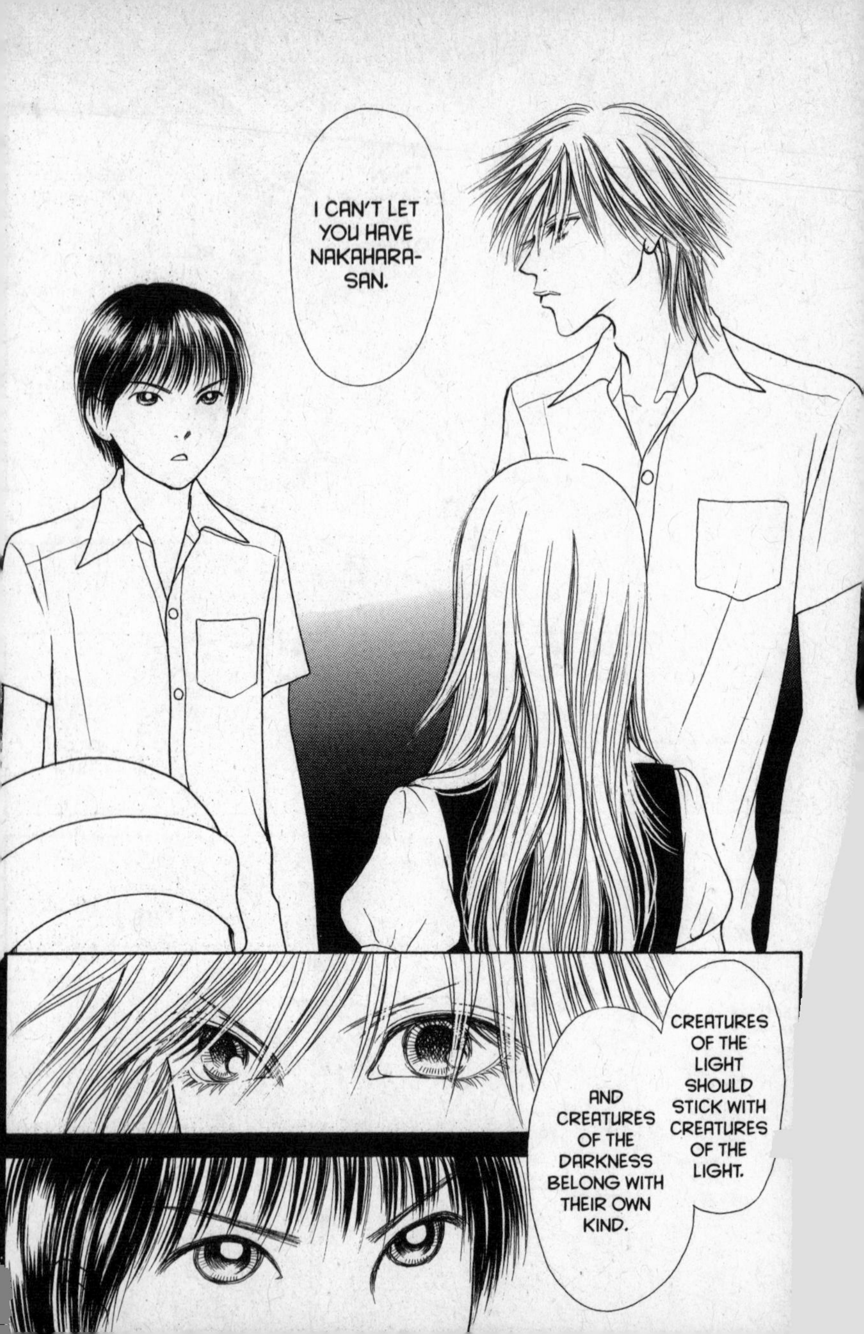
I CAN'T LET YOU HAVE NAKAHARA-SAN.
CREATURES OF THE LIGHT SHOULD STICK WITH CREATURES OF THE LIGHT.
AND CREATURES OF THE DARKNESS BELONG WITH THEIR OWN KIND.

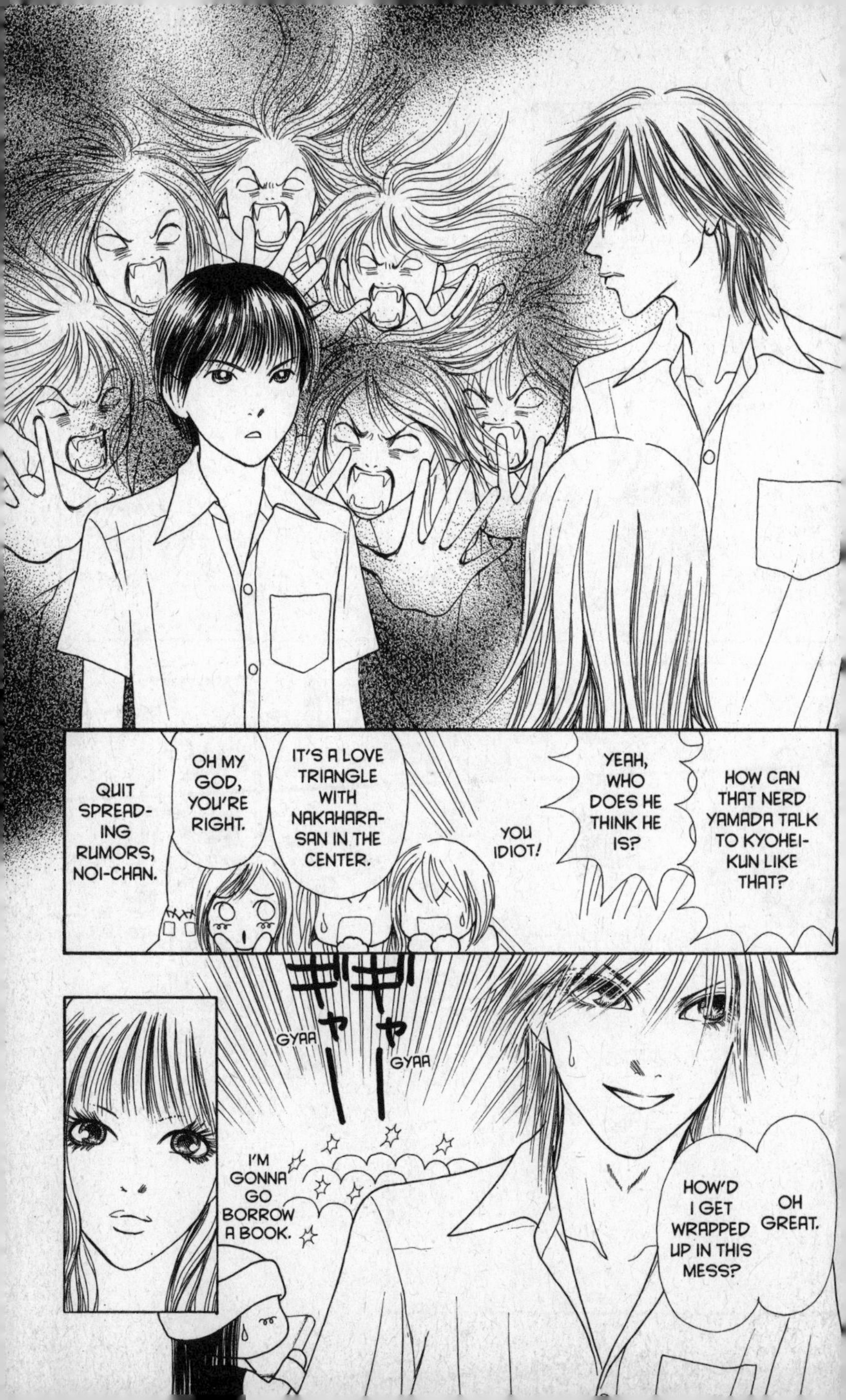
HOW CAN THAT NERD YAMADA TALK TO KYOHEI-KUN LIKE THAT?
YEAH, WHO DOES HE THINK HE IS?
YOU IDIOT!
IT'S A LOVE TRIANGLE WITH NAKAHARA-SAN IN THE CENTER.
OH MY GOD, YOU'RE RIGHT.
QUIT SPREADING-ING RUMORS, NOI-CHAN.
OH GREAT.
HOW'D I GET WRAPPED UP IN THIS MESS?
ギャー ギャー
GYAA GYAA
I'M GONNA GO BORROW A BOOK.

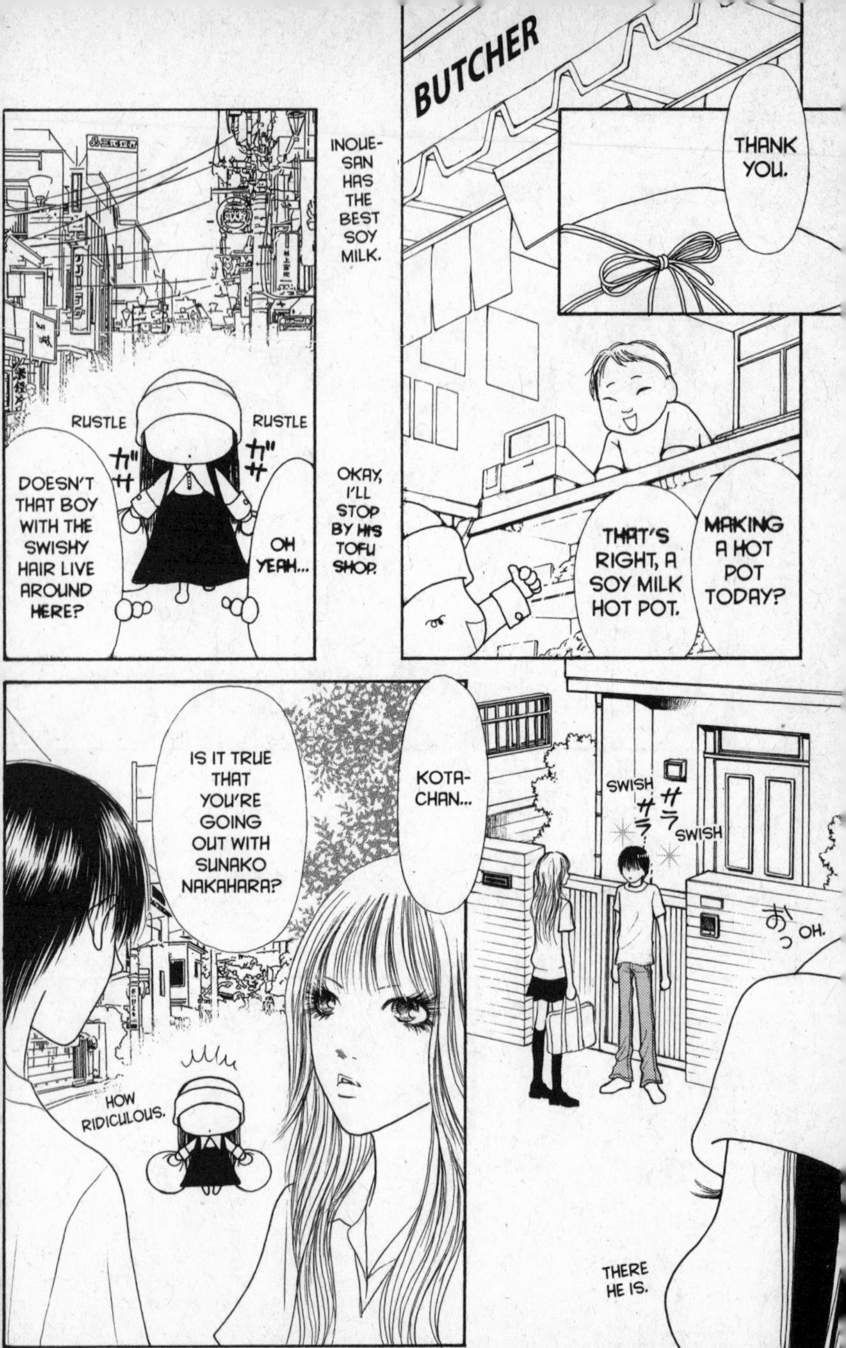
BUTCHER
THANK YOU.
MAKING A HOT POT TODAY?
THAT'S RIGHT, A SOY MILK HOT POT.
INOUE-SAN HAS THE BEST SOY MILK.
RUSTLE ガサ
RUSTLE ガサ
OKAY, I'LL STOP BY HIS TOFU SHOP.
OH YEAH...
DOESN'T THAT BOY WITH THE SWISHY HAIR LIVE AROUND HERE?
おっ OH.
THERE HE IS.
SWISH サラ
サラ SWISH
KOTA-CHAN...
IS IT TRUE THAT YOU'RE GOING OUT WITH SUNAKO NAKAHARA?
HOW RIDICULOUS.

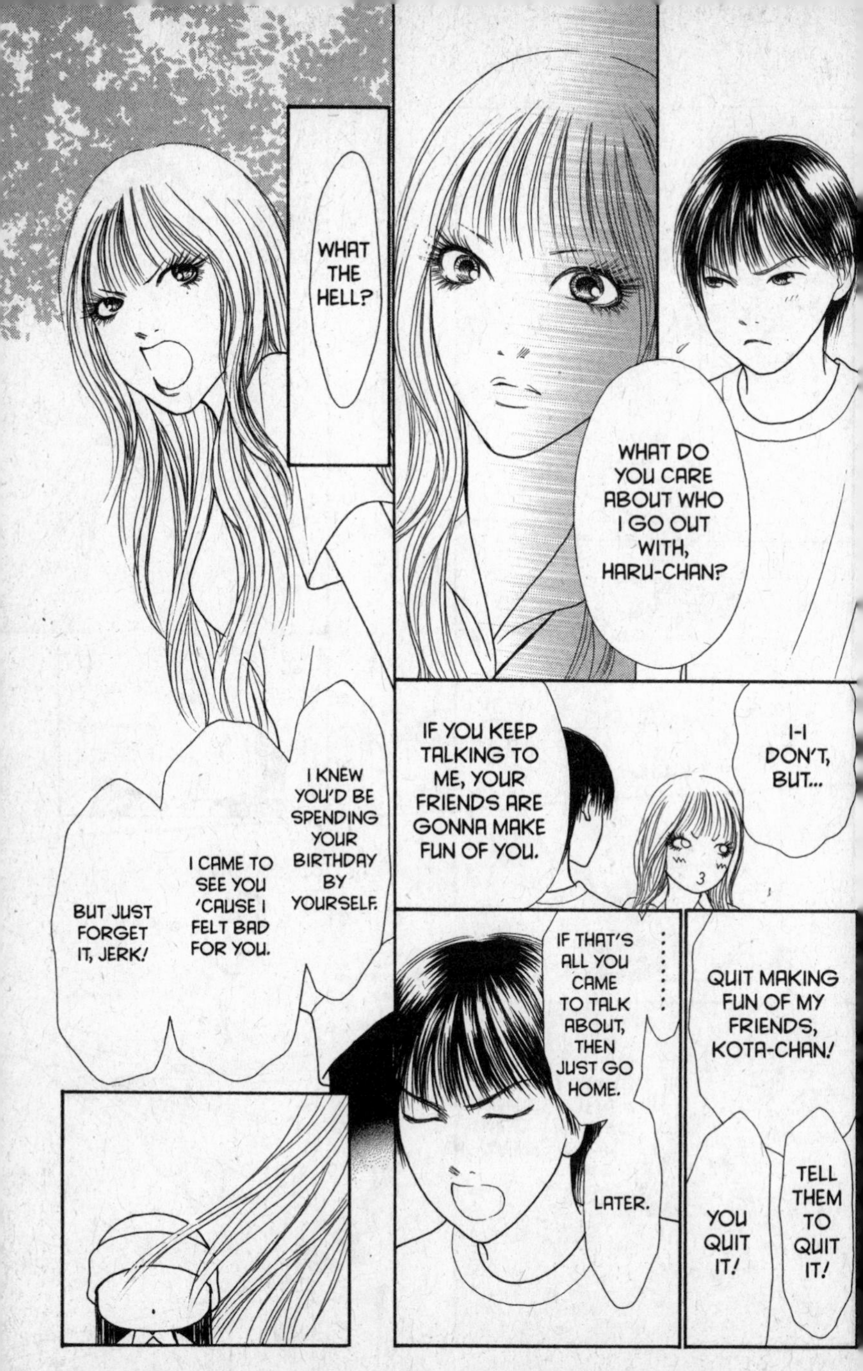
WHAT DO YOU CARE ABOUT WHO I GO OUT WITH, HARU-CHAN?
I-I DON'T, BUT...
IF YOU KEEP TALKING TO ME, YOUR FRIENDS ARE GONNA MAKE FUN OF YOU.
QUIT MAKING FUN OF MY FRIENDS, KOTA-CHAN!
TELL THEM TO QUIT IT!
YOU QUIT IT!
......
IF THAT'S ALL YOU CAME TO TALK ABOUT, THEN JUST GO HOME.
LATER.
WHAT THE HELL?
I KNEW YOU'D BE SPENDING YOUR BIRTHDAY BY YOURSELF.
I CAME TO SEE YOU 'CAUSE I FELT BAD FOR YOU.
BUT JUST FORGET IT, JERK!

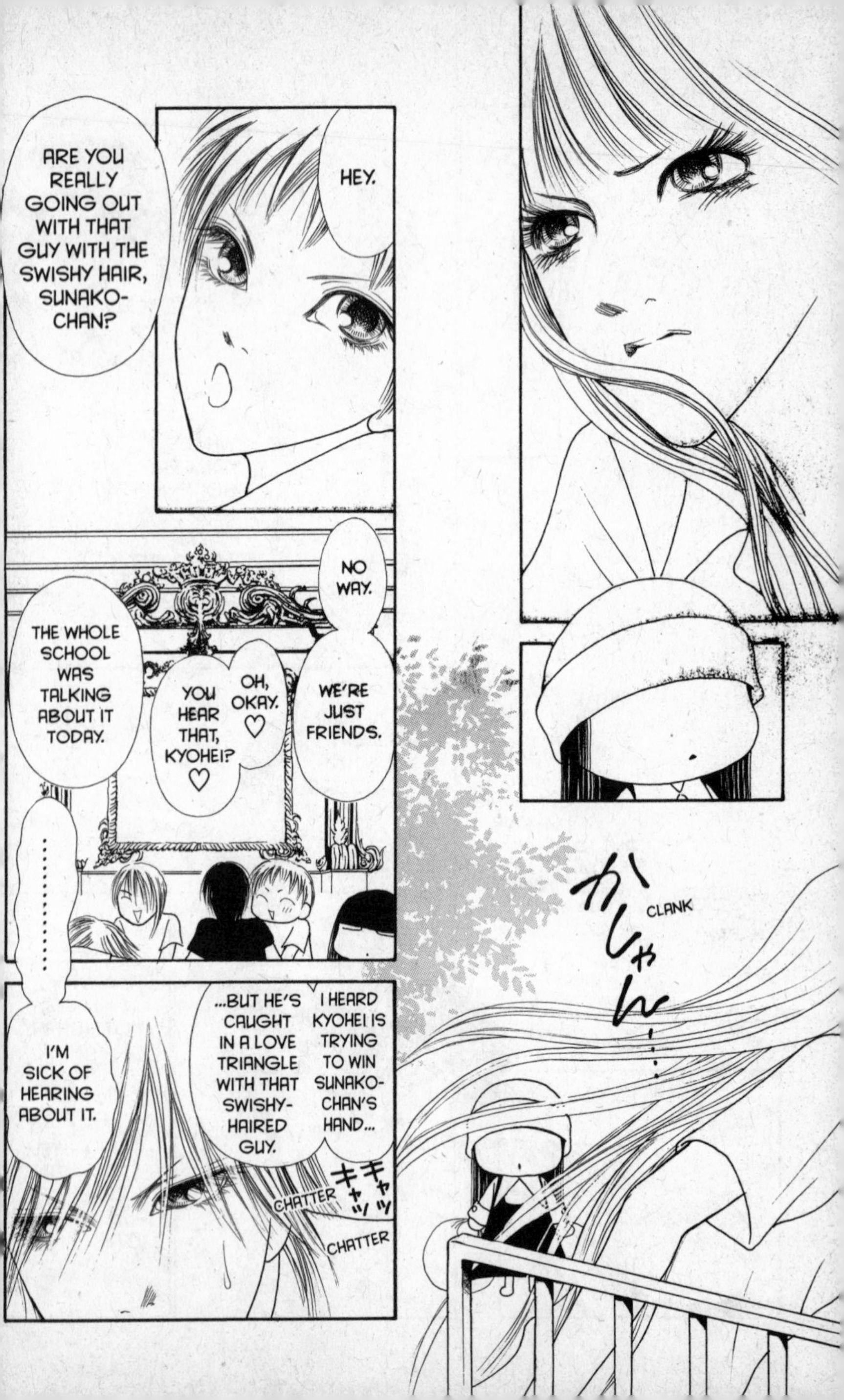
HEY.
ARE YOU REALLY GOING OUT WITH THAT GUY WITH THE SWISHY HAIR, SUNAKO-CHAN?
NO WAY.
WE'RE JUST FRIENDS.
OH, OKAY. ♡
YOU HEAR THAT, KYOHEI? ♡
THE WHOLE SCHOOL WAS TALKING ABOUT IT TODAY.
....
I HEARD KYOHEI IS TRYING TO WIN SUNAKO-CHAN'S HAND...
...BUT HE'S CAUGHT IN A LOVE TRIANGLE WITH THAT SWISHY-HAIRED GUY.
キャッキャッ
CHATTER
キャッ
CHATTER
I'M SICK OF HEARING ABOUT IT.
かしゃん…
CLANK

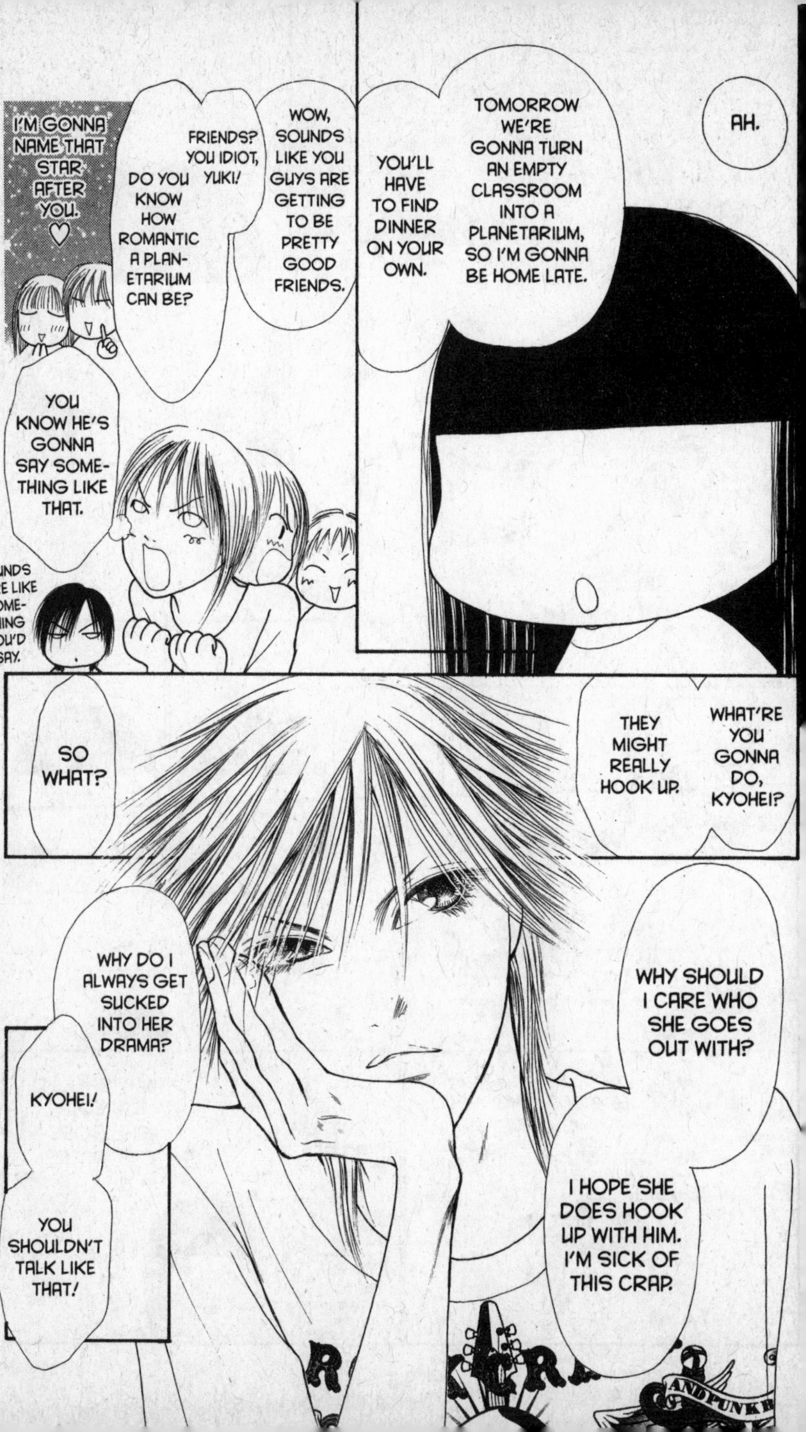
AH.
TOMORROW WE'RE GONNA TURN AN EMPTY CLASSROOM INTO A PLANETARIUM, SO I'M GONNA BE HOME LATE.
YOU'LL HAVE TO FIND DINNER ON YOUR OWN.
WOW, SOUNDS LIKE YOU GUYS ARE GETTING TO BE PRETTY GOOD FRIENDS.
FRIENDS? YOU IDIOT, YUKI!
DO YOU KNOW HOW ROMANTIC A PLAN-ETARIUM CAN BE?
I'M GONNA NAME THAT STAR AFTER YOU. ♡
YOU KNOW HE'S GONNA SAY SOME-THING LIKE THAT.
SOUNDS MORE LIKE SOME-THING YOU'D SAY.
WHAT'RE YOU GONNA DO, KYOHEI?
THEY MIGHT REALLY HOOK UP.
SO WHAT?
WHY SHOULD I CARE WHO SHE GOES OUT WITH?
I HOPE SHE DOES HOOK UP WITH HIM. I'M SICK OF THIS CRAP.
WHY DO I ALWAYS GET SUCKED INTO HER DRAMA?
KYOHEI!
YOU SHOULDN'T TALK LIKE THAT!

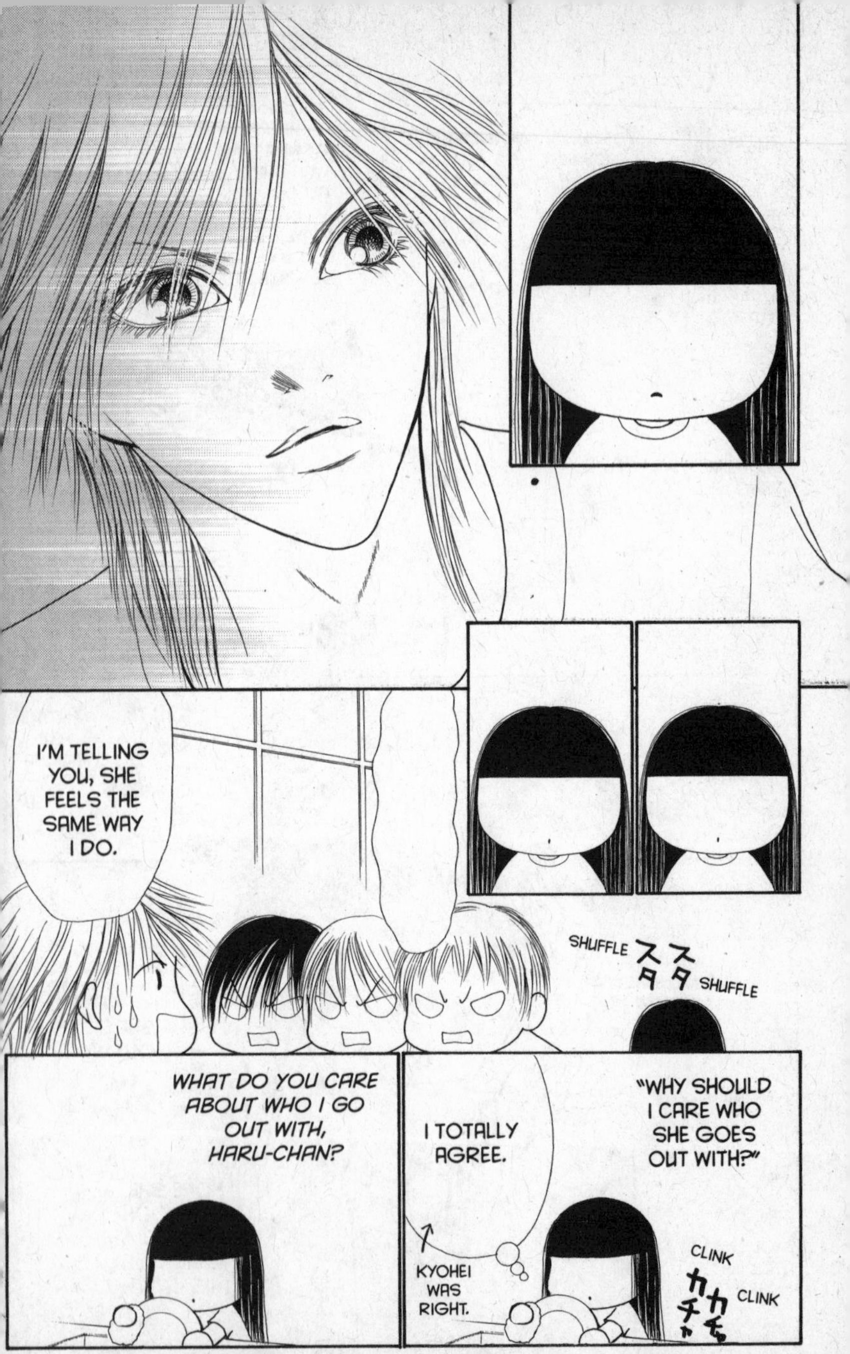
I'M TELLING YOU, SHE FEELS THE SAME WAY I DO.
SHUFFLE スタスタ SHUFFLE
"WHY SHOULD I CARE WHO SHE GOES OUT WITH?"
I TOTALLY AGREE.
KYOHEI WAS RIGHT.
CLINK カチャカチャ CLINK
WHAT DO YOU CARE ABOUT WHO I GO OUT WITH, HARU-CHAN?

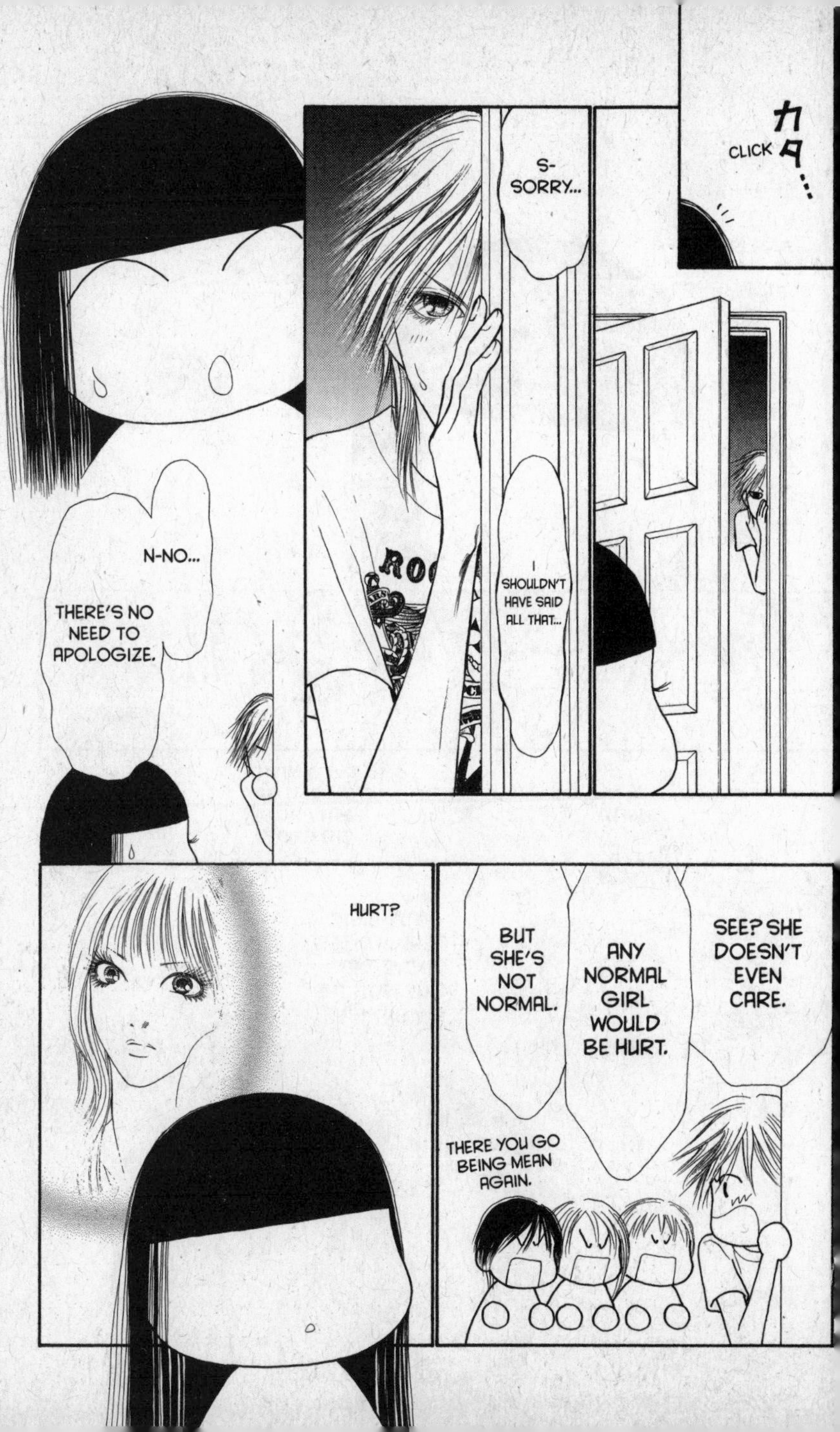
カタ…
CLICK
S-SORRY...
I SHOULDN'T HAVE SAID ALL THAT...
N-NO...
THERE'S NO NEED TO APOLOGIZE.
SEE? SHE DOESN'T EVEN CARE.
ANY NORMAL GIRL WOULD BE HURT.
BUT SHE'S NOT NORMAL.
THERE YOU GO BEING MEAN AGAIN.
HURT?

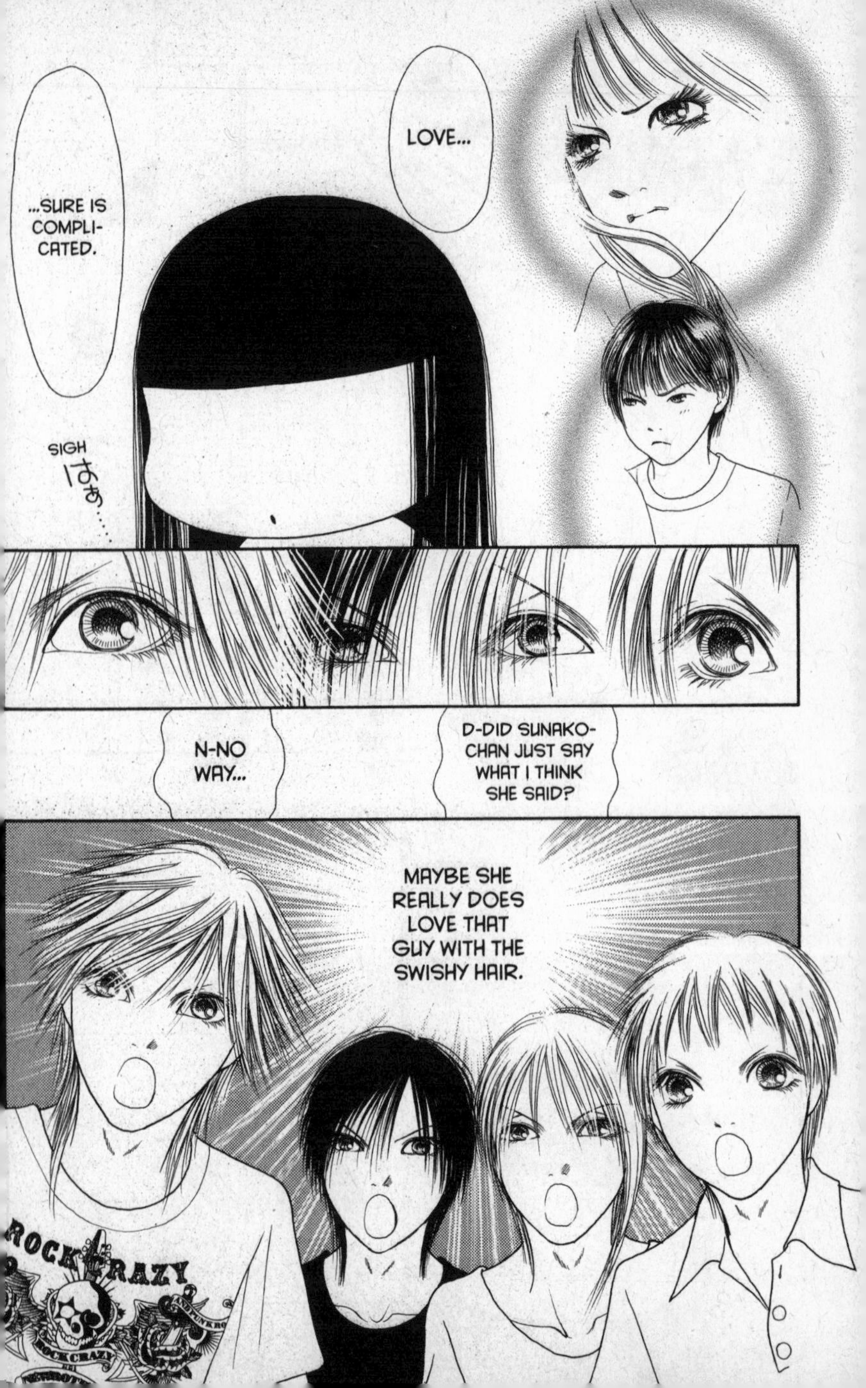
LOVE...
...SURE IS COMPLI-CATED.
SIGH
はぁ…
D-DID SUNAKO-CHAN JUST SAY WHAT I THINK SHE SAID?
N-NO WAY...
MAYBE SHE REALLY DOES LOVE THAT GUY WITH THE SWISHY HAIR.
ROCK CRAZY

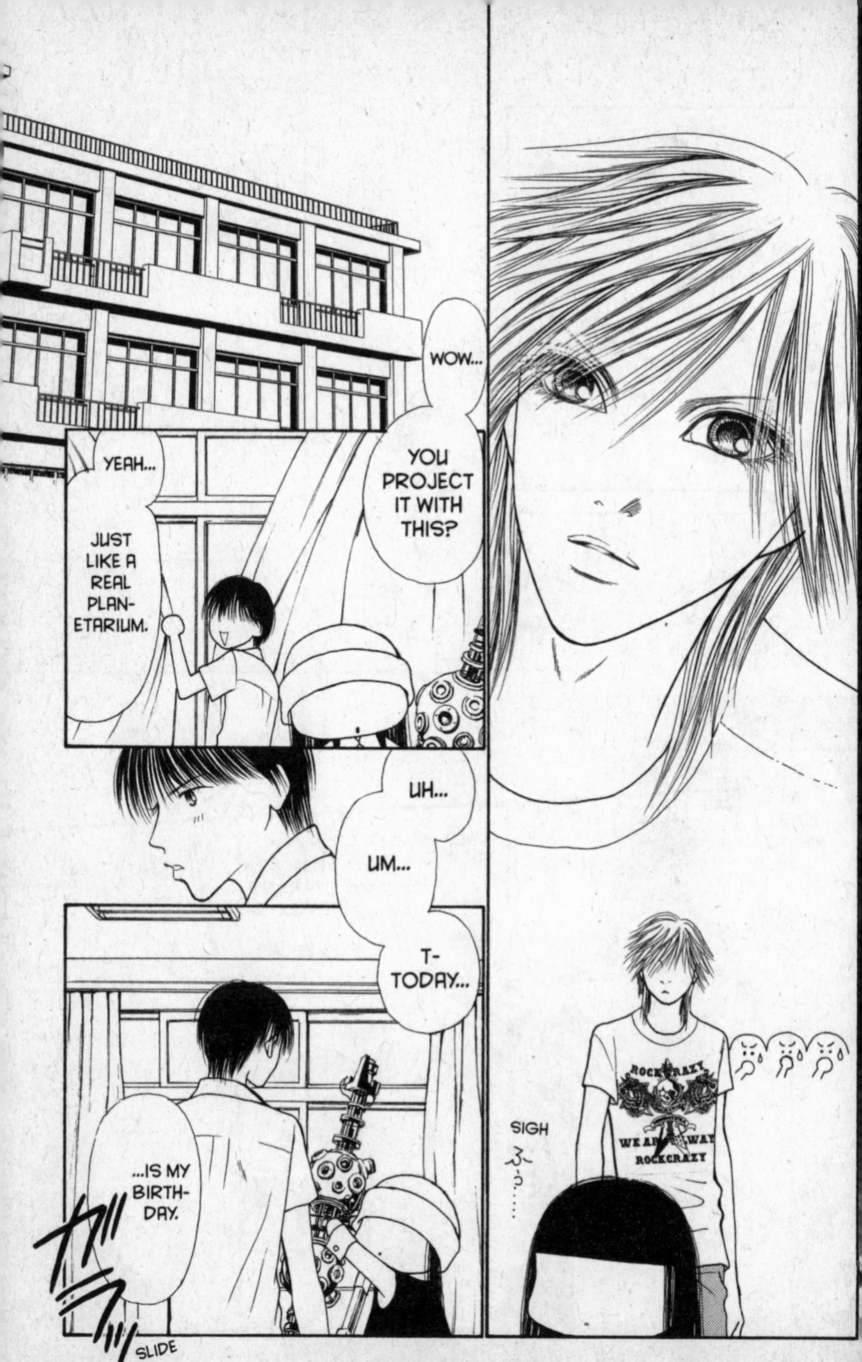

ROCKCRAZY
SIGH
ふ～っ……
WOW...
YOU PROJECT IT WITH THIS?
YEAH...
JUST LIKE A REAL PLAN-ETARIUM.
UH...
UM...
T-TODAY...
...IS MY BIRTH-DAY.
SLIDE

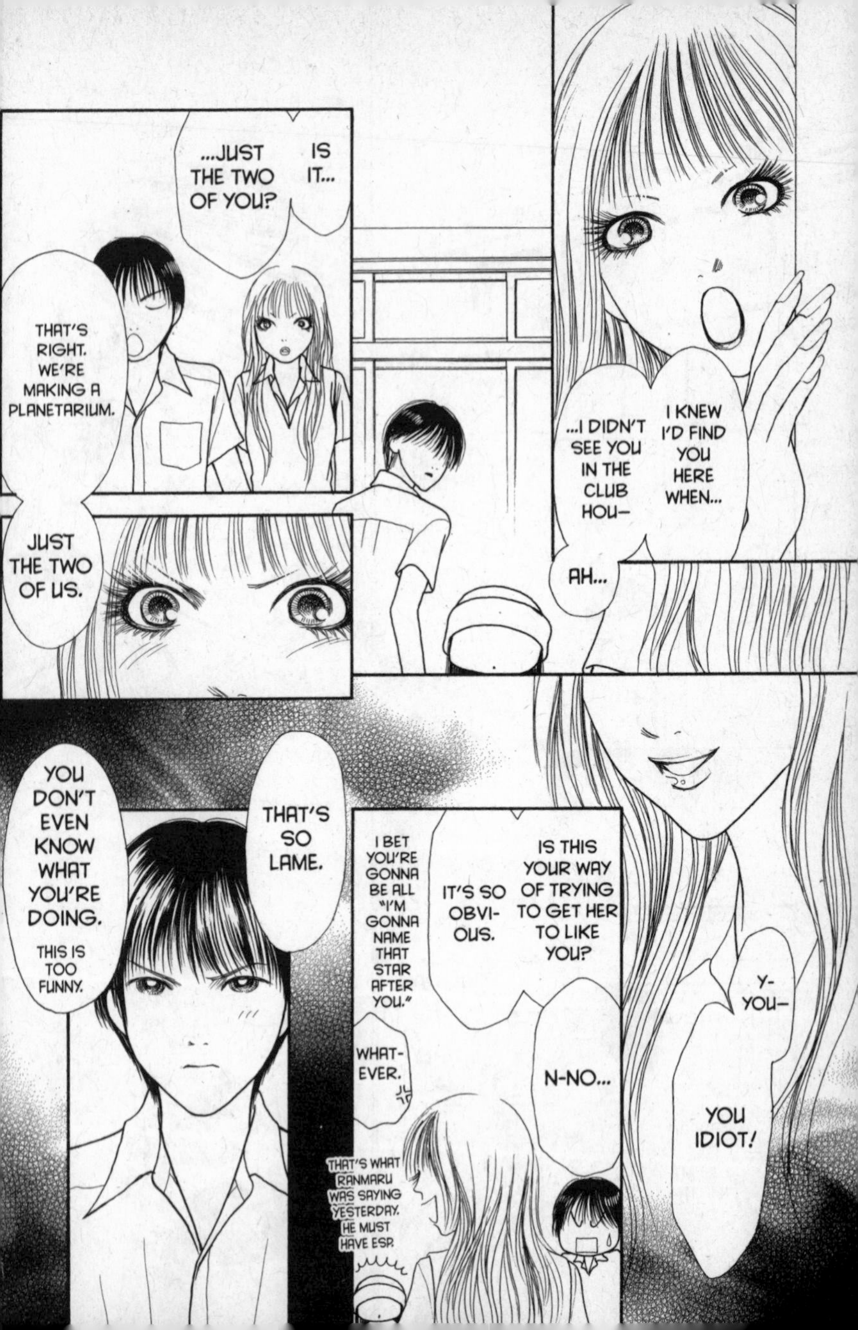
I KNEW I'D FIND YOU HERE WHEN...
...I DIDN'T SEE YOU IN THE CLUB HOU—
AH...
IS IT...
...JUST THE TWO OF YOU?
THAT'S RIGHT. WE'RE MAKING A PLANETARIUM.
JUST THE TWO OF US.
IS THIS YOUR WAY OF TRYING TO GET HER TO LIKE YOU?
IT'S SO OBVIOUS.
I BET YOU'RE GONNA BE ALL "I'M GONNA NAME THAT STAR AFTER YOU."
Y-YOU—
YOU IDIOT!
N-NO...
WHATEVER.
THAT'S WHAT RANMARU WAS SAYING YESTERDAY. HE MUST HAVE ESP.
THAT'S SO LAME.
YOU DON'T EVEN KNOW WHAT YOU'RE DOING.
THIS IS TOO FUNNY.

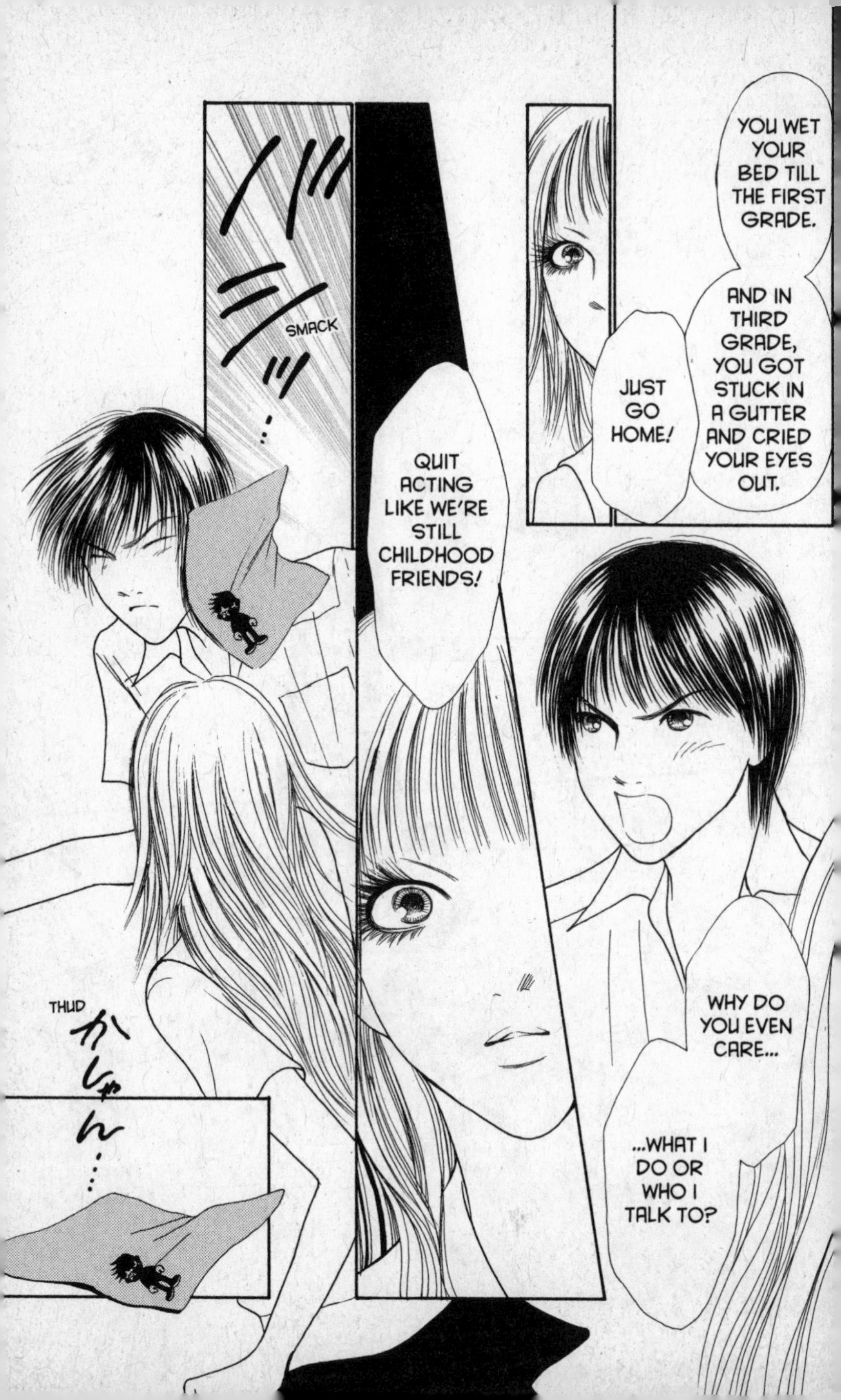
YOU WET YOUR BED TILL THE FIRST GRADE.
AND IN THIRD GRADE, YOU GOT STUCK IN A GUTTER AND CRIED YOUR EYES OUT.
JUST GO HOME!
QUIT ACTING LIKE WE'RE STILL CHILDHOOD FRIENDS!
WHY DO YOU EVEN CARE...
...WHAT I DO OR WHO I TALK TO?
バシッ
SMACK
THUD
かしゃん…

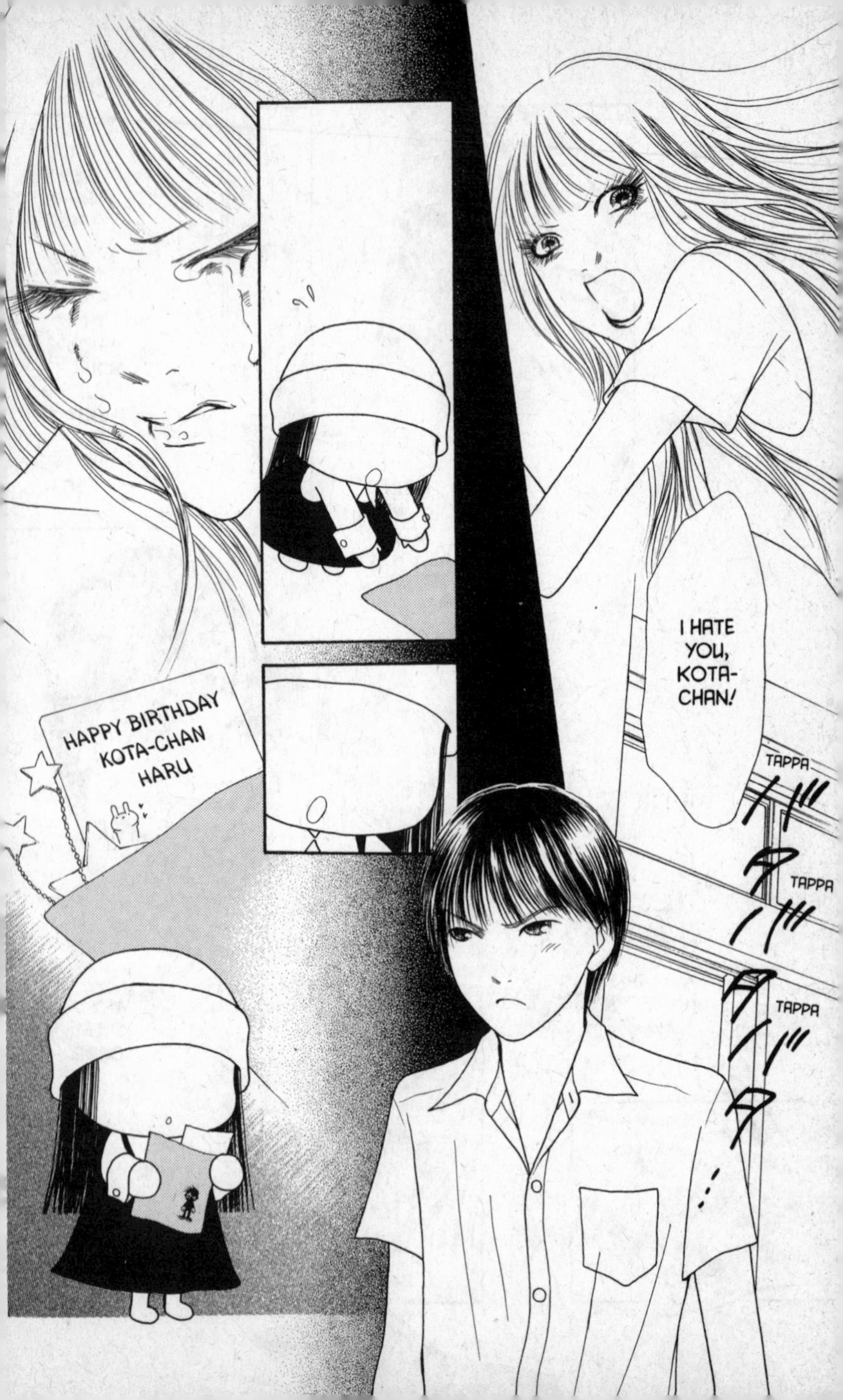
I HATE YOU, KOTA-CHAN!
TAPPA
TAPPA
TAPPA
HAPPY BIRTHDAY KOTA-CHAN HARU

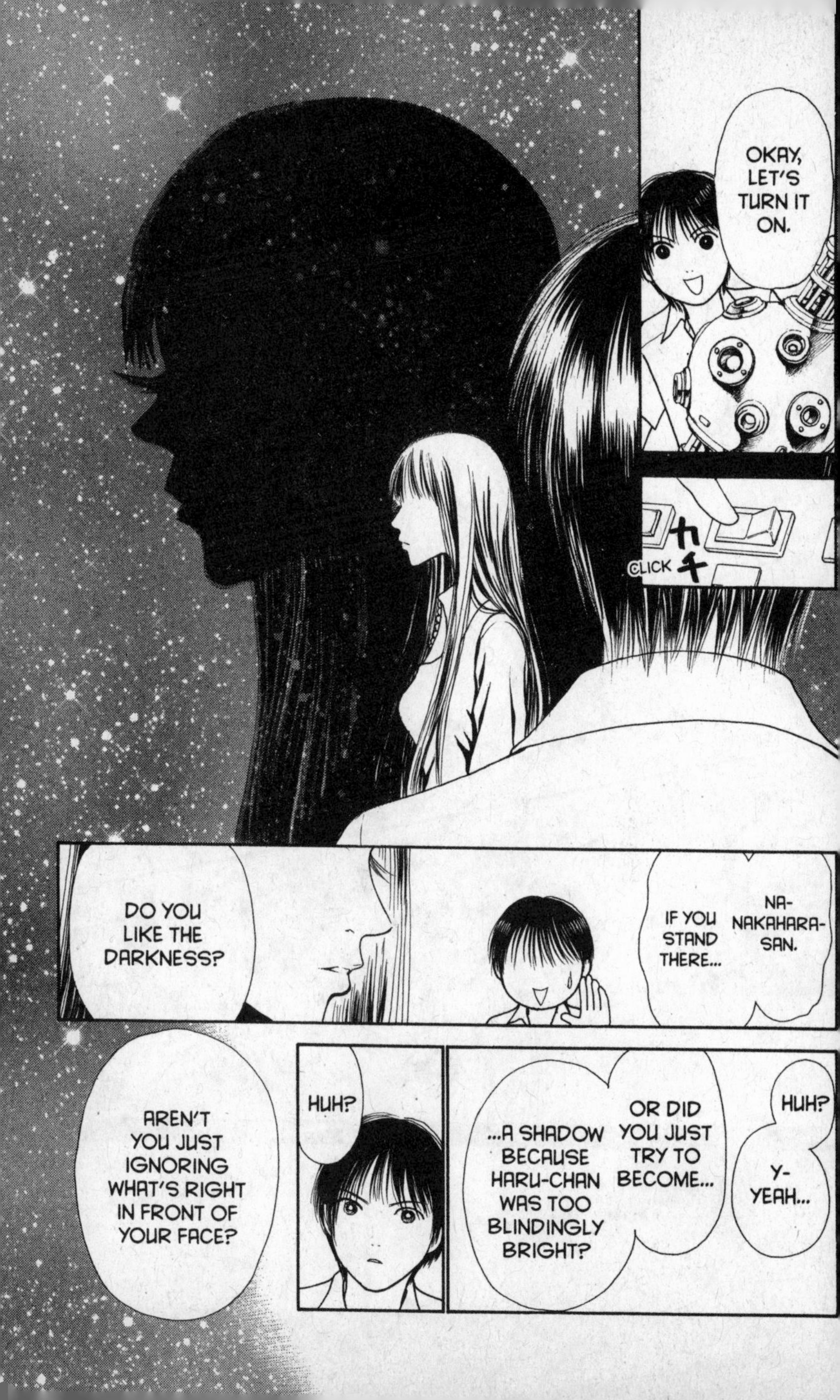

OKAY, LET'S TURN IT ON.
カチ
CLICK
NA- NAKAHARA- SAN.
IF YOU STAND THERE...
DO YOU LIKE THE DARKNESS?
HUH?
Y- YEAH...
OR DID YOU JUST TRY TO BECOME...
...A SHADOW BECAUSE HARU-CHAN WAS TOO BLINDINGLY BRIGHT?
HUH?
AREN'T YOU JUST IGNORING WHAT'S RIGHT IN FRONT OF YOUR FACE?

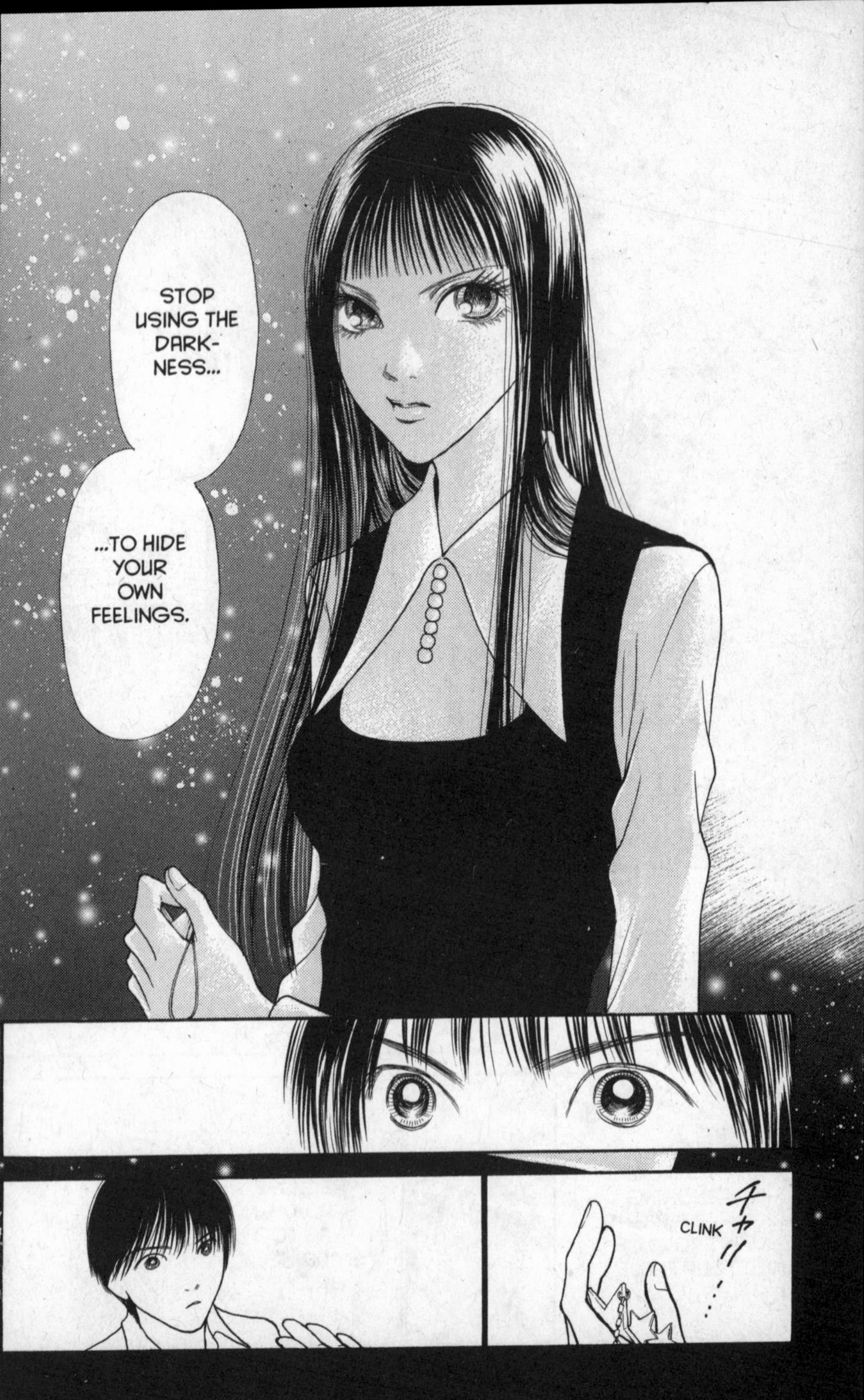
STOP USING THE DARK-NESS...
...TO HIDE YOUR OWN FEELINGS.
CLINK
チャリ…

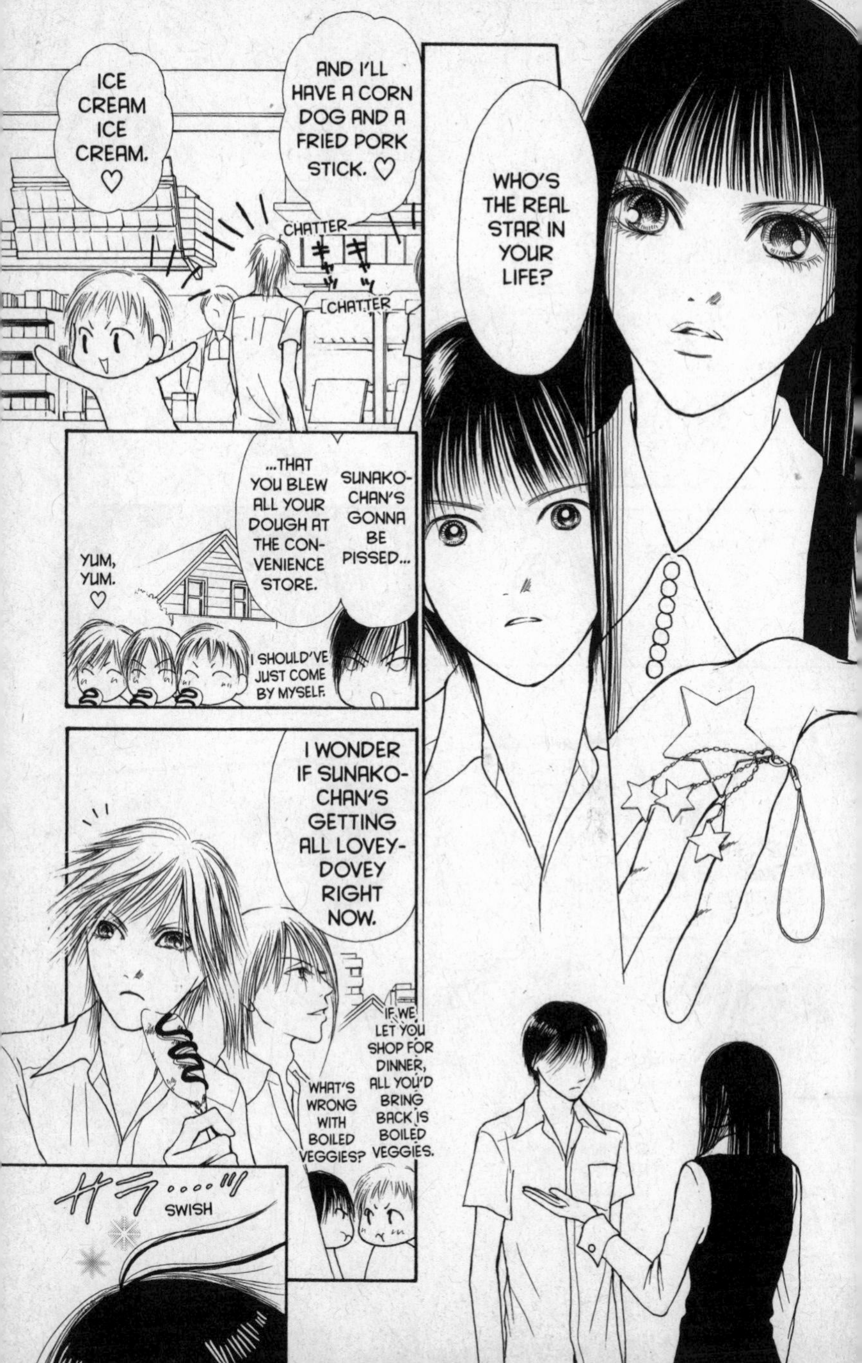

WHO'S THE REAL STAR IN YOUR LIFE?
AND I'LL HAVE A CORN DOG AND A FRIED PORK STICK. ♡
ICE CREAM ICE CREAM. ♡
CHATTER
キャッ キャッ
CHATTER
SUNAKO-CHAN'S GONNA BE PISSED...
...THAT YOU BLEW ALL YOUR DOUGH AT THE CON-VENIENCE STORE.
YUM, YUM. ♡
I SHOULD'VE JUST COME BY MYSELF.
I WONDER IF SUNAKO-CHAN'S GETTING ALL LOVEY-DOVEY RIGHT NOW.
IF WE LET YOU SHOP FOR DINNER, ALL YOU'D BRING BACK IS BOILED VEGGIES.
WHAT'S WRONG WITH BOILED VEGGIES?
サラ.....
SWISH

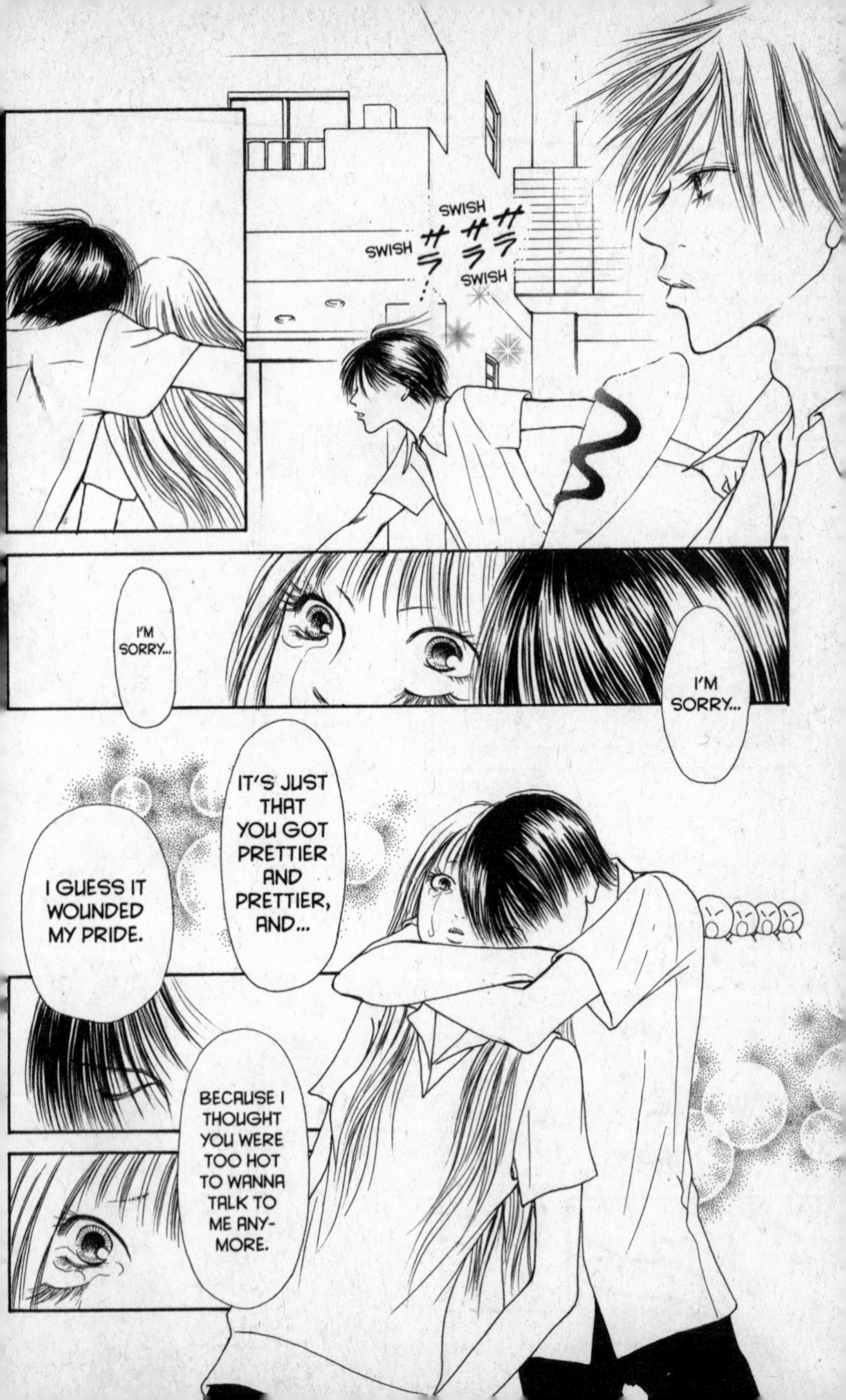

SWISH
サラ サラ サラ
SWISH
SWISH
I'M SORRY...
I'M SORRY...
IT'S JUST THAT YOU GOT PRETTIER AND PRETTIER, AND...
I GUESS IT WOUNDED MY PRIDE.
BECAUSE I THOUGHT YOU WERE TOO HOT TO WANNA TALK TO ME ANY-MORE.

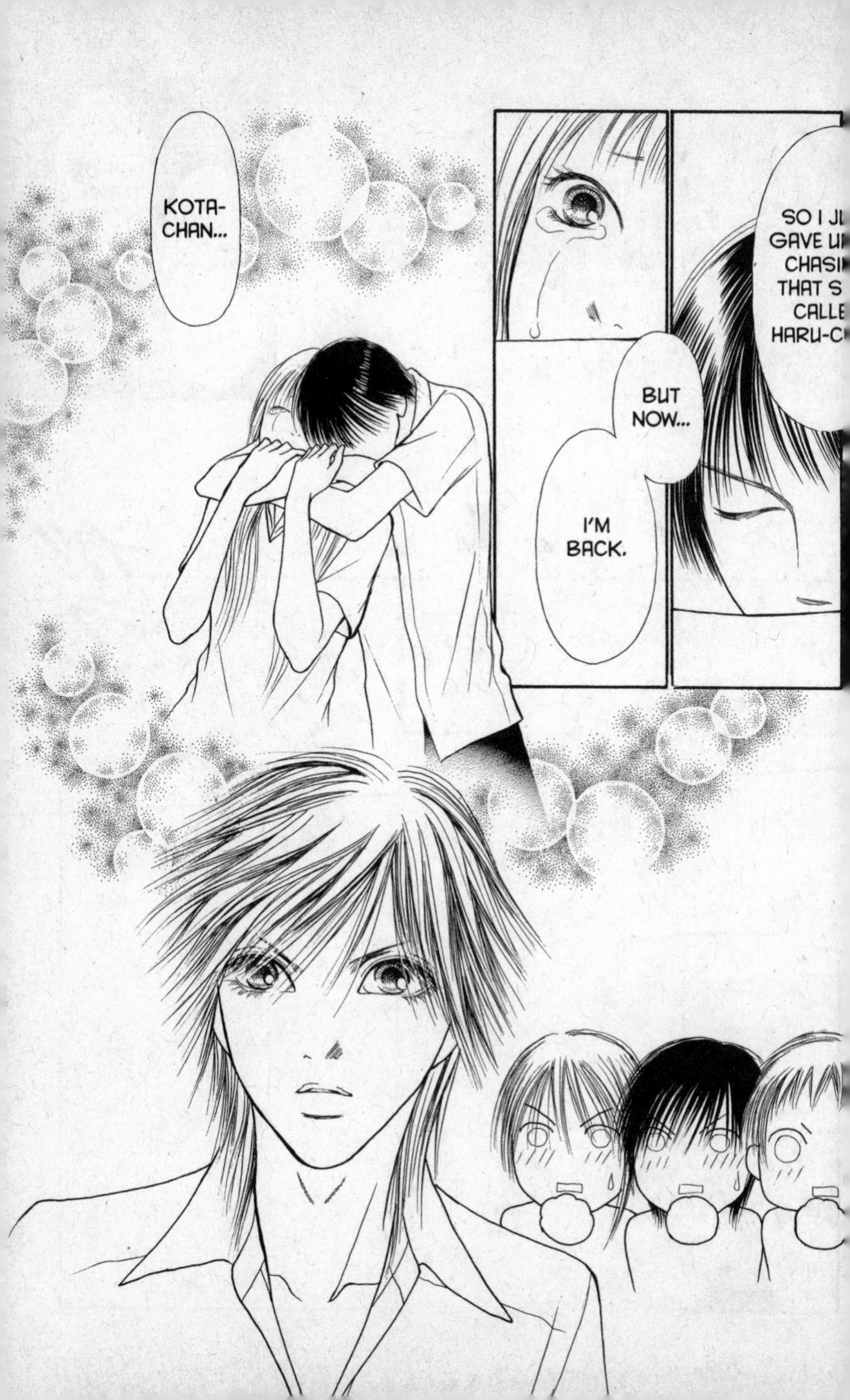

SO I J
GAVE U
CHASI
THAT S
CALLE
HARU-C
BUT NOW...
I'M BACK.
KOTA-CHAN...

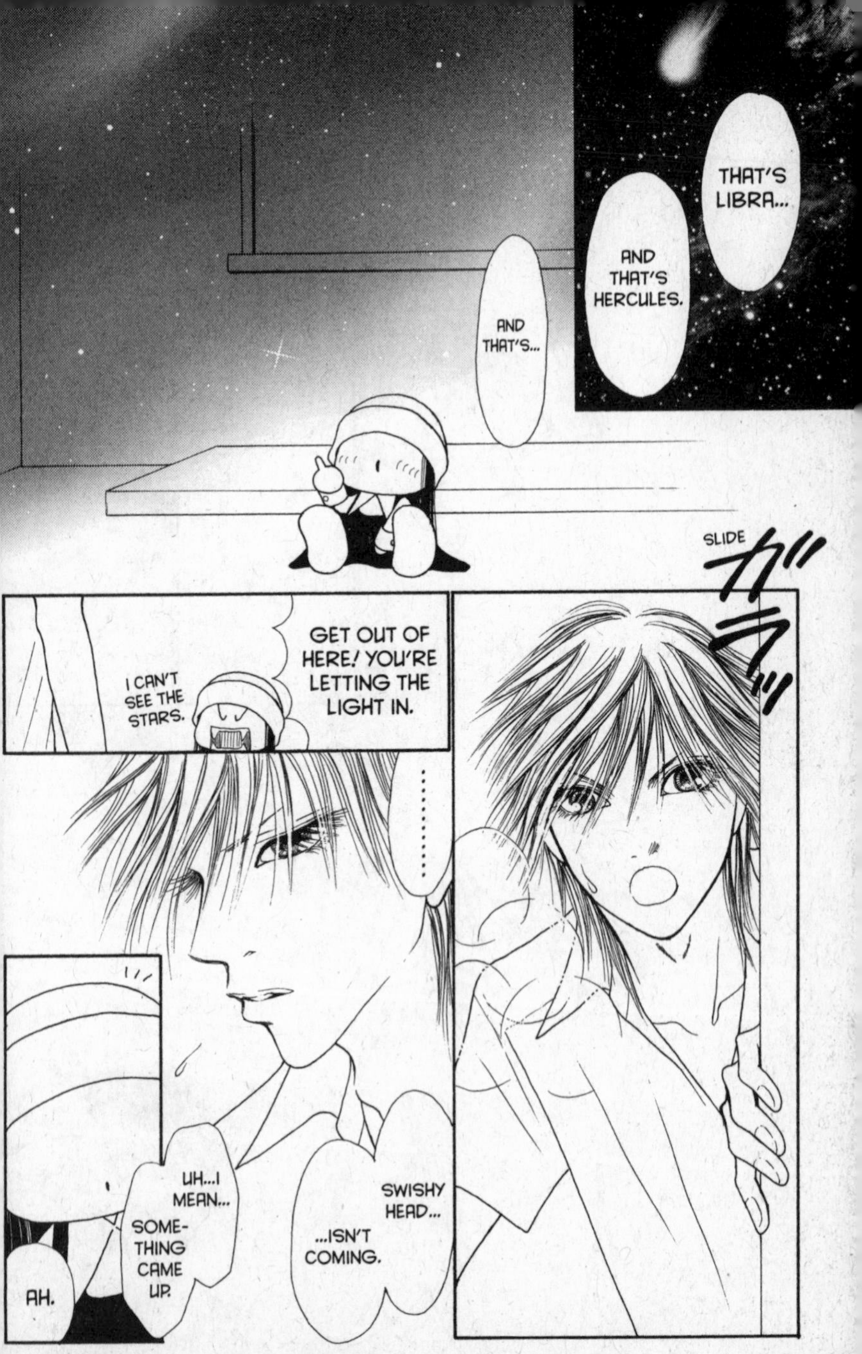
THAT'S LIBRA...
AND THAT'S HERCULES.
AND THAT'S...
SLIDE
GET OUT OF HERE! YOU'RE LETTING THE LIGHT IN.
I CAN'T SEE THE STARS.
......
SWISHY HEAD...
...ISN'T COMING.
UH...I MEAN...
SOME-THING CAME UP.
AH.

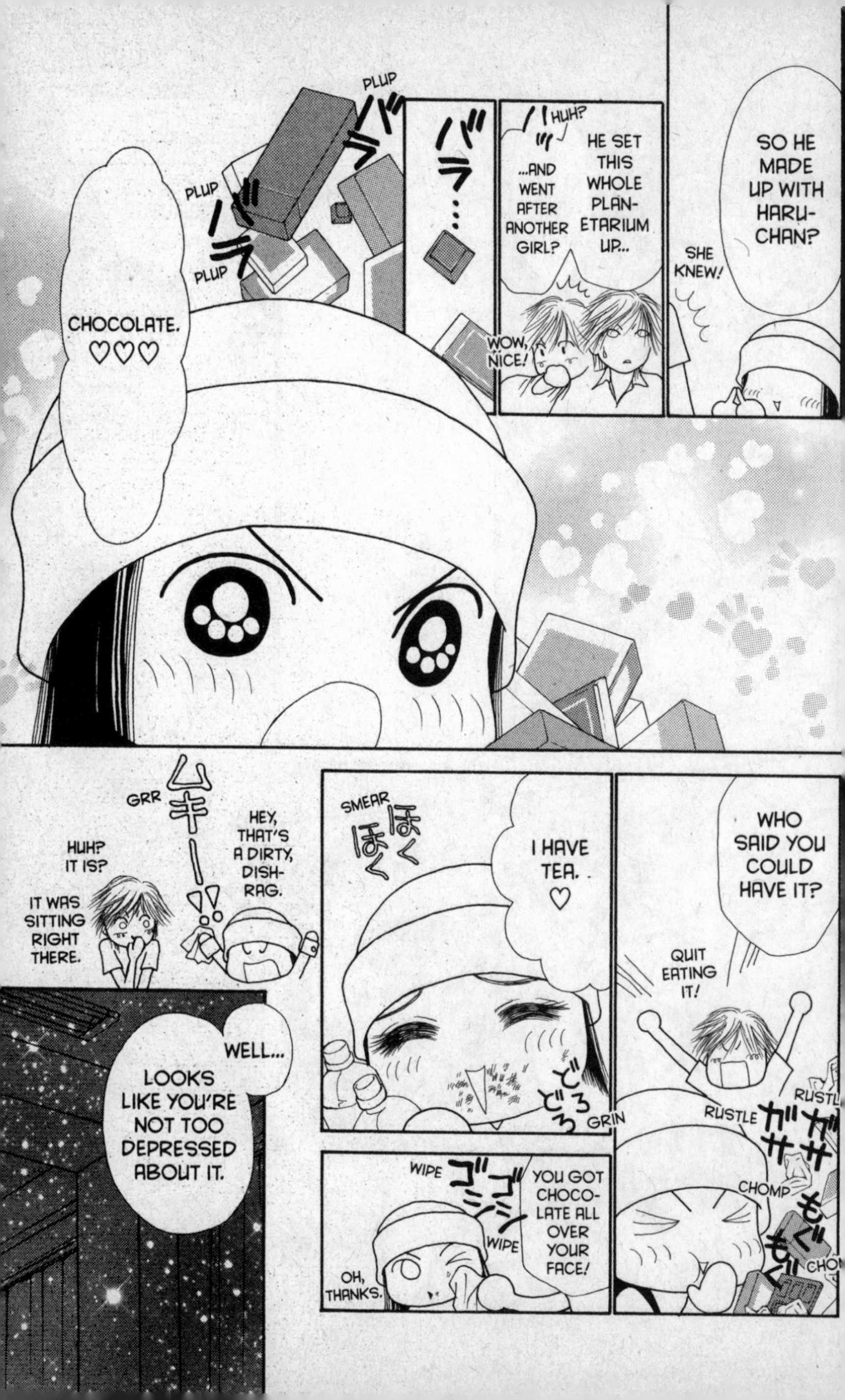
SO HE MADE UP WITH HARU-CHAN?
SHE KNEW!
HE SET THIS WHOLE PLAN-ETARIUM UP...
...AND WENT AFTER ANOTHER GIRL?
HUH?
WOW, NICE!
バラ…
PLUP
バラ
PLUP
バラ
PLUP
CHOCOLATE. ♡♡♡
WHO SAID YOU COULD HAVE IT?
QUIT EATING IT!
RUSTLE
ガサ
RUSTLE
ガサ
CHOMP
もぐもぐ
I HAVE TEA. ♡
SMEAR
ほくほく
どろどろ
GRIN
YOU GOT CHOCO-LATE ALL OVER YOUR FACE!
WIPE
ゴシゴシ
WIPE
OH, THANKS.
HEY, THAT'S A DIRTY, DISH-RAG.
GRR
ムキー!!
HUH? IT IS?
IT WAS SITTING RIGHT THERE.
WELL...
LOOKS LIKE YOU'RE NOT TOO DEPRESSED ABOUT IT.

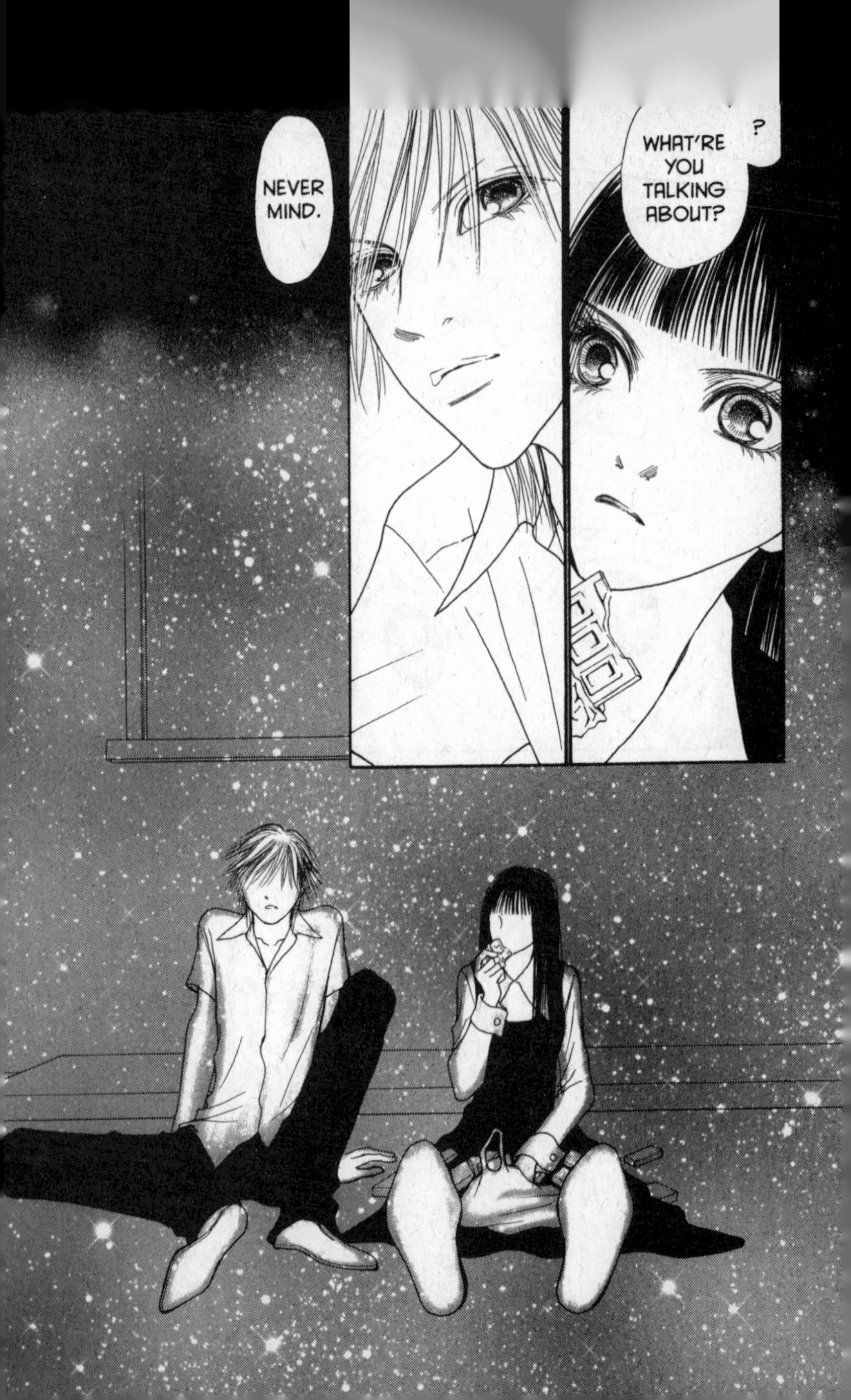
?
WHAT'RE YOU TALKING ABOUT?
NEVER MIND.

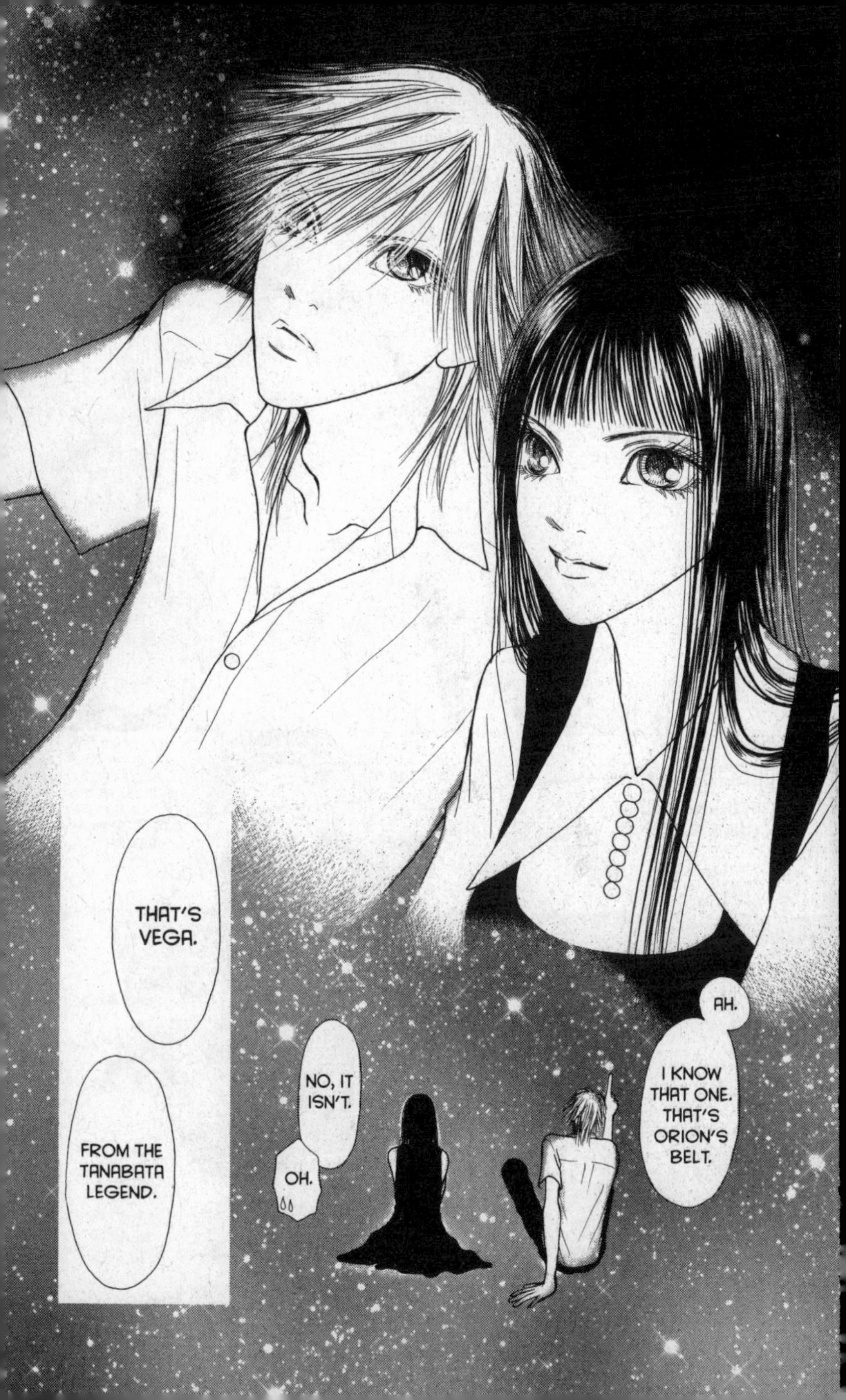
AH.
I KNOW THAT ONE. THAT'S ORION'S BELT.
NO, IT ISN'T.
OH.
THAT'S VEGA.
FROM THE TANABATA LEGEND.

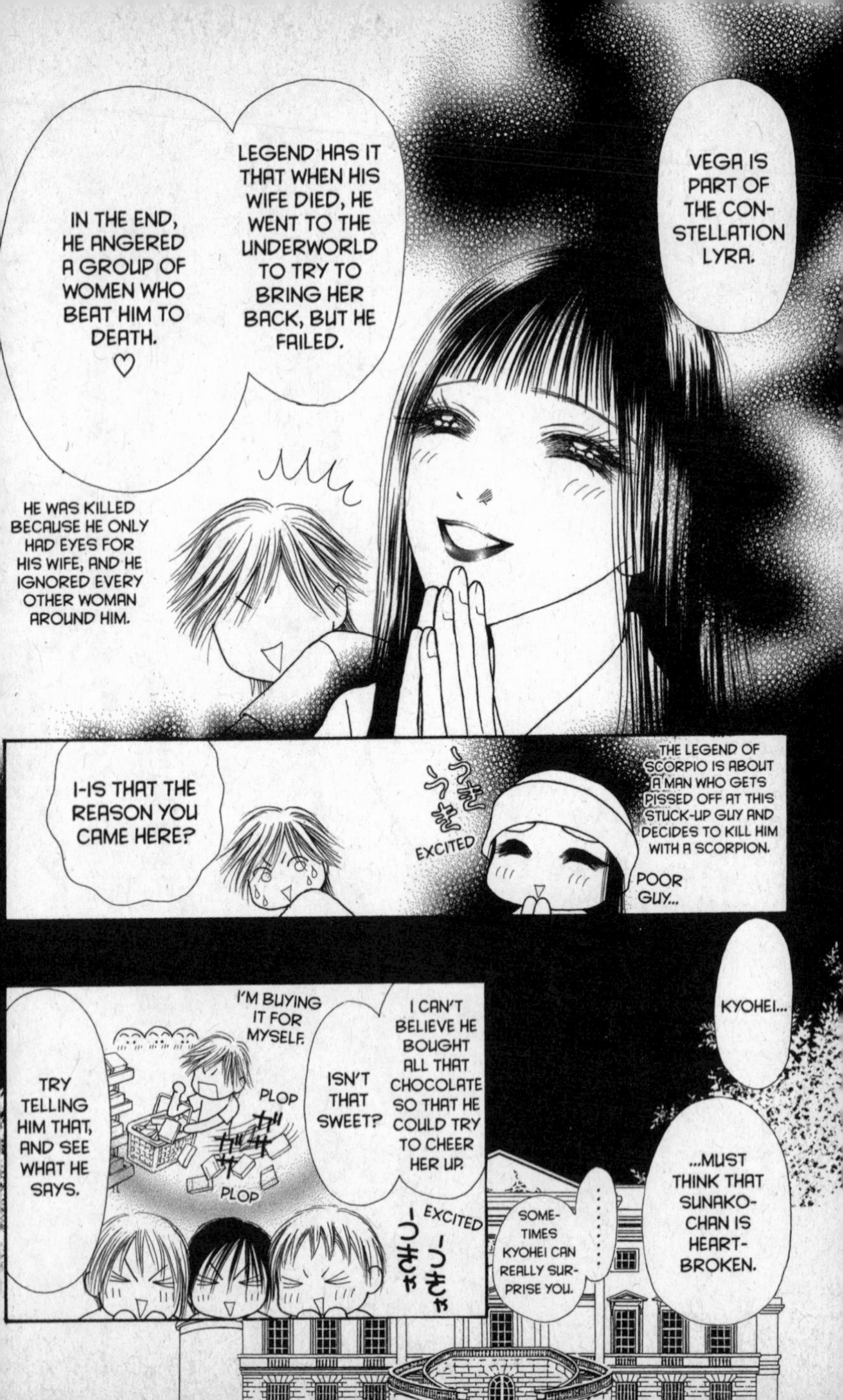
VEGA IS PART OF THE CON-STELLATION LYRA.
LEGEND HAS IT THAT WHEN HIS WIFE DIED, HE WENT TO THE UNDERWORLD TO TRY TO BRING HER BACK, BUT HE FAILED.
IN THE END, HE ANGERED A GROUP OF WOMEN WHO BEAT HIM TO DEATH. ♡
HE WAS KILLED BECAUSE HE ONLY HAD EYES FOR HIS WIFE, AND HE IGNORED EVERY OTHER WOMAN AROUND HIM.
THE LEGEND OF SCORPIO IS ABOUT A MAN WHO GETS PISSED OFF AT THIS STUCK-UP GUY AND DECIDES TO KILL HIM WITH A SCORPION.
POOR GUY...
EXCITED
I-IS THAT THE REASON YOU CAME HERE?
KYOHEI...
...MUST THINK THAT SUNAKO-CHAN IS HEART-BROKEN.
SOME-TIMES KYOHEI CAN REALLY SUR-PRISE YOU.
EXCITED
I CAN'T BELIEVE HE BOUGHT ALL THAT CHOCOLATE SO THAT HE COULD TRY TO CHEER HER UP.
ISN'T THAT SWEET?
I'M BUYING IT FOR MYSELF.
PLOP
PLOP
TRY TELLING HIM THAT, AND SEE WHAT HE SAYS.

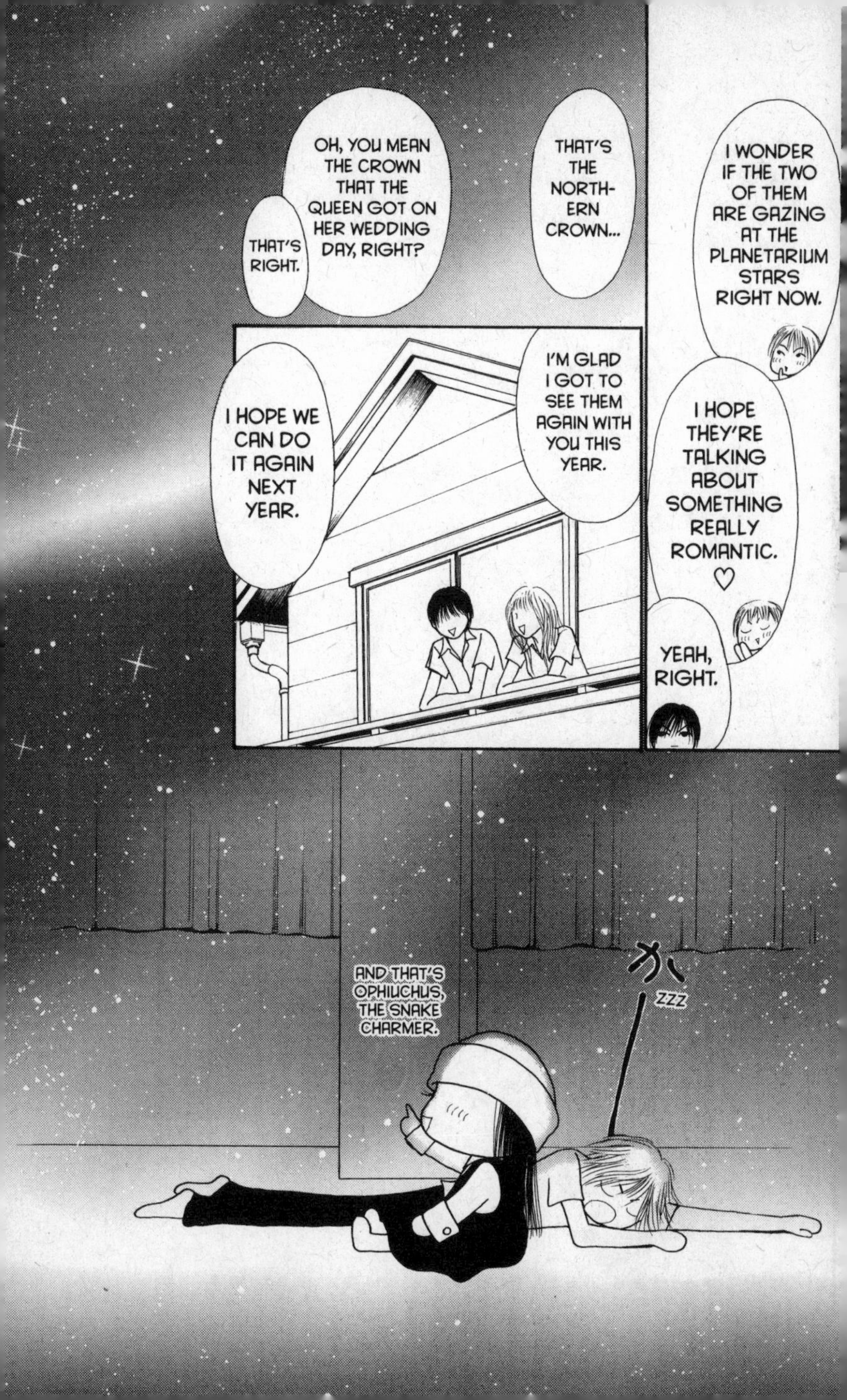
I WONDER IF THE TWO OF THEM ARE GAZING AT THE PLANETARIUM STARS RIGHT NOW.
I HOPE THEY'RE TALKING ABOUT SOMETHING REALLY ROMANTIC. ♡
YEAH, RIGHT.
THAT'S THE NORTHERN-ERN CROWN...
OH, YOU MEAN THE CROWN THAT THE QUEEN GOT ON HER WEDDING DAY, RIGHT?
THAT'S RIGHT.
I'M GLAD I GOT TO SEE THEM AGAIN WITH YOU THIS YEAR.
I HOPE WE CAN DO IT AGAIN NEXT YEAR.
AND THAT'S OPHIUCHUS, THE SNAKE CHARMER.
ZZZ

Chapter 91

HOW TO BE A PRINCESS OF DARKNESS (PART 1)

A LONG TIME AGO, THERE WAS A BEAUTIFUL PRINCESS NAMED ELIZABETH.

THE PRINCESS WAS A VAMPIRE. THE ONLY WAY FOR HER TO LIVE WAS TO FEED ON HUMAN BLOOD.

ONE DAY, SHE FOUND A VERY HANDSOME GENTLEMAN, AND...

SHE DECIDED TO FEAST ON HIM LATER THAT EVENING.

BUT SHE JUST COULDN'T BRING HERSELF TO FEED ON THE HANDSOME GENTLEMAN'S BLOOD.

FINALLY, SHE PASSED AWAY, AND DISAPPEARED.

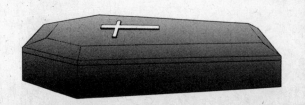

THAT'S RIGHT...

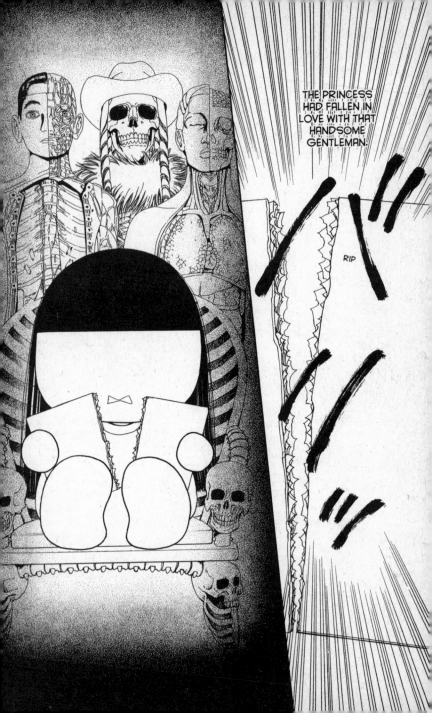

THE PRINCESS HAD FALLEN IN LOVE WITH THAT HANDSOME GENTLEMAN.

RIP

WHAT A CRAPPY BOOK.

WHY WOULD A VAMPIRE WHO LIVES IN DARKNESS FALL FOR A HANDSOME GENTLEMAN?

CLICK
YOU SEEM EVEN DARKER THAN USUAL.
SOMETHING MUST'VE REALLY PISSED YOU OFF.
THE DARKNESS COULD NEVER LOSE TO A HANDSOME CREATURE.
GRR
ギギギ
ラララ
ROAR

Chapter 91

HOW TO BE A PRINCESS OF DARKNESS (PART 1)

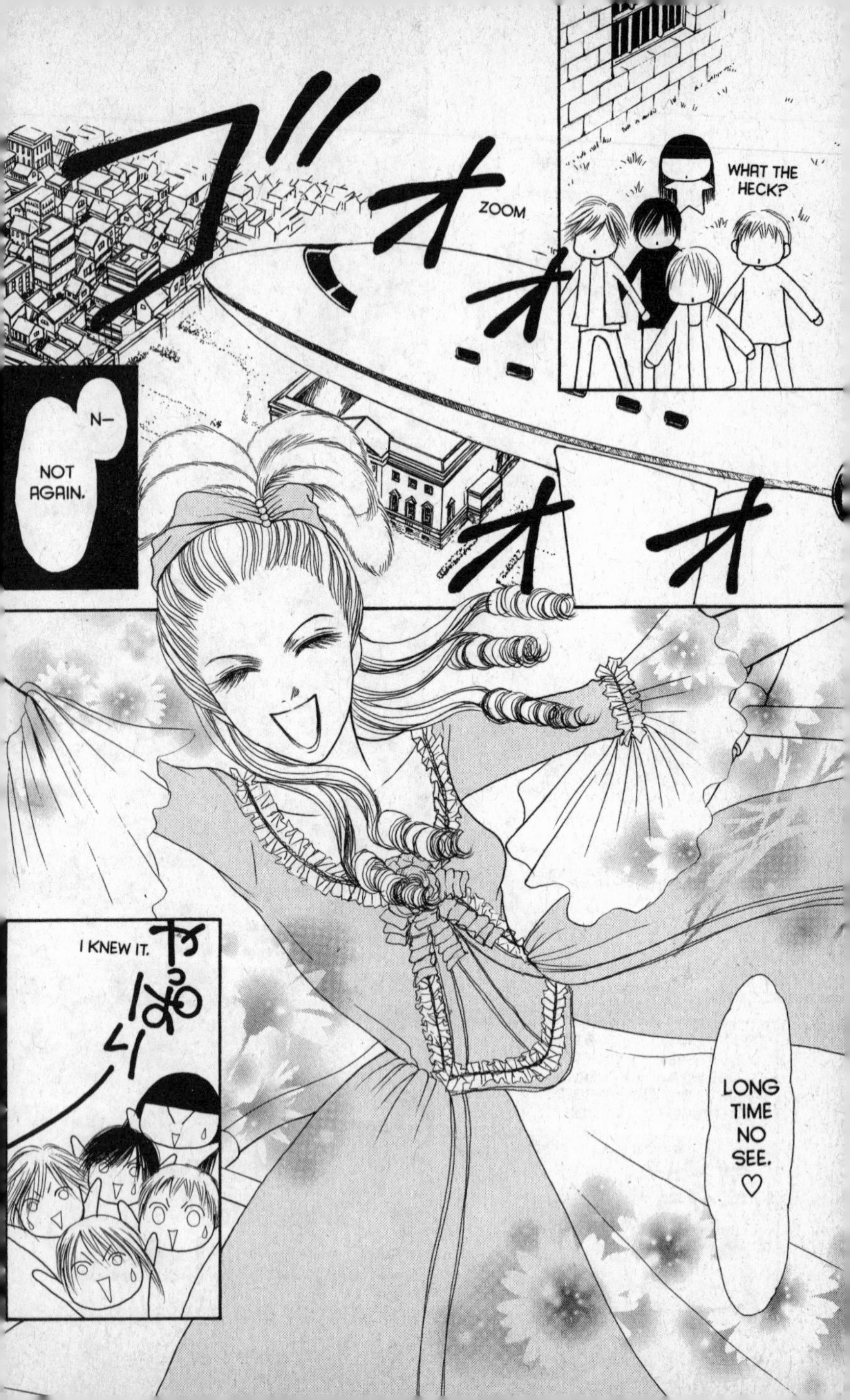
WHAT THE HECK?
ゴオオオオ
ZOOM
N—
NOT AGAIN.
LONG TIME NO SEE. ♡
I KNEW IT.
やっぱりー

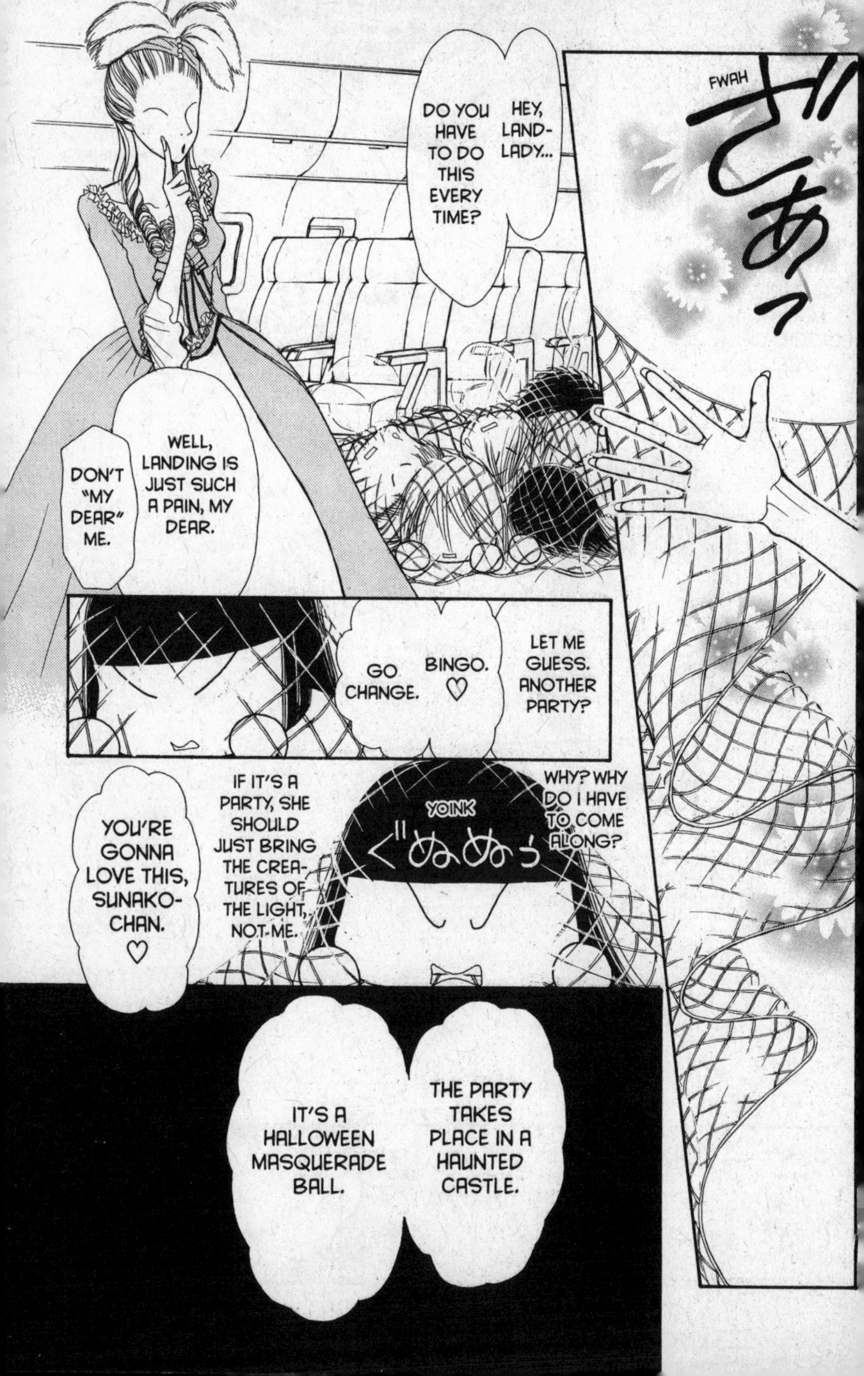

FWAH
ざあっ
HEY, LAND-LADY...
DO YOU HAVE TO DO THIS EVERY TIME?
WELL, LANDING IS JUST SUCH A PAIN, MY DEAR.
DON'T "MY DEAR" ME.
LET ME GUESS. ANOTHER PARTY?
BINGO. ♡
GO CHANGE.
WHY? WHY DO I HAVE TO COME ALONG?
YOINK
ぐぬぬっ
IF IT'S A PARTY, SHE SHOULD JUST BRING THE CREA-TURES OF THE LIGHT, NOT ME.
YOU'RE GONNA LOVE THIS, SUNAKO-CHAN. ♡
THE PARTY TAKES PLACE IN A HAUNTED CASTLE.
IT'S A HALLOWEEN MASQUERADE BALL.

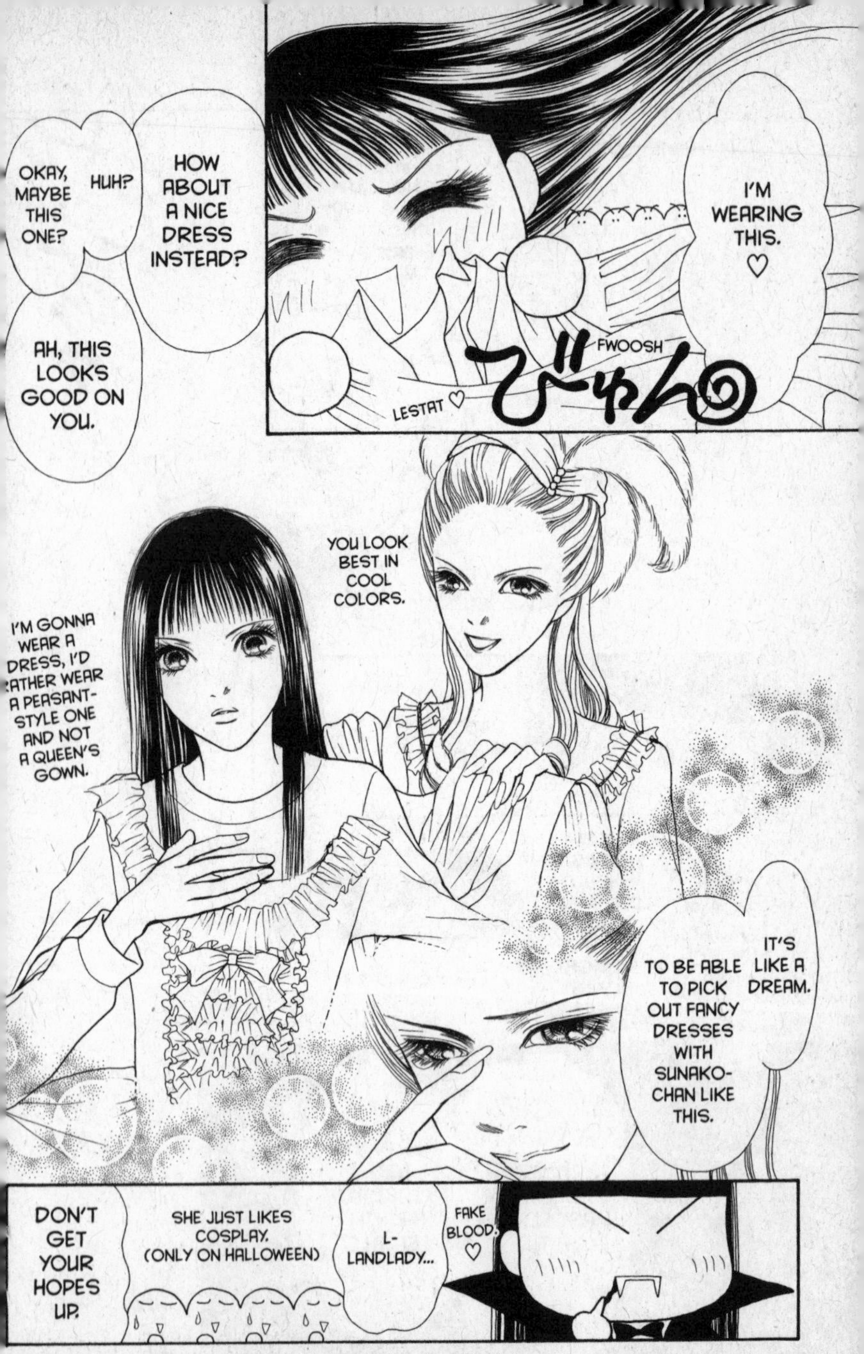

I'M WEARING THIS. ♡
FWOOSH
LESTAT ♡
HOW ABOUT A NICE DRESS INSTEAD?
HUH?
OKAY, MAYBE THIS ONE?
AH, THIS LOOKS GOOD ON YOU.
YOU LOOK BEST IN COOL COLORS.
I'M GONNA WEAR A DRESS, I'D RATHER WEAR A PEASANT-STYLE ONE AND NOT A QUEEN'S GOWN.
IT'S LIKE A DREAM.
TO BE ABLE TO PICK OUT FANCY DRESSES WITH SUNAKO-CHAN LIKE THIS.
FAKE BLOOD. ♡
L-LANDLADY...
SHE JUST LIKES COSPLAY. (ONLY ON HALLOWEEN)
DON'T GET YOUR HOPES UP.

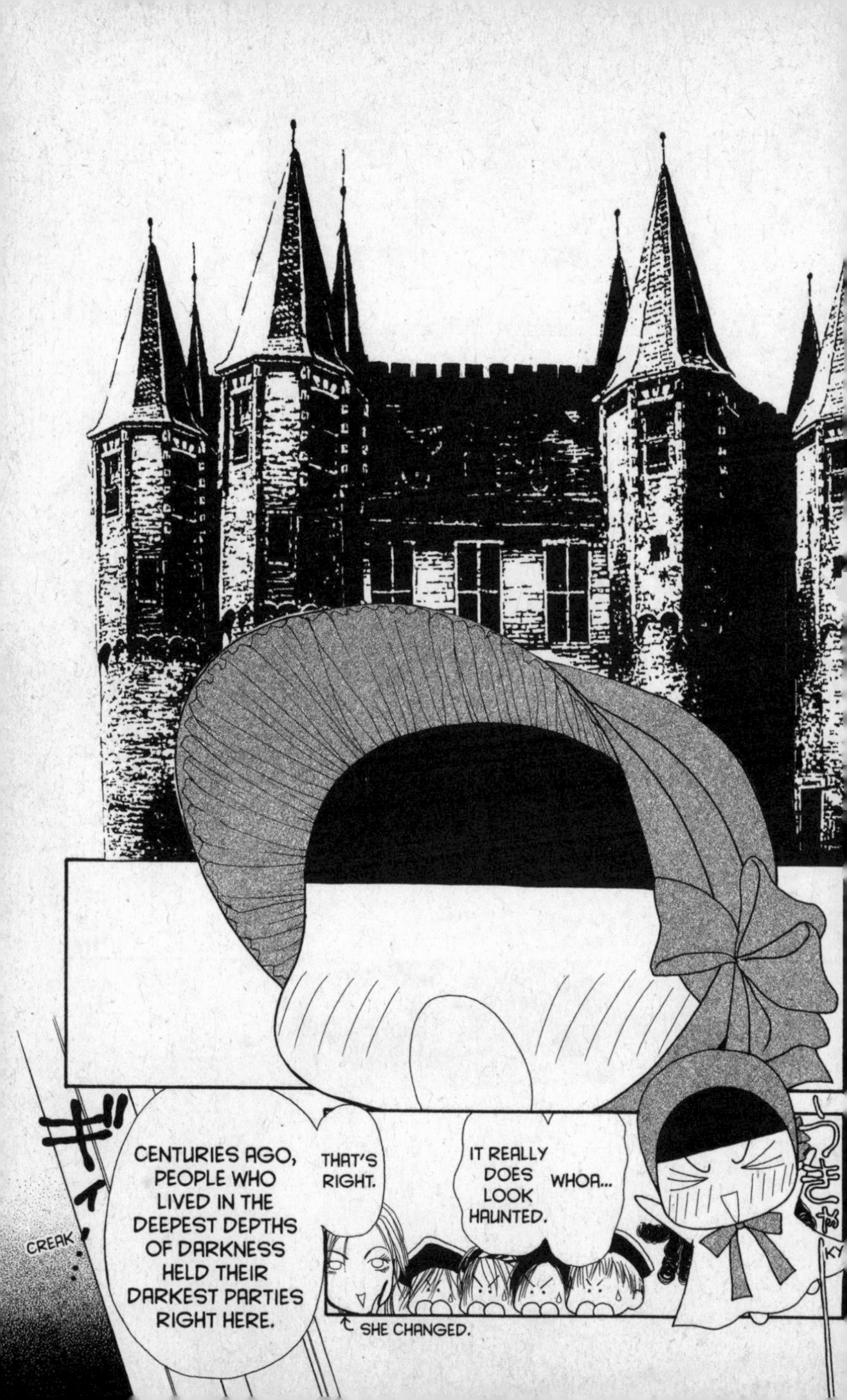
KY
WHOA...
IT REALLY DOES LOOK HAUNTED.
THAT'S RIGHT.
SHE CHANGED.
CENTURIES AGO, PEOPLE WHO LIVED IN THE DEEPEST DEPTHS OF DARKNESS HELD THEIR DARKEST PARTIES RIGHT HERE.
CREAK

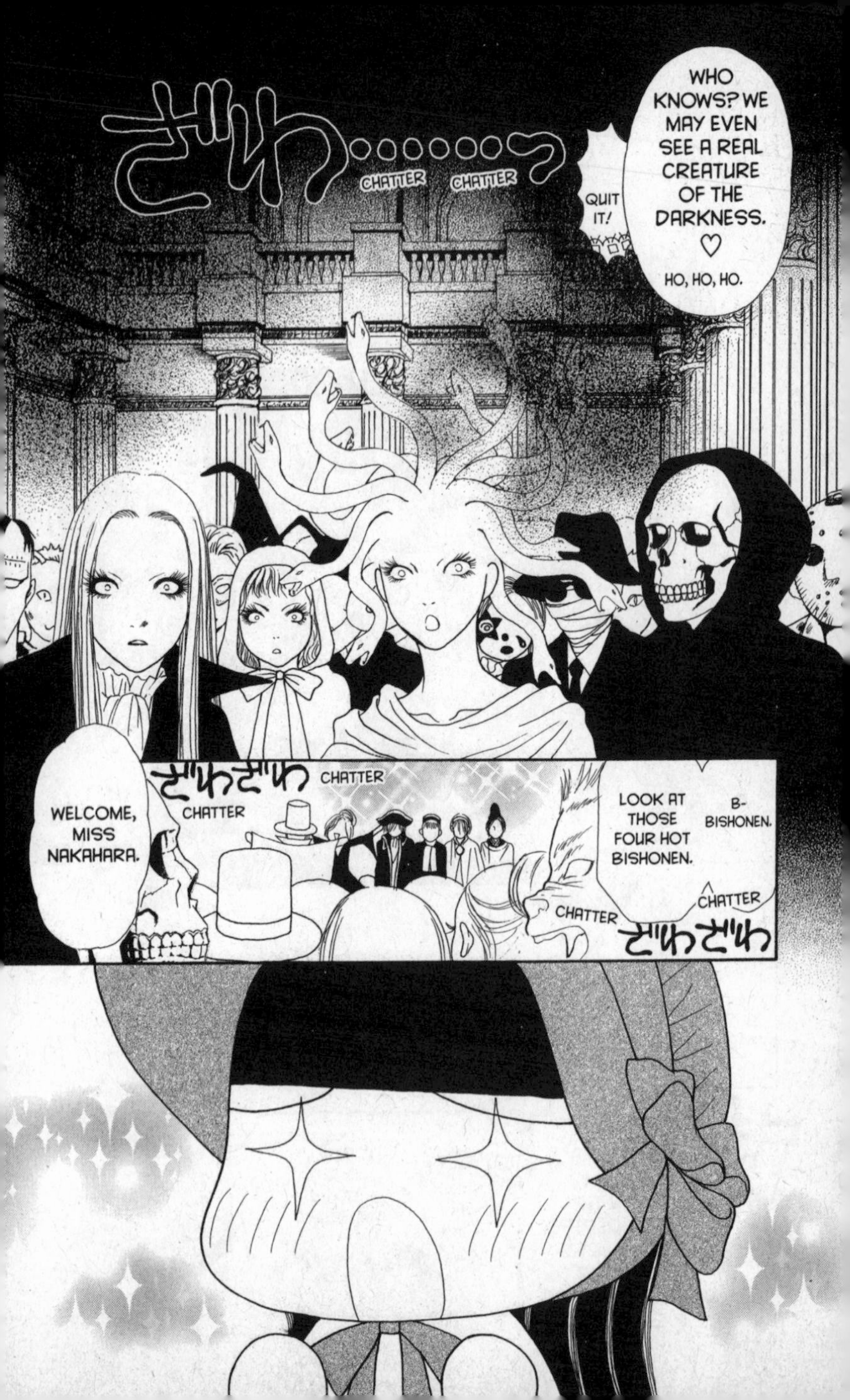
WHO KNOWS? WE MAY EVEN SEE A REAL CREATURE OF THE DARKNESS. ♡
HO, HO, HO.
QUIT IT!
ざわ……………っ
CHATTER CHATTER
B-BISHONEN.
LOOK AT THOSE FOUR HOT BISHONEN.
ざわざわ
CHATTER
CHATTER
ざわざわ
CHATTER
CHATTER
WELCOME, MISS NAKAHARA.

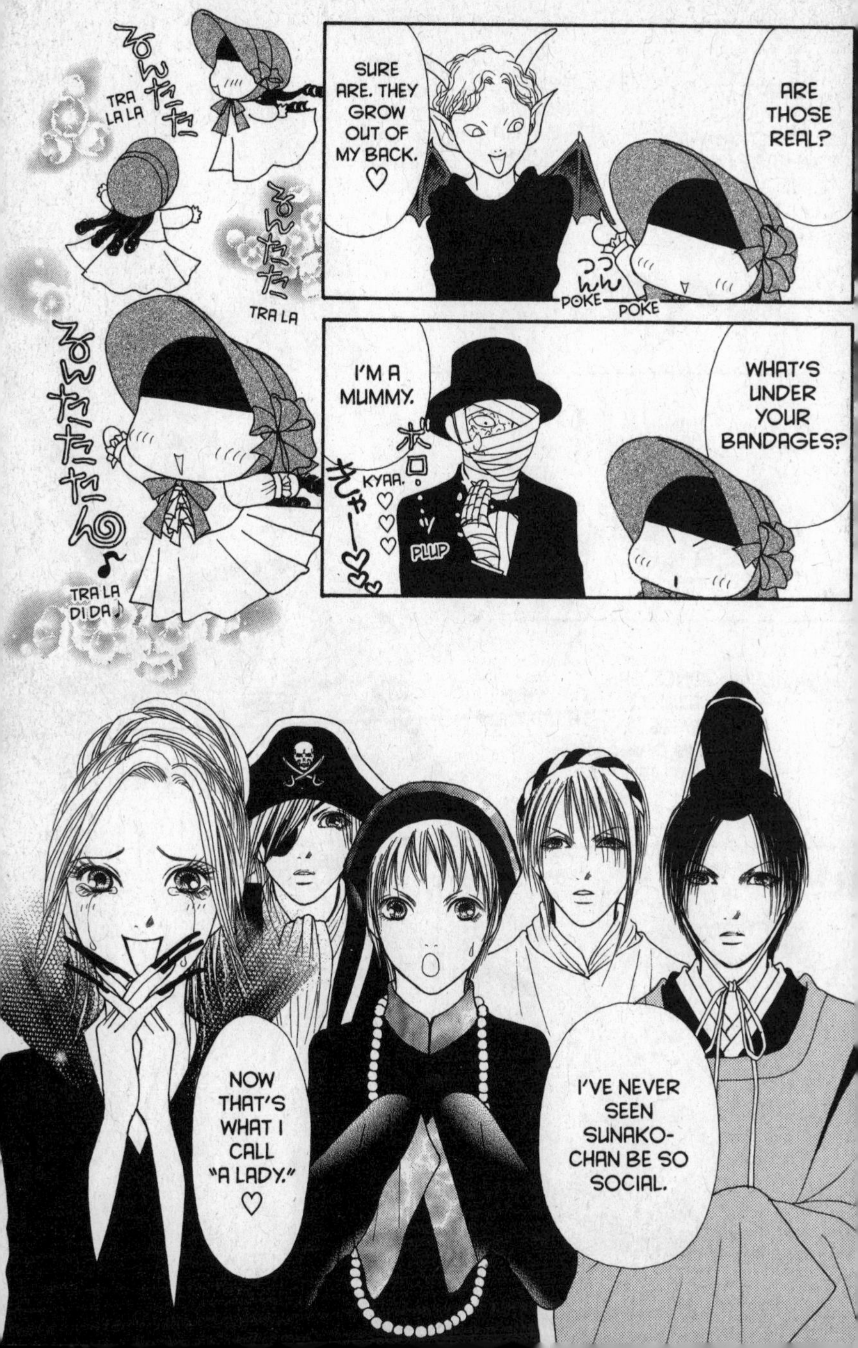
ARE THOSE REAL?
SURE ARE. THEY GROW OUT OF MY BACK. ♡
POKE POKE
WHAT'S UNDER YOUR BANDAGES?
I'M A MUMMY.
KYAA. ♡
PLUP
TRA LA LA
TRA LA
TRA LA DI DA♪
I'VE NEVER SEEN SUNAKO-CHAN BE SO SOCIAL.
NOW THAT'S WHAT I CALL "A LADY." ♡

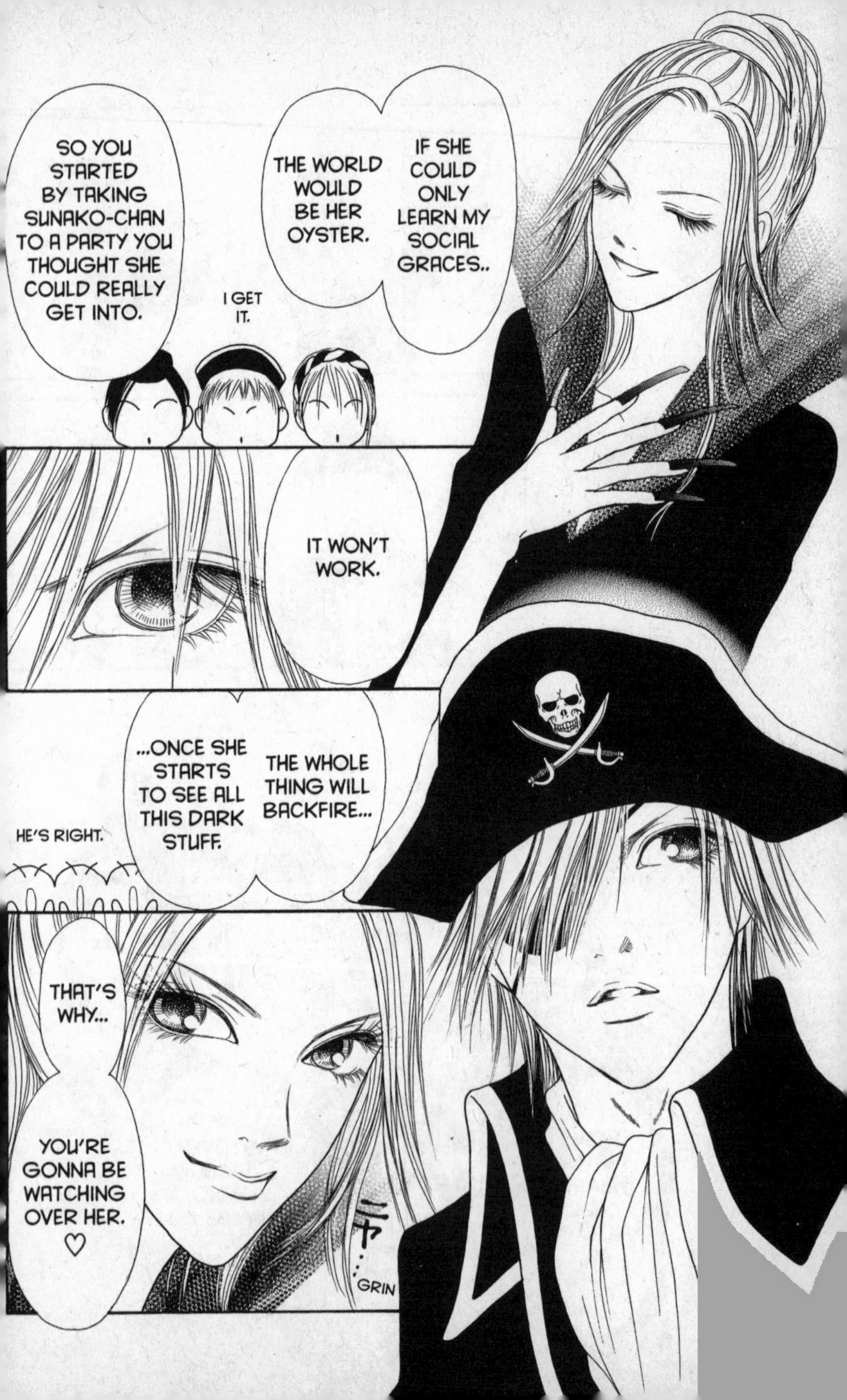
IF SHE COULD ONLY LEARN MY SOCIAL GRACES..
THE WORLD WOULD BE HER OYSTER.
SO YOU STARTED BY TAKING SUNAKO-CHAN TO A PARTY YOU THOUGHT SHE COULD REALLY GET INTO.
I GET IT.
IT WON'T WORK.
THE WHOLE THING WILL BACKFIRE...
...ONCE SHE STARTS TO SEE ALL THIS DARK STUFF.
HE'S RIGHT.
THAT'S WHY...
YOU'RE GONNA BE WATCHING OVER HER. ♡
GRIN

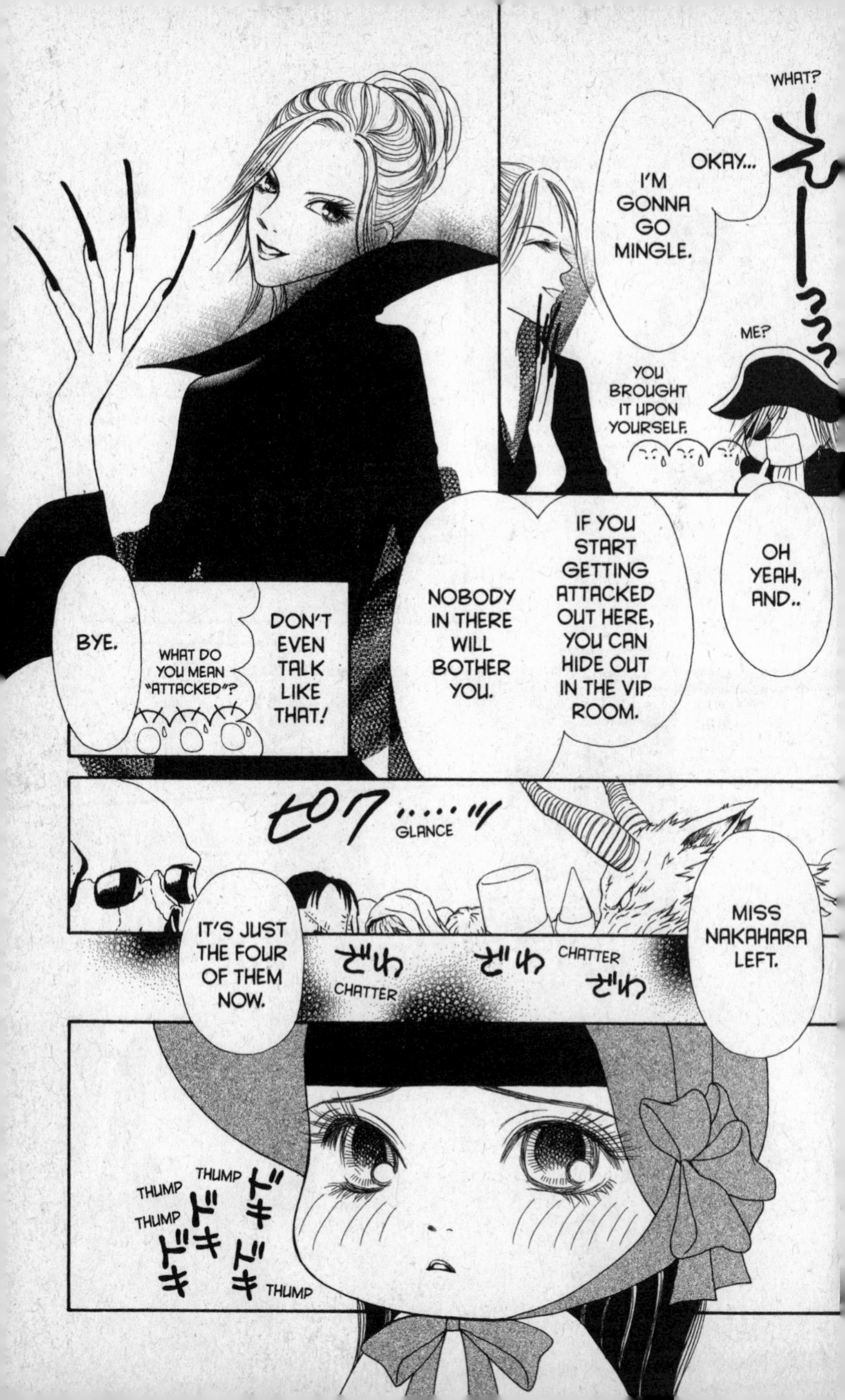
WHAT?
OKAY... I'M GONNA GO MINGLE.
ME?
YOU BROUGHT IT UPON YOURSELF.
OH YEAH, AND..
IF YOU START GETTING ATTACKED OUT HERE, YOU CAN HIDE OUT IN THE VIP ROOM.
NOBODY IN THERE WILL BOTHER YOU.
DON'T EVEN TALK LIKE THAT!
WHAT DO YOU MEAN "ATTACKED"?
BYE.
GLANCE
MISS NAKAHARA LEFT.
IT'S JUST THE FOUR OF THEM NOW.
ざわ CHATTER
ざわ
ざわ CHATTER
ドキ THUMP
ドキ THUMP
ドキ THUMP
ドキ THUMP

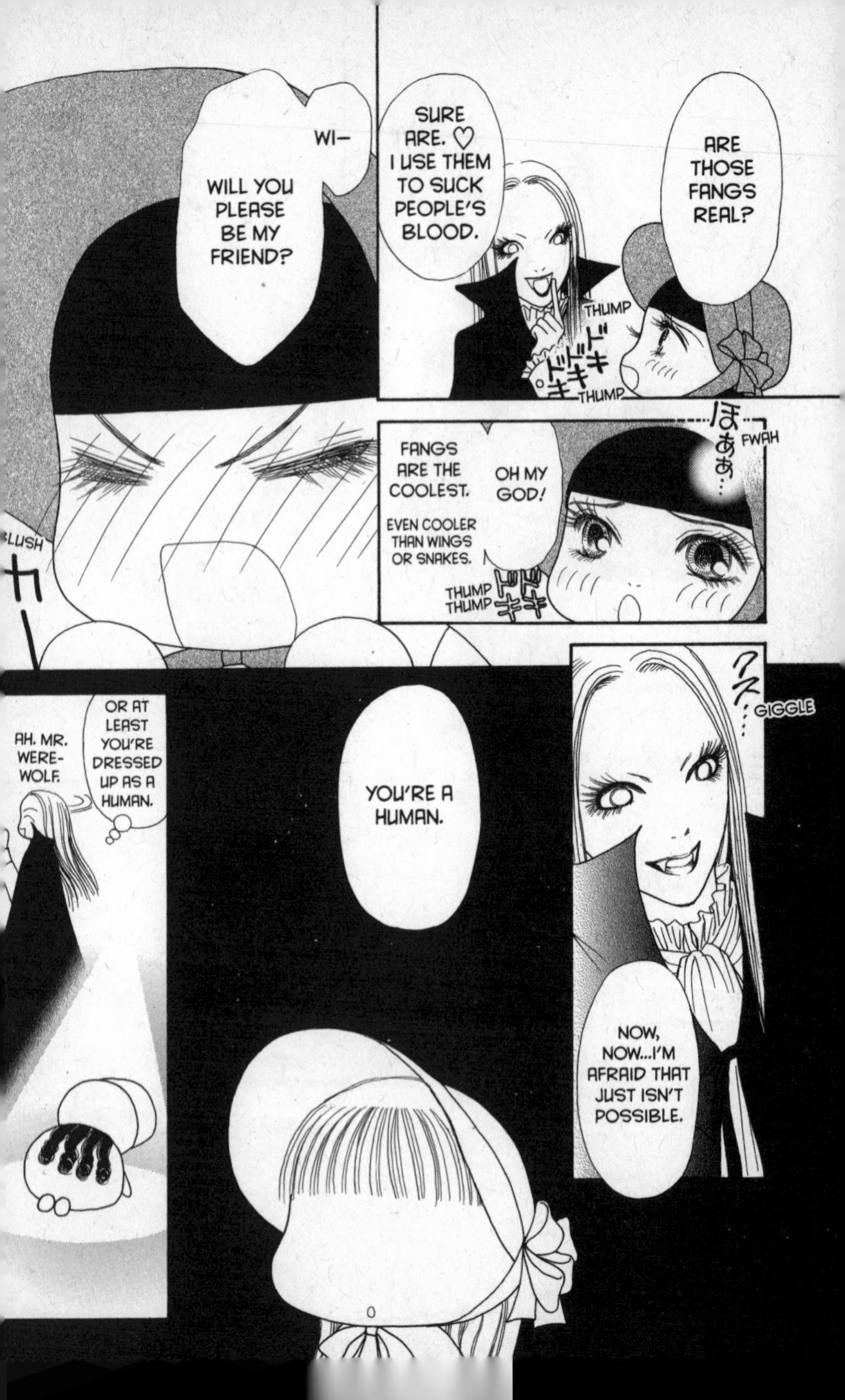
ARE THOSE FANGS REAL?
SURE ARE. ♡ I USE THEM TO SUCK PEOPLE'S BLOOD.
THUMP
THUMP
FWAH
OH MY GOD!
FANGS ARE THE COOLEST.
EVEN COOLER THAN WINGS OR SNAKES.
THUMP THUMP
WI—
WILL YOU PLEASE BE MY FRIEND?
BLUSH
GIGGLE
NOW, NOW...I'M AFRAID THAT JUST ISN'T POSSIBLE.
YOU'RE A HUMAN.
AH. MR. WERE-WOLF.
OR AT LEAST YOU'RE DRESSED UP AS A HUMAN.

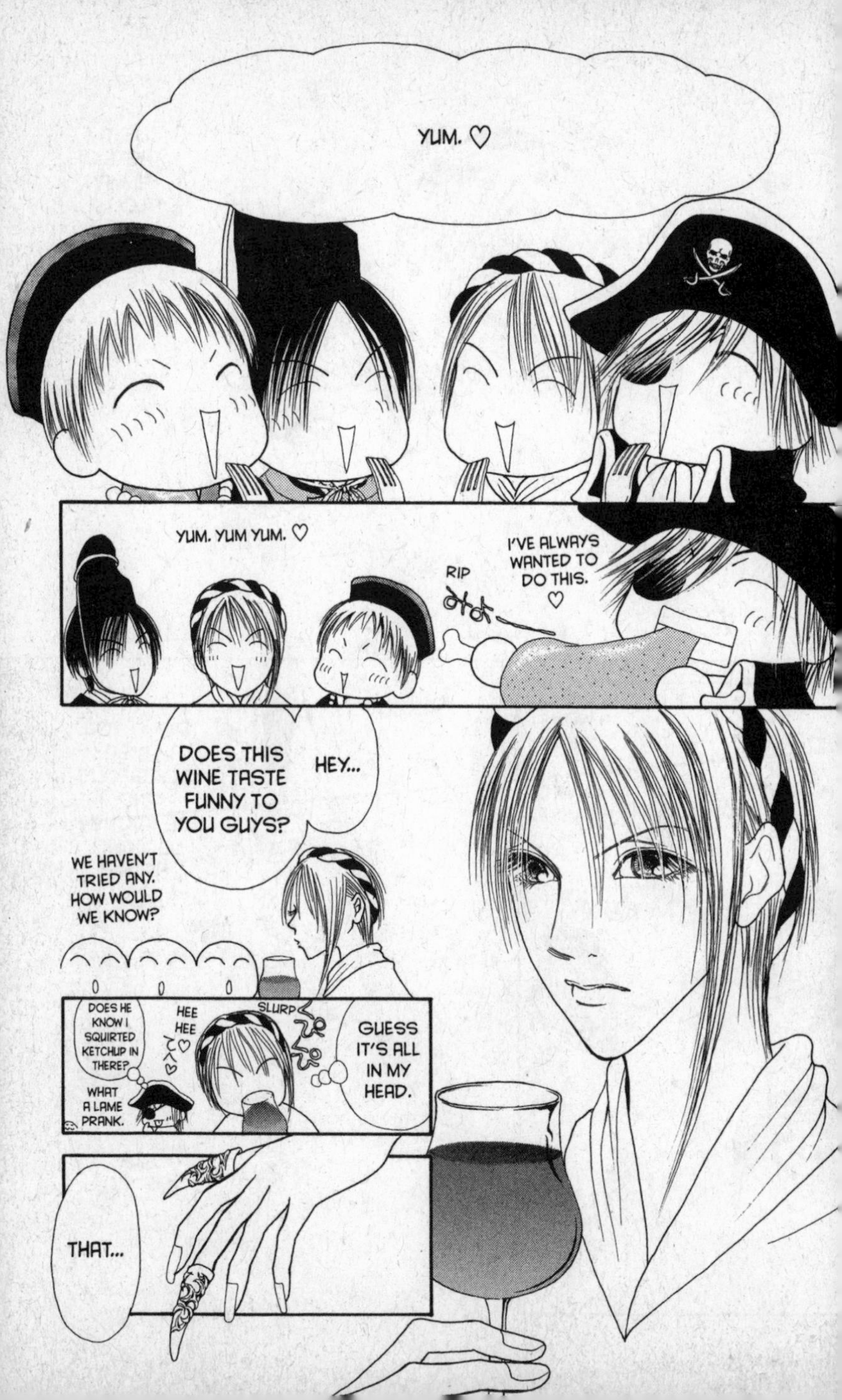

YUM. ♡
I'VE ALWAYS WANTED TO DO THIS. ♡
RIP
YUM. YUM YUM. ♡
HEY...
DOES THIS WINE TASTE FUNNY TO YOU GUYS?
WE HAVEN'T TRIED ANY. HOW WOULD WE KNOW?
GUESS IT'S ALL IN MY HEAD.
SLURP
HEE HEE ♡
DOES HE KNOW I SQUIRTED KETCHUP IN THERE?
WHAT A LAME PRANK.
THAT...

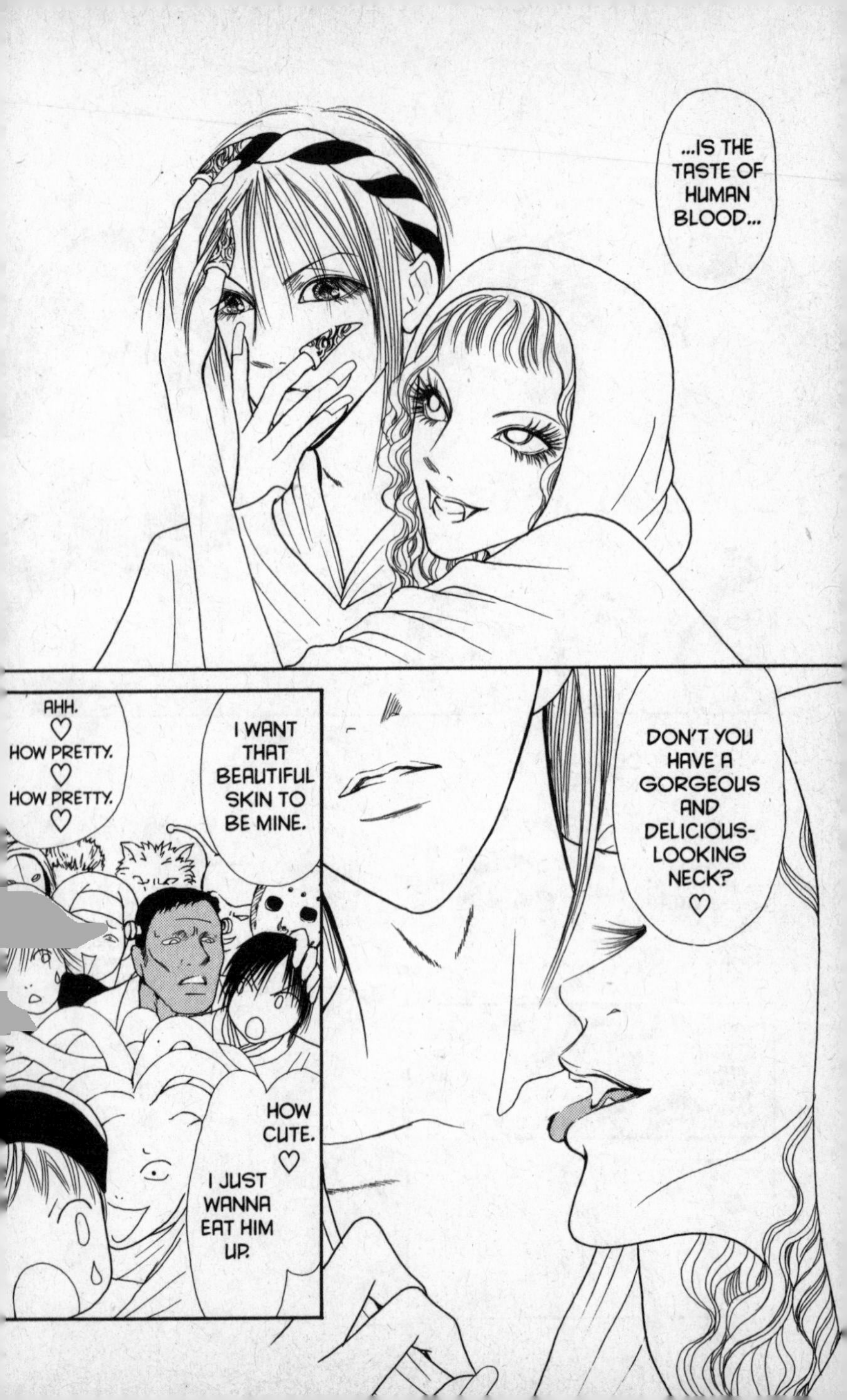

...IS THE TASTE OF HUMAN BLOOD...
DON'T YOU HAVE A GORGEOUS AND DELICIOUS-LOOKING NECK? ♡
I WANT THAT BEAUTIFUL SKIN TO BE MINE.
AHH. ♡ HOW PRETTY. ♡ HOW PRETTY. ♡
HOW CUTE. ♡ I JUST WANNA EAT HIM UP.

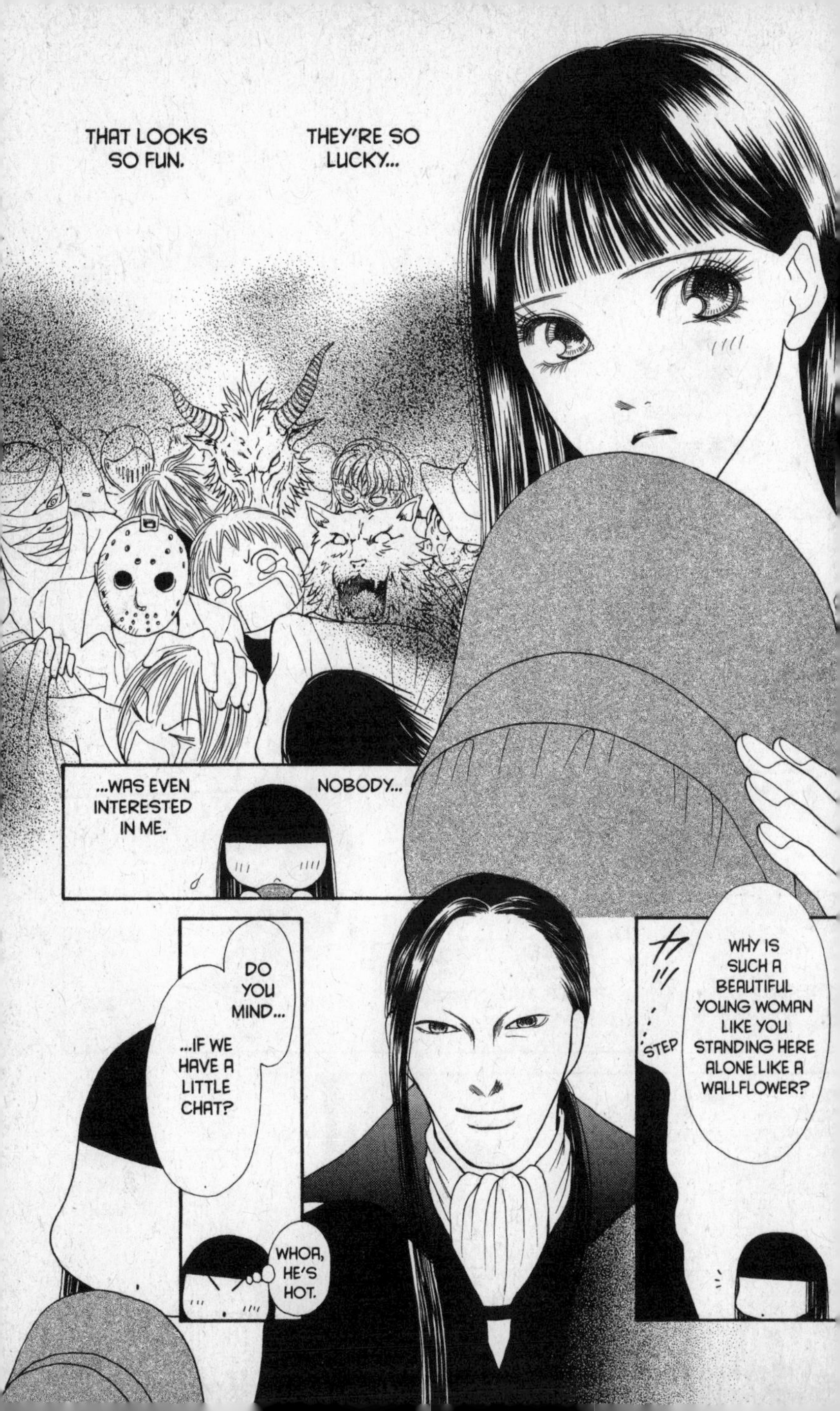
THEY'RE SO LUCKY...
THAT LOOKS SO FUN.
NOBODY...
...WAS EVEN INTERESTED IN ME.
STEP
WHY IS SUCH A BEAUTIFUL YOUNG WOMAN LIKE YOU STANDING HERE ALONE LIKE A WALLFLOWER?
DO YOU MIND...
...IF WE HAVE A LITTLE CHAT?
WHOA, HE'S HOT.

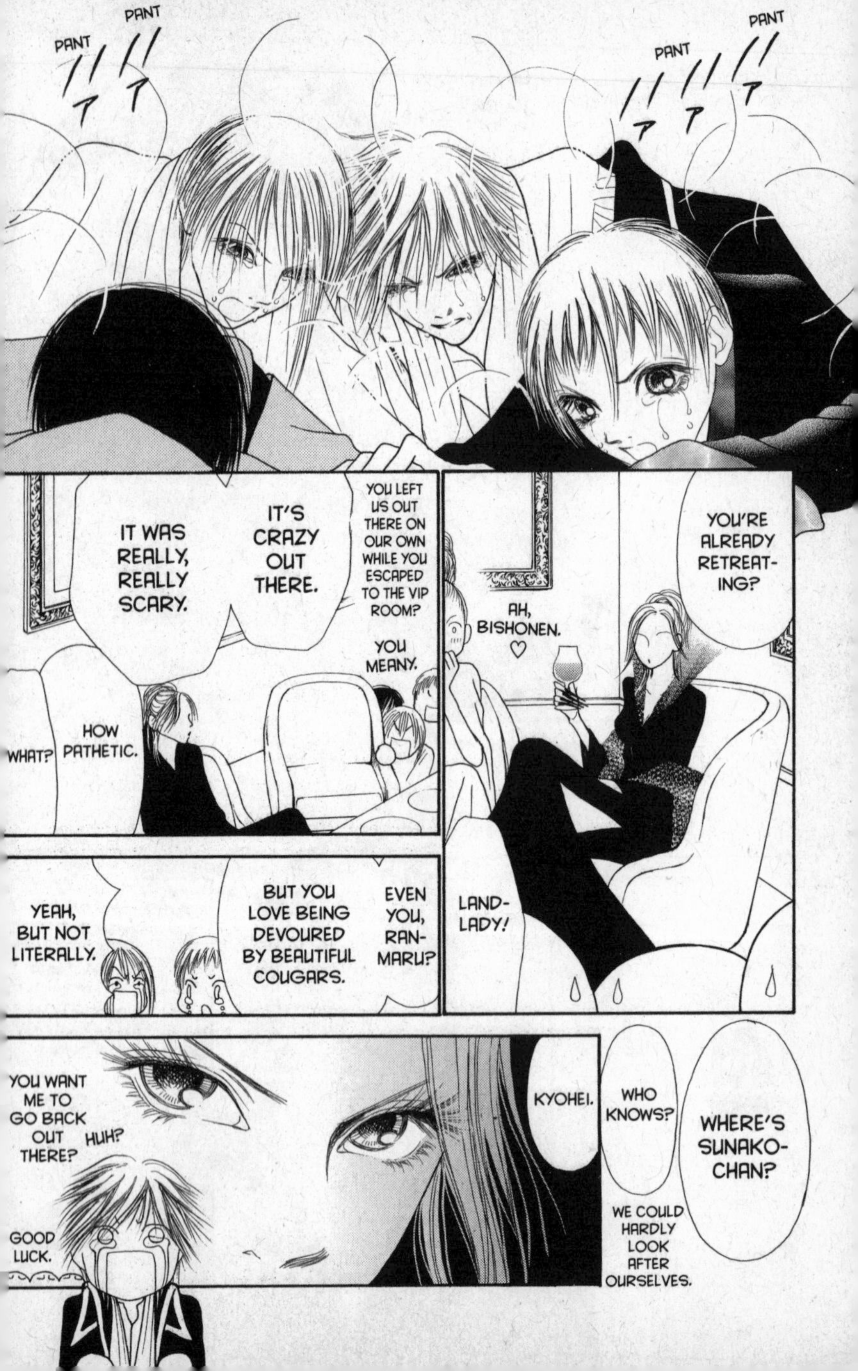
PANT
PANT
PANT
PANT
YOU'RE ALREADY RETREAT-ING?
AH, BISHONEN. ♡
LAND-LADY!
YOU LEFT US OUT THERE ON OUR OWN WHILE YOU ESCAPED TO THE VIP ROOM?
YOU MEANY.
IT'S CRAZY OUT THERE.
IT WAS REALLY, REALLY SCARY.
HOW PATHETIC.
WHAT?
EVEN YOU, RAN-MARU?
BUT YOU LOVE BEING DEVOURED BY BEAUTIFUL COUGARS.
YEAH, BUT NOT LITERALLY.
WHERE'S SUNAKO-CHAN?
WHO KNOWS?
WE COULD HARDLY LOOK AFTER OURSELVES.
KYOHEI.
HUH?
YOU WANT ME TO GO BACK OUT THERE?
GOOD LUCK.

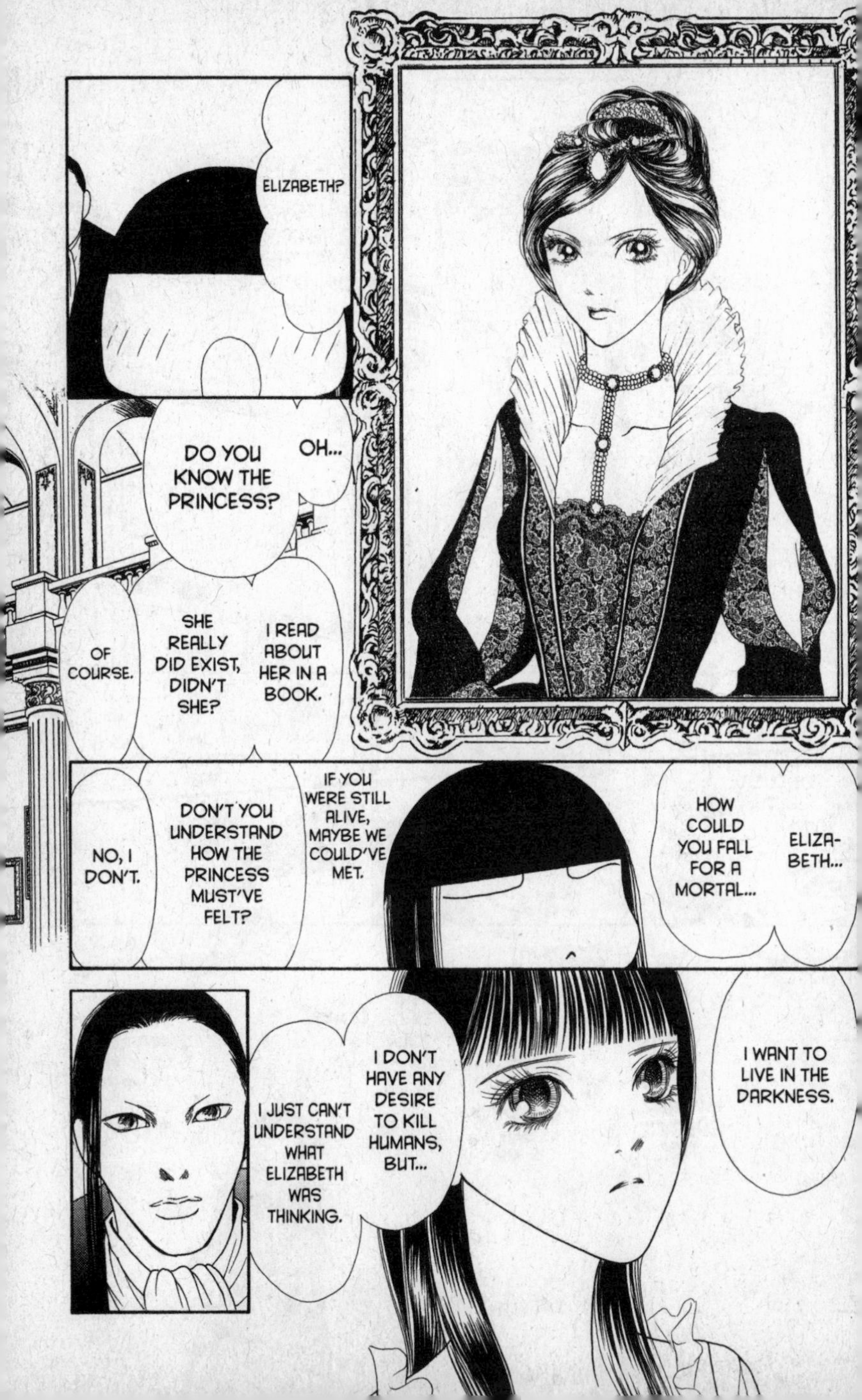
ELIZABETH?
OH...
DO YOU KNOW THE PRINCESS?
I READ ABOUT HER IN A BOOK.
SHE REALLY DID EXIST, DIDN'T SHE?
OF COURSE.
ELIZA-BETH...
HOW COULD YOU FALL FOR A MORTAL...
IF YOU WERE STILL ALIVE, MAYBE WE COULD'VE MET.
DON'T YOU UNDERSTAND HOW THE PRINCESS MUST'VE FELT?
NO, I DON'T.
I WANT TO LIVE IN THE DARKNESS.
I DON'T HAVE ANY DESIRE TO KILL HUMANS, BUT...
I JUST CAN'T UNDERSTAND WHAT ELIZABETH WAS THINKING.

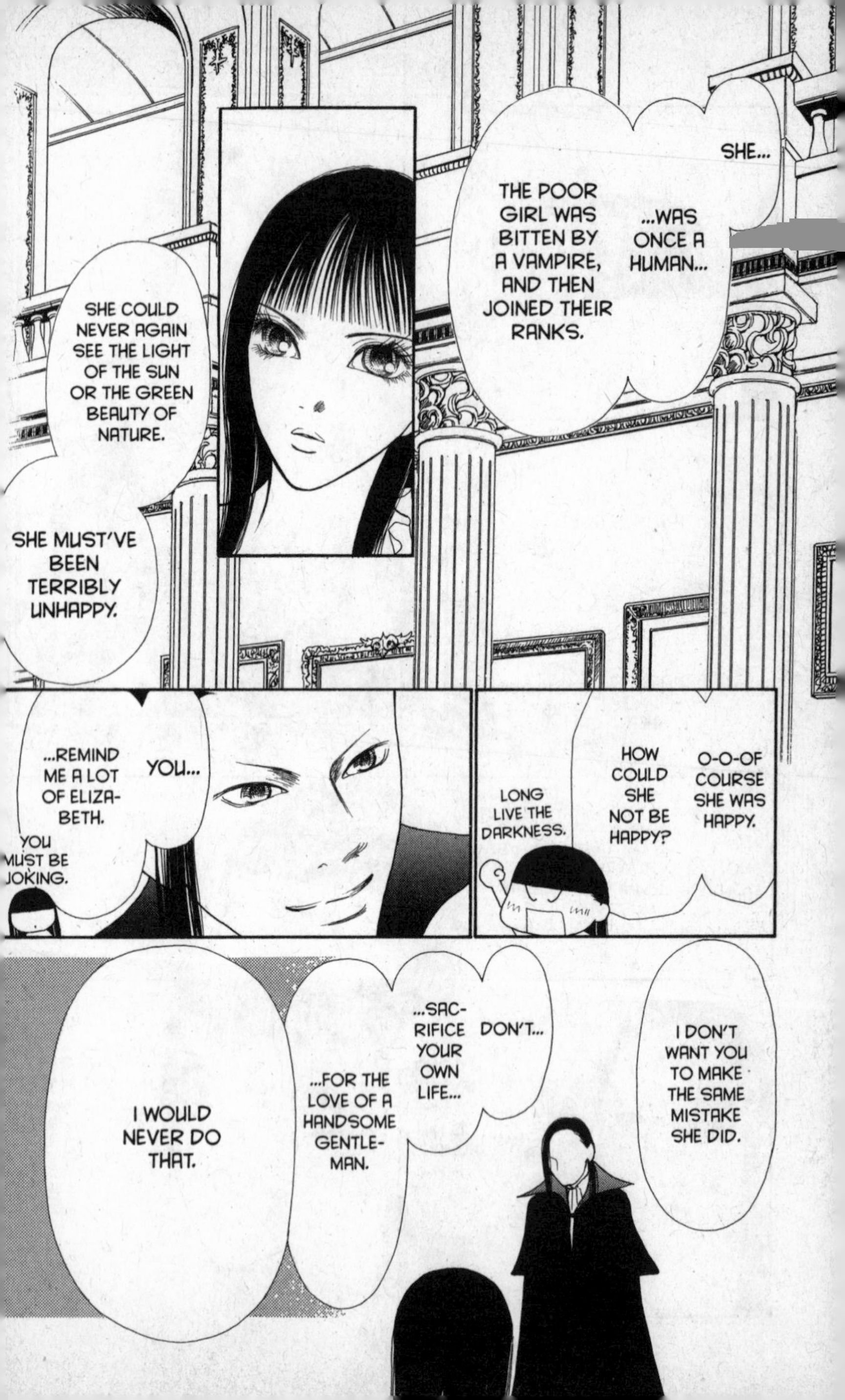
SHE...
...WAS ONCE A HUMAN...
THE POOR GIRL WAS BITTEN BY A VAMPIRE, AND THEN JOINED THEIR RANKS.
SHE COULD NEVER AGAIN SEE THE LIGHT OF THE SUN OR THE GREEN BEAUTY OF NATURE.
SHE MUST'VE BEEN TERRIBLY UNHAPPY.
O-O-OF COURSE SHE WAS HAPPY.
HOW COULD SHE NOT BE HAPPY?
LONG LIVE THE DARKNESS.
YOU...
...REMIND ME A LOT OF ELIZA-BETH.
YOU MUST BE JOKING.
I DON'T WANT YOU TO MAKE THE SAME MISTAKE SHE DID.
DON'T...
...SAC-RIFICE YOUR OWN LIFE...
...FOR THE LOVE OF A HANDSOME GENTLE-MAN.
I WOULD NEVER DO THAT.

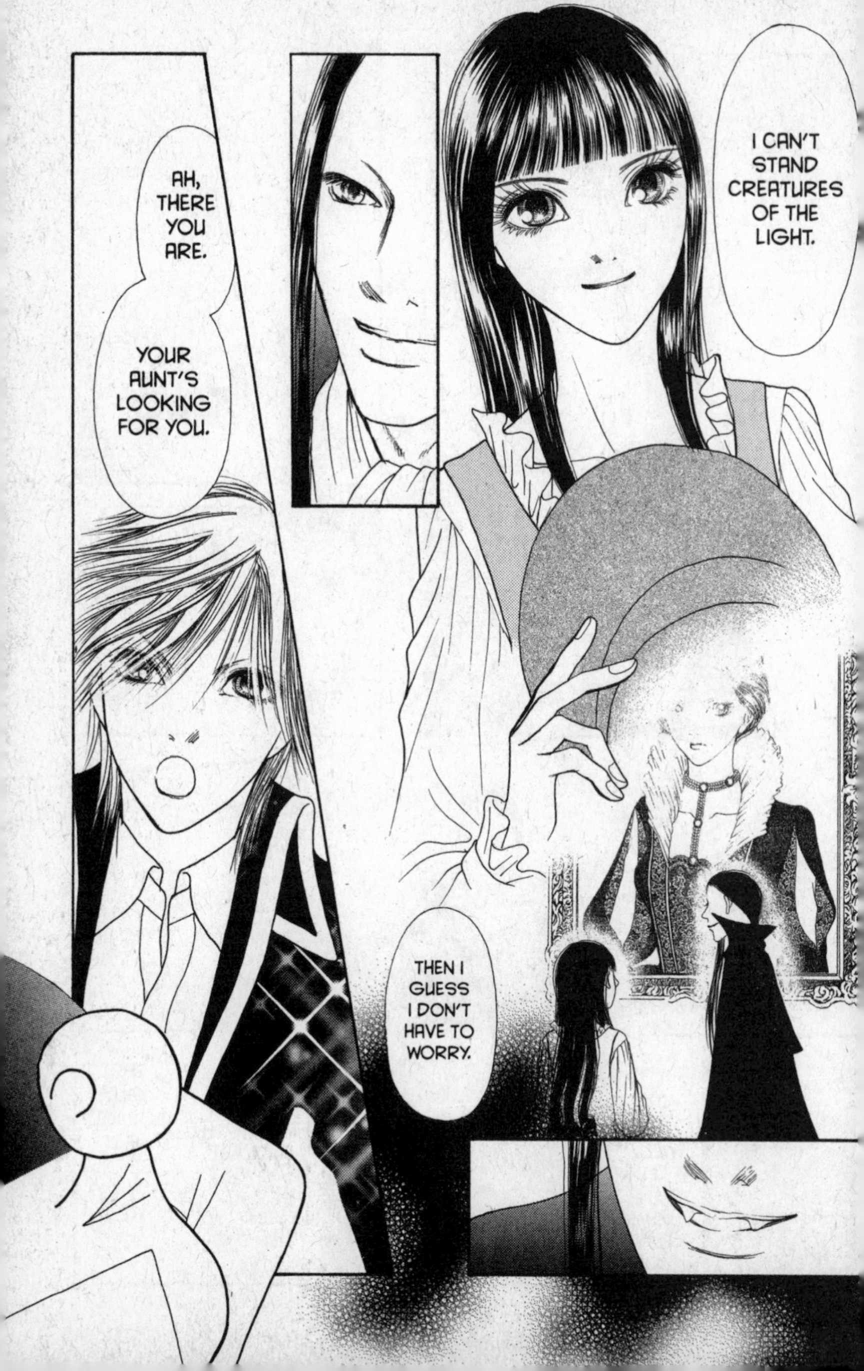
I CAN'T STAND CREATURES OF THE LIGHT.
AH, THERE YOU ARE.
YOUR AUNT'S LOOKING FOR YOU.
THEN I GUESS I DON'T HAVE TO WORRY.

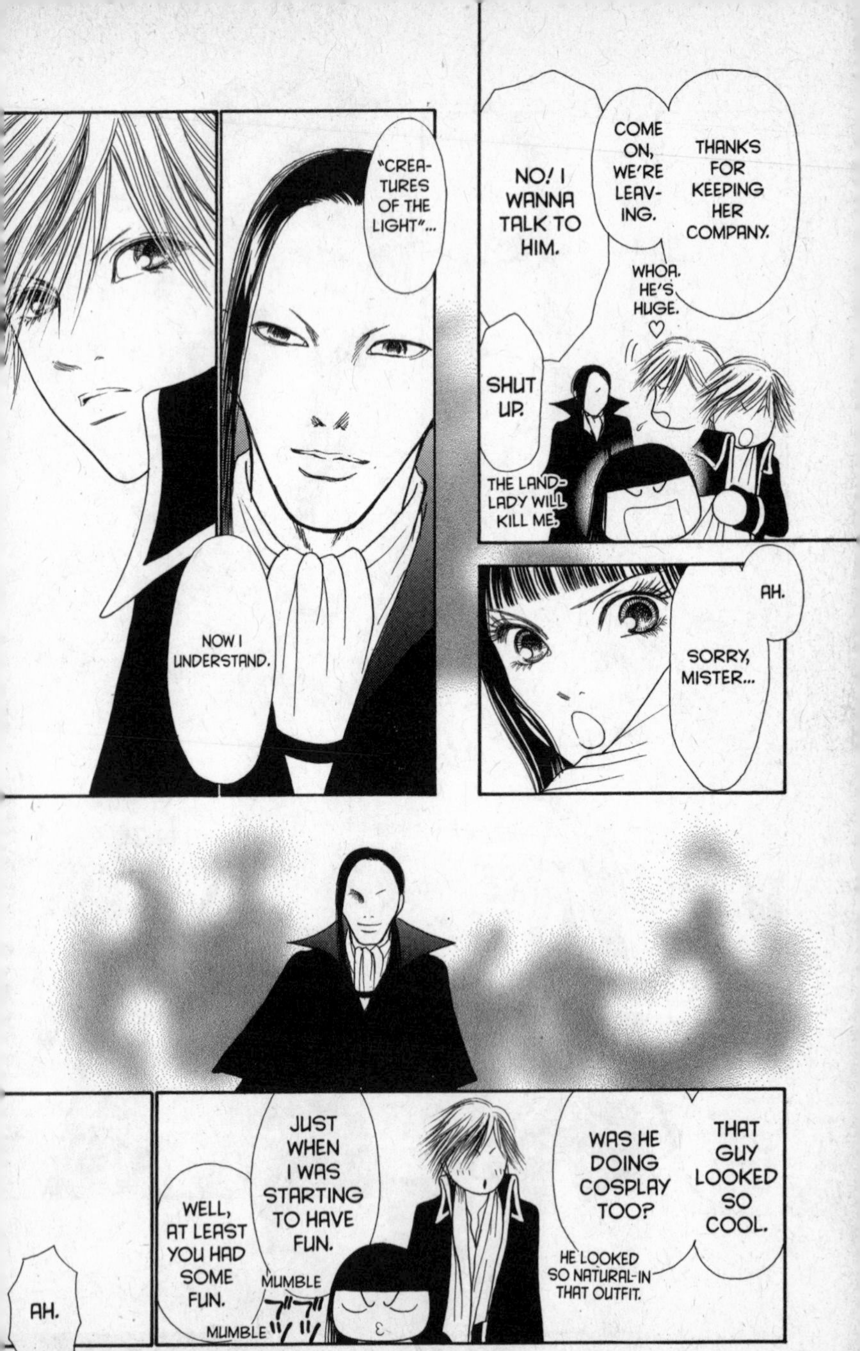
THANKS FOR KEEPING HER COMPANY.
COME ON, WE'RE LEAVING.
WHOA. HE'S HUGE. ♡
NO! I WANNA TALK TO HIM.
SHUT UP.
THE LANDLADY WILL KILL ME.
AH.
SORRY, MISTER...
"CREATURES OF THE LIGHT"...
NOW I UNDERSTAND.
THAT GUY LOOKED SO COOL.
WAS HE DOING COSPLAY TOO?
HE LOOKED SO NATURAL IN THAT OUTFIT.
JUST WHEN I WAS STARTING TO HAVE FUN.
MUMBLE
MUMBLE
WELL, AT LEAST YOU HAD SOME FUN.
AH.

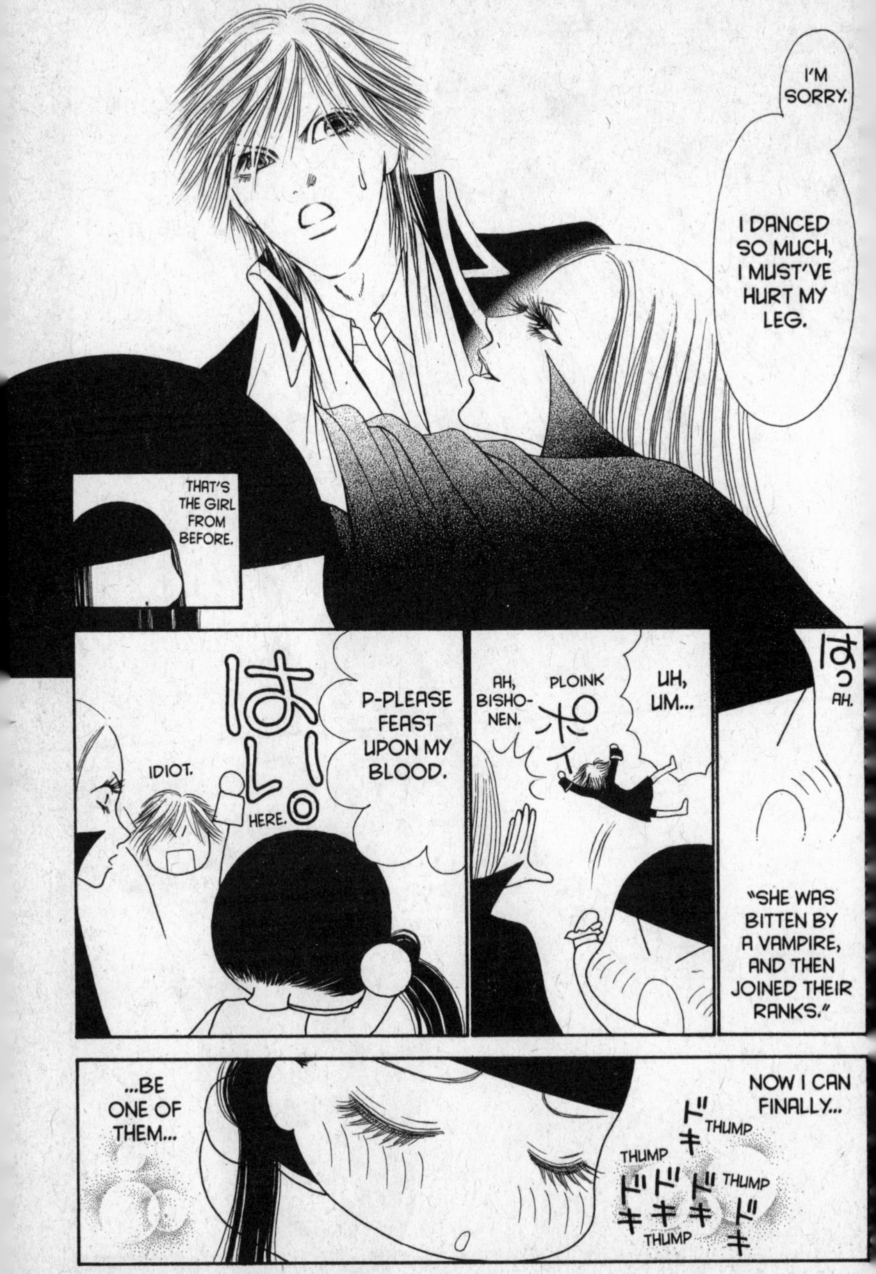
I'M SORRY.
I DANCED SO MUCH, I MUST'VE HURT MY LEG.
THAT'S THE GIRL FROM BEFORE.
はっ
AH.
"SHE WAS BITTEN BY A VAMPIRE, AND THEN JOINED THEIR RANKS."
UH, UM...
ポイ
PLOINK
AH, BISHO-NEN.
P-PLEASE FEAST UPON MY BLOOD.
はーい。
HERE.
IDIOT.
NOW I CAN FINALLY...
ドキ
THUMP
ドキ
THUMP
ドキ
THUMP
ドキ
THUMP
ドキ
...BE ONE OF THEM...

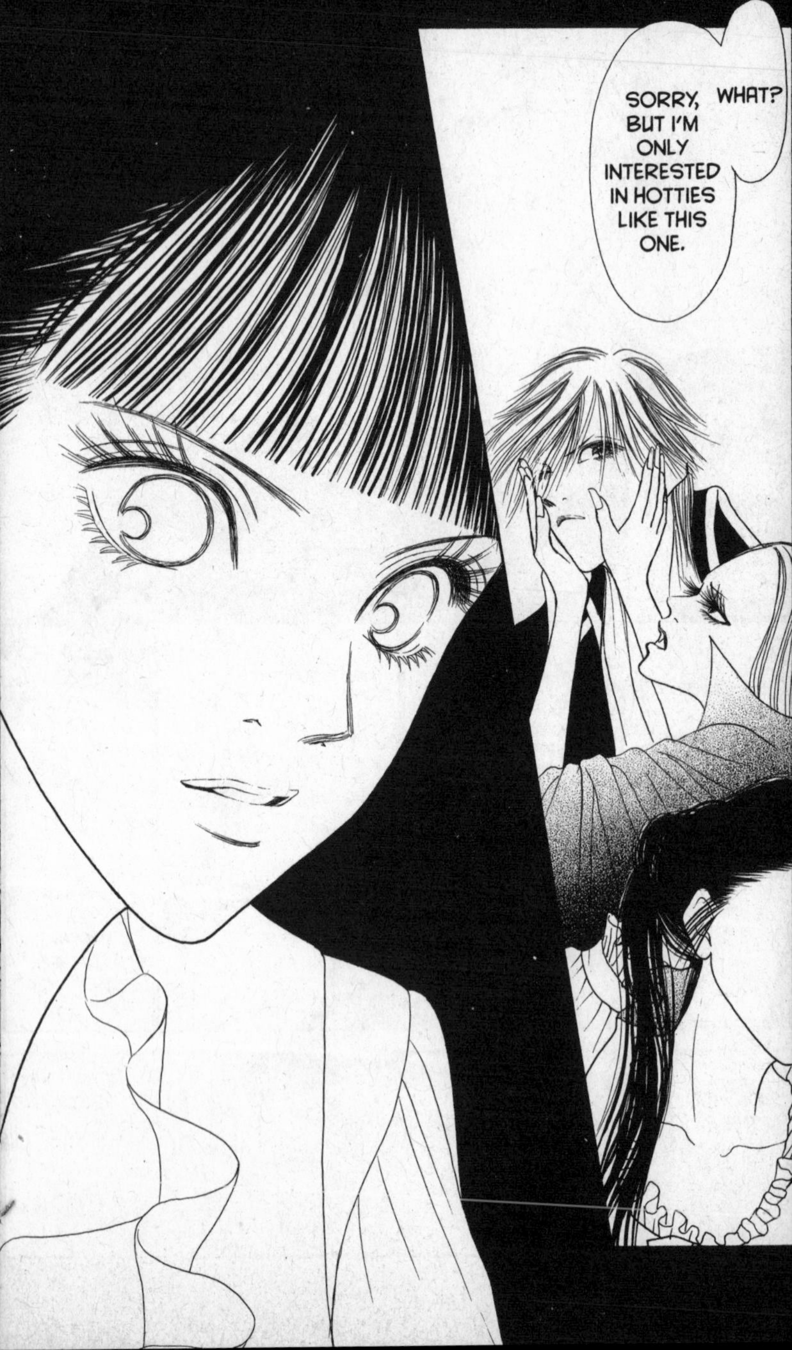
WHAT?
SORRY, BUT I'M ONLY INTERESTED IN HOTTIES LIKE THIS ONE.

KYAAA!
I'VE HAD MY EYES ON HIM ALL NIGHT!
HE'S MINE!
NO, MINE!
NO. HE'S MINE!
Q-QUIT IT!
SO YOU CAN'T BECOME A RESIDENT OF THE DARKNESS...
...UNLESS YOU'RE BEAUTIFUL?
AAAAAHHH

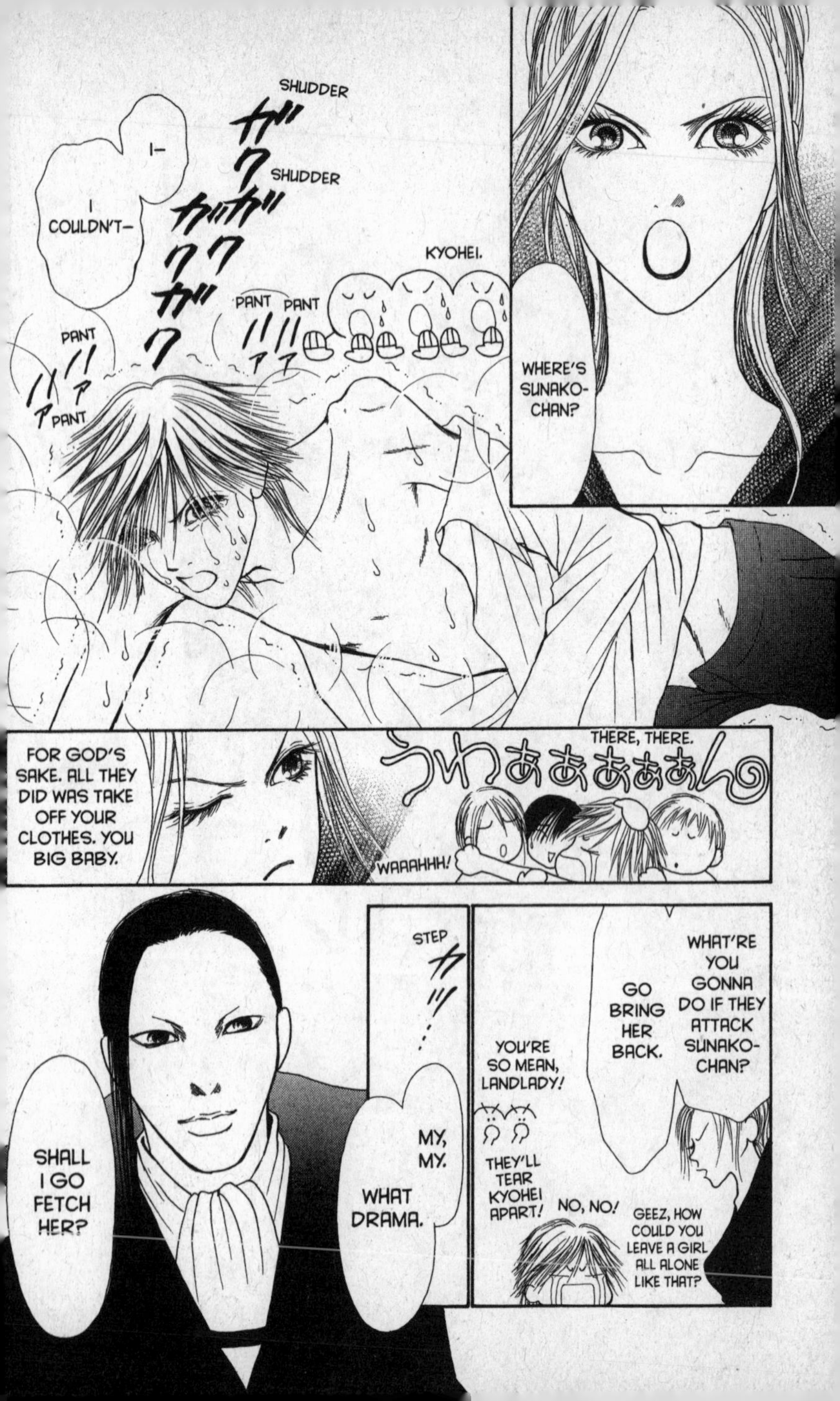
WHERE'S SUNAKO-CHAN?
SHUDDER
SHUDDER
KYOHEI.
I—
I COULDN'T—
PANT PANT
PANT
PANT
THERE, THERE.
うわあああああん
WAAAHHH!
FOR GOD'S SAKE. ALL THEY DID WAS TAKE OFF YOUR CLOTHES. YOU BIG BABY.
WHAT'RE YOU GONNA DO IF THEY ATTACK SUNAKO-CHAN?
GO BRING HER BACK.
YOU'RE SO MEAN, LANDLADY!
THEY'LL TEAR KYOHEI APART!
NO, NO!
GEEZ, HOW COULD YOU LEAVE A GIRL ALL ALONE LIKE THAT?
STEP
MY, MY.
WHAT DRAMA.
SHALL I GO FETCH HER?

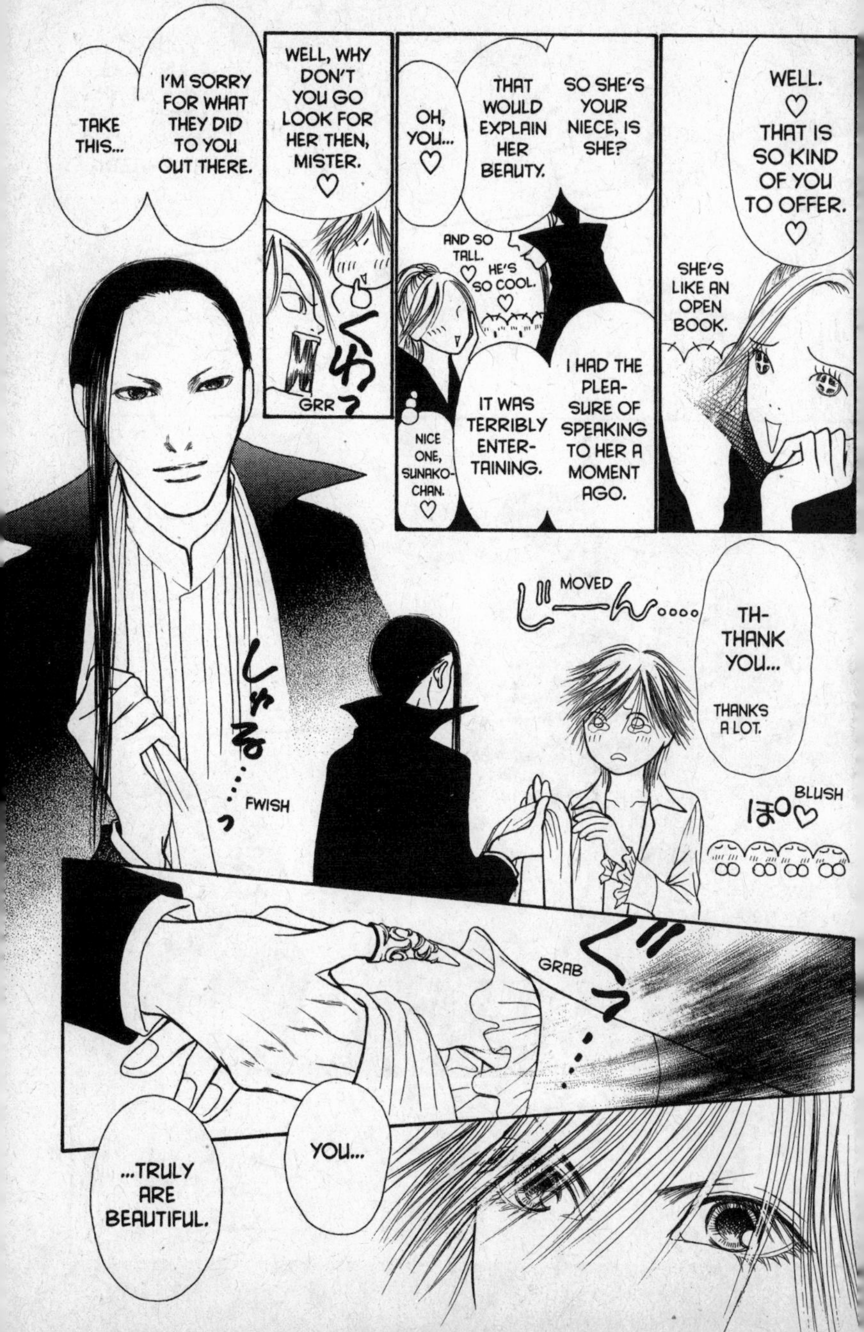
WELL. ♡ THAT IS SO KIND OF YOU TO OFFER. ♡
SHE'S LIKE AN OPEN BOOK.
SO SHE'S YOUR NIECE, IS SHE?
THAT WOULD EXPLAIN HER BEAUTY.
I HAD THE PLEA-SURE OF SPEAKING TO HER A MOMENT AGO.
IT WAS TERRIBLY ENTER-TAINING.
AND SO TALL. ♡ HE'S SO COOL. ♡
OH, YOU... ♡
NICE ONE, SUNAKO-CHAN. ♡
WELL, WHY DON'T YOU GO LOOK FOR HER THEN, MISTER. ♡
くわっ
GRR
I'M SORRY FOR WHAT THEY DID TO YOU OUT THERE.
TAKE THIS...
しゅる...っ
FWISH
じーん....
MOVED
TH-THANK YOU...
THANKS A LOT.
ぽっ♡
BLUSH
ぐっ...
GRAB
YOU...
...TRULY ARE BEAUTIFUL.

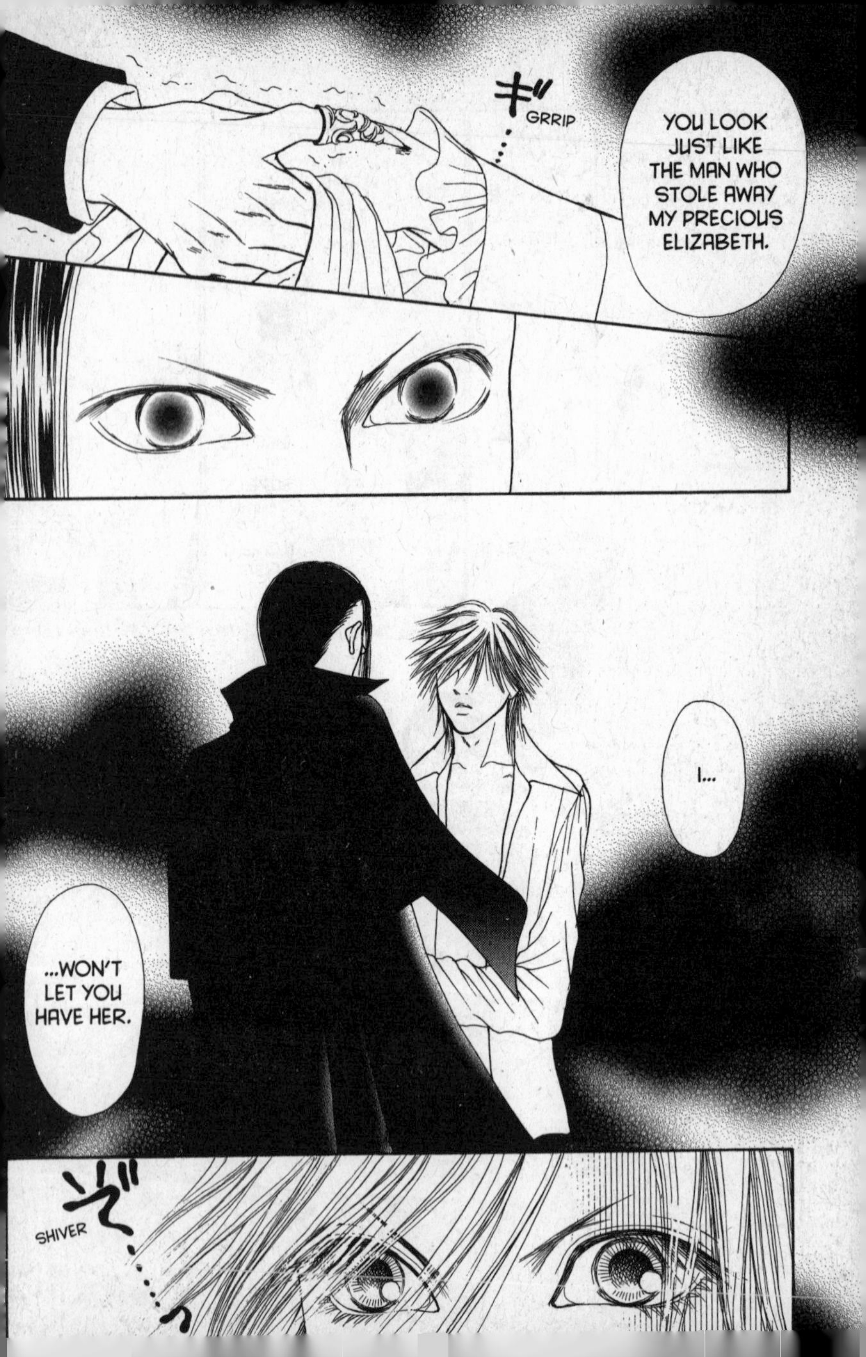
YOU LOOK JUST LIKE THE MAN WHO STOLE AWAY MY PRECIOUS ELIZABETH.
GRRIP
I...
...WON'T LET YOU HAVE HER.
SHIVER

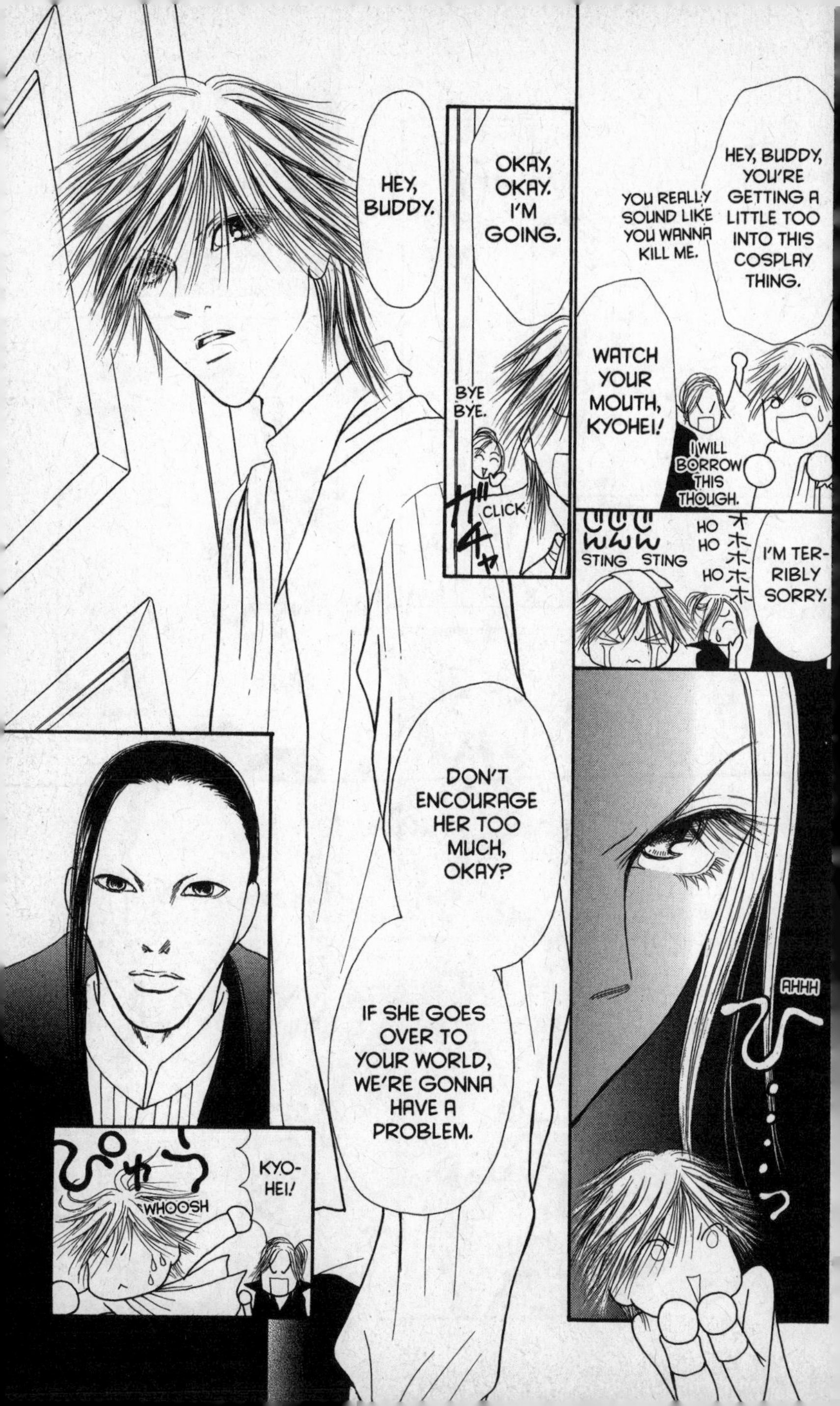
HEY, BUDDY, YOU'RE GETTING A LITTLE TOO INTO THIS COSPLAY THING.
YOU REALLY SOUND LIKE YOU WANNA KILL ME.
WATCH YOUR MOUTH, KYOHEI!
I WILL BORROW THIS THOUGH.
I'M TERRIBLY SORRY.
HO HO HO
オホホホ
じじじんんん
STING STING
OKAY, OKAY. I'M GOING.
BYE BYE.
ガチャ
CLICK
HEY, BUDDY.
DON'T ENCOURAGE HER TOO MUCH, OKAY?
IF SHE GOES OVER TO YOUR WORLD, WE'RE GONNA HAVE A PROBLEM.
AHHH
KYO-HEI!
ぴゅう
WHOOSH

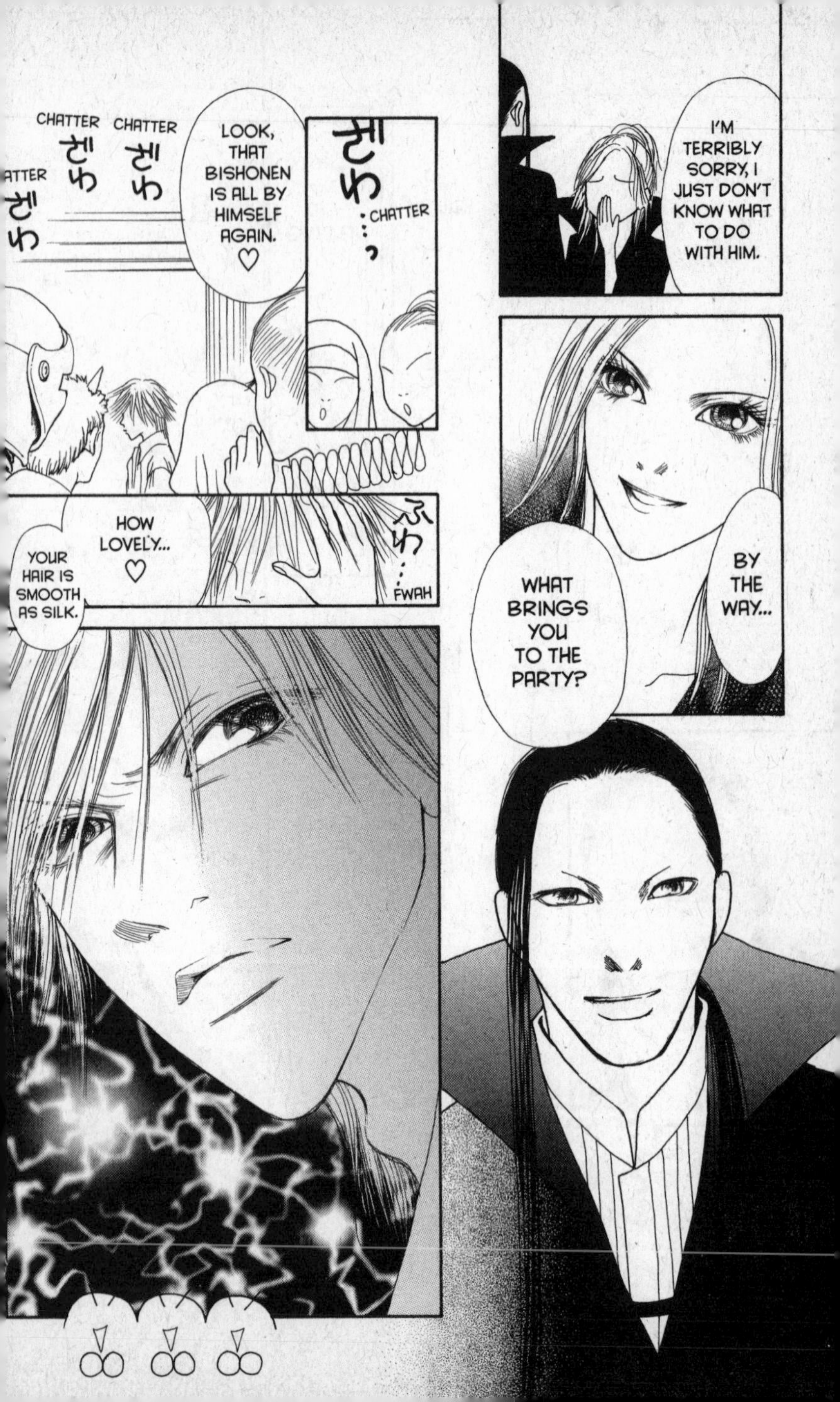

I'M TERRIBLY SORRY, I JUST DON'T KNOW WHAT TO DO WITH HIM.
ざわ…っ
CHATTER
LOOK, THAT BISHONEN IS ALL BY HIMSELF AGAIN. ♡
CHATTER
ざわ
CHATTER
ざわ
ATTER
ざわ
BY THE WAY...
WHAT BRINGS YOU TO THE PARTY?
ふわ…
FWAH
HOW LOVELY... ♡
YOUR HAIR IS SMOOTH AS SILK.

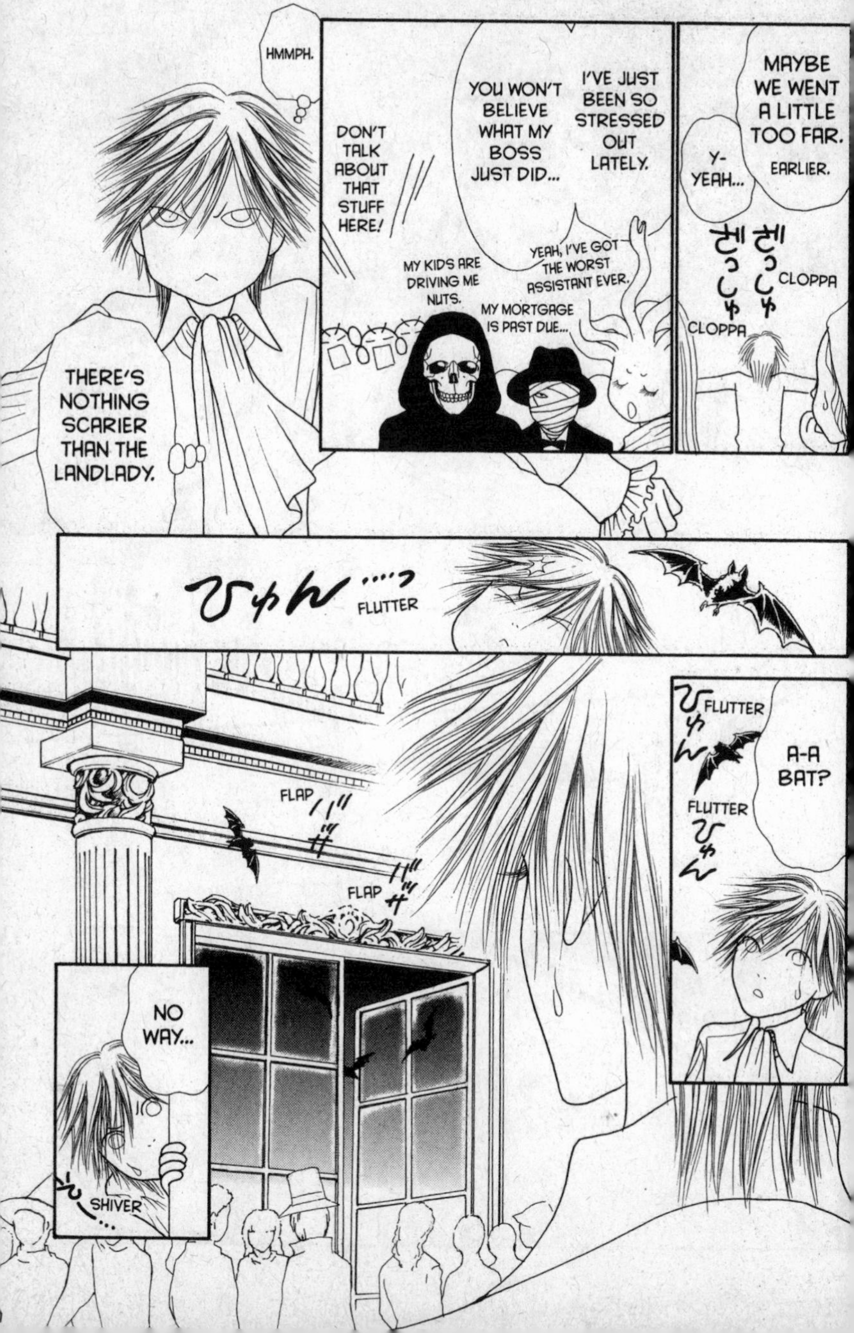

MAYBE WE WENT A LITTLE TOO FAR.
EARLIER.
Y-YEAH...
CLOPPA
CLOPPA
I'VE JUST BEEN SO STRESSED OUT LATELY.
YOU WON'T BELIEVE WHAT MY BOSS JUST DID...
DON'T TALK ABOUT THAT STUFF HERE!
YEAH, I'VE GOT THE WORST ASSISTANT EVER.
MY KIDS ARE DRIVING ME NUTS.
MY MORTGAGE IS PAST DUE...
HMMPH.
THERE'S NOTHING SCARIER THAN THE LANDLADY.
ひゅん....
FLUTTER
A-A BAT?
ひゅん
FLUTTER
ひゅん
FLUTTER
FLAP
FLAP
NO WAY...
SHIVER

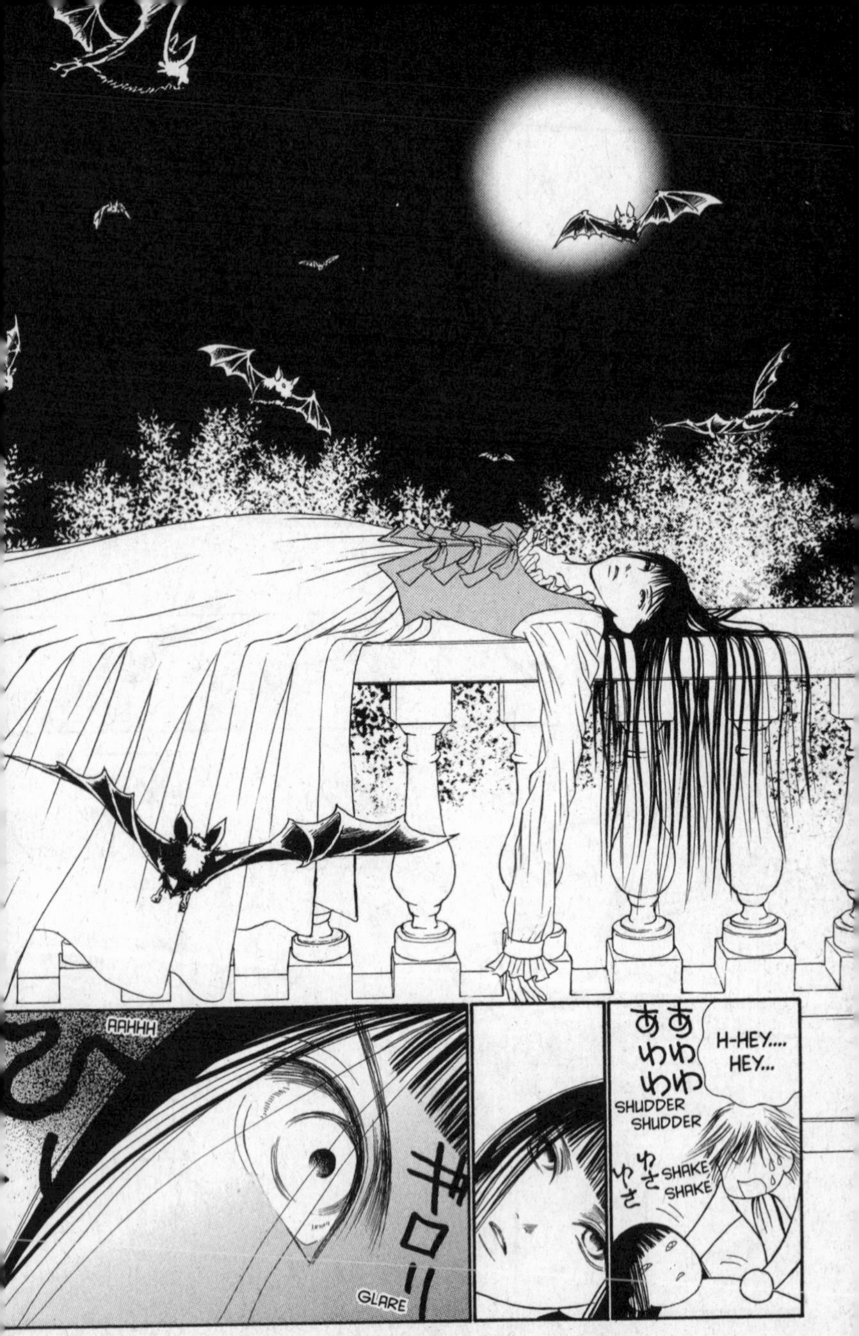
あわわ
あわわ
H-HEY.... HEY...
SHUDDER SHUDDER
ゆさゆさ
SHAKE SHAKE
ギロリ
GLARE
AAHHH

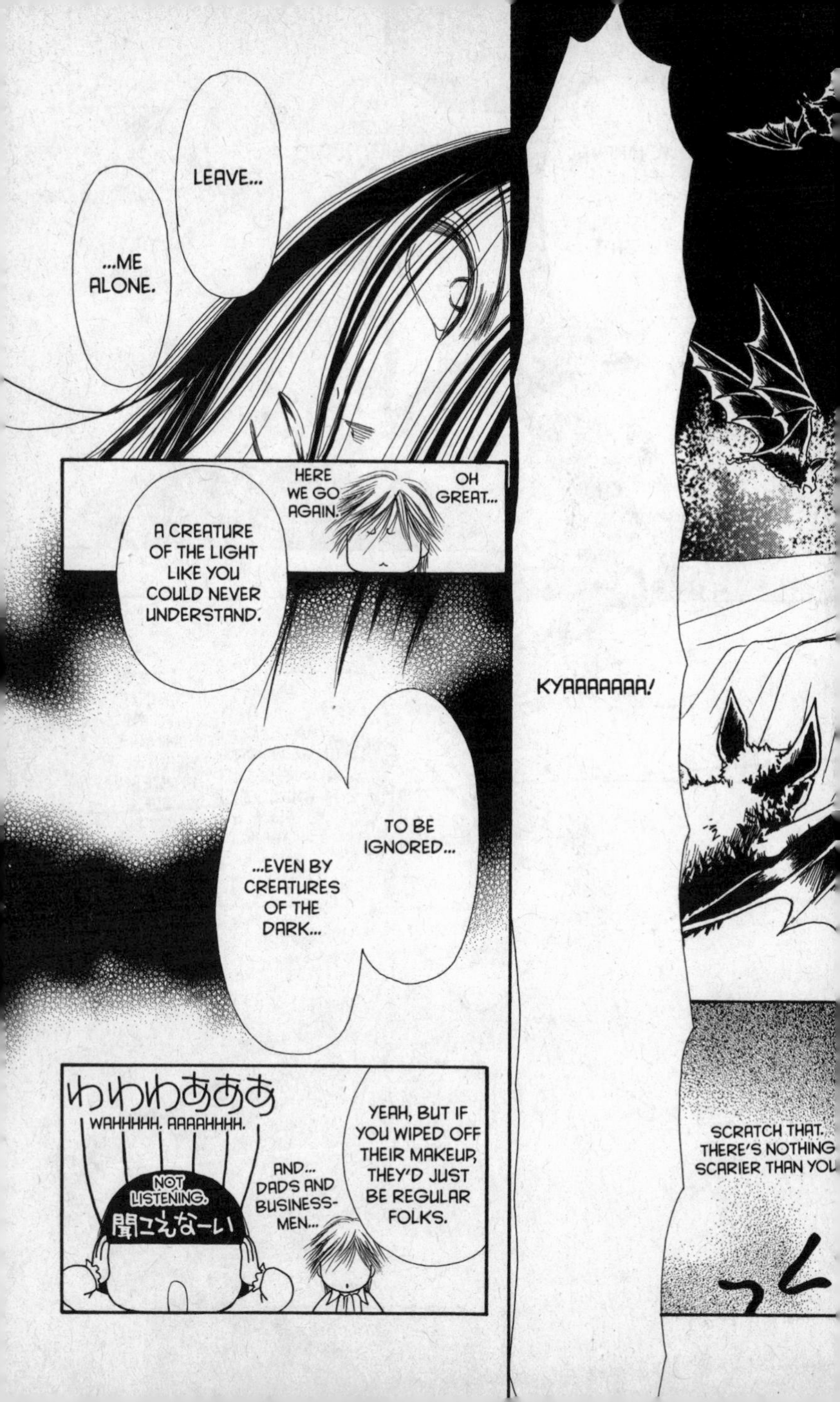
KYAAAAAAA!
SCRATCH THAT. THERE'S NOTHING SCARIER THAN YOU
LEAVE...
...ME ALONE.
OH GREAT...
HERE WE GO AGAIN.
A CREATURE OF THE LIGHT LIKE YOU COULD NEVER UNDERSTAND.
TO BE IGNORED...
...EVEN BY CREATURES OF THE DARK...
YEAH, BUT IF YOU WIPED OFF THEIR MAKEUP, THEY'D JUST BE REGULAR FOLKS.
AND... DADS AND BUSINESS-MEN...
わわわあああ
WAHHHHH. AAAAHHHH.
NOT LISTENING.
聞こえなーい

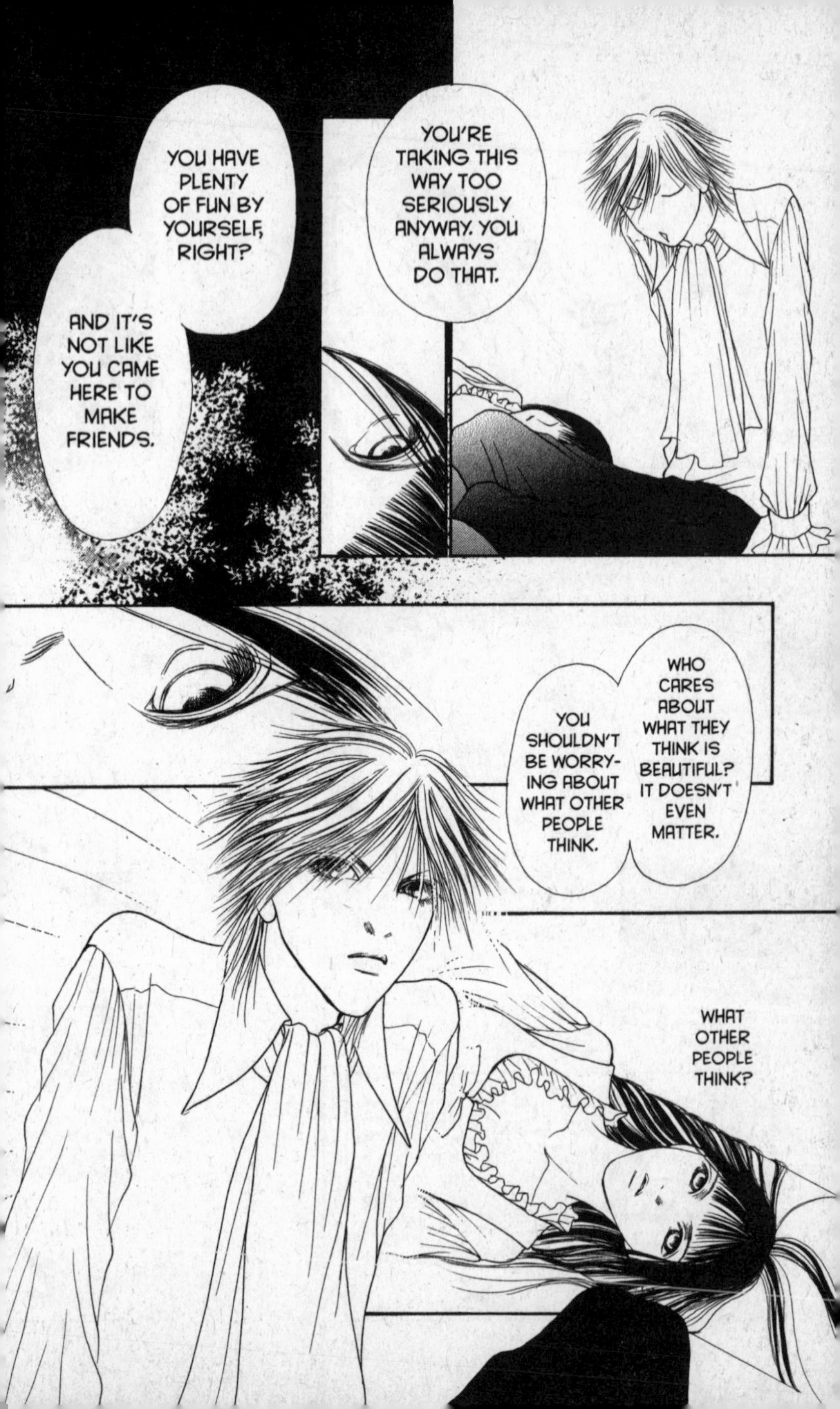
YOU'RE TAKING THIS WAY TOO SERIOUSLY ANYWAY. YOU ALWAYS DO THAT.
YOU HAVE PLENTY OF FUN BY YOURSELF, RIGHT?
AND IT'S NOT LIKE YOU CAME HERE TO MAKE FRIENDS.
WHO CARES ABOUT WHAT THEY THINK IS BEAUTIFUL? IT DOESN'T EVEN MATTER.
YOU SHOULDN'T BE WORRY-ING ABOUT WHAT OTHER PEOPLE THINK.
WHAT OTHER PEOPLE THINK?

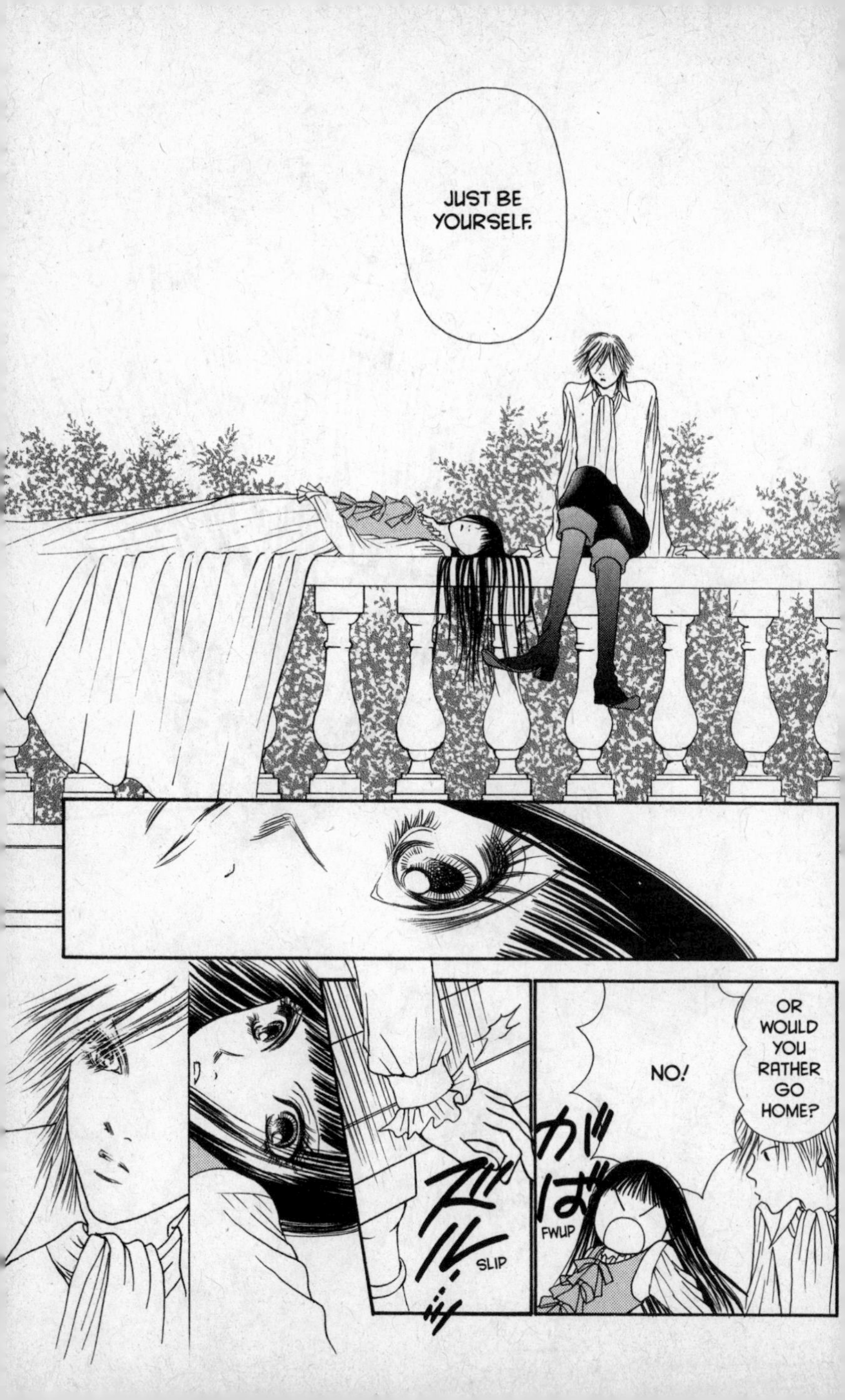
JUST BE YOURSELF.
OR WOULD YOU RATHER GO HOME?
NO!
FWUP
SLIP

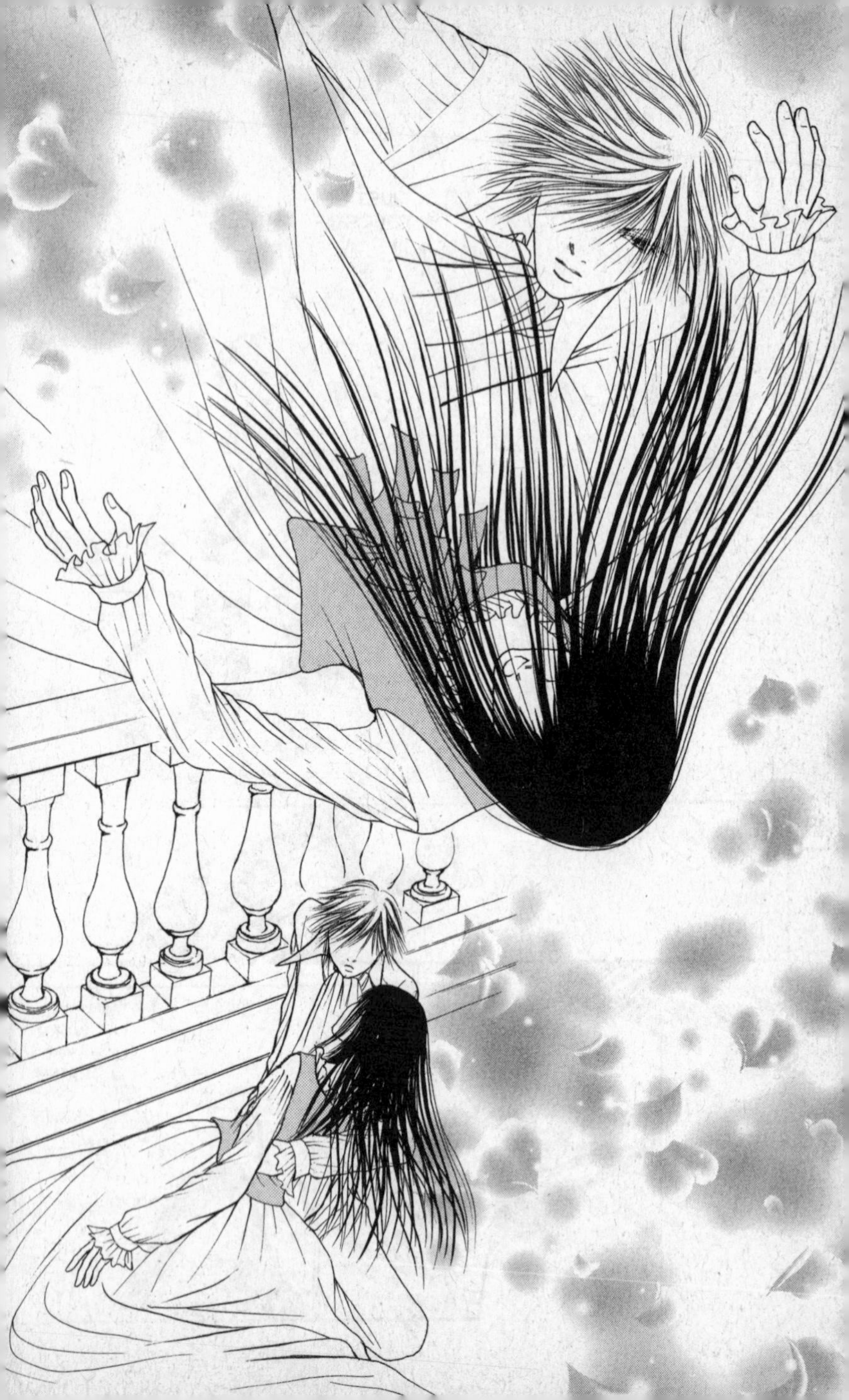

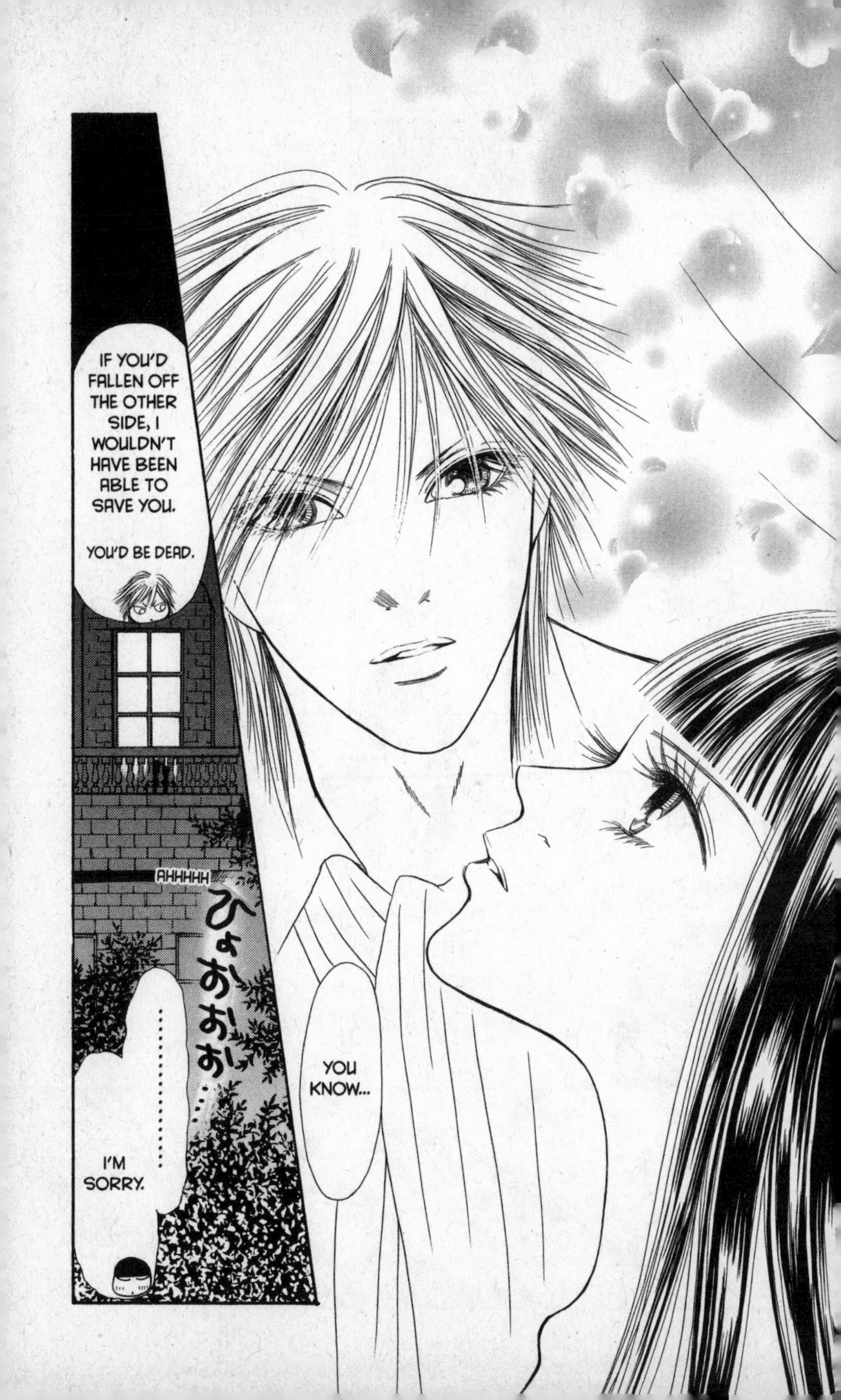
IF YOU'D FALLEN OFF THE OTHER SIDE, I WOULDN'T HAVE BEEN ABLE TO SAVE YOU.
YOU'D BE DEAD.
AHHHHH
ひょおおお
....
I'M SORRY.
YOU KNOW...

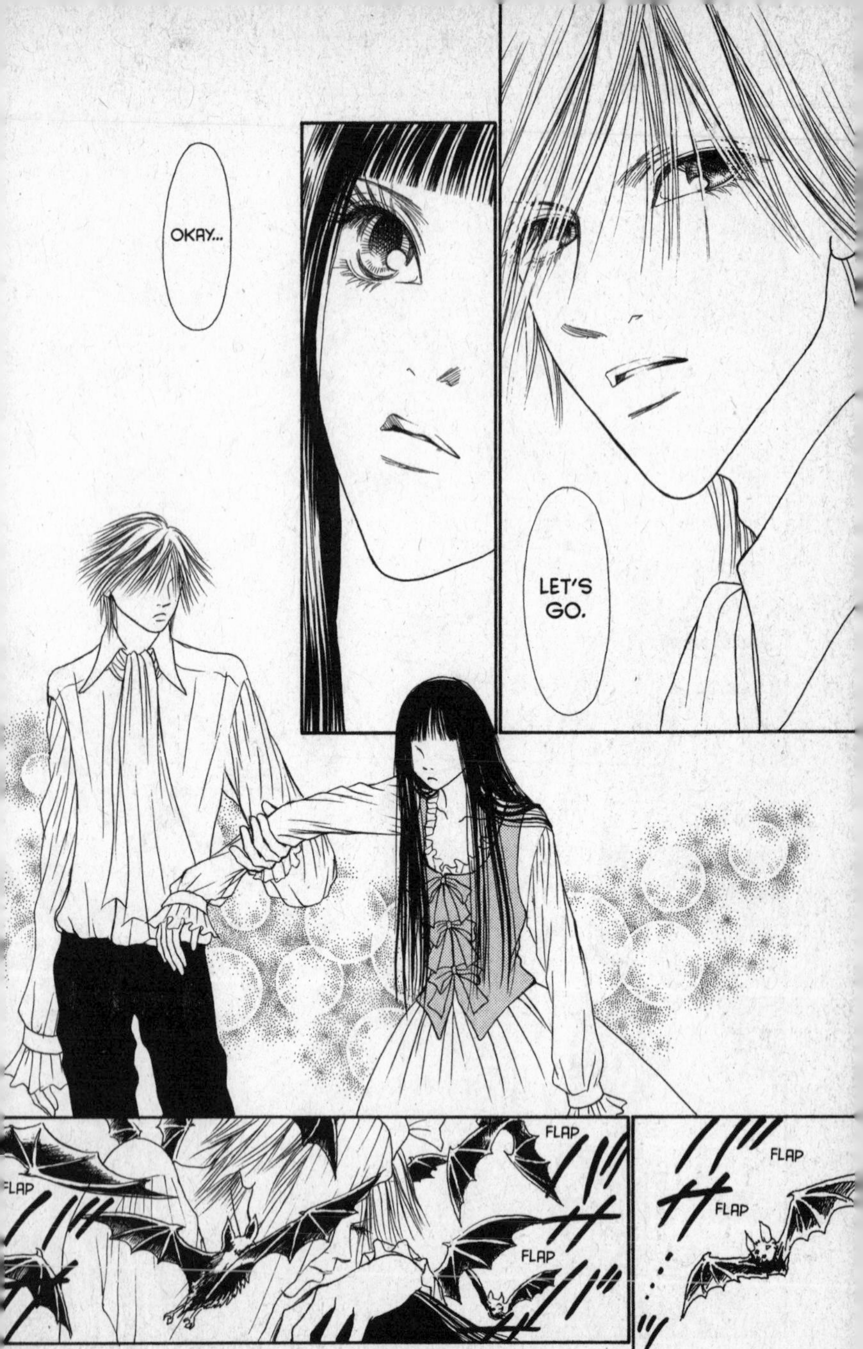
LET'S GO.
OKAY...
FLAP
FLAP
FLAP
FLAP
FLAP

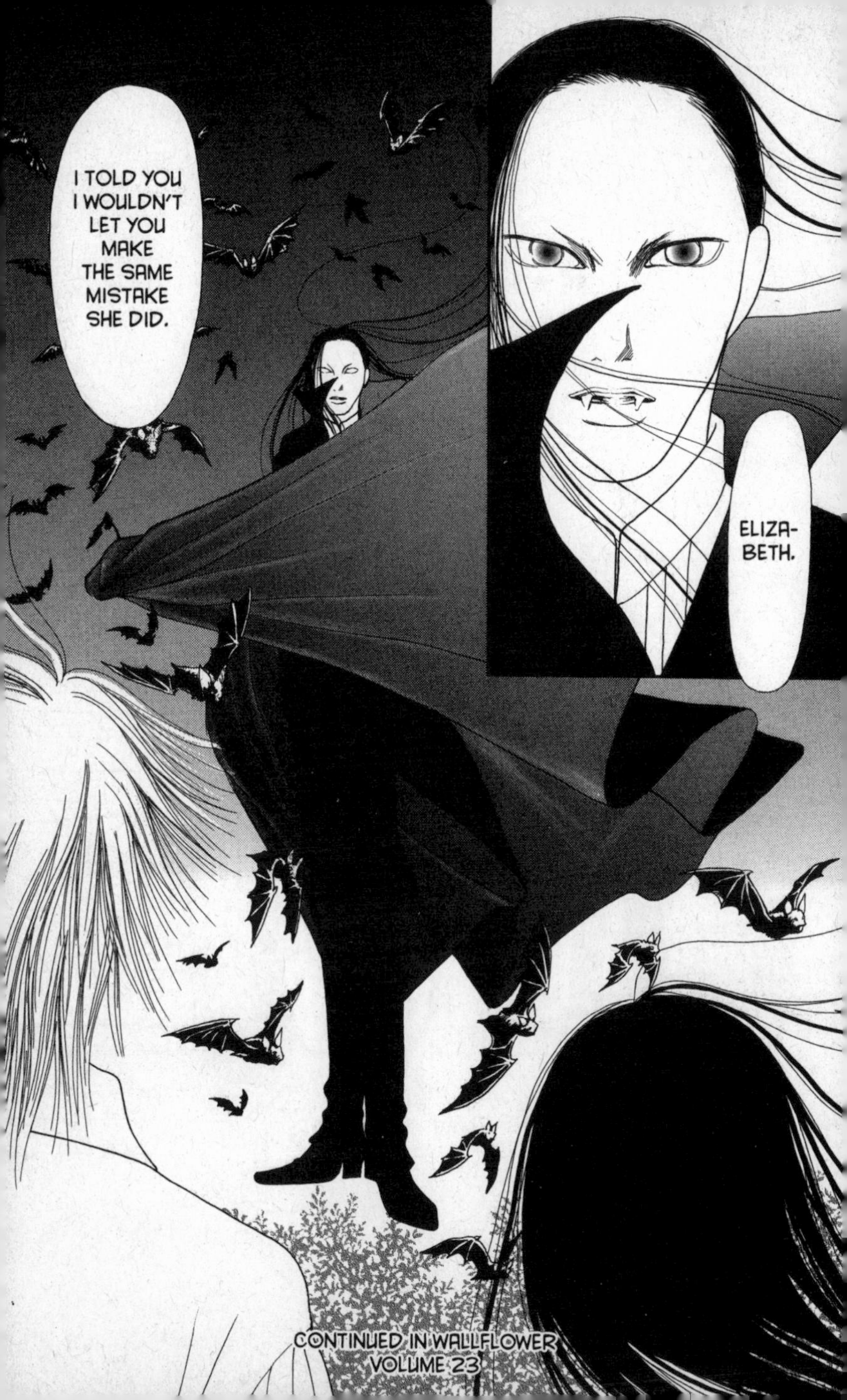
ELIZA-BETH.
I TOLD YOU I WOULDN'T LET YOU MAKE THE SAME MISTAKE SHE DID.
CONTINUED IN WALLFLOWER VOLUME 23

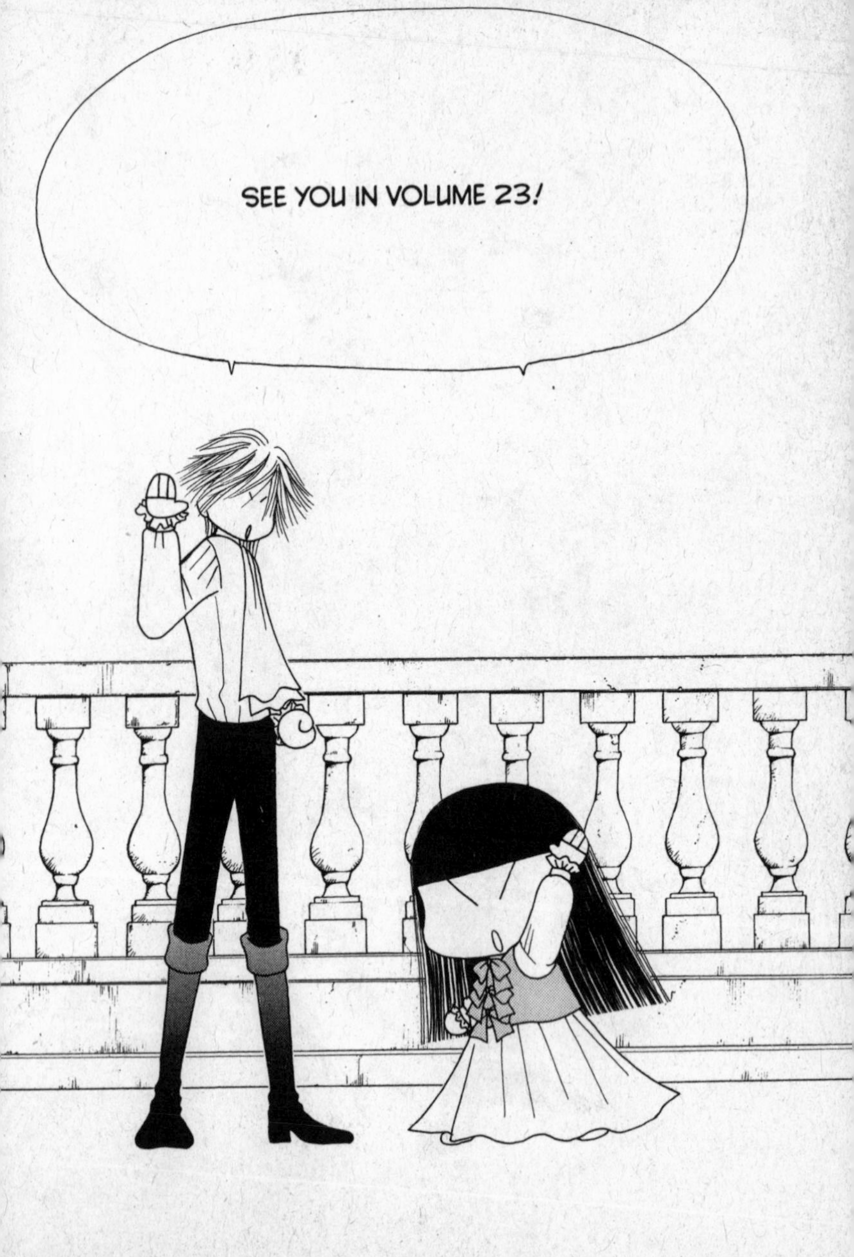
SEE YOU IN VOLUME 23!

THANK YOU FOR BUYING KODANSHA COMICS. ♥

PURR

IN MY BEHIND-THE-SCENES SECTION, ALL I DID WAS TALK ABOUT HOW DEPRESSED I WAS. IT MUST'VE SOUNDED REALLY ANNOYING . . . SORRY. I FINALLY WORKED THROUGH ALL MY PROBLEMS, AND NOW I'M *FEELING GREAT.* ♥

I'M SO HAPPY. FOR A MOMENT THERE, I WASN'T SURE IF I'D MAKE IT.

I'M FEELING MUCH BETTER, BUT WHILE I WAS WORKING ON THE FOURTH STORY IN THIS BOOK (CHAPTER 91), *I HURT MY BACK.* IT WAS SUPER PAINFUL. IT HURT TO SIT, TO STAND, AND EVEN TO SLEEP. IT HURT JUST TO BREATHE. I WAS LIKE, "SOMETHING'S WRONG HERE. THIS IS NO ORDINARY BACK PAIN." SO I WENT TO THE HOSPITAL, AND THEY TOLD ME TO REST. IT WAS SO PAINFUL, AND THAT'S ALL THEY COULD SAY . . . BUT I RESTED AND IT DID GET BETTER.

LATE AT NIGHT, IT HURT SO BAD I COULDN'T SLEEP. MACHIKO SAKURAI HAPPENED TO BE STAYING OVER, AND I WOKE HER UP AND MADE HER PUT MUSCLE CREAM ALL OVER MY BACK. SORRY, SAKURAI . . .

SEE? DOESN'T IT FEEL LIKE WE'RE HANGING OUT ON THE BEACH? ♥

JUST IMAGINE WE'RE ON THE BEACH IN OKINAWA, AND YOU'RE RUBBING SUNTAN OIL ON ME.

NO, MORE LIKE WE'RE HANGING OUT AT A NURSING HOME.

THE BONUS PAGES ARE COMING UP!

GO !!

I'VE BEEN TALKING ABOUT NEW ROTE'KA A LOT LATELY, AND I'VE RECEIVED A BUNCH OF LETTERS ASKING "WHAT DO THE NEW ROTE'KA GUYS LOOK LIKE?" SO HERE YOU GO...

NEW ROTE'KA

THEY LOOK LIKE THIS. ♥ ♥ ♥

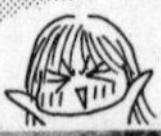
KYAA! I LOVE THEM. ♥

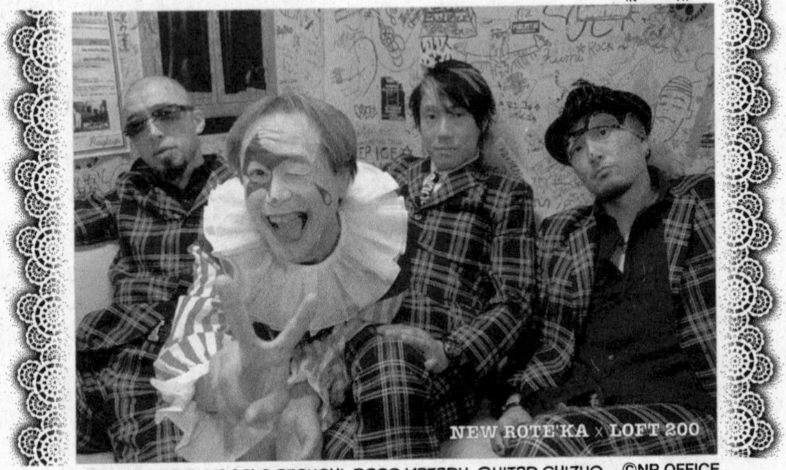
NEW ROTE'KA x LOFT 200

DRUMS NABO, VOCALS ATSUSHI, BASS KATARU, GUITAR SHIZUO ©NR OFFICE

I WENT TO SEE THEIR SHOW WHEN I WAS EXTREMELY DEPRESSED, AND COULDN'T EVEN GET UP ON MY OWN. I KNEW THAT NEW ROTE'KA-SAN'S SHOW WOULD BE PURE ENTERTAINMENT, AND I WAS HOPING THAT IT WOULD CHEER ME UP...*I WAS COMPLETELY RIGHT!*

THE SHOW WAS SO AWESOME. I COULDN'T GET ENOUGH. ♥ ♥ ♥ ♥ ♥ ♥
I WAS IN A *GOOD MOOD* FOR A FEW DAYS. I'M SO *ADDICTED* TO THEM. ♥ ♥ ♥

WHEN I WAS TOO BUSY TO GO TO SEE THEM LIVE, I LISTENED TO THEIR CDS AND WATCHED THEIR CONCERT DVDS. I LISTENED TO SONGS LIKE "ORETACHI AMIGO (WE'RE AMIGO)" AND "DAINAMAITO DE BUTTOBASE! (BLOW UP THE DYNAMITE!)" WHILE WORKING AND CRYING AT THE SAME TIME. THEY HAVE SO MANY EMOTIONAL SONGS. THEY'RE NOT JUST FUNNY! THEY MAKE YOU *LAUGH AND CRY* . . . THEY'RE *THE BEST!* KATARU-SAN IS A GENIUS SONG-WRITER, AND A-CHAN'S LYRICS ARE AMAZING! THEIR LIVE SHOWS ARE EVEN BETTER! *THEY ALWAYS GIVE ME TONS OF HAPPINESS!*

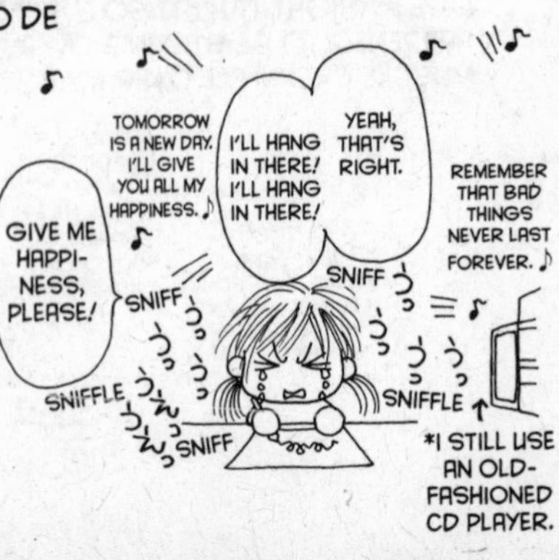
REMEMBER THAT BAD THINGS NEVER LAST FOREVER. ♪
YEAH, THAT'S RIGHT.
I'LL HANG IN THERE! I'LL HANG IN THERE!
TOMORROW IS A NEW DAY. I'LL GIVE YOU ALL MY HAPPINESS. ♪
GIVE ME HAPPI-NESS, PLEASE!
SNIFF
SNIFF
SNIFFLE
SNIFFLE
SNIFF
*I STILL USE AN OLD-FASHIONED CD PLAYER.

KIYOHARU-SAMA

I PUT A LOT OF EFFORT INTO GETTING READY WHENEVER I GO TO ONE OF KIYOHARU-SAMA'S CONCERTS. I GET MY HAIR DYED, AND PUT EXTRA MAKEUP ON . . . BUT I WAS SO DEPRESSED AROUND THAT TIME THAT I JUST COULDN'T DO ANYTHING. I COULDN'T EVEN MAKE IT TO HIS CONCERT. AND WHEN I FINALLY RECOVERED I HAD SO MUCH WORK TO DO! BUT I'M BACK TO NORMAL NOW, SO I'M GONNA START GOING TO HIS SHOWS AS MUCH AS POSSIBLE!

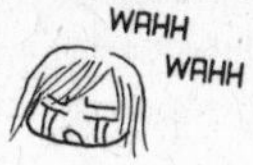
WAHH
WAHH

EVEN THOUGH I WASN'T ABLE TO GO SEE HIS SHOWS FOR A WHILE, I WAS STILL CHECKING OUT HIS BLOG, AND I NOTICED THAT HE WROTE ABOUT *VOLUME 21!*

KI-KI-KI-KIYOHARU-SAMA WROTE ABOUT MY MANGA . . . ! THANK YOU, THANK YOU, THANK YOU SOOOO MUCH! I'M SO HAPPY. I'M SO GLAD I BECAME A MANGA ARTIST! I KNOW I'VE SAID THIS MANY TIMES, BUT *I'LL BE YOUR FAN FOREVER!*

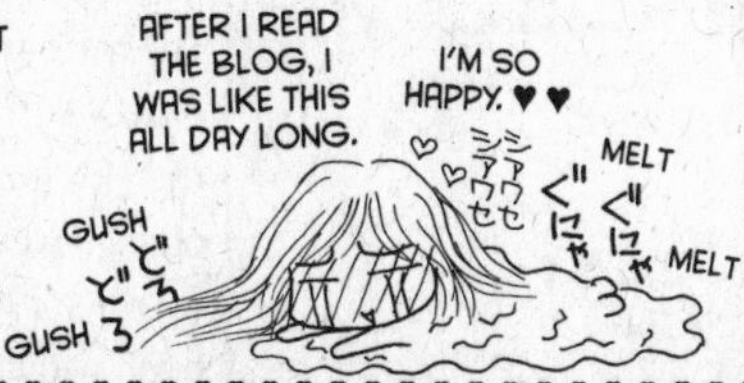
AFTER I READ THE BLOG, I WAS LIKE THIS ALL DAY LONG.
I'M SO HAPPY. ♥ ♥
MELT
MELT
GUSH
GUSH

CQA

THIS IS *YUMI-CHAN'S (OF PUFFY)* BAND.

KATARU-KUN, THE BASSIST FROM NEW ROTE'KA, IS IN THE BAND, AND HE WRITES THE SONGS. KATARU-SAN IS SUCH A GENIUS. THEIR SONGS ARE AWESOME. I LOVE YUMI-CHAN'S VOICE. ♥ AMAZING SONGS. I REALLY ENJOYED THEIR SHOW. ♥ I WANNA SEE THEM AGAIN. ♥ I WANNA SEE PUFFY TOO. ♥ YUMI-CHAN LOOKED *AMAZINGLY BEAUTIFUL.* ♥ ♥ ♥ SHE'S GOT A SMALL FACE AND BIG EYES. HER SKIN IS FLAWLESS, AND HER HAIR IS SO FLUFFY . . . ♥ ♥ ♥ OH MY GOD, I'M *IN LOVE.* ♥ ♥ ♥

D'ERLANGER

I STARTED GOING TO THEIR SHOWS BECAUSE I WANTED TO HEAR THEIR OLD SONGS, BUT I'M TOTALLY IN LOVE WITH THEIR NEW SONGS NOW. THEY'RE AMAZING. "ZAKURO" IS A BRILLIANT SONG. ♥ ♥ ♥ AND "XXX FOR YOU," "KAGEMAI" . . . THEY'VE GOT TONS OF GREAT SONGS!

TASUKU ITAYA-SAMA

IT WAS AN AWESOME SHOW! I WASN'T EXPECTING TO HEAR ZI-KILL'S SIGNATURE SONG "NO MORE TO SAY." ♥ HIS VOICE IS SO SEXY. I REALLY ENJOYED THE COVER SONGS TOO. ♥

MERRY

THEIR SONGS ARE ALWAYS SO AMAZING. ♥ ALL OF THEIR SONGS ARE REALLY GREAT. THEIR SHOWS ARE AWESOME TOO. ♥ ♥ ♥ I'M DEFINITELY GONNA GO SEE THEM AGAIN.

AFTER I'M DONE WRITING THIS, I'M GONNA GO SEE D'ESPAIRS RAY.

SPECIAL THANKS♥

TOMMY,
KAI-CHAN.
MORI-SAN

NABEKO
KOIZUMI-SAMA

INNAN-SAMA,
INO-SAMA

THE EDITOR IN CHIEF-SAMA

EVERYBODY IN THE EDITING DEPARTMENT

EVERYBODY WHO'S READING THIS RIGHT NOW ♥

Translation Notes

Japanese is a tricky language for most Westerners, and translation is often more art than science. For your edification and reading pleasure, here are notes on some of the places where we could have gone in a different direction in our translation of the work, or where a Japanese cultural reference is used.

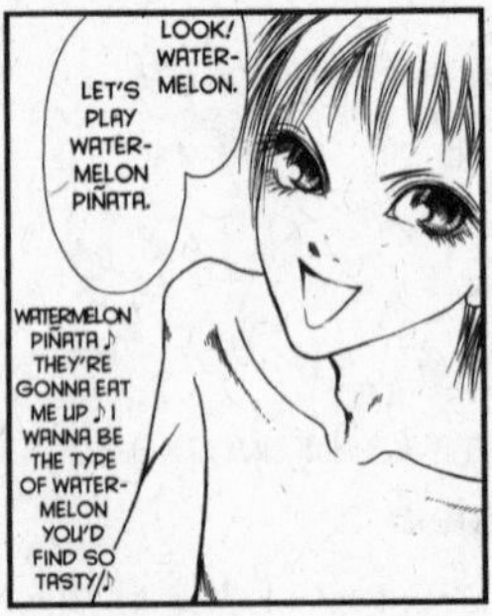
LOOK! WATER-MELON.
LET'S PLAY WATER-MELON PIÑATA.
WATERMELON PIÑATA ♪ THEY'RE GONNA EAT ME UP ♪ I WANNA BE THE TYPE OF WATER-MELON YOU'D FIND SO TASTY ♪

Watermelon Piñata, page 21

The guys are playing the game known as *suika wari*. *Suika wari* is a popular summer pastime much like the Mexican tradition of the piñata. In *suika wari*, players wear a blindfold and try to hit a watermelon with a stick. The first person to split the watermelon open wins the game.

Octopus Ears, page 43

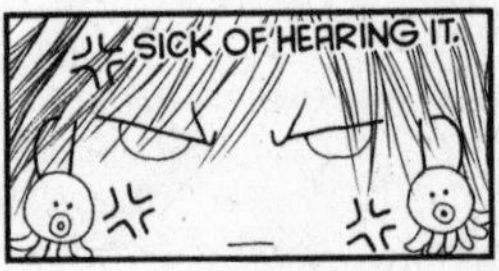
SICK OF HEARING IT.

Perhaps you're wondering why Kyohei has octopi in his ears. The Japanese phrase, *mimi ni tako*, literally means "calluses on the ears" and means that one has heard something so much that their ears are getting callused. The word for calluses *tako* also means "octopus." Hence the visual pun of octopi clinging to Kyohei's ears.

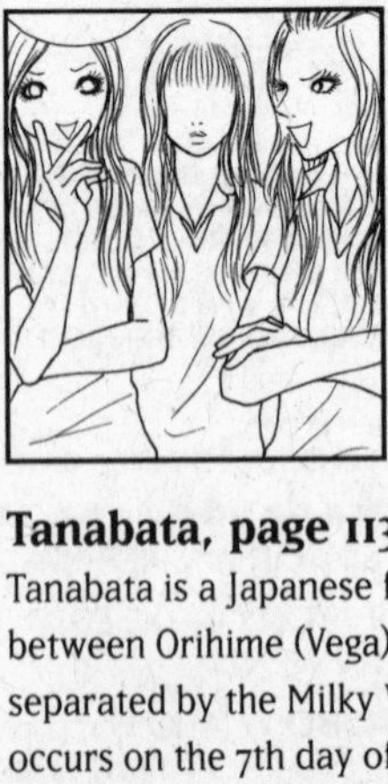

Altered uniforms, page 87

Nearly all Japanese schools require uniforms. Teens sometimes rebel by altering their uniforms, as these girls have done here.

Tanabata, page 113

Tanabata is a Japanese festival celebrating the Chinese legend of the meeting between Orihime (Vega) and Hikoboshi (Altair). The lovers are said to be separated by the Milky Way, and can only meet one night a year. The celebration occurs on the 7th day of the 7th lunar month. It's usually celebrated on August 7th in Japan.

THE
wallflower
YAMATONADESHIKO SHICHIHENGE

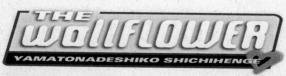

Volume 23

A Note from the Author

MY BODY HAS BEEN IN REALLY BAD SHAPE LATELY, SO I'VE BEEN TRYING TO GET BACK TO BASICS. (EARLY TO BED, EARLY TO RISE) I HAVE TO TRY REALLY HARD, BECAUSE IF I LET UP FOR A MINUTE, I END UP STAYING UP SUPER LATE. GOING TO BED EARLY AND GETTING UP EARLY IS SUPER COOL. I FEEL SO GOOD, BUT WHEN I'M GOING TO BED AT 9 PM, AND GETTING UP AT 4 AM, I NEVER GET TO HANG OUT WITH MY FRIENDS. A LOT OF DAYS, I GIVE IN TO TEMPTATION AND STAY UP ALL NIGHT.

—Tomoko Hayakawa

THE wallFLOWER

YAMATONADESHIKO SHICHIHENGE

ヤマトナデシコ七変化♡

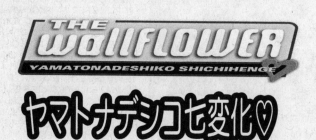

CONTENTS

KYOHEI TAKANO—
A STRONG FIGHTER,
"I'M THE KING"

TAKENAGA ODA—
A CARING FEMINIST

RANMARU MORII—
A TRUE LADY'S MAN

YUKINOJO TOYAMA—
A GENTLE, CHEERFUL, AND
VERY EMOTIONAL GUY

SUNAKO NAKAHARA

WALLFLOWER'S BEAUTIFUL CAST OF CHARACTERS (?)

SUNAKO IS A DARK LONER WHO LOVES HORROR MOVIES. WHEN HER AUNT, THE LANDLADY, LEAVES TOWN, SUNAKO IS FORCED TO LIVE WITH FOUR HANDSOME GUYS. SUNAKO'S AUNT MAKES A DEAL WITH THE BOYS, WHICH CAUSES NOTHING BUT HEADACHES FOR SUNAKO. "MAKE SUNAKO INTO A LADY, AND YOU CAN LIVE RENT FREE." THE ROAD TO LOVE IS LONG AND PERILOUS, AND IT LOOKS LIKE SUNAKO AND KYOHEI'S RELATIONSHIP WILL NEVER MAKE IT THERE. AFTER SUNAKO'S AUNTIE DRAGS HER TO A MASQUERADE BALL, SHE MEETS A GENTLEMAN DRESSED AS A VAMPIRE. OR PERHAPS HE REALLY IS A VAMPIRE…?

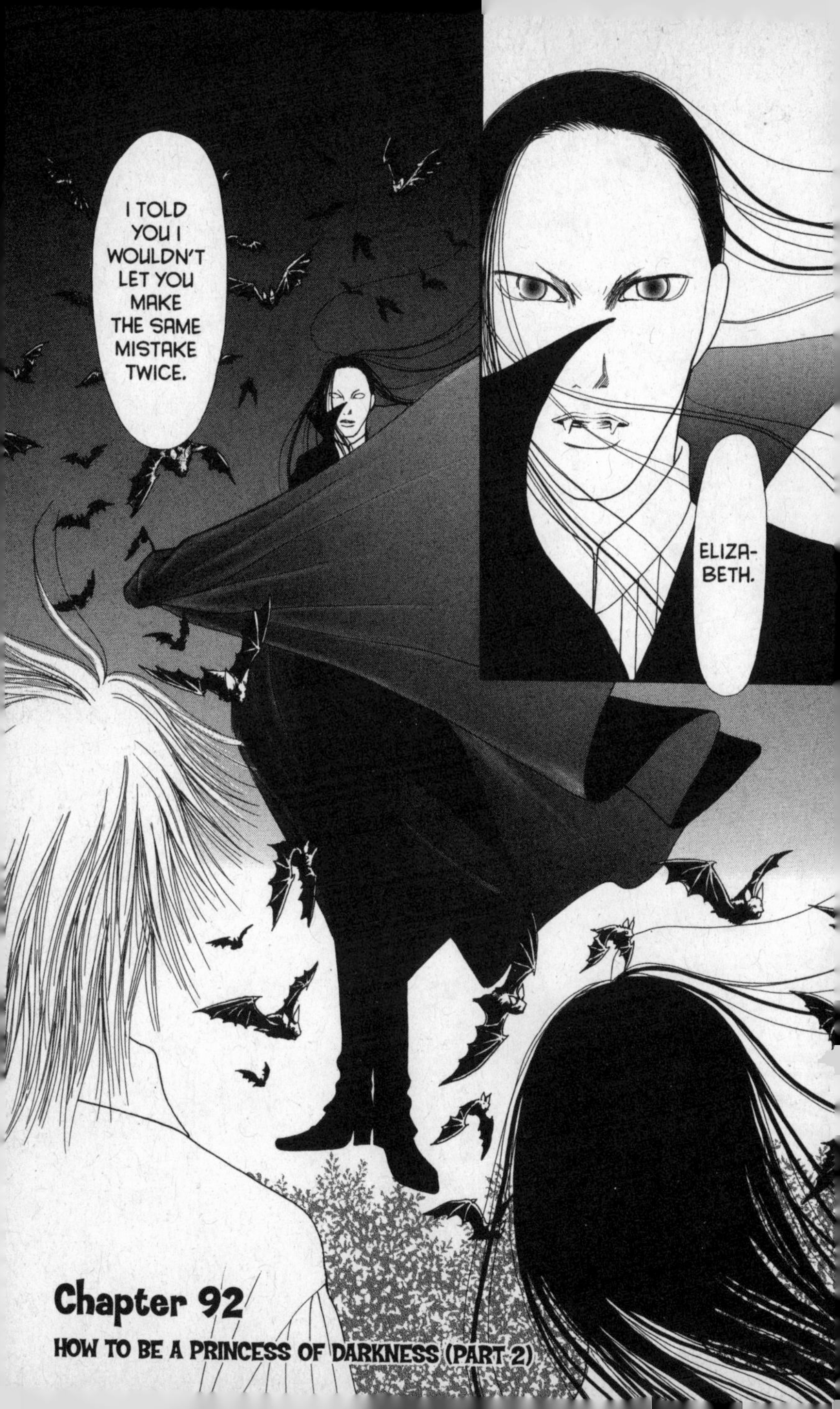
ELIZA-BETH.
I TOLD YOU I WOULDN'T LET YOU MAKE THE SAME MISTAKE TWICE.

Chapter 92

HOW TO BE A PRINCESS OF DARKNESS (PART 2)

Chapter 92
HOW TO BE A PRINCESS OF DARKNESS (PART 2)

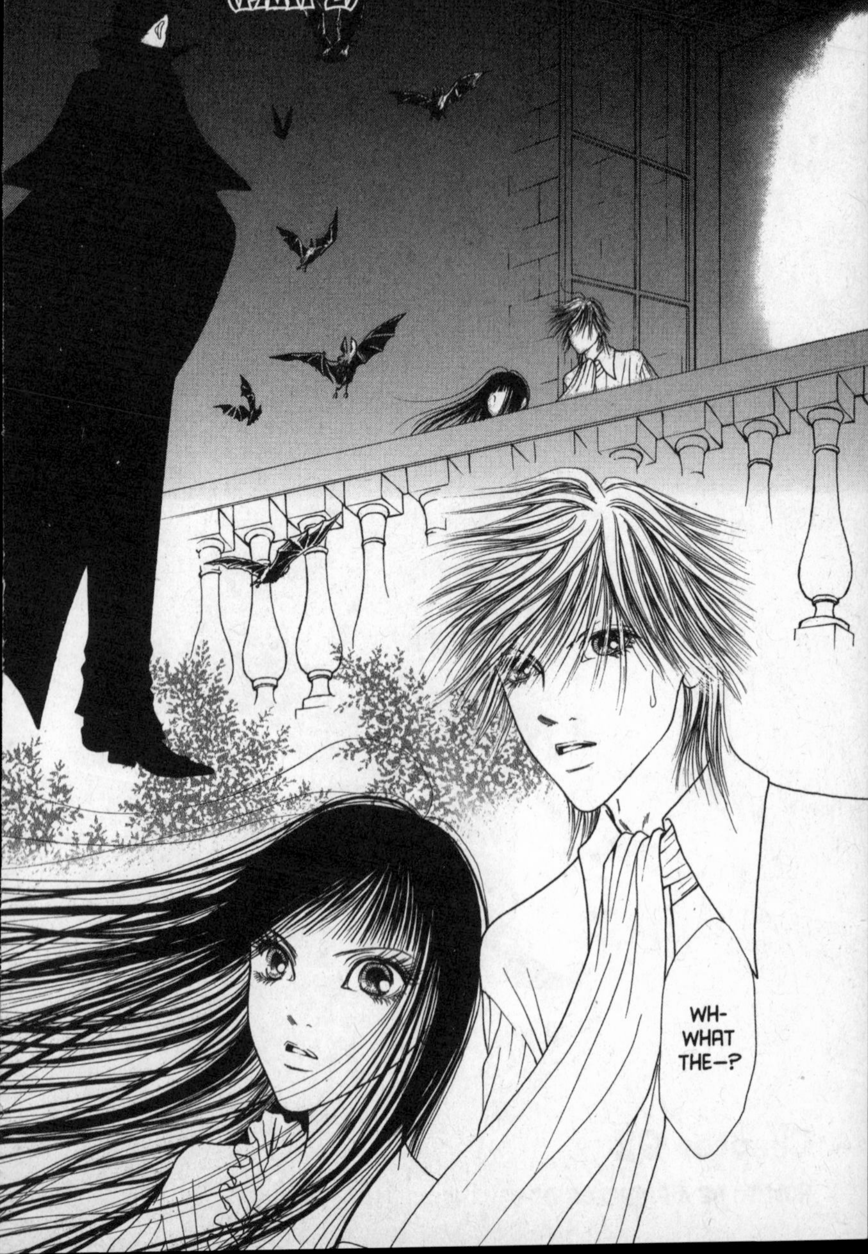
WH- WHAT THE—?

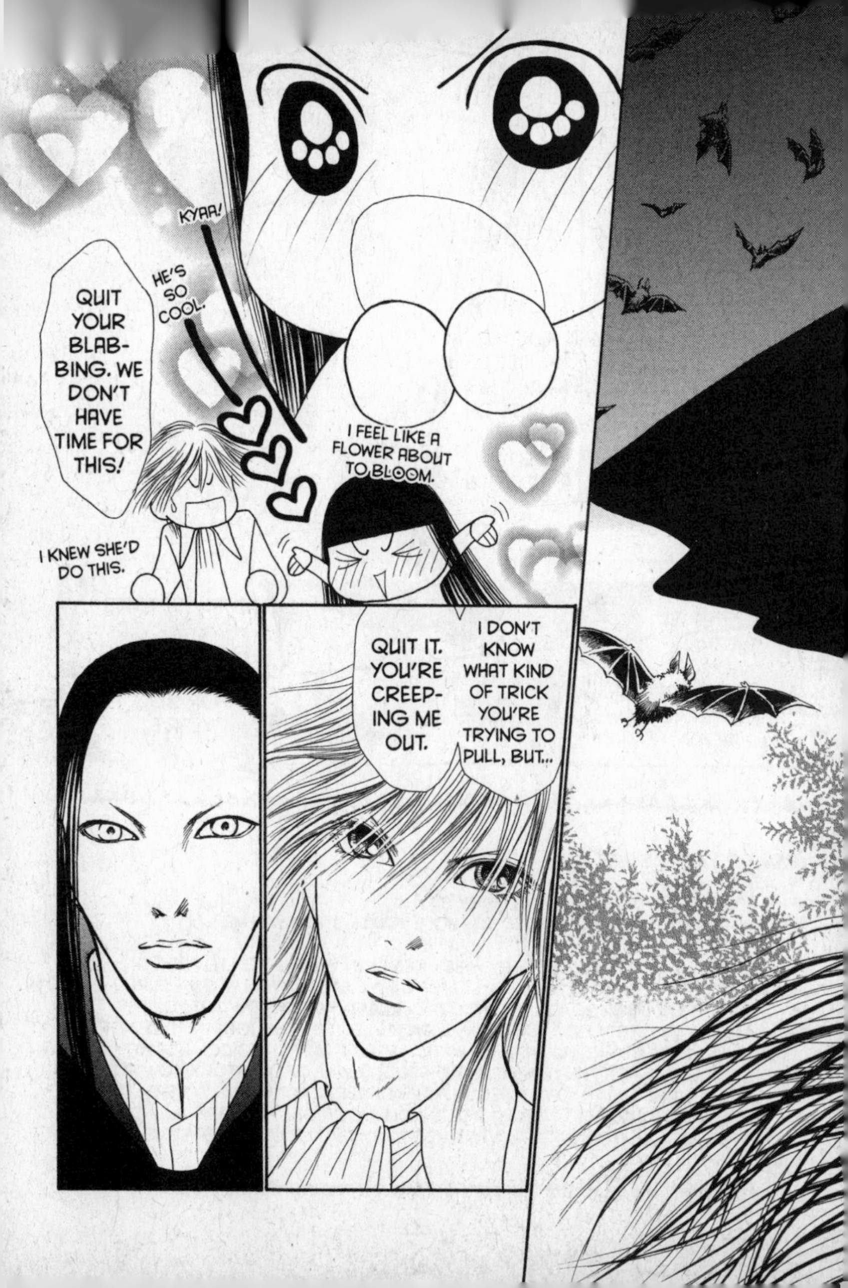
KYAA!
HE'S SO COOL.
I FEEL LIKE A FLOWER ABOUT TO BLOOM.
QUIT YOUR BLAB-BING. WE DON'T HAVE TIME FOR THIS!
I KNEW SHE'D DO THIS.
I DON'T KNOW WHAT KIND OF TRICK YOU'RE TRYING TO PULL, BUT...
QUIT IT. YOU'RE CREEP-ING ME OUT.

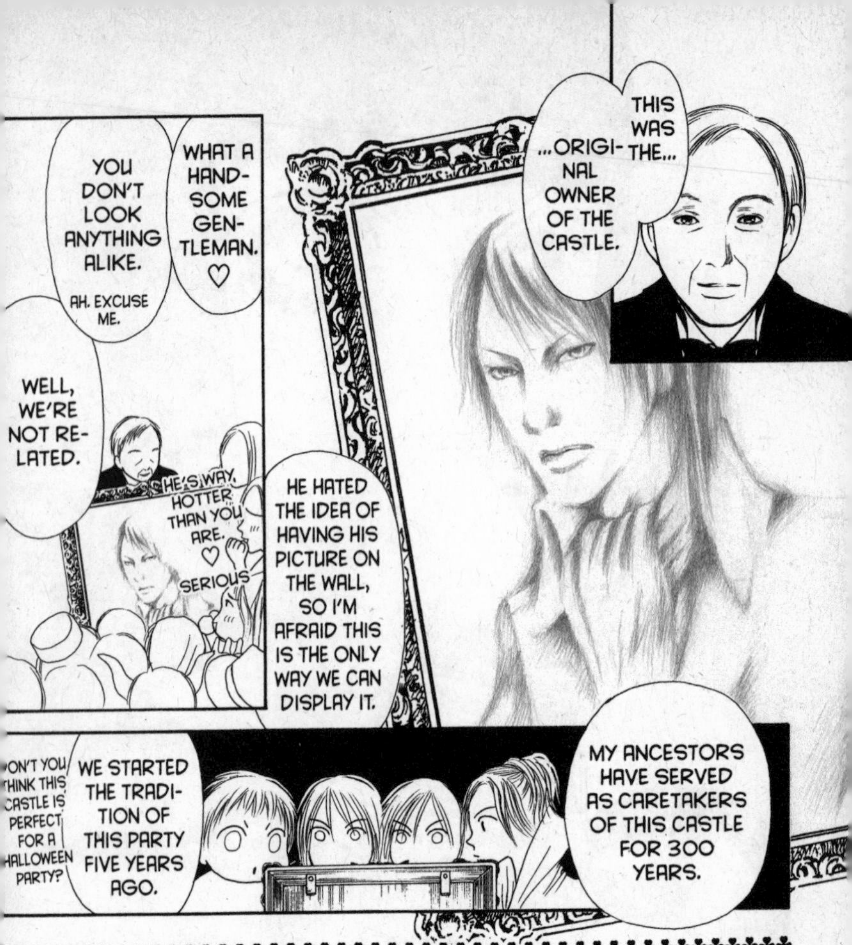
THIS WAS THE...
...ORIGINAL OWNER OF THE CASTLE.
HE HATED THE IDEA OF HAVING HIS PICTURE ON THE WALL, SO I'M AFRAID THIS IS THE ONLY WAY WE CAN DISPLAY IT.
WHAT A HANDSOME GENTLEMAN. ♡
YOU DON'T LOOK ANYTHING ALIKE.
AH. EXCUSE ME.
WELL, WE'RE NOT RELATED.
HE'S WAY HOTTER THAN YOU ARE. ♡
SERIOUS
MY ANCESTORS HAVE SERVED AS CARETAKERS OF THIS CASTLE FOR 300 YEARS.
WE STARTED THE TRADITION OF THIS PARTY FIVE YEARS AGO.
ON'T YOU THINK THIS CASTLE IS PERFECT FOR A HALLOWEEN PARTY?

BEHIND THE SCENES

THANK YOU FOR BUYING KODANSHA COMICS♡
I'M GONNA KEEP ON WORKING HARD, SO I HOPE YOU'LL STICK WITH ME.♡

THIS IS THE CONTINUATION OF A STORY WHICH BEGAN IN VOLUME 22. I FELT LIKE I OPENED UP A CAN OF WORMS IN THE FIRST HALF OF THE STORY, AND I WASN'T SURE WHAT TO DO. IT ENDED UP BECOMING THE CRAZY ROMANTIC COMEDY THAT YOU SEE HERE. THIS WAS MY FIRST TIME EVER WRITING A LOVE LETTER. I THOUGHT I'D NEVER GET IT RIGHT. LOVE LETTERS ARE SO HARD TO WRITE. I REALLY WANTED TO COME UP WITH A GOOD BACK STORY FOR THE VAMPIRE IN THE SECOND HALF OF THE STORY. SO I TRIED BASING HIS CHARACTER ON VLAD TEPES, BUT THEN MY EDITOR TOLD ME I WAS GETTING TOO CARRIED AWAY, AND THAT I COULD DO A WHOLE BOOK ON THAT TOPIC ALONE. I WAS SO HAPPY ABOUT DOING A REAL VAMPIRE STORY THAT I ENDED UP GETTING OFF TRACK. [SIGH]

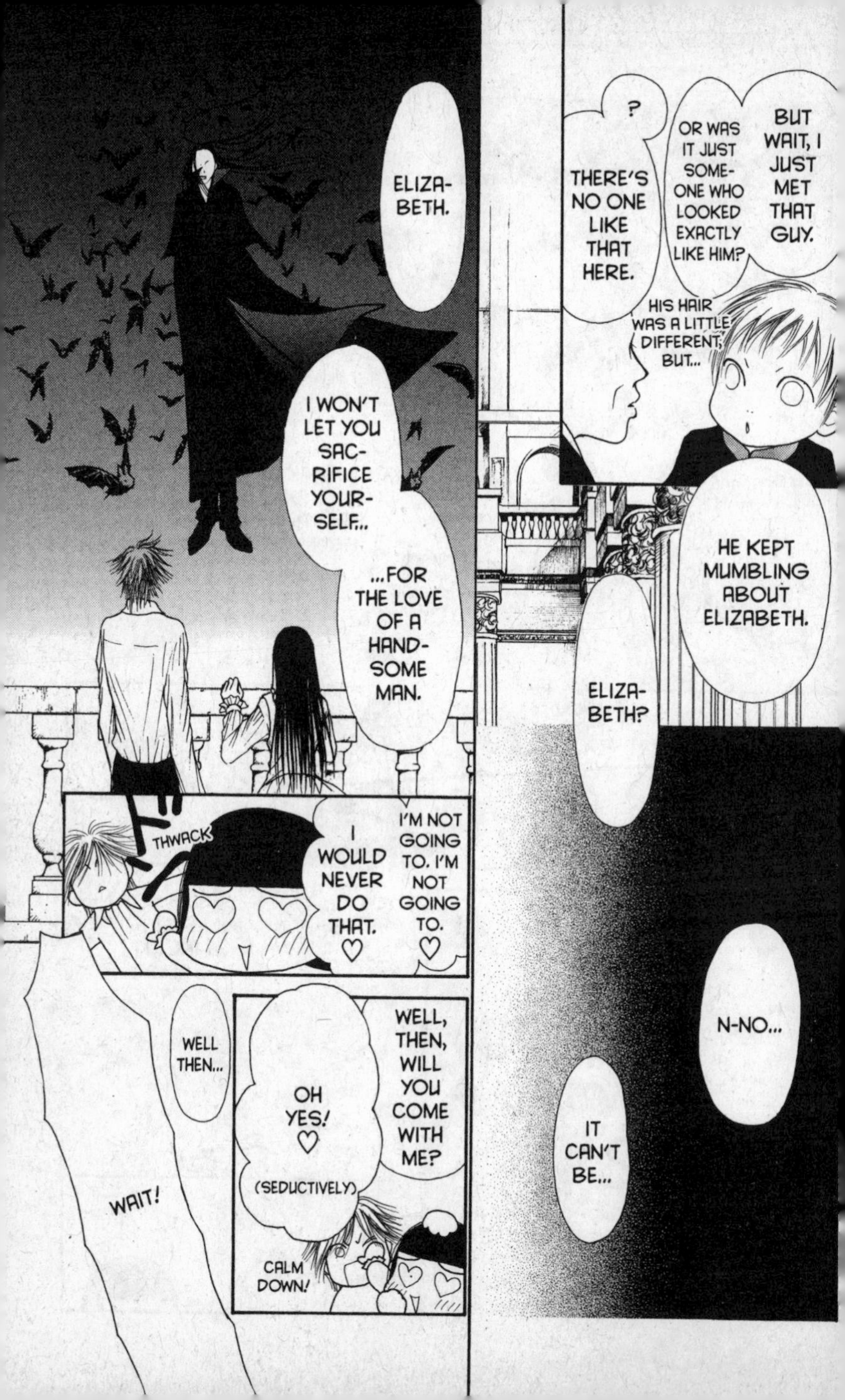
BUT WAIT, I JUST MET THAT GUY.
OR WAS IT JUST SOME-ONE WHO LOOKED EXACTLY LIKE HIM?
?
THERE'S NO ONE LIKE THAT HERE.
HIS HAIR WAS A LITTLE DIFFERENT, BUT...
HE KEPT MUMBLING ABOUT ELIZABETH.
ELIZA-BETH?
N-NO...
IT CAN'T BE...
ELIZA-BETH.
I WON'T LET YOU SAC-RIFICE YOUR-SELF...
...FOR THE LOVE OF A HAND-SOME MAN.
I'M NOT GOING TO. I'M NOT GOING TO. ♡
I WOULD NEVER DO THAT. ♡
THWACK
WELL, THEN, WILL YOU COME WITH ME?
OH YES! ♡
(SEDUCTIVELY)
CALM DOWN!
WELL THEN...
WAIT!

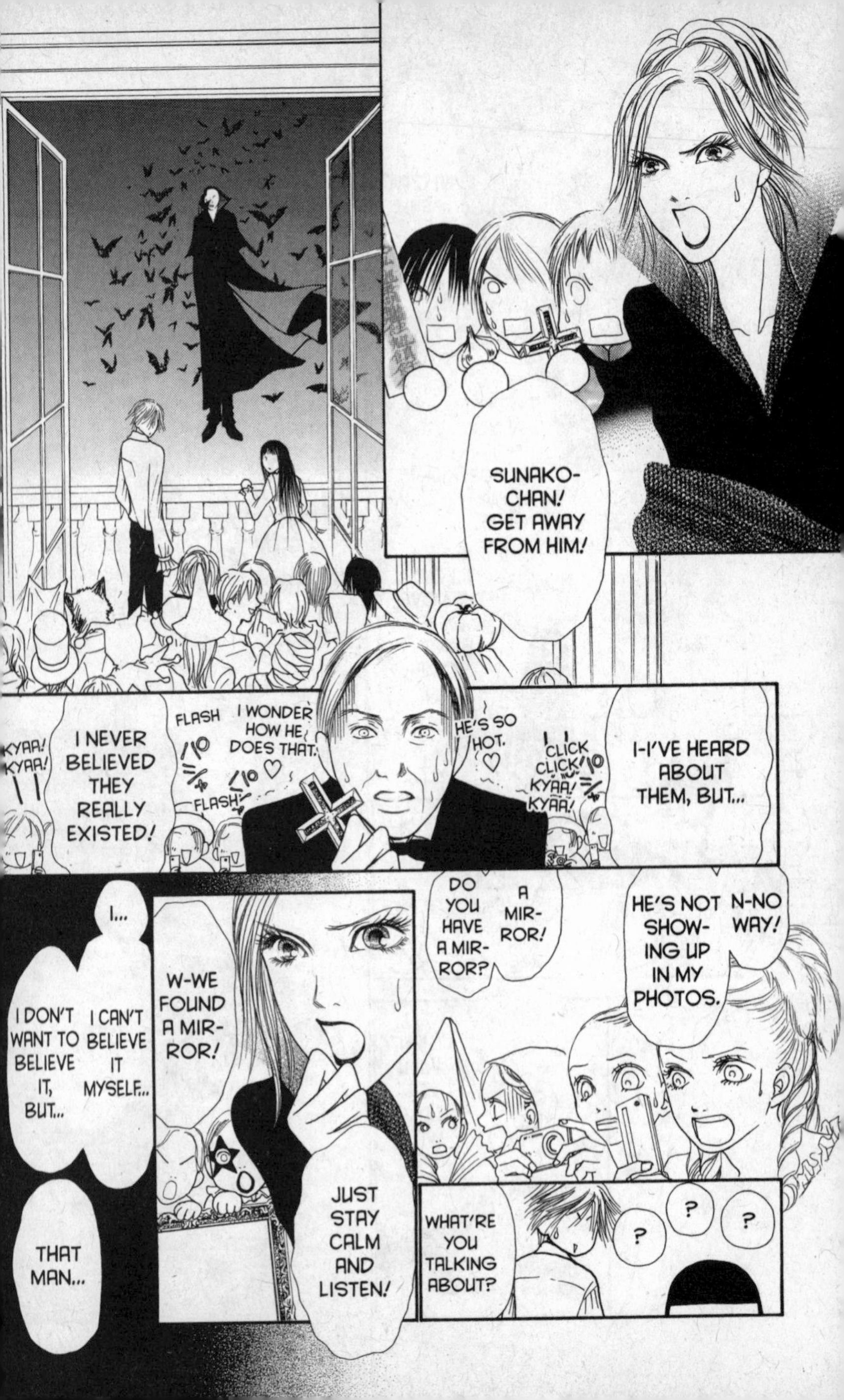
SUNAKO-CHAN! GET AWAY FROM HIM!
I-I'VE HEARD ABOUT THEM, BUT...
CLICK CLICK
KYAA! KYAA!
HE'S SO HOT. ♡
I WONDER HOW HE DOES THAT. ♡
FLASH
FLASH
I NEVER BELIEVED THEY REALLY EXISTED!
KYAA! KYAA!
N-NO WAY!
HE'S NOT SHOWING UP IN MY PHOTOS.
A MIRROR!
DO YOU HAVE A MIRROR?
?
?
?
WHAT'RE YOU TALKING ABOUT?
W-WE FOUND A MIRROR!
JUST STAY CALM AND LISTEN!
I...
I CAN'T BELIEVE IT MYSELF...
I DON'T WANT TO BELIEVE IT, BUT...
THAT MAN...

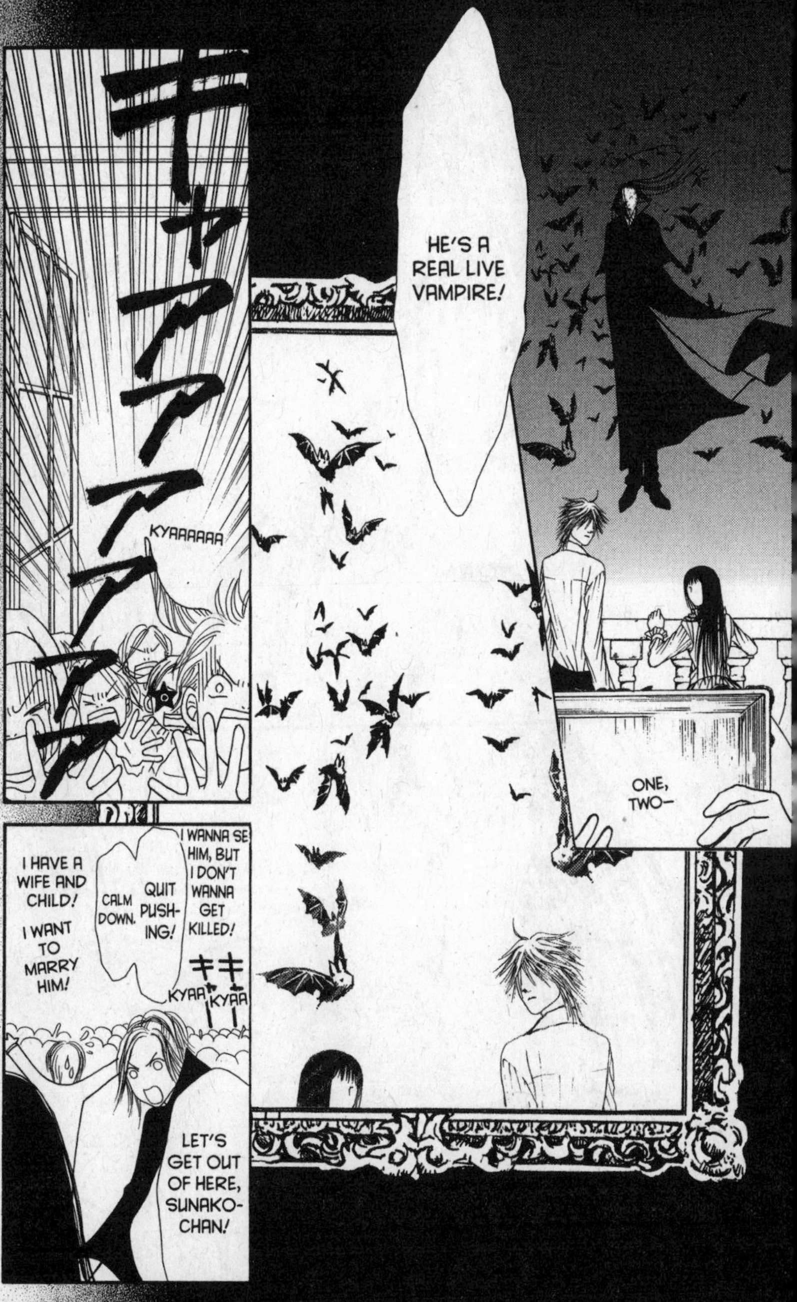
HE'S A REAL LIVE VAMPIRE!
ONE, TWO-
キャアアアアア
KYAAAAAA
I WANNA SE HIM, BUT I DON'T WANNA GET KILLED!
QUIT PUSHING!
CALM DOWN.
I HAVE A WIFE AND CHILD!
I WANT TO MARRY HIM!
キャ キャ
KYAA KYAA
LET'S GET OUT OF HERE, SUNAKO-CHAN!

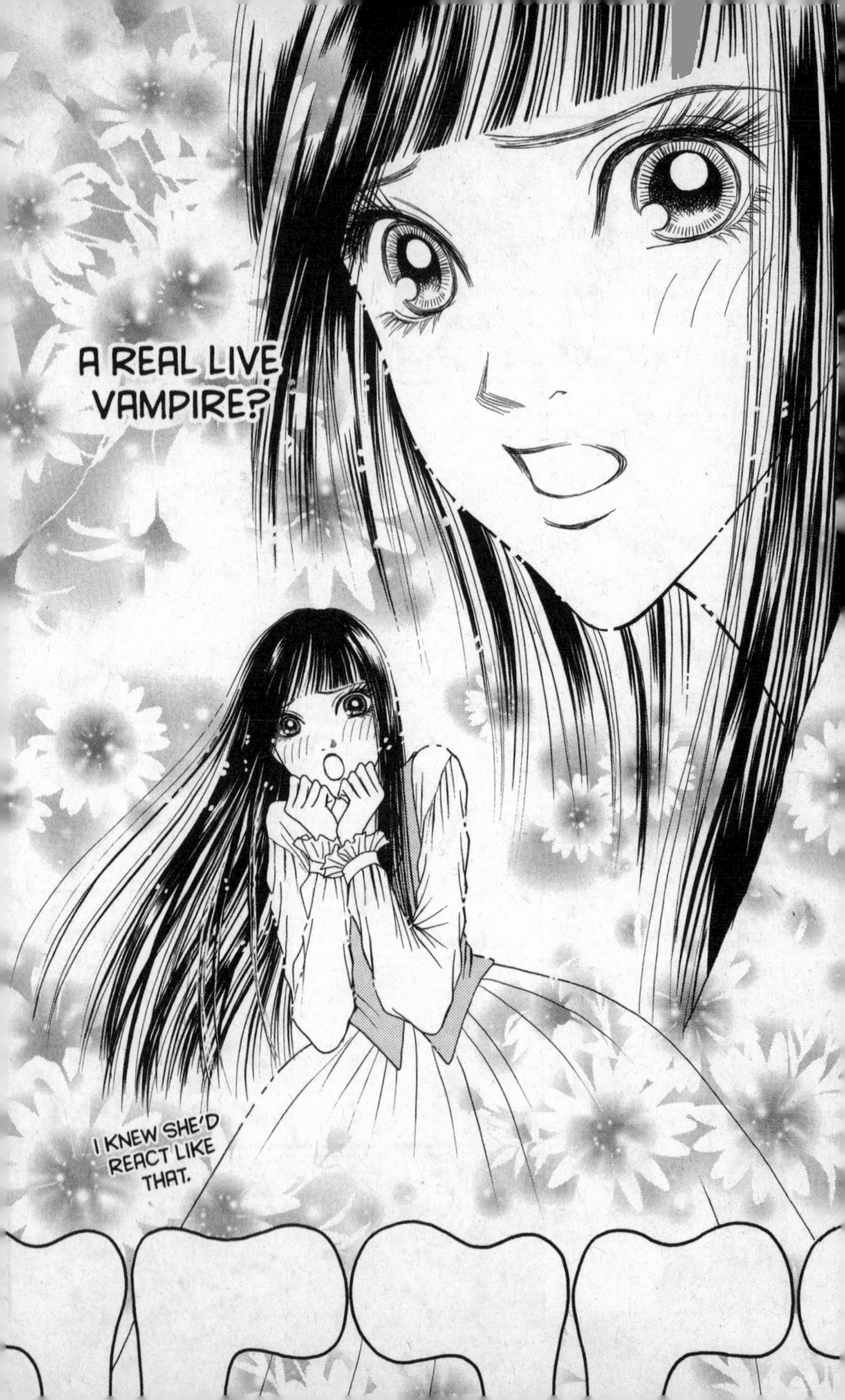
A REAL LIVE VAMPIRE?
I KNEW SHE'D REACT LIKE THAT.

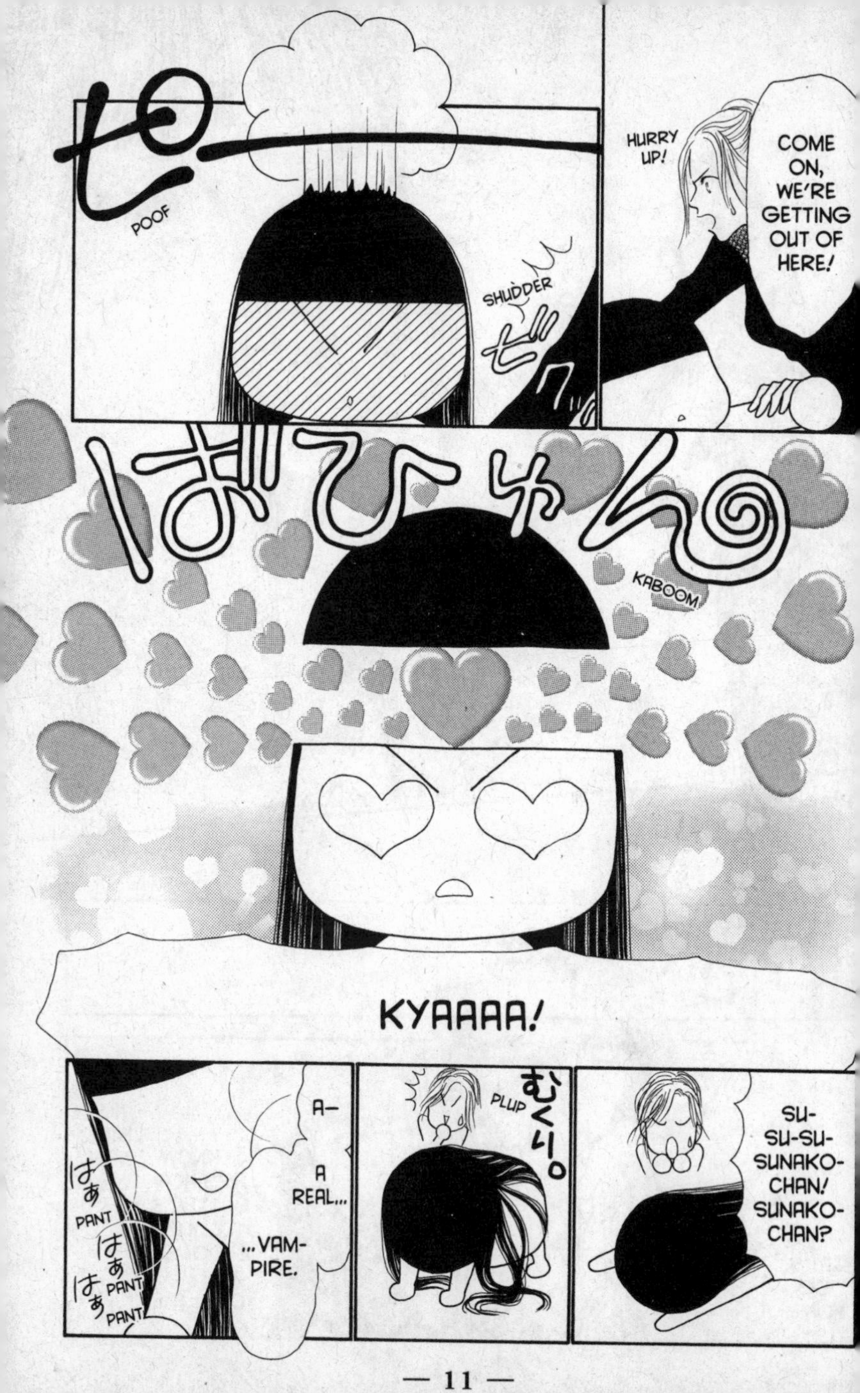
COME ON, WE'RE GETTING OUT OF HERE!
HURRY UP!
SHUDDER
ビク
POOF
ぜー
はひゅん
KABOOM
KYAAAA!
SU-SU-SU-SUNAKO-CHAN! SUNAKO-CHAN?
むくり。
PLUP
A—
A REAL...
...VAMPIRE.
はぁ
PANT
はぁ
PANT
はぁ
PANT

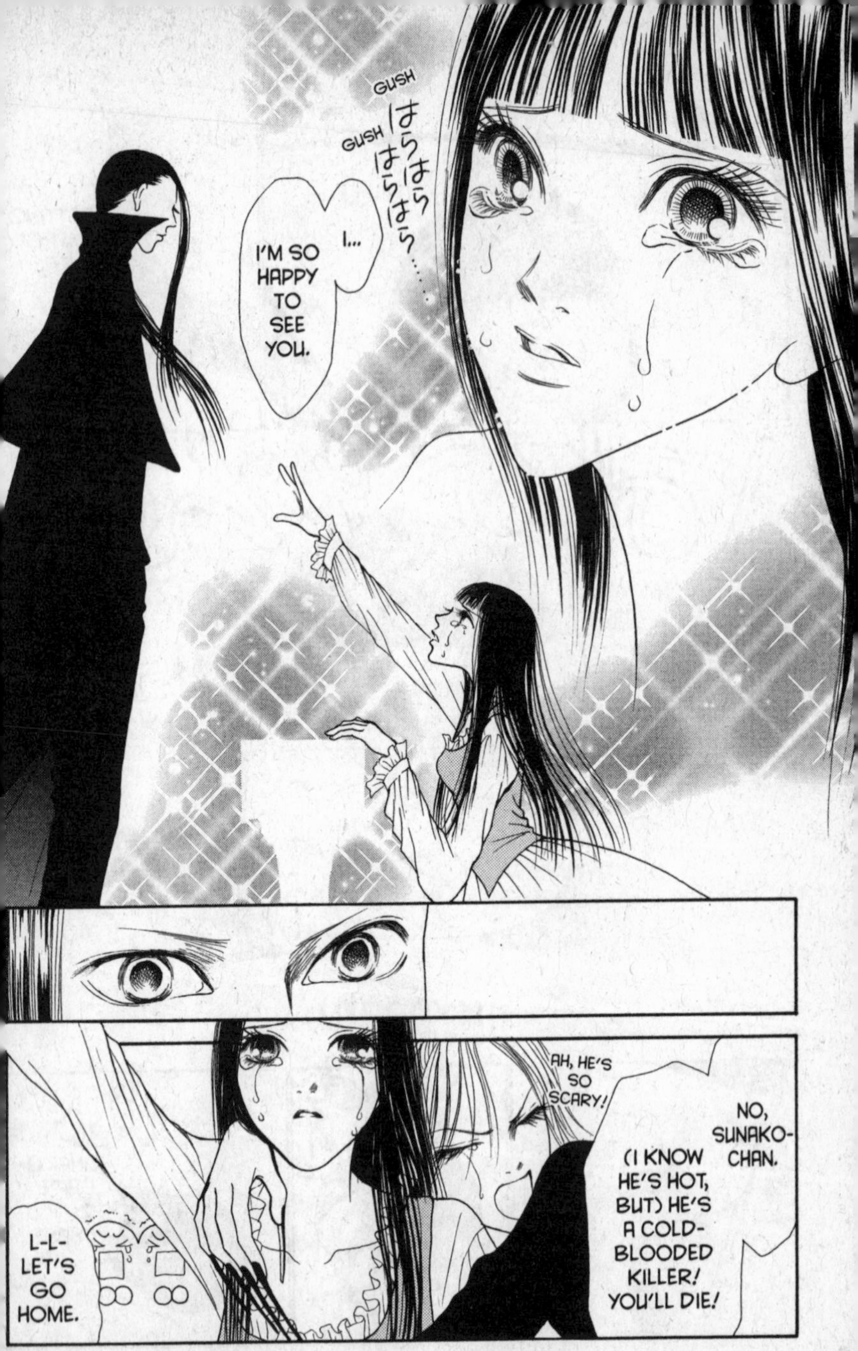
GUSH
GUSH
はらはら
はらはら……
I…
I'M SO HAPPY TO SEE YOU.
NO, SUNAKO-CHAN.
(I KNOW HE'S HOT, BUT) HE'S A COLD-BLOODED KILLER! YOU'LL DIE!
AH, HE'S SO SCARY!
L-L-LET'S GO HOME.

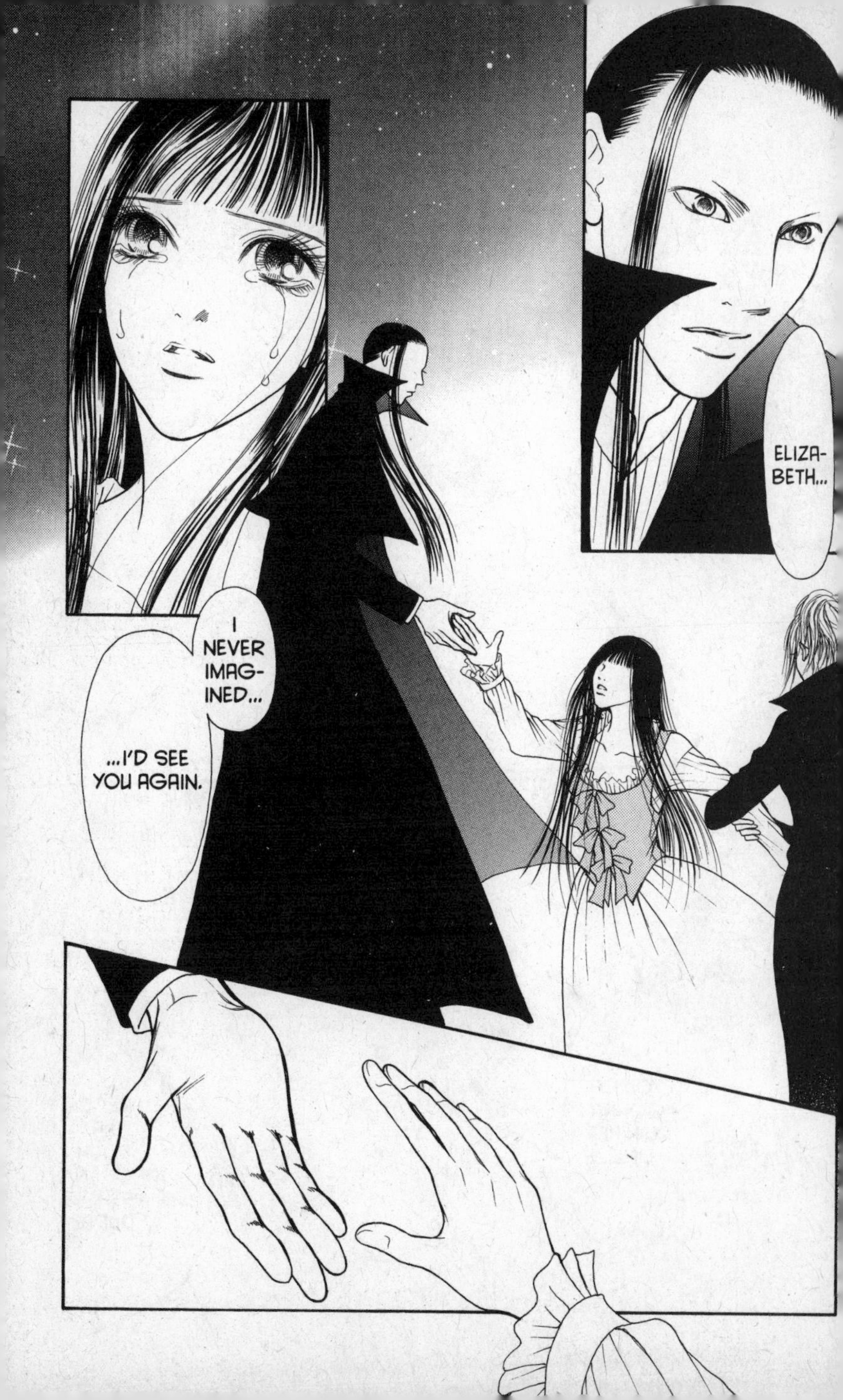
ELIZA-
BETH...
I NEVER IMAG-
INED...
...I'D SEE YOU AGAIN.

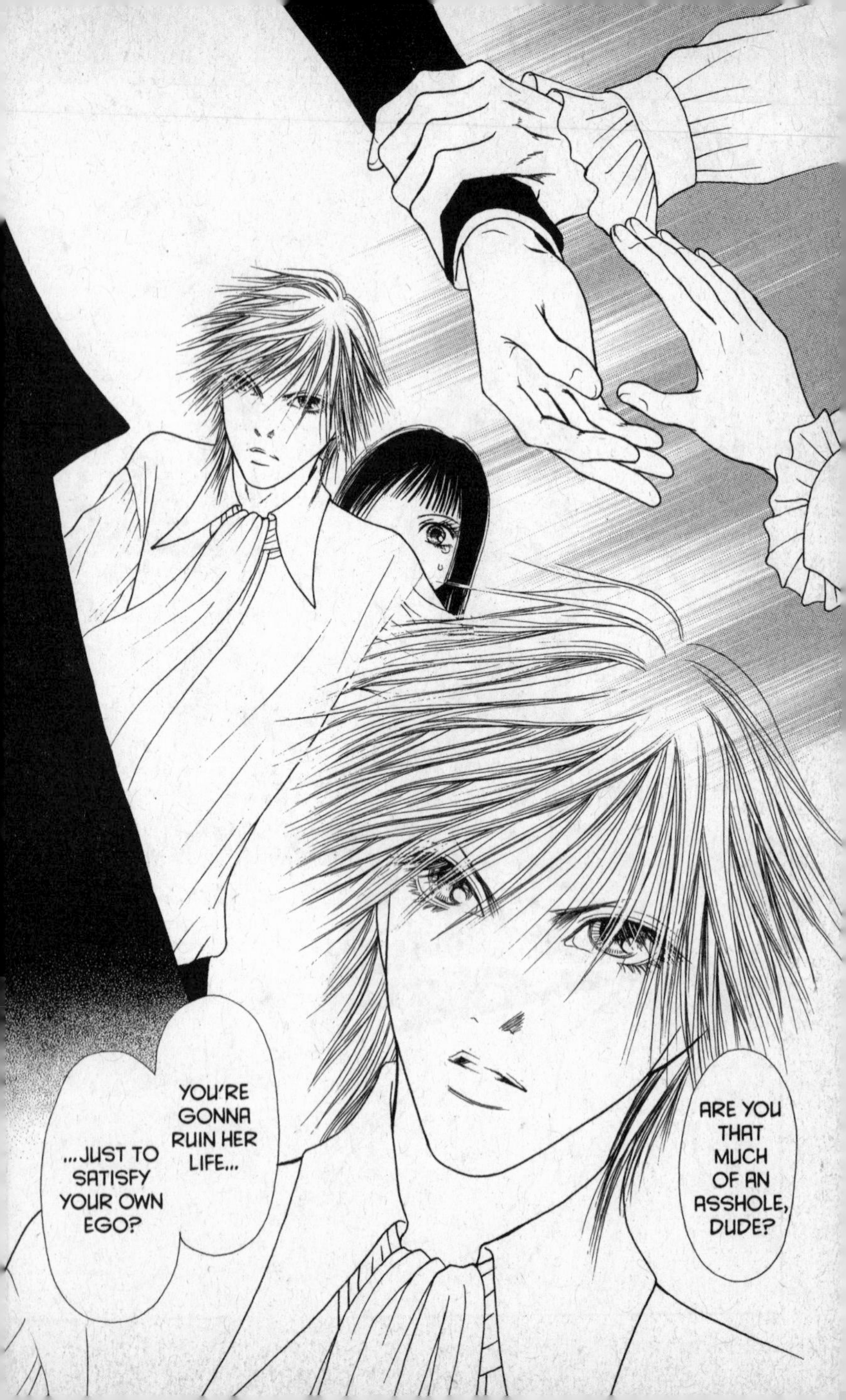
ARE YOU THAT MUCH OF AN ASSHOLE, DUDE?
YOU'RE GONNA RUIN HER LIFE...
...JUST TO SATISFY YOUR OWN EGO?

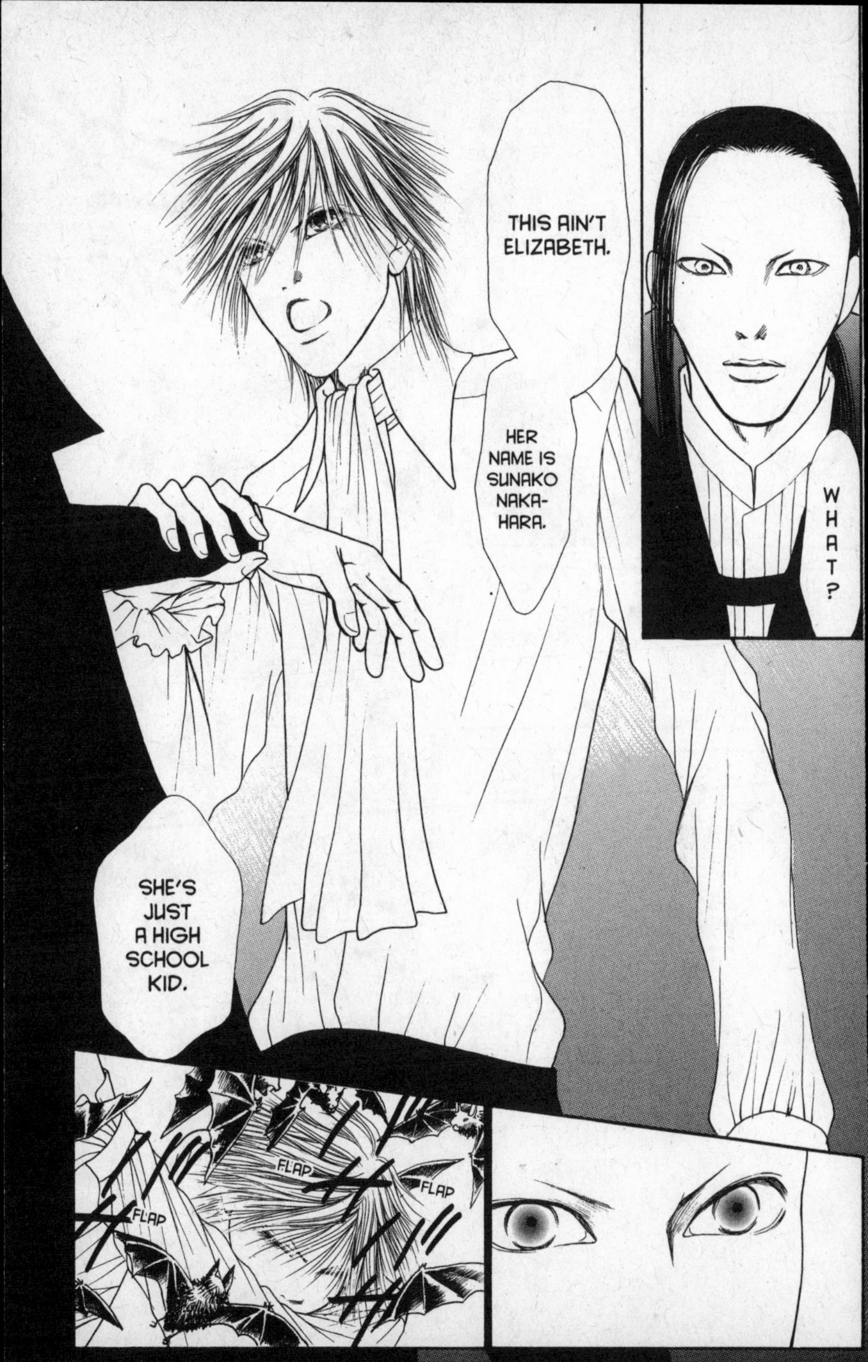
THIS AIN'T ELIZABETH.
WHAT?
HER NAME IS SUNAKO NAKA-HARA.
SHE'S JUST A HIGH SCHOOL KID.
FLAP
FLAP
FLAP

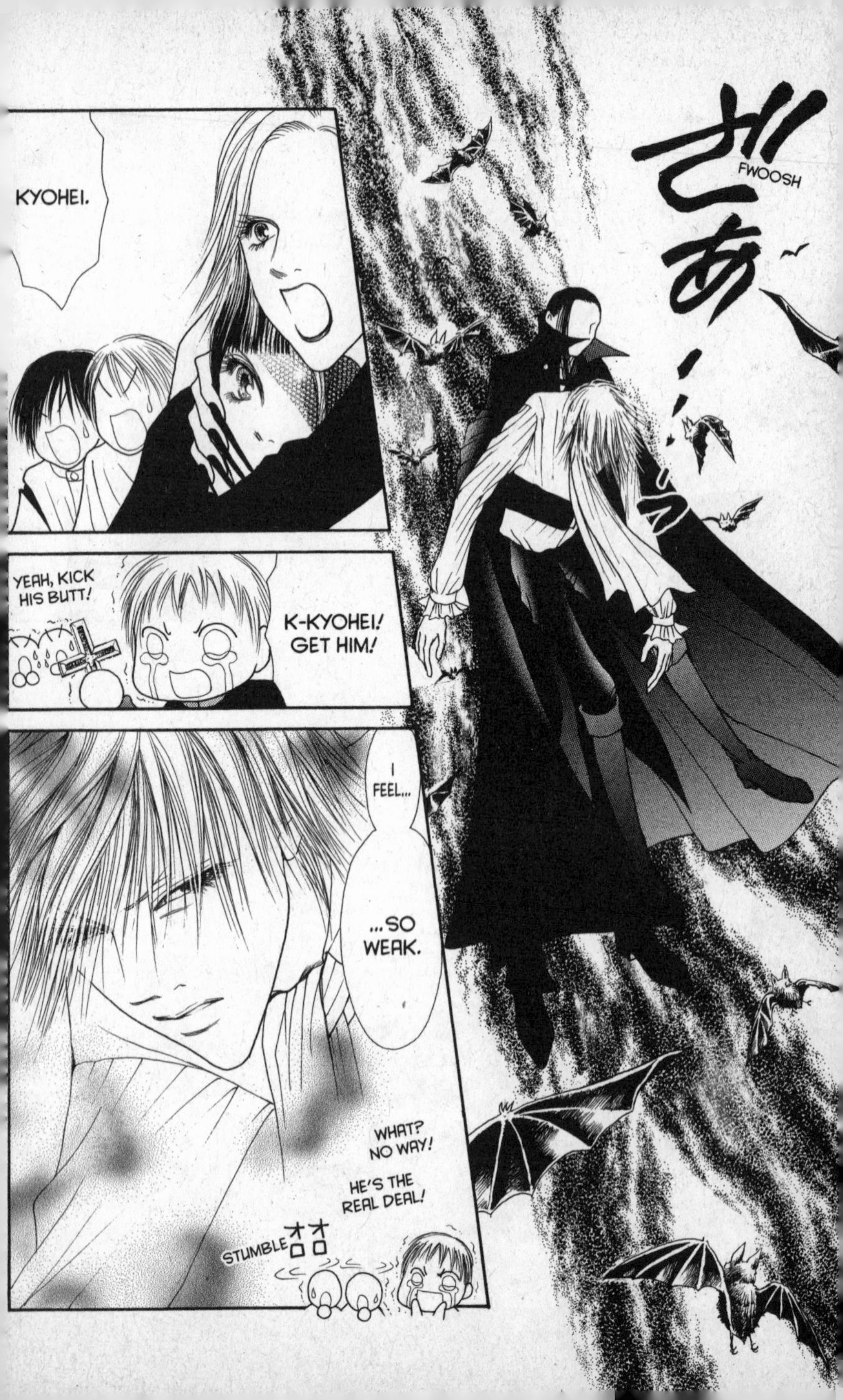
ざあ
FWOOSH
KYOHEI.
K-KYOHEI! GET HIM!
YEAH, KICK HIS BUTT!
I FEEL...
...SO WEAK.
WHAT? NO WAY!
HE'S THE REAL DEAL!
STUMBLE

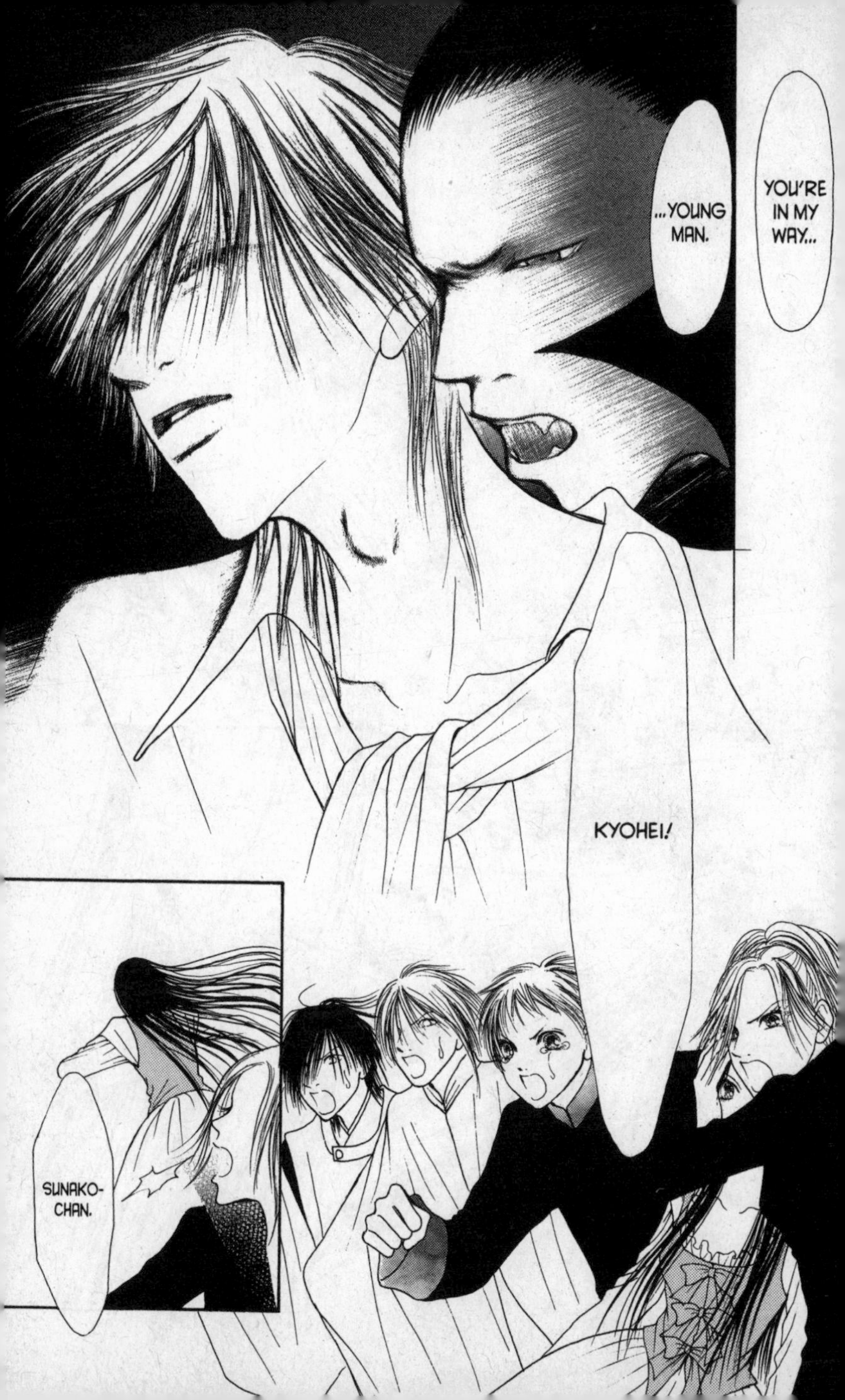
YOU'RE IN MY WAY...
...YOUNG MAN.
KYOHEI!
SUNAKO-CHAN.

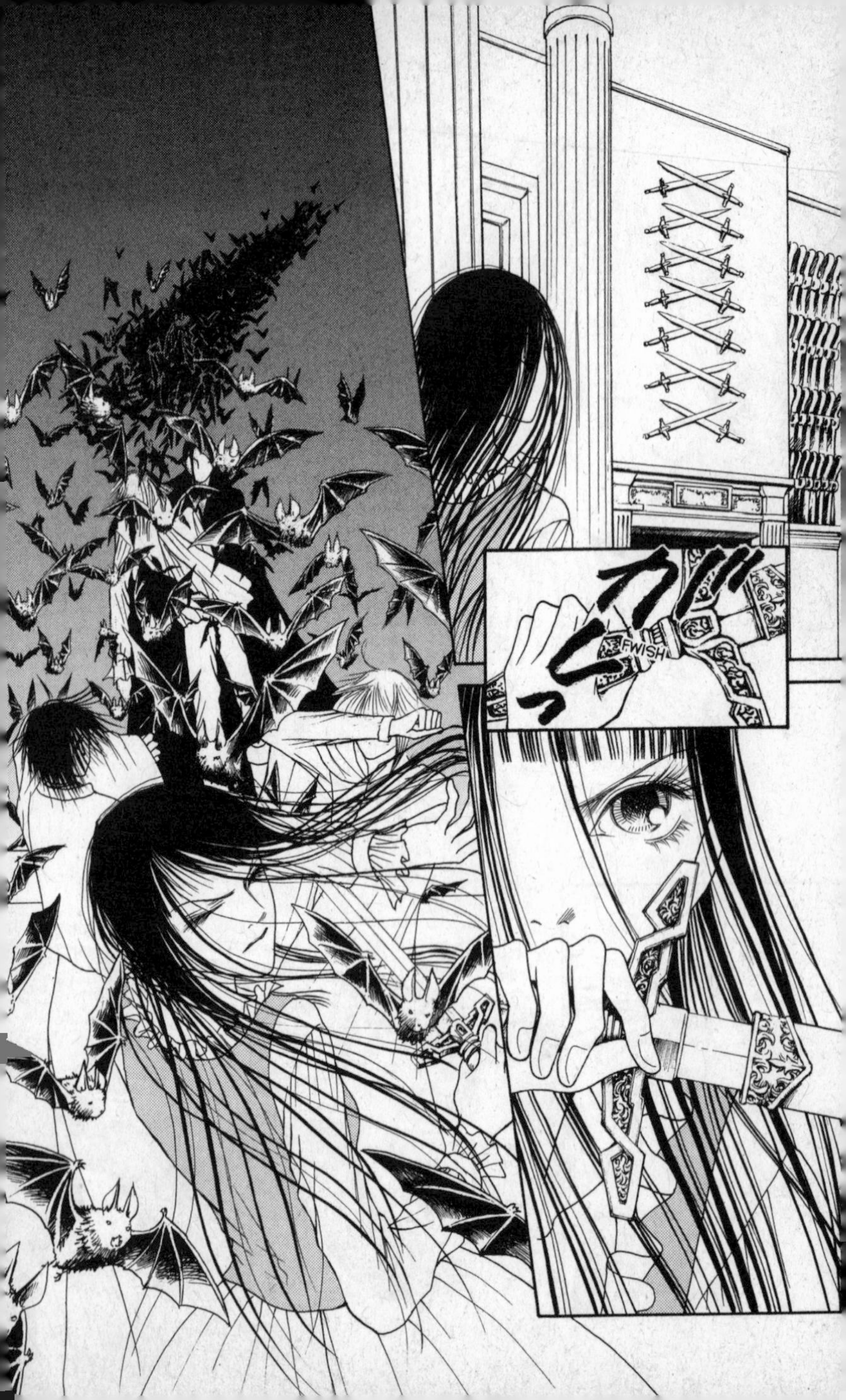
カッ
FWISH

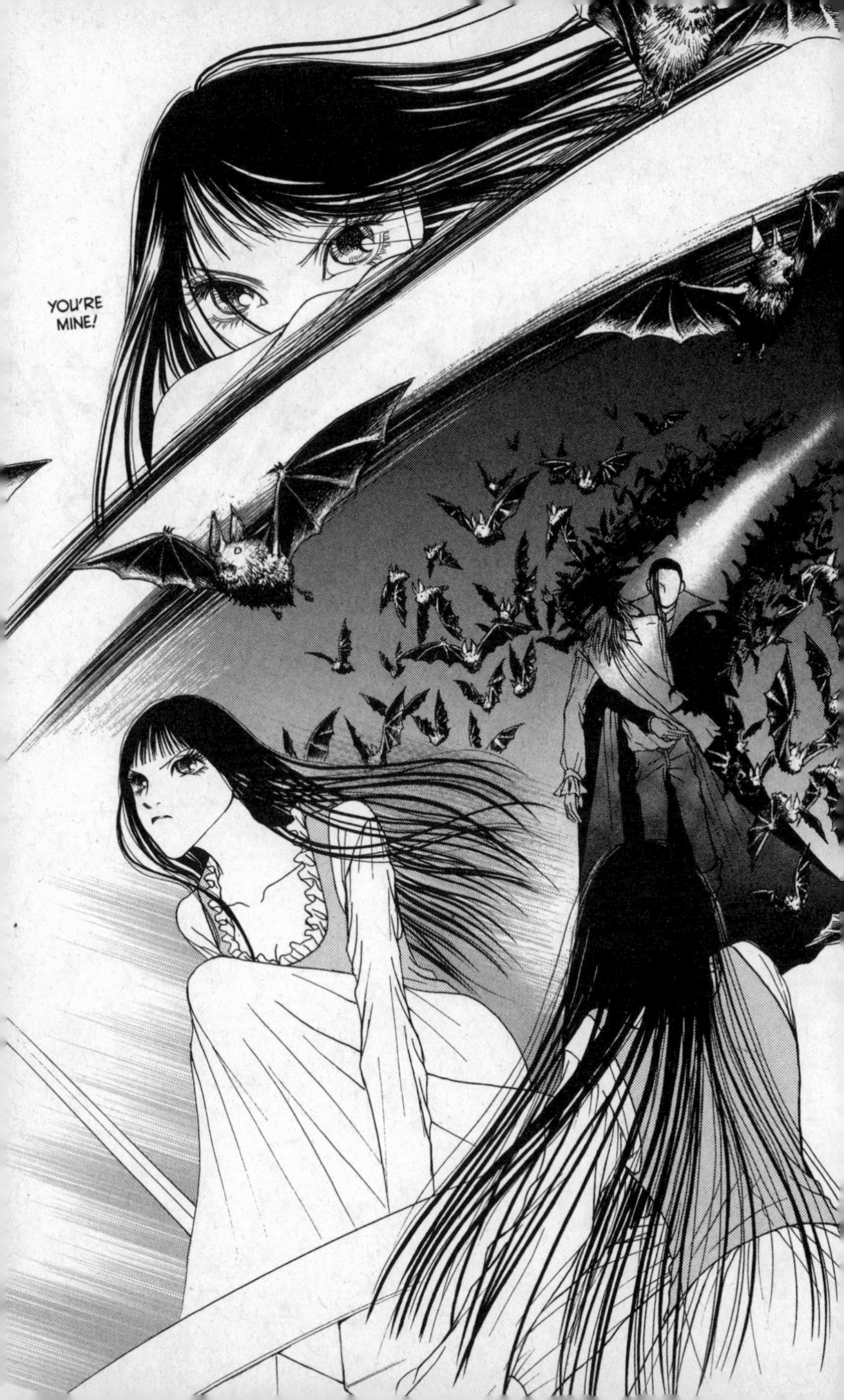
YOU'RE MINE!

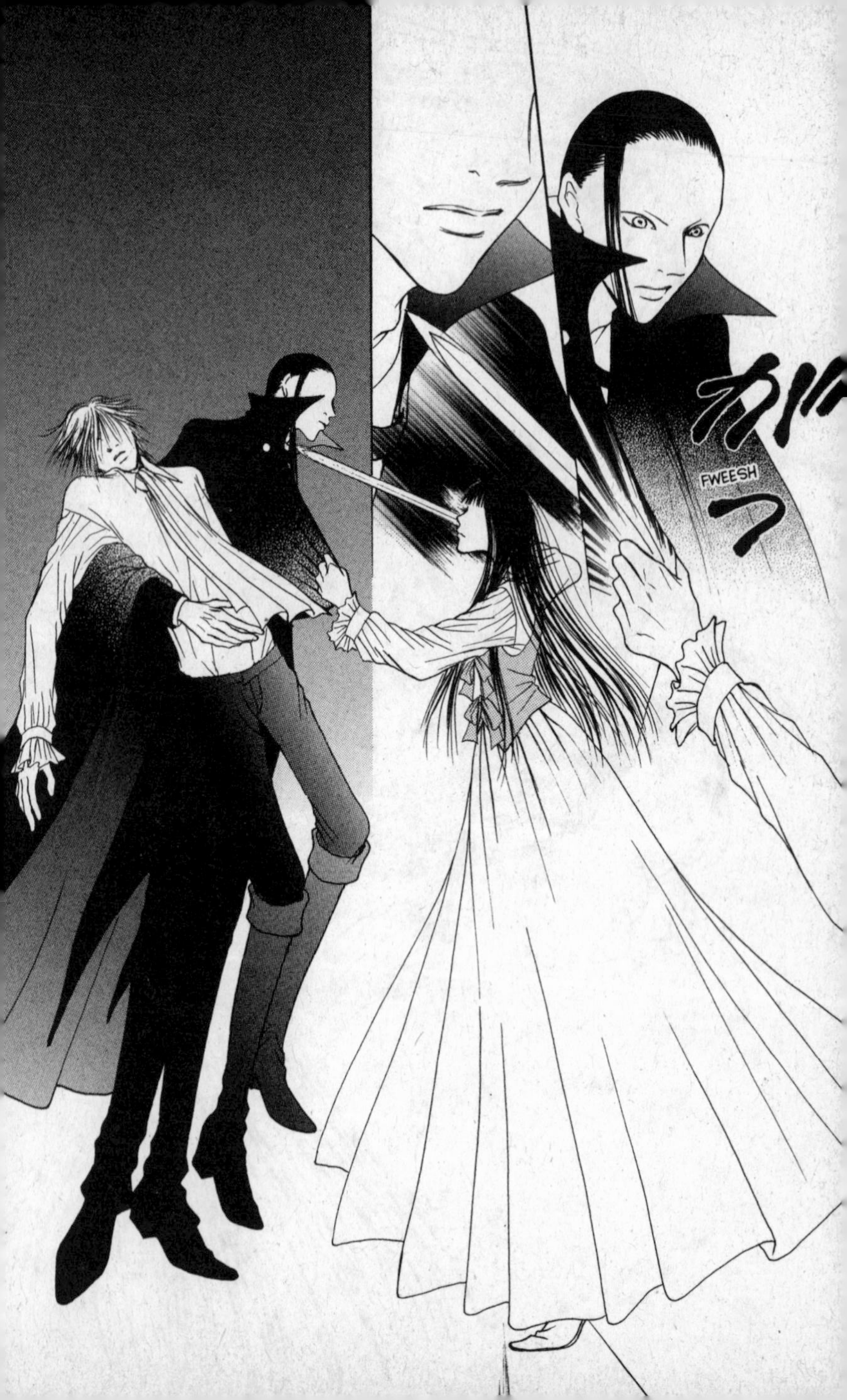

カッ
FWEESH

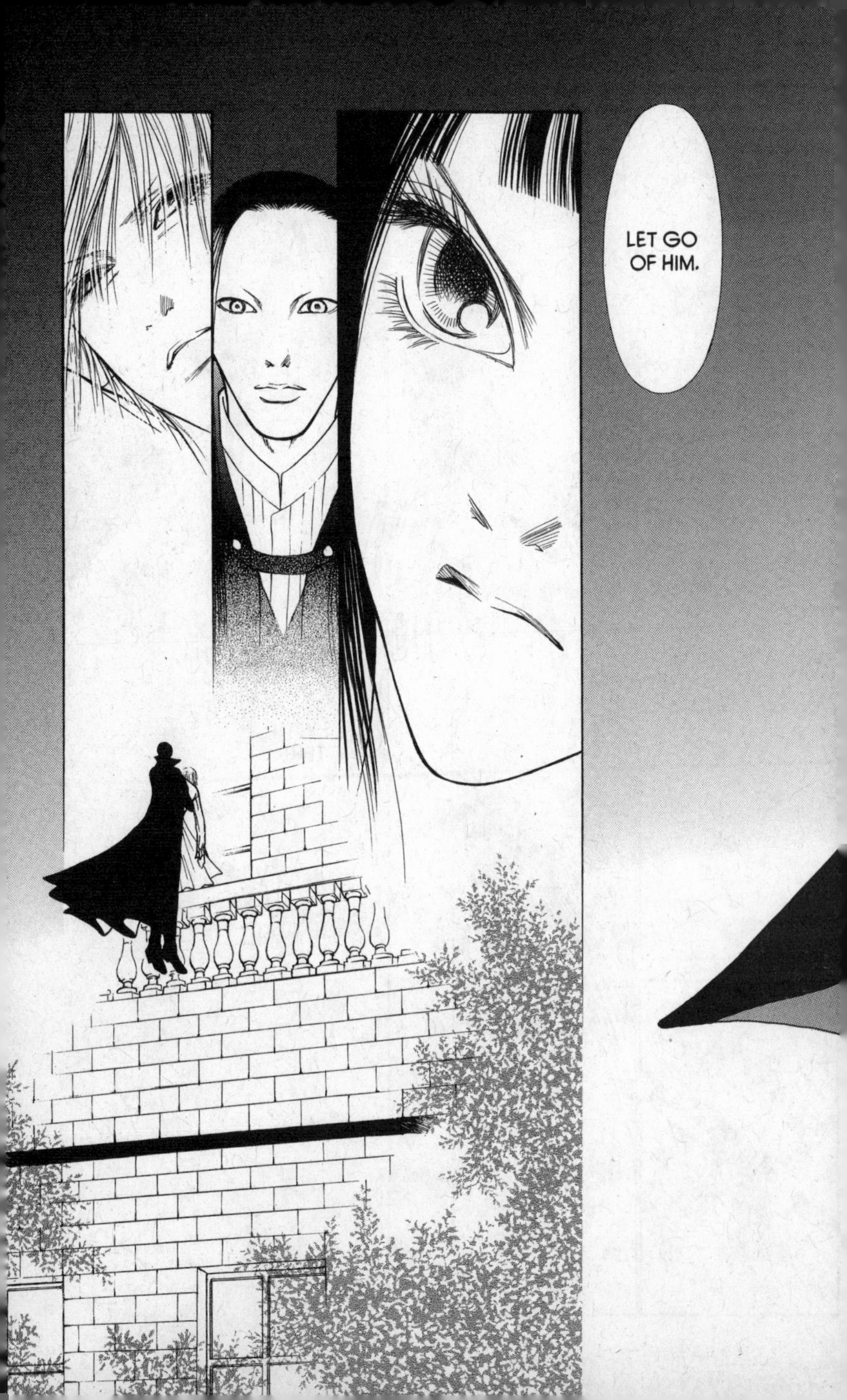
LET GO OF HIM.

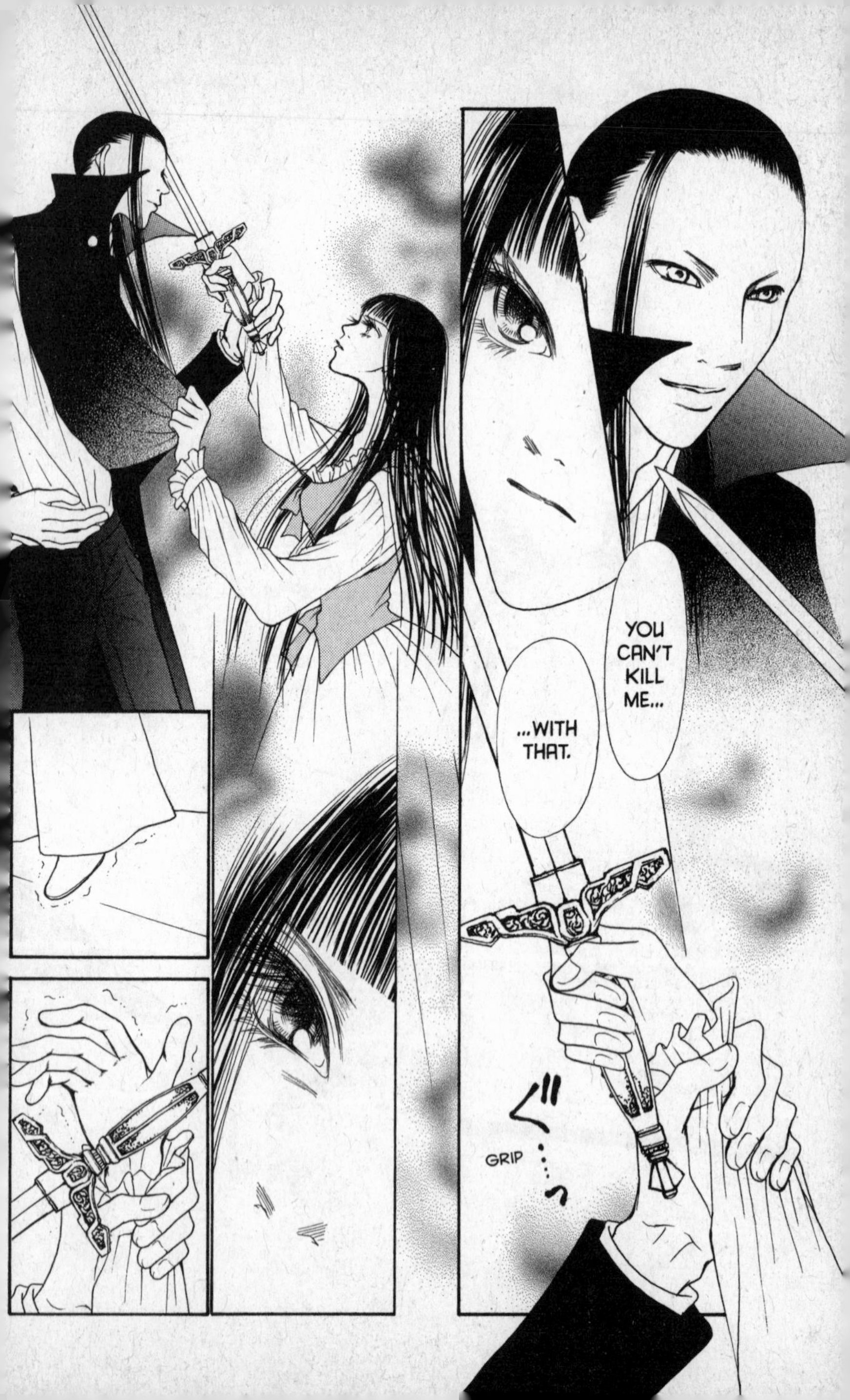

YOU CAN'T KILL ME...
...WITH THAT.
GRIP

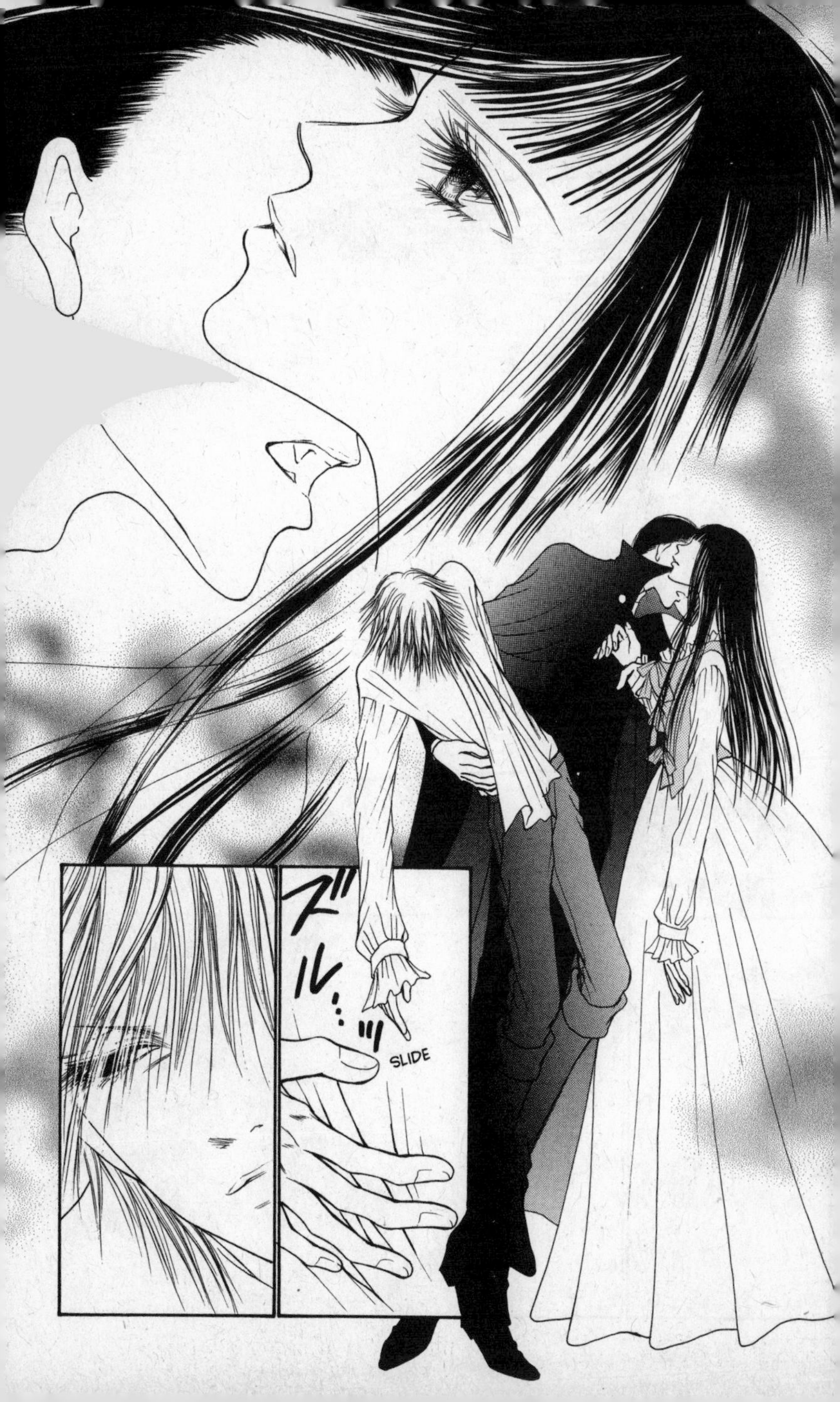
ズル…ッ
SLIDE

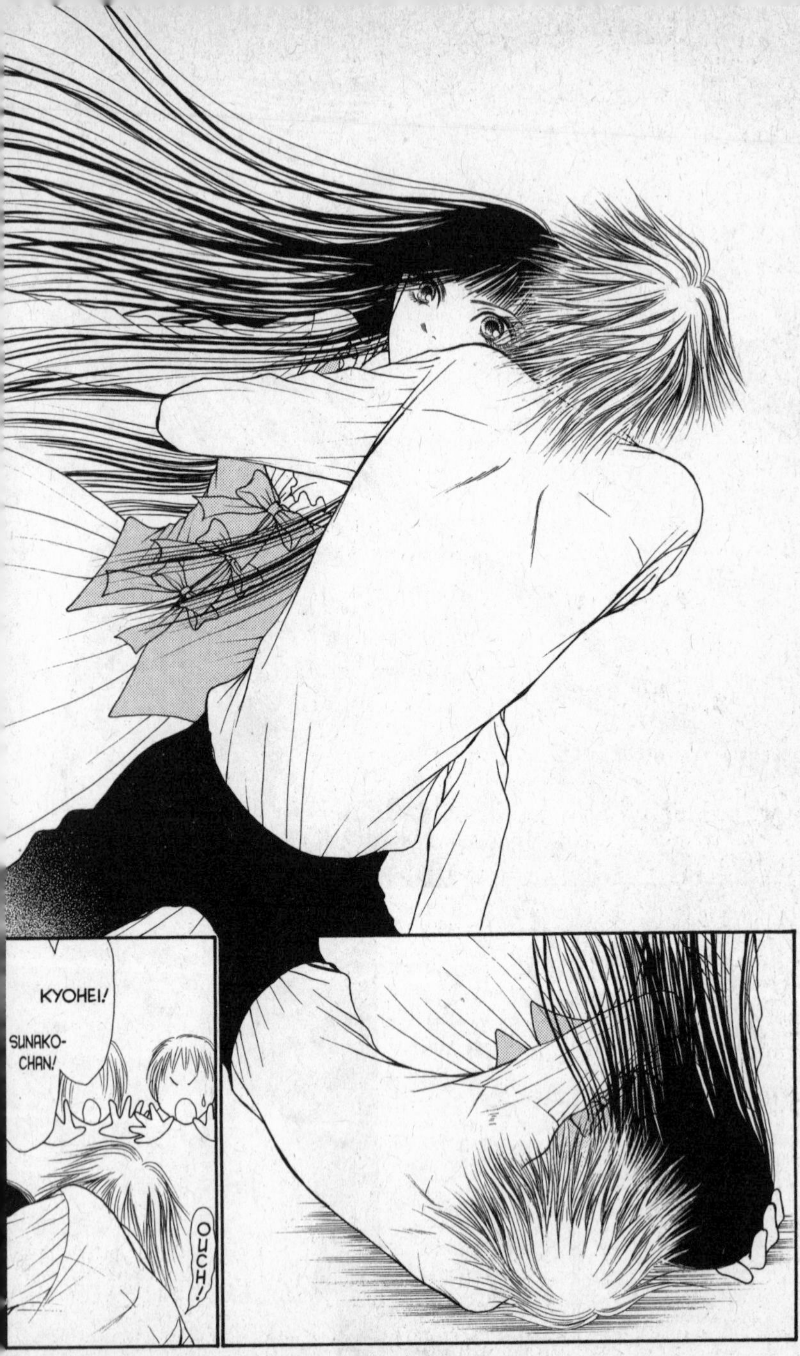
KYOHEI!
SUNAKO-CHAN!
OUCH!

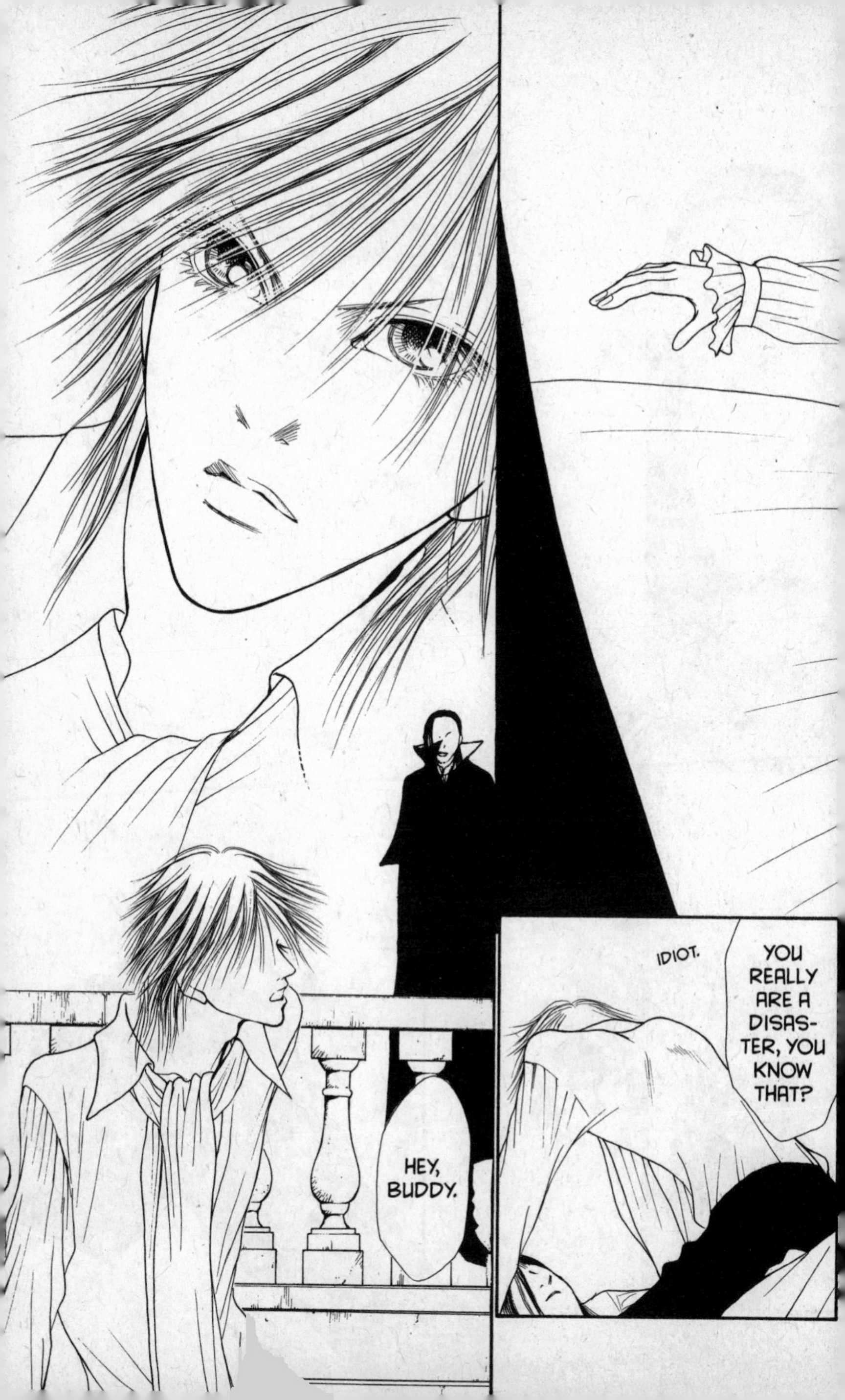
YOU REALLY ARE A DISASTER, YOU KNOW THAT?
IDIOT.
HEY, BUDDY.

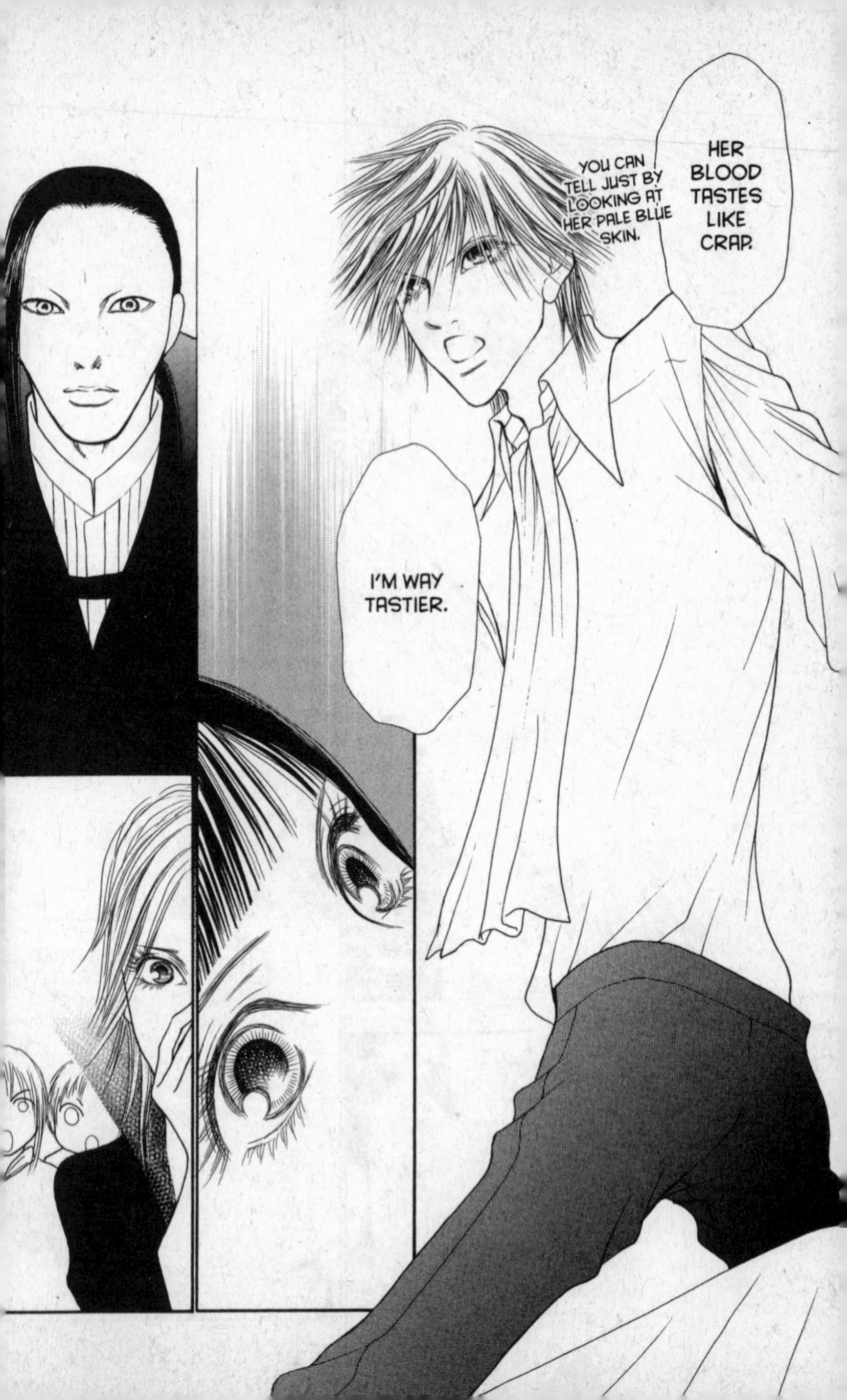
HER BLOOD TASTES LIKE CRAP.
YOU CAN TELL JUST BY LOOKING AT HER PALE BLUE SKIN.
I'M WAY TASTIER.

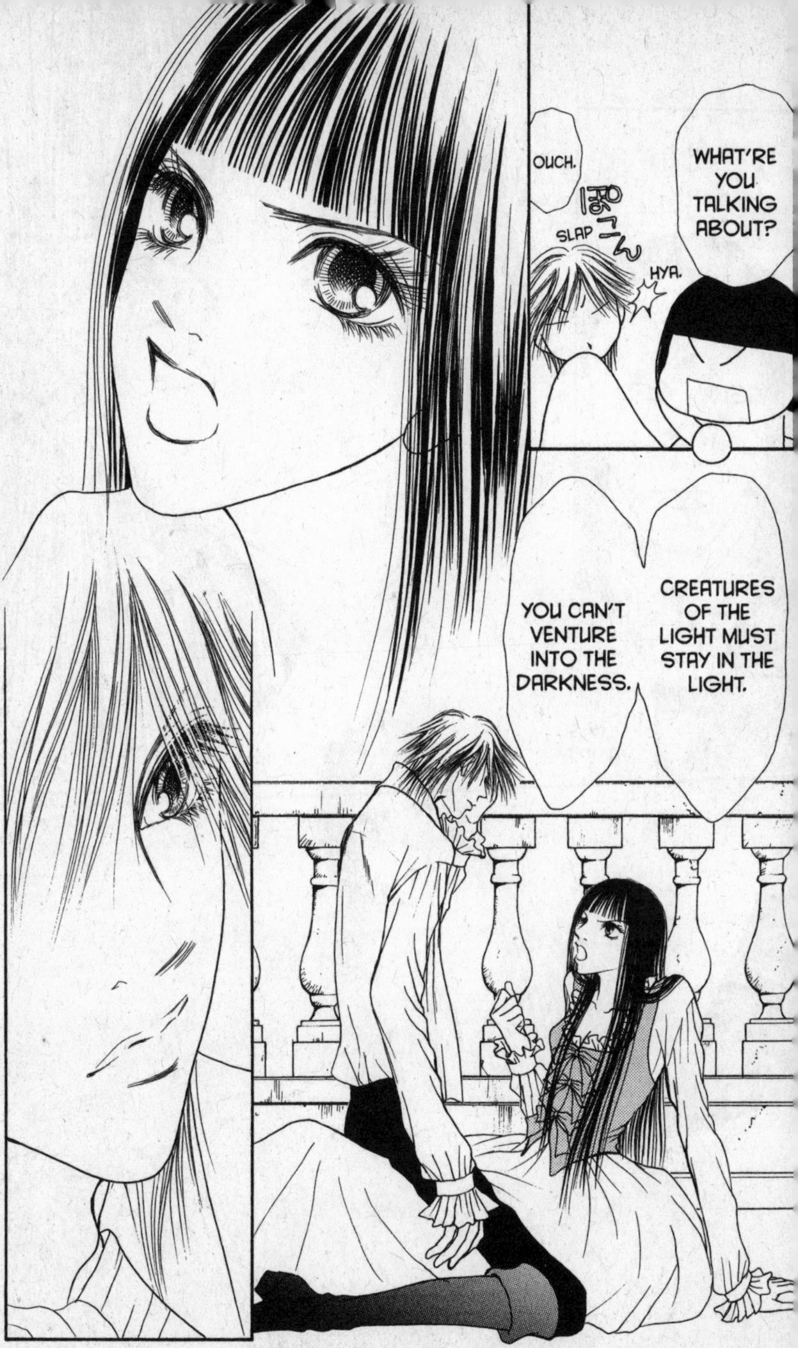
WHAT'RE YOU TALKING ABOUT?
HYA.
SLAP
OUCH.
CREATURES OF THE LIGHT MUST STAY IN THE LIGHT.
YOU CAN'T VENTURE INTO THE DARKNESS.

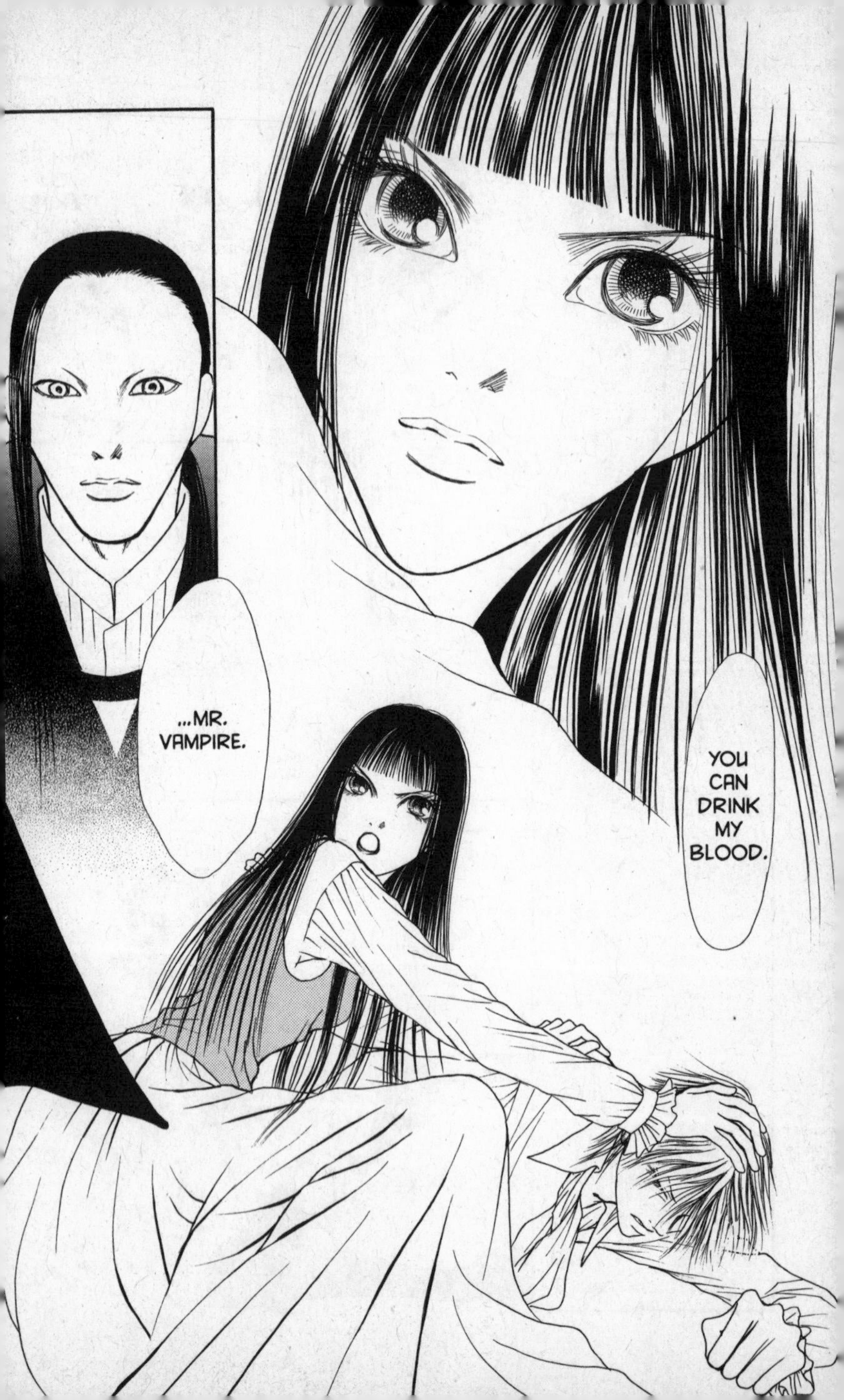
YOU CAN DRINK MY BLOOD.
...MR. VAMPIRE.

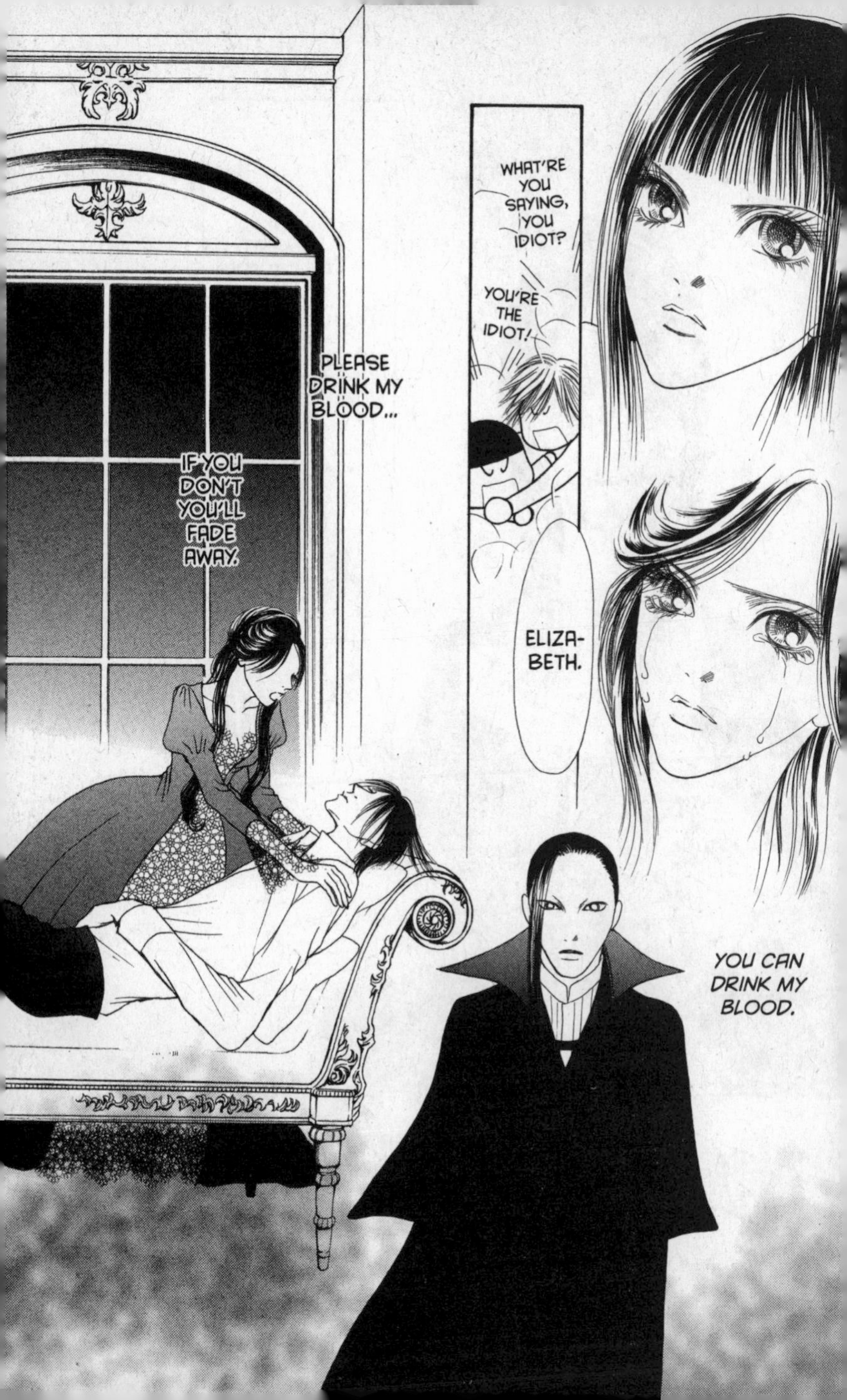
WHAT'RE YOU SAYING, YOU IDIOT?
YOU'RE THE IDIOT!
ELIZA-BETH.
YOU CAN DRINK MY BLOOD.
PLEASE DRINK MY BLOOD...
IF YOU DON'T YOU'LL FADE AWAY.

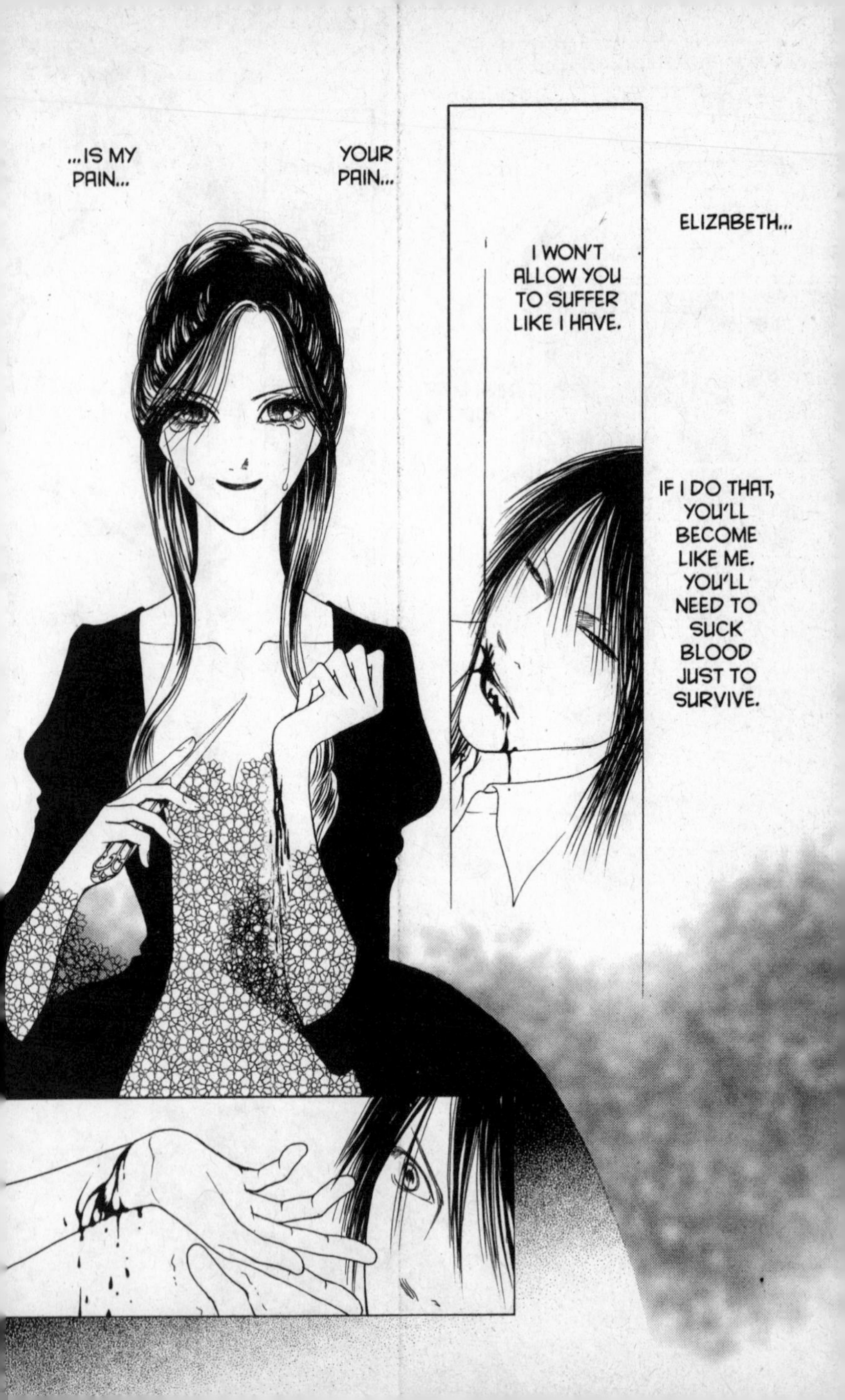
ELIZABETH...
I WON'T ALLOW YOU TO SUFFER LIKE I HAVE.
IF I DO THAT, YOU'LL BECOME LIKE ME. YOU'LL NEED TO SUCK BLOOD JUST TO SURVIVE.
YOUR PAIN...
...IS MY PAIN...

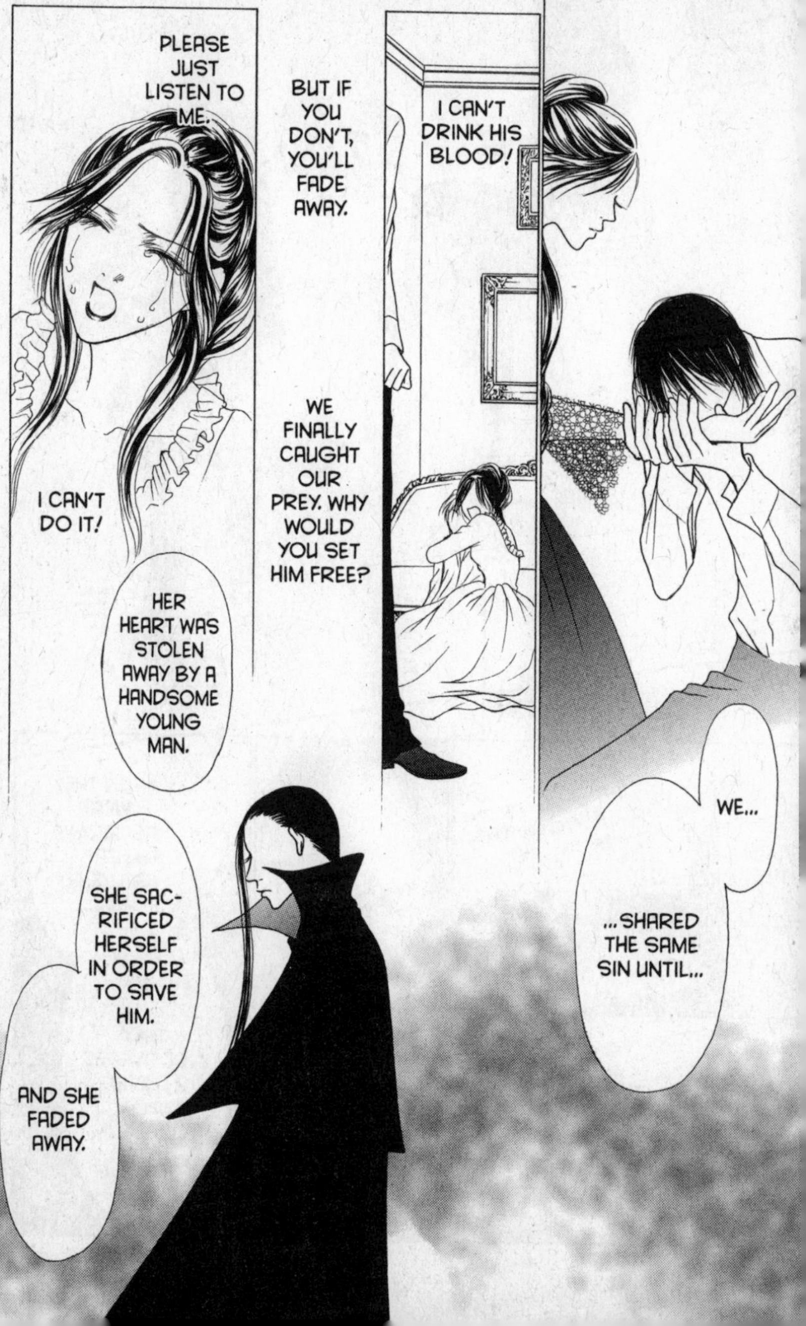
I CAN'T DRINK HIS BLOOD!
BUT IF YOU DON'T, YOU'LL FADE AWAY.
WE FINALLY CAUGHT OUR PREY. WHY WOULD YOU SET HIM FREE?
PLEASE JUST LISTEN TO ME.
I CAN'T DO IT!
HER HEART WAS STOLEN AWAY BY A HANDSOME YOUNG MAN.
WE...
...SHARED THE SAME SIN UNTIL...
SHE SACRIFICED HERSELF IN ORDER TO SAVE HIM.
AND SHE FADED AWAY.

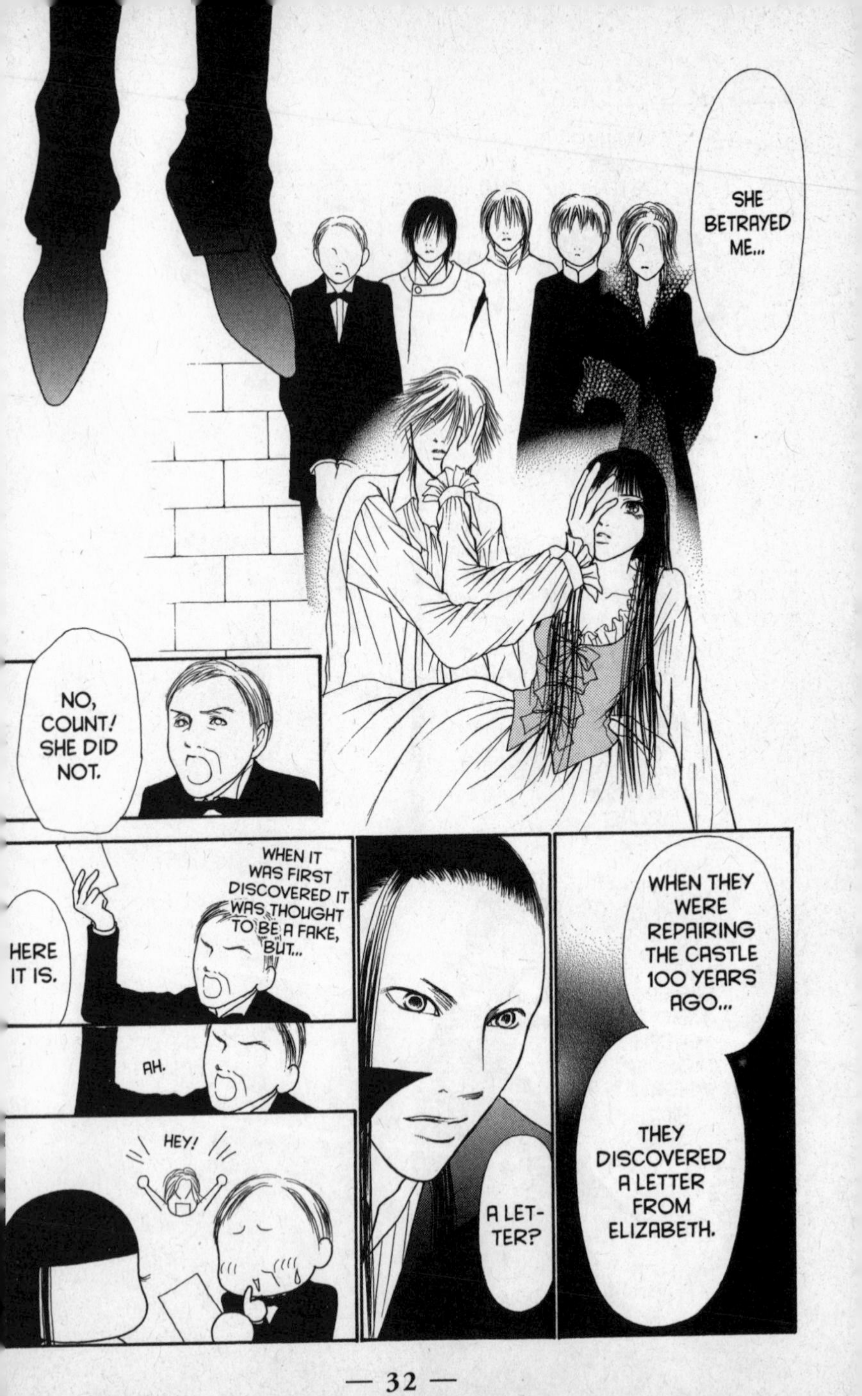
SHE BETRAYED ME...
NO, COUNT! SHE DID NOT.
WHEN THEY WERE REPAIRING THE CASTLE 100 YEARS AGO...
THEY DISCOVERED A LETTER FROM ELIZABETH.
A LET-TER?
WHEN IT WAS FIRST DISCOVERED IT WAS THOUGHT TO BE A FAKE, BUT...
HERE IT IS.
AH.
HEY!

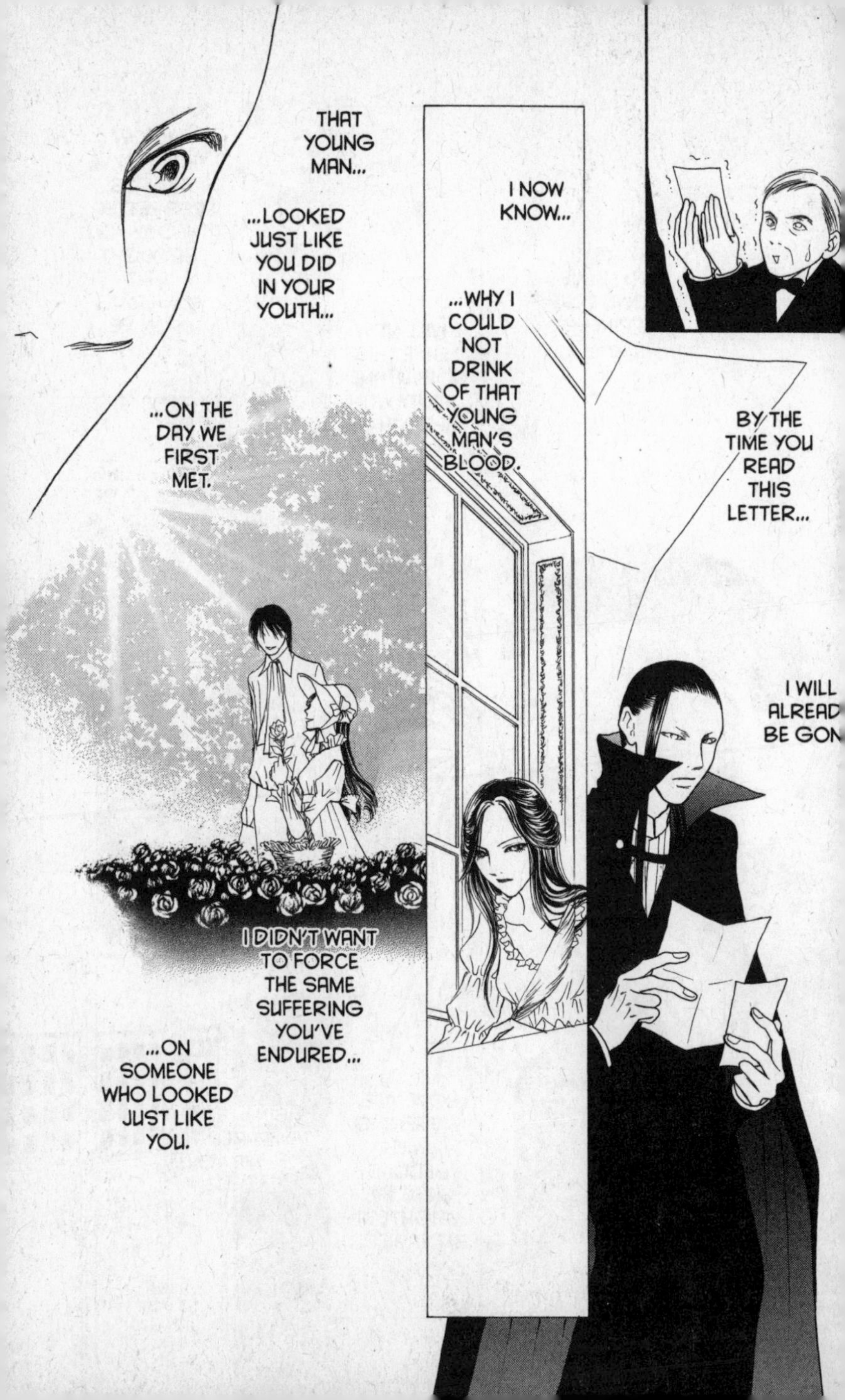
BY THE TIME YOU READ THIS LETTER...
I WILL ALREAD BE GON
I NOW KNOW...
...WHY I COULD NOT DRINK OF THAT YOUNG MAN'S BLOOD.
THAT YOUNG MAN...
...LOOKED JUST LIKE YOU DID IN YOUR YOUTH...
...ON THE DAY WE FIRST MET.
I DIDN'T WANT TO FORCE THE SAME SUFFERING YOU'VE ENDURED...
...ON SOMEONE WHO LOOKED JUST LIKE YOU.

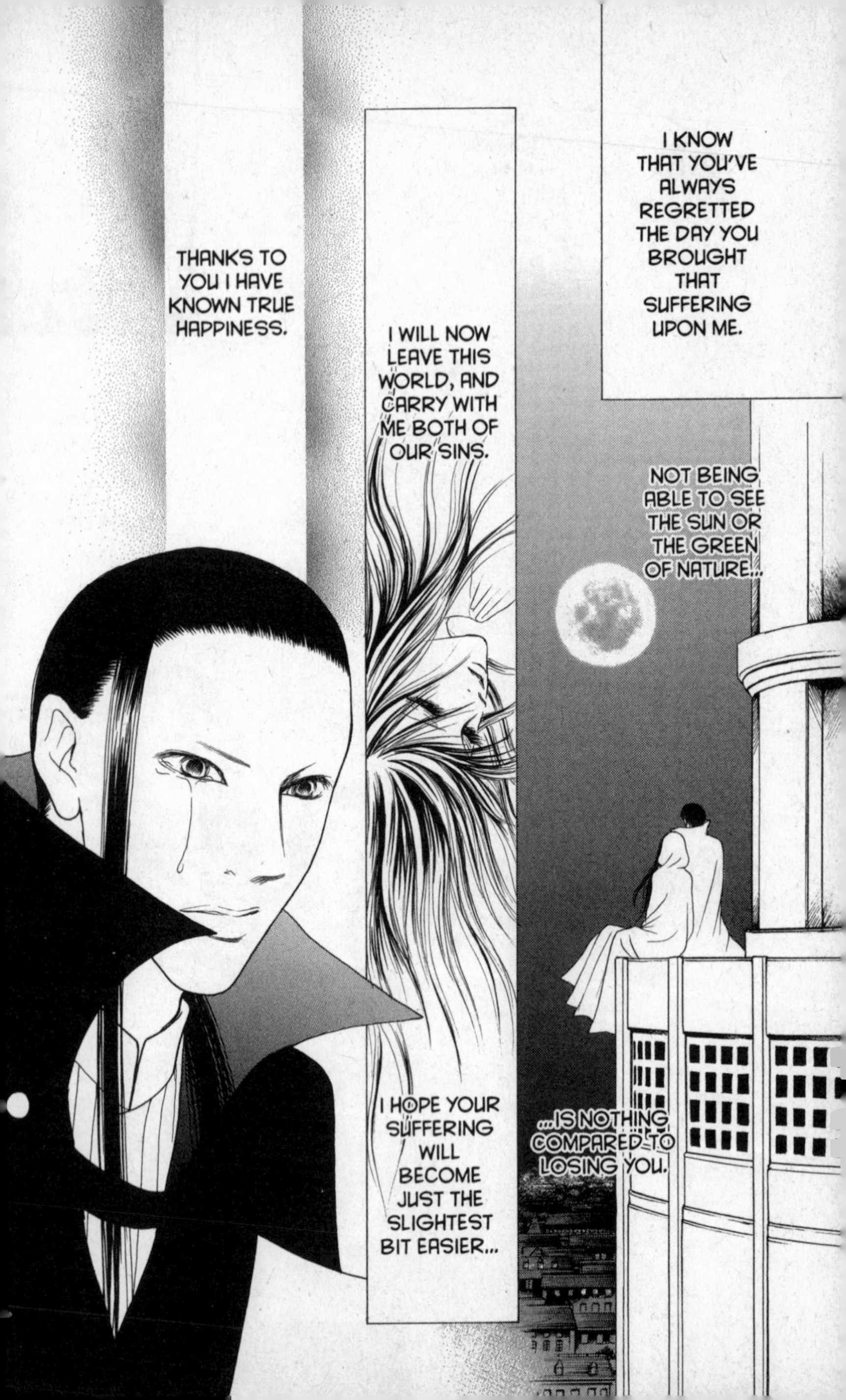
I KNOW THAT YOU'VE ALWAYS REGRETTED THE DAY YOU BROUGHT THAT SUFFERING UPON ME.
NOT BEING ABLE TO SEE THE SUN OR THE GREEN OF NATURE...
...IS NOTHING COMPARED TO LOSING YOU.
I WILL NOW LEAVE THIS WORLD, AND CARRY WITH ME BOTH OF OUR SINS.
I HOPE YOUR SUFFERING WILL BECOME JUST THE SLIGHTEST BIT EASIER...
THANKS TO YOU I HAVE KNOWN TRUE HAPPINESS.

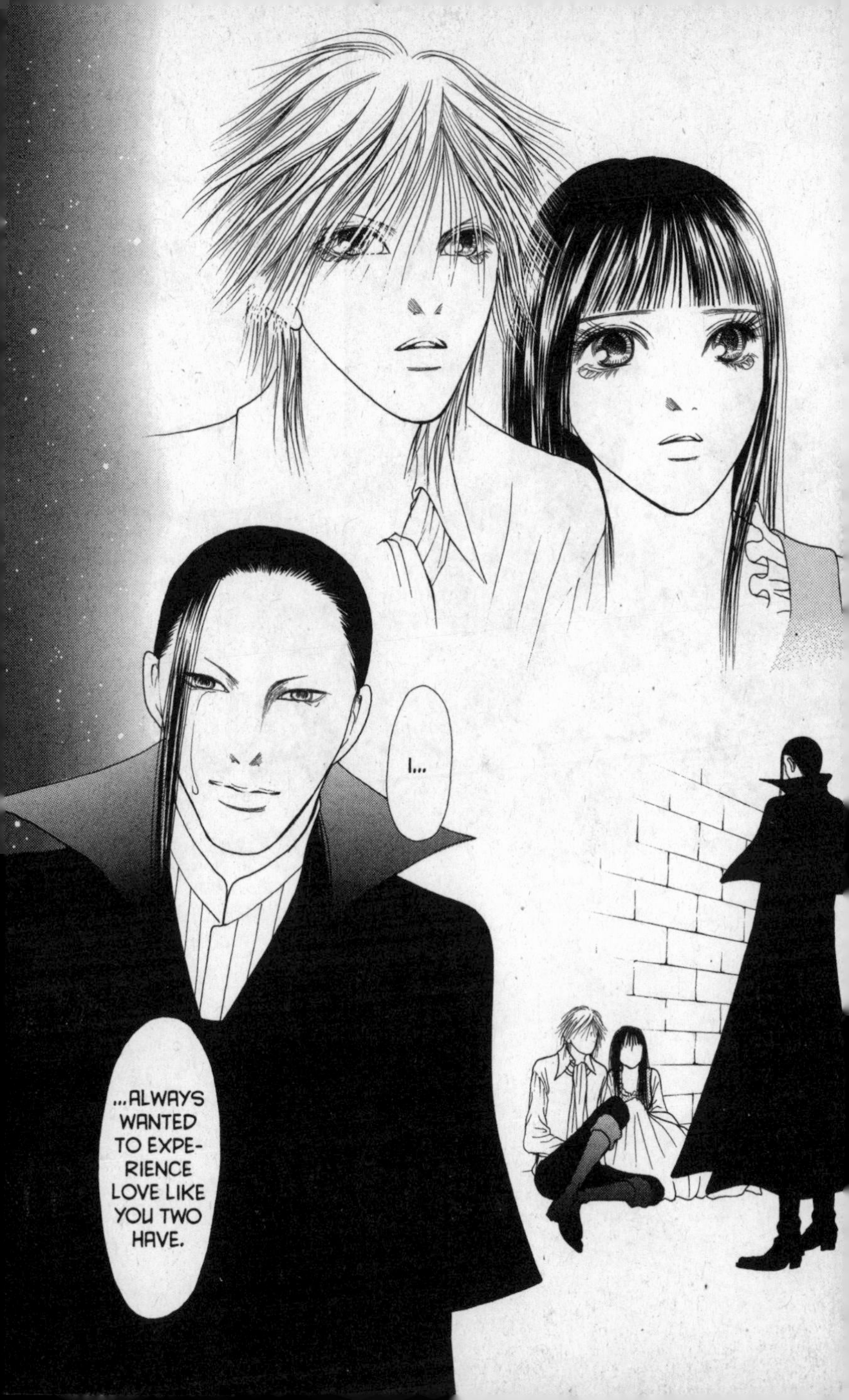
I...
...ALWAYS WANTED TO EXPE-RIENCE LOVE LIKE YOU TWO HAVE.

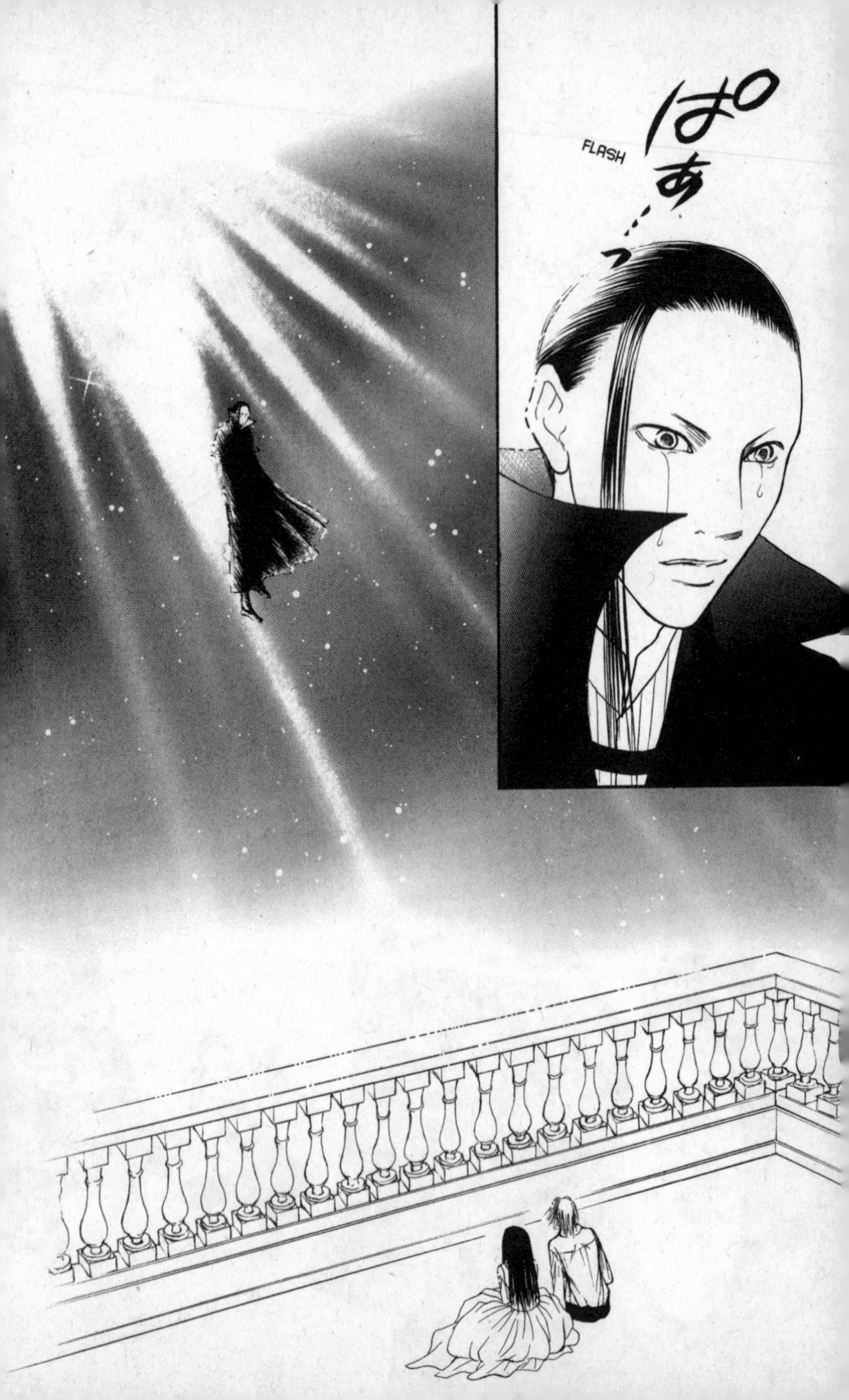
ぱぁ…っ
FLASH

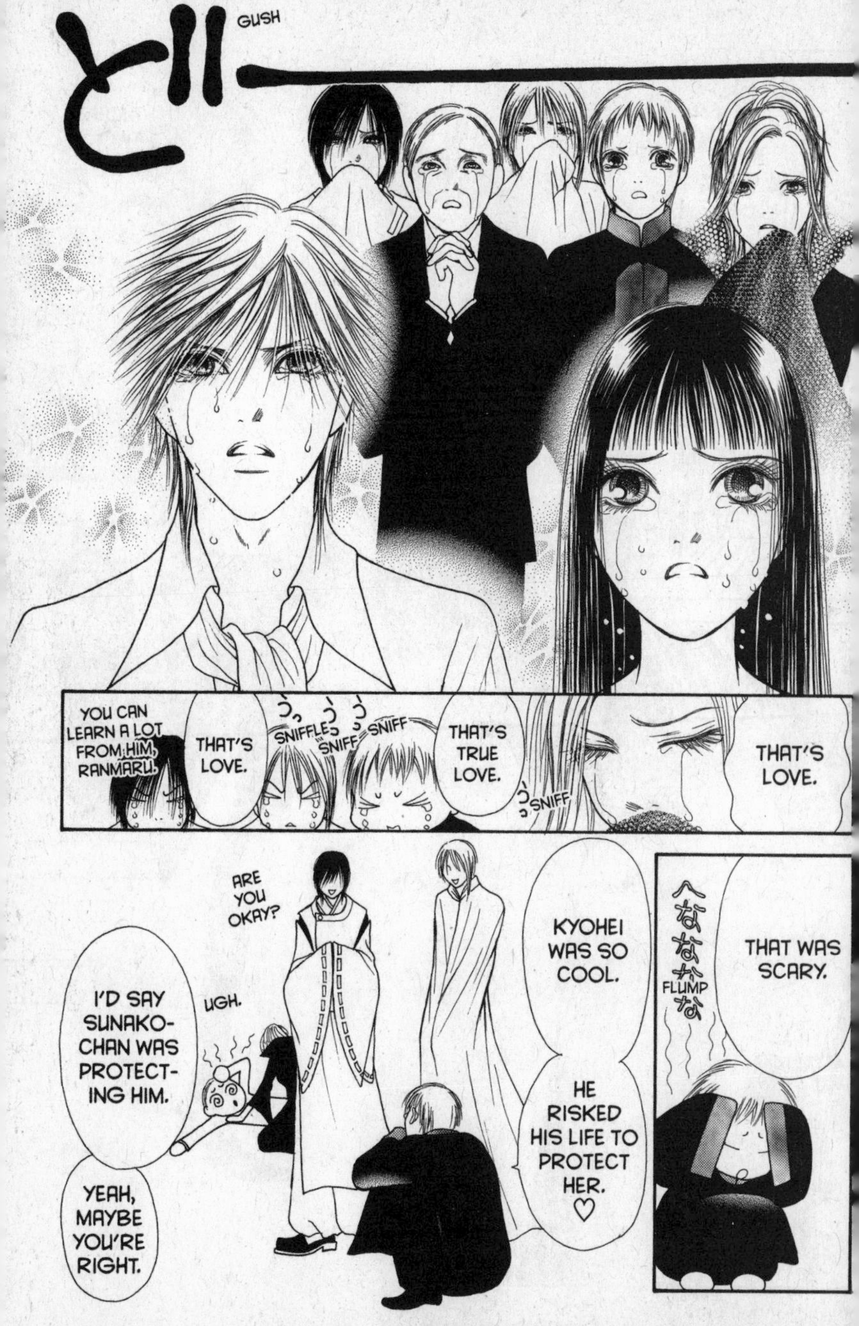

とーー
GUSH
THAT'S LOVE.
SNIFF
THAT'S TRUE LOVE.
SNIFFLE SNIFF SNIFF
THAT'S LOVE.
YOU CAN LEARN A LOT FROM HIM, RANMARU.
THAT WAS SCARY.
へなななな
FLUMP
KYOHEI WAS SO COOL.
HE RISKED HIS LIFE TO PROTECT HER. ♡
ARE YOU OKAY?
I'D SAY SUNAKO-CHAN WAS PROTECTING HIM.
UGH.
YEAH, MAYBE YOU'RE RIGHT.

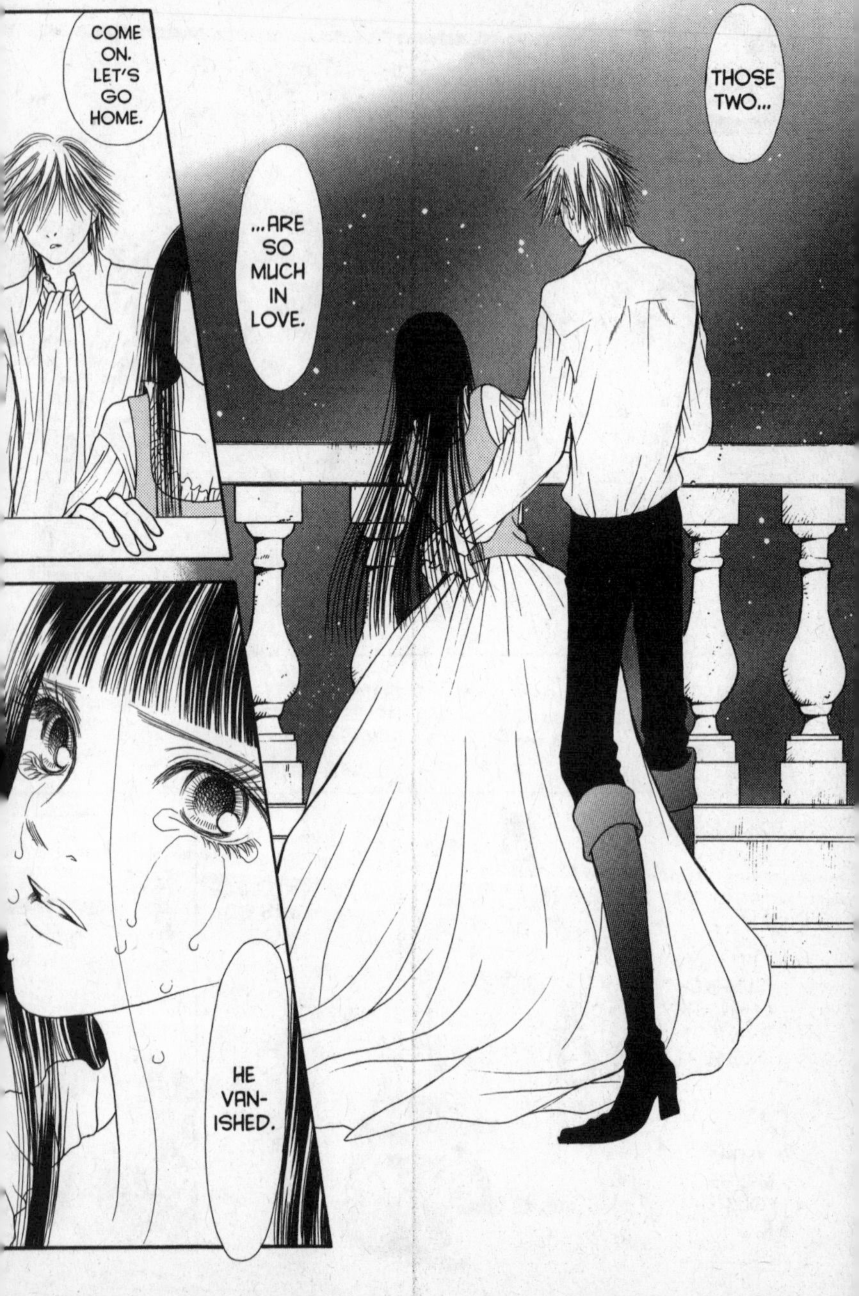
THOSE TWO...
...ARE SO MUCH IN LOVE.
COME ON. LET'S GO HOME.
HE VAN-ISHED.

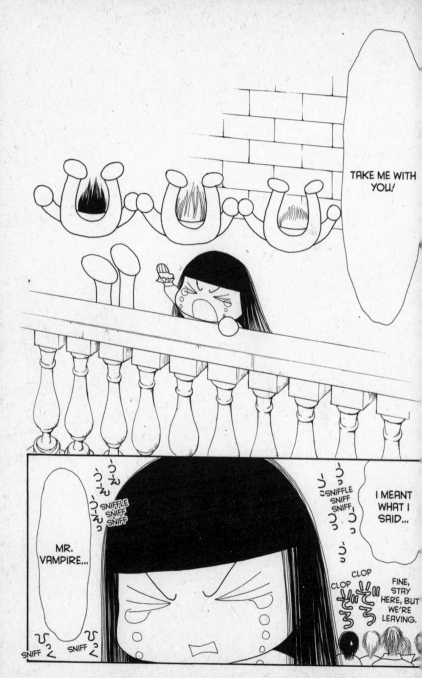

TAKE ME WITH YOU!

MR. VAMPIRE...

SNIFFLE SNIFF SNIFF

SNIFFLE SNIFF SNIFF

I MEANT WHAT I SAID...

SNIFF

SNIFF

CLOP CLOP

FINE, STAY HERE, BUT WE'RE LEAVING.

Chapter 93

WELCOME FUCKIN' XMAS NIGHT

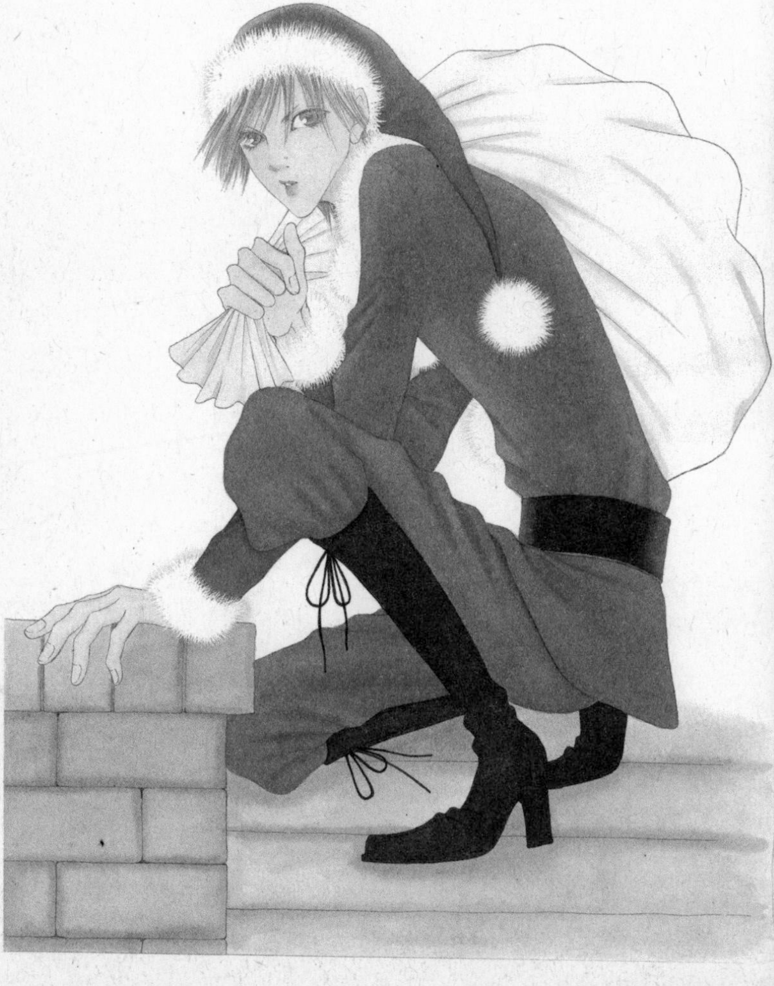

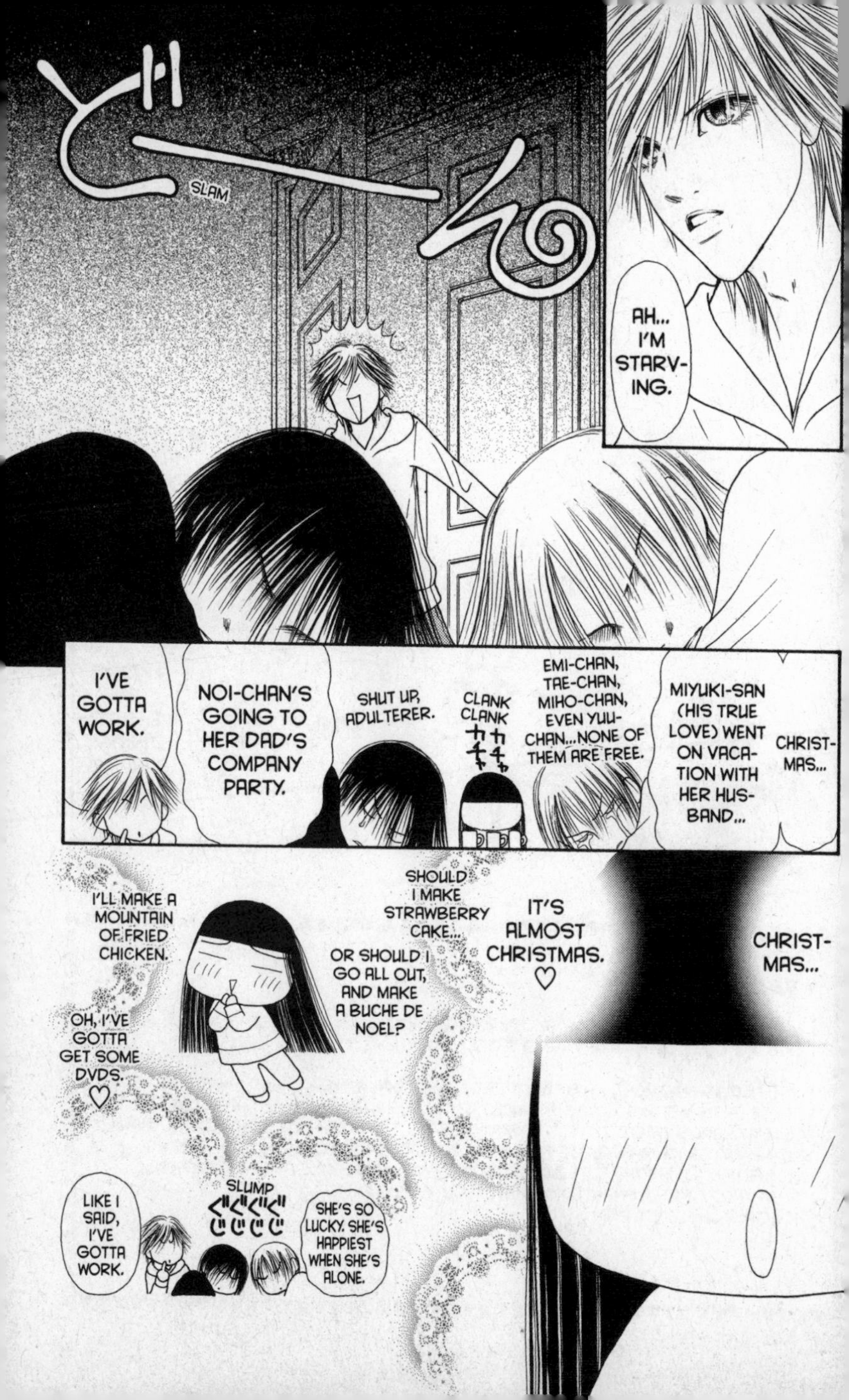
AH... I'M STARVING.
SLAM
CHRISTMAS...
MIYUKI-SAN (HIS TRUE LOVE) WENT ON VACATION WITH HER HUSBAND...
EMI-CHAN, TAE-CHAN, MIHO-CHAN, EVEN YUU-CHAN...NONE OF THEM ARE FREE.
CLANK CLANK
SHUT UP, ADULTERER.
NOI-CHAN'S GOING TO HER DAD'S COMPANY PARTY.
I'VE GOTTA WORK.
CHRISTMAS...
IT'S ALMOST CHRISTMAS. ♡
SHOULD I MAKE STRAWBERRY CAKE...
OR SHOULD I GO ALL OUT, AND MAKE A BUCHE DE NOEL?
I'LL MAKE A MOUNTAIN OF FRIED CHICKEN.
OH, I'VE GOTTA GET SOME DVDS. ♡
SHE'S SO LUCKY. SHE'S HAPPIEST WHEN SHE'S ALONE.
SLUMP
LIKE I SAID, I'VE GOTTA WORK.

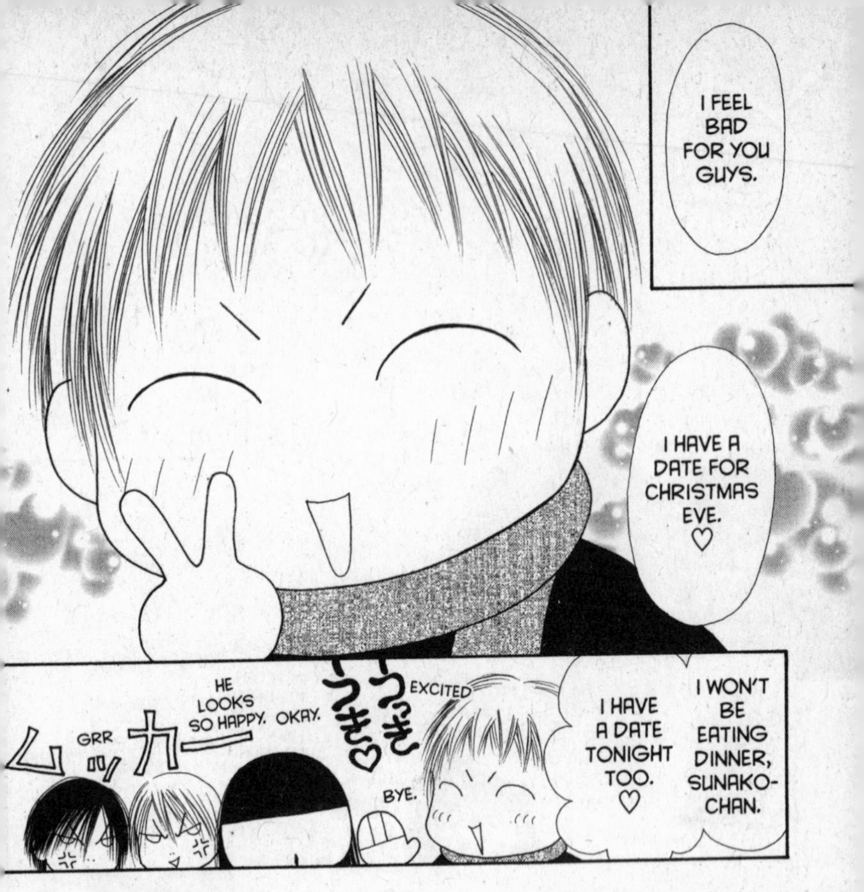
I FEEL BAD FOR YOU GUYS.
I HAVE A DATE FOR CHRISTMAS EVE. ♡
I WON'T BE EATING DINNER, SUNAKO-CHAN.
I HAVE A DATE TONIGHT TOO. ♡
うっきうっき♡
EXCITED
BYE.
OKAY.
HE LOOKS SO HAPPY.
ムッカー
GRR

BEHIND THE SCENES

I WAS TRYING TO THINK OF A CHRISTMAS STORY TO GO WITH THE SEASON, BUT I JUST COULDN'T COME UP WITH ANYTHING GOOD. BUT THEN...

I LISTENED TO NEW ROTE'KA'S "WELCOME FUCKIN' XMAS NIGHT," AND I WAS LIKE "THAT'S IT! THAT'S EXACTLY WHAT I NEEDED." AND SUDDENLY THE STORY FLOWED FROM MY HANDS EFFORTLESSLY. ♥ WHAT GREAT LYRICS. WHAT A GREAT SONG. THANK YOU, NEW ROTE'KA-SAN. I LOVE YOU. ♥ ♥ ♥ THE CHRISTMAS CAKE IN THIS STORY WAS INFLUENCED BY THE CUTE BIRTHDAY CAKE NEW ROTE'KA'S A-CHAN GOT FOR HIS BIRTHDAY PARTY. I WANTED TO HAVE A CLOWN ON THE CAKE INSTEAD OF SANTA THOUGH. ♥ JUST KIDDING.

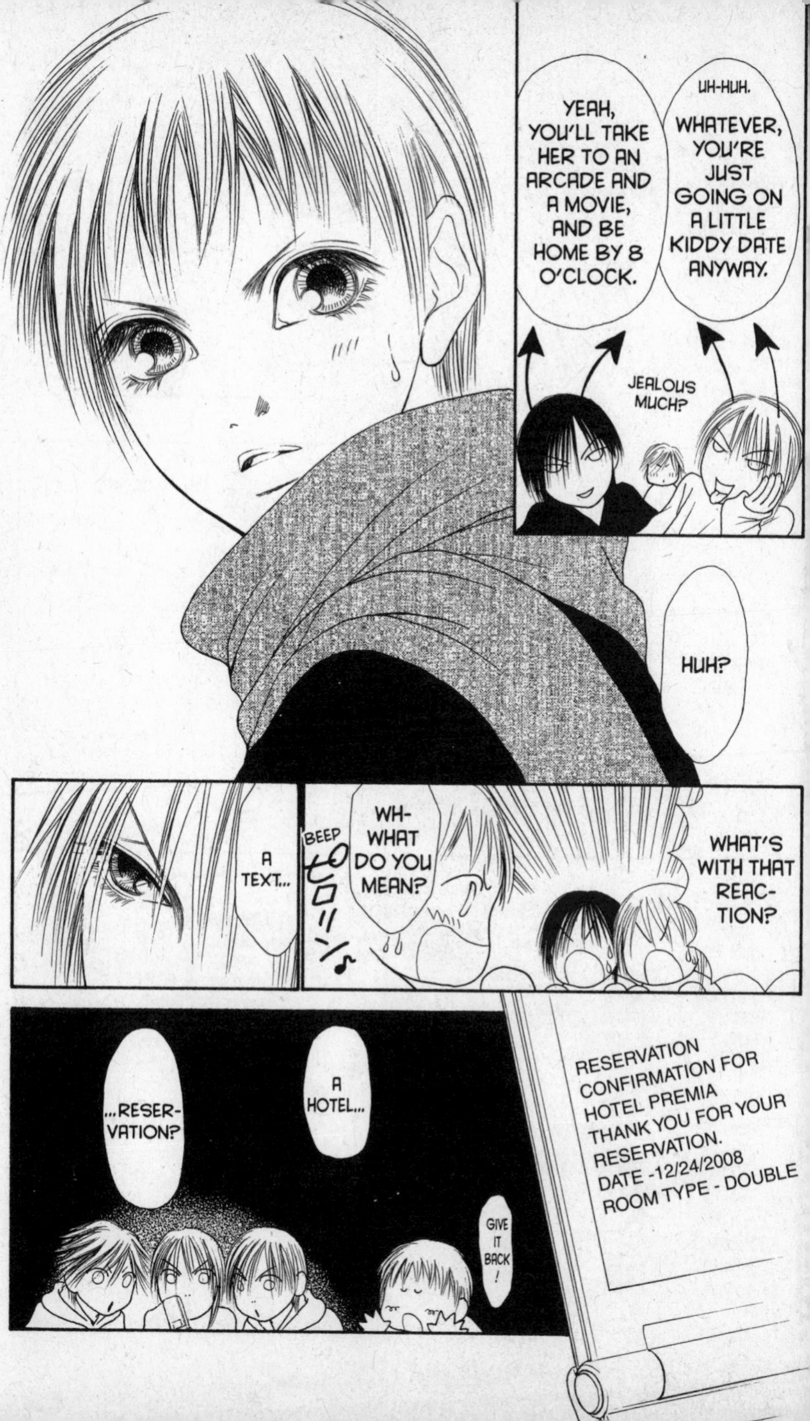
UH-HUH.
WHATEVER, YOU'RE JUST GOING ON A LITTLE KIDDY DATE ANYWAY.
YEAH, YOU'LL TAKE HER TO AN ARCADE AND A MOVIE, AND BE HOME BY 8 O'CLOCK.
JEALOUS MUCH?
HUH?
WHAT'S WITH THAT REAC-TION?
WH- WHAT DO YOU MEAN?
BEEP
A TEXT...
RESERVATION CONFIRMATION FOR HOTEL PREMIA THANK YOU FOR YOUR RESERVATION. DATE -12/24/2008 ROOM TYPE - DOUBLE
GIVE IT BACK!
A HOTEL...
...RESER-VATION?

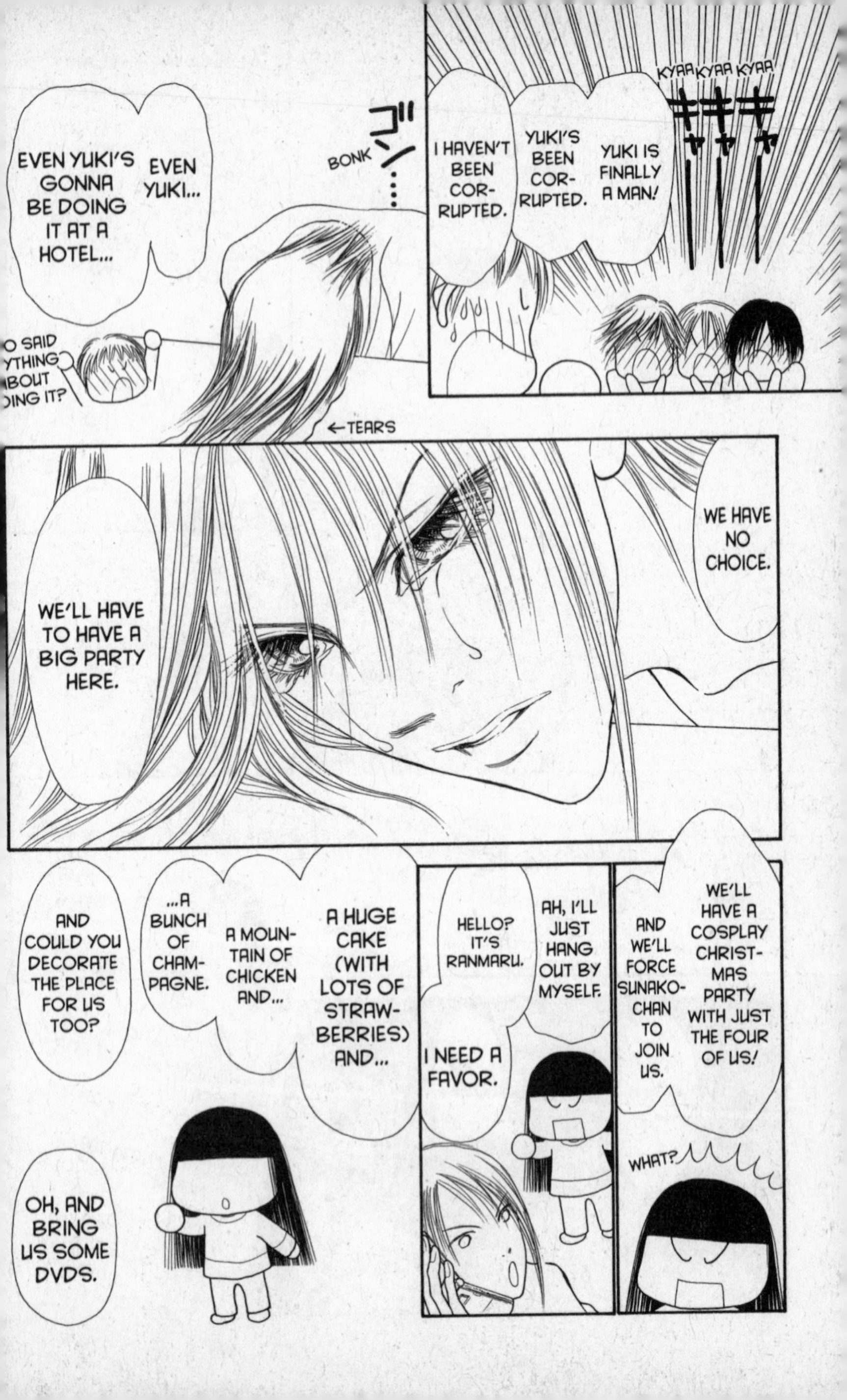
KYAA KYAA KYAA
YUKI IS FINALLY A MAN!
YUKI'S BEEN COR-RUPTED.
I HAVEN'T BEEN COR-RUPTED.
BONK
EVEN YUKI...
EVEN YUKI'S GONNA BE DOING IT AT A HOTEL...
O SAID YTHING BOUT OING IT?
←TEARS
WE HAVE NO CHOICE.
WE'LL HAVE TO HAVE A BIG PARTY HERE.
WE'LL HAVE A COSPLAY CHRIST-MAS PARTY WITH JUST THE FOUR OF US!
AND WE'LL FORCE SUNAKO-CHAN TO JOIN US.
WHAT?
AH, I'LL JUST HANG OUT BY MYSELF.
HELLO? IT'S RANMARU.
I NEED A FAVOR.
A HUGE CAKE (WITH LOTS OF STRAW-BERRIES) AND...
A MOUN-TAIN OF CHICKEN AND...
...A BUNCH OF CHAM-PAGNE.
AND COULD YOU DECORATE THE PLACE FOR US TOO?
OH, AND BRING US SOME DVDS.

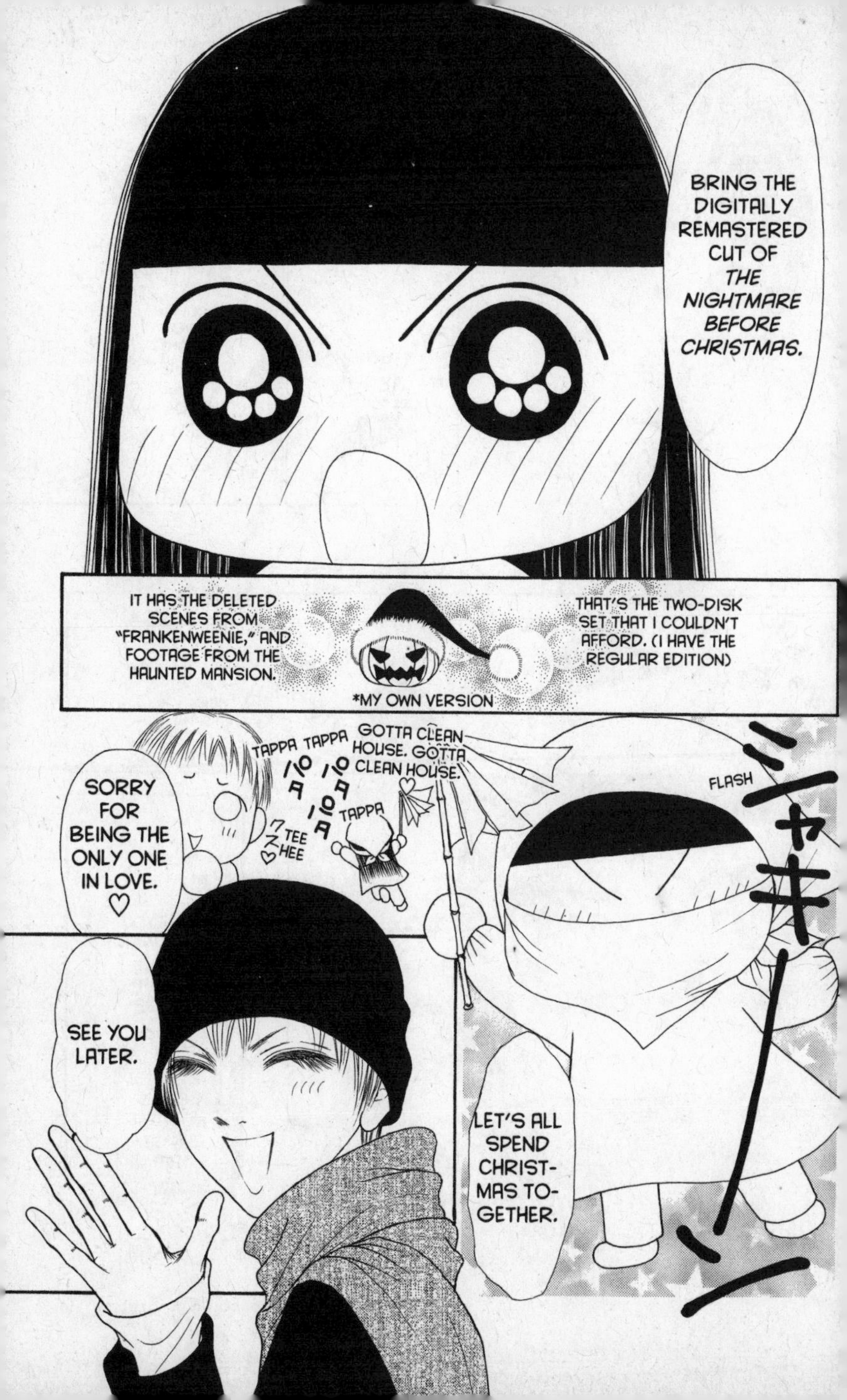
BRING THE DIGITALLY REMASTERED CUT OF *THE NIGHTMARE BEFORE CHRISTMAS.*
THAT'S THE TWO-DISK SET THAT I COULDN'T AFFORD. (I HAVE THE REGULAR EDITION)
IT HAS THE DELETED SCENES FROM "FRANKENWEENIE," AND FOOTAGE FROM THE HAUNTED MANSION.
*MY OWN VERSION
FLASH
シャキーン
LET'S ALL SPEND CHRIST-MAS TO-GETHER.
GOTTA CLEAN HOUSE. GOTTA CLEAN HOUSE.
TAPPA TAPPA
パタパタ
パタ
TAPPA
クス♡
TEE HEE
SORRY FOR BEING THE ONLY ONE IN LOVE. ♡
SEE YOU LATER.

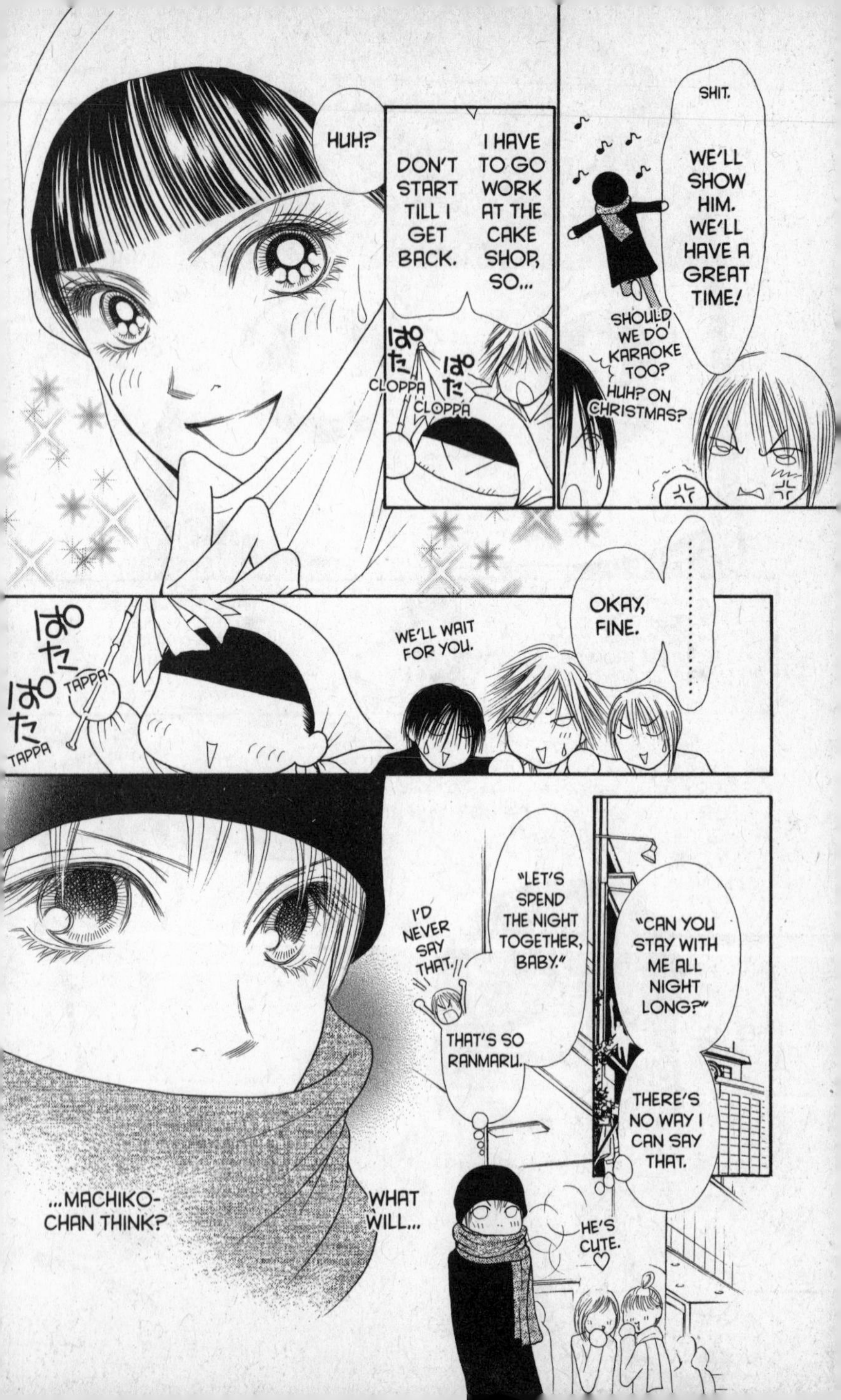
SHIT.
WE'LL SHOW HIM. WE'LL HAVE A GREAT TIME!
SHOULD WE DO KARAOKE TOO?
HUH? ON CHRISTMAS?
I HAVE TO GO WORK AT THE CAKE SHOP, SO...
DON'T START TILL I GET BACK.
ぱた
CLOPPA
ぱた
CLOPPA
HUH?
......
OKAY, FINE.
WE'LL WAIT FOR YOU.
ぱた
TAPPA
ぱた
TAPPA
"CAN YOU STAY WITH ME ALL NIGHT LONG?"
THERE'S NO WAY I CAN SAY THAT.
HE'S CUTE.
"LET'S SPEND THE NIGHT TOGETHER, BABY."
I'D NEVER SAY THAT.
THAT'S SO RANMARU.
WHAT WILL...
...MACHIKO-CHAN THINK?

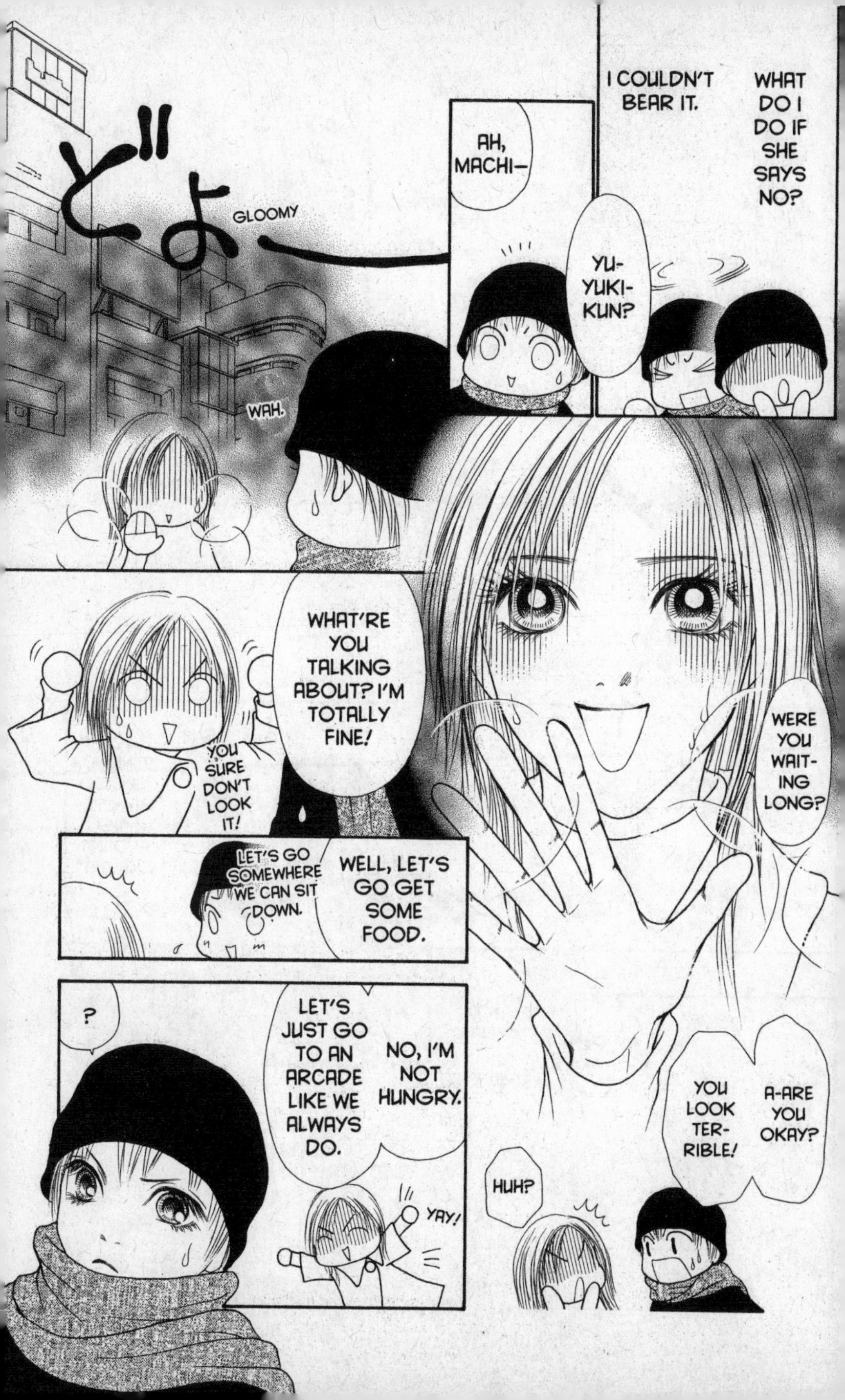
WHAT DO I DO IF SHE SAYS NO?
I COULDN'T BEAR IT.
AH, MACHI—
YU-YUKI-KUN?
どよ〜
GLOOMY
WAH.
WERE YOU WAITING LONG?
A-ARE YOU OKAY?
YOU LOOK TERRIBLE!
HUH?
WHAT'RE YOU TALKING ABOUT? I'M TOTALLY FINE!
YOU SURE DON'T LOOK IT!
WELL, LET'S GO GET SOME FOOD.
LET'S GO SOMEWHERE WE CAN SIT DOWN.
NO, I'M NOT HUNGRY.
LET'S JUST GO TO AN ARCADE LIKE WE ALWAYS DO.
?
YAY!

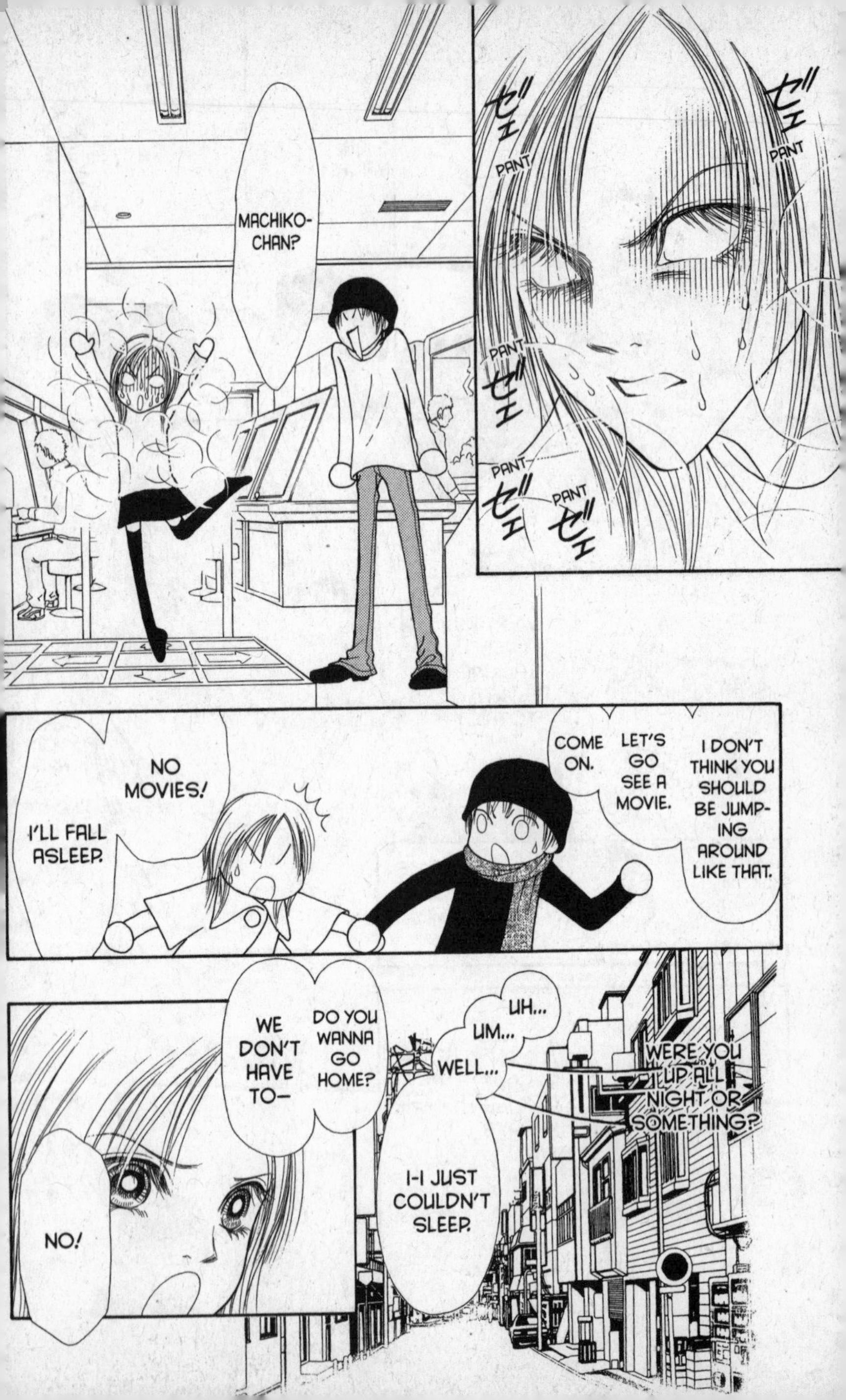
ゼェ
PANT
ゼェ
PANT
PANT
ゼェ
PANT
ゼェ
PANT
ゼェ
MACHIKO-CHAN?
I DON'T THINK YOU SHOULD BE JUMP-ING AROUND LIKE THAT.
LET'S GO SEE A MOVIE.
COME ON.
NO MOVIES!
I'LL FALL ASLEEP.
WERE YOU UP ALL NIGHT OR SOMETHING?
UH...
UM...
WELL...
I-I JUST COULDN'T SLEEP.
DO YOU WANNA GO HOME?
WE DON'T HAVE TO—
NO!

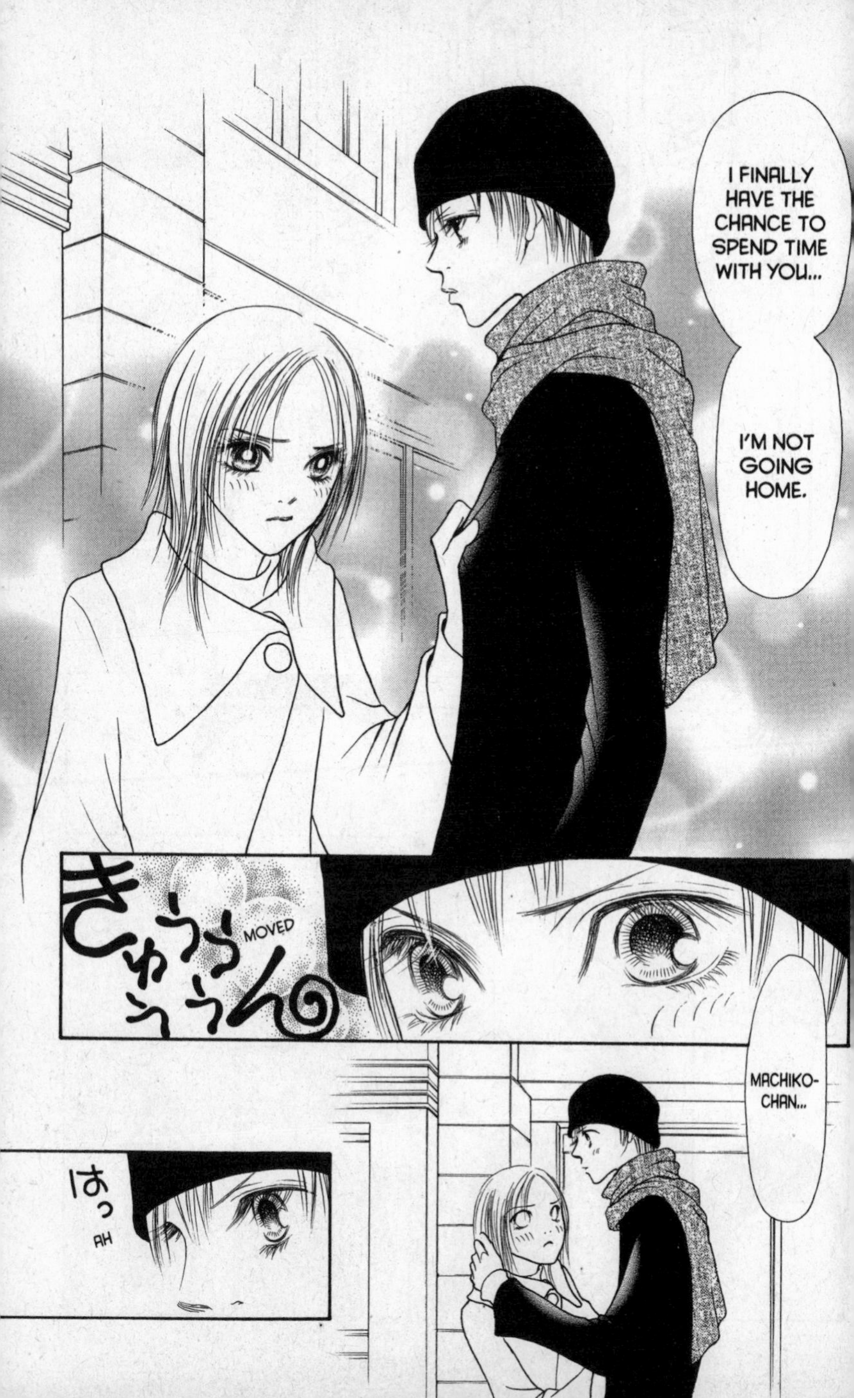
I FINALLY HAVE THE CHANCE TO SPEND TIME WITH YOU...
I'M NOT GOING HOME.
きゅううん
MOVED
MACHIKO-CHAN...
はっ
AH

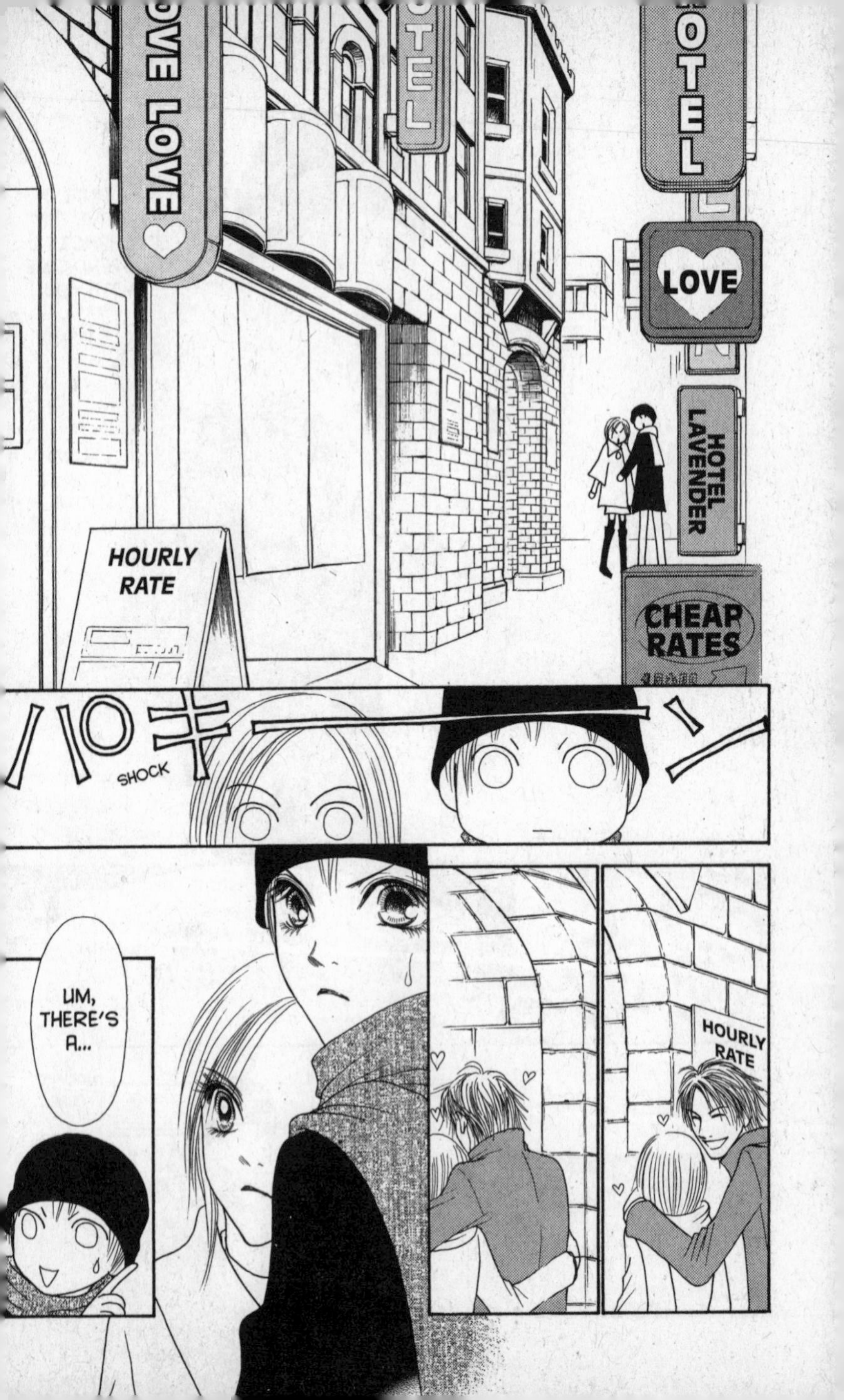
HOTEL
LOVE
HOTEL LAVENDER
CHEAP RATES
OVE LOVE
HOURLY RATE
SHOCK
HOURLY RATE
UM, THERE'S A...

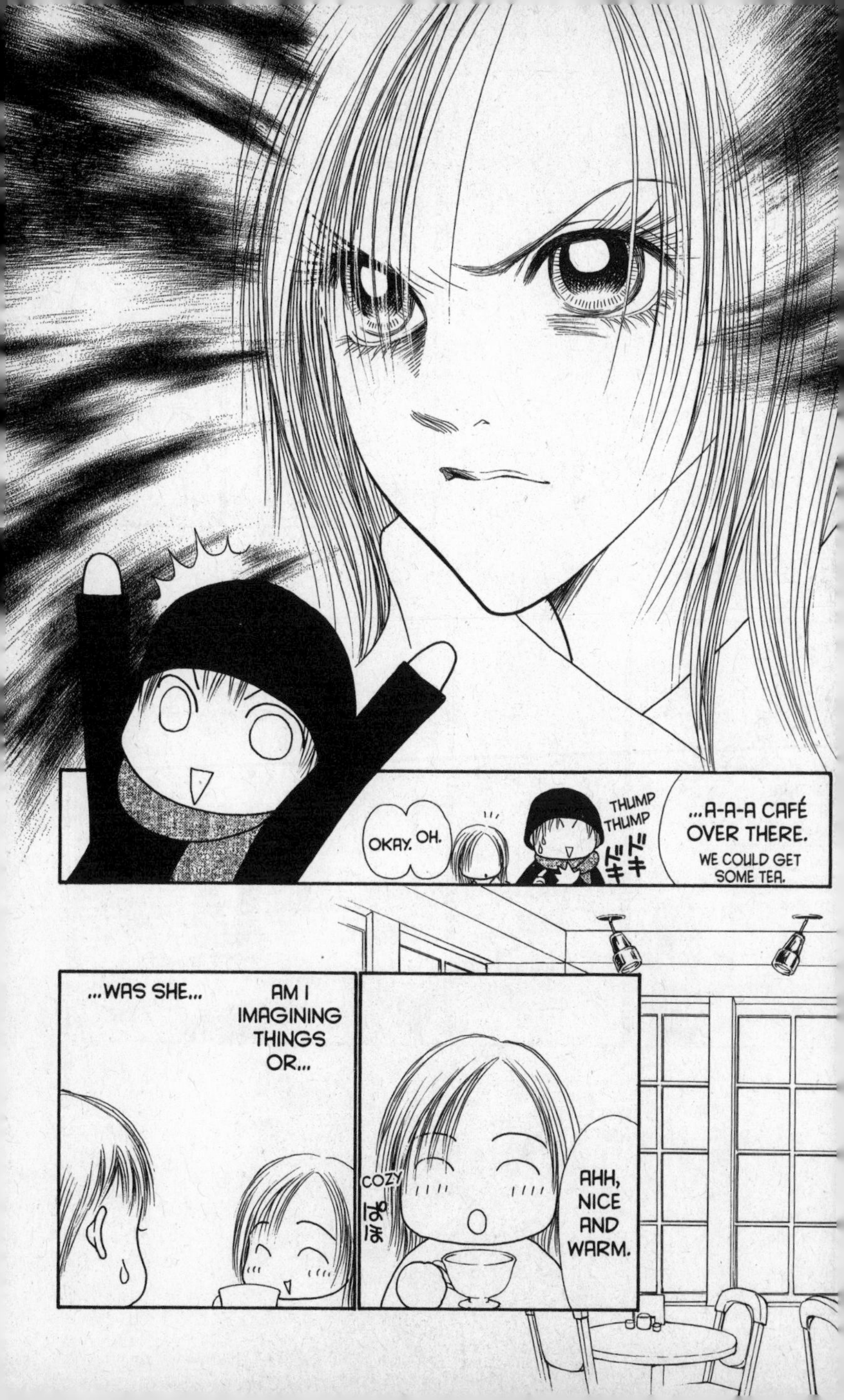
...A-A-A CAFÉ OVER THERE.
WE COULD GET SOME TEA.
THUMP THUMP
ドキドキ
OH.
OKAY.
AHH, NICE AND WARM.
COZY
ぽほ
AM I IMAGINING THINGS OR...
...WAS SHE...

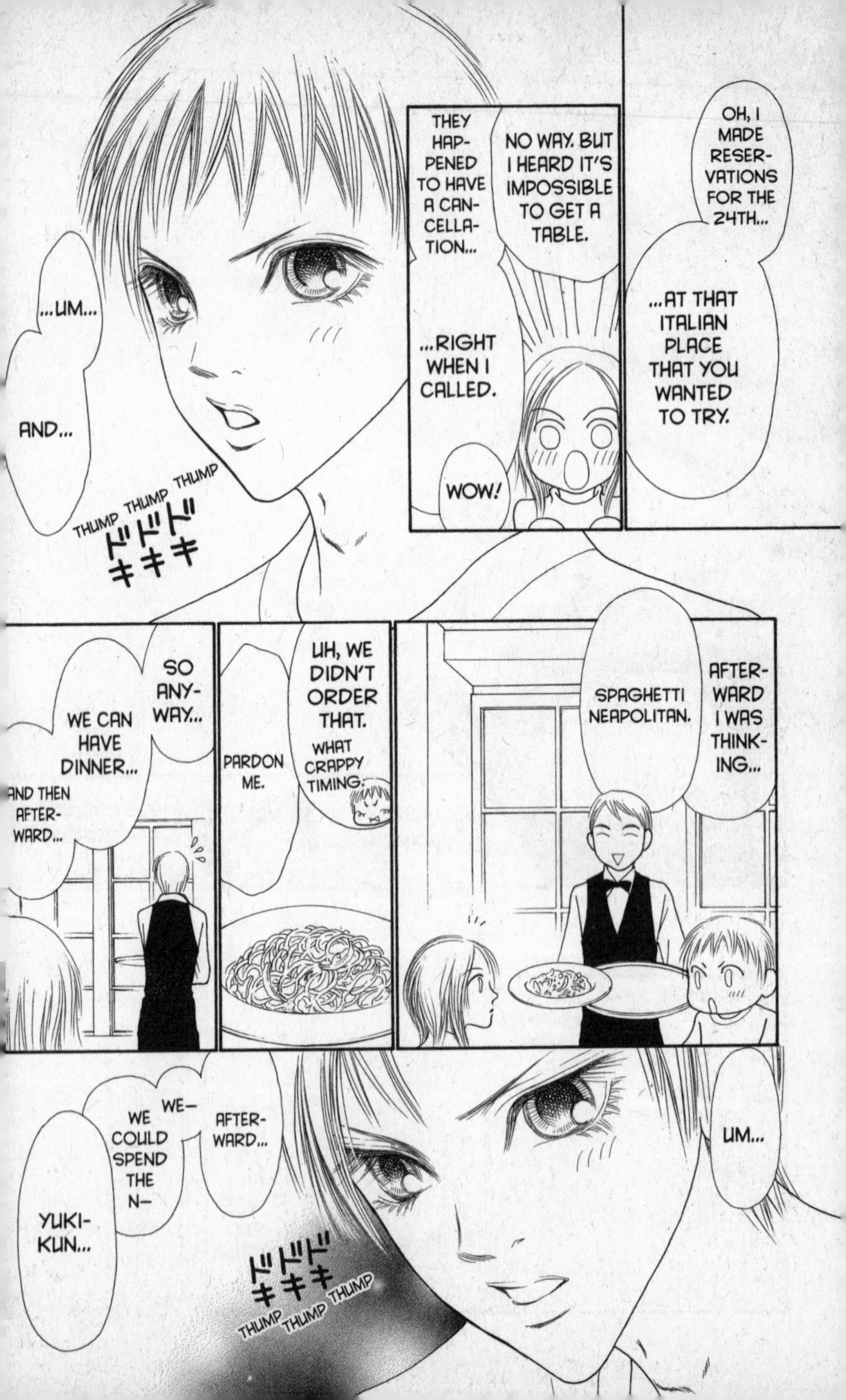
OH, I MADE RESER-VATIONS FOR THE 24TH...
...AT THAT ITALIAN PLACE THAT YOU WANTED TO TRY.
NO WAY. BUT I HEARD IT'S IMPOSSIBLE TO GET A TABLE.
THEY HAP-PENED TO HAVE A CAN-CELLA-TION...
...RIGHT WHEN I CALLED.
WOW!
...UM...
AND...
ドドドキキキ
THUMP THUMP THUMP
AFTER-WARD I WAS THINK-ING...
SPAGHETTI NEAPOLITAN.
UH, WE DIDN'T ORDER THAT.
WHAT CRAPPY TIMING.
PARDON ME.
SO ANY-WAY...
WE CAN HAVE DINNER...
AND THEN AFTER-WARD...
UM...
AFTER-WARD...
WE-
WE COULD SPEND THE N-
YUKI-KUN...
ドドドキキキ
THUMP THUMP THUMP

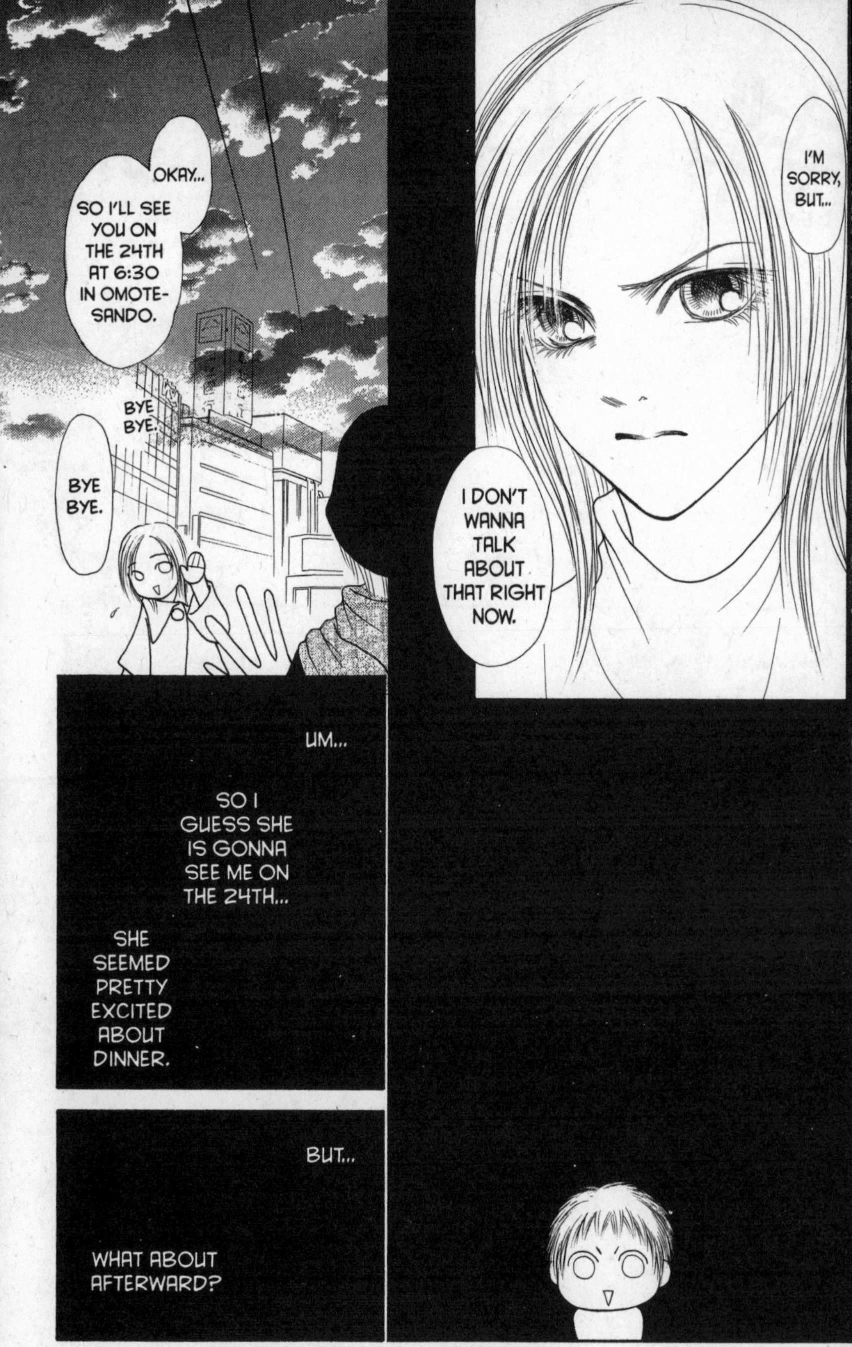
I'M SORRY, BUT...
I DON'T WANNA TALK ABOUT THAT RIGHT NOW.
OKAY...
SO I'LL SEE YOU ON THE 24TH AT 6:30 IN OMOTE-SANDO.
BYE BYE.
BYE BYE.
UM...
SO I GUESS SHE IS GONNA SEE ME ON THE 24TH...
SHE SEEMED PRETTY EXCITED ABOUT DINNER.
BUT...
WHAT ABOUT AFTERWARD?

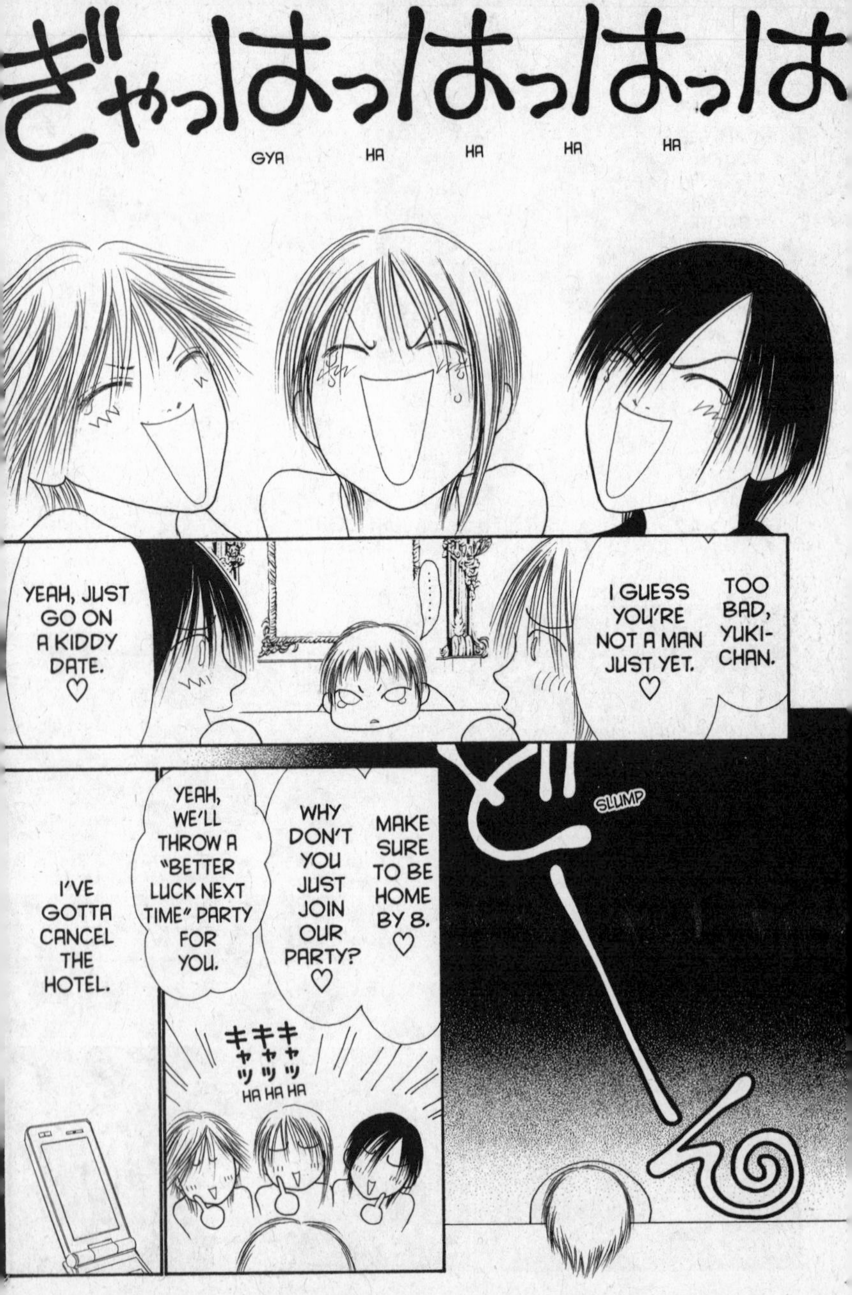
ぎゃっはっはっはっは
GYA HA HA HA HA
TOO BAD, YUKI-CHAN.
I GUESS YOU'RE NOT A MAN JUST YET. ♡
. . . . .
YEAH, JUST GO ON A KIDDY DATE. ♡
どーん
SLUMP
MAKE SURE TO BE HOME BY 8. ♡
WHY DON'T YOU JUST JOIN OUR PARTY? ♡
YEAH, WE'LL THROW A "BETTER LUCK NEXT TIME" PARTY FOR YOU.
キャッ キャッ キャッ
HA HA HA
I'VE GOTTA CANCEL THE HOTEL.

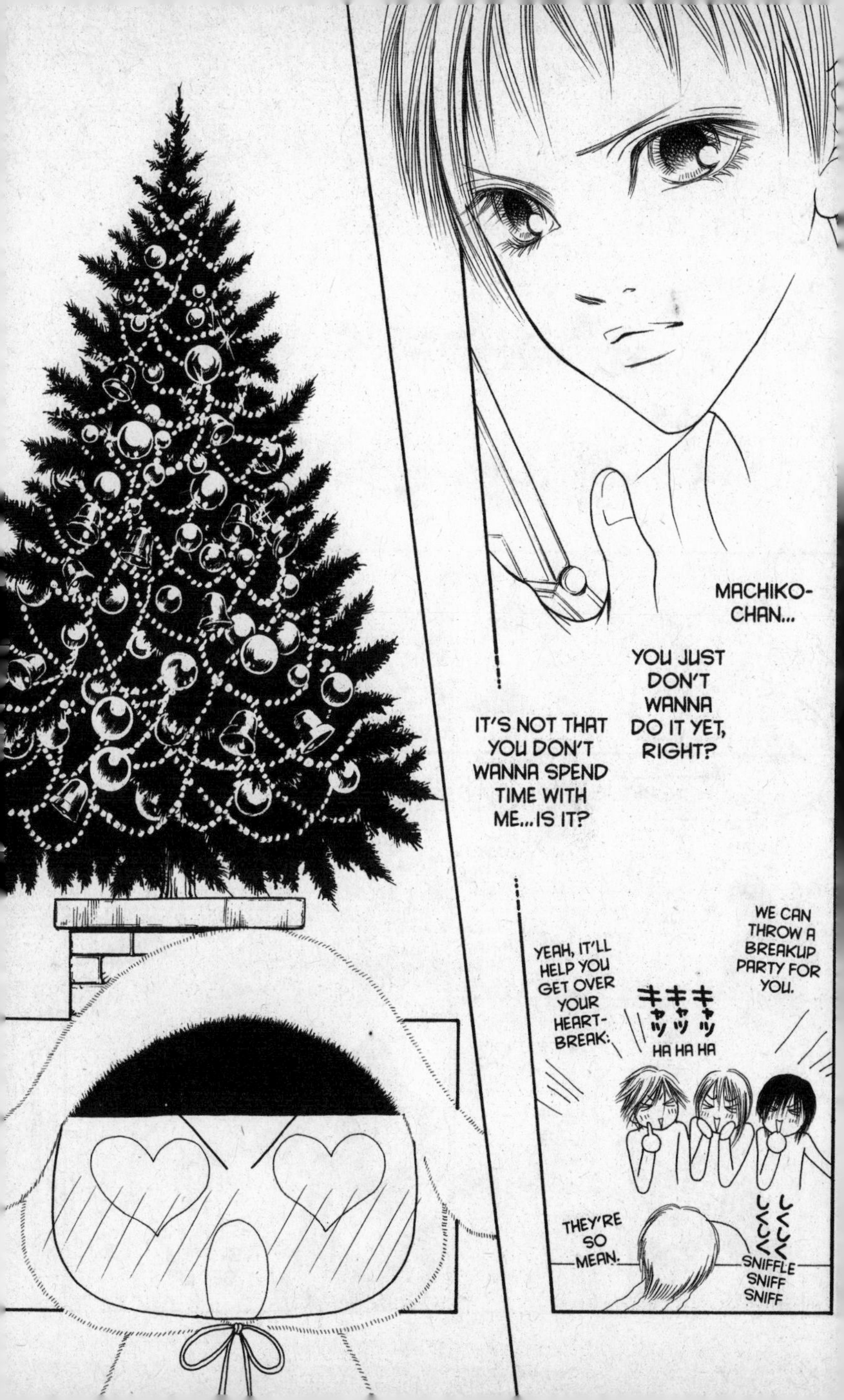
MACHIKO-CHAN...
YOU JUST DON'T WANNA DO IT YET, RIGHT?
IT'S NOT THAT YOU DON'T WANNA SPEND TIME WITH ME...IS IT?
WE CAN THROW A BREAKUP PARTY FOR YOU.
キャッ キャッ キャッ
HA HA HA
YEAH, IT'LL HELP YOU GET OVER YOUR HEART-BREAK.
しくしく しくしく
SNIFFLE SNIFF SNIFF
THEY'RE SO MEAN.

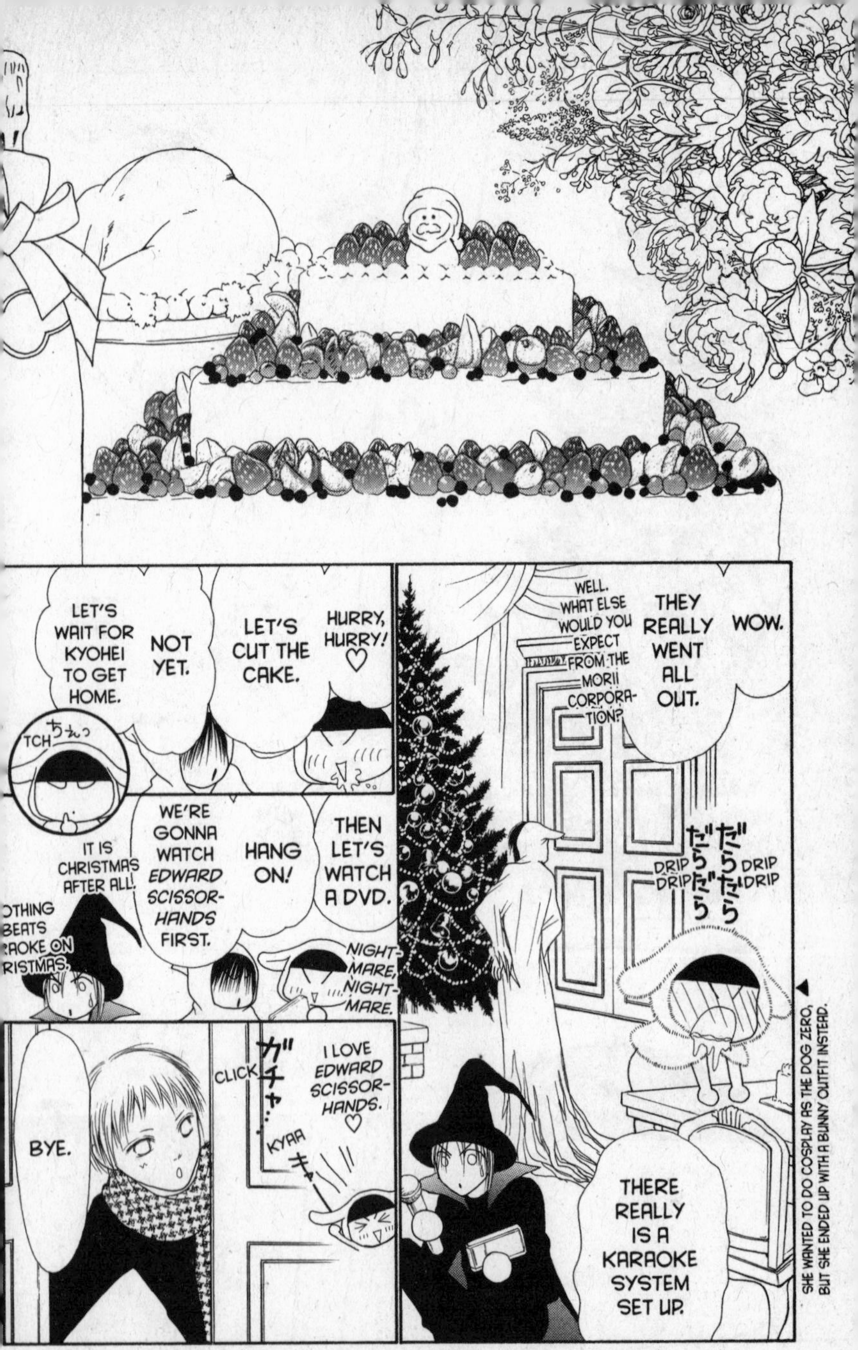
WOW.
THEY REALLY WENT ALL OUT.
WELL. WHAT ELSE WOULD YOU EXPECT FROM THE MORII CORPORATION?
DRIP DRIP だらだら
DRIP DRIP だらだら
THERE REALLY IS A KARAOKE SYSTEM SET UP.
HURRY, HURRY! ♡
LET'S CUT THE CAKE.
NOT YET.
LET'S WAIT FOR KYOHEI TO GET HOME.
TCH ちぇっ
THEN LET'S WATCH A DVD.
HANG ON!
WE'RE GONNA WATCH EDWARD SCISSORHANDS FIRST.
NIGHTMARE, NIGHTMARE.
IT IS CHRISTMAS AFTER ALL!
OTHING BEATS RAOKE ON RISTMAS.
I LOVE EDWARD SCISSORHANDS. ♡
CLICK ガチャ
KYAA キャ
BYE.

▲ SHE WANTED TO DO COSPLAY AS THE DOG ZERO, BUT SHE ENDED UP WITH A BUNNY OUTFIT INSTEAD.

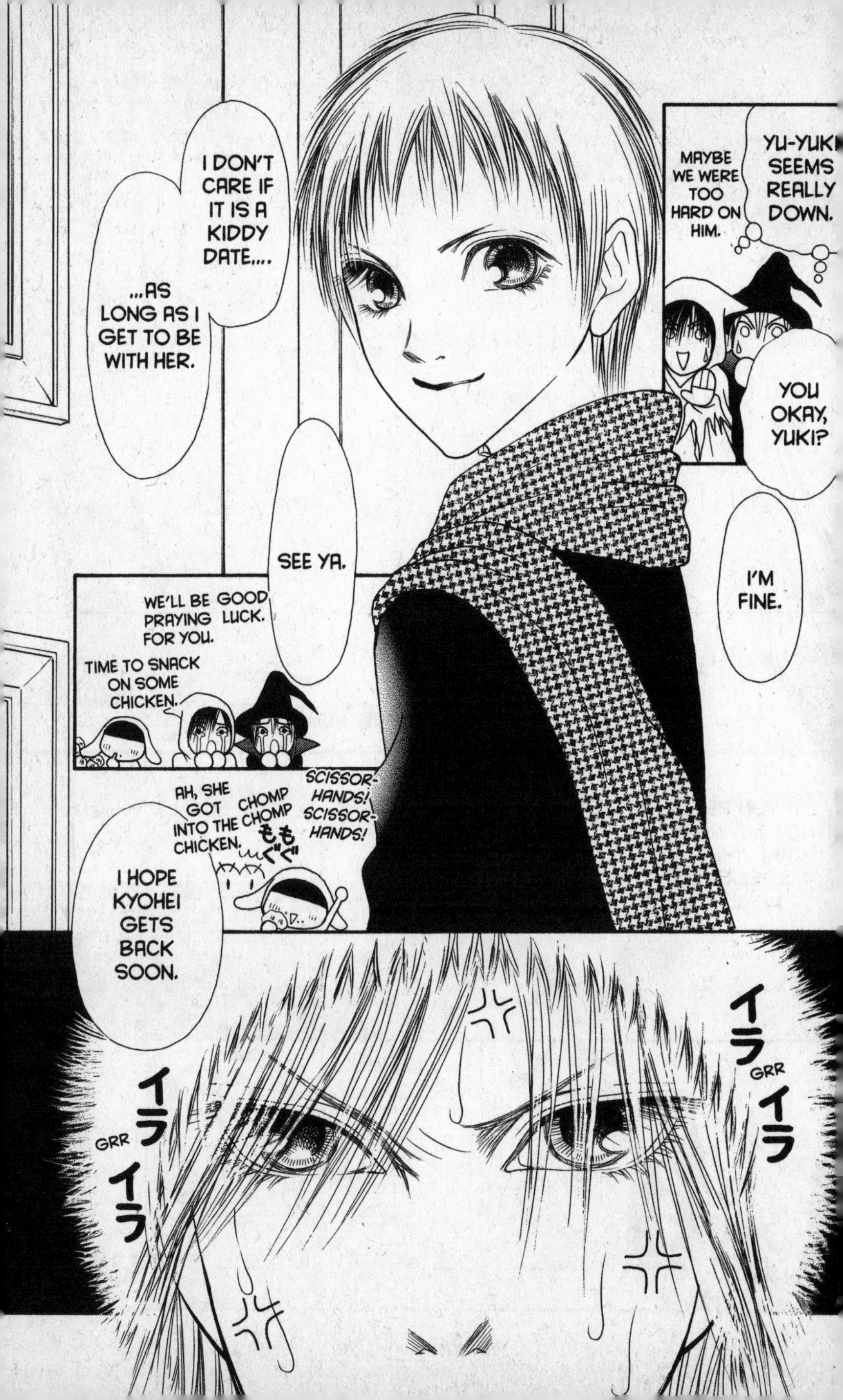
YU-YUKI SEEMS REALLY DOWN.
MAYBE WE WERE TOO HARD ON HIM.
YOU OKAY, YUKI?
I'M FINE.
I DON'T CARE IF IT IS A KIDDY DATE....
...AS LONG AS I GET TO BE WITH HER.
SEE YA.
GOOD LUCK.
WE'LL BE PRAYING FOR YOU.
TIME TO SNACK ON SOME CHICKEN.
SCISSOR-HANDS! SCISSOR-HANDS!
CHOMP CHOMP
もぐもぐ
AH, SHE GOT INTO THE CHICKEN.
I HOPE KYOHEI GETS BACK SOON.
イラ GRR イラ
イラ GRR イラ

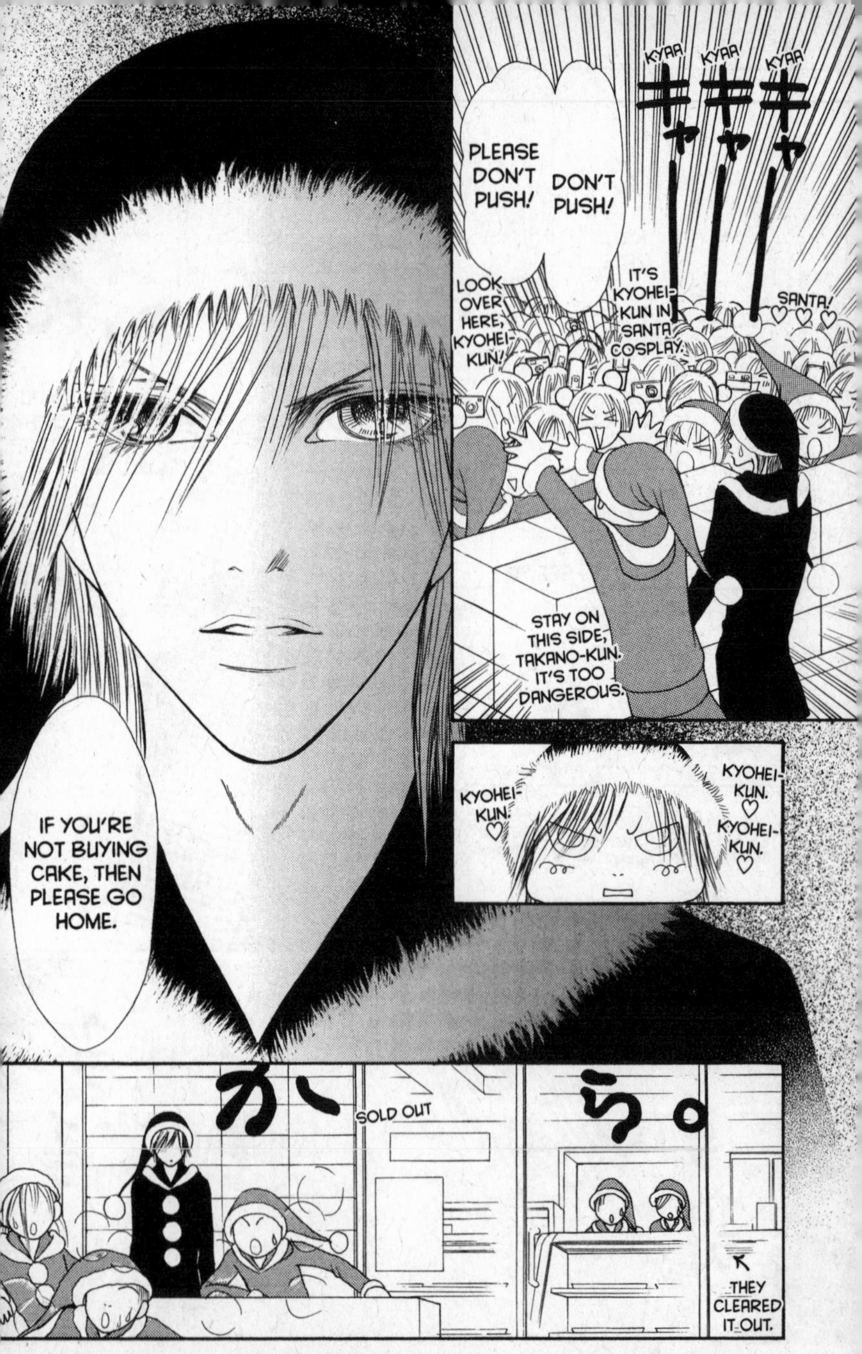
KYAA
KYAA
KYAA
キャーキャーキャー
DON'T PUSH!
PLEASE DON'T PUSH!
SANTA!
IT'S KYOHEI-KUN IN SANTA COSPLAY.
LOOK OVER HERE, KYOHEI-KUN!
STAY ON THIS SIDE, TAKANO-KUN. IT'S TOO DANGEROUS.
KYOHEI-KUN.
KYOHEI-KUN.
KYOHEI-KUN.
IF YOU'RE NOT BUYING CAKE, THEN PLEASE GO HOME.
から。
SOLD OUT
THEY CLEARED IT OUT.

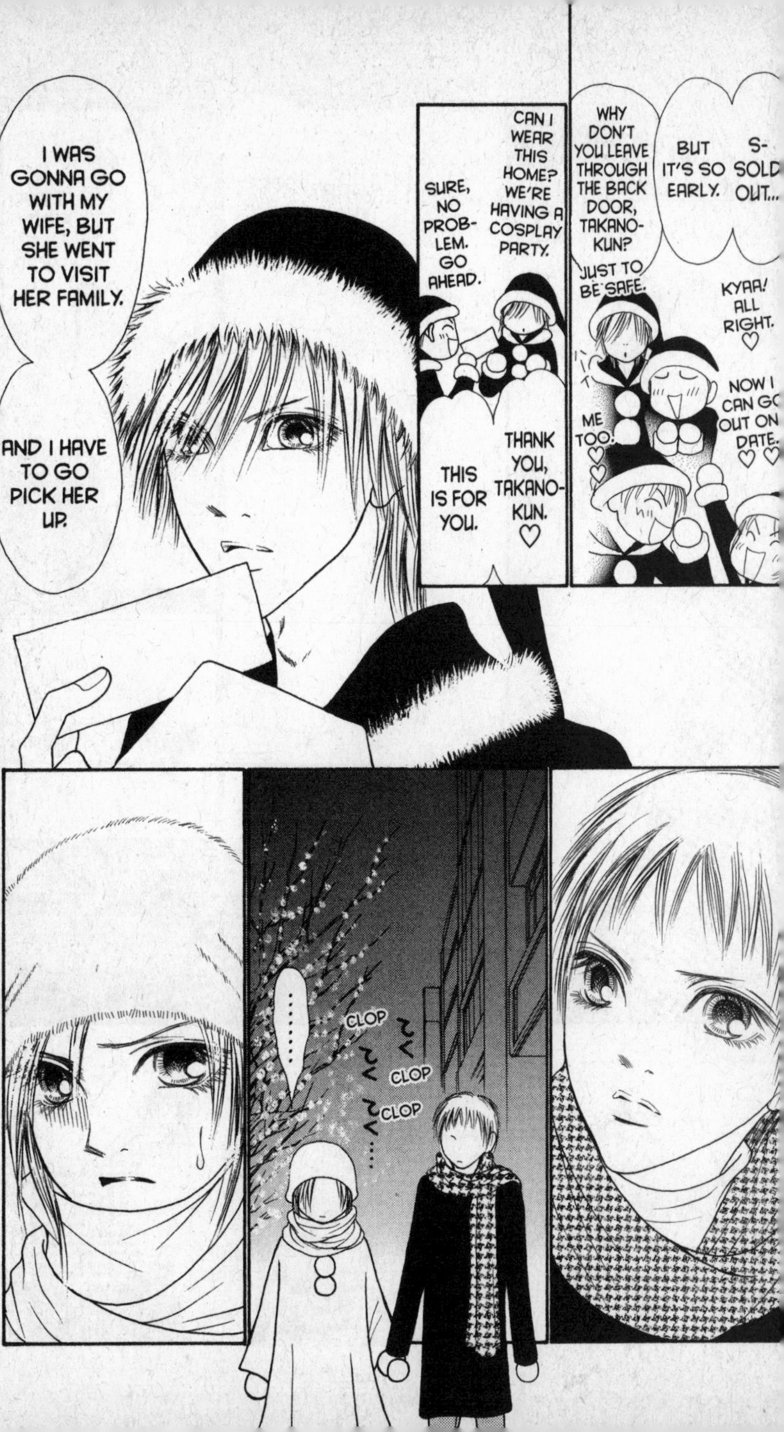

S-SOLD OUT...
BUT IT'S SO EARLY.
WHY DON'T YOU LEAVE THROUGH THE BACK DOOR, TAKANO-KUN? JUST TO BE SAFE.
KYAA! ALL RIGHT. ♡
NOW I CAN GO OUT ON DATE. ♡♡
ME TOO. ♡♡
CAN I WEAR THIS HOME? WE'RE HAVING A COSPLAY PARTY.
SURE, NO PROBLEM. GO AHEAD.
THANK YOU, TAKANO-KUN. ♡
THIS IS FOR YOU.
I WAS GONNA GO WITH MY WIFE, BUT SHE WENT TO VISIT HER FAMILY.
AND I HAVE TO GO PICK HER UP.
......
CLOP
CLOP
CLOP

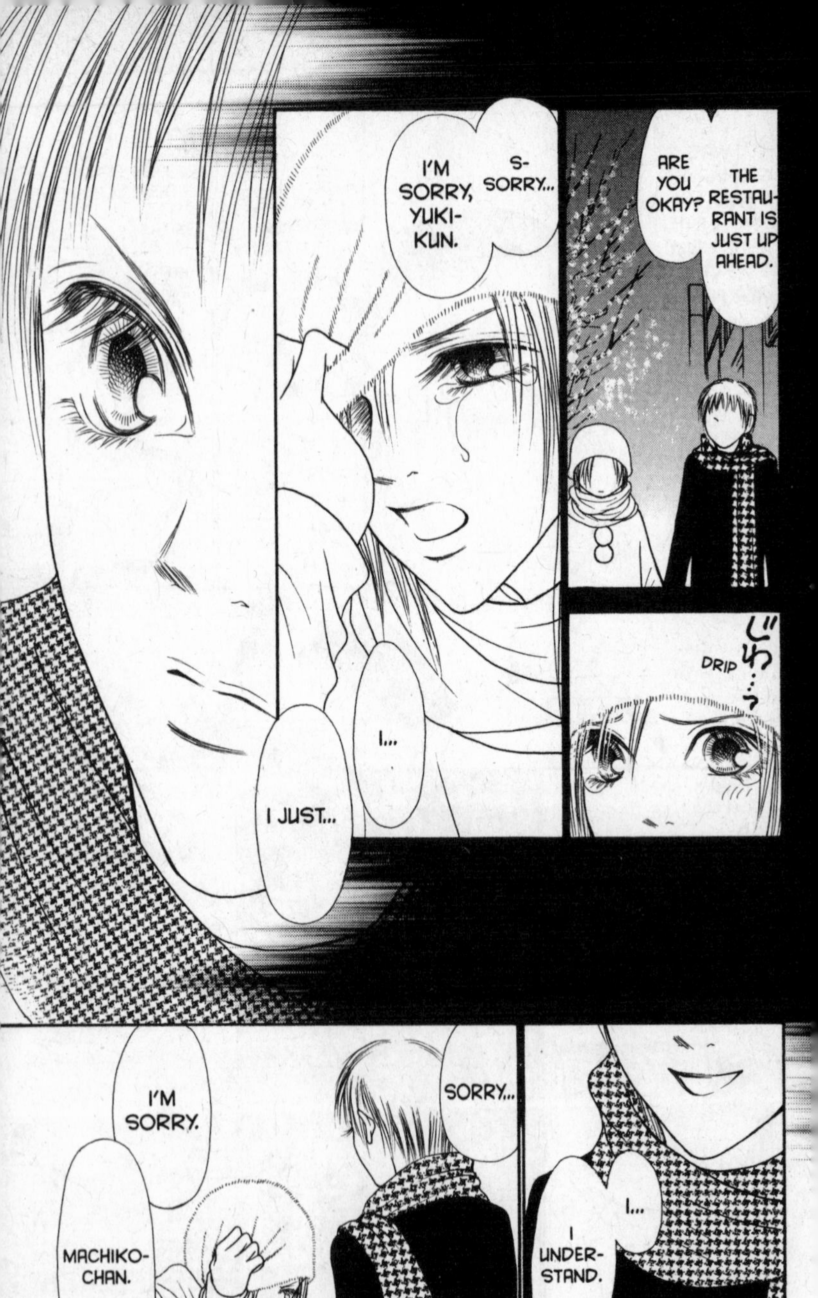
ARE YOU OKAY?
THE RESTAU-RANT IS JUST UP AHEAD.
DRIP
S-SORRY...
I'M SORRY, YUKI-KUN.
I...
I JUST...
I...
I UNDER-STAND.
SORRY...
I'M SORRY.
MACHIKO-CHAN.

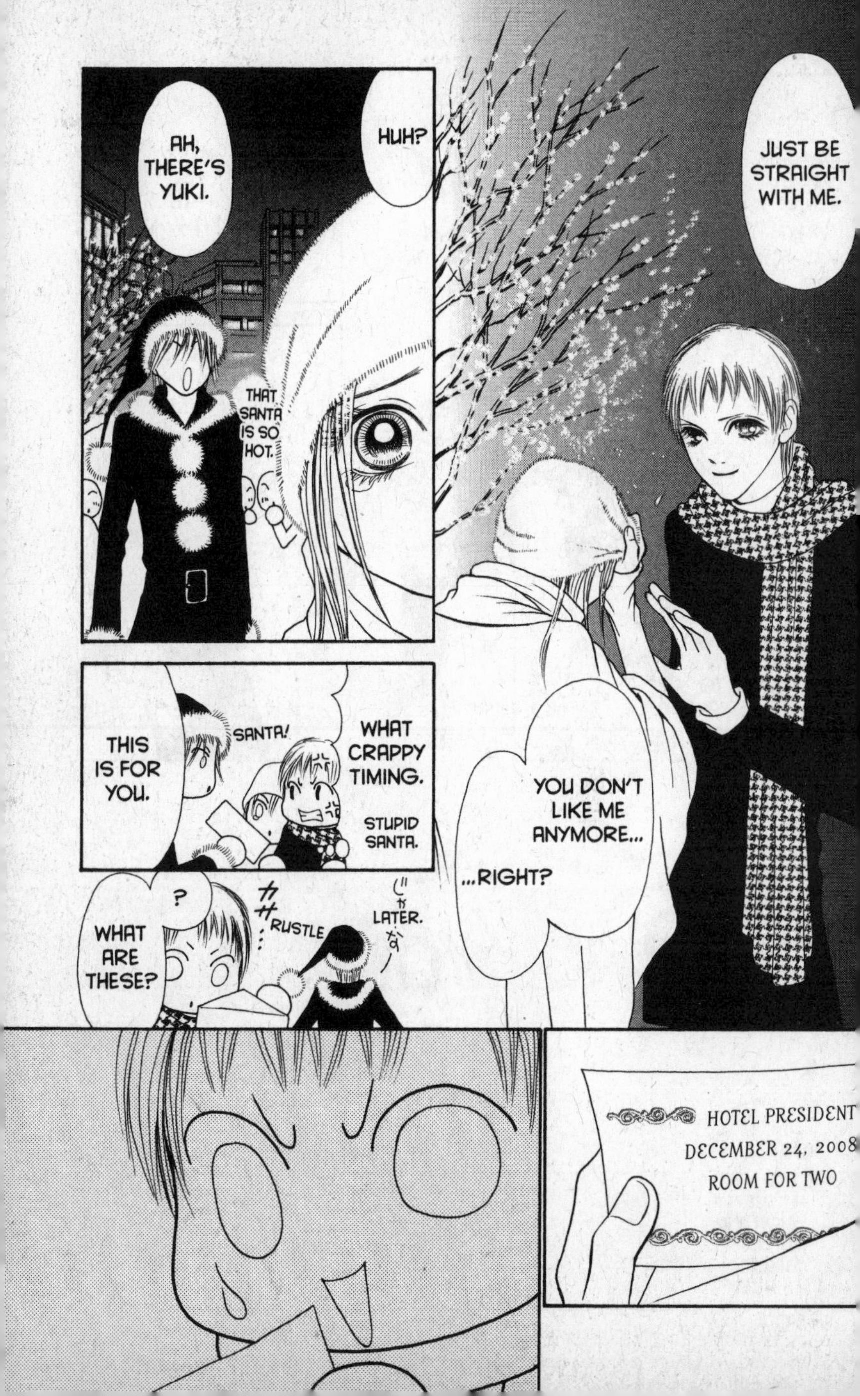
JUST BE STRAIGHT WITH ME.
YOU DON'T LIKE ME ANYMORE...
...RIGHT?
HUH?
AH, THERE'S YUKI.
THAT SANTA IS SO HOT.
WHAT CRAPPY TIMING.
SANTA!
THIS IS FOR YOU.
STUPID SANTA.
LATER.
じゃなー
ガサ
RUSTLE
?
WHAT ARE THESE?
HOTEL PRESIDENT
DECEMBER 24, 2008
ROOM FOR TWO

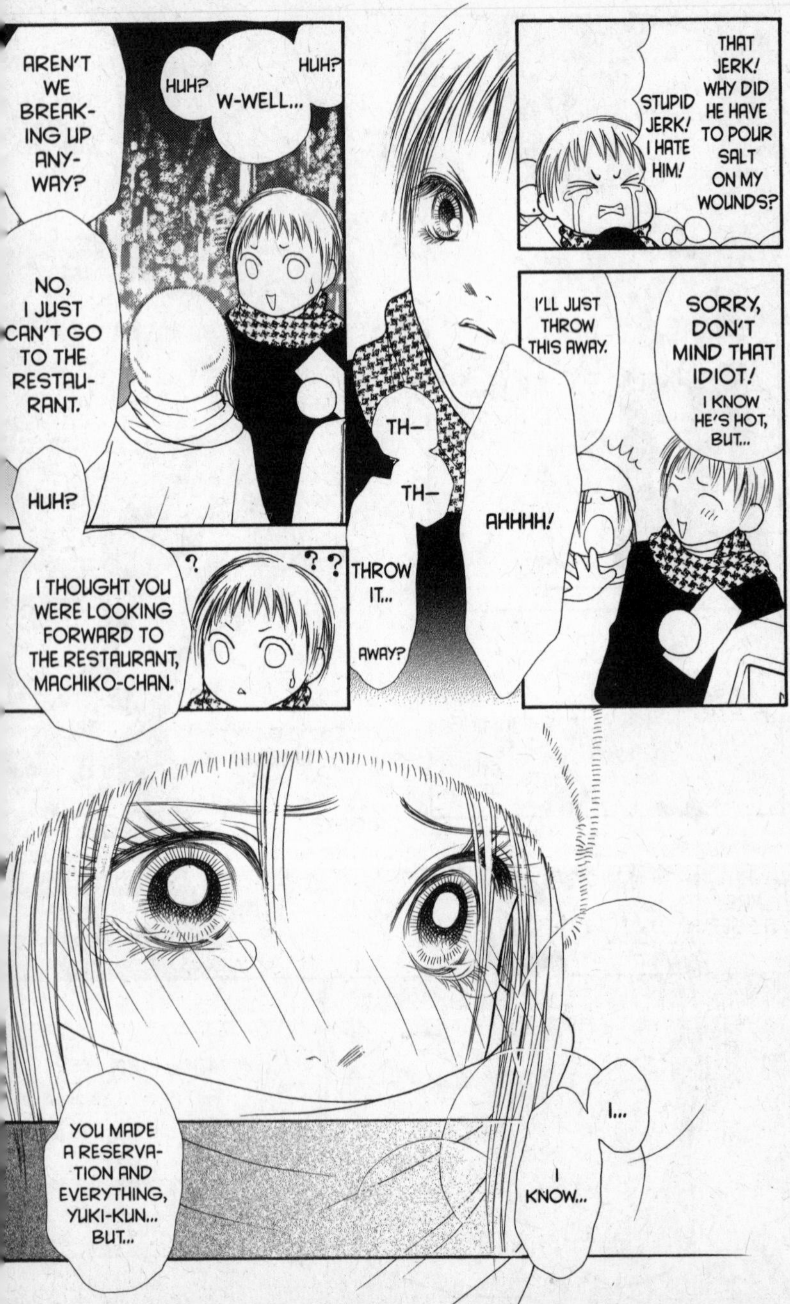

THAT JERK! WHY DID HE HAVE TO POUR SALT ON MY WOUNDS?
STUPID JERK! I HATE HIM!
SORRY, DON'T MIND THAT IDIOT!
I KNOW HE'S HOT, BUT...
I'LL JUST THROW THIS AWAY.
TH-
TH-
AHHHH!
THROW IT...
AWAY?
HUH?
HUH?
W-WELL...
AREN'T WE BREAKING-UP ANYWAY?
NO, I JUST CAN'T GO TO THE RESTAURANT.
HUH?
I THOUGHT YOU WERE LOOKING FORWARD TO THE RESTAURANT, MACHIKO-CHAN.
I...
I KNOW...
YOU MADE A RESERVATION AND EVERYTHING, YUKI-KUN... BUT...

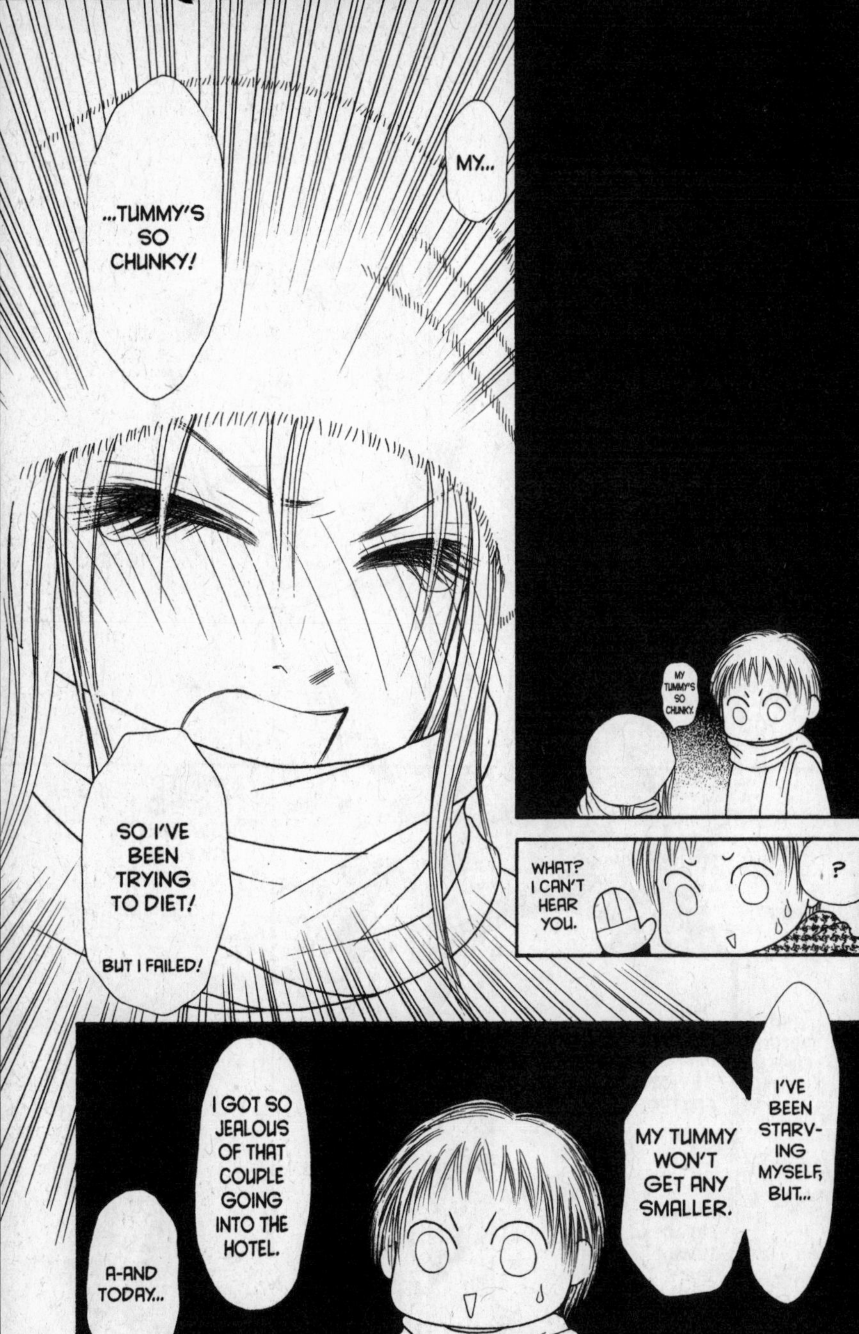
MY TUMMY'S SO CHUNKY.
WHAT? I CAN'T HEAR YOU.
?
MY...
...TUMMY'S SO CHUNKY!
SO I'VE BEEN TRYING TO DIET!
BUT I FAILED!
I'VE BEEN STARV-ING MYSELF, BUT...
MY TUMMY WON'T GET ANY SMALLER.
I GOT SO JEALOUS OF THAT COUPLE GOING INTO THE HOTEL.
A-AND TODAY...

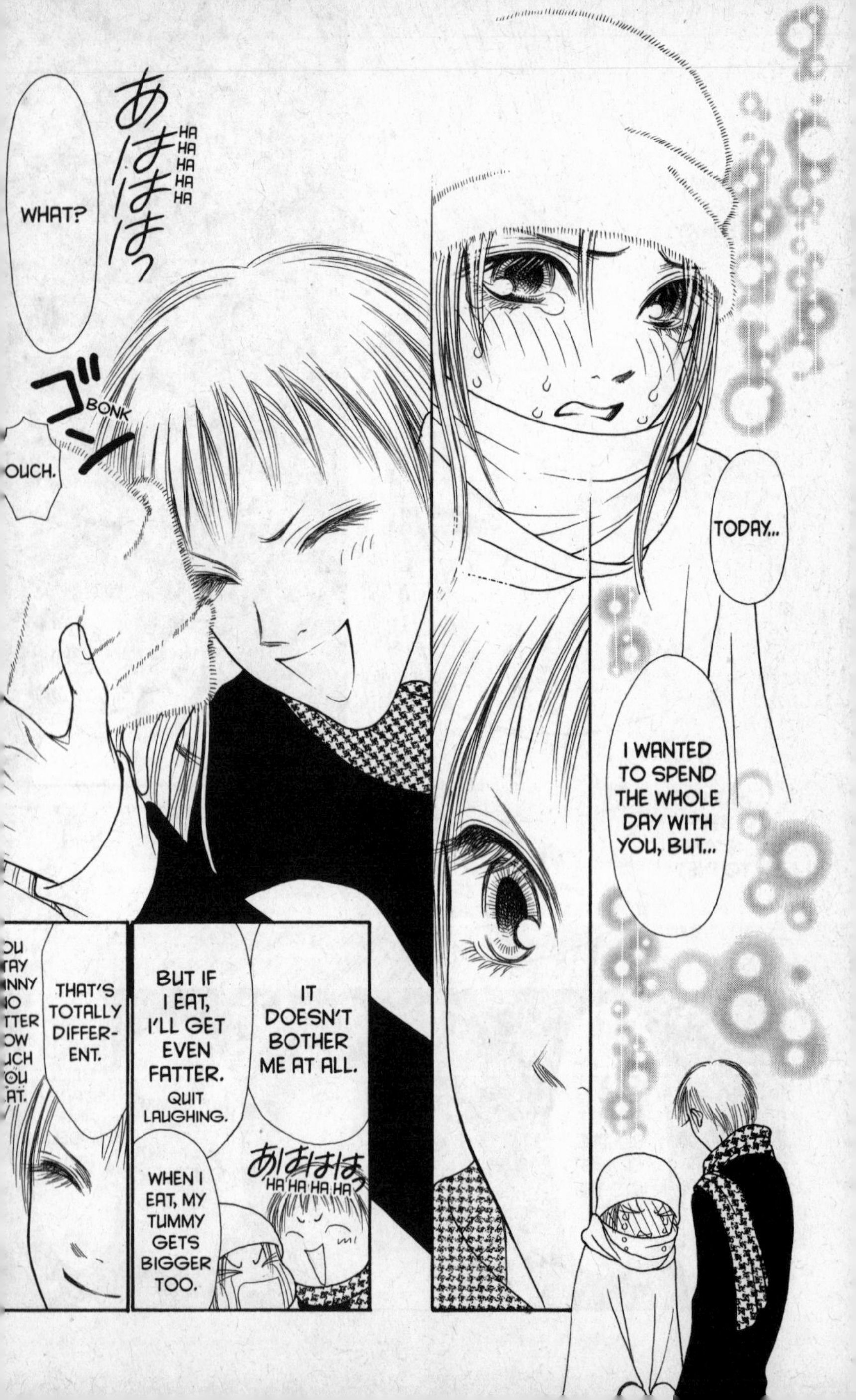
TODAY...
I WANTED TO SPEND THE WHOLE DAY WITH YOU, BUT...
あははっ
HA HA HA HA HA
WHAT?
ゴン
BONK
OUCH.
IT DOESN'T BOTHER ME AT ALL.
BUT IF I EAT, I'LL GET EVEN FATTER.
QUIT LAUGHING.
WHEN I EAT, MY TUMMY GETS BIGGER TOO.
あははは
HA HA HA HA
THAT'S TOTALLY DIFFER-ENT.
OU TAY INNY IO TTER OW UCH OU AT.

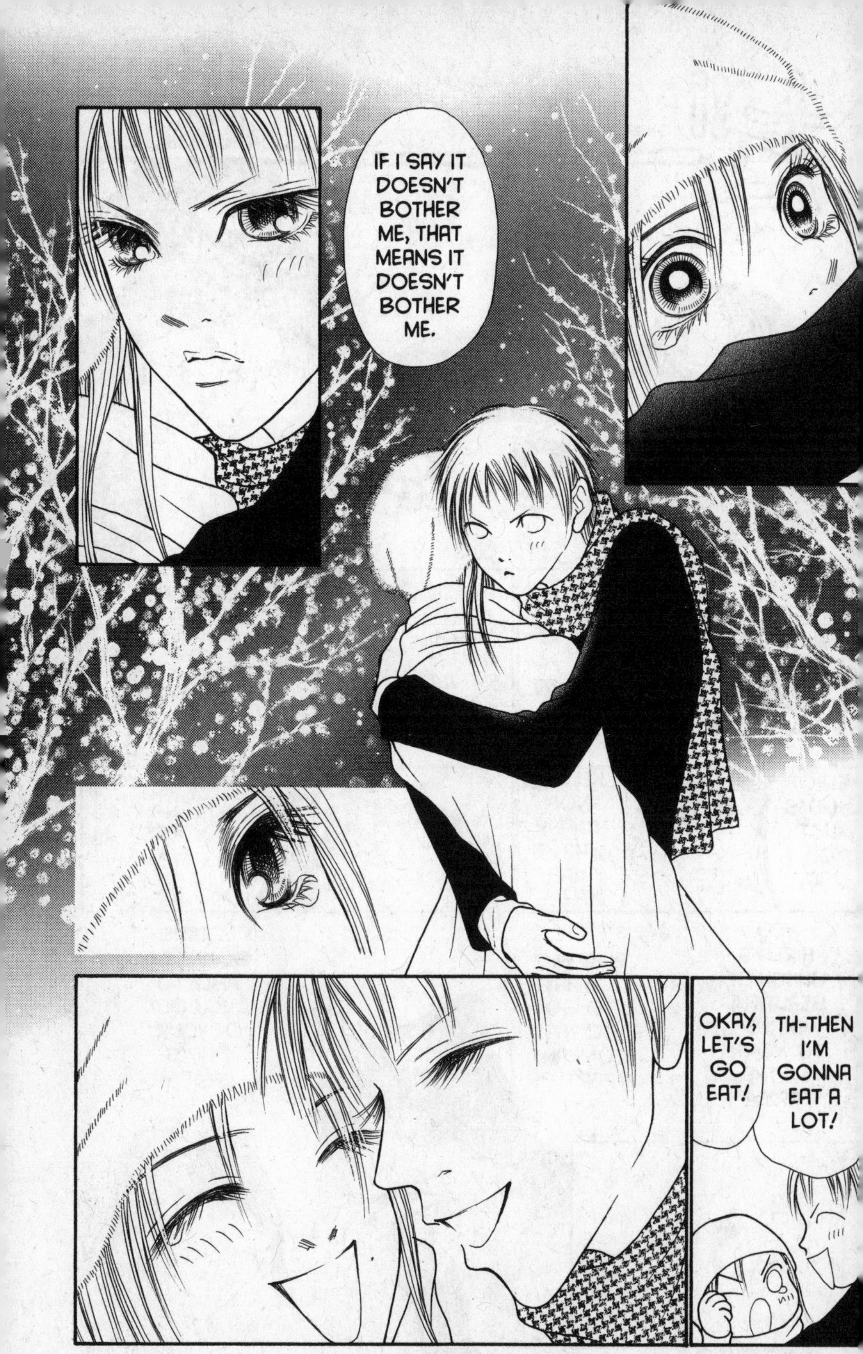
IF I SAY IT DOESN'T BOTHER ME, THAT MEANS IT DOESN'T BOTHER ME.
TH-THEN I'M GONNA EAT A LOT!
OKAY, LET'S GO EAT!

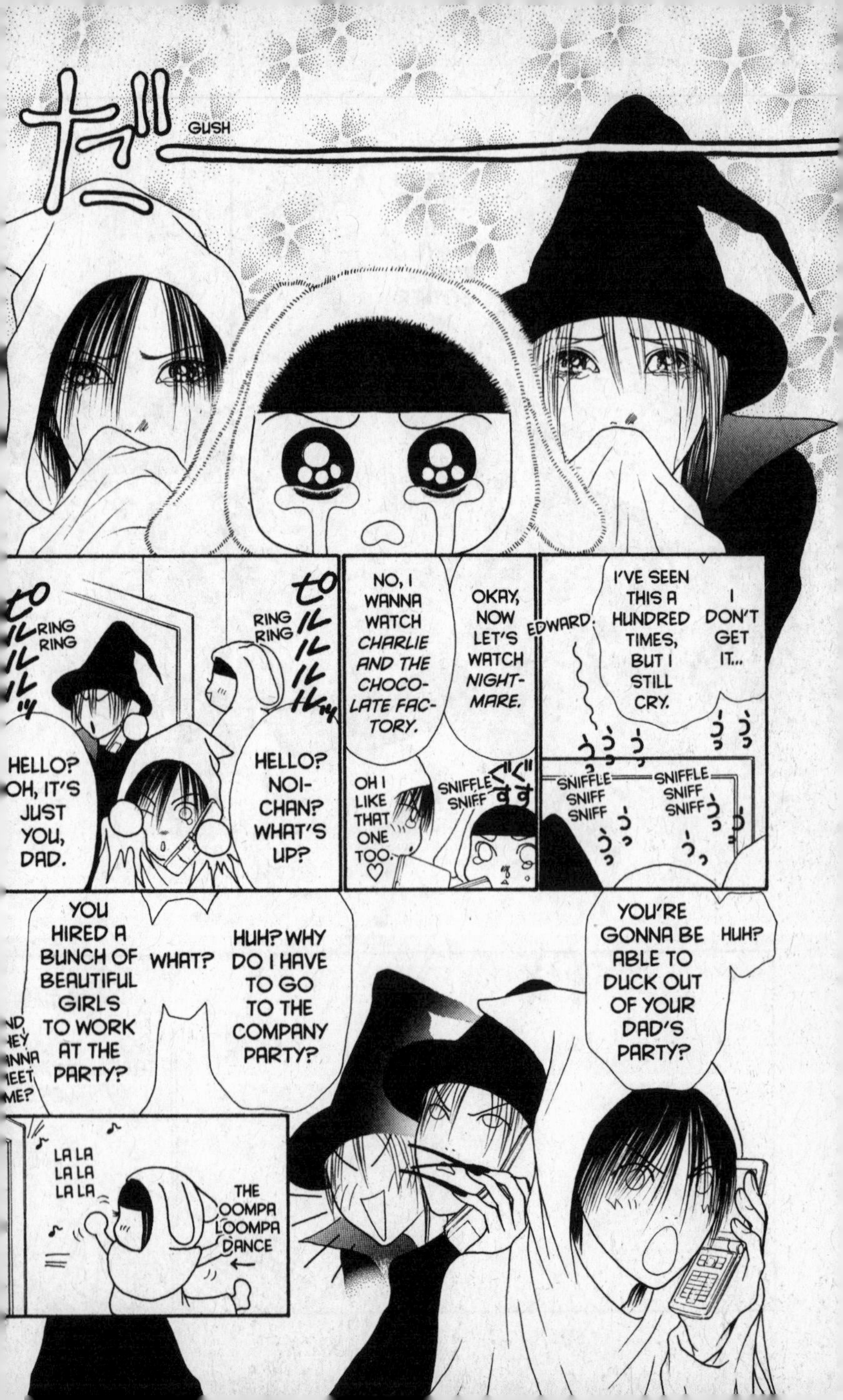
ナダー
GUSH
I DON'T GET IT...
I'VE SEEN THIS A HUNDRED TIMES, BUT I STILL CRY.
EDWARD.
SNIFFLE SNIFF SNIFF
SNIFFLE SNIFF SNIFF
OKAY, NOW LET'S WATCH NIGHTMARE.
NO, I WANNA WATCH CHARLIE AND THE CHOCOLATE FACTORY.
ぐすっ
SNIFFLE SNIFF
OH I LIKE THAT ONE TOO.♡
RING RING
HELLO? NOI-CHAN? WHAT'S UP?
RING RING
HELLO? OH, IT'S JUST YOU, DAD.
HUH?
YOU'RE GONNA BE ABLE TO DUCK OUT OF YOUR DAD'S PARTY?
HUH? WHY DO I HAVE TO GO TO THE COMPANY PARTY?
WHAT?
YOU HIRED A BUNCH OF BEAUTIFUL GIRLS TO WORK AT THE PARTY?
LA LA LA LA LA LA
THE OOMPA LOOMPA DANCE

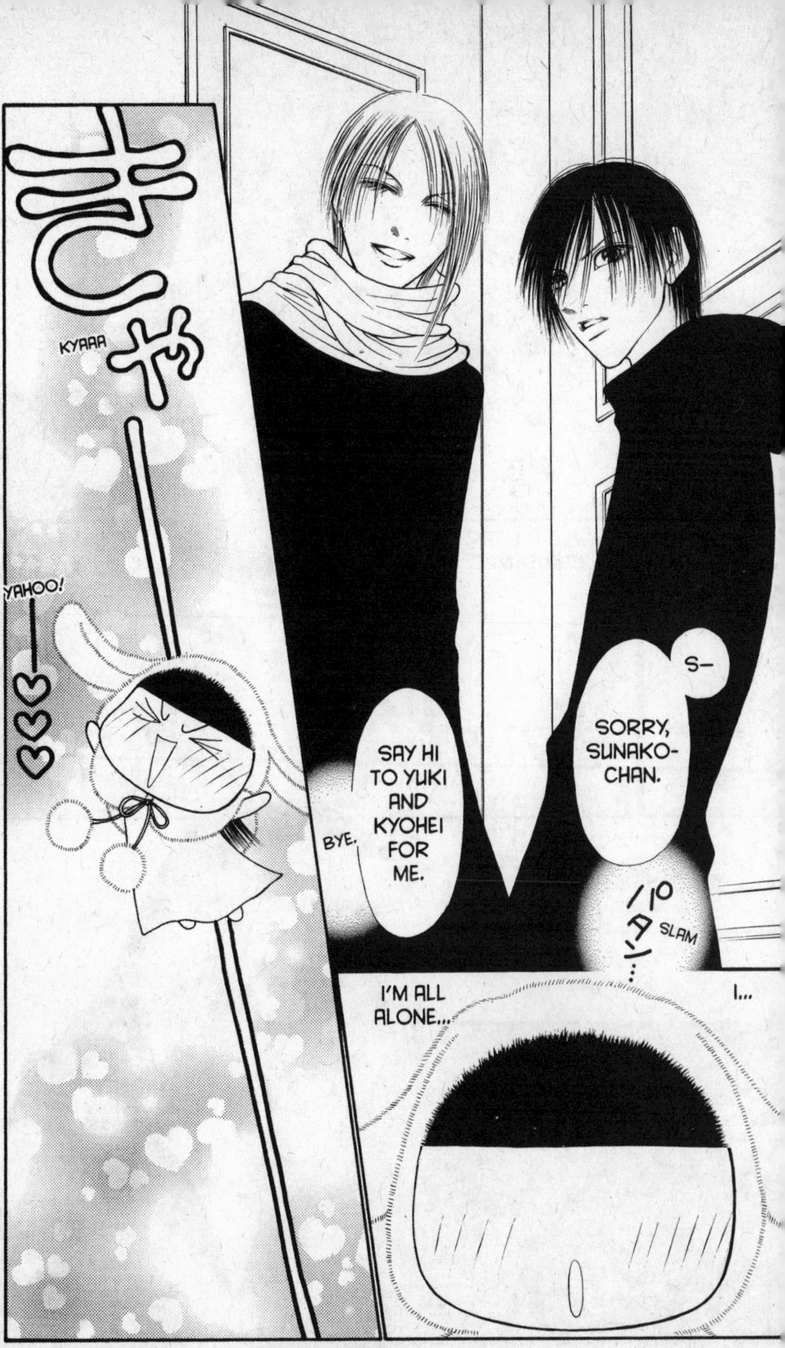
S—
SORRY, SUNAKO-CHAN.
SAY HI TO YUKI AND KYOHEI FOR ME.
BYE.
パタン…
SLAM
I...
I'M ALL ALONE...
きゃー
KYAAA
YAHOO!
♥♥♥

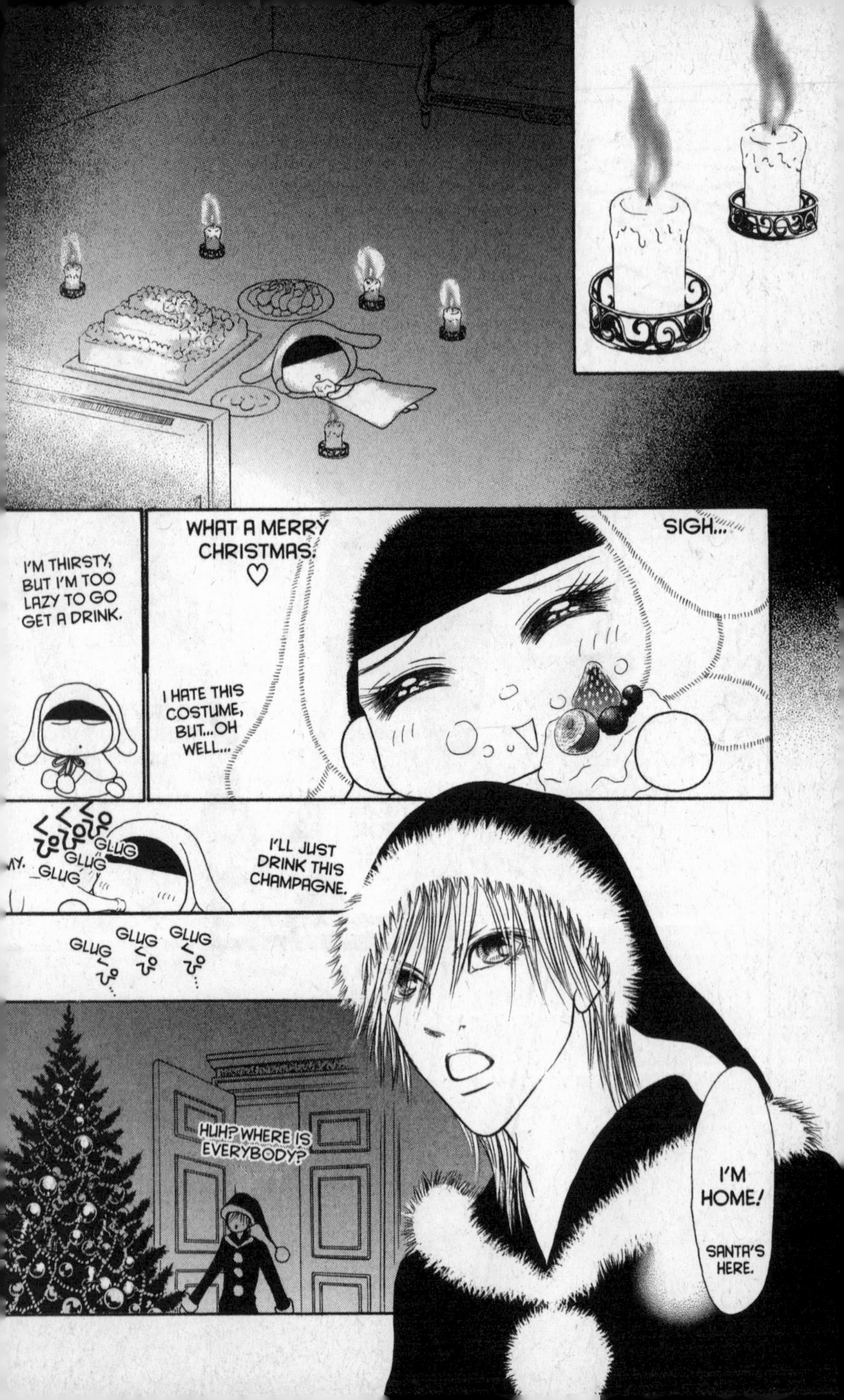
SIGH...
WHAT A MERRY CHRISTMAS. ♡
I HATE THIS COSTUME, BUT...OH WELL...
I'M THIRSTY, BUT I'M TOO LAZY TO GO GET A DRINK.
I'LL JUST DRINK THIS CHAMPAGNE.
くぴくぴくぴ
GLUG GLUG GLUG
GLUG くぴ GLUG くぴ GLUG くぴ…
I'M HOME!
SANTA'S HERE.
HUH? WHERE IS EVERYBODY?

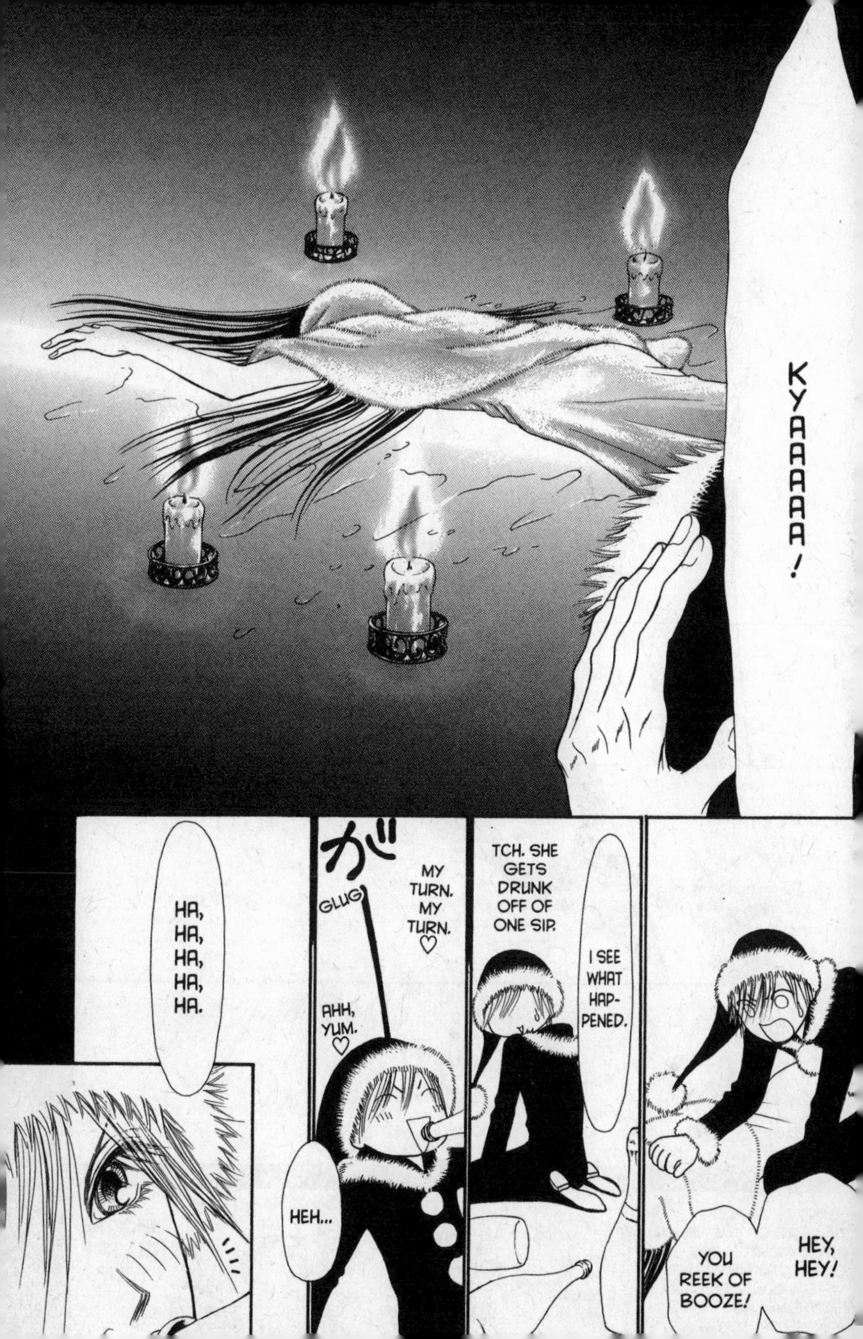

KYAAAAA!
HEY, HEY!
YOU REEK OF BOOZE!
I SEE WHAT HAP-PENED.
TCH. SHE GETS DRUNK OFF OF ONE SIP.
が
MY TURN. MY TURN. ♡
GLUG
AHH, YUM. ♡
HEH...
HA, HA, HA, HA, HA.

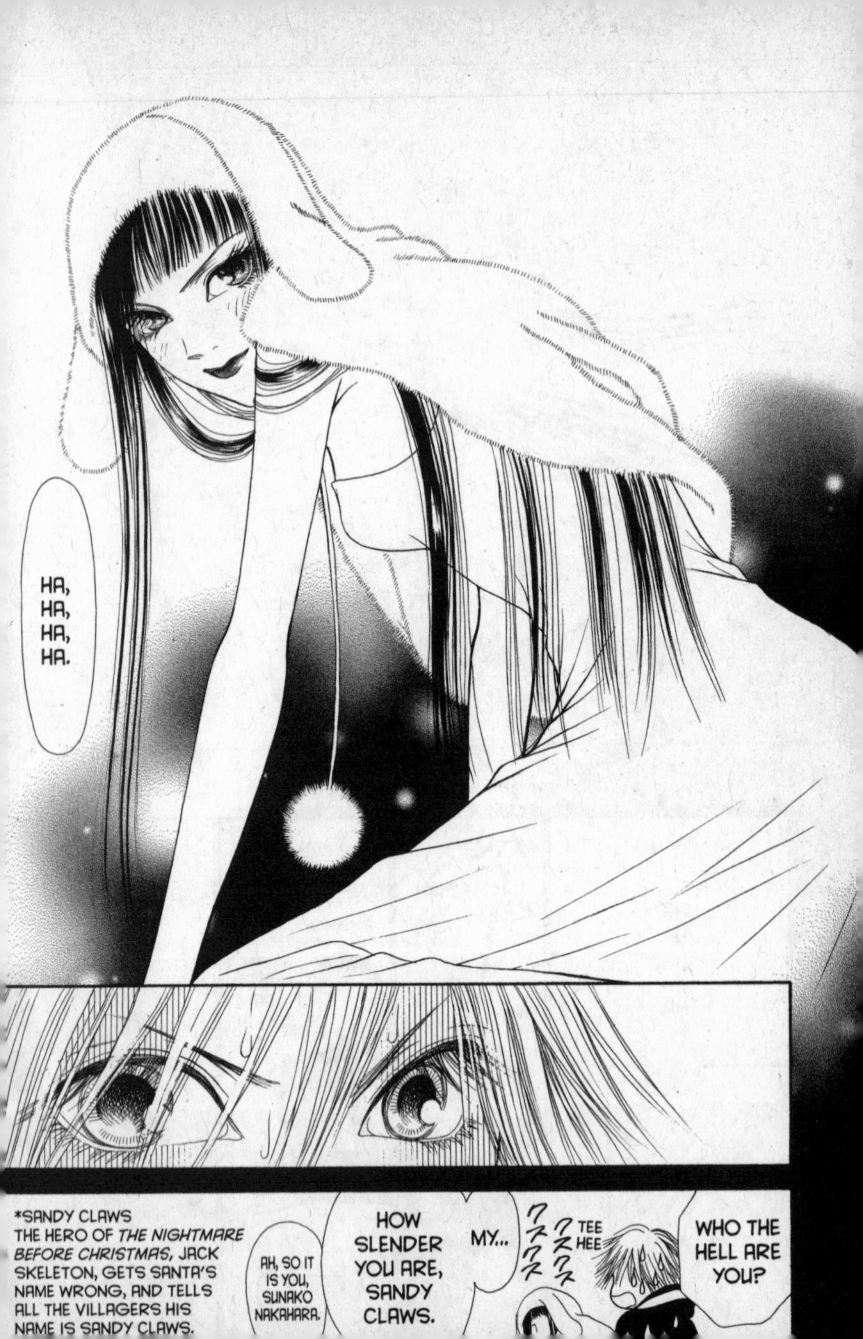
HA, HA, HA, HA.
WHO THE HELL ARE YOU?
TEE HEE
MY...
HOW SLENDER YOU ARE, SANDY CLAWS.
AH, SO IT IS YOU, SUNAKO NAKAHARA.

*SANDY CLAWS
THE HERO OF *THE NIGHTMARE BEFORE CHRISTMAS,* JACK SKELETON, GETS SANTA'S NAME WRONG, AND TELLS ALL THE VILLAGERS HIS NAME IS SANDY CLAWS.

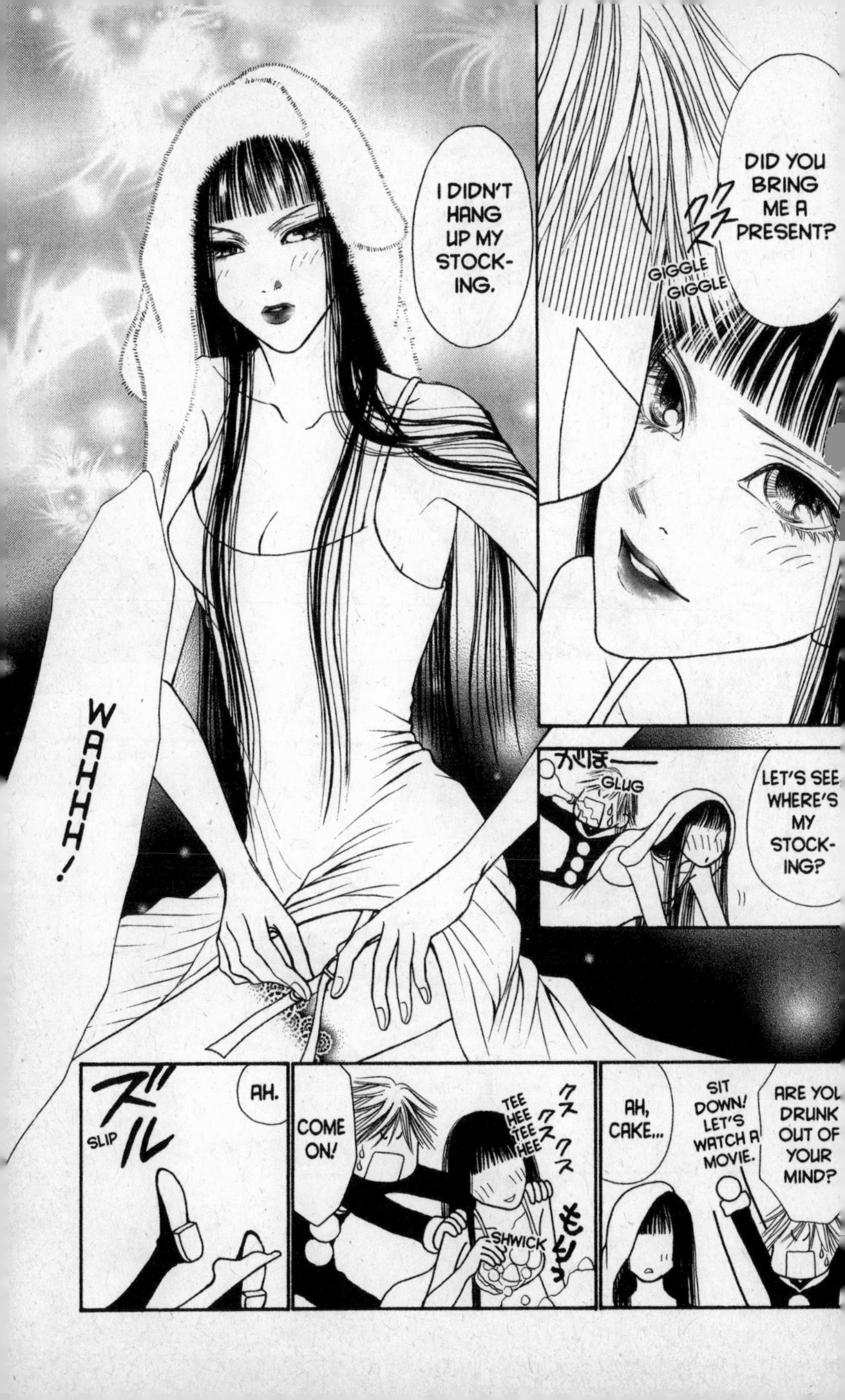
DID YOU BRING ME A PRESENT?
GIGGLE GIGGLE
GLUG
LET'S SEE WHERE'S MY STOCK-ING?
I DIDN'T HANG UP MY STOCK-ING.
WAHHHH!
ARE YOU DRUNK OUT OF YOUR MIND?
SIT DOWN! LET'S WATCH A MOVIE.
AH, CAKE...
TEE HEE TEE HEE
COME ON!
SHWICK
AH.
ズル
SLIP

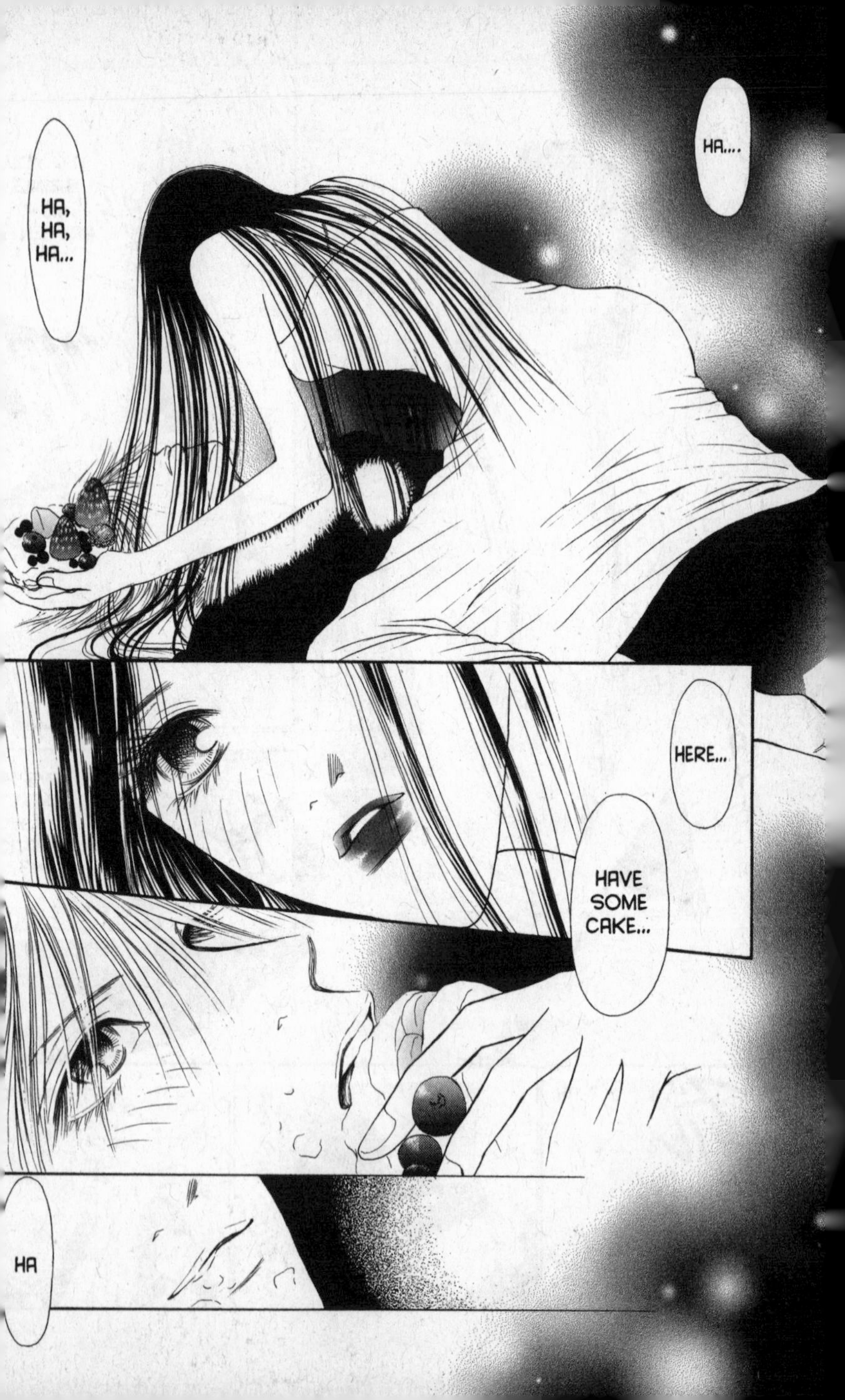
HA....
HA, HA, HA...
HERE...
HAVE SOME CAKE...
HA

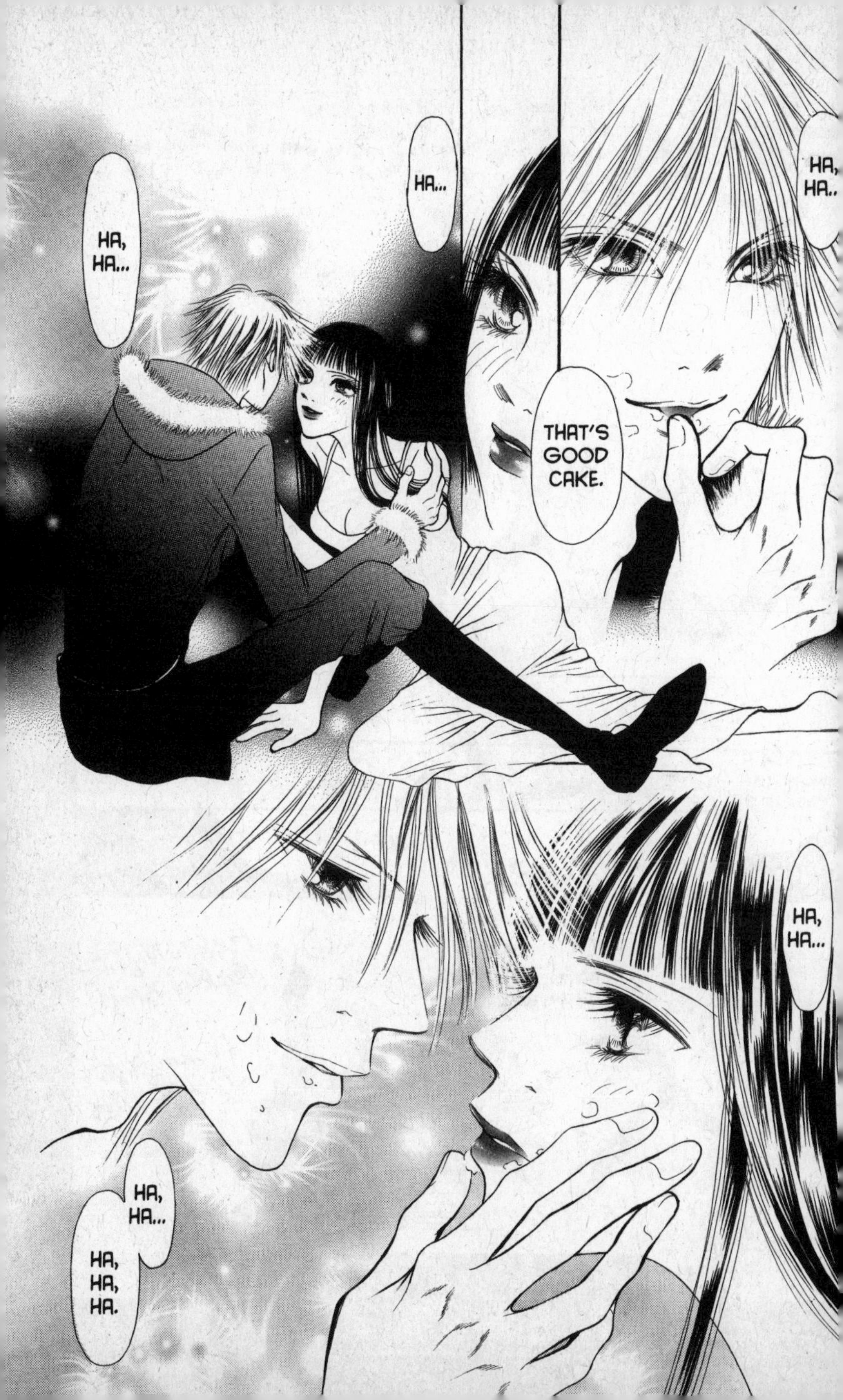
HA, HA..
THAT'S GOOD CAKE.
HA...
HA, HA...
HA, HA...
HA, HA...
HA, HA, HA.

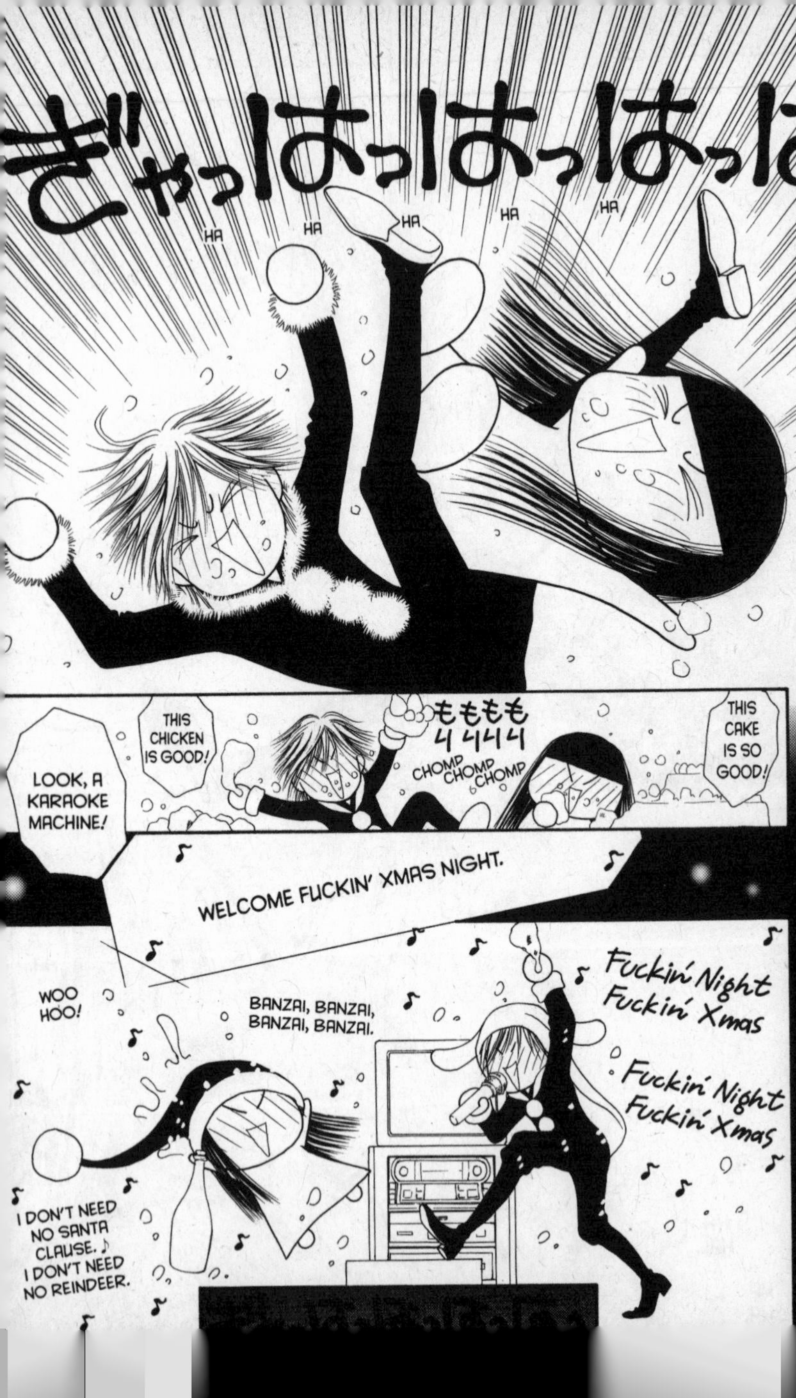
ぎゃっはっはっはっは
HA
HA
HA
HA
HA
THIS CAKE IS SO GOOD!
もももも
CHOMP CHOMP CHOMP
THIS CHICKEN IS GOOD!
LOOK, A KARAOKE MACHINE!
WELCOME FUCKIN' XMAS NIGHT.
Fuckin' Night Fuckin' Xmas
Fuckin' Night Fuckin' Xmas
BANZAI, BANZAI, BANZAI, BANZAI.
WOO HOO!
I DON'T NEED NO SANTA CLAUSE.♪ I DON'T NEED NO REINDEER.

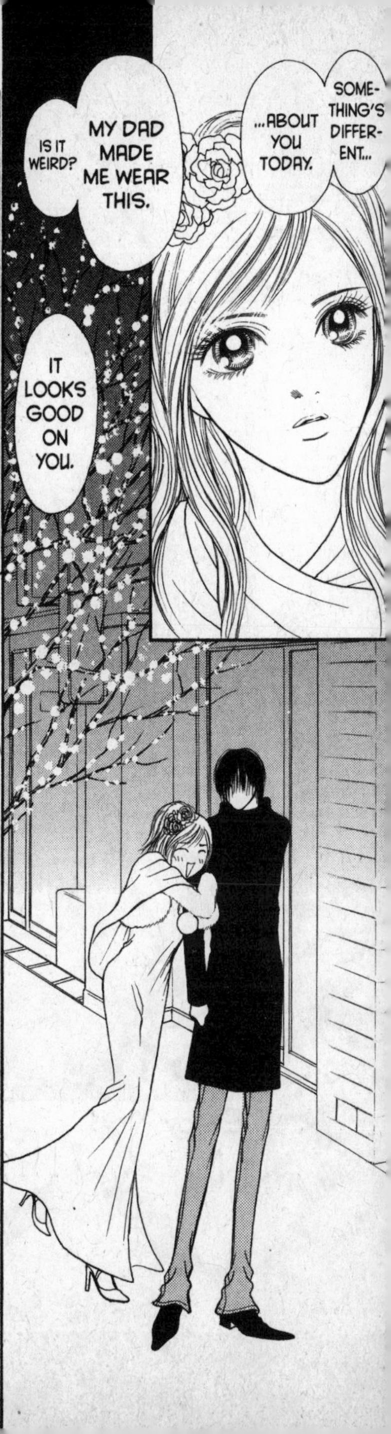
SOME-THING'S DIFFER-ENT...
...ABOUT YOU TODAY.
MY DAD MADE ME WEAR THIS.
IS IT WEIRD?
IT LOOKS GOOD ON YOU.
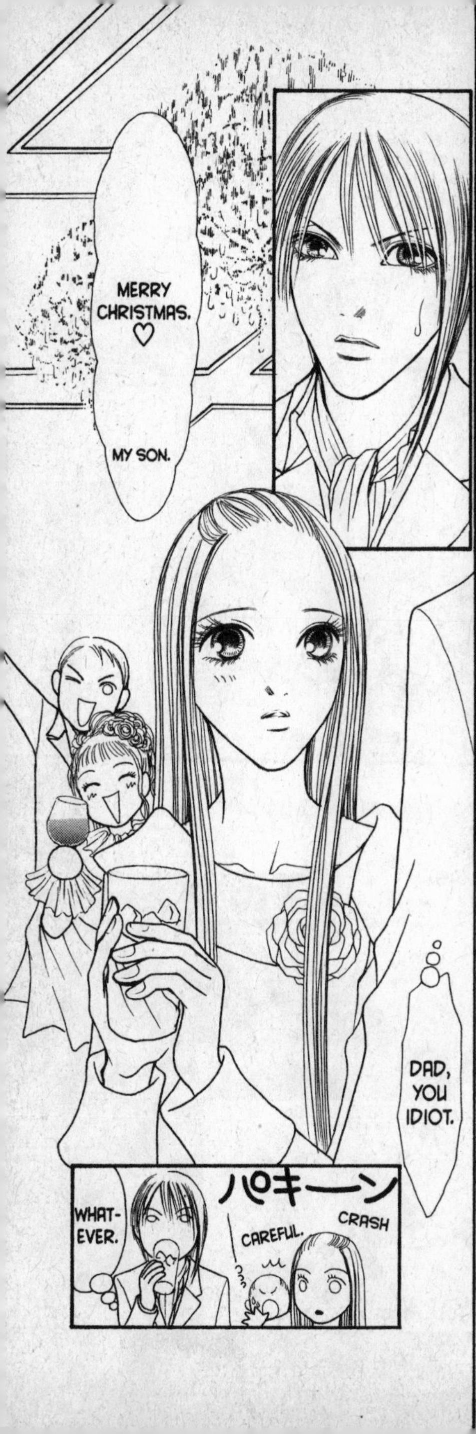
MERRY CHRISTMAS. ♡
MY SON.
DAD, YOU IDIOT.
パキーン
CRASH
CAREFUL.
WHAT-EVER.

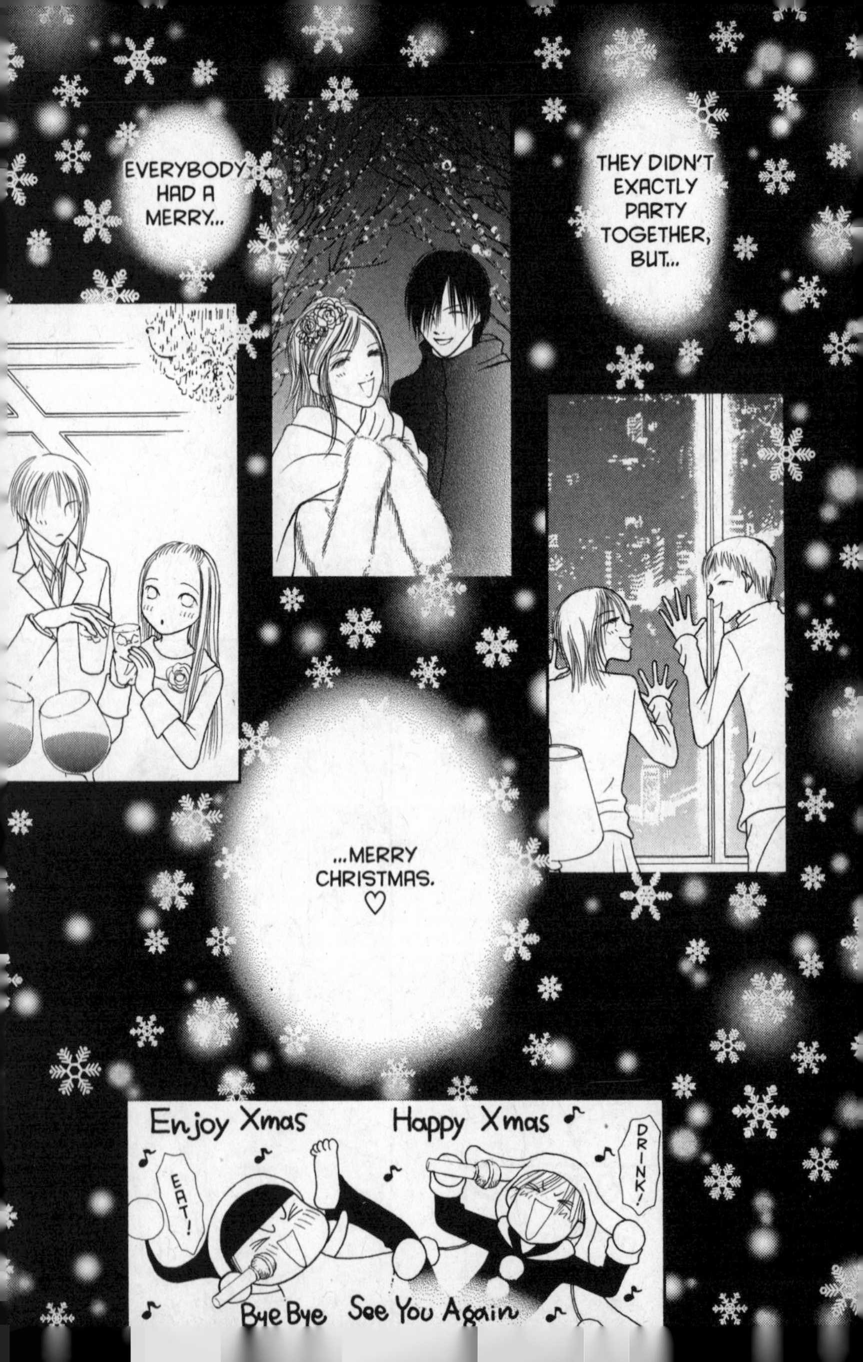
THEY DIDN'T EXACTLY PARTY TOGETHER, BUT...
EVERYBODY HAD A MERRY...
...MERRY CHRISTMAS. ♡
Happy Xmas
DRINK!
Enjoy Xmas
EAT!
See You Again
Bye Bye

Chapter 94

A PLAYBOY'S PARADISE

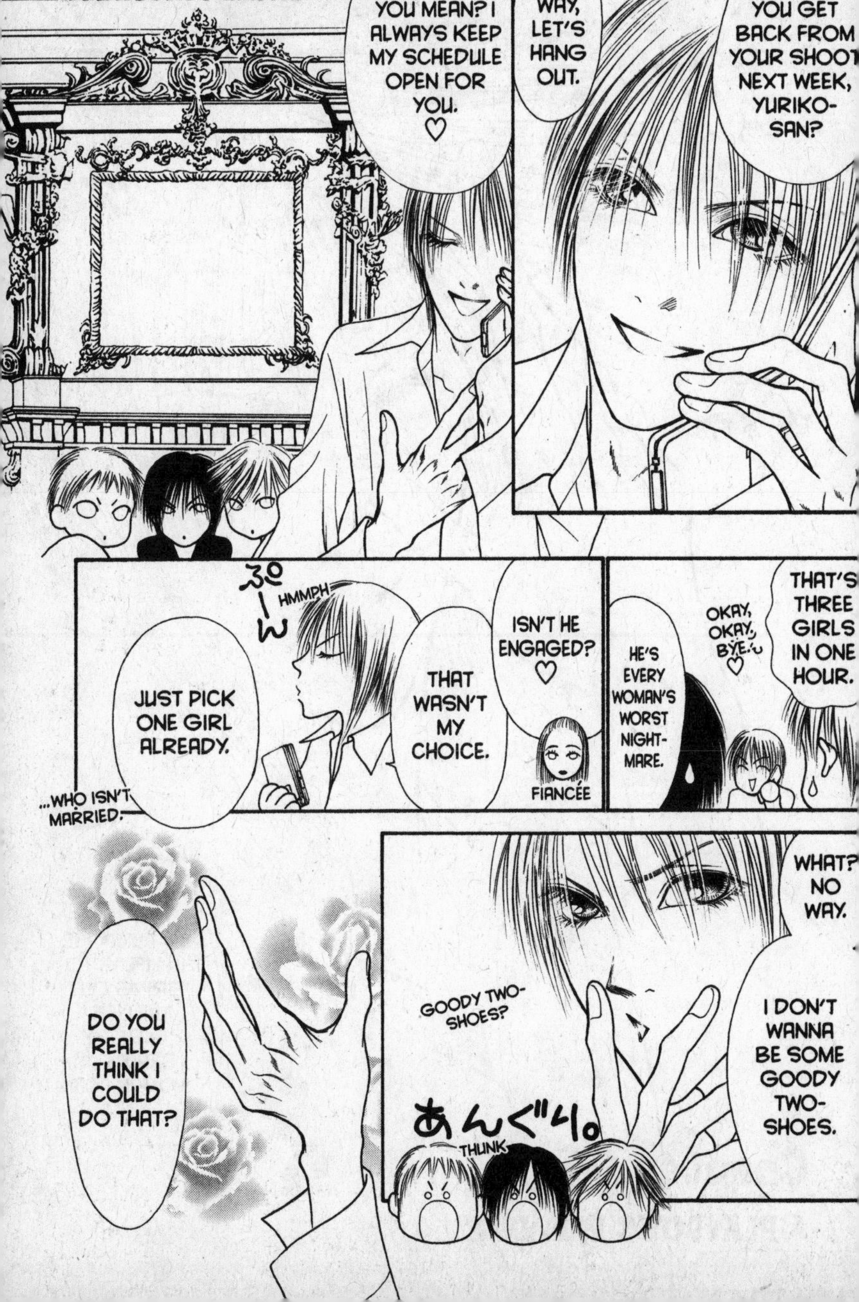

WHAT? ♡ YOU GET BACK FROM YOUR SHOOT NEXT WEEK, YURIKO-SAN?
NO WAY, LET'S HANG OUT.
WHAT DO YOU MEAN? I ALWAYS KEEP MY SCHEDULE OPEN FOR YOU. ♡
THAT'S THREE GIRLS IN ONE HOUR.
OKAY, OKAY, BYE. ♡
HE'S EVERY WOMAN'S WORST NIGHT-MARE.
ISN'T HE ENGAGED? ♡
FIANCÉE
THAT WASN'T MY CHOICE.
ぷーん
HMMPH
JUST PICK ONE GIRL ALREADY.
...WHO ISN'T MARRIED.
WHAT? NO WAY.
I DON'T WANNA BE SOME GOODY TWO-SHOES.
GOODY TWO-SHOES?
あんぐり。
THUNK
DO YOU REALLY THINK I COULD DO THAT?

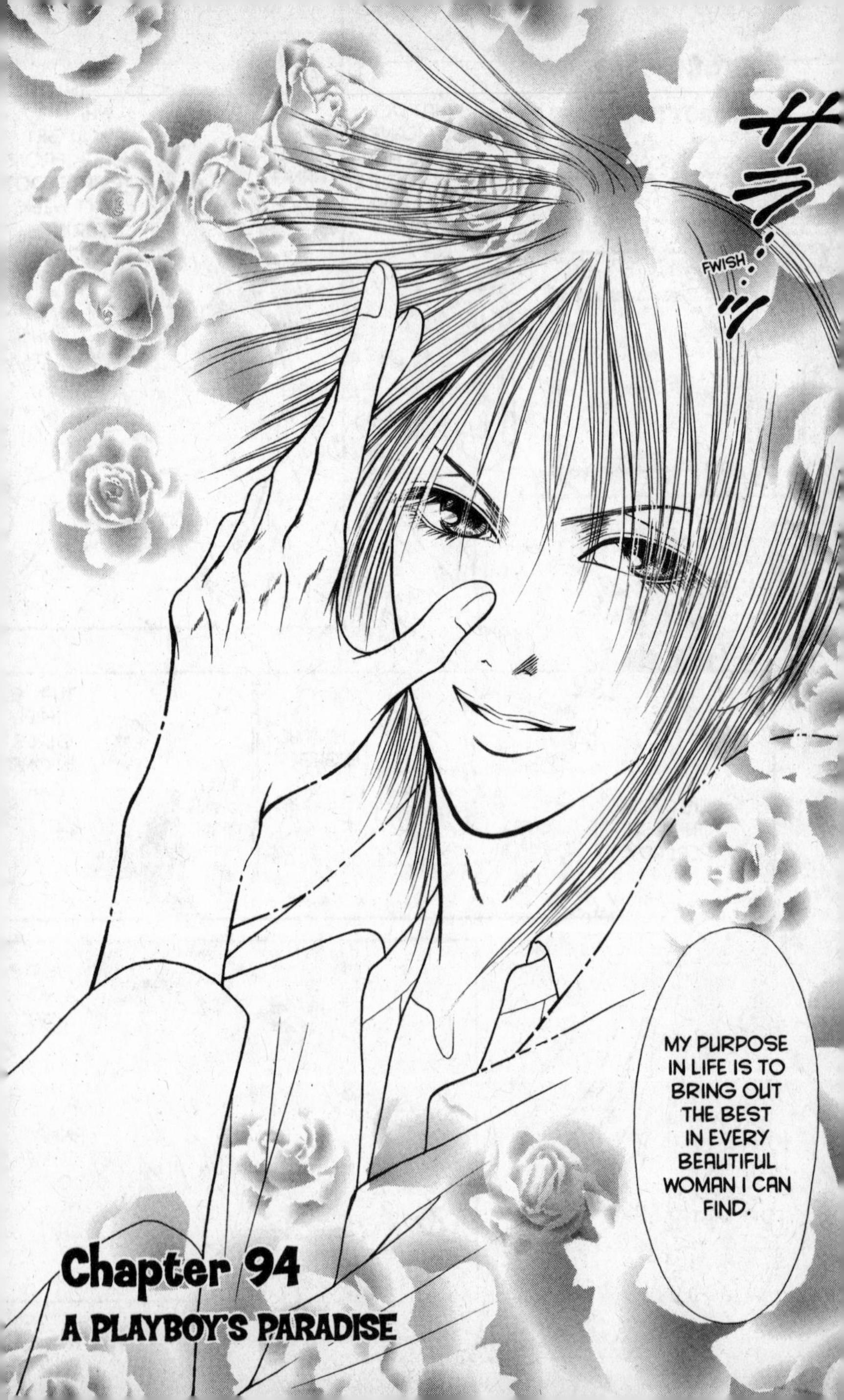
サラ…ッ
FWISH
MY PURPOSE IN LIFE IS TO BRING OUT THE BEST IN EVERY BEAUTIFUL WOMAN I CAN FIND.
Chapter 94
A PLAYBOY'S PARADISE

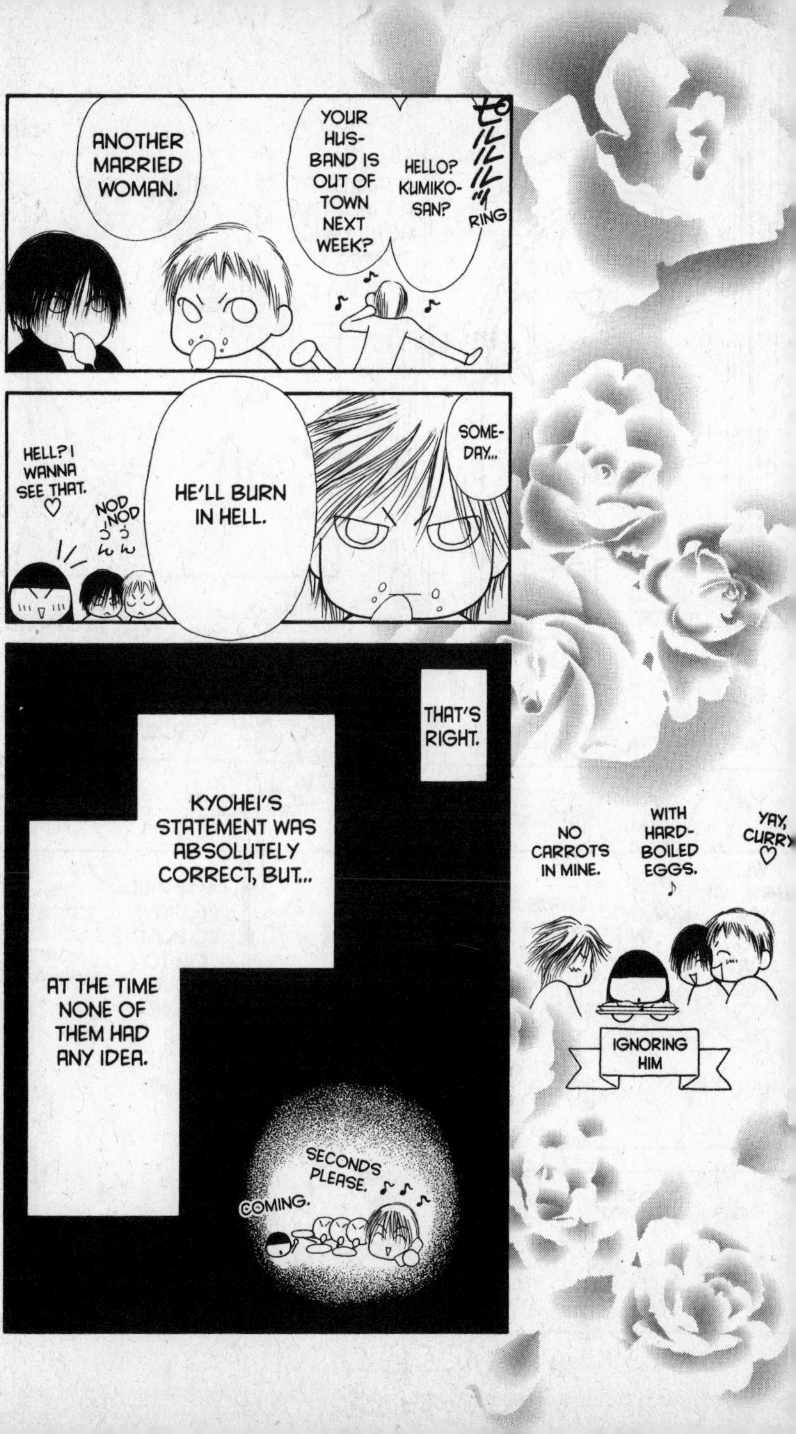
YAY, CURRY ♡
WITH HARD-BOILED EGGS. ♪
NO CARROTS IN MINE.
IGNORING HIM
RING
HELLO? KUMIKO-SAN?
YOUR HUS-BAND IS OUT OF TOWN NEXT WEEK?
ANOTHER MARRIED WOMAN.
SOME-DAY...
HE'LL BURN IN HELL.
NOD NOD
HELL? I WANNA SEE THAT. ♡
THAT'S RIGHT.
KYOHEI'S STATEMENT WAS ABSOLUTELY CORRECT, BUT...
AT THE TIME NONE OF THEM HAD ANY IDEA.
SECONDS PLEASE. ♪♪♪
COMING.

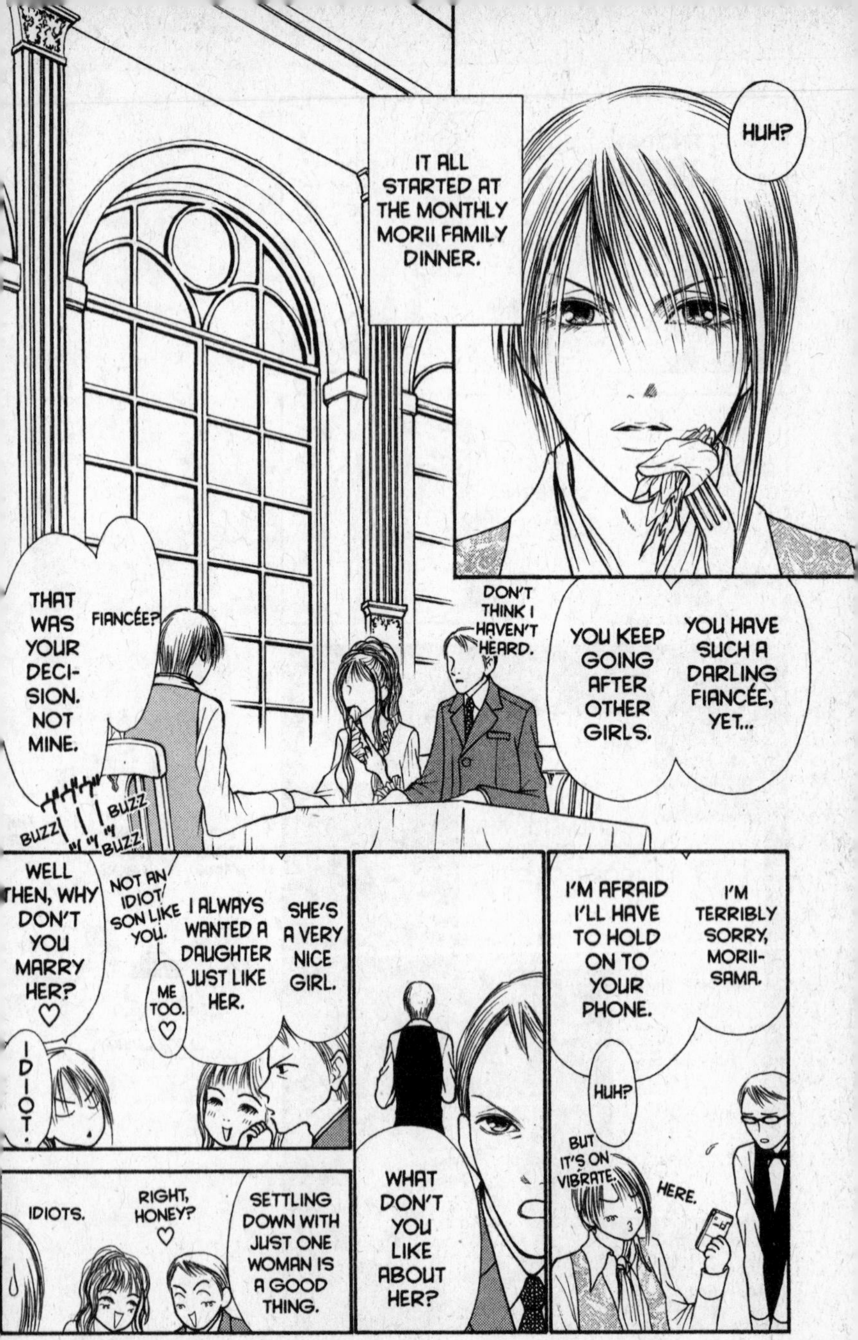
HUH?
IT ALL STARTED AT THE MONTHLY MORII FAMILY DINNER.
YOU HAVE SUCH A DARLING FIANCÉE, YET...
YOU KEEP GOING AFTER OTHER GIRLS.
DON'T THINK I HAVEN'T HEARD.
FIANCÉE?
THAT WAS YOUR DECI-SION. NOT MINE.
BUZZ BUZZ BUZZ
I'M TERRIBLY SORRY, MORII-SAMA.
I'M AFRAID I'LL HAVE TO HOLD ON TO YOUR PHONE.
HUH?
BUT IT'S ON VIBRATE.
HERE.
WHAT DON'T YOU LIKE ABOUT HER?
SHE'S A VERY NICE GIRL.
I ALWAYS WANTED A DAUGHTER JUST LIKE HER.
ME TOO. ♡
NOT AN IDIOT SON LIKE YOU.
WELL THEN, WHY DON'T YOU MARRY HER? ♡
IDIOT.
SETTLING DOWN WITH JUST ONE WOMAN IS A GOOD THING.
RIGHT, HONEY? ♡
IDIOTS.

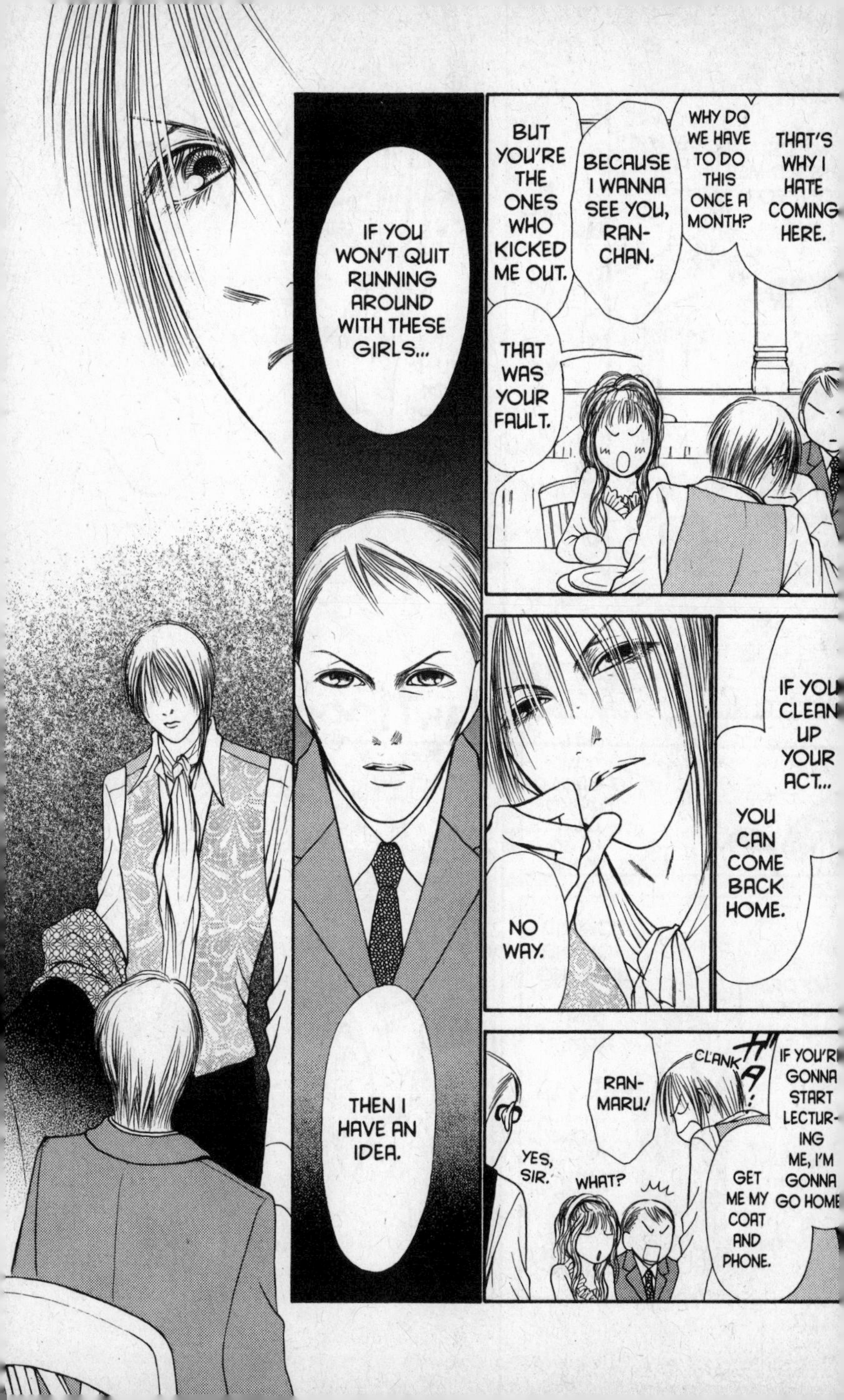
THAT'S WHY I HATE COMING HERE.
WHY DO WE HAVE TO DO THIS ONCE A MONTH?
BECAUSE I WANNA SEE YOU, RAN-CHAN.
BUT YOU'RE THE ONES WHO KICKED ME OUT.
THAT WAS YOUR FAULT.
IF YOU CLEAN UP YOUR ACT...
YOU CAN COME BACK HOME.
NO WAY.
IF YOU'R GONNA START LECTURING ME, I'M GONNA GO HOME
GET ME MY COAT AND PHONE.
HA HA!
CLANK
RAN-MARU!
WHAT?
YES, SIR.
IF YOU WON'T QUIT RUNNING AROUND WITH THESE GIRLS...
THEN I HAVE AN IDEA.

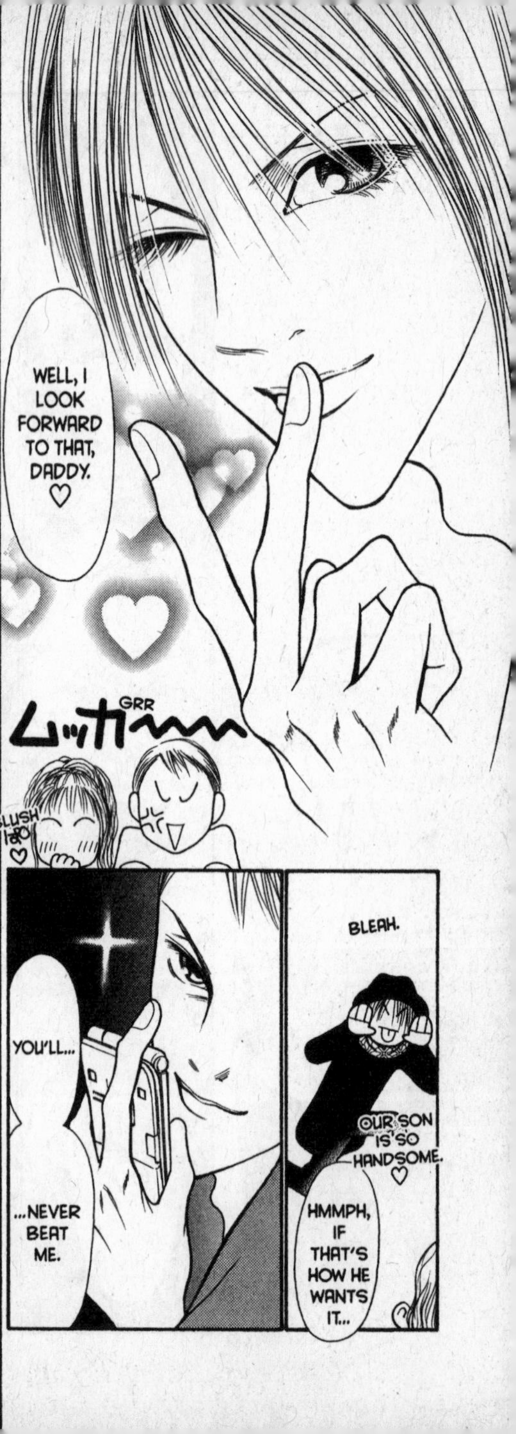
WELL, I LOOK FORWARD TO THAT, DADDY. ♡
GRR
BLUSH ♡
BLEAH.
OUR SON IS SO HANDSOME. ♡
HMMPH, IF THAT'S HOW HE WANTS IT...
YOU'LL...
...NEVER BEAT ME.

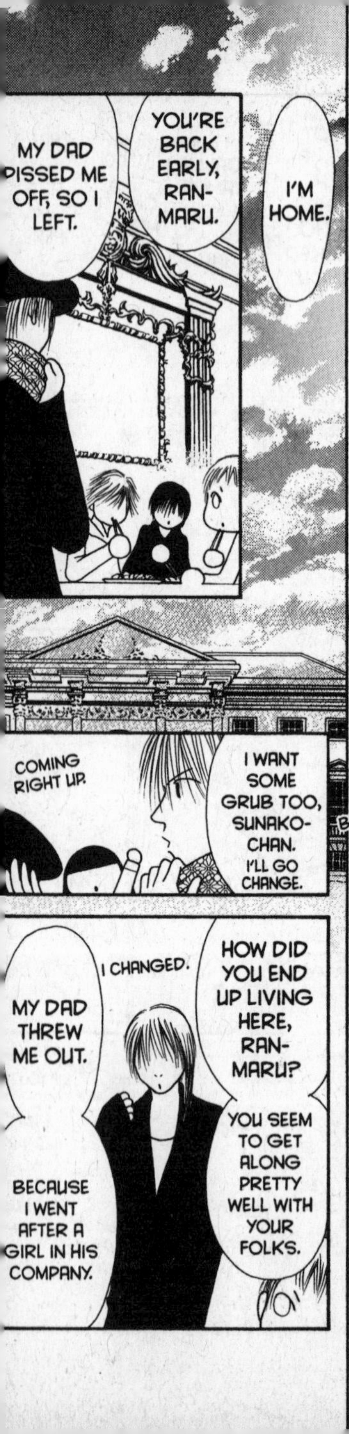
I'M HOME.
YOU'RE BACK EARLY, RAN-MARU.
MY DAD PISSED ME OFF, SO I LEFT.
I WANT SOME GRUB TOO, SUNAKO-CHAN.
I'LL GO CHANGE.
COMING RIGHT UP.
HOW DID YOU END UP LIVING HERE, RAN-MARU?
I CHANGED.
MY DAD THREW ME OUT.
YOU SEEM TO GET ALONG PRETTY WELL WITH YOUR FOLKS.
BECAUSE I WENT AFTER A GIRL IN HIS COMPANY.

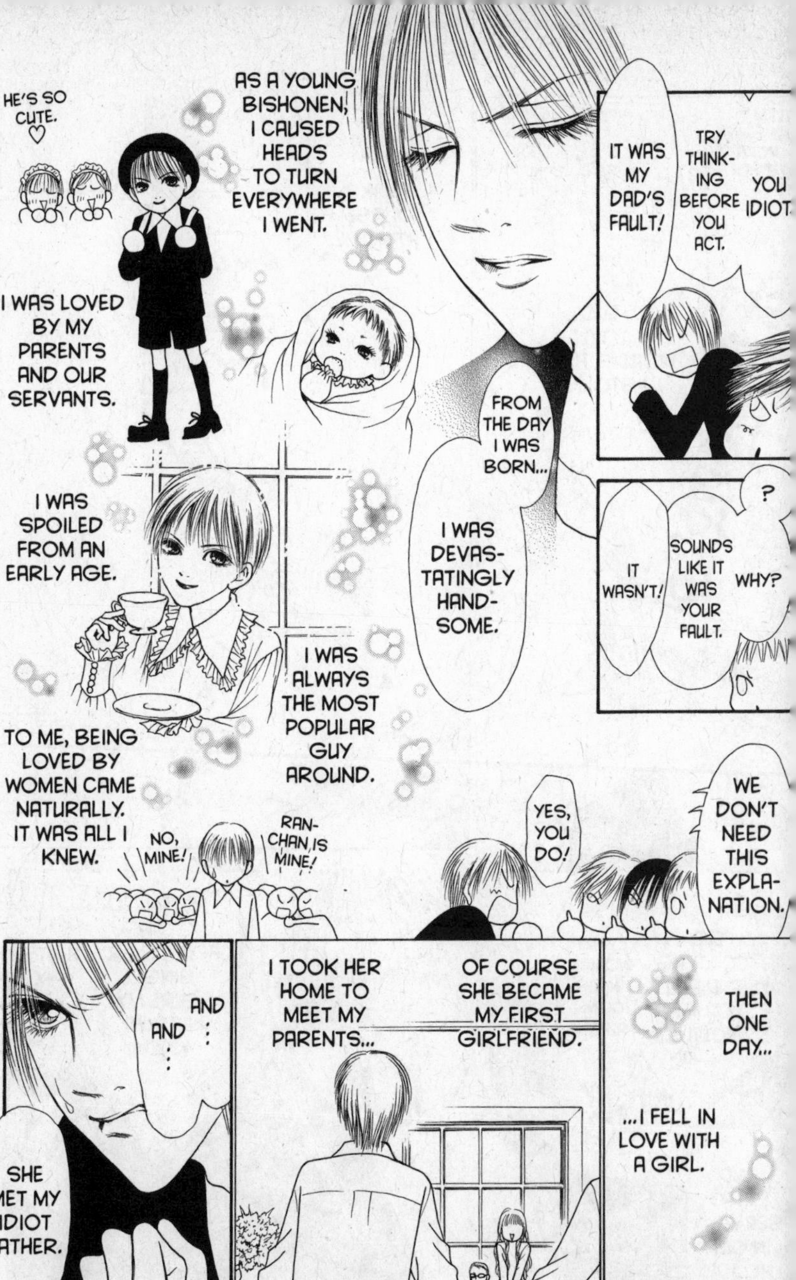
YOU IDIOT.
TRY THINKING BEFORE YOU ACT.
IT WAS MY DAD'S FAULT!
?
WHY?
SOUNDS LIKE IT WAS YOUR FAULT.
IT WASN'T!
FROM THE DAY I WAS BORN...
I WAS DEVASTATINGLY HANDSOME.
AS A YOUNG BISHONEN, I CAUSED HEADS TO TURN EVERYWHERE I WENT.
HE'S SO CUTE. ♡
I WAS LOVED BY MY PARENTS AND OUR SERVANTS.
I WAS ALWAYS THE MOST POPULAR GUY AROUND.
I WAS SPOILED FROM AN EARLY AGE.
TO ME, BEING LOVED BY WOMEN CAME NATURALLY. IT WAS ALL I KNEW.
RAN-CHAN IS MINE!
NO, MINE!
WE DON'T NEED THIS EXPLANATION.
YES, YOU DO!
THEN ONE DAY...
...I FELL IN LOVE WITH A GIRL.
OF COURSE SHE BECAME MY FIRST GIRLFRIEND.
I TOOK HER HOME TO MEET MY PARENTS...
AND...
AND...
SHE MET MY IDIOT FATHER.

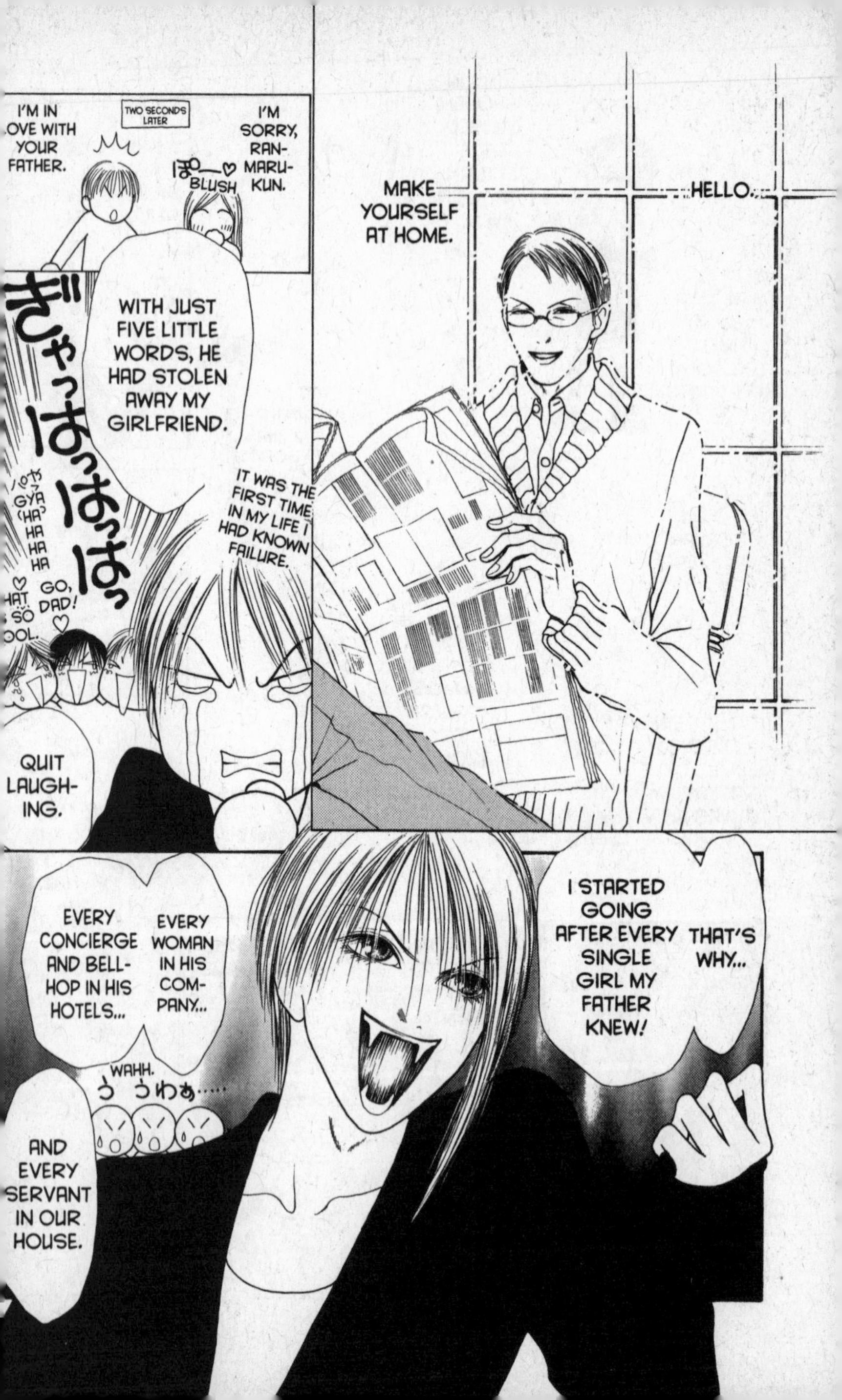
HELLO.
MAKE YOURSELF AT HOME.
I'M SORRY, RAN-MARU-KUN.
ぽー♡ BLUSH
TWO SECONDS LATER
I'M IN LOVE WITH YOUR FATHER.
IT WAS THE FIRST TIME IN MY LIFE I HAD KNOWN FAILURE.
WITH JUST FIVE LITTLE WORDS, HE HAD STOLEN AWAY MY GIRLFRIEND.
ぎゃっはっはっはっ
GYA HA HA HA HA
GO, DAD!
HAT 'S SO OOL.
QUIT LAUGHING.
THAT'S WHY...
I STARTED GOING AFTER EVERY SINGLE GIRL MY FATHER KNEW!
EVERY WOMAN IN HIS COMPANY...
EVERY CONCIERGE AND BELL-HOP IN HIS HOTELS...
うわぁ…… WAHH.
AND EVERY SERVANT IN OUR HOUSE.

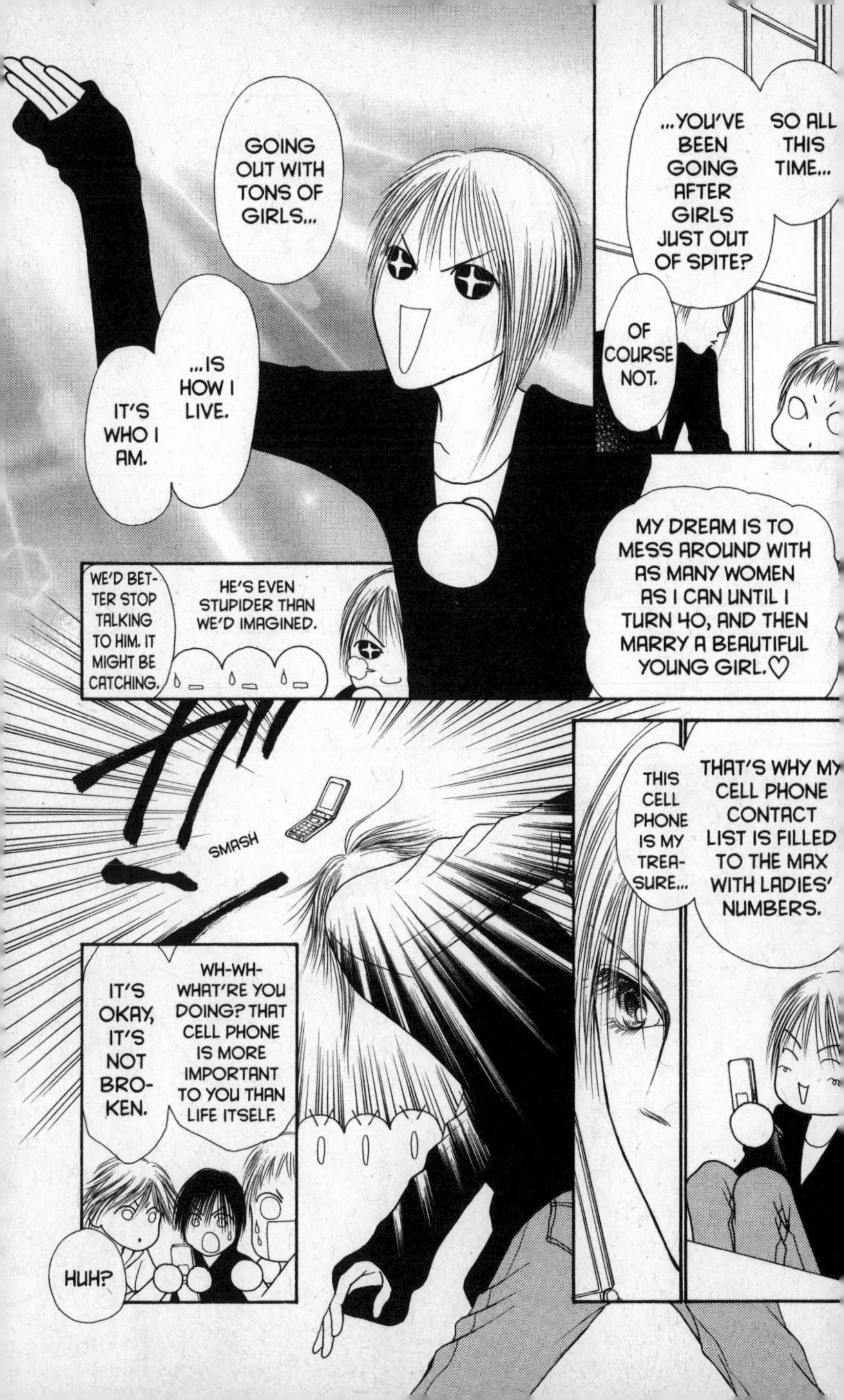
SO ALL THIS TIME...
...YOU'VE BEEN GOING AFTER GIRLS JUST OUT OF SPITE?
OF COURSE NOT.
MY DREAM IS TO MESS AROUND WITH AS MANY WOMEN AS I CAN UNTIL I TURN 40, AND THEN MARRY A BEAUTIFUL YOUNG GIRL.♡
GOING OUT WITH TONS OF GIRLS...
...IS HOW I LIVE.
IT'S WHO I AM.
HE'S EVEN STUPIDER THAN WE'D IMAGINED.
WE'D BETTER STOP TALKING TO HIM. IT MIGHT BE CATCHING.
THAT'S WHY MY CELL PHONE CONTACT LIST IS FILLED TO THE MAX WITH LADIES' NUMBERS.
THIS CELL PHONE IS MY TREASURE...
SMASH
WH-WH-WHAT'RE YOU DOING? THAT CELL PHONE IS MORE IMPORTANT TO YOU THAN LIFE ITSELF.
IT'S OKAY, IT'S NOT BRO-KEN.
HUH?

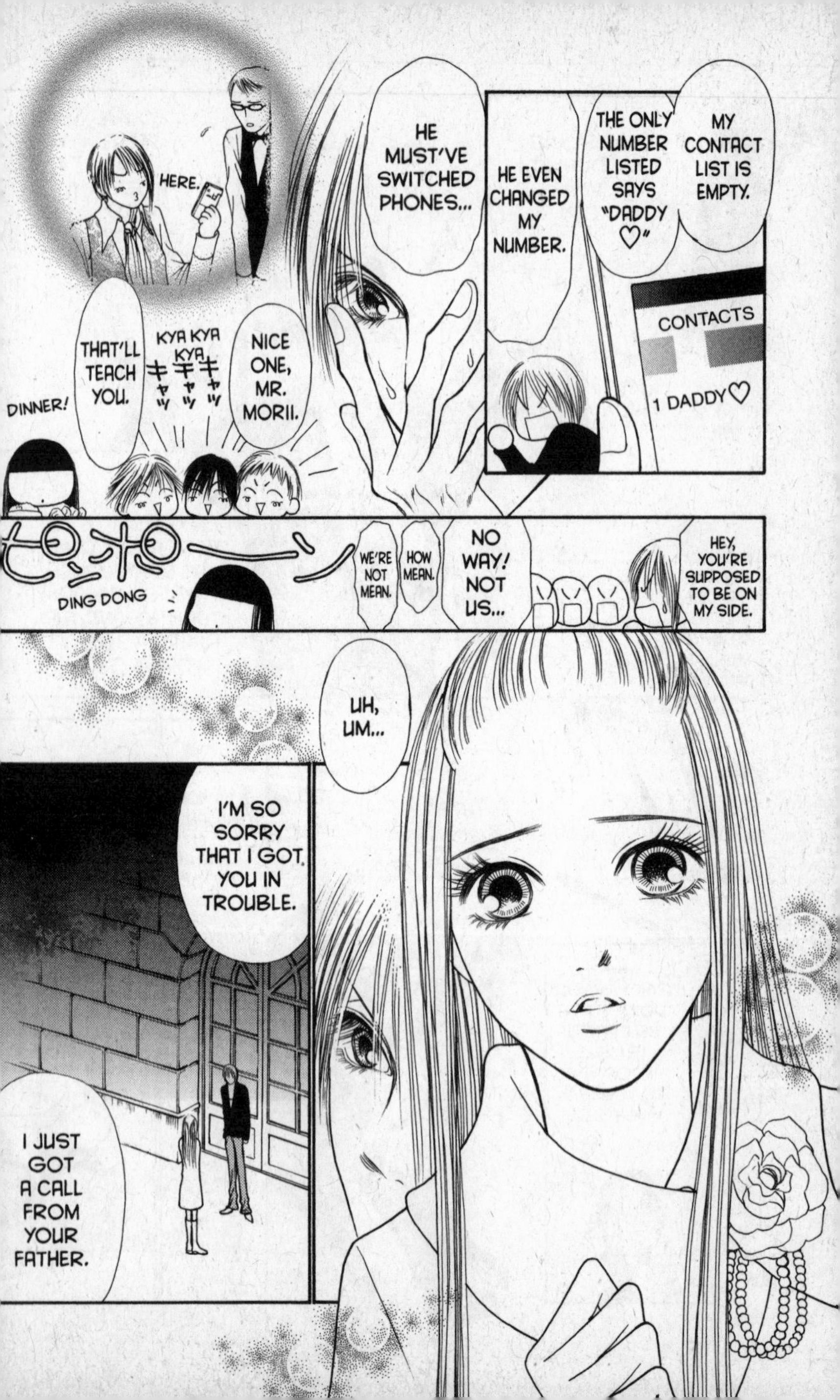
MY CONTACT LIST IS EMPTY.
THE ONLY NUMBER LISTED SAYS "DADDY ♡"
HE EVEN CHANGED MY NUMBER.
CONTACTS
1 DADDY♡
HE MUST'VE SWITCHED PHONES...
HERE.
NICE ONE, MR. MORII.
KYA KYA KYA
キャッ キャッ キャッ
THAT'LL TEACH YOU.
DINNER!
HEY, YOU'RE SUPPOSED TO BE ON MY SIDE.
NO WAY! NOT US...
HOW MEAN.
WE'RE NOT MEAN.
ピンポーン
DING DONG
UH, UM...
I'M SO SORRY THAT I GOT YOU IN TROUBLE.
I JUST GOT A CALL FROM YOUR FATHER.

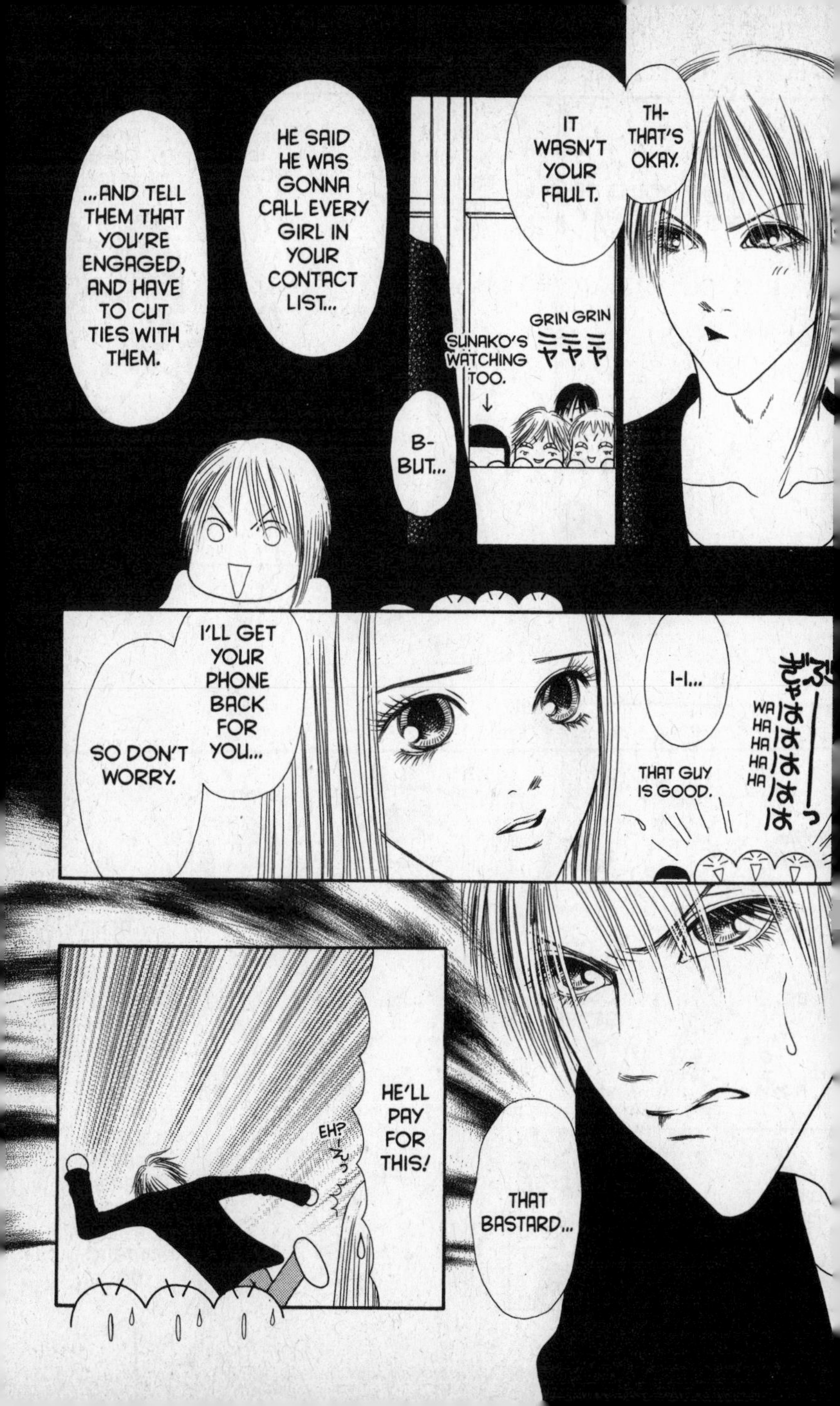
TH- THAT'S OKAY.
IT WASN'T YOUR FAULT.
GRIN GRIN
ニヤニヤ
SUNAKO'S WATCHING TOO.
B- BUT...
HE SAID HE WAS GONNA CALL EVERY GIRL IN YOUR CONTACT LIST...
...AND TELL THEM THAT YOU'RE ENGAGED, AND HAVE TO CUT TIES WITH THEM.
ぶーーっ
ぎゃははははは
WA HA HA HA HA
THAT GUY IS GOOD.
I-I...
I'LL GET YOUR PHONE BACK FOR YOU...
SO DON'T WORRY.
THAT BASTARD...
HE'LL PAY FOR THIS!
EH?

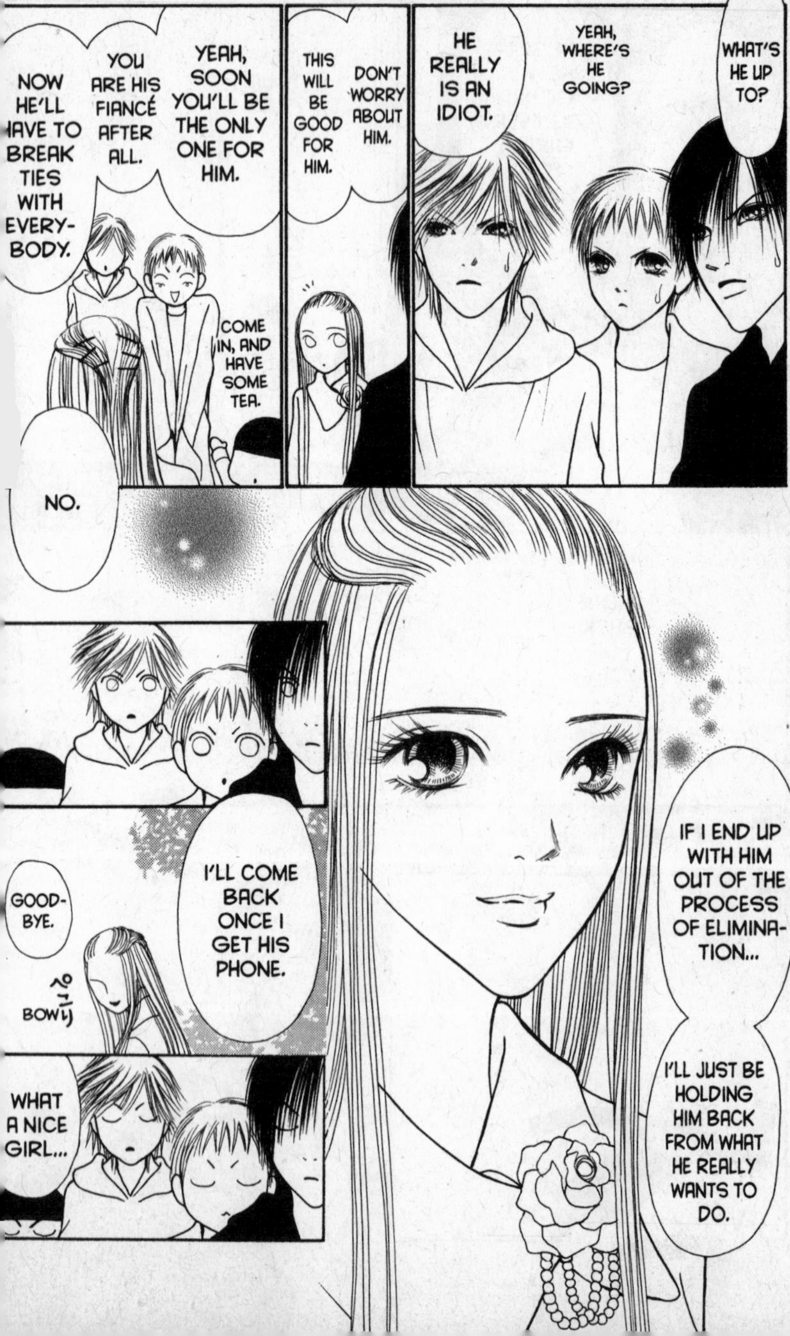

WHAT'S HE UP TO?
YEAH, WHERE'S HE GOING?
HE REALLY IS AN IDIOT.
DON'T WORRY ABOUT HIM.
THIS WILL BE GOOD FOR HIM.
YEAH, SOON YOU'LL BE THE ONLY ONE FOR HIM.
YOU ARE HIS FIANCÉ AFTER ALL.
NOW HE'LL HAVE TO BREAK TIES WITH EVERY-BODY.
COME IN, AND HAVE SOME TEA.
NO.
IF I END UP WITH HIM OUT OF THE PROCESS OF ELIMINA-TION...
I'LL JUST BE HOLDING HIM BACK FROM WHAT HE REALLY WANTS TO DO.
I'LL COME BACK ONCE I GET HIS PHONE.
GOOD-BYE.
BOW
WHAT A NICE GIRL...

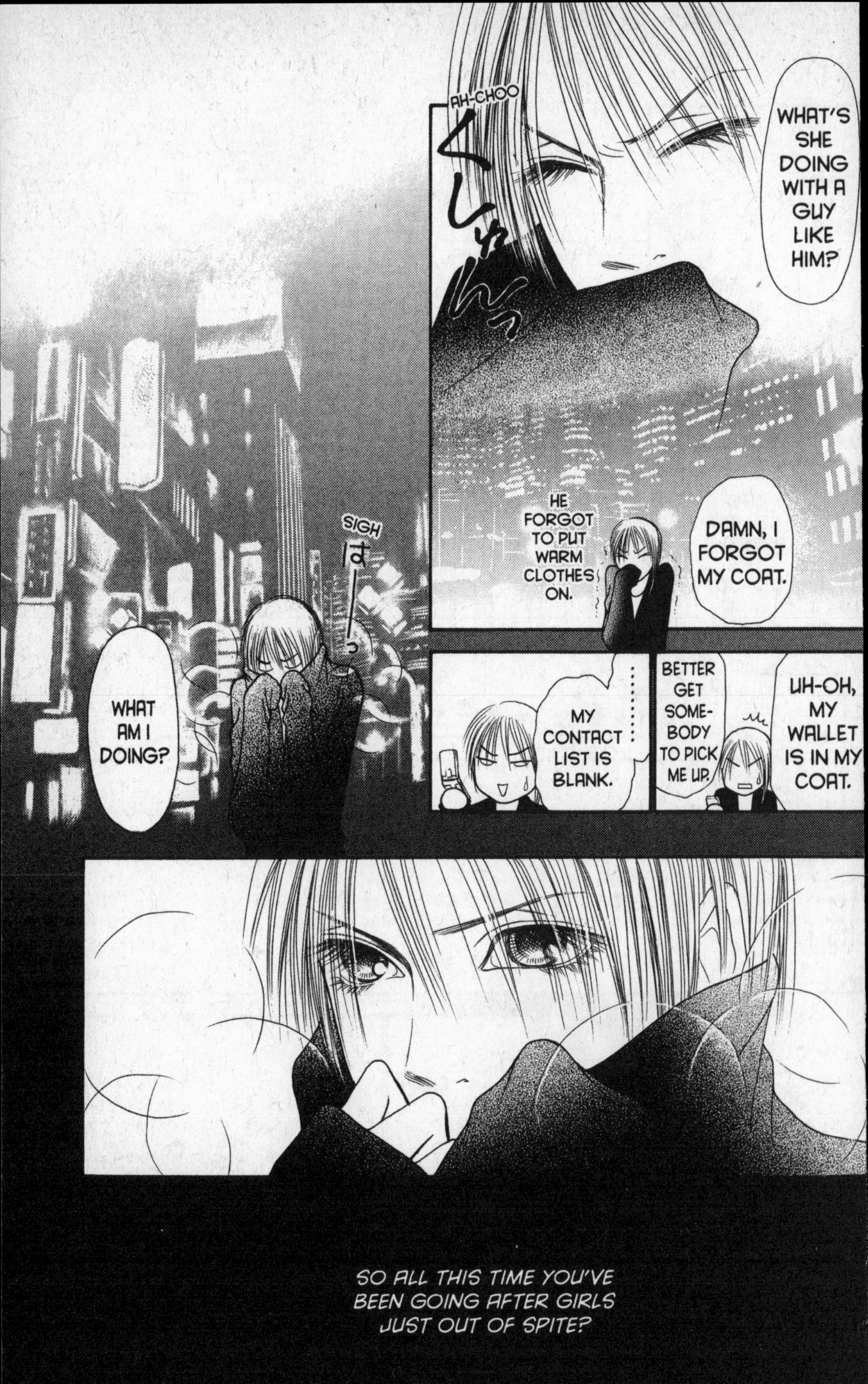

WHAT'S SHE DOING WITH A GUY LIKE HIM?
AH-CHOO
DAMN, I FORGOT MY COAT.
HE FORGOT TO PUT WARM CLOTHES ON.
UH-OH, MY WALLET IS IN MY COAT.
BETTER GET SOMEBODY TO PICK ME UP.
MY CONTACT LIST IS BLANK.
......
SIGH
WHAT AM I DOING?
SO ALL THIS TIME YOU'VE BEEN GOING AFTER GIRLS JUST OUT OF SPITE?

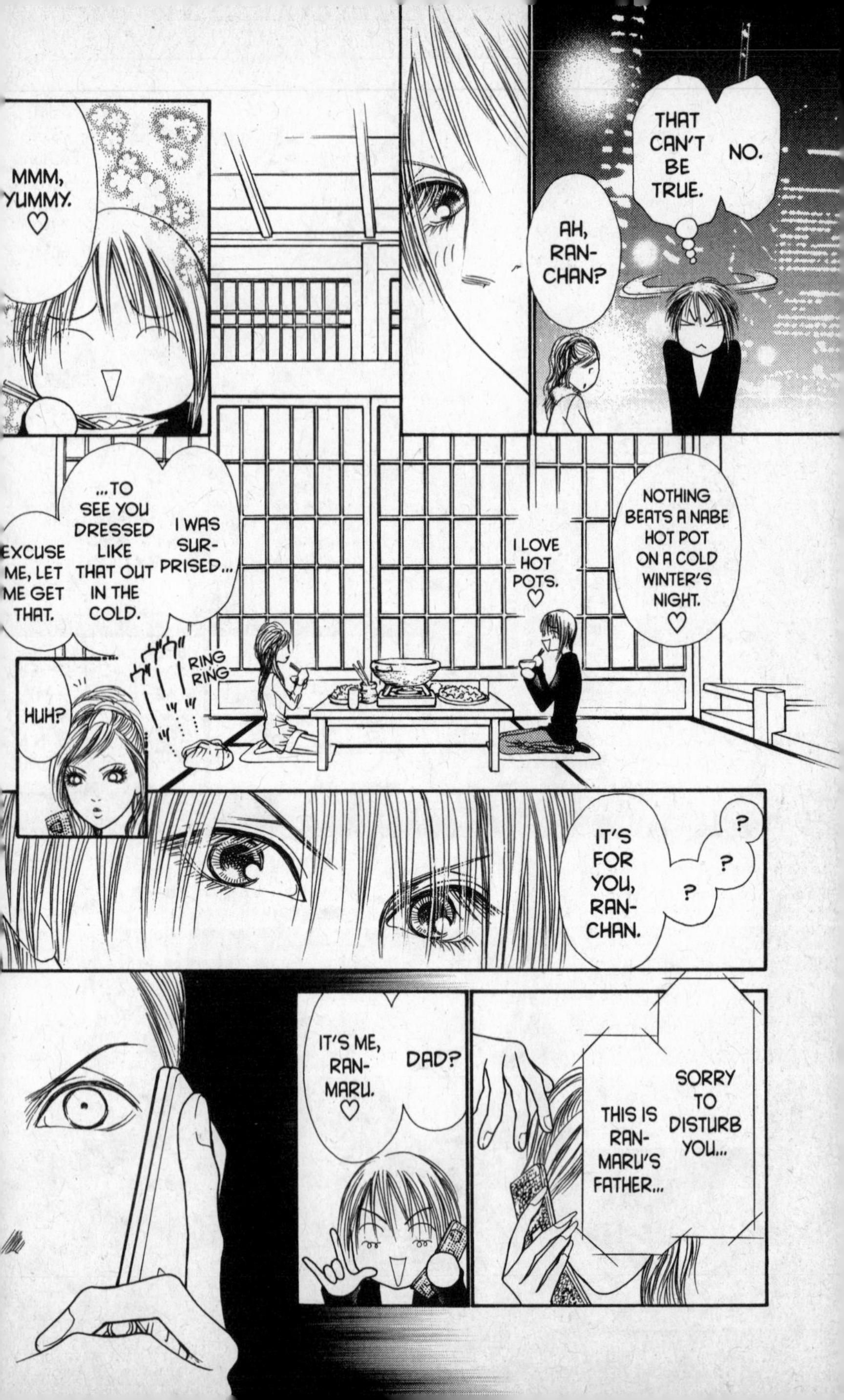
NO.
THAT CAN'T BE TRUE.
AH, RAN-CHAN?
MMM, YUMMY. ♡
NOTHING BEATS A NABE HOT POT ON A COLD WINTER'S NIGHT. ♡
I LOVE HOT POTS. ♡
I WAS SUR-PRISED...
...TO SEE YOU DRESSED LIKE THAT OUT IN THE COLD.
EXCUSE ME, LET ME GET THAT.
RING RING
HUH?
? ? ?
IT'S FOR YOU, RAN-CHAN.
SORRY TO DISTURB YOU...
THIS IS RAN-MARU'S FATHER...
DAD?
IT'S ME, RAN-MARU. ♡

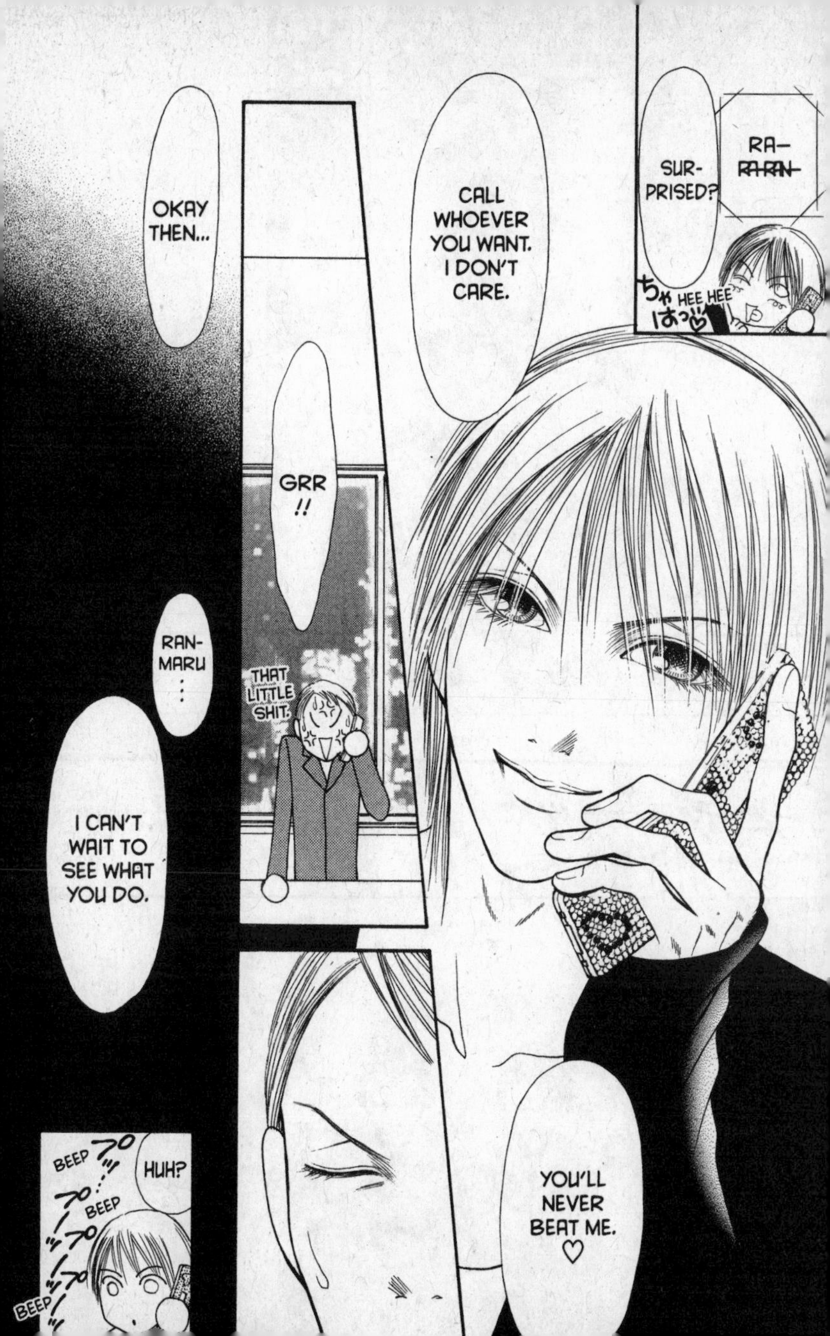
RA-RA-RAN
SUR-PRISED?
HEE HEE
CALL WHOEVER YOU WANT. I DON'T CARE.
GRR!!
THAT LITTLE SHIT.
OKAY THEN...
YOU'LL NEVER BEAT ME. ♡
RAN-MARU...
I CAN'T WAIT TO SEE WHAT YOU DO.
HUH?
BEEP
BEEP
BEEP

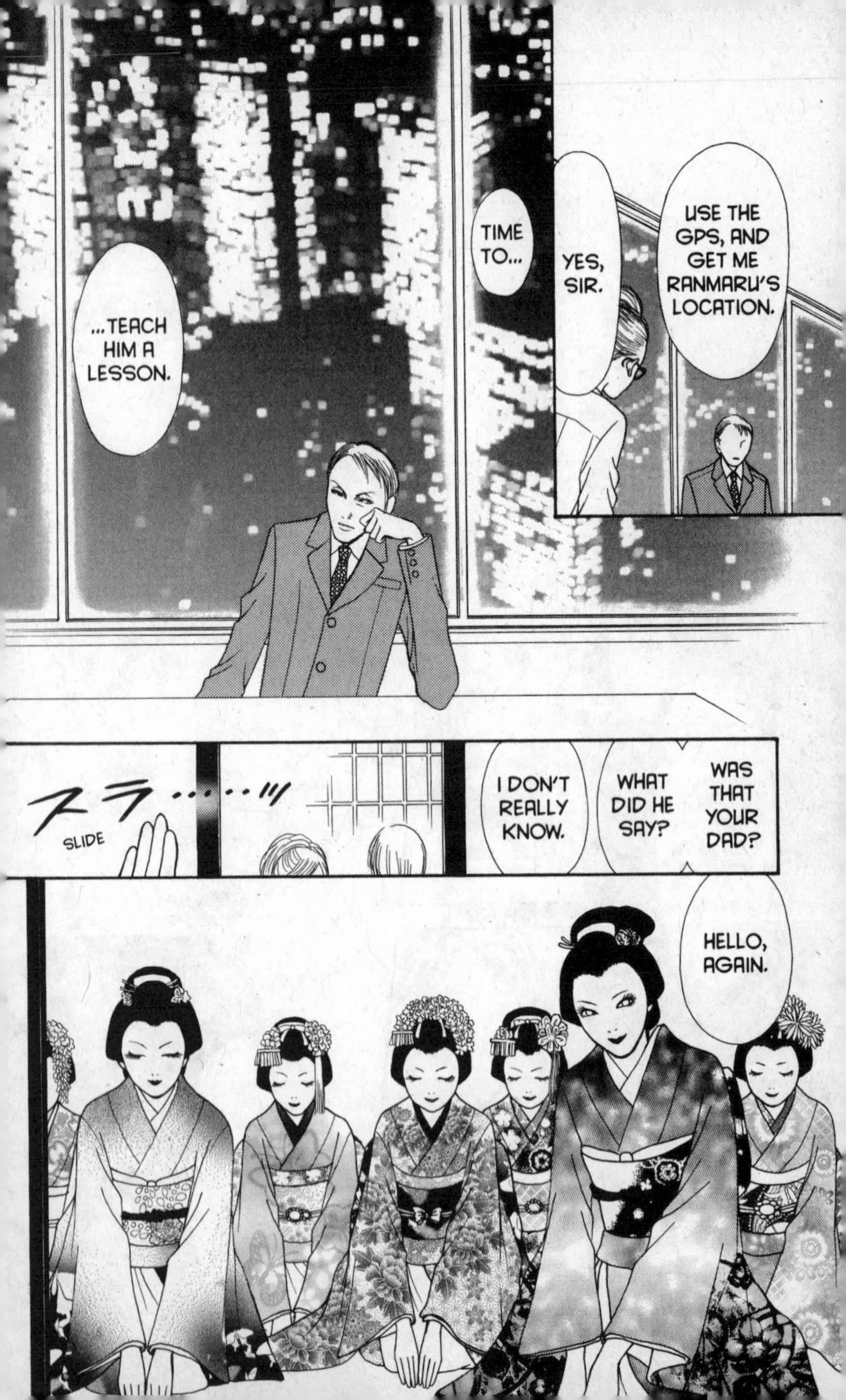
USE THE GPS, AND GET ME RANMARU'S LOCATION.
YES, SIR.
TIME TO...
...TEACH HIM A LESSON.
WAS THAT YOUR DAD?
WHAT DID HE SAY?
I DON'T REALLY KNOW.
スラ……ッ
SLIDE
HELLO, AGAIN.

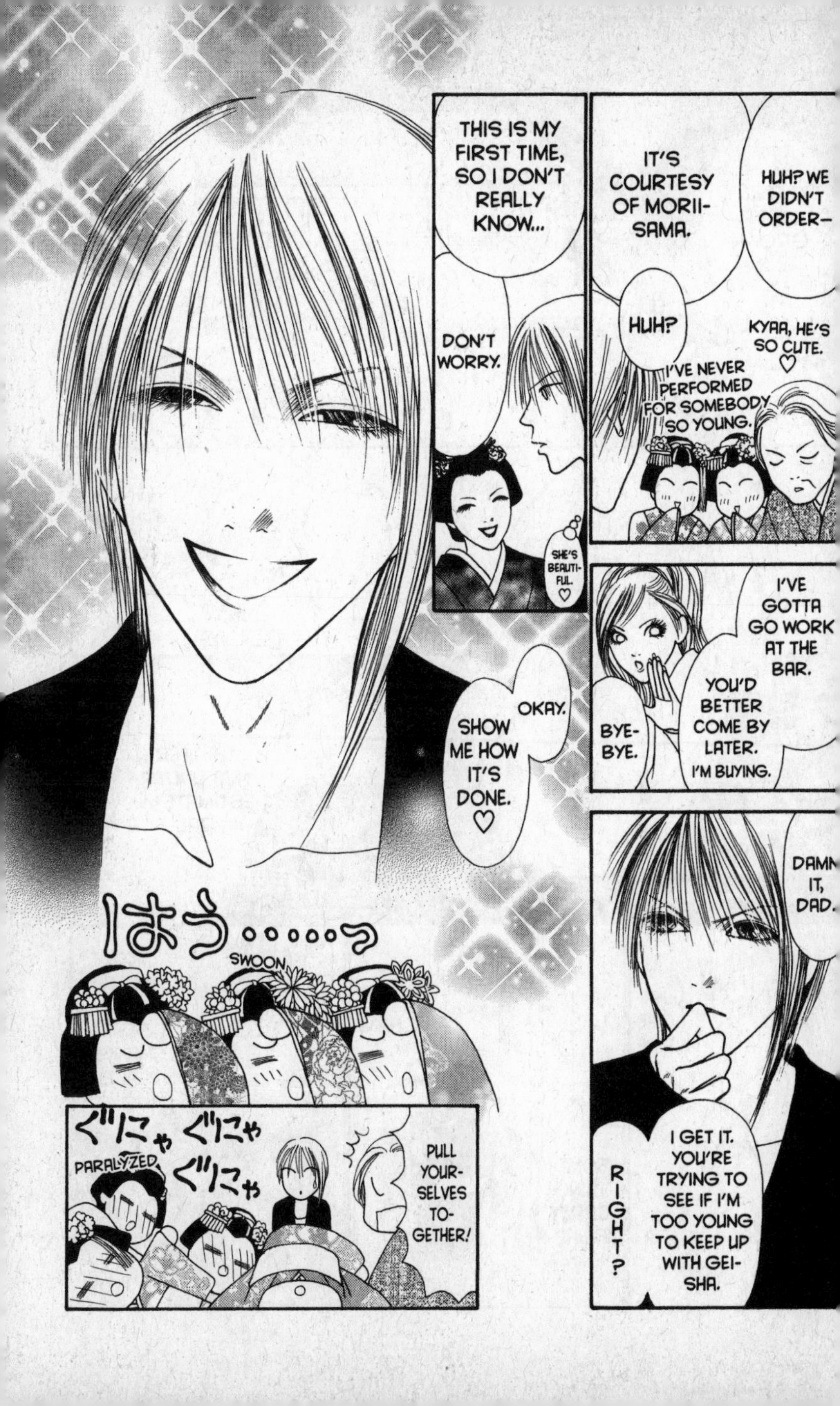

HUH? WE DIDN'T ORDER—
IT'S COURTESY OF MORII-SAMA.
HUH?
KYAA, HE'S SO CUTE. ♡
I'VE NEVER PERFORMED FOR SOMEBODY SO YOUNG.
THIS IS MY FIRST TIME, SO I DON'T REALLY KNOW...
DON'T WORRY.
SHE'S BEAUTIFUL. ♡
I'VE GOTTA GO WORK AT THE BAR.
YOU'D BETTER COME BY LATER. I'M BUYING.
BYE-BYE.
DAMN IT, DAD.
I GET IT. YOU'RE TRYING TO SEE IF I'M TOO YOUNG TO KEEP UP WITH GEISHA.
RIGHT?
OKAY.
SHOW ME HOW IT'S DONE. ♡
はう。。。。。っ
SWOON
ぐにゃ ぐにゃ ぐにゃ
PARALYZED
PULL YOURSELVES TOGETHER!

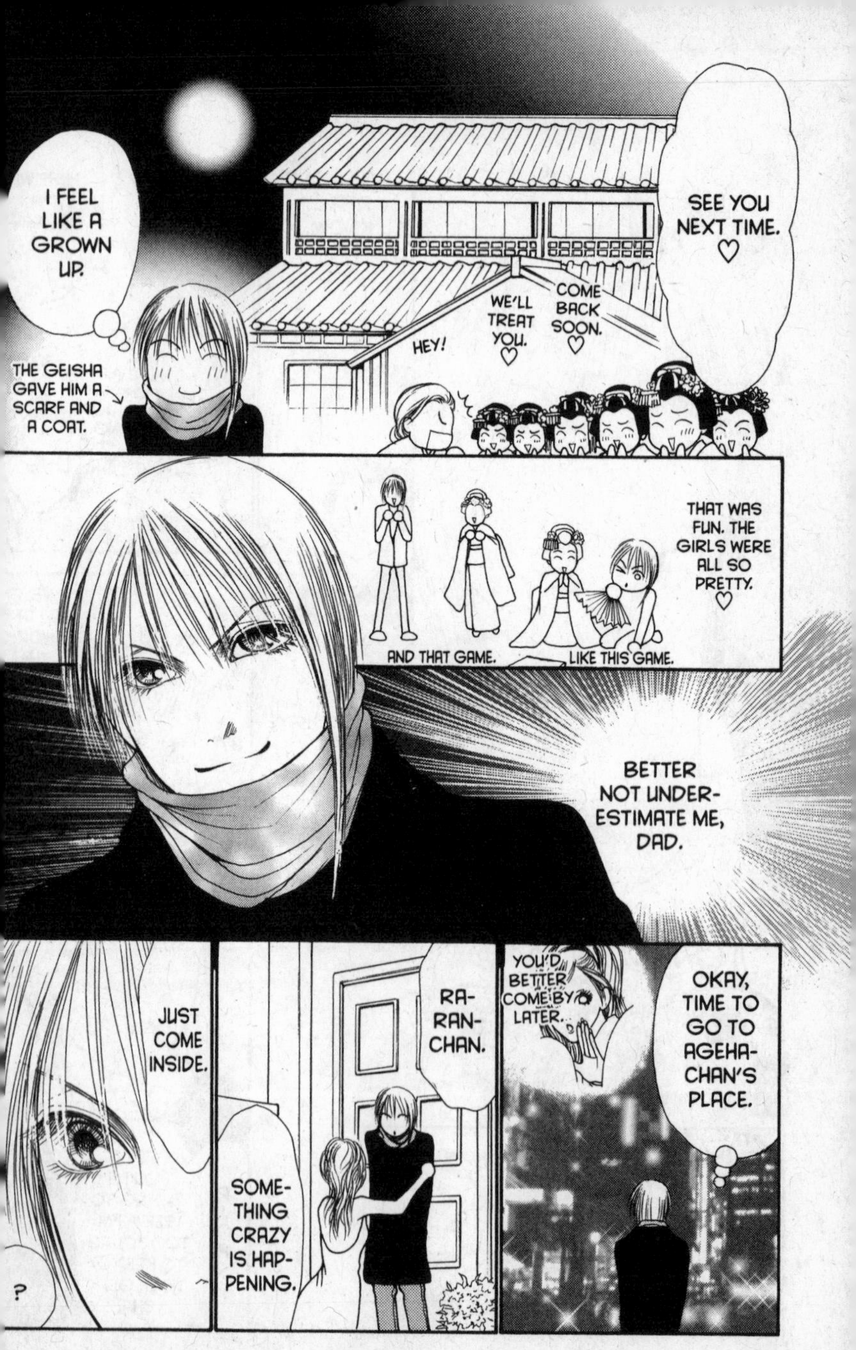
SEE YOU NEXT TIME. ♡
COME BACK SOON. ♡
WE'LL TREAT YOU. ♡
HEY!
I FEEL LIKE A GROWN UP.
THE GEISHA GAVE HIM A SCARF AND A COAT.
THAT WAS FUN. THE GIRLS WERE ALL SO PRETTY. ♡
LIKE THIS GAME.
AND THAT GAME.
BETTER NOT UNDER-ESTIMATE ME, DAD.
OKAY, TIME TO GO TO AGEHA-CHAN'S PLACE.
YOU'D BETTER COME BY LATER...
RA-RAN-CHAN.
SOMETHING CRAZY IS HAPPENING.
JUST COME INSIDE.
?

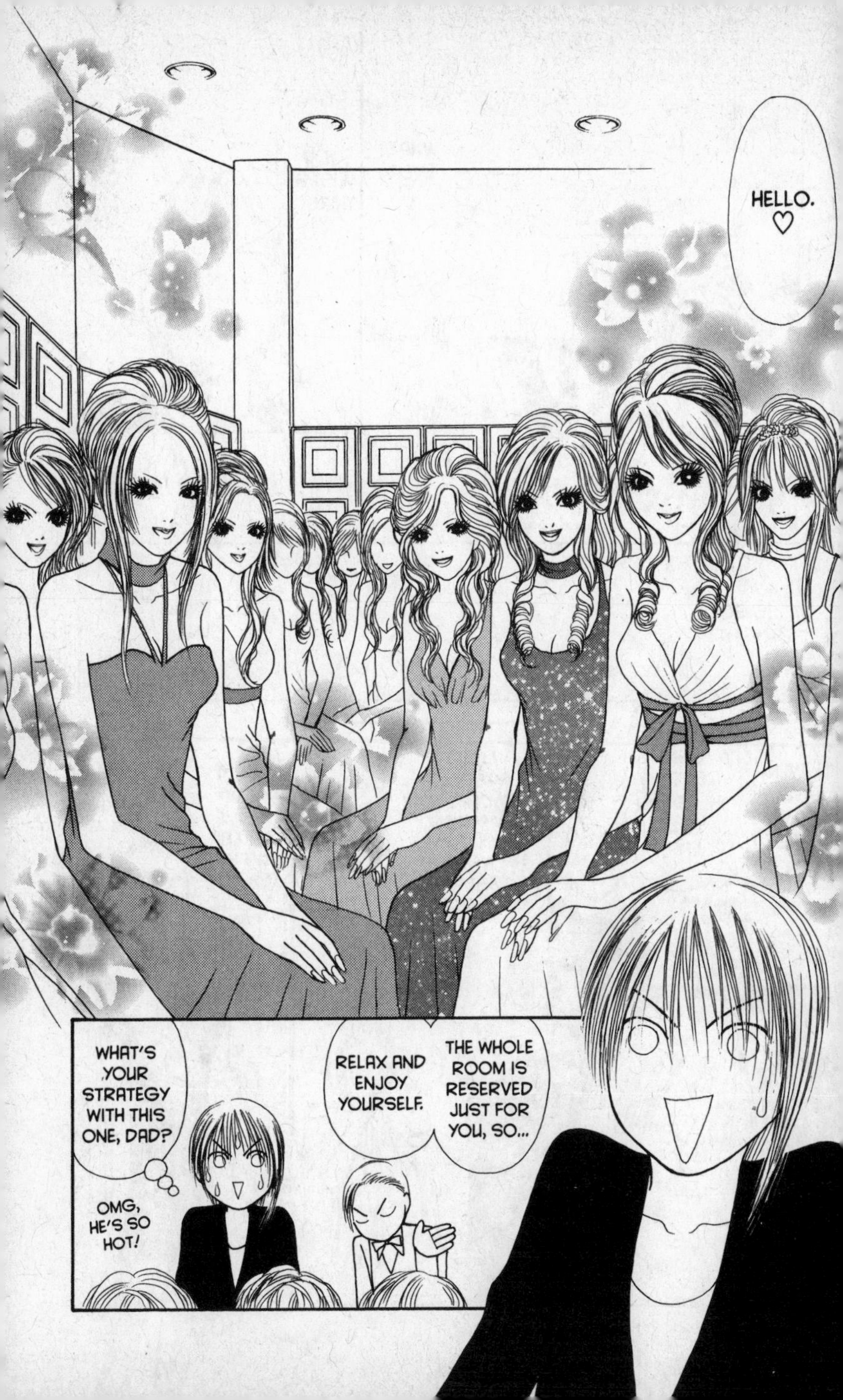
HELLO. ♡
THE WHOLE ROOM IS RESERVED JUST FOR YOU, SO...
RELAX AND ENJOY YOURSELF.
WHAT'S YOUR STRATEGY WITH THIS ONE, DAD?
OMG, HE'S SO HOT!

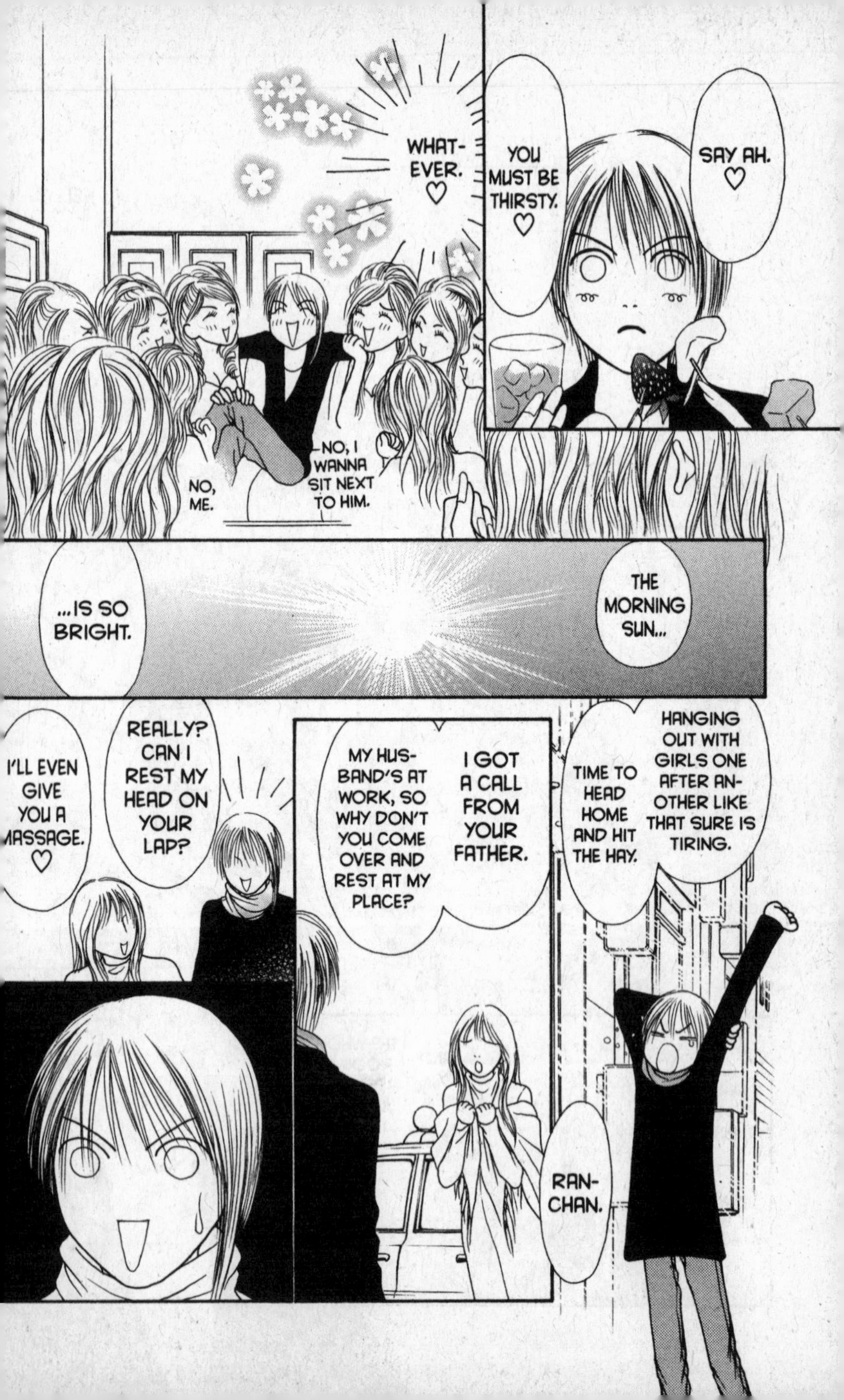
SAY AH. ♡
YOU MUST BE THIRSTY. ♡
WHAT-EVER. ♡
NO, I WANNA SIT NEXT TO HIM.
NO, ME.
THE MORNING SUN...
...IS SO BRIGHT.
HANGING OUT WITH GIRLS ONE AFTER AN-OTHER LIKE THAT SURE IS TIRING.
TIME TO HEAD HOME AND HIT THE HAY.
RAN-CHAN.
I GOT A CALL FROM YOUR FATHER.
MY HUS-BAND'S AT WORK, SO WHY DON'T YOU COME OVER AND REST AT MY PLACE?
REALLY? CAN I REST MY HEAD ON YOUR LAP?
I'LL EVEN GIVE YOU A MASSAGE. ♡

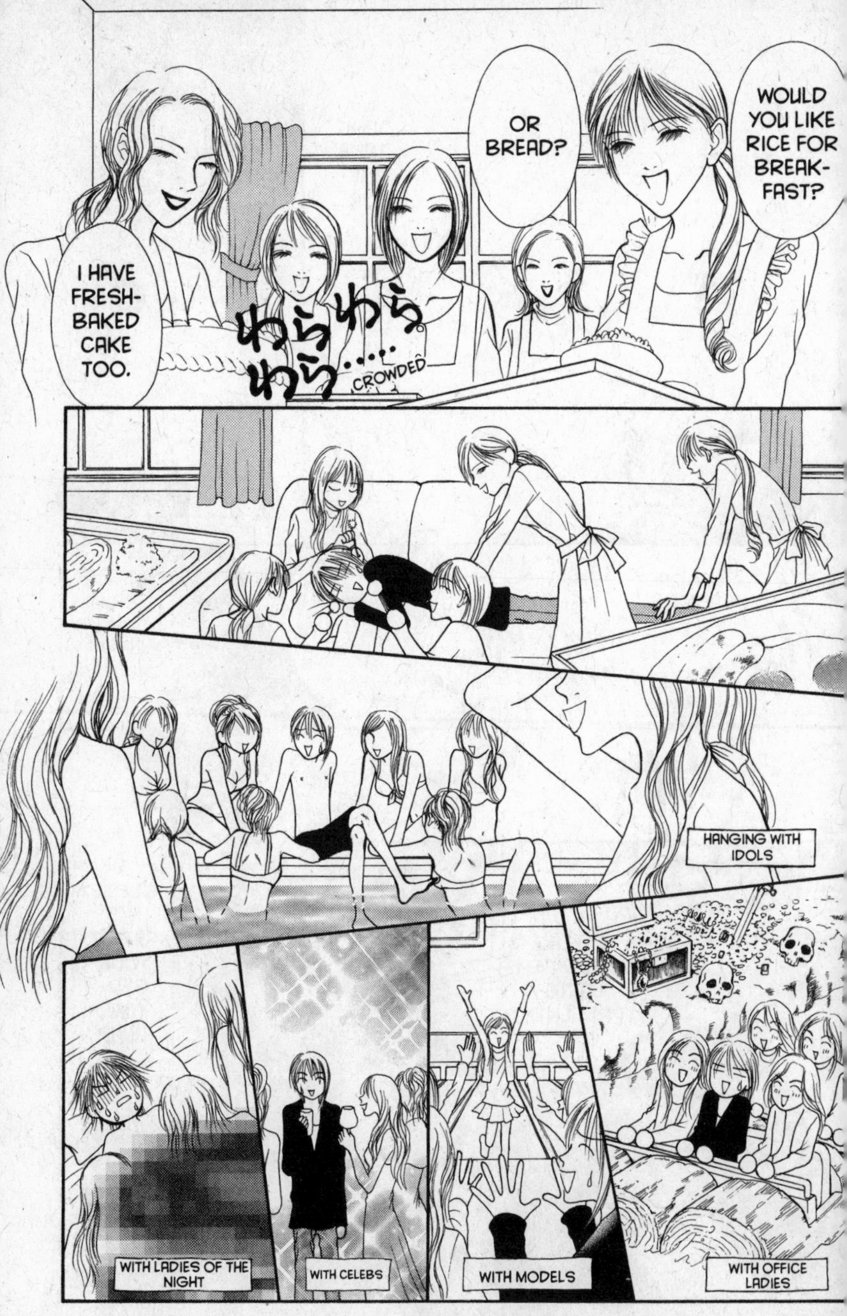
WOULD YOU LIKE RICE FOR BREAK-FAST?
OR BREAD?
わらわら わら……
CROWDED
I HAVE FRESH-BAKED CAKE TOO.
HANGING WITH IDOLS
WITH OFFICE LADIES
WITH MODELS
WITH CELEBS
WITH LADIES OF THE NIGHT

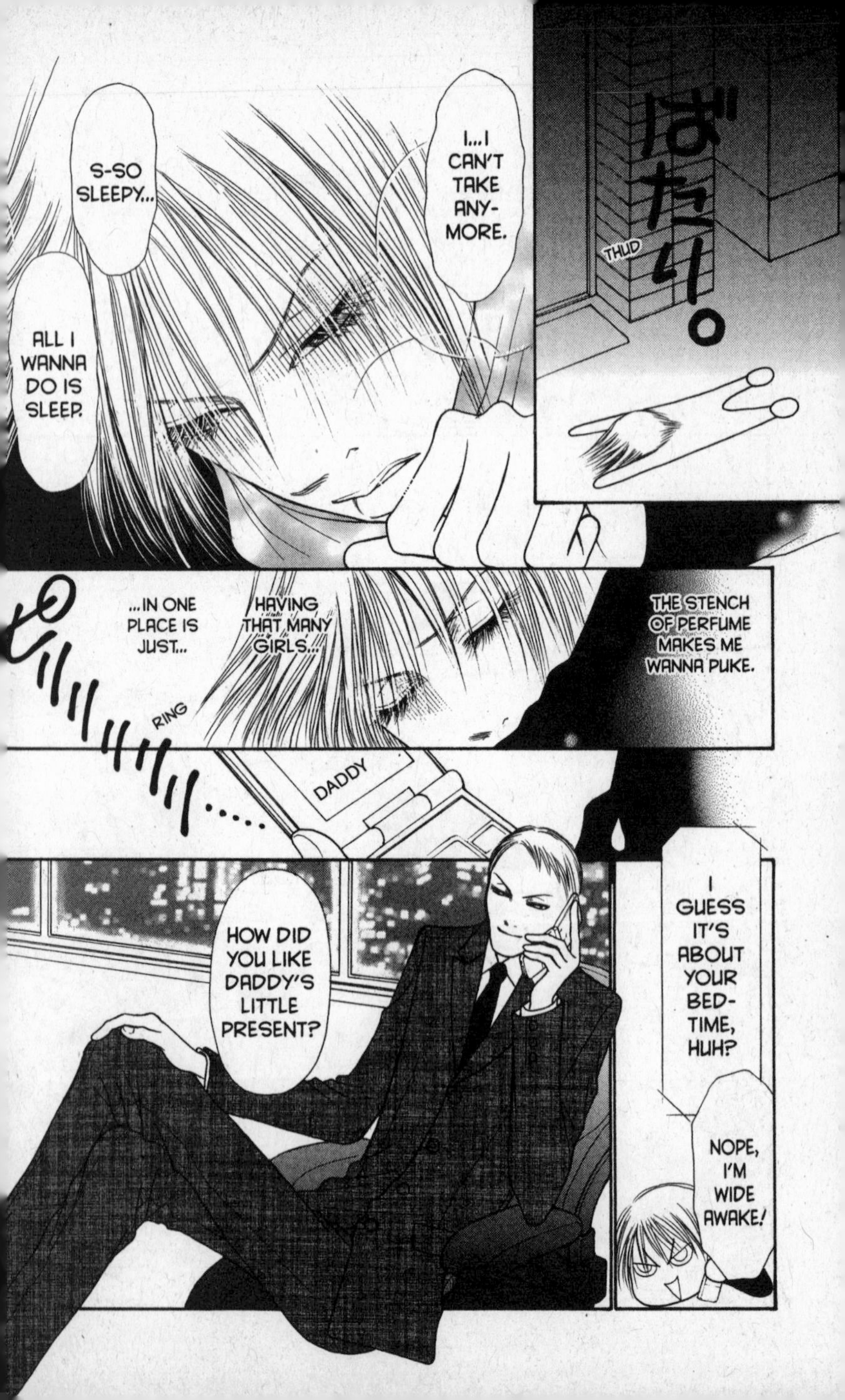
ばたーり。
THUD
I...I CAN'T TAKE ANY-MORE.
S-SO SLEEPY...
ALL I WANNA DO IS SLEEP.
THE STENCH OF PERFUME MAKES ME WANNA PUKE.
HAVING THAT MANY GIRLS...
...IN ONE PLACE IS JUST...
ぴりりりり.....
RING
DADDY
I GUESS IT'S ABOUT YOUR BED-TIME, HUH?
NOPE, I'M WIDE AWAKE!
HOW DID YOU LIKE DADDY'S LITTLE PRESENT?

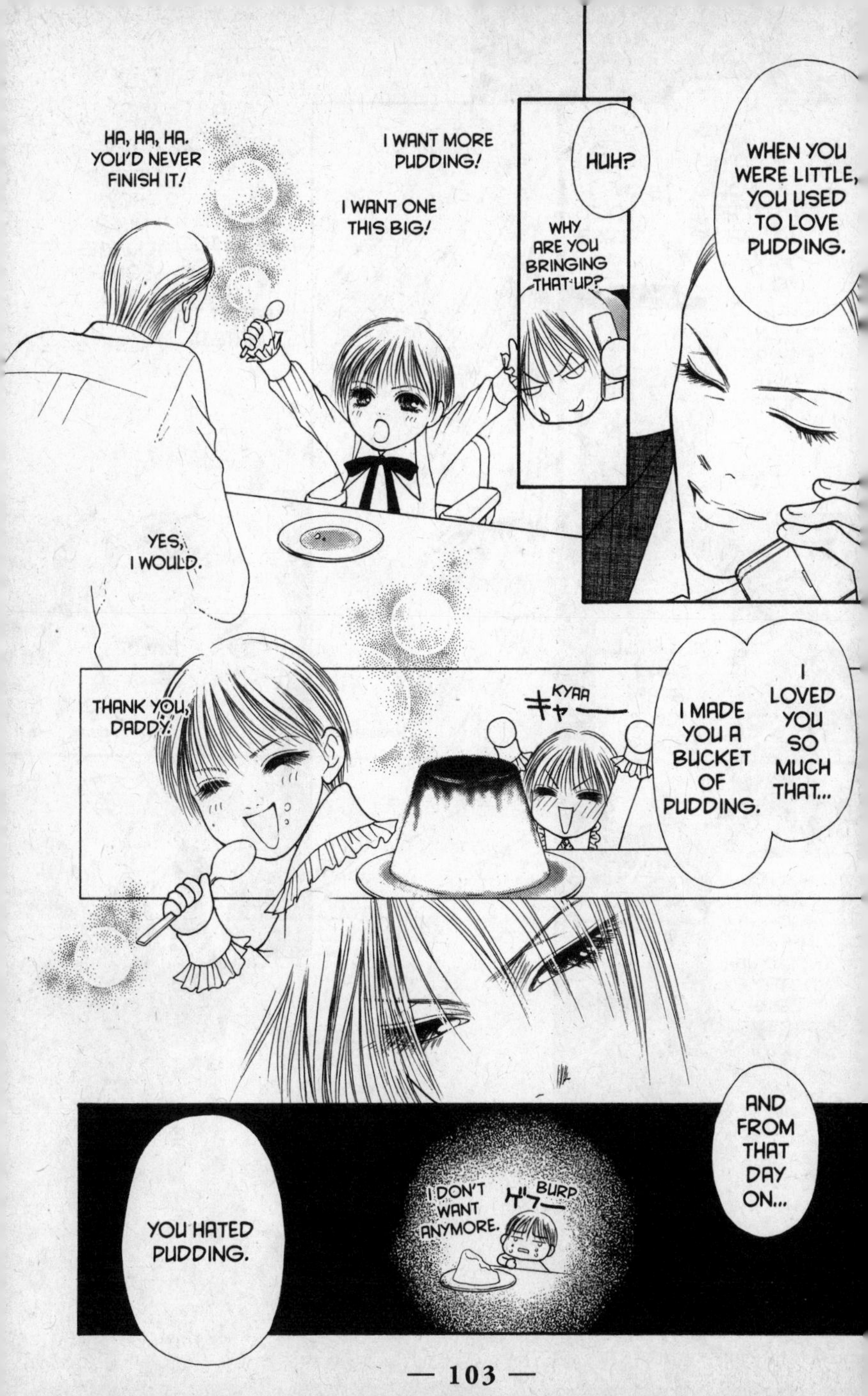
WHEN YOU WERE LITTLE, YOU USED TO LOVE PUDDING.
HUH?
WHY ARE YOU BRINGING THAT UP?
I WANT MORE PUDDING!
I WANT ONE THIS BIG!
HA, HA, HA. YOU'D NEVER FINISH IT!
YES, I WOULD.
I LOVED YOU SO MUCH THAT...
I MADE YOU A BUCKET OF PUDDING.
キャー KYAA
THANK YOU, DADDY.
AND FROM THAT DAY ON...
BURP ゲフー
I DON'T WANT ANYMORE.
YOU HATED PUDDING.

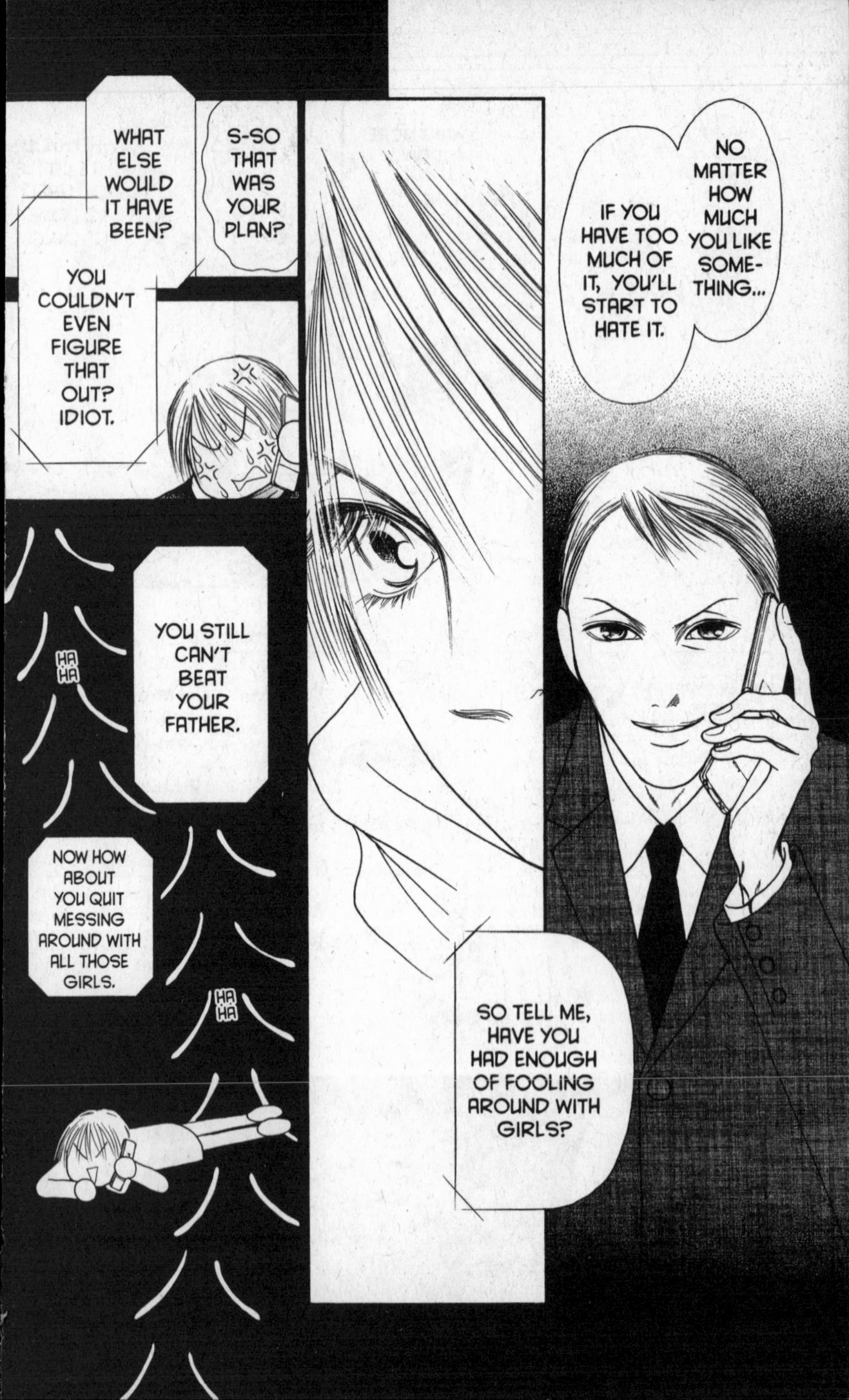
NO MATTER HOW MUCH YOU LIKE SOME-THING...
IF YOU HAVE TOO MUCH OF IT, YOU'LL START TO HATE IT.
SO TELL ME, HAVE YOU HAD ENOUGH OF FOOLING AROUND WITH GIRLS?
S-SO THAT WAS YOUR PLAN?
WHAT ELSE WOULD IT HAVE BEEN?
YOU COULDN'T EVEN FIGURE THAT OUT? IDIOT.
YOU STILL CAN'T BEAT YOUR FATHER.
HA HA
NOW HOW ABOUT YOU QUIT MESSING AROUND WITH ALL THOSE GIRLS.
HA HA

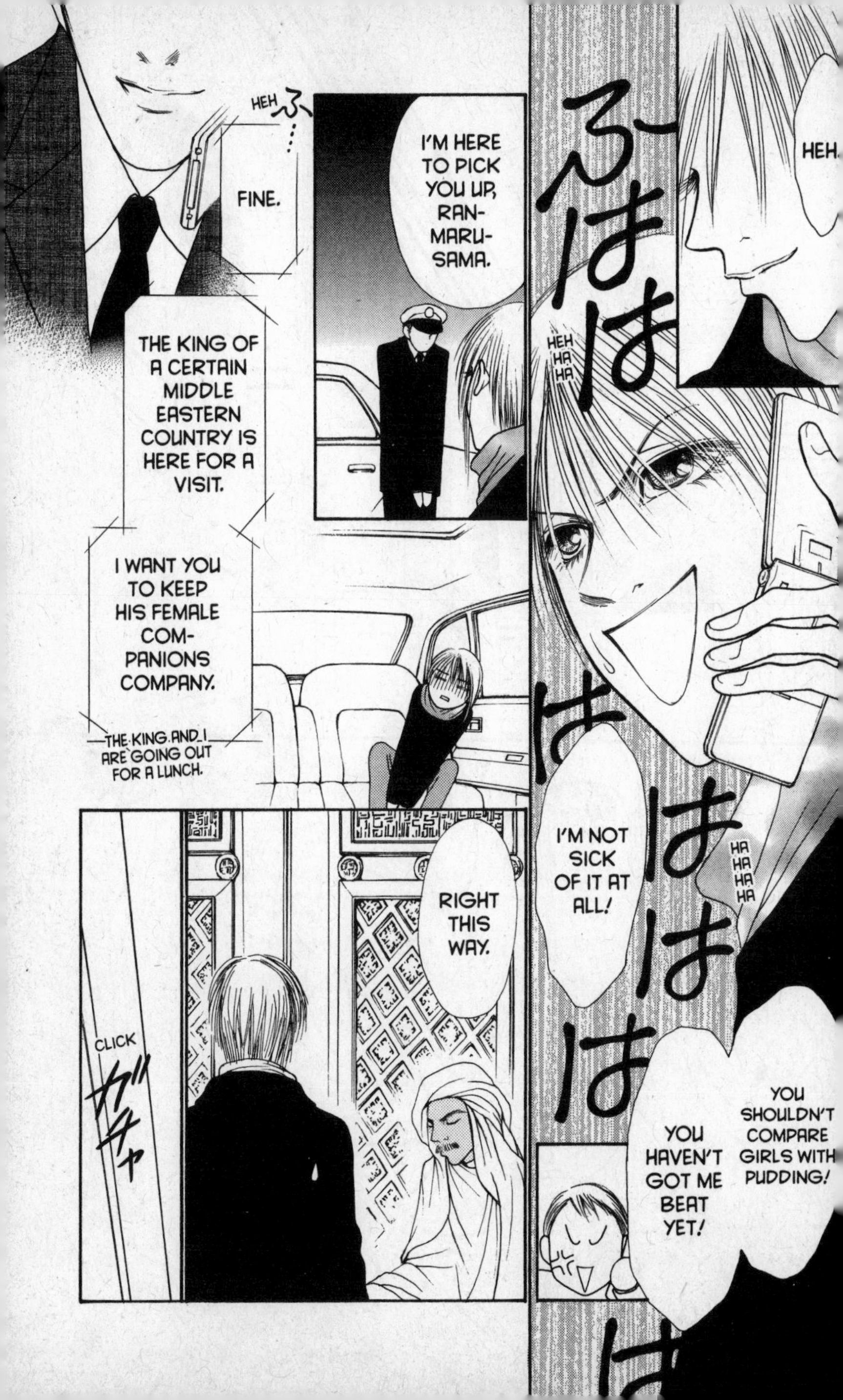

HEH.
ふ〜ははははは
HEH HA HA
I'M NOT SICK OF IT AT ALL!
HA HA HA HA
YOU SHOULDN'T COMPARE GIRLS WITH PUDDING!
YOU HAVEN'T GOT ME BEAT YET!
I'M HERE TO PICK YOU UP, RAN-MARU-SAMA.
HEH ふ...
FINE.
THE KING OF A CERTAIN MIDDLE EASTERN COUNTRY IS HERE FOR A VISIT.
I WANT YOU TO KEEP HIS FEMALE COM-PANIONS COMPANY.
—THE KING AND I ARE GOING OUT FOR A LUNCH.
RIGHT THIS WAY.
CLICK
ガチャ

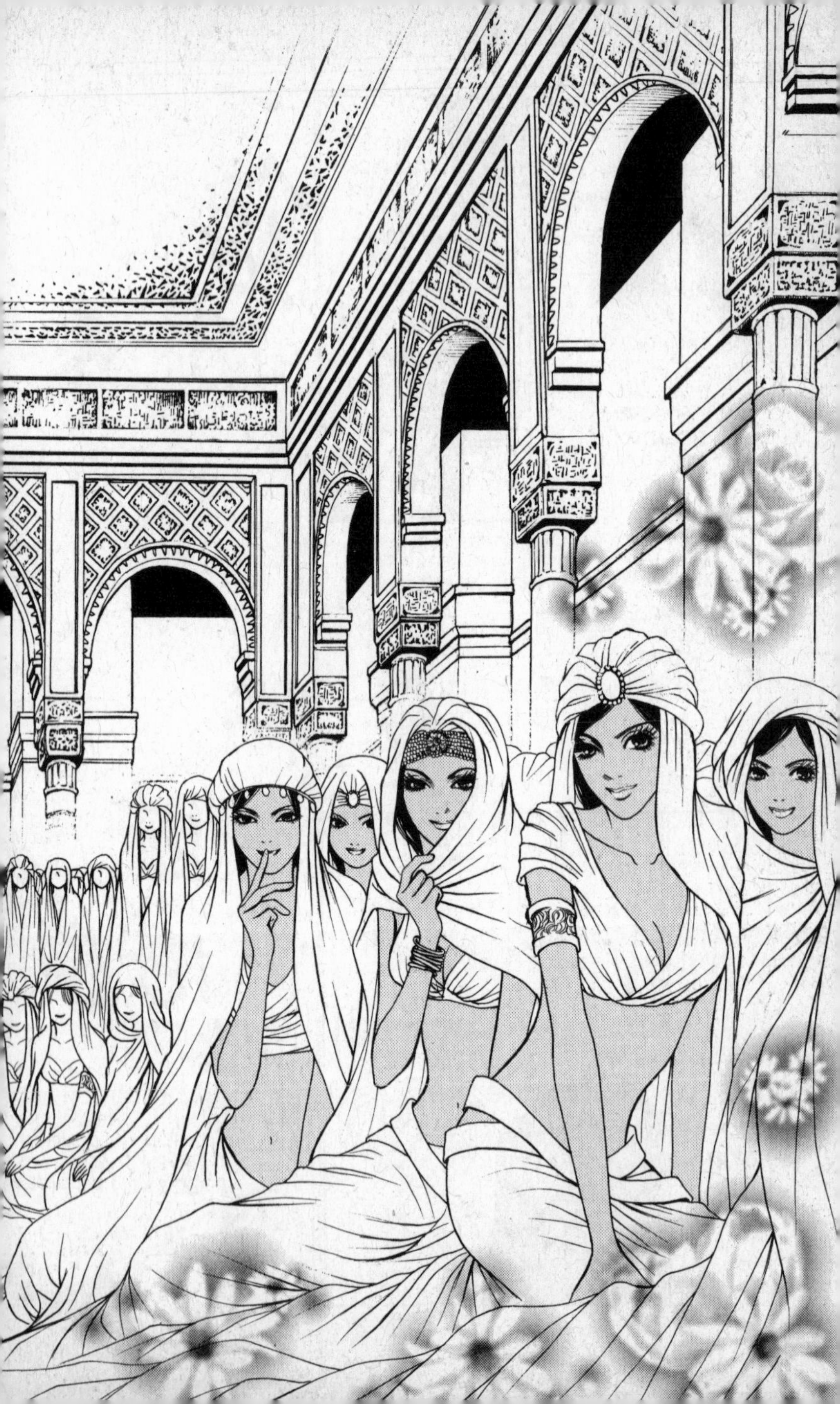

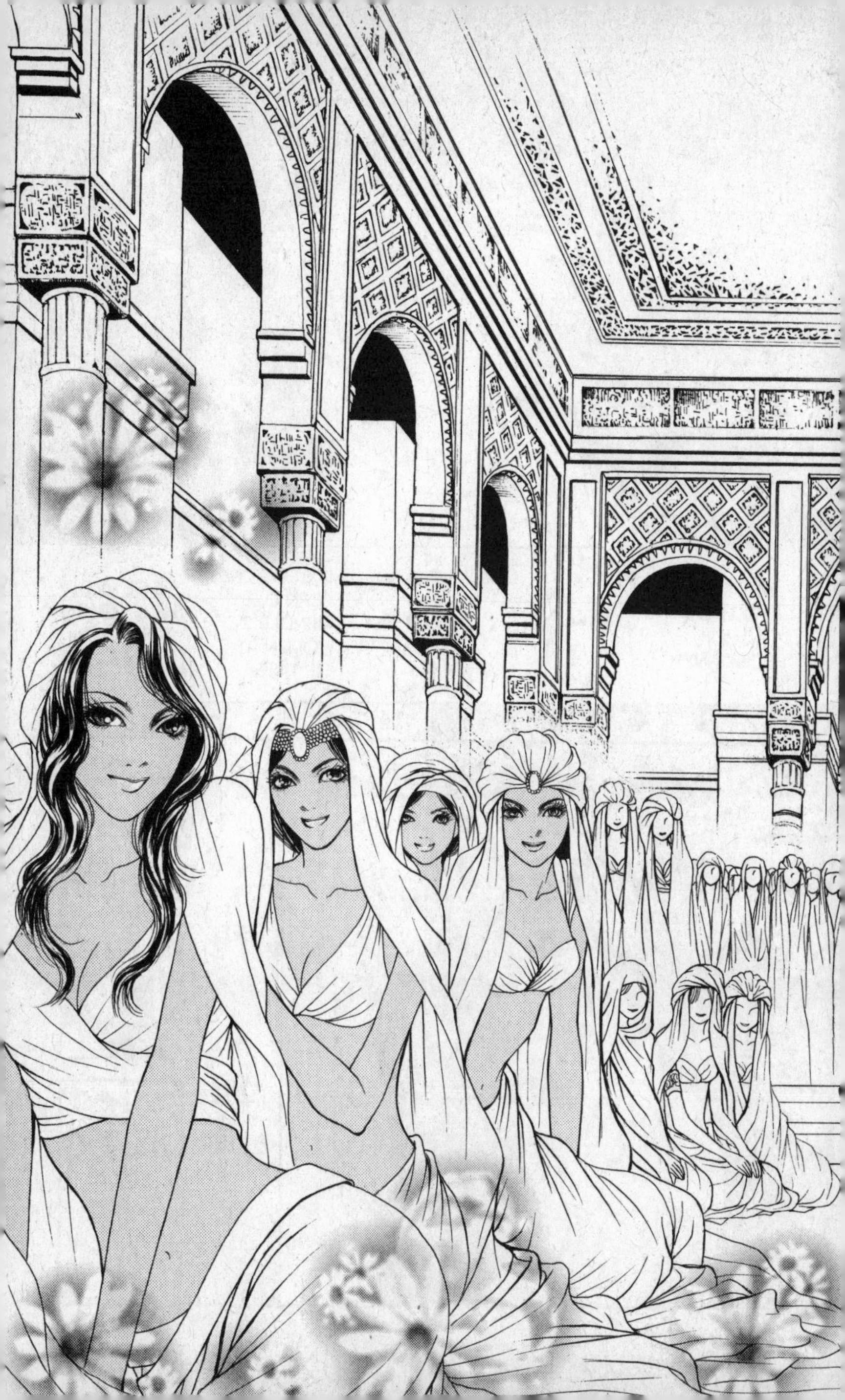

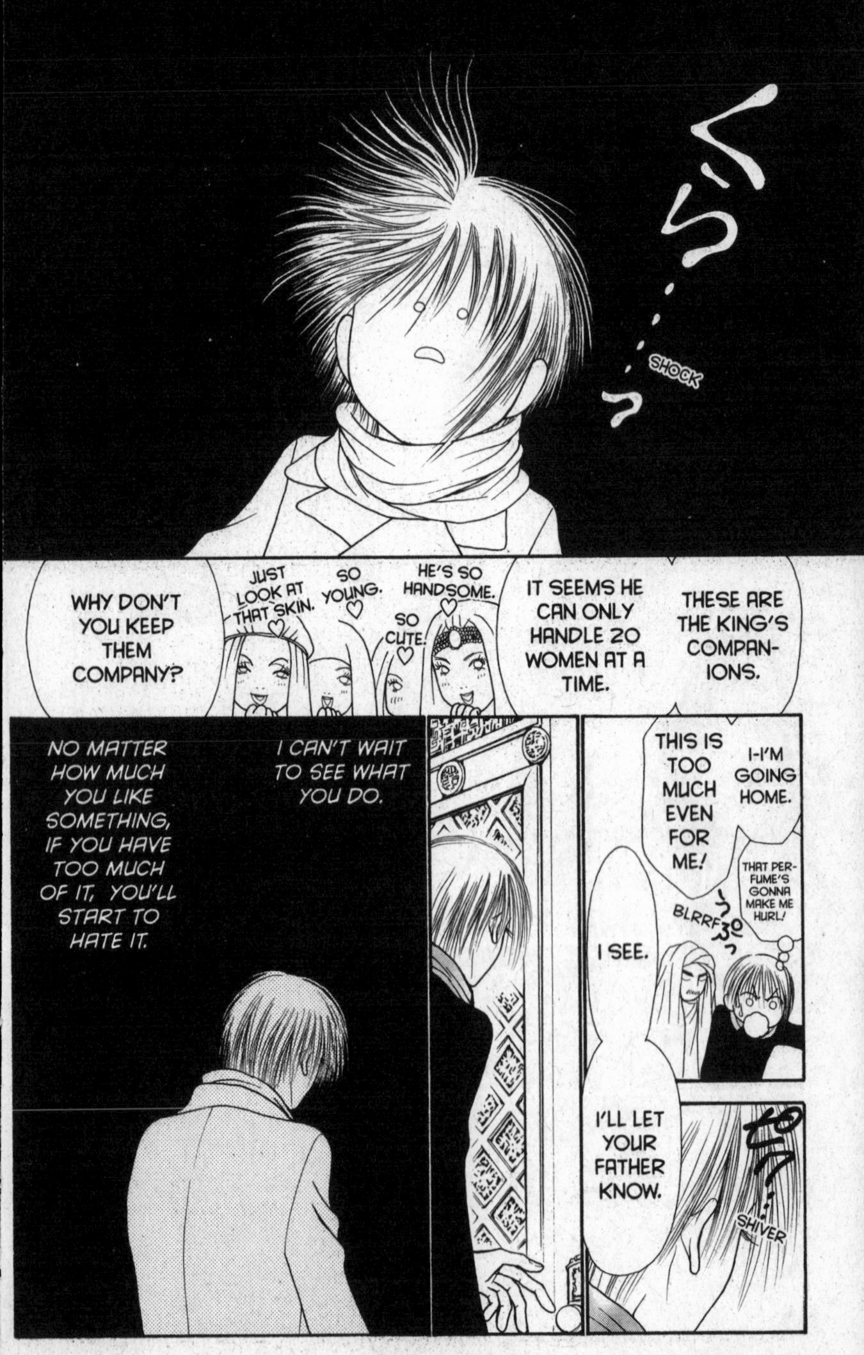
SHOCK
THESE ARE THE KING'S COMPANIONS.
IT SEEMS HE CAN ONLY HANDLE 20 WOMEN AT A TIME.
HE'S SO HANDSOME.
SO CUTE.
SO YOUNG.
JUST LOOK AT THAT SKIN.
WHY DON'T YOU KEEP THEM COMPANY?
I-I'M GOING HOME.
THIS IS TOO MUCH EVEN FOR ME!
THAT PERFUME'S GONNA MAKE ME HURL!
BLRRF
I SEE.
I'LL LET YOUR FATHER KNOW.
SHIVER
I CAN'T WAIT TO SEE WHAT YOU DO.
NO MATTER HOW MUCH YOU LIKE SOMETHING, IF YOU HAVE TOO MUCH OF IT, YOU'LL START TO HATE IT.

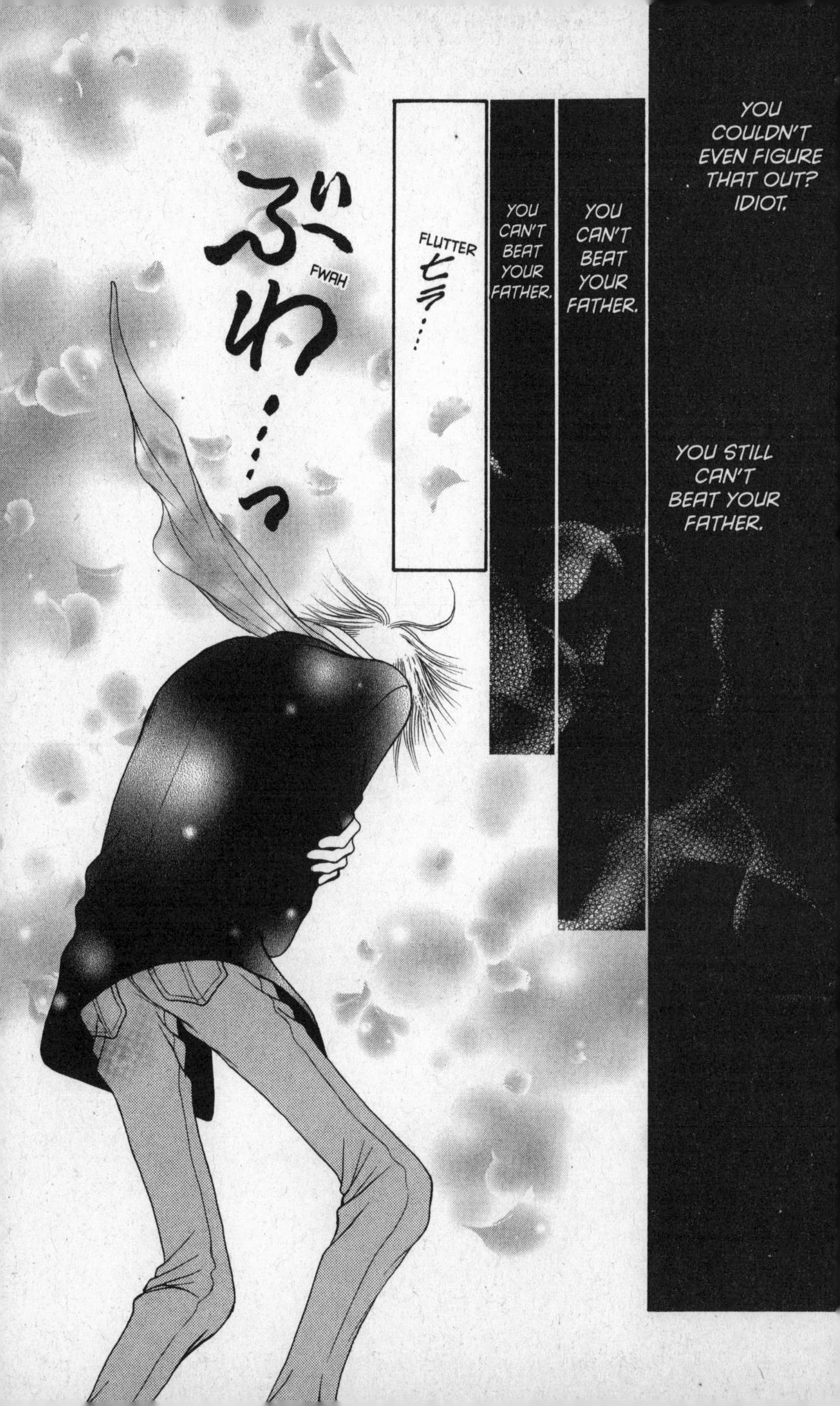
YOU COULDN'T EVEN FIGURE THAT OUT? IDIOT.
YOU STILL CAN'T BEAT YOUR FATHER.
YOU CAN'T BEAT YOUR FATHER.
YOU CAN'T BEAT YOUR FATHER.
FLUTTER
ヒラ…
FWAH
ふわ…っ

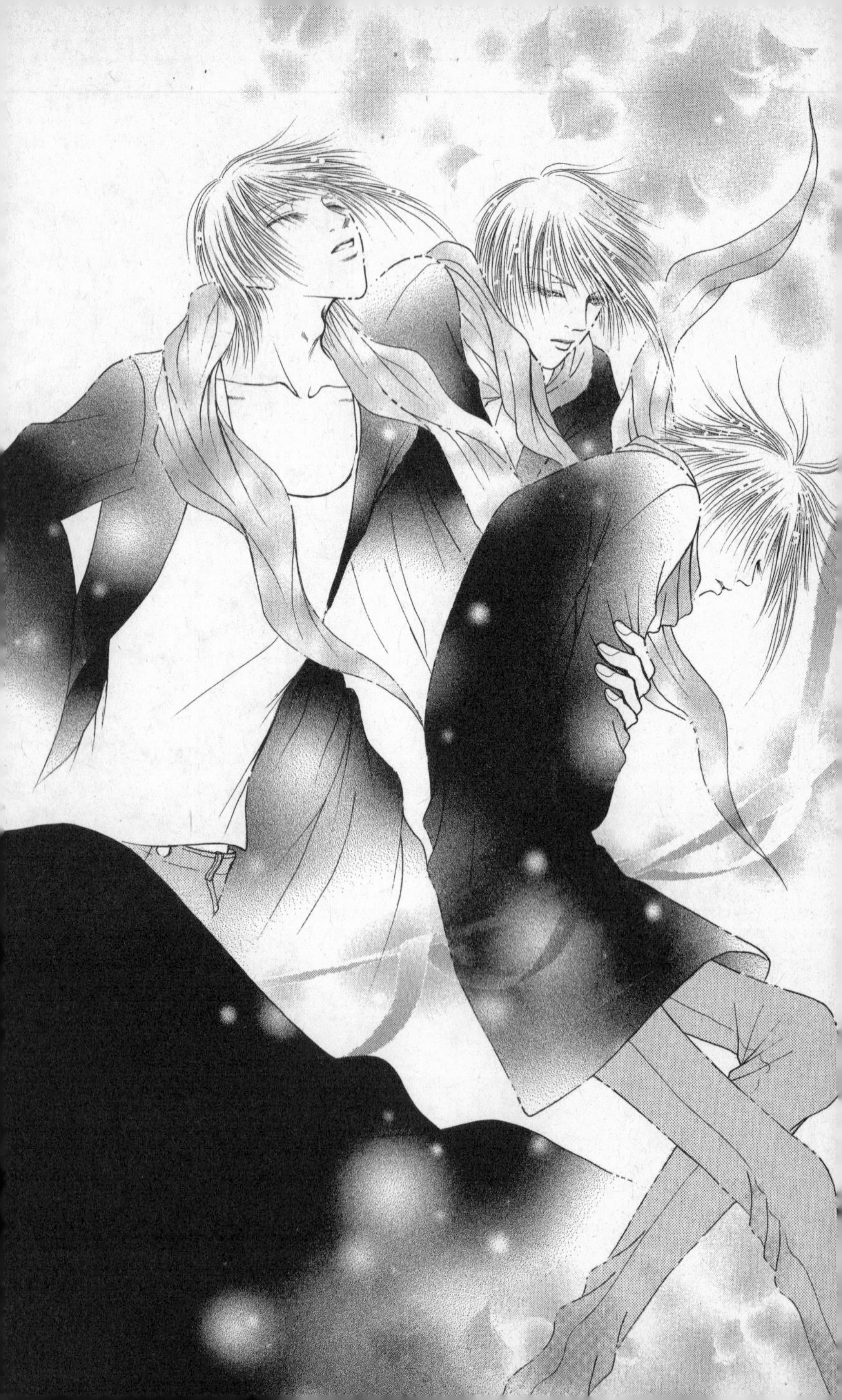

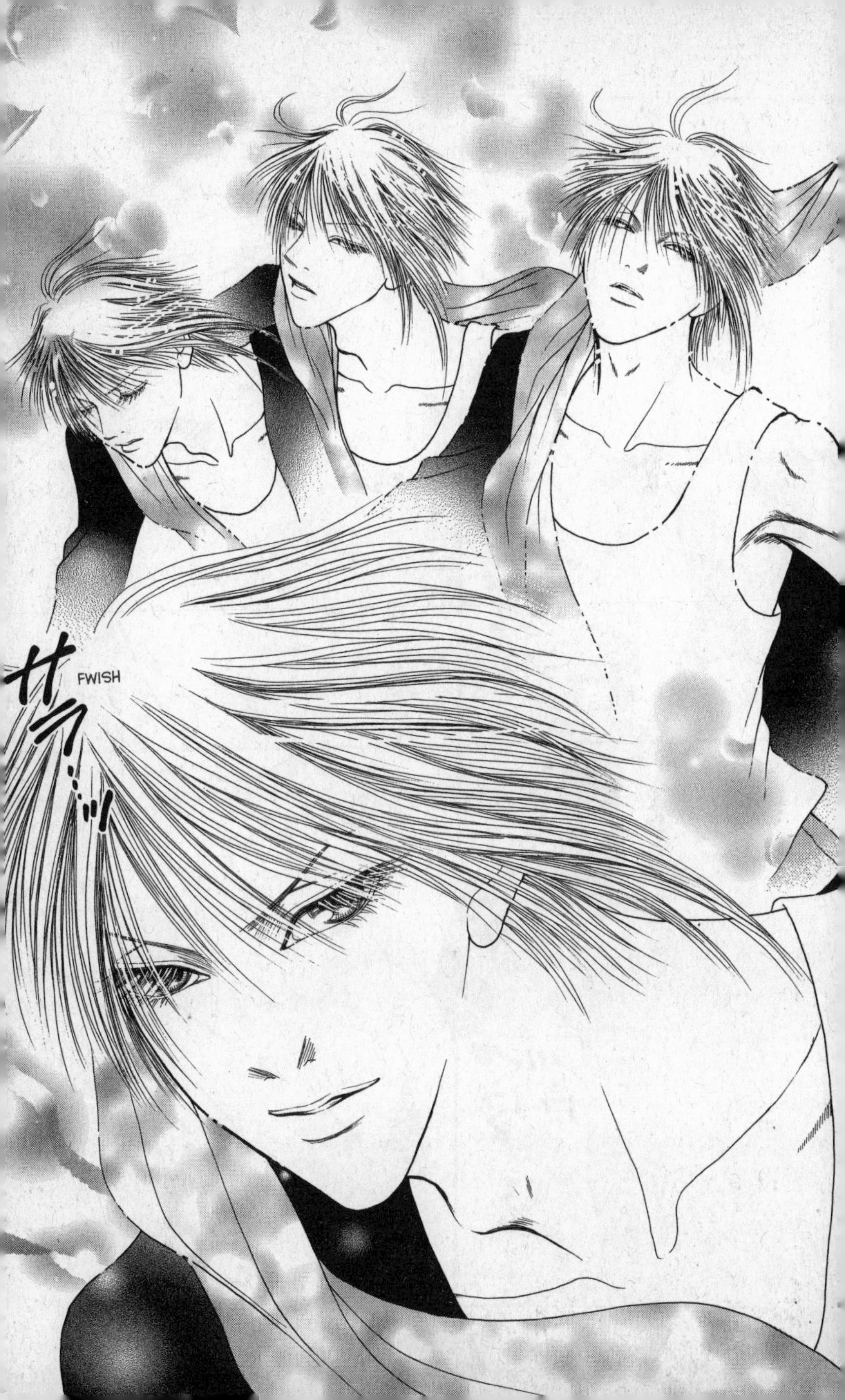
サラ…ッ
FWISH

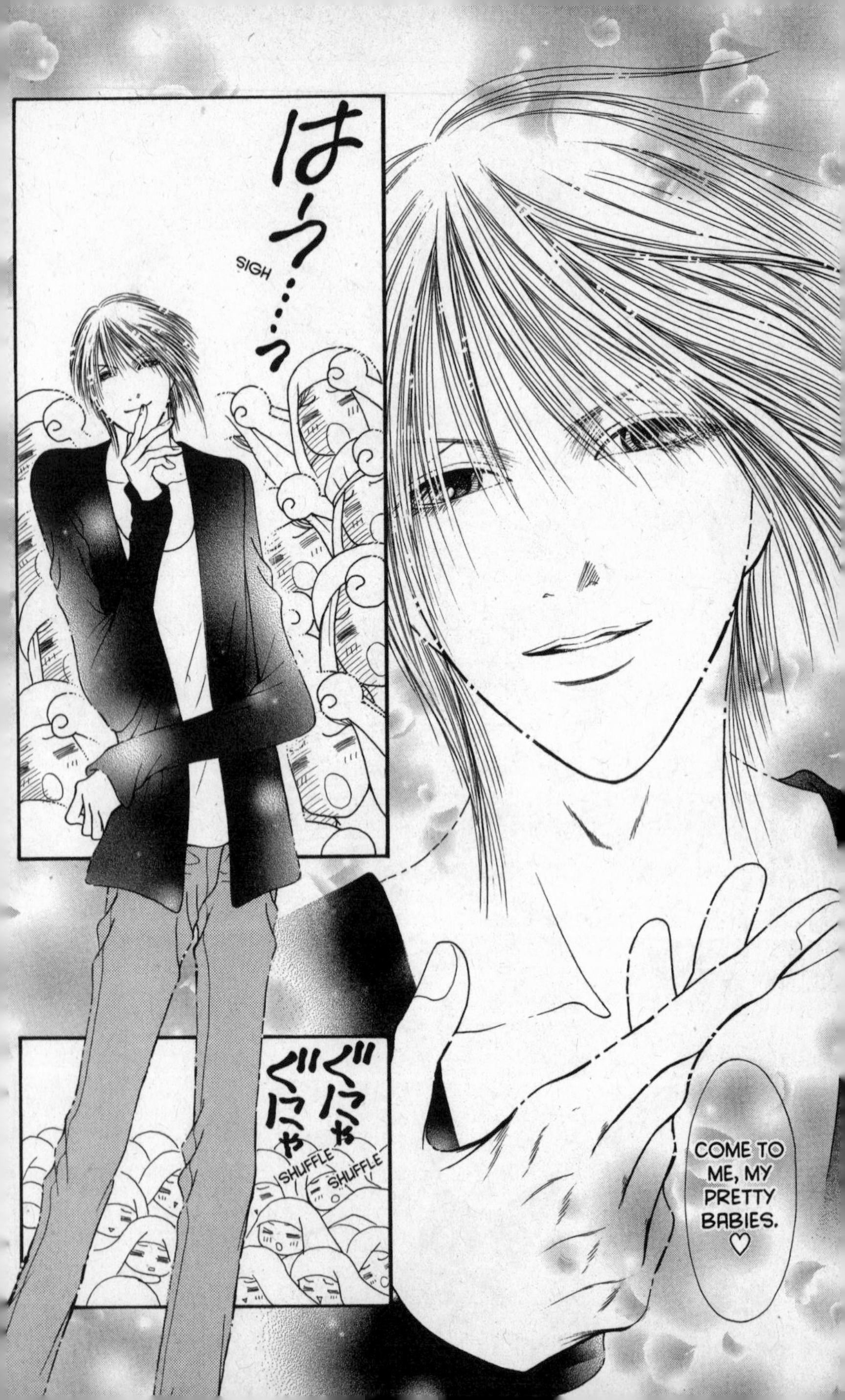
COME TO ME, MY PRETTY BABIES. ♡
はう…っ
SIGH
ぐにゃぐにゃ
SHUFFLE SHUFFLE

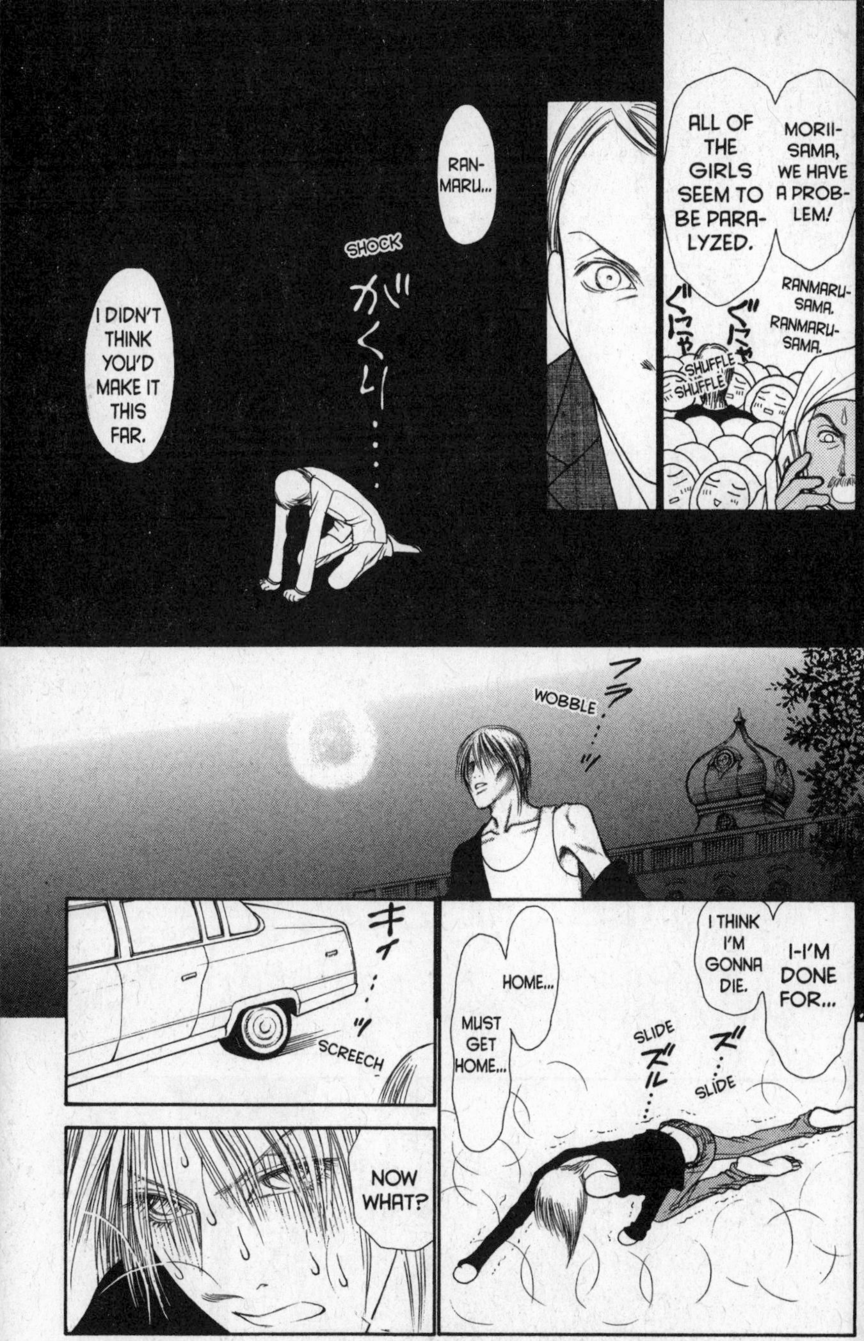

MORII-SAMA, WE HAVE A PROBLEM!
ALL OF THE GIRLS SEEM TO BE PARA-LYZED.
ぐにゃ
ぐにゃ
RANMARU-SAMA. RANMARU-SAMA.
SHUFFLE SHUFFLE
RAN-MARU...
SHOCK
がくり...
I DIDN'T THINK YOU'D MAKE IT THIS FAR.
WOBBLE
フラ...ッ
I-I'M DONE FOR...
I THINK I'M GONNA DIE.
HOME...
MUST GET HOME...
SLIDE
ズ...
ズル...
SLIDE
キイ...ッ
SCREECH
NOW WHAT?

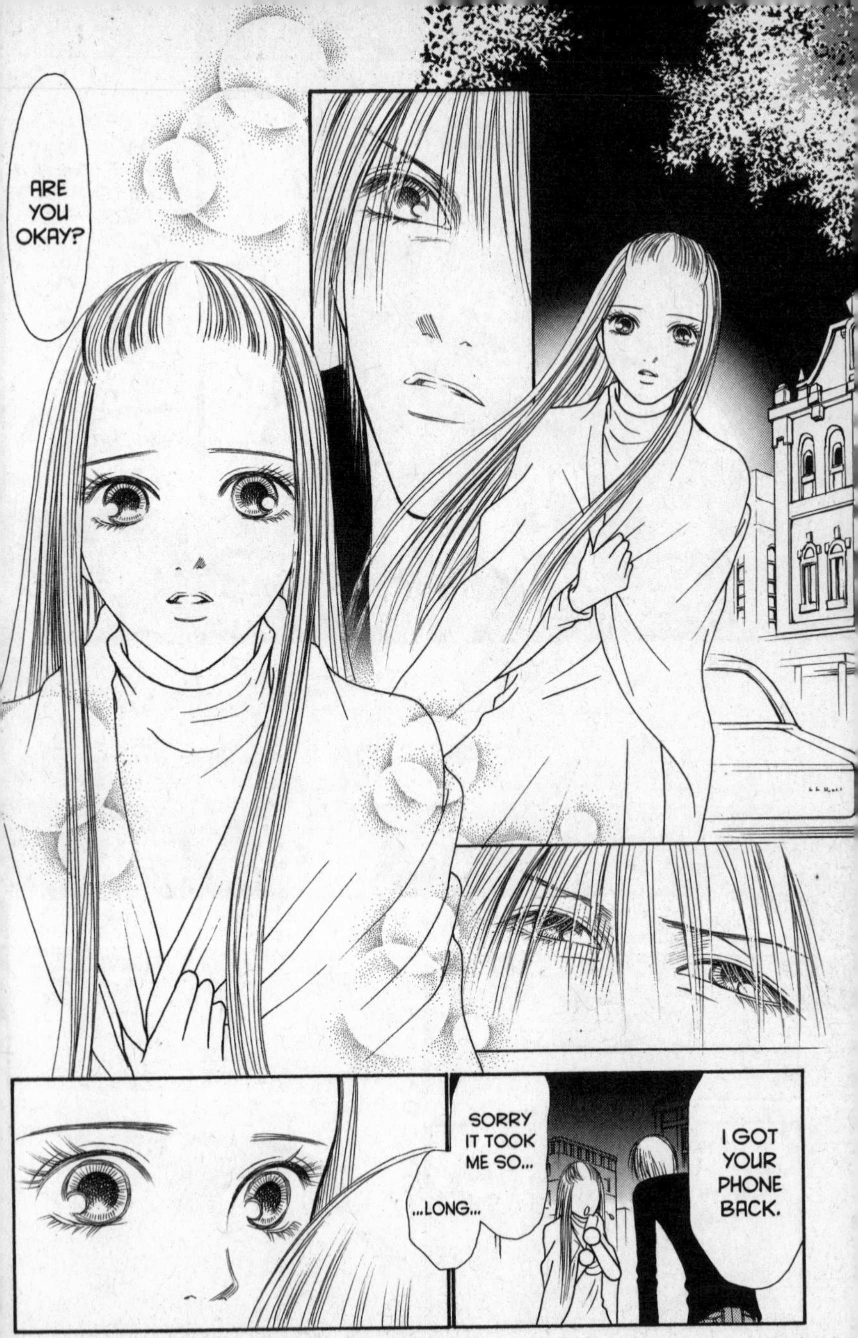
ARE YOU OKAY?
I GOT YOUR PHONE BACK.
SORRY IT TOOK ME SO...
...LONG...

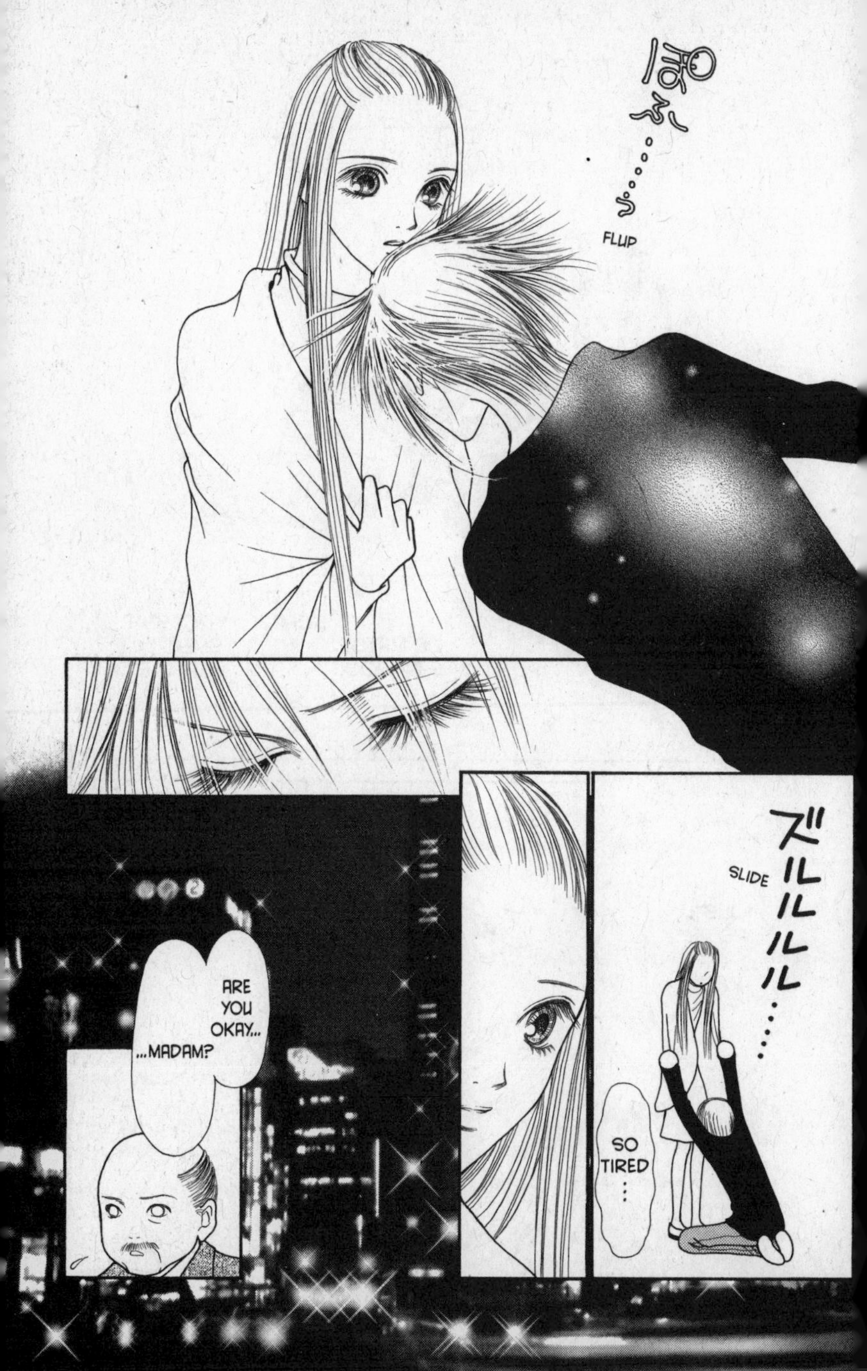
ぽふ…っ
FLUP
ズルルル…
SLIDE
SO TIRED…
ARE YOU OKAY… …MADAM?

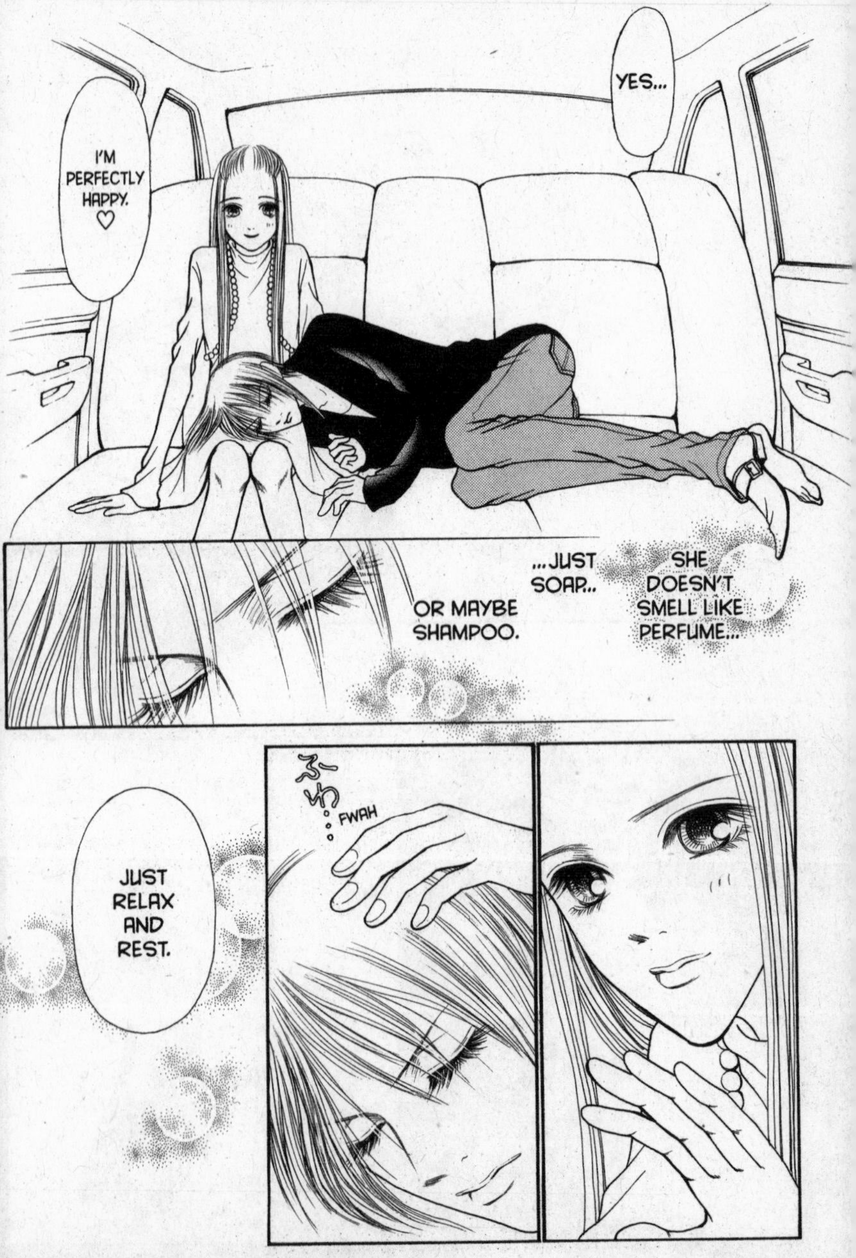
YES...
I'M PERFECTLY HAPPY. ♡
SHE DOESN'T SMELL LIKE PERFUME...
...JUST SOAP...
OR MAYBE SHAMPOO.
ふわ・・・
FWAH
JUST RELAX AND REST.

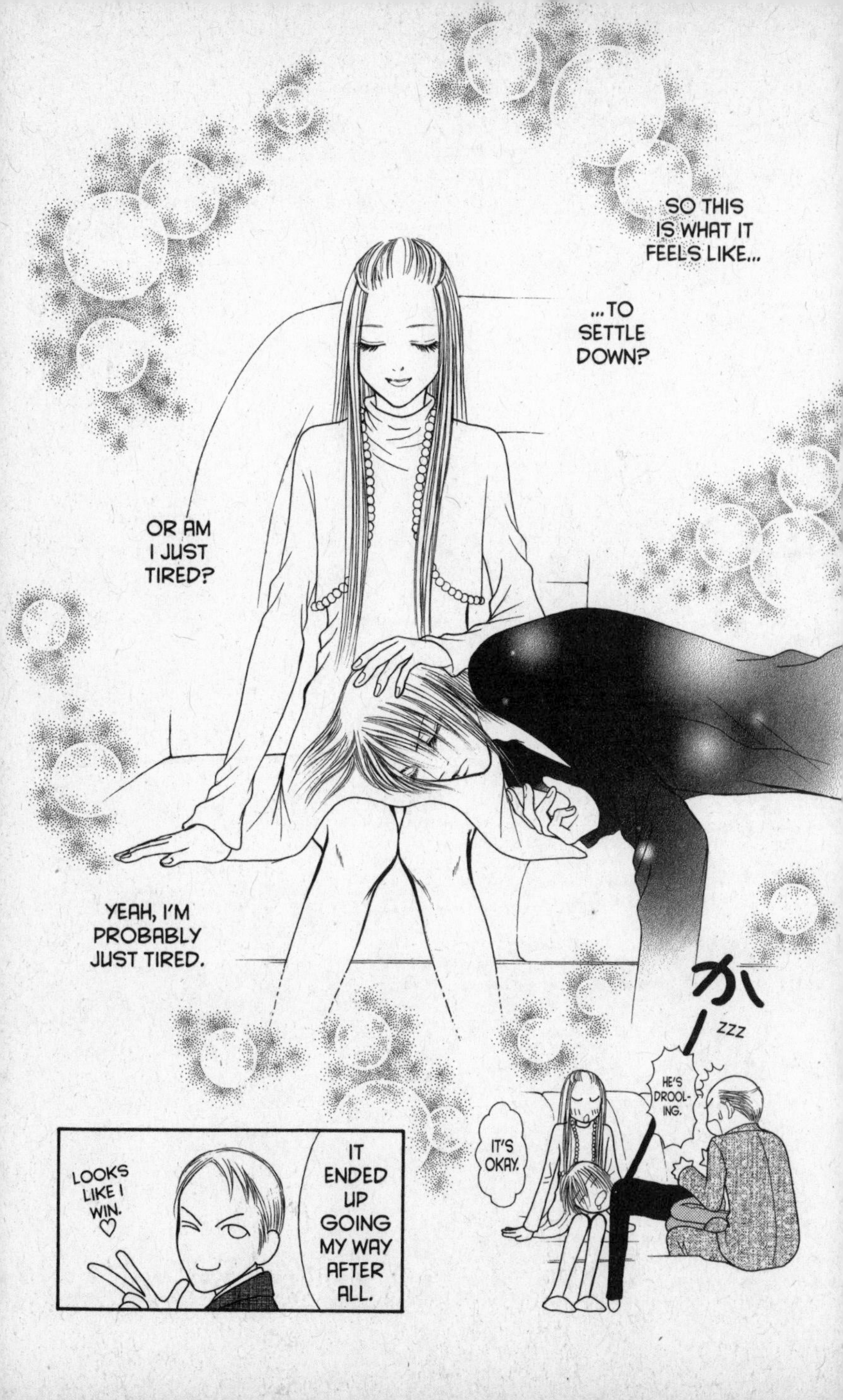
SO THIS IS WHAT IT FEELS LIKE...
...TO SETTLE DOWN?
OR AM I JUST TIRED?
YEAH, I'M PROBABLY JUST TIRED.
かー
ZZZ
HE'S DROOL-ING.
IT'S OKAY.
IT ENDED UP GOING MY WAY AFTER ALL.
LOOKS LIKE I WIN. ♡

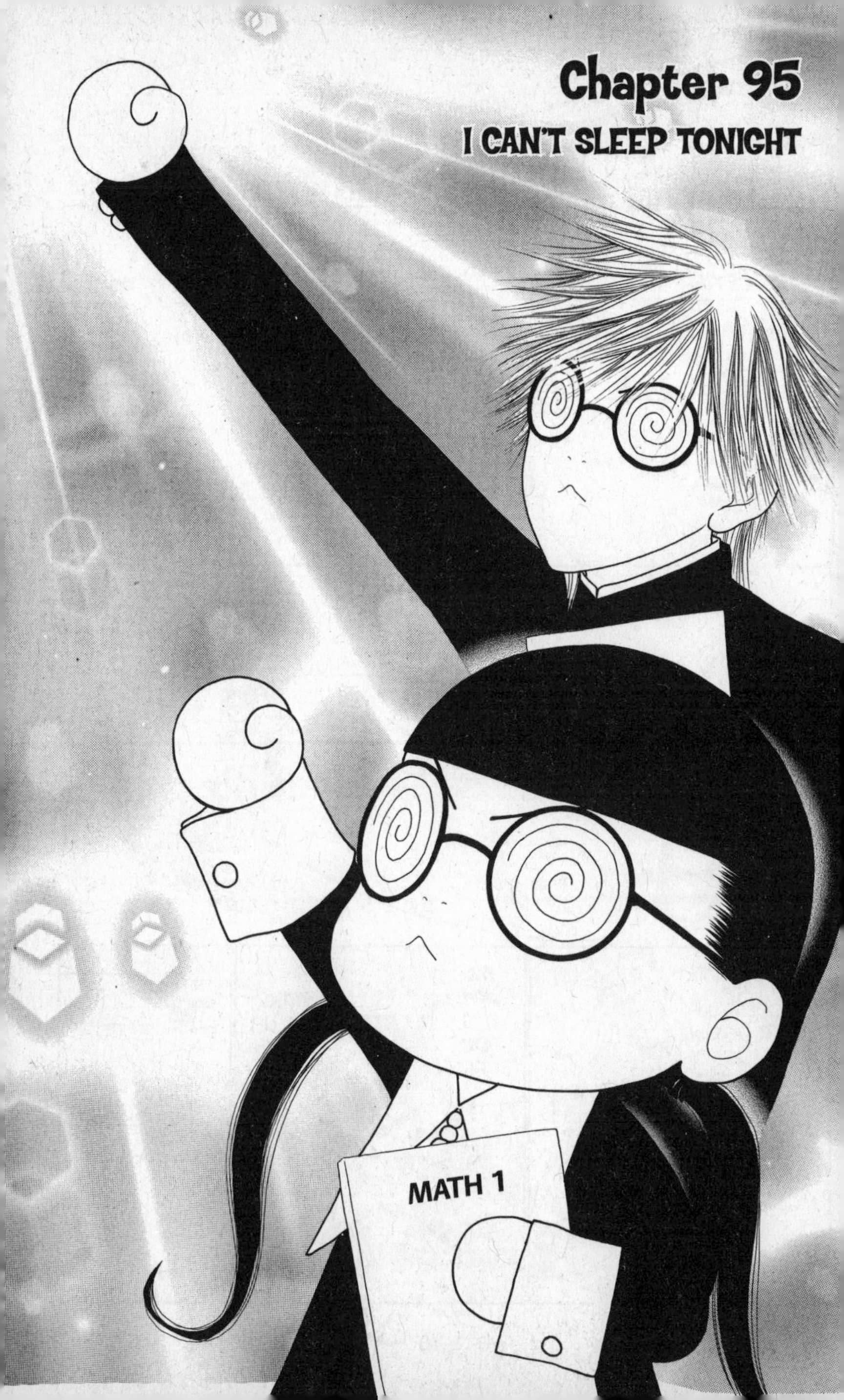
Chapter 95
I CAN'T SLEEP TONIGHT
MATH 1

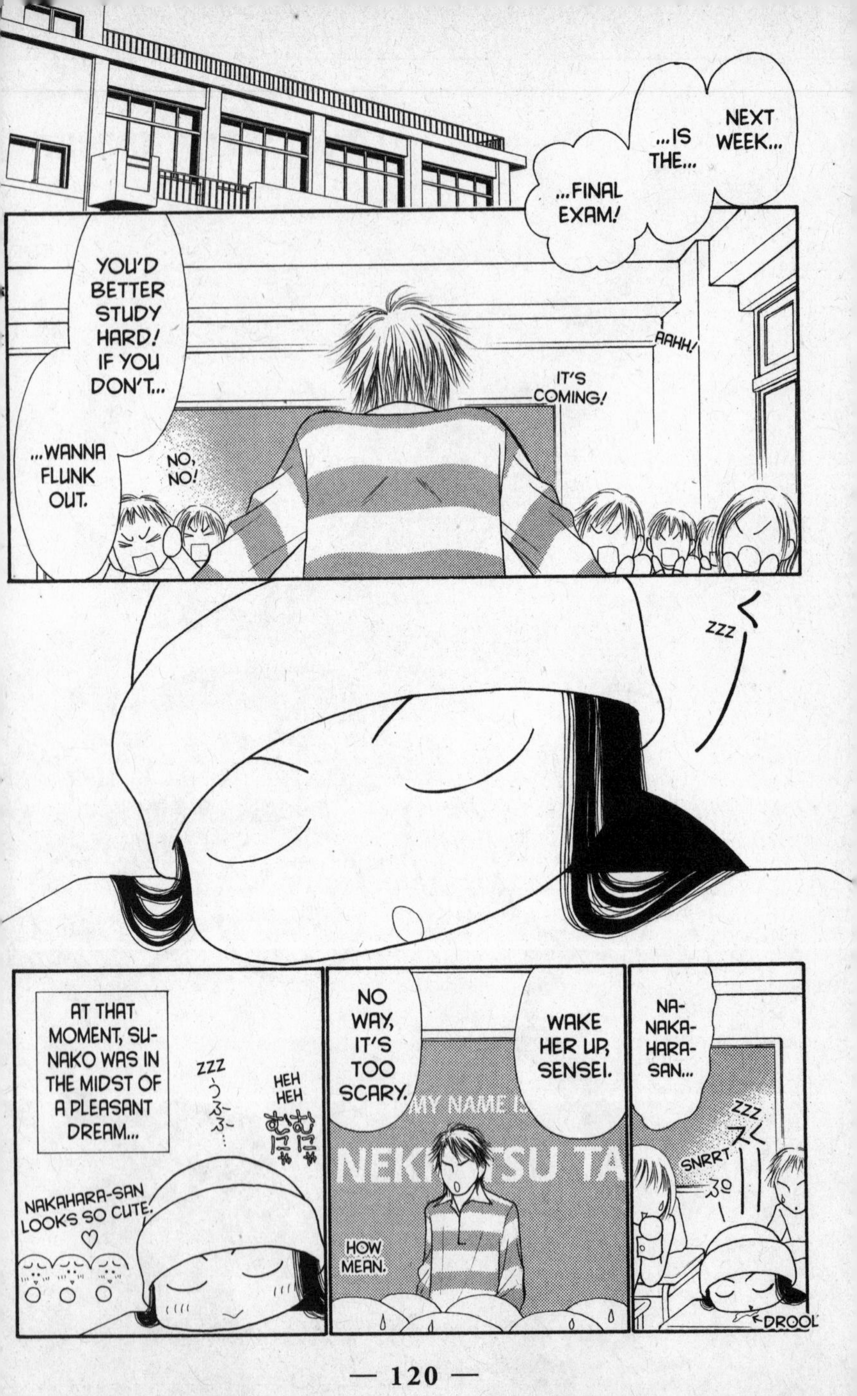
NEXT WEEK...
...IS THE...
...FINAL EXAM!
AAHH!
IT'S COMING!
YOU'D BETTER STUDY HARD! IF YOU DON'T...
NO, NO!
...WANNA FLUNK OUT.
ZZZ
NA-NAKA-HARA-SAN...
ZZZ
SNRRT
ぷー
DROOL
WAKE HER UP, SENSEI.
NO WAY, IT'S TOO SCARY.
MY NAME IS
HOW MEAN.
AT THAT MOMENT, SU-NAKO WAS IN THE MIDST OF A PLEASANT DREAM...
ZZZ
うふふー...
HEH HEH
むにゃむにゃ
NAKAHARA-SAN LOOKS SO CUTE.

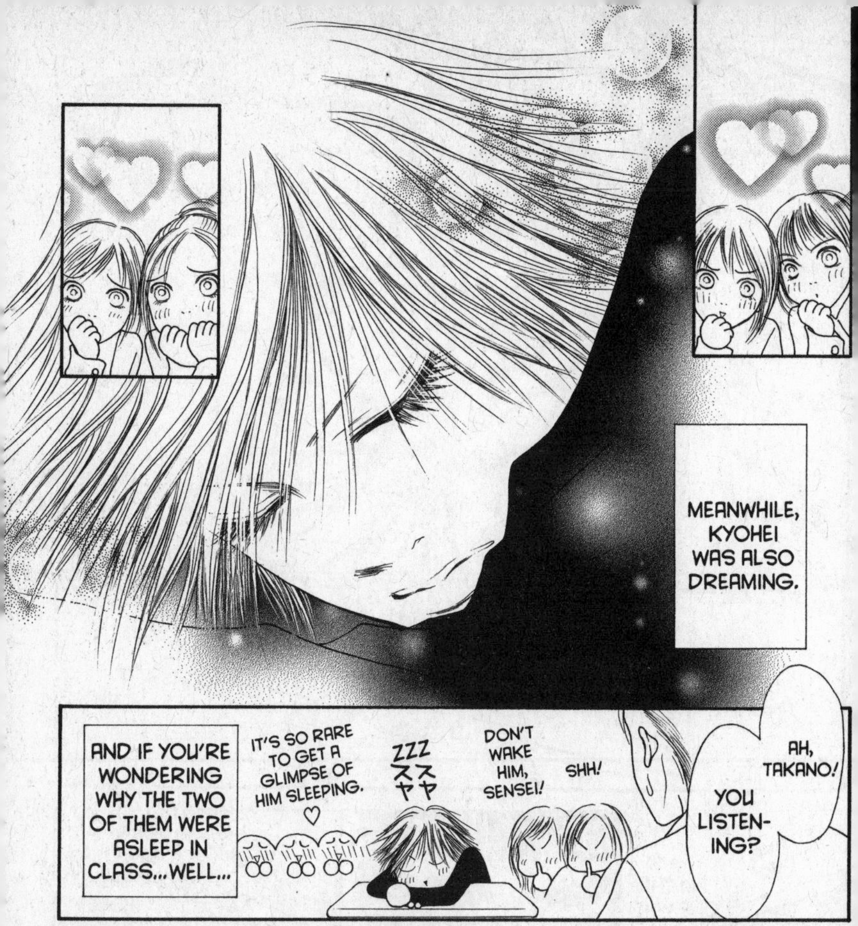
MEANWHILE, KYOHEI WAS ALSO DREAMING.
AH, TAKANO!
YOU LISTENING?
SHH!
DON'T WAKE HIM, SENSEI!
ZZZ
スヤスヤ
IT'S SO RARE TO GET A GLIMPSE OF HIM SLEEPING. ♡
AND IF YOU'RE WONDERING WHY THE TWO OF THEM WERE ASLEEP IN CLASS...WELL...

BEHIND THE SCENES

FOR THE FIRST TIME IN QUITE A WHILE, ALL OF MY STORY BOARDS WERE REJECTED. HOW MANY YEARS HAVE I BEEN A MANGA ARTIST? I HAVE TO GET BETTER. AND RIGHT AFTER THE DEADLINE OF THIS STORY, ***KUROYUME*** WAS PLAYING LIVE AT THE BUDOUKAN! THE SAME PLACE I FIRST FELL IN LOVE WITH THEM 10 YEARS AGO. AND IT WAS A ONE-NIGHT-ONLY REUNION CONCERT! JUST THINKING ABOUT IT MADE ME SO EXCITED THAT MY HANDS WOULD SHAKE, I COULDN'T EVEN LISTEN TO THE CD. THE NIGHT OF THE SHOW I WAITED IN LINE OUTSIDE FOR OVER AN HOUR. I COULDN'T GET IN ON TIME. WHEN I HEARD THEIR FIRST SONG STARTING, I BURST INTO TEARS. I FELT LIKE THE WORLD WAS ENDING. I WAS ALL ALONE CRYING MY EYES OUT IN FRONT OF THE BUDOUKAN. ONCE I MADE IT INSIDE I THOUGHT I'D BE CRYING THE WHOLE TIME, BUT I ENDED UP GOING WILD. I DANCED LIKE CRAZY ALL BY MYSELF. I GUESS I CRIED OUT ALL MY TEARS OUTSIDE. ***KIYOHARA-SAMA*** IS DEFINITELY THE ***HOTTEST MAN IN THE WHOLE WORLD!*** ♡ I WANTED TO HEAR THE SONG "FAKE STAR."

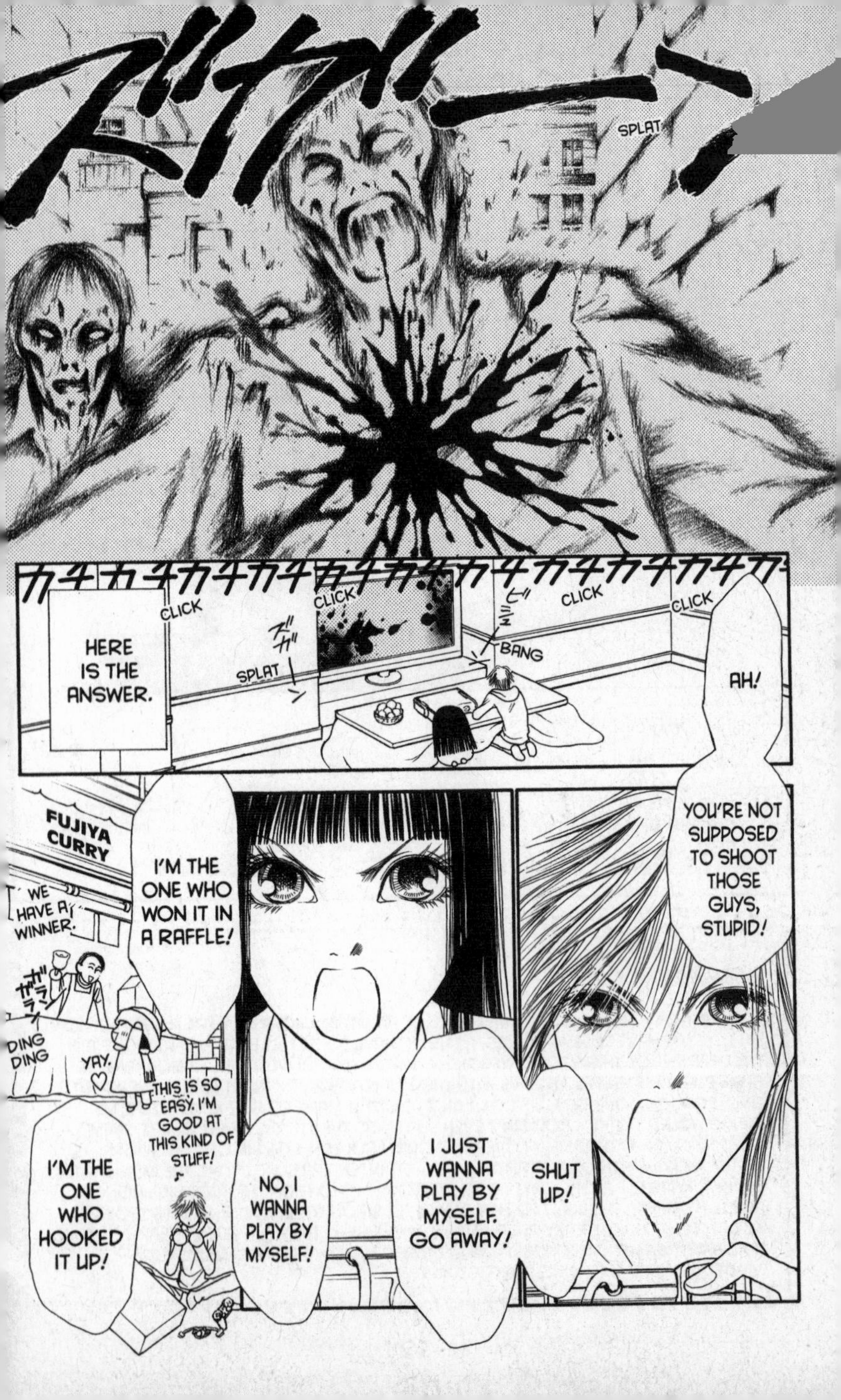
SPLAT
AH!
CLICK
CLICK
BANG
CLICK
SPLAT
CLICK
HERE IS THE ANSWER.
YOU'RE NOT SUPPOSED TO SHOOT THOSE GUYS, STUPID!
SHUT UP!
I JUST WANNA PLAY BY MYSELF. GO AWAY!
I'M THE ONE WHO WON IT IN A RAFFLE!
NO, I WANNA PLAY BY MYSELF!
FUJIYA CURRY
WE HAVE A WINNER.
DING DING
YAY.
THIS IS SO EASY. I'M GOOD AT THIS KIND OF STUFF!
I'M THE ONE WHO HOOKED IT UP!

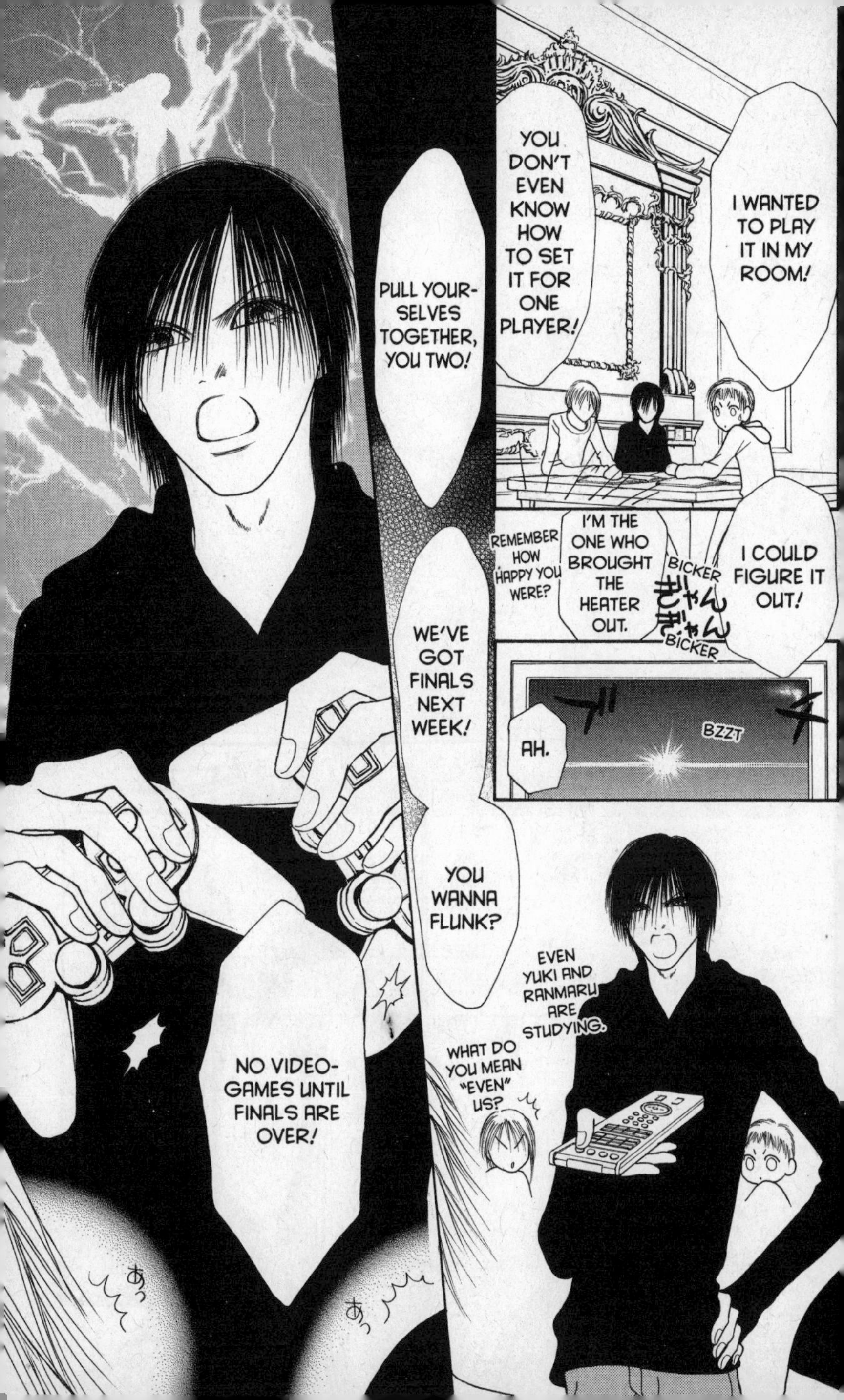

I WANTED TO PLAY IT IN MY ROOM!
YOU DON'T EVEN KNOW HOW TO SET IT FOR ONE PLAYER!
I COULD FIGURE IT OUT!
BICKER ぎゃんぎゃん BICKER
I'M THE ONE WHO BROUGHT THE HEATER OUT.
REMEMBER HOW HAPPY YOU WERE?
BZZT
AH.
EVEN YUKI AND RANMARU ARE STUDYING.
WHAT DO YOU MEAN "EVEN" US?
PULL YOURSELVES TOGETHER, YOU TWO!
WE'VE GOT FINALS NEXT WEEK!
YOU WANNA FLUNK?
NO VIDEO-GAMES UNTIL FINALS ARE OVER!

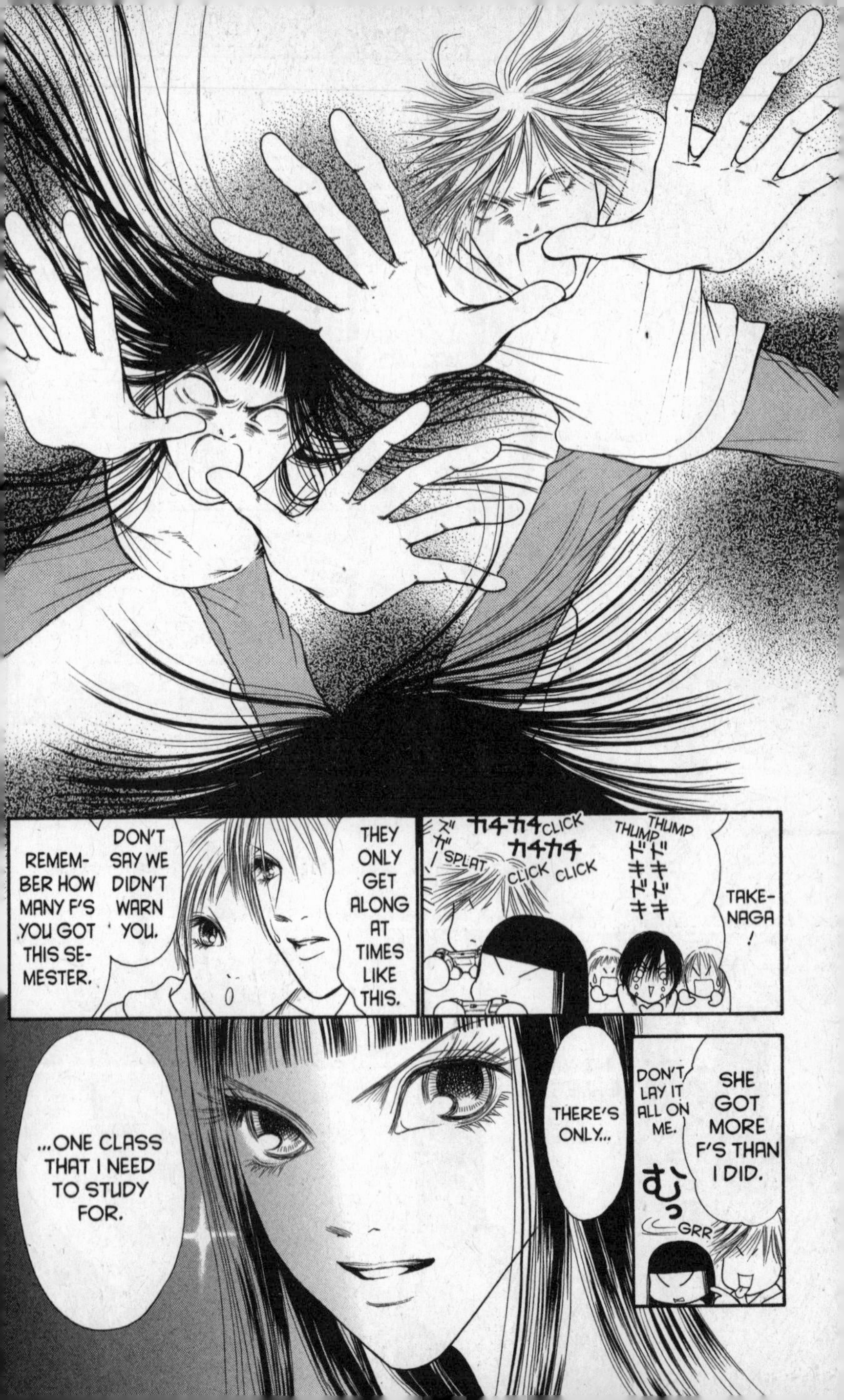
TAKE-NAGA!
THUMP THUMP
ドキドキ ドキドキ
カチカチ CLICK
カチカチ CLICK CLICK
ズガ! SPLAT
THEY ONLY GET ALONG AT TIMES LIKE THIS.
DON'T SAY WE DIDN'T WARN YOU.
REMEMBER HOW MANY F'S YOU GOT THIS SEMESTER.
SHE GOT MORE F'S THAN I DID.
DON'T LAY IT ALL ON ME.
むっ GRR
THERE'S ONLY...
...ONE CLASS THAT I NEED TO STUDY FOR.

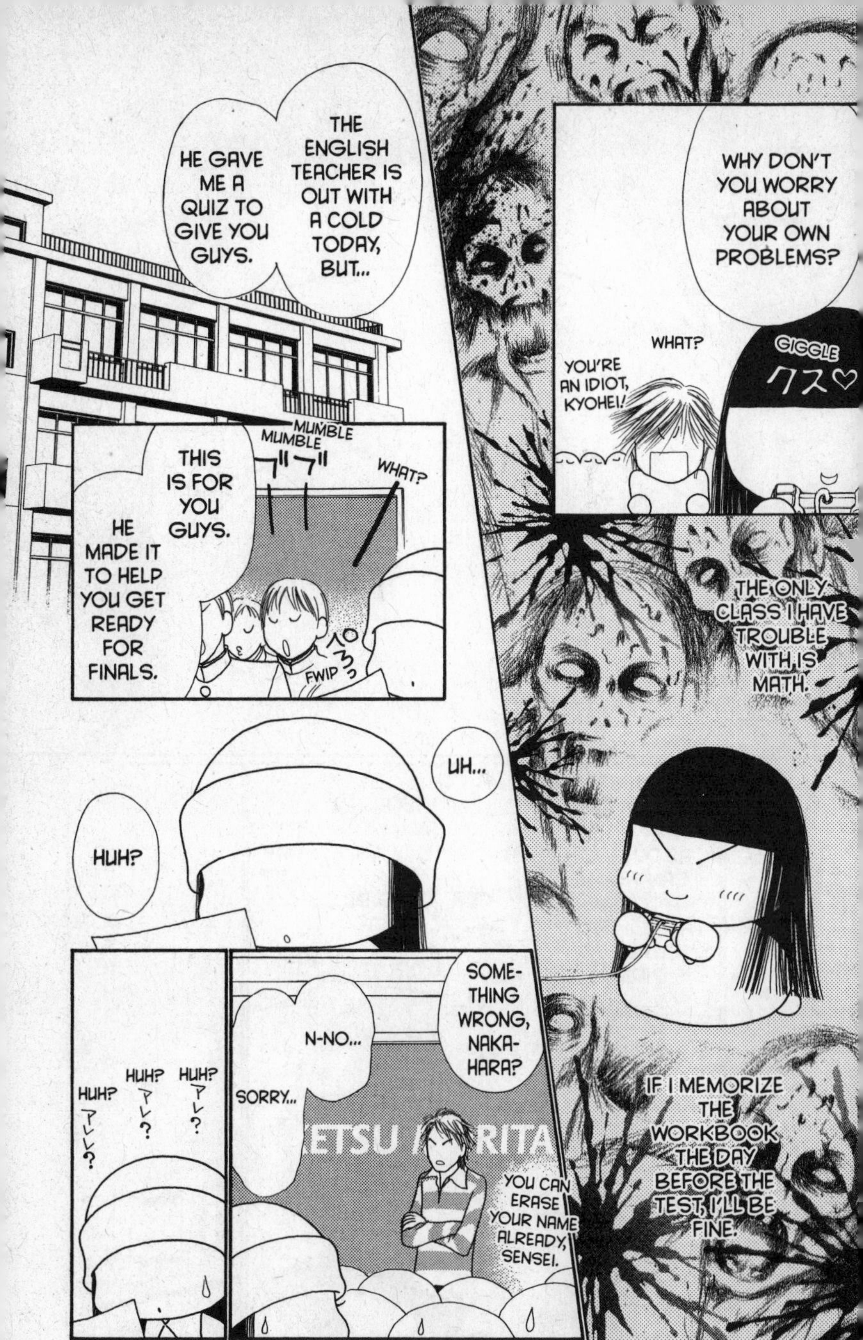
WHY DON'T YOU WORRY ABOUT YOUR OWN PROBLEMS?
WHAT?
GIGGLE
クス♡
YOU'RE AN IDIOT, KYOHEI!
THE ONLY CLASS I HAVE TROUBLE WITH IS MATH.
IF I MEMORIZE THE WORKBOOK THE DAY BEFORE THE TEST, I'LL BE FINE.
THE ENGLISH TEACHER IS OUT WITH A COLD TODAY, BUT...
HE GAVE ME A QUIZ TO GIVE YOU GUYS.
WHAT?
MUMBLE MUMBLE
THIS IS FOR YOU GUYS.
HE MADE IT TO HELP YOU GET READY FOR FINALS.
FWIP
UH...
HUH?
SOMETHING WRONG, NAKAHARA?
N-NO...
SORRY...
YOU CAN ERASE YOUR NAME ALREADY, SENSEI.
HUH? アレ?
HUH? アレ?
HUH? アレレ?

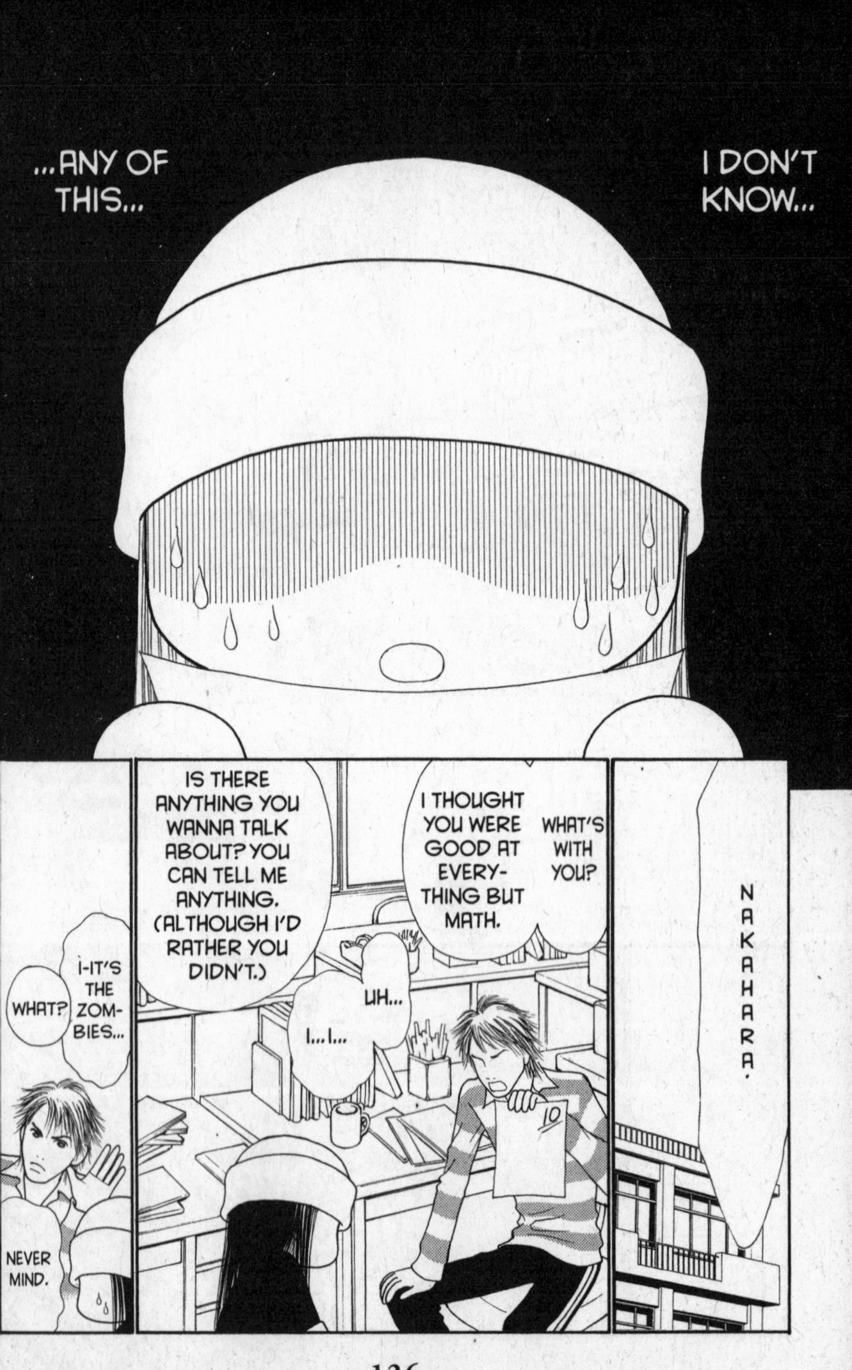
I DON'T KNOW...
...ANY OF THIS...
NAKAHARA.
WHAT'S WITH YOU?
I THOUGHT YOU WERE GOOD AT EVERYTHING BUT MATH.
IS THERE ANYTHING YOU WANNA TALK ABOUT? YOU CAN TELL ME ANYTHING. (ALTHOUGH I'D RATHER YOU DIDN'T.)
UH...
I... I...
I-IT'S THE ZOMBIES...
WHAT?
NEVER MIND.

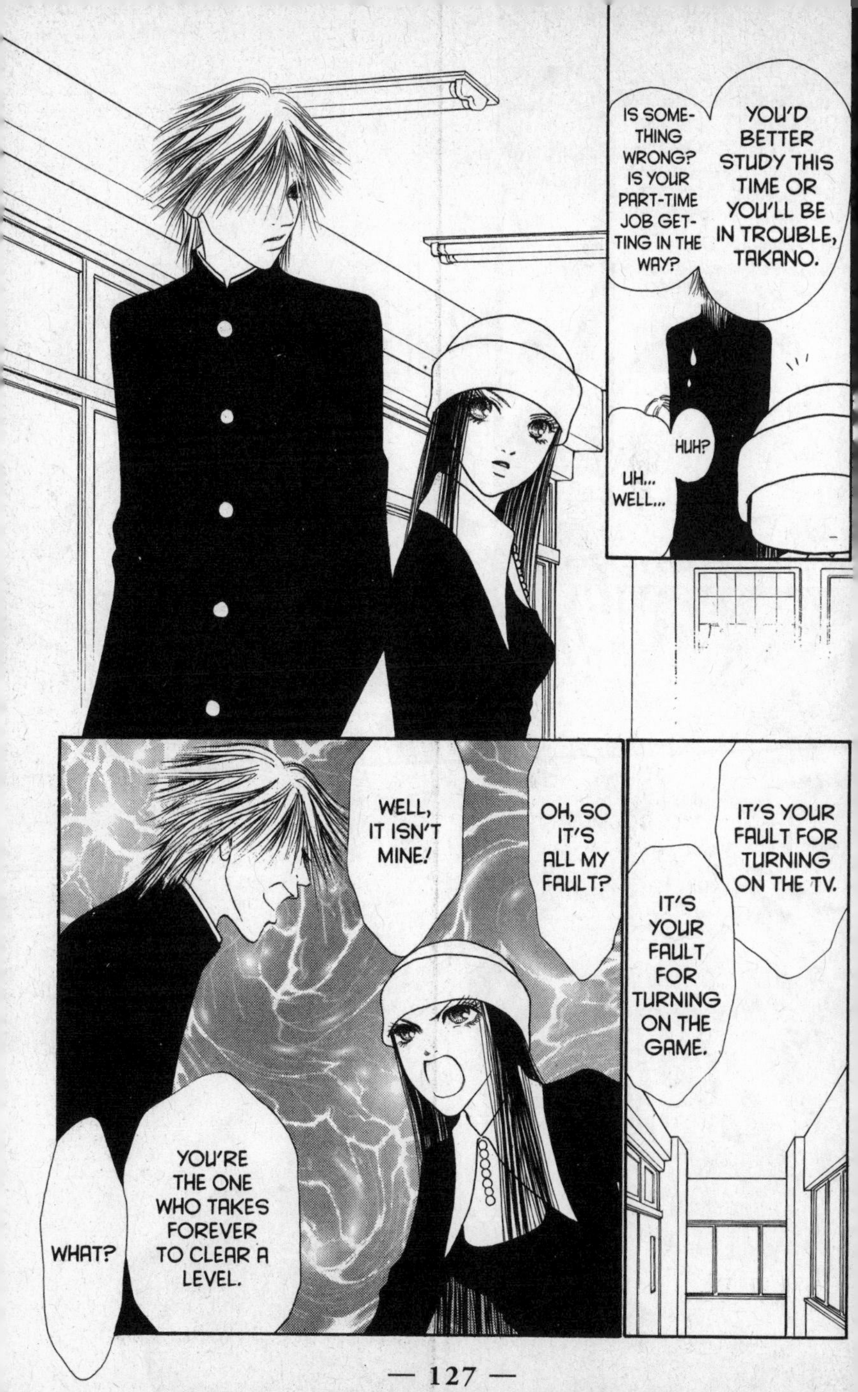
YOU'D BETTER STUDY THIS TIME OR YOU'LL BE IN TROUBLE, TAKANO.
IS SOME-THING WRONG? IS YOUR PART-TIME JOB GET-TING IN THE WAY?
HUH?
UH... WELL...
IT'S YOUR FAULT FOR TURNING ON THE TV.
IT'S YOUR FAULT FOR TURNING ON THE GAME.
OH, SO IT'S ALL MY FAULT?
WELL, IT ISN'T MINE!
YOU'RE THE ONE WHO TAKES FOREVER TO CLEAR A LEVEL.
WHAT?

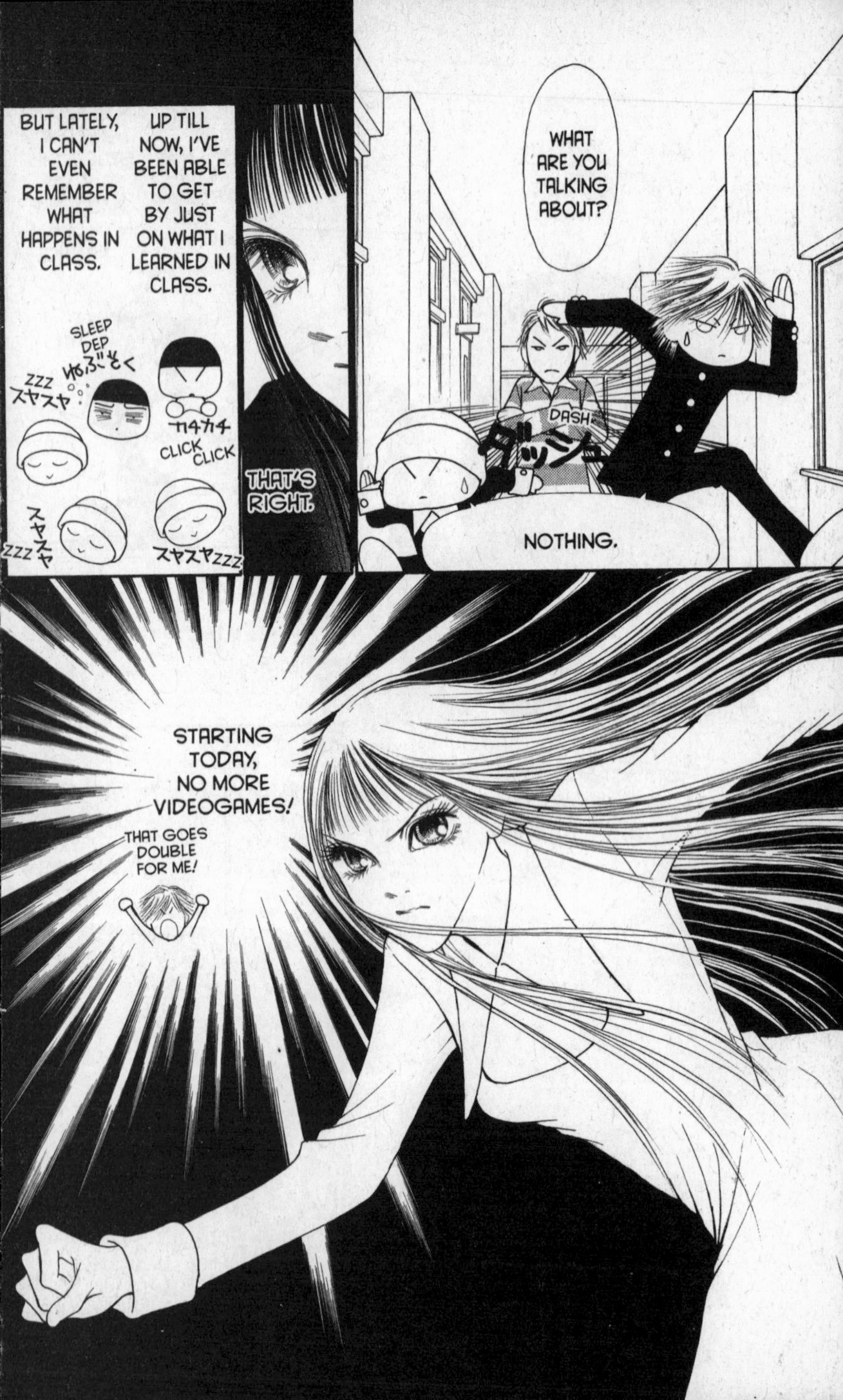

WHAT ARE YOU TALKING ABOUT?
DASH
ダッシュ
NOTHING.
THAT'S RIGHT.
UP TILL NOW, I'VE BEEN ABLE TO GET BY JUST ON WHAT I LEARNED IN CLASS.
BUT LATELY, I CAN'T EVEN REMEMBER WHAT HAPPENS IN CLASS.
SLEEP DEP
ねぶそく
カチカチ
CLICK CLICK
ZZZ
スヤスヤ
スヤスヤ ZZZ
スヤスヤ ZZZ
STARTING TODAY, NO MORE VIDEOGAMES!
THAT GOES DOUBLE FOR ME!

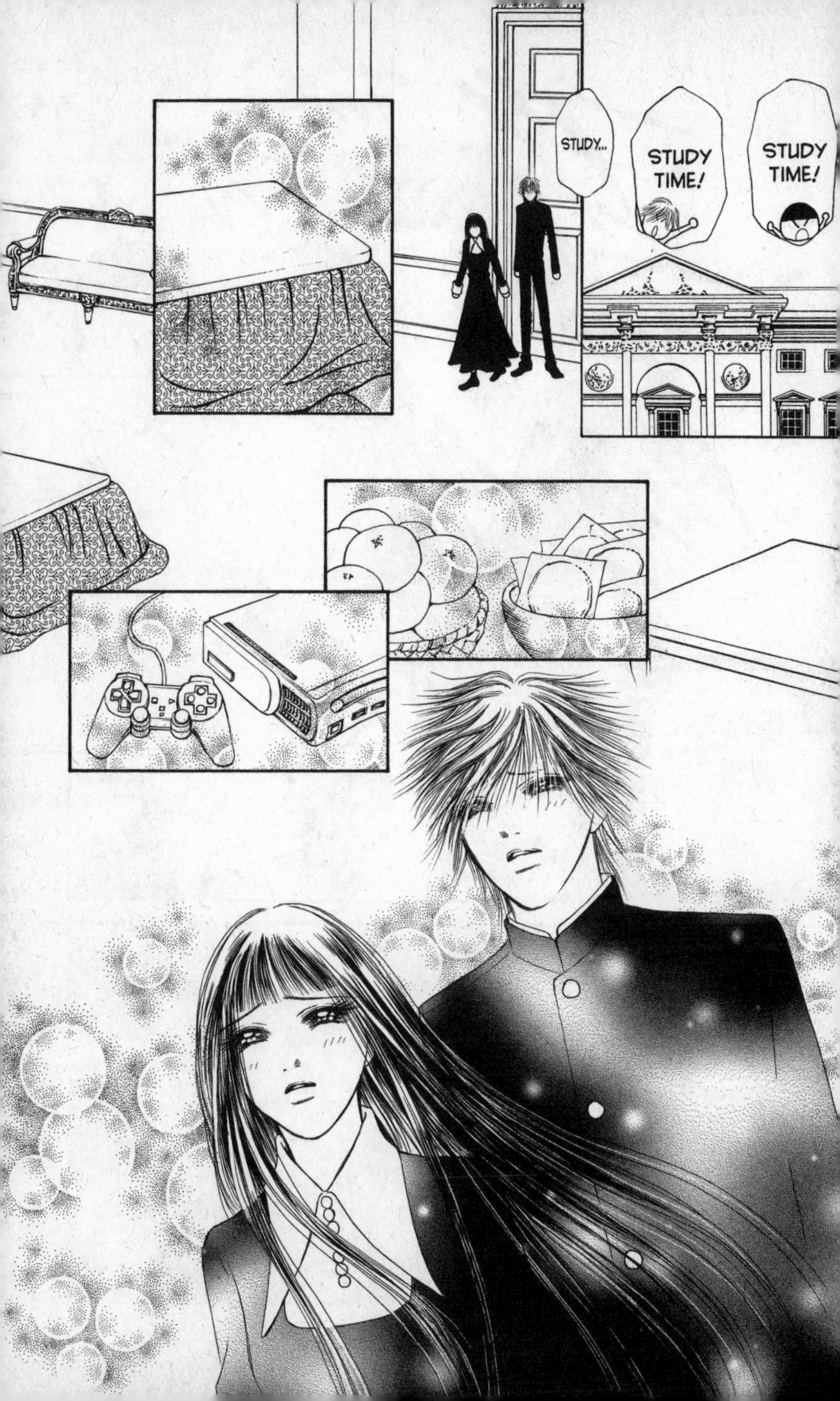
STUDY TIME!
STUDY TIME!
STUDY...

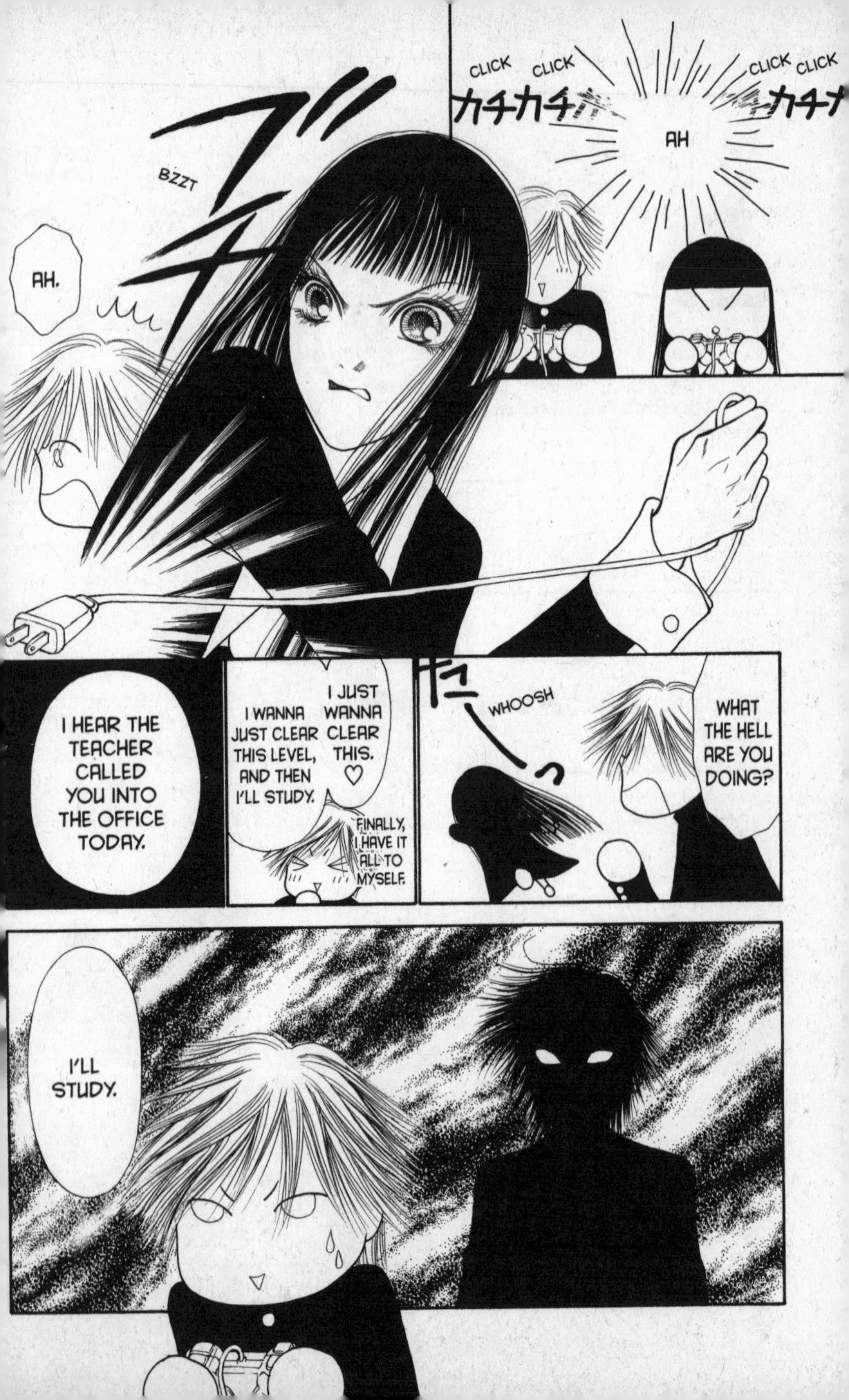

CLICK CLICK
CLICK CLICK
AH
BZZT
AH.
WHOOSH
WHAT THE HELL ARE YOU DOING?
I JUST WANNA CLEAR THIS. ♡
I WANNA JUST CLEAR THIS LEVEL, AND THEN I'LL STUDY.
FINALLY, I HAVE IT ALL TO MYSELF.
I HEAR THE TEACHER CALLED YOU INTO THE OFFICE TODAY.
I'LL STUDY.

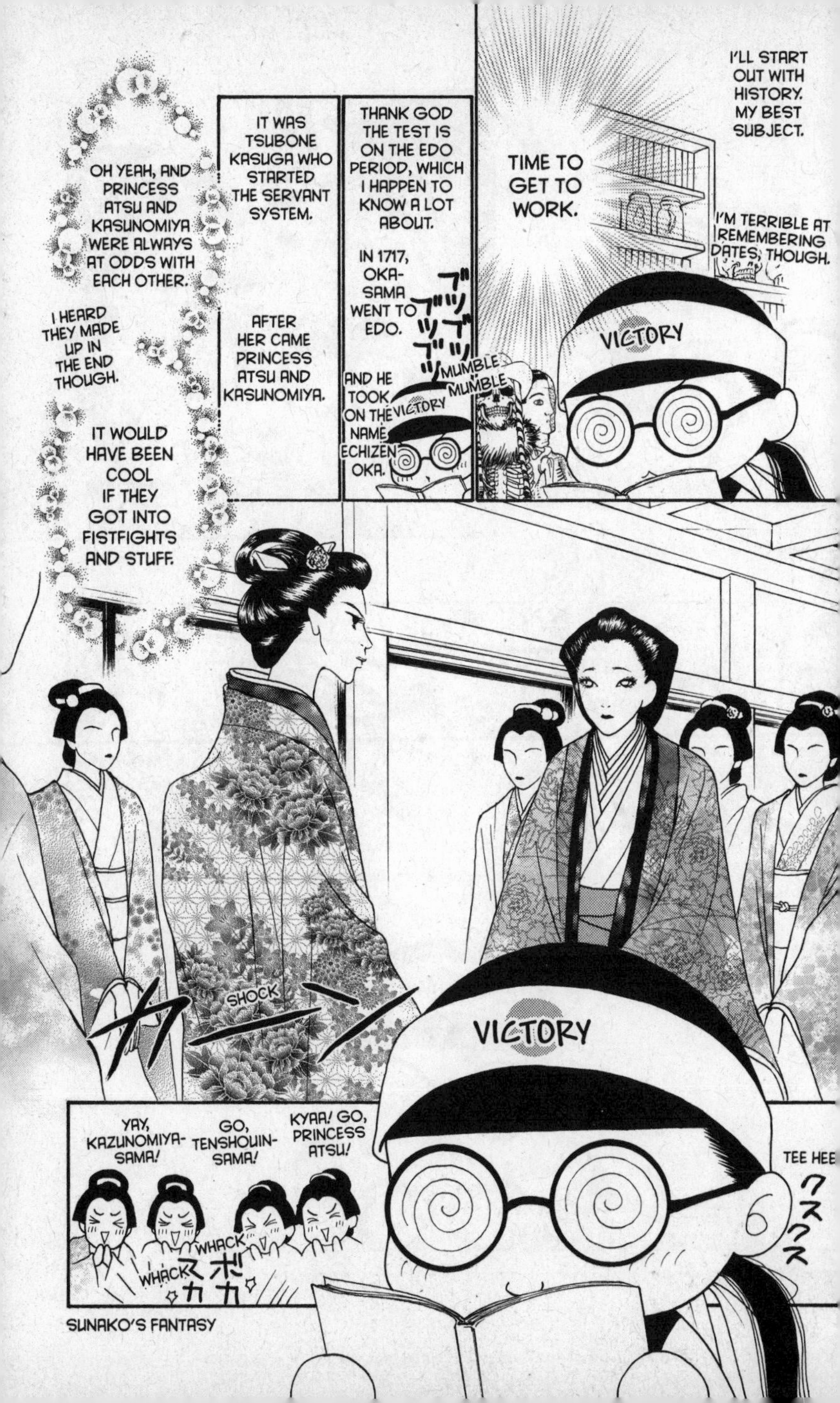
I'LL START OUT WITH HISTORY. MY BEST SUBJECT.
TIME TO GET TO WORK.
I'M TERRIBLE AT REMEMBERING DATES, THOUGH.
VICTORY
THANK GOD THE TEST IS ON THE EDO PERIOD, WHICH I HAPPEN TO KNOW A LOT ABOUT.
IN 1717, OKA-SAMA WENT TO EDO.
ブツブツ
MUMBLE MUMBLE
AND HE TOOK ON THE NAME ECHIZEN OKA.
VICTORY
IT WAS TSUBONE KASUGA WHO STARTED THE SERVANT SYSTEM.
AFTER HER CAME PRINCESS ATSU AND KASUNOMIYA.
OH YEAH, AND PRINCESS ATSU AND KASUNOMIYA WERE ALWAYS AT ODDS WITH EACH OTHER.
I HEARD THEY MADE UP IN THE END THOUGH.
IT WOULD HAVE BEEN COOL IF THEY GOT INTO FISTFIGHTS AND STUFF.
TEE HEE
クスクス
VICTORY
SHOCK
カーッ
KYAA! GO, PRINCESS ATSU!
GO, TENSHOUIN-SAMA!
YAY, KAZUNOMIYA-SAMA!
WHACK
ポカ
WHACK
ポカ
SUNAKO'S FANTASY

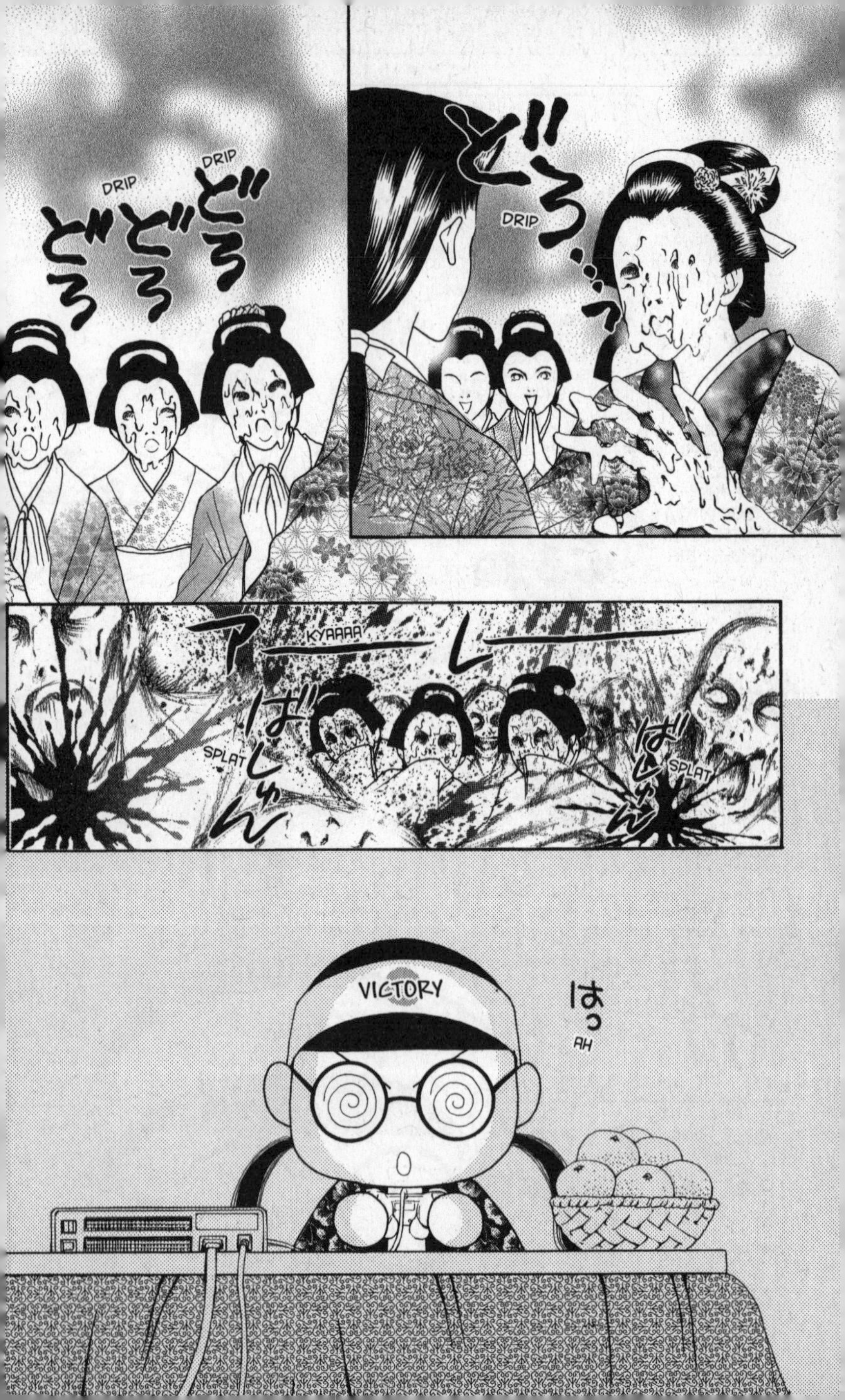
どろ…っ
DRIP
どろ
DRIP
どろ
DRIP
どろ
アーレー
KYAAAA
ばしゃん
SPLAT
ばしゃん
SPLAT
VICTORY
はっ
AH

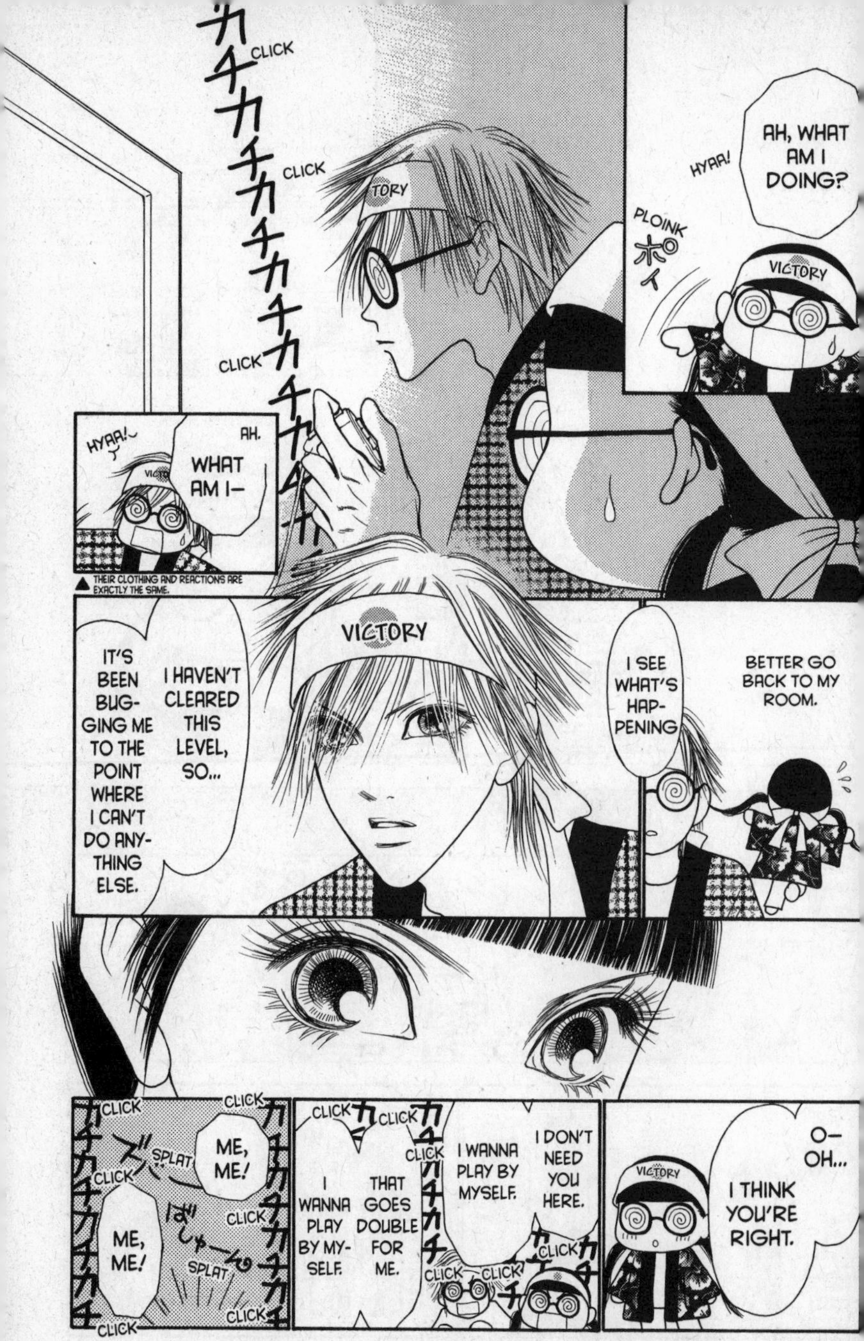
HYAA!
AH, WHAT AM I DOING?
PLOINK
ポイ
CLICK
CLICK
CLICK
HYAA!
AH.
WHAT AM I—
THEIR CLOTHING AND REACTIONS ARE EXACTLY THE SAME.
BETTER GO BACK TO MY ROOM.
I SEE WHAT'S HAP-PENING
I HAVEN'T CLEARED THIS LEVEL, SO...
IT'S BEEN BUG-GING ME TO THE POINT WHERE I CAN'T DO ANY-THING ELSE.
O—OH...
I THINK YOU'RE RIGHT.
I DON'T NEED YOU HERE.
I WANNA PLAY BY MYSELF.
THAT GOES DOUBLE FOR ME.
I WANNA PLAY BY MY-SELF.
CLICK
CLICK
CLICK
CLICK
CLICK
CLICK
ME, ME!
ME, ME!
SPLAT
SPLAT
CLICK
CLICK
CLICK
CLICK
CLICK

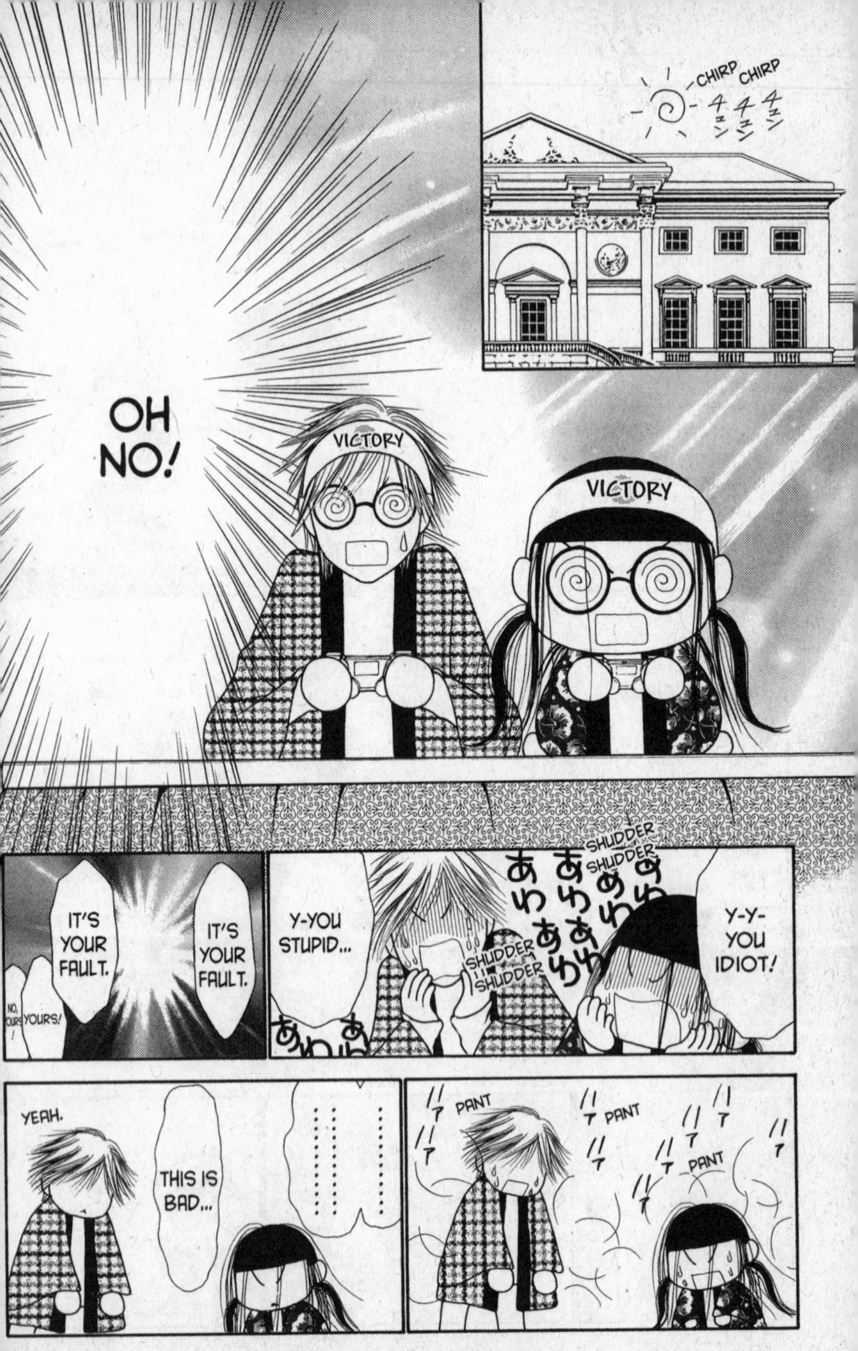
CHIRP CHIRP
チュンチュンチュン
OH NO!
VICTORY
VICTORY
Y-Y-YOU IDIOT!
SHUDDER SHUDDER
あわわあわわ
あわわあわわ
Y-YOU STUPID...
SHUDDER SHUDDER
あわわ
IT'S YOUR FAULT.
IT'S YOUR FAULT.
YOURS!
NO, YOURS!
PANT
PANT
PANT
ハァハァ
......
THIS IS BAD...
YEAH.

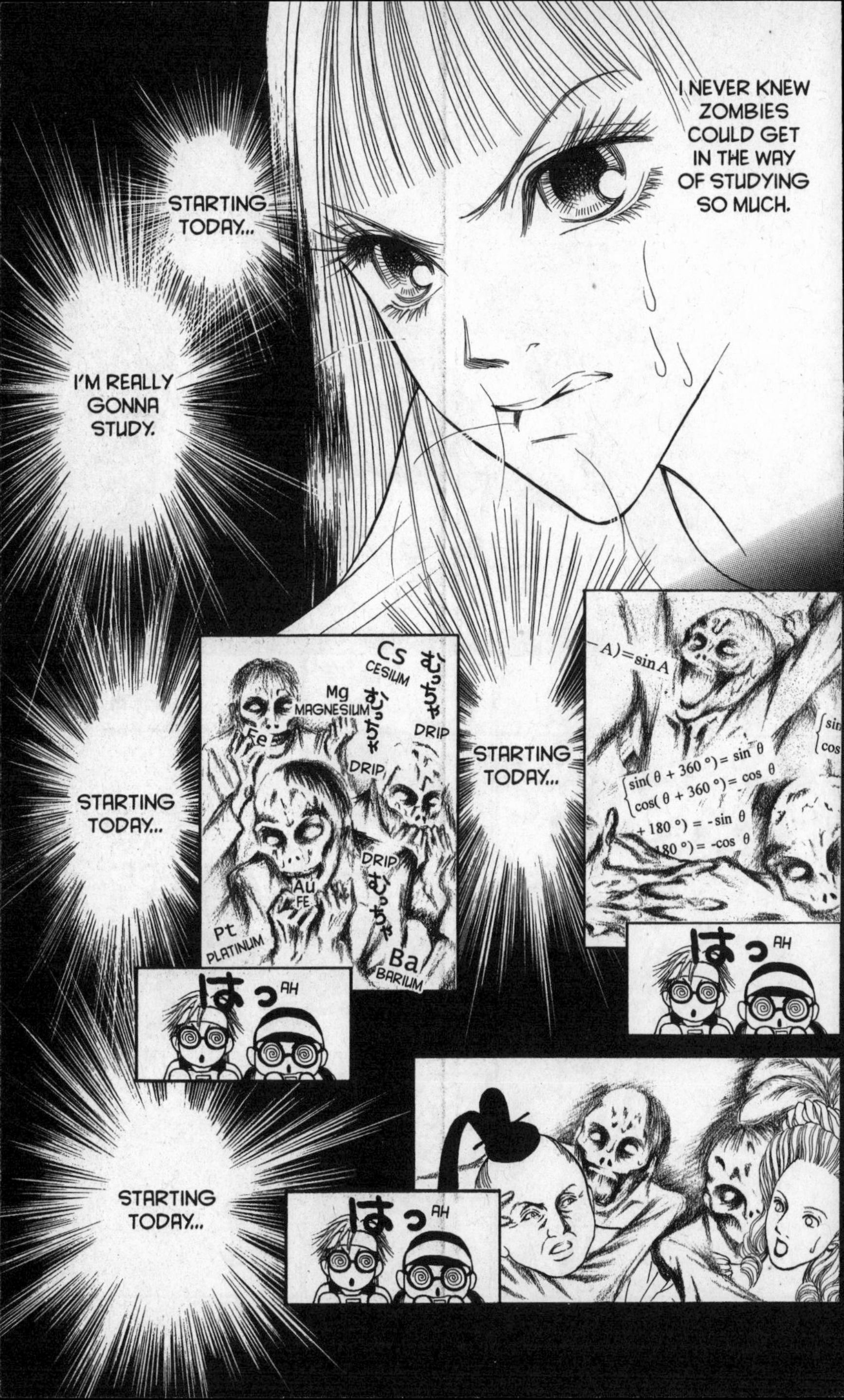
I NEVER KNEW ZOMBIES COULD GET IN THE WAY OF STUDYING SO MUCH.
STARTING TODAY...
I'M REALLY GONNA STUDY.
A)=sin A
sin(θ + 360 °)= sin θ
cos(θ + 360 °)= cos θ
+ 180 °) = -sin θ
180 °) = -cos θ
はっ AH
STARTING TODAY...
Cs CESIUM
むっちゃ
Mg MAGNESIUM
むっちゃ
DRIP
Fe
DRIP
DRIP
むっちゃ
Au FE
Pt PLATINUM
Ba BARIUM
はっ AH
STARTING TODAY...
はっ AH
STARTING TODAY...

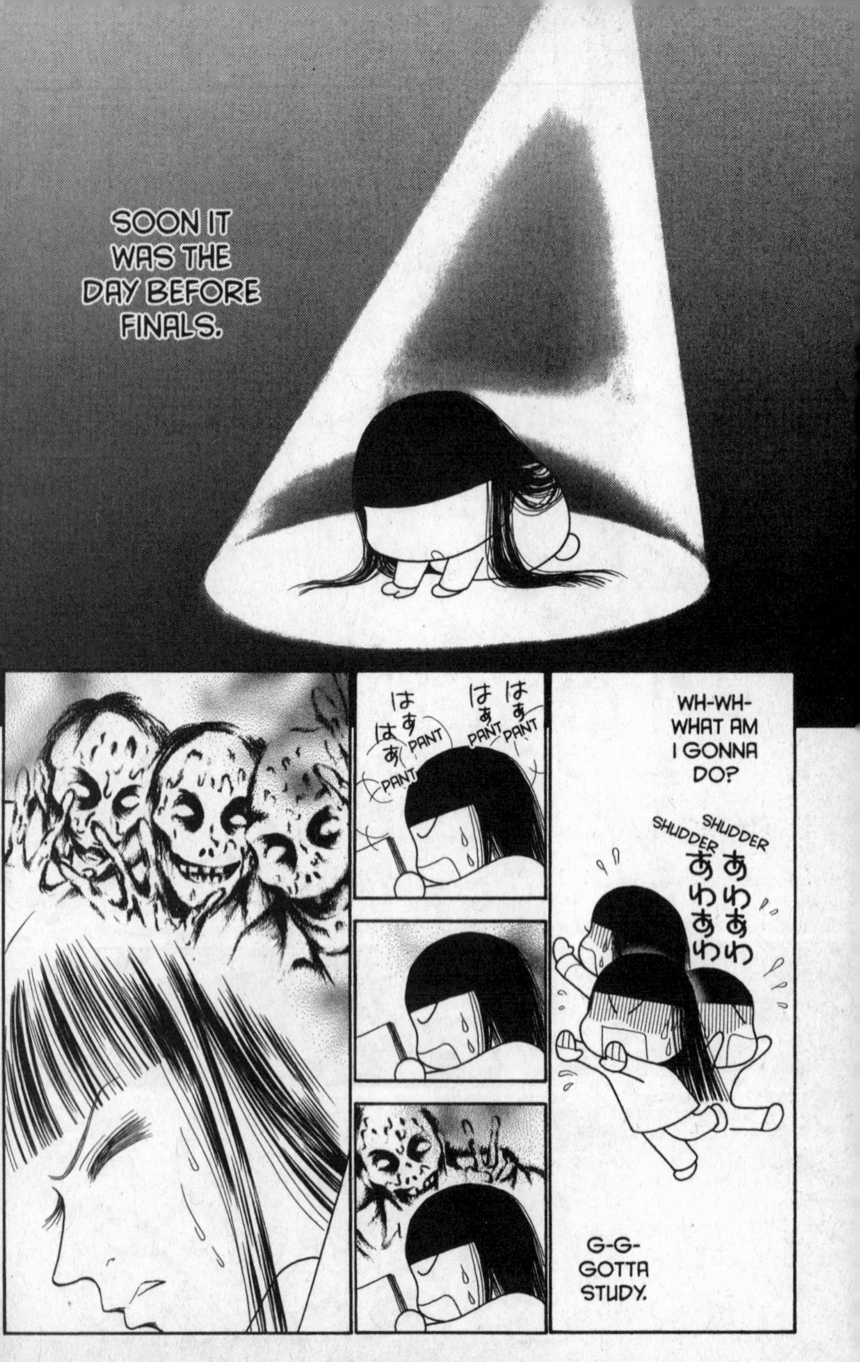
SOON IT WAS THE DAY BEFORE FINALS.
WH-WH-WHAT AM I GONNA DO?
SHUDDER SHUDDER
あわあわ
あわあわ
G-G-GOTTA STUDY.
PANT PANT
はぁはぁ
PANT PANT
はぁはぁ

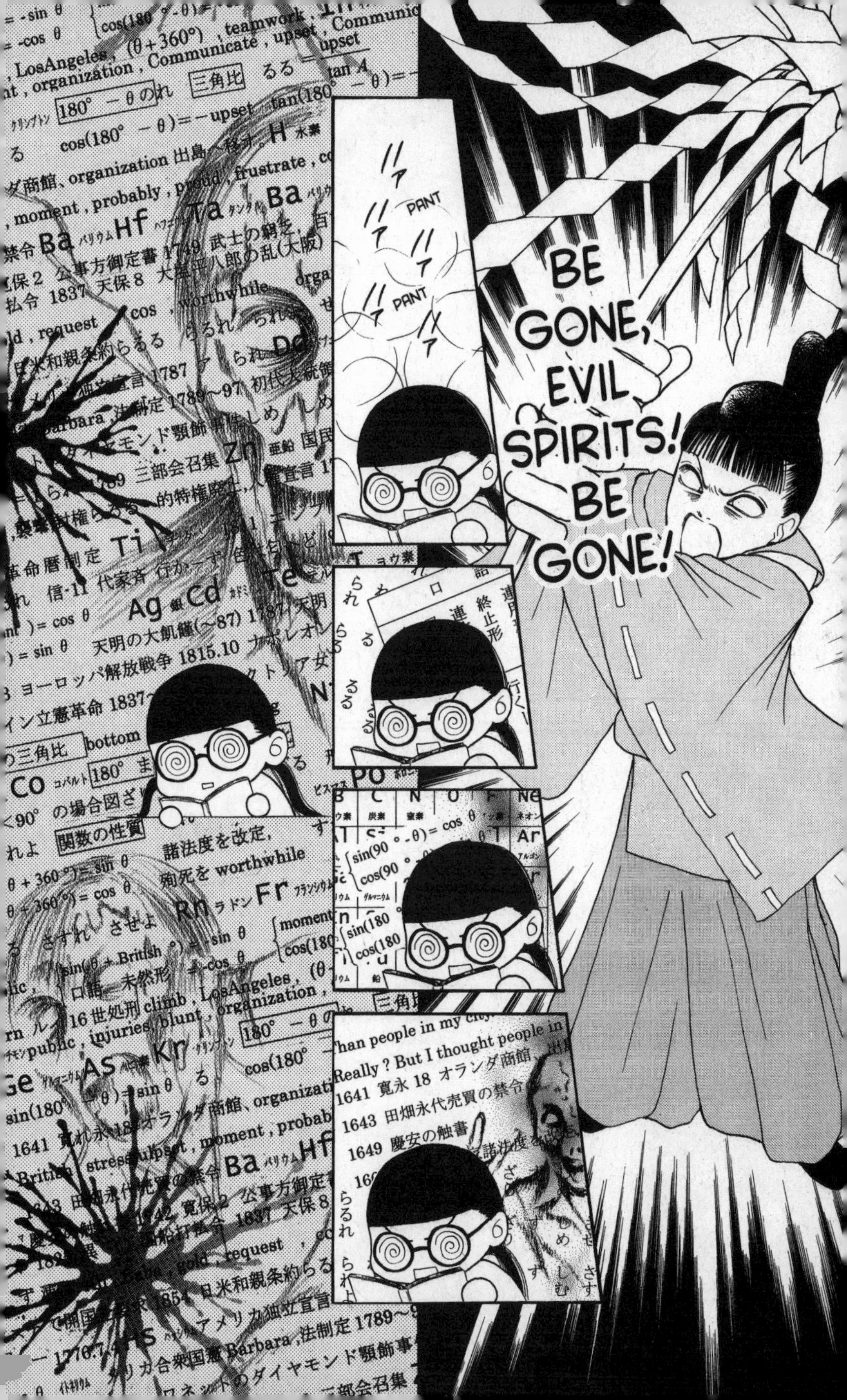
BE GONE, EVIL SPIRITS! BE GONE!
PANT
PANT

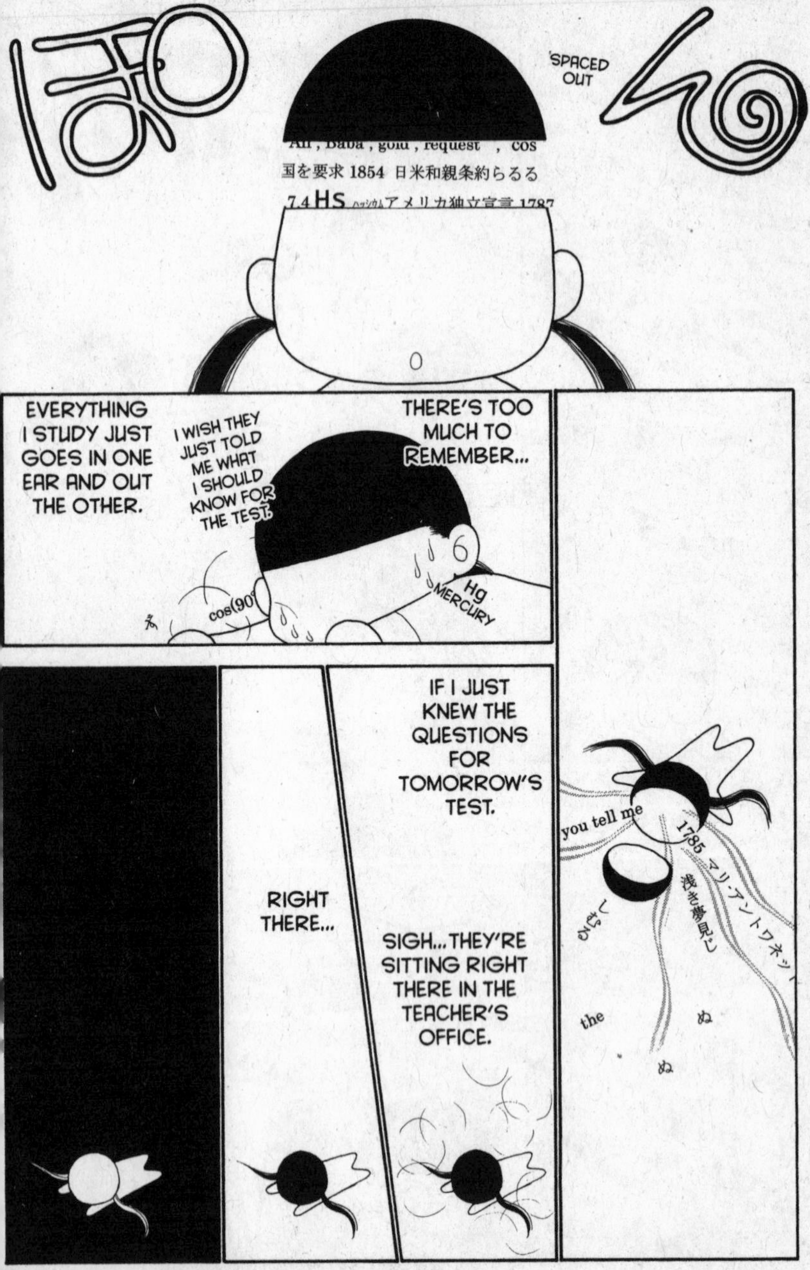
SPACED OUT
Ali, Baba, gold, request , cos
国を要求 1854 日米和親条約らるる
74HS ハッシウムアメリカ独立宣言 1787
you tell me
1785 マリ・アントワネッ
浅き夢見じ
しむる
the
ぬ
ぬ
THERE'S TOO MUCH TO REMEMBER...
I WISH THEY JUST TOLD ME WHAT I SHOULD KNOW FOR THE TEST.
EVERYTHING I STUDY JUST GOES IN ONE EAR AND OUT THE OTHER.
Hg MERCURY
cos(90
IF I JUST KNEW THE QUESTIONS FOR TOMORROW'S TEST.
SIGH...THEY'RE SITTING RIGHT THERE IN THE TEACHER'S OFFICE.
RIGHT THERE...

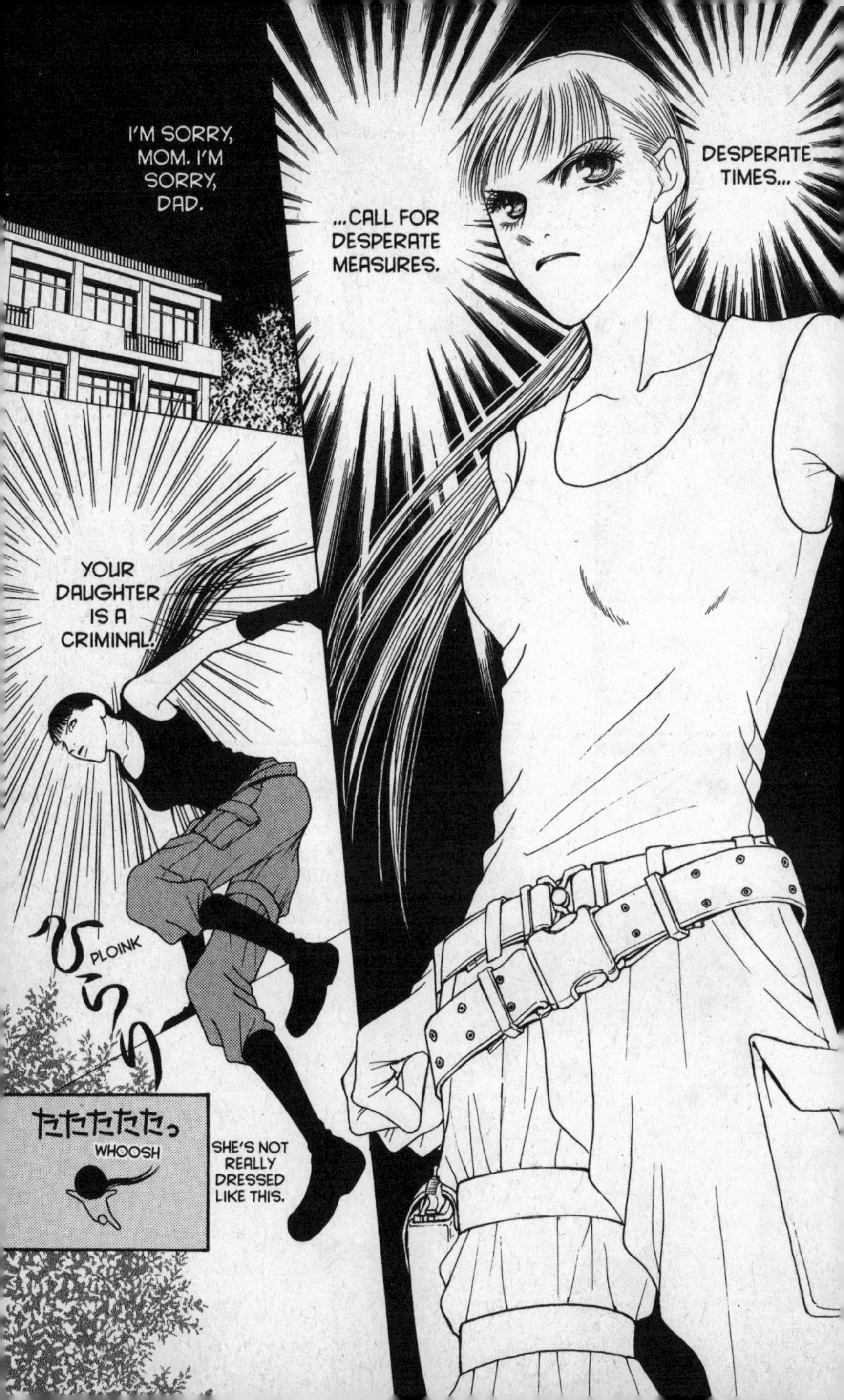
DESPERATE TIMES...
...CALL FOR DESPERATE MEASURES.
I'M SORRY, MOM. I'M SORRY, DAD.
YOUR DAUGHTER IS A CRIMINAL!
ひらり
PLOINK
たたたたたっ
WHOOSH
SHE'S NOT REALLY DRESSED LIKE THIS.

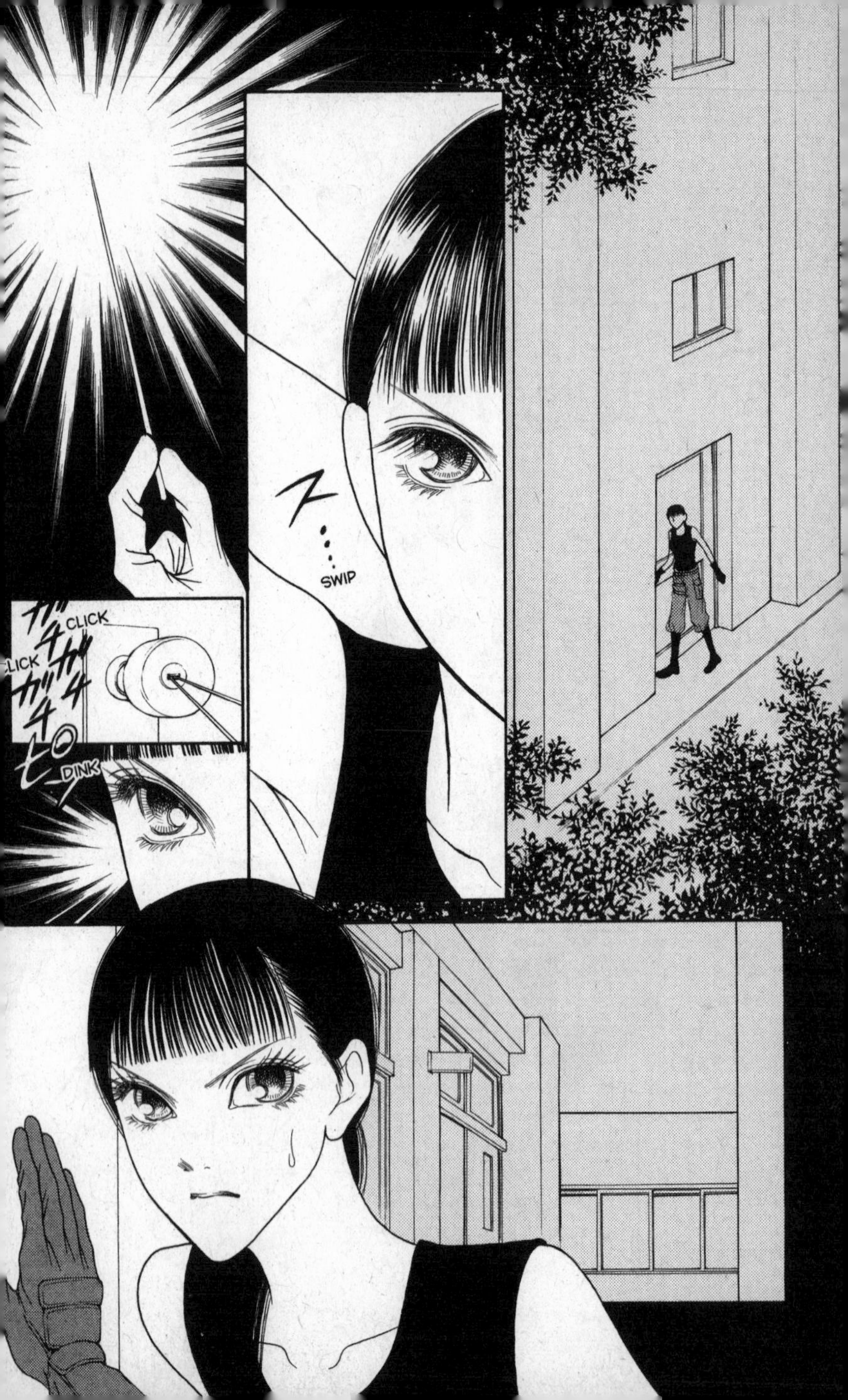

SWIP
CLICK
LICK
DINK

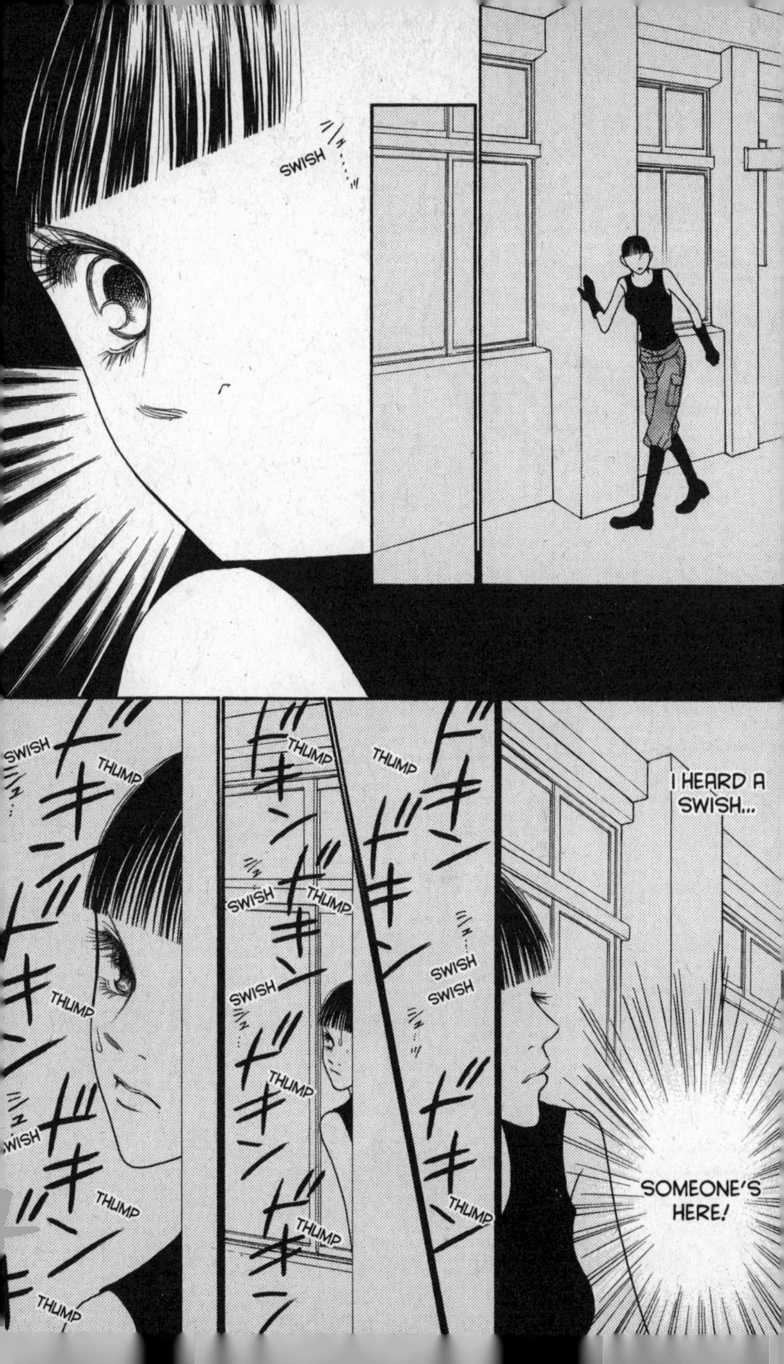
SWISH
I HEARD A SWISH...
SOMEONE'S HERE!
THUMP
SWISH
SWISH
THUMP
THUMP
SWISH
THUMP
SWISH
THUMP
THUMP
SWISH
THUMP
THUMP
SWISH
THUMP
THUMP

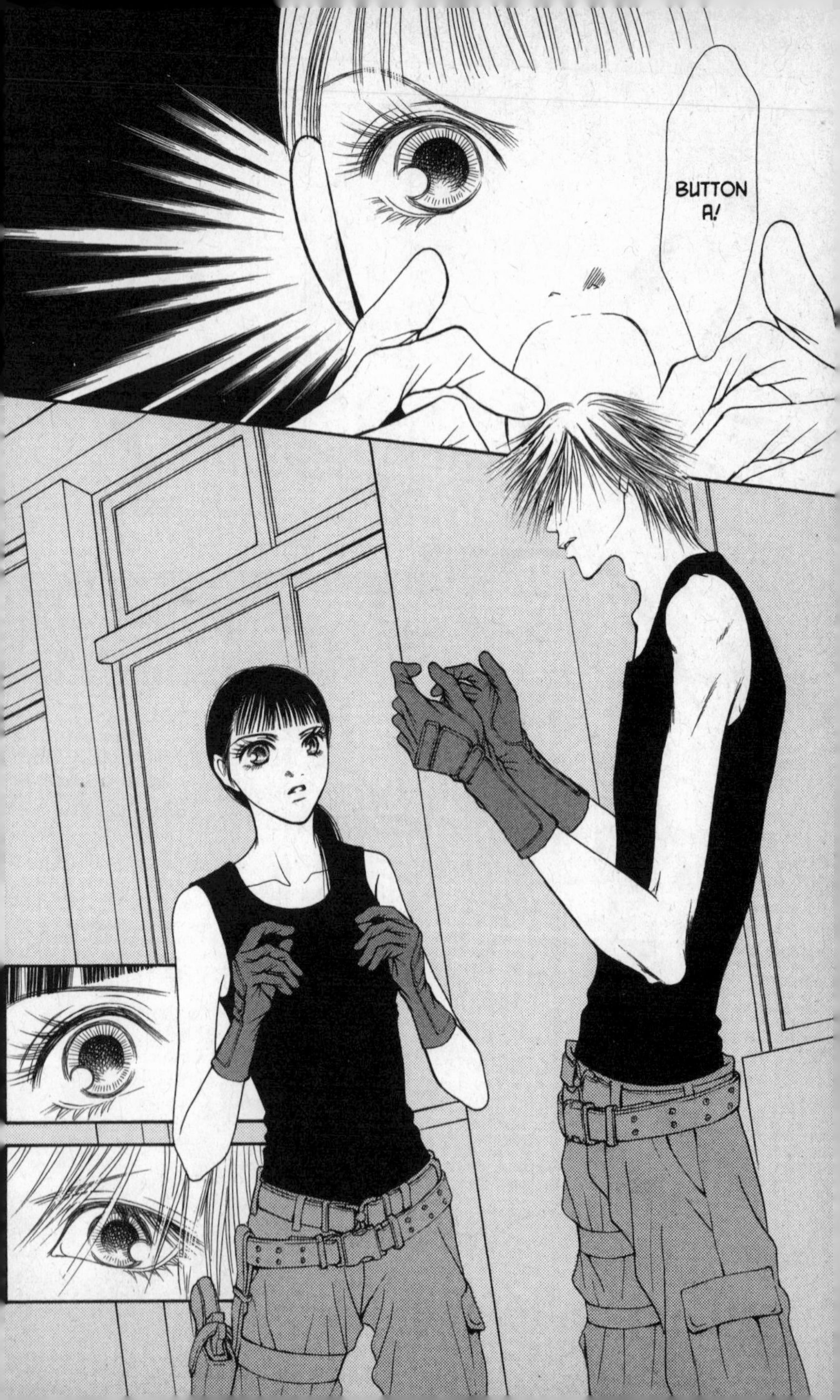
BUTTON A!

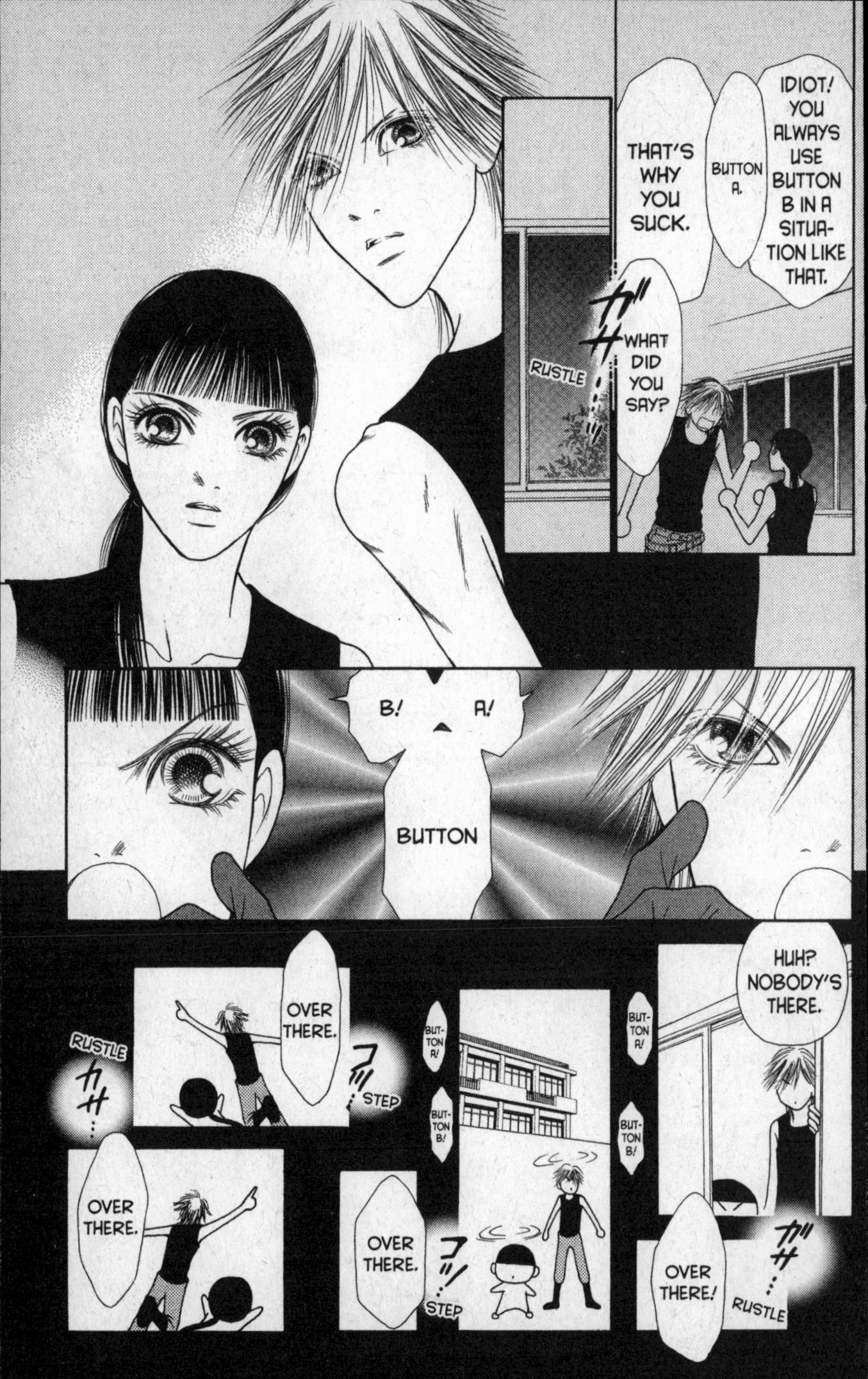
IDIOT! YOU ALWAYS USE BUTTON B IN A SITUATION LIKE THAT.
BUTTON A.
THAT'S WHY YOU SUCK.
WHAT DID YOU SAY?
RUSTLE
A!
B!
BUTTON
HUH? NOBODY'S THERE.
BUTTON A!
BUTTON B!
BUTTON A!
BUTTON B!
OVER THERE.
STEP
RUSTLE
OVER THERE!
RUSTLE
OVER THERE.
STEP
OVER THERE.

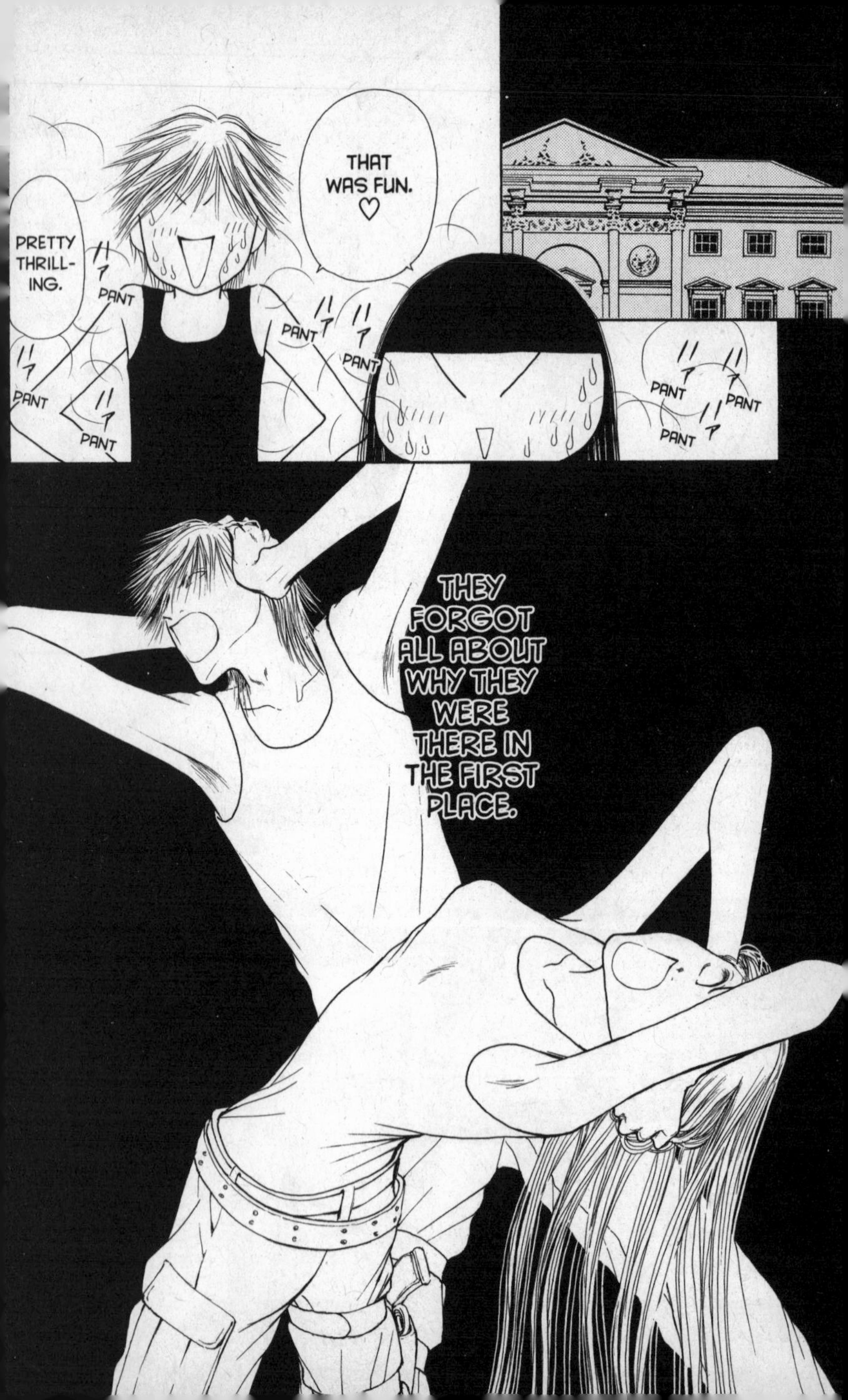
PANT
PANT
PANT
THAT WAS FUN. ♡
PANT
PANT
PRETTY THRILL-ING.
PANT
PANT
PANT
THEY FORGOT ALL ABOUT WHY THEY WERE THERE IN THE FIRST PLACE.

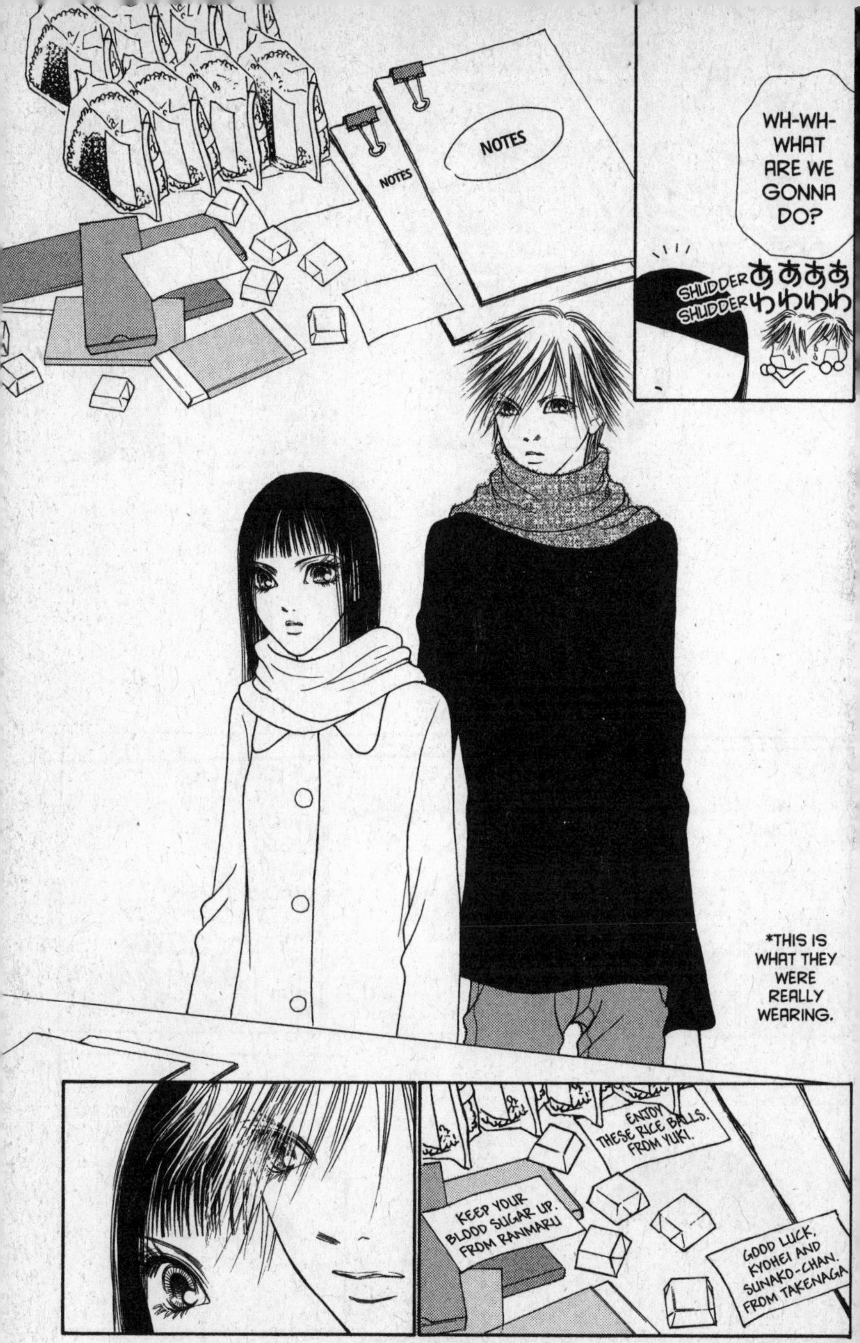
WH-WH-WHAT ARE WE GONNA DO?
SHUDDER あああ
SHUDDER わわわ
NOTES
NOTES
*THIS IS WHAT THEY WERE REALLY WEARING.
ENJOY THESE RICE BALLS. FROM YUKI.
GOOD LUCK, KYOHEI AND SUNAKO-CHAN. FROM TAKENAGA
KEEP YOUR BLOOD SUGAR UP. FROM RANMARU

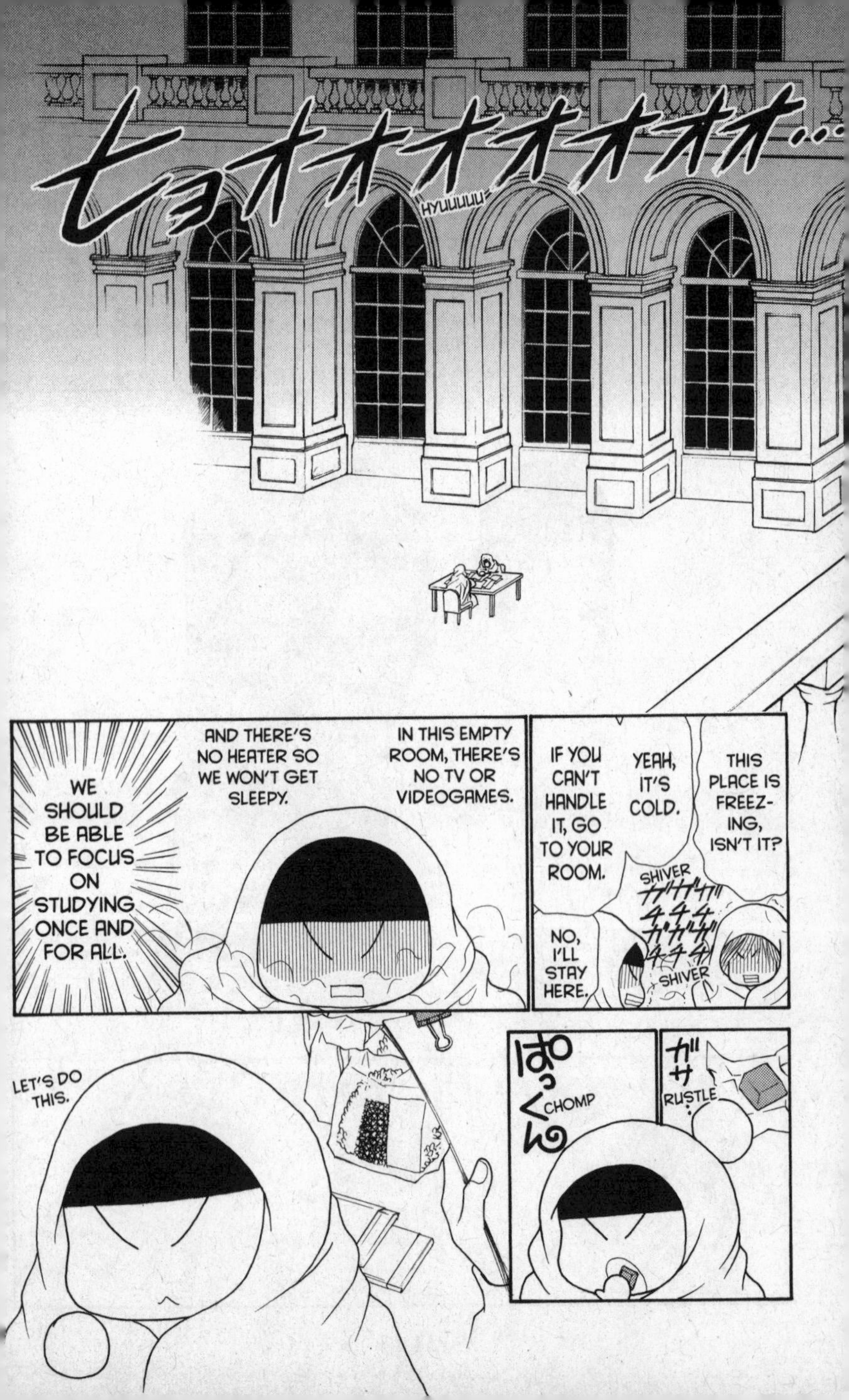
ヒョオオオオオオオ…
HYUUUUUU
THIS PLACE IS FREEZING, ISN'T IT?
YEAH, IT'S COLD.
IF YOU CAN'T HANDLE IT, GO TO YOUR ROOM.
SHIVER
SHIVER
NO, I'LL STAY HERE.
IN THIS EMPTY ROOM, THERE'S NO TV OR VIDEOGAMES.
AND THERE'S NO HEATER SO WE WON'T GET SLEEPY.
WE SHOULD BE ABLE TO FOCUS ON STUDYING ONCE AND FOR ALL.
ガサ
RUSTLE
ぱっくん
CHOMP
LET'S DO THIS.

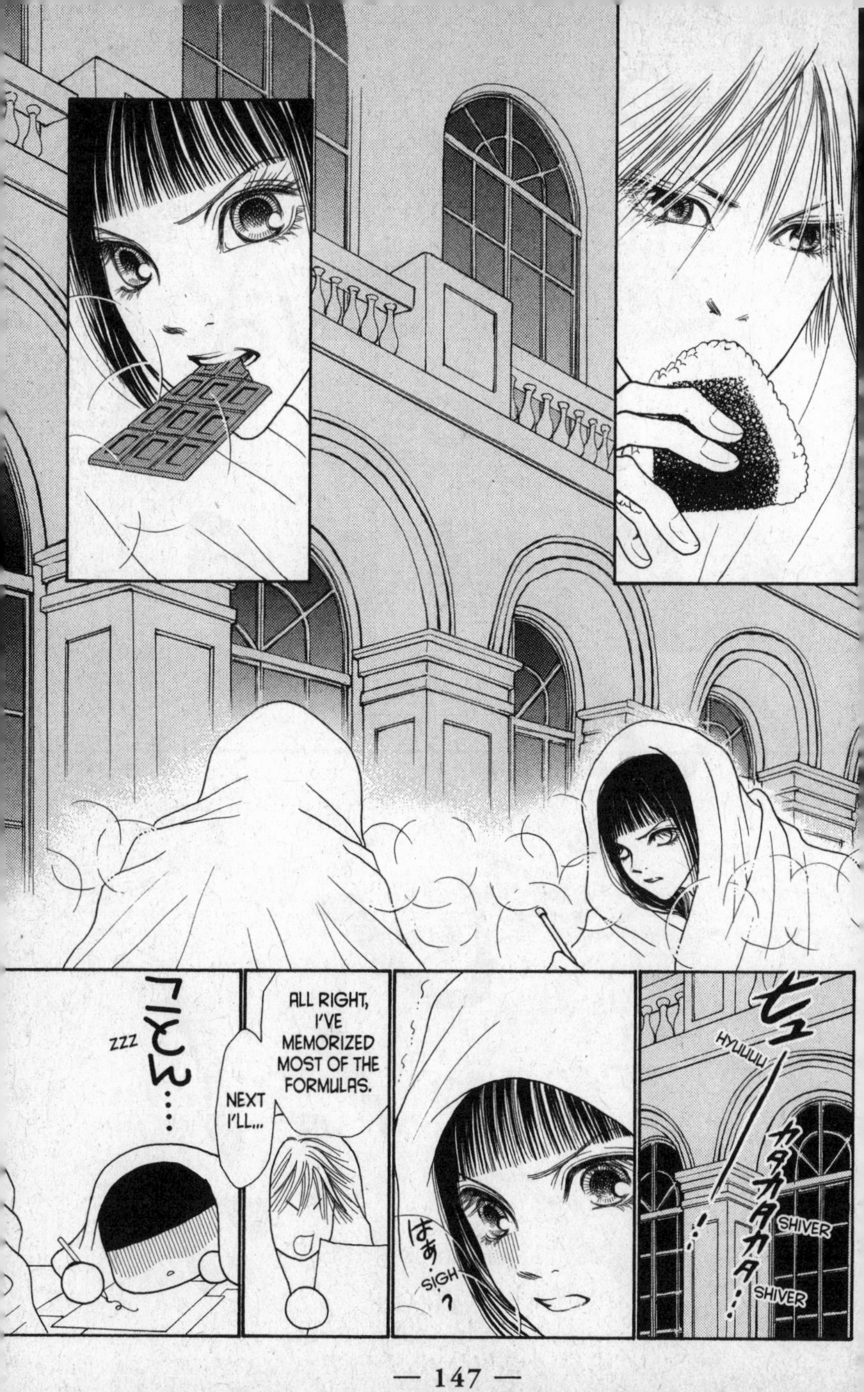

ヒュー
HYUUUU
カタカタカタ…
SHIVER
SHIVER
はぁ
SIGH
ALL RIGHT, I'VE MEMORIZED MOST OF THE FORMULAS.
NEXT I'LL...
ことん…
ZZZ

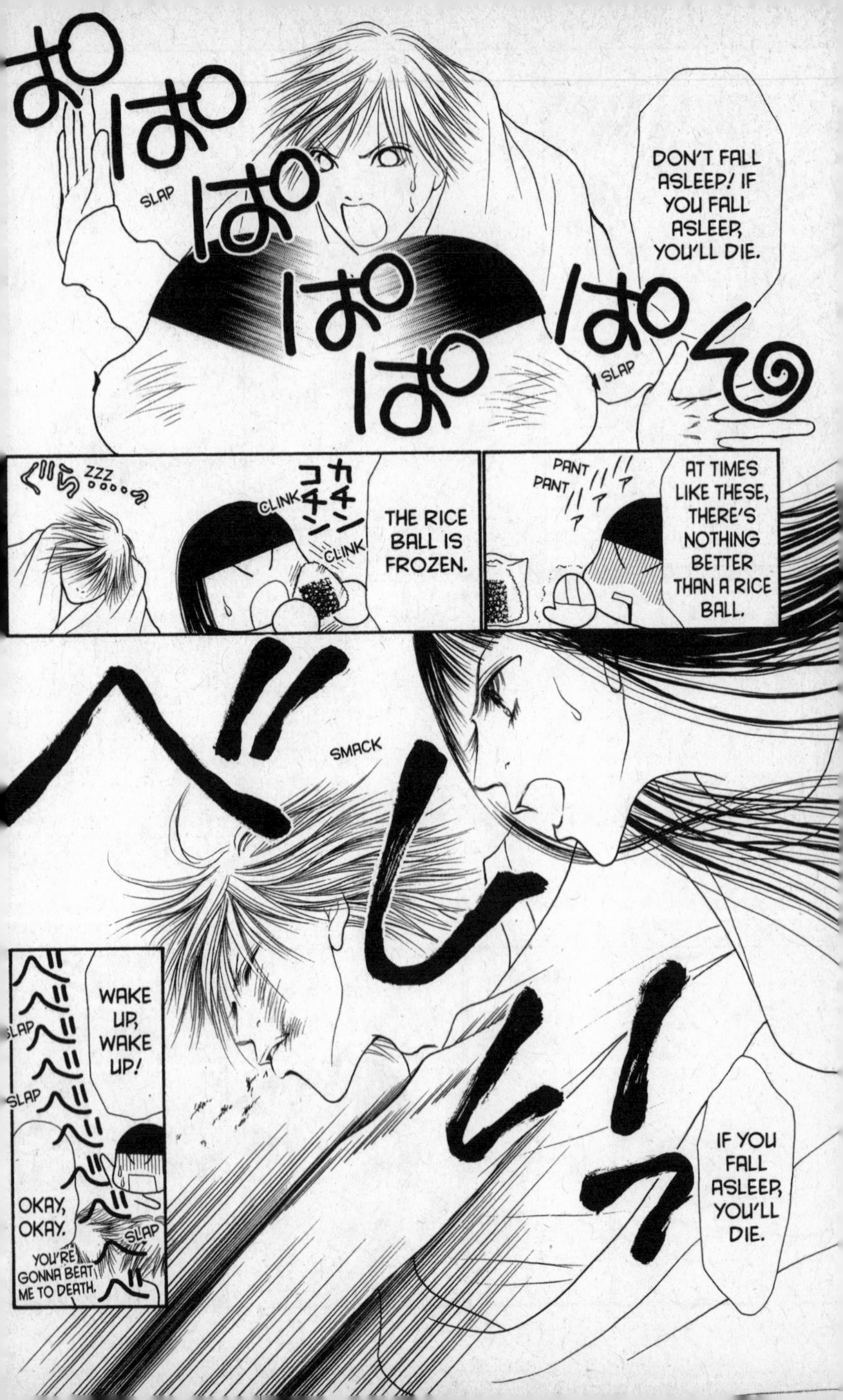

DON'T FALL ASLEEP! IF YOU FALL ASLEEP, YOU'LL DIE.
SLAP
SLAP
AT TIMES LIKE THESE, THERE'S NOTHING BETTER THAN A RICE BALL.
PANT PANT
ハァハァ
THE RICE BALL IS FROZEN.
カチンコチン
CLINK
CLINK
ZZZ
SMACK
IF YOU FALL ASLEEP, YOU'LL DIE.
WAKE UP, WAKE UP!
SLAP
SLAP
SLAP
OKAY, OKAY.
YOU'RE GONNA BEAT ME TO DEATH.

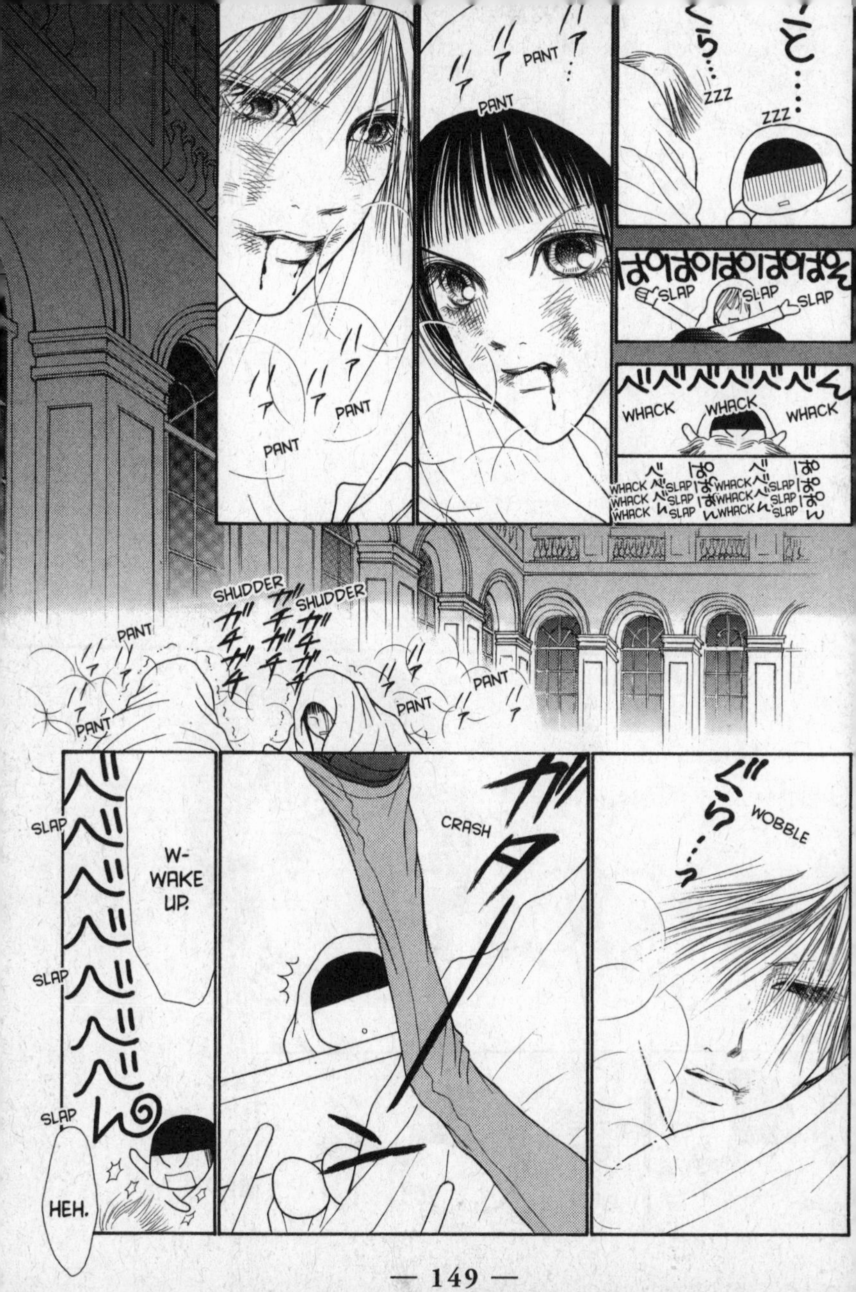

と…
ZZZ
くら…
ZZZ
ぱぱぱぱぱ
SLAP
SLAP
SLAP
べべべべべん
WHACK
WHACK
WHACK
ぱぱぱん
SLAP
SLAP
SLAP
べべべん
WHACK
WHACK
WHACK
ぱぱぱん
SLAP
SLAP
SLAP
べべべん
WHACK
WHACK
WHACK
ハァ…
PANT
ハァ
ハァ
PANT
ハァ
ハァ
PANT
ハァ
PANT
SHUDDER
ガチガチガチ
SHUDDER
ガチガチガチ
ハァ
PANT
ハァ
PANT
ハァ
PANT
ハァ
PANT
ぐら…
WOBBLE
ガタ
CRASH
べべべべべべん
SLAP
W-WAKE UP.
SLAP
SLAP
HEH.

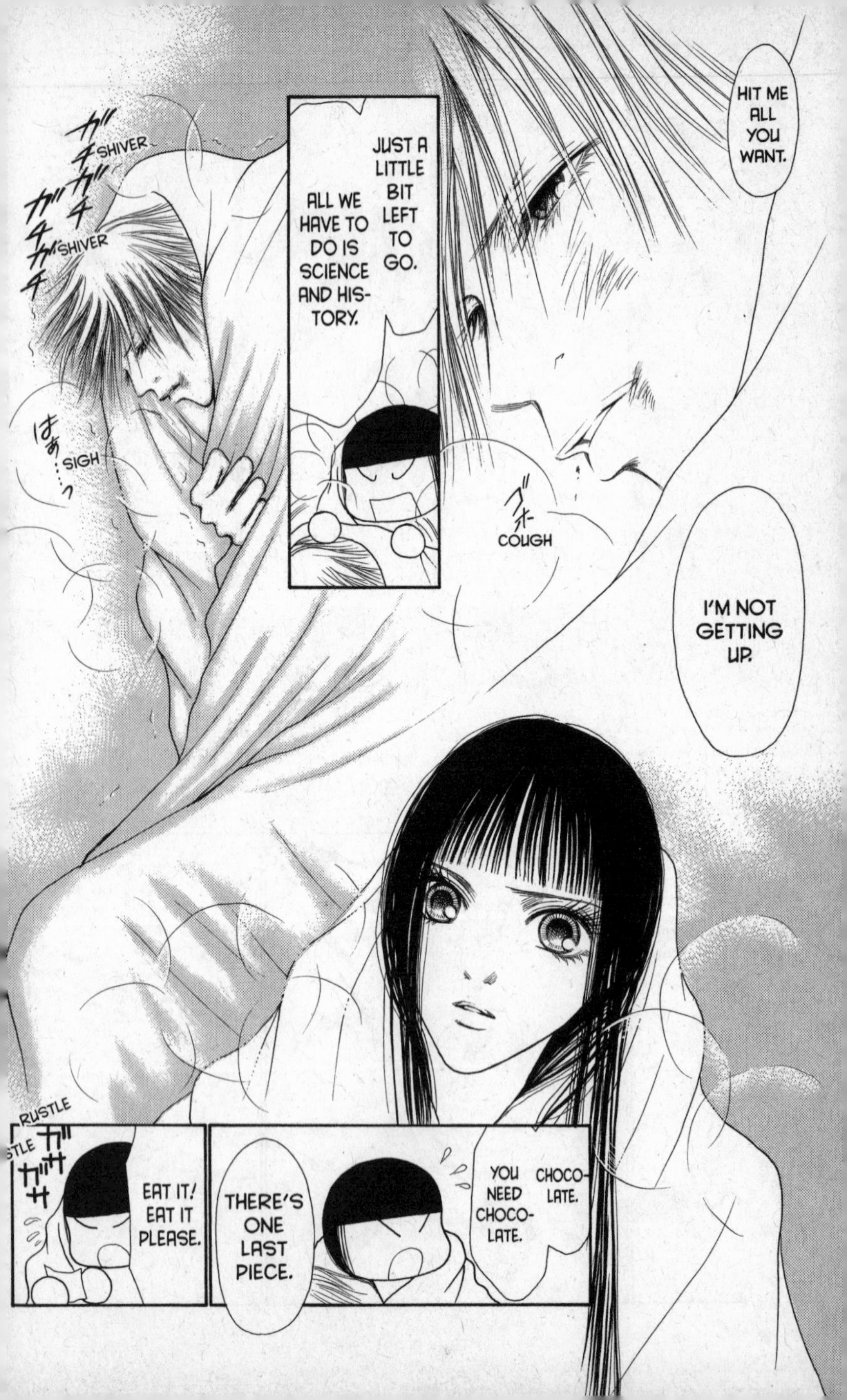
HIT ME ALL YOU WANT.
I'M NOT GETTING UP.
COUGH
JUST A LITTLE BIT LEFT TO GO.
ALL WE HAVE TO DO IS SCIENCE AND HIS-TORY.
SHIVER
SHIVER
SIGH
CHOCO-LATE.
YOU NEED CHOCO-LATE.
THERE'S ONE LAST PIECE.
EAT IT! EAT IT PLEASE.
RUSTLE

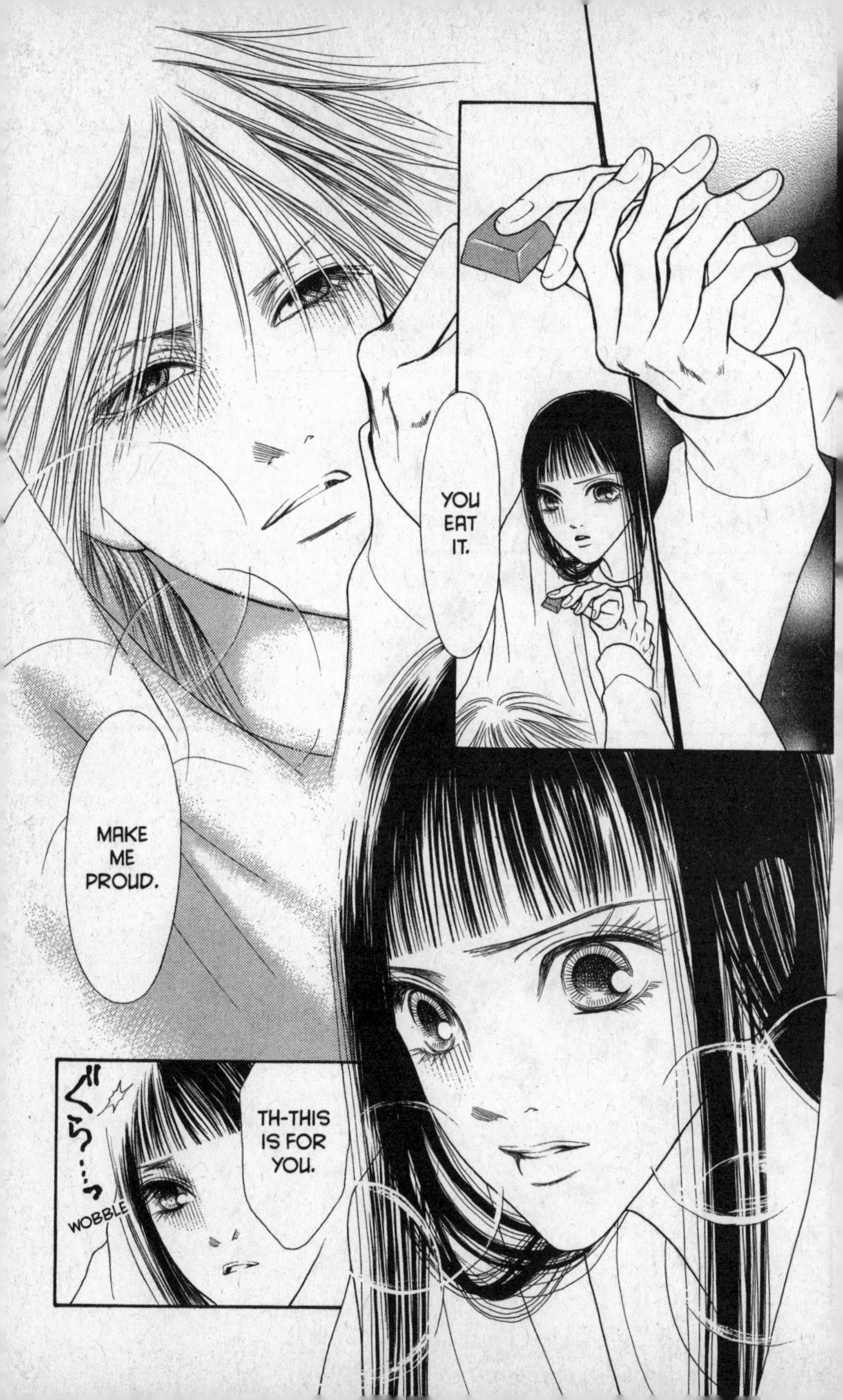
YOU EAT IT.
MAKE ME PROUD.
TH-THIS IS FOR YOU.
ぐら…っ
WOBBLE

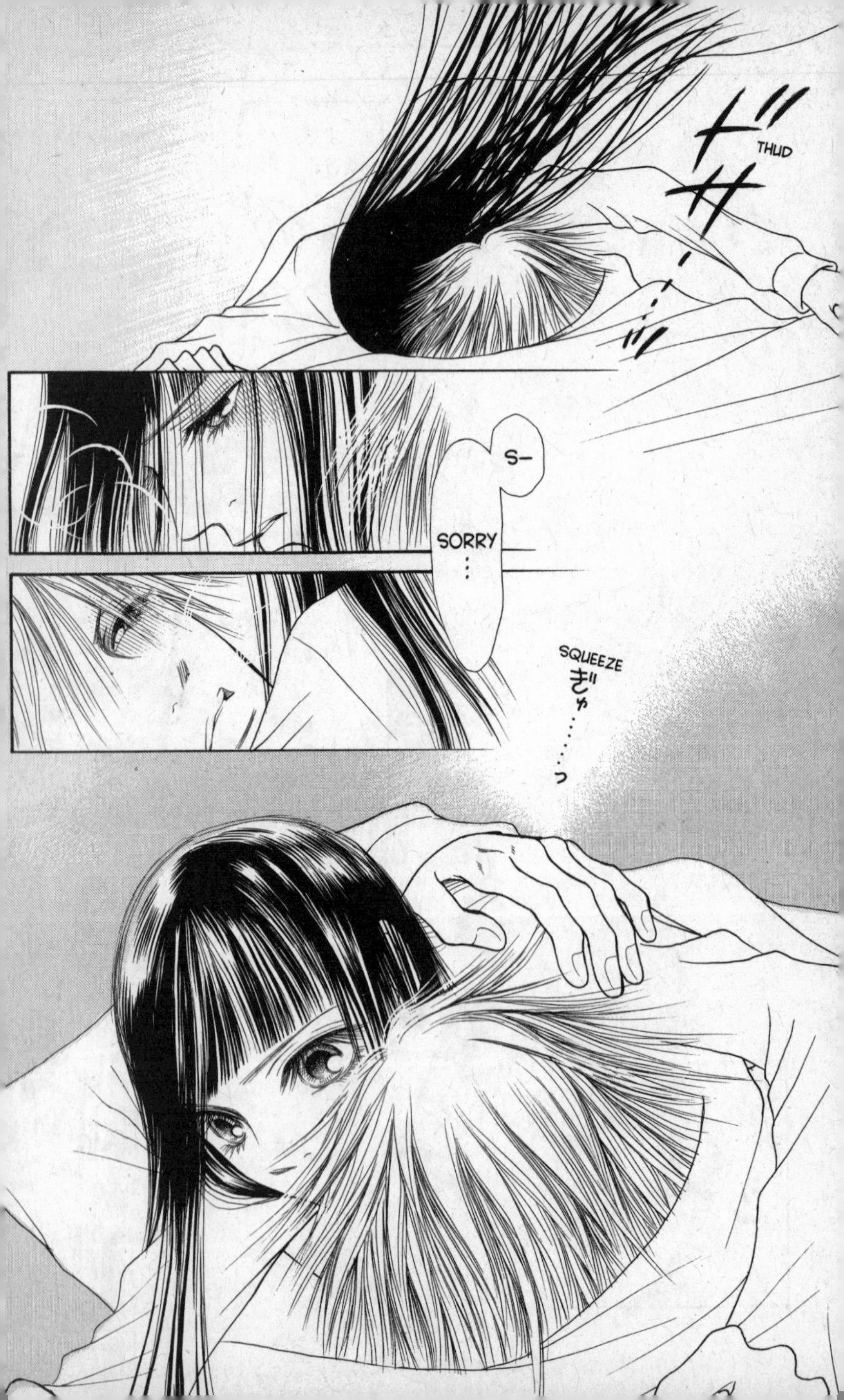
ドサー…ッ
THUD
S-
SORRY
…
SQUEEZE
ぎゅ……っ

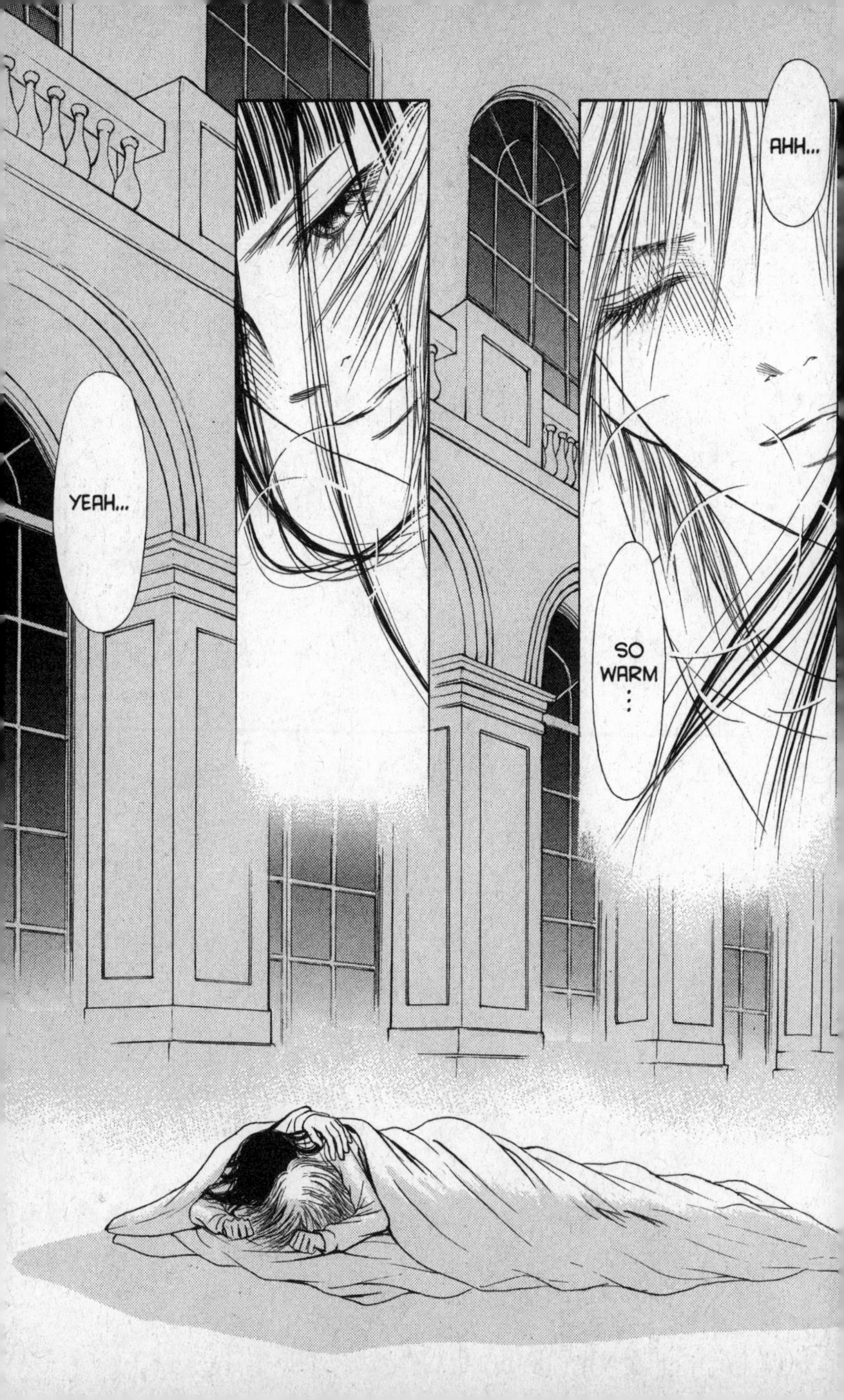
AHH...
SO WARM ...
YEAH...

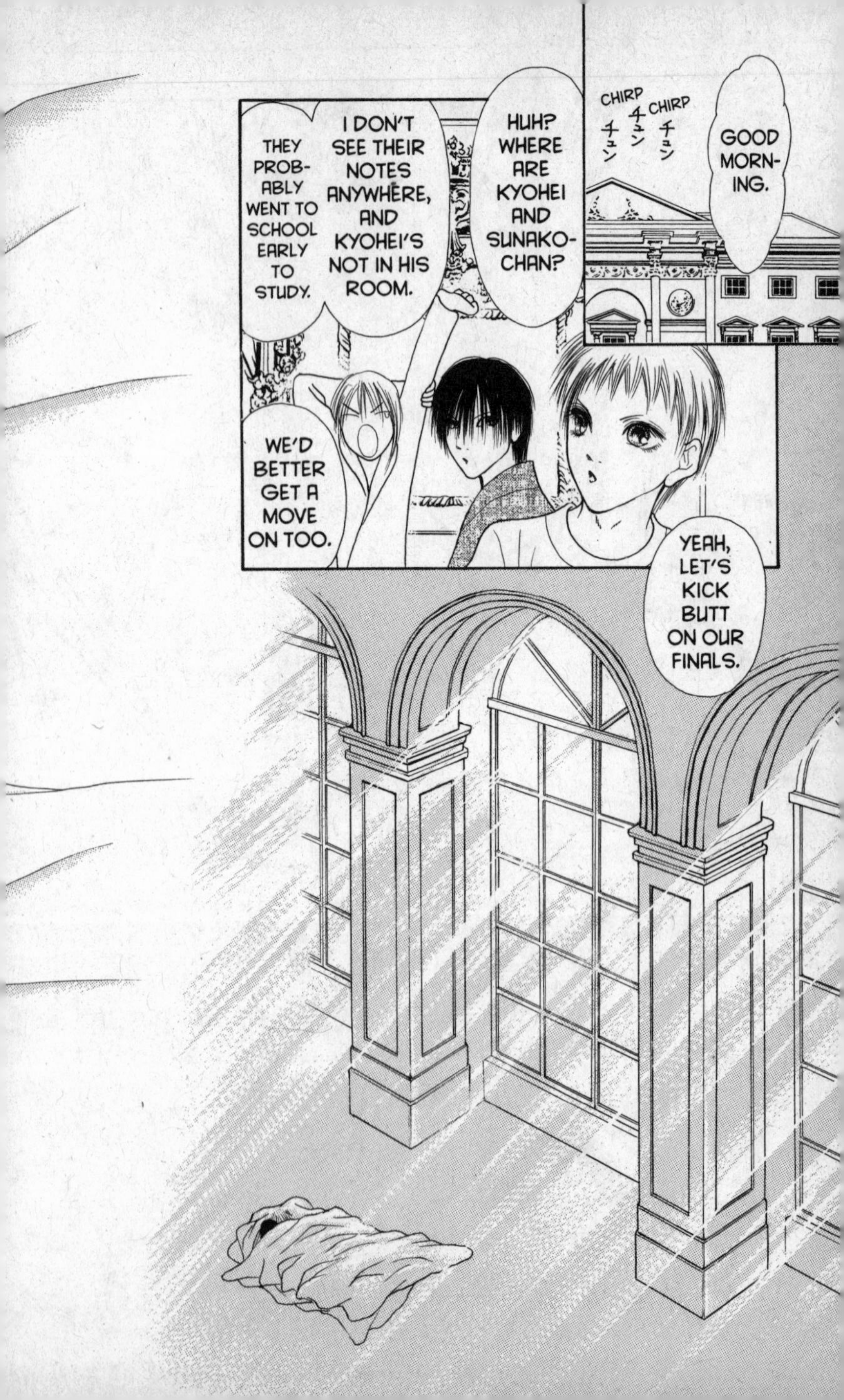
GOOD MORNING.
CHIRP チュン
CHIRP チュン チュン
HUH? WHERE ARE KYOHEI AND SUNAKO-CHAN?
I DON'T SEE THEIR NOTES ANYWHERE, AND KYOHEI'S NOT IN HIS ROOM.
THEY PROBABLY WENT TO SCHOOL EARLY TO STUDY.
WE'D BETTER GET A MOVE ON TOO.
YEAH, LET'S KICK BUTT ON OUR FINALS.

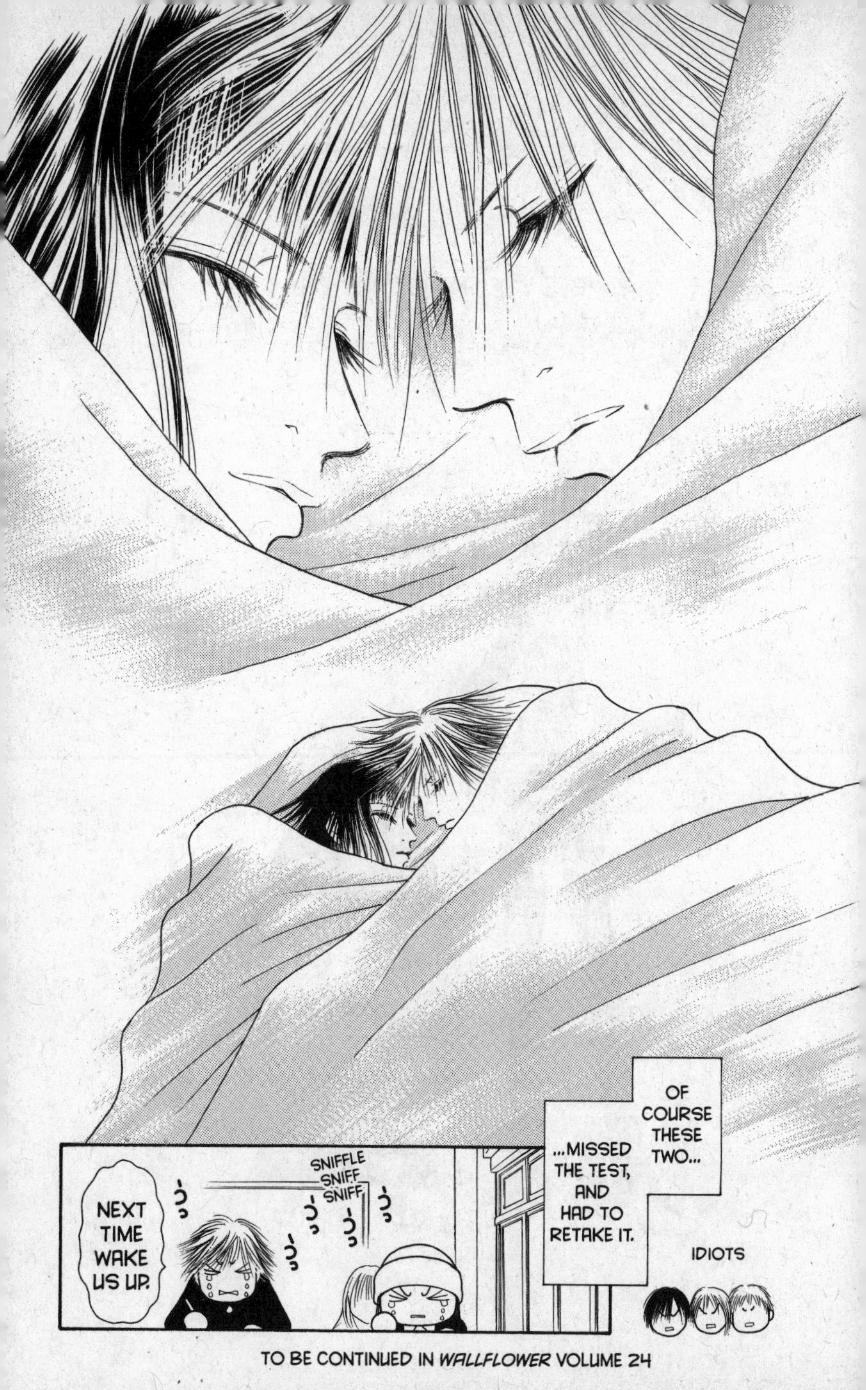
OF COURSE THESE TWO...
...MISSED THE TEST, AND HAD TO RETAKE IT.
IDIOTS
SNIFFLE SNIFF SNIFF
NEXT TIME WAKE US UP.

TO BE CONTINUED IN *WALLFLOWER* VOLUME 24

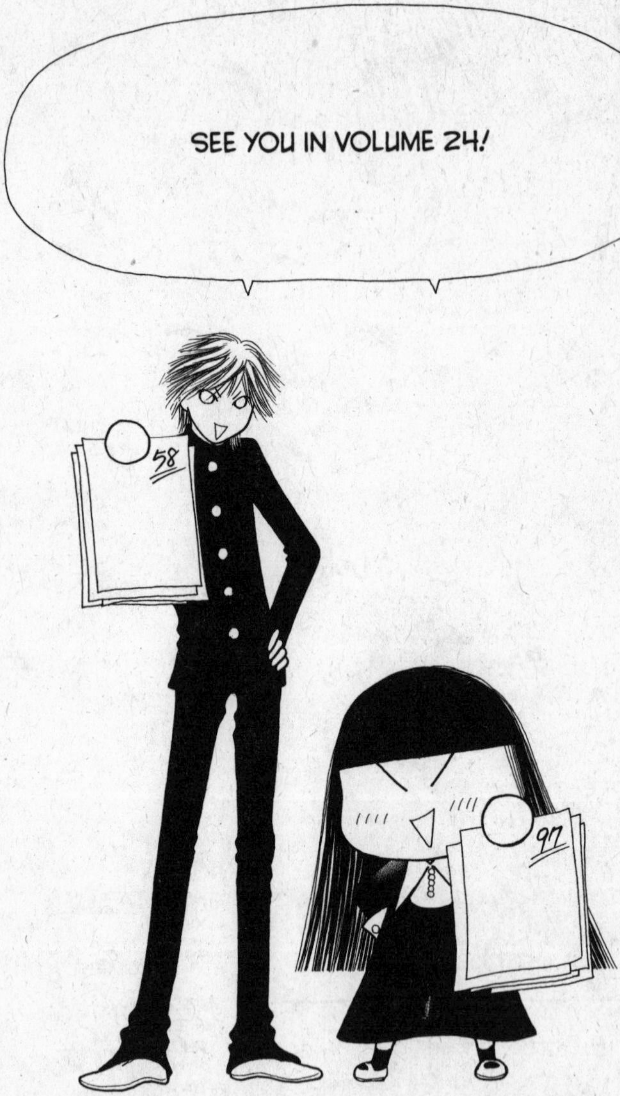
SEE YOU IN VOLUME 24!
58
97

THANK YOU FOR BUYING KODANSHA COMICS. ♥

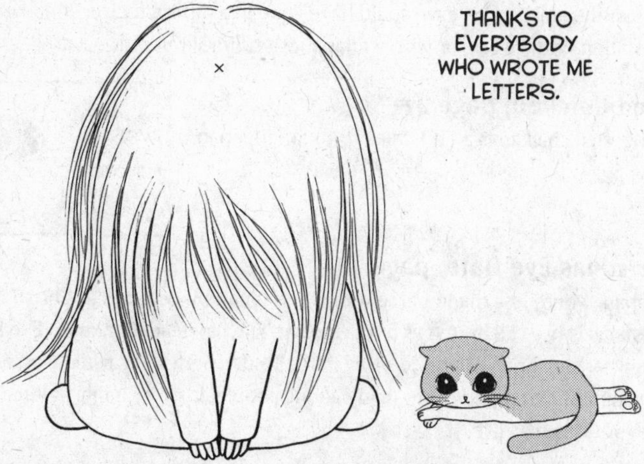

THANKS TO EVERYBODY WHO WROTE ME LETTERS.

RIGHT NOW I'M HAVING MYSTERY SHOULDER PAIN, AND IT'S REALLY TERRIBLE. IN BOOK 22, MY BACK HURT, AND NOW IT'S MY SHOULDERS. WHAT THE HECK? IT HURTS THE MOST WHEN I SNEEZE, AND NOW IT'S SPRING... YEP, YOU GUESSED IT, IT'S ALLERGY SEASON.

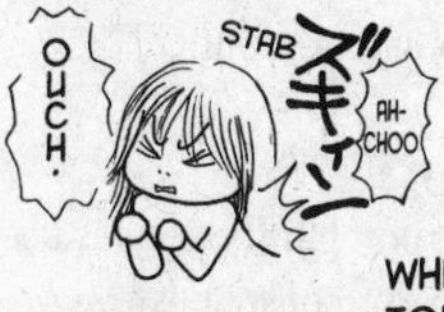
AH-CHOO
STAB
ズキーン
OUCH.

THAT'S WHAT KEEPS HAPPENING.

MY EYES ITCH, AND
MY NOSE IS RUNNY, AND
MY BACK IS SWOLLEN, AND
MY SHOULDERS AND BACK HURT...
SIGH...

WHEN I GOT MY PALM READ, THE PALM READER TOLD ME THAT MY INTERNAL ORGANS WERE IN BAD SHAPE. I NEED TO GO IN FOR A FULL PHYSICAL.

I'LL KEEP WHIPPING MY AGING BODY INTO SHAPE, AND I'LL SEE YOU IN VOLUME 24. ♥

SPECIAL THANKS

TOMMY YOUICHIROU TOMITA-SAMA
KAI-CHAN (MY FRIEND)
HITOSHI (MY REAL BROTHER)

MACHIKO SAKURAI-SAMA
REN KOIZUMI-SAMA
IYU KOZAKURA-SAMA

MY EDITOR IN CHIEF
INO-SAMA
INNAN-SAMA
EVERYBODY IN THE EDITING DEPARTMENT

EVERYBODY WHO'S READING THIS RIGHT NOW

Translation Notes

Japanese is a tricky language for most Westerners, and translation is often more art than science. For your edification and reading pleasure, here are notes on some of the places where we could have gone in a different direction in our translation of the work, or where a Japanese cultural reference is used.

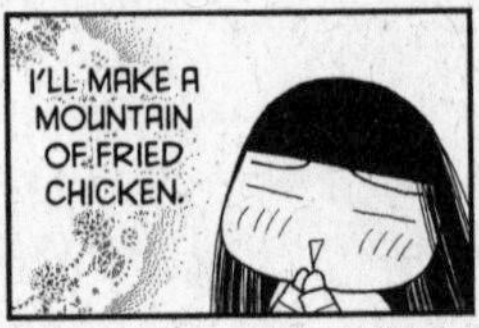
I'LL MAKE A MOUNTAIN OF FRIED CHICKEN.

Fried Chicken, page 43

Eating fried chicken is a Christmas tradition in Japan.

Christmas Eve Date, page 44

In Japan, where less than 1 percent of the population identifies as Christian, Christmas is not celebrated as a religious holiday. Instead, Christmas Eve is somewhat similar to Valentine's Day in the United States. It's usually associated with couples and romance. To many young people, it's very important to have a date for Christmas Eve.

Love Hotels, page 52

Love hotels are specifically designed for couples seeking privacy. They can be rented by the night or by the hour during the daytime. They often have gaudy, Las Vegas–style designs and themed rooms. In metropolitan areas, love hotels tend to be clustered together to form little love hotel neighborhoods.

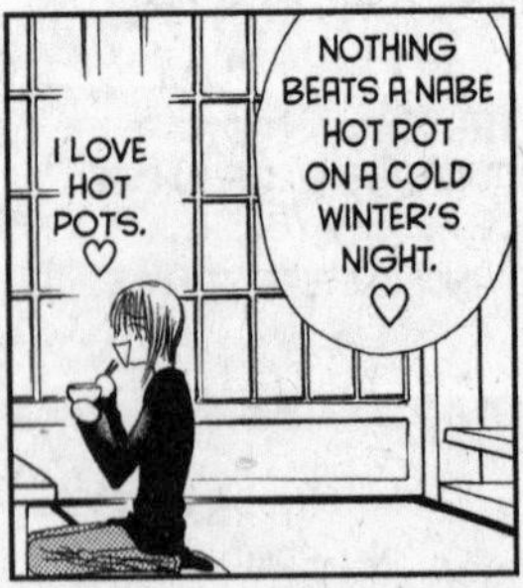
NOTHING BEATS A NABE HOT POT ON A COLD WINTER'S NIGHT. ♡
I LOVE HOT POTS. ♡

Nabe Hot Pot, page 94

A "nabe" is literally a large pot, but the term is used generically to describe any kind of soup, stew, or boiled dish made in a hot pot. Generally, the hot pot sits in the middle of the table, and each diner serves herself. It's a popular winter food.

Geisha Games, page 98

Geisha have a variety of ways to entertain their guests such as dance, music, and playing traditional games.

THE wallflower

YAMATONADESHIKO SHICHIHENGE

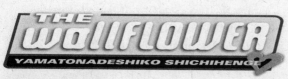

Volume 24

A Note from the Author

I'M STILL TRYING TO FOLLOW MY NEW MANTRA "EARLY TO
BED, EARLY TO RISE," BUT I ALWAYS END UP TAKING NAPS
(FOR HOURS) AND THEN I FALL RIGHT BACK INTO BEING A
NIGHT OWL. I'M WORKING REALLY HARD EVERY DAY, AND
I'VE ALSO BEEN EXERCISING. I DO A STRENGTH-TRAINING
WORKOUT AT HOME. I'VE ALWAYS HATED EXERCISE, SO
KEEPING MYSELF MOTIVATED IS NO EASY TASK, BUT I'M
GONNA KEEP IT UP.

—Tomoko Hayakawa

THE wallFLOWER

YAMATONADESHIKO SHICHIHENGE

ヤマトナデシコ七変化♡

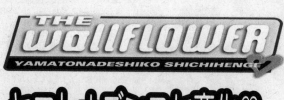

CONTENTS

WALLFLOWER'S BEAUTIFUL CAST OF CHARACTERS (?)

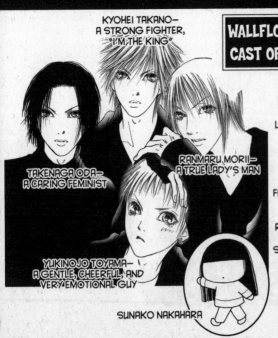

KYOHEI TAKANO—
A STRONG FIGHTER,
"I'M THE KING"
RANMARU MORII—
A TRUE LADY'S MAN
TAKENAGA ODA—
A CARING FEMINIST
YUKINOJO TOYAMA—
A GENTLE, CHEERFUL, AND
VERY EMOTIONAL GUY
SUNAKO NAKAHARA

SUNAKO IS A DARK LONER WHO LOVES HORROR MOVIES. WHEN HER AUNT, THE LANDLADY, LEAVES TOWN, SUNAKO IS FORCED TO LIVE WITH FOUR HANDSOME GUYS. SUNAKO'S AUNT MAKES A DEAL WITH THE BOYS, WHICH CAUSES NOTHING BUT HEADACHES FOR SUNAKO. "MAKE SUNAKO INTO A LADY, AND YOU CAN LIVE RENT FREE." THE ROAD TO LOVE IS LONG AND PERILOUS, AND IT LOOKS LIKE SUNAKO AND KYOHEI'S RELATIONSHIP WILL NEVER MAKE IT THERE. AS RANMARU BEGINS TO SHOW HIS SOFT SIDE TO A CERTAIN LADY, KYOHEI AND SUNAKO TEAM UP TO STUDY FOR FINALS. THEIR STUDIES PROGRESS AT AN EVEN SLOWER PACE THAN THEIR RELATIONSHIP, AND SUNAKO AND KYOHEI END UP HAVING TO DO A MAKEUP TEST. (💧)

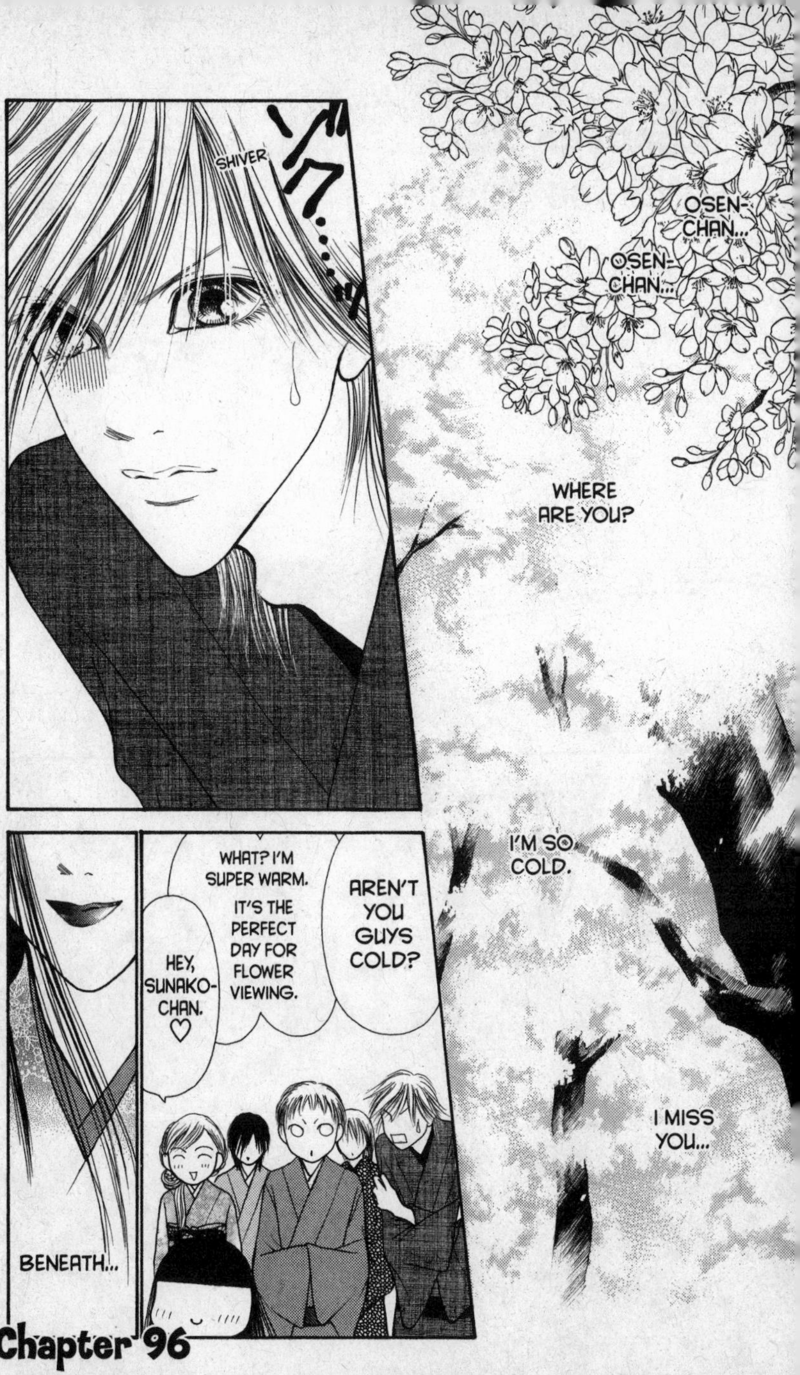
OSEN-CHAN...
OSEN-CHAN...
WHERE ARE YOU?
I'M SO COLD.
I MISS YOU...
SHIVER
AREN'T YOU GUYS COLD?
WHAT? I'M SUPER WARM.
IT'S THE PERFECT DAY FOR FLOWER VIEWING.
HEY, SUNAKO-CHAN. ♡
BENEATH...

Chapter 96

I MISS YOU (PART 1)

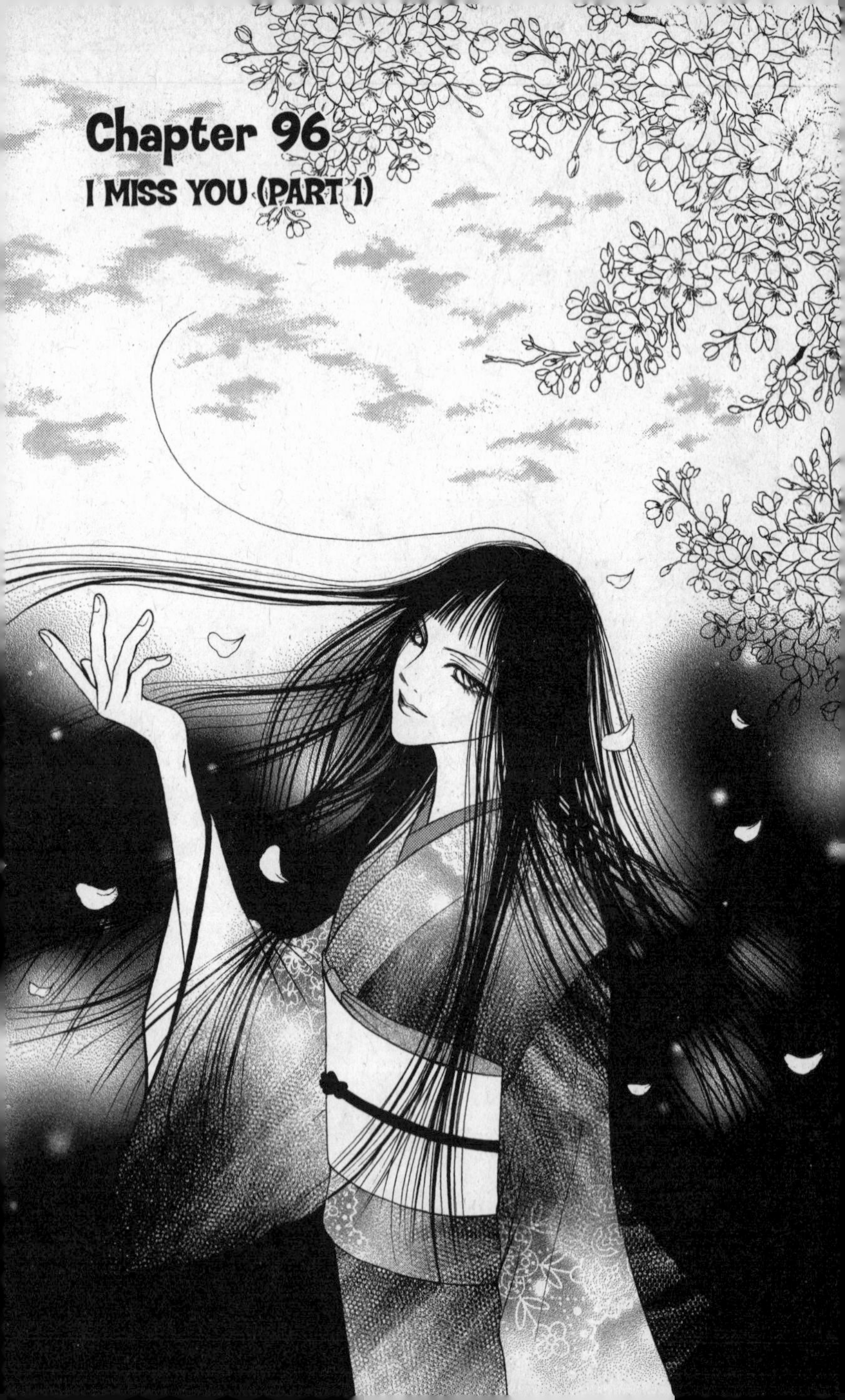
Chapter 96
I MISS YOU (PART 1)

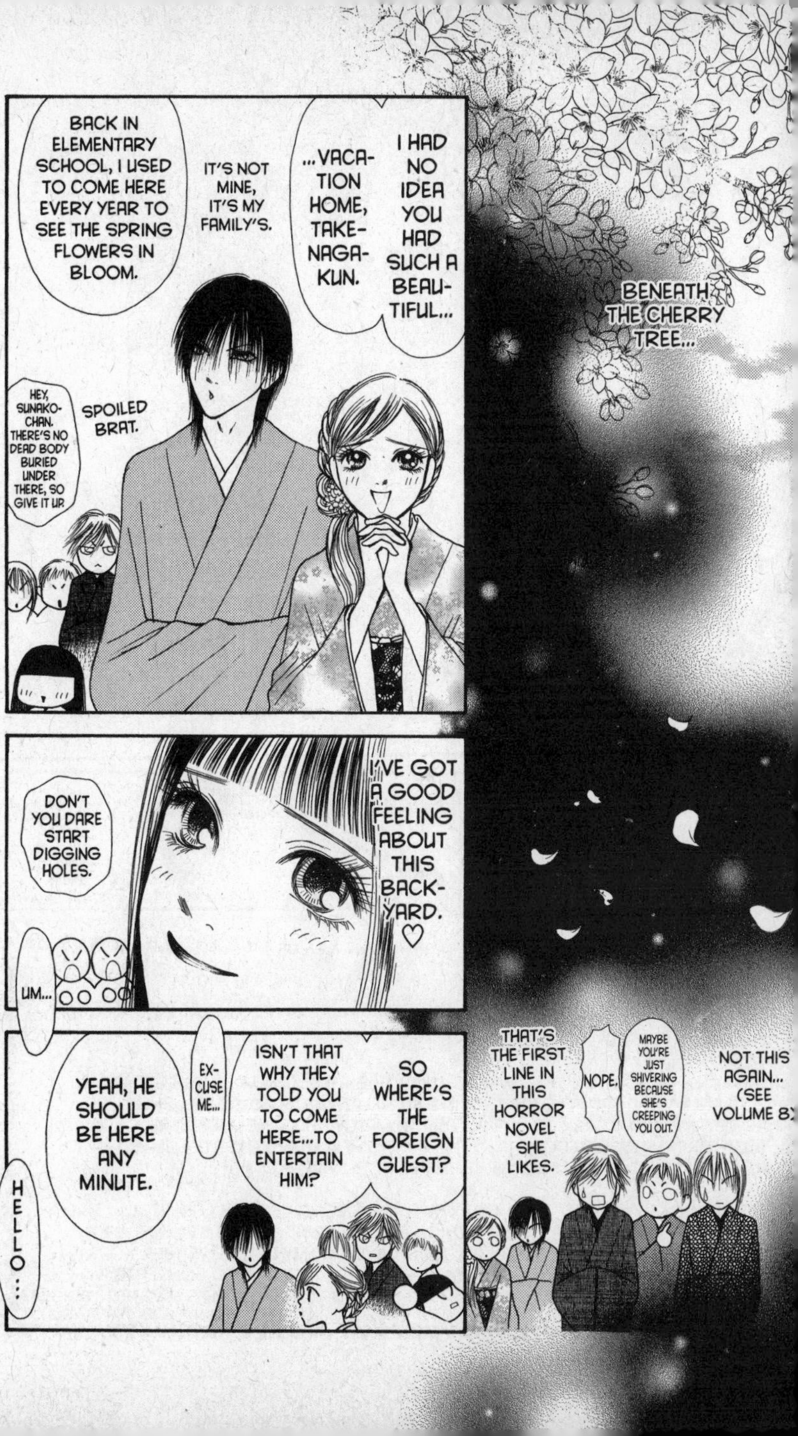
BENEATH THE CHERRY TREE...
I HAD NO IDEA YOU HAD SUCH A BEAUTIFUL...
...VACATION HOME, TAKENAGA-KUN.
IT'S NOT MINE, IT'S MY FAMILY'S.
BACK IN ELEMENTARY SCHOOL, I USED TO COME HERE EVERY YEAR TO SEE THE SPRING FLOWERS IN BLOOM.
SPOILED BRAT.
HEY, SUNAKO-CHAN. THERE'S NO DEAD BODY BURIED UNDER THERE, SO GIVE IT UP.
I'VE GOT A GOOD FEELING ABOUT THIS BACKYARD. ♡
DON'T YOU DARE START DIGGING HOLES.
UM...
SO WHERE'S THE FOREIGN GUEST?
ISN'T THAT WHY THEY TOLD YOU TO COME HERE...TO ENTERTAIN HIM?
EXCUSE ME...
YEAH, HE SHOULD BE HERE ANY MINUTE.
HELLO...
NOT THIS AGAIN... (SEE VOLUME 8)
MAYBE YOU'RE JUST SHIVERING BECAUSE SHE'S CREEPING YOU OUT.
NOPE.
THAT'S THE FIRST LINE IN THIS HORROR NOVEL SHE LIKES.

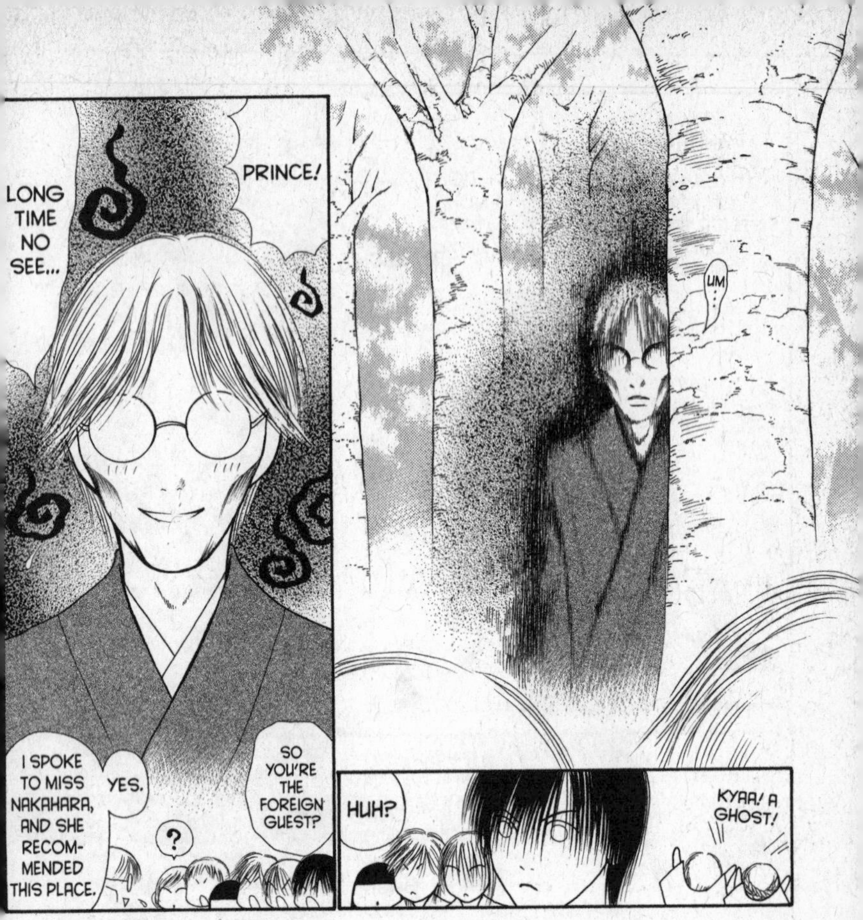
UM...
KYAA! A GHOST!
HUH?
PRINCE!
LONG TIME NO SEE...
SO YOU'RE THE FOREIGN GUEST?
YES.
?
I SPOKE TO MISS NAKAHARA, AND SHE RECOMMENDED THIS PLACE.

BEHIND THE SCENES

THANK YOU FOR BUYING KODANSHA COMICS. ♥

STARTING AROUND THE TIME I WAS WRITING THIS STORY, I NEEDED ASSISTANTS SO BADLY THAT I HAD TO START ASKING MY RELATIVES. SOME OF MY LONGTIME ASSISTANTS WENT BACK TO LIVE IN THEIR HOMETOWNS. COME BACK HERE, CHOBIN! SOME OF THEM HAVE BECOME VERY BUSY WITH THEIR OWN MANGA CAREERS, AND I'M REALLY HAPPY FOR THEM. KEEP UP THE HARD WORK, NABEKO. ♥

I'VE HAD TO GIVE TOMMY A LOT OF EXTRA WORK. SORRY, TOMMY. I FEEL REALLY BAD ABOUT IT. I REALLY NEED PEOPLE TO DRAW BACKGROUNDS. I WAS SERIOUS WHEN I SAID I HAD TO START ASKING MY RELATIVES. I'VE GOT MY LITTLE BROTHER WORKING FOR ME NOW. AND MY FRIEND KAI-CHAN WHO'S ALWAYS GOING TO CONCERTS WITH ME. SHE COMES BY WHEN SHE'S NOT TOO BUSY WITH HER REGULAR JOB. THANK YOU.

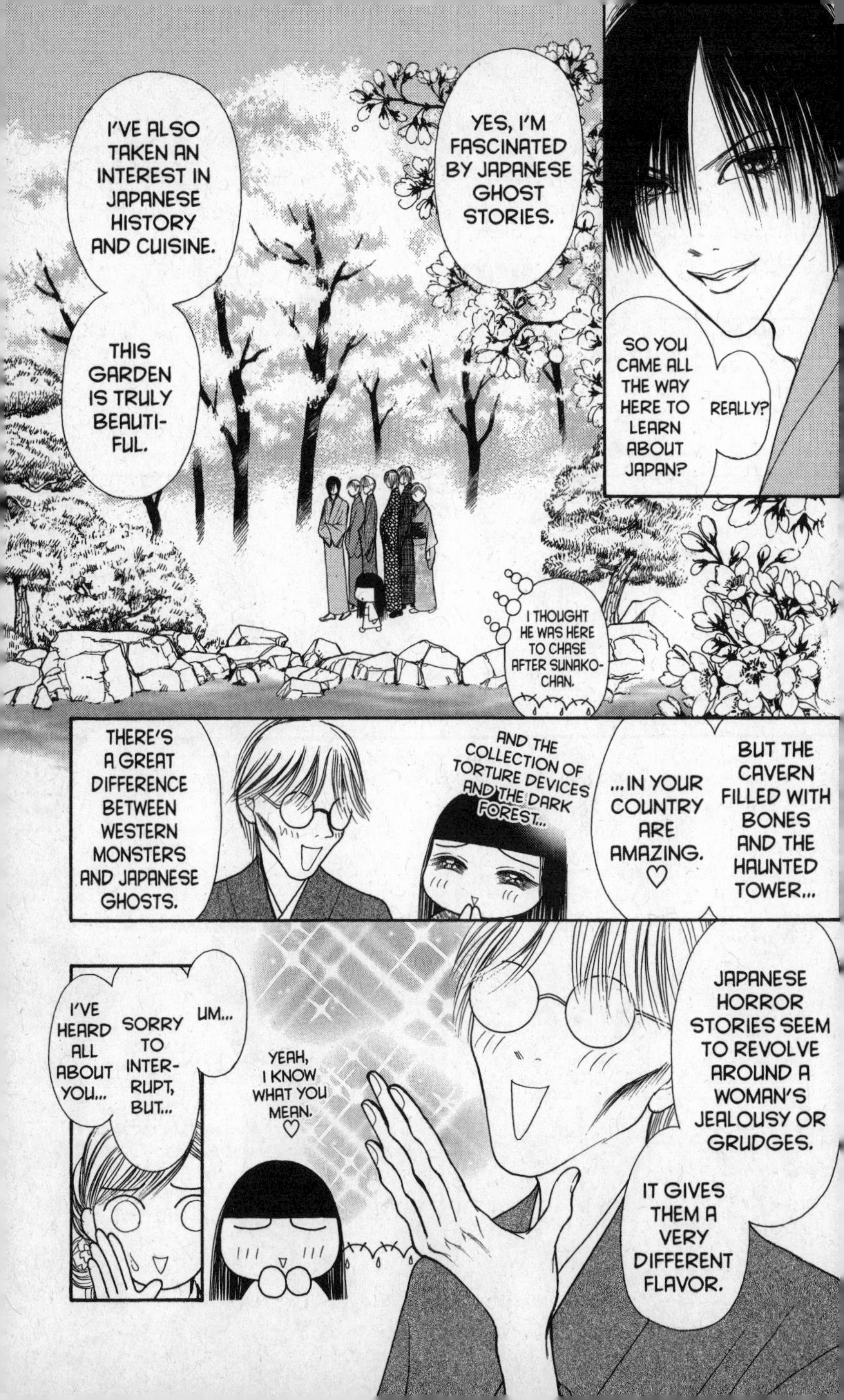
SO YOU CAME ALL THE WAY HERE TO LEARN ABOUT JAPAN?
REALLY?
YES, I'M FASCINATED BY JAPANESE GHOST STORIES.
I'VE ALSO TAKEN AN INTEREST IN JAPANESE HISTORY AND CUISINE.
THIS GARDEN IS TRULY BEAUTI-FUL.
I THOUGHT HE WAS HERE TO CHASE AFTER SUNAKO-CHAN.
BUT THE CAVERN FILLED WITH BONES AND THE HAUNTED TOWER...
...IN YOUR COUNTRY ARE AMAZING. ♡
AND THE COLLECTION OF TORTURE DEVICES AND THE DARK FOREST...
THERE'S A GREAT DIFFERENCE BETWEEN WESTERN MONSTERS AND JAPANESE GHOSTS.
JAPANESE HORROR STORIES SEEM TO REVOLVE AROUND A WOMAN'S JEALOUSY OR GRUDGES.
IT GIVES THEM A VERY DIFFERENT FLAVOR.
YEAH, I KNOW WHAT YOU MEAN. ♡
UM...
SORRY TO INTER-RUPT, BUT...
I'VE HEARD ALL ABOUT YOU...

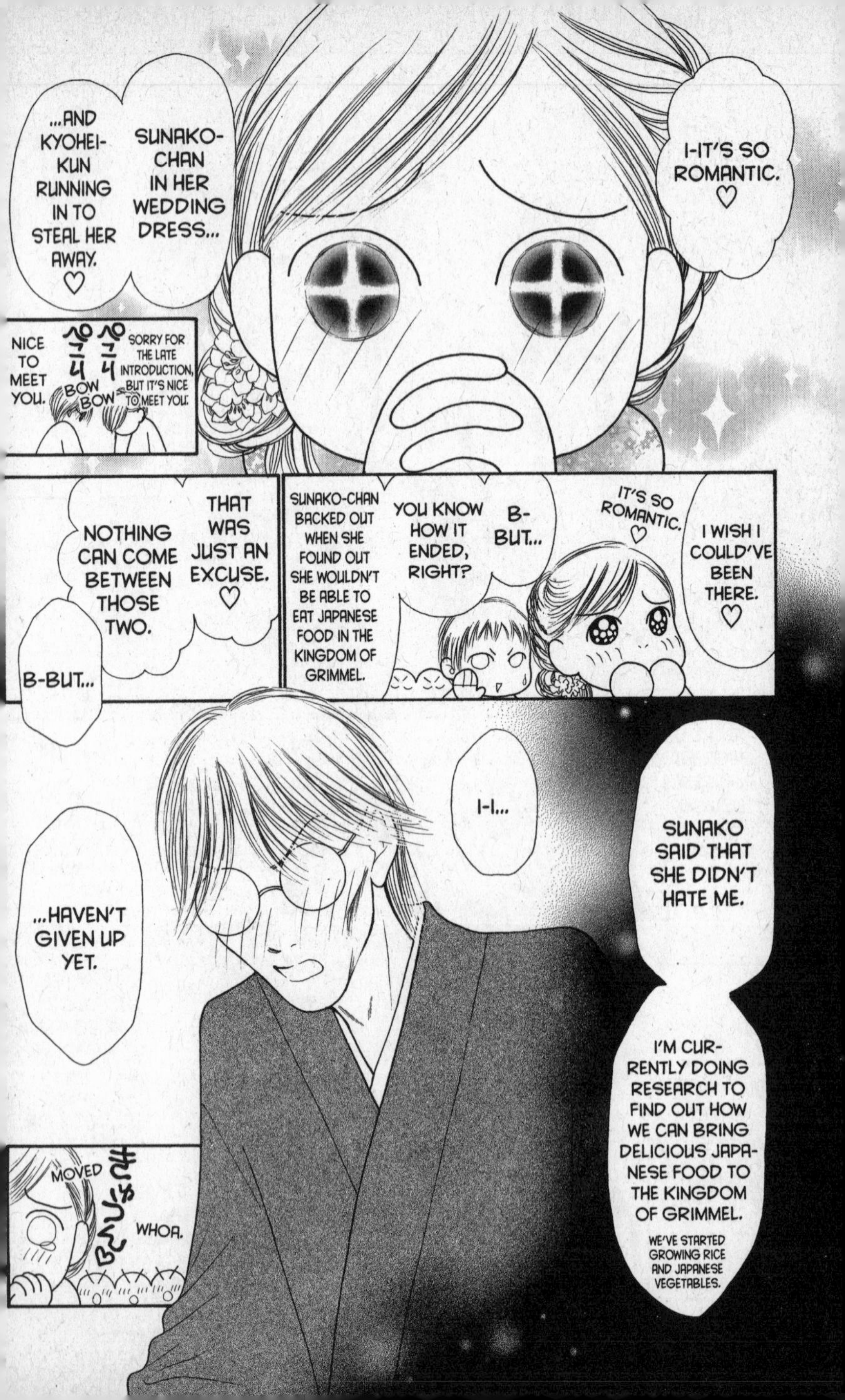
I-IT'S SO ROMANTIC. ♡
SUNAKO-CHAN IN HER WEDDING DRESS...
...AND KYOHEI-KUN RUNNING IN TO STEAL HER AWAY. ♡
SORRY FOR THE LATE INTRODUCTION, BUT IT'S NICE TO MEET YOU.
BOW
NICE TO MEET YOU.
BOW
I WISH I COULD'VE BEEN THERE. ♡
IT'S SO ROMANTIC. ♡
B-BUT...
YOU KNOW HOW IT ENDED, RIGHT?
SUNAKO-CHAN BACKED OUT WHEN SHE FOUND OUT SHE WOULDN'T BE ABLE TO EAT JAPANESE FOOD IN THE KINGDOM OF GRIMMEL.
THAT WAS JUST AN EXCUSE. ♡
NOTHING CAN COME BETWEEN THOSE TWO.
B-BUT...
SUNAKO SAID THAT SHE DIDN'T HATE ME.
I'M CURRENTLY DOING RESEARCH TO FIND OUT HOW WE CAN BRING DELICIOUS JAPANESE FOOD TO THE KINGDOM OF GRIMMEL.
WE'VE STARTED GROWING RICE AND JAPANESE VEGETABLES.
I-I...
...HAVEN'T GIVEN UP YET.
MOVED
WHOA.

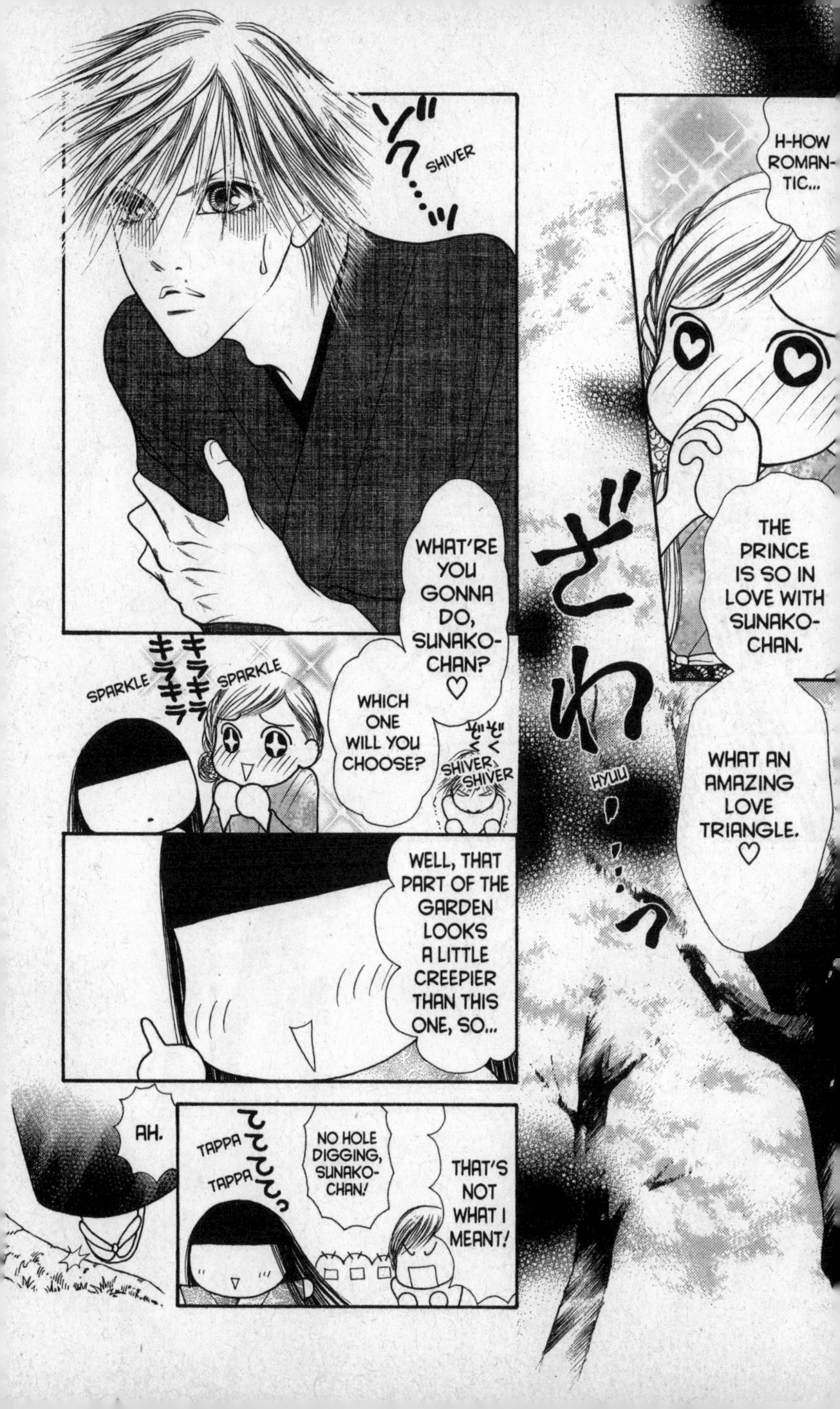
H-HOW ROMANTIC...
THE PRINCE IS SO IN LOVE WITH SUNAKO-CHAN.
WHAT AN AMAZING LOVE TRIANGLE. ♡
ざわ
HYUU
ゾク…ッ
SHIVER
WHAT'RE YOU GONNA DO, SUNAKO-CHAN? ♡
キラキラ
SPARKLE
キラキラ
SPARKLE
WHICH ONE WILL YOU CHOOSE?
ぞくぞく
SHIVER SHIVER
WELL, THAT PART OF THE GARDEN LOOKS A LITTLE CREEPIER THAN THIS ONE, SO...
THAT'S NOT WHAT I MEANT!
NO HOLE DIGGING, SUNAKO-CHAN!
てててて
TAPPA TAPPA
AH.

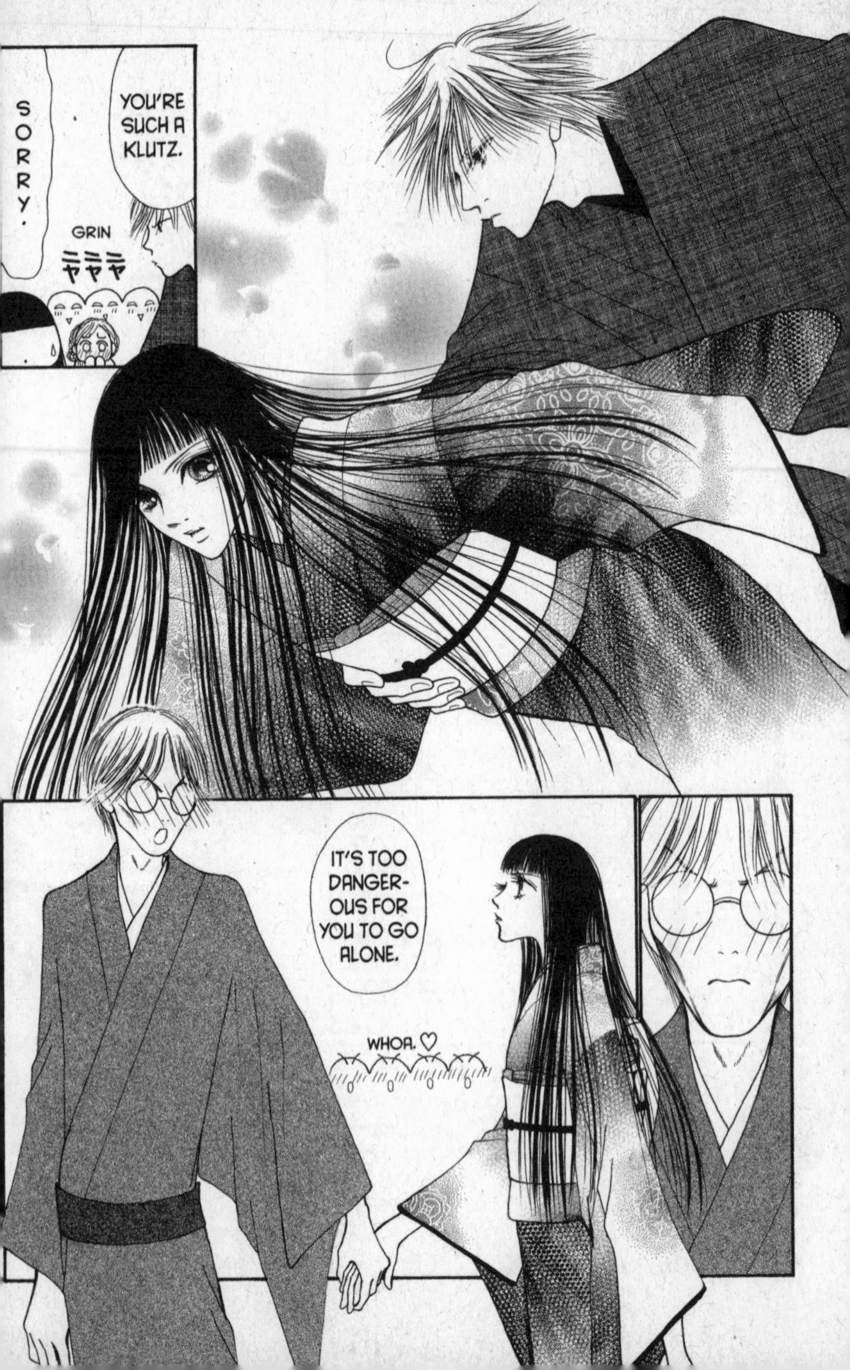
YOU'RE SUCH A KLUTZ.
SORRY.
GRIN
IT'S TOO DANGER-OUS FOR YOU TO GO ALONE.
WHOA. ♡

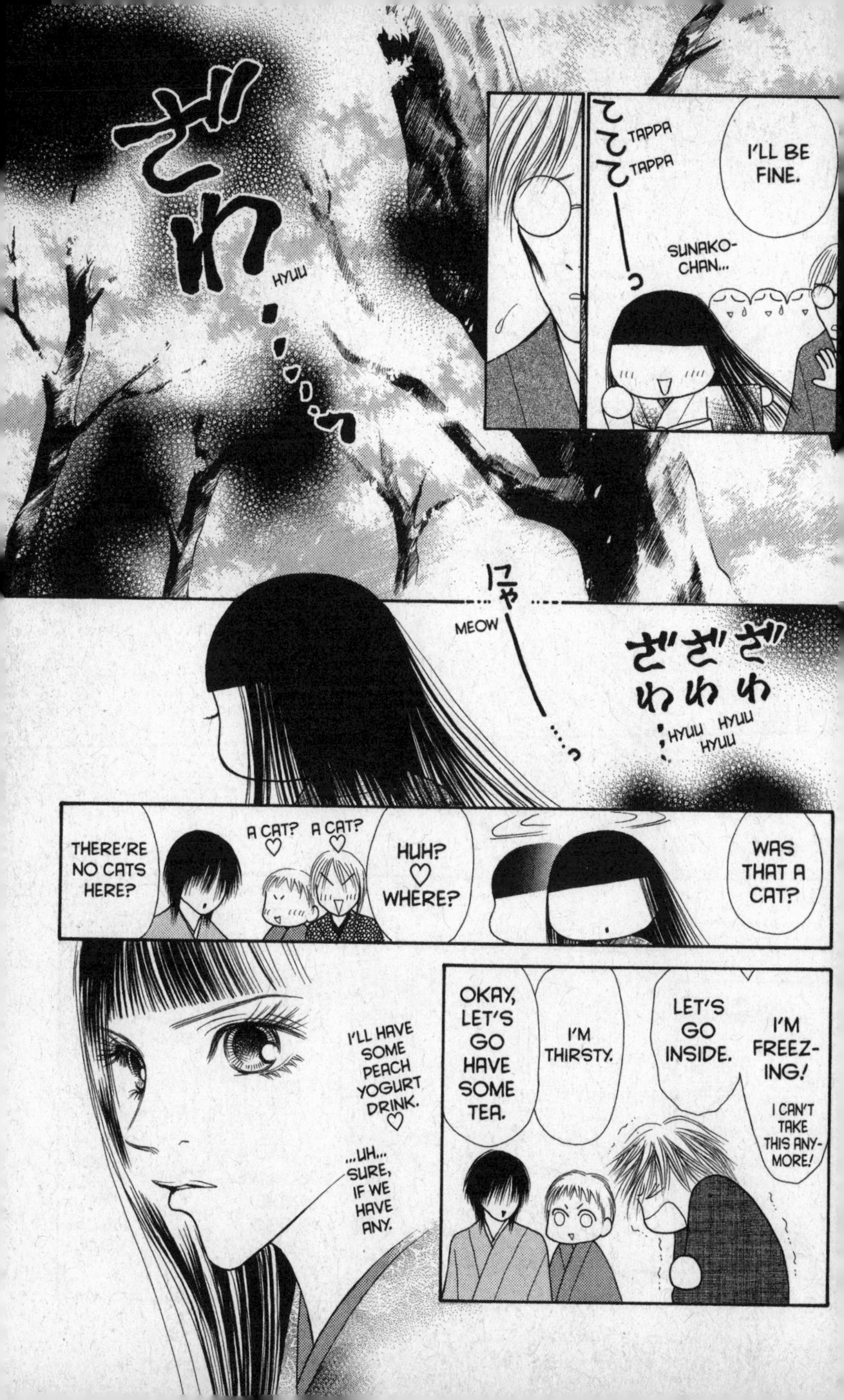I'LL BE FINE.
てててーっ
TAPPA TAPPA
SUNAKO-CHAN...
ざわ......っ
HYUU
にゃー...っ
MEOW
ざざざ わわわ
HYUU HYUU HYUU
WAS THAT A CAT?
HUH? ♡ WHERE?
A CAT? ♡
A CAT? ♡
THERE'RE NO CATS HERE?
I'M FREEZING!
I CAN'T TAKE THIS ANYMORE!
LET'S GO INSIDE.
I'M THIRSTY.
OKAY, LET'S GO HAVE SOME TEA.
I'LL HAVE SOME PEACH YOGURT DRINK. ♡
...UH... SURE, IF WE HAVE ANY.

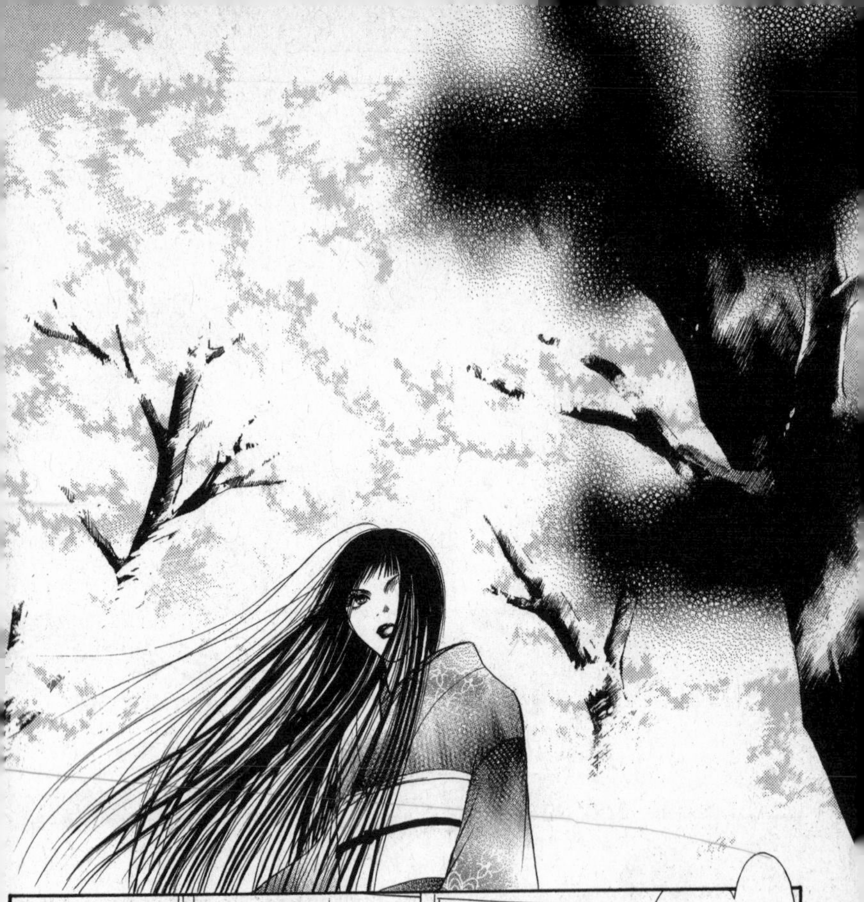

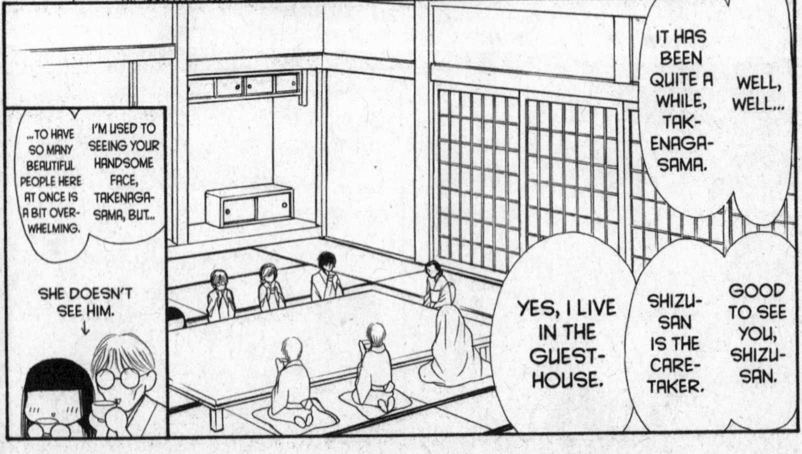
WELL, WELL...
IT HAS BEEN QUITE A WHILE, TAKENAGA-SAMA.
GOOD TO SEE YOU, SHIZU-SAN.
SHIZU-SAN IS THE CARETAKER.
YES, I LIVE IN THE GUEST-HOUSE.
I'M USED TO SEEING YOUR HANDSOME FACE, TAKENAGA-SAMA, BUT...
...TO HAVE SO MANY BEAUTIFUL PEOPLE HERE AT ONCE IS A BIT OVERWHELMING.
SHE DOESN'T SEE HIM.

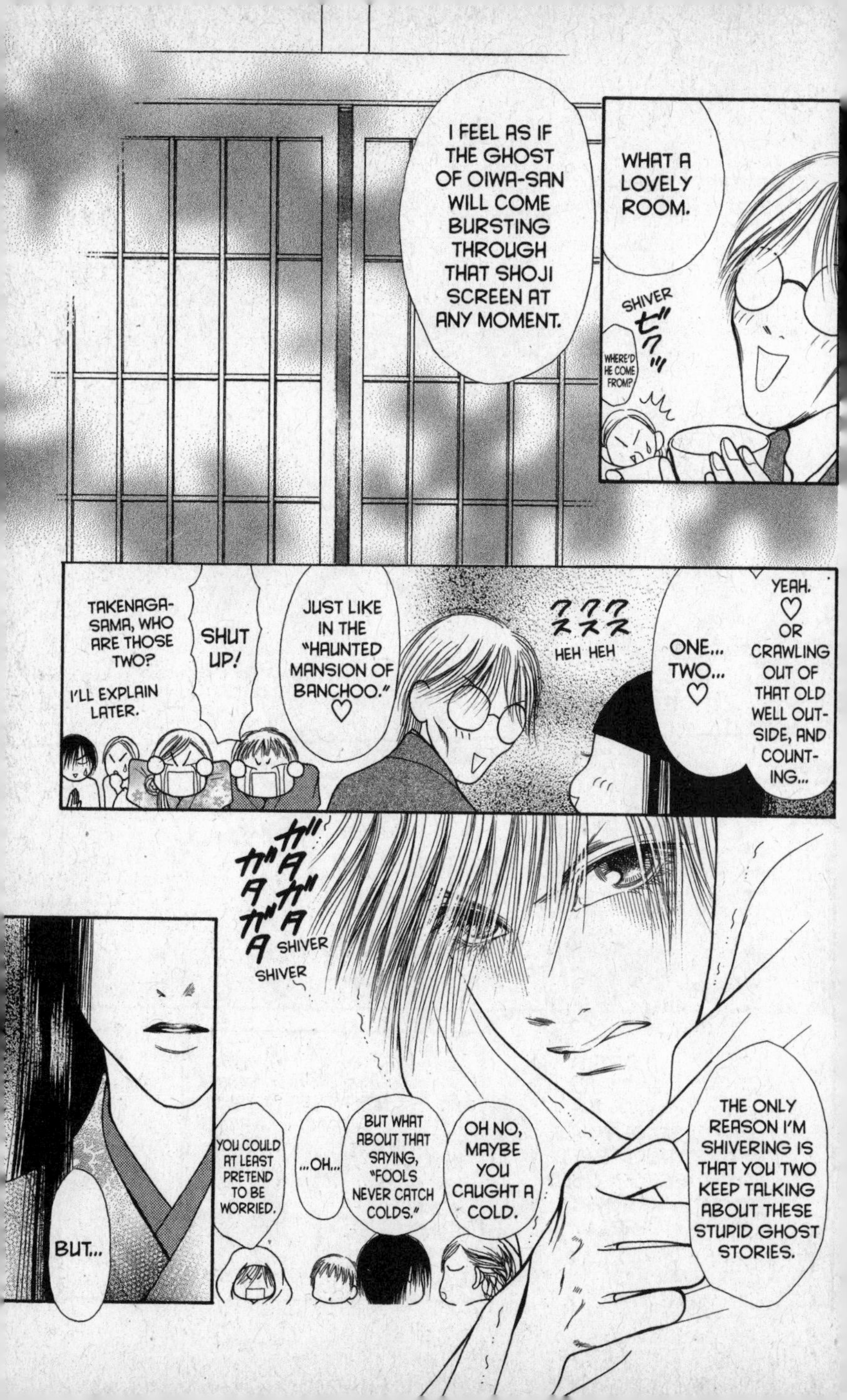
WHAT A LOVELY ROOM.
SHIVER
WHERE'D HE COME FROM?
I FEEL AS IF THE GHOST OF OIWA-SAN WILL COME BURSTING THROUGH THAT SHOJI SCREEN AT ANY MOMENT.
YEAH. ♡ OR CRAWLING OUT OF THAT OLD WELL OUT-SIDE, AND COUNT-ING...
ONE... TWO... ♡
HEH HEH
JUST LIKE IN THE "HAUNTED MANSION OF BANCHOO." ♡
SHUT UP!
TAKENAGA-SAMA, WHO ARE THOSE TWO?
I'LL EXPLAIN LATER.
SHIVER
SHIVER
THE ONLY REASON I'M SHIVERING IS THAT YOU TWO KEEP TALKING ABOUT THESE STUPID GHOST STORIES.
OH NO, MAYBE YOU CAUGHT A COLD.
BUT WHAT ABOUT THAT SAYING, "FOOLS NEVER CATCH COLDS."
...OH...
YOU COULD AT LEAST PRETEND TO BE WORRIED.
BUT...

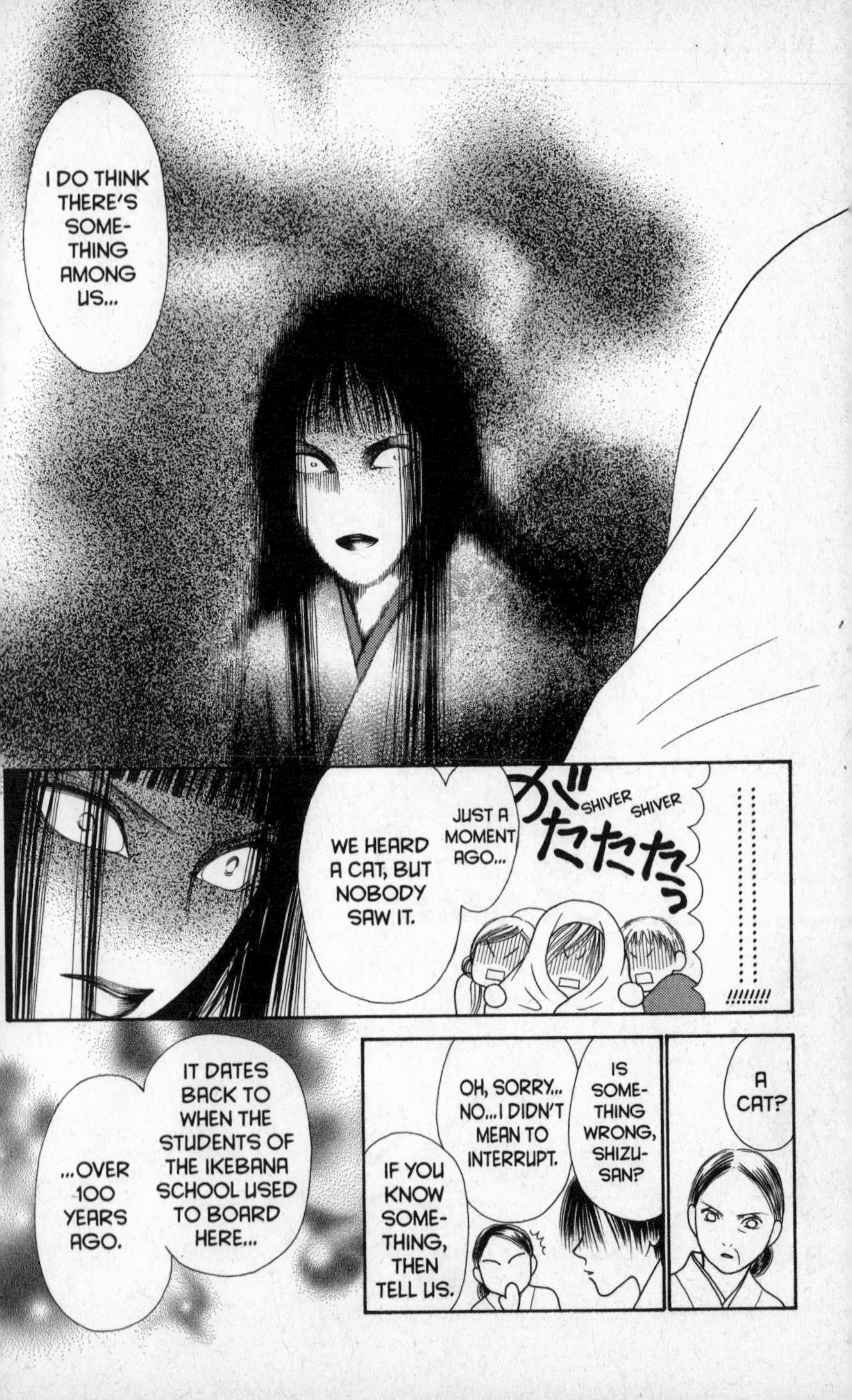
I DO THINK THERE'S SOME-THING AMONG US...
......
!!!!!!!!
がたたたっ
SHIVER SHIVER
JUST A MOMENT AGO...
WE HEARD A CAT, BUT NOBODY SAW IT.
A CAT?
IS SOME-THING WRONG, SHIZU-SAN?
OH, SORRY... NO...I DIDN'T MEAN TO INTERRUPT.
IF YOU KNOW SOME-THING, THEN TELL US.
IT DATES BACK TO WHEN THE STUDENTS OF THE IKEBANA SCHOOL USED TO BOARD HERE...
...OVER 100 YEARS AGO.

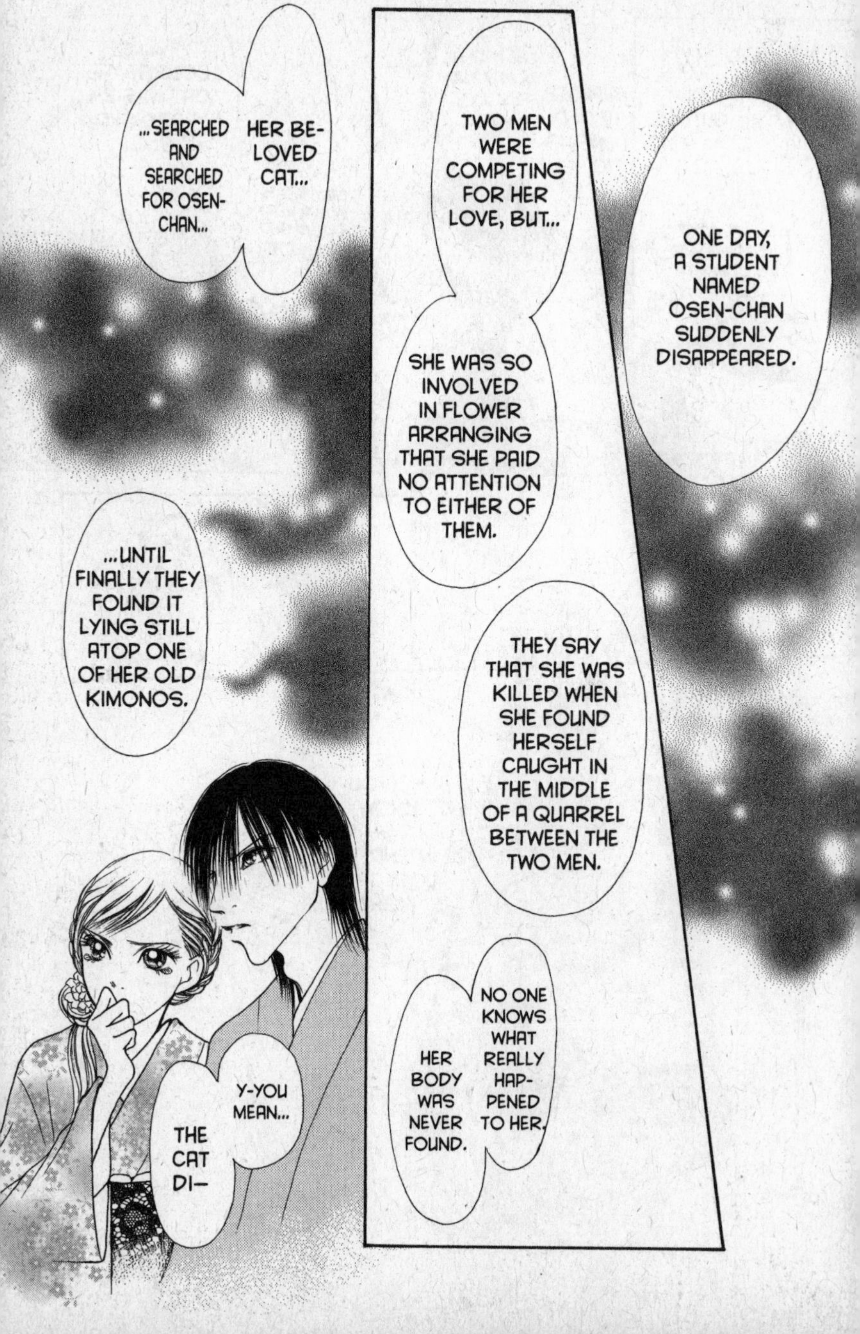
ONE DAY, A STUDENT NAMED OSEN-CHAN SUDDENLY DISAPPEARED.
TWO MEN WERE COMPETING FOR HER LOVE, BUT...
SHE WAS SO INVOLVED IN FLOWER ARRANGING THAT SHE PAID NO ATTENTION TO EITHER OF THEM.
THEY SAY THAT SHE WAS KILLED WHEN SHE FOUND HERSELF CAUGHT IN THE MIDDLE OF A QUARREL BETWEEN THE TWO MEN.
NO ONE KNOWS WHAT REALLY HAP-PENED TO HER.
HER BODY WAS NEVER FOUND.
HER BE-LOVED CAT...
...SEARCHED AND SEARCHED FOR OSEN-CHAN...
...UNTIL FINALLY THEY FOUND IT LYING STILL ATOP ONE OF HER OLD KIMONOS.
Y-YOU MEAN...
THE CAT DI—

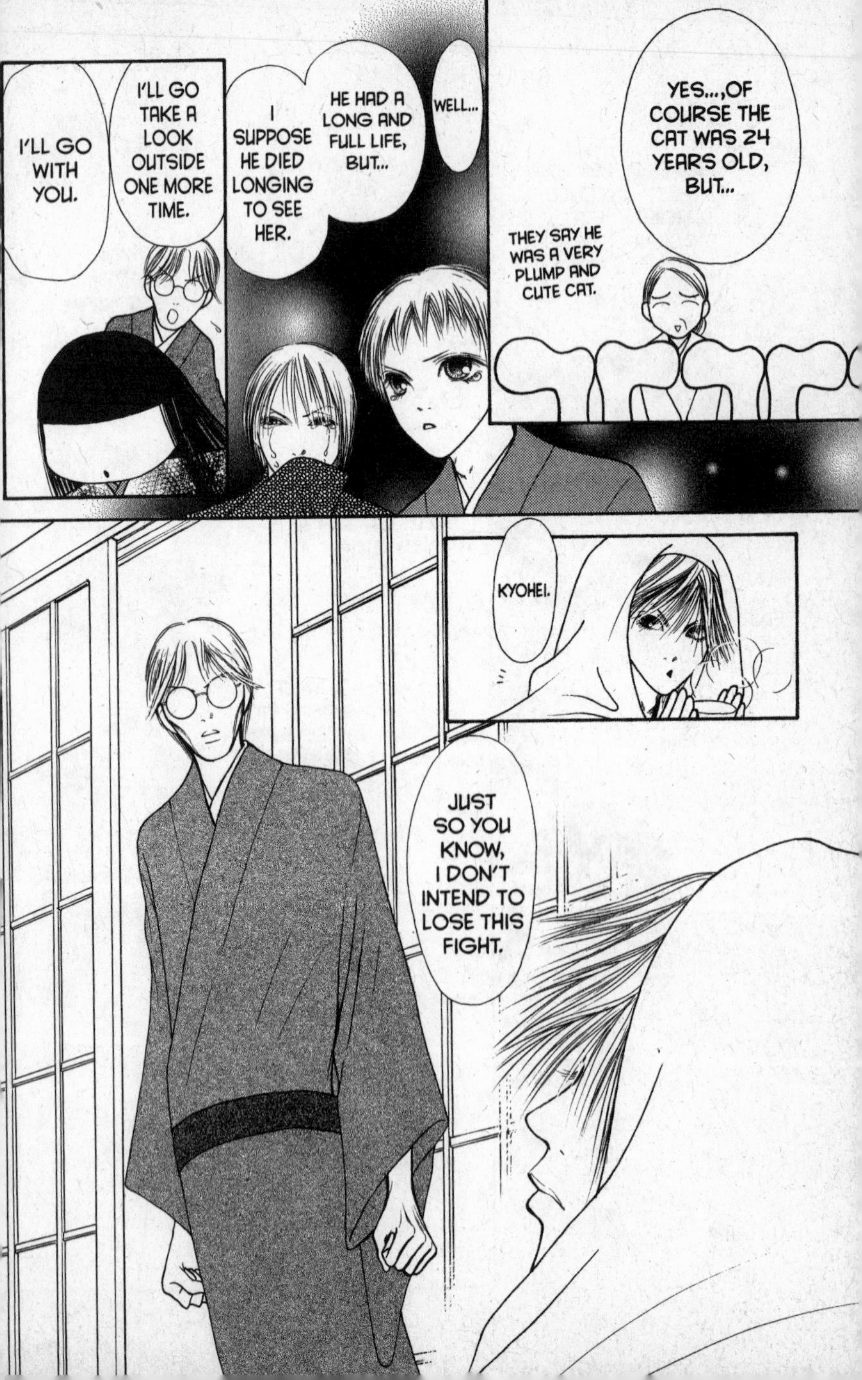
YES...,OF COURSE THE CAT WAS 24 YEARS OLD, BUT...
THEY SAY HE WAS A VERY PLUMP AND CUTE CAT.
WELL...
HE HAD A LONG AND FULL LIFE, BUT...
I SUPPOSE HE DIED LONGING TO SEE HER.
I'LL GO TAKE A LOOK OUTSIDE ONE MORE TIME.
I'LL GO WITH YOU.
KYOHEI.
JUST SO YOU KNOW, I DON'T INTEND TO LOSE THIS FIGHT.

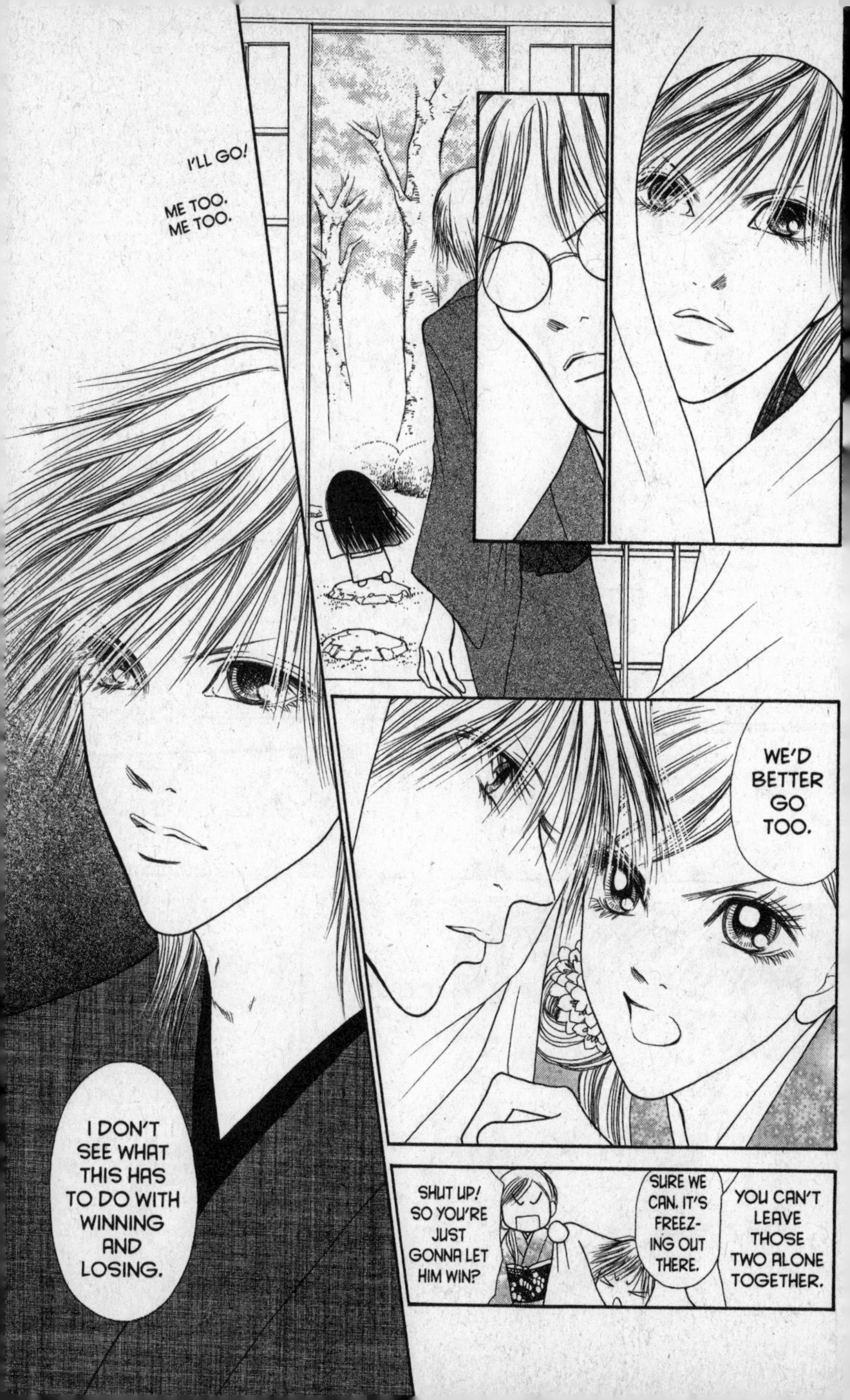
I'LL GO!
ME TOO. ME TOO.
WE'D BETTER GO TOO.
YOU CAN'T LEAVE THOSE TWO ALONE TOGETHER.
SURE WE CAN. IT'S FREEZ-ING OUT THERE.
SHUT UP! SO YOU'RE JUST GONNA LET HIM WIN?
I DON'T SEE WHAT THIS HAS TO DO WITH WINNING AND LOSING.

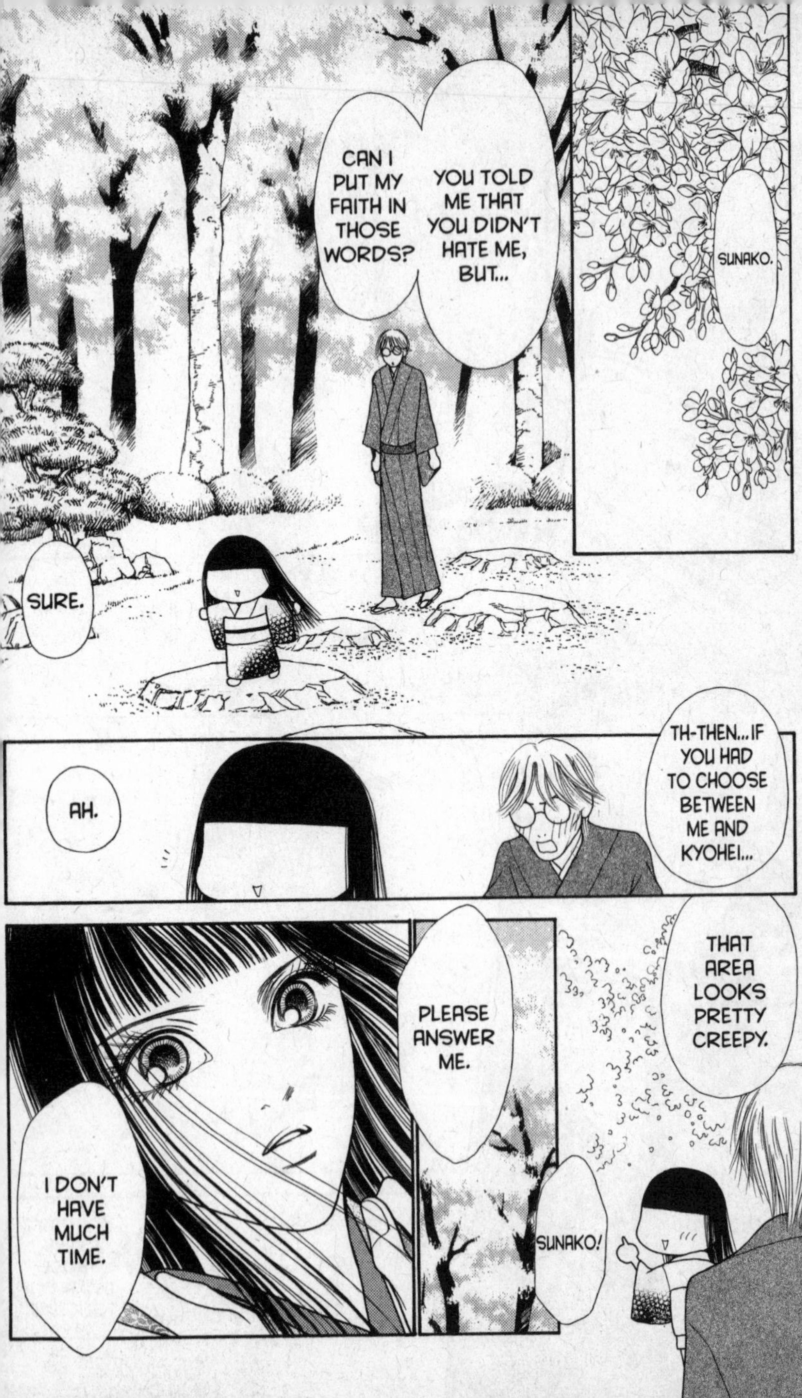
SUNAKO.
YOU TOLD ME THAT YOU DIDN'T HATE ME, BUT...
CAN I PUT MY FAITH IN THOSE WORDS?
SURE.
TH-THEN...IF YOU HAD TO CHOOSE BETWEEN ME AND KYOHEI...
AH.
THAT AREA LOOKS PRETTY CREEPY.
SUNAKO!
PLEASE ANSWER ME.
I DON'T HAVE MUCH TIME.

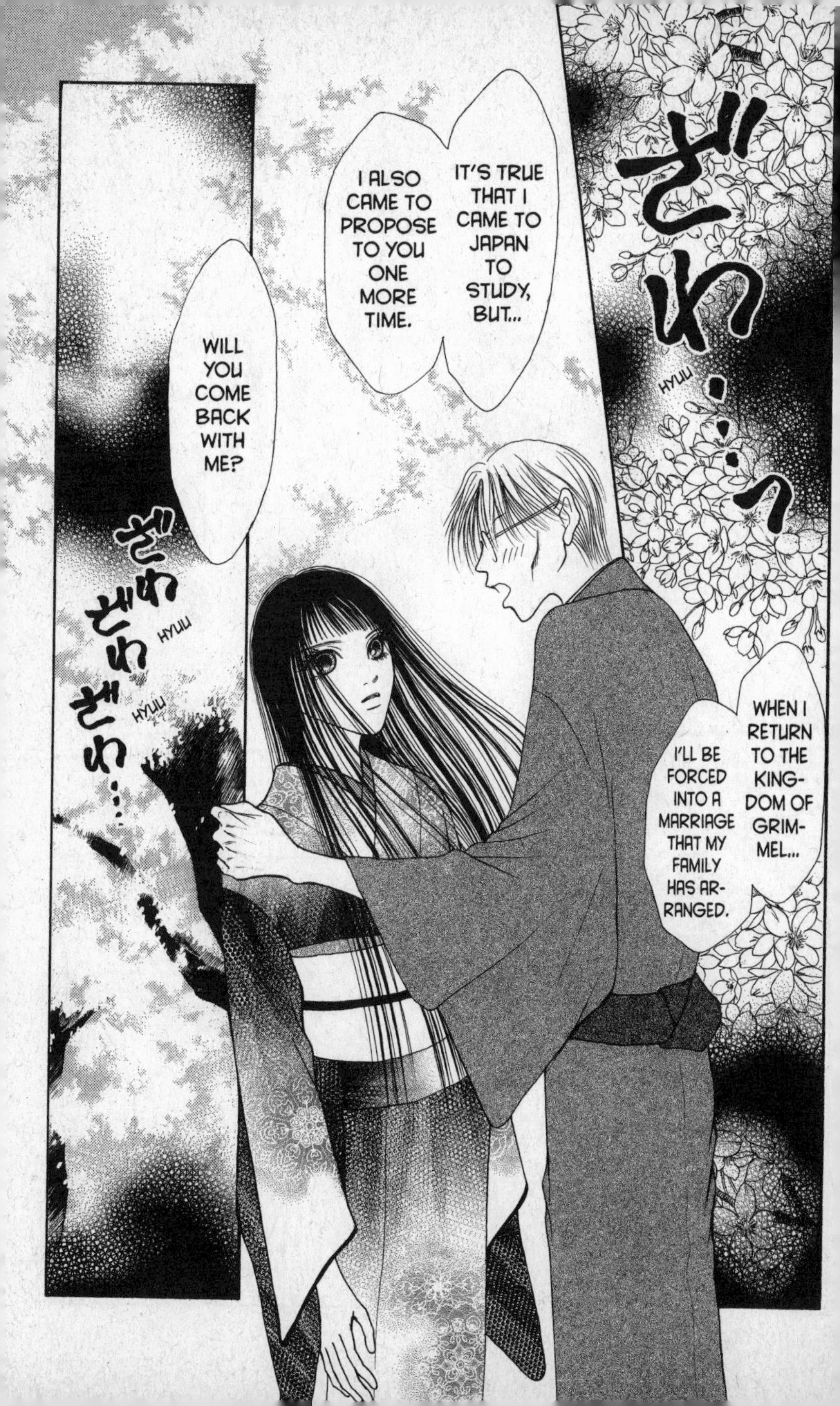
ざわ…っ
HYUU
IT'S TRUE THAT I CAME TO JAPAN TO STUDY, BUT...
I ALSO CAME TO PROPOSE TO YOU ONE MORE TIME.
WILL YOU COME BACK WITH ME?
ざわざわざわ…
HYUU
HYUU
WHEN I RETURN TO THE KING-DOM OF GRIM-MEL...
I'LL BE FORCED INTO A MARRIAGE THAT MY FAMILY HAS AR-RANGED.

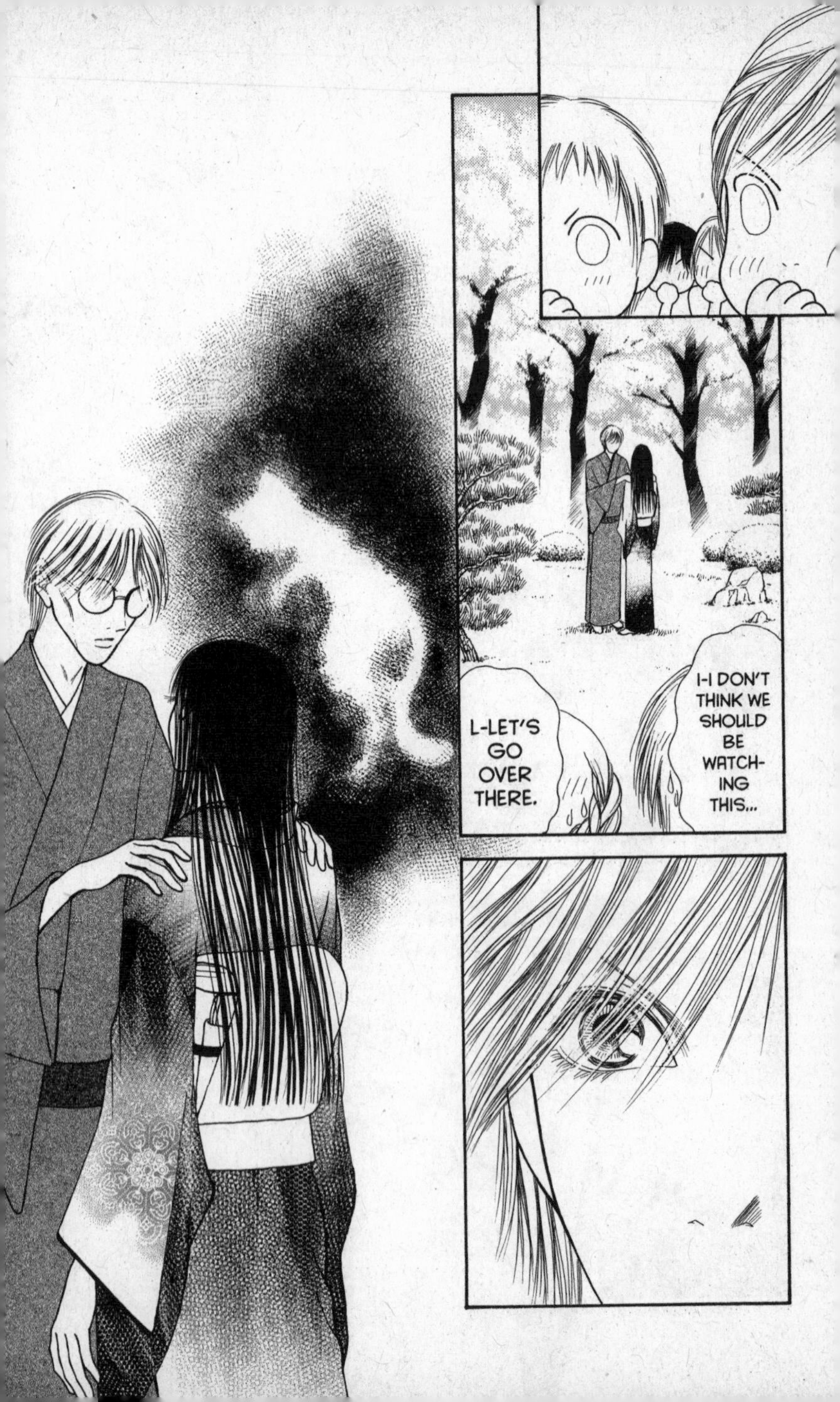
I-I DON'T THINK WE SHOULD BE WATCHING THIS...
L-LET'S GO OVER THERE.

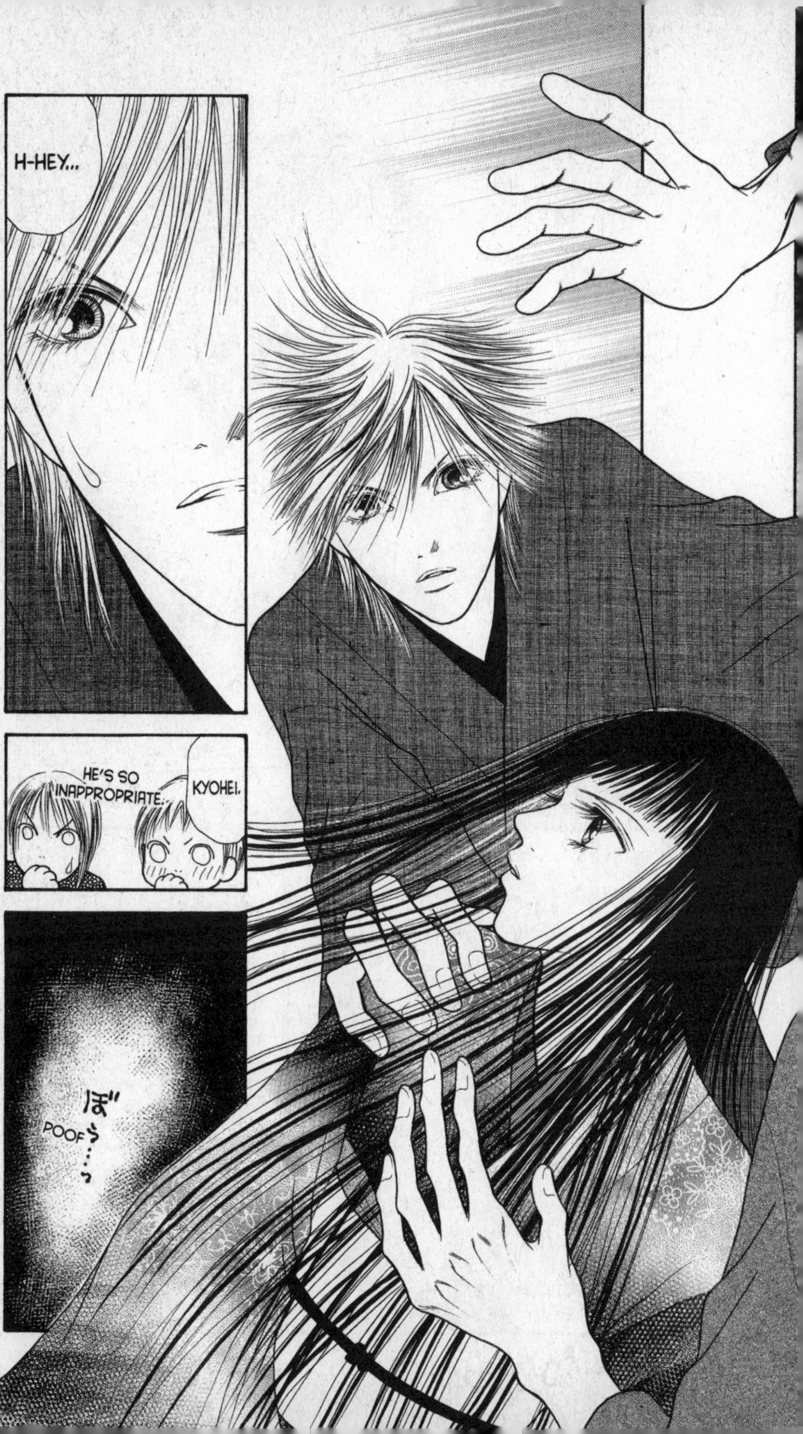
H-HEY...
KYOHEI.
HE'S SO INAPPROPRIATE...
ぼう…
POOF

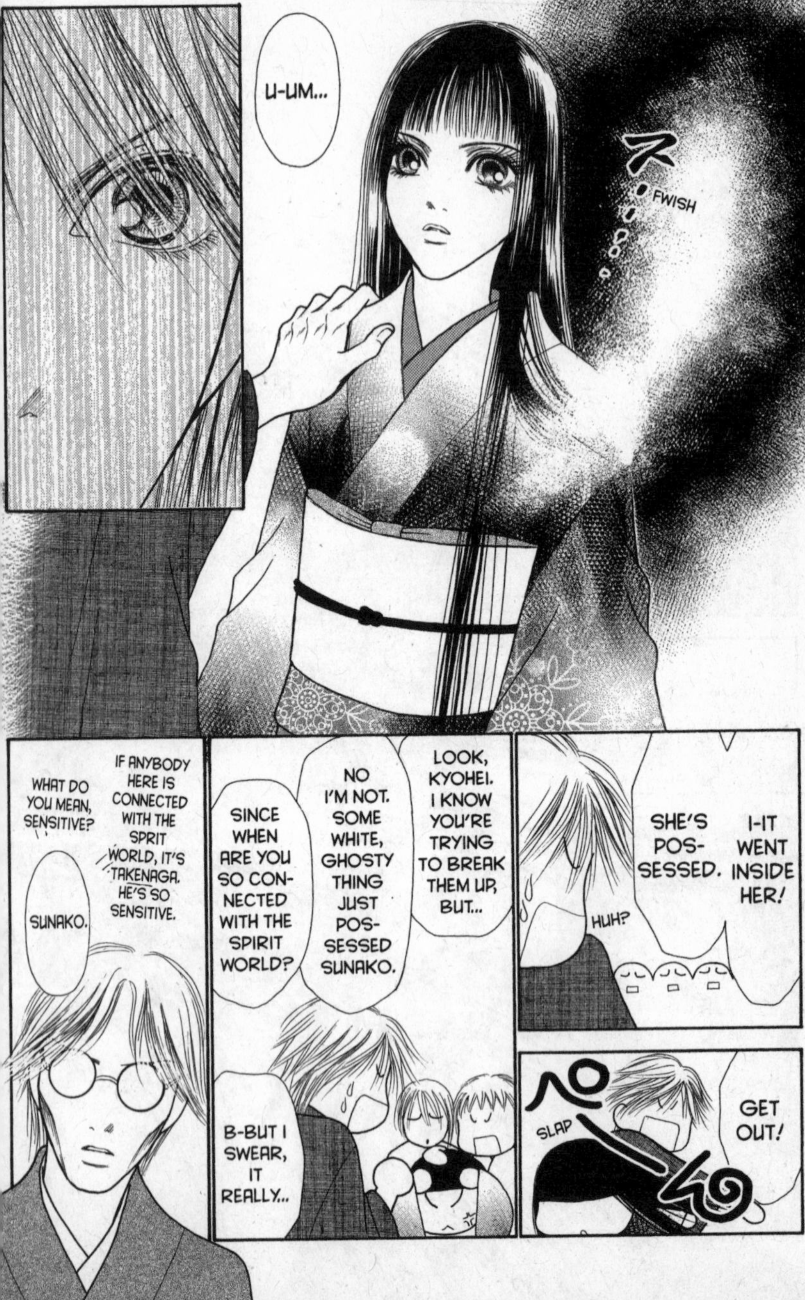
U-UM...
FWISH
I-IT WENT INSIDE HER!
SHE'S POS-SESSED.
HUH?
GET OUT!
SLAP
LOOK, KYOHEI. I KNOW YOU'RE TRYING TO BREAK THEM UP, BUT...
NO I'M NOT. SOME WHITE, GHOSTY THING JUST POS-SESSED SUNAKO.
SINCE WHEN ARE YOU SO CON-NECTED WITH THE SPIRIT WORLD?
B-BUT I SWEAR, IT REALLY...
IF ANYBODY HERE IS CONNECTED WITH THE SPRIT WORLD, IT'S TAKENAGA. HE'S SO SENSITIVE.
WHAT DO YOU MEAN, SENSITIVE?
SUNAKO.

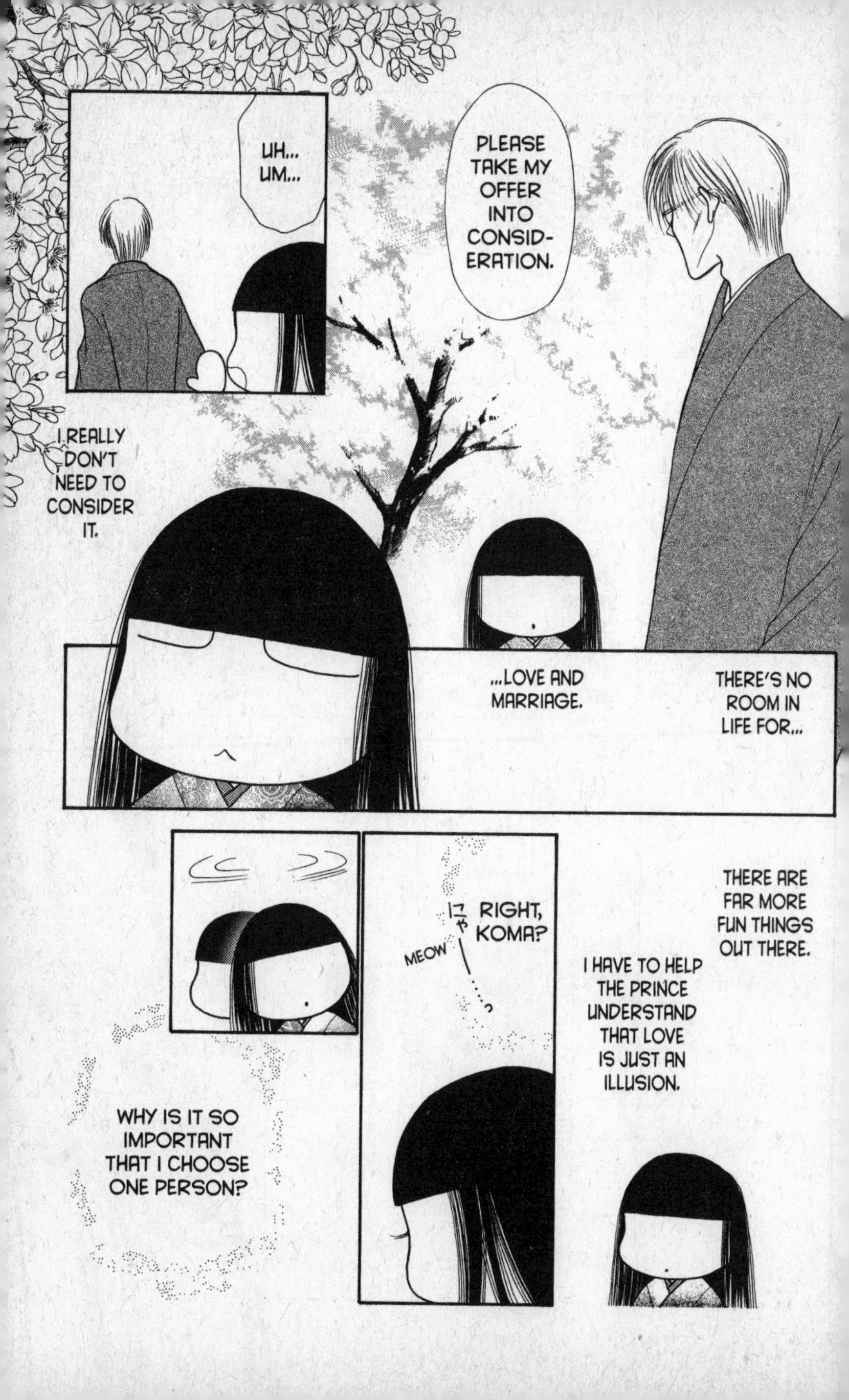
PLEASE TAKE MY OFFER INTO CONSIDERATION.
UH... UM...
I REALLY DON'T NEED TO CONSIDER IT.
THERE'S NO ROOM IN LIFE FOR...
...LOVE AND MARRIAGE.
THERE ARE FAR MORE FUN THINGS OUT THERE.
I HAVE TO HELP THE PRINCE UNDERSTAND THAT LOVE IS JUST AN ILLUSION.
RIGHT, KOMA?
にゃ
MEOW
...?
WHY IS IT SO IMPORTANT THAT I CHOOSE ONE PERSON?

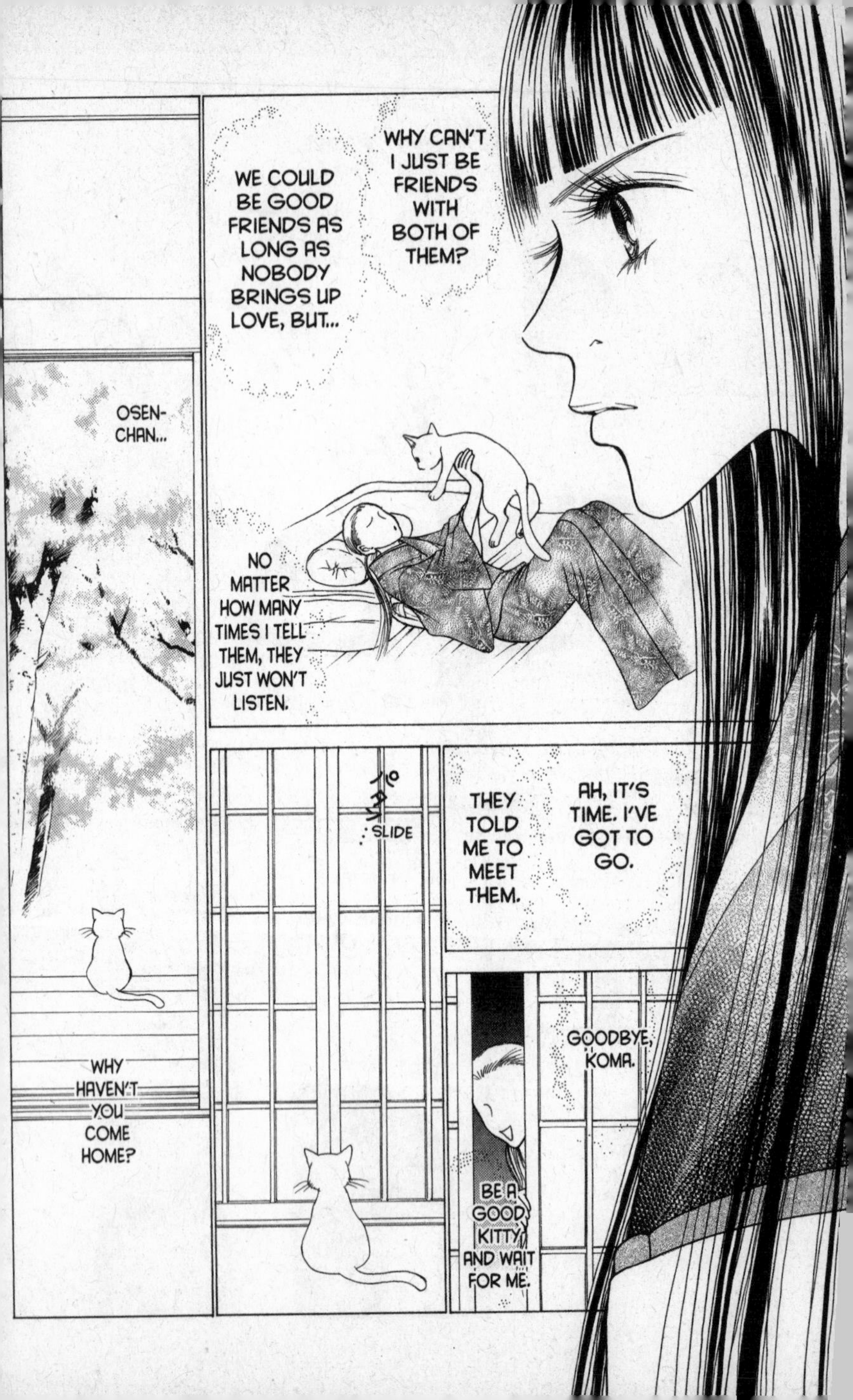
WHY CAN'T I JUST BE FRIENDS WITH BOTH OF THEM?
WE COULD BE GOOD FRIENDS AS LONG AS NOBODY BRINGS UP LOVE, BUT...
NO MATTER HOW MANY TIMES I TELL THEM, THEY JUST WON'T LISTEN.
AH, IT'S TIME. I'VE GOT TO GO.
THEY TOLD ME TO MEET THEM.
GOODBYE, KOMA.
BE A GOOD KITTY AND WAIT FOR ME.
SLIDE
OSEN-CHAN...
WHY HAVEN'T YOU COME HOME?

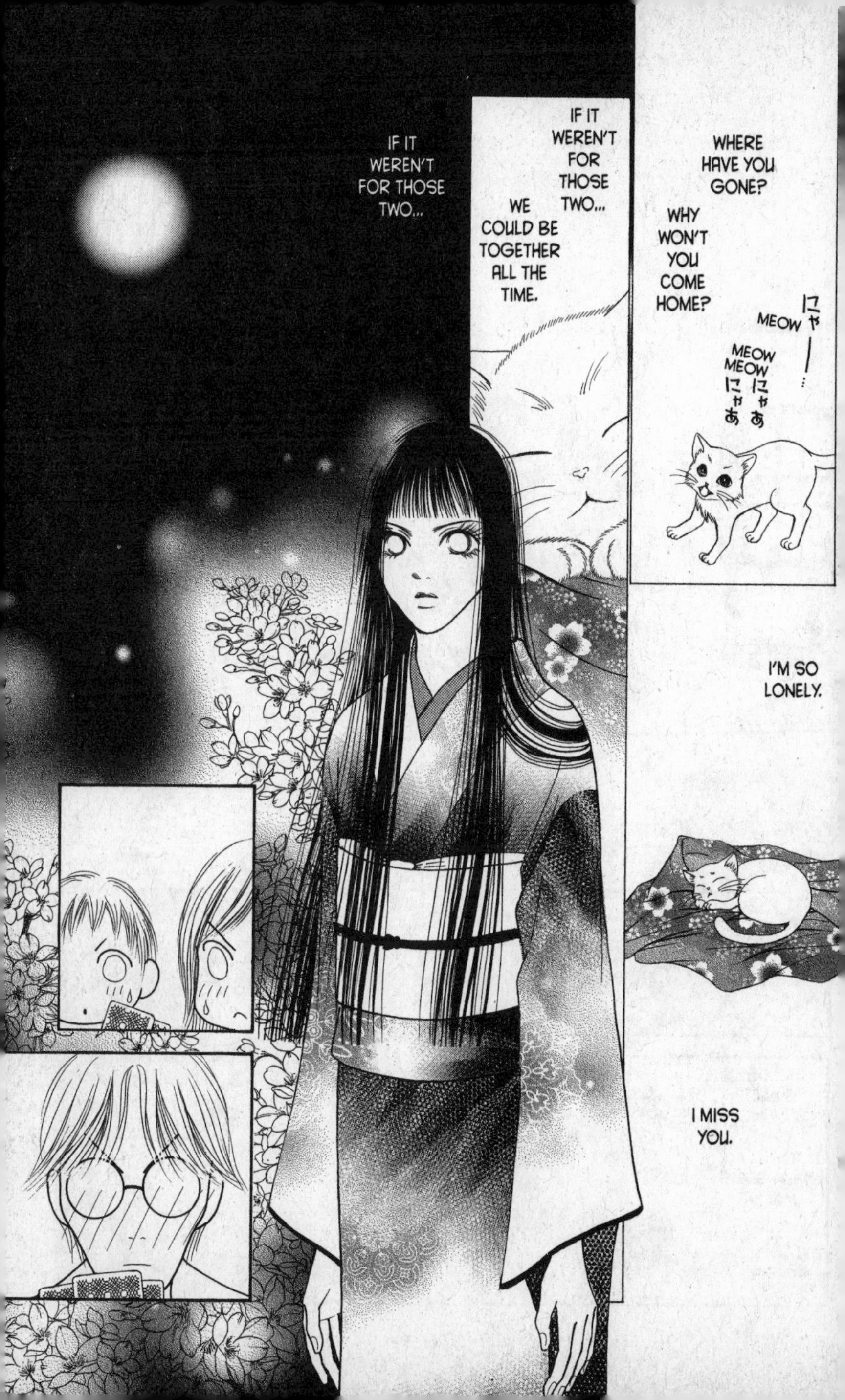
WHERE HAVE YOU GONE?
WHY WON'T YOU COME HOME?
にゃー…!
MEOW
にゃあ にゃあ
MEOW MEOW
IF IT WEREN'T FOR THOSE TWO...
WE COULD BE TOGETHER ALL THE TIME.
IF IT WEREN'T FOR THOSE TWO...
I'M SO LONELY.
I MISS YOU.

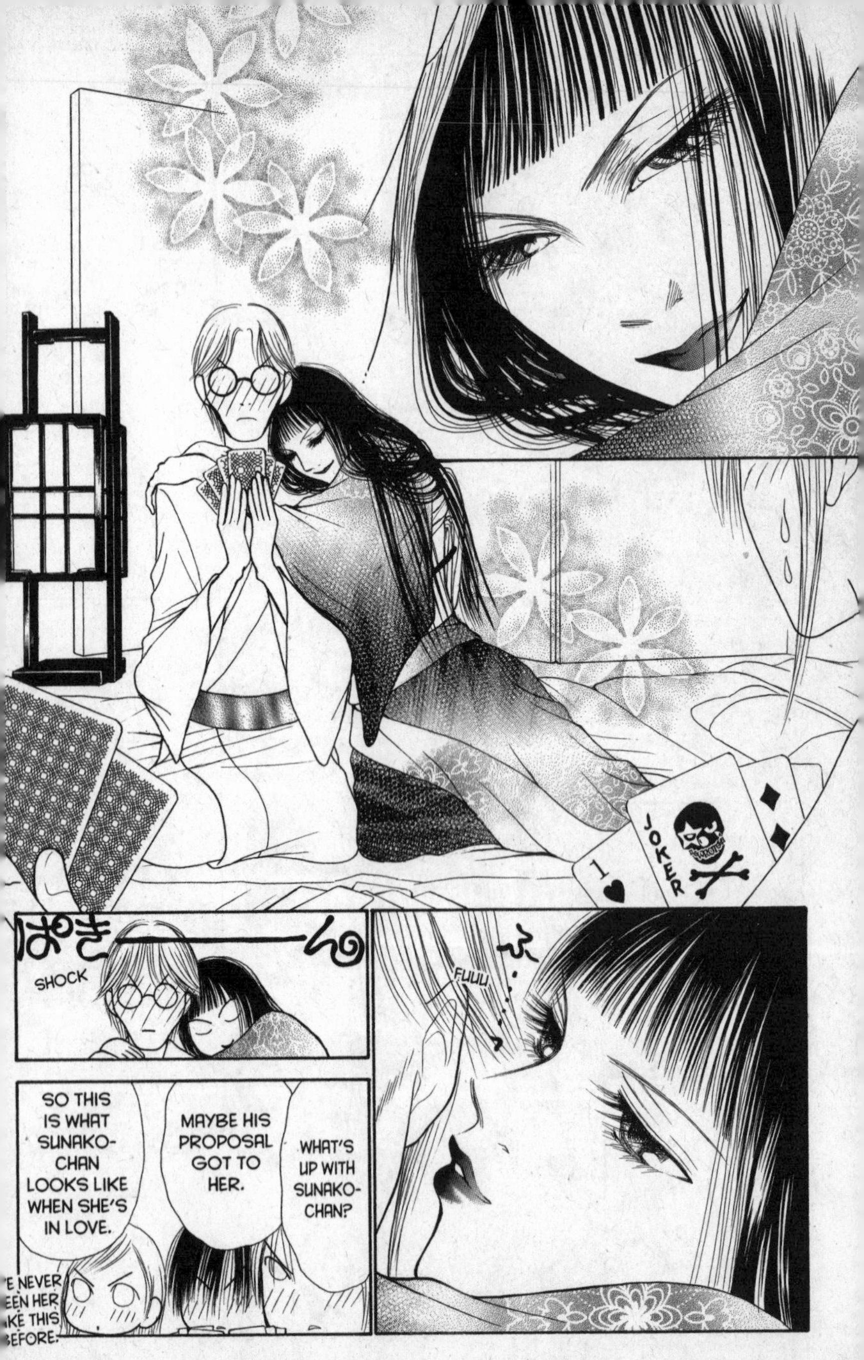
ふ…
FUUU
ぱき——ん
SHOCK
WHAT'S UP WITH SUNAKO-CHAN?
MAYBE HIS PROPOSAL GOT TO HER.
SO THIS IS WHAT SUNAKO-CHAN LOOKS LIKE WHEN SHE'S IN LOVE.
'E NEVER EEN HER IKE THIS BEFORE.
JOKER

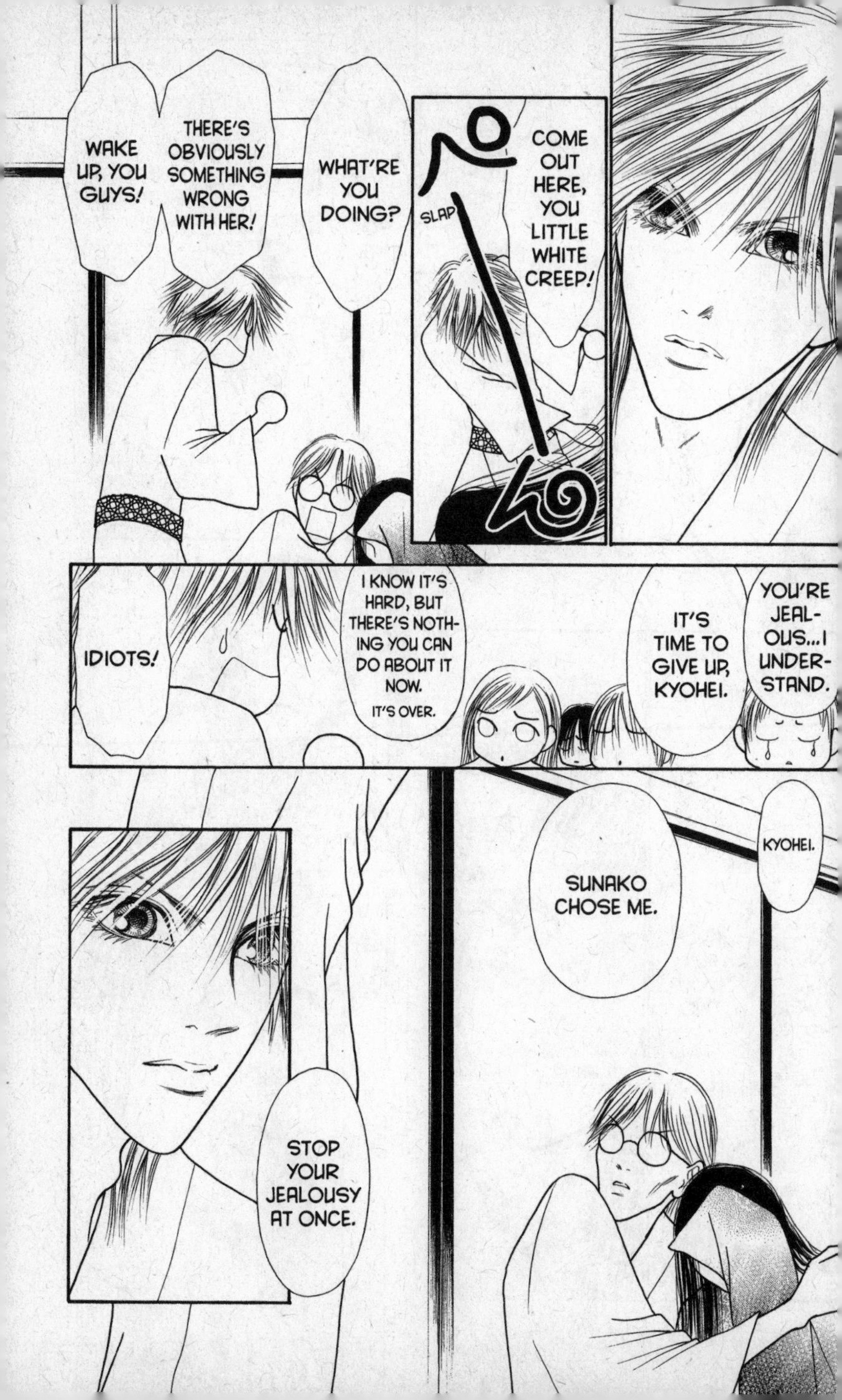
COME OUT HERE, YOU LITTLE WHITE CREEP!
SLAP
WHAT'RE YOU DOING?
THERE'S OBVIOUSLY SOMETHING WRONG WITH HER!
WAKE UP, YOU GUYS!
YOU'RE JEAL-OUS...I UNDER-STAND.
IT'S TIME TO GIVE UP, KYOHEI.
I KNOW IT'S HARD, BUT THERE'S NOTH-ING YOU CAN DO ABOUT IT NOW.
IT'S OVER.
IDIOTS!
KYOHEI.
SUNAKO CHOSE ME.
STOP YOUR JEALOUSY AT ONCE.

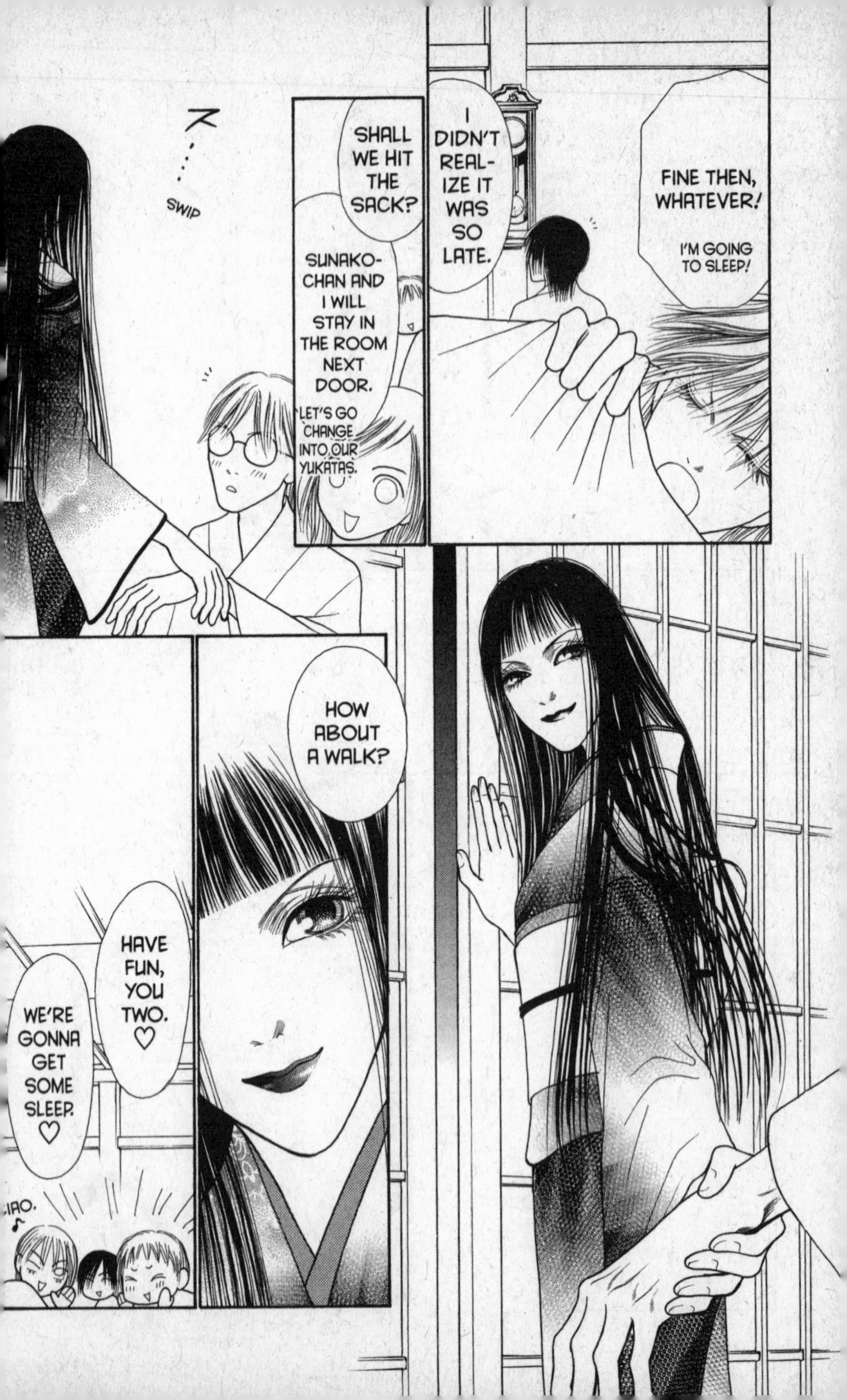
FINE THEN, WHATEVER!
I'M GOING TO SLEEP!
I DIDN'T REAL-IZE IT WAS SO LATE.
SHALL WE HIT THE SACK?
SUNAKO-CHAN AND I WILL STAY IN THE ROOM NEXT DOOR.
LET'S GO CHANGE INTO OUR YUKATAS.
SWIP
HOW ABOUT A WALK?
HAVE FUN, YOU TWO. ♡
WE'RE GONNA GET SOME SLEEP. ♡
IAO. ♪

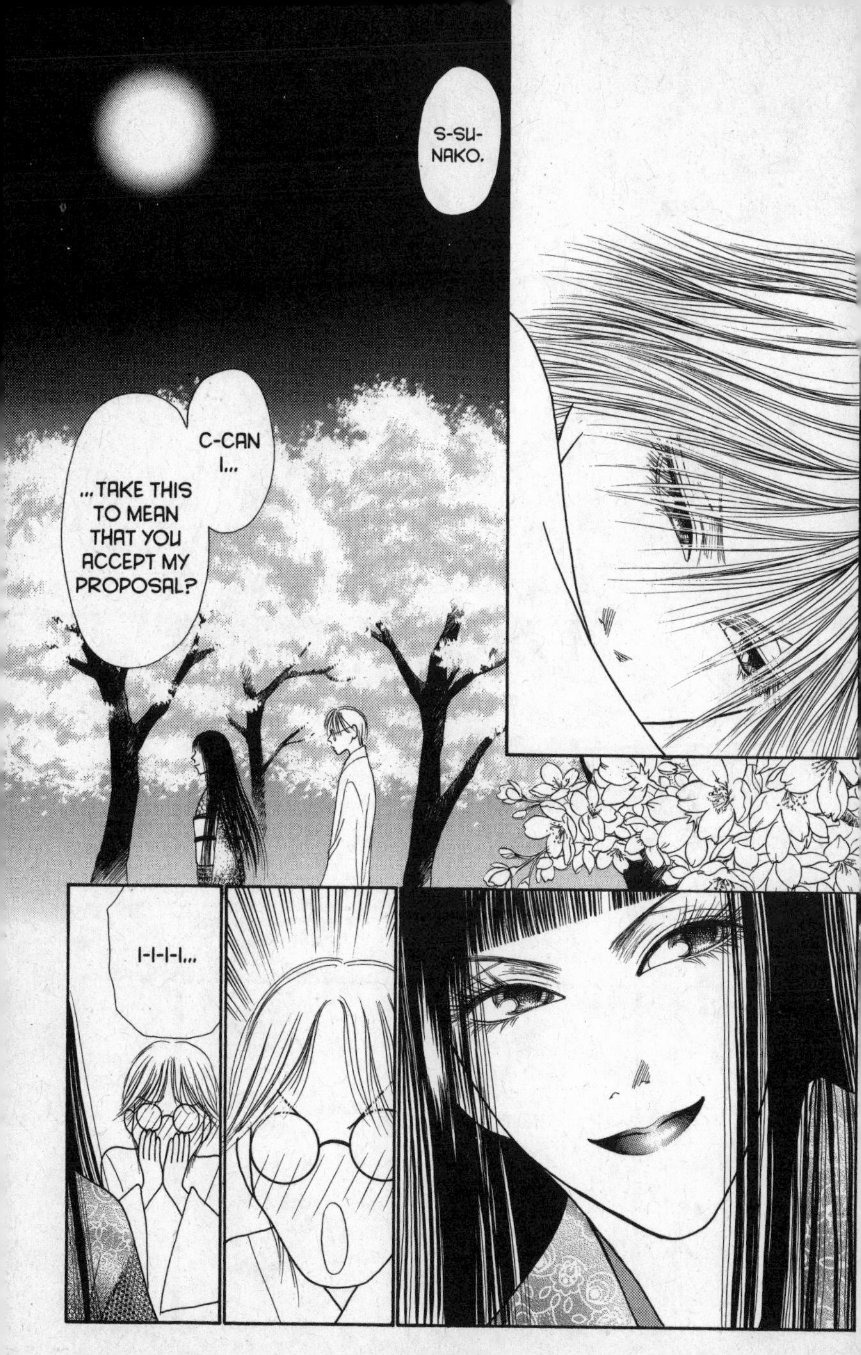
S-SU-NAKO.
C-CAN I...
...TAKE THIS TO MEAN THAT YOU ACCEPT MY PROPOSAL?
I-I-I-I...

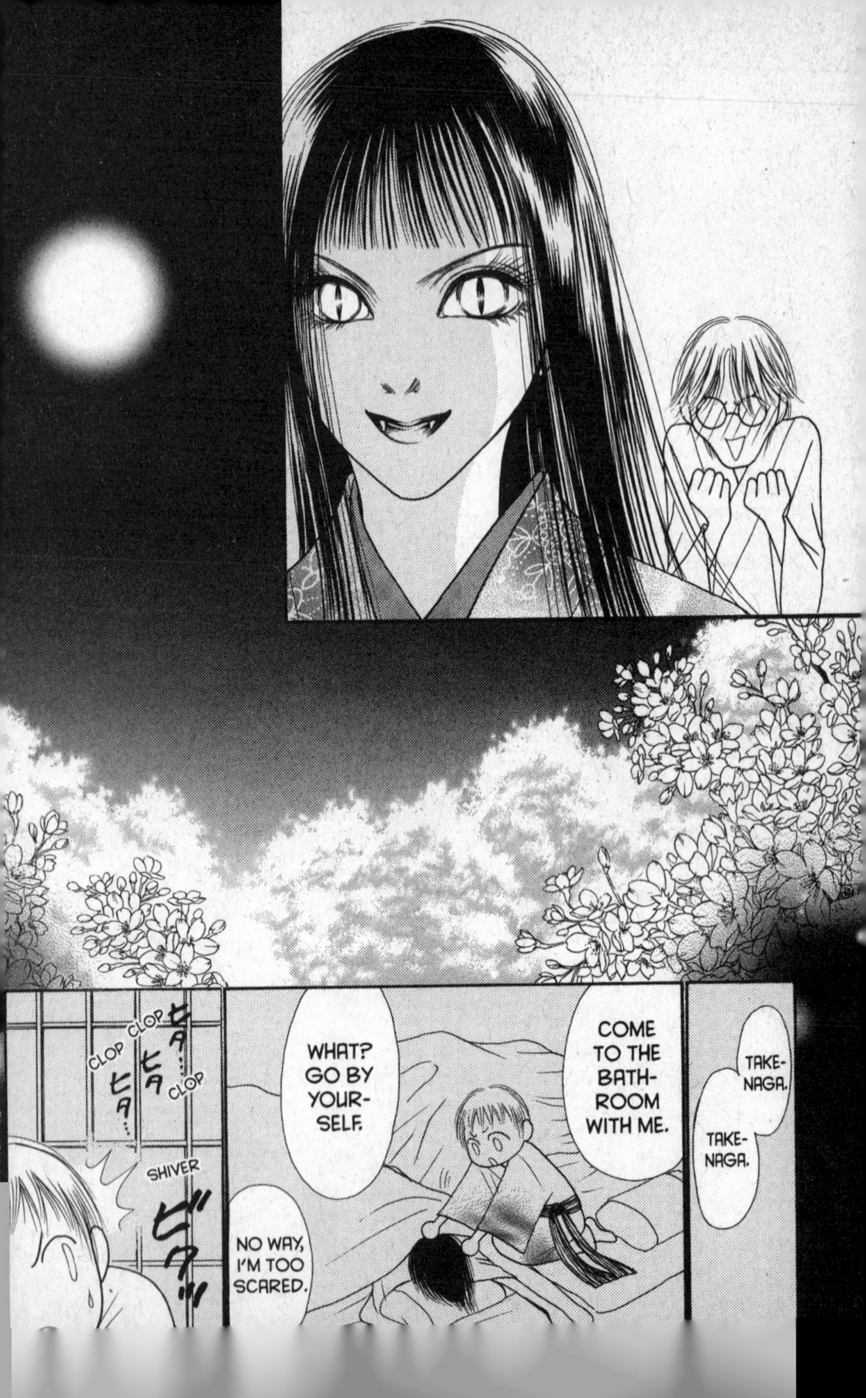
TAKE-NAGA.
TAKE-NAGA.
COME TO THE BATH-ROOM WITH ME.
WHAT? GO BY YOUR-SELF.
NO WAY, I'M TOO SCARED.
ヒタ… ヒタ ヒタ…
CLOP CLOP
CLOP
SHIVER
ビクッ

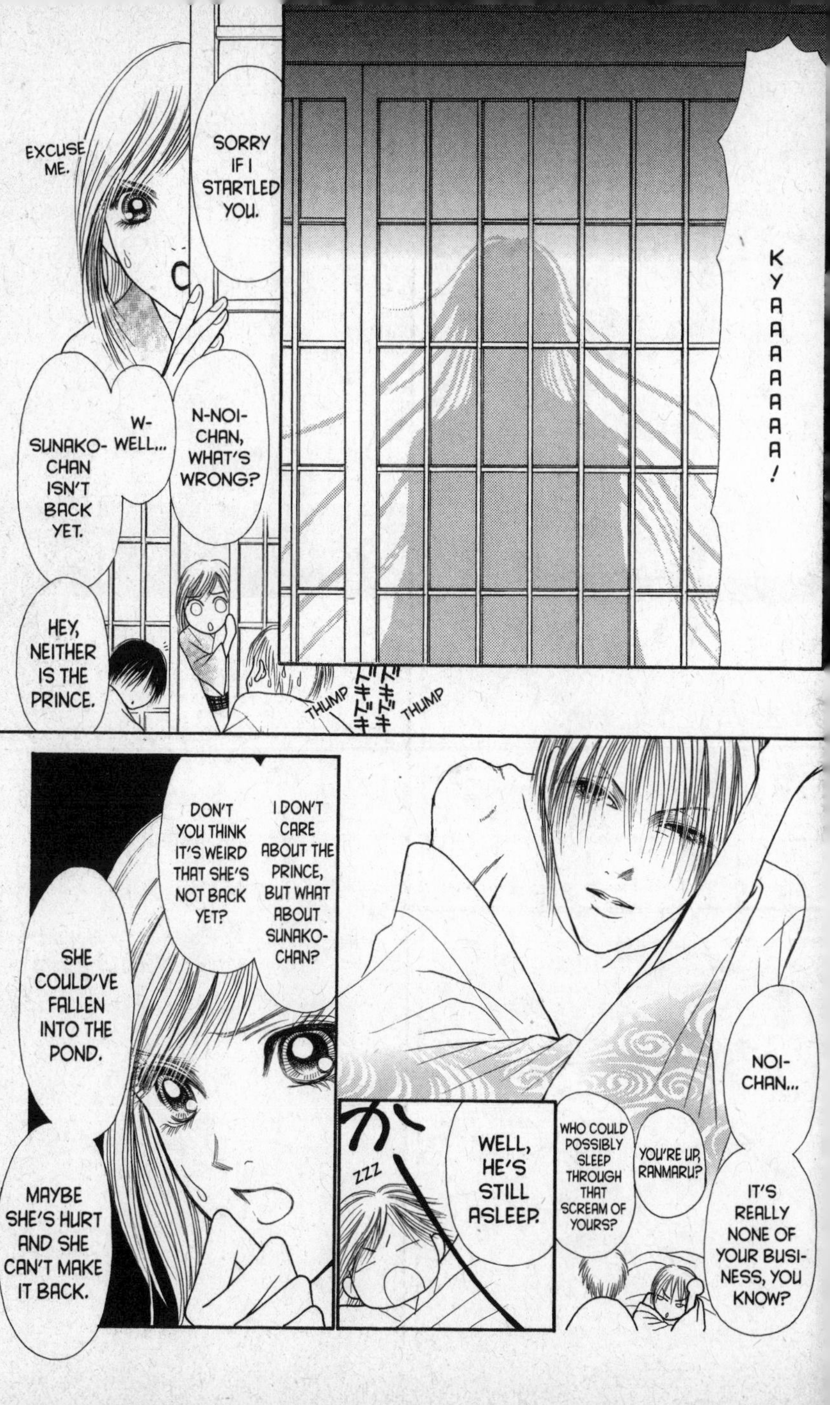
KYAAAAAAAA!
SORRY IF I STARTLED YOU.
EXCUSE ME.
N-NOI-CHAN, WHAT'S WRONG?
W-WELL...
SUNAKO-CHAN ISN'T BACK YET.
HEY, NEITHER IS THE PRINCE.
ドキドキ THUMP
ドキドキ THUMP
NOI-CHAN...
IT'S REALLY NONE OF YOUR BUSI-NESS, YOU KNOW?
YOU'RE UP, RANMARU?
WHO COULD POSSIBLY SLEEP THROUGH THAT SCREAM OF YOURS?
WELL, HE'S STILL ASLEEP.
ZZZ
I DON'T CARE ABOUT THE PRINCE, BUT WHAT ABOUT SUNAKO-CHAN?
DON'T YOU THINK IT'S WEIRD THAT SHE'S NOT BACK YET?
SHE COULD'VE FALLEN INTO THE POND.
MAYBE SHE'S HURT AND SHE CAN'T MAKE IT BACK.

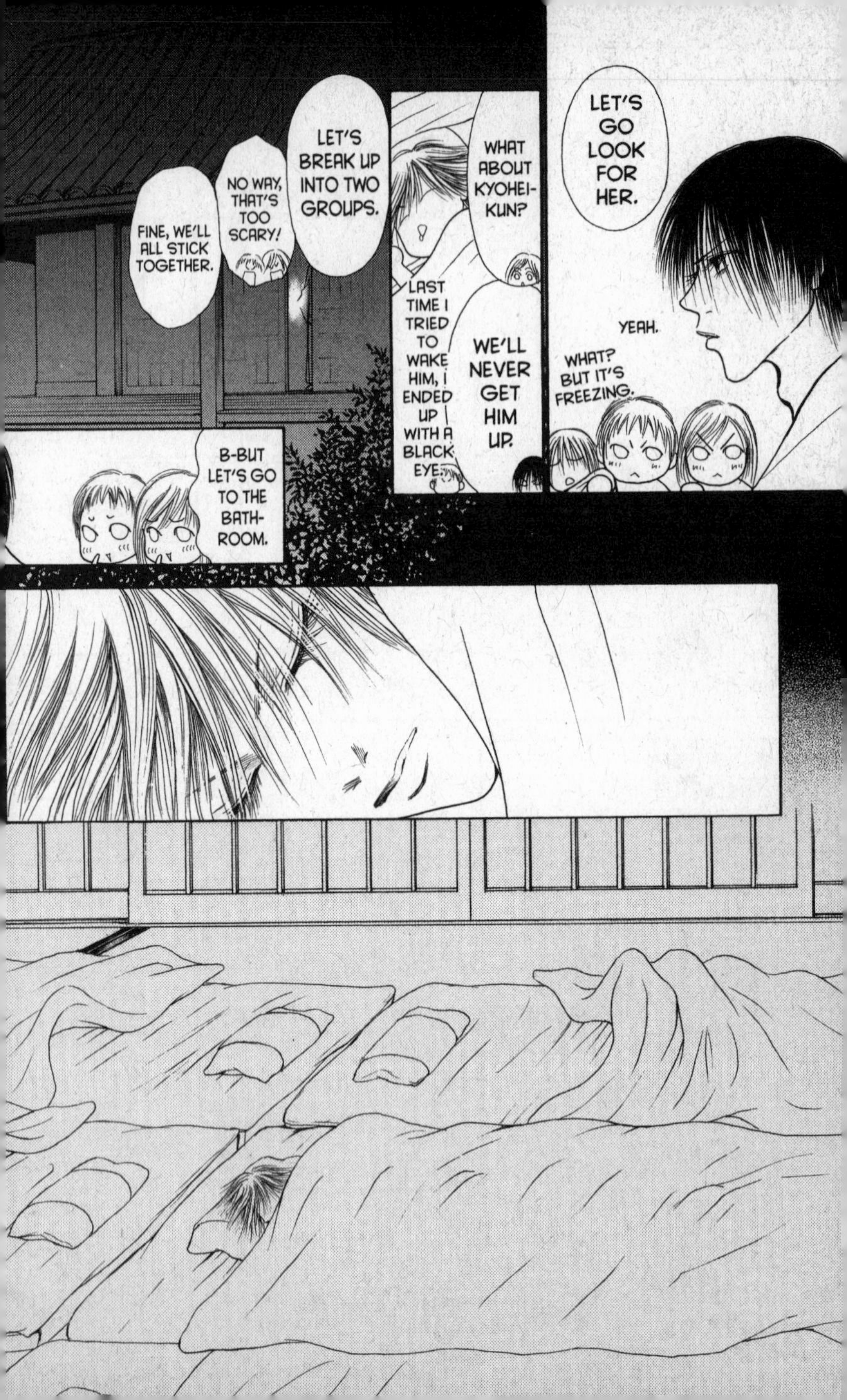
LET'S GO LOOK FOR HER.
YEAH.
WHAT? BUT IT'S FREEZING.
WHAT ABOUT KYOHEI-KUN?
WE'LL NEVER GET HIM UP.
LAST TIME I TRIED TO WAKE HIM, I ENDED UP WITH A BLACK EYE.
LET'S BREAK UP INTO TWO GROUPS.
NO WAY, THAT'S TOO SCARY!
FINE, WE'LL ALL STICK TOGETHER.
B-BUT LET'S GO TO THE BATHROOM.

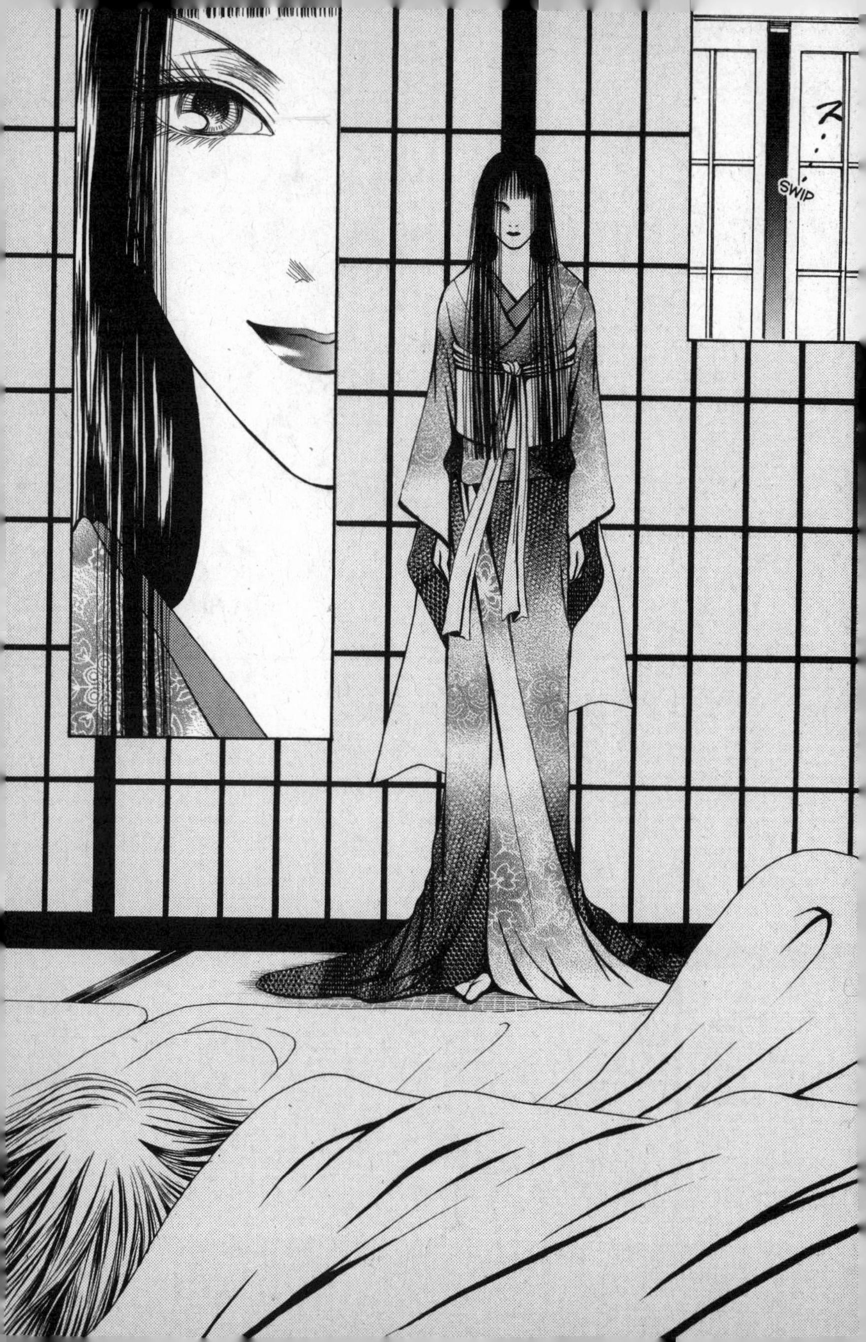
ス…
SWIP

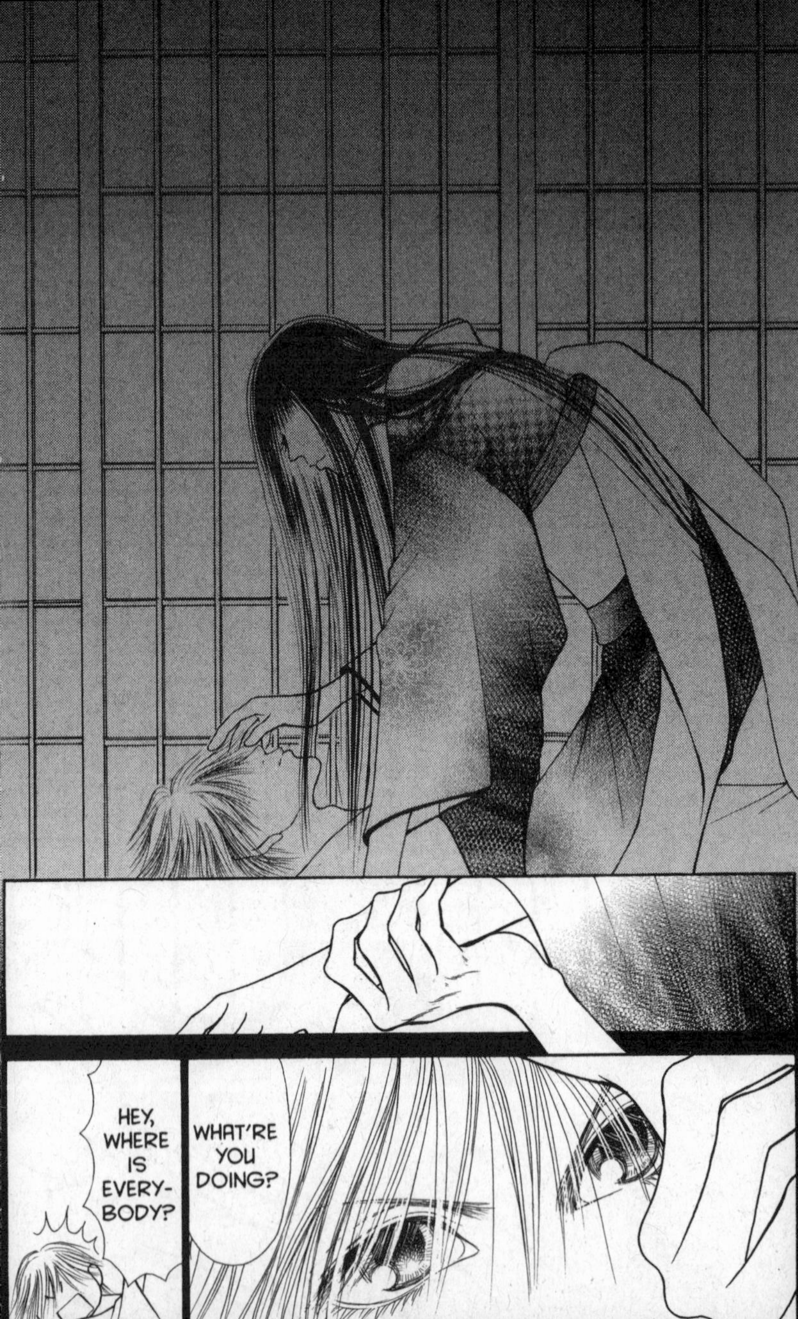
WHAT'RE YOU DOING?
HEY, WHERE IS EVERY-BODY?

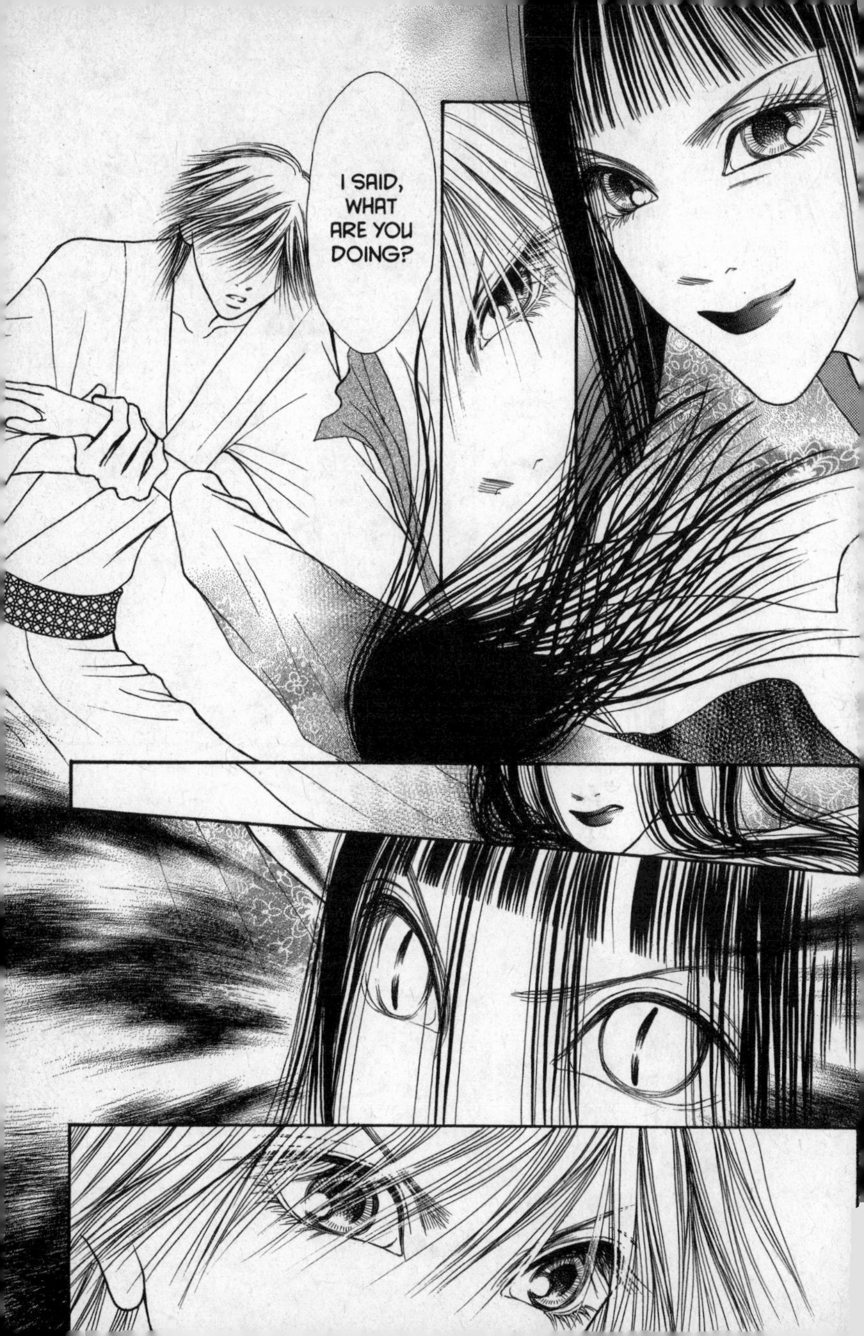
I SAID, WHAT ARE YOU DOING?

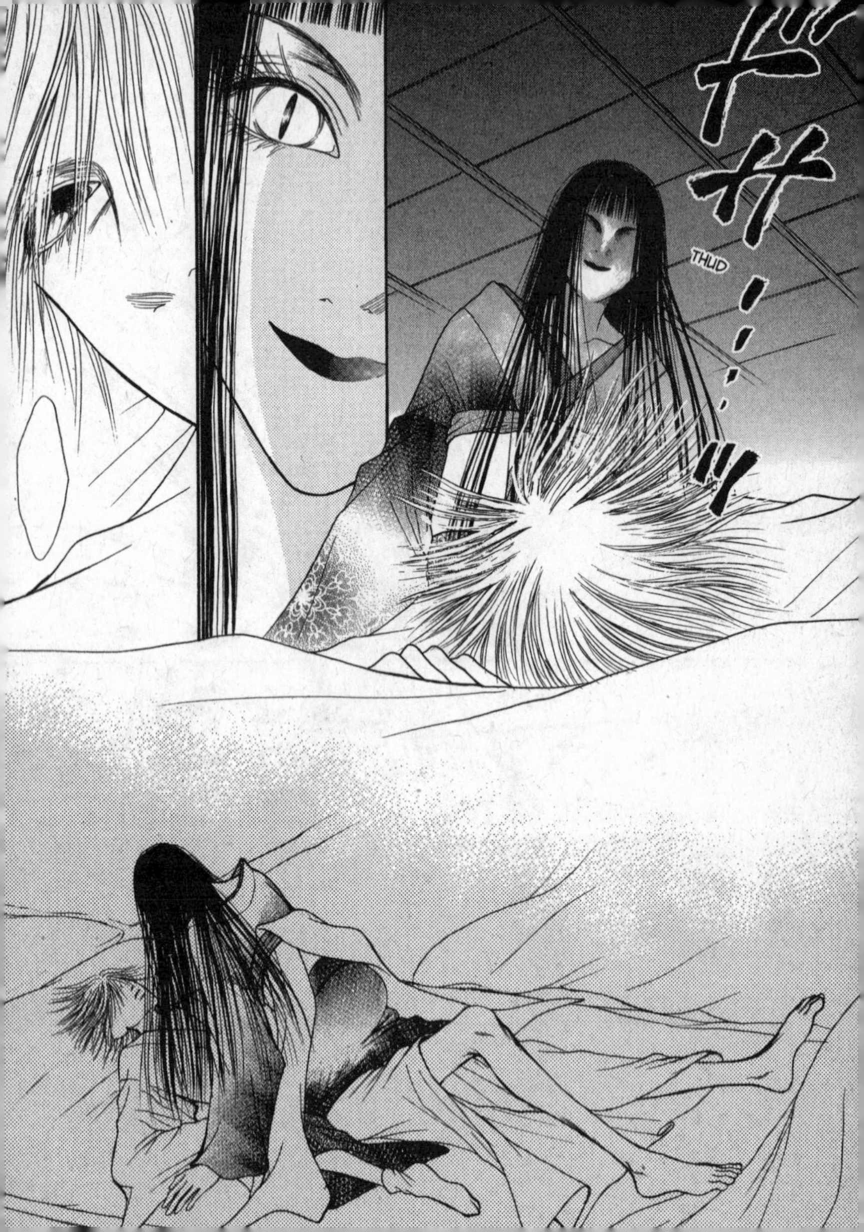
ドサッ
THUD

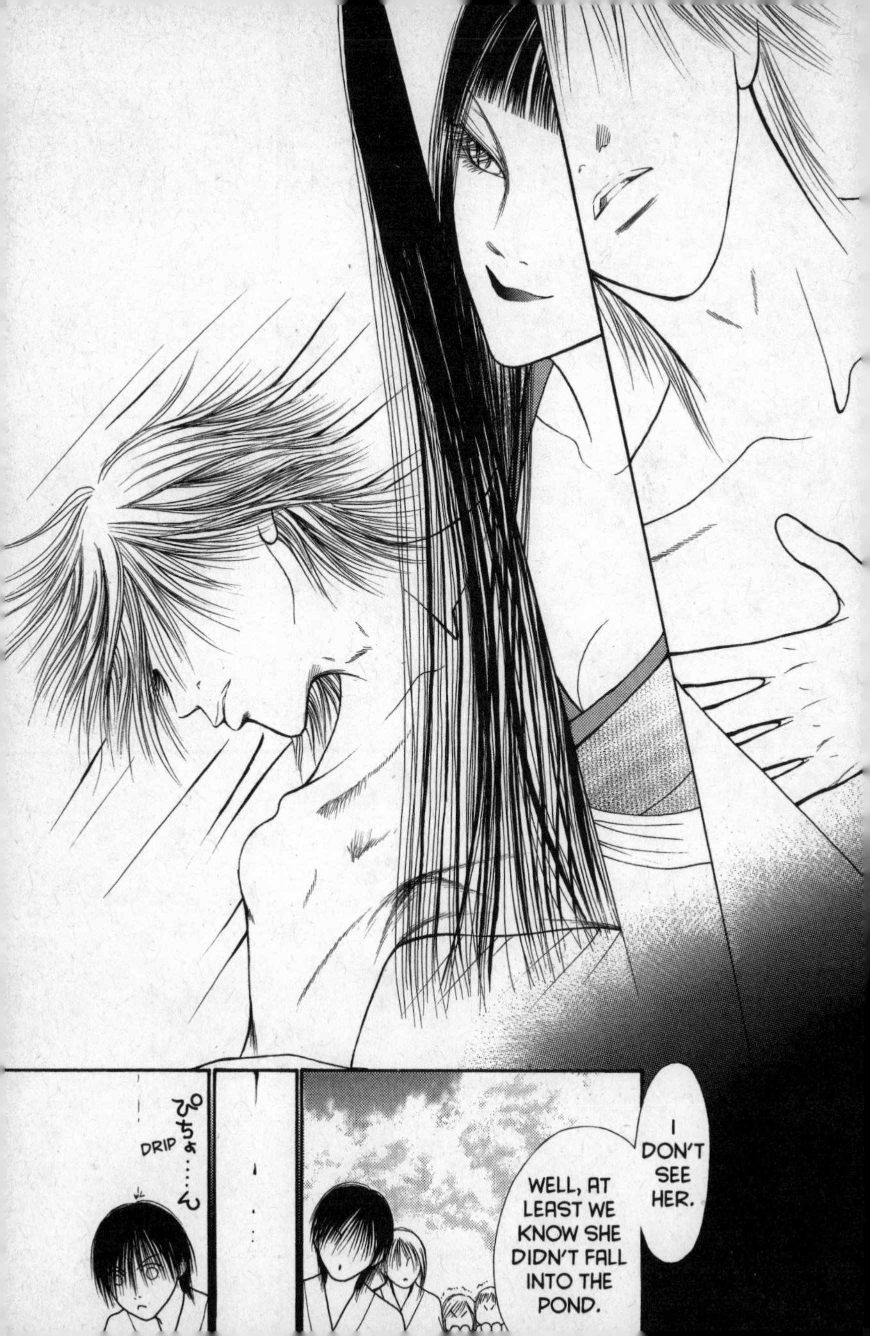
I DON'T SEE HER.
WELL, AT LEAST WE KNOW SHE DIDN'T FALL INTO THE POND.
. . .
ぴちょ…ん
DRIP

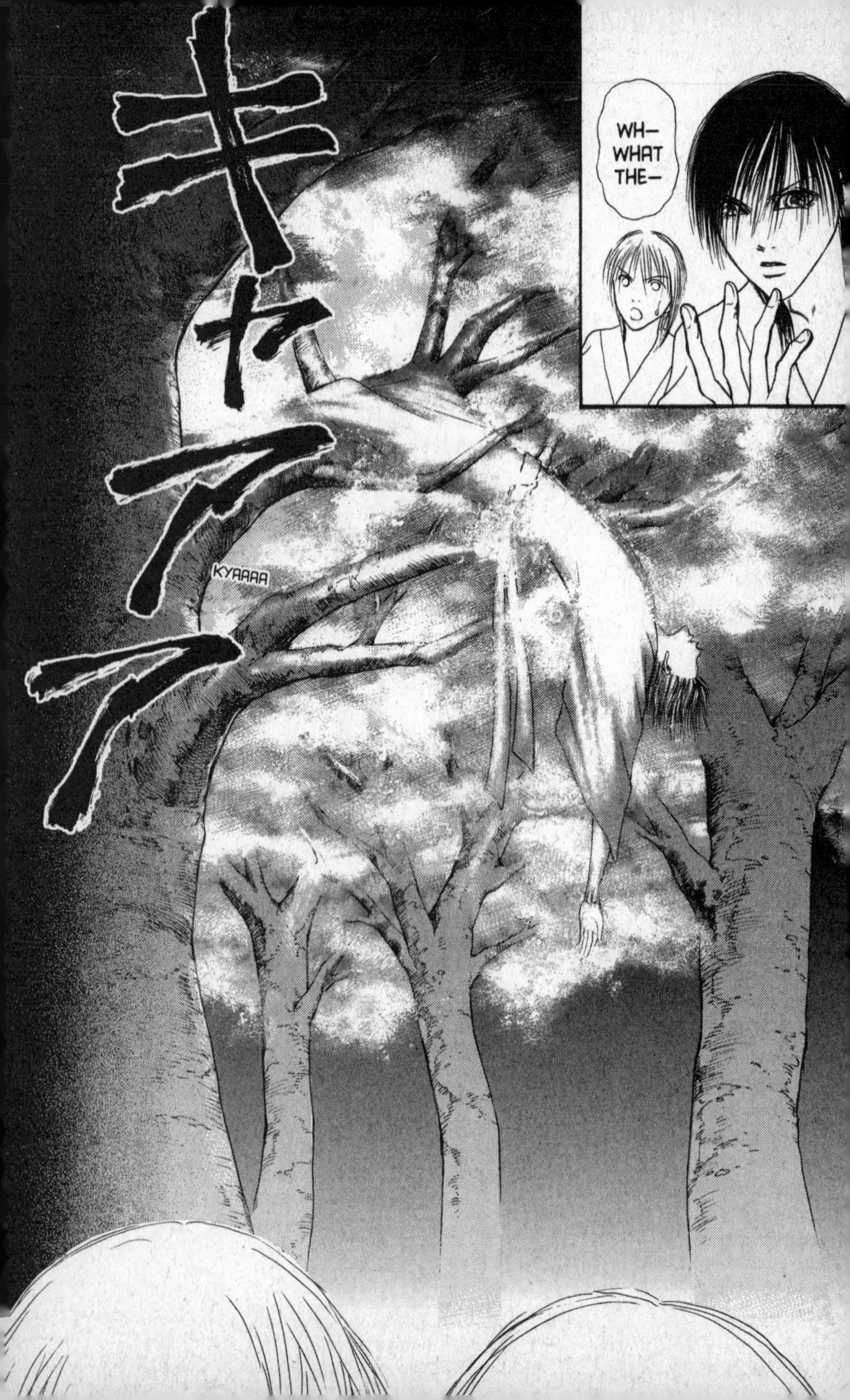
WH— WHAT THE—
キャアアア
KYAAAA

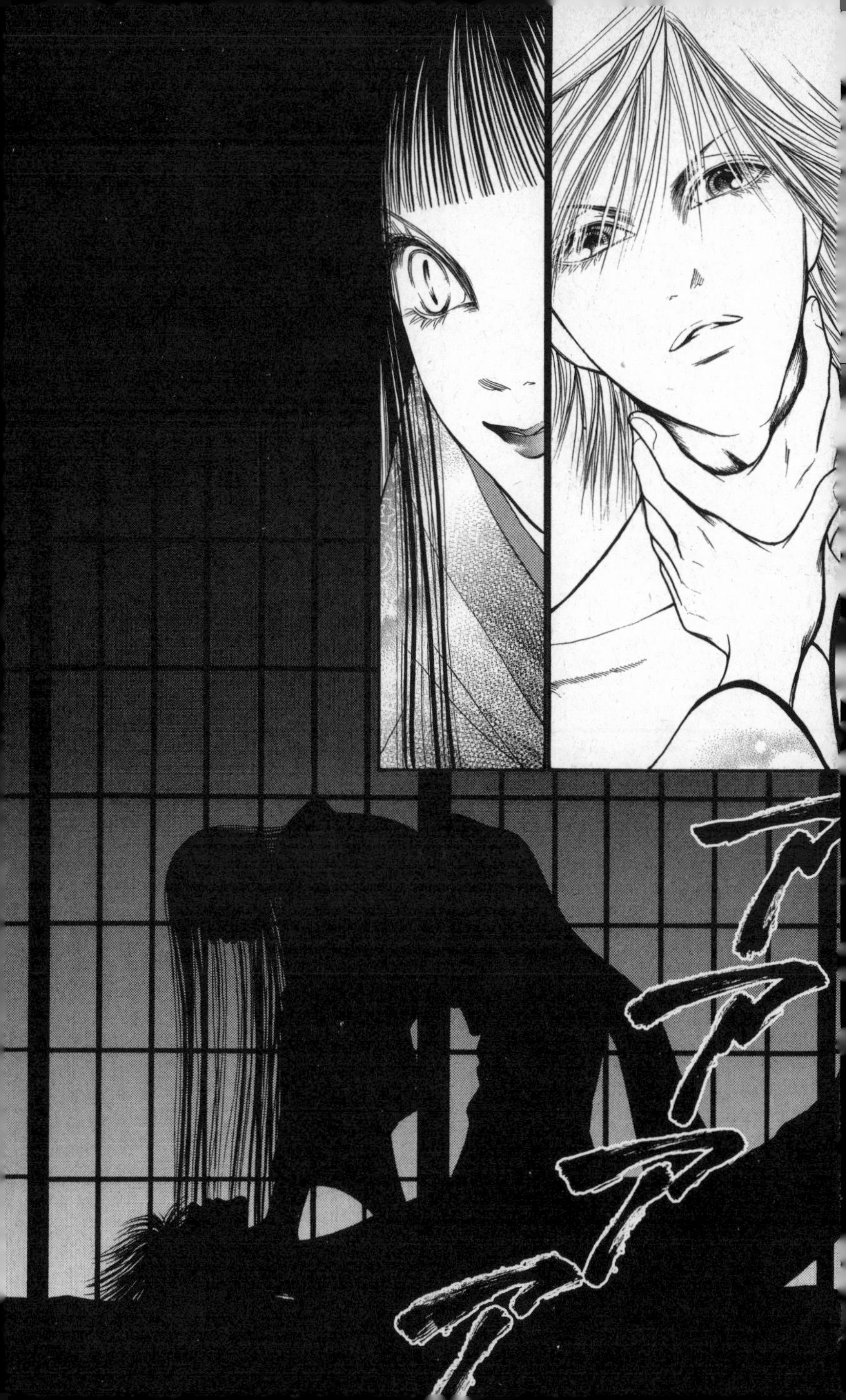
アアアア

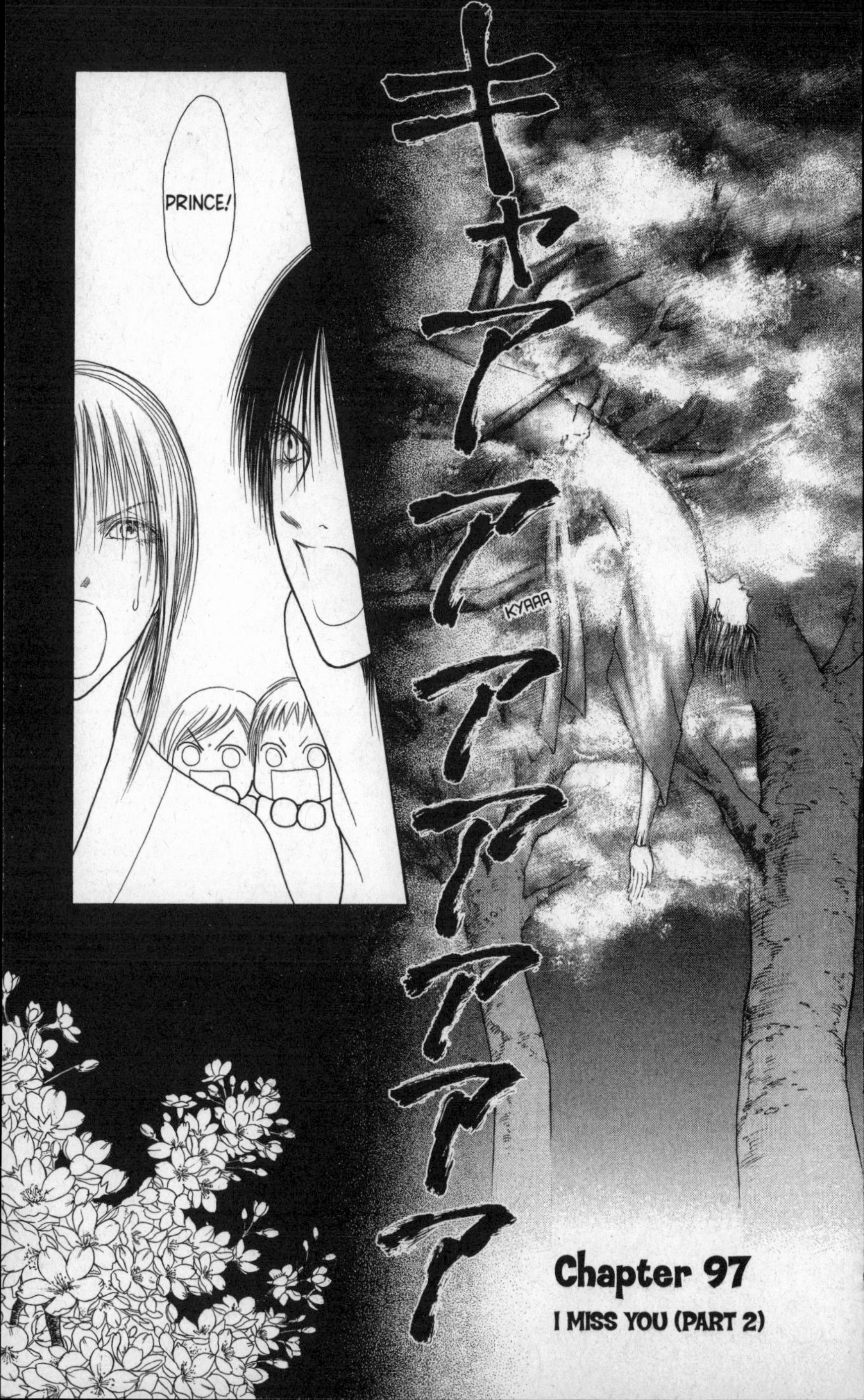
KYAAA
PRINCE!

Chapter 97

I MISS YOU (PART 2)

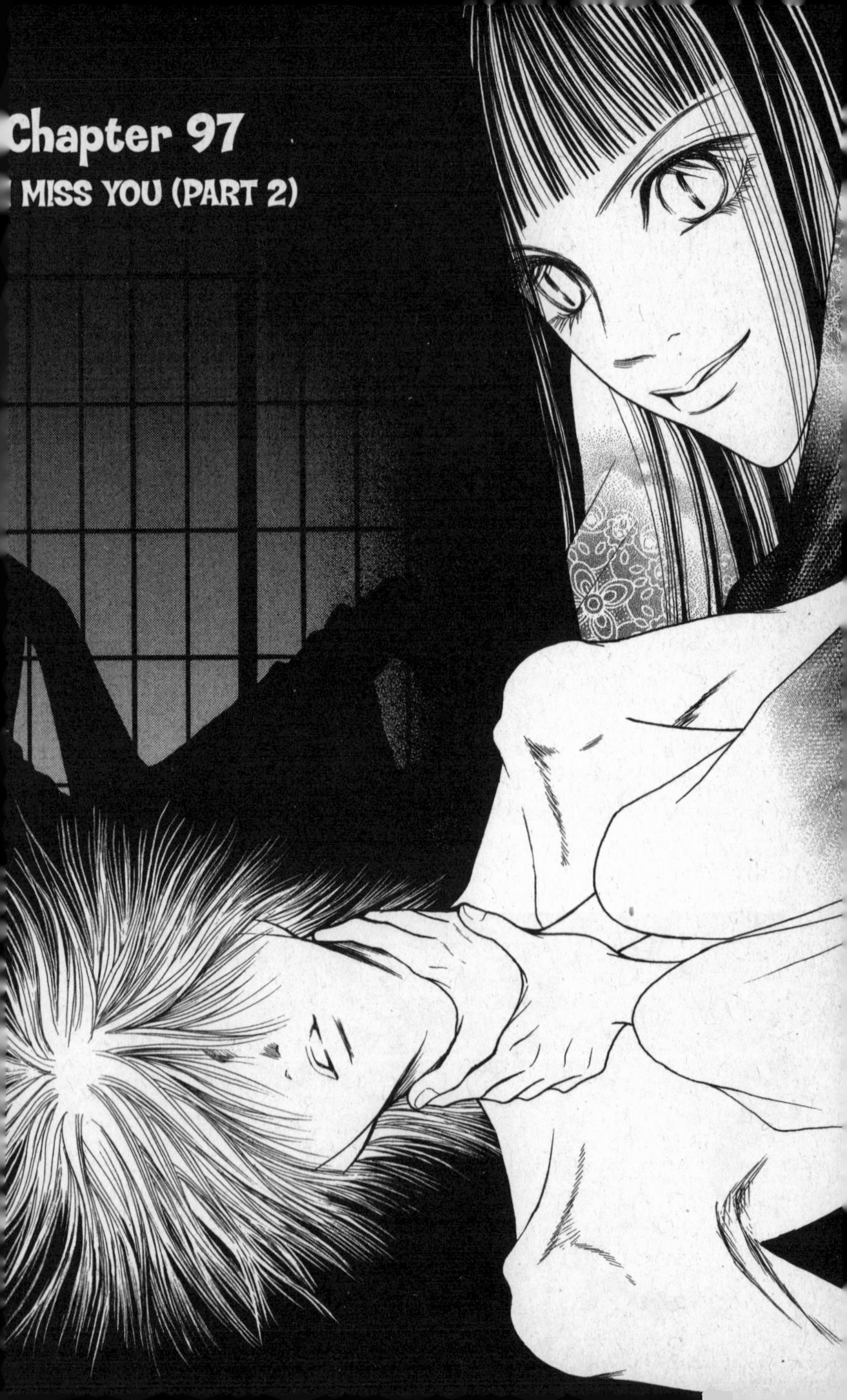
Chapter 97
I MISS YOU (PART 2)

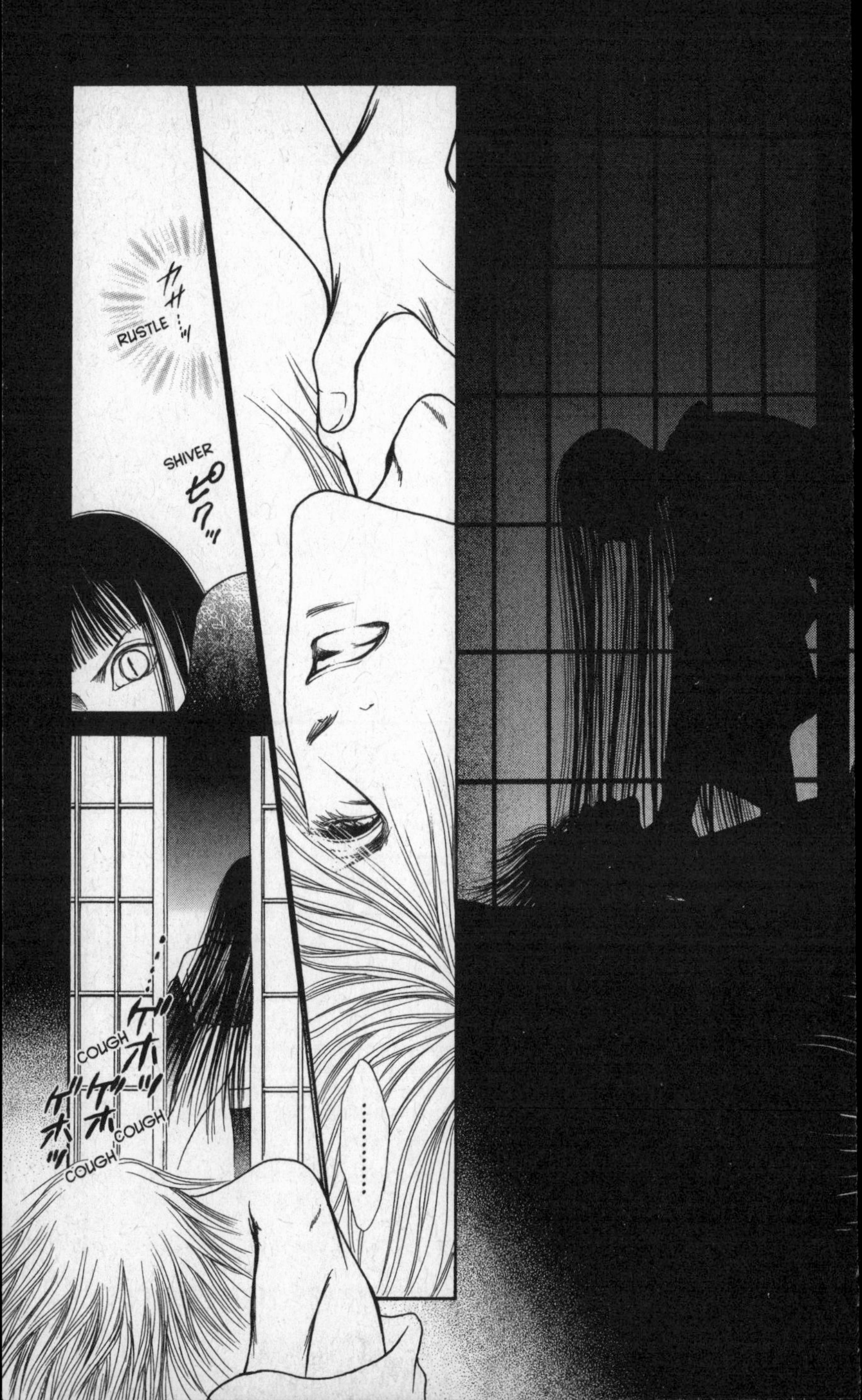
カサ…ッ
RUSTLE
ピクッ
SHIVER
……
ゲホッ
COUGH
ゲホッ
COUGH
ゲホッ
COUGH
……

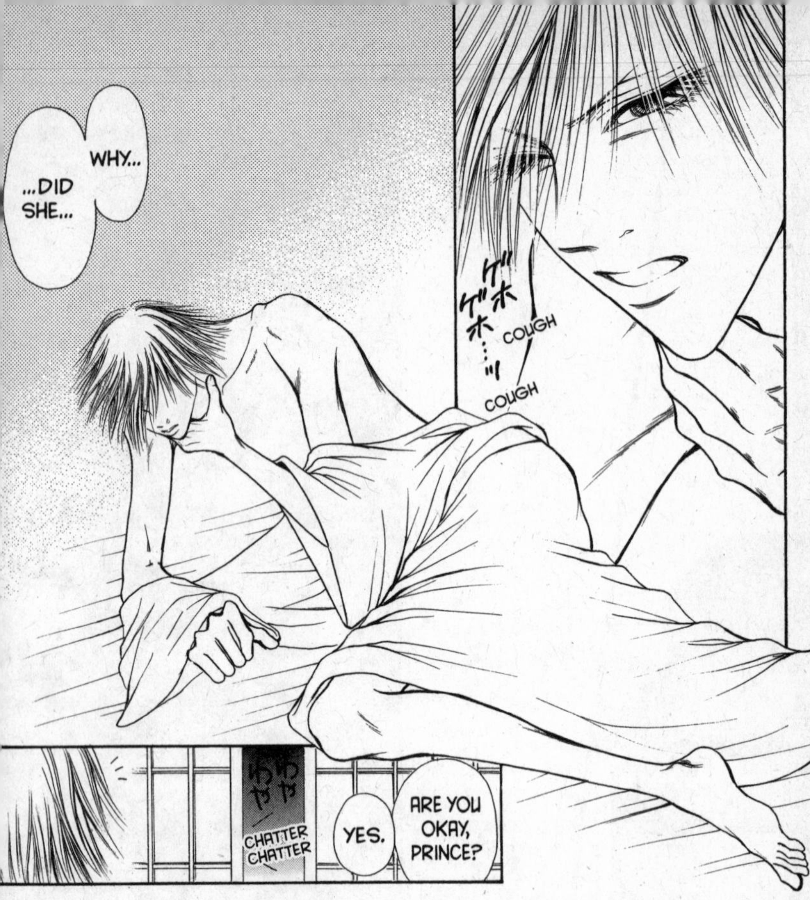
ゲホゲホ…ッ
COUGH
COUGH
WHY...
...DID SHE...
ARE YOU OKAY, PRINCE?
YES.
CHATTER CHATTER

BEHIND THE SCENES

IT'S ANOTHER TWO-PART SERIES.

THIS TIME I PLOTTED OUT PART 1 AND PART 2 BEFORE I STARTED WRITING THEM, SO IT WAS MUCH EASIER. (WHY DON'T I DO THAT EVERY TIME?) I WROTE THIS DURING GOLDEN WEEK. I DIDN'T HAVE MUCH TIME, SO IT WAS REALLY TOUGH. ON THE DAY OF THE DEADLINE, I HAD TO LEAVE MY TWO MALE ASSISTANTS BEHIND TO FINISH UP WHILE I WENT TO A MEETING ABOUT THE NEXT STORY. SORRY, GUYS...

I'D ALWAYS WANTED TO DO A STORY ABOUT SUNAKO BEING POSSESSED BY A CAT, SO IT WAS REALLY FUN. I'D LIKE TO DO IT AGAIN, BUT IT'S NOT THE SORT OF STORY LINE YOU CAN REPEAT.

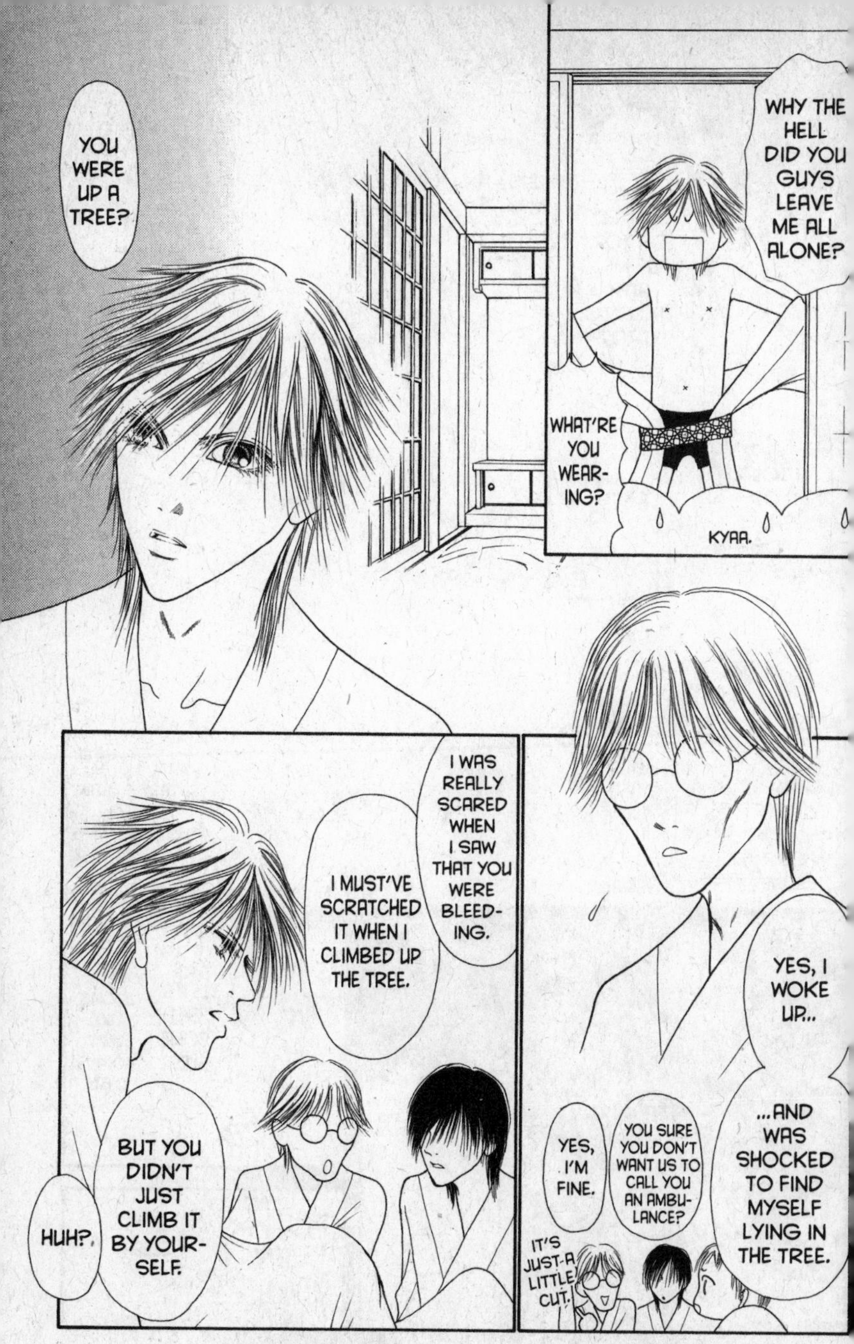
WHY THE HELL DID YOU GUYS LEAVE ME ALL ALONE?
WHAT'RE YOU WEAR-ING?
KYAA.
YOU WERE UP A TREE?
YES, I WOKE UP...
...AND WAS SHOCKED TO FIND MYSELF LYING IN THE TREE.
YOU SURE YOU DON'T WANT US TO CALL YOU AN AMBU-LANCE?
YES, I'M FINE.
IT'S JUST A LITTLE CUT.
I WAS REALLY SCARED WHEN I SAW THAT YOU WERE BLEED-ING.
I MUST'VE SCRATCHED IT WHEN I CLIMBED UP THE TREE.
BUT YOU DIDN'T JUST CLIMB IT BY YOUR-SELF.
HUH?

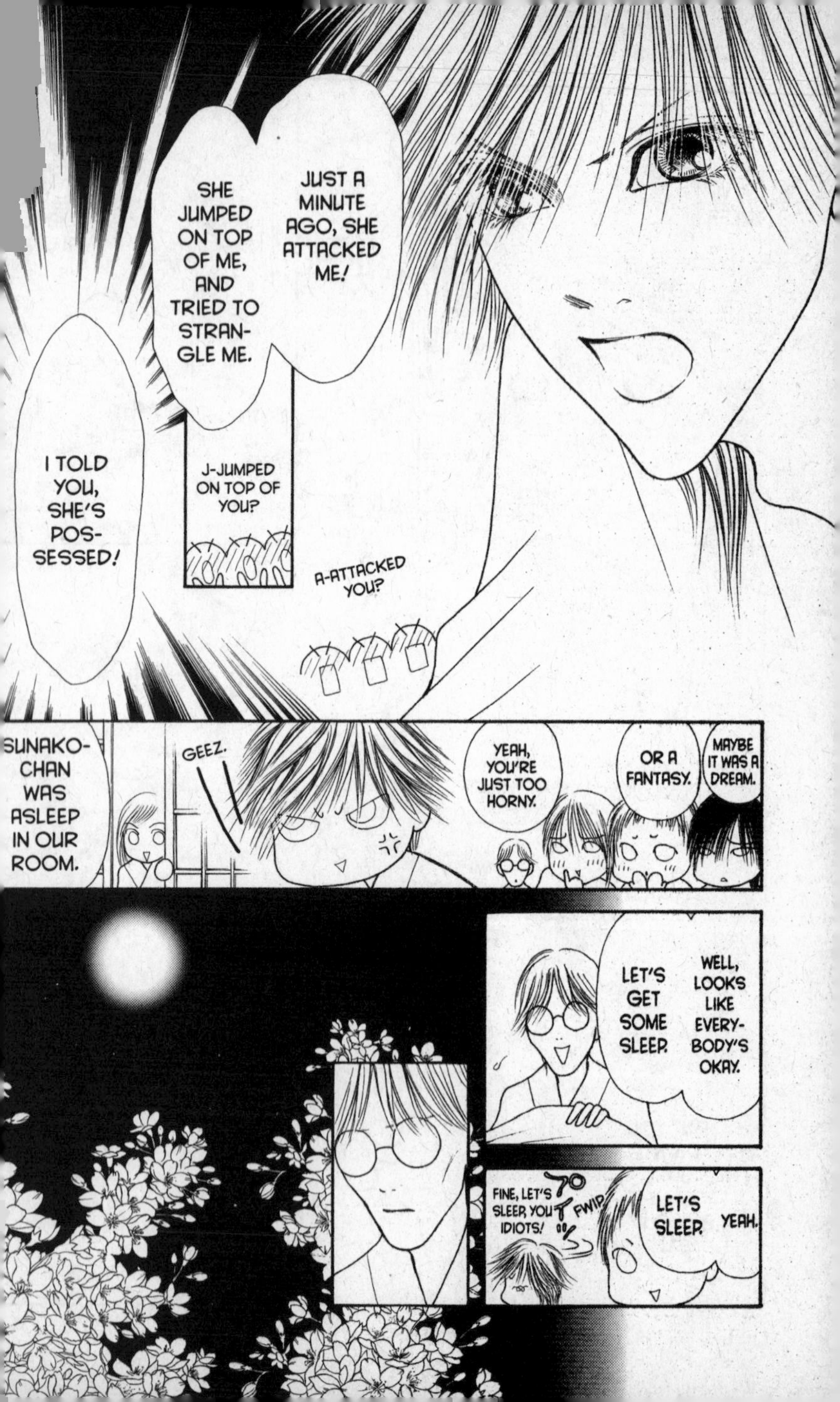
JUST A MINUTE AGO, SHE ATTACKED ME!
SHE JUMPED ON TOP OF ME, AND TRIED TO STRANGLE ME.
A-ATTACKED YOU?
J-JUMPED ON TOP OF YOU?
I TOLD YOU, SHE'S POSSESSED!
MAYBE IT WAS A DREAM.
OR A FANTASY.
YEAH, YOU'RE JUST TOO HORNY.
GEEZ.
SUNAKO-CHAN WAS ASLEEP IN OUR ROOM.
WELL, LOOKS LIKE EVERYBODY'S OKAY.
LET'S GET SOME SLEEP.
YEAH.
LET'S SLEEP.
FWIP
FINE, LET'S SLEEP, YOU IDIOTS!

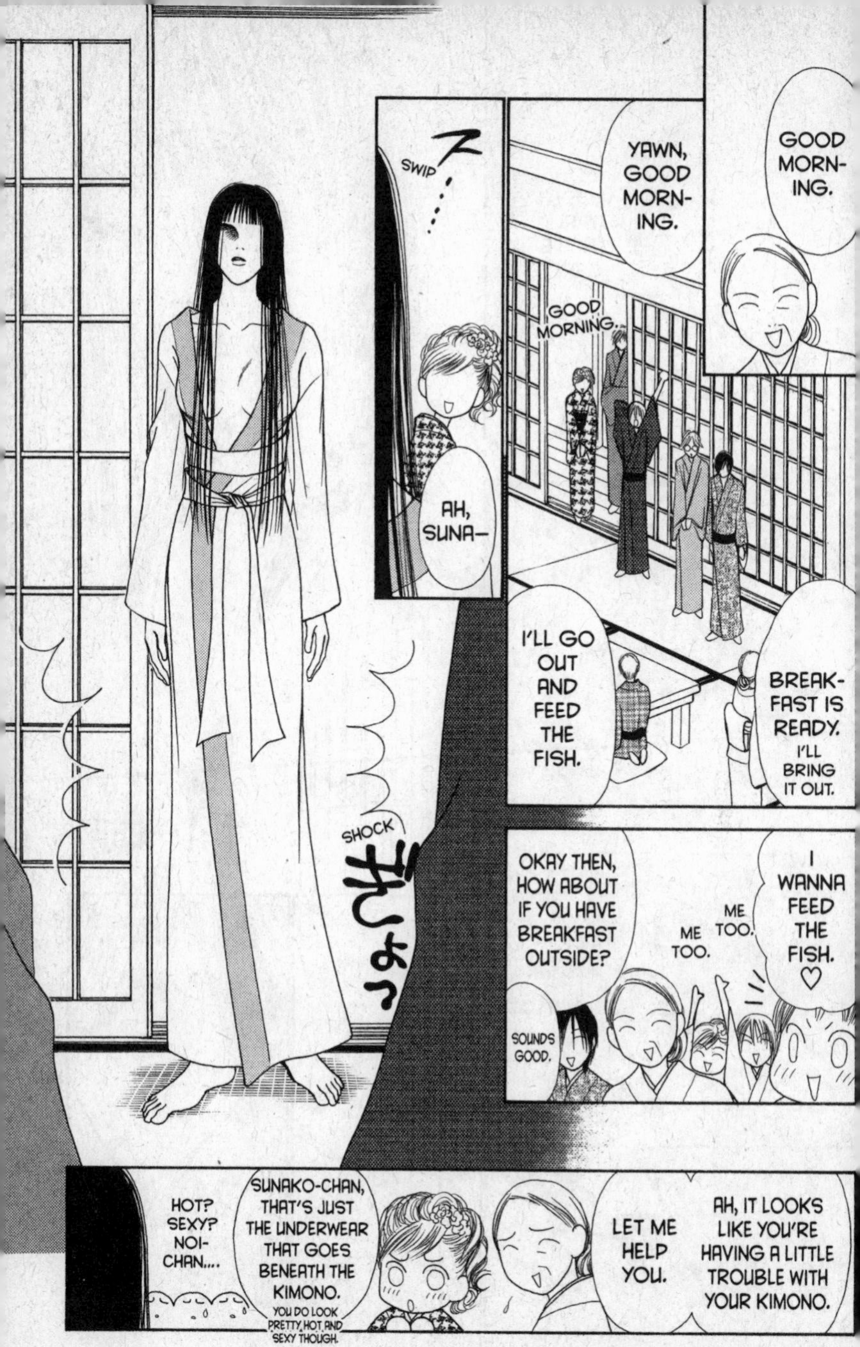
GOOD MORNING.
YAWN, GOOD MORNING.
GOOD MORNING...
BREAKFAST IS READY.
I'LL BRING IT OUT.
I'LL GO OUT AND FEED THE FISH.
SWIP
AH, SUNA–
I WANNA FEED THE FISH. ♡
ME TOO.
ME TOO.
OKAY THEN, HOW ABOUT IF YOU HAVE BREAKFAST OUTSIDE?
SOUNDS GOOD.
SHOCK
AH, IT LOOKS LIKE YOU'RE HAVING A LITTLE TROUBLE WITH YOUR KIMONO.
LET ME HELP YOU.
SUNAKO-CHAN, THAT'S JUST THE UNDERWEAR THAT GOES BENEATH THE KIMONO.
YOU DO LOOK PRETTY, HOT, AND SEXY THOUGH.
HOT? SEXY? NOI-CHAN....

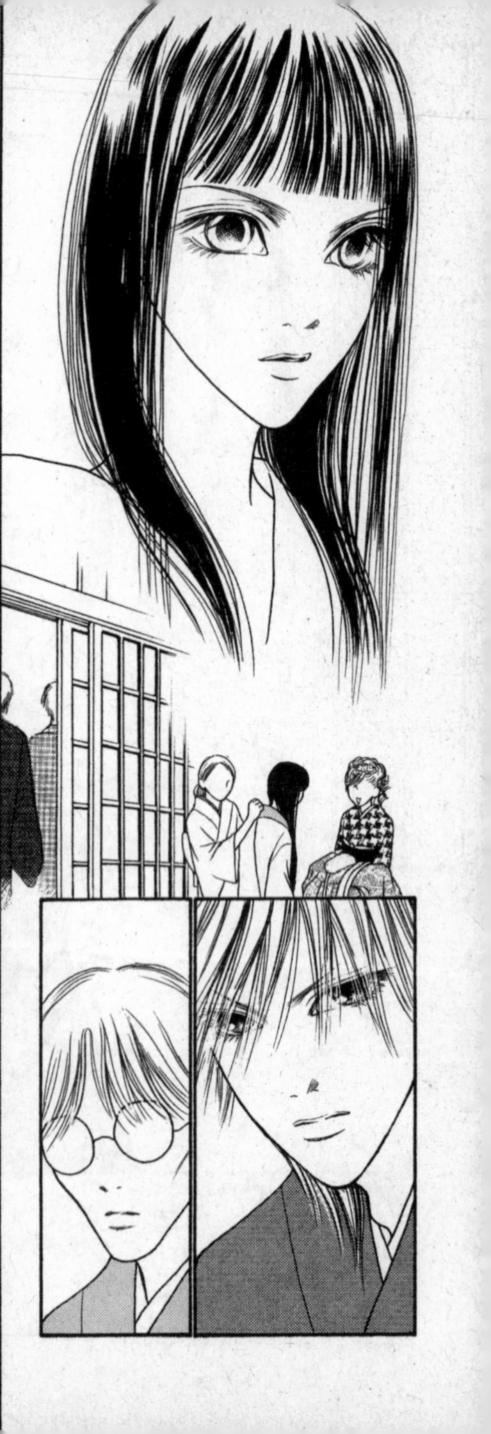

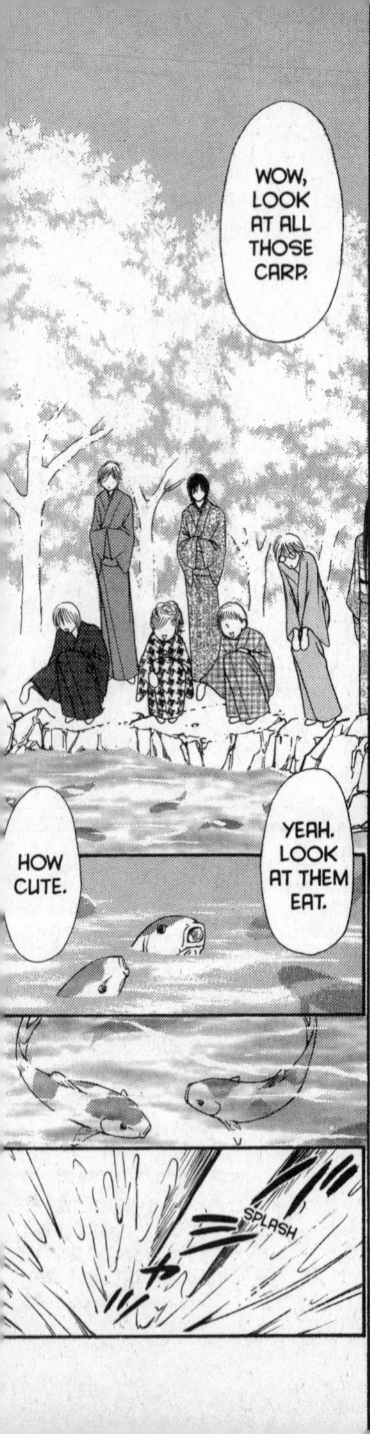

WOW, LOOK AT ALL THOSE CARP.
YEAH. LOOK AT THEM EAT.
HOW CUTE.
SPLASH

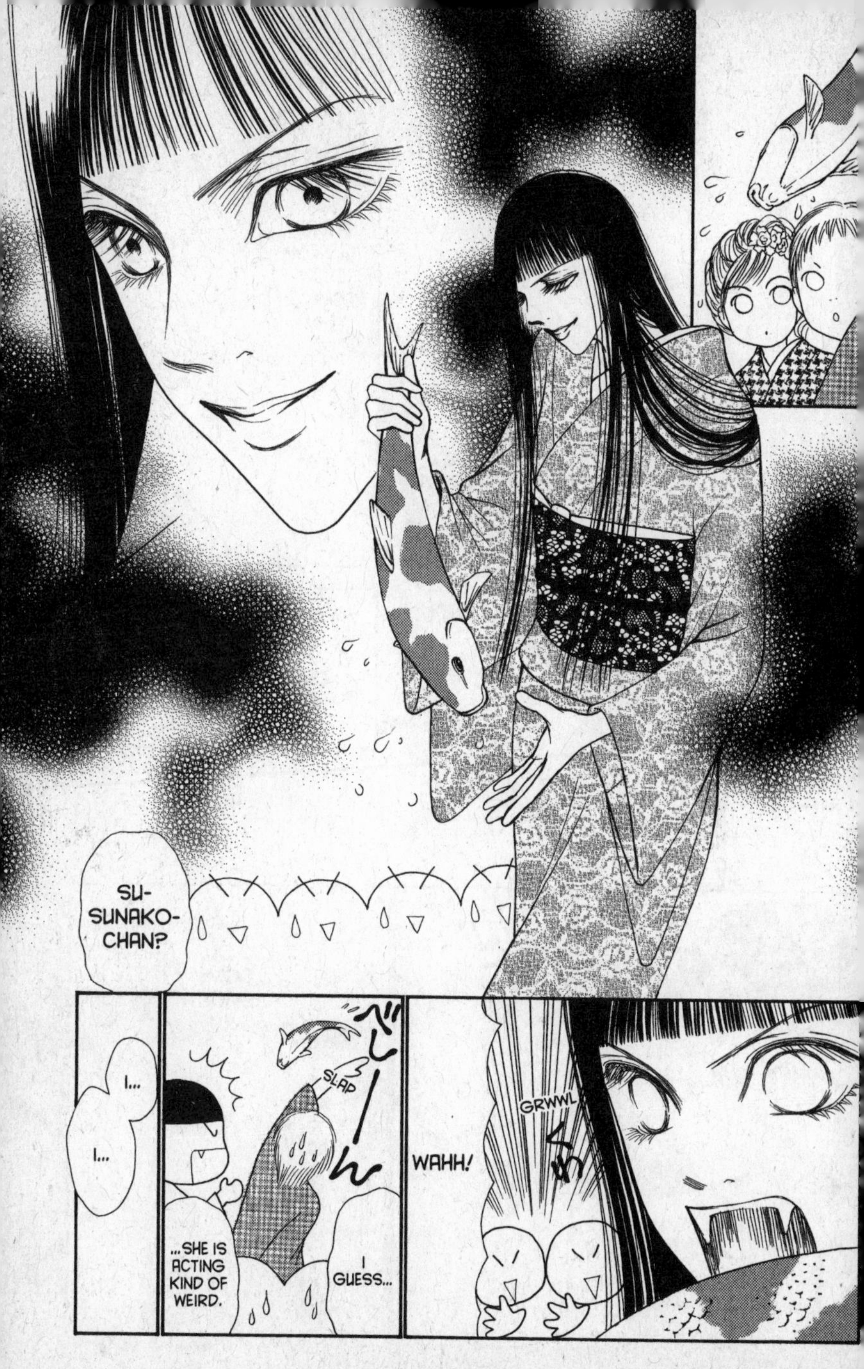
SU-SUNAKO-CHAN?
GRWWL
WAHH!
SLAP
I GUESS...
...SHE IS ACTING KIND OF WEIRD.
I...
I...

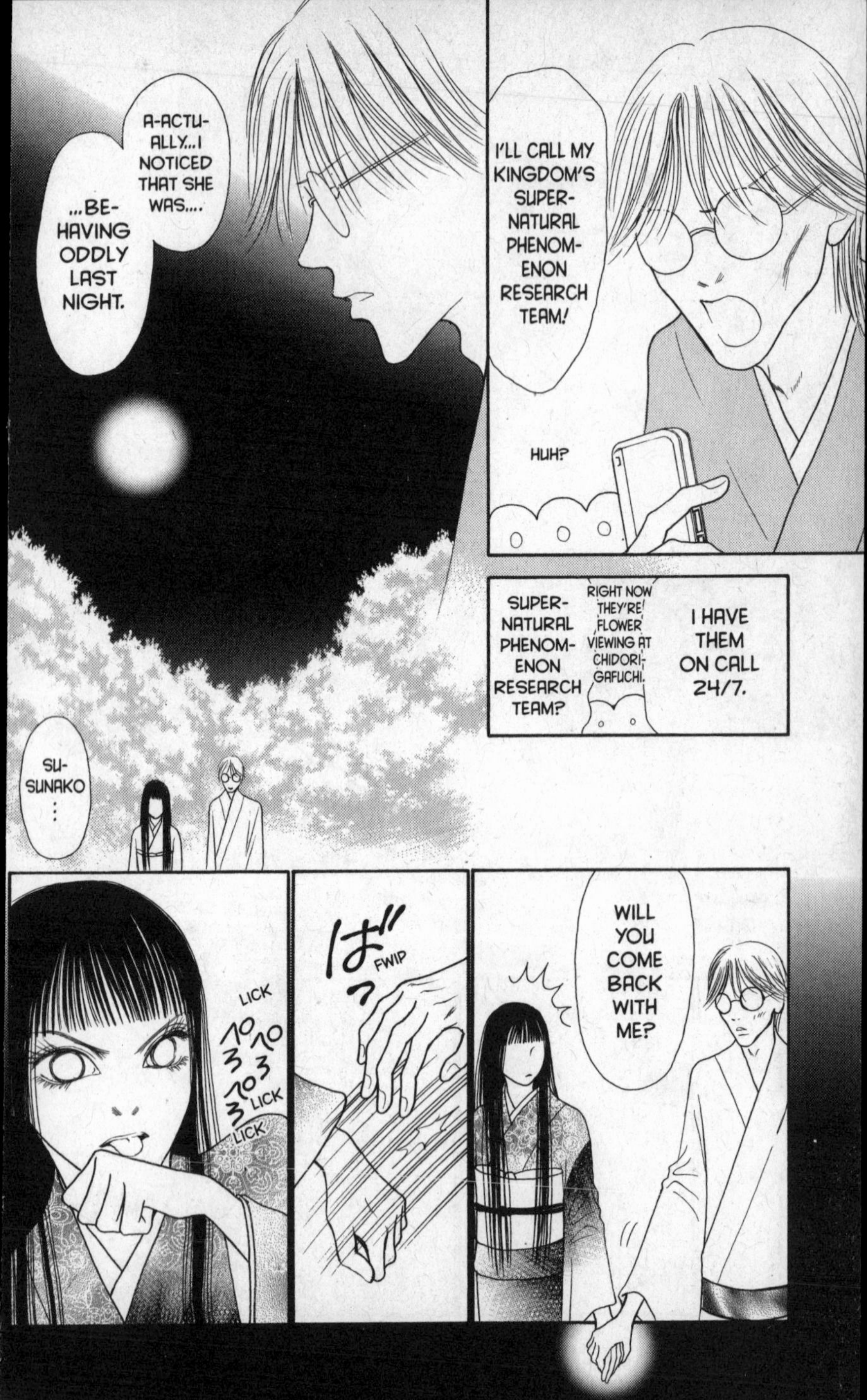
I'LL CALL MY KINGDOM'S SUPER-NATURAL PHENOM-ENON RESEARCH TEAM!
HUH?
I HAVE THEM ON CALL 24/7.
RIGHT NOW THEY'RE FLOWER VIEWING AT CHIDORI-GAFUCHI.
SUPER-NATURAL PHENOM-ENON RESEARCH TEAM?
A-ACTU-ALLY...I NOTICED THAT SHE WAS....
...BE-HAVING ODDLY LAST NIGHT.
SU-SUNAKO...
WILL YOU COME BACK WITH ME?
ぱっ
FWIP
LICK
ぺろぺろぺろ
LICK
LICK

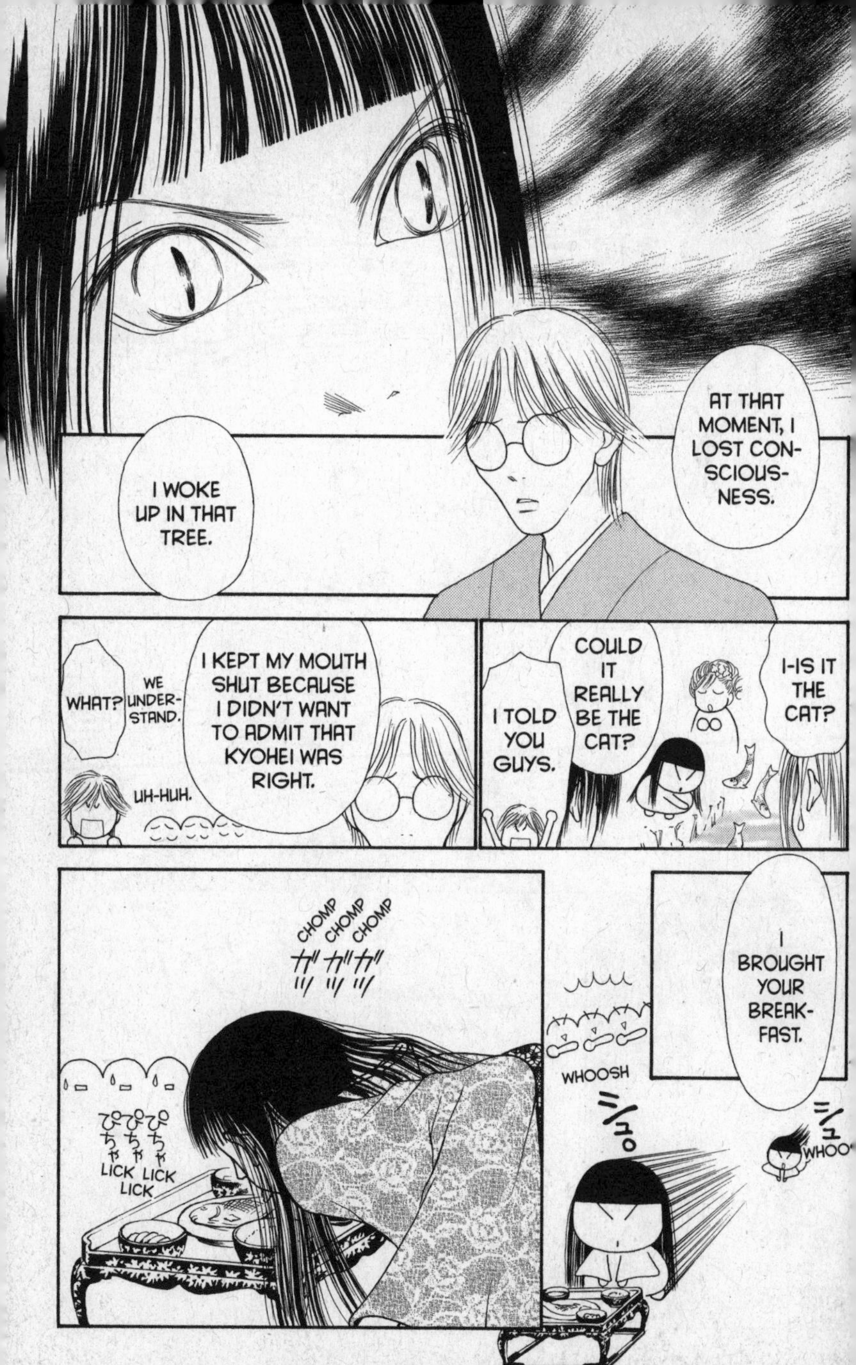
AT THAT MOMENT, I LOST CONSCIOUSNESS.
I WOKE UP IN THAT TREE.
I-IS IT THE CAT?
COULD IT REALLY BE THE CAT?
I TOLD YOU GUYS.
I KEPT MY MOUTH SHUT BECAUSE I DIDN'T WANT TO ADMIT THAT KYOHEI WAS RIGHT.
WE UNDERSTAND.
WHAT?
UH-HUH.
I BROUGHT YOUR BREAKFAST.
シュ
WHOO
シュッ
WHOOSH
ガツガツガツ
CHOMP CHOMP CHOMP
ぴちゃぴちゃぴちゃ
LICK LICK LICK

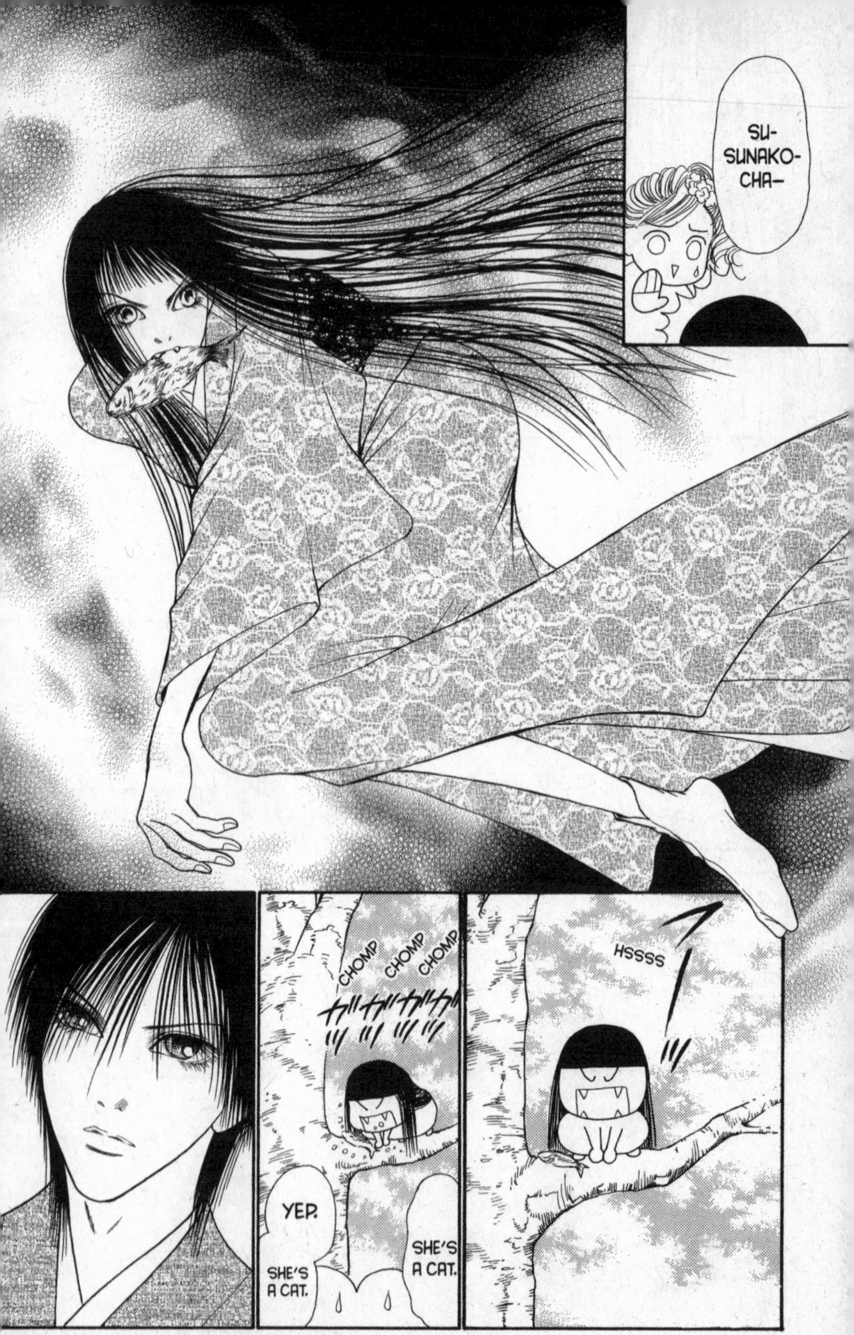
SU-SUNAKO-CHA-
HSSSS
CHOMP CHOMP CHOMP
SHE'S A CAT.
YEP.
SHE'S A CAT.

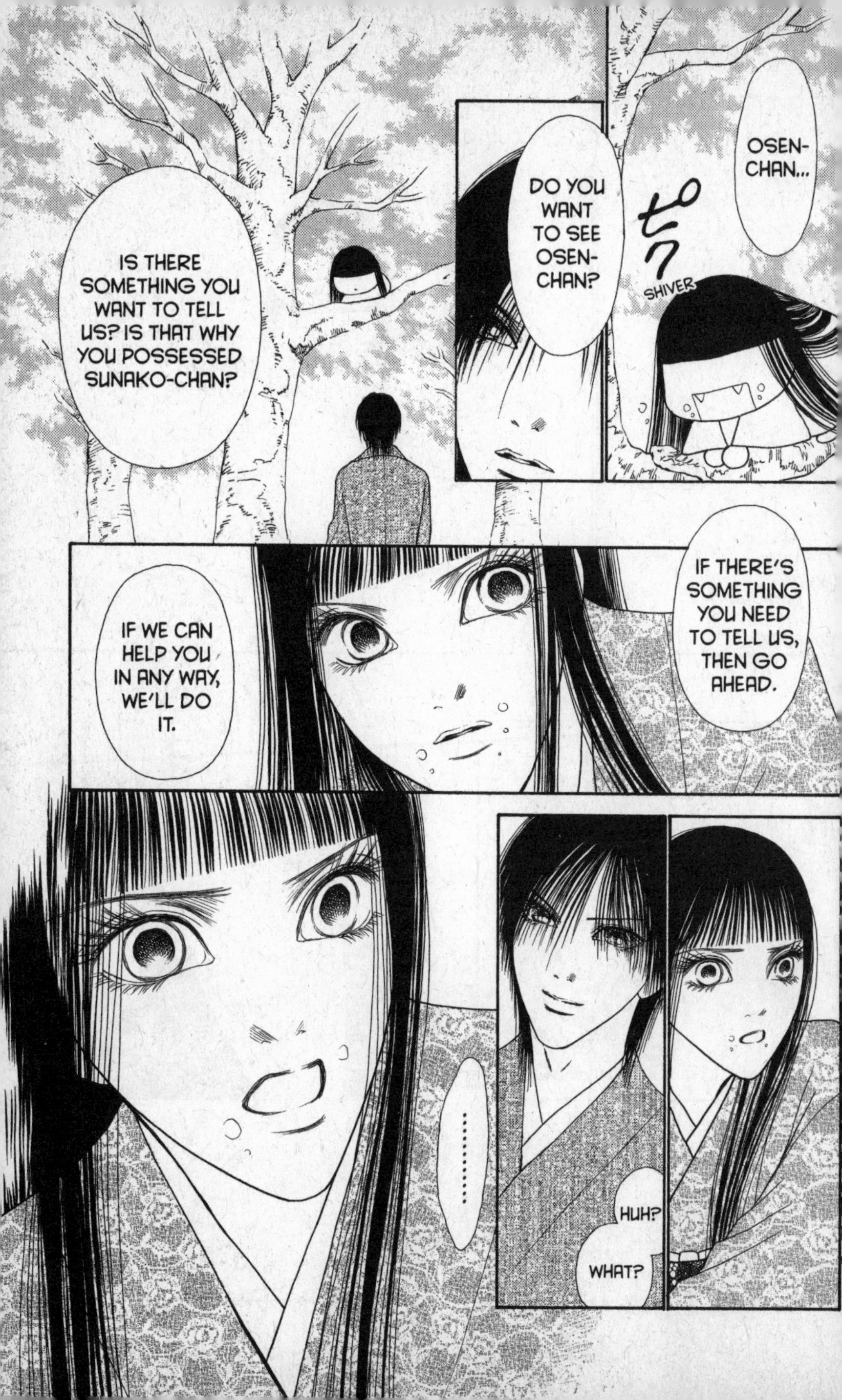

OSEN-CHAN...
SHIVER
DO YOU WANT TO SEE OSEN-CHAN?
IS THERE SOMETHING YOU WANT TO TELL US? IS THAT WHY YOU POSSESSED SUNAKO-CHAN?
IF THERE'S SOMETHING YOU NEED TO TELL US, THEN GO AHEAD.
IF WE CAN HELP YOU IN ANY WAY, WE'LL DO IT.
HUH?
WHAT?
......

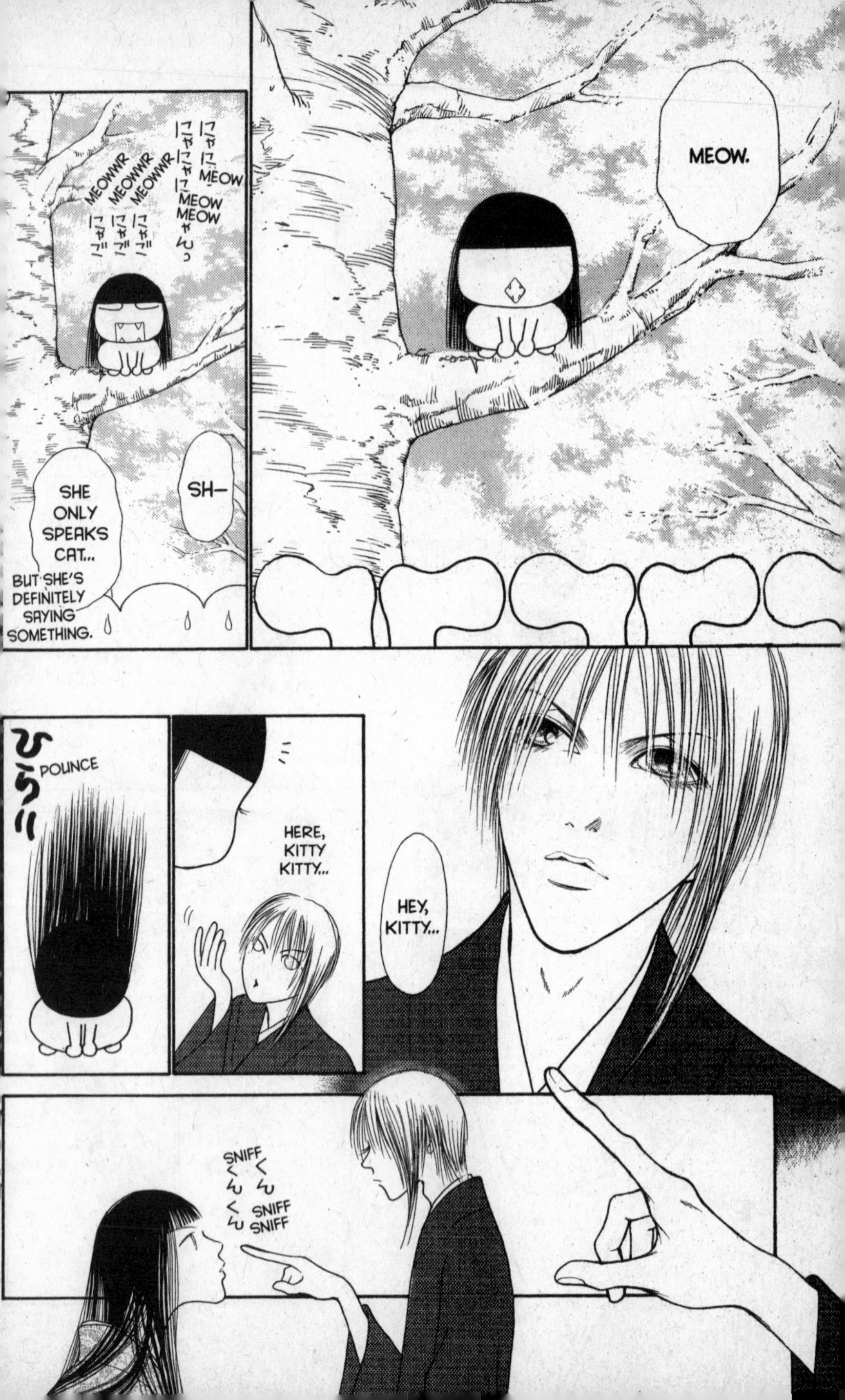
MEOW.
MEOW
MEOW MEOW
MEOWWR MEOWWR MEOWWR
SH—
SHE ONLY SPEAKS CAT...
BUT SHE'S DEFINITELY SAYING SOMETHING.
HEY, KITTY...
HERE, KITTY KITTY...
POUNCE
SNIFF
SNIFF SNIFF

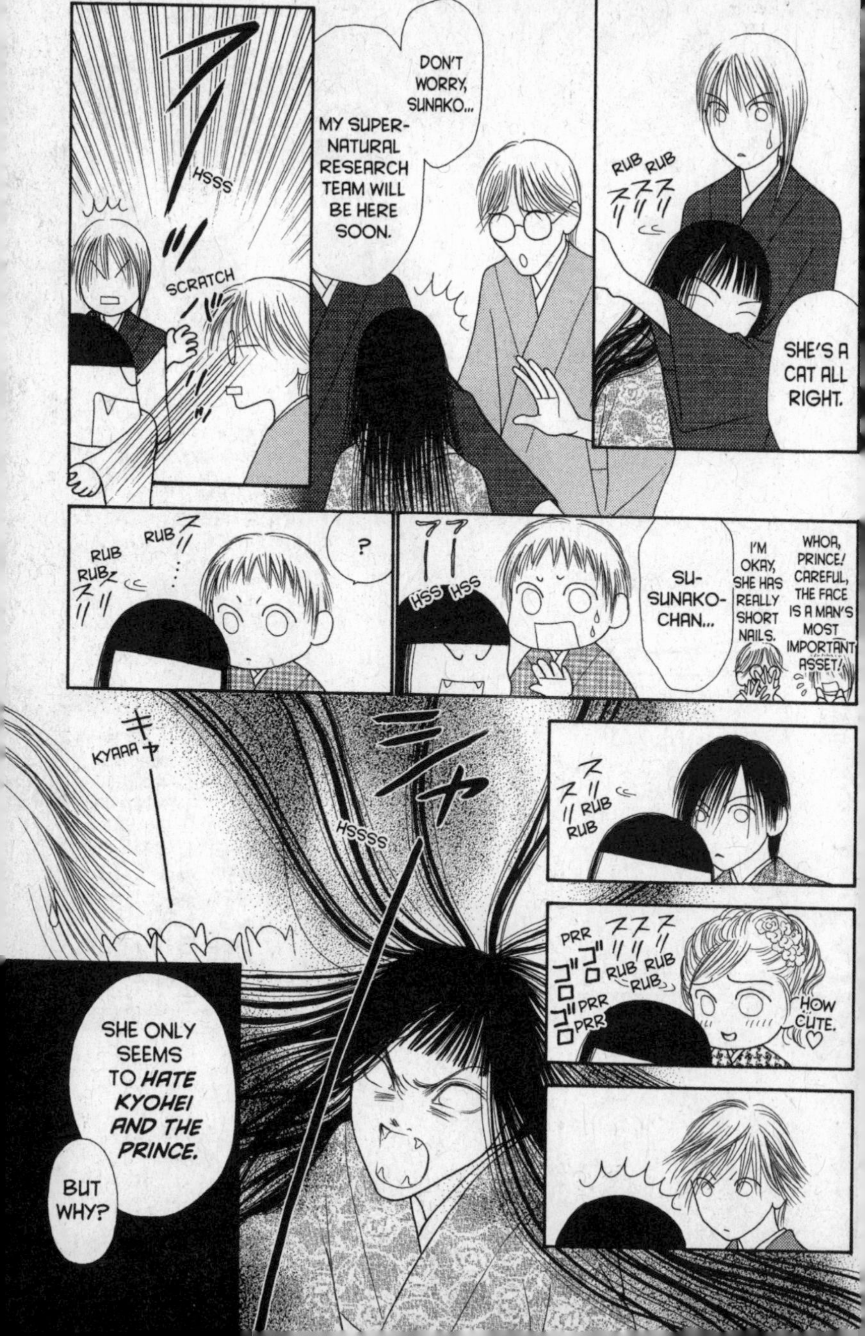
RUB RUB
SHE'S A CAT ALL RIGHT.
DON'T WORRY, SUNAKO...
MY SUPER-NATURAL RESEARCH TEAM WILL BE HERE SOON.
HSSS
SCRATCH
HSS HSS
SU-SUNAKO-CHAN...
WHOA, PRINCE! CAREFUL, THE FACE IS A MAN'S MOST IMPORTANT ASSET!
I'M OKAY, SHE HAS REALLY SHORT NAILS.
RUB RUB RUB
?
RUB RUB
PRR PRR PRR RUB RUB RUB
HOW CUTE.
KYAAA
HSSSS
SHE ONLY SEEMS TO *HATE KYOHEI AND THE PRINCE.*
BUT WHY?

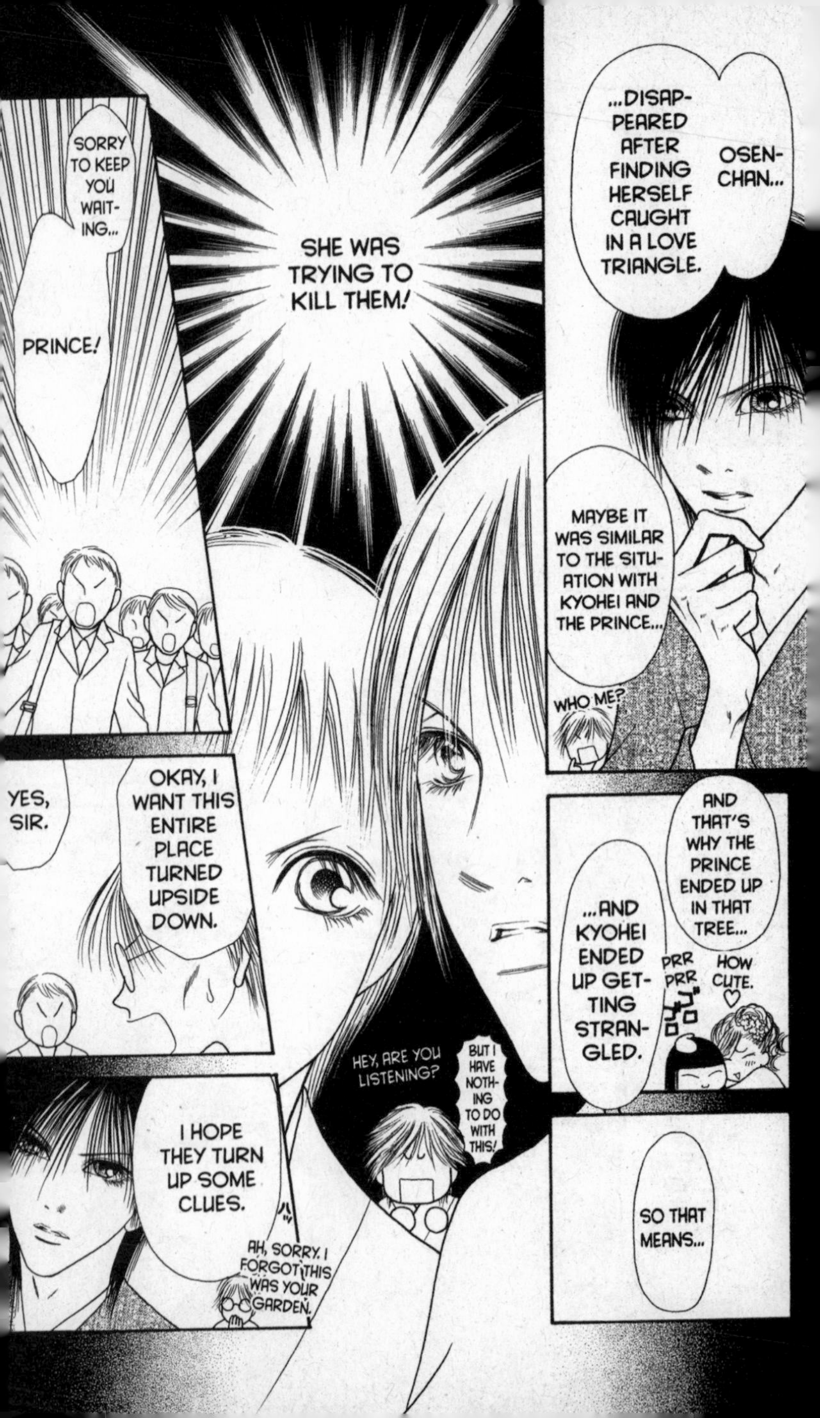

OSEN-CHAN...
...DISAPPEARED AFTER FINDING HERSELF CAUGHT IN A LOVE TRIANGLE.
MAYBE IT WAS SIMILAR TO THE SITUATION WITH KYOHEI AND THE PRINCE...
WHO ME?
AND THAT'S WHY THE PRINCE ENDED UP IN THAT TREE...
...AND KYOHEI ENDED UP GETTING STRANGLED.
HOW CUTE.
PRR PRR
SO THAT MEANS...
BUT I HAVE NOTHING TO DO WITH THIS!
HEY, ARE YOU LISTENING?
SHE WAS TRYING TO KILL THEM!
SORRY TO KEEP YOU WAITING...
PRINCE!
OKAY, I WANT THIS ENTIRE PLACE TURNED UPSIDE DOWN.
YES, SIR.
I HOPE THEY TURN UP SOME CLUES.
AH, SORRY. I FORGOT THIS WAS YOUR GARDEN.

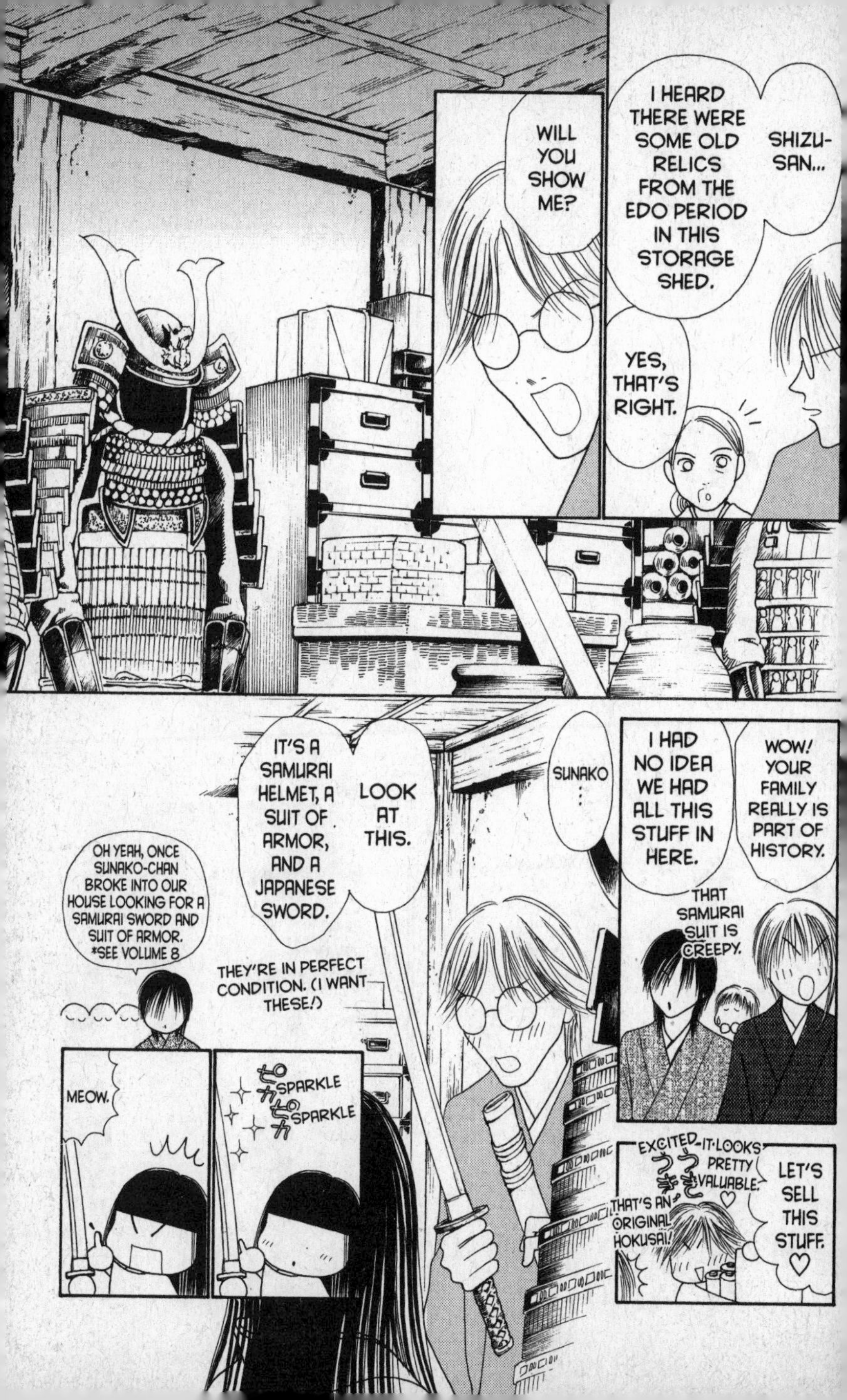

SHIZU-SAN...
I HEARD THERE WERE SOME OLD RELICS FROM THE EDO PERIOD IN THIS STORAGE SHED.
YES, THAT'S RIGHT.
WILL YOU SHOW ME?
WOW! YOUR FAMILY REALLY IS PART OF HISTORY.
I HAD NO IDEA WE HAD ALL THIS STUFF IN HERE.
THAT SAMURAI SUIT IS CREEPY.
SUNAKO...
LOOK AT THIS.
IT'S A SAMURAI HELMET, A SUIT OF ARMOR, AND A JAPANESE SWORD.
THEY'RE IN PERFECT CONDITION. (I WANT THESE!)
OH YEAH, ONCE SUNAKO-CHAN BROKE INTO OUR HOUSE LOOKING FOR A SAMURAI SWORD AND SUIT OF ARMOR. *SEE VOLUME 8
LET'S SELL THIS STUFF. ♡
IT LOOKS PRETTY VALUABLE. ♡
EXCITED
THAT'S AN ORIGINAL HOKUSAI!
SPARKLE SPARKLE
MEOW.

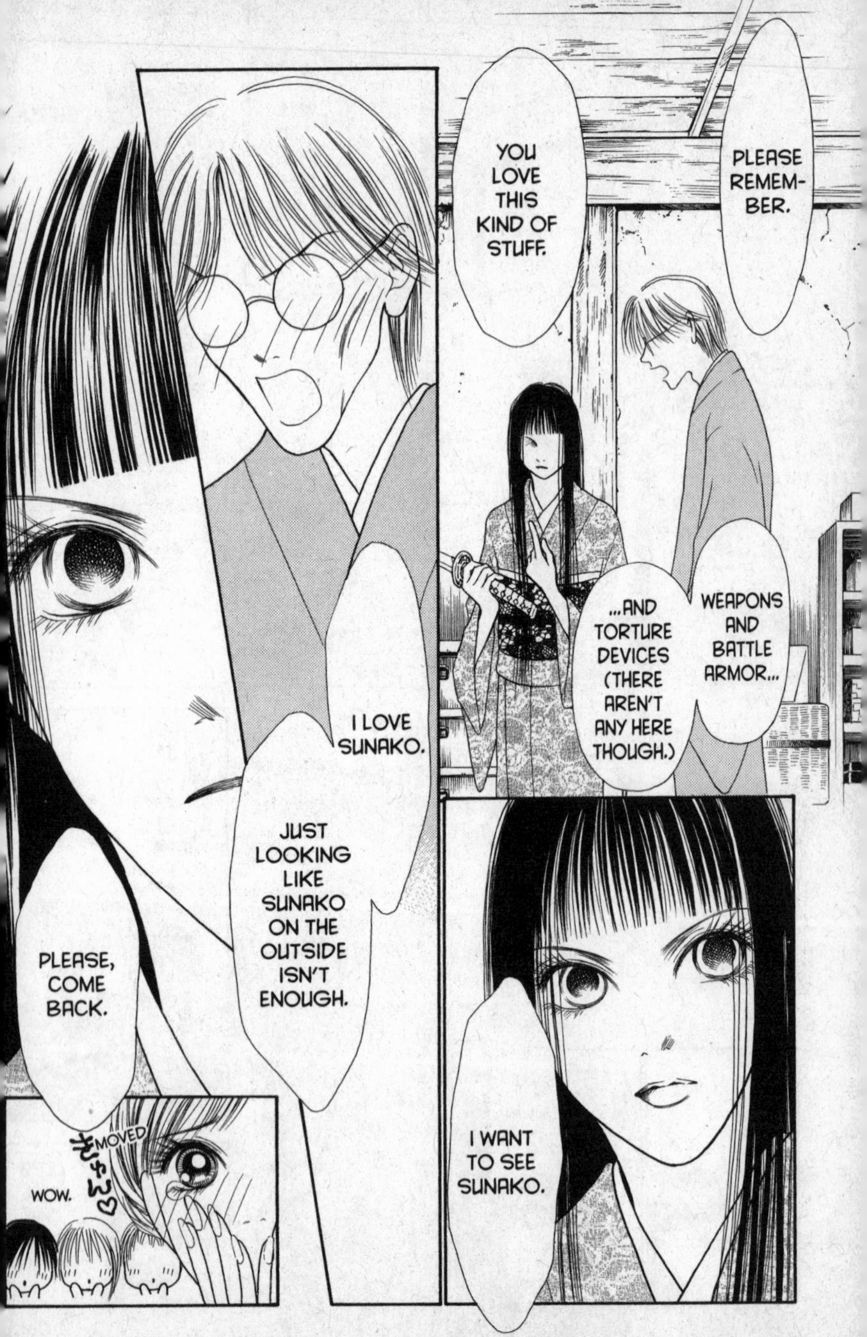
PLEASE REMEMBER.
YOU LOVE THIS KIND OF STUFF.
WEAPONS AND BATTLE ARMOR...
...AND TORTURE DEVICES (THERE AREN'T ANY HERE THOUGH.)
I LOVE SUNAKO.
JUST LOOKING LIKE SUNAKO ON THE OUTSIDE ISN'T ENOUGH.
I WANT TO SEE SUNAKO.
PLEASE, COME BACK.
MOVED
WOW.

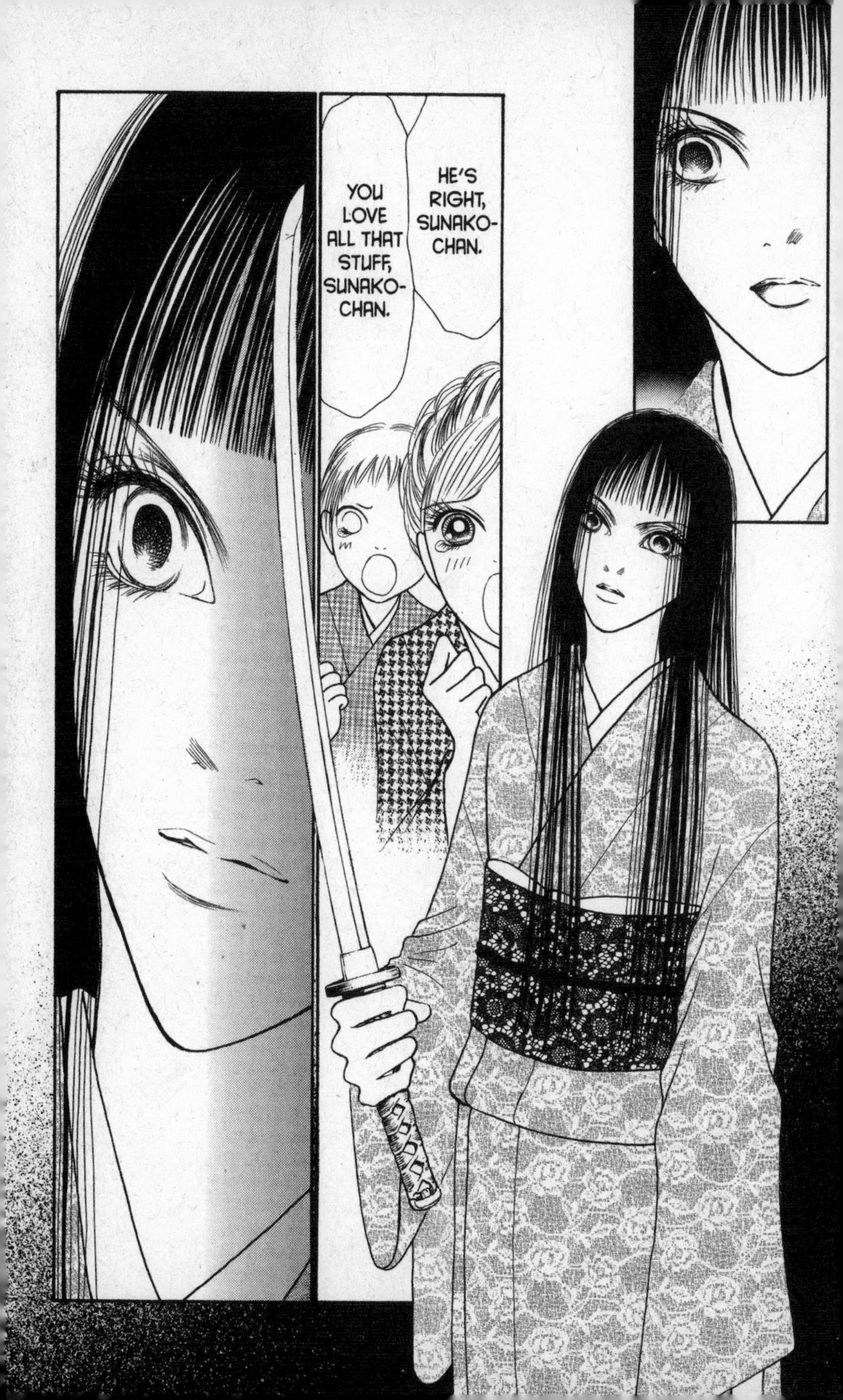
HE'S RIGHT, SUNAKO-CHAN.
YOU LOVE ALL THAT STUFF, SUNAKO-CHAN.

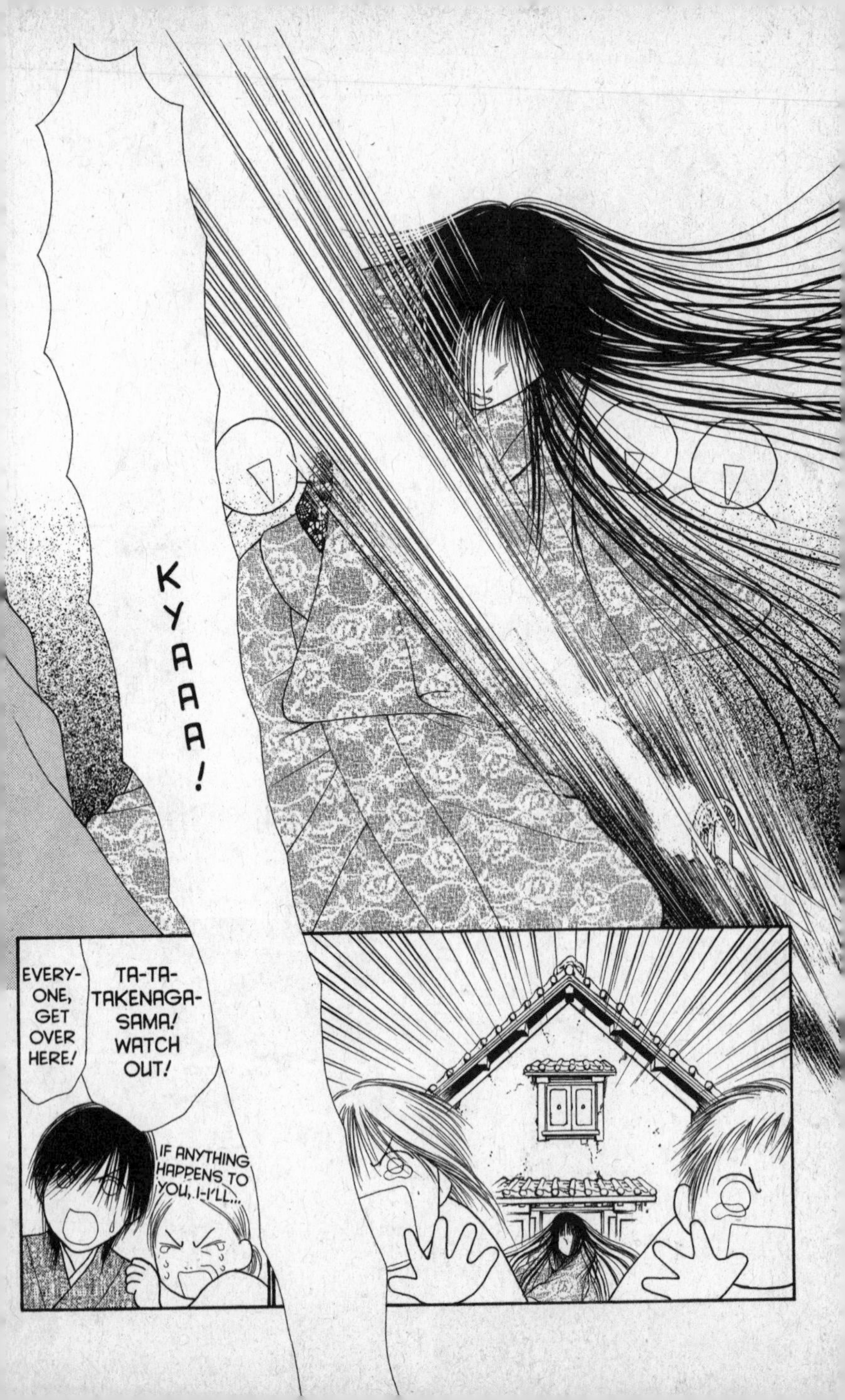
KYAAA!
TA-TA-TAKENAGA-SAMA! WATCH OUT!
EVERYONE, GET OVER HERE!
IF ANYTHING HAPPENS TO YOU, I-I'LL...

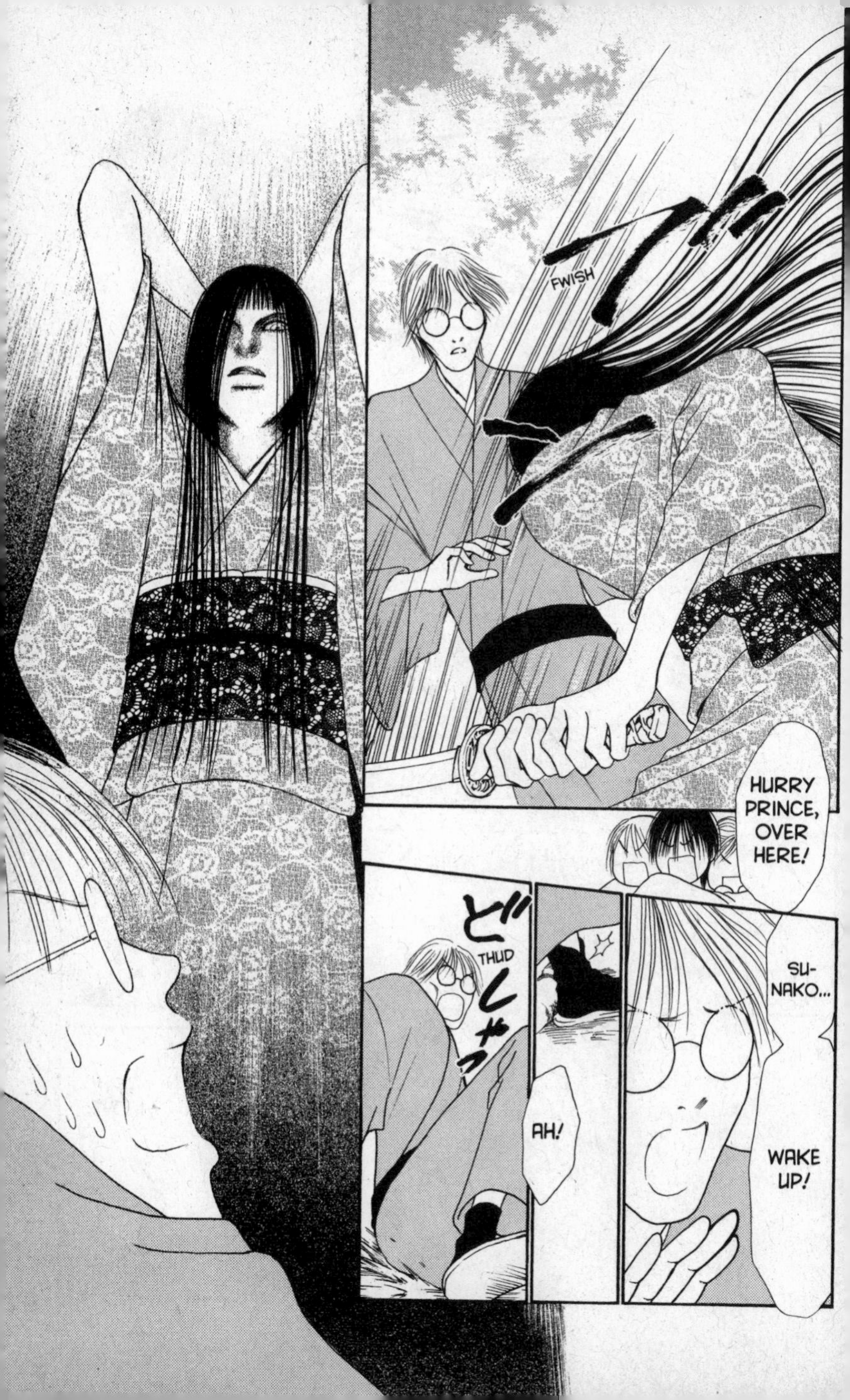
FWISH
HURRY PRINCE, OVER HERE!
SU-NAKO...
WAKE UP!
AH!
どしゃっ
THUD

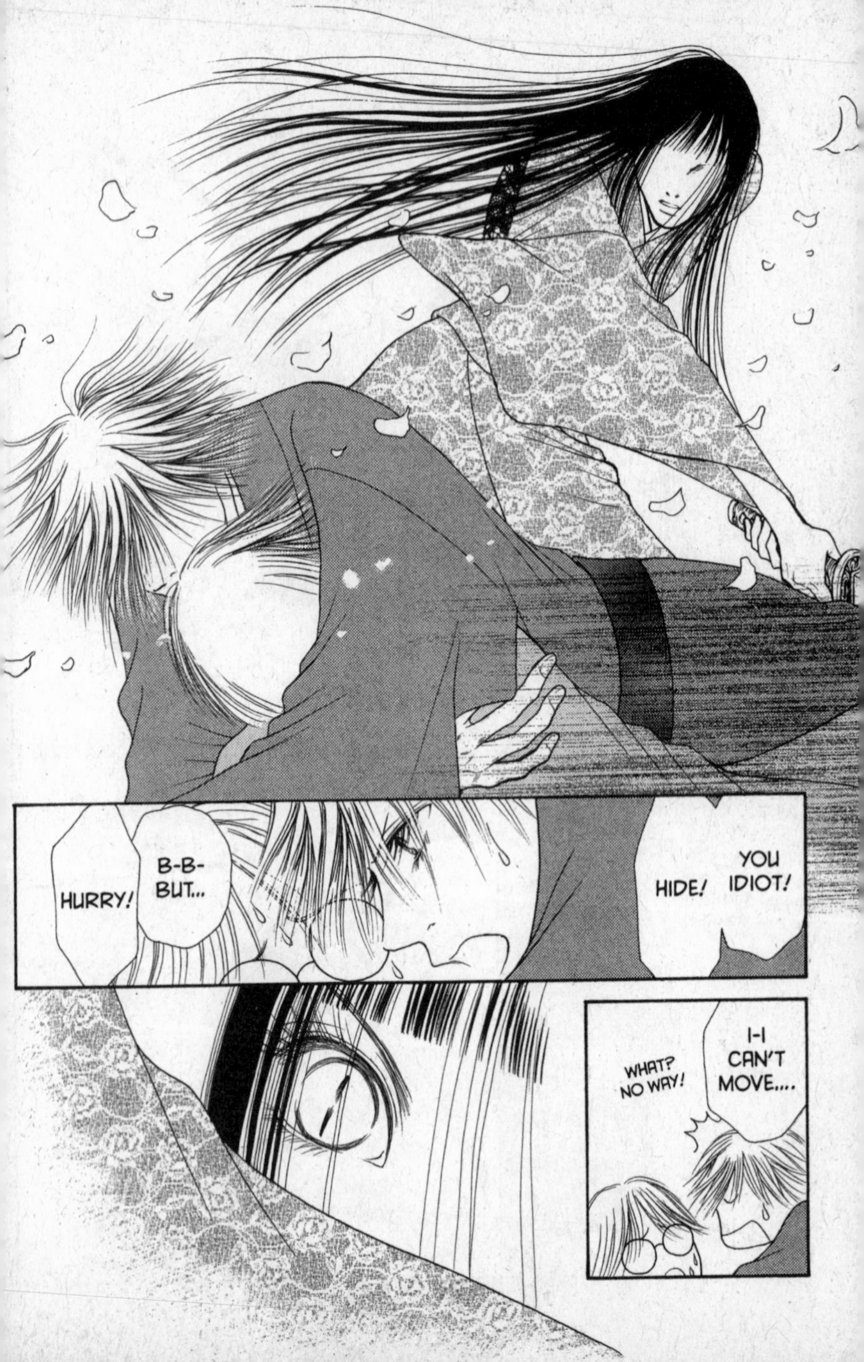
YOU IDIOT!
HIDE!
B-B-BUT...
HURRY!
I-I CAN'T MOVE....
WHAT? NO WAY!

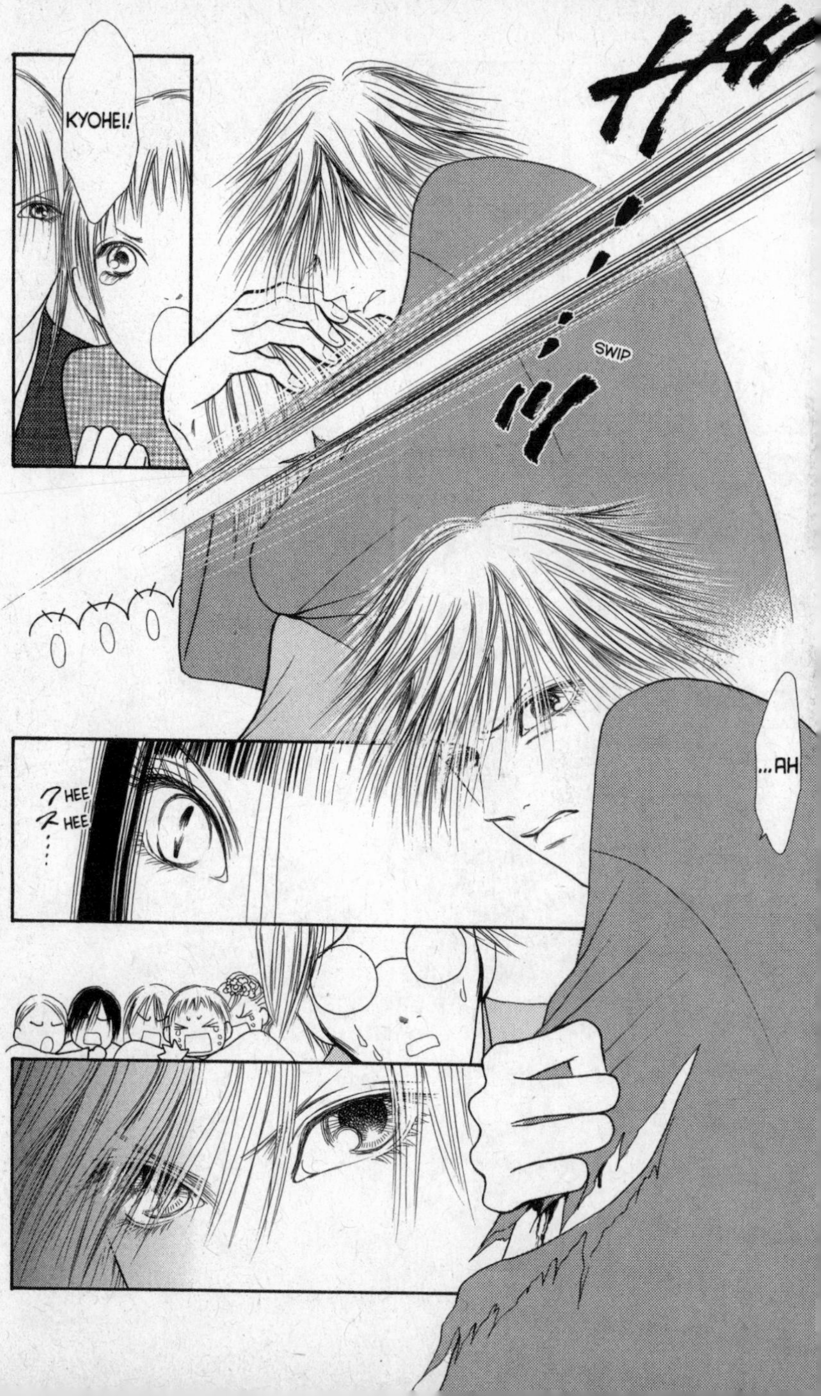

SWIP
KYOHEI!
...AH
HEE HEE

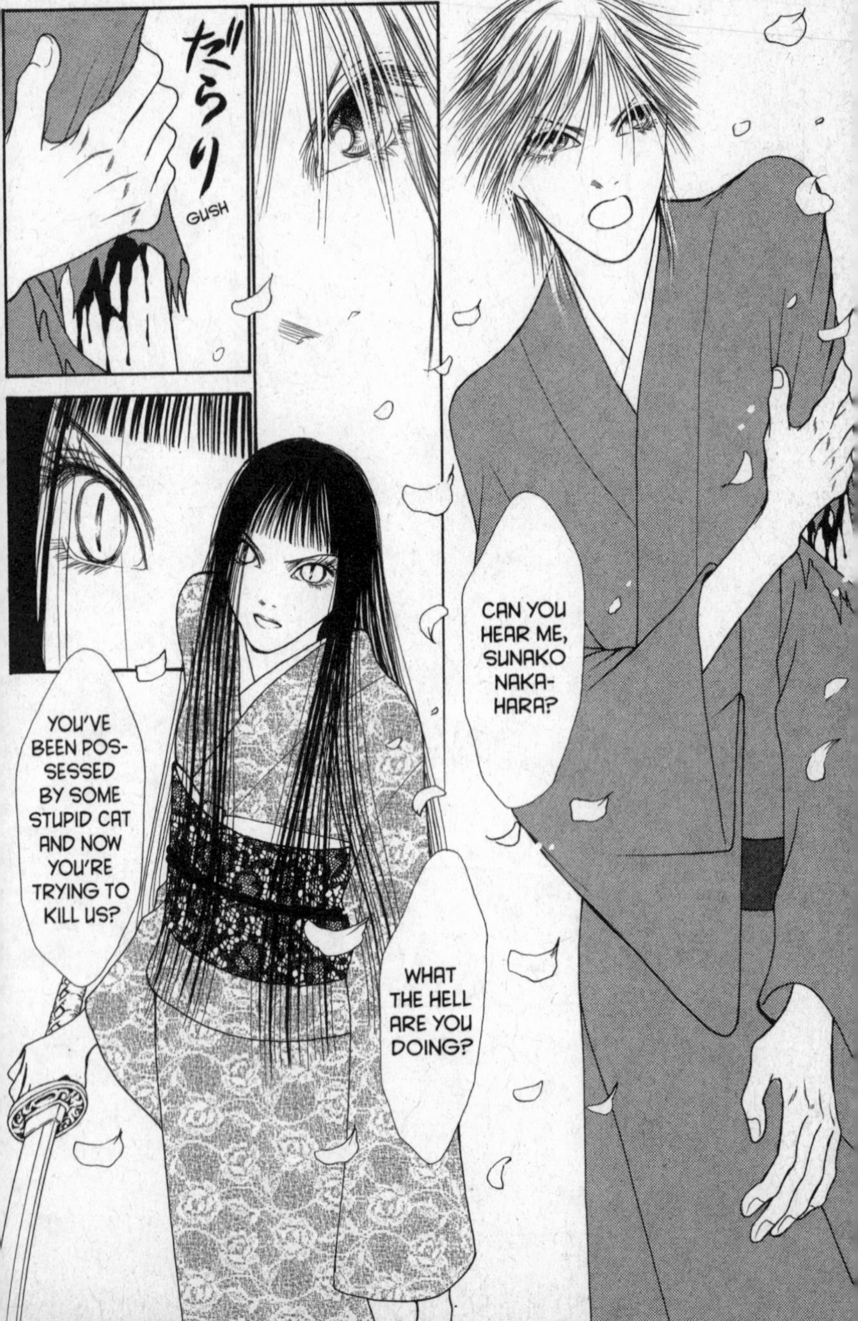
だらり
GUSH
CAN YOU HEAR ME, SUNAKO NAKA-HARA?
YOU'VE BEEN POS-SESSED BY SOME STUPID CAT AND NOW YOU'RE TRYING TO KILL US?
WHAT THE HELL ARE YOU DOING?

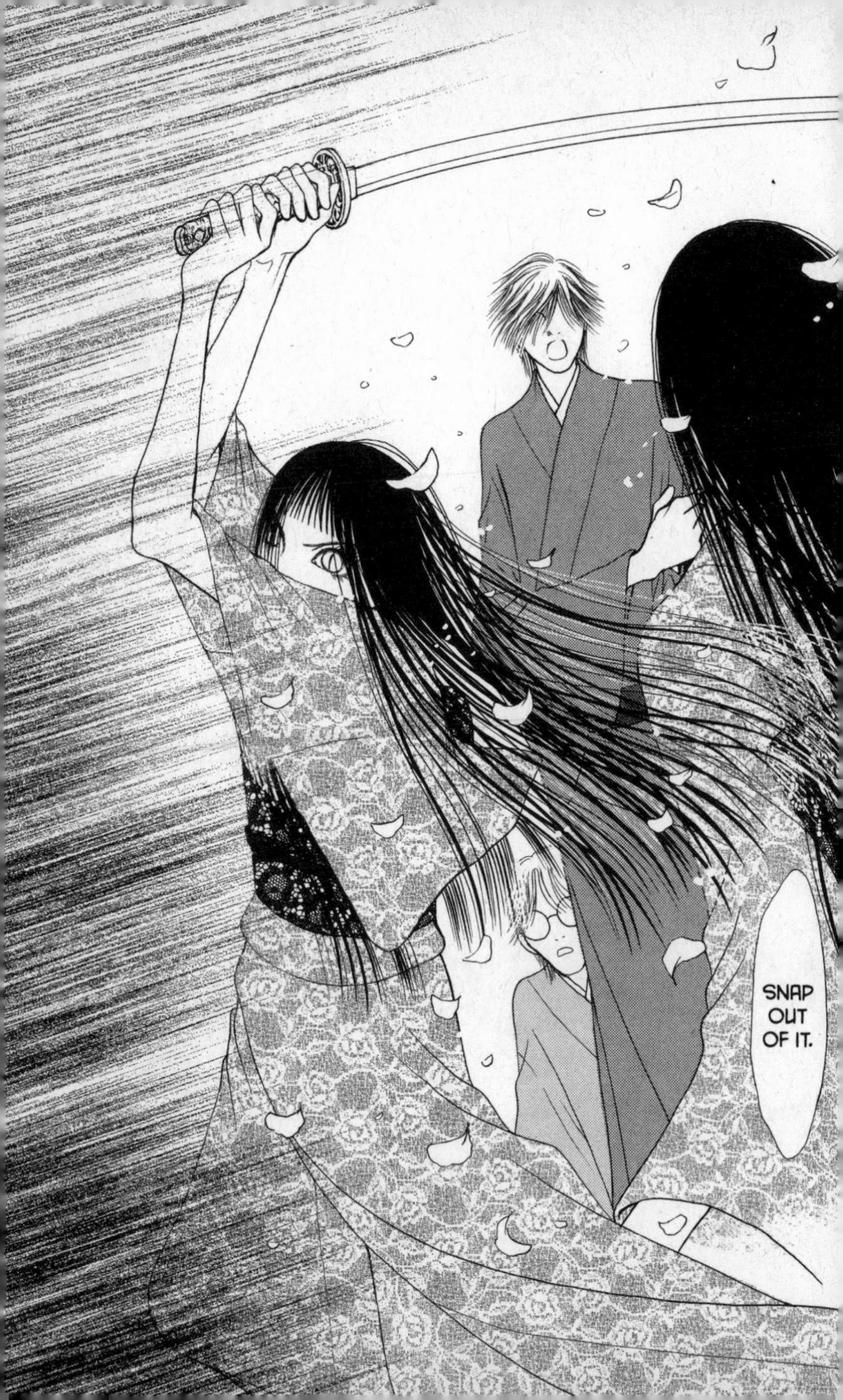
SNAP OUT OF IT.

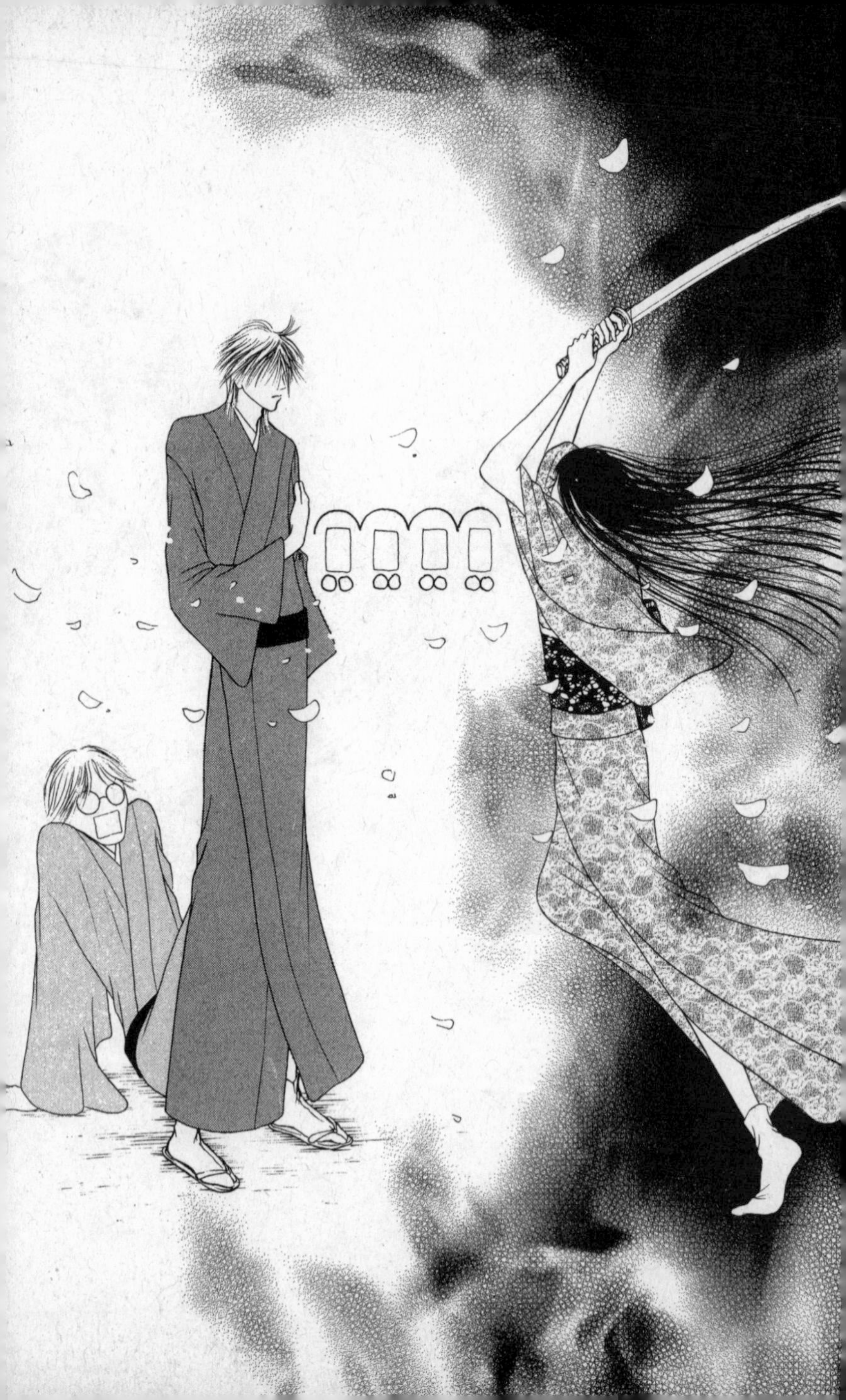

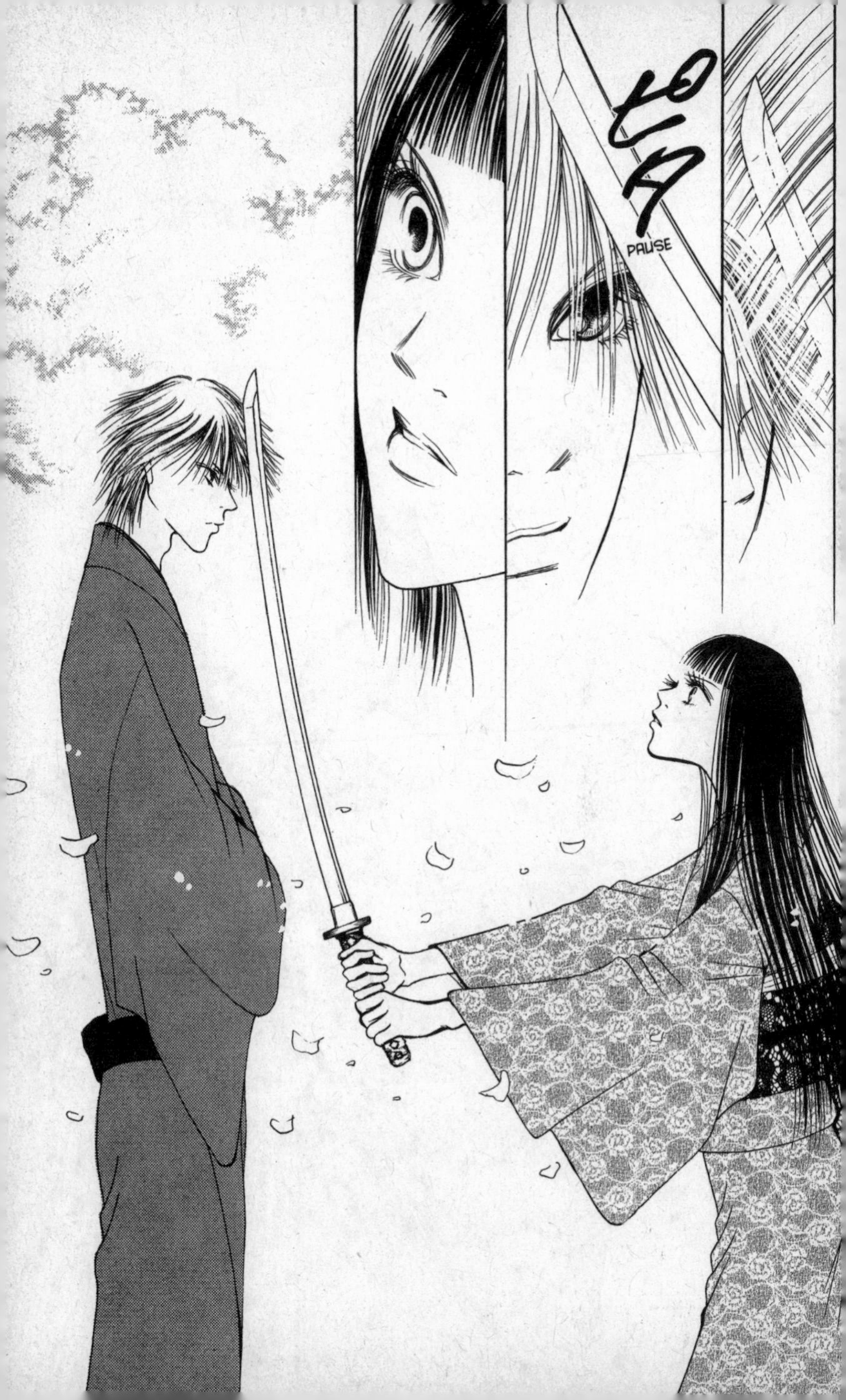
ピタ
PAUSE

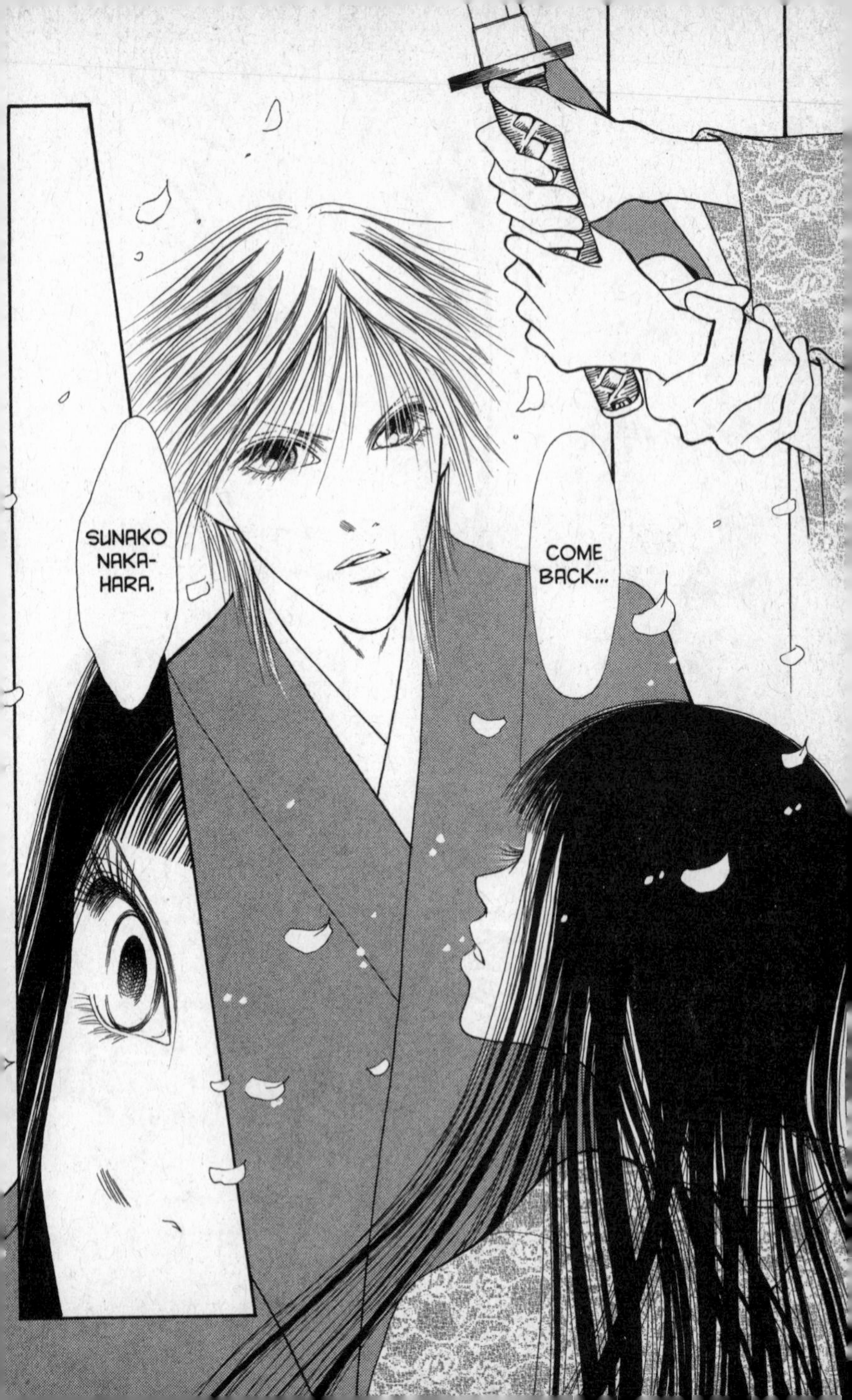
COME BACK...
SUNAKO NAKA-HARA.

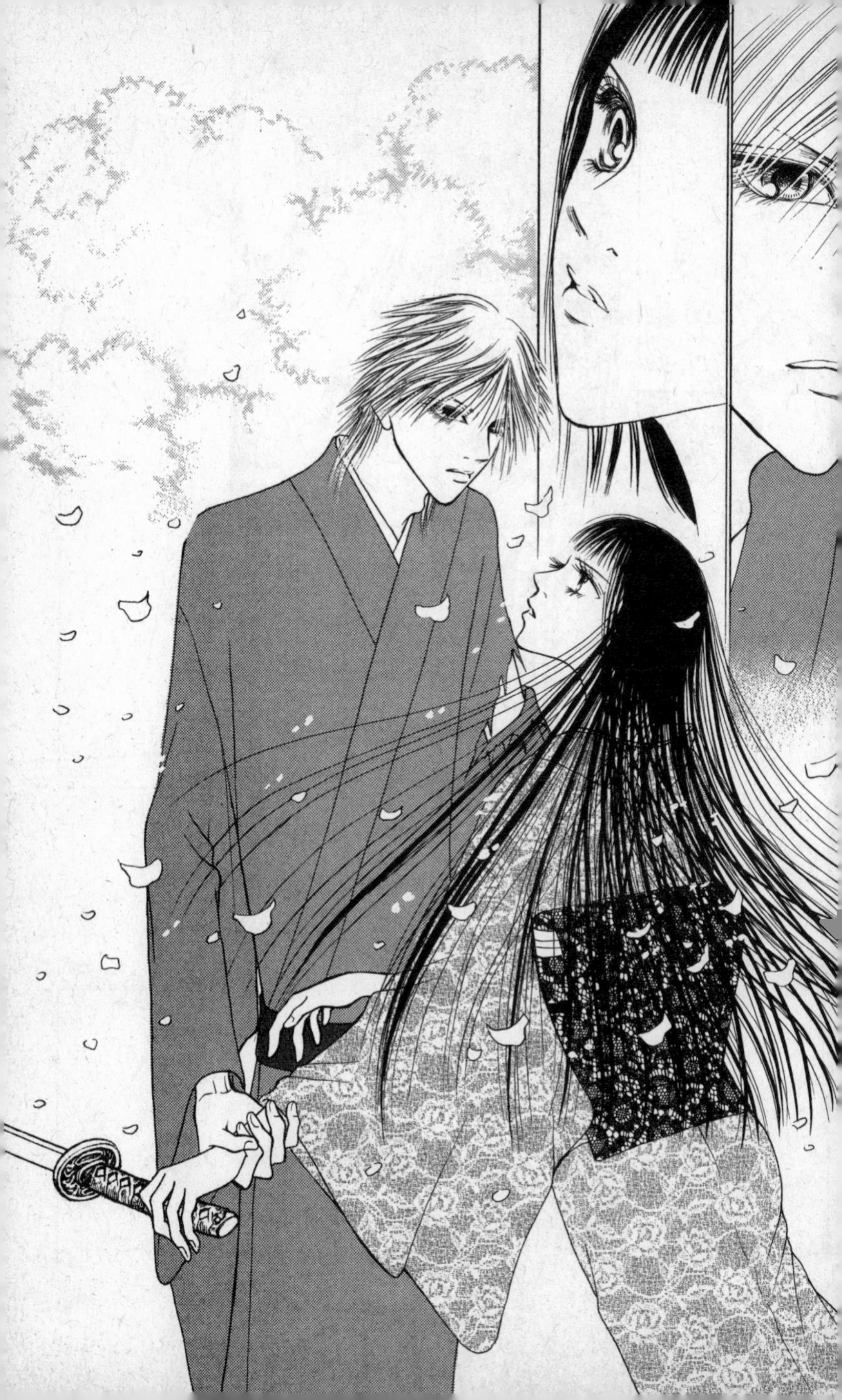

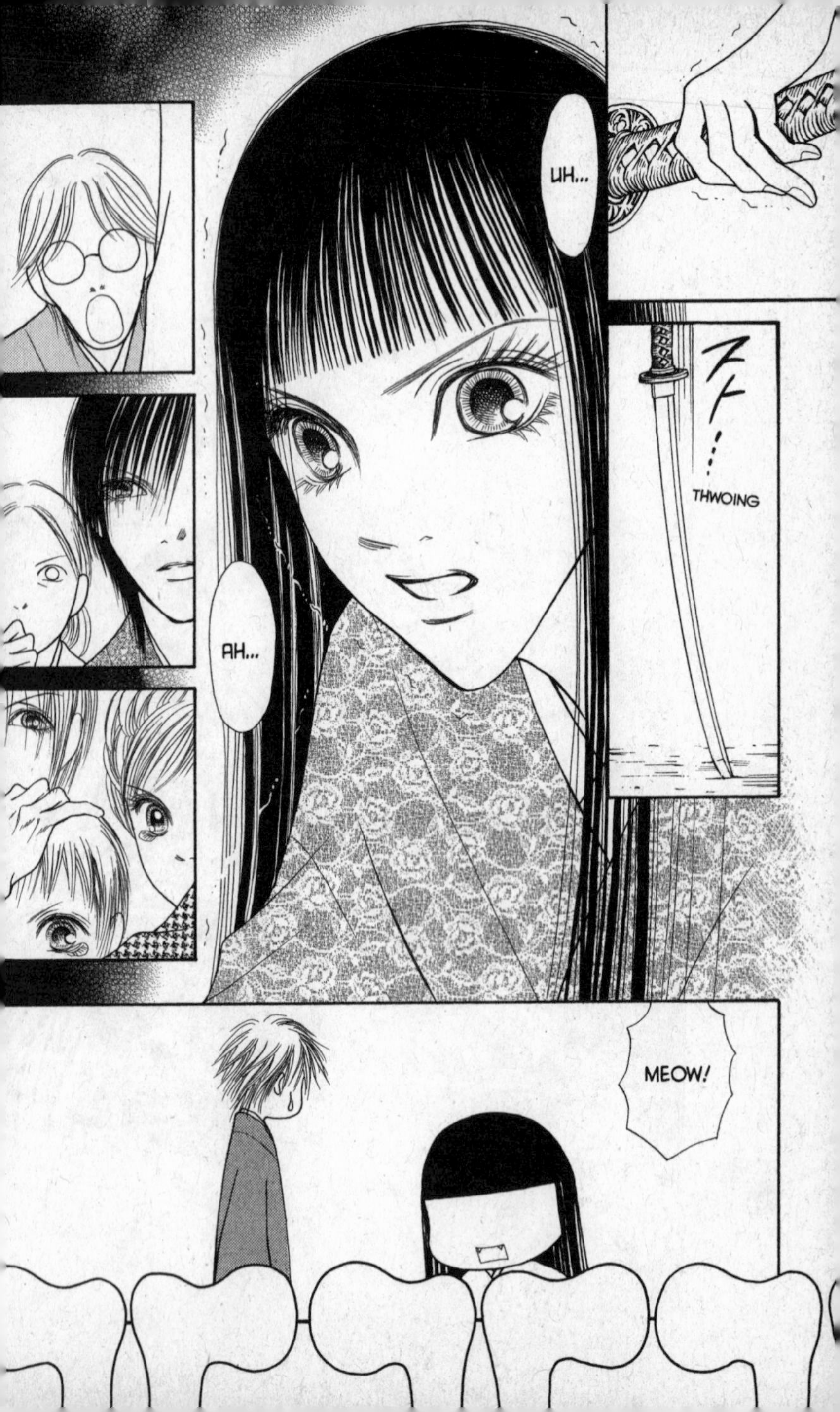
THWOING
UH...
AH...
MEOW!

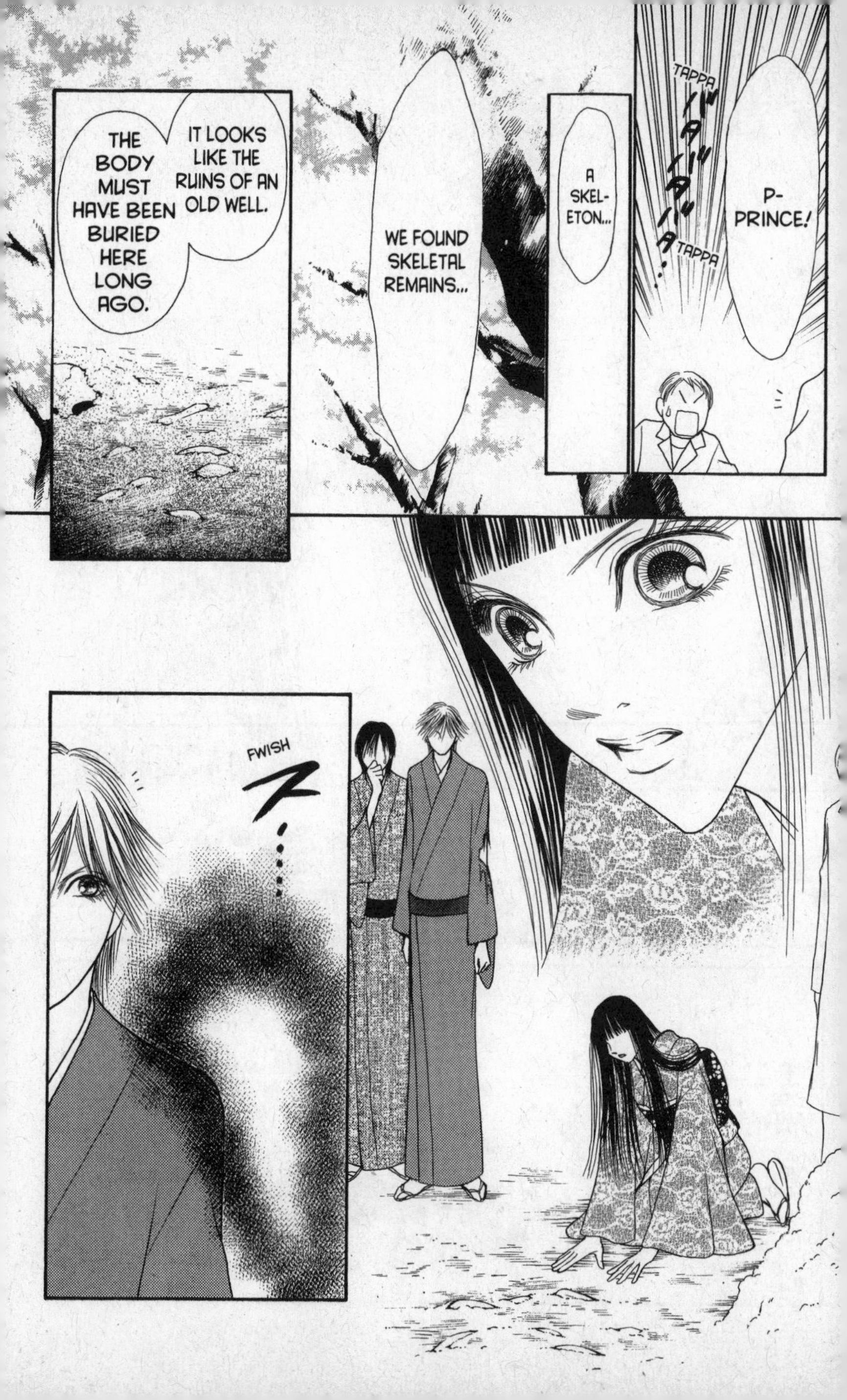
TAPPA
P-PRINCE!
TAPPA
A SKEL-ETON...
WE FOUND SKELETAL REMAINS...
IT LOOKS LIKE THE RUINS OF AN OLD WELL.
THE BODY MUST HAVE BEEN BURIED HERE LONG AGO.
FWISH

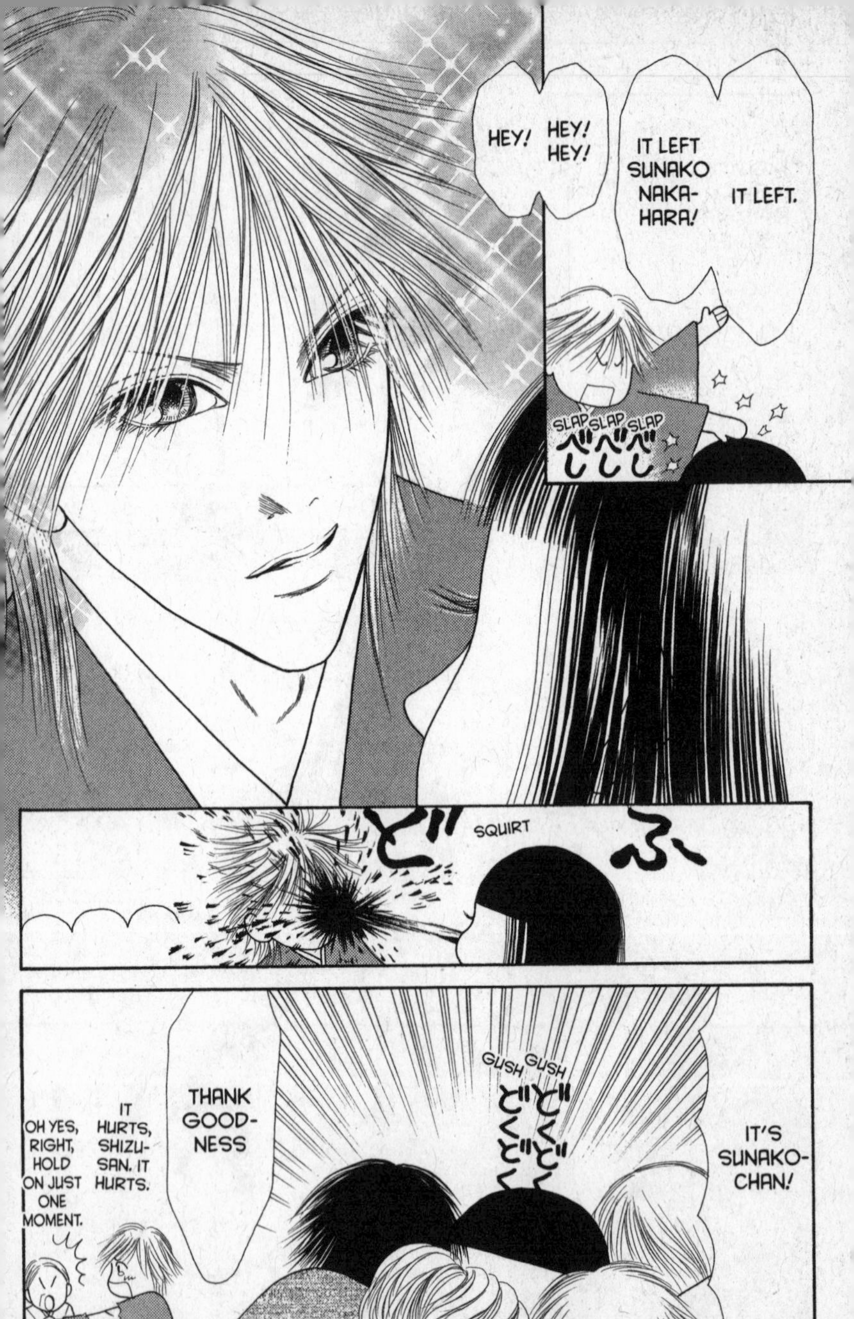
IT LEFT.
IT LEFT SUNAKO NAKA-HARA!
HEY! HEY!
HEY!
SLAP SLAP SLAP
べしべしべし
ふ
SQUIRT
ど
IT'S SUNAKO-CHAN!
GUSH GUSH
どくどく
THANK GOOD-NESS
IT HURTS, SHIZU-SAN. IT HURTS.
OH YES, RIGHT, HOLD ON JUST ONE MOMENT.

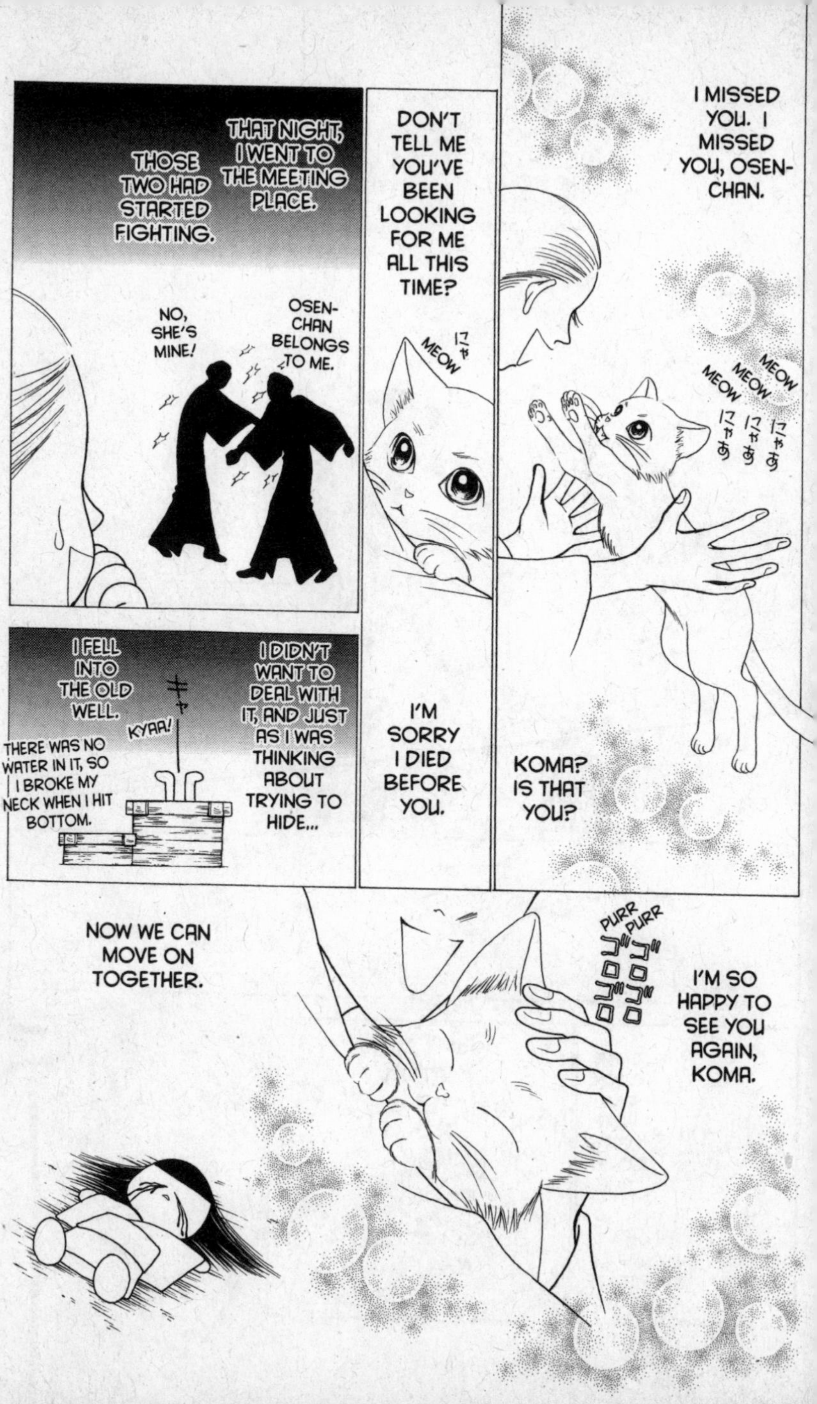
I MISSED YOU. I MISSED YOU, OSEN-CHAN.
MEOW MEOW MEOW
にゃあ にゃあ にゃあ
KOMA? IS THAT YOU?
DON'T TELL ME YOU'VE BEEN LOOKING FOR ME ALL THIS TIME?
MEOW
にゃ
I'M SORRY I DIED BEFORE YOU.
THAT NIGHT, I WENT TO THE MEETING PLACE.
THOSE TWO HAD STARTED FIGHTING.
OSEN-CHAN BELONGS TO ME.
NO, SHE'S MINE!
I DIDN'T WANT TO DEAL WITH IT, AND JUST AS I WAS THINKING ABOUT TRYING TO HIDE...
KYAA!
キャ
I FELL INTO THE OLD WELL.
THERE WAS NO WATER IN IT, SO I BROKE MY NECK WHEN I HIT BOTTOM.
I'M SO HAPPY TO SEE YOU AGAIN, KOMA.
PURR PURR
ゴロゴロ ゴロゴロ
NOW WE CAN MOVE ON TOGETHER.

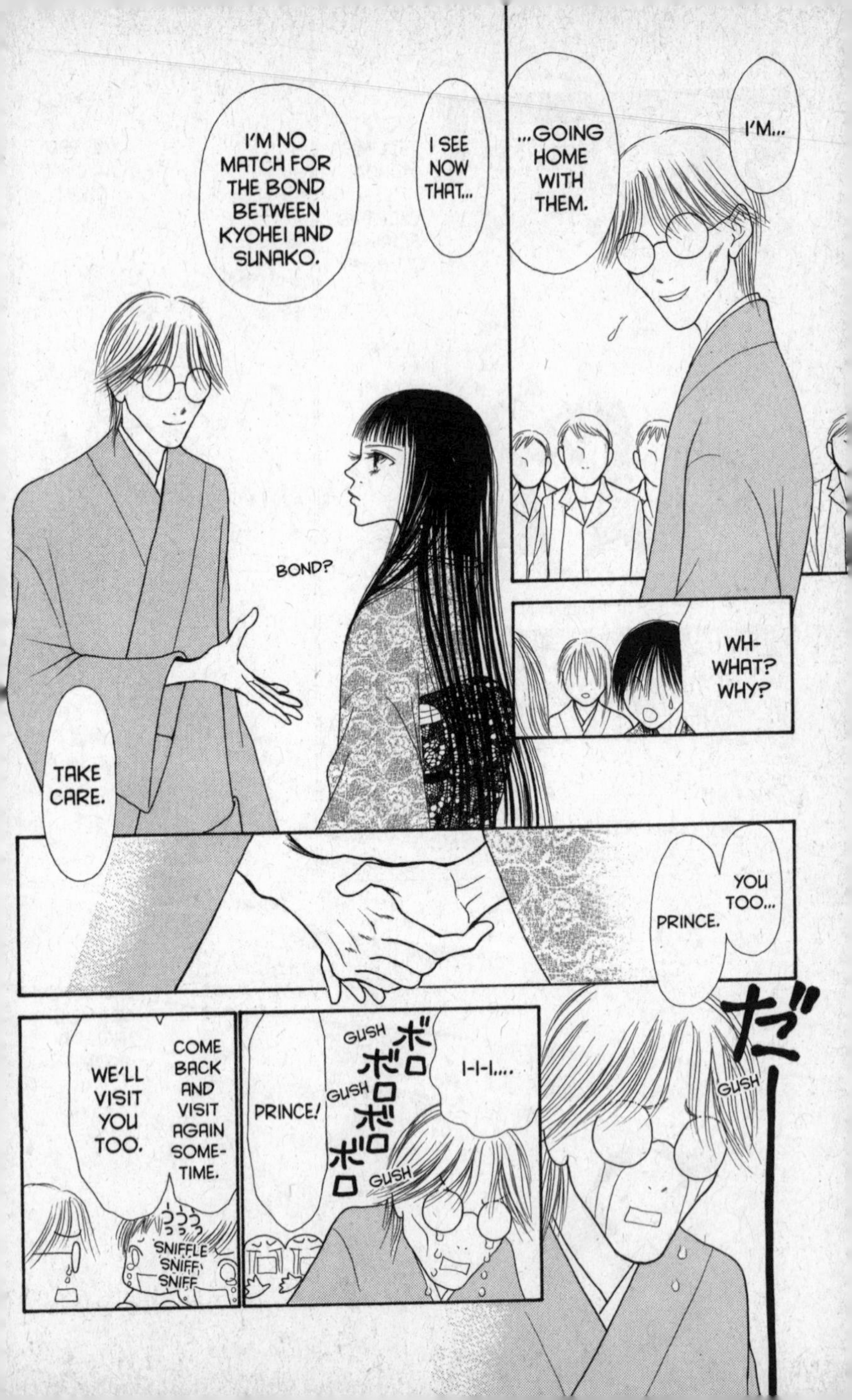
I'M...
...GOING HOME WITH THEM.
WH-WHAT? WHY?
I SEE NOW THAT...
I'M NO MATCH FOR THE BOND BETWEEN KYOHEI AND SUNAKO.
BOND?
TAKE CARE.
YOU TOO...
PRINCE.
だっ
GUSH
I-I-I....
ボロボロボロボロ
GUSH
GUSH
GUSH
PRINCE!
COME BACK AND VISIT AGAIN SOMETIME.
WE'LL VISIT YOU TOO.
うううう
SNIFFLE SNIFF SNIFF

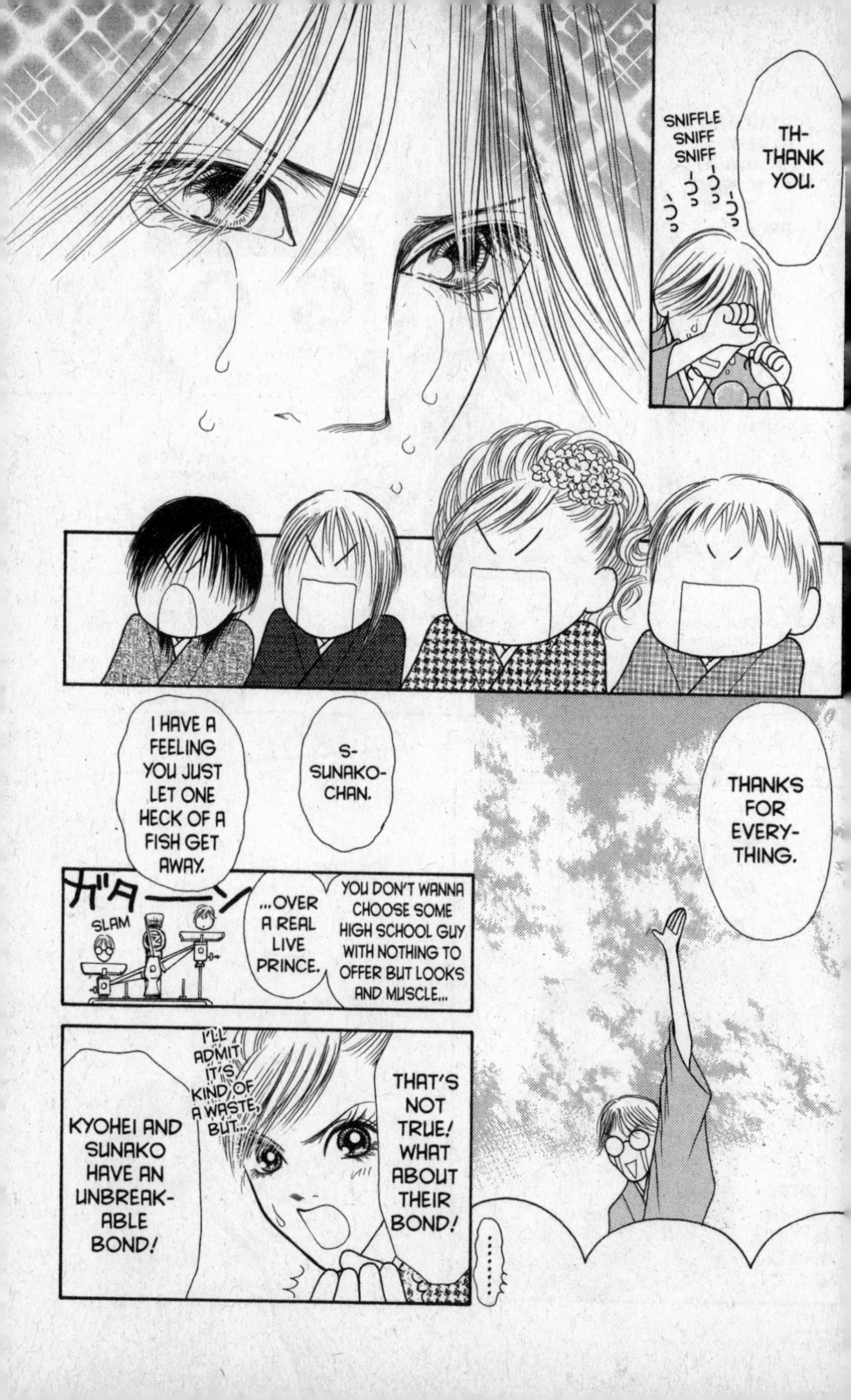
TH- THANK YOU.
SNIFFLE SNIFF SNIFF
THANKS FOR EVERY- THING.
S- SUNAKO- CHAN.
I HAVE A FEELING YOU JUST LET ONE HECK OF A FISH GET AWAY.
YOU DON'T WANNA CHOOSE SOME HIGH SCHOOL GUY WITH NOTHING TO OFFER BUT LOOKS AND MUSCLE...
...OVER A REAL LIVE PRINCE.
ガターン
SLAM
......
THAT'S NOT TRUE! WHAT ABOUT THEIR BOND!
I'LL ADMIT IT'S KIND OF A WASTE, BUT...
KYOHEI AND SUNAKO HAVE AN UNBREAK- ABLE BOND!

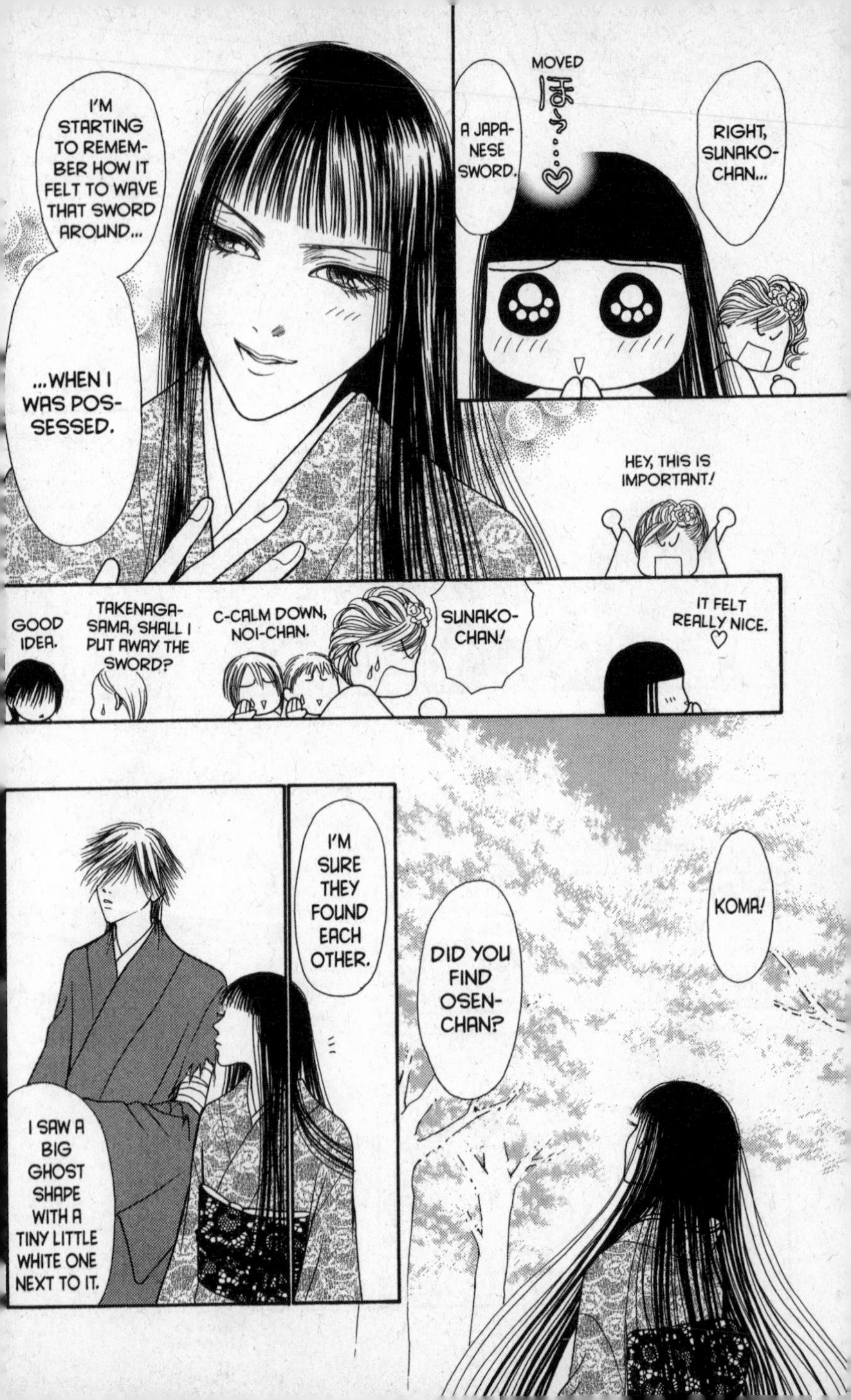
RIGHT, SUNAKO-CHAN...
MOVED
ほぅ…♡
A JAPANESE SWORD.
I'M STARTING TO REMEMBER HOW IT FELT TO WAVE THAT SWORD AROUND...
...WHEN I WAS POSSESSED.
HEY, THIS IS IMPORTANT!
IT FELT REALLY NICE. ♡
SUNAKO-CHAN!
C-CALM DOWN, NOI-CHAN.
TAKENAGA-SAMA, SHALL I PUT AWAY THE SWORD?
GOOD IDEA.
KOMA!
DID YOU FIND OSEN-CHAN?
I'M SURE THEY FOUND EACH OTHER.
I SAW A BIG GHOST SHAPE WITH A TINY LITTLE WHITE ONE NEXT TO IT.

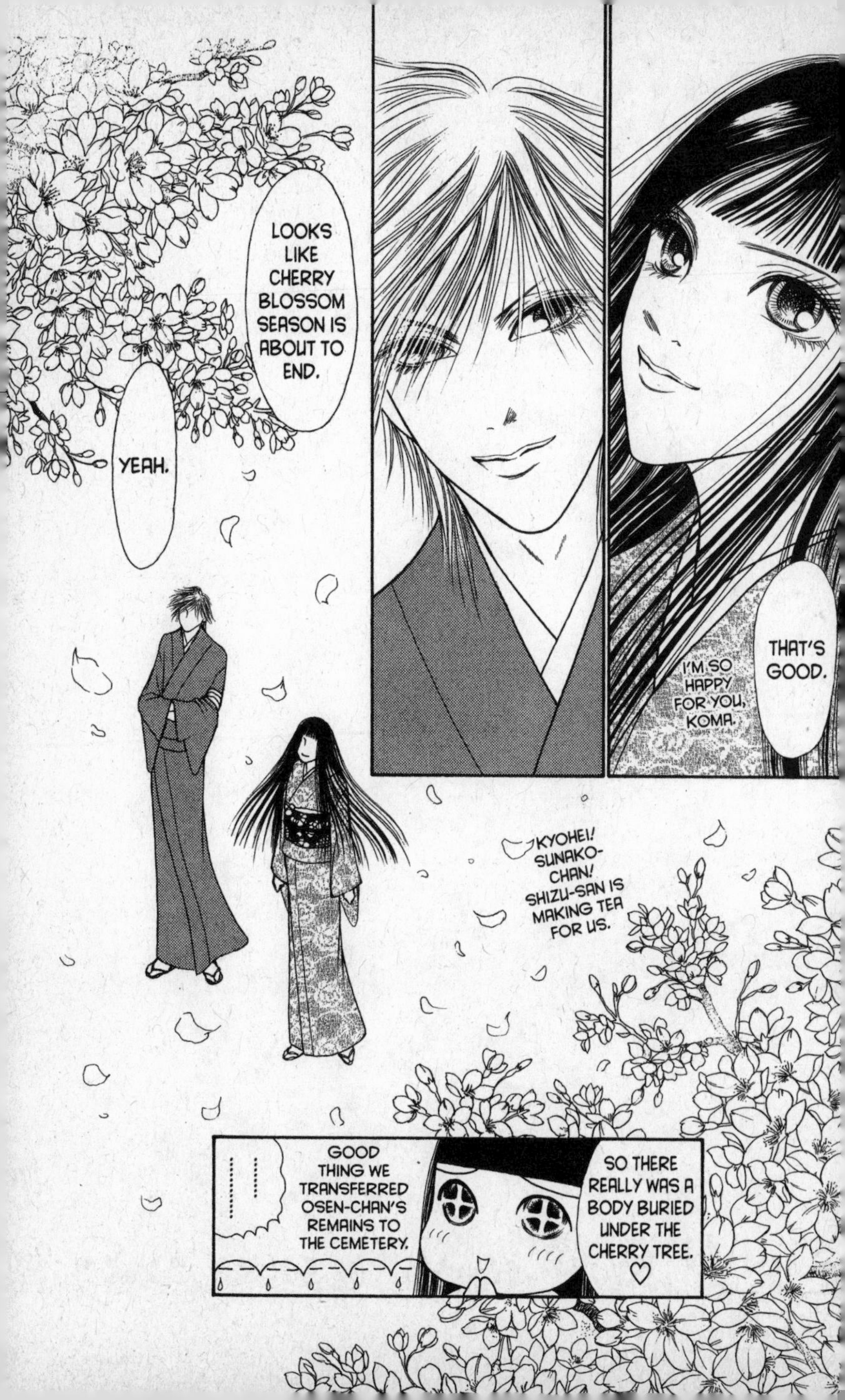
THAT'S GOOD.
I'M SO HAPPY FOR YOU, KOMA.
LOOKS LIKE CHERRY BLOSSOM SEASON IS ABOUT TO END.
YEAH.
KYOHEI! SUNAKO-CHAN! SHIZU-SAN IS MAKING TEA FOR US.
SO THERE REALLY WAS A BODY BURIED UNDER THE CHERRY TREE. ♡
GOOD THING WE TRANSFERRED OSEN-CHAN'S REMAINS TO THE CEMETERY.
......

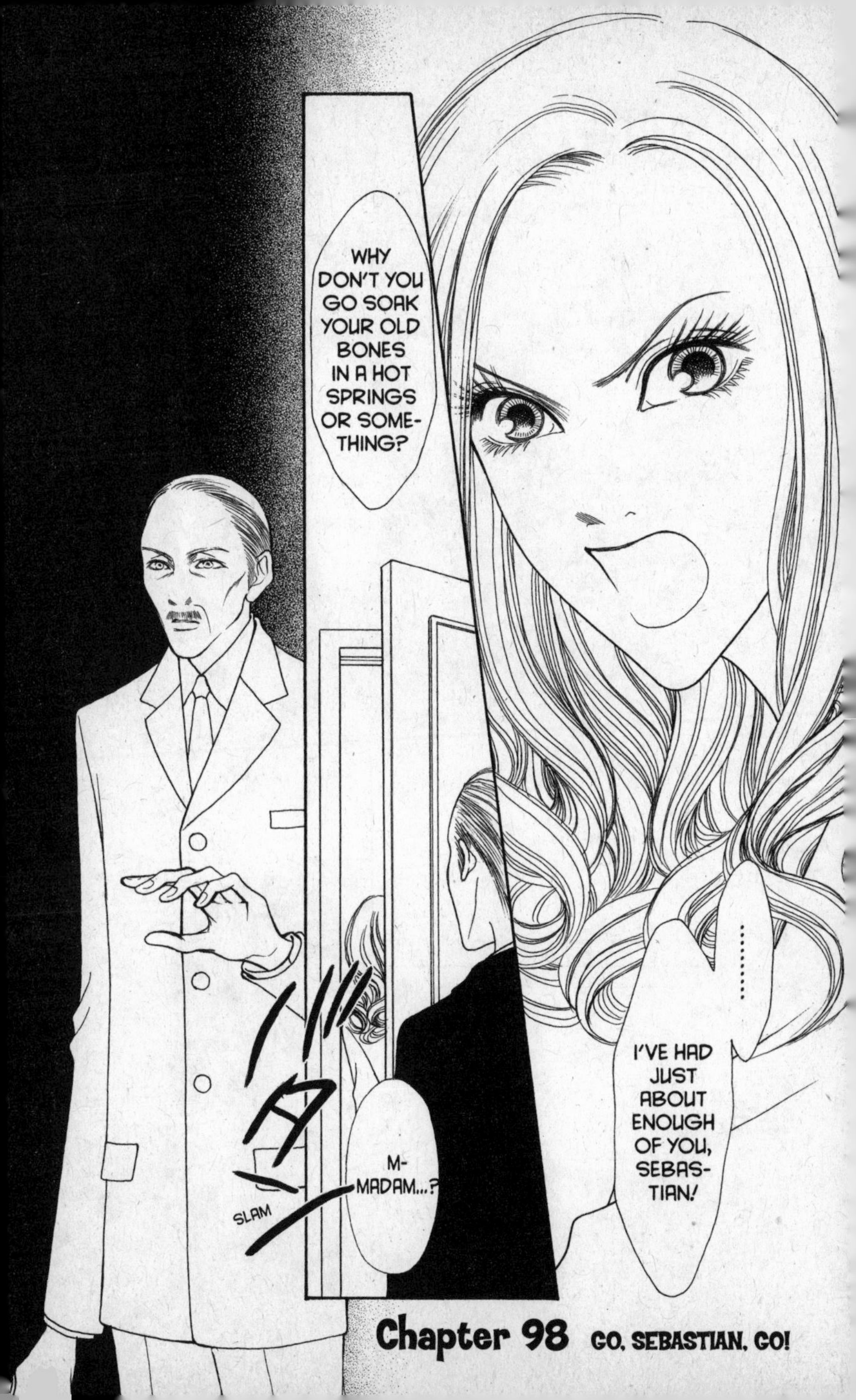
WHY DON'T YOU GO SOAK YOUR OLD BONES IN A HOT SPRINGS OR SOME-THING?
......
I'VE HAD JUST ABOUT ENOUGH OF YOU, SEBAS-TIAN!
M-MADAM...?
SLAM

Chapter 98 GO, SEBASTIAN, GO!

Chapter 98
GO, SEBASTIAN, GO!

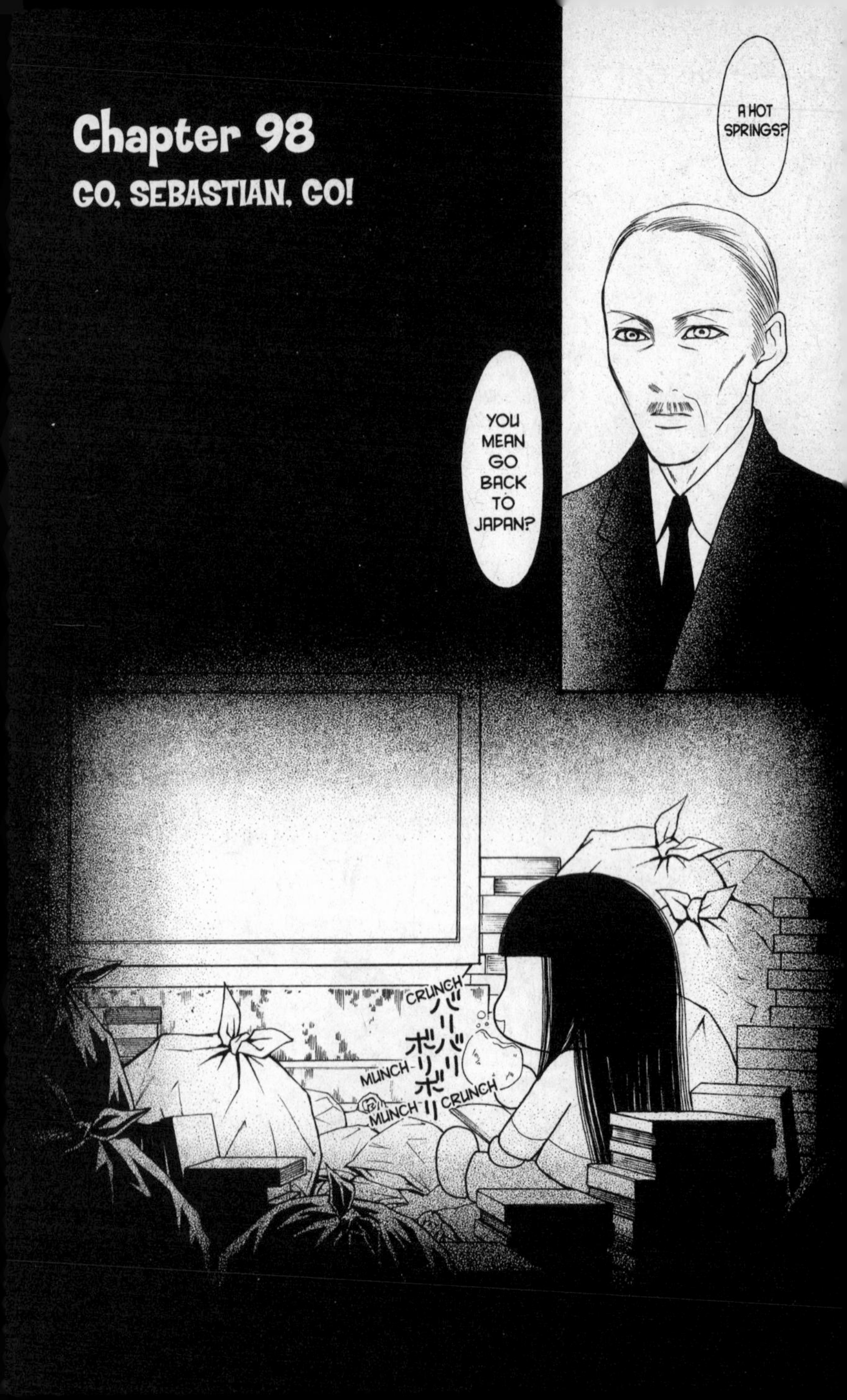
A HOT SPRINGS?
YOU MEAN GO BACK TO JAPAN?
CRUNCH バリバリ
CRUNCH
MUNCH ボリボリ
MUNCH

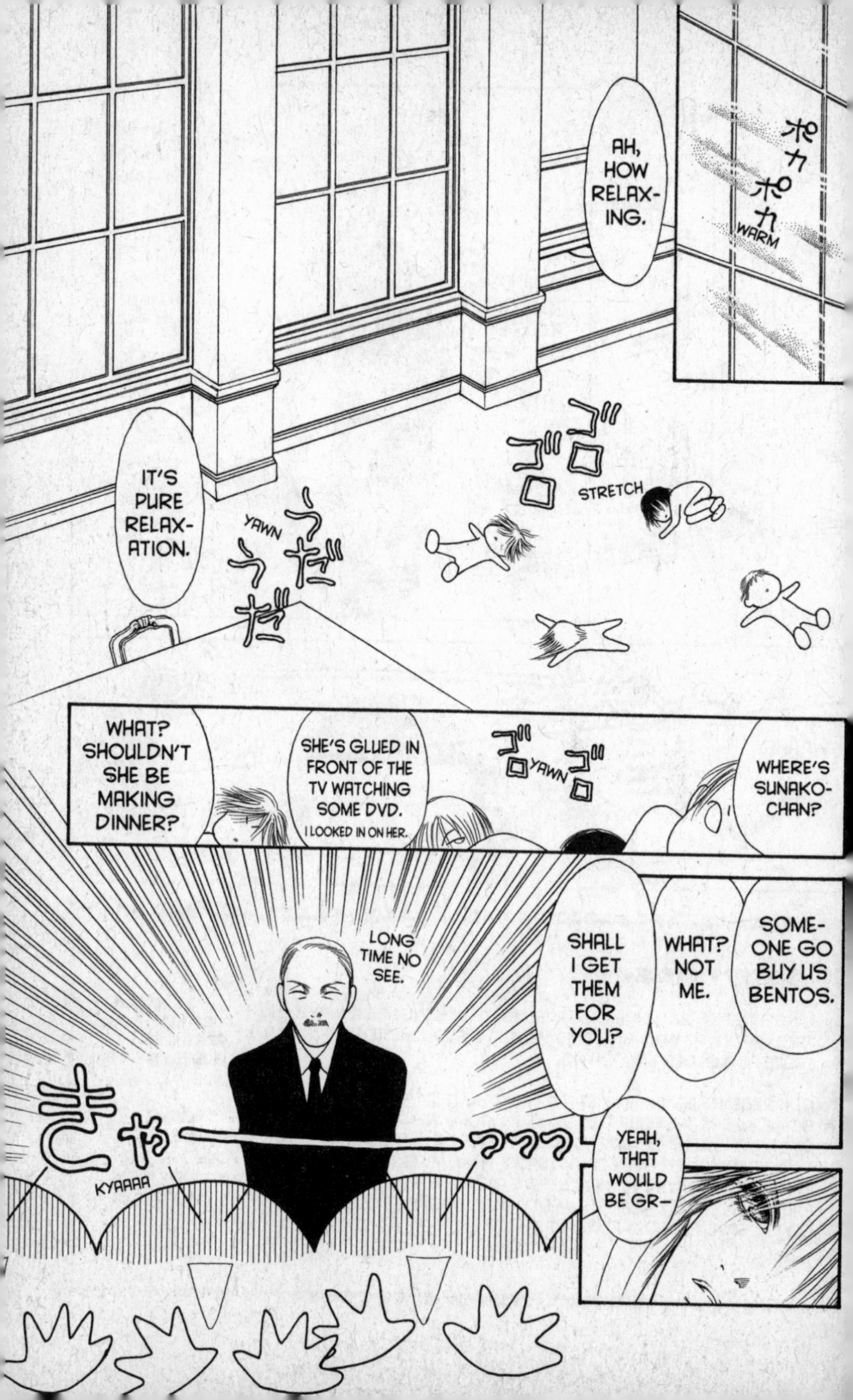

ポカポカ
WARM
AH, HOW RELAXING.
ゴロゴロ
STRETCH
うだうだ
YAWN
IT'S PURE RELAXATION.
WHERE'S SUNAKO-CHAN?
ゴロゴロ
YAWN
SHE'S GLUED IN FRONT OF THE TV WATCHING SOME DVD.
I LOOKED IN ON HER.
WHAT? SHOULDN'T SHE BE MAKING DINNER?
SOME-ONE GO BUY US BENTOS.
WHAT? NOT ME.
SHALL I GET THEM FOR YOU?
YEAH, THAT WOULD BE GR–
LONG TIME NO SEE.
きゃーーっっっ
KYAAAA

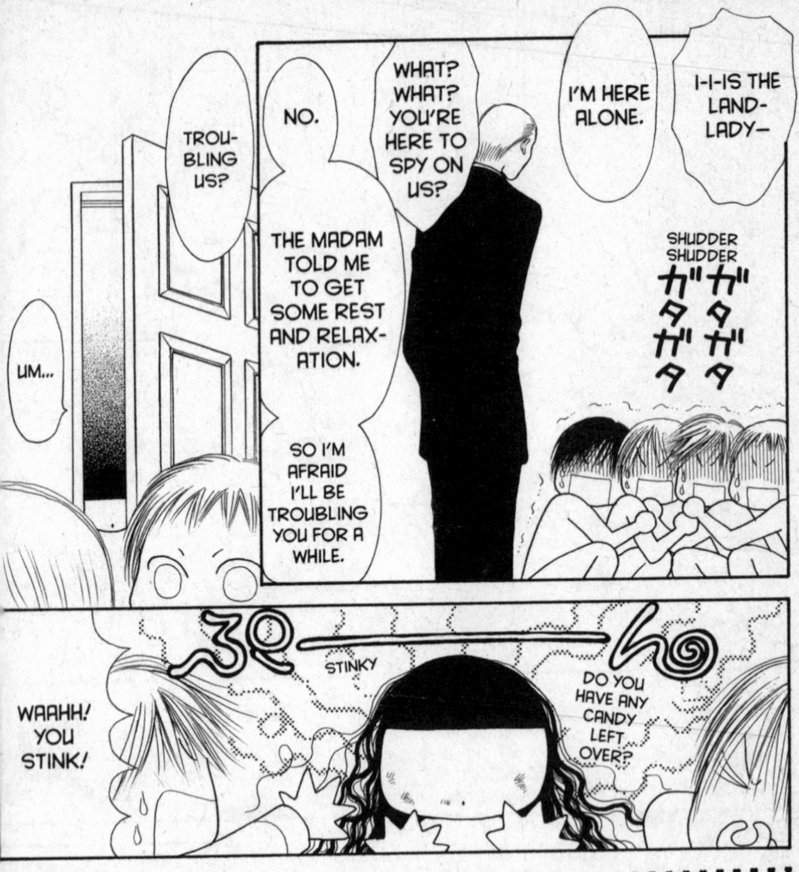
I-I-IS THE LANDLADY—
I'M HERE ALONE.
WHAT? WHAT? YOU'RE HERE TO SPY ON US?
NO.
THE MADAM TOLD ME TO GET SOME REST AND RELAXATION.
SO I'M AFRAID I'LL BE TROUBLING YOU FOR A WHILE.
TROUBLING US?
UM...
SHUDDER SHUDDER
ガタガタ ガタガタ
DO YOU HAVE ANY CANDY LEFT OVER?
STINKY
WAAHH! YOU STINK!

BEHIND THE SCENES

MY SECRET'S OUT. I LIKE OLDER GUYS. THAT'S RIGHT, I ALWAYS THOUGHT I WAS INTO BISHONEN, BUT I'VE SUDDENLY DEVELOPED A TASTE FOR OLDER MEN. OH NO.

BUT I STILL LIKE AIBA-KUN FROM ARASHI, SO I GUESS I'M SAFE.

AT A RECENT MEETING, MY EDITOR SUGGESTED THAT I HAVE A SCENE WHERE THE FOUR GUYS IMPART SOME WISDOM UPON SEBASTIAN. I FOUND MYSELF ANSWERING "WHAT COULD A PERFECT MAN LIKE SEBASTIAN POSSIBLY LEARN FROM A BUNCH OF BOYS?" ACTUALLY, I LIKE MY GUYS TO BE A LITTLE YOUNGER THAN SEBASTIAN...MAYBE IN THEIR 50S. ♥ RIGHT BEFORE MY DEADLINE FOR THIS STORY, I HAD TO GO TO MY FRIEND'S WEDDING. IT WAS PRETTY CRAZY, BUT I'M OUT OF ROOM, SO I'LL SAVE THE REST FOR LATER.

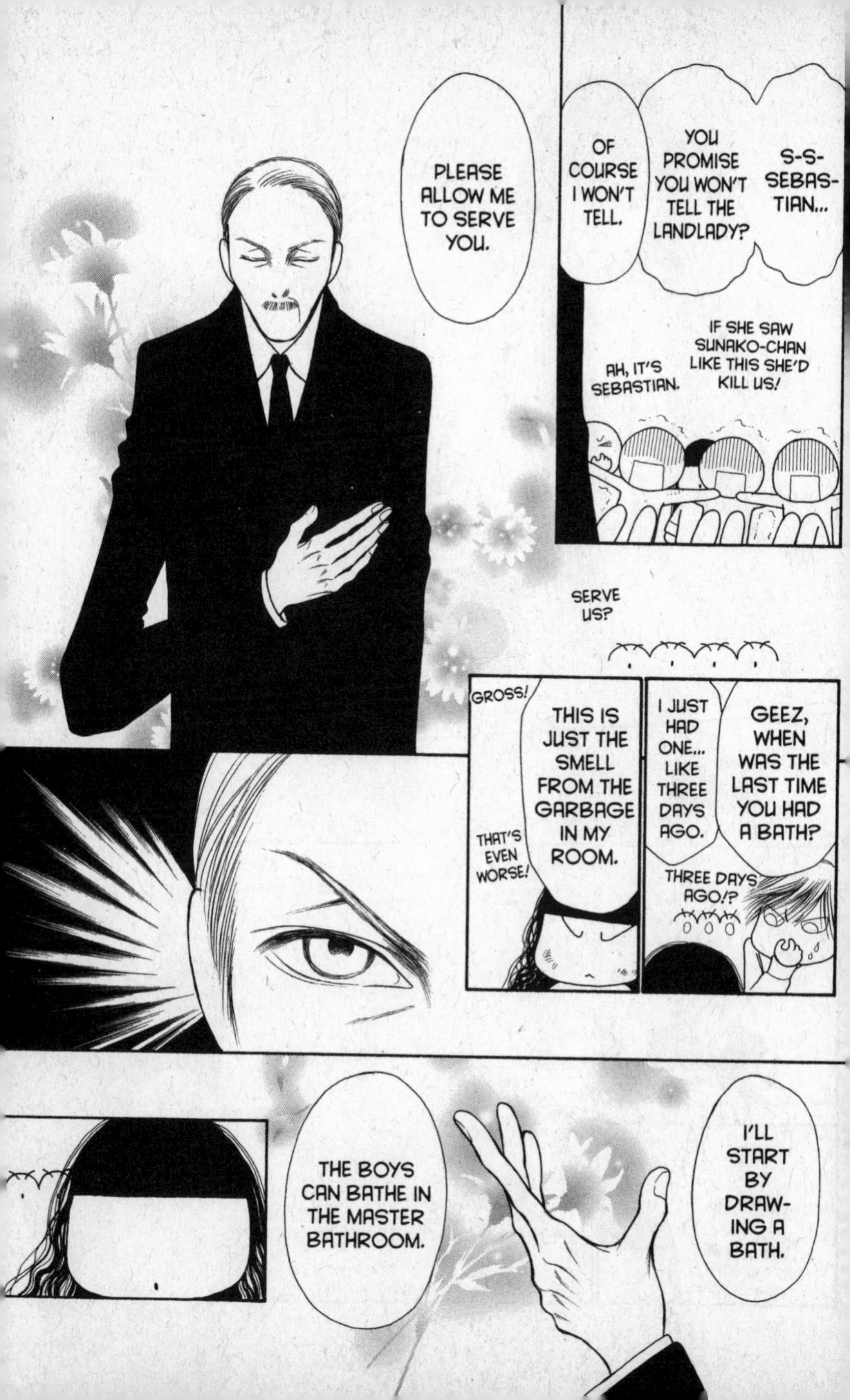
S-S-SEBASTIAN...
YOU PROMISE YOU WON'T TELL THE LANDLADY?
OF COURSE I WON'T TELL.
IF SHE SAW SUNAKO-CHAN LIKE THIS SHE'D KILL US!
AH, IT'S SEBASTIAN.
SERVE US?
GEEZ, WHEN WAS THE LAST TIME YOU HAD A BATH?
I JUST HAD ONE... LIKE THREE DAYS AGO.
THREE DAYS AGO!?
THIS IS JUST THE SMELL FROM THE GARBAGE IN MY ROOM.
GROSS!
THAT'S EVEN WORSE!
PLEASE ALLOW ME TO SERVE YOU.
I'LL START BY DRAWING A BATH.
THE BOYS CAN BATHE IN THE MASTER BATHROOM.

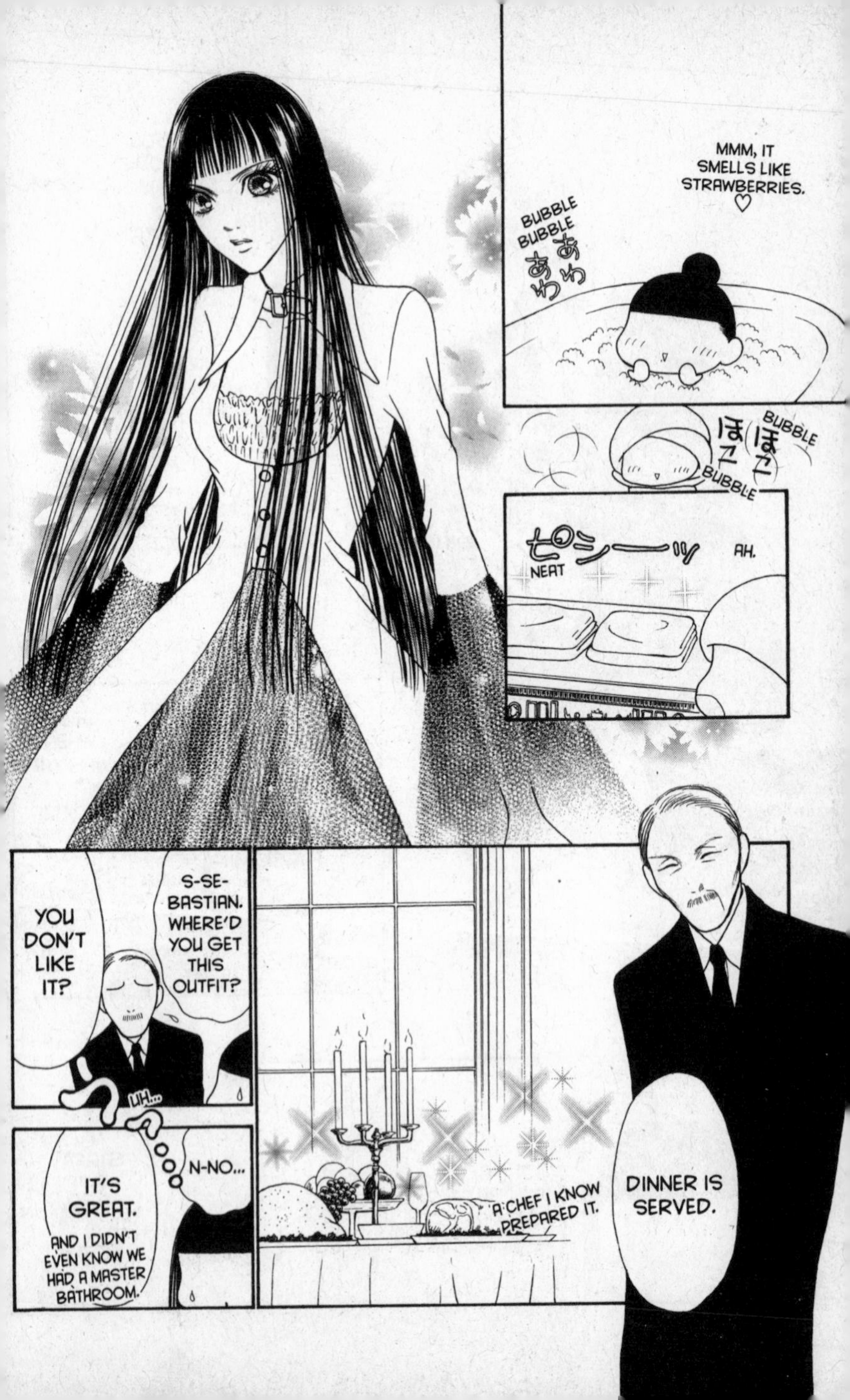

MMM, IT SMELLS LIKE STRAWBERRIES. ♡
BUBBLE BUBBLE
あわあわ
ほこほこ
BUBBLE BUBBLE
ピシーーッ
NEAT
AH.
DINNER IS SERVED.
A CHEF I KNOW PREPARED IT.
S-SE-BASTIAN. WHERE'D YOU GET THIS OUTFIT?
YOU DON'T LIKE IT?
UH...
N-NO...
IT'S GREAT.
AND I DIDN'T EVEN KNOW WE HAD A MASTER BATHROOM.

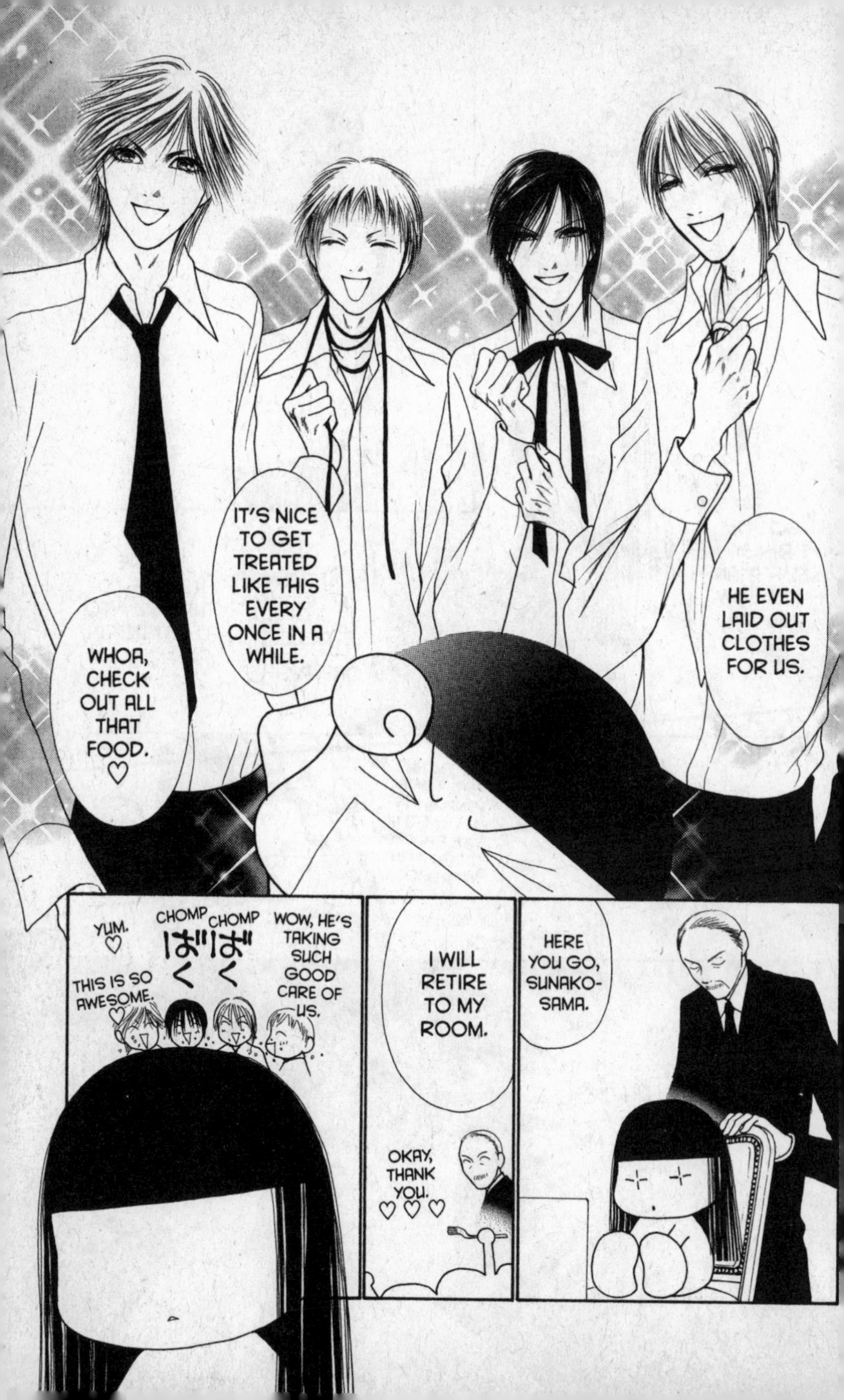
HE EVEN LAID OUT CLOTHES FOR US.
IT'S NICE TO GET TREATED LIKE THIS EVERY ONCE IN A WHILE.
WHOA, CHECK OUT ALL THAT FOOD. ♡
HERE YOU GO, SUNAKO-SAMA.
I WILL RETIRE TO MY ROOM.
OKAY, THANK YOU. ♡♡♡
WOW, HE'S TAKING SUCH GOOD CARE OF US.
CHOMP CHOMP
ばくばく
YUM. ♡
THIS IS SO AWESOME. ♡

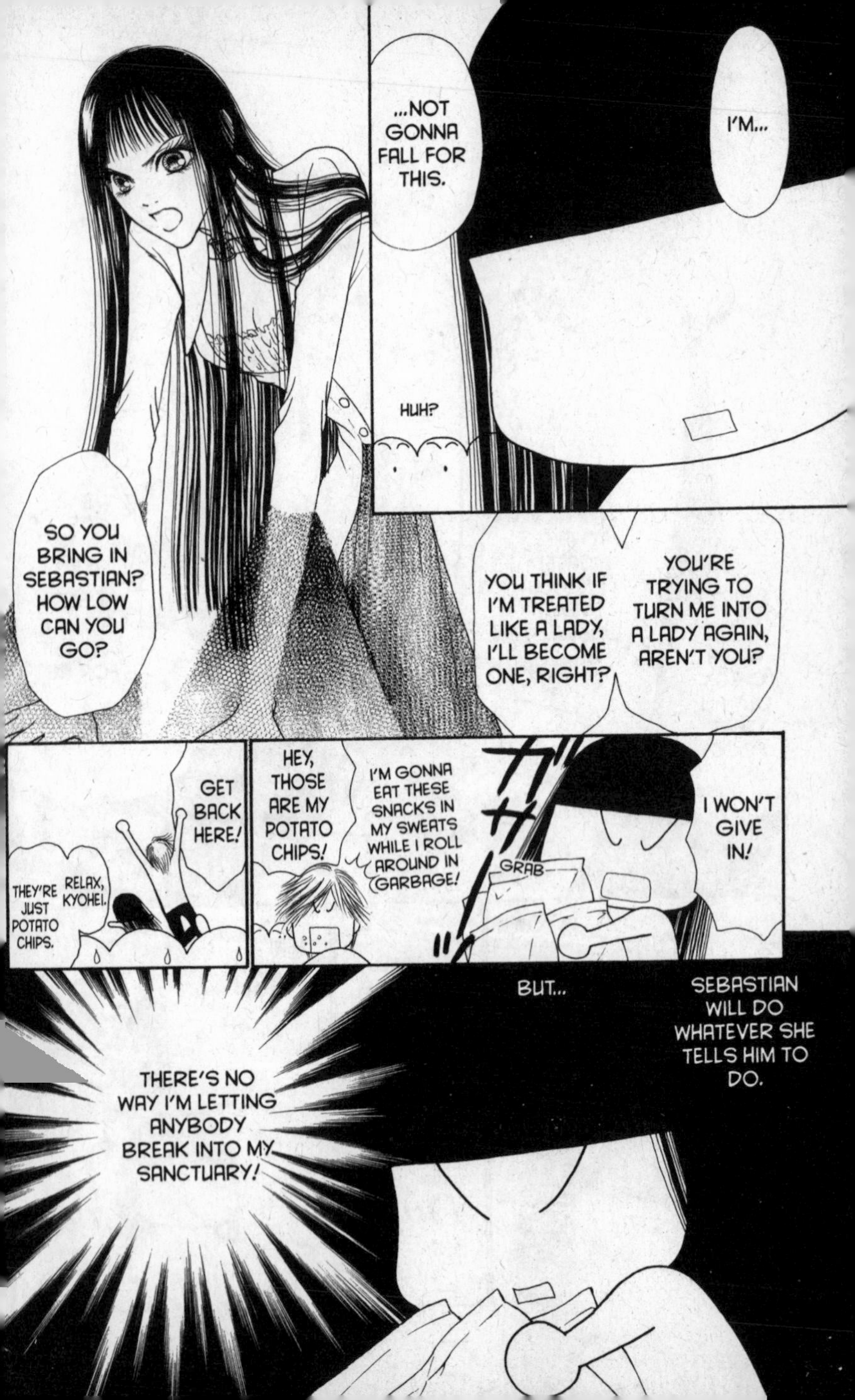
I'M...
...NOT GONNA FALL FOR THIS.
HUH?
YOU'RE TRYING TO TURN ME INTO A LADY AGAIN, AREN'T YOU?
YOU THINK IF I'M TREATED LIKE A LADY, I'LL BECOME ONE, RIGHT?
SO YOU BRING IN SEBASTIAN? HOW LOW CAN YOU GO?
I WON'T GIVE IN!
GRAB
I'M GONNA EAT THESE SNACKS IN MY SWEATS WHILE I ROLL AROUND IN GARBAGE!
HEY, THOSE ARE MY POTATO CHIPS!
GET BACK HERE!
RELAX, KYOHEI.
THEY'RE JUST POTATO CHIPS.
SEBASTIAN WILL DO WHATEVER SHE TELLS HIM TO DO.
BUT...
THERE'S NO WAY I'M LETTING ANYBODY BREAK INTO MY SANCTUARY!

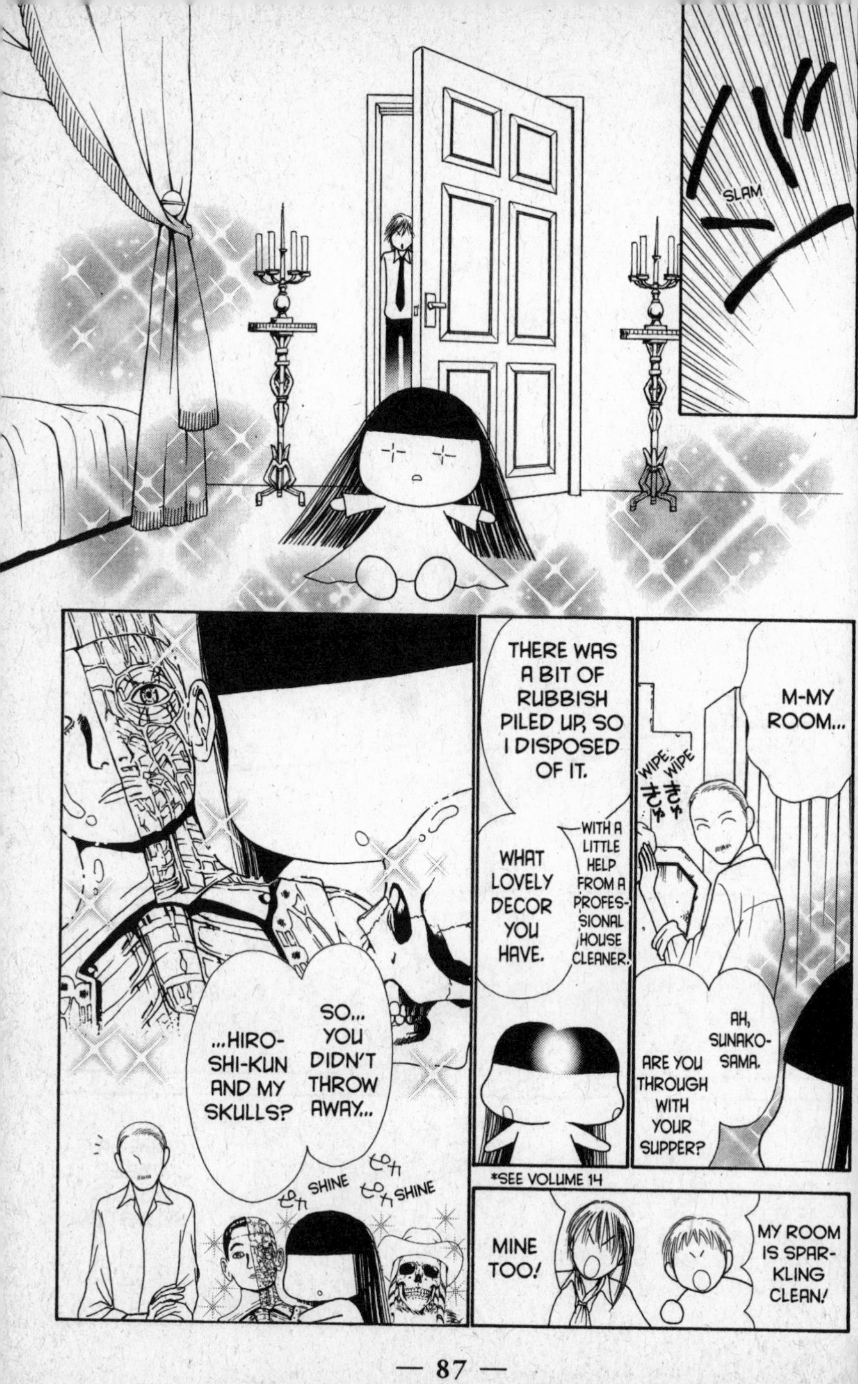
SLAM
M-MY ROOM...
WIPE, WIPE
AH, SUNAKO-SAMA.
ARE YOU THROUGH WITH YOUR SUPPER?
THERE WAS A BIT OF RUBBISH PILED UP, SO I DISPOSED OF IT.
WITH A LITTLE HELP FROM A PROFES-SIONAL HOUSE CLEANER.
WHAT LOVELY DECOR YOU HAVE.
*SEE VOLUME 14
MY ROOM IS SPAR-KLING CLEAN!
MINE TOO!
SO... YOU DIDN'T THROW AWAY...
...HIRO-SHI-KUN AND MY SKULLS?
SHINE
SHINE

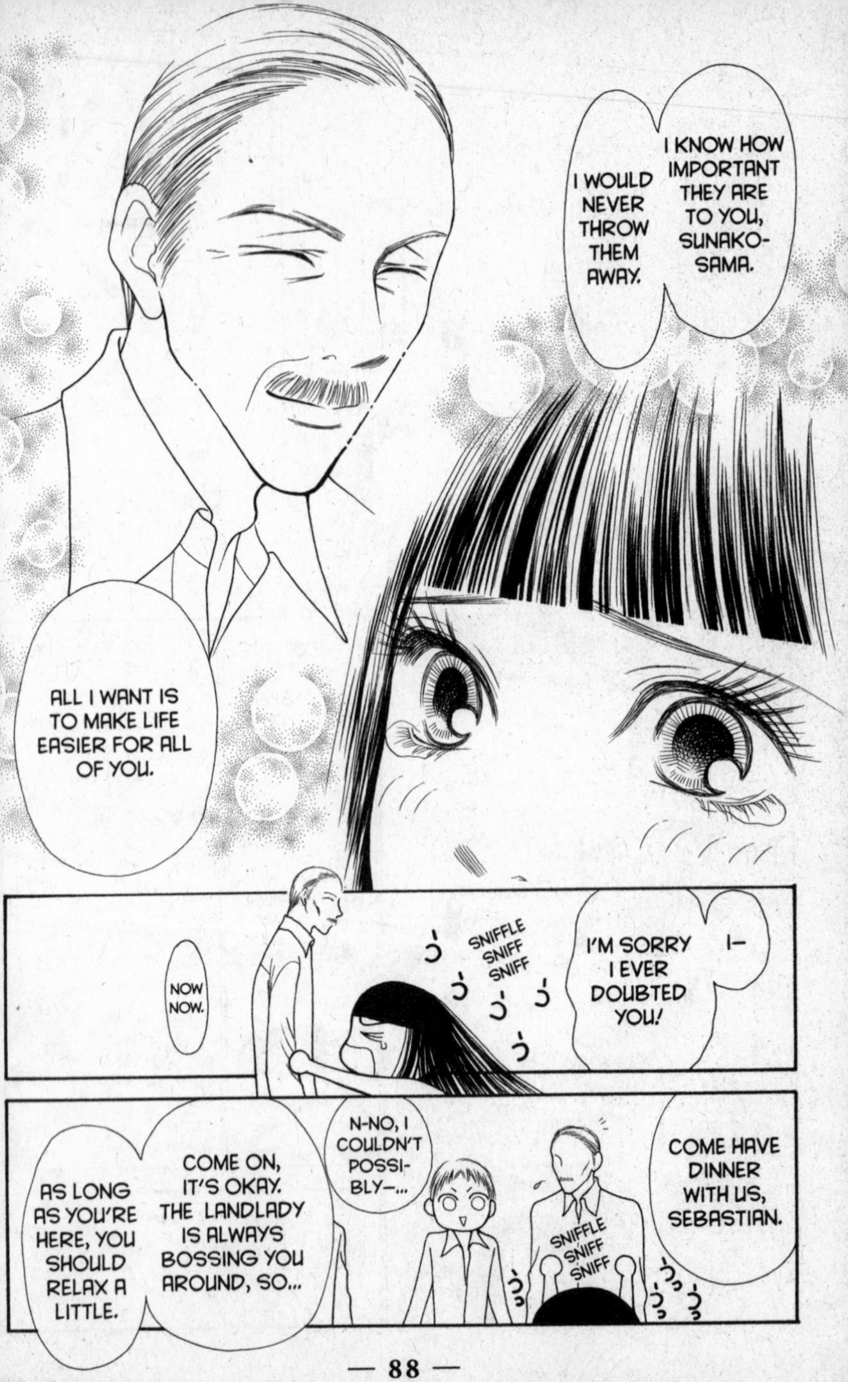
I KNOW HOW IMPORTANT THEY ARE TO YOU, SUNAKO-SAMA.
I WOULD NEVER THROW THEM AWAY.
ALL I WANT IS TO MAKE LIFE EASIER FOR ALL OF YOU.
I— I'M SORRY I EVER DOUBTED YOU!
SNIFFLE SNIFF SNIFF
NOW NOW.
COME HAVE DINNER WITH US, SEBASTIAN.
SNIFFLE SNIFF SNIFF
N-NO, I COULDN'T POSSI-BLY—...
COME ON, IT'S OKAY. THE LANDLADY IS ALWAYS BOSSING YOU AROUND, SO...
AS LONG AS YOU'RE HERE, YOU SHOULD RELAX A LITTLE.

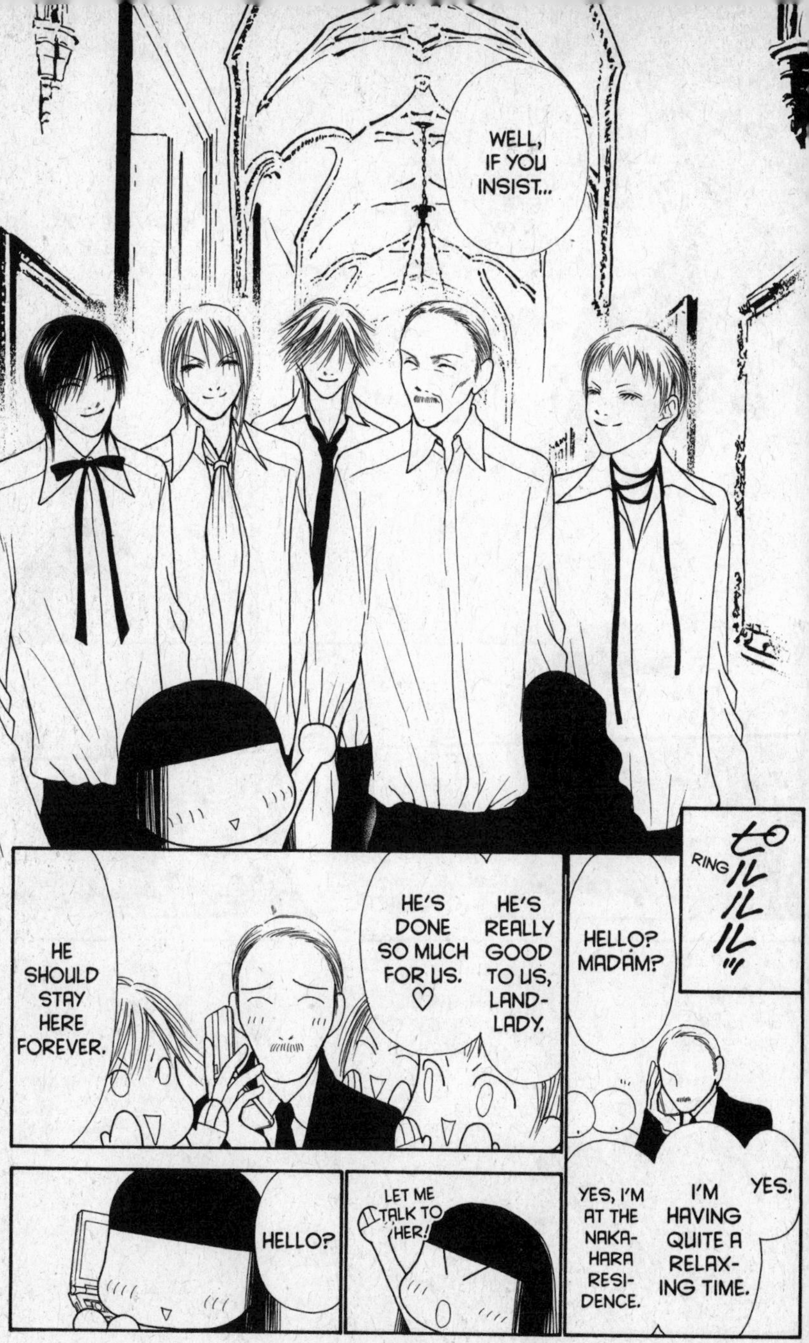
WELL, IF YOU INSIST...
RING
ピルルル
HELLO? MADAM?
YES.
I'M HAVING QUITE A RELAX-ING TIME.
YES, I'M AT THE NAKA-HARA RESI-DENCE.
HE'S REALLY GOOD TO US, LAND-LADY.
HE'S DONE SO MUCH FOR US. ♡
HE SHOULD STAY HERE FOREVER.
LET ME TALK TO HER!
HELLO?

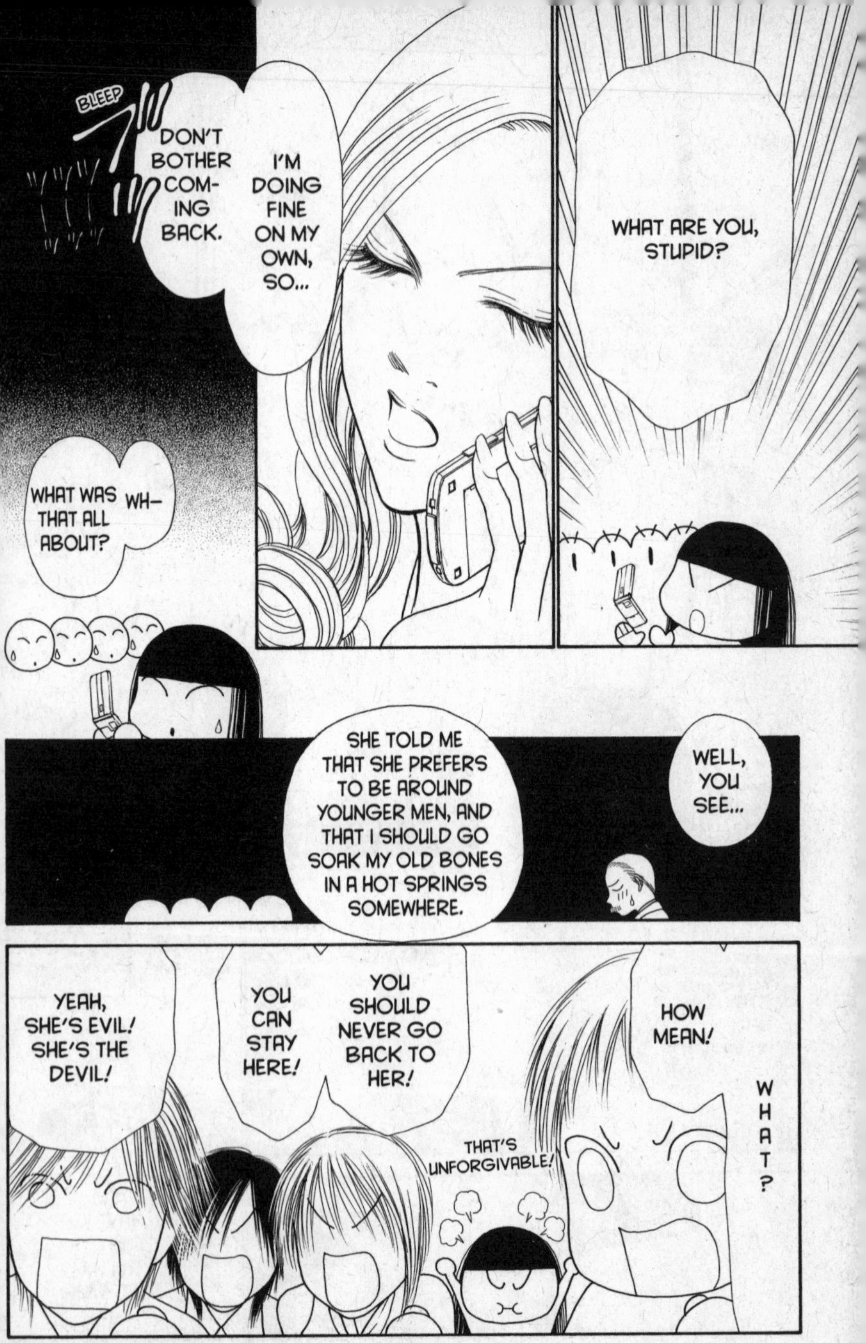
WHAT ARE YOU, STUPID?
I'M DOING FINE ON MY OWN, SO...
DON'T BOTHER COMING BACK.
BLEEP
WH-
WHAT WAS THAT ALL ABOUT?
WELL, YOU SEE...
SHE TOLD ME THAT SHE PREFERS TO BE AROUND YOUNGER MEN, AND THAT I SHOULD GO SOAK MY OLD BONES IN A HOT SPRINGS SOMEWHERE.
WHAT?
HOW MEAN!
THAT'S UNFORGIVABLE!
YOU SHOULD NEVER GO BACK TO HER!
YOU CAN STAY HERE!
YEAH, SHE'S EVIL! SHE'S THE DEVIL!

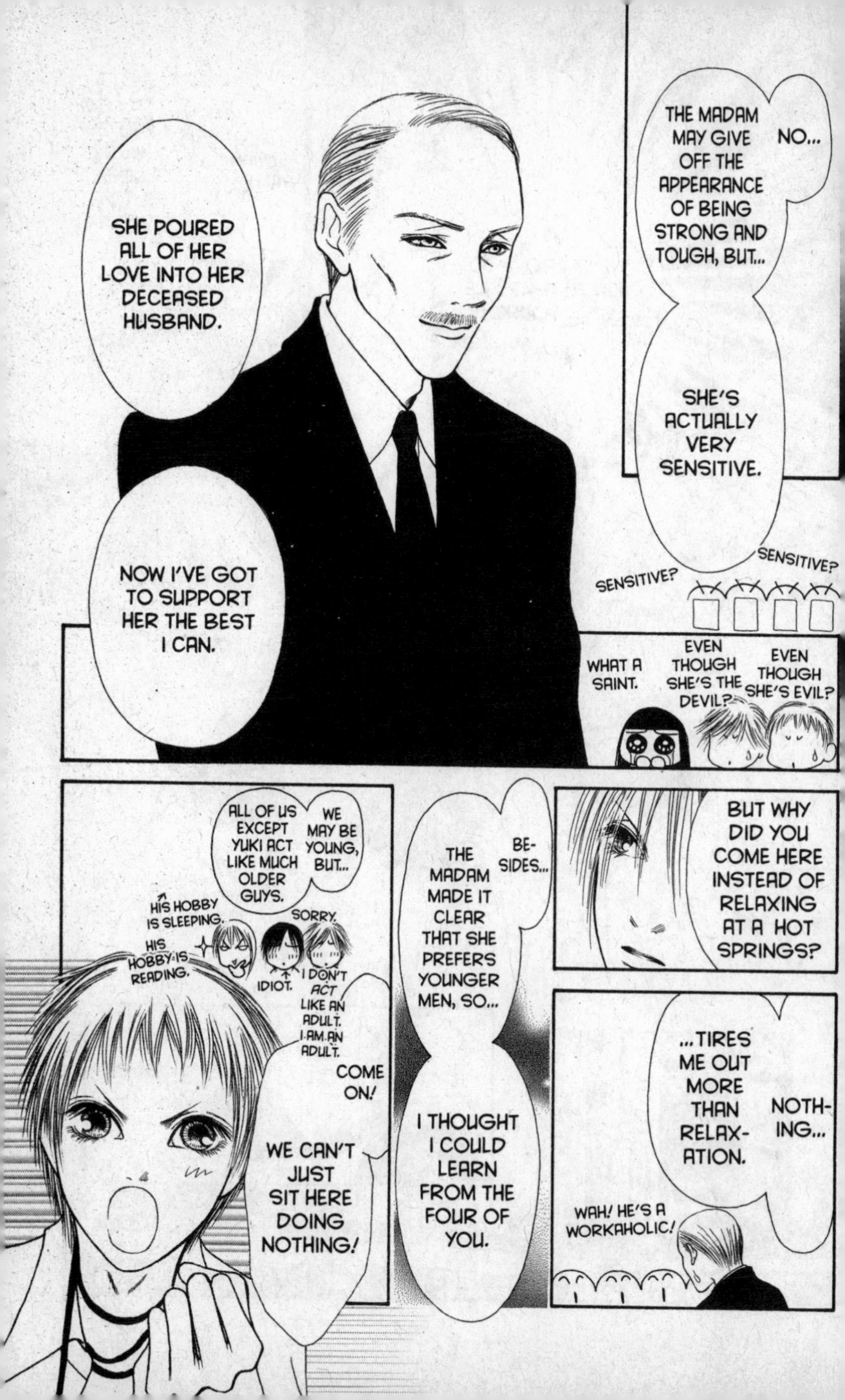
NO...
THE MADAM MAY GIVE OFF THE APPEARANCE OF BEING STRONG AND TOUGH, BUT...
SHE'S ACTUALLY VERY SENSITIVE.
SENSITIVE?
SENSITIVE?
EVEN THOUGH SHE'S EVIL?
EVEN THOUGH SHE'S THE DEVIL?
WHAT A SAINT.
SHE POURED ALL OF HER LOVE INTO HER DECEASED HUSBAND.
NOW I'VE GOT TO SUPPORT HER THE BEST I CAN.
BUT WHY DID YOU COME HERE INSTEAD OF RELAXING AT A HOT SPRINGS?
NOTHING...
...TIRES ME OUT MORE THAN RELAXATION.
WAH! HE'S A WORKAHOLIC!
BESIDES...
THE MADAM MADE IT CLEAR THAT SHE PREFERS YOUNGER MEN, SO...
I THOUGHT I COULD LEARN FROM THE FOUR OF YOU.
WE MAY BE YOUNG, BUT...
ALL OF US EXCEPT YUKI ACT LIKE MUCH OLDER GUYS.
SORRY.
I DON'T ACT LIKE AN ADULT. I AM AN ADULT.
IDIOT.
HIS HOBBY IS SLEEPING.
HIS HOBBY IS READING.
COME ON!
WE CAN'T JUST SIT HERE DOING NOTHING!

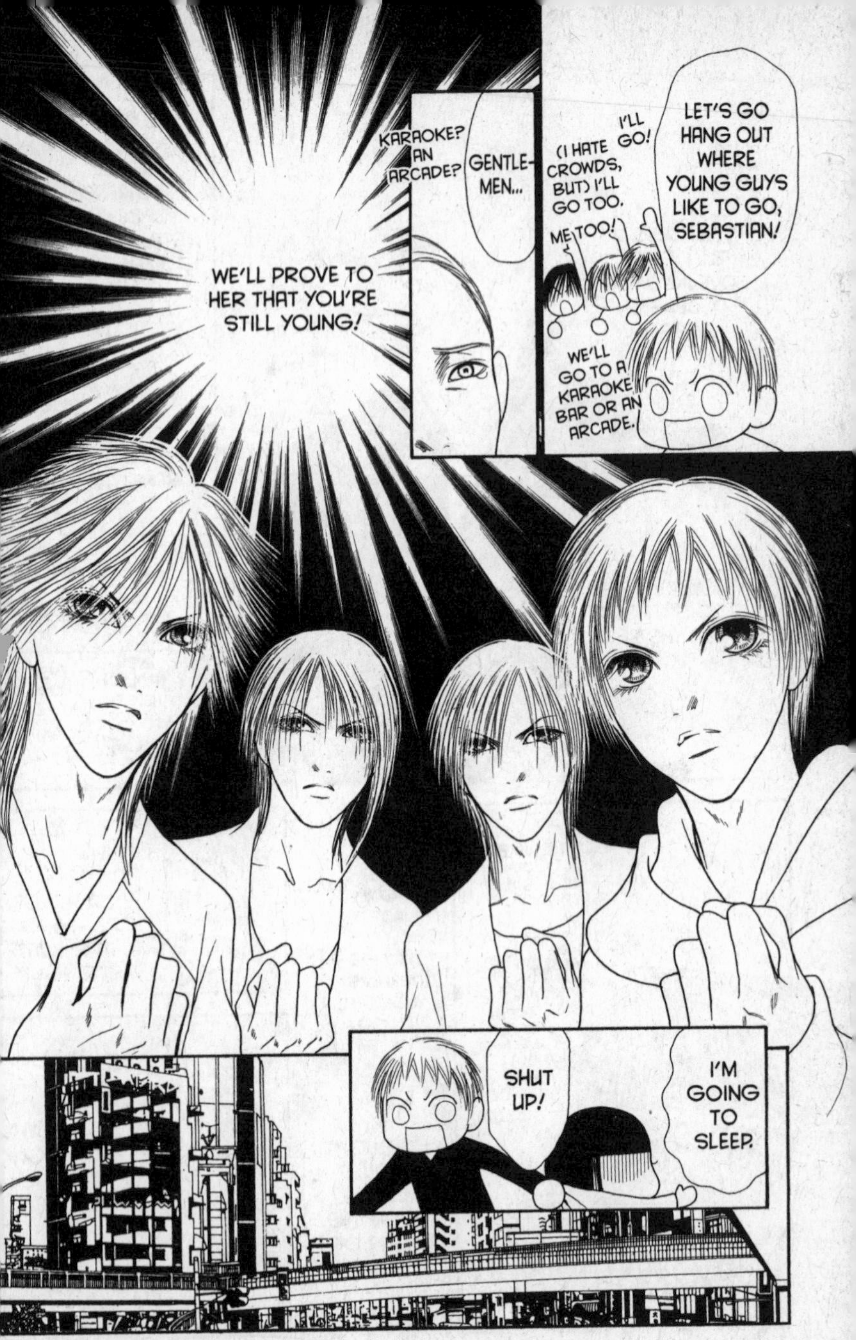
LET'S GO HANG OUT WHERE YOUNG GUYS LIKE TO GO, SEBASTIAN!
I'LL GO!
(I HATE CROWDS, BUT) I'LL GO TOO.
ME TOO!
WE'LL GO TO A KARAOKE BAR OR AN ARCADE.
GENTLE-MEN...
KARAOKE? AN ARCADE?
WE'LL PROVE TO HER THAT YOU'RE STILL YOUNG!
I'M GOING TO SLEEP.
SHUT UP!

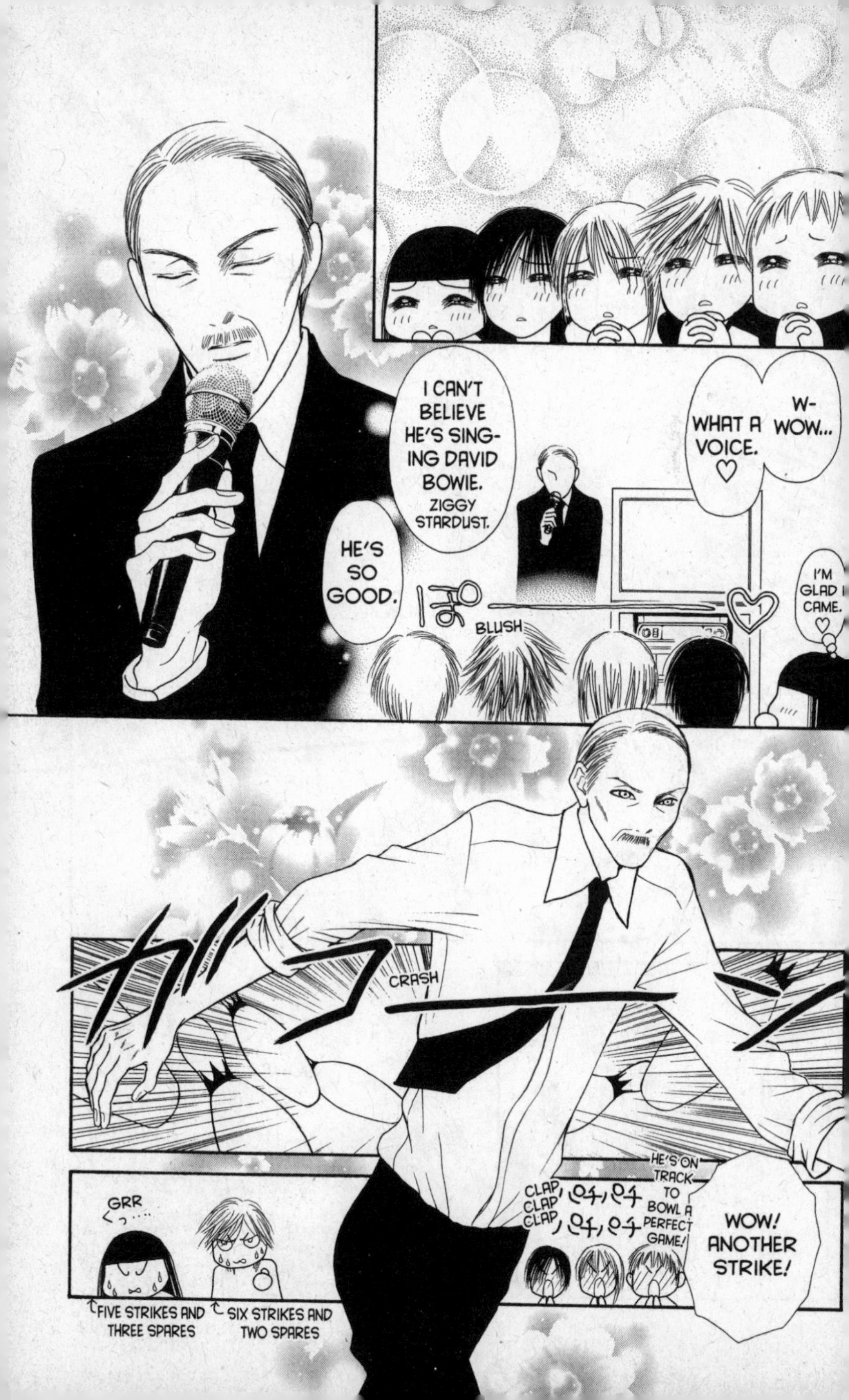
W-WOW...
WHAT A VOICE. ♡
I'M GLAD I CAME. ♡
I CAN'T BELIEVE HE'S SING-ING DAVID BOWIE.
ZIGGY STARDUST.
BLUSH
HE'S SO GOOD.
CRASH
WOW! ANOTHER STRIKE!
HE'S ON TRACK TO BOWL A PERFECT GAME!
CLAP, CLAP CLAP
GRR
SIX STRIKES AND TWO SPARES
FIVE STRIKES AND THREE SPARES

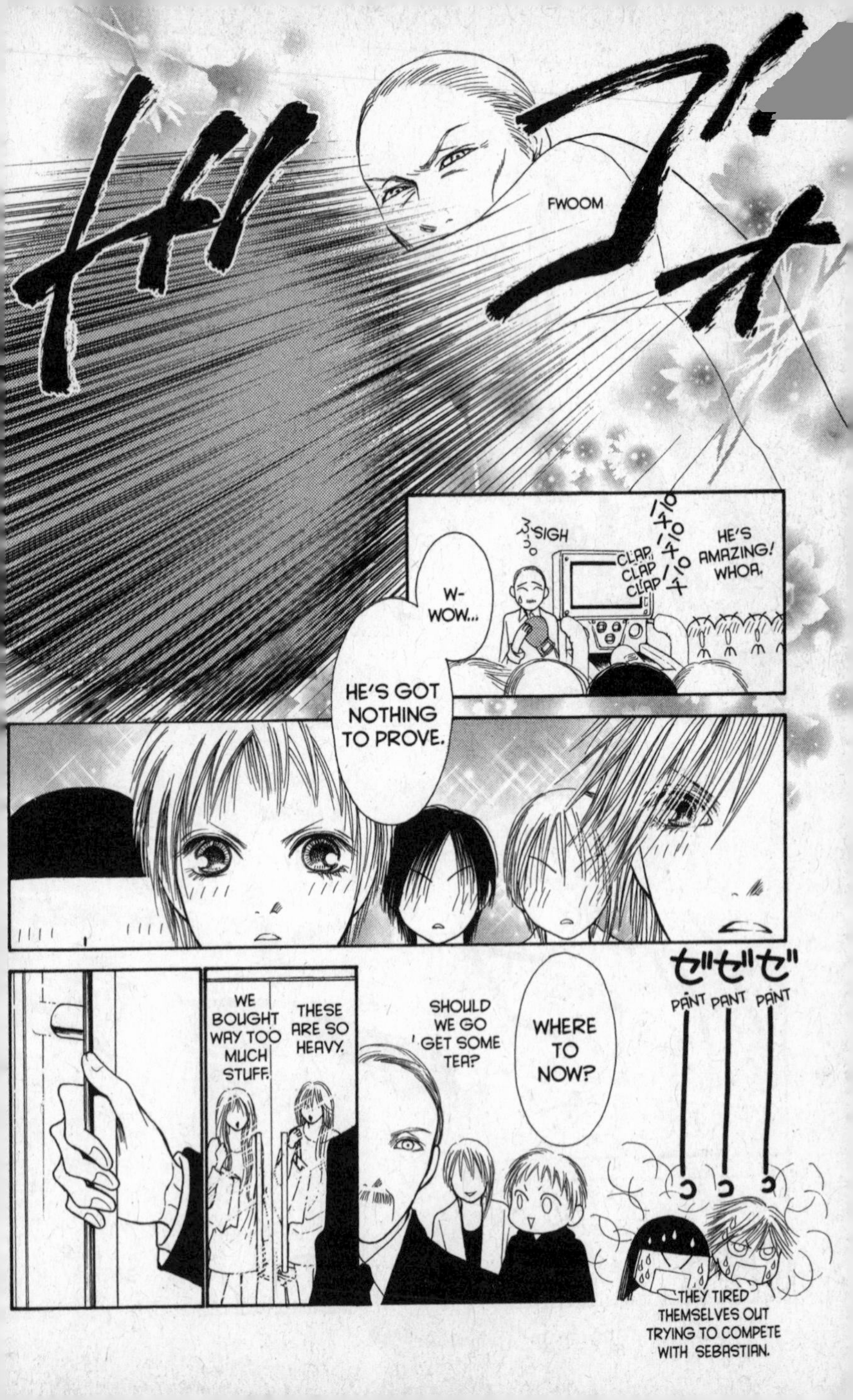
FWOOM
HE'S AMAZING! WHOA.
CLAP, CLAP CLAP
SIGH
W-WOW...
HE'S GOT NOTHING TO PROVE.
ゼゼゼ
PANT PANT PANT
THEY TIRED THEMSELVES OUT TRYING TO COMPETE WITH SEBASTIAN.
WHERE TO NOW?
SHOULD WE GO GET SOME TEA?
THESE ARE SO HEAVY.
WE BOUGHT WAY TOO MUCH STUFF.

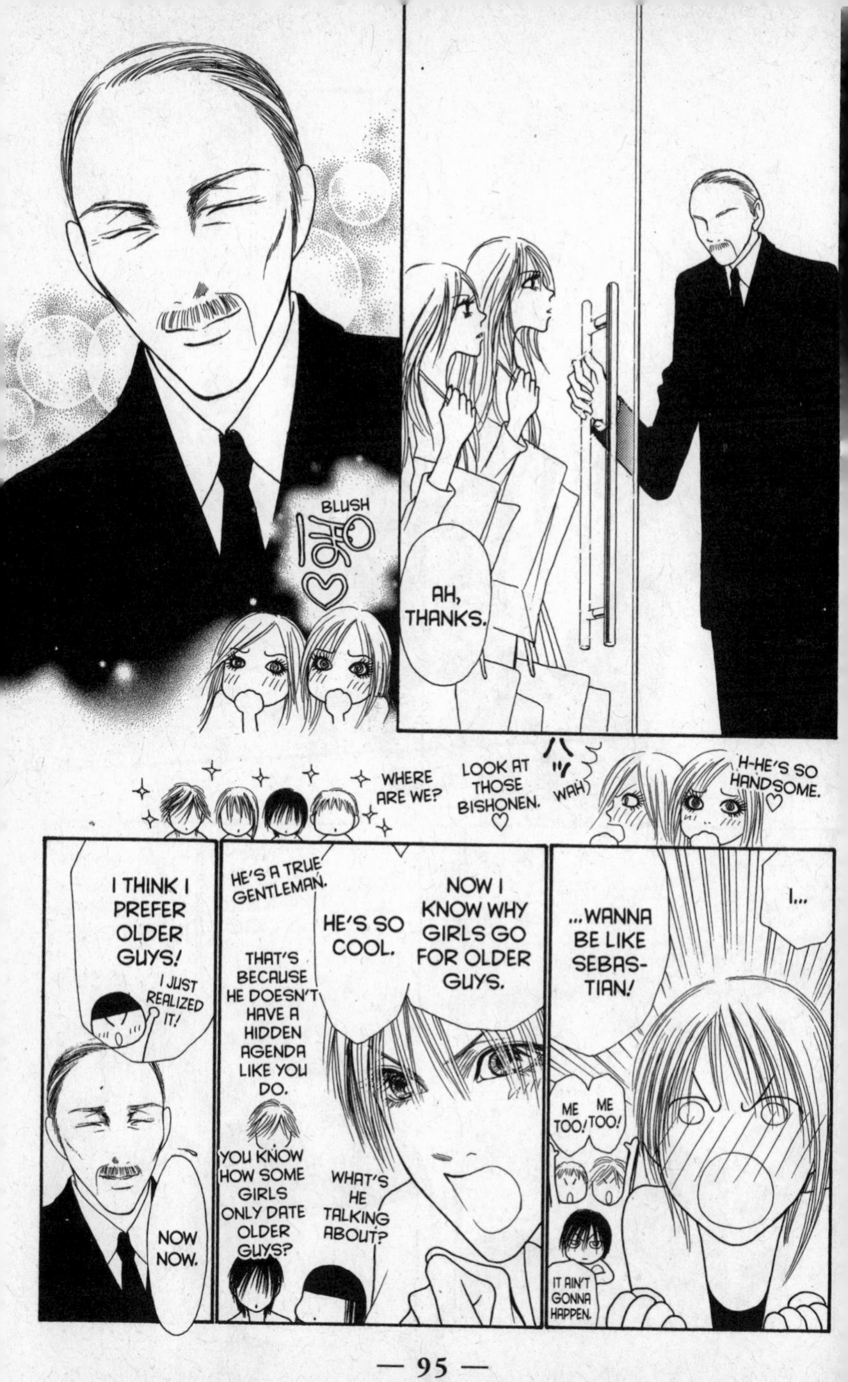
AH, THANKS.
BLUSH
ぽ ♡
H-HE'S SO HANDSOME. ♡
WAH
ハッ
LOOK AT THOSE BISHONEN. ♡
WHERE ARE WE?
I...
...WANNA BE LIKE SEBAS-TIAN!
ME TOO!
ME TOO!
IT AIN'T GONNA HAPPEN.
NOW I KNOW WHY GIRLS GO FOR OLDER GUYS.
HE'S SO COOL.
HE'S A TRUE GENTLEMAN.
THAT'S BECAUSE HE DOESN'T HAVE A HIDDEN AGENDA LIKE YOU DO.
WHAT'S HE TALKING ABOUT?
YOU KNOW HOW SOME GIRLS ONLY DATE OLDER GUYS?
I THINK I PREFER OLDER GUYS!
I JUST REALIZED IT!
NOW NOW.

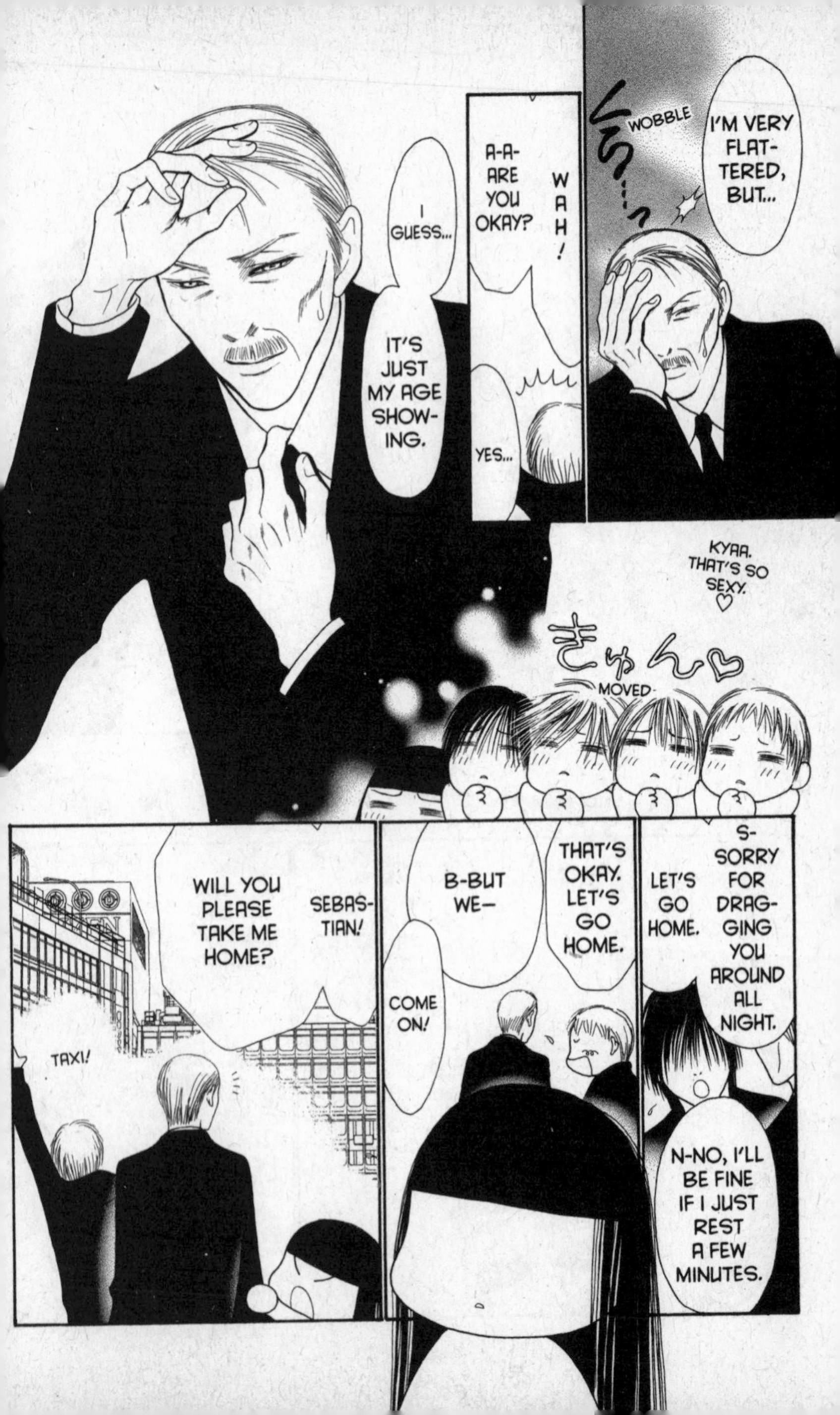
くら…
WOBBLE
I'M VERY FLAT-TERED, BUT...
WAH!
A-A-ARE YOU OKAY?
YES...
I GUESS...
IT'S JUST MY AGE SHOWING.
KYAA. THAT'S SO SEXY. ♡
きゅん♡
MOVED
S-SORRY FOR DRAG-GING YOU AROUND ALL NIGHT.
LET'S GO HOME.
N-NO, I'LL BE FINE IF I JUST REST A FEW MINUTES.
THAT'S OKAY. LET'S GO HOME.
B-BUT WE—
COME ON!
SEBAS-TIAN!
WILL YOU PLEASE TAKE ME HOME?
TAXI!

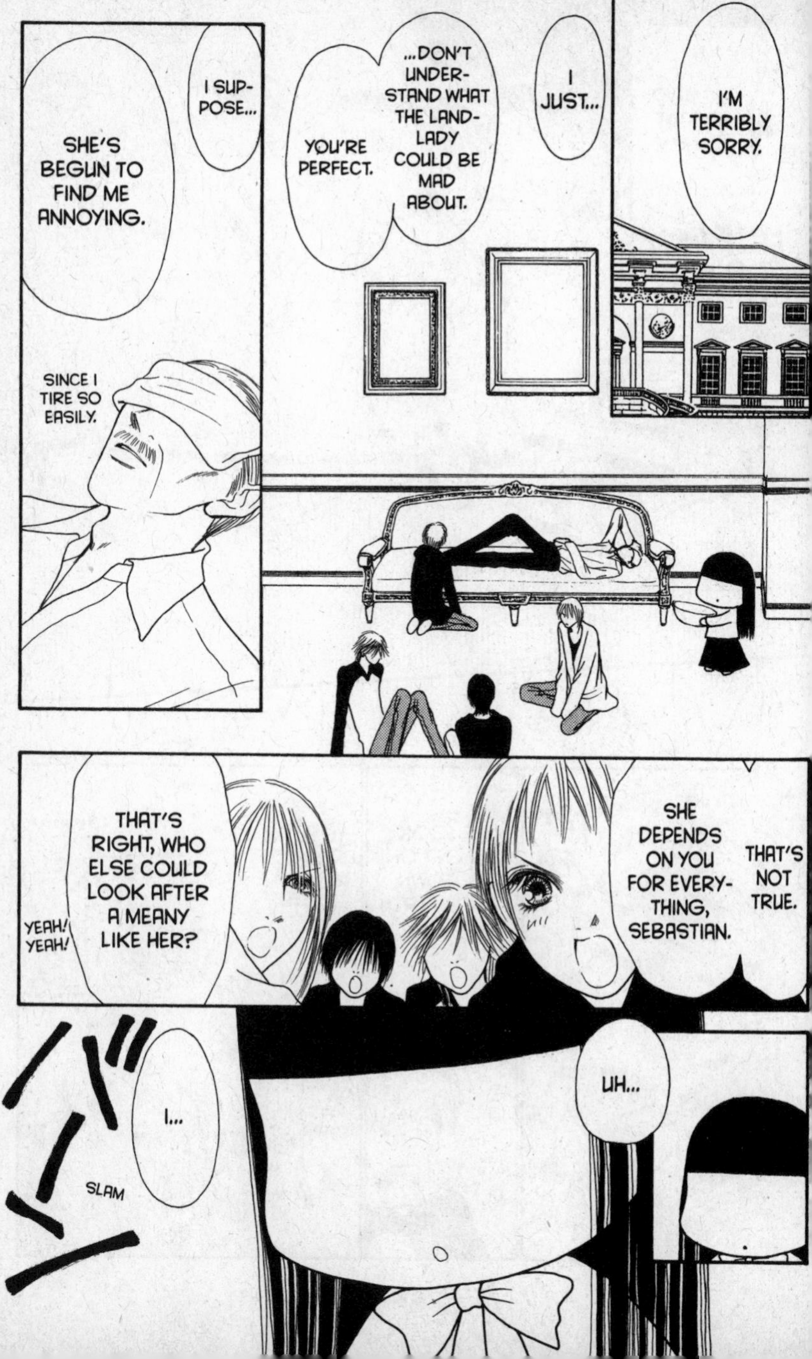
I'M TERRIBLY SORRY.
I JUST...
...DON'T UNDERSTAND WHAT THE LANDLADY COULD BE MAD ABOUT.
YOU'RE PERFECT.
I SUPPOSE...
SHE'S BEGUN TO FIND ME ANNOYING.
SINCE I TIRE SO EASILY.
THAT'S NOT TRUE.
SHE DEPENDS ON YOU FOR EVERYTHING, SEBASTIAN.
THAT'S RIGHT, WHO ELSE COULD LOOK AFTER A MEANY LIKE HER?
YEAH! YEAH!
UH...
I...
SLAM

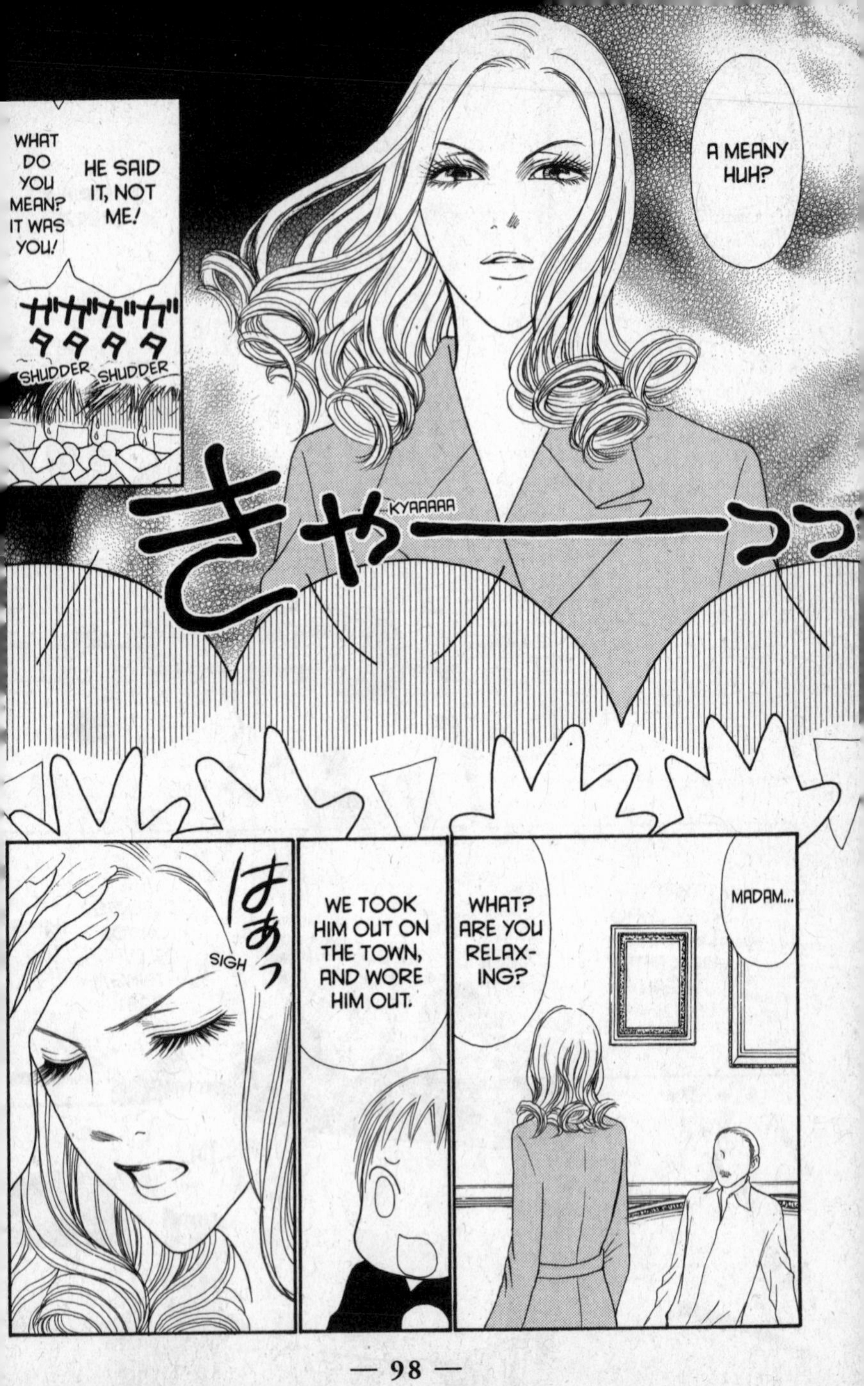
A MEANY HUH?
HE SAID IT, NOT ME!
WHAT DO YOU MEAN? IT WAS YOU!
ガガガガ タタタタ
SHUDDER SHUDDER
きゃーーっっ
KYAAAAA
MADAM...
WHAT? ARE YOU RELAXING?
WE TOOK HIM OUT ON THE TOWN, AND WORE HIM OUT.
はあっ
SIGH

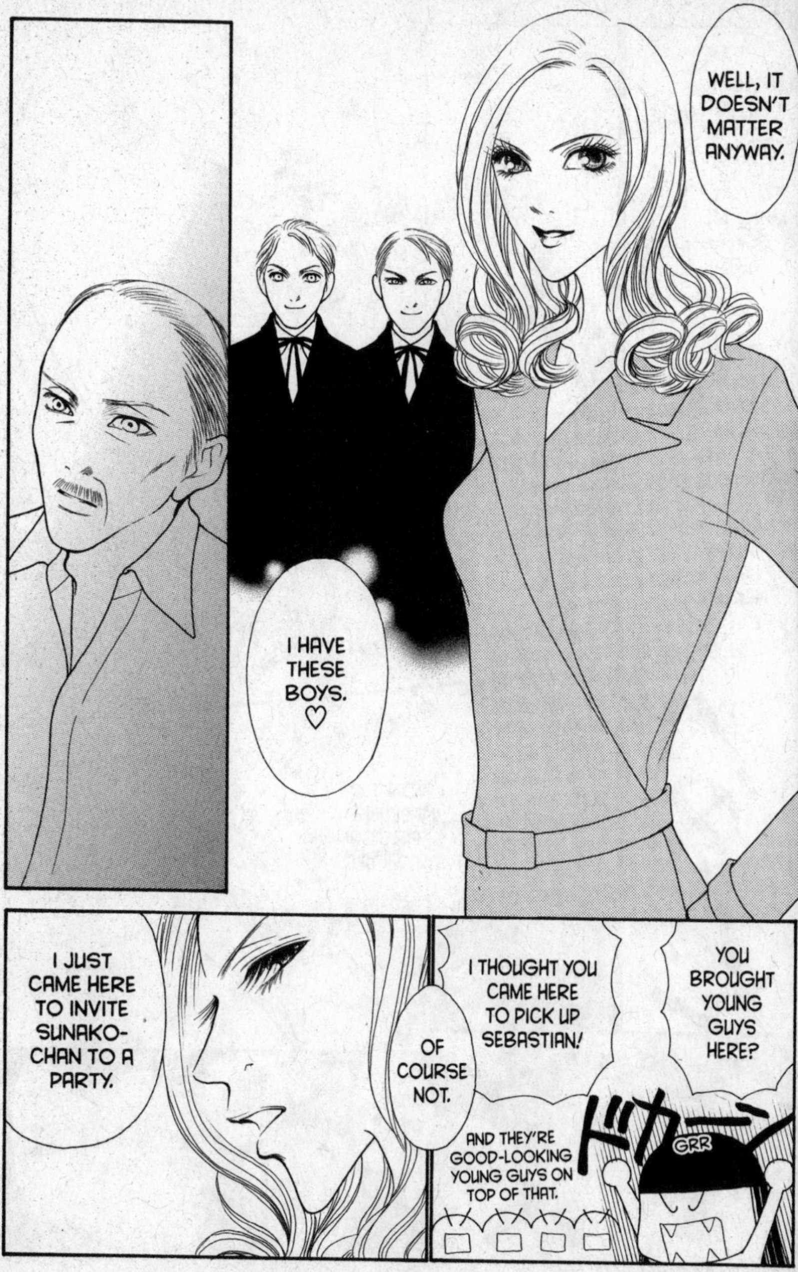
WELL, IT DOESN'T MATTER ANYWAY.
I HAVE THESE BOYS. ♡
YOU BROUGHT YOUNG GUYS HERE?
I THOUGHT YOU CAME HERE TO PICK UP SEBASTIAN!
ドカーン
GRR
AND THEY'RE GOOD-LOOKING YOUNG GUYS ON TOP OF THAT.
OF COURSE NOT.
I JUST CAME HERE TO INVITE SUNAKO-CHAN TO A PARTY.

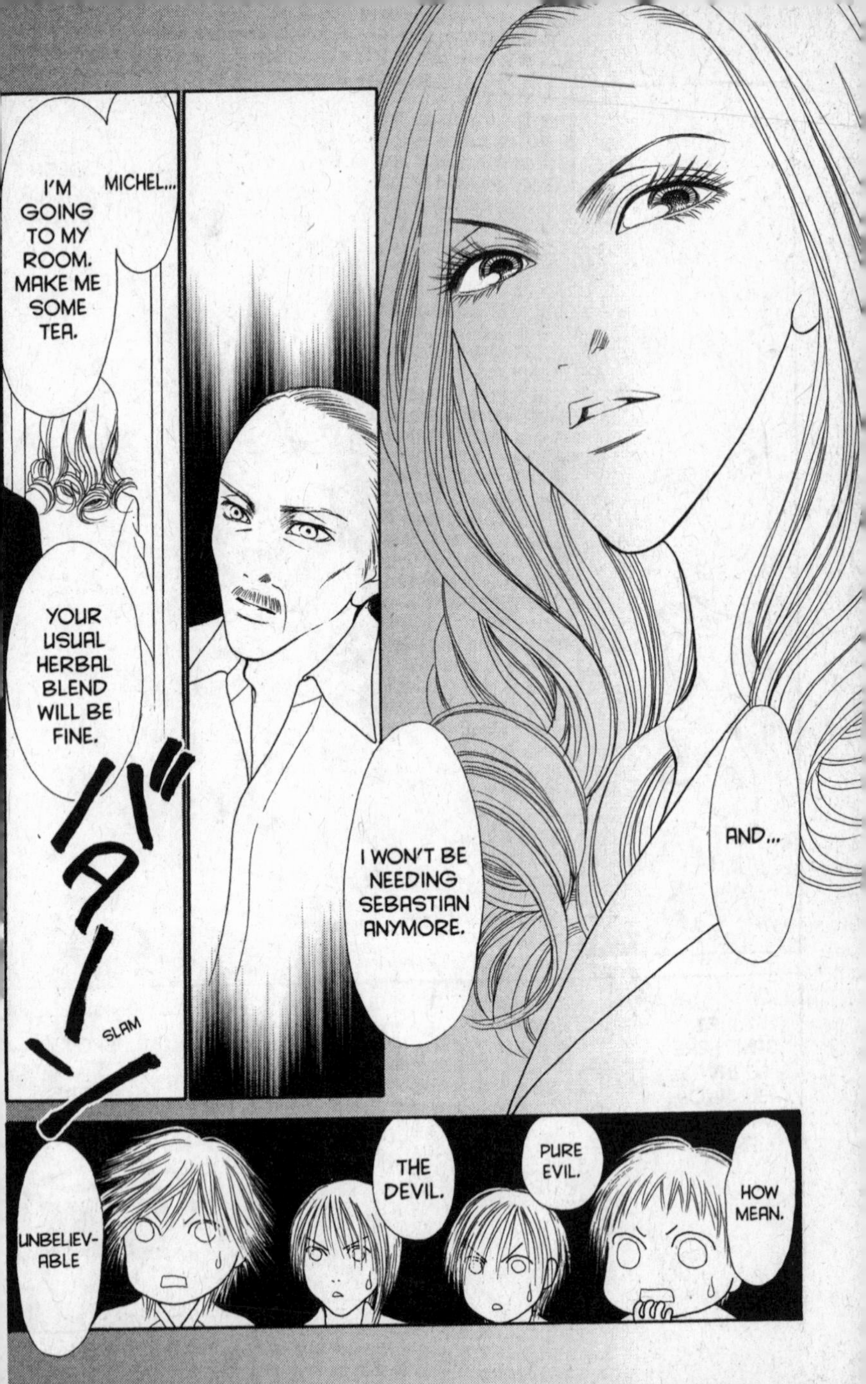
AND...
I WON'T BE NEEDING SEBASTIAN ANYMORE.
MICHEL...
I'M GOING TO MY ROOM. MAKE ME SOME TEA.
YOUR USUAL HERBAL BLEND WILL BE FINE.
バターン
SLAM
HOW MEAN.
PURE EVIL.
THE DEVIL.
UNBELIEV-ABLE

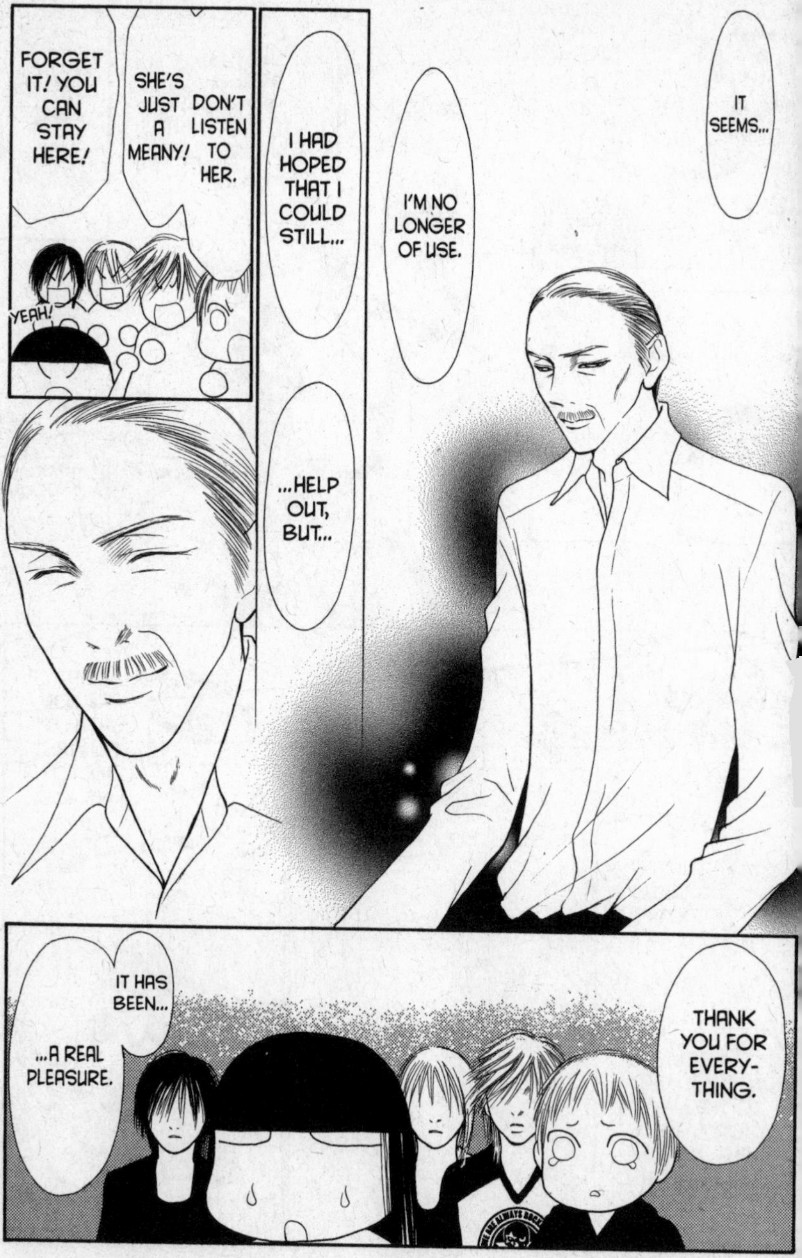
IT SEEMS...
I'M NO LONGER OF USE.
I HAD HOPED THAT I COULD STILL...
...HELP OUT, BUT...
DON'T LISTEN TO HER.
SHE'S JUST A MEANY!
FORGET IT! YOU CAN STAY HERE!
YEAH!
THANK YOU FOR EVERY-THING.
IT HAS BEEN...
...A REAL PLEASURE.

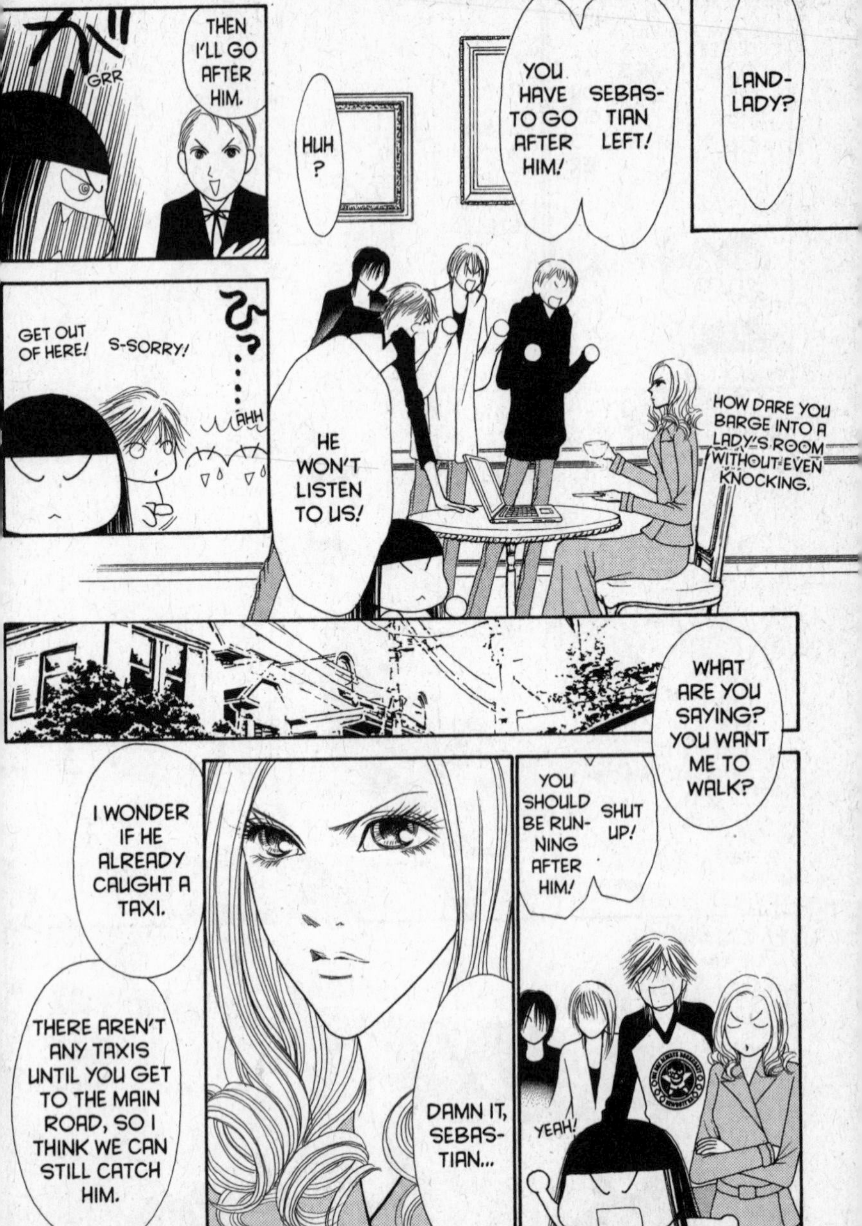
LAND-LADY?
SEBASTIAN LEFT!
YOU HAVE TO GO AFTER HIM!
HUH?
HOW DARE YOU BARGE INTO A LADY'S ROOM WITHOUT EVEN KNOCKING.
HE WON'T LISTEN TO US!
THEN I'LL GO AFTER HIM.
GRR
S-SORRY!
GET OUT OF HERE!
AHH
WHAT ARE YOU SAYING? YOU WANT ME TO WALK?
SHUT UP!
YOU SHOULD BE RUNNING AFTER HIM!
YEAH!
DAMN IT, SEBASTIAN...
I WONDER IF HE ALREADY CAUGHT A TAXI.
THERE AREN'T ANY TAXIS UNTIL YOU GET TO THE MAIN ROAD, SO I THINK WE CAN STILL CATCH HIM.

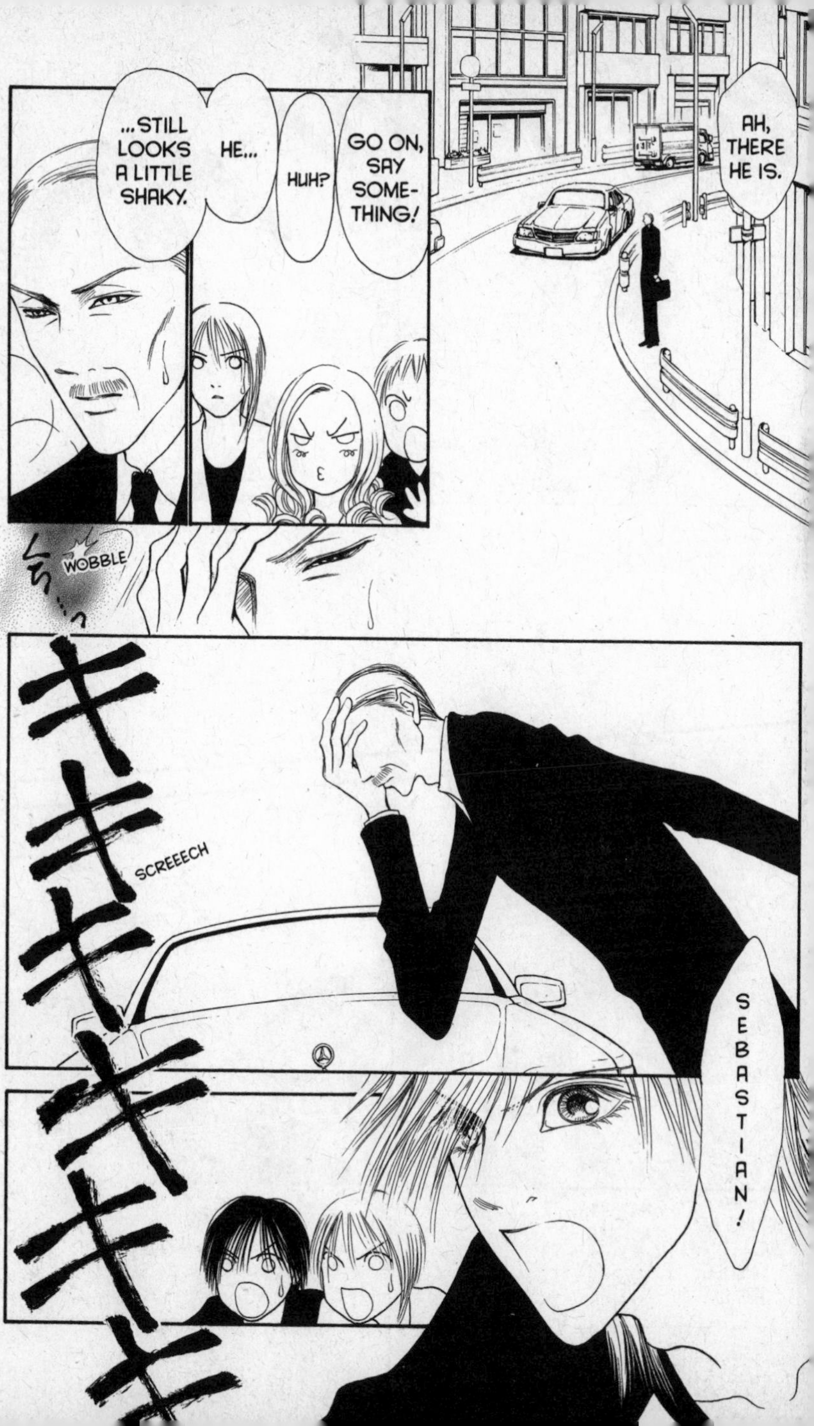
AH, THERE HE IS.
GO ON, SAY SOMETHING!
HUH?
HE...
...STILL LOOKS A LITTLE SHAKY.
WOBBLE
SCREEECH
SEBASTIAN!

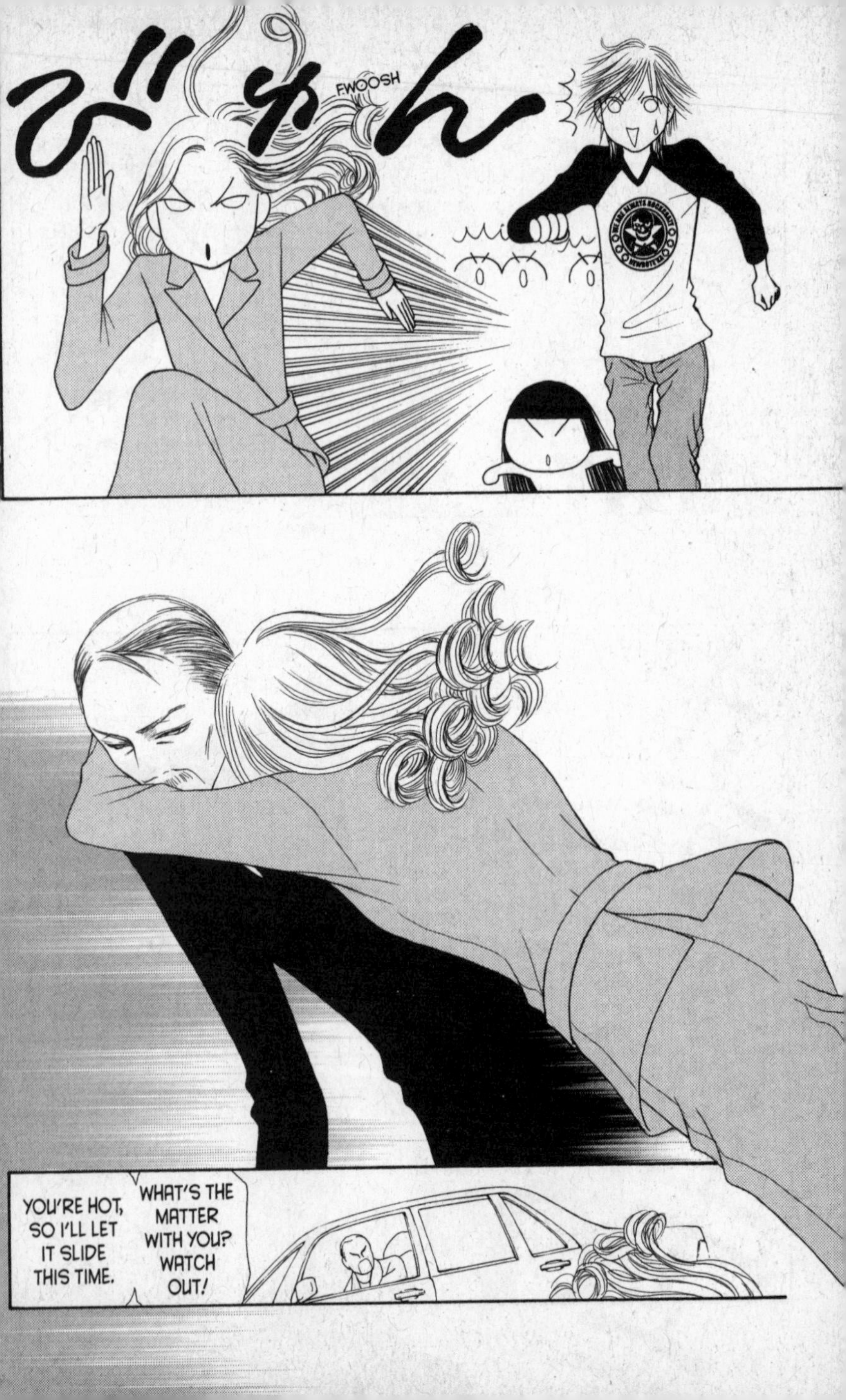
びゅん
FWOOSH
WHAT'S THE MATTER WITH YOU? WATCH OUT!
YOU'RE HOT, SO I'LL LET IT SLIDE THIS TIME.

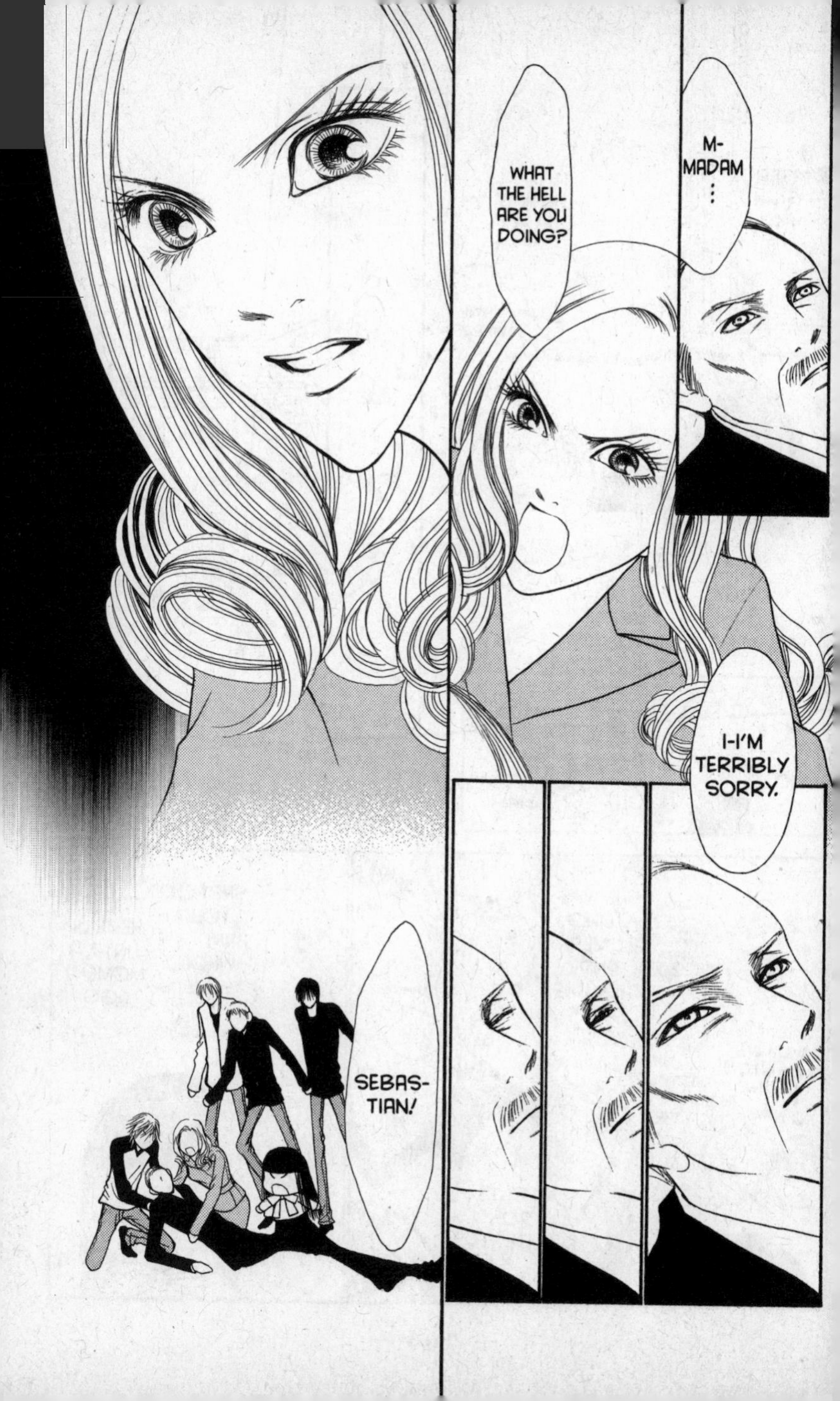
M-MADAM...
WHAT THE HELL ARE YOU DOING?
I-I'M TERRIBLY SORRY.
SEBASTIAN!

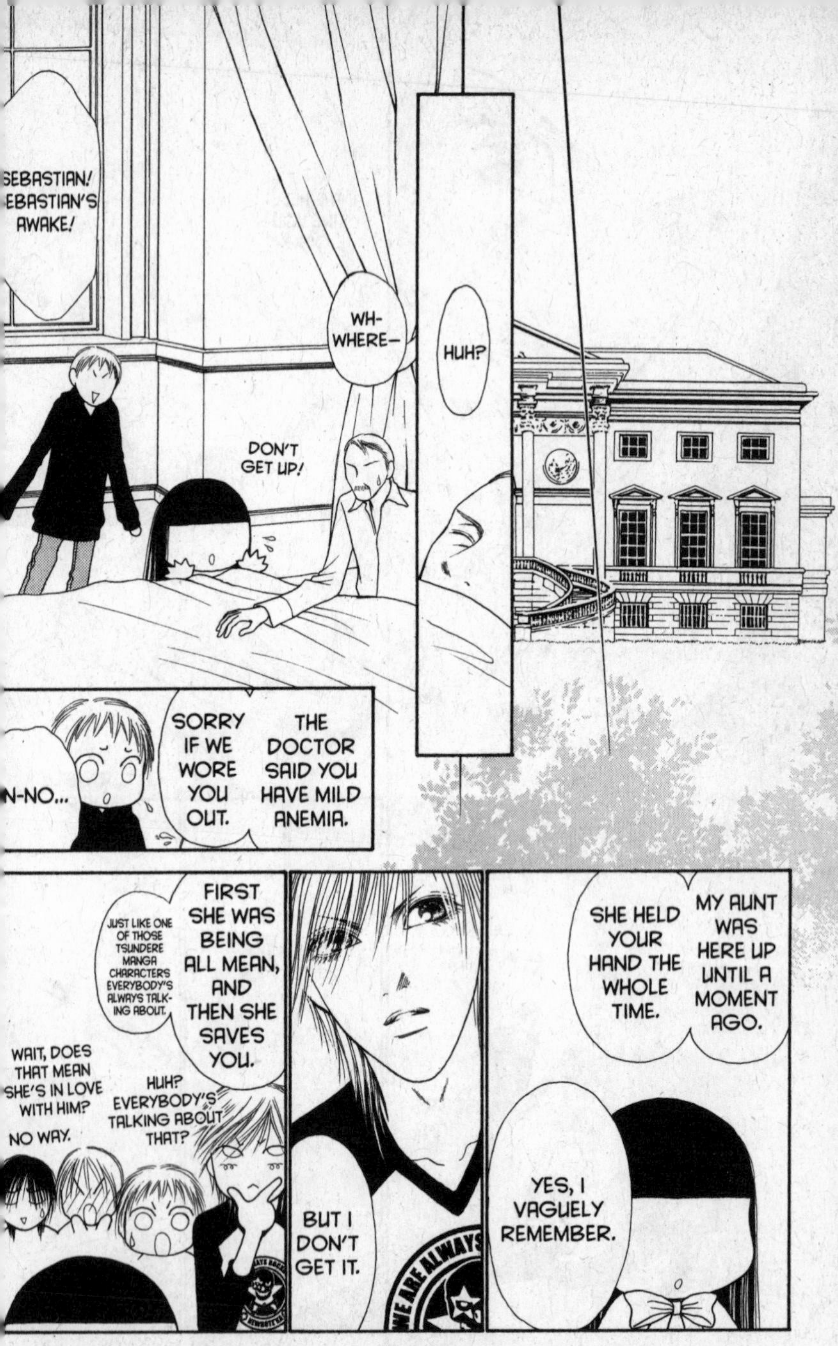
HUH?
WH- WHERE-
SEBASTIAN! SEBASTIAN'S AWAKE!
DON'T GET UP!
THE DOCTOR SAID YOU HAVE MILD ANEMIA.
SORRY IF WE WORE YOU OUT.
N-NO...
MY AUNT WAS HERE UP UNTIL A MOMENT AGO.
SHE HELD YOUR HAND THE WHOLE TIME.
YES, I VAGUELY REMEMBER.
BUT I DON'T GET IT.
FIRST SHE WAS BEING ALL MEAN, AND THEN SHE SAVES YOU.
JUST LIKE ONE OF THOSE TSUNDERE MANGA CHARACTERS EVERYBODY'S ALWAYS TALKING ABOUT.
HUH? EVERYBODY'S TALKING ABOUT THAT?
WAIT, DOES THAT MEAN SHE'S IN LOVE WITH HIM?
NO WAY.

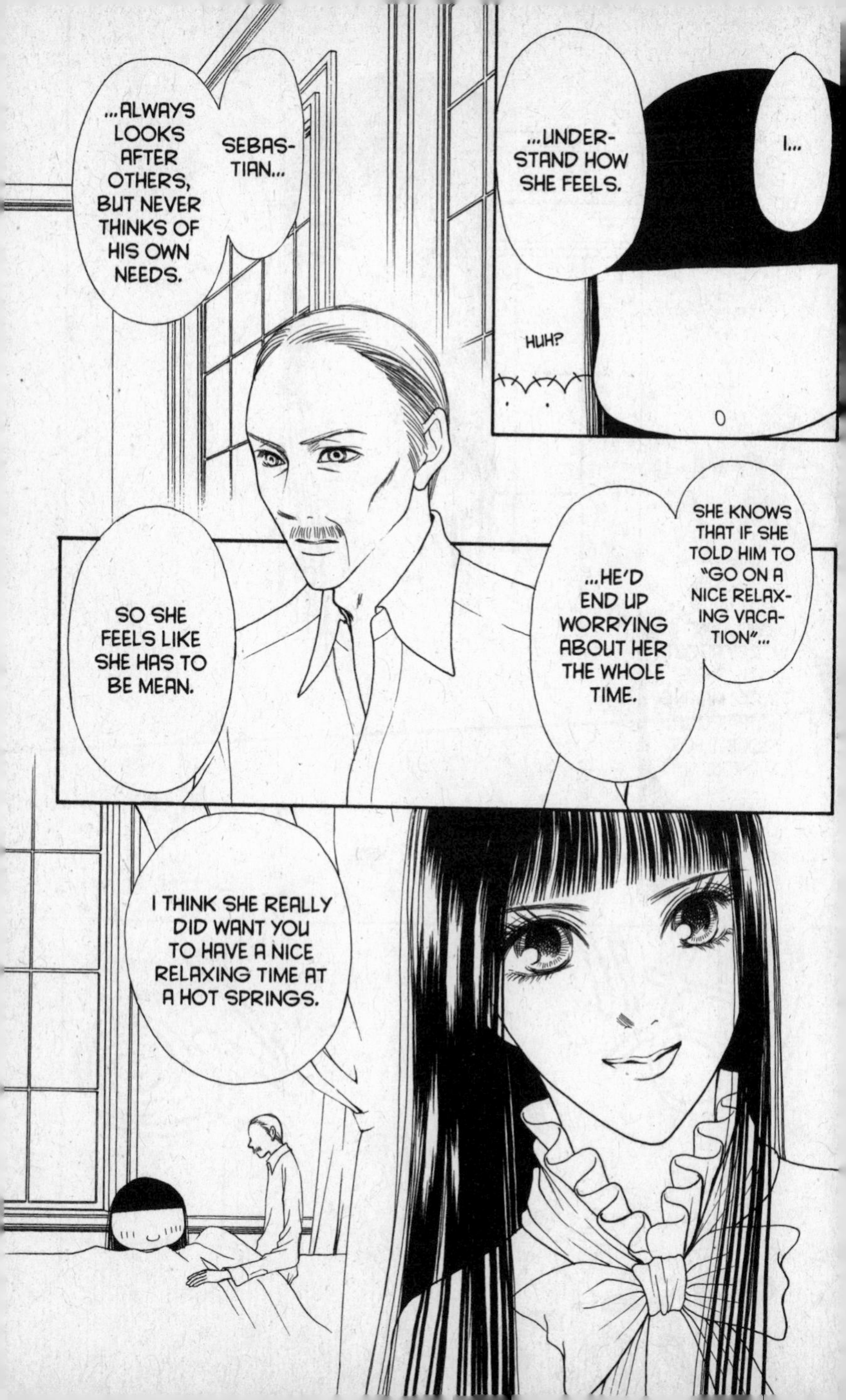
I...
...UNDERSTAND HOW SHE FEELS.
HUH?
SEBASTIAN...
...ALWAYS LOOKS AFTER OTHERS, BUT NEVER THINKS OF HIS OWN NEEDS.
SHE KNOWS THAT IF SHE TOLD HIM TO "GO ON A NICE RELAXING VACATION"...
...HE'D END UP WORRYING ABOUT HER THE WHOLE TIME.
SO SHE FEELS LIKE SHE HAS TO BE MEAN.
I THINK SHE REALLY DID WANT YOU TO HAVE A NICE RELAXING TIME AT A HOT SPRINGS.

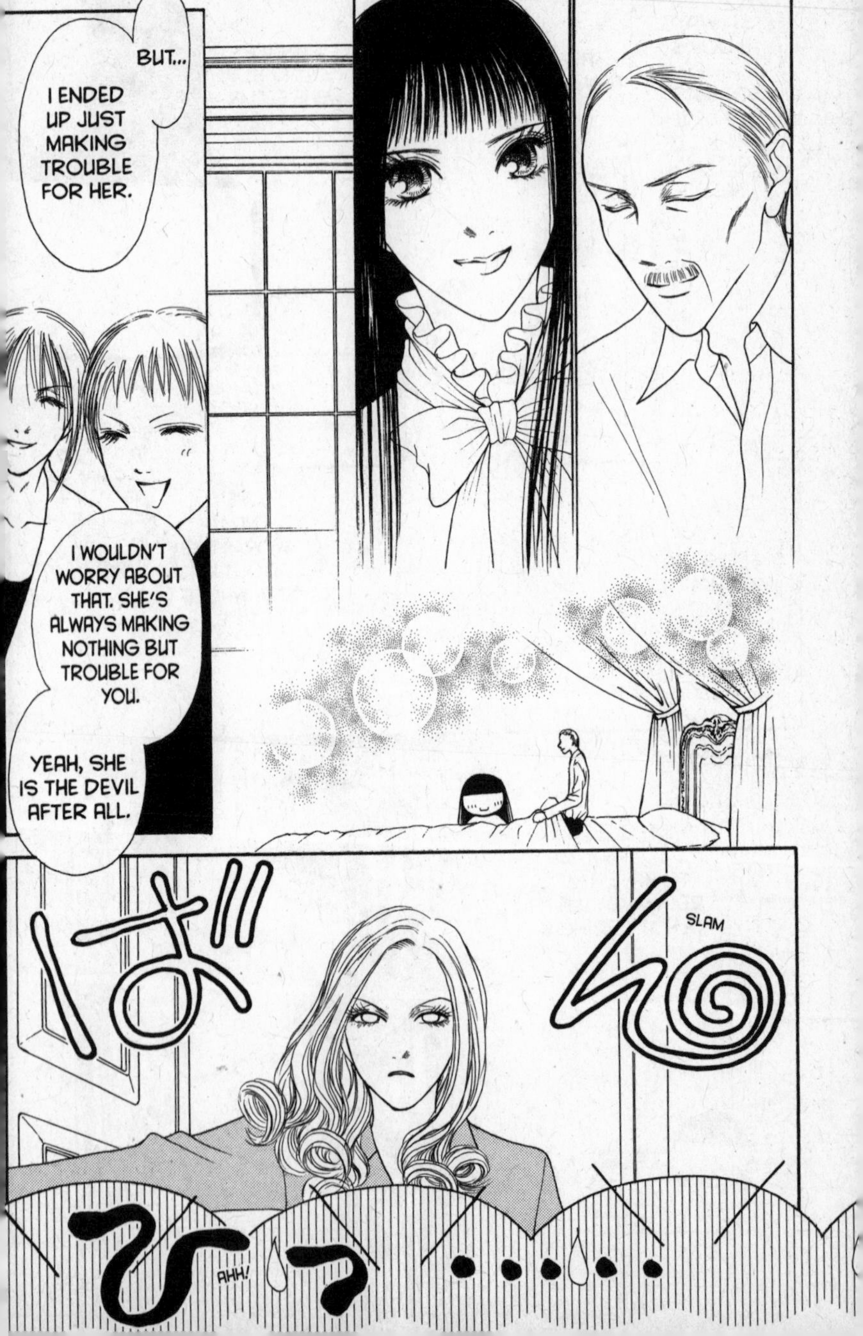
BUT...
I ENDED UP JUST MAKING TROUBLE FOR HER.
I WOULDN'T WORRY ABOUT THAT. SHE'S ALWAYS MAKING NOTHING BUT TROUBLE FOR YOU.
YEAH, SHE IS THE DEVIL AFTER ALL.
ばん
SLAM
ひっ......
AHH!

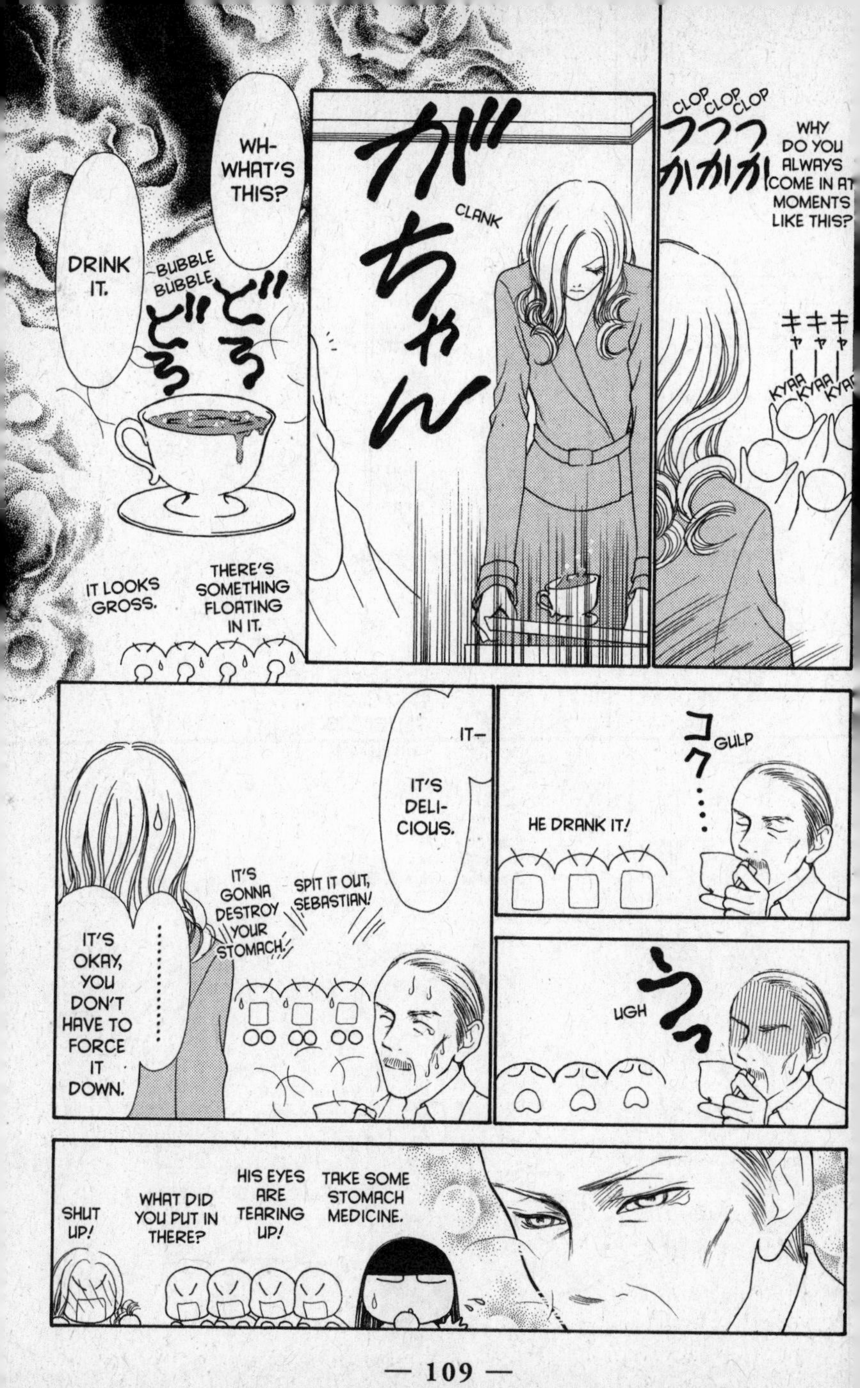
CLOP CLOP CLOP
WHY DO YOU ALWAYS COME IN AT MOMENTS LIKE THIS?
キャーキャーキャー
KYAA KYAA KYAA
がちゃん
CLANK
WH-WHAT'S THIS?
DRINK IT.
どろどろ
BUBBLE BUBBLE
THERE'S SOMETHING FLOATING IN IT.
IT LOOKS GROSS.
コク…
GULP
HE DRANK IT!
うっ
UGH
IT—
IT'S DELICIOUS.
SPIT IT OUT, SEBASTIAN!
IT'S GONNA DESTROY YOUR STOMACH.
……
IT'S OKAY, YOU DON'T HAVE TO FORCE IT DOWN.
TAKE SOME STOMACH MEDICINE.
HIS EYES ARE TEARING UP!
WHAT DID YOU PUT IN THERE?
SHUT UP!

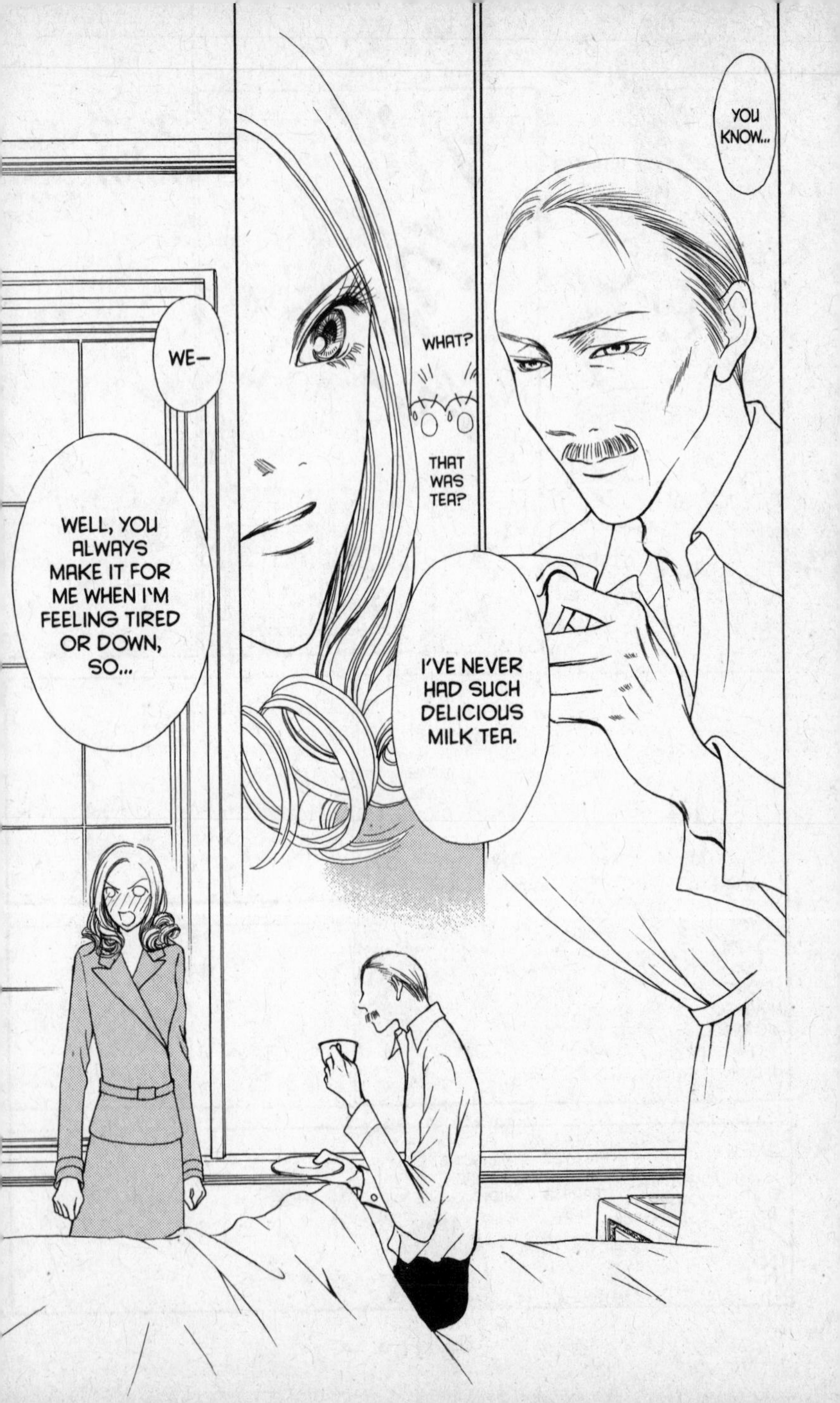
YOU KNOW...
I'VE NEVER HAD SUCH DELICIOUS MILK TEA.
WHAT?
THAT WAS TEA?
WE—
WELL, YOU ALWAYS MAKE IT FOR ME WHEN I'M FEELING TIRED OR DOWN, SO...

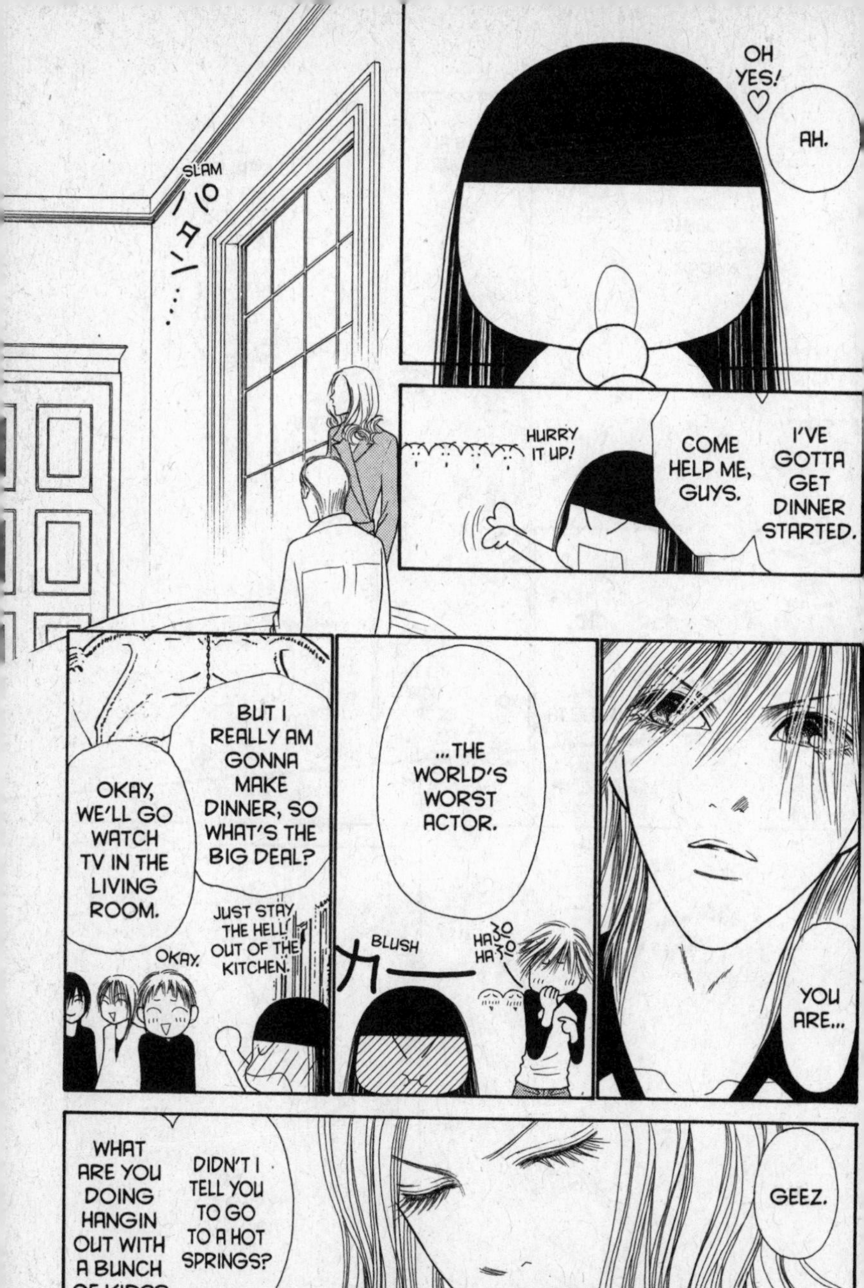
OH YES! ♡
AH.
I'VE GOTTA GET DINNER STARTED.
COME HELP ME, GUYS.
HURRY IT UP!
SLAM
YOU ARE...
...THE WORLD'S WORST ACTOR.
BLUSH
HA HA
BUT I REALLY AM GONNA MAKE DINNER, SO WHAT'S THE BIG DEAL?
OKAY, WE'LL GO WATCH TV IN THE LIVING ROOM.
JUST STAY THE HELL OUT OF THE KITCHEN.
OKAY.
GEEZ.
DIDN'T I TELL YOU TO GO TO A HOT SPRINGS?
WHAT ARE YOU DOING HANGIN OUT WITH A BUNCH OF KIDS?

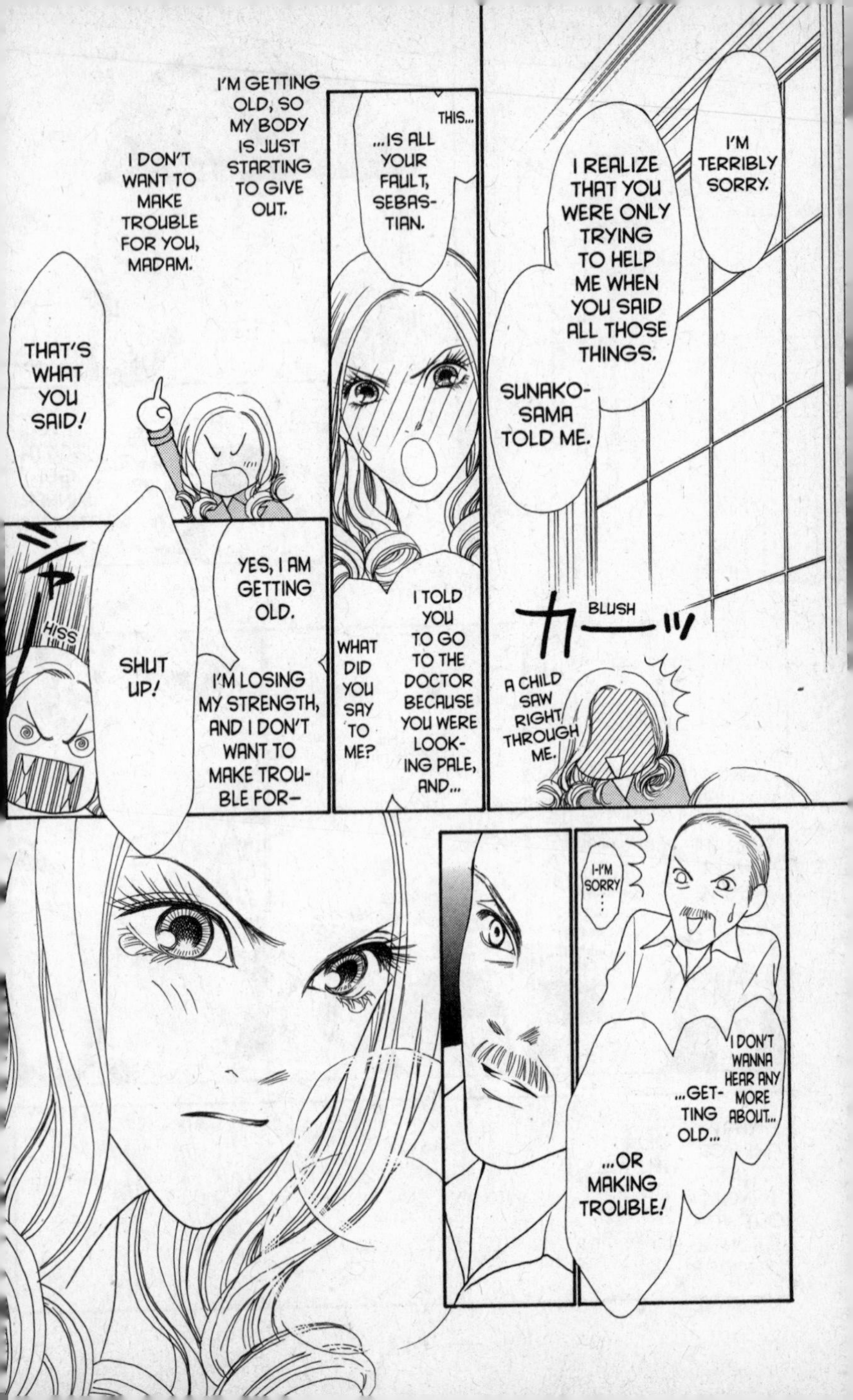
I'M TERRIBLY SORRY.
I REALIZE THAT YOU WERE ONLY TRYING TO HELP ME WHEN YOU SAID ALL THOSE THINGS.
SUNAKO-SAMA TOLD ME.
THIS...
...IS ALL YOUR FAULT, SEBASTIAN.
I'M GETTING OLD, SO MY BODY IS JUST STARTING TO GIVE OUT.
I DON'T WANT TO MAKE TROUBLE FOR YOU, MADAM.
THAT'S WHAT YOU SAID!
BLUSH
A CHILD SAW RIGHT THROUGH ME.
I TOLD YOU TO GO TO THE DOCTOR BECAUSE YOU WERE LOOKING PALE, AND...
WHAT DID YOU SAY TO ME?
YES, I AM GETTING OLD.
I'M LOSING MY STRENGTH, AND I DON'T WANT TO MAKE TROUBLE FOR—
HISS
SHUT UP!
I-I'M SORRY...
I DON'T WANNA HEAR ANY MORE ABOUT...
...GETTING OLD...
...OR MAKING TROUBLE!

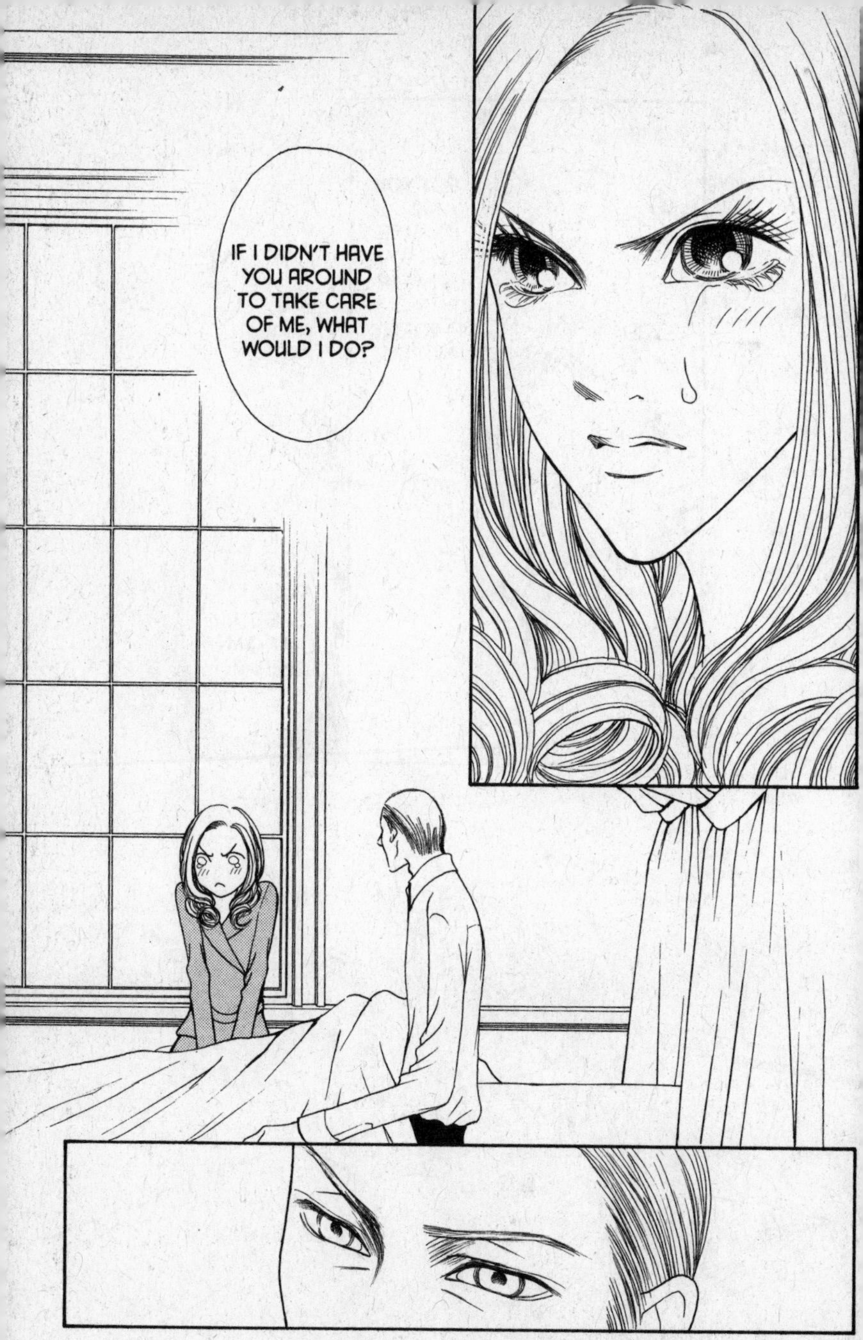
IF I DIDN'T HAVE YOU AROUND TO TAKE CARE OF ME, WHAT WOULD I DO?

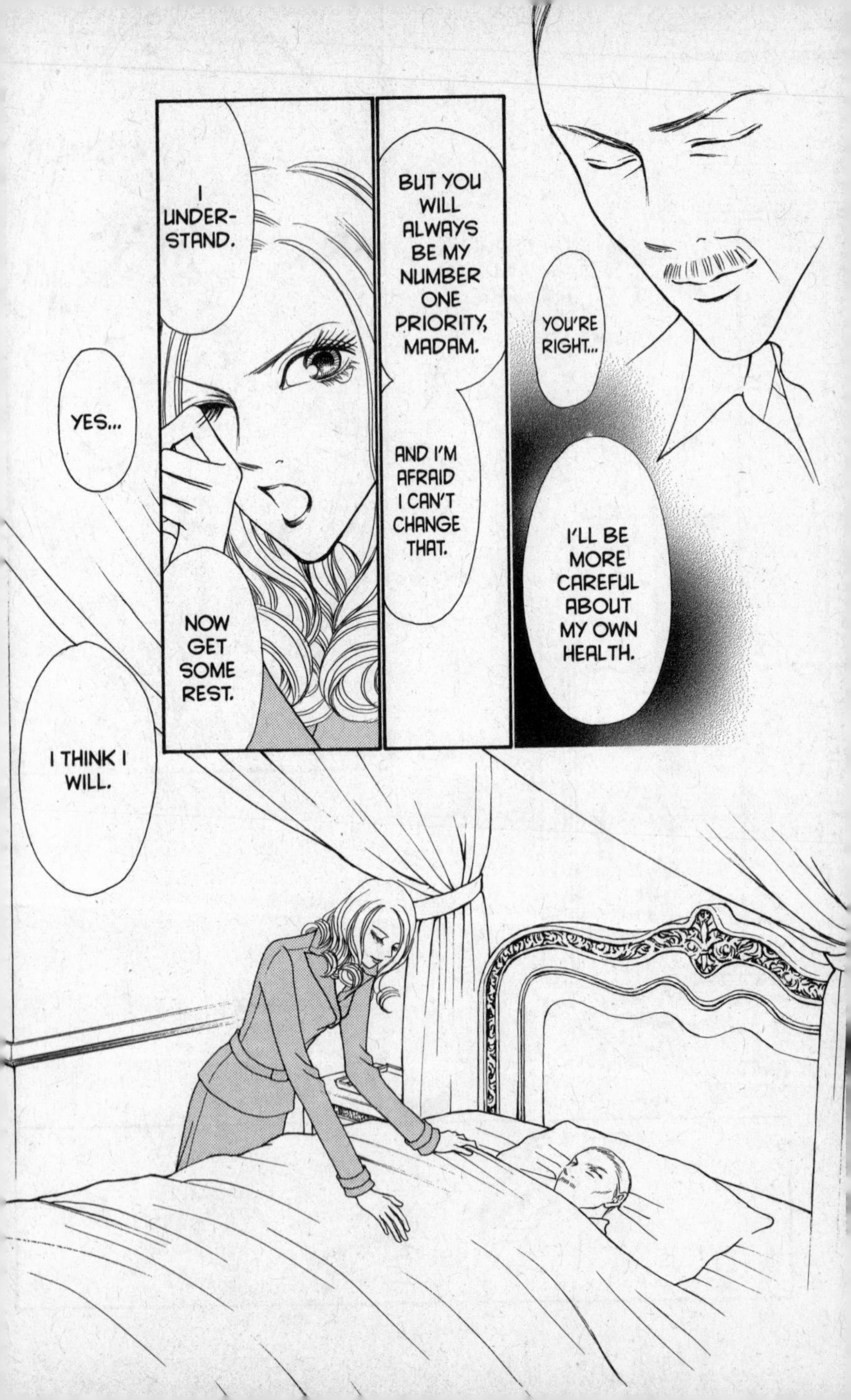

YOU'RE RIGHT...
I'LL BE MORE CAREFUL ABOUT MY OWN HEALTH.
BUT YOU WILL ALWAYS BE MY NUMBER ONE PRIORITY, MADAM.
AND I'M AFRAID I CAN'T CHANGE THAT.
I UNDER-STAND.
NOW GET SOME REST.
YES...
I THINK I WILL.

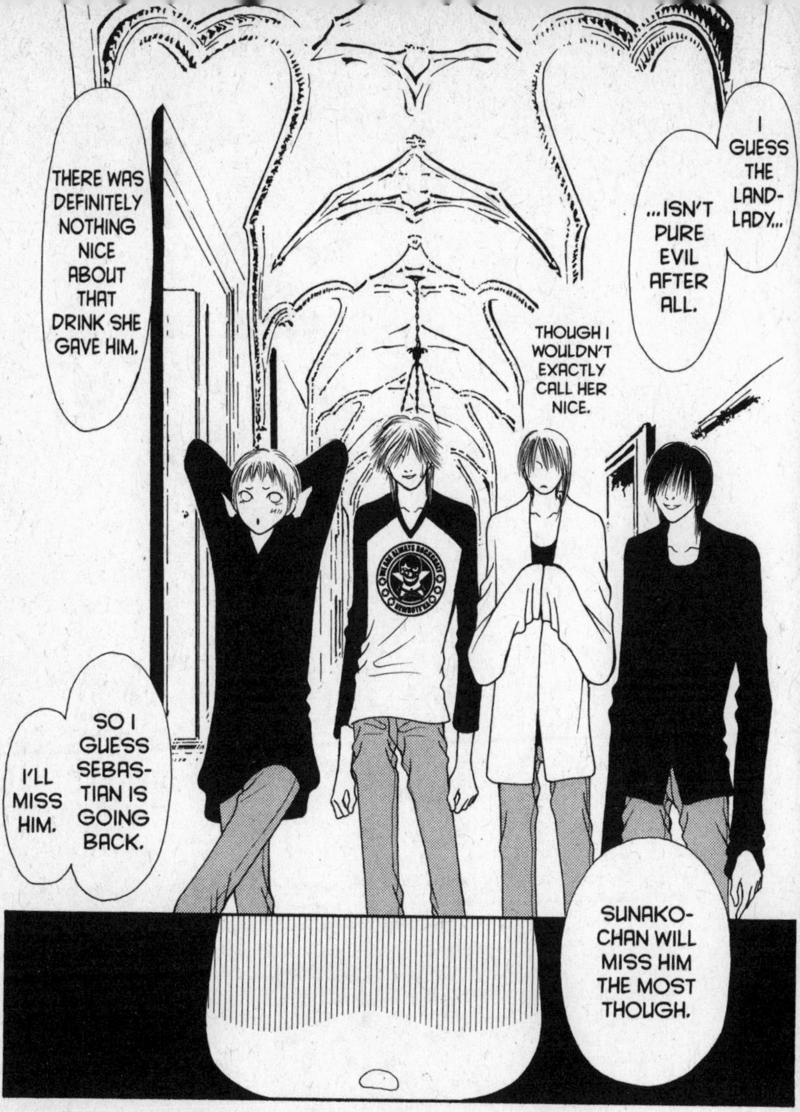
I GUESS THE LANDLADY...
...ISN'T PURE EVIL AFTER ALL.
THOUGH I WOULDN'T EXACTLY CALL HER NICE.
THERE WAS DEFINITELY NOTHING NICE ABOUT THAT DRINK SHE GAVE HIM.
SO I GUESS SEBASTIAN IS GOING BACK.
I'LL MISS HIM.
SUNAKO-CHAN WILL MISS HIM THE MOST THOUGH.
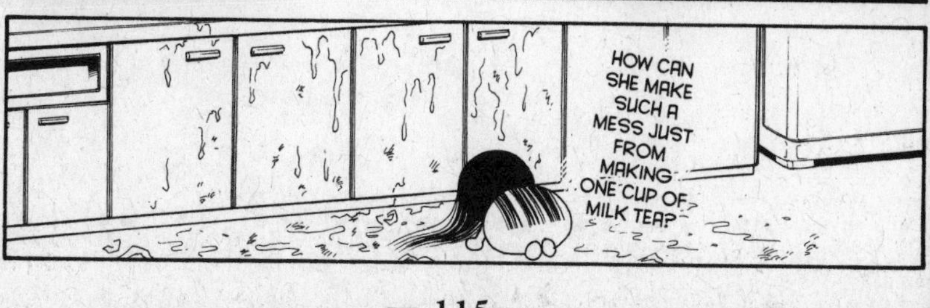
HOW CAN SHE MAKE SUCH A MESS JUST FROM MAKING ONE CUP OF MILK TEA?

Chapter 99 THE BRILLIANT BOND

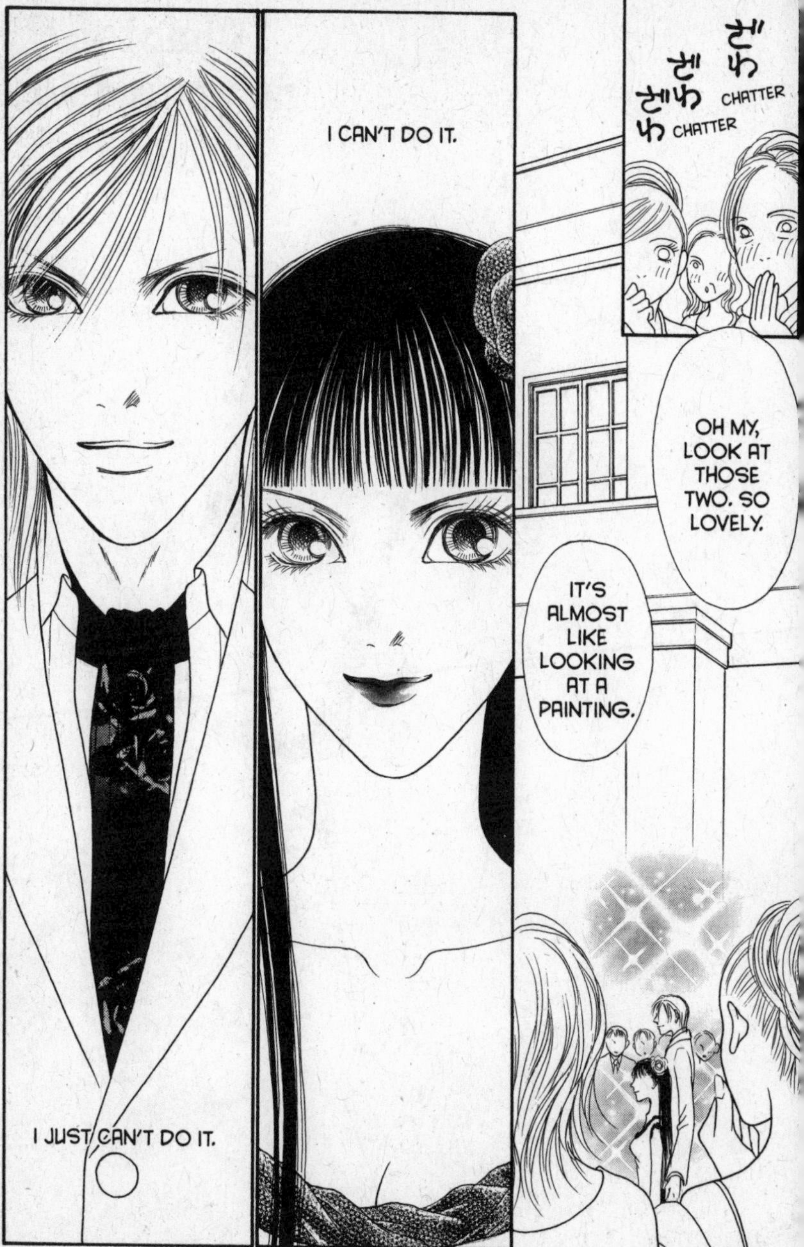
ざわ
CHATTER
ざわざわ
CHATTER
OH MY, LOOK AT THOSE TWO. SO LOVELY.
IT'S ALMOST LIKE LOOKING AT A PAINTING.
I CAN'T DO IT.
I JUST CAN'T DO IT.

Chapter 99

THE BRILLIANT BOND

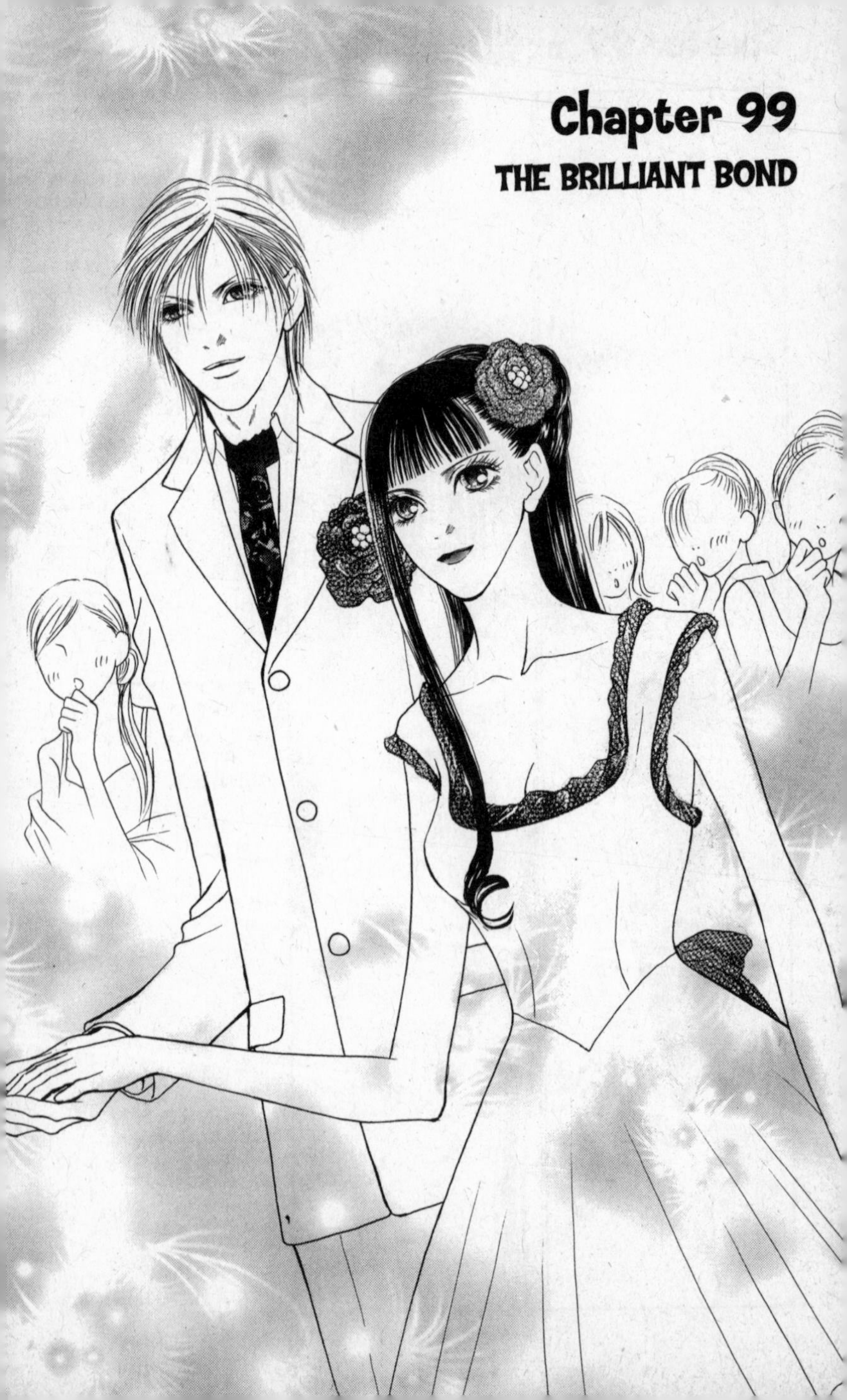

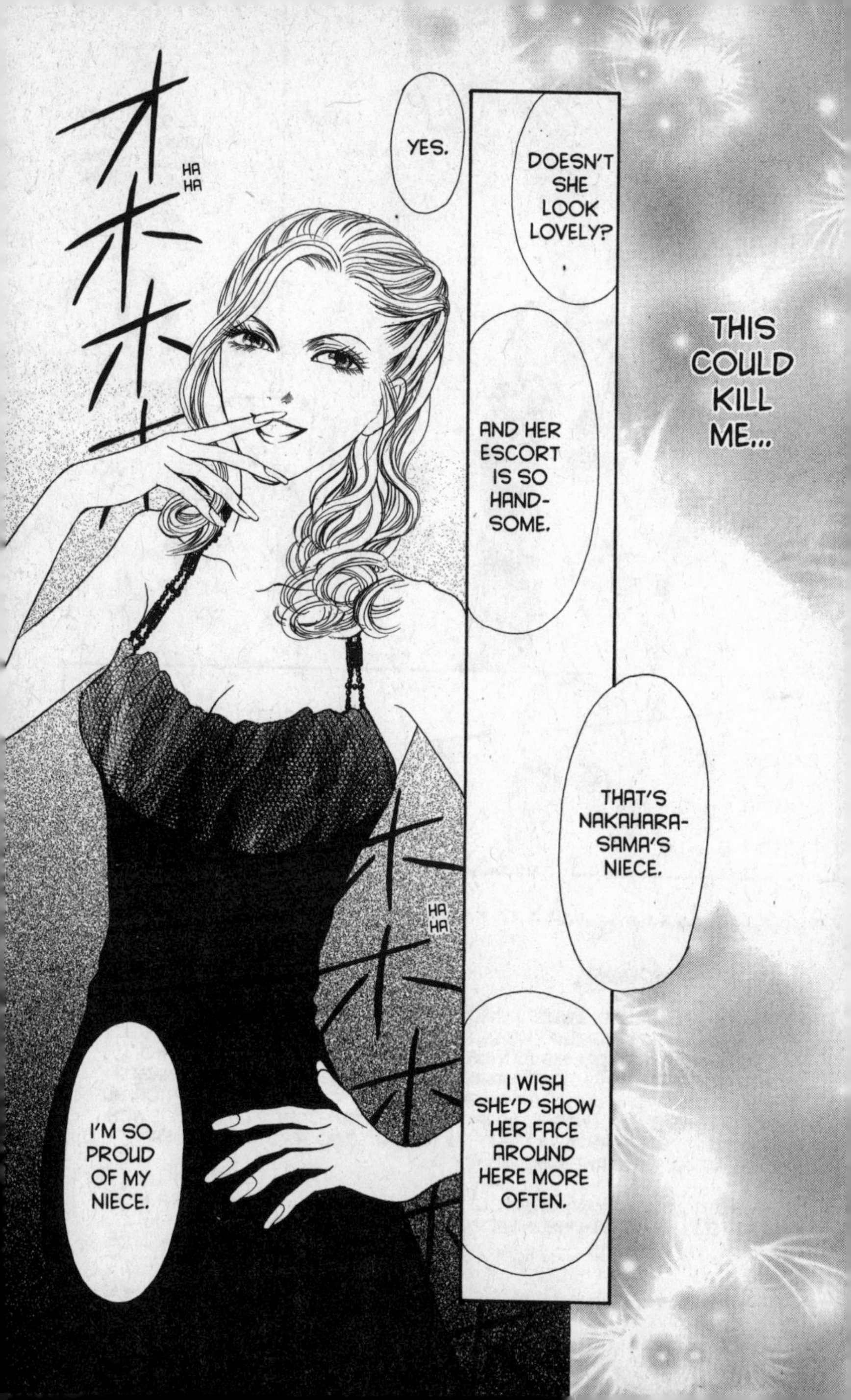
THIS COULD KILL ME...
DOESN'T SHE LOOK LOVELY?
YES.
AND HER ESCORT IS SO HANDSOME.
THAT'S NAKAHARA-SAMA'S NIECE.
I WISH SHE'D SHOW HER FACE AROUND HERE MORE OFTEN.
HA HA
HA HA
I'M SO PROUD OF MY NIECE.

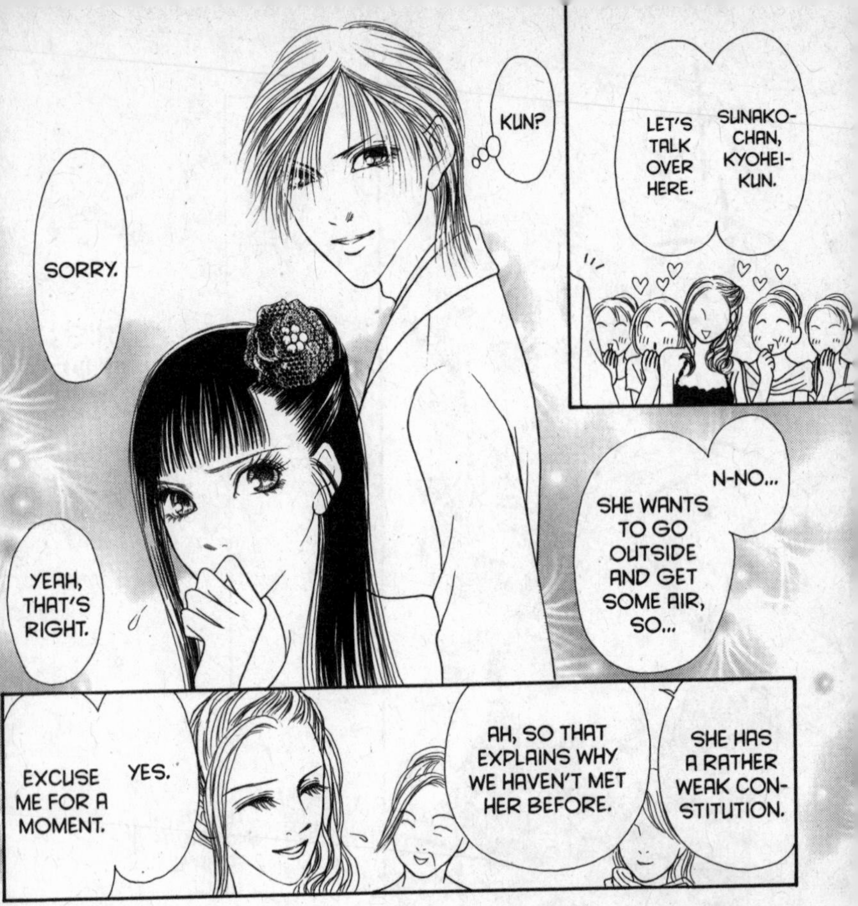
SUNAKO-CHAN, KYOHEI-KUN.
LET'S TALK OVER HERE.
N-NO...
SHE WANTS TO GO OUTSIDE AND GET SOME AIR, SO...
KUN?
SORRY.
YEAH, THAT'S RIGHT.
SHE HAS A RATHER WEAK CON-STITUTION.
AH, SO THAT EXPLAINS WHY WE HAVEN'T MET HER BEFORE.
YES.
EXCUSE ME FOR A MOMENT.

BEHIND THE SCENES

THE STORY OF MY FRIEND'S WEDDING—CONTINUED... ONE OF MY REALLY CLOSE GUY FRIENDS, MAKO, GOT MARRIED. (HIS REAL NAME IS MAKOTO.) I WENT TO HACHIOUJI. I HAD TO LEAVE IN THE MORNING TO MAKE IT TO THE CEREMONY. HIS BRIDE RIEKO LOOKED SO PRETTY. ♥♥♥ I GOT ALL TEARY-EYED AT THE CEREMONY, BUT I MANAGED TO KEEP MYSELF FROM FULL-ON BAWLING. I TRIED NOT TO CRY AT THE RECEPTION, BUT I JUST COULDN'T HELP IT. I WAS SO HAPPY THAT HE FOUND SUCH A PRETTY BRIDE WITH SUCH A GREAT PERSONALITY WHO IS TRULY DEDICATED TO HER JOB. I'M SO HAPPY FOR YOU, MAKO. SHE IS AWESOME.

I ALSO GOT TO SEE SO MANY OF MY OLD FRIENDS. IT WAS LIKE A REUNION. IT ALMOST MADE ME FEEL LIKE I WAS LIVING IN HACHIOUJI AGAIN. IT'S SUCH A NICE TOWN.

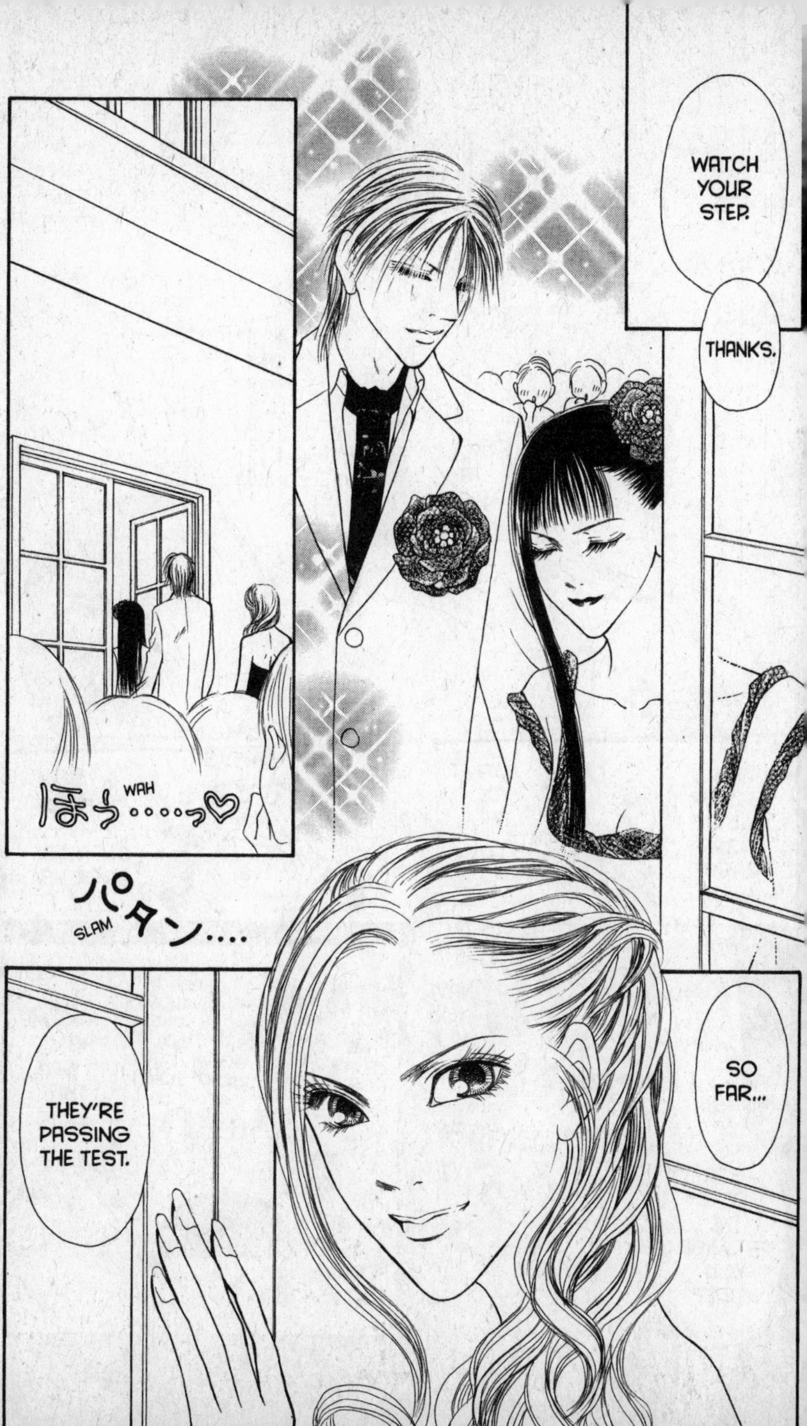
WATCH YOUR STEP.
THANKS.
ほぅ……っ♡ WAH
パタン…. SLAM
SO FAR...
THEY'RE PASSING THE TEST.

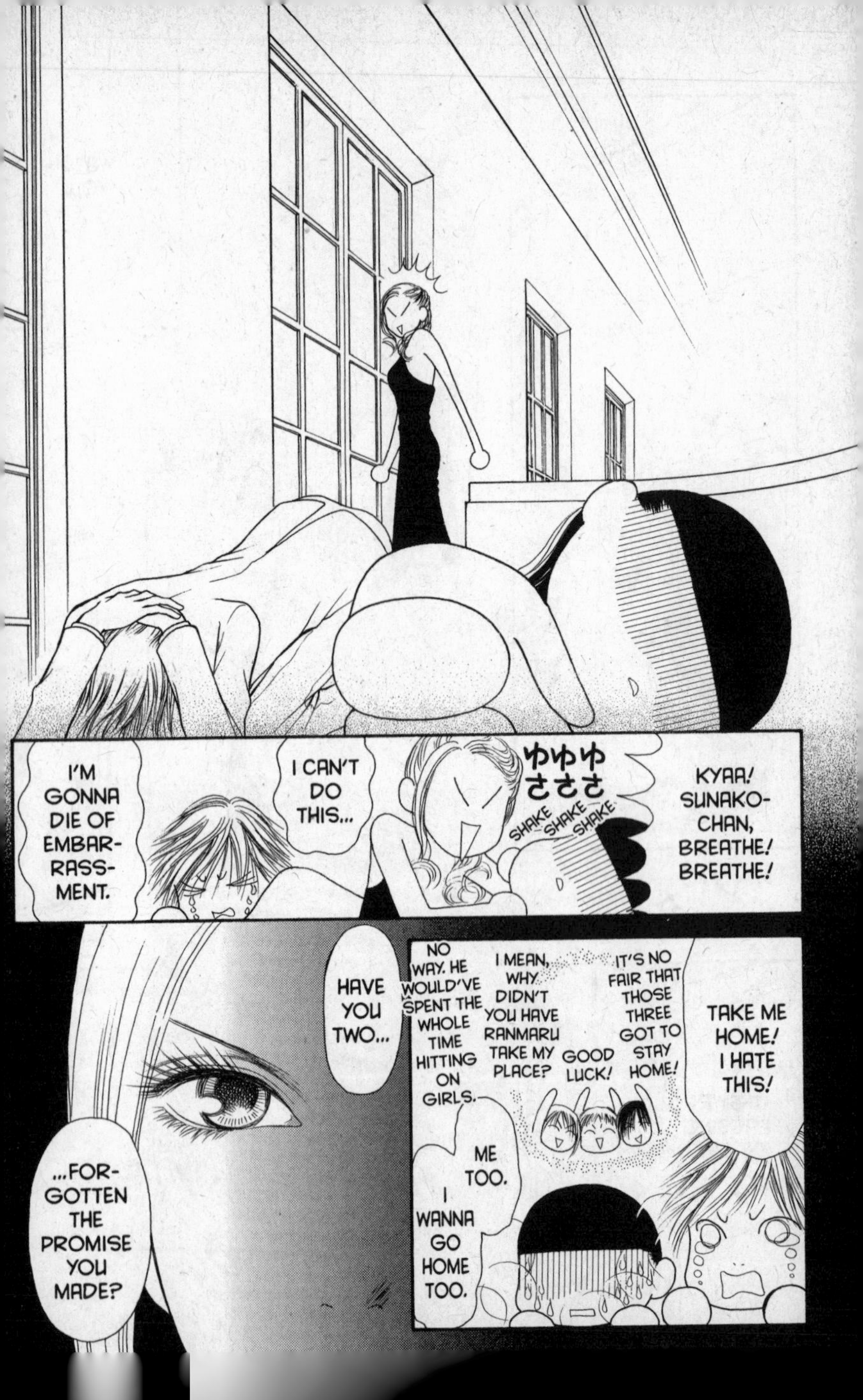
KYAA! SUNAKO-CHAN, BREATHE! BREATHE!
ゆさゆさゆさ
SHAKE SHAKE SHAKE
I CAN'T DO THIS...
I'M GONNA DIE OF EMBARRASSMENT.
TAKE ME HOME! I HATE THIS!
IT'S NO FAIR THAT THOSE THREE GOT TO STAY HOME!
GOOD LUCK!
I MEAN, WHY DIDN'T YOU HAVE RANMARU TAKE MY PLACE?
NO WAY. HE WOULD'VE SPENT THE WHOLE TIME HITTING ON GIRLS.
ME TOO.
I WANNA GO HOME TOO.
HAVE YOU TWO...
...FORGOTTEN THE PROMISE YOU MADE?

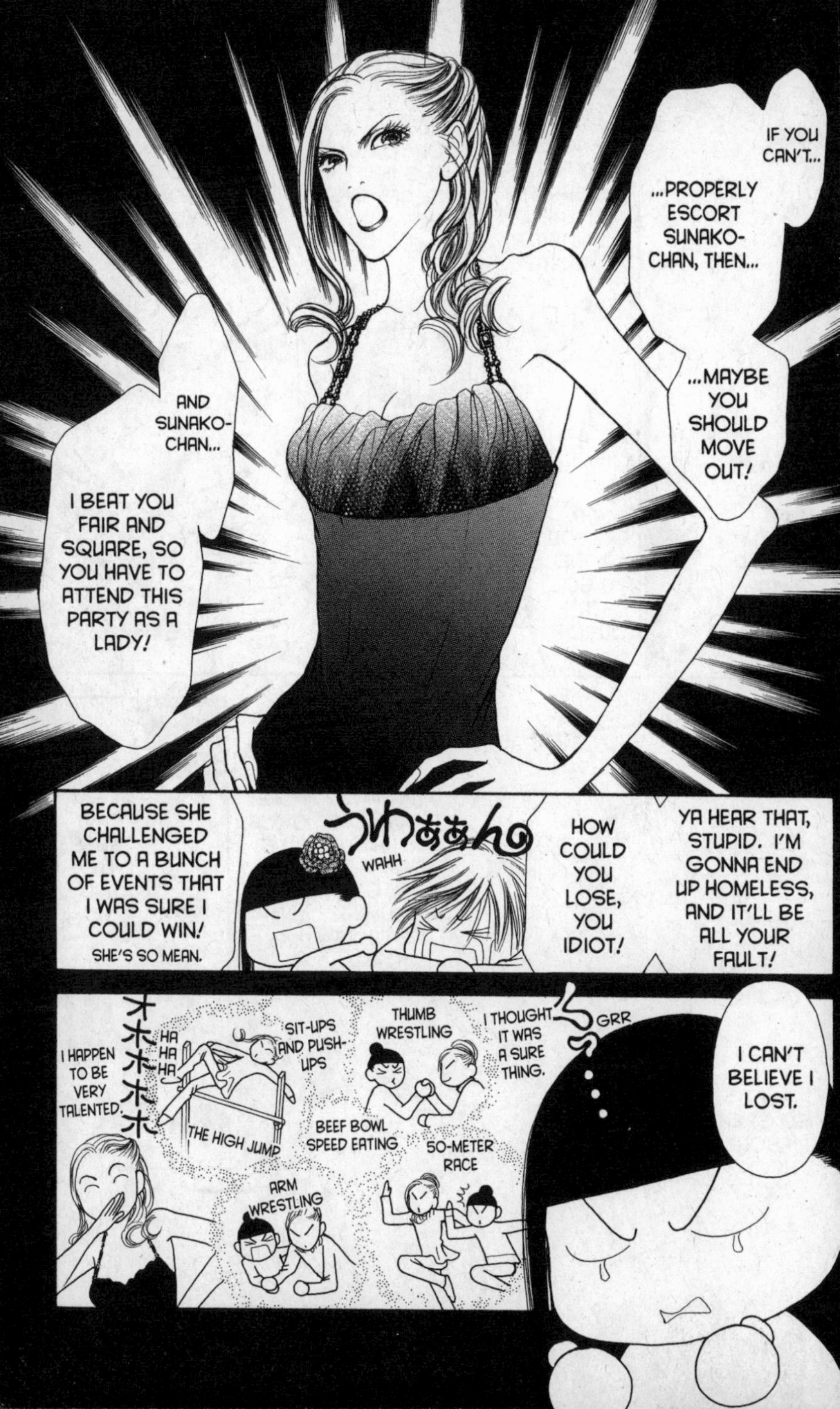
IF YOU CAN'T...
...PROPERLY ESCORT SUNAKO-CHAN, THEN...
...MAYBE YOU SHOULD MOVE OUT!
AND SUNAKO-CHAN...
I BEAT YOU FAIR AND SQUARE, SO YOU HAVE TO ATTEND THIS PARTY AS A LADY!
YA HEAR THAT, STUPID. I'M GONNA END UP HOMELESS, AND IT'LL BE ALL YOUR FAULT!
HOW COULD YOU LOSE, YOU IDIOT!
うわあぁん
WAHH
BECAUSE SHE CHALLENGED ME TO A BUNCH OF EVENTS THAT I WAS SURE I COULD WIN!
SHE'S SO MEAN.
I CAN'T BELIEVE I LOST.
GRR
I THOUGHT IT WAS A SURE THING.
THUMB WRESTLING
SIT-UPS AND PUSH-UPS
HA HA HA
オホホホホ
I HAPPEN TO BE VERY TALENTED.
THE HIGH JUMP
BEEF BOWL SPEED EATING
50-METER RACE
ARM WRESTLING

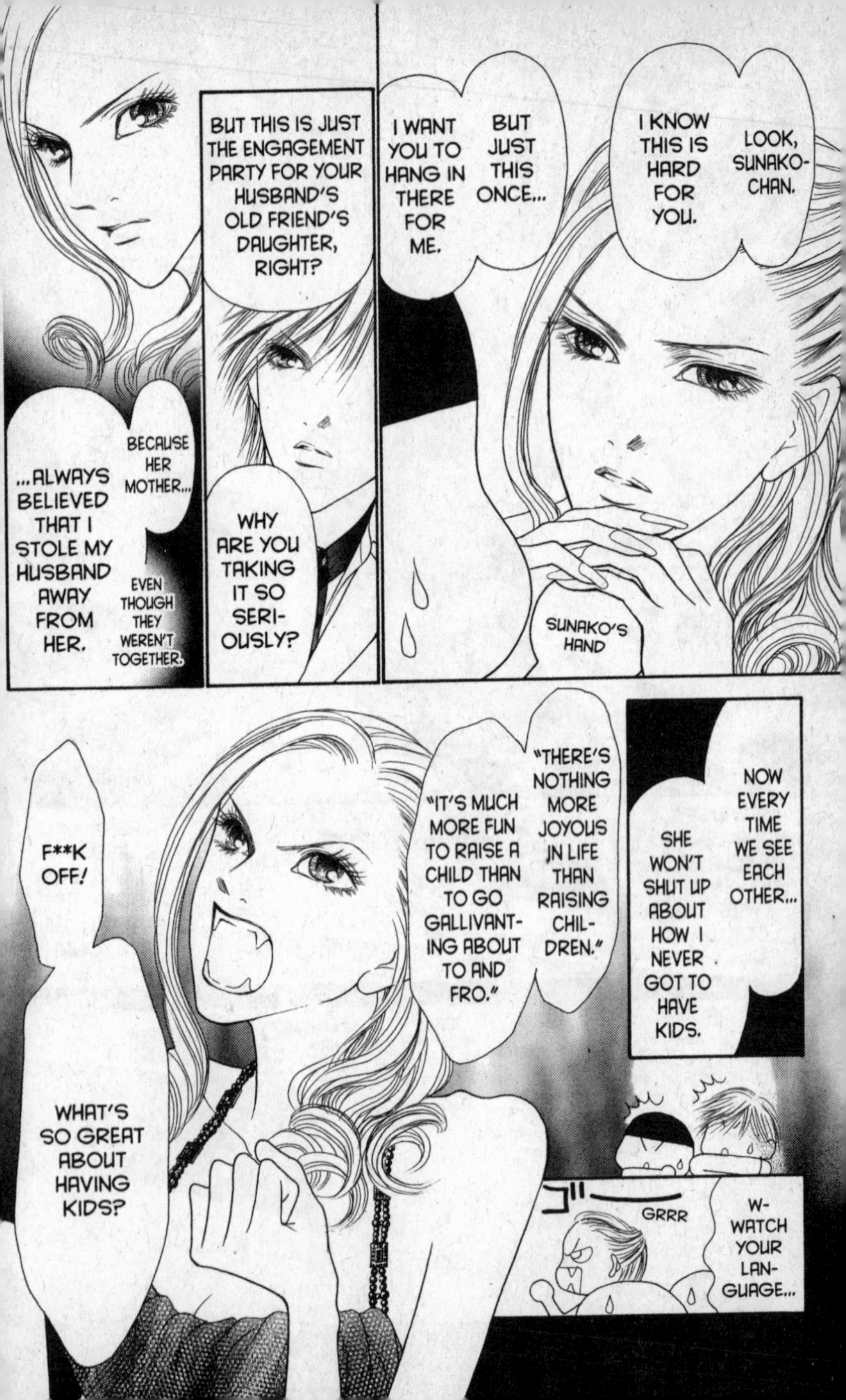
LOOK, SUNAKO-CHAN.
I KNOW THIS IS HARD FOR YOU.
BUT JUST THIS ONCE...
I WANT YOU TO HANG IN THERE FOR ME.
SUNAKO'S HAND
BUT THIS IS JUST THE ENGAGEMENT PARTY FOR YOUR HUSBAND'S OLD FRIEND'S DAUGHTER, RIGHT?
WHY ARE YOU TAKING IT SO SERIOUSLY?
BECAUSE HER MOTHER...
...ALWAYS BELIEVED THAT I STOLE MY HUSBAND AWAY FROM HER.
EVEN THOUGH THEY WEREN'T TOGETHER.
NOW EVERY TIME WE SEE EACH OTHER...
SHE WON'T SHUT UP ABOUT HOW I NEVER GOT TO HAVE KIDS.
"THERE'S NOTHING MORE JOYOUS IN LIFE THAN RAISING CHILDREN."
"IT'S MUCH MORE FUN TO RAISE A CHILD THAN TO GO GALLIVANTING ABOUT TO AND FRO."
F**K OFF!
WHAT'S SO GREAT ABOUT HAVING KIDS?
GRRR
W-WATCH YOUR LANGUAGE...

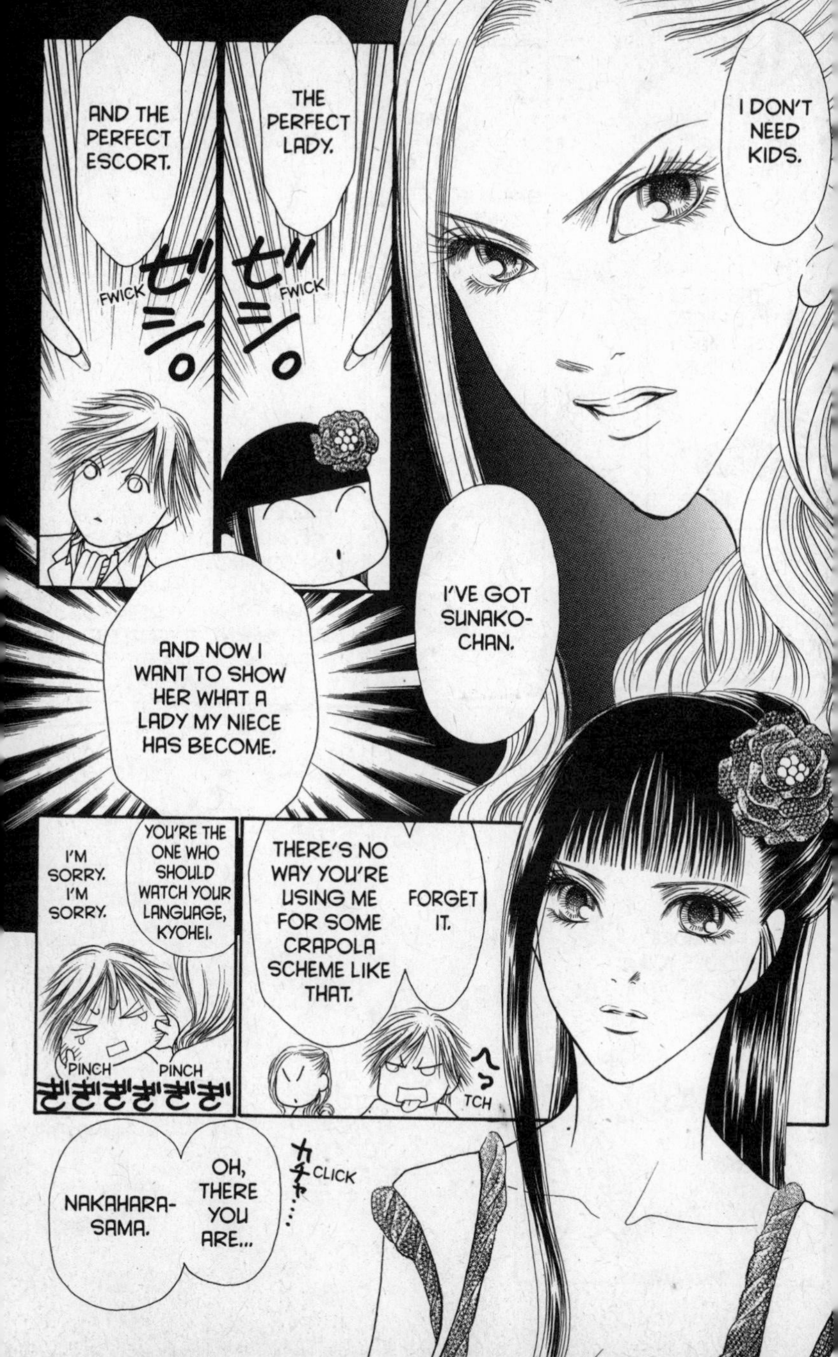
I DON'T NEED KIDS.
I'VE GOT SUNAKO-CHAN.
THE PERFECT LADY.
FWICK
AND THE PERFECT ESCORT.
FWICK
AND NOW I WANT TO SHOW HER WHAT A LADY MY NIECE HAS BECOME.
FORGET IT.
THERE'S NO WAY YOU'RE USING ME FOR SOME CRAPOLA SCHEME LIKE THAT.
TCH
YOU'RE THE ONE WHO SHOULD WATCH YOUR LANGUAGE, KYOHEI.
I'M SORRY. I'M SORRY.
PINCH
PINCH
CLICK
OH, THERE YOU ARE...
NAKAHARA-SAMA.

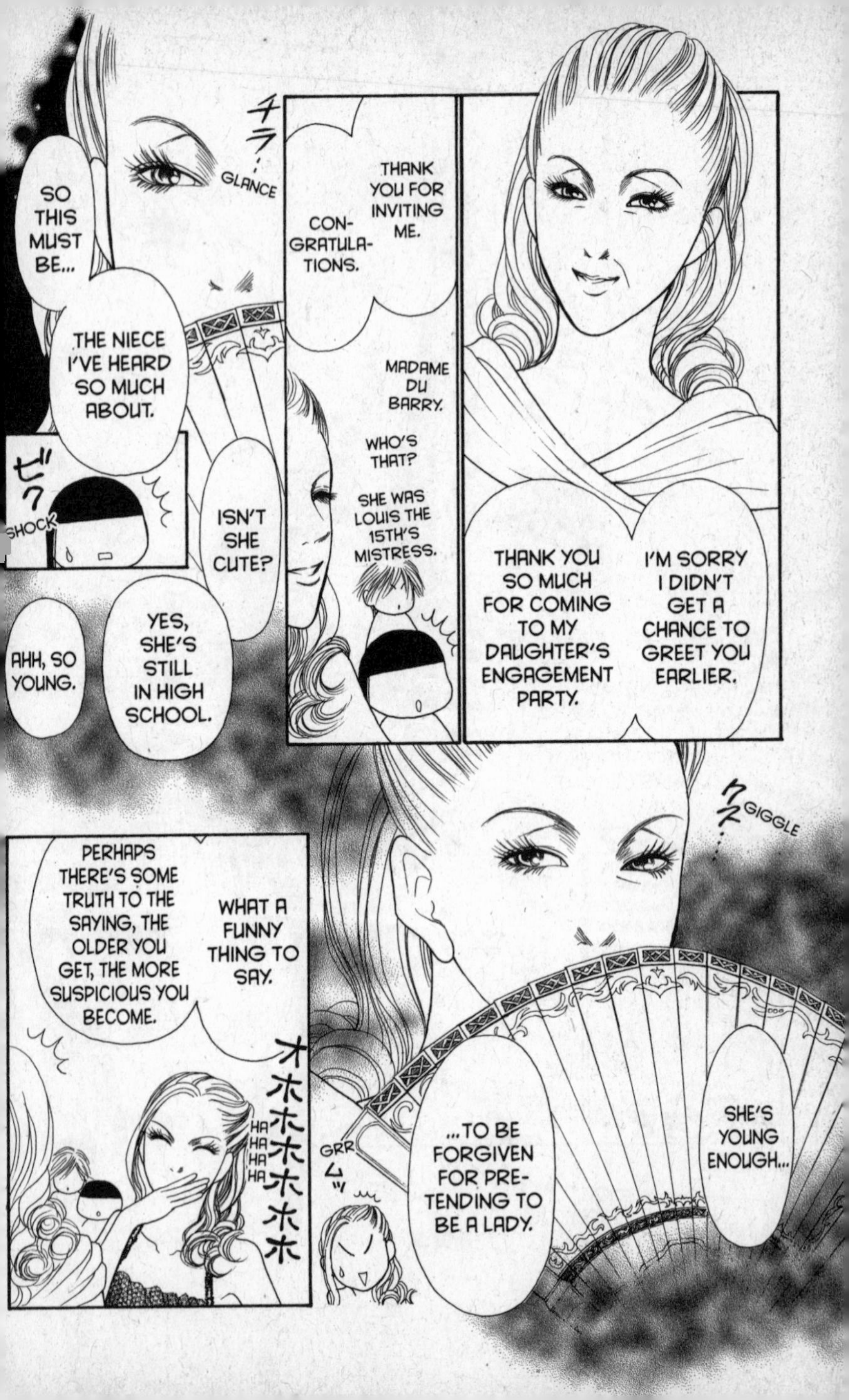
I'M SORRY I DIDN'T GET A CHANCE TO GREET YOU EARLIER.
THANK YOU SO MUCH FOR COMING TO MY DAUGHTER'S ENGAGEMENT PARTY.
THANK YOU FOR INVITING ME.
CON-GRATULA-TIONS.
MADAME DU BARRY.
WHO'S THAT?
SHE WAS LOUIS THE 15TH'S MISTRESS.
チラ… GLANCE
SO THIS MUST BE...
THE NIECE I'VE HEARD SO MUCH ABOUT.
ビク SHOCK
ISN'T SHE CUTE?
YES, SHE'S STILL IN HIGH SCHOOL.
AHH, SO YOUNG.
クス… GIGGLE
SHE'S YOUNG ENOUGH...
...TO BE FORGIVEN FOR PRE-TENDING TO BE A LADY.
ムッ GRR
WHAT A FUNNY THING TO SAY.
PERHAPS THERE'S SOME TRUTH TO THE SAYING, THE OLDER YOU GET, THE MORE SUSPICIOUS YOU BECOME.
オホホホホホ HA HA HA HA

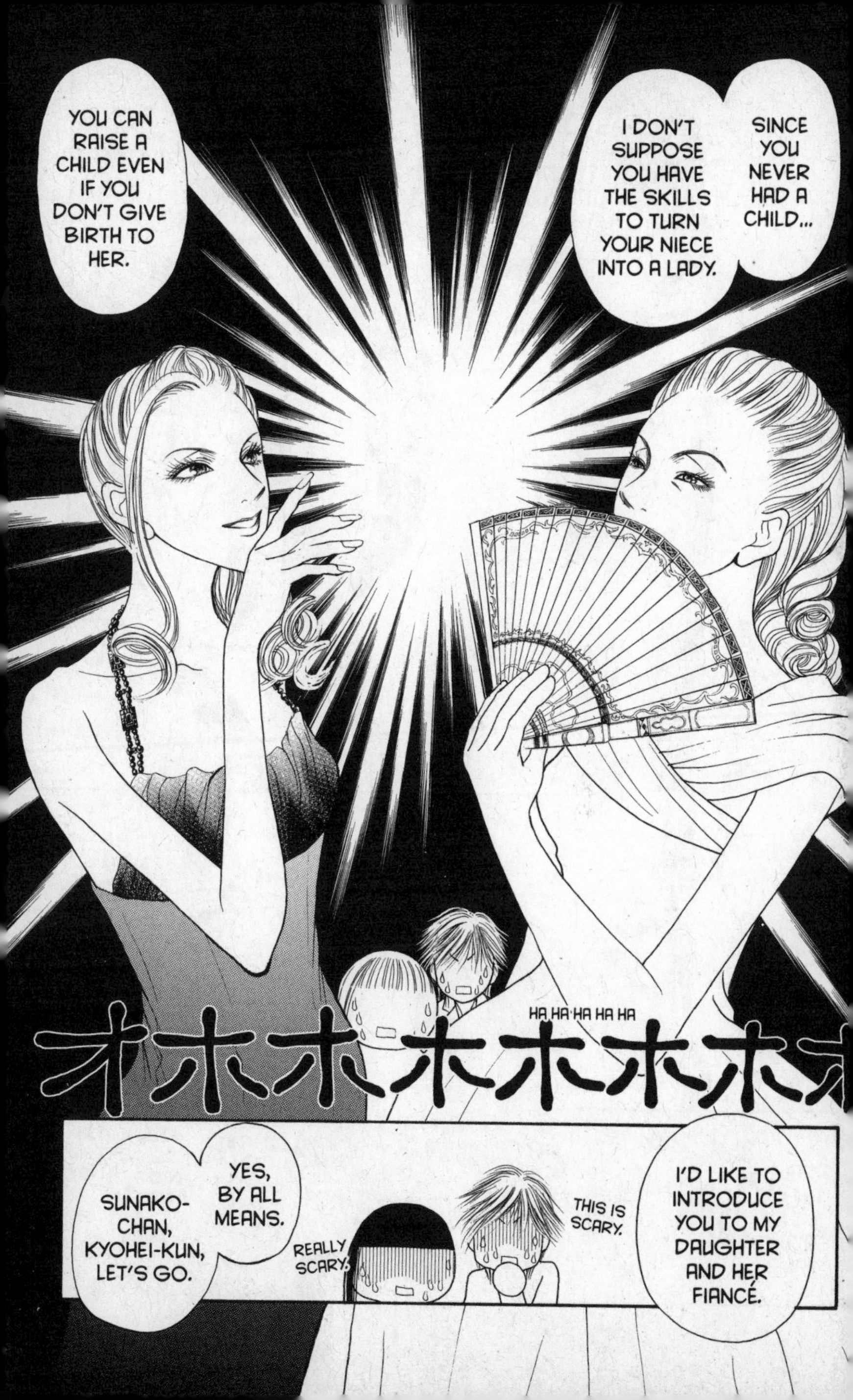
SINCE YOU NEVER HAD A CHILD...
I DON'T SUPPOSE YOU HAVE THE SKILLS TO TURN YOUR NIECE INTO A LADY.
YOU CAN RAISE A CHILD EVEN IF YOU DON'T GIVE BIRTH TO HER.
オホホホホホホホ
HA HA HA HA HA
I'D LIKE TO INTRODUCE YOU TO MY DAUGHTER AND HER FIANCÉ.
THIS IS SCARY.
REALLY SCARY.
YES, BY ALL MEANS.
SUNAKO-CHAN, KYOHEI-KUN, LET'S GO.

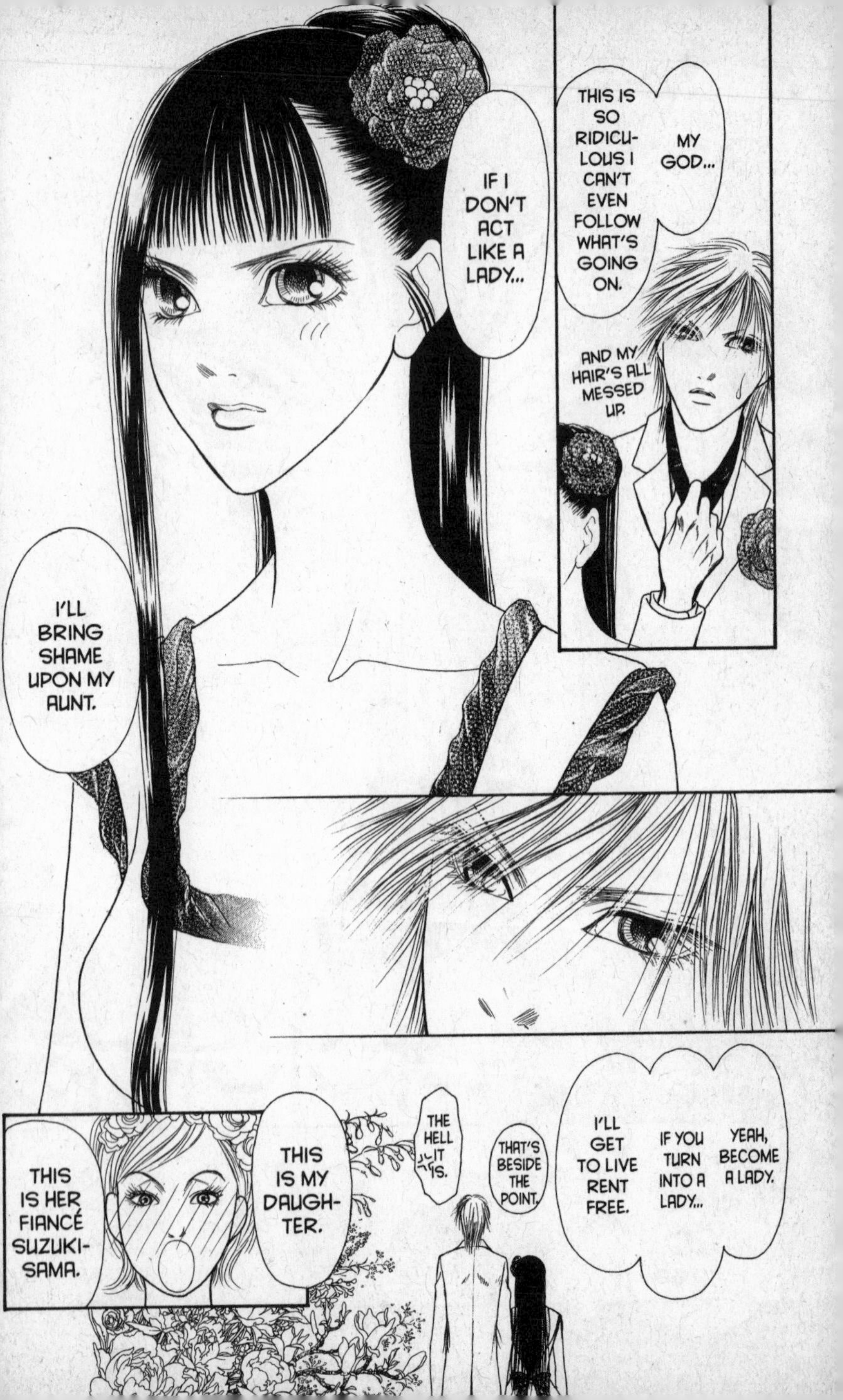
MY GOD...
THIS IS SO RIDICULOUS I CAN'T EVEN FOLLOW WHAT'S GOING ON.
AND MY HAIR'S ALL MESSED UP.
IF I DON'T ACT LIKE A LADY...
I'LL BRING SHAME UPON MY AUNT.
YEAH, BECOME A LADY.
IF YOU TURN INTO A LADY...
I'LL GET TO LIVE RENT FREE.
THAT'S BESIDE THE POINT.
THE HELL IT IS.
THIS IS MY DAUGHTER.
THIS IS HER FIANCÉ SUZUKI-SAMA.

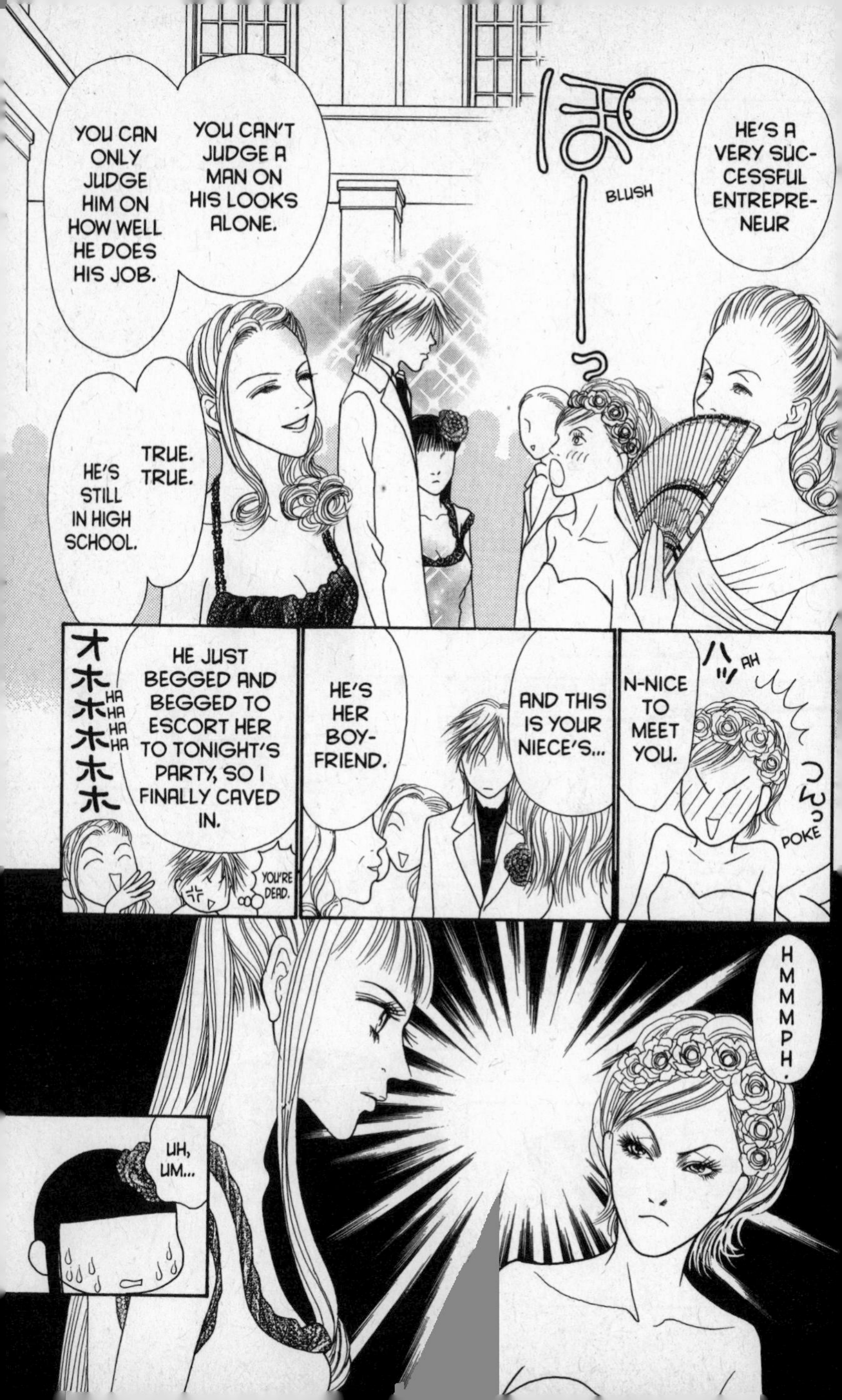
HE'S A VERY SUCCESSFUL ENTREPRENEUR
ぽーっ
BLUSH
YOU CAN'T JUDGE A MAN ON HIS LOOKS ALONE.
YOU CAN ONLY JUDGE HIM ON HOW WELL HE DOES HIS JOB.
TRUE. TRUE.
HE'S STILL IN HIGH SCHOOL.
ハッ
AH
N-NICE TO MEET YOU.
つんっ
POKE
AND THIS IS YOUR NIECE'S...
HE'S HER BOYFRIEND.
オホホホホホ
HA HA HA HA
HE JUST BEGGED AND BEGGED TO ESCORT HER TO TONIGHT'S PARTY, SO I FINALLY CAVED IN.
YOU'RE DEAD.
HMMMPH.
UH, UM...

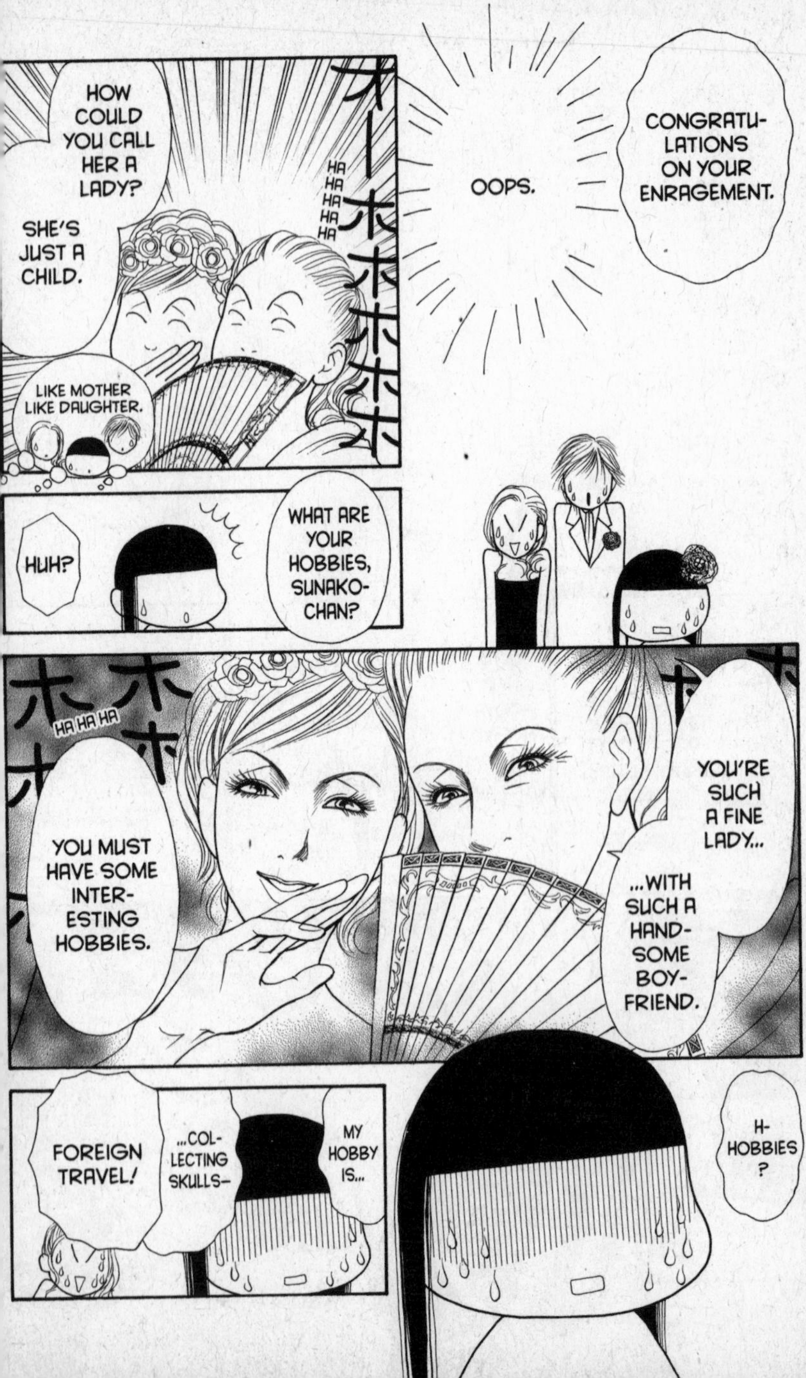

CONGRATULATIONS ON YOUR ENRAGEMENT.
OOPS.
HOW COULD YOU CALL HER A LADY?
オーホホホホ
HA HA HA HA HA
SHE'S JUST A CHILD.
LIKE MOTHER LIKE DAUGHTER.
WHAT ARE YOUR HOBBIES, SUNAKO-CHAN?
HUH?
YOU'RE SUCH A FINE LADY...
...WITH SUCH A HANDSOME BOYFRIEND.
HA HA HA
YOU MUST HAVE SOME INTERESTING HOBBIES.
H-HOBBIES?
MY HOBBY IS...
...COLLECTING SKULLS-
FOREIGN TRAVEL!

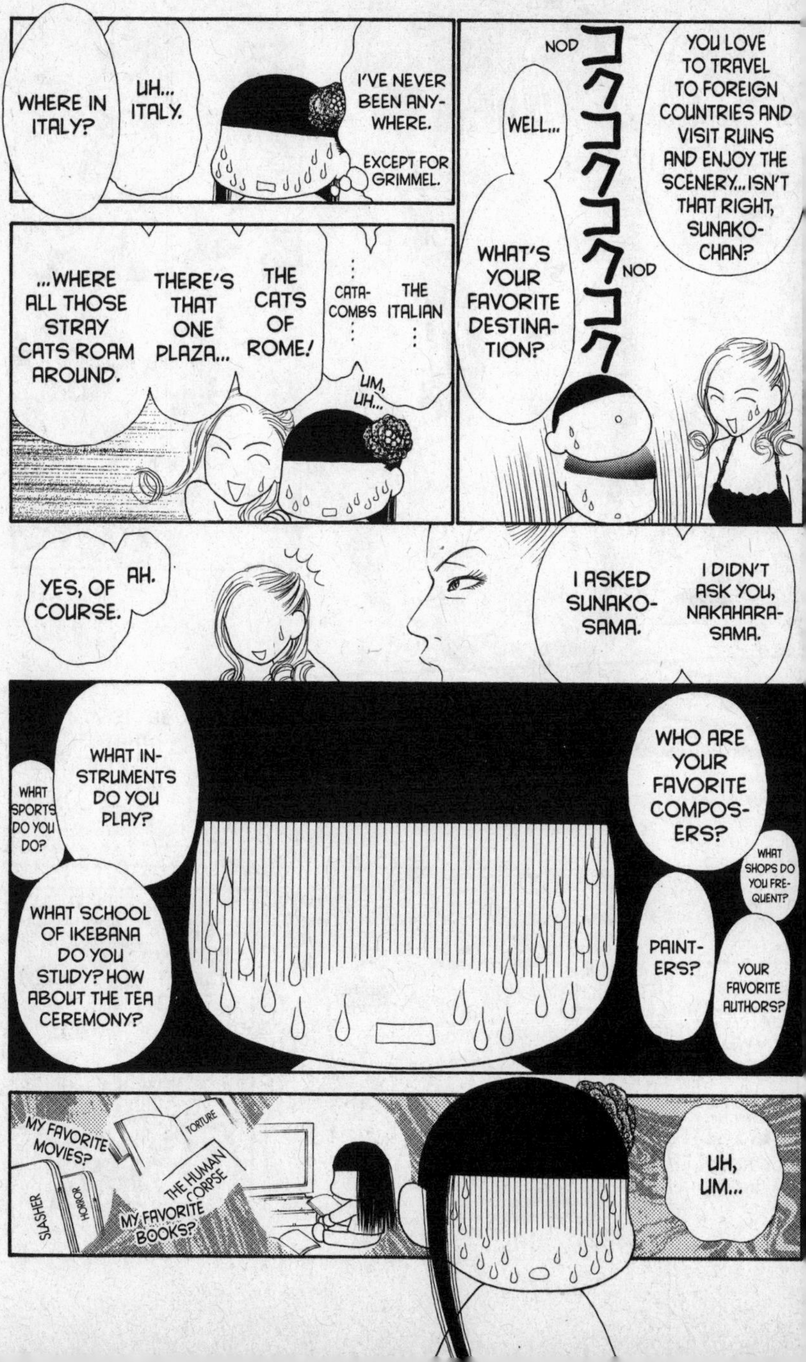
YOU LOVE TO TRAVEL TO FOREIGN COUNTRIES AND VISIT RUINS AND ENJOY THE SCENERY...ISN'T THAT RIGHT, SUNAKO-CHAN?
NOD
コクコクコクコク
NOD
WELL...
WHAT'S YOUR FAVORITE DESTINATION?
I'VE NEVER BEEN ANYWHERE.
EXCEPT FOR GRIMMEL.
UH... ITALY.
WHERE IN ITALY?
THE ITALIAN ...
CATACOMBS ...
UM, UH...
THE CATS OF ROME!
THERE'S THAT ONE PLAZA...
...WHERE ALL THOSE STRAY CATS ROAM AROUND.
I DIDN'T ASK YOU, NAKAHARA-SAMA.
I ASKED SUNAKO-SAMA.
AH.
YES, OF COURSE.
WHO ARE YOUR FAVORITE COMPOSERS?
WHAT SHOPS DO YOU FREQUENT?
PAINTERS?
YOUR FAVORITE AUTHORS?
WHAT INSTRUMENTS DO YOU PLAY?
WHAT SPORTS DO YOU DO?
WHAT SCHOOL OF IKEBANA DO YOU STUDY? HOW ABOUT THE TEA CEREMONY?
UH, UM...
TORTURE
THE HUMAN CORPSE
MY FAVORITE MOVIES?
HORROR
SLASHER
MY FAVORITE BOOKS?

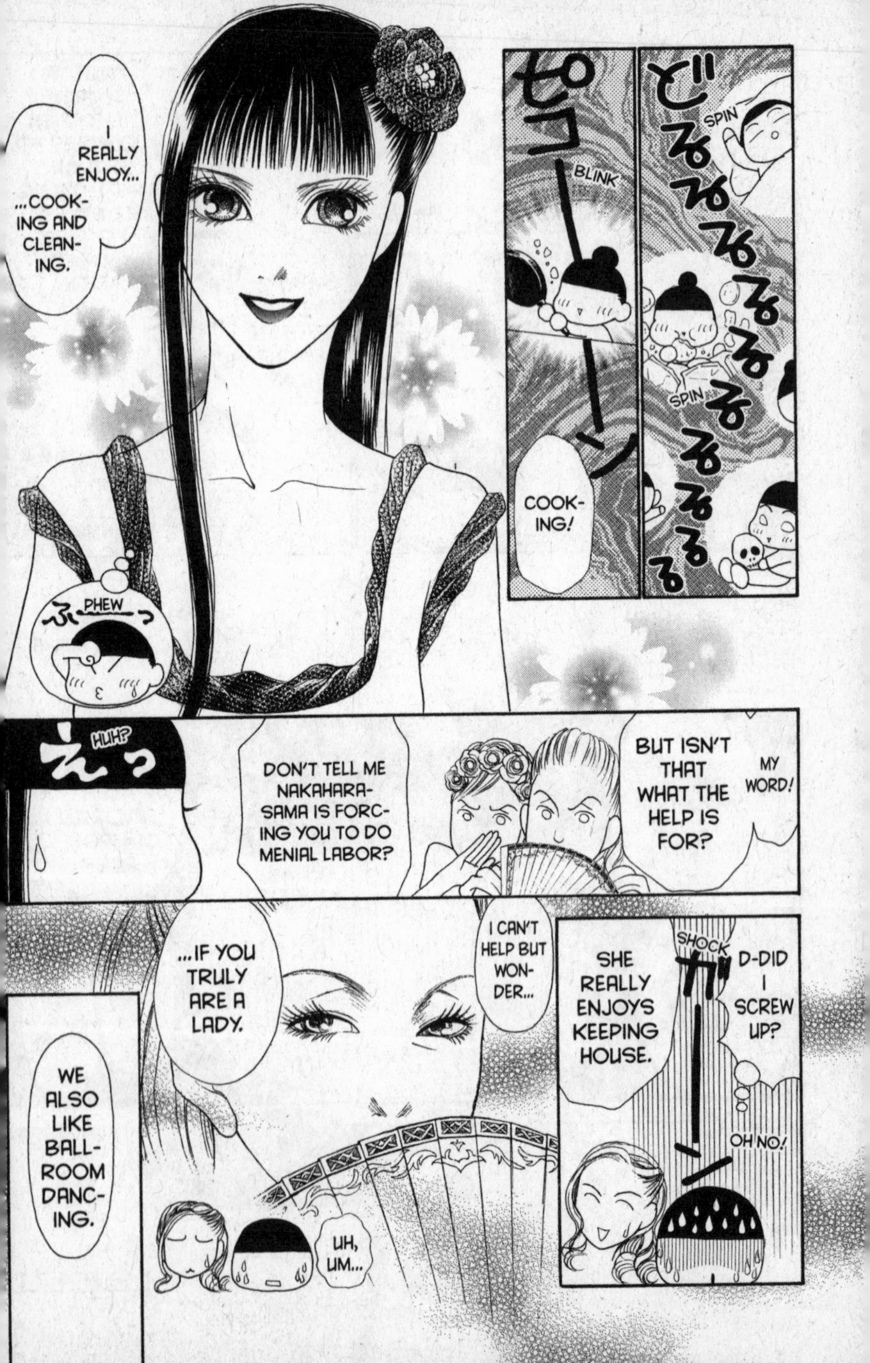
SPIN
SPIN
ピコーン
BLINK
COOKING!
I REALLY ENJOY...
...COOKING AND CLEANING.
ふーっ
PHEW
MY WORD!
BUT ISN'T THAT WHAT THE HELP IS FOR?
DON'T TELL ME NAKAHARA-SAMA IS FORCING YOU TO DO MENIAL LABOR?
えっ
HUH?
D-DID I SCREW UP?
SHOCK
SHE REALLY ENJOYS KEEPING HOUSE.
OH NO!
I CAN'T HELP BUT WONDER...
...IF YOU TRULY ARE A LADY.
WE ALSO LIKE BALLROOM DANCING.
UH, UM...

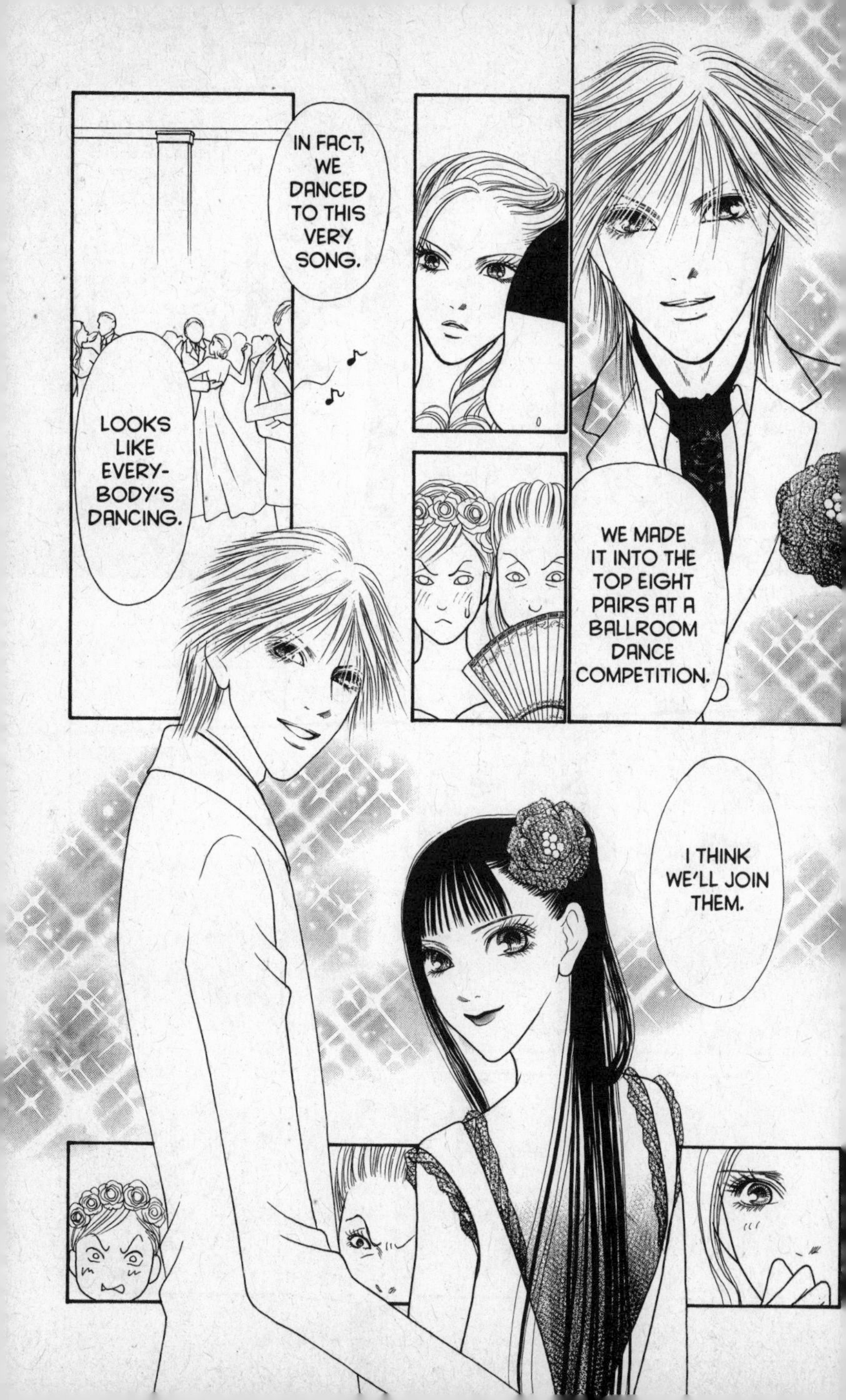
LOOKS LIKE EVERY-BODY'S DANCING.
IN FACT, WE DANCED TO THIS VERY SONG.
WE MADE IT INTO THE TOP EIGHT PAIRS AT A BALLROOM DANCE COMPETITION.
I THINK WE'LL JOIN THEM.

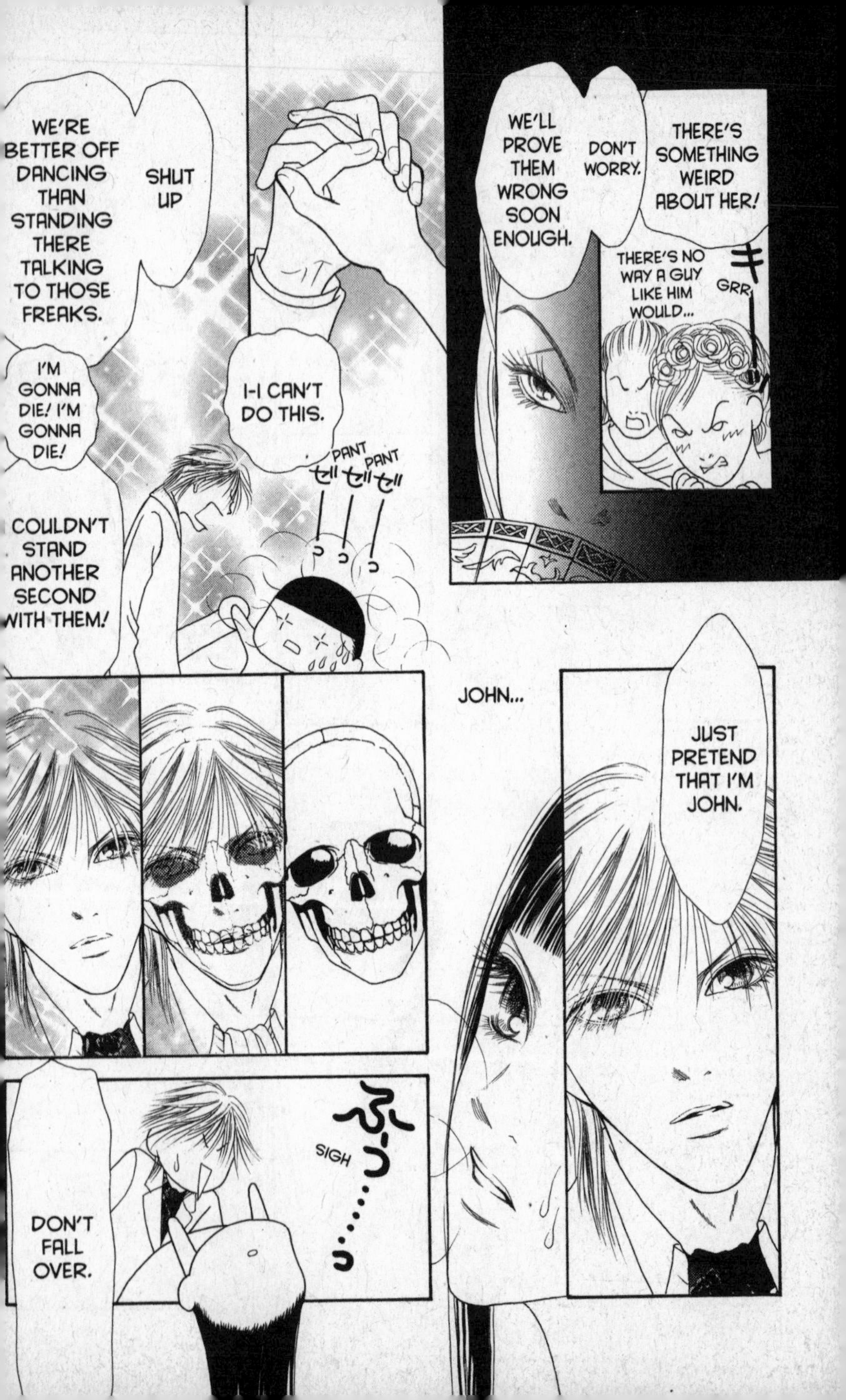
THERE'S SOMETHING WEIRD ABOUT HER!
DON'T WORRY.
WE'LL PROVE THEM WRONG SOON ENOUGH.
THERE'S NO WAY A GUY LIKE HIM WOULD...
GRR
I-I CAN'T DO THIS.
PANT PANT
WE'RE BETTER OFF DANCING THAN STANDING THERE TALKING TO THOSE FREAKS.
SHUT UP
I'M GONNA DIE! I'M GONNA DIE!
COULDN'T STAND ANOTHER SECOND WITH THEM!
JUST PRETEND THAT I'M JOHN.
JOHN...
SIGH
DON'T FALL OVER.

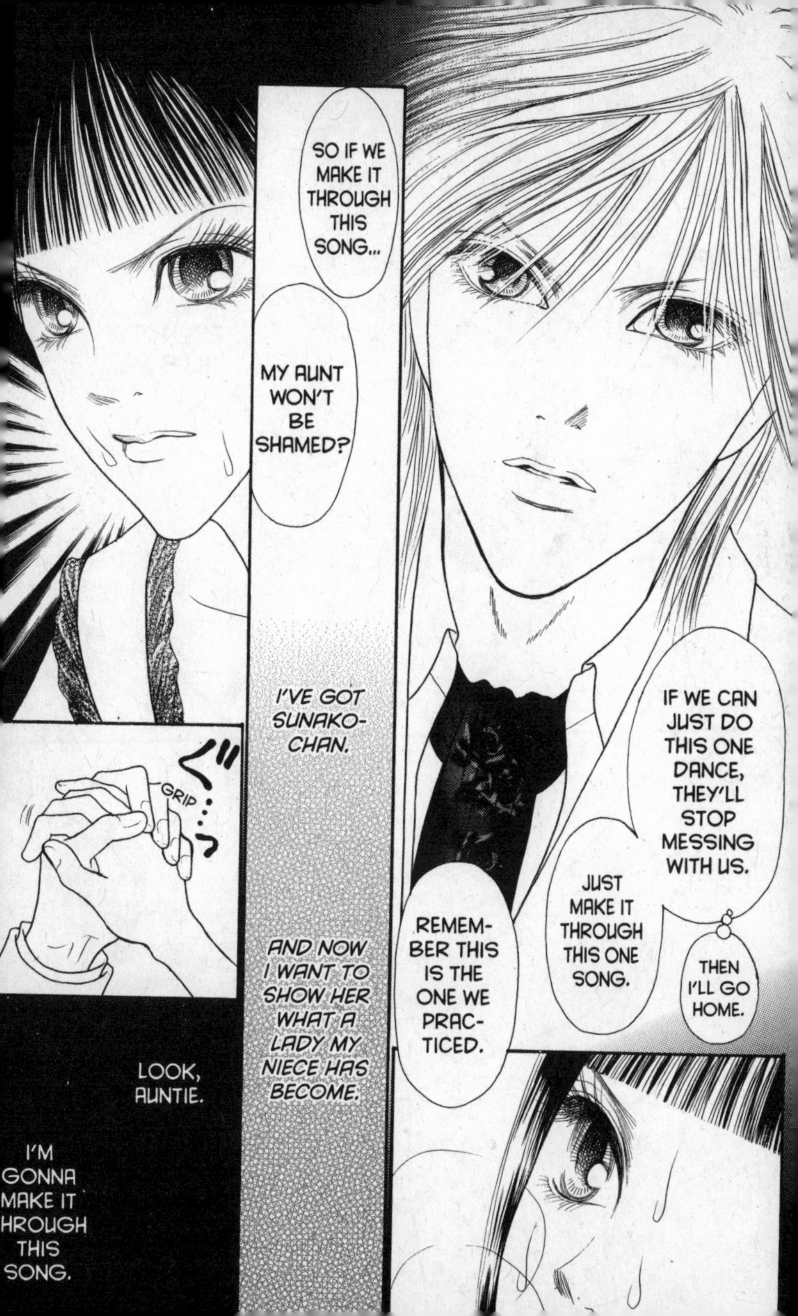

IF WE CAN JUST DO THIS ONE DANCE, THEY'LL STOP MESSING WITH US.
JUST MAKE IT THROUGH THIS ONE SONG.
REMEMBER THIS IS THE ONE WE PRACTICED.
THEN I'LL GO HOME.
SO IF WE MAKE IT THROUGH THIS SONG...
MY AUNT WON'T BE SHAMED?
I'VE GOT SUNAKO-CHAN.
AND NOW I WANT TO SHOW HER WHAT A LADY MY NIECE HAS BECOME.
GRIP
LOOK, AUNTIE.
I'M GONNA MAKE IT THROUGH THIS SONG.

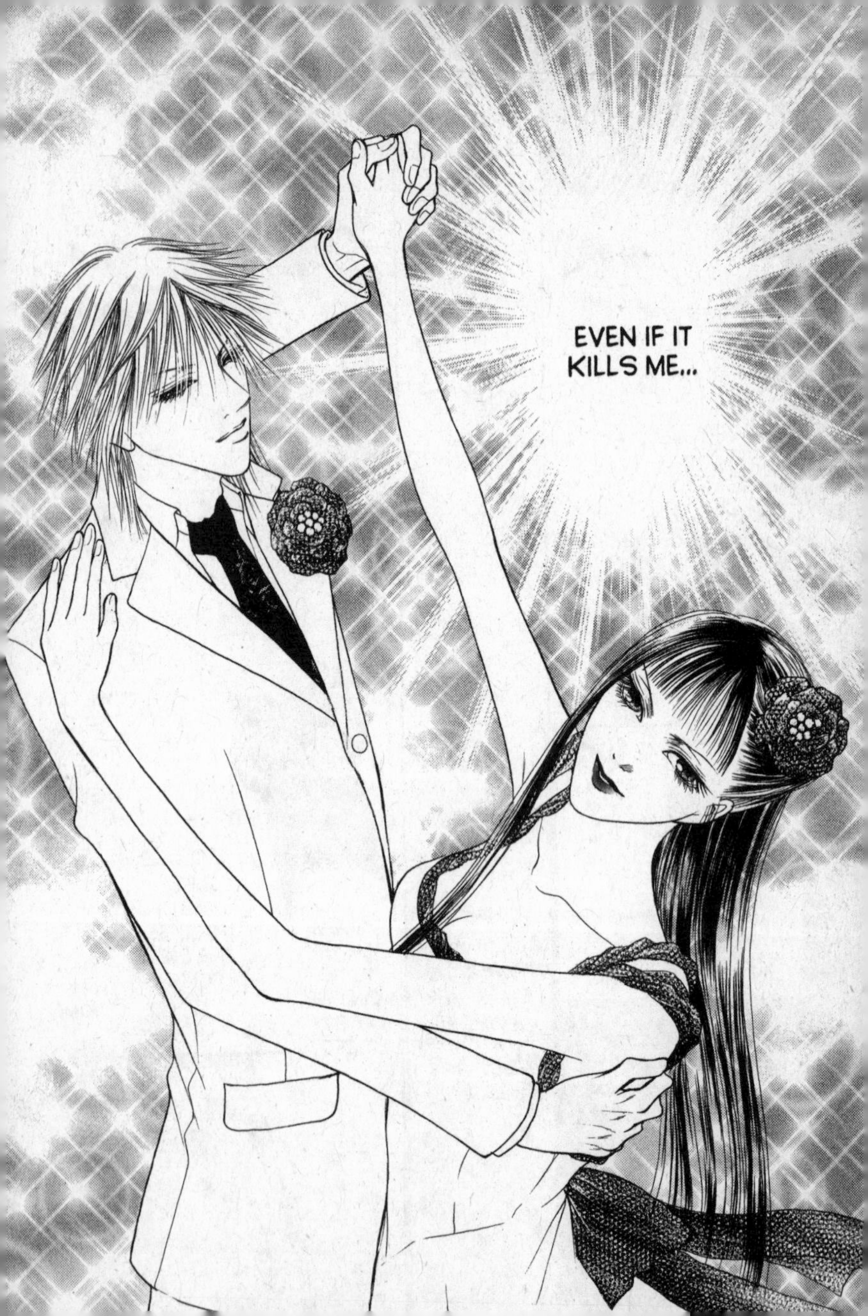
EVEN IF IT
KILLS ME...

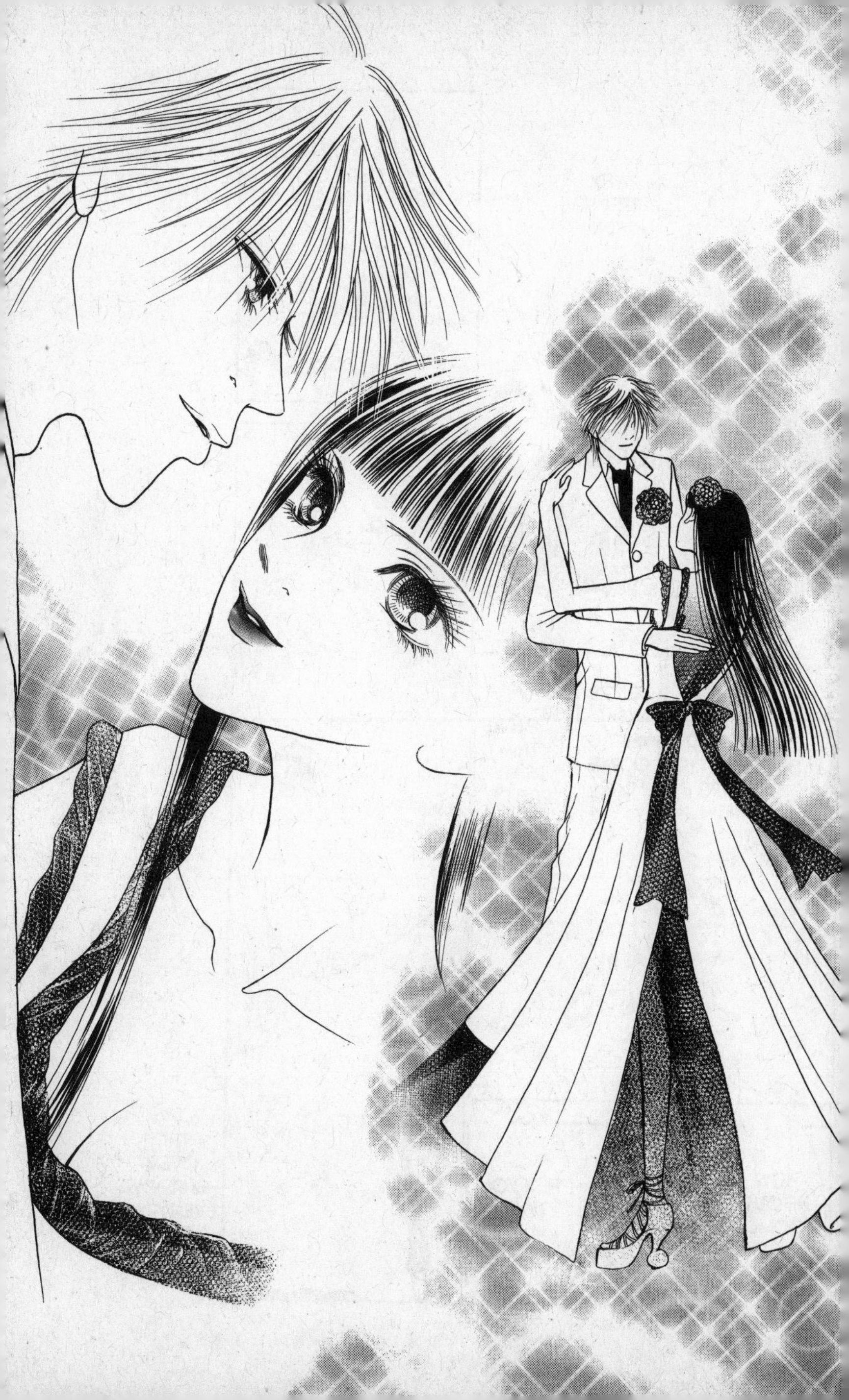

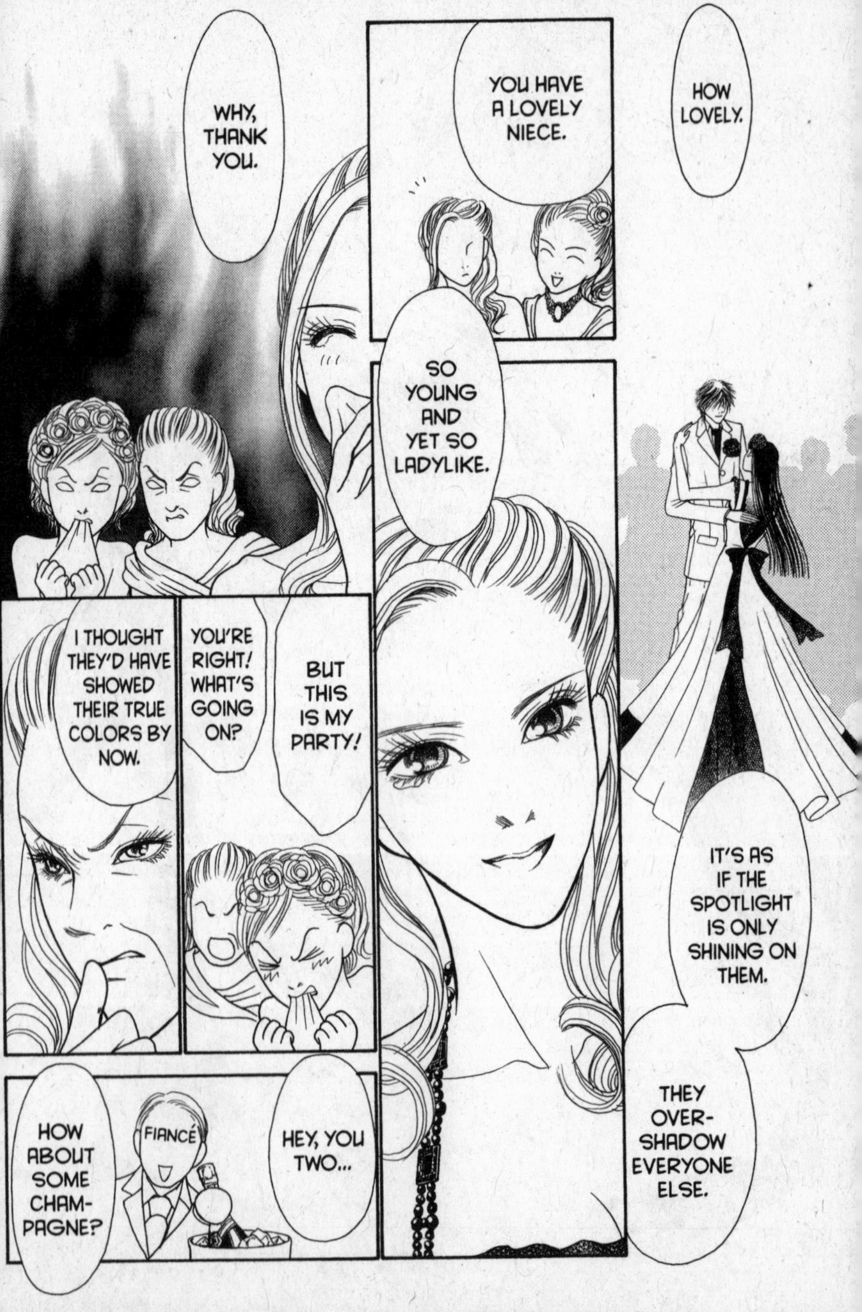
HOW LOVELY.
IT'S AS IF THE SPOTLIGHT IS ONLY SHINING ON THEM.
THEY OVER-SHADOW EVERYONE ELSE.
YOU HAVE A LOVELY NIECE.
SO YOUNG AND YET SO LADYLIKE.
WHY, THANK YOU.
BUT THIS IS MY PARTY!
YOU'RE RIGHT! WHAT'S GOING ON?
I THOUGHT THEY'D HAVE SHOWED THEIR TRUE COLORS BY NOW.
HEY, YOU TWO...
FIANCÉ
HOW ABOUT SOME CHAM-PAGNE?

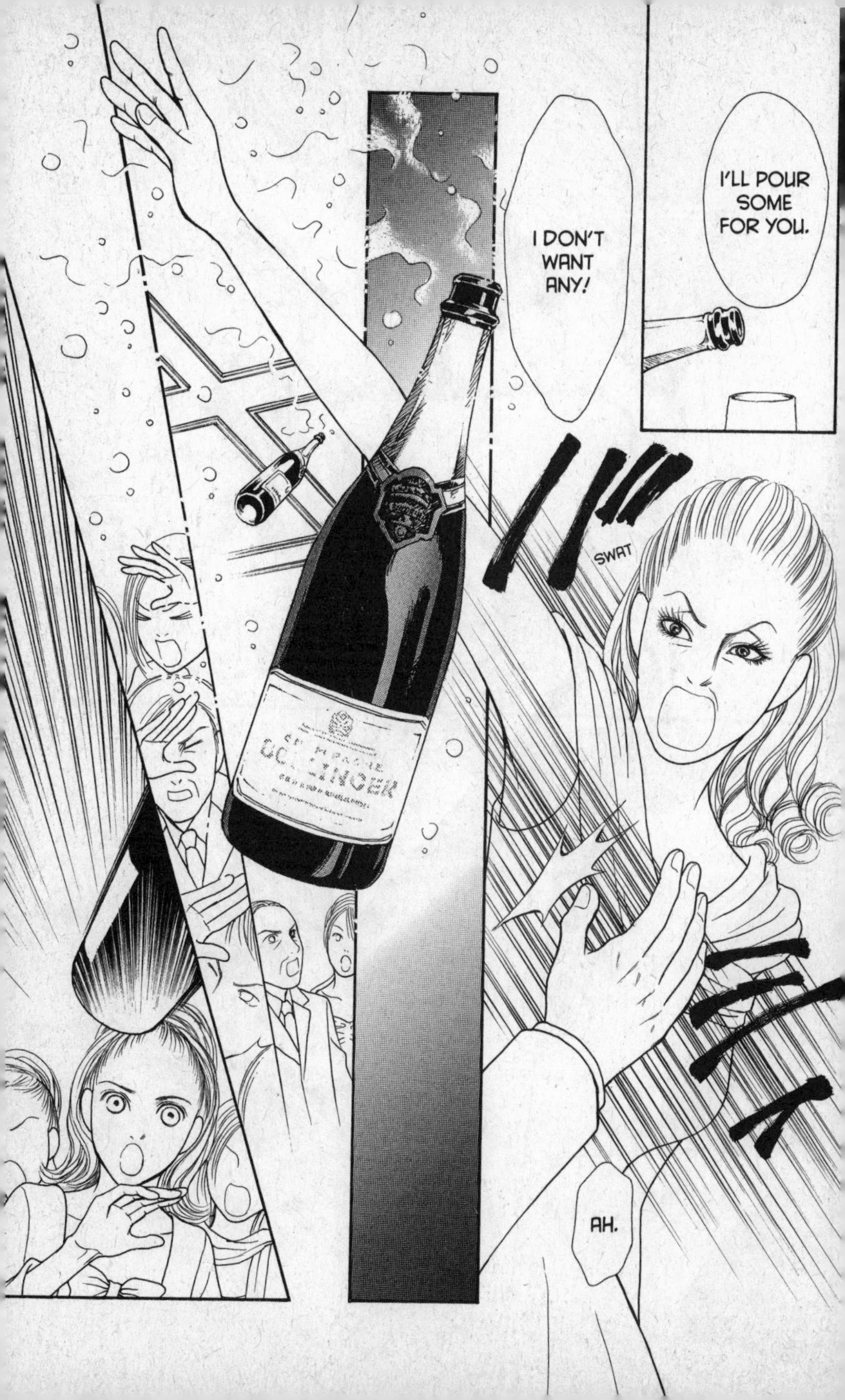
I'LL POUR SOME FOR YOU.
I DON'T WANT ANY!
SWAT
AH.

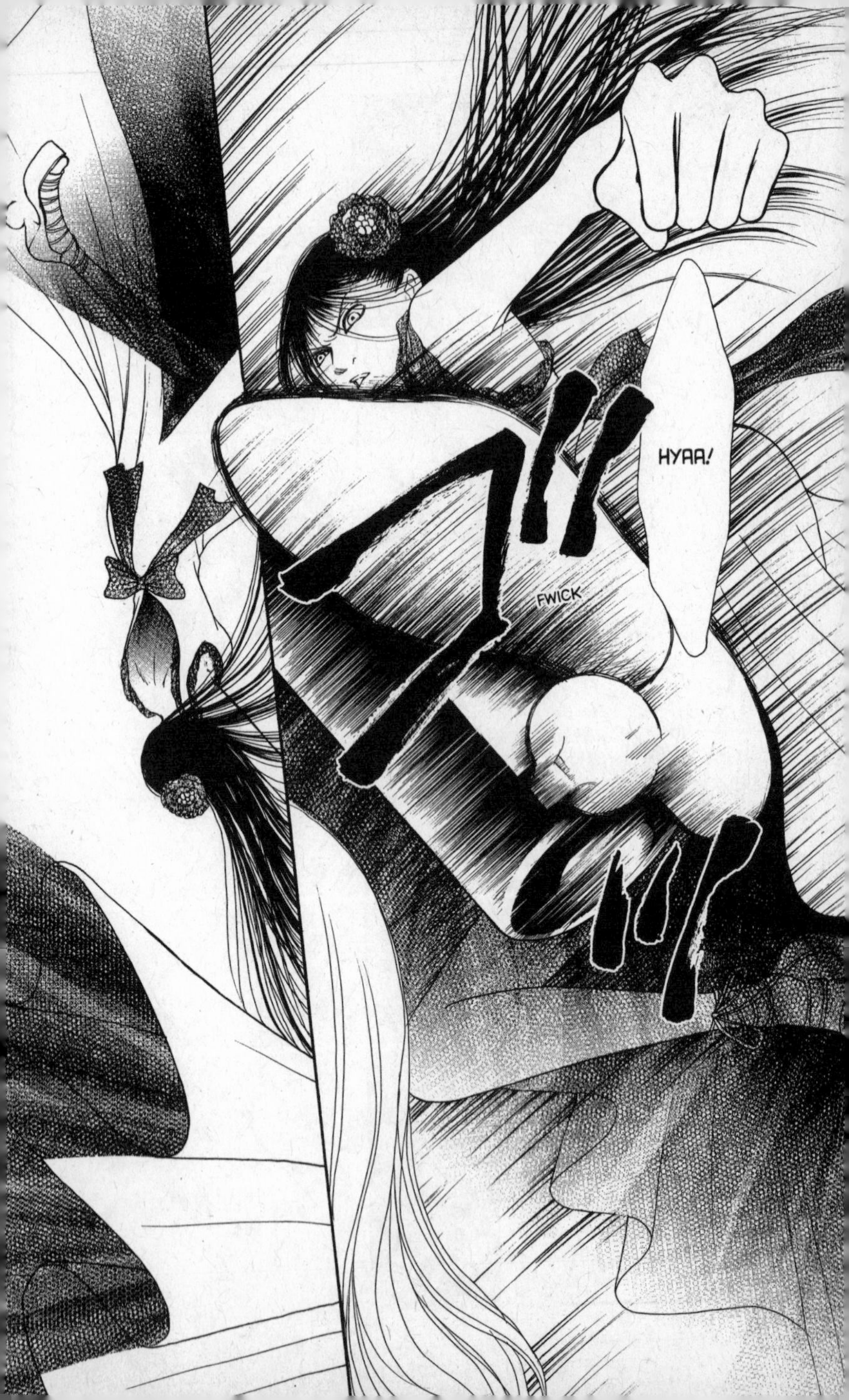
HYAA!
FWICK

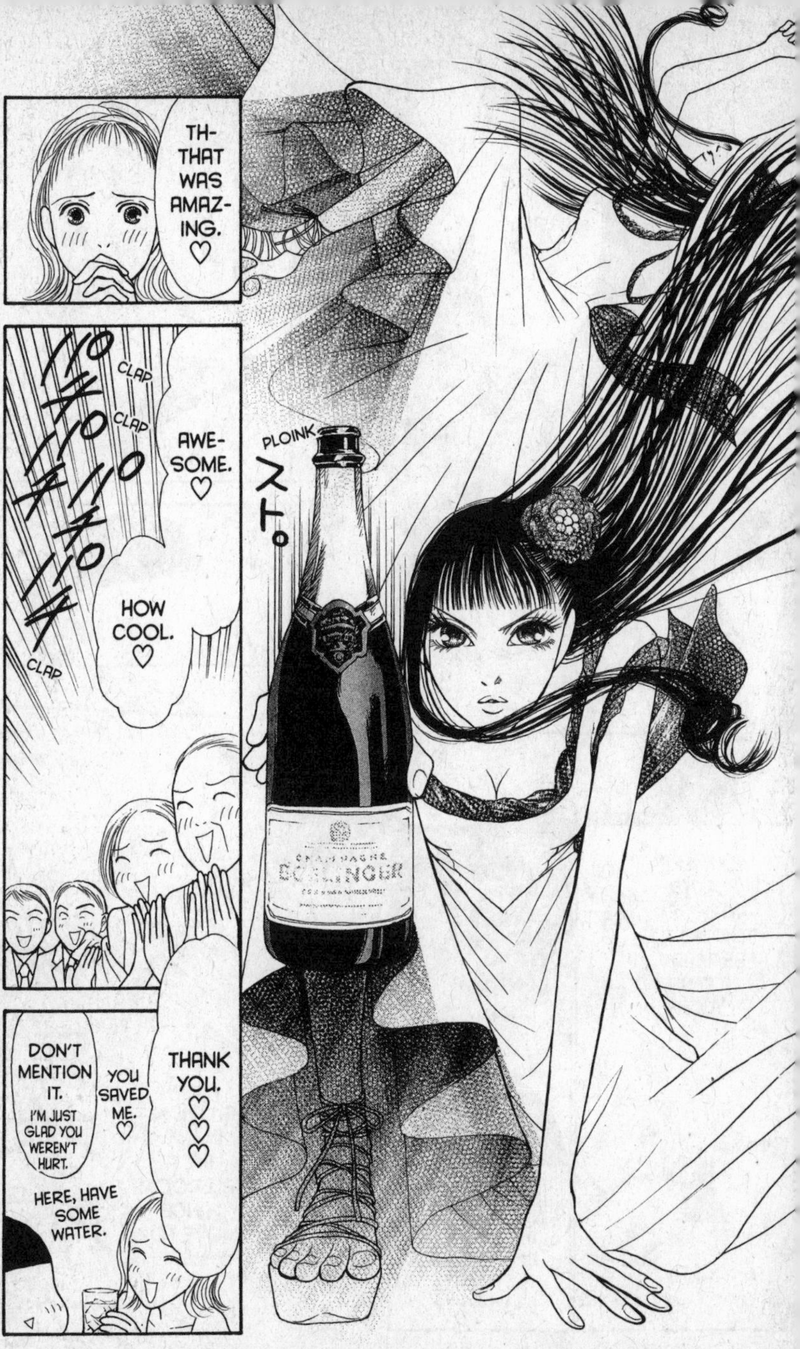
PLOINK
スト。
TH-THAT WAS AMAZING. ♡
CLAP
CLAP
CLAP
AWESOME. ♡
HOW COOL. ♡
THANK YOU. ♡♡♡
YOU SAVED ME. ♡
DON'T MENTION IT.
I'M JUST GLAD YOU WEREN'T HURT.
HERE, HAVE SOME WATER.

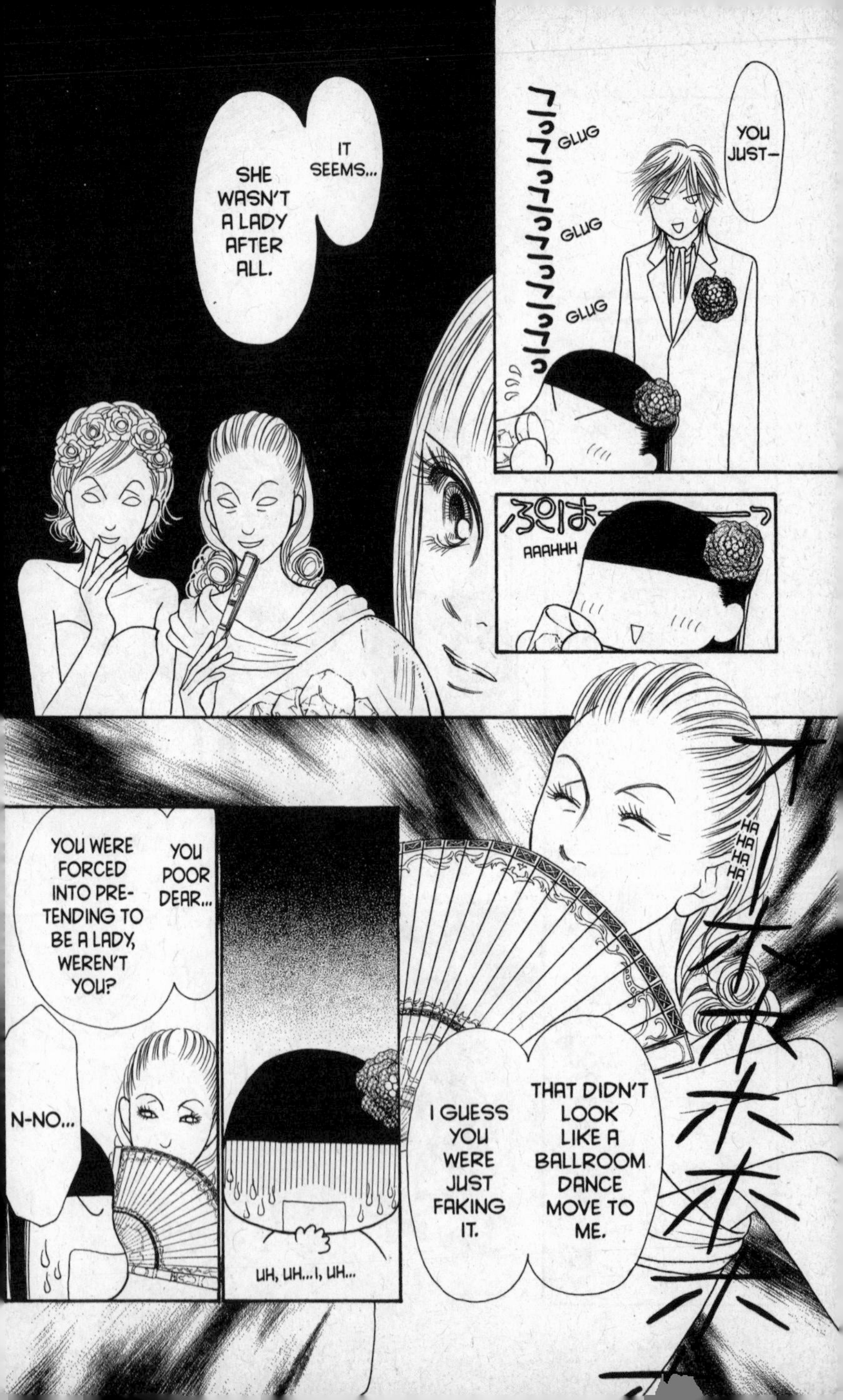
YOU JUST—
GLUG
GLUG
GLUG
ぷはーーーっ
AAAHHH
IT SEEMS...
SHE WASN'T A LADY AFTER ALL.
HA HA HA HA
THAT DIDN'T LOOK LIKE A BALLROOM DANCE MOVE TO ME.
I GUESS YOU WERE JUST FAKING IT.
UH, UH... I, UH...
YOU POOR DEAR...
YOU WERE FORCED INTO PRE-TENDING TO BE A LADY, WEREN'T YOU?
N-NO...

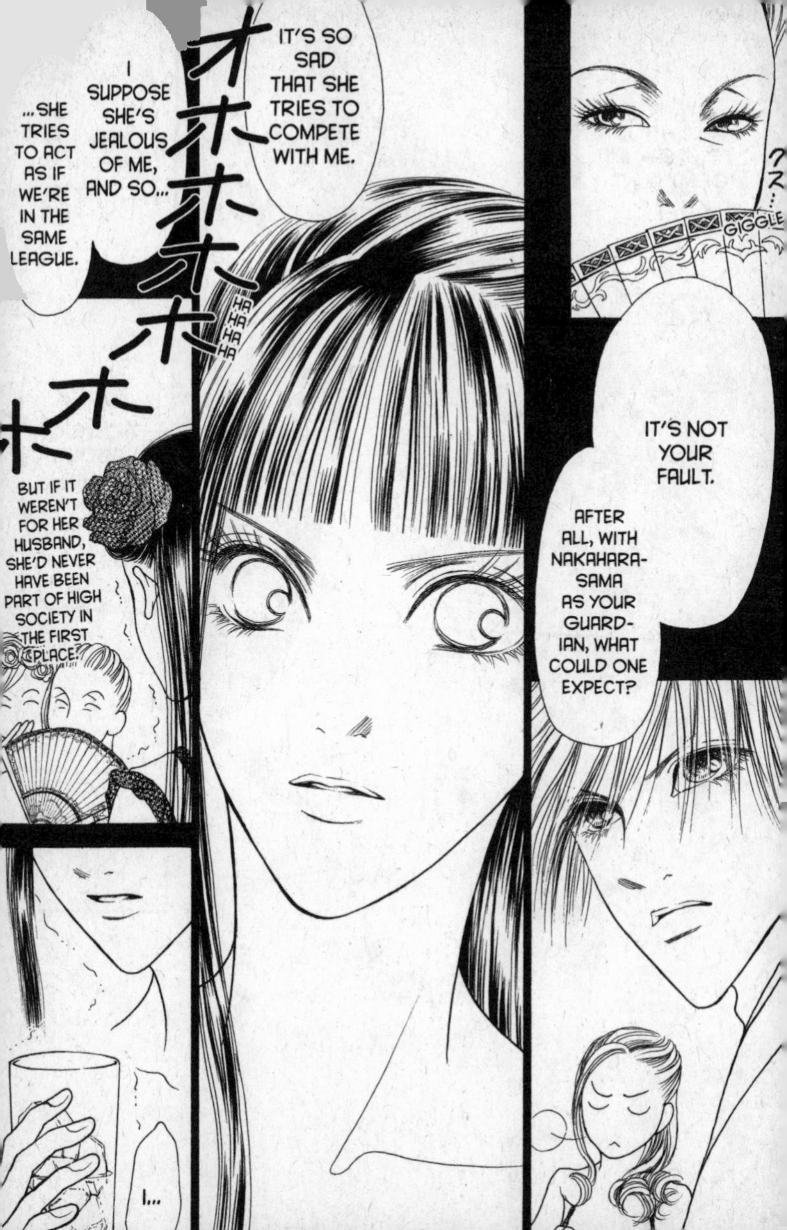
クス…
GIGGLE
IT'S NOT YOUR FAULT.
AFTER ALL, WITH NAKAHARA-SAMA AS YOUR GUARDIAN, WHAT COULD ONE EXPECT?
IT'S SO SAD THAT SHE TRIES TO COMPETE WITH ME.
オホホホホホホ
HA HA HA HA
I SUPPOSE SHE'S JEALOUS OF ME, AND SO...
...SHE TRIES TO ACT AS IF WE'RE IN THE SAME LEAGUE.
BUT IF IT WEREN'T FOR HER HUSBAND, SHE'D NEVER HAVE BEEN PART OF HIGH SOCIETY IN THE FIRST PLACE!
I...

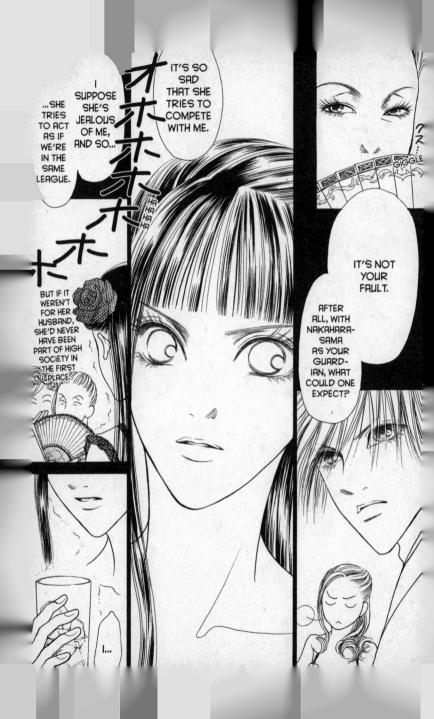

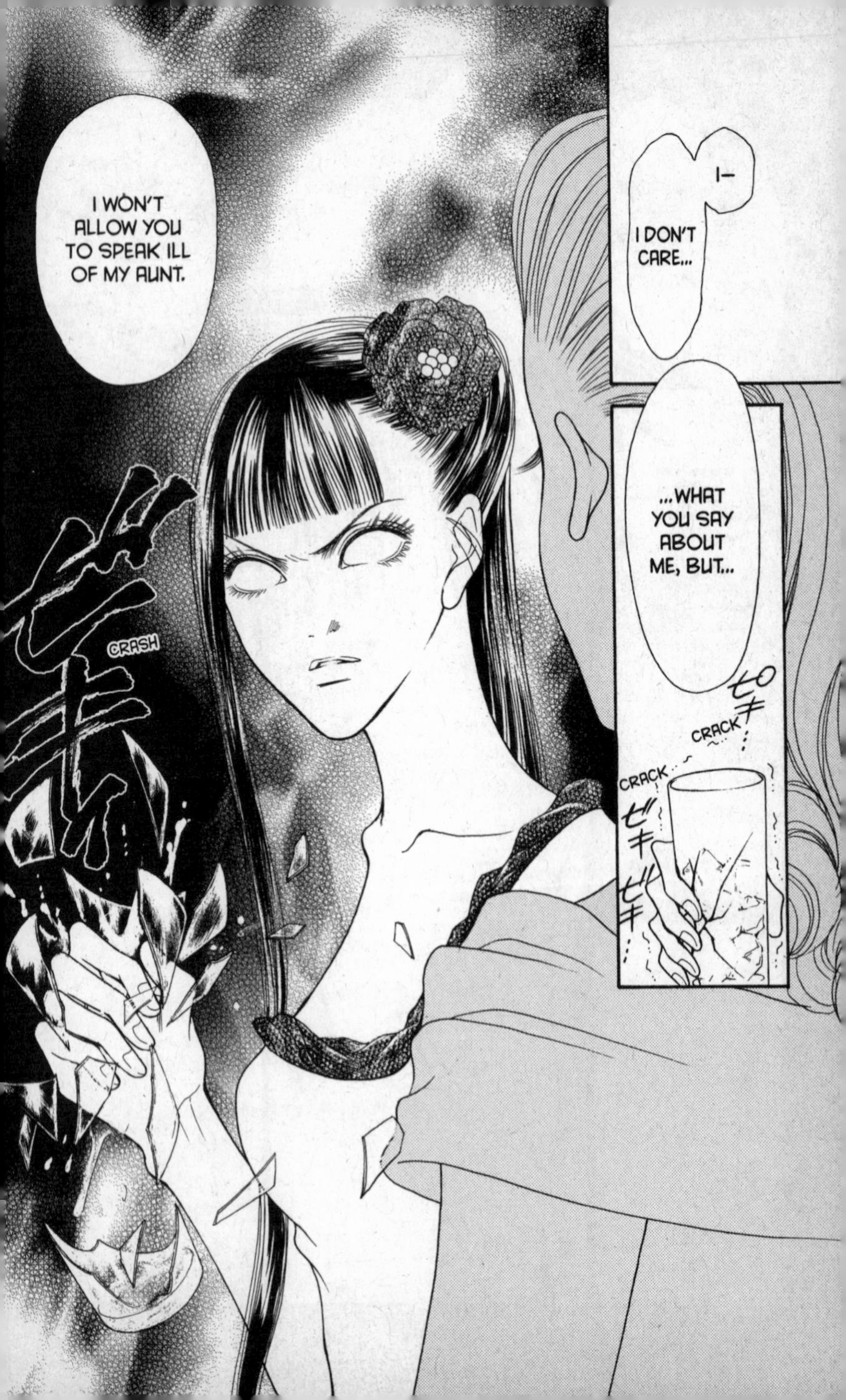
I—
I DON'T CARE...
...WHAT YOU SAY ABOUT ME, BUT...
CRACK
CRACK
I WON'T ALLOW YOU TO SPEAK ILL OF MY AUNT.
CRASH

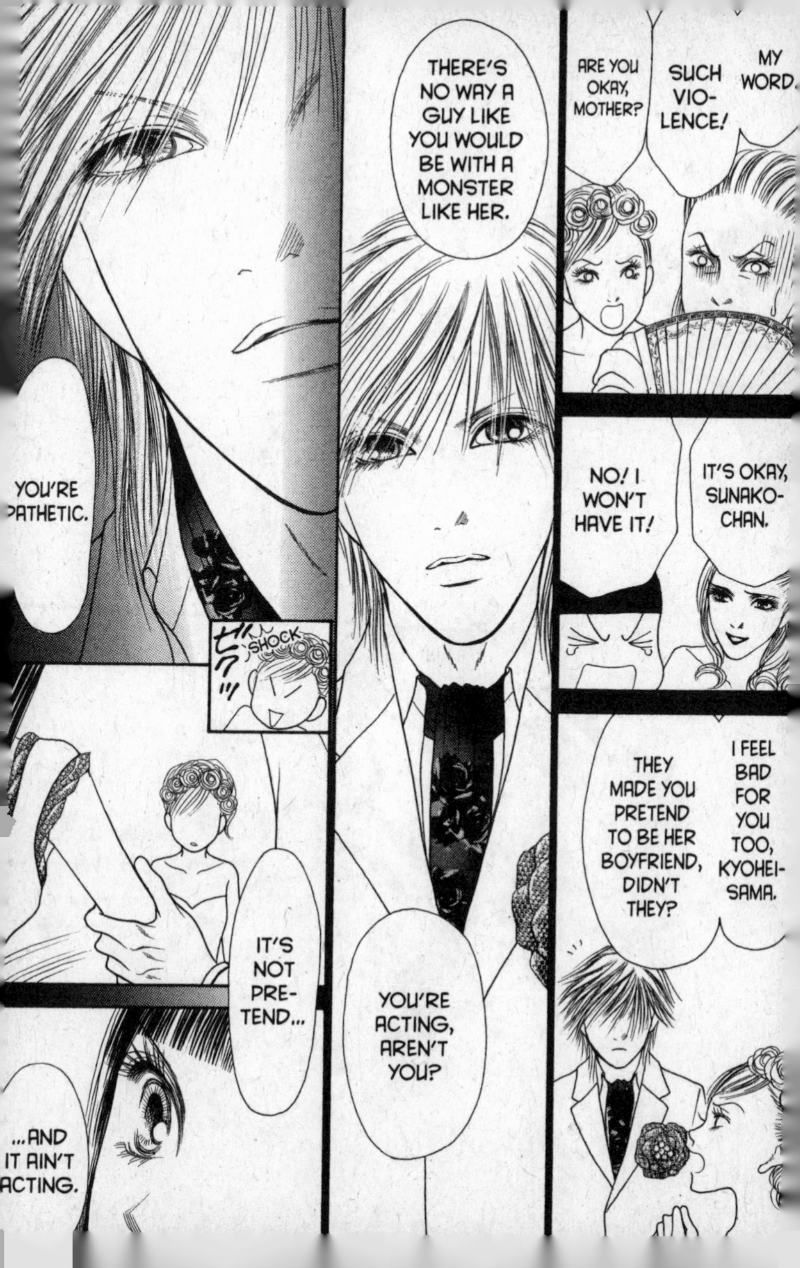
MY WORD.
SUCH VIO-LENCE!
ARE YOU OKAY, MOTHER?
IT'S OKAY, SUNAKO-CHAN.
NO! I WON'T HAVE IT!
I FEEL BAD FOR YOU TOO, KYOHEI-SAMA.
THEY MADE YOU PRETEND TO BE HER BOYFRIEND, DIDN'T THEY?
THERE'S NO WAY A GUY LIKE YOU WOULD BE WITH A MONSTER LIKE HER.
YOU'RE ACTING, AREN'T YOU?
YOU'RE PATHETIC.
SHOCK
IT'S NOT PRE-TEND...
...AND IT AIN'T ACTING.

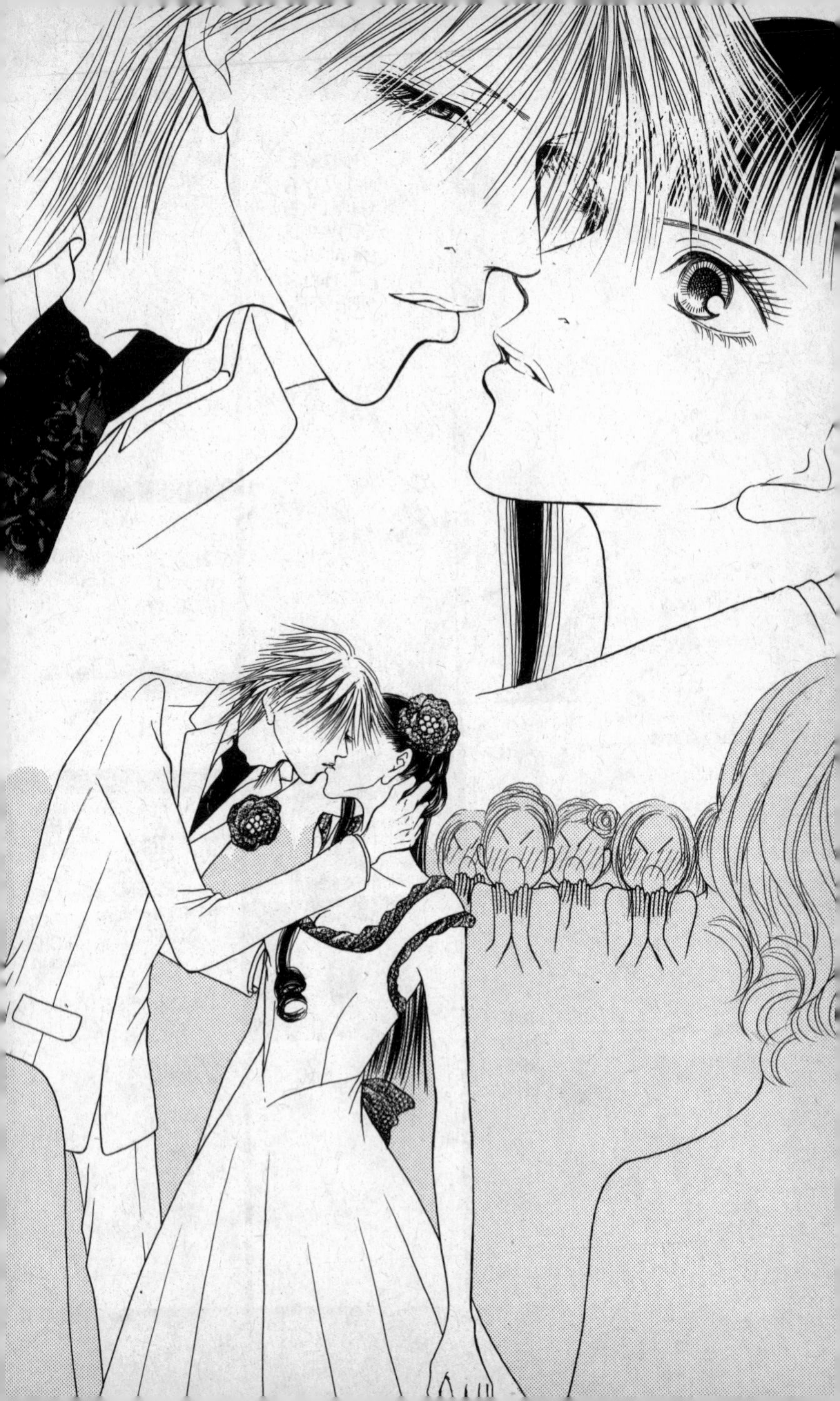

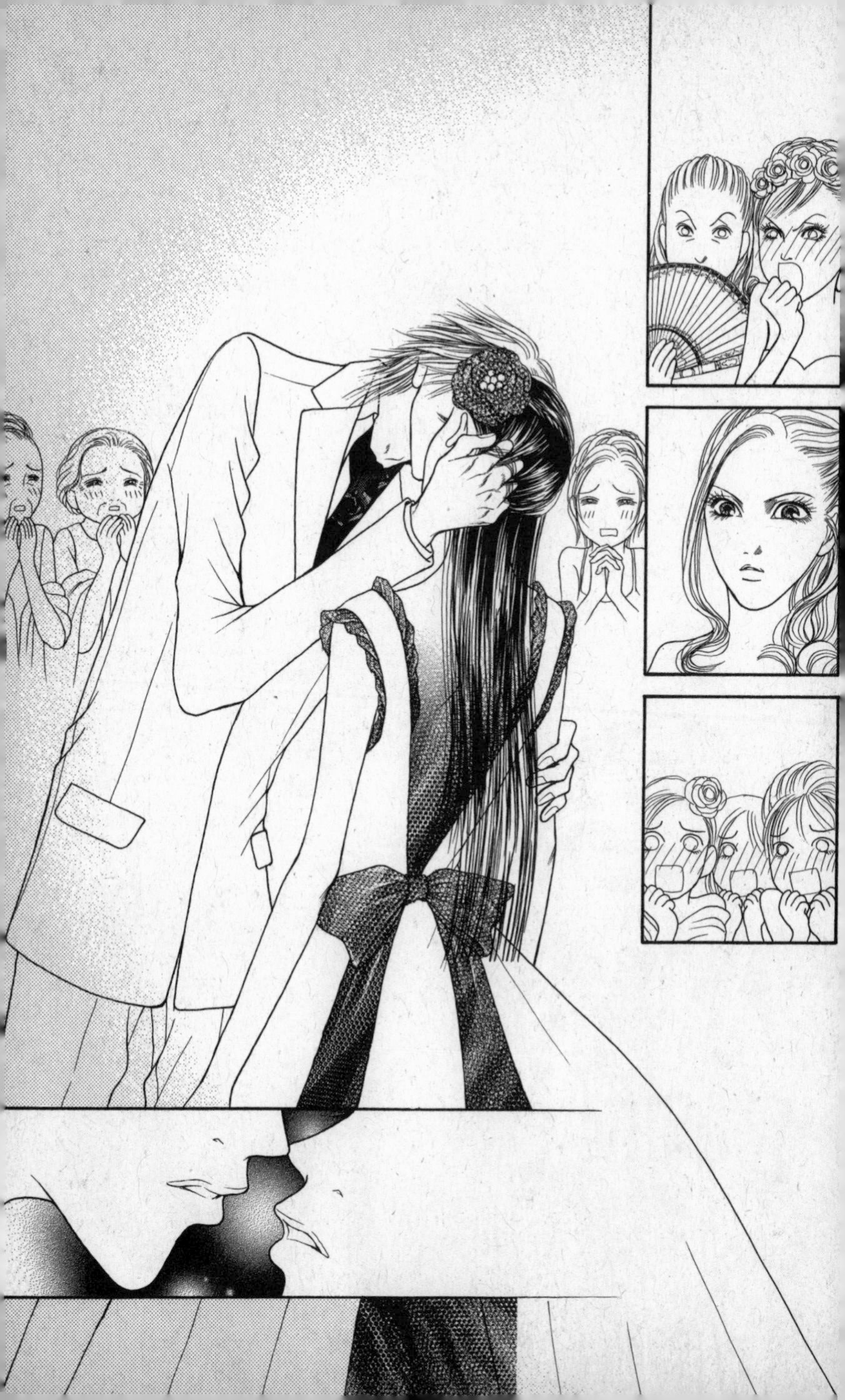

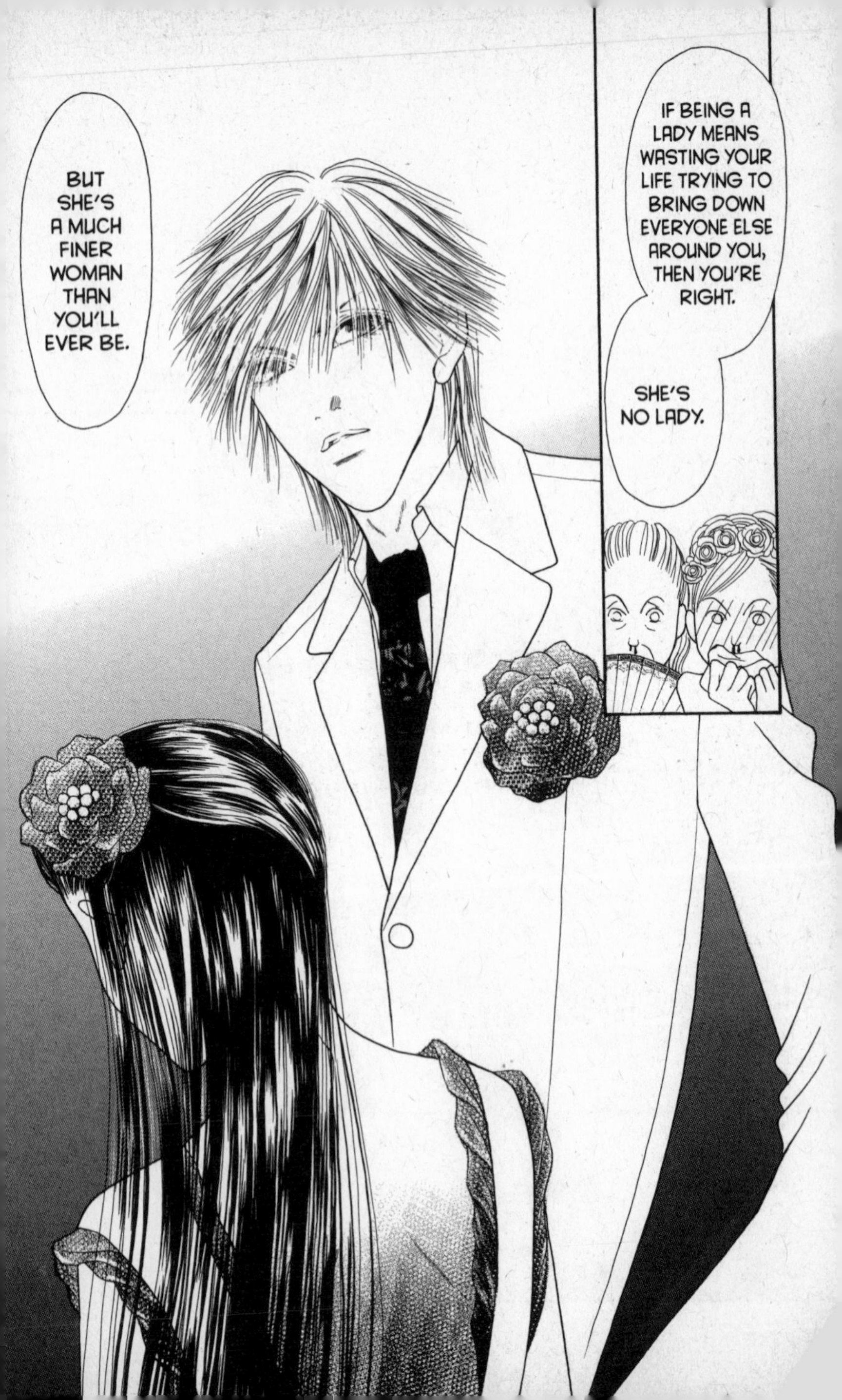
IF BEING A LADY MEANS WASTING YOUR LIFE TRYING TO BRING DOWN EVERYONE ELSE AROUND YOU, THEN YOU'RE RIGHT.
SHE'S NO LADY.
BUT SHE'S A MUCH FINER WOMAN THAN YOU'LL EVER BE.

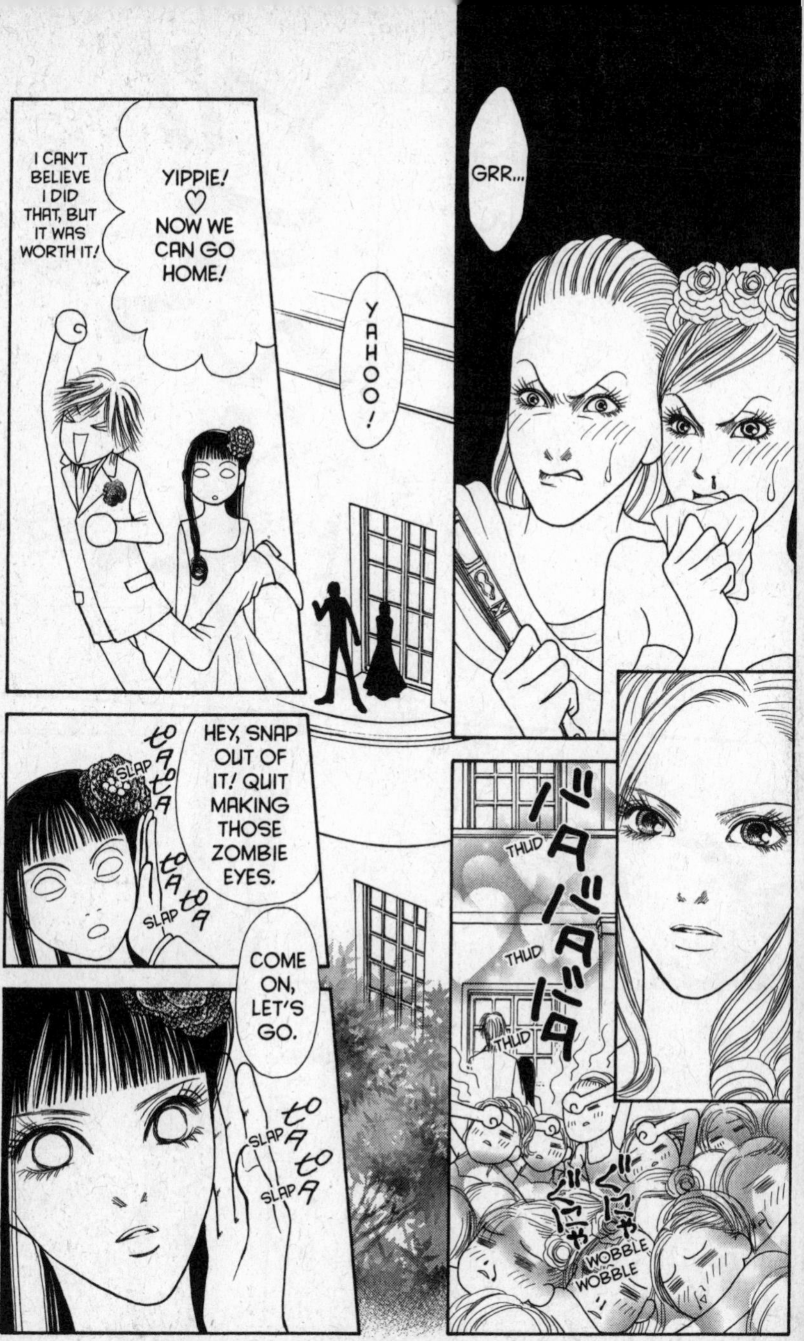
GRR...
THUD
THUD
THUD
WOBBLE
WOBBLE
I CAN'T BELIEVE I DID THAT, BUT IT WAS WORTH IT!
YIPPIE! ♡ NOW WE CAN GO HOME!
YAHOO!
HEY, SNAP OUT OF IT! QUIT MAKING THOSE ZOMBIE EYES.
SLAP
SLAP
COME ON, LET'S GO.
SLAP
SLAP

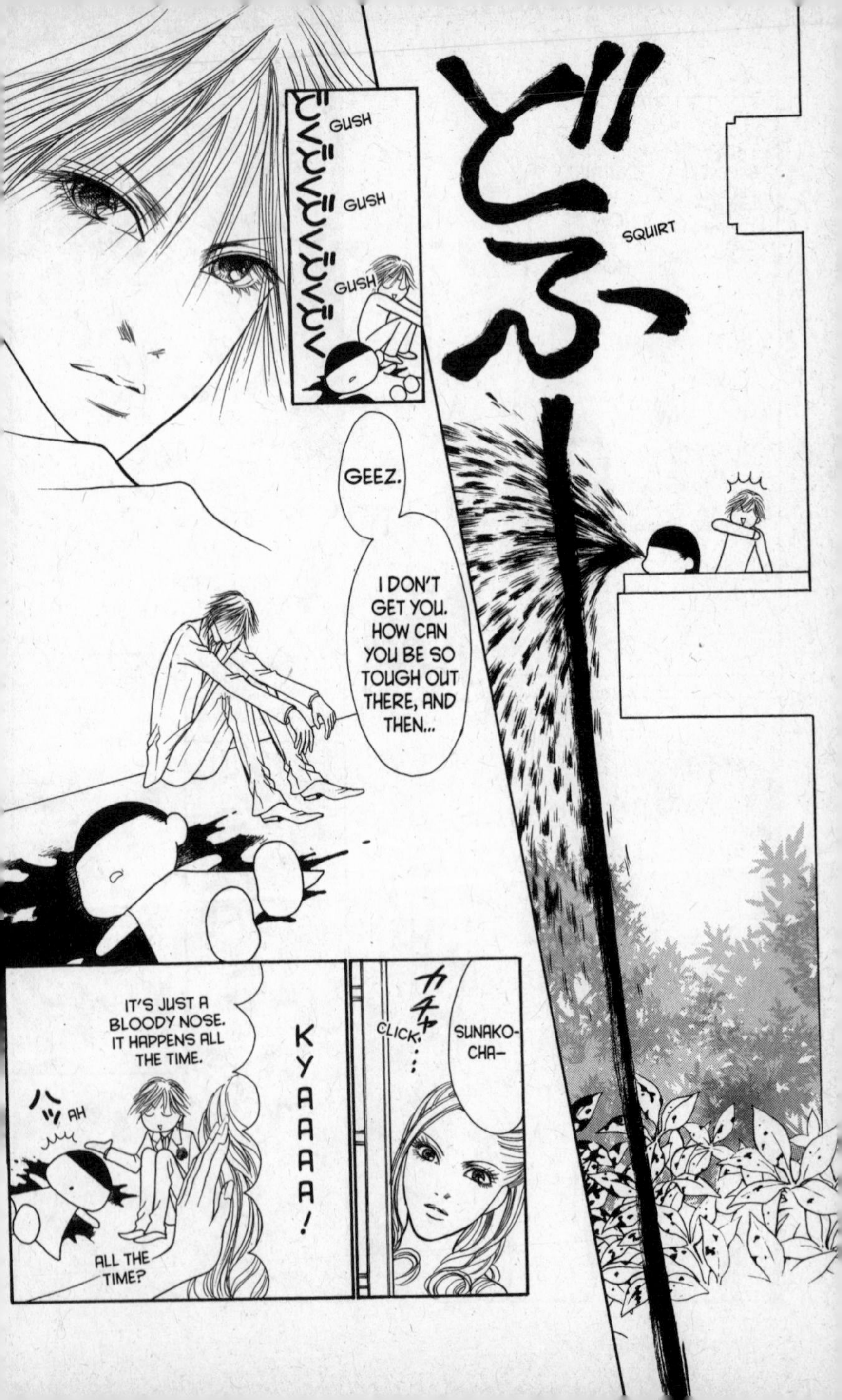
どぶっ
SQUIRT
GUSH
GUSH
GUSH
GEEZ.
I DON'T GET YOU. HOW CAN YOU BE SO TOUGH OUT THERE, AND THEN...
カチャ
CLICK...
SUNAKO-CHA-
KYAAAAA!
IT'S JUST A BLOODY NOSE. IT HAPPENS ALL THE TIME.
ハッ
AH
ALL THE TIME?

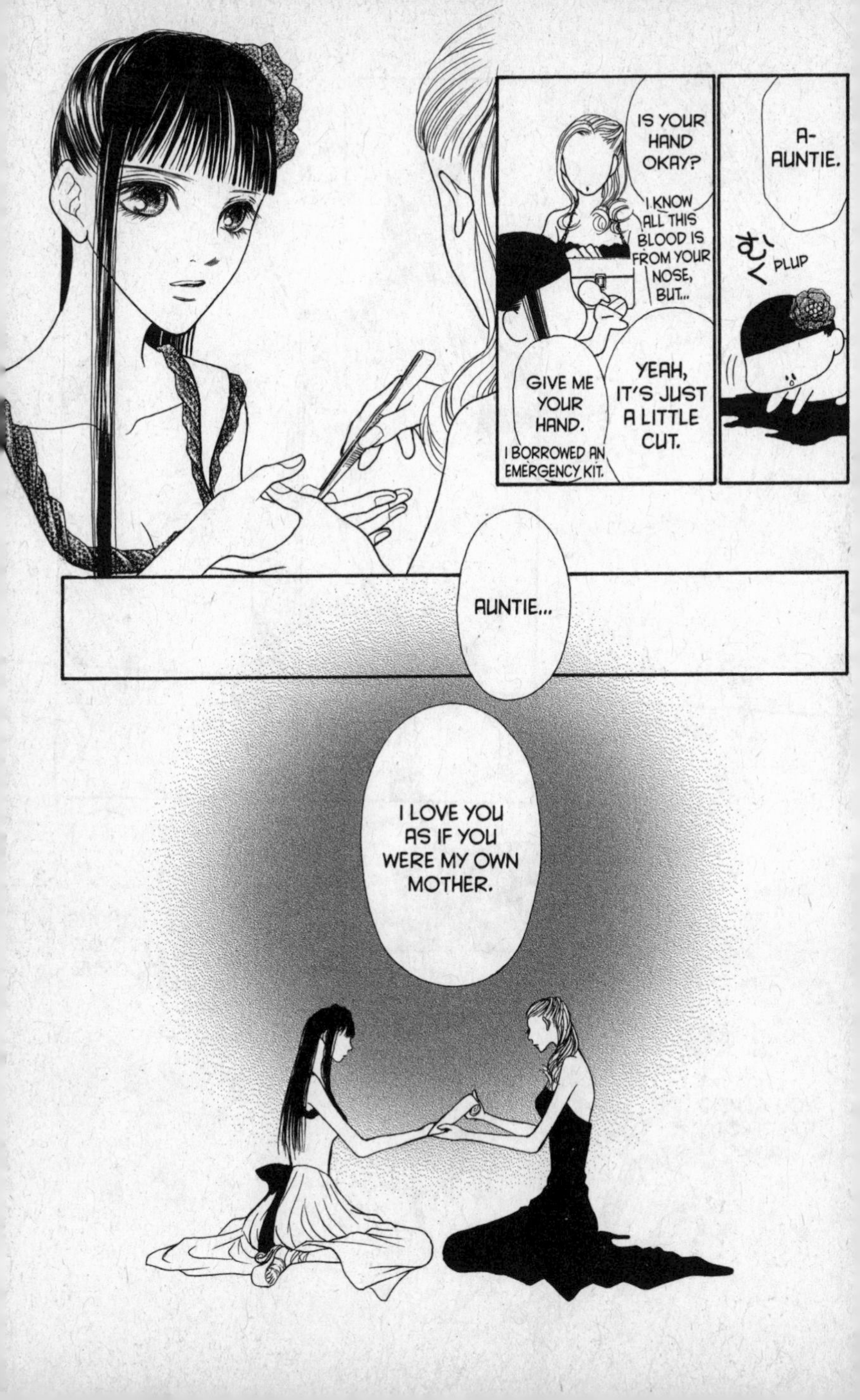
A- AUNTIE.
むく PLUP
IS YOUR HAND OKAY?
I KNOW ALL THIS BLOOD IS FROM YOUR NOSE, BUT...
YEAH, IT'S JUST A LITTLE CUT.
GIVE ME YOUR HAND.
I BORROWED AN EMERGENCY KIT.
AUNTIE...
I LOVE YOU AS IF YOU WERE MY OWN MOTHER.

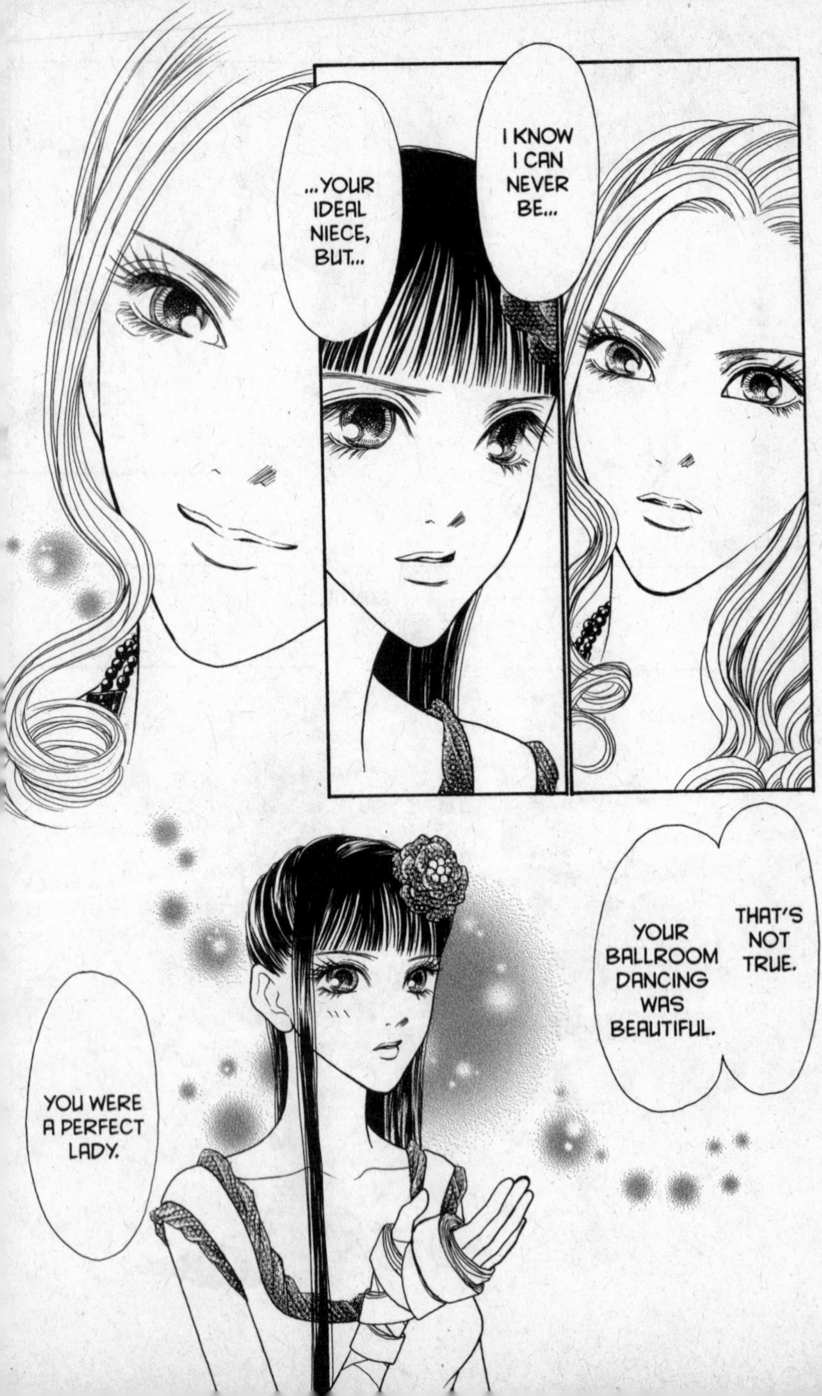
I KNOW I CAN NEVER BE...
...YOUR IDEAL NIECE, BUT...
THAT'S NOT TRUE.
YOUR BALLROOM DANCING WAS BEAUTIFUL.
YOU WERE A PERFECT LADY.

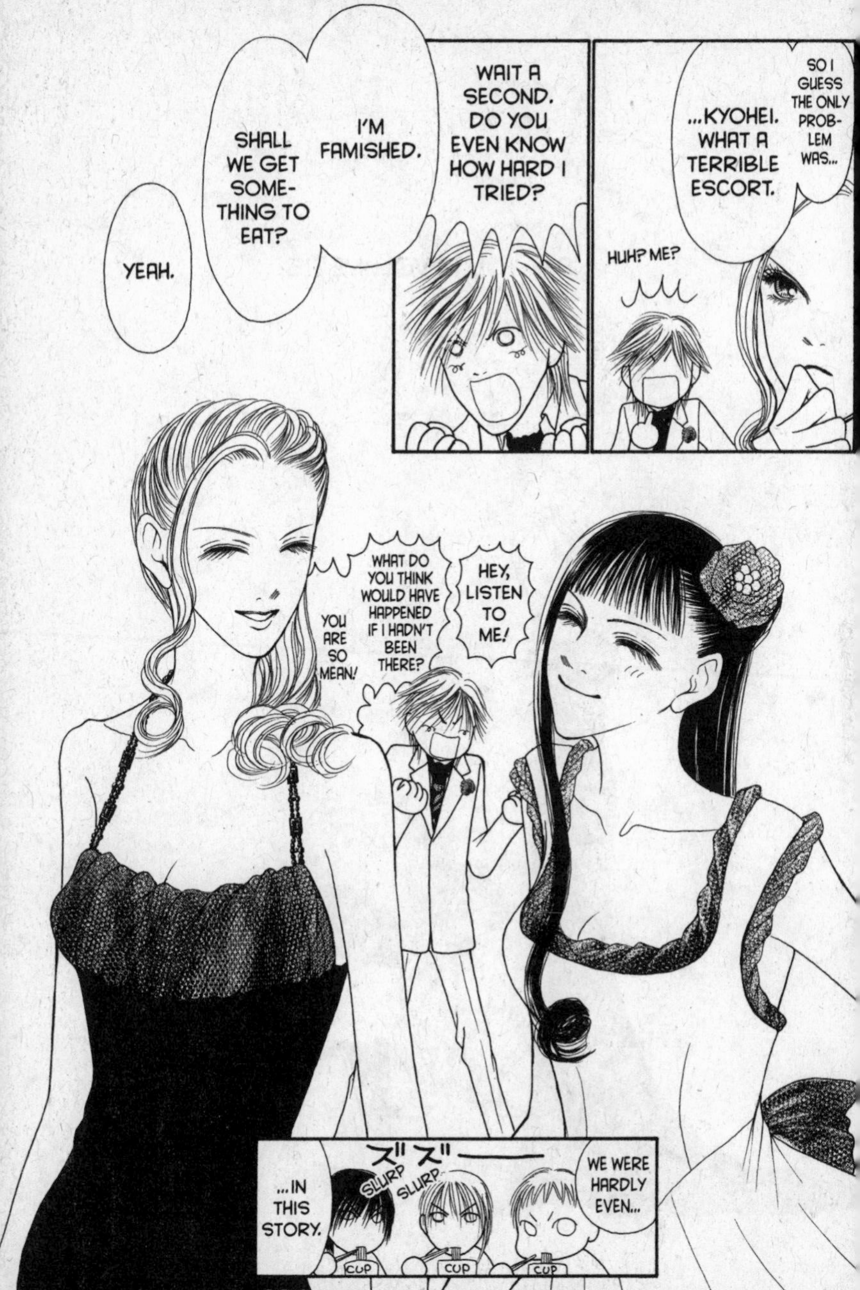
SO I GUESS THE ONLY PROB-LEM WAS...
...KYOHEI. WHAT A TERRIBLE ESCORT.
HUH? ME?
WAIT A SECOND. DO YOU EVEN KNOW HOW HARD I TRIED?
I'M FAMISHED.
SHALL WE GET SOME-THING TO EAT?
YEAH.
HEY, LISTEN TO ME!
WHAT DO YOU THINK WOULD HAVE HAPPENED IF I HADN'T BEEN THERE?
YOU ARE SO MEAN!
WE WERE HARDLY EVEN...
ズズー
SLURP
SLURP
CUP
CUP
CUP
...IN THIS STORY.

CONTINUED IN *WALLFLOWER* VOLUME 25

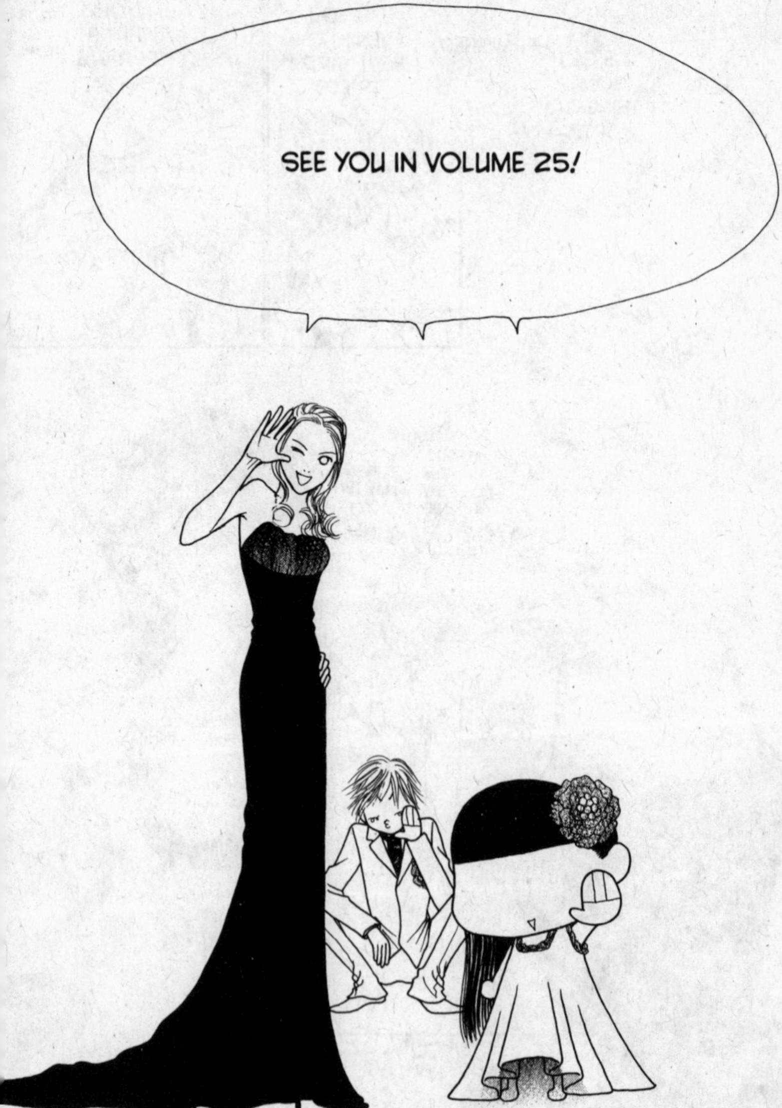
SEE YOU IN VOLUME 25!

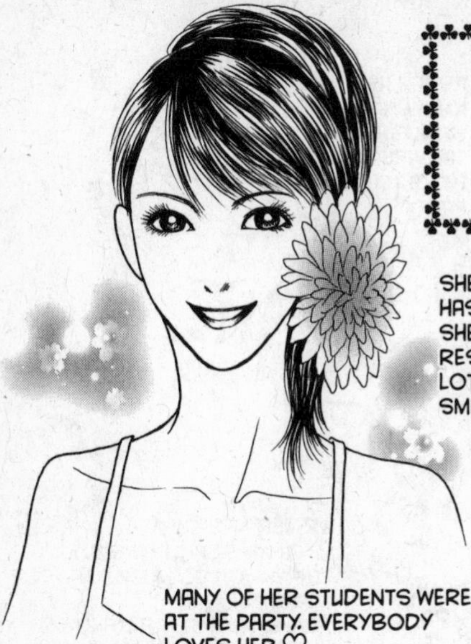

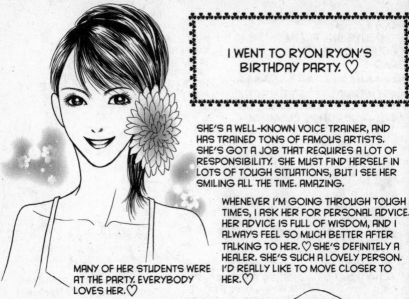

I WENT TO RYON RYON'S BIRTHDAY PARTY. ♡

SHE'S A WELL-KNOWN VOICE TRAINER, AND HAS TRAINED TONS OF FAMOUS ARTISTS. SHE'S GOT A JOB THAT REQUIRES A LOT OF RESPONSIBILITY. SHE MUST FIND HERSELF IN LOTS OF TOUGH SITUATIONS, BUT I SEE HER SMILING ALL THE TIME. AMAZING.

WHENEVER I'M GOING THROUGH TOUGH TIMES, I ASK HER FOR PERSONAL ADVICE. HER ADVICE IS FULL OF WISDOM, AND I ALWAYS FEEL SO MUCH BETTER AFTER TALKING TO HER. ♡ SHE'S DEFINITELY A HEALER. SHE'S SUCH A LOVELY PERSON. I'D REALLY LIKE TO MOVE CLOSER TO HER. ♡

MANY OF HER STUDENTS WERE AT THE PARTY. EVERYBODY LOVES HER. ♡

MEMBERS OF MY FAVORITE BAND NEW ROTE'KA WERE THERE TOO. ♡

SHIZUO-SAN AND NABO-CHAN WEREN'T THERE. 💔

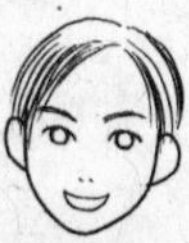

VO. A-CHAN ♡

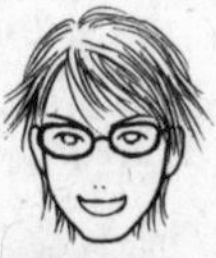

BA. KATARU-KUN ♡

LOLITA NUMBER 18 TO-BU-CHAN ♡
(TO-BU-CHAN ISN'T RYON RYON'S STUDENT. HE'S JUST A FRIEND OF HERS.)

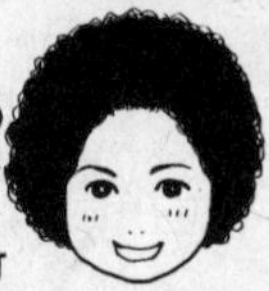

TO-BU-CHAN IS SO CUTE. ♡
LOVE ♡ ♡
I LOVE HIM. ♡
I BET EVERYBODY LOVES HIM. ♡ ♡

THESE TWO ARE HER FRIENDS TOO.
XL MAN NISHIO-SAN

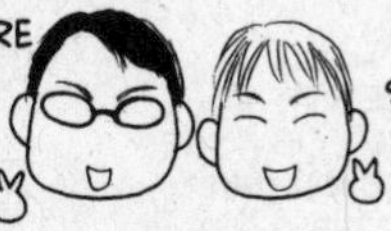

SUDOU-KUN

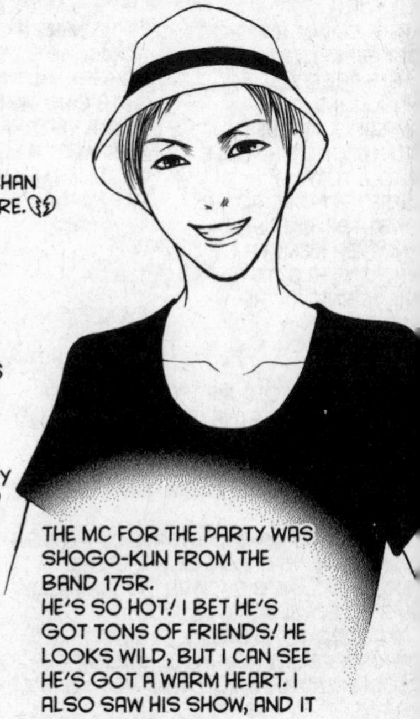

THE MC FOR THE PARTY WAS SHOGO-KUN FROM THE BAND 175R.
HE'S SO HOT! I BET HE'S GOT TONS OF FRIENDS! HE LOOKS WILD, BUT I CAN SEE HE'S GOT A WARM HEART. I ALSO SAW HIS SHOW, AND IT WAS AWESOME!

ROTE'KA BIG TEAM
THANKS FOR YOUR SUPPORT.
I'D LIKE TO THANK NAO-SAN FROM THE BAND MAXIM THE HORMONE. ♡ ♡

A LOT OF HER STUDENTS ARE FROM "VISUAL-KEI" GLAM BANDS.

✿✿✿✿✿✿✿✿✿✿✿✿✿✿✿✿✿✿✿

THERE WERE A LOT OF THEM AT THE PARTY, BUT I'M GONNA FOCUS ON THESE TWO FROM PS COMPANY.

AS FAR AS I KNOW, N-SAMA BROUGHT ALL THE VISUAL-KEI BOYS TO THE PARTY.

WRITER N-SAMA ♡
(I ALWAYS CALL HER SISTER.)
THANK YOU SO MUCH FOR YOUR SUPPORT. ♡
SHE'S SO BEAUTIFUL AND MASCULINE. MANY YOUNG BOYS THINK OF HER AS THEIR BIG SISTER. I ASK HER FOR ADVICE ABOUT RELATIONSHIPS AND OTHER STUFF ALL THE TIME. ♡
♡ HER ADVICE IS ALWAYS VERY STRAIGHTFORWARD. THANKS TO HER, I'VE GOTTEN TO MEET SO MANY PEOPLE. ♡ (INCLUDING MICHII WHO APPEARS 2 PAGES AFTER THIS ONE ♡)

VOCALIST ISSHI-KUN FROM THE BAND KAGURA
HE'S SMART AND HOT. I BET GIRLS LOVE HIM. HE'S PRETTY MASCULINE. IT'S AMAZING HOW HE TRANSFORMS HIMSELF INTO A TOTALLY DIFFERENT CHARACTER ONSTAGE. AKIYA-KUN, ANOTHER MEMBER OF KAGURA, IS CUTE TOO. (HE WASN'T AT THE PARTY.)

VOCALIST KEIYUU-KUN FROM THE BAND KRA
HE'S AMAZINGLY CUTE. ♡
IF HE WERE A GIRL, HE WOULD BE SUPER HOT. HE'S SO CUTE, BUT WHEN HE GETS ONSTAGE, HE TURNS INTO A VERY HANDSOME MAN. WHAT A MYSTERY. ALL OF THE MEMBERS OF KRA ARE REALLY NICE.

RYON RYON TOLD ME THAT VISUAL-KEI BAND MEMBERS ALWAYS HANG OUT TOGETHER IN ONE GROUP WHEN THEY GO TO PARTIES, BUT THEY WERE MOSTLY TALKING TO A-CHAN FROM NEW ROTE'KA ♡ THAT DAY.
A-CHAN WAS MAKING EVERYBODY LAUGH NO MATTER WHAT TYPE OF BAND THEY PLAYED IN. ♡ HE'S SUCH AN AMAZING GUY. HE'S SO LOVELY. ♡ ♡ ♡ ♡ ♡
IT'S HARD TO STOP ONCE I START TALKING ABOUT NEW ROTE'KA, SO I RECOMMEND THAT YOU READ VOLUME 22. (SHAMELESS PLUG ♡)

A-CHAN. ♡ A-CHAN. ♡

PEOPLE WERE A LITTLE PUT OFF BY MY OBVIOUS AFFECTION FOR A-CHAN. (I USUALLY BEHAVE LIKE AN OLD MAN, BUT I TURN INTO A GIRL WHEN I'M IN FRONT OF A-CHAN.)

THIS IS WHAT A-CHAN LOOKS LIKE IN MY MIND.

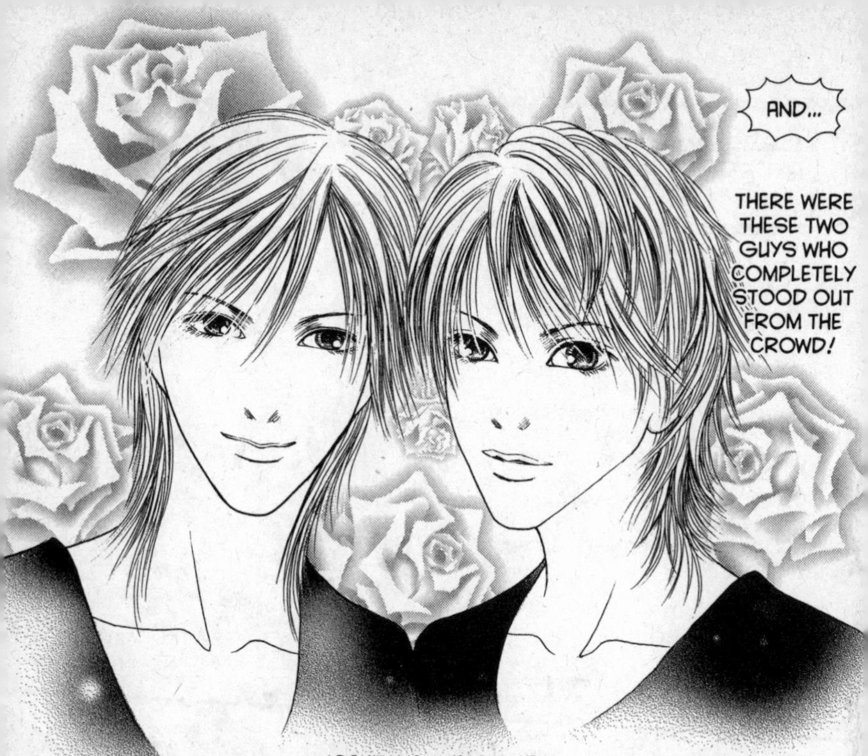
AND...
THERE WERE THESE TWO GUYS WHO COMPLETELY STOOD OUT FROM THE CROWD!

TETSU-SAN FROM THE BAND L'ARC~EN~CIEL.

WHEN I MET HIM, HE SAID, "I'M TETSU FROM L'ARC~EN~CIEL." I WAS LIKE, "OF COURSE I KNOW WHO YOU ARE! I'VE BEEN TO SO MANY OF YOUR SHOWS!" HE WAS A REALLY NICE, LAID-BACK PERSON. HE HAD A STRONGER PRESENCE IN PERSON THAN ON TV. I DON'T KNOW QUITE HOW TO PUT THIS BUT... I FEEL LIKE HE HAS WHAT IT TAKES TO BE A REAL MAN. SORRY MY VOCABULARY IS SO LIMITED. ANYWAY, HE WAS REALLY COOL.

I DON'T KNOW WHY, BUT THEY ASKED ME TO DRAW THEM AS IF THEY WERE A GAY COUPLE, SO HERE YOU GO. N-SAMA IS FRIENDS WITH THEM, SO I GOT A CHANCE TO TALK TO THEM FOR A LITTLE BIT.

AND...

NISHIKAWA-KUN WROTE A BLURB FOR VOLUME 24! THANK YOU SO MUCH. YOU REALLY ARE A GREAT GUY!

TAKAYOSHI NISHIKAWA-SAMA FROM THE BAND T.M. REVOLUTION

NISHIKAWA-KUN ISN'T A STUDENT OF RYON RYON'S, BUT HE'S A FRIEND OF HERS. I'M SHOCKED BY HOW WELL HE CAN SING WITHOUT ANY VOICE TRAINING. THAT'S PRETTY AMAZING! HIS SHOW WAS AWESOME! HE WAS 100 TIMES HOTTER THAN HE LOOKS ON TV, BUT HE WAS JUST AS FRIENDLY IN PERSON AS HE SEEMS ON TV.

I HAD LOTS OF FUN AT RYON RYON'S BIRTHDAY PARTY. ♡ IT WAS SUCH A COZY AND LOVELY PARTY. IT WAS THE PERFECT REFLECTION OF HER PERSONALITY. ♡

THANKS FOR READING ♡ ♡ ♡
HAPPY BIRTHDAY, RYON RYON. ♡

IT'S SUMMER! MICHII FESTIVAL TIME!
IN RYOUGOKU STADIUM
I WENT.♡

THIS SHOW WAS DIFFERENT FROM HIS USUAL CONCERTS (HIS SOLO ACT). IT WAS MORE LIKE A FESTIVAL! I HAD SO MUCH FUN. ♡ MICHII IS AWESOME. ♡ ♡ ♡

THE CONCERT WAS AMAZING AS USUAL, BUT...

THE BEST PART WAS SEEING HIM DRESSED IN A *YUKATA*. (AFTER THE SHOW) ♡ ♡ ♡

HOW COULD I RESIST WRITING ABOUT THIS?

(IF HIS FANS HAD GOTTEN TO SEE HIM, THEY WOULD'VE BEEN BLOWN AWAY.)

I GOT SO EXCITED AND CAUSED SO MUCH TROUBLE.

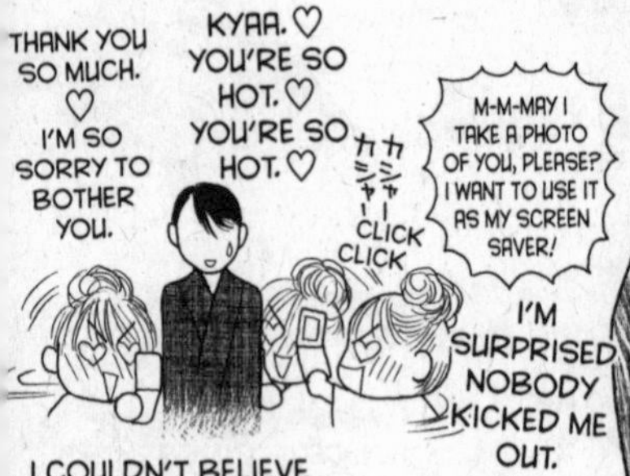
THANK YOU SO MUCH. ♡ I'M SO SORRY TO BOTHER YOU.
KYAA. ♡ YOU'RE SO HOT. ♡ YOU'RE SO HOT. ♡
カシャー カシャー
CLICK CLICK
M-M-MAY I TAKE A PHOTO OF YOU, PLEASE? I WANT TO USE IT AS MY SCREEN SAVER!
I'M SURPRISED NOBODY KICKED ME OUT.

I COULDN'T BELIEVE I FORGOT MY DIGITAL CAMERA THAT DAY. I WAS SO EXCITED THAT MY CELL PHONE PICS WERE ALL OUT OF FOCUS. I'M SUCH AN IDIOT!

BELIEVE IT OR NOT, I EVEN HAD A CHANCE TO TAKE A PICTURE WITH HIM. ♡

OH MY GOD.

WHO'S THIS CHUNKY CHICK WITH THE BIG HEAD STANDING NEXT TO MICHII? WHAT THE HELL?

IT'S HARD TO BELIEVE THAT WE BOTH BELONG TO THE SAME SPECIES.

I TOTALLY LOOKED LIKE A RUSSIAN BABUSHKA DOLL.

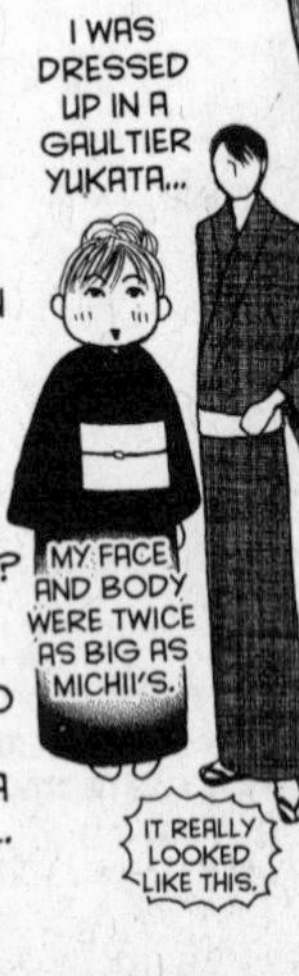
I WAS DRESSED UP IN A GAULTIER YUKATA...
MY FACE AND BODY WERE TWICE AS BIG AS MICHII'S.
IT REALLY LOOKED LIKE THIS.

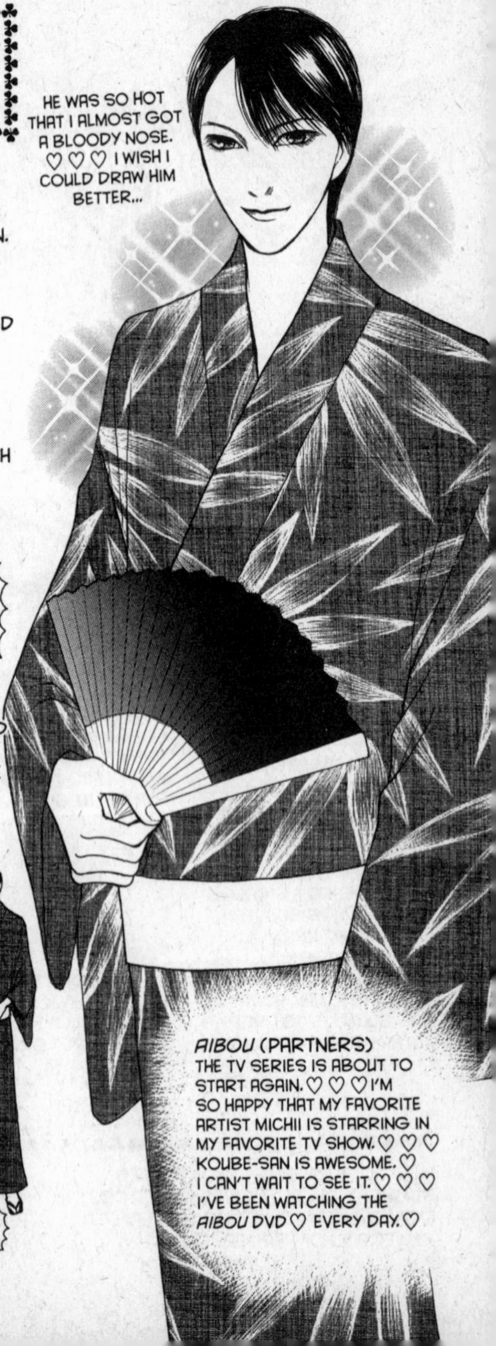
HE WAS SO HOT THAT I ALMOST GOT A BLOODY NOSE. ♡ ♡ ♡ I WISH I COULD DRAW HIM BETTER...

AIBOU (PARTNERS)
THE TV SERIES IS ABOUT TO START AGAIN. ♡ ♡ ♡ I'M SO HAPPY THAT MY FAVORITE ARTIST MICHII IS STARRING IN MY FAVORITE TV SHOW. ♡ ♡ ♡ KOUBE-SAN IS AWESOME. ♡ I CAN'T WAIT TO SEE IT. ♡ ♡ ♡ I'VE BEEN WATCHING THE *AIBOU* DVD ♡ EVERY DAY. ♡

THANK YOU FOR BUYING KODANSHA COMICS. ♥

IT'S BEEN A LONG TIME SINCE I WROTE SO MANY BONUS PAGES AND SO MANY ILLUSTRATIONS. IT SURE WAS A LOT OF WORK. PHEW.

OH, I'M NOT REALLY GOOD AT DRAWING PORTRAITS. IF ANY OF YOU THOUGHT, "THE ILLUSTRATIONS LOOK NOTHING LIKE THE REAL PEOPLE," I SINCERELY APOLOGIZE.

I HOPE YOU CAN STILL GIVE ME SOME CREDIT FOR MY HARD WORK AND EFFORT.

GEEZ, I HAVEN'T BEEN TO ANY CONCERTS LATELY...

AND THAT INCLUDES KIYOHARU-SAMA CONCERTS (THE LOVE OF MY LIFE)...

IT'S JUST PHYSICALLY IMPOSSIBLE. I'VE BEEN SO BUSY, ALL I DO IS WORK.

IT'S BEEN 10 YEARS SINCE I STARTED WORKING AS A MANGA ARTIST. I'VE REALLY BEEN ENJOYING DRAWING MANGA THESE DAYS. BUT WHO KNOWS HOW LONG THAT FEELING WILL LAST? LAST YEAR WAS PRETTY TOUGH, YOU KNOW?

I MIGHT FALL APART AGAIN, BUT I WANNA KEEP MOVING FORWARD, AND I HOPE YOU'LL STICK AROUND.

I'D LIKE TO THANK EVERYONE WHO SENT ME LETTERS.♥ THEY ARE THE SOURCE OF MY POWER. ♥ ♥ ♥

TEN IS ADORABLE AS EVER. ♡ I KNOW I LOVE HIM WAY TOO MUCH.

OKAY, SEE YOU IN VOLUME 25. ♥ ♥ ♥

SPECIAL THANKS

TOMMY YOUICHIROU
TOMITA-SAMA

KAI-CHAN (MY FRIEND)

HITOSHI (MY BROTHER)

MIEKO SUZUKI-SAMA

THE EDITOR IN CHIEF-SAMA

NARIKIYO-SAMA

INO-SAMA

INAMI-SAMA

EVERYBODY WHO'S READING THIS RIGHT NOW ♡

Translation Notes

Japanese is a tricky language for most Westerners, and translation is often more art than science. For your edification and reading pleasure, here are notes on some of the places where we could have gone in a different direction in our translation of the work, or where a Japanese cultural reference is used.

Flower Viewing, page 3

Springtime flower viewing is a popular leisure activity in Japan. People head to local parks and nature areas, lay out blankets, and eat and drink as they sit beneath the blossoming plum and cherry trees.

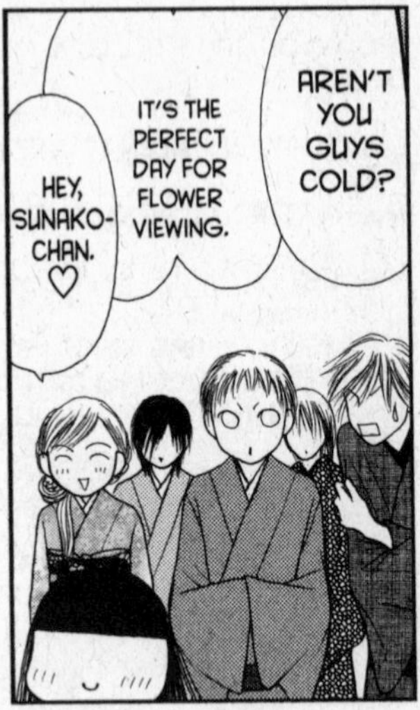
AREN'T YOU GUYS COLD?
IT'S THE PERFECT DAY FOR FLOWER VIEWING.
HEY, SUNAKO-CHAN. ♡

Hokusai, page 57

Hokusai is one of Japan's most famous artists from the 19th century. He was a master of the woodblock print, and his work is known throughout the world. Although you may not know the name, you've surely seen his work. The most famous of his works is the giant wave, with Mt. Fuji in the backdrop. It's part of his series entitled "36 Views of Mt. Fuji."

Tsundere, page 106

A *Tsundere* is a type of manga or anime character that starts out mean, but later turns lovey-dovey.

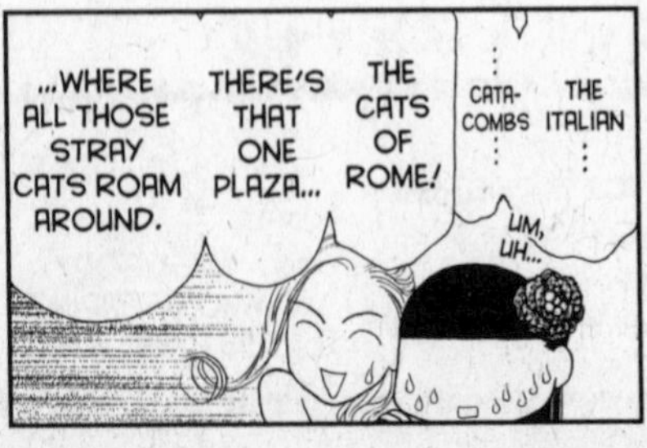
THE ITALIAN ...
CATA-COMBS ...
THE CATS OF ROME!
THERE'S THAT ONE PLAZA...
...WHERE ALL THOSE STRAY CATS ROAM AROUND.
UM, UH...

Italian Catacombs, page 131

The catacombs are an ancient underground burial site located in Rome.

About the Creator

Tomoko Hayakawa was born on March 4.

Since her debut as a manga creator, Tomoko Hayakawa has worked on many shojo titles with the theme of romantic love—only to realize that she could write about other subjects as well. She decided to pack her newest story with the things she likes most, which led to her current, enormously popular series, *The Wallflower*.

Her favorite things are: Tim Burton's *The Nightmare Before Christmas*, Jean-Paul Gaultier, and samurai dramas on TV. Her hobbies are collecting items with skull designs and watching bishonen (beautiful boys). Her dream is to build a mansion like the one the Addams family lives in. Her favorite pastime is to lie around at home with her cat, Ten (whose full name is Tennosuke).

Her zodiac sign is Pisces, and her blood group is AB.

Preview of Volume 25

We're pleased to present you a preview from volume 25. Please check our website (www.delreymanga.com) to see when this volume will be available in English. For now you'll have to make do with Japanese!

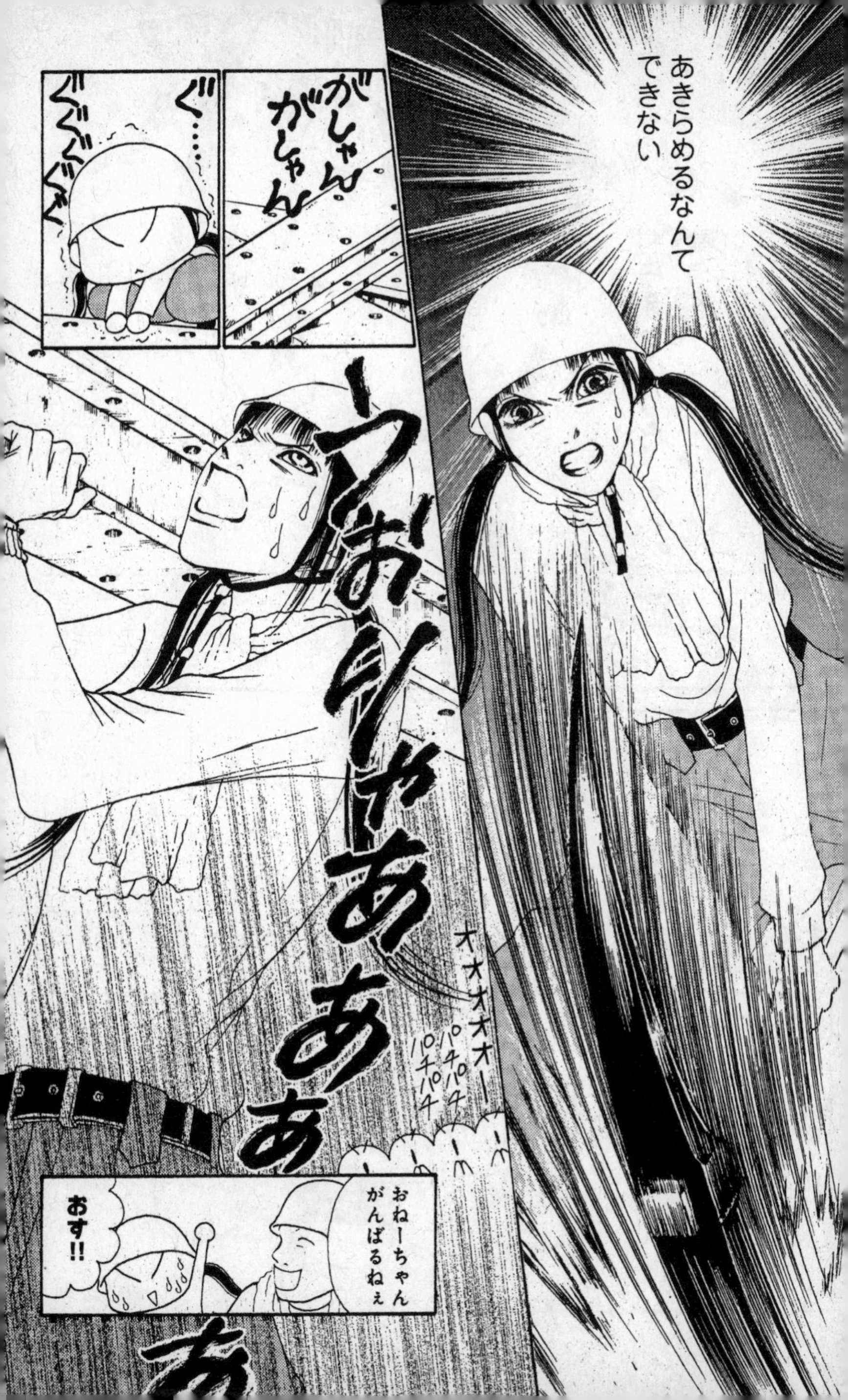
あきらめるなんて
できない
がしゃん
がしゃん
ぐ……
ぐぐぐぐぐ
うおりゃあああ
あ
オオオオオー
パチパチ
パチパチ
おねーちゃん
がんばるねぇ
おす!!

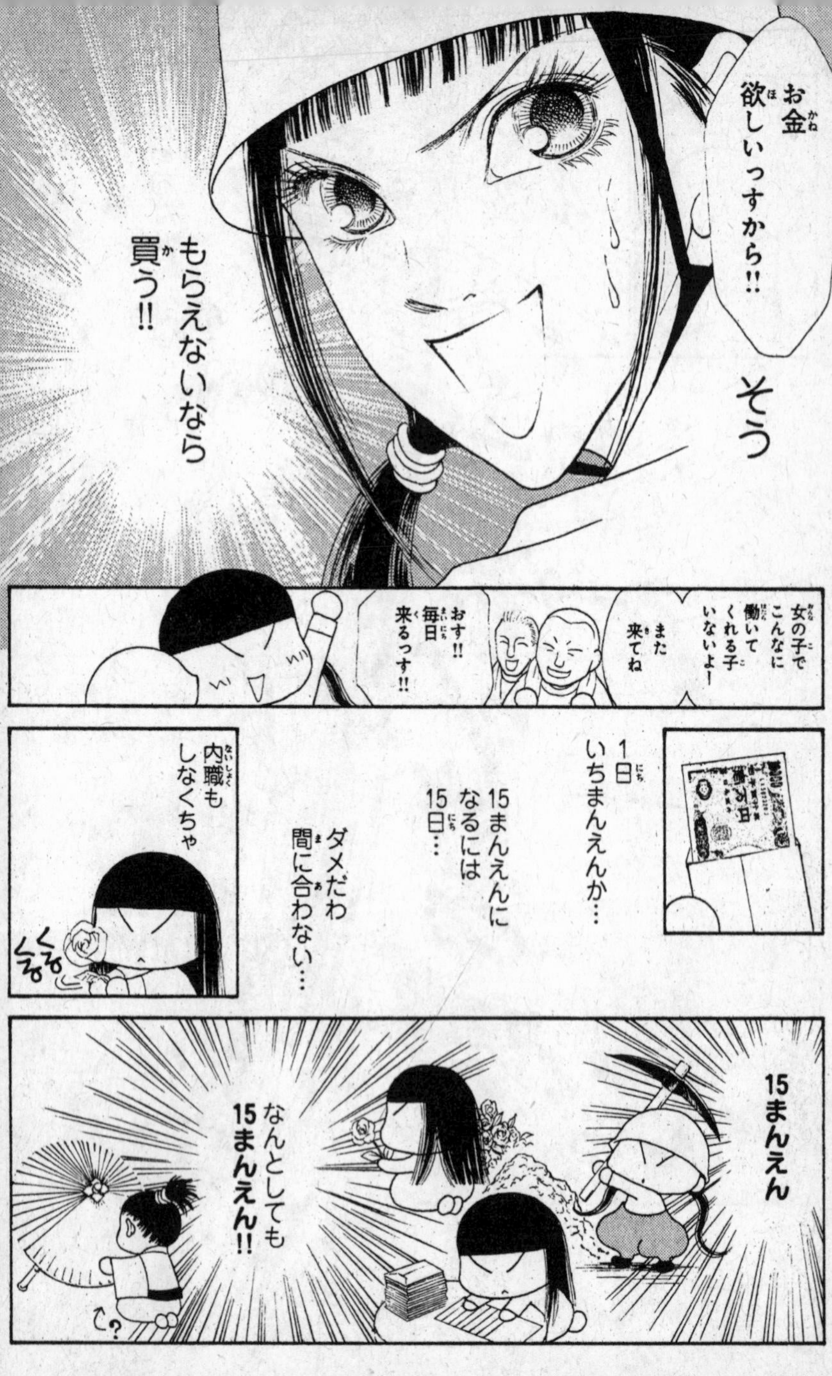
お金欲しいっすから!!
そう
もらえないなら買う!!
女の子でこんなに働いてくれる子いないよー
また来てね
おす!! 毎日来るっす!!
1日いちまんえんか…
15まんえんになるには15日…
ダメだわ間に合わない…
内職もしなくちゃ
15まんえん
なんとしても15まんえん!!
?

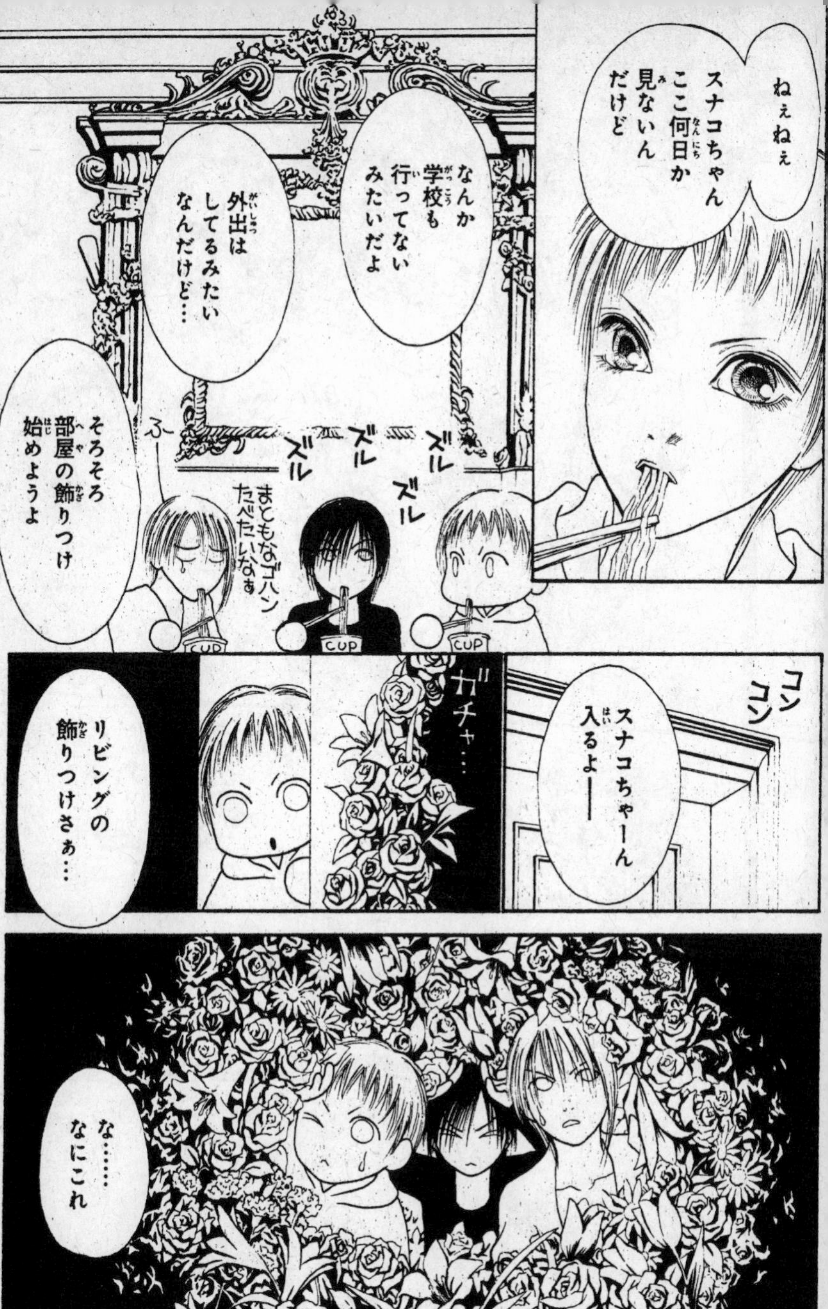
ねぇねぇ
スナコちゃんここ何日か見ないんだけど
なんか学校も行ってないみたいだよ
外出はしてるみたいなんだけど…
ズル
ズル
ズル
ズル
まともなゴハンたべたいなぁ
ふー
そろそろ部屋の飾りつけ始めようよ
コンコン
スナコちゃーん入るよー
ガチャ…
リビングの飾りつけさぁ…
な……なにこれ

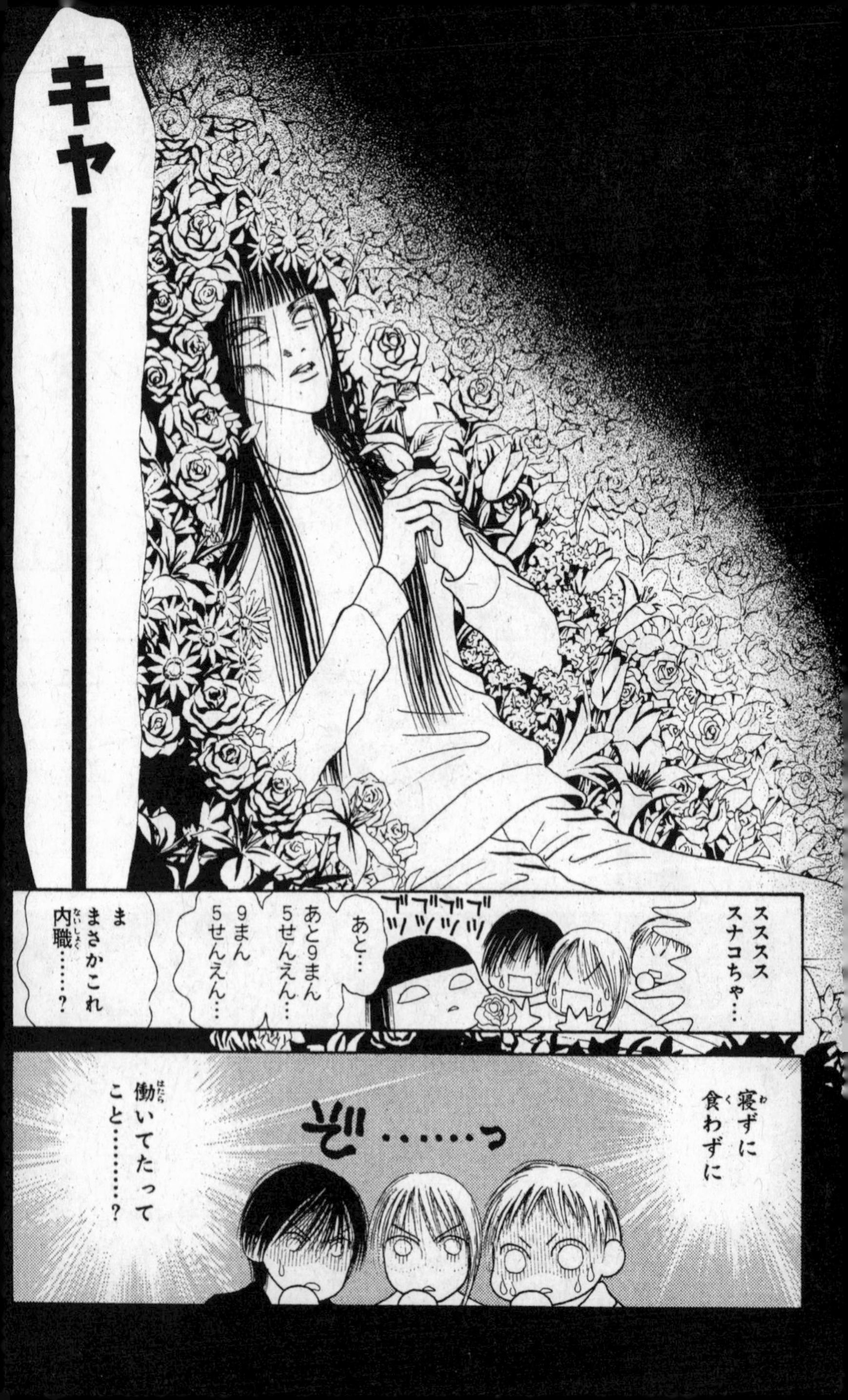
キャー
スススス
スナコちゃ…
ブブブブ
ツツツツ
あと…
あと9まん
5せんえん…
9まん
5せんえん…
ま
まさかこれ
内職……？
寝ずに
食わずに
ぞ……っ
働いてたって
こと……？

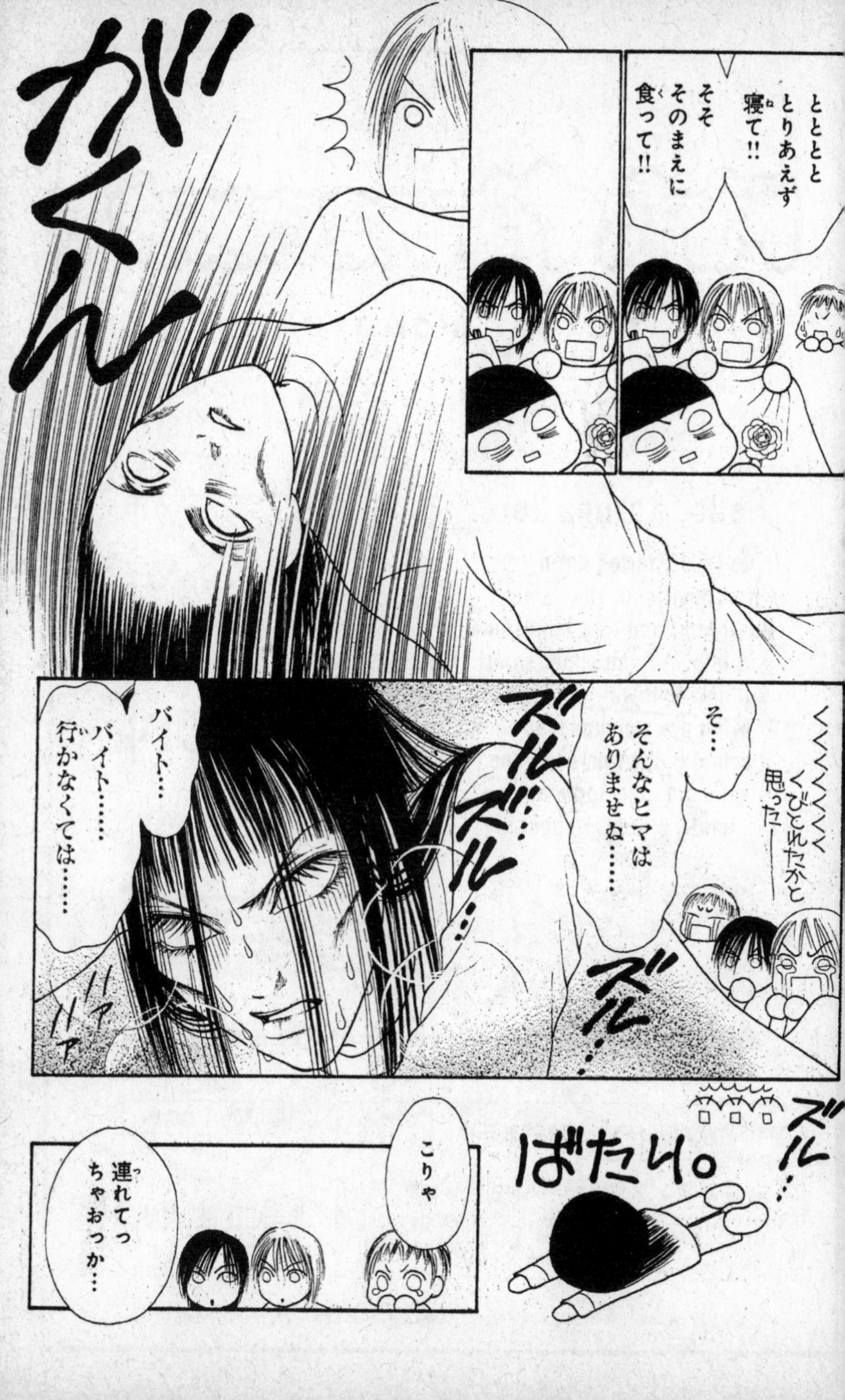
とととと
とりあえず
寝て!!
そそ
そのまえに
食って!!
がくん
くくくくくく
くびとれたかと
思った――
そ…
そんなヒマは
ありませぬ……
ズル…
ズル…
ズル…
バイト…
バイト……
行かなくては……
ハァ
ハァ
ズル…
ばたり。
こりゃ
連れてっ
ちゃおっか…

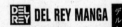

TOMARE!

[STOP!]

You're going the wrong way!

Manga is a completely different type of reading experience.

To start at the *beginning*,
go to the *end*!

That's right! Authentic manga is read the traditional Japanese way—from right to left. Exactly the *opposite* of how American books are read. It's easy to follow: Just go to the other end of the book, and read each page—and each panel—from right side to left side, starting at the top right. Now you're experiencing manga as it was meant to be!